BARRON'S

SAT®

25TH EDITION

Sharon Weiner Green, M.A.
Former Instructor in English
Merritt College
Oakland, California

Ira K. Wolf, Ph.D.
President, PowerPrep, Inc.
Former High School Teacher, College Professor,
and University Director of Teacher Preparation

BARRON'S

DEDICATION

In memory of Mitchel Weiner and Samuel Brownstein, who first brought
college entrance test preparation to the high school students of America.

S.W.G.

To Elaine, my wife and best friend, for all of your support and love.

I.K.W.

ABOUT THE AUTHORS

Sharon Green started helping prepare students for the PSAT and SAT as a 13-year-old
assistant at her father's college entrance tutoring course; she has never stopped since.
A National Merit Scholar, she holds degrees from Harvard College, New York University School of Education, and the University of California at Berkeley. Her test preparation books, all published by Barron's, run the gamut from the California High School
Proficiency Examination to the GRE. Whenever she can dig her way out from under
multiple dictionaries, Sharon enjoys folk dancing, reading Jane Austen and science
fiction, and watching Little League baseball.

Dr. Ira Wolf has had a long career in math education. In addition to teaching math at
the high school level for several years, he was a professor of mathematics at Brooklyn
College and the Director of the Mathematics Teacher Preparation program at SUNY
Stony Brook.

Dr. Wolf has been helping students prepare for the PSAT, SAT, and SAT Subject
Tests in Math for more than 35 years. He is the founder and president of PowerPrep,
a test preparation company on Long Island that currently works with more than
1,000 high school students each year.

© Copyright 2010, 2008 by Barron's Educational Series, Inc.

Previous editions © copyright 2006, 2005, 2001, 1998, 1997, 1994, 1993, 1991, 1989, 1987, 1986,
1984, 1982, 1980, 1978, 1975, 1974, 1973, 1972, 1971, 1969, 1966, 1965, 1964, 1962, 1958, 1955,
1954 by Barron's Educational Series, Inc., under the titles *How to Prepare for the SAT, How to Prepare
for the SAT I,* and *How to Prepare for the Scholastic Aptitude Test.*

Critical Reading sections adapted from previous editions of *How to Prepare for the SAT I* by Samuel C.
Brownstein, Mitchel Weiner, and Sharon Weiner Green, published by Barron's Educational Series, Inc.

All inquiries should be addressed to:
Barron's Educational Series, Inc.
250 Wireless Boulevard
Hauppauge, NY 11788
www.barronseduc.com

ISBN-13: 978-0-7641-4436-3
ISBN-10: 0-7641-4436-7
ISBN-13 (with CD-ROM): 978-0-7641-9722-2
ISBN-10 (with CD-ROM): 0-7641-9722-3
International Standard Serial No. (print): 1941-6180
International Standard Serial No. (print with CD-ROM): 1941-6474

PRINTED IN THE UNITED STATES OF AMERICA
9 8 7 6 5 4 3

FSC
Mixed Sources
Product group from well-managed
forests and other controlled sources

Cert no. SW-COC-002507
www.fsc.org
© 1996 Forest Stewardship Council

Contents

MATHEMATICS

PART FOUR: TEST YOURSELF

Preface

In writing this edition of Barron's *SAT*, we have aimed to give you the advantages on the SAT that the students we tutor and teach in classes have enjoyed for decades. Therefore, we'd like you to think of this study guide as your personal SAT tutor, because that's precisely what it is. Like any good tutor, it will work closely with you, prompting you and giving you pointers to improve your testing skills. It will help you pinpoint your trouble spots and show you how to work on them, and it will point out your strengths as well. After working with your tutor, you should see marked improvement in your performance.

Your personal tutor will be available to work with you whenever you like, for as long or short a time as you like. Working with your tutor, you can go as quickly or as slowly as you like, repeating sections as often as you need, skipping over sections you already know well. Your tutor will give you explanations, not just correct answers, when you make mistakes, and will be infinitely patient and adaptable.

Here are just a few of the things your tutor offers you:

- It takes you step by step through thousands of critical reading, writing, and mathematical questions, showing you how to solve them and how to avoid going wrong.
- It offers you dozens of clear-cut Testing Tactics and shows you how to use them to attack every question type you will find on the new SAT.
- It enables you to simulate actual testing conditions, providing you with a diagnostic test and five model tests—all with answers fully explained—each of which follows the format of the SAT exactly.
- It provides comprehensive mathematics review in arithmetic, algebra, and geometry— the three math areas you need to know to do well on the SAT.
- It gives you the 365-word High-Frequency Word List, 365 words from *abridge* to *zealot* that have been shown by computer analysis to occur and reoccur on actual published SATs, plus Barron's 3,500 Basic Word List, your best chance to acquaint yourself with the whole range of college-level vocabulary you will face on the SAT.
- It even gives you your own set of high-frequency word list flash cards in a convenient tear-out section at the back of the book. More than 200 words that have appeared regularly on previous SAT exams are presented, each with its part of speech, pronunciation, definition, and illustrative sentence. Separate the cards and carry some with you to study in spare moments. Or devise a competitive game, and use them with a partner.

No other book offers you as much. Your personal tutor embodies Barron's ongoing commitment to provide you with the best possible coaching for the SAT and every other important test you take. It has benefited from the dedicated labors of Linda Turner and other members of the editorial staff of Barron's, all of whom wish you the best as you settle down with your tutor to work on the SAT.

SAT Format and Test Dates

SAT Format

Total Time: 4 Hours and 5 Minutes (including two breaks)

Section 1: Essay
Time—25 minutes

Section 2: Critical Reading—24 Questions
Time—25 minutes

8 Sentence Completion
4 Reading Comprehension (2 short passages)
12 Reading Comprehension (1 long passage)

Section 3: Mathematics—20 Questions
Time—25 minutes

20 Standard Multiple-Choice

Break
Time—10 minutes

Section 4: Writing Skills—35 Questions
Time—25 minutes

11 Improving Sentences
18 Identifying Sentence Errors
6 Improving Paragraphs

Section 5: Experimental
Time—25 minutes

This section can be Critical Reading, Mathematics, or Writing Skills

Section 6: Critical Reading—24 Questions
Time—25 minutes

5 Sentence Completion
4 Reading Comprehension (paired short passages)
15 Reading Comprehension (2 long passages)

Break
Time—10 minutes

Section 7: Mathematics—18 Questions
Time—25 minutes

8 Standard Multiple-Choice
10 Student-Produced Response (Grid-in)

Section 8: Critical Reading—19 Questions
Time—20 minutes

6 Sentence Completion
13 Reading Comprehension (paired long passages)

Section 9: Mathematics—16 Questions
Time—20 minutes

16 Standard Multiple-Choice

Section 10: Writing Skills—14 Questions
Time—10 minutes

14 Improving Sentences

Note: As stated above, the "experimental" section can be an extra 25-minute Critical Reading, Mathematics, or Writing Skills section. This section, which permits the test-makers to try out new questions, does not count in your score; but because there is no way to know which section is the experimental one, you must do your best on every section.

Section 1 is *always* the essay. Sections 2–7, which are each 25-minutes long, can come *in any order*. In particular, the experimenal section is not necessarily Section 5—it can be any of Sections 2–7. Sections 8 and 9 are *always* a 20-minute Mathematics section and a 20-minute Critical Reading section—*in either order*. Section 10 is always the 10-minute Writing Skills section.

The above format is used in all the tests in this book, except that the tests don't have an experimental section. Therefore, the tests in the book take 25 minutes less than an actual SAT.

SAT Test Dates

Test Dates*	Registration Deadlines	
	Regular*	**Late***
2010		
October 9	September 10	September 24
November 6	October 8	October 14
December 4	November 5	November 12
2011		
January 22	December 23	December 29
March 12	February 11	February 17
May 7	April 8	April 14
June 4	May 6	May 12

*Check the College Board's website (*www.collegeboard.com*) periodically for updates and additional information.

Countdown to the SAT

The day before you take the test, don't do practice tests. Do look over all the tactics listed below so they will be fresh in your mind.

BEFORE THE TEST

If the test location is unfamiliar to you, drive there before the test day so that you will know exactly where you're going on the day you take the test.

Set out your test kit the night before. You will need your admission ticket, a photo ID (a driver's license or a non-driver picture ID, a passport, or a school ID), your calculator, four or five sharp No. 2 pencils (with erasers), plus a map or directions showing how to get to the test center.

Get a good night's sleep so you are well rested and alert.

Wear comfortable clothes. Dress in layers. Bring a sweater in case the room is cold.

Bring an accurate watch—not one that beeps—in case the room has no clock. You'll want to use the same watch or small clock that you've been using during your practice sessions.

Bring a small snack for quick energy.

Don't be late. Allow plenty of time for getting to the test site. You want to be in your seat, relaxed, before the test begins.

DURING THE TEST

First answer all the easy questions; then tackle the hard ones if you have time.

Remember which sorts of questions you do well on. Aim for them.

Pace yourself. Don't work so fast that you start making careless errors. On the other hand, don't get bogged down on any one question.

Feel free to skip back and forth between questions within a section.

Play the percentages: guess whenever you can eliminate one or more of the answers.

Make educated guesses, not random ones. As a rule, don't fill in answers when you haven't even looked at the questions.

Watch out for eye-catchers, answer choices that are designed to tempt you into guessing wrong.

Change answers only if you have a reason for doing so; don't change them on a last-minute hunch or whim.

Check your assumptions. Make sure you are answering the question asked and not the one you *thought* was going to be asked.

Remember that you are allowed to write anything you want in your test booklet. Make full use of it.

- Do math calculations and draw diagrams.
- Underline key words in reading passages and sentence completions.

- Cross out answer choices you are *sure* are wrong.
- Circle questions you want to come back to.

Be careful not to make any stray marks on your answer sheet. The test is graded by a machine, and a machine cannot always tell the difference between an accidental mark and an intentionally filled-in answer.

Check frequently to make sure you are answering the questions in the right spots.

Remember that you don't have to answer every question to do well.

TIPS FOR THE CRITICAL READING QUESTIONS

Read all the answer choices before you decide which is best.

Think of a context for an unfamiliar word; the context may help you come up with the word's meaning.

Break down unfamiliar words into recognizable parts—prefixes, suffixes, roots.

Consider secondary meanings of words. If none of the answer choices seems right to you, take another look. A word may have more than one meaning.

Sentence Completion Questions

First, read the sentence carefully to get a feel for its meaning.

Before you look at the choices, think of a word that makes sense.

Watch for words that signal a contrast (*but, although, however*) or indicate the continuation of a thought (*also, additionally, besides, furthermore*). These signal words are clues that can help you figure out what a sentence actually means.

Look for words that signal the unexpected, such as *abnormal, illogical,* and *ironic.* These words indicate that something unexpected, possibly even unwanted, exists or has occurred.

In double-blank sentences, test one blank at a time, not two.

Reading Passage Questions

When you have a choice, tackle reading passages with familiar subjects before passages with unfamiliar ones.

Make use of the introductions to acquaint yourself with the text.

Read as rapidly as you can with understanding, but do not force yourself.

As you read the opening sentence, try to predict what the passage is about.

When you tackle the questions, use any line references given to help in the passage.

Base your answer only on what is written in the passage, not on what you know from other books or courses.

In answering questions on the long paired reading passages, first read one passage and answer the questions based on it; then read the second passage and tackle the remaining questions.

Try to answer *all* the questions on a particular passage.

TIPS FOR THE MATHEMATICS QUESTIONS

Whenever you know how to answer a question directly, just do it. The tactics that are reviewed below should be used only when you need them.

Memorize all the formulas you need to know. Even though some of them are printed on the first page of each math section, during the test you do not want to waste any time referring to that reference material.

Be sure to bring a calculator, but use it only when you need it. Don't use it for simple arithmetic that you can easily do in your head.

Remember that no problem requires lengthy or difficult computations. If you find yourself doing a lot of arithmetic, stop and reread the question. You are probably not answering the question asked.

Answer every question you attempt. Even if you can't solve it, you can almost always eliminate two or more choices. Often you know that an answer must be negative, but two or three of the choices are positive, or an answer must be even, and some of the choices are odd.

Unless a diagram is labeled "<u>Note</u>: Figure not drawn to scale," it is perfectly accurate, and you can trust it in making an estimate.

When a diagram has not been provided, draw one, especially on a geometry problem.

If a diagram has been provided, feel free to label it, and mark it up in any way, including adding line segments, if necessary.

Answer any question for which you can estimate the answer, even if you are not sure you are correct.

Don't panic when you see a strange symbol in a question; it will always be defined. Getting the correct answer just involves using the information given in the definition.

When a question involves two equations, either add them or subtract them. If there are three or more, just add them.

Never make unwarranted assumptions. Do not assume numbers are positive or integers. If a question refers to two numbers, do not assume that they have to be different. If you know a figure has four sides, do not assume that it is a rectangle.

Be sure to work in consistent units. If the width and length of a rectangle are 8 inches and 2 feet, respectively, either convert the 2 feet to 24 inches or the 8 inches to two-thirds of a foot before calculating the area or perimeter.

Standard Multiple-Choice Questions

Whenever you answer a question by backsolving, start with Choice C.

When you replace variables with numbers, choose easy-to-use numbers, whether or not they are realistic.

Choose appropriate numbers. The best number to use in percent problems is 100. In problems involving fractions, the best number to use is the least common denominator.

When you have no idea how to solve a problem, eliminate all of the absurd choices and guess.

Student-Produced Response (Grid-in) Questions

Write your answer in the four spaces at the top of the grid, and *carefully* grid in your answer below. No credit is given for a correct answer if it has been gridded improperly.

Remember that the answer to a grid-in question can never be negative.

You can never grid in a mixed number—you must convert it to an improper fraction or a decimal.

Never round off your answers. If a fraction can fit in the four spaces of the grid, enter it. If not, use your calculator to convert it to a decimal (by dividing) and enter a decimal point followed by the first three decimal digits.

When gridding a decimal, do not write a zero before the decimal point.

If a question has more than one possible answer, grid in only one of them.

There is no penalty for wrong answers on grid-in questions, so you should grid in anything that seems reasonable, rather than omit a question.

TIPS FOR THE WRITING SKILLS QUESTIONS

Read all the answer choices before you decide which is correct.

Use your ear for the language to help you decide whether something is wrong.

Pay particular attention to the shorter answer choices. Good prose is economical. Often the correct answer choice will be the shortest, most direct way of making a point.

Remember that not every sentence contains an error or needs to be improved.

Identifying Sentence Error Questions

First read the sentence to get a feel for its structure and sense.

Remember that the error, if there is one, must be in an underlined part of the sentence.

Look first for the most common errors (lack of subject–verb agreement, pronoun–antecedent problems, faulty diction, incorrect verb tense).

Improving Sentence Questions

If you immediately spot an error in the underlined section, eliminate any answer choice that also contains the error.

If you don't spot an error in the underlined section, look at the answer choices to see what is changed in each one. The nature of the changes may reveal what kind of error is present.

Make sure that all parts of the sentence are logically connected.

Make sure that all sentence parts arranged as a series are similar in form. If they are not, the sentence suffers from a lack of parallel structure.

Improving Paragraph Questions

First read the passage; then read the questions.

First tackle the questions that ask you to improve individual sentences; then tackle the ones that ask you to strengthen the passage as a whole.

Consider whether the addition of signal words or phrases—transitions—would strengthen the passage or particular sentences within it.

When you tackle the questions, *go back to the passage* to verify each answer choice.

Tips for the Essay

First, read and re-read the prompt with care. Be sure you understand the topic.

Decide on your thesis, the main point you want to make.

Pace yourself: keep to your essay-writing plan.

Allow yourself 4 minutes *at most* for pre-writing and outlining.

Keep careful track of your time. Allow yourself time to come to a conclusion.

Write as legibly as you can.

Length counts: write as much as you can (while still making sense) within the allotted time.

Follow traditional essay-writing conventions. Write 4 to 5 paragraphs. Indent them. Use transitions.

Upgrade your vocabulary judiciously. Avoid throwing in big words that you don't understand.

Acknowledgments

The authors gratefully acknowledge the following copyright holders for permission to reprint material used in the reading passages.

Page 6: From *A Handbook to Literature* by C. Hugh Holman, ©1995. Reprinted by permission of Prentice Hall, Inc.

Pages 37–38: "Introduction" from *Bury My Heart at Wounded Knee: An Indian History of the American West* by Dee Brown ©1970 by Dee Brown. Reprinted by arrangement with Henry Holt and Company, LLC.

Page 52: From *Black Boy* by Richard Wright. Copyright 1937, 1942, 1944, 1945 by Richard Wright; renewed © 1973 by Ellen Wright. Reprinted by permission of HarperCollins Publishers.

Page 53: Excerpt from pp. 17–19 from *King Solomon's Ring* by Konrad Z. Lorenz. Copyright ©1952 by Harper & Row, Publishers, Inc. Reprinted with permission of HarperCollins Publishers.

Page 60: From "Let's Say You Wrote Badly This Morning" in *The Writing Habit* by David Huddle, ©1989, 1994 University Press of New England, Lebanon, NH. Reprinted with permission. Page 47.

Pages 60–61: From "My Two One-Eyed Coaches" by George Garrett. © Copyright George Garrett. Originally published in the *Virginia Quarterly Review,* Spring 1987, Vol. 63, No. 2.

Pages 120–121: Excerpt from pp. 42–4 from *Summer of '49* by David Halberstam. Copyright ©1989 by David Halberstam. Reprinted by permission of HarperCollins Publishers, William Morrow.

Page 121: From *Take Time For Paradise* ©1989 by the Estate of A. Bartlett Giamatti. Reprinted by permission of Estate of A. Bartlett Giamatti.

Page 130: From *Sculpture/Inuit,* ©1971. Reprinted with permission of the Canadian Eskimo Arts Council and James Houston.

Page 133: From "Renaissance to Modern Tapestries in the Metropolitan Museum of Art" in the *Metropolitan Museum of Art Bulletin*, Spring 1987, by Edith Appleton Standen, copyright ©1987 by the Metropolitan Museum of Art. Reprinted courtesy of the Metropolitan Museum of Art.

Page 135: From "African Sculpture Speaks," by Ladislas Segy, ©1958 by permission of Dover Publications.

Pages 135–136: From "Yonder Peasant, Who Is He?" in *Memories of a Catholic Girlhood,* ©1948 and renewed 1975 by Mary McCarthy. Reprinted with permission by Houghton Mifflin Harcourt Publishing Company.

Page 136: From *Reinventing Womanhood* by Caroline G. Heilbrun. Copyright ©1979 by Carolyn G. Heilbrun. Used by permission of W. W. Norton & Co., Inc.

Page 640: Excerpts from pp. 119, 123–6 from *Teaching a Stone to Talk: Expeditions and Encounters* by Annie Dillard. Copyright ©1982 by Annie Dillard. Reprinted by permission of HarperCollins Publishers.

Page 654: From *The Waning of the Middle Ages* by J. Huizinga. Reprinted with permission of Edward Arnold.

Page 655: From *Hunger of Memory: The Education of Richard Rodriguez* by Richard Rodriguez. Reprinted by permission of David R. Godine, Publisher, Inc. Copyright ©1982 by Richard Rodriguez.

Page 662: From "The Guilty Vicarage," copyright 1948 by W.H. Auden, from *The Dyer's Hand and Other Essays* by W.H. Auden. Used by permission of Random House, Inc.

Pages 662–663: From *Modus Operandi: An Excursion into Detective Fiction* by Robin W. Winks, ©1982, pp. 118–119. Reprinted by permission of Robin W. Winks.

Pages 712–713: From *Athabasca* by Alistair MacLean. Copyright ©1980 by Alistair MacLean. Used by permission of Doubleday, a division of Random House, Inc.

Page 714: From *The Uses of Enchantment* by Bruno Bettelheim. Copyright ©1975, 1976 by Bruno

ON THE CD-ROM
Practice Test 1

Practice Test 2

PART ONE

GET ACQUAINTED
WITH THE SAT

Introduction:
Let's Look at the SAT

- **What Is the SAT?**
- **The Critical Reading Sections**
- **The Mathematics Sections**
- **The Use of Calculators on the SAT**
- **The Writing Skills Sections**
- **Winning Tactics for the SAT**

WHAT IS THE SAT?

The SAT is a standardized exam that most high school students take before applying for college. Genereally, students take the SAT for the first time as high school juniors. If they do very well, they are through. If they want to try to boost their scores, they can take the test a second or even a third time.

The SAT tests you in three areas: reading, writing, and mathematical reasoning. As a result, each time you take the test you get three separate scores: a critical reading score, a writing score, and a math score. Each of these scores will fall somewhere between 200 and 800. For all three tests, the median score is 500: about 50 percent of all students score below 500 and about 50 percent score 500 or above. In talking about their results, students often add the three scores and say, "Ron got a 1560," or "Hermione got a 2400." (Total scores range from 600 to 2400, with a median of about 1500.)

WHAT IS SCORE CHOICE?

In 2009, the College Board instituted a Score Choice policy for the SAT. Now, you may be able to take the SAT as many times as you want, receive your scores, and then choose which scores the colleges to which you eventually apply will see. In fact, you don't have to make that choice until your senior year when you actually send in your college applications.

Here's How Score Choice Works

Suppose you take the SAT in May of your junior year and again in October of your senior year, and your October scores are higher than your May scores. Through Score Choice you can send the colleges only your October scores; not only will the colleges *not* see your May scores, they won't even know that you took the test in May. The importance of the Score Choice policy is that it can significantly lessen your anxiety anytime you take the SAT. If you have a bad day

---

HOW DO I SIGN UP TO TAKE THE SAT?

Online: Go to *www.collegeboard.com*
   Have available your social security number and/or date of birth.
   Pay with a major credit card.
   Note: If you are signing up for Sunday testing, or if you have a visual, hearing, or learning disability and plan to sign up for the Services for Students with Disabilities Program, you *cannot* register online. You must register by mail well in advance.

By mail: Get a copy of the SAT Program Registration Bulletin from your high school guidance office or from the College Board. (Write to College Board SAT, P.O. Box 6200, Princeton, NJ 08541-6200, or phone the College Board office in Princeton at 866-756-7346.)
   Pay by check, money order, fee waiver, or credit card.

CAUTION

Some colleges allow you to use Score Choice; others do not. Some want to see all of your scores. Be sure to go to *http://sat.collegeboard.com/register/sat-score-choice* to check the score-use policy of the colleges to which you hope to apply.

when you take the SAT for the first time, and your scores aren't as high as you had hoped, relax: you can retake it at a later date, and if your scores improve, you will never have to report the lower scores. Even if you do very well the first time you take the SAT, you can still retake it in an attempt to earn even higher scores. If your scores do improve, terrific—those are the scores you will report. If your scores happen to go down, don't worry—you can send only your original scores to the colleges and they will never even know that you retook the test. In fact, you can take the test more than twice. No matter how many times you take the SAT, because of Score Choice, you can send in only the scores that you want the colleges to see.

CHECKLIST: WHAT SHOULD I BRING TO THE TEST CENTER?

- ☐ admission ticket
- ☐ photo ID (driver's license, passport, official school photo ID)
- ☐ calculator (*Note*: Check the batteries the day before!)
- ☐ 4 or 5 sharpened No. 2 pencils (with erasers)
- ☐ wristwatch or small clock (*not* one that beeps!)
- ☐ map and directions to the test center
- ☐ sweater
- ☐ a drink and a small snack for quick energy

WHAT IS THE FORMAT OF THE SAT?

The SAT is a 4-hour plus exam divided into ten sections; but because you should arrive a little early and because time is required to pass out materials, read instructions, collect the test, and give you two 10-minute breaks between sections, you should assume that you will be in the testing room for 4½ to 5 hours.

Although the SAT contains ten sections, your scores will be based on only nine of them: five 25-minute multiple-choice sections (two math, two critical reading, and one writing skills); two 20-minute multiple-choice sections (one math and one critical reading); one 10-minute multiple-choice section (writing skills); and one 25-minute essay-writing section. The tenth section is an additional 25-minute multiple-choice section that may be on math, critical reading, or writing skills. It is what ETS calls an "equating" section, but most people call it the "experimental" section. ETS uses it to test new questions for use on future exams. However, because this section typically is identical in format to one of the other sections, you have no way of knowing which section is the experimental one, and so you must do your best on all ten sections.

THE CRITICAL READING SECTIONS

There are two types of questions on the critical reading portion of the SAT: sentence completion questions and reading comprehension questions.

Examples of each type appear in this chapter. Later, in Chapters 1 and 2, you will learn important strategies for handling both types. The 67 sentence completion and reading comprehension questions are divided into three sections, each of which has its own format. Below is one typical format for the SAT. You should expect to see something like the following on your test, although not necessarily in this order:

24-Question Critical Reading Section
Questions 1–8	sentence completion
Questions 9–12	reading comprehension (short passages)
Questions 13–24	reading comprehension (long passage)

24-Question Critical Reading Section
Questions 1–5	sentence completion
Questions 6–9	reading comprehension (short passages)
Questions 10–24	reading comprehension (long passages)

19-Question Critical Reading Section
Questions 1–6	sentence completion
Questions 7–19	reading comprehension (long passages)

As you see, most of the critical reading questions on the SAT directly test your reading skills.

Pay particular attention to how the sections described above are organized. These sections contain groups of sentence completion questions arranged roughly in order of difficulty: they start out with easy warm-up questions and get more difficult as they go along. The critical reading questions, however, are not arranged in order of difficulty. Instead, they follow the organization of the passage on which they are based: questions about material found early in the passage precede questions about material occurring later. This information can help you pace yourself during the test.

Here are examples of the specific types of critical reading questions you can expect.

NOTE

If the 25-minute experimental section on your SAT is a critical reading section, it will follow exactly the same format as one of the two 25-minute sections described above. Since, however, there will be no way for you to know which one of the 25-minute critical reading sections on your test is experimental, *you must do your best on each one.*

Sentence Completions

Sentence completion questions ask you to fill in the blanks. In each case, your job is to find the word or phrase that best completes the sentence and conveys its meaning.

> **Directions:** Choose the word or set of words that, when inserted in the sentence, *best* fits the meaning of the sentence as a whole.

> Brown, this biography suggests, was an _____ employer, giving generous bonuses one day, ordering pay cuts the next.
>
> (A) indifferent
> (B) objective
> (C) unpredictable
> (D) ineffectual
> (E) unobtrusive

Note how the phrases immediately following the word *employer* give you an idea of Brown's character and help you select the missing word. Clearly, someone who switches back and forth in this manner would be a difficult employer, but the test-makers want the *precise* word that characterizes Brown's arbitrary behavior.

Insert the different answer choices in the sentence to see which make the most sense.

(A) Was Brown an indifferent (uncaring or mediocre) employer? Not necessarily: he may or may not have cared about what sort of job he did.

(B) Was Brown an objective (fair and impartial) employer? You don't know: you have no information about his fairness and impartiality.

(C) Was Brown an unpredictable employer? Definitely. A man who gives bonuses one day and orders pay cuts the next clearly is *unpredictable*—no one can tell what he's going to do next. The correct answer appears to be Choice C.

To confirm your answer, check the remaining two choices.

(D) Was Brown an ineffectual (weak and ineffective) employer. Not necessarily: though his employees probably disliked not knowing from one day to the next how much pay they would receive, he still may have been an effective boss.

(E) Was Brown an unobtrusive (hardly noticeable; low-profile) employer? You don't know: you have no information about his visibility in the company.

The best answer definitely is Choice C.

Sometimes sentence completion questions contain two blanks rather than one. In answering these double-blank sentences, you must be sure that *both words* in your answer choice make sense in the original sentence.

For a complete discussion of all the tactics used in handling sentence completion questions, turn to Chapter 1.

Reading Comprehension

Critical reading questions ask about a passage's main idea or specific details, the author's attitude to the subject, the author's logic and techniques, the implications of the discussion, or the meaning of specific words.

> **Directions:** The passage below is followed by questions based on its content. Answer the questions on the basis of what is *stated* or *implied* in that passage.

Certain qualities common to the sonnet should be noted. Its definite restrictions make it a challenge to the artistry of the poet and call for all the technical skill at the poet's command. The more or less set rhyme pat-
Line terns occurring regularly within the short space of fourteen lines afford a
(5) pleasant effect on the ear of the reader, and can create truly musical effects. The rigidity of the form precludes too great economy or too great prodigality of words. Emphasis is placed on exactness and perfection of expression. The brevity of the form favors concentrated expression of ideas or passion.

1. The author's primary purpose is to

    (A) contrast different types of sonnets
    (B) criticize the limitations of the sonnet
    (C) identify the characteristics of the sonnet
    (D) explain why the sonnet has lost popularity as a literary form
    (E) encourage readers to compose formal sonnets

NOTE

Even if you felt uneasy about eliminating all four of these incorrect answer choices, you should have been comfortable eliminating two or three of them. Thus, even if you were not absolutely sure of the correct answer, you would have been in an excellent position to guess.

The first question asks you to find the author's main idea. In the opening sentence, the author says certain qualities of the sonnet should be noted. In other words, he intends to call attention to certain of its characteristics, identifying them. The correct answer is Choice C.

You can eliminate the other answers with ease. The author is upbeat about the sonnet: he doesn't say that the sonnet has limitations or that it has become less popular. You can eliminate Choices B and D.

Similarly the author doesn't mention any different types of sonnets; therefore, he cannot be contrasting them. You can eliminate Choice A.

And although the author talks about the challenge of composing formal sonnets, he never invites his readers to try to write them. You can eliminate Choice E.

2. The word "afford" in line 4 means

    (A) initiate
    (B) exaggerate
    (C) are able to pay for
    (D) change into
    (E) provide

NOTE

Because you can eliminate at least one of the answer choices, you are in a good position to guess the correct answer to this question.

The second question asks you to figure out a word's meaning from its context. Substitute each of the answer choices in the original sentence and see which word or phrase makes most sense. Some make no sense at all: the rhyme patterns that the reader hears certainly are not *able to pay for* any pleasant effect. You can definitely eliminate Choice C. What is it exactly that these rhyme patterns do? The rhyme patterns have a pleasant effect on the ear of the listener; indeed, they *provide* (furnish or afford) this effect. The correct answer is Choice E.

3. The author's attitude toward the sonnet form can best be described as one of
   (A) amused toleration
   (B) grudging admiration
   (C) strong disapprobation
   (D) effusive enthusiasm
   (E) scholarly appreciation

The third question asks you to figure out how the author feels about his subject. All the author's comments about the sonnet are positive: he approves of this poetic form. You can immediately eliminate Choice C, *strong disapprobation* or disapproval.

You can also eliminate Choice A, *amused toleration* or forbearance: the author is not simply putting up with the sonnet form in a good-humored, somewhat patronizing way; he thinks well of it.

Choices B and D are somewhat harder to eliminate. The author does seem to admire the sonnet form. However, his admiration is unforced: it is not *grudging* or reluctant. You can eliminate Choice B. Likewise, the author is enthusiastic about the sonnet. However, he doesn't go so far as to gush: he's not *effusive*. You can eliminate Choice D.

The only answer that properly reflects the author's attitude is Choice E, *scholarly appreciation.*

See Chapter 2 for tactics that will help you handle the entire range of critical reading questions.

THE MATHEMATICS SECTIONS

There are two types of questions on the mathematics portion of the SAT: multiple-choice questions and grid-in questions.

Examples of both types appear in this chapter. Later, in Chapter 8, you will learn several important strategies for handling each type.

There are 54 math questions in all, divided into three sections, each of which has its own format. You should expect to see, although not necessarily in this order:

- a 25-minute section with 20 multiple-choice questions
- a 25-minute section with 8 multiple-choice questions followed by 10 student-produced response questions (grid-ins)
- a 20-minute section with 16 multiple-choice questions

> **NOTE**
>
> If the 25-minute experimental section on your SAT is a mathematics section, it will follow exactly the same format as one of the two 25-minute sections described at left. Since, however, there will be no way for you to know which section is experimental, you must do your best on each one.

> Within each of the three math sections, the questions are arranged in order of increasing difficulty. The first few multiple-choice questions are quite easy; they are followed by several of medium difficulty; and the last few are considered hard. The grid-ins also proceed from easy to difficult. As a result, the amount of time you spend on any one question will vary greatly.
>
> Note that, in the section that contains eight multiple-choice questions followed by ten grid-in questions, questions 7 and 8 are hard multiple-choice questions, whereas questions 9–11 and 12–15 are easy and medium grid-in questions, respectively. Therefore, for many students, it is advisable to skip questions 7 and 8 and to move on to the easy and medium grid-in questions.

Multiple-Choice Questions

On the SAT, all but 10 of the questions are multiple-choice questions. Although you have certainly taken multiple-choice tests before, the SAT uses a few different types of questions, and you must become familiar with all of them. By far, the most common type of question is one in which you are asked to solve a problem. The straightforward way to answer such a question is to do the necessary work, get the solution, look at the five choices, and choose the one that corresponds to your answer. In Chapter 8 other techniques for answering these questions are discussed, but now let's look at a couple of examples.

EXAMPLE 1

What is the average (arithmetic mean) of all the even integers between –5 and 7?

(A) 0   (B) $\frac{5}{6}$ (C) 1   (D) $\frac{6}{5}$ (E) 3

To solve this problem requires only that you know how to find the average of a set of numbers. Ignore the fact that this is a multiple-choice question. *Don't even look at the choices.*

- List the even integers whose average you need: –4, –2, 0, 2, 4, 6. (Be careful not to leave out 0, which *is* an even integer.)
- Calculate the average by adding the six integers and dividing by 6.

$$\frac{(-4)+(-2)+0+2+4+6}{6} = \frac{6}{6} = \mathbf{1}.$$

- Having found the average to be 1, look at the five choices, see that 1 is Choice C, and blacken **C** on your answer sheet.

EXAMPLE 2

A necklace is formed by stringing 133 colored beads on a thin wire in the following order: red, orange, yellow, green, blue, indigo, violet; red, orange, yellow, green, blue, indigo, violet. If this pattern continues, what will be the color of the 101st bead on the string?

(A) Orange   (B) Yellow   (C) Green   (D) Blue   (E) Indigo

Again, you are not helped by the fact that the question, which is less a test of your arithmetic skills than of your ability to reason, is a multiple-choice question. You need to determine the color of the 101st bead, and then select the choice that matches your answer.

The seven colors keep repeating in exactly the same order.

Color: red orange yellow green blue indigo violet

Bead
number: 1   2   3   4   5   6   7

          8   9   10   11   12   13   14 etc.

- The violet beads are in positions 7, 14, 21, . . . , 70, . . . , that is, the multiples of 7.
- If 101 were a multiple of 7, the 101st bead would be violet.
- But when 101 is divided by 7, the quotient is 14 and the remainder is 3.
- Since $14 \times 7 = 98$, the 98th bead completes the 14th cycle, and hence is violet.
- The 99th bead starts the next cycle; it is red. The 100th bead is orange, and the 101st bead is yellow.
- The answer is **B.**

In contrast to Examples 1 and 2, some questions *require* you to look at all five choices in order to find the answer. Consider Example 3.

> **NOTE**
>
> Did you notice that the solution didn't use the fact that the necklace consisted of 133 beads? This is unusual; occasionally, but not often, a problem contains information you don't need.

EXAMPLE 3

If a and b are both odd integers, which of the following could be an odd integer?

(A) $a + b$ (B) $a^2 + b^2$ (C) $(a + 1)^2 + (b - 1)^2$

(D) $(a + 1)(b - 1)$ (E) $\dfrac{a+1}{b-1}$

The words *Which of the following* alert you to the fact that you will have to examine each of the five choices to determine which one satisfies the stated condition, in this case that the quantity *could* be odd. Check each choice.

- The sum of two odd integers is always even. Eliminate A.
- The square of an odd integer is odd; so a^2 and b^2 are each odd, and their sum is even. Eliminate B.
- Since a and b are odd, $(a + 1)$ and $(b - 1)$ are even; so $(a + 1)^2$ and $(b - 1)^2$ are also even, as is their sum. Eliminate C.
- The product of two even integers is even. Eliminate D.
- Having eliminated A, B, C, and D, you know that *the answer must be* E. Check to be sure:

  $\dfrac{a+1}{b-1}$ need not even be an integer (e.g., if $a = 1$ and $b = 5$), but it *could be*. For example, if $a = 3$ and $b = 5$, then

$$\frac{a+1}{b-1} = \frac{3+1}{5-1} = \frac{4}{4} = 1,$$

which *is* an odd integer. The answer is **E**.

Another kind of multiple-choice question that appears on the SAT is the Roman numeral-type question. These questions actually consist of three statements labeled I, II, and III. The five answer choices give various possibilities for which statement or statements are true. Here is a typical example.

EXAMPLE 4

If x is negative, which of the following *must* be true?

$$\text{I. } x^3 < x^2$$

$$\text{II. } x + \frac{1}{x} < 0$$

$$\text{III. } x = \sqrt{x^2}$$

(A) I only   (B) II only   (C) I and II only
(D) II and III only   (E) I, II, and III

- To solve this problem, examine each statement independently to determine if it is true or false.

  I. If x is negative, then x^3 is negative and so must be less than x^2, which is positive. (I is true.)

  II. If x is negative, so is $\dfrac{1}{x}$, and the sum of two negative numbers is negative. (II is true.)

  III. The square root of a number is *never* negative, and so $\sqrt{x^2}$ could not possibly equal x. (III is false.)

- Only I and II are true. The answer is **C.**

NOTE

You should almost never leave out a Roman numeral-type question. Even if you can't solve the problem completely, there should be *at least one* of the three Roman numeral statements that you *know* to be true or false. On the basis of that information, you should be able to eliminate two or three of the answer choices. For instance, in Example 4, if all you know for sure is that statement I is true, you can eliminate choices B and D. Similarly, if all you know is that statement III is false, you can eliminate choices D and E. Then, as you will learn, you *must* guess between the remaining choices.

Grid-in Questions

Ten of the mathematics questions on the SAT are what the College Board calls student-produced response questions. Since the answers to these questions are entered on a special grid, they are usually referred to as *grid-in* questions. Except for the method of entering your answer, this type of question is probably the one with which you are most familiar. In your math class, most of your homework problems and test questions require you to determine an answer and write it down, and this is what you will do on the grid-in problems. The only difference is that, once you have figured out an answer, it must be recorded on a special grid, such as the one shown at the right, so that it can be read by a computer. Here is a typical grid-in question.

EXAMPLE 5

At the diner, John ordered a sandwich for $3.95 and a soda for 85¢. A sales tax of 5% was added to his bill, and he left the waitress a $1 tip. What was the total cost, in dollars, of John's lunch?

- Calculate the cost of the food: $3.95 + $0.85 = $4.80
- Calculate the tax (5% of $4.80): .05 × $4.80 = $0.24
- Add the cost of the food, tax, and tip: $4.80 + $0.24 + $1.00 = $6.04

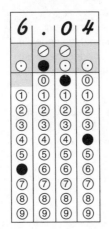

To enter this answer, you write 6.04 (*without* the dollar sign) in the four spaces at the top of the grid, and blacken the appropriate oval under each space. In the first column, under the 6, you blacken the oval marked 6; in the second column, under the decimal point, you blacken the oval with the decimal point; in the third column, under the 0, you blacken the oval marked 0; and, finally, in the fourth column, under the 4, you blacken the oval marked 4.

Always read each grid-in question very carefully. Example 5 might have asked for the total cost of John's lunch *in cents.* In that case, the correct answer would have been 604, which would be gridded in, without a decimal point, using only three of the four columns (see below).

Note that the only symbols that appear in the grid are the digits from 0 to 9, a decimal point, and a fraction bar (/). The grid does not have a minus sign, so *answers to grid-in problems can never be negative.* In Introduction to the Math Sections, in Part Three, you will learn some important tactics for answering grid-in questions and will be able to practice filling in grids. You will also learn the special rules concerning the proper way to grid in fractions, mixed numbers, and decimals that won't fit in the grid's four columns. When you take the diagnostic test, just enter your answers to the grid-in questions exactly as was done in Example 5.

> **NOTE**
>
> Any multiple-choice question whose answer is a positive number less than 10,000 could be a grid-in question. If Example 1 had been a grid-in question, you would have solved it in exactly the same way: you would have determined that the average of the six numbers is 1; but then, instead of looking for 1 among the five choices, you would have entered the number 1 on a grid. The mathematics is no harder on grid-in questions than on multiple-choice questions. However, if you don't know how to solve a problem correctly, it is harder to guess at the right answer, since there are no choices to eliminate.

CALCULATOR TIPS

- Bring a calculator to the test: it's not required, but it sometimes can help.

- *Don't* buy a new calculator the night before the SAT. If you need one, *buy one now* and become familiar with it. Do all the practice exams in this book with the calculator you plan to take to the test—probably the same calculator you use in school.

- The College Board recommends a scientific calculator with parentheses keys, ( ); a reciprocal key, $\frac{1}{x}$; and an exponent key, y or ^.

- Use your calculator when you *need* to; ignore it when you don't. Most students use calculators more than they should. You can solve many problems without doing *any* calculations—mental, written, or calculator-assisted.

- Throughout this book, the icon [calculator icon] will be placed next to a problem where the use of a calculator is recommended. As you will see, this judgment is subjective. Sometimes a question can be answered in a few seconds, with no calculations whatsoever, *if* you see the best approach. In that case, the use of a calculator is not recommended. If you don't see the easy way, however, and have to do some arithmetic, you may prefer to use a calculator.

- No SAT problem ever requires a lot of tedious calculation. However, if you don't see how to avoid calculating, just do it—*don't spend a lot of time looking for a shortcut that will save you a little time!*

THE WRITING SKILLS SECTIONS

There are three types of questions on the writing skills section of the SAT:

1. Improving sentences
2. Identifying sentence errors
3. Improving paragraphs

Examples of each type of question appear in this section. Later, in Chapter 6, you will find some tips on how to handle each one.

The writing skills section on your test will contain 49 questions. The two sections break down as follows:

35-Question Writing Skills Section (25 minutes)

Questions 1–11   Improving sentences
Questions 12–29   Identifying sentence errors
Questions 30–35   Improving paragraphs

14-Question Writing Skills Section (10 minutes)

Questions 1–14   Improving sentences

Here are examples of the specific types of writing skills questions you can expect.

Identifying Sentence Errors

Identifying sentence errors questions ask you to spot something wrong. Your job is to find the error in the sentence, not to fix it.

> **Directions:** These sentences may contain errors in grammar, usage, choice of words, or idioms. Either there is just one error in a sentence or the sentence is correct. Some words or phrases are underlined and lettered; everything else in the sentence is correct.
>
> If an underlined word or phrase is incorrect, choose that letter; if the sentence is correct, select <u>No error</u>.

Example:

After the incident was over, <u>neither</u> the passengers nor the bus driver
  A   B

<u>were</u> able to identify the youngster who <u>had created</u> the disturbance.
 C   D

<u>No error</u>
 E

The error here is lack of agreement between the subject and the verb. In a *neither-nor* construction, the verb agrees in number with the noun or pronoun that comes immediately before it. Here, the noun that immediately precedes the verb is the singular noun *driver.* Therefore, the correct verb form is the singular verb *was.* The error is in C.

Improving Sentences

Improving sentences questions ask you to spot the form of a sentence that works best. Your job is to select the most effective version of a sentence.

> **Directions:** Some or all parts of the following sentences are underlined. The first answer choice, (A), simply repeats the underlined part of the sentence. The other four choices present four alternative ways to phrase the underlined part. Select the answer choice that produces the most effective sentence, one that is clear and exact.

Example:

<u>Walking out the hotel door, the Danish village with its charming stores and bakeries beckons you to enjoy a memorable day.</u>

- (A) Walking out the hotel door, the Danish village with its charming stores and bakeries beckons you to enjoy a memorable day.
- (B) Walking out the hotel door, the Danish village with its charming stores and bakeries is beckoning you to enjoy a memorable day.
- (C) While you were walking out the hotel door, the Danish village with its charming stores and bakeries beckons you to enjoy a memorable day.
- (D) As you walk out the hotel door, the Danish village with its charming stores and bakeries beckons you to enjoy a memorable day.
- (E) Walking out the hotel door, the Danish village with its charming stores and bakeries beckon you to enjoy a memorable day.

The underlined sentence begins with a participial phrase, *Walking out the hotel door.* In such cases, be on the lookout for a possible dangling modifier. A dangling participial phrase is a phrase that does not refer clearly to another word in the sentence. Ask yourself who or what is walking out the hotel door. Certainly not the village! To improve the sentence, you must fix the dangling modifier, replacing the initial participial phrase with a clause. Both Choices C and D do so. However, Choice C introduces an error involving the sequence of tenses: the verb *were walking* is in the past tense, not the present. Only Choice D corrects the dangling participial phrase without introducing any fresh errors. It is the correct answer.

To reach the answer above, you took a shortcut. You suspected the presence of a dangling participial phrase, focused on the two answer choices that replaced the participial phrase *Walking out the hotel door* with different wording, and selected the answer choice that produced a clear, effective sentence. Even if you had not taken this shortcut, however, you could have figured out the correct answer by working your way through all the answer choices, noting any changes to the original sentence.

Improving Paragraphs

Improving paragraphs questions require you to correct the flaws in a student essay. Some questions involve rewriting or combining separate sentences to come up with a more effective wording. Other questions involve reordering sentences to produce a better organized argument.

> **Directions:** The passage below is the unedited draft of a student's essay. Parts of the essay need to be rewritten to make the meaning clearer and more precise. Read the essay carefully.
>
> The essay is followed by six questions about changes that might improve all or part of the organization, development, sentence structure, use of language, appropriateness to the audience, or use of standard written English. Choose the answer that most clearly and effectively expresses the student's intended meaning.

> **NOTE**
>
> Remember, this essay is a rough draft. It is likely to contain grammatical errors and awkward phrasing. Do not assume it is exemplary prose.

(1) This fall I am supposed to vote for the first time. (2) However, I do not know whether my vote will count. (3) Ever since the 2000 presidential election, I have been reading in the newspapers about problems in our voting system. (4) Some days I ask myself whether there is any point in me voting at all. (5) From the papers, I know our methods of counting votes are seriously flawed. (6) We use many different kinds of technology in voting, and none of them work perfectly. (7) And the newest method, electronic voting technology, is the worst of all.

Sentence 3 would make the most sense if placed after

(A) Sentence 1
(B) Sentence 4
(C) Sentence 5
(D) Sentence 6
(E) Sentence 7

The best way to improve this opening paragraph is to place sentence 3 immediately after sentence 4. The opening section would then read: *This fall I am supposed to vote for the first time. However, I do not know whether my vote will count. Some days I ask myself whether there is any point in me voting at all. Ever since the 2000 presidential election, I have been reading in the newspapers about problems in our voting system. From the papers, I know our methods of counting votes are seriously flawed.* Rewritten in this fashion, the paragraph moves from the general ("voting") to the specific ("problems in our voting system"). The student author is gradually introducing her topic, the problems inherent in today's electronic voting technology. Her opening paragraph still contains errors, but its organization is somewhat improved.

WINNING TACTICS FOR THE SAT

You now know the basic framework of the SAT. It's time for the big question: How can you become a winner on the SAT?

- First, you have to decide just what winning is for you. For one student, winning means breaking 1500; for another, only a total score of 2100 will do. Therefore, the first thing you have to do is set *your* goal.
- Second, you must learn to pace yourself during the test. You need to know how many questions to attempt to answer, how many to spend a little extra time on, and how many simply to skip.
- Third, you need to understand the rewards of guessing—how *educated guesses* can boost your scores dramatically. Educated guessing is a key strategy in helping you to reach your goal.

Here are your winning tactics for the SAT.

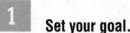

Set your goal.

Before you begin studying for the SAT, you need to set a realistic goal for yourself. Here's what to do.

1. Establish your **baseline score**. You need to know your math, critical reading, and writing scores on one actual PSAT or SAT to use as your starting point.

   - If you have already taken an SAT, use your actual scores from that test.
   - If you have already taken the PSAT but have not yet taken the SAT, use your most recent actual PSAT scores, adding a zero to the end of each score (55 on the PSAT = 550 on the SAT).
   - If you have not yet taken an actual PSAT or SAT, do the following:

     □ Go to: *http://www.collegeboard.com/student/testing/sat/prep_one/prep_one.html* and click on the link to the Official SAT Practice Test. Print a copy.

     OR

     Get a hard copy of the College Board's SAT preparation booklet from your school guidance office. (The online practice test and the test in the preparation booklet are the same.)

     □ Find a quiet place where you can work for 3¾ hours without interruptions.

     □ Take the SAT under true exam conditions:

     Time yourself on each section.
     Take no more than a 2-minute break between sections.
     After finishing three sections, take a 10-minute break.
     Take another 10-minute break after section 7.

     □ Follow the instructions to grade the test and convert your total raw scores on each part to a scaled score.

     □ Use these scores as your baseline.

2. Look up the average SAT scores for the most recent freshman class at each of the colleges to which you're applying. (College admissions offices have this information. You can find it online.) You want to beat that average, if you can.

3. Now **set your goals**. Challenge yourself, but be realistic. If you earned 470 on the critical reading portion of the PSAT, for example, you might like to get 700 on the SAT, but that's unrealistic. On the other hand, don't wimp out. Aim for 550, not 490.

General Guidelines for Setting Your Initial Goals

Current Score	Goal	Current Score	Goal
300	400	550	620
350	450	600	660
400	500	650	700
450	540	700	740
500	580	750	780

TACTIC

2   Know how many questions you should try to answer.

Why is it so important to set a goal? Why not just try to get the highest score you can by correctly answering as many questions as possible? The answer is that *your goal tells you how many questions you should try to answer.* The most common tactical error that students make is trying to answer too many questions. Therefore, surprising as it may be, the following statement is true for almost all students:

THE BEST WAY TO INCREASE YOUR SCORE ON THE SAT
IS TO ANSWER FEWER QUESTIONS.

Why is slowing down and answering fewer questions the best way to increase your score on the SAT? To understand that, you first need to know how the SAT is scored. There are two types of scores associated with the SAT: raw scores and scaled scores. First, three raw scores are calculated—one for each part of the test. Each raw score is then converted to a scaled score between 200 and 800. On the SAT, every question is worth exactly the same amount: 1 raw score point. You get no more credit for a correct answer to the hardest math question than you do for the easiest. For each question that you answer correctly, you receive 1 raw score point. For each multiple-choice question that you answer incorrectly, you lose ¼ point. Questions that you leave out have no effect on your score. On each of the SAT's three parts—Critical Reading, Math, and Writing Skills—the raw score is calculated as follows:

$$\text{\# of correct answers} - \frac{\text{\# of incorrect multiple-choice answers}}{4} = \text{Raw Score}$$

On every SAT, one math section has 20 multiple-choice questions. The questions in this section are presented in order of difficulty. Although this varies slightly from test to test, typically questions 1–6 are considered easy, questions 7–14 are considered medium, and questions 15–20 are considered hard. Even within the groups, the questions increase in difficulty: questions 7 and 14, for example, may both be ranked medium, but question 14 will definitely be harder than question 7. Of course, this depends slightly on each student's math skills. Some students might find question 8 or 9 or even 10 to be easier than question 7, but everyone will find questions 11 and 12 to be harder than questions 1 and 2, and questions 19 and 20 to be harder than questions 13 and 14.

However, all questions have the same value: 1 raw score point. You earn 1 point for a correct answer to question 1, which might take you only 15 seconds to solve, and 1 point for a correct answer to question 20, which might take 2 or 3 minutes to solve. Knowing that it will probably take at least 10 minutes to answer the last 5 questions, many students try to race through the first 15 questions in 15 minutes or less and, as a result, miss many questions that they could have answered correctly, had they slowed down.

Suppose a student rushed through questions 1–15 and got 9 right answers and 6 wrong ones and then worked on the 5 hardest questions and answered 2 more correctly and 3 more incorrectly. His raw score would be 8¾: 11 points for the 11 correct answers minus 2¼ points for the 9 wrong answers. Had he gone slowly and carefully, and not made any careless errors on the easy and medium questions, he might have run out of time and not even answered any of the 5 hardest questions at the end. But if spending all 25 minutes on the first 15 questions meant that he answered 13 correctly, 2 incorrectly, and omitted 5, his raw score would have been 12½. If he had a similar improvement on the other math sections, his raw score would have been about 10 points higher, an increase of approximately 80 SAT points.

In this hypothetical scenario, a student increased his score significantly by answering fewer questions, but eliminating careless errors.

Now, let's see how slowing down improved the scores of two actual students.

Student 1: John

Class standing: midrange
Grade point average: low 80s
Expected SAT score: 500s
Goal: 60th percentile

Here's how John did on the 25-minute math section with 20 questions.

Time Spent	Questions Answered	# Right	# Wrong
13 minutes	1–13	9	4
12 minutes	14–20	2	5

Total: 11 right, 9 wrong

Raw score: $11 - 2\dfrac{1}{4} = 8\dfrac{3}{4}$, which rounds off to 9

OUR ADVICE TO JOHN: Slow down. Don't even try the hard problems at the end of the section. Spend all 25 minutes on the first 13 questions so that you *avoid all careless mistakes*.

John then took another 20-question math section:

Time Spent	Questions Answered	# Right	# Wrong
25 minutes	1–13	12	1

Total: 12 right, 1 wrong

Raw score: $12 - \dfrac{1}{4} = 11\dfrac{3}{4}$, which rounds off to 12

John's raw score went up 3 points on just one section. Similar improvements in the other two math sections resulted in a total increase of 8 raw score points, which raised his math scaled score by 70 points.

OUTCOME: With practice, John learned he could get the first 13 questions right in about 21 minutes, rather than 25. He used his extra 4 minutes to work on just one or two of the remaining questions in the section, selecting questions he had the best chance of answering correctly. As a result, his math score improved by more than 100 points!

Student 2: Mary

Class standing: top 10–15%
Grade point average: low 90s
Junior year SAT math score: 710
Junior year SAT reading score: 620
Goal: 1400 total in reading and math

PROBLEMS:
• slow reader
• raced through sentence completions to have more time for reading passages
• skimmed some reading passages instead of reading them

OUR ADVICE TO MARY: Slow down. On the reading section with two long passages, skip the 5-question passage and focus on reading the 10-question passage slowly and carefully.

OUTCOME: At first, Mary strongly resisted the idea of leaving out questions on the SAT, but she agreed to take our advice. When she retook the SAT her senior year, she answered just 59 reading questions and left out 8. Mary's senior year reading score: 700.

What did John and Mary learn?

THE BEST WAY TO INCREASE YOUR SCORE ON THE SAT IS TO ANSWER FEWER QUESTIONS.

How many questions should *you* try to answer?

First, set your goal based on your original scores. For example, using the table on page 15, if your original reading score was 540, your goal should be 610.

Next, look at an actual SAT score conversion table on the College Board's web site or in its *Official SAT Study Guide*. Find the raw scores that correspond to your scaled score goals.

CRITICAL READING CONVERSION TABLE

Raw Score	Scaled Score
51	640
50	630
49	620
48	620
47	610
46	610
45	600
44	590
43	580
42	580

You need a raw score of about 46 to reach your goal of 600 in critical reading. One way to do that is to get 46 questions correct, and no questions wrong. But probably, even going slowly, you'll miss a few, so answer about 6 more.

How many reading questions should you answer?

$$46 + 6 = 52$$

Remember, for each question you answer incorrectly, you lose ¼ point. You need to answer 52 questions so that, even if you miss 5, your raw score will still be 46.

$$47 - \frac{5}{4} = 45\frac{3}{4} = 46 \text{ (rounded raw score)}$$

How does that work out for each of the three reading sections?

24-question critical reading sections   Try to answer 19 questions on each

19-question critical reading section   Try to answer 14 questions

$$19 + 19 + 14 = 52$$

TACTIC 3

Know how to pace yourself, section by section. Never get bogged down on any one question, and never rush.

Go quickly but carefully through the easy questions, slowly but steadily through the harder ones. Always keep moving.

Here is one pattern to follow:

20-Question Math Section (25 minutes total)

Questions 1–5	1 minute each
Questions 6–10	2 minutes each
Questions 11–14	2½ minutes each
Questions 15–20	Don't even read them!

Unless you are consistently getting at least 12 of the first 14 questions right, *do not go any faster.*

What if you finish all 14 questions in 22 or 23 minutes, and still have 2 or 3 minutes left? Here's what to do. Take 30 seconds to read questions 15 and 16. Quickly decide which one you have the better chance of getting right or making an educated guess on. Use your remaining time on that one question.

What if you finish all 14 questions in just 20 minutes, and have 5 minutes left? You have time to answer two more questions at most. Do *not* automatically try to answer questions 15 and 16. Take a quick look at the remaining questions and pick the 2 questions that *you* like best. It's like cherry-picking: pick the questions that look good to you. If you like geometry questions, try those. If you like algebra questions, try those instead. Skip around. Just be sure to mark your answer choices in the correct spots.

TACTIC

Know how to guess, and when.

The rule is, if you have worked on a problem and have eliminated even one of the choices, you *must* guess. This is what is called an *educated* guess. You are not guessing wildly, marking answers at random. You are working on the problem, ruling out answers that make no sense. The more choices you can rule out, the better your chance is of picking the right answer and earning one more point.

You should almost always be able to rule out some answer choices. Most math questions contain at least one or two answer choices that are absurd (for example, negative choices when you know the answer must be positive). In the critical reading section, once you have read a passage, you can always eliminate some of the answer choices. Cross out any choices that you *know* are incorrect, and go for that educated guess.

Unconvinced? If you are still not persuaded that educated guessing will work for you, turn to the end of this introduction for a detailed analysis of guessing on the SAT.

TACTIC

5

Keep careful track of your time.

Bring a watch. Even if there is a clock in the room, it is better for you to have a watch on your desk. Before you start each section, set your watch to 12:00. It is easier to know that a section will be over when your watch reads 12:25 than to have a section start at 9:37 and have to remember that it will be over at 10:02. Your job will be even easier if you have a digital stopwatch that you start at the beginning of each section; either let it count down to zero, or start it at zero and know that your time will be up after the allotted number of minutes.

TACTIC

6

Don't read the directions or look at the sample questions.

For each section of the SAT, the directions given in this book are identical to the directions you will see on your actual exam. Learn them now. Do not waste even a few seconds of your valuable test time reading them.

TACTIC

7

Remember, each question, easy or hard, is worth just 1 point.

Concentrate on questions that don't take you tons of time to answer.

TACTIC

8

Answer the easy questions first; then tackle the hard ones.

Because the questions in each section (except the critical reading questions) proceed from easy to hard, usually you should answer the questions in the order in which they appear.

9   Be aware of the difficulty level of each question.

Easy questions (the first few in each section or group) can usually be answered very quickly. Don't read too much into them. On these questions, your first hunch is probably right. Difficult questions (the last few in a section or group) usually require a bit of thought. On these questions, be wary of an answer that strikes you immediately. You may have made an incorrect assumption or fallen into a trap. Reread the question and check the other choices before answering too quickly.

10   Feel free to skip back and forth between questions within a section or group.

Remember that you're in charge. You don't have to answer everything in order. You should skip the hard sentence completions at the end and go straight to the reading questions on the next page. You can temporarily skip a question that's taking you too long and come back to it if you have time. Just be sure to mark your answers in the correct spot on the answer sheet.

11   Remember which sorts of questions you do well on. Aim for them.

As you go through the model tests, note which question types are best for you. Then, when you take the SAT, head for questions you are comfortable with. If you have time, you can always go back to the others.

12   In the critical reading and writing sections, read each choice before choosing your answer.

In comparison to math questions, which always have exactly one correct answer, critical reading questions are more subjective. You are looking for the *best* choice. Even if A or B looks good, check out the others; D or E may be better.

13   Fill in the answers on your answer sheet in blocks.

This is an important time-saving technique. For example, suppose that the first page of a math section has four questions. As you answer each question, circle the correct answer in your question book. Then, before going on to the next page, enter your four answers on your answer sheet. This is more efficient than moving back and forth between your question booklet and answer sheet after each question. This technique is particularly valuable on the critical reading sections, where entering your answer after each question may interrupt your train of thought about the passage.

CAUTION: When you get to the last two or three minutes of each section, enter your answers as you go. You don't want to be left with a block of questions that you have answered but not yet entered when the proctor announces that time is up.

Make sure that you answer the question asked.

Sometimes a math question requires you to solve an equation, but instead of asking for the value of x, the question asks for the value of x^2 or $x - 5$. Similarly, sometimes a critical reading question requires you to determine the LEAST likely outcome of an action; still another may ask you to find the exception to something, as in "The author uses all of the following EXCEPT." To avoid answering the wrong question, circle or underline what you have been asked for.

Base your answers only on the information provided— never on what you think you already know.

On critical reading questions, base your answers only on the material in the passage, not on what you think you know about the subject matter. On data interpretation questions, base your answers only on the information given in the chart or table.

Remember that you are allowed to write anything you want in your test booklet.

Circle questions you skip, and put big question marks next to questions you answer but are unsure about. If you have time left at the end, you want to be able to locate those questions quickly to go over them. In sentence completion questions, circle or underline key words such as *although, therefore,* and *not.* In reading passages, underline or put a mark in the margin next to any important point. On math questions, mark up diagrams, adding lines when necessary. And, of course, use all the space provided to solve the problem. In every section, math, reading, and writing, cross out every choice that you *know* is wrong. In short, write anything that will help you, using whatever symbols you like. But remember: the only thing that counts is what you enter on your answer sheet. No one but you will ever see anything that you write in your booklet.

Be careful not to make any stray pencil marks on your answer sheet.

The SAT is scored by a computer that cannot distinguish between an accidental mark and a filled-in answer. If the computer registers two answers where there should be only one, it will mark that question wrong.

Don't change answers capriciously.

If you have time to return to a question and realize that you made a mistake, by all means correct it, making sure you *completely* erase the first mark you made. However, don't change answers on a last-minute hunch or whim, or for fear you have chosen too many A's and not enough B's. In such cases, more often than not, students change right answers to wrong ones.

TACTIC

19

Use your calculator only when you need to.

Many students actually waste time using their calculators on questions that do not require them. Use your calculator whenever you feel it will help, but don't overuse it. And remember: no problem on the SAT requires lengthy, tedious calculations.

TACTIC

20

When you use your calculator, don't go too quickly.

Your calculator leaves no trail. If you accidentally hit the wrong button and get a wrong answer, you have no way to look at your work and find your mistake. You just have to do it all over.

TACTIC

21

Remember that you don't have to answer every question to do well.

You have learned about setting goals and pacing. You know you don't have to answer all the questions to do well. It is possible to omit more than half of the questions and still be in the top half of all students taking the test; similarly, you can omit more than 40 questions and earn a top score. After you set your final goal, pace yourself to reach it.

TACTIC

22

Don't be nervous: if your scores aren't as high as you would like, you can always take the SAT again.

Relax. The biggest reason that some students do worse on the actual SAT than they did on their practice tests is that they are nervous. You can't do your best if your hands are shaking and you're worried that your whole future is riding on this one test. First of all, your SAT scores are only one of many factors that influence the admissions process, and many students are accepted at their first-choice colleges even if their SAT scores are lower than they had expected. But more important, because of Score Choice, you can always retake the SAT if you don't do well enough the first or second time. So, give yourself the best chance for success: prepare conscientiously and then stay calm while actually taking the test.

Now you have an overview of the general tactics you'll need to deal with the SAT. In the next section, apply them: take the diagnostic test and see how you do. Then move on to Part Three, where you will learn tactics for handling each specific question type.

An Afterword: More on Guessing

Are you still worried about whether you should guess on the SAT? If so, read through the following analysis of how guessing affects your scores. The bottom line is, even if you don't know the answer to a question, whenever you can eliminate one or more answer choices, you *must* guess.

In general, it pays to guess. To understand why this is so and why so many people are confused about guessing, you must consider what you know about how the SAT is scored.

Consider the following scenario. Suppose you work very slowly and carefully, answer only 32 of the critical reading questions (omitting 35), and get each of them correct. Your raw score will be converted to a scaled score of about 520. If that were the whole story, you should use the last minute of the test to quickly fill in an answer to each of the other questions. Because each question has 5 choices, you should get about one-fifth of them right. Surely, you would get *some* of them right—most likely about 7. If you did that, your raw score would go up 7 points, and your scaled score would then be about 560. Your critical reading score would increase 40 points because of 1 minute of wild guessing! Clearly, this is not what the College Board wants to happen. To counter this possibility, there is a so-called *guessing penalty,* which adjusts your scores for wrong answers and makes it unlikely that you will profit from wild guessing.

The penalty for each incorrect answer on the critical reasoning sections is a reduction of $\frac{1}{4}$ point of raw score. What effect would this penalty have in the example just discussed? Say that by wildly guessing you got 7 right and 28 wrong. Those 7 extra right answers caused your raw score to go up by 7 points. But now you lose $\frac{1}{4}$ point for each of the 28 problems you missed—a total reduction of $\frac{28}{4}$ or 7 points. As a result, you broke even: you gained 7 points and lost 7 points. Your raw score, and hence your scaled score, didn't change at all.

Notice that the guessing *penalty* didn't actually penalize you. It prevented you from making a big gain that you didn't deserve, but it didn't punish you by lowering your score. It's not a very harsh penalty after all. In fairness, however, it should be pointed out that wild guessing *could* have lowered your score. It is possible that, instead of getting 7 correct answers, you were unlucky and got only 5 or 6, and as a result, your scaled score dropped from 520 to 510. On the other hand, it is equally likely that you would have been lucky and gotten 8 or 9 rather than 7 right, and that your scaled score would have increased from 520 to 530 or 540.

Educated guessing, on the other hand, can have an enormous effect on your score: it can increase it dramatically! Let's look at what is meant by educated guessing and see how it can improve your score on the SAT.

Consider the following sentence completion question.

> In Victorian times, countless Egyptian mummies were ground up to produce dried mummy powder, hailed by quacks as a near-magical ----, able to cure a wide variety of ailments.
>
> (A) toxin
> (B) diagnosis
> (C) symptom
> (D) panacea
> (E) placebo

Clearly, what is needed is a word such as *medicine*—something capable of curing ailments. Let's assume that you know that *toxin* means poison, so you immediately eliminate Choice A. You also know that, although *diagnosis* and *symptom* are medical terms, neither means a medicine or a cure, so you eliminate Choices B and C. You now know that the correct answer must be Choice D or E, but unfortunately you have no idea what either *panacea* or *placebo* means.

You *could* guess, but you don't want to be wrong; after all, there's that penalty for incorrect answers. Then should you leave the question out? Absolutely not! *You must guess!* We'll explain why and how in a moment, but first let's look at one more example, this time a math question.

NOTE

On average, *wild guessing does not affect your score on the SAT.*

What is the slope of line ℓ in the figure to the right?

(A) $-\dfrac{2}{3}$

(B) $-\dfrac{3}{2}$

(C) 0

(D) $\dfrac{2}{3}$

(E) $\dfrac{3}{2}$

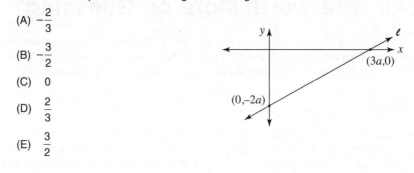

Suppose that you have completely forgotten how to calculate the slope of a line, but you do remember that lines that go up ($\nearrow$) have positive slopes and that lines that go down ($\searrow$) have negative slopes. Then you know the answer must be Choice D or E. What do you do? Do you guess and risk incurring the guessing penalty, or do you omit the question because you're not sure which answer is correct? *You must guess!*

Suppose that you are still working slowly and carefully on the critical reading sections, and that you are sure of the answers to 32 questions. Of the 35 questions you planned to omit, there are 15 in which you are able to eliminate 3 of the choices, but you have no idea which of the remaining 2 choices is correct; and the remaining 20 questions you don't even look at. You already know what would happen if you guessed wildly on those 20 questions—you would probably break even. But what about the 15 questions you narrowed down to 2 choices? If you guess on those, you should get about half right and half wrong. Is that good or bad? *It's very good!* Assume you got 7 right and 8 wrong. For the 7 correct answers, you would receive 7 points, and for the 8 incorrect answers, you would lose $^8/_4 = 2$ points. This is a net gain of 5 raw score points, raising your critical reading SAT score from 520 to 560. It would be a shame to throw away those 40 points just because you were afraid of the guessing penalty.

At this point, many students protest that they are unlucky and that they never guess right. They are wrong. *There is no such thing as a poor guesser,* as we'll prove in a minute. For the sake of argument, however, suppose you were a poor guesser, and that when you guessed on those 15 questions, you got twice as many wrong (10) as you got right (5). In that case you would have received 5 points for the correct ones and lost $^{10}/_4 = 2^1/_2$ points for the incorrect ones. Your raw score would have increased by $2^1/_2$ points, which would be rounded up to 3, and your scaled score would still have increased: from 520 to 540. Therefore, even if you think you're a poor guesser, you should guess.

Actually, the real guessing penalty is not the one that the College Board uses to prevent you from profiting from wild guesses. **The real guessing penalty is the one you impose on yourself by not guessing when you should.**

Occasionally, you can even eliminate 4 of the 5 choices! Suppose that in the sentence completion question given above, you realize that you do know what *placebo* means, and that it can't be the answer. You still have no idea about *panacea,* and you may be hesitant to answer a question with a word you never heard of; but you must. If, in the preceding math question, only one of the choices were positive, it would have to be correct. In that case, don't omit the question because you can't verify the answer by calculating the slope yourself. Choose the only answer you haven't eliminated.

What if you can't eliminate 3 or 4 of the choices? You should guess if you can eliminate even 1 choice. Assume that there are 20 questions whose answers you are unsure of. The following table indicates the most likely outcome if you guess at each of them.

On an actual test, there would be some questions on which you could eliminate 1 or 2 choices and others where you could eliminate 3 or 4. No matter what the mix, guessing pays.

Number of choices eliminated	Most Likely Effect				
	Number correct	Number wrong	Raw score	Scaled Score Verbal	Math
0	4	16	+0	+0	+0
1	5	15	+1.25	+10	+15
2	7	13	+3.75	+30	+40
3	10	10	+7.50	+50	+70
4	20	0	+20	+120	+150

The scoring of the math sections is somewhat different from the scoring of the critical reading. The multiple-choice math questions have the same $1/4$-point penalty for incorrect answers as do all the critical reading and writing skills questions. There is *no penalty,* however, on grid-in questions, so you can surely guess on those. Of course, because you can grid in any number from .001 to 9999, it is very unlikely that a wild guess will be correct. But, as you will see, sometimes a grid-in question will ask for the smallest integer that satisfies a certain property (the length of the side of a particular triangle, for example), and you know that the answer must be greater than 1 and less than 10. Then guess.

It's time to prove to you that you are not a poor guesser; in fact, no one is. Take out a sheet of paper and number from 1 to 20. This is your answer sheet. Assume that for each of 20 questions you have eliminated three of the five choices (B, C, and E), so you know that the correct answer is either A or D. Now guess. Next to each number write either A or D. When you are done, turn to page 26. Tests 1, 2, and 3 list the order in which the first 20 A's and D's appeared on three actual SATs. Check to see how many right answers you would have had. On each test, if you got 10 out of 20 correct, your SAT score would have risen by about 60 points as a result of your guessing. If you had more than 10 right, add an additional 10 points for each extra question you got correct; if you had fewer than 10 right, subtract 10 points from 60 for each extra one you missed. If you had 13 right, your SAT score increased by 90 points; if you got only 7 right, it still increased by 30 points. Probably, for the three tests, your average number of correct answers was very close to 10. You couldn't have missed all of the questions if you wanted to. You simply cannot afford not to guess.

You can repeat this experiment as often as you like. Ask a friend to write down a list of 20 A's and D's, and then compare your list and his. Or just go to the answer keys for the model tests in the back of the book, and read down any column, ignoring the B's, C's, and E's.

Would you like to see how well you do if you can eliminate only two choices? Do the same thing, except this time eliminate B and D and choose A, C, or E. Check your answers against the correct answers in Tests 4, 5, and 6 on page 26. Give yourself 1 raw score point for each correct answer and deduct $1/4$ point for each wrong answer. Multiply your raw score by 8 to learn approximately how many points you gained by guessing.

A few final comments about guessing are in order.

- If it is really a guess, don't agonize over it. Don't spend 30 seconds thinking, "Should I pick A? The last time I guessed, I chose A; maybe this time I should pick D. I'm really not sure. But I haven't had too many A answers lately; so, maybe it's time." STOP! A guess is just that—a guess.
- You can decide right now how you are going to guess on the actual SAT you take. For example, you could just always guess the letter closest to A: if A is in the running, choose it; if not, pick B, and so on. If you'd rather start with E, that's OK, too.
- If you are down to two choices and you have a hunch, play it. But if you have no idea and it is truly a guess, do not take more than two seconds to choose. Then move on to the next question.

Answer Key for Guessing

TEST 1

1. A	11. D
2. D	12. D
3. D	13. A
4. A	14. D
5. A	15. A
6. D	16. D
7. D	17. A
8. A	18. D
9. A	19. A
10. A	20. D

TEST 2

1. D	11. D
2. A	12. A
3. D	13. D
4. A	14. D
5. D	15. A
6. A	16. A
7. A	17. D
8. D	18. D
9. A	19. D
10. A	20. A

TEST 3

1. A	11. D
2. D	12. D
3. D	13. D
4. A	14. A
5. D	15. A
6. D	16. D
7. D	17. A
8. A	18. A
9. A	19. D
10. D	20. D

TEST 4

1. A	11. E
2. C	12. A
3. A	13. E
4. C	14. E
5. E	15. C
6. E	16. C
7. C	17. C
8. A	18. E
9. E	19. E
10. C	20. A

TEST 5

1. C	11. C
2. A	12. E
3. A	13. E
4. A	14. E
5. C	15. A
6. E	16. E
7. A	17. C
8. C	18. C
9. C	19. C
10. C	20. E

TEST 6

1. C	11. C
2. C	12. E
3. E	13. A
4. E	14. C
5. A	15. A
6. A	16. A
7. C	17. A
8. E	18. C
9. E	19. E
10. A	20. E

PART TWO

PINPOINT YOUR TROUBLE SPOTS

A Diagnostic Test

> - **Diagnostic Test**
> - **Answer Key**
> - **Self-Evaluation**
> - **Answer Explanations**

The diagnostic test in this chapter is a multipurpose tool.

- First, it will help you identify your problem areas and skills. Take the test and evaluate your results, following the charts provided. You will discover your strengths and weaknesses, and you will know what to study.
- Second, this test will help you design a study plan that's right for you. Use the information you get from your result to tailor a study plan to fit your particular needs. If you need extra time on a certain topic, build time in. You are in charge of your study program—make it work for you.
- Third, this test is your introduction to the format and content of the SAT. There is nothing like working your way through actual SAT-type questions for 3 hours and 20 minutes to teach you how much stamina you need and how much speed.
- Finally, this test is your chance to learn how to profit from your mistakes. It will expose you to the sorts of traps the test-makers set for you and the sorts of shortcuts that you should take. Read the answer explanation for every question you miss or omit. You'll be amazed to see how much you'll learn.

As shown in the chart on pages vii–viii, an actual SAT has ten sections and takes a little more than 4 hours to complete, including two 10-minute breaks. One of those ten sections is an experimental section that is not included in your scores. This diagnostic test, as well as all the model tests in this book, has only nine sections—it does not have the experimental section—and so it takes about 3 hours and 45 minutes to complete: 3 hours and 20 minutes of actual time working on the test, plus six 1-minute breaks between sections and two 10-minute breaks, after Sections 3 and 7.

You are about to take a diagnostic test that can change the way you do on the SAT. You have 3 hours and 45 minutes to get through the nine sections (numbered 1–4 and 6–10; there is no Section 5), with breaks. Make every minute count.

Answer Sheet–Diagnostic Test

Section 1   ESSAY

Diagnostic Test

Essay (continued)

If a section has fewer questions than answer spaces, leave the extra spaces blank.

Section 2

1 Ⓐ Ⓑ Ⓒ Ⓓ Ⓔ	8 Ⓐ Ⓑ Ⓒ Ⓓ Ⓔ	15 Ⓐ Ⓑ Ⓒ Ⓓ Ⓔ	22 Ⓐ Ⓑ Ⓒ Ⓓ Ⓔ	29 Ⓐ Ⓑ Ⓒ Ⓓ Ⓔ
2 Ⓐ Ⓑ Ⓒ Ⓓ Ⓔ	9 Ⓐ Ⓑ Ⓒ Ⓓ Ⓔ	16 Ⓐ Ⓑ Ⓒ Ⓓ Ⓔ	23 Ⓐ Ⓑ Ⓒ Ⓓ Ⓔ	30 Ⓐ Ⓑ Ⓒ Ⓓ Ⓔ
3 Ⓐ Ⓑ Ⓒ Ⓓ Ⓔ	10 Ⓐ Ⓑ Ⓒ Ⓓ Ⓔ	17 Ⓐ Ⓑ Ⓒ Ⓓ Ⓔ	24 Ⓐ Ⓑ Ⓒ Ⓓ Ⓔ	31 Ⓐ Ⓑ Ⓒ Ⓓ Ⓔ
4 Ⓐ Ⓑ Ⓒ Ⓓ Ⓔ	11 Ⓐ Ⓑ Ⓒ Ⓓ Ⓔ	18 Ⓐ Ⓑ Ⓒ Ⓓ Ⓔ	25 Ⓐ Ⓑ Ⓒ Ⓓ Ⓔ	32 Ⓐ Ⓑ Ⓒ Ⓓ Ⓔ
5 Ⓐ Ⓑ Ⓒ Ⓓ Ⓔ	12 Ⓐ Ⓑ Ⓒ Ⓓ Ⓔ	19 Ⓐ Ⓑ Ⓒ Ⓓ Ⓔ	26 Ⓐ Ⓑ Ⓒ Ⓓ Ⓔ	33 Ⓐ Ⓑ Ⓒ Ⓓ Ⓔ
6 Ⓐ Ⓑ Ⓒ Ⓓ Ⓔ	13 Ⓐ Ⓑ Ⓒ Ⓓ Ⓔ	20 Ⓐ Ⓑ Ⓒ Ⓓ Ⓔ	27 Ⓐ Ⓑ Ⓒ Ⓓ Ⓔ	34 Ⓐ Ⓑ Ⓒ Ⓓ Ⓔ
7 Ⓐ Ⓑ Ⓒ Ⓓ Ⓔ	14 Ⓐ Ⓑ Ⓒ Ⓓ Ⓔ	21 Ⓐ Ⓑ Ⓒ Ⓓ Ⓔ	28 Ⓐ Ⓑ Ⓒ Ⓓ Ⓔ	35 Ⓐ Ⓑ Ⓒ Ⓓ Ⓔ

Section 3

1 Ⓐ Ⓑ Ⓒ Ⓓ Ⓔ	8 Ⓐ Ⓑ Ⓒ Ⓓ Ⓔ	15 Ⓐ Ⓑ Ⓒ Ⓓ Ⓔ	22 Ⓐ Ⓑ Ⓒ Ⓓ Ⓔ	29 Ⓐ Ⓑ Ⓒ Ⓓ Ⓔ
2 Ⓐ Ⓑ Ⓒ Ⓓ Ⓔ	9 Ⓐ Ⓑ Ⓒ Ⓓ Ⓔ	16 Ⓐ Ⓑ Ⓒ Ⓓ Ⓔ	23 Ⓐ Ⓑ Ⓒ Ⓓ Ⓔ	30 Ⓐ Ⓑ Ⓒ Ⓓ Ⓔ
3 Ⓐ Ⓑ Ⓒ Ⓓ Ⓔ	10 Ⓐ Ⓑ Ⓒ Ⓓ Ⓔ	17 Ⓐ Ⓑ Ⓒ Ⓓ Ⓔ	24 Ⓐ Ⓑ Ⓒ Ⓓ Ⓔ	31 Ⓐ Ⓑ Ⓒ Ⓓ Ⓔ
4 Ⓐ Ⓑ Ⓒ Ⓓ Ⓔ	11 Ⓐ Ⓑ Ⓒ Ⓓ Ⓔ	18 Ⓐ Ⓑ Ⓒ Ⓓ Ⓔ	25 Ⓐ Ⓑ Ⓒ Ⓓ Ⓔ	32 Ⓐ Ⓑ Ⓒ Ⓓ Ⓔ
5 Ⓐ Ⓑ Ⓒ Ⓓ Ⓔ	12 Ⓐ Ⓑ Ⓒ Ⓓ Ⓔ	19 Ⓐ Ⓑ Ⓒ Ⓓ Ⓔ	26 Ⓐ Ⓑ Ⓒ Ⓓ Ⓔ	33 Ⓐ Ⓑ Ⓒ Ⓓ Ⓔ
6 Ⓐ Ⓑ Ⓒ Ⓓ Ⓔ	13 Ⓐ Ⓑ Ⓒ Ⓓ Ⓔ	20 Ⓐ Ⓑ Ⓒ Ⓓ Ⓔ	27 Ⓐ Ⓑ Ⓒ Ⓓ Ⓔ	34 Ⓐ Ⓑ Ⓒ Ⓓ Ⓔ
7 Ⓐ Ⓑ Ⓒ Ⓓ Ⓔ	14 Ⓐ Ⓑ Ⓒ Ⓓ Ⓔ	21 Ⓐ Ⓑ Ⓒ Ⓓ Ⓔ	28 Ⓐ Ⓑ Ⓒ Ⓓ Ⓔ	35 Ⓐ Ⓑ Ⓒ Ⓓ Ⓔ

Section 4

1 Ⓐ Ⓑ Ⓒ Ⓓ Ⓔ	8 Ⓐ Ⓑ Ⓒ Ⓓ Ⓔ	15 Ⓐ Ⓑ Ⓒ Ⓓ Ⓔ	22 Ⓐ Ⓑ Ⓒ Ⓓ Ⓔ	29 Ⓐ Ⓑ Ⓒ Ⓓ Ⓔ
2 Ⓐ Ⓑ Ⓒ Ⓓ Ⓔ	9 Ⓐ Ⓑ Ⓒ Ⓓ Ⓔ	16 Ⓐ Ⓑ Ⓒ Ⓓ Ⓔ	23 Ⓐ Ⓑ Ⓒ Ⓓ Ⓔ	30 Ⓐ Ⓑ Ⓒ Ⓓ Ⓔ
3 Ⓐ Ⓑ Ⓒ Ⓓ Ⓔ	10 Ⓐ Ⓑ Ⓒ Ⓓ Ⓔ	17 Ⓐ Ⓑ Ⓒ Ⓓ Ⓔ	24 Ⓐ Ⓑ Ⓒ Ⓓ Ⓔ	31 Ⓐ Ⓑ Ⓒ Ⓓ Ⓔ
4 Ⓐ Ⓑ Ⓒ Ⓓ Ⓔ	11 Ⓐ Ⓑ Ⓒ Ⓓ Ⓔ	18 Ⓐ Ⓑ Ⓒ Ⓓ Ⓔ	25 Ⓐ Ⓑ Ⓒ Ⓓ Ⓔ	32 Ⓐ Ⓑ Ⓒ Ⓓ Ⓔ
5 Ⓐ Ⓑ Ⓒ Ⓓ Ⓔ	12 Ⓐ Ⓑ Ⓒ Ⓓ Ⓔ	19 Ⓐ Ⓑ Ⓒ Ⓓ Ⓔ	26 Ⓐ Ⓑ Ⓒ Ⓓ Ⓔ	33 Ⓐ Ⓑ Ⓒ Ⓓ Ⓔ
6 Ⓐ Ⓑ Ⓒ Ⓓ Ⓔ	13 Ⓐ Ⓑ Ⓒ Ⓓ Ⓔ	20 Ⓐ Ⓑ Ⓒ Ⓓ Ⓔ	27 Ⓐ Ⓑ Ⓒ Ⓓ Ⓔ	34 Ⓐ Ⓑ Ⓒ Ⓓ Ⓔ
7 Ⓐ Ⓑ Ⓒ Ⓓ Ⓔ	14 Ⓐ Ⓑ Ⓒ Ⓓ Ⓔ	21 Ⓐ Ⓑ Ⓒ Ⓓ Ⓔ	28 Ⓐ Ⓑ Ⓒ Ⓓ Ⓔ	35 Ⓐ Ⓑ Ⓒ Ⓓ Ⓔ

Section 6

1 Ⓐ Ⓑ Ⓒ Ⓓ Ⓔ	8 Ⓐ Ⓑ Ⓒ Ⓓ Ⓔ	15 Ⓐ Ⓑ Ⓒ Ⓓ Ⓔ	22 Ⓐ Ⓑ Ⓒ Ⓓ Ⓔ	29 Ⓐ Ⓑ Ⓒ Ⓓ Ⓔ
2 Ⓐ Ⓑ Ⓒ Ⓓ Ⓔ	9 Ⓐ Ⓑ Ⓒ Ⓓ Ⓔ	16 Ⓐ Ⓑ Ⓒ Ⓓ Ⓔ	23 Ⓐ Ⓑ Ⓒ Ⓓ Ⓔ	30 Ⓐ Ⓑ Ⓒ Ⓓ Ⓔ
3 Ⓐ Ⓑ Ⓒ Ⓓ Ⓔ	10 Ⓐ Ⓑ Ⓒ Ⓓ Ⓔ	17 Ⓐ Ⓑ Ⓒ Ⓓ Ⓔ	24 Ⓐ Ⓑ Ⓒ Ⓓ Ⓔ	31 Ⓐ Ⓑ Ⓒ Ⓓ Ⓔ
4 Ⓐ Ⓑ Ⓒ Ⓓ Ⓔ	11 Ⓐ Ⓑ Ⓒ Ⓓ Ⓔ	18 Ⓐ Ⓑ Ⓒ Ⓓ Ⓔ	25 Ⓐ Ⓑ Ⓒ Ⓓ Ⓔ	32 Ⓐ Ⓑ Ⓒ Ⓓ Ⓔ
5 Ⓐ Ⓑ Ⓒ Ⓓ Ⓔ	12 Ⓐ Ⓑ Ⓒ Ⓓ Ⓔ	19 Ⓐ Ⓑ Ⓒ Ⓓ Ⓔ	26 Ⓐ Ⓑ Ⓒ Ⓓ Ⓔ	33 Ⓐ Ⓑ Ⓒ Ⓓ Ⓔ
6 Ⓐ Ⓑ Ⓒ Ⓓ Ⓔ	13 Ⓐ Ⓑ Ⓒ Ⓓ Ⓔ	20 Ⓐ Ⓑ Ⓒ Ⓓ Ⓔ	27 Ⓐ Ⓑ Ⓒ Ⓓ Ⓔ	34 Ⓐ Ⓑ Ⓒ Ⓓ Ⓔ
7 Ⓐ Ⓑ Ⓒ Ⓓ Ⓔ	14 Ⓐ Ⓑ Ⓒ Ⓓ Ⓔ	21 Ⓐ Ⓑ Ⓒ Ⓓ Ⓔ	28 Ⓐ Ⓑ Ⓒ Ⓓ Ⓔ	35 Ⓐ Ⓑ Ⓒ Ⓓ Ⓔ

Section 7

1 Ⓐ Ⓑ Ⓒ Ⓓ Ⓔ 　 3 Ⓐ Ⓑ Ⓒ Ⓓ Ⓔ 　 5 Ⓐ Ⓑ Ⓒ Ⓓ Ⓔ 　 7 Ⓐ Ⓑ Ⓒ Ⓓ Ⓔ
2 Ⓐ Ⓑ Ⓒ Ⓓ Ⓔ 　 4 Ⓐ Ⓑ Ⓒ Ⓓ Ⓔ 　 6 Ⓐ Ⓑ Ⓒ Ⓓ Ⓔ 　 8 Ⓐ Ⓑ Ⓒ Ⓓ Ⓔ

9   10   11   12   13

14   15   16   17   18

Section 8

1 Ⓐ Ⓑ Ⓒ Ⓓ Ⓔ 　 5 Ⓐ Ⓑ Ⓒ Ⓓ Ⓔ 　 9 Ⓐ Ⓑ Ⓒ Ⓓ Ⓔ 　 13 Ⓐ Ⓑ Ⓒ Ⓓ Ⓔ 　 17 Ⓐ Ⓑ Ⓒ Ⓓ Ⓔ
2 Ⓐ Ⓑ Ⓒ Ⓓ Ⓔ 　 6 Ⓐ Ⓑ Ⓒ Ⓓ Ⓔ 　 10 Ⓐ Ⓑ Ⓒ Ⓓ Ⓔ 　 14 Ⓐ Ⓑ Ⓒ Ⓓ Ⓔ 　 18 Ⓐ Ⓑ Ⓒ Ⓓ Ⓔ
3 Ⓐ Ⓑ Ⓒ Ⓓ Ⓔ 　 7 Ⓐ Ⓑ Ⓒ Ⓓ Ⓔ 　 11 Ⓐ Ⓑ Ⓒ Ⓓ Ⓔ 　 15 Ⓐ Ⓑ Ⓒ Ⓓ Ⓔ 　 19 Ⓐ Ⓑ Ⓒ Ⓓ Ⓔ
4 Ⓐ Ⓑ Ⓒ Ⓓ Ⓔ 　 8 Ⓐ Ⓑ Ⓒ Ⓓ Ⓔ 　 12 Ⓐ Ⓑ Ⓒ Ⓓ Ⓔ 　 16 Ⓐ Ⓑ Ⓒ Ⓓ Ⓔ 　 20 Ⓐ Ⓑ Ⓒ Ⓓ Ⓔ

Section 9

1 Ⓐ Ⓑ Ⓒ Ⓓ Ⓔ 　 5 Ⓐ Ⓑ Ⓒ Ⓓ Ⓔ 　 9 Ⓐ Ⓑ Ⓒ Ⓓ Ⓔ 　 13 Ⓐ Ⓑ Ⓒ Ⓓ Ⓔ 　 17 Ⓐ Ⓑ Ⓒ Ⓓ Ⓔ
2 Ⓐ Ⓑ Ⓒ Ⓓ Ⓔ 　 6 Ⓐ Ⓑ Ⓒ Ⓓ Ⓔ 　 10 Ⓐ Ⓑ Ⓒ Ⓓ Ⓔ 　 14 Ⓐ Ⓑ Ⓒ Ⓓ Ⓔ 　 18 Ⓐ Ⓑ Ⓒ Ⓓ Ⓔ
3 Ⓐ Ⓑ Ⓒ Ⓓ Ⓔ 　 7 Ⓐ Ⓑ Ⓒ Ⓓ Ⓔ 　 11 Ⓐ Ⓑ Ⓒ Ⓓ Ⓔ 　 15 Ⓐ Ⓑ Ⓒ Ⓓ Ⓔ 　 19 Ⓐ Ⓑ Ⓒ Ⓓ Ⓔ
4 Ⓐ Ⓑ Ⓒ Ⓓ Ⓔ 　 8 Ⓐ Ⓑ Ⓒ Ⓓ Ⓔ 　 12 Ⓐ Ⓑ Ⓒ Ⓓ Ⓔ 　 16 Ⓐ Ⓑ Ⓒ Ⓓ Ⓔ 　 20 Ⓐ Ⓑ Ⓒ Ⓓ Ⓔ

Section 10

1 Ⓐ Ⓑ Ⓒ Ⓓ Ⓔ 　 5 Ⓐ Ⓑ Ⓒ Ⓓ Ⓔ 　 9 Ⓐ Ⓑ Ⓒ Ⓓ Ⓔ 　 13 Ⓐ Ⓑ Ⓒ Ⓓ Ⓔ 　 17 Ⓐ Ⓑ Ⓒ Ⓓ Ⓔ
2 Ⓐ Ⓑ Ⓒ Ⓓ Ⓔ 　 6 Ⓐ Ⓑ Ⓒ Ⓓ Ⓔ 　 10 Ⓐ Ⓑ Ⓒ Ⓓ Ⓔ 　 14 Ⓐ Ⓑ Ⓒ Ⓓ Ⓔ 　 18 Ⓐ Ⓑ Ⓒ Ⓓ Ⓔ
3 Ⓐ Ⓑ Ⓒ Ⓓ Ⓔ 　 7 Ⓐ Ⓑ Ⓒ Ⓓ Ⓔ 　 11 Ⓐ Ⓑ Ⓒ Ⓓ Ⓔ 　 15 Ⓐ Ⓑ Ⓒ Ⓓ Ⓔ 　 19 Ⓐ Ⓑ Ⓒ Ⓓ Ⓔ
4 Ⓐ Ⓑ Ⓒ Ⓓ Ⓔ 　 8 Ⓐ Ⓑ Ⓒ Ⓓ Ⓔ 　 12 Ⓐ Ⓑ Ⓒ Ⓓ Ⓔ 　 16 Ⓐ Ⓑ Ⓒ Ⓓ Ⓔ 　 20 Ⓐ Ⓑ Ⓒ Ⓓ Ⓔ

Diagnostic Test   1 1 1 1 1 1   1

SECTION **1**   **Time—25 Minutes**   **ESSAY**

> The excerpt appearing below makes a point about a particular topic. Read the passage carefully, and think about the assignment that follows.

Since the invention of television, the medium has had its ups and downs. At first, television watching was a communal affair; the first television set owners in a neighborhood would proudly invite the neighbors in to view the marvelous box. In time, however, television came to have an isolating effect on viewers; as the painter Andy Warhol once said, "When I got my first television set, I stopped caring so much about having close relationships."

ASSIGNMENT: What are your thoughts on the idea that television has turned out to isolate people instead of bringing them together? Compose an essay in which you express your views on this topic. Your essay may support, refute, or qualify the views expressed in the excerpt. What you write, however, must be relevant to the topic under discussion. Additionally, you must support your viewpoint, explaining your reasoning and providing examples based on your studies and/or experience.

2 2 2 2 2 2 2 2 2 2 2

SECTION 2 | Time—25 Minutes 24 Questions | Select the best answer to each of the following questions; then blacken the appropriate space on your answer sheet.

Each of the following sentences contains one or two blanks; each blank indicates that a word or set of words has been left out. Below the sentence are five words or phrases, lettered A through E. Select the word or set of words that best completes the sentence.

Example:

Fame is ----; today's rising star is all too soon tomorrow's washed-up has-been.

(A) rewarding   (B) gradual
 (C) essential   (D) spontaneous
  (E) transitory

Ⓐ Ⓑ Ⓒ Ⓓ ●

1. Because of their frequent disarray, confusion, and loss of memory, those hit by lightning while alone are sometimes ---- victims of assault.

   (A) mistaken for
   (B) attracted to
   (C) unaware of
   (D) avoided by
   (E) useful to

2. Having published more than three hundred books in less than fifty years, science fiction writer Isaac Asimov may well be the most ---- author of our day.

   (A) fastidious
   (B) insecure
   (C) outmoded
   (D) prolific
   (E) indigenous

3. Because his time was limited, Weng decided to read the ---- novel *War and Peace* in ---- edition.

   (A) wordy..an unedited
   (B) lengthy..an abridged
   (C) famous..a modern
   (D) romantic..an autographed
   (E) popular..a complete

4. In giving a speech, the speaker's goal is to communicate ideas clearly and ----, so that the audience will be in no ---- about the meaning of the speech.

   (A) effectively..haste
   (B) indirectly..distress
   (C) vigorously..discomfort
   (D) unambiguously..confusion
   (E) tactfully..suspense

5. Although gregarious by nature, Lisa became quiet and ---- after she was unexpectedly laid off from work.

   (A) autonomous   (B) susceptible   (C) assertive
    (D) withdrawn   (E) composed

6. The increasingly popular leader of America's second largest tribe, Cherokee Chief Wilma Mankiller, has ---- the myth that only males can be leaders in American Indian government.

   (A) shattered   (B) perpetuated   (C) exaggerated
    (D) confirmed   (E) venerated

7. The commission of inquiry censured the senator for his ---- expenditure of public funds, which they found to be ----.

   (A) flagrant..cursory
   (B) improper..vindicated
   (C) lavish..unjustifiable
   (D) judicious..blameworthy
   (E) arbitrary..critical

8. Despite their ---- of Twain's *Huckleberry Finn* for its stereotyped portrait of the slave Jim, even the novel's ---- agreed that it is a masterpiece of American prose.

   (A) admiration..critics
   (B) denunciation..supporters
   (C) criticism..detractors
   (D) defense..censors
   (E) praise..advocates

GO ON TO THE NEXT PAGE ➡

2 2 2 2 2 2 2 2 2 2 2

Read each of the passages below, and then answer the questions that follow the passage. The correct response may be stated outright or merely suggested in the passage.

Questions 9 and 10 are based on the following passage.

Consider the humble jellyfish. Headless, spine-less, without a heart or brain, it has such a simple exterior that it seems the most primitive of crea-
Line tures. Unlike its sessile (attached to a surface, as
(5) an oyster is attached to its shell) relatives whose stalks cling to seaweed or tropical coral reefs, the free-swimming jellyfish, or medusa, drifts along the ocean shore, propelling itself by pulsing, mus-cular contractions of its bell-shaped body. Yet
(10) beneath the simple surface of this aimlessly drift-ing, supposedly primitive creature is an unusually sophisticated set of genes, as recent studies of the invertebrate animal phylum Cnidaria (pronounced nih-DARE-ee-uh) reveal.

9. Which assertion about jellyfish is supported by the passage?

(A) They move at a rapid rate.
(B) They are cowardly.
(C) They lack mobility.
(D) They have a certain degree of intelligence.
(E) They are unexpectedly complex.

10. The last sentence of the passage serves primarily to

(A) explain the origin of a term
(B) contradict an assumption
(C) provide an example
(D) cite a well-known fact
(E) describe a process

Questions 11 and 12 are based on the following passage.

The passage below is excerpted from Somerset Maugham's The Moon and Sixpence, *first published in 1919.*

The faculty for myth is innate in the human race. It seizes with avidity upon any incidents, surprising or mysterious, in the career of those
Line who have at all distinguished themselves from
(5) their fellows, and invents a legend. It is the protest of romance against the commonplace of life. The incidents of the legend become the hero's surest passport to immortality. The ironic philosopher reflects with a smile that Sir Walter
(10) Raleigh is more safely enshrined in the memory of mankind because he set his cloak for the Virgin Queen to walk on than because he carried the English name to undiscovered countries.

11. As used in the passage, the word "faculty" (line 1) most nearly means

(A) capacity
(B) distinction
(C) authority
(D) teaching staff
(E) branch of learning

12. In lines 8–13, the author mentions Sir Walter Raleigh primarily to

(A) demonstrate the importance of Raleigh's voyages of discovery
(B) mock Raleigh's behavior in casting down his cloak to protect the queen's feet from the mud
(C) illustrate how legendary events outshine historical achievements in the public's mind
(D) distinguish between Raleigh the courtier and Raleigh the seafarer
(E) remind us that historical figures may act in idiosyncratic ways

Questions 13–24 are based on the following passage.

The passage below is excerpted from the introduction to Bury My Heart at Wounded Knee, *written in 1970 by the Native American historian Dee Brown.*

Since the exploratory journey of Lewis and Clark to the Pacific Coast early in the nineteenth century, the number of published accounts
Line describing the "opening" of the American West
(5) has risen into the thousands. The greatest concen-tration of recorded experience and observation came out of the thirty-year span between 1860 and 1890—the period covered by this book. It was an incredible era of violence, greed, audacity,
(10) sentimentality, undirected exuberance, and an almost reverential attitude toward the ideal of per-sonal freedom for those who already had it.
During that time the culture and civilization of the American Indian was destroyed, and out of
(15) that time came virtually all the great myths of the American West—tales of fur traders, mountain men, steamboat pilots, goldseekers, gamblers, gunmen, cavalrymen, cowboys, harlots, mission-aries, schoolmarms, and homesteaders. Only
(20) occasionally was the voice of the Indian heard,

GO ON TO THE NEXT PAGE

and then more often than not it was recorded by the pen of a white man. The Indian was the dark menace of the myths, and even if he had known how to write in English, where would he have
(25) found a printer or a publisher?

Yet they are not all lost, those Indian voices of the past. A few authentic accounts of American western history were recorded by Indians either in pictographs or in translated English, and some
(30) managed to get published in obscure journals, pamphlets, or books of small circulation. In the late nineteenth century, when the white man's curiosity about Indian survivors of the wars reached a high point, enterprising newspaper
(35) reporters frequently interviewed warriors and chiefs and gave them an opportunity to express their opinions on what was happening in the West. The quality of these interviews varied greatly, depending upon the abilities of the inter-
(40) preters, or upon the inclination of the Indians to speak freely. Some feared reprisals for telling the truth, while others delighted in hoaxing reporters with tall tales and shaggy-dog stories. Contemporary newspaper statements by Indians
(45) must therefore be read with skepticism, although some of them are masterpieces of irony and others burn with outbursts of poetic fury.

Among the richest sources of first-person statements by Indians are the records of treaty
(50) councils and other formal meetings with civilian and military representatives of the United States government. Isaac Pitman's new stenographic system was coming into vogue in the second half of the nineteenth century, and when Indians spoke
(55) in council a recording clerk sat beside the official interpreter.

Even when the meetings were in remote parts of the West, someone usually was available to write down the speeches, and because of the
(60) slowness of the translation process, much of what was said could be recorded in longhand. Interpreters quite often were half-bloods who knew spoken languages but seldom could read or write. Like most oral peoples they and the Indians
(65) depended upon imagery to express their thoughts, so that the English translations were filled with graphic similes and metaphors of the natural world. If an eloquent Indian had a poor inter- preter, his words might be transformed to flat
(70) prose, but a good interpreter could make a poor speaker sound poetic.

Most Indian leaders spoke freely and candidly in councils with white officials, and as they became more sophisticated in such matters during
(75) the 1870s and 1880s, they demanded the right to choose their own interpreters and recorders. In

this latter period, all members of the tribes were free to speak, and some of the older men chose such opportunities to recount events they had wit-
(80) nessed in the past, or sum up the histories of their peoples. Although the Indians who lived through this doom period of their civilization have van- ished from the earth, millions of their words are preserved in official records. Many of the more
(85) important council proceedings were published in government documents and reports.

Out of all these sources of almost forgotten oral history, I have tried to fashion a narrative of the conquest of the American West as the victims
(90) experienced it, using their own words whenever possible. Americans who have always looked westward when reading about this period should read this book facing eastward.

This is not a cheerful book, but history has a
(95) way of intruding upon the present, and perhaps those who read it will have a clearer understand- ing of what the American Indian is, by knowing what he was. They may learn something about their own relationship to the earth from a people
(100) who were true conservationists. The Indians knew that life was equated with the earth and its resources, that America was a paradise, and they could not comprehend why the intruders from the East were determined to destroy all that was
(105) Indian as well as America itself.

13. The author finds the period of 1860–1890 notewor- thy because

   (A) the journals of the Lewis and Clark expedition were made public during this time
   (B) in that period the bulk of original accounts of the "winning of the West" were produced
   (C) during these years American Indians made great strides in regaining their lands
   (D) only a very few documents dating from this period are still extant
   (E) people still believed in personal freedom as an ideal

GO ON TO THE NEXT PAGE

2 2 2 2 2 2 2 2 2 2

14. The author most likely uses quotation marks around the word "opening" (line 4) because

(A) the West was closed rather than opened during this period of time
(B) the American West actually was opened for settlement much earlier in the century
(C) from a Native American perspective it is an inaccurate term
(D) he is citing an authoritative source
(E) he has employed the word in its figurative sense

15. A main concern of the author in this passage is to

(A) denounce the white man for his untrustworthi-ness and savagery
(B) evaluate the effectiveness of the military treaty councils
(C) argue for the improved treatment of Indians today
(D) suggest that Indian narratives of the conquest of the West are similar to white accounts
(E) introduce the background of the original source materials for his text

16. The word "concentration" in lines 5 and 6 means

(A) memory
(B) attention
(C) diligence
(D) imprisonment
(E) accumulation

17. In describing the ideal of freedom revered by the pioneers as "personal freedom for those who already had it" (lines 11 and 12), the author is being

(A) enthusiastic
(B) ironic
(C) prosaic
(D) redundant
(E) lyrical

18. According to the passage, nineteenth-century news-paper accounts of interviews with Indians may con-tain inaccuracies for which of the following reasons?

  I. Lack of skill on the part of the translators
 II. The tendency of the reporters to overstate what they were told by the Indians
III. The Indians' misgivings about possible retaliations

(A) I only
(B) III only
(C) I and II only
(D) I and III only
(E) I, II, and III

19. The author's tone in describing the Indian survivors can best be described as

(A) skeptical
(B) detached
(C) elegiac
(D) obsequious
(E) impatient

20. The author is most impressed by which aspect of the English translations of Indian speeches?

(A) Their vividness of imagery
(B) Their lack of frankness
(C) The inefficiency of the process
(D) Their absence of sophistication
(E) Their brevity of expression

21. The word "flat" in line 69 means

(A) smooth
(B) level
(C) pedestrian
(D) horizontal
(E) unequivocal

22. In treaty councils before 1870, most Indians did not ask for their own interpreters and recorders because

(A) they could not afford to hire people to take down their words
(B) the white officials provided these services as a matter of course
(C) they were unaware that they had the option to demand such services
(D) they preferred speaking for themselves without the help of translators
(E) they were reluctant to have their words recorded for posterity

23. The author most likely suggests that Americans should read this book facing eastward (lines 91–93)

(A) in an inappropriate attempt at levity
(B) out of respect for Western superstitions
(C) in order to read by natural light
(D) because the Indians came from the East
(E) to identify with the Indians' viewpoint

24. The phrase "equated with" in line 101 means

(A) reduced to an average with
(B) necessarily tied to
(C) numerically equal to
(D) fulfilled by
(E) differentiated by

YOU MAY GO BACK AND REVIEW THIS SECTION IN THE REMAINING TIME, BUT DO NOT WORK IN ANY OTHER SECTION UNTIL TOLD TO DO SO.

S T O P

Diagnostic Test

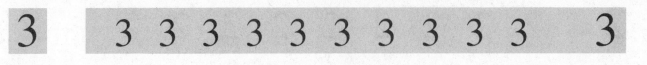

SECTION 3

Time—25 Minutes
20 Questions

For each problem in this section determine which of the five choices is correct and blacken the corresponding choice on your answer sheet. You may use any blank space on the page for your work.

Notes:

- You may use a calculator whenever you think it will be helpful.
- Only real numbers are used. No question or answer on this test involves a complex or imaginary number.
- Use the diagrams provided to help you solve the problems. Unless you see the words "Note: Figure not drawn to scale" under a diagram, it has been drawn as accurately as possible. Unless it is stated that a figure is three-dimensional, you may assume it lies in a plane.
- For any function, f, the domain, unless specifically restricted, is the set of all real numbers for which $f(x)$ is also a real number.

Reference Information

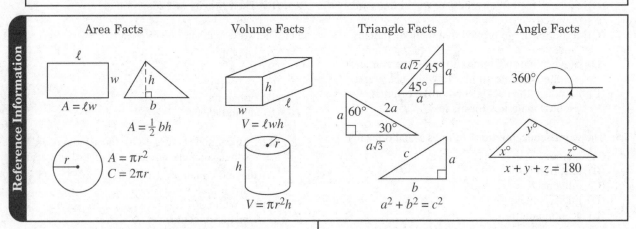

Area Facts

$A = \ell w$

$A = \frac{1}{2} bh$

$A = \pi r^2$
$C = 2\pi r$

Volume Facts

$V = \ell wh$

$V = \pi r^2 h$

Triangle Facts

$a^2 + b^2 = c^2$

Angle Facts

$x + y + z = 180$

1. Every Sunday Greg jogs 3 miles. For the rest of the week, each day he jogs 1 mile more than the preceding day. How many miles does Greg jog in 2 weeks?

   (A) 42
   (B) 63
   (C) 84
   (D) 98
   (E) 117

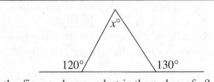

2. In the figure above, what is the value of x?

   (A) 50
   (B) 60
   (C) 70
   (D) 110
   (E) It cannot be determined from the information given.

3. The following table lists the prices of eight types of sandwiches:

Sandwich	Price	Sandwich	Price
Roast beef	$5.25	Tuna fish	$4.25
Corned beef	$5.00	Salami	$4.50
BLT	$4.00	Grilled cheese	$3.95
Egg salad	$3.50	Club	$5.75

If the price of a tuna fish sandwich is increased 75¢ and the price of every other sandwich is increased 50¢, how many sandwiches will be more expensive than the tuna fish?

   (A) 0
   (B) 1
   (C) 2
   (D) 3
   (E) 4

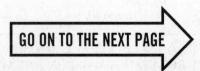
GO ON TO THE NEXT PAGE

4. When a gymnast competes at the Olympics, each of six judges awards a score between 0 and 10. The highest and lowest scores are discarded, and the gymnast's final mark is the average (arithmetic mean) of the remaining scores. What would be a gymnast's mark if the judges' scores were 9.6, 9.4, 9.5, 9.7, 9.2, and 9.6?

(A) 9.5
(B) 9.525
(C) 9.55
(D) 9.575
(E) 9.6

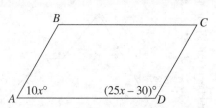

5. In parallelogram *ABCD* above, what is the value of *x*?

(A) 2
(B) 4
(C) 6
(D) 20
(E) 60

6. Three lines are drawn in a plane. Which of the following CANNOT be the total number of points of intersection?

(A) 0
(B) 1
(C) 2
(D) 3
(E) They all could.

7. If $a - b = 10$, and $a^2 - b^2 = 20$, what is the value of *b*?

(A) –6
(B) –4
(C) 4
(D) 6
(E) It cannot be determined from the information given.

8. A dealer in rare metals owns 1000 ounces of silver. If every year she sells half of the silver she owns and doesn't acquire any more, which of the following is an expression for the number of ounces of silver she will own *t* years from now where *t* is a positive integer?

(A) $\dfrac{1000}{2t}$

(B) $1000 \times 2t$

(C) 1000×2^{-t}

(D) $\dfrac{1000}{2^{-t}}$

(E) 1000×2^{t}

9. If $x = 9$ is a solution of the equation $x^2 - a = 0$, which of the following is a solution of $x^4 - a = 0$?

(A) –81
(B) –3
(C) 0
(D) 9
(E) 81

10. The following table shows the hourly wages earned by the 16 employees of a small company and the number of employees who earn each wage.

Wages per Hour	Number of Employees
$6	3
8	5
10	4
13	4

What is the average (arithmetic mean) of the median and the mode of this set of data?

(A) 4.5
(B) 8
(C) 8.5
(D) 9
(E) 9.5

GO ON TO THE NEXT PAGE

3   3   3   3   3   3   3   3   3   3   3   3

11. The degree measure of each of the three angles of a triangle is an integer. Which of the following CANNOT be the ratio of their measures?

(A) 2:3:4
(B) 3:4:5
(C) 4:5:6
(D) 5:6:7
(E) 6:7:8

12. If $3x + 2y = 11$ and $2x + 3y = 17$, what is the average (arithmetic mean) of x and y?

(A) 2.5
(B) 2.8
(C) 5.6
(D) 5.8
(E) 14

Questions 13 and 14 refer to the following definition.

W	X
Y	Z

is a *number square* if $W + Z = X + Y$ and $2W = 3X$.

13. If

3	X
Y	7

is a *number square*, what is the value of Y?

(A) 0
(B) 2
(C) 4
(D) 6
(E) 8

14. If

W	X
Y	W

is a *number square*, $Y =$

(A) $\frac{3}{4}W$

(B) W

(C) $\frac{4}{3}W$

(D) $3W$

(E) $4W$

15. When the price of gold went up, a jeweler raised the prices on certain rings by 60%. On one ring, however, the price was accidentally reduced by 60%. By what percent must the incorrect price be increased to reflect the proper new price?

(A) 60%
(B) 120%
(C) 300%
(D) 400%
(E) It depends on the original price of the ring

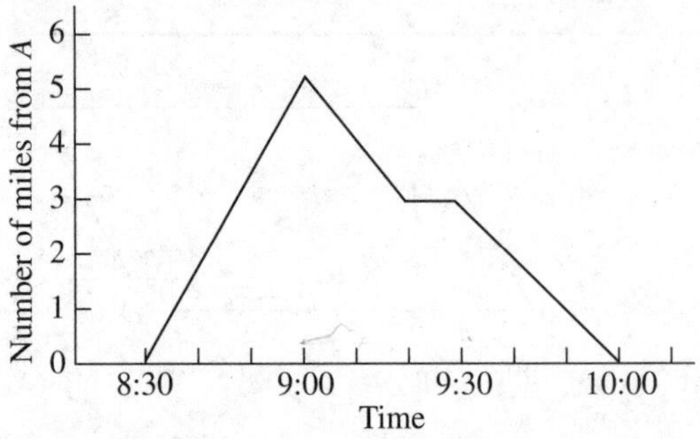

16. John rode his bicycle 5 miles along a straight road from *A* to *B* and back. The graph above shows how far he was from *A* at any given time. Not counting the time he stopped, what was John's average speed, in miles per hour, for the round trip?

(A) $6\frac{2}{3}$

(B) $7\frac{1}{2}$

(C) $8\frac{4}{7}$

(D) 10

(E) It cannot be determined from the graph.

GO ON TO THE NEXT PAGE

3   3 3 3 3 3 3 3 3 3 3   3

17. Let A, B, and C be three points in a plane such that $AB:BC = 3:5$. Which of the following can be the ratio $AB:AC$?

   I. 1:2
  II. 1:3
 III. 3:8

(A) I only
(B) II only
(C) III only
(D) I and III only
(E) I, II, and III

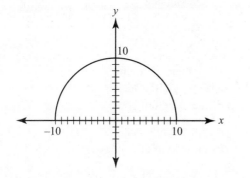

18. The semicircle above is the graph of the function $f(x) = \sqrt{100 - x^2}$. If $g(x)$ is defined by $g(x) = f(3x) + 3$, what is $g(2)$?

(A) $\sqrt{19} + 3$
(B) $\sqrt{96} + 3$
(C) 5
(D) 9
(E) 11

19. A right circular cylinder has a radius of 8 and a height of π^2. If a cube has the same volume as the cylinder, what is the length of an edge of the cube?

(A) $4\sqrt{\pi}$
(B) $8\sqrt{\pi}$
(C) $4\pi\sqrt{\pi}$
(D) 4π
(E) 8π

20. On the critical reading portion of the SAT, the raw score is calculated as follows: 1 point is awarded for each correct answer, and $\frac{1}{4}$ point is deducted for each wrong answer. If Ellen answered all q questions on the test and earned a raw score of 10, how many questions did she answer correctly?

(A) $q - 10$

(B) $\dfrac{q}{5}$

(C) $\dfrac{q}{5} - 10$

(D) $\dfrac{q - 10}{5}$

(E) $8 + \dfrac{q}{5}$

YOU MAY GO BACK AND REVIEW THIS SECTION IN THE REMAINING TIME,
BUT DO NOT WORK IN ANY OTHER SECTION UNTIL TOLD TO DO SO.

S T O P

4 4 4 4 4 4 4 4 4 4 4 4   **4**

SECTION 4	Time—25 Minutes 35 Questions	Select the best answer to each of the following questions; then blacken the appropriate space on your answer sheet.

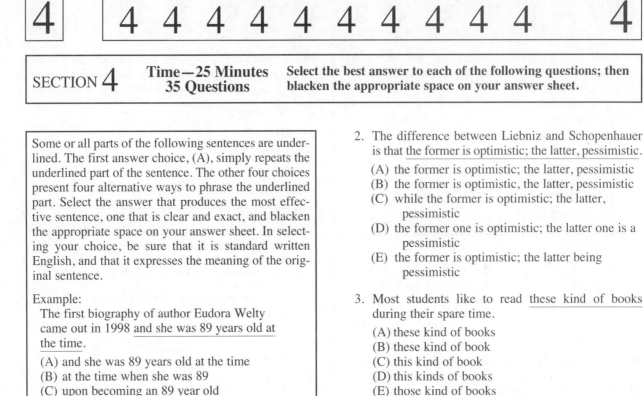

Some or all parts of the following sentences are under-lined. The first answer choice, (A), simply repeats the underlined part of the sentence. The other four choices present four alternative ways to phrase the underlined part. Select the answer that produces the most effec-tive sentence, one that is clear and exact, and blacken the appropriate space on your answer sheet. In select-ing your choice, be sure that it is standard written English, and that it expresses the meaning of the orig-inal sentence.

Example:

The first biography of author Eudora Welty came out in 1998 <u>and she was 89 years old at the time</u>.

(A) and she was 89 years old at the time
(B) at the time when she was 89
(C) upon becoming an 89 year old
(D) when she was 89
(E) at the age of 89 years old

Ⓐ Ⓑ Ⓒ ● Ⓔ

1. <u>Because he spoke out against Hitler's policies was why Dietrich Bonhoeffer, a Lutheran pastor in Nazi Germany, was arrested and eventually hanged by the Gestapo.</u>

   (A) Because he spoke out against Hitler's policies was why Dietrich Bonhoeffer, a Lutheran pastor in Nazi Germany, was arrested and eventually hanged by the Gestapo.
   (B) Dietrich Bonhoeffer, a Lutheran pastor in Nazi Germany, was arrested and eventually hanged by the Gestapo because he spoke out against Hitler's policies.
   (C) Because he spoke out against Hitler's policies, Dietrich Bonhoeffer, a Lutheran pastor in Nazi Germany, was arrested and eventually hung by the Gestapo.
   (D) Dietrich Bonhoeffer, a Lutheran pastor in Nazi Germany, being arrested and eventually hung because he spoke out against Hitler's policies.
   (E) A Lutheran pastor in Nazi Germany, Dietrich Bonhoeffer, spoke out against Hitler's poli-cies so that he arrested and eventually hung.

2. The difference between Liebniz and Schopenhauer is that <u>the former is optimistic; the latter, pessimistic.</u>

   (A) the former is optimistic; the latter, pessimistic
   (B) the former is optimistic, the latter, pessimistic
   (C) while the former is optimistic; the latter, pessimistic
   (D) the former one is optimistic; the latter one is a pessimistic
   (E) the former is optimistic; the latter being pessimistic

3. Most students like to read <u>these kind of books</u> during their spare time.

   (A) these kind of books
   (B) these kind of book
   (C) this kind of book
   (D) this kinds of books
   (E) those kind of books

4. John was <u>imminently qualified for the position because he had studied computer programming and how to operate an IBM machine.</u>

   (A) imminently qualified for the position because he had studied computer programming and how to operate an IBM machine
   (B) imminently qualified for the position since studying computer programming and the operation of an IBM machine
   (C) eminently qualified for the position because he had studied computer programming and how to operate an IBM machine
   (D) eminently qualified for the position because he had studied computer programming and the operation of an IBM machine
   (E) eminently qualified for the position because he has studied computer programming and how to operate an IBM machine

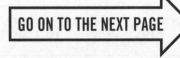
GO ON TO THE NEXT PAGE

4 4 4 4 4 4 4 4 4 4 4 4

5. The idea of inoculating people with smallpox to protect them from later attacks was introduced into
Europe by <u>Mary Wortley Montagu, who learned of
it in Asia</u>.

(A) Mary Wortley Montagu, who learned of it in
Asia
(B) Mary Wortley Montagu, who learned of them
in Asia
(C) Mary Wortley Montagu, who learned it of
those in Asia
(D) Mary Wortley Montagu, learning of it in Asia
(E) Mary Wortley Montagu, because she learned
of it in Asia

6. In general, the fate of Latin American or East Asian
countries <u>will affect America more than it does</u>
Britain or France.

(A) will affect America more than it does
(B) will effect America more than it does
(C) will affect America more than they do
(D) will effect America more than they do
(E) will affect America more than they would

7. While campaigning for President, Dole nearly
<u>exhausted his funds and must raise money so that he
could pay</u> for last-minute television commercials.

(A) exhausted his funds and must raise money so
that he could pay
(B) would exhaust his funds to raise money so that
he could pay
(C) exhausted his funds and had to raise money so
that he can pay
(D) exhausted his funds and had to raise money so
that he could pay
(E) exhausted his funds and must raise money so
that he can pay

8. Athletic coaches stress <u>not only eating nutritious
meals but also to get</u> adequate sleep.

(A) not only eating nutritious meals but also to get
(B) to not only eat nutritious meals but also
getting
(C) not only to eat nutritious meals but also
getting
(D) not only the eating of nutritious meals but also
getting
(E) not only eating nutritious meals but also
getting

9. The goal of the remedial program was <u>that it enables</u>
the students to master the basic skills they need to
succeed in regular coursework.

(A) that it enables
(B) by enabling
(C) to enable
(D) where students are enabled
(E) where it enables

10. Having revised her dissertation with some care,
<u>that her thesis advisor rejected the changes
distressed her greatly</u>.

(A) that her thesis advisor rejected the changes distressed her greatly
(B) she found her thesis advisor's rejection of the
changes greatly distressing
(C) her thesis advisor's rejection of the changes
was a great distress
(D) she was greatly distressed about her thesis
advisor rejecting the changes
(E) her distress at her thesis advisor's rejection of
the changes was great

11. Running an insurance agency left Charles Ives little
time for composition, yet he <u>nevertheless developed
a unique musical idiom</u>.

(A) nevertheless developed a unique musical idiom
(B) nevertheless developed a very unique musical
idiom
(C) therefore developed a uniquely musical idiom
(D) nevertheless developed his musical idiom
uniquely
(E) however developed a very unique and
idiomatic music

GO ON TO THE NEXT PAGE

The sentences in this section may contain errors in grammar, usage, choice of words, or idioms. Either there is just one error in a sentence or the sentence is correct. Some words or phrases are underlined and lettered; everything else in the sentence is correct.

If an underlined word or phrase is incorrect, choose that letter; if the sentence is correct, select <u>No error</u>. Then blacken the appropriate space on your answer sheet.

Example:

The region has a climate <u>so severe that</u> plants
                                        A

<u>growing there</u> rarely <u>had been</u> more than twelve
      B   C

inches <u>high</u>. <u>No error</u>
        D   E

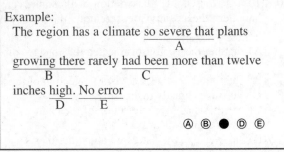

12. I <u>have been thinking</u> lately about the monsters—
          A

   or fantasies <u>or</u> whatever— <u>that</u> frightened
                  B   C

   <u>myself</u> as a child. <u>No error</u>
      D   E

13. Postoperative patients <u>who fail</u> <u>to exercise</u> as
                              A   B

   <u>regular</u> as their doctors recommend take longer to
      C

   <u>recover from</u> surgery than more active patients do.
      D

   <u>No error</u>
      E

14. He worked in the lumber camps <u>during</u> the summer
                                     A

   not <u>because of</u> the money <u>but</u> because he wanted to
        B   C

   strengthen his muscles by doing <u>hard</u> physical
                                     D

   labor. <u>No error</u>
           E

15. That book is <u>liable</u> to become a best seller because
      A   B

   it is well written, <u>full of suspense</u>, and <u>very</u>
                          C   D

   entertaining. <u>No error</u>
                   E

16. <u>According to</u> a random poll <u>taken by</u> *National*
      A   B

   Wildlife, the top three threats to the environment <u>is</u>
                                                          C

   water pollution, air pollution, and <u>hazardous</u>
                                         D

   wastes. <u>No error</u>
             E

17. His three children, Ruth, Frank, and Ellis, are very

   talented youngsters, <u>but</u> the <u>latter</u> <u>shows</u> the <u>most</u>
                          A   B   C   D

   promise. <u>No error</u>
              E

18. <u>Passing</u> antidrug legislation, calling for more
      A

   education, and <u>to aid</u> Bolivia in raids on cocaine
                    B

   dealers are <u>all ways</u> that the United States is
                 C

   fighting back <u>against</u> "crack" use. <u>No error</u>
                   D   E

19. Cajun cooking, which uses <u>special prepared</u> spices,
                                A

   has always been popular in Louisiana, <u>but</u>
                                           B

   it is <u>only</u> now becoming known in other
          C

   <u>parts of</u> the country. <u>No error</u>
      D   E

20. It seems strange <u>to realize that</u>, when Harvey
                       A

   Firestone <u>organized</u> the Firestone Tire and Rubber
                B

   Company in <u>1900, rubber</u> tires <u>had been</u> a novelty.
                C   D

   <u>No error</u>
      E

GO ON TO THE NEXT PAGE

21. The same laser technology that is <u>being used</u> on
                                        A
    compact discs <u>is</u> also <u>under application</u> to
                   B   C
    computers <u>to achieve</u> additional memory.
              D
    <u>No error</u>
    E

22. The Philippine government <u>changed hands</u> <u>when</u>
                               A   B
    Marcos failed <u>satisfying</u> his countrymen that he had
                  C
    won the presidential election, and Corazon Aquino

    <u>took over</u>. <u>No error</u>
    D   E

23. <u>Was</u> <u>it</u> <u>they</u> who were involved in last week's
    A   B   C
    <u>unruly</u> demonstration? <u>No error</u>
    D   E

24. We <u>must regard</u> any statement about this
       A
    controversy, <u>whatever</u> the source, <u>as</u> gossip until
                 B   C
    <u>they are</u> confirmed. <u>No error</u>
    D   E

25. She is the <u>only</u> one of the applicants <u>who</u> <u>are</u>
               A   B   C
    <u>fully qualified</u> for the position. <u>No error</u>
    D   E

26. <u>In order to</u> meet publication schedules, publishers
    A
    often <u>find</u> <u>it necessary</u> to trim everyone's schedule
          B   C
    and <u>leaving room for</u> unexpected problems.
        D
    <u>No error</u>
    E

27. There are <u>probably</u> <u>few comeback stories</u>
              A   B
    as moving as cycling's <u>stalwart champion</u>, Lance
                           C   D
    Armstrong. <u>No error</u>
               E

28. A hotel's <u>ability for winning</u> the loyalty of
              A
    its guests <u>is primarily determined by the</u>
               B
    friendliness and courtesy of the employees

    who are <u>stationed</u> at the front desk. <u>No error</u>
    C   D   E

29. While some scientists are <u>absorbed</u> <u>by the</u>
    A   B
    philosophical question of what consciousness is,

    but others restrict <u>themselves</u> to trying to
                        C
    understand what is going on at the neurological

    level <u>when</u> consciousness is present. <u>No error</u>
    D   E

GO ON TO THE NEXT PAGE

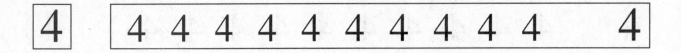

The passage below is the unedited draft of a student's essay. Parts of the essay need to be rewritten to make the meaning clearer and more precise. Read the essay carefully.

The essay is followed by six questions about changes that might improve all or part of the organization, development, sentence structure, use of language, appropriateness to the audience, or use of standard written English. In each case, choose the answer that most clearly and effectively expresses the student's intended meaning. Indicate your choice by blackening the corresponding space on the answer sheet.

[1] When you turn on the radio or pop in a tape while the house is quiet or going to work or school in your car, you have several choices of music to listen to. [2] Although, in recent years, CDs have become the medium of choice over records and even tapes. [3] On the radio you have your rap on one station, your classical on another, your New Wave music on another, and then you have your Country. [4] Some young people feel that country is for fat old people, but it isn't. [5] It is music for all ages, fat or thin.

[6] Country music is "fun" music. [7] It has an unmistakable beat and sound that gets you up and ready to move. [8] You can really get into country, even if it is just the clapping of the hands or the stamping of the feet. [9] You can't help feeling cheerful watching the country performers, who all seem so happy to be entertaining their close "friends," although there may be 10,000 of them in the stadium or concert hall. [10] The musicians love it, and audience flips out with delight. [11] The interpersonal factors in evidence cause a sudden psychological bond to develop into a temporary, but nevertheless tightly knit, family unit. [12] For example, you can imagine June Carter Cash as your favorite aunt and Randy Travis as your long lost cousin.

[13] Some people spurn country music. [14] Why, they ask, would anyone want to listen to singers whine about their broken marriages or their favorite pet that was run over by an 18-wheeler? [15] They claim that Willie Nelson, one of today's country legends, can't even keep his income taxes straight. [16] Another "dynamic" performer is Dolly Parton, whose most famous feature is definitely not her voice. [17] How talented could she be if her body is more famous than her singing?

[18] Loretta Lynn is the greatest. [19] Anyone's negative feelings towards country music would change after hearing Loretta's strong, emotional, and haunting voice. [20] Look, it can't hurt to give a listen. [21] You never know, you might even like it so much that you will go out, pick up a secondhand guitar and learn to strum a few chords.

30. Which is the best revision of the underlined segment of sentence 1 below?

    When you turn on the radio or pop in a tape while the house is quiet or going to work or school in your car, you have several choices of music to listen to.

    (A) while the house is quiet or in your car going to work or school
    (B) driving to work or school while the house is quiet
    (C) while the house is quiet or you are driving to work or school
    (D) while driving to work or school in your car, and the house is quiet
    (E) while there's quiet in the house or you go to work or school in your car

31. To improve the coherence of paragraph 1, which of the following sentences should be deleted?

    (A) Sentence 1
    (B) Sentence 2
    (C) Sentence 3
    (D) Sentence 4
    (E) Sentence 5

GO ON TO THE NEXT PAGE

4   4 4 4 4 4 4 4 4 4 4 4   4

32. In the context of the sentences that precede and fol-
    low sentence 8, which of the following is the best
    revision of sentence 8?

    (A) Clap your hands and stamp your feet is what to
        do to easily get into country.
    (B) You're really into country, even if it is just
        clapping of the hands or stamping of the feet.
    (C) You can easily get into country just by clap-
        ping your hands or stamping your feet.
    (D) One can get into country music rather easily;
        one must merely clap one's hands or stamp
        one's feet.
    (E) Getting into country is easy, just clap your
        hands and stamp your feet.

33. Given the writing style and tone of the essay, which
    is the best revision of sentence 11?

    (A) The interpersonal relationship that develops
        suddenly creates a temporary, but neverthe-
        less a closely knit, family unit.
    (B) A family-like relationship develops quickly
        and rapidly.
    (C) A close family-type relation is suddenly very
        much in evidence between the performer and
        his or her audience.
    (D) All of a sudden you feel like a member of a
        huge, but tight, family.
    (E) A sudden bond develops between the enter-
        tainer and the audience that might most suit-
        ably be described as a "family," in the best
        sense of the term.

34. Which of the following best describes the function of
    paragraph 3 in the essay as a whole?

    (A) To present some objective data in support of
        another viewpoint
    (B) To offer a more balanced view of the essay's
        subject matter
    (C) To ridicule readers who disagree with the
        writer
    (D) To lend further support to the essay's main
        idea
    (E) To divert the reader's attention from the main
        idea of the essay

35. Which of the following revisions of sentence 18 pro-
    vides the smoothest transition between paragraphs 3
    and 4?

    (A) Loretta Lynn is one of the great singers of
        country music.
    (B) Loretta Lynn, however, is the greatest country
        singer yet.
    (C) But you can bet they've never heard Loretta
        Lynn sing.
    (D) The sounds of Loretta Lynn tells a different
        story, however.
    (E) Loretta Lynn, on the other hand, is superb.

YOU MAY GO BACK AND REVIEW THIS SECTION IN THE REMAINING TIME,
BUT DO NOT WORK IN ANY OTHER SECTION UNTIL TOLD TO DO SO.   **S T O P**

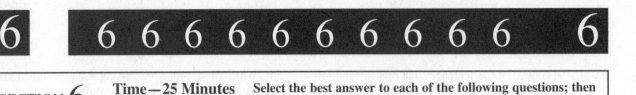

SECTION 6   Time—25 Minutes   Select the best answer to each of the following questions; then
24 Questions   blacken the appropriate space on your answer sheet.

Each of the following sentences contains one or two blanks; each blank indicates that a word or set of words has been left out. Below the sentence are five words or phrases, lettered A through E. Select the word or set of words that best completes the sentence.

Example:

Fame is ----; today's rising star is all too soon tomorrow's washed-up has-been.

(A) rewarding   (B) gradual
(C) essential   (D) spontaneous
(E) transitory

Ⓐ Ⓑ Ⓒ Ⓓ ●

1. Despite the ---- of the materials with which Tiffany worked, many of his glass masterpieces have survived for more than seventy years.
   (A) beauty
   (B) translucence
   (C) abundance
   (D) majesty
   (E) fragility

2. No summary of the behavior of animals toward reflected images is given, but not much else that is ---- seems missing from this comprehensive yet compact study of mirrors and mankind.
   (A) redundant
   (B) contemplative
   (C) relevant
   (D) peripheral
   (E) disputable

3. Pain is the body's early warning system: loss of ---- in the extremities leaves a person ---- injuring himself unwittingly.
   (A) agony..incapable of
   (B) sensation..vulnerable to
   (C) consciousness..desirous of
   (D) feeling..habituated to
   (E) movement..prone to

4. Much of the clown's success may be attributed to the contrast between the ---- manner he adopts and the general ---- that characterizes the circus.
   (A) giddy..sobriety
   (B) lugubrious..hilarity
   (C) gaudy..clamor
   (D) joyful..hysteria
   (E) frenetic..excitement

5. Fortunately, she was ---- her accomplishments, properly unwilling to ---- them before her friends.
   (A) excited by..parade
   (B) immodest about..discuss
   (C) deprecatory about..flaunt
   (D) uncertain of..concede
   (E) unaware of..conceal

GO ON TO THE NEXT PAGE ⟹

Read the passages below, and then answer the questions that follow them. The correct response may be stated outright or merely suggested in the passages.

Questions 6–9 are based on the following passages.

Passage 1

Pioneering conservationist Marjory Stoneman Douglas called it the River of Grass. Stretching south from Lake Okeechobee, fed by the rain-
Line drenched Kissimmee River basin, the Everglades
(5) is a water marsh, a slow-moving river of swamps and sawgrass flowing southward to the Gulf of Mexico. It is a unique ecosystem, whose enduring value has come from its being home to countless species of plants and animals: cypress trees and
(10) mangroves, wood storks and egrets, snapping turtles and crocodiles. For the past 50 years, however, this river has been shrinking. Never a torrent, it has dwindled as engineering projects have diverted the waters feeding it to meet agricultural
(15) and housing needs.

Passage 2

Today South Florida's sugar industry is in serious trouble. Responding to the concerns of the scientific community and to the mandates of the Everglades Forever Act, local sugar producers
(20) have spent millions of dollars since 1994 to minimize the runoff of phosphorus from sugar cane fields into the Everglades. (Phosphorus runoff, scientists maintain, has encouraged an invasion of cattails, which overrun the native sawgrass and
(25) choke the flow of water through what was once a vast sawgrass marsh.) Sugar producers have adopted ecologically sound farming practices and at great cost have dramatically reduced phosphorus levels to help save the Everglades' fragile
(30) ecosystem. But who or what will help save Florida's imperiled sugar industry?

6. The author of Passage 1 cites the conservationist Marjory Stoneman Douglas in order to

(A) present a viewpoint
(B) challenge an opinion
(C) introduce a metaphor
(D) correct a misapprehension
(E) honor a pioneer

7. In Passage 1, the word "enduring" (line 7) most nearly means

(A) tolerating
(B) noteworthy
(C) hard-won
(D) lasting
(E) serene

8. In lines 22–26, the author of Passage 2 uses a parenthetic remark to

(A) cast doubt on the credibility of a statement
(B) provide background on the reasons for a concern
(C) demonstrate support for the scientific community
(D) explain the usage of a technical term
(E) justify the efforts of the sugar industry

9. On the basis of the final sentence ("But…industry") of Passage 2, the author of this passage would most likely appear to the author of Passage 1 as

(A) strongly opposed to the Everglades cleanup
(B) well informed concerning specific requirements of the Everglades Forever Act
(C) inclined to overestimate the importance of the sugar industry
(D) having a deep sympathy for environmental causes
(E) having little understanding of scientific methods

GO ON TO THE NEXT PAGE

Questions 10–15 are based on the following passage.

In this excerpt from Richard Wright's 1937 novel Black Boy, *the young African-American narrator confronts a new world in the books he illegally borrows from the "whites-only" public library.*

That night in my rented room, while letting the hot water run over my can of pork and beans in the sink, I opened Mencken's *A Book of*
Line *Prejudices* and began to read. I was jarred and
(5) shocked by the style, the clear, clean, sweeping sentences. Why did he write like that? And how did one write like that? I pictured the man as a raging demon, slashing with his pen, consumed with hate, denouncing everything American,
(10) extolling everything European, laughing at the weaknesses of people, mocking God, authority. What was this? I stood up, trying to realize what reality lay behind the meaning of the words. Yes, this man was fighting, fighting with words. He
(15) was using words as a weapon, using them as one would use a club. Could words be weapons? Well, yes, for here they were. Then, maybe, per-haps, a Negro could use them as a weapon? No. It frightened me. I read on, and what amazed me
(20) was not what he said, but how on earth anybody had the courage to say it.

What strange world was this? I concluded the book with the conviction that I had somehow overlooked something terribly important in life. I
(25) had once tried to write, had once reveled in feel-ing, had let my crude imagination roam, but the impulse to dream had been slowly beaten out of me by experience. Now it surged up again and I hungered for books, new ways of looking and
(30) seeing. It was not a matter of believing or disbe-lieving what I read, but of feeling something new, of being affected by something that made the look of the world different.

As dawn broke I ate my pork and beans, feel-
(35) ing dopey, sleepy. I went to work, but the mood of the book would not die; it lingered, coloring everything I saw, heard, did. I now felt that I knew what the white men were feeling. Merely because I had read a book that had spoken of how
(40) they lived and thought, I identified myself with that book. I felt vaguely guilty. Would I, filled with bookish notions, act in a manner that would make the whites dislike me?

I forged more notes and my trips to the library
(45) became frequent. Reading grew into a passion. My first serious novel was Sinclair Lewis's *Main Street*. It made me see my boss, Mr. Gerald, and identify him as an American type. I would smile when I saw him lugging his golf bags into the
(50) office. I had always felt a vast distance separating me from the boss, and now I felt closer to him,

though still distant. I felt now that I knew him, that I could feel the very limits of his narrow life. This had happened because I had read a novel
(55) about a mythical man called George F. Babbitt. But I could not conquer my sense of guilt, my feeling that the white men around me knew that I was changing, that I had begun to regard them differently.

10. The narrator's initial reaction to Mencken's prose can best be described as one of

   (A) wrath
   (B) disbelief
   (C) remorse
   (D) laughter
   (E) disdain

11. To the narrator, Mencken appeared to be all of the following EXCEPT

   (A) intrepid
   (B) articulate
   (C) satiric
   (D) reverent
   (E) opinionated

12. As used in line 36, "coloring" most nearly means

   (A) reddening
   (B) sketching
   (C) blushing
   (D) affecting
   (E) lying

13. The narrator's attitude in lines 28–30 is best described as one of

   (A) dreamy indifference
   (B) sullen resentment
   (C) impatient ardor
   (D) wistful anxiety
   (E) quiet resolve

14. The passage suggests that, when he saw Mr. Gerald carrying the golf clubs, the narrator smiled out of a sense of

   (A) relief
   (B) duty
   (C) recognition
   (D) disbelief
   (E) levity

GO ON TO THE NEXT PAGE

15. The passage as a whole is best characterized as

    (A) an impassioned argument in favor of increased literacy for blacks
    (B) a description of a youth's gradual introduction to racial prejudice
    (C) a comparison of the respective merits of Mencken's and Lewis's literary styles
    (D) an analysis of the impact of ordinary life on art
    (E) a portrait of a youth's response to expanding intellectual horizons

Questions 16–24 are based on the following passage.

The following passage about pond-dwellers is excerpted from a classic essay on natural history written by the zoologist Konrad Lorenz.

There are some terrible robbers in the pond world, and, in our aquarium, we may witness all the cruelties of an embittered struggle for exis-
Line tence enacted before our very eyes. If you have
(5) introduced to your aquarium a mixed catch, you will soon see an example of such conflicts, for, amongst the new arrivals, there will probably be a larva of the water-beetle *Dytiscus*. Considering their relative size, the voracity and cunning with
(10) which these animals destroy their prey eclipse the methods of even such notorious robbers as tigers, lions, wolves, or killer whales. These are all as lambs compared with the *Dytiscus* larva.

It is a slim, streamlined insect, rather more
(15) than two inches long. Its six legs are equipped with stout fringes of bristles, which form broad oar-like blades that propel the animal quickly and surely through the water. The wide, flat head bears an enormous, pincer-shaped pair of jaws
(20) that are hollow and serve not only as syringes for injecting poison, but also as orifices of ingestion. The animal lies in ambush on some waterplant; suddenly it shoots at lightning speed towards its prey, darts underneath it, then quickly jerks up its
(25) head and grabs the victim in its jaws. "Prey," for these creatures, is all that moves or that smells of "animal" in any way. It has often happened to me that, while standing quietly in the water of a pond, I have been "eaten" by a *Dytiscus* larva.
(30) Even for man, an injection of the poisonous digestive juice of this insect is extremely painful.

These beetle larvae are among the few animals that digest "out of doors." The glandular secretion that they inject, through their hollow forceps, into
(35) their prey, dissolves the entire inside of the latter into a liquid soup, which is then sucked in through the same channel by the attacker. Even large victims, such as fat tadpoles or dragon-fly larvae, which have been bitten by a *Dytiscus*

(40) larva, stiffen after a few defensive moments, and their inside, which, as in most water animals, is more or less transparent, becomes opaque as though fixed by formalin. The animal swells up first, then gradually shrinks to a limp bundle of
(45) skin that hangs from the deadly jaws, and is finally allowed to drop. In the confines of an aquarium, a few large *Dytiscus* larvae will, within days, eat all living things over a quarter of an inch long. What happens then? They will eat each other, if
(50) they have not already done so; this depends less on who is bigger and stronger than upon who succeeds in seizing the other first. I have often seen two nearly equal sized *Dytiscus* larvae each seize the other simultaneously and both die a quick
(55) death by inner dissolution. Very few animals, even when threatened with starvation, will attack an equal sized animal of their own species with the intention of devouring it. I only know this to be definitely true of rats and a few related
(60) rodents; that wolves do the same thing, I am much inclined to doubt, on the strength of some observations of which I shall speak later. But *Dytiscus* larvae devour animals of their own breed and size, even when other nourishment is at hand, and that
(65) is done, as far as I know, by no other animal.

16. By robbers (line 1), the author refers to

    (A) thieves
    (B) plagiarists
    (C) people who steal fish
    (D) creatures that devour their prey
    (E) unethical scientific observers

17. As used in line 5, a "mixed catch" most likely is

    (A) a device used to shut the aquarium lid temporarily
    (B) a disturbed group of water beetle larvae
    (C) a partially desirable prospective denizen of the aquarium
    (D) a random batch of creatures taken from a pond
    (E) a theoretical drawback that may have positive results

GO ON TO THE NEXT PAGE

18. The presence of Dytiscus larvae in an aquarium most likely would be of particular interest to naturalists studying

    (A) means of exterminating water-beetle larvae
    (B) predatory patterns within a closed environment
    (C) genetic characteristics of a mixed catch
    (D) the effect of captivity on aquatic life
    (E) the social behavior of dragon-fly larvae

19. The author's primary purpose in lines 14–21 is to

    (A) depict the typical victim of a Dytiscus larva
    (B) point out the threat to humans represented by Dytiscus larvae
    (C) describe the physical appearance of an aquatic predator
    (D) refute the notion of the aquarium as a peaceful habitat
    (E) clarify the method the Dytiscus larva uses to dispatch its prey

20. The passage mentions all of the following facts about Dytiscus larvae EXCEPT that they

    (A) secrete digestive juices
    (B) attack their fellow larvae
    (C) are attracted to motion
    (D) provide food for amphibians
    (E) have ravenous appetites

21. By digesting "out of doors" (line 33), the author is referring to the Dytiscus larva's

    (A) preference for open-water ponds over confined spaces
    (B) metabolic elimination of waste matter
    (C) amphibious method of locomotion
    (D) extreme voraciousness of appetite
    (E) external conversion of food into absorbable form

22. According to the author, which of the following is (are) true of the victim of a Dytiscus larva?

    I. Its interior increases in opacity.
    II. It shrivels as it is drained of nourishment.
    III. It is beheaded by the larva's jaws.

    (A) I only
    (B) II only
    (C) III only
    (D) I and II only
    (E) II and III only

23. In the final paragraph, the author mentions rats and related rodents in order to emphasize which point about Dytiscus larvae?

    (A) Unless starvation drives them, they will not resort to eating members of their own species.
    (B) They are reluctant to attack equal-sized members of their own breed.
    (C) They are capable of resisting attacks from much larger animals.
    (D) They are one of extremely few species given to devouring members of their own breed.
    (E) Although they are noted predators, Dytiscus larvae are less savage than rats.

24. The author indicates that in subsequent passages he will discuss

    (A) the likelihood of cannibalism among wolves
    (B) the metamorphosis of dragon-fly larvae into dragon-flies
    (C) antidotes to cases of Dytiscus poisoning
    (D) the digestive processes of killer whales
    (E) the elimination of Dytiscus larvae from aquariums

YOU MAY GO BACK AND REVIEW THIS SECTION IN THE REMAINING TIME, BUT DO NOT WORK IN ANY OTHER SECTION UNTIL TOLD TO DO SO.

STOP

7

SECTION 7
Time—25 Minutes
18 Questions

You have 25 minutes to answer the 8 multiple-choice questions and 10 student-produced response questions in this section. For each multiple-choice question, determine which of the five choices is correct and blacken the corresponding choice on your answer sheet. You may use any blank space on the page for your work.

Notes:

- You may use a calculator whenever you think it will be helpful.
- Only real numbers are used. No question or answer on this test involves a complex or imaginary number.
- Use the diagrams provided to help you solve the problems. Unless you see the words "Note: Figure not drawn to scale" under a diagram, it has been drawn as accurately as possible. Unless it is stated that a figure is three-dimensional, you may assume it lies in a plane.
- For any function, f, the domain, unless specifically restricted, is the set of all real numbers for which $f(x)$ is also a real number.

Reference Information

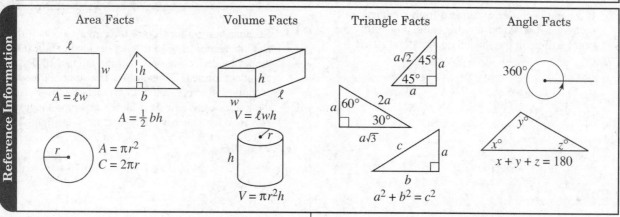

Area Facts   Volume Facts   Triangle Facts   Angle Facts

$A = \ell w$

$A = \frac{1}{2}bh$

$A = \pi r^2$
$C = 2\pi r$

$V = \ell w h$

$V = \pi r^2 h$

$a^2 + b^2 = c^2$

$x + y + z = 180$

1. How many integers are solutions of the inequality $3|x| + 2 < 17$?

   (A) 0
   (B) 4
   (C) 8
   (D) 9
   (E) Infinitely many

2. If a speed of 1 meter per second is equal to a speed of k kilometers per hour, what is the value of k?

   (1 kilometer = 1000 meters)

   (A) 0.036
   (B) 0.06
   (C) 0.36
   (D) 0.6
   (E) 3.6

3. If $f(x) = x^2 + \sqrt[3]{x}$, what is the value of $f(-8)$?

   (A) −66
   (B) −62
   (C) 62
   (D) 64
   (E) 66

4. In 2000, twice as many boys as girls at Adams High School earned varsity letters. From 2000 to 2010, the number of girls earning varsity letters increased by 25% while the number of boys earning varsity letters decreased by 25%. What was the ratio in 2010 of the number of girls to the number of boys who earned varsity letters?

   (A) $\frac{5}{3}$

   (B) $\frac{6}{5}$

   (C) $\frac{1}{1}$

   (D) $\frac{5}{6}$

   (E) $\frac{3}{5}$

GO ON TO THE NEXT PAGE

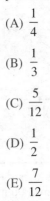

5. If today is Saturday, what day will it be 500 days from today?

   (A) Saturday
   (B) Sunday
   (C) Tuesday
   (D) Wednesday
   (E) Friday

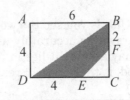

6. If a point is chosen at random from the interior of rectangle *ABCD* above, what is the probability the point will be in the shaded quadrilateral *BDEF*?

   (A) $\dfrac{1}{4}$

   (B) $\dfrac{1}{3}$

   (C) $\dfrac{5}{12}$

   (D) $\dfrac{1}{2}$

   (E) $\dfrac{7}{12}$

7. If the average (arithmetic mean) of a, b, c, and d is equal to the average of a, b, and c, what is d in terms of a, b, and c?

   (A) $a + b + c$

   (B) $\dfrac{a+b+c}{3}$

   (C) $\dfrac{4(a+b+c)}{3}$

   (D) $\dfrac{3(a+b+c)}{4}$

   (E) $\dfrac{(a+b+c)}{4}$

8. Because her test turned out to be more difficult than she intended it to be, a teacher decided to adjust the grades by deducting only half the number of points a student missed. For example, if a student missed 10 points, she received a 95 instead of a 90. Before the grades were adjusted, Meri's grade on the test was A. What was her grade after the adjustment?

   (A) $50 + \dfrac{A}{2}$

   (B) $\dfrac{50 + A}{2}$

   (C) $100 - \dfrac{A}{2}$

   (D) $\dfrac{100 - A}{2}$

   (E) $A + 25$

Directions for Student-Produced Response Questions (Grid-ins)

In questions 9–18, first solve the problem, and then enter your answer on the grid provided on the answer sheet. The instructions for entering your answers are as follows:

- First, write your answer in the boxes at the top of the grid.
- Second, grid your answer in the columns below the boxes.
- Use the fraction bar in the first row or the decimal point in the second row to enter fractions and decimal answers.

Answer: $\frac{8}{15}$ Answer: 1.75

Write your → answer in the boxes.

Grid in → your answer.

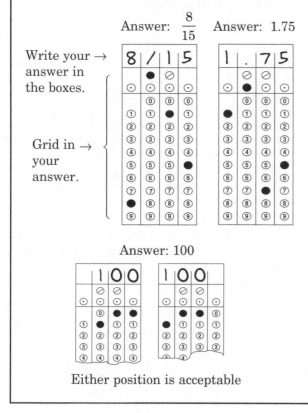

Answer: 100

Either position is acceptable

- Grid only one space in each column.
- Entering the answer in the boxes is recommended as an aid in gridding, but is not required.
- The machine scoring your exam can read only what you grid, so you **must grid in your answers correctly to get credit.**
- If a question has more than one correct answer, grid in only one of these answers.
- The grid does not have a minus sign, so no answer can be negative.
- A mixed number *must* be converted to an improper fraction or a decimal before it is gridded. Enter $1\frac{1}{4}$ as 5/4 or 1.25; the machine will interpret 1 1/4 as $\frac{11}{4}$ and mark it wrong.
- **All decimals must be entered as accurately as possible.** Here are the three acceptable ways of gridding

$$\frac{3}{11} = 0.272727...$$

3/11   .272   .273

- Note that rounding to .273 is acceptable, because you are using the full grid, but you would receive **no credit** for .3 or .27, because these answers are less accurate.

9. Pencils that were selling at three for 25 cents are now on sale at five for 29 cents. How much money, in cents, would you save by buying 60 pencils at the sale price?

10. If $1 < 3x - 5 < 2$, what is one possible value for *x*?

7

11. What is the largest integer, x, such that $x < 10,000$ and $\dfrac{\sqrt{x}}{5}$ is an even integer?

12. Ellie is dropping marbles into a box one at a time in the following order: red, white, white, blue, blue, blue; red, white, white, blue, blue, blue; .... How many marbles will be in the box right after the 100th blue one is put in?

13. Four 3-4-5 right triangles and a square whose sides are 5 are arranged to form a second square. What is the perimeter of that square?

Questions 14 and 15 refer to the following definition.

For any positive integer a: $\langle\langle a \rangle\rangle = \dfrac{1}{2^{a+1}}$.

14. What is the value of $\langle\langle 3 \rangle\rangle - \langle\langle 4 \rangle\rangle$?

15. What is the ratio of $\langle\langle a + 3 \rangle\rangle$ to $\langle\langle a \rangle\rangle$?

16. Each of 100 cards has none, one, or two of the letters A and C written on it. If 75 cards have the letter A, 30 have the letter C, and fewer than 15 are blank, what is the largest possible number of cards that have both A and C written on them?

17. To use a certain cash machine, you need a Personal Identification Code (PIC). If each PIC consists of two letters followed by one of the digits from 1 to 9 (such as AQ7 or BB3) or one letter followed by two digits (such as Q37 or J88), how many different PIC's can be assigned?

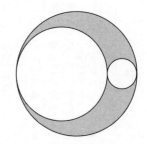

18. In the figure above, the three circles are tangent to one another. If the ratio of the diameter of the large white circle to the diameter of the small white circle is 3:1, what fraction of the largest circle has been shaded?

| YOU MAY GO BACK AND REVIEW THIS SECTION IN THE REMAINING TIME, BUT DO NOT WORK IN ANY OTHER SECTION UNTIL TOLD TO DO SO. | **S T O P** |

8 8 8 8 8 8 8 8 8 8 8

SECTION 8 | **Time—20 Minutes** **19 Questions** | **Select the best answer to each of the following questions; then blacken the appropriate space on your answer sheet.**

Each of the following sentences contains one or two blanks; each blank indicates that a word or set of words has been left out. Below the sentence are five words or phrases, lettered A through E. Select the word or set of words that best completes the sentence.

Example:

Fame is ----; today's rising star is all too soon tomorrow's washed-up has-been.

(A) rewarding (B) gradual
 (C) essential (D) spontaneous
  (E) transitory

Ⓐ Ⓑ Ⓒ Ⓓ ●

---

1. Although similar to mice in many physical characteristics, voles may be ---- mice by the shortness of their tails.

   (A) distinguished from
   (B) classified with
   (C) related to
   (D) categorized as
   (E) enumerated with

2. Dr. Charles Drew's technique for preserving and storing blood plasma for emergency use proved so ---- that it became the ---- for the present blood bank system used by the American Red Cross.

   (A) irrelevant..inspiration
   (B) urgent..pattern
   (C) effective..model
   (D) innocuous..excuse
   (E) complex..blueprint

3. The likenesses of language around the Mediterranean were sufficiently marked to ---- ease of movement both of men and ideas: it took relatively few alterations to make a Spanish song intelligible in Italy, and an Italian trader could, without much difficulty, make himself at home in France.

   (A) eliminate
   (B) facilitate
   (C) hinder
   (D) clarify
   (E) aggravate

4. Because he saw no ---- to the task assigned him, he worked at it in a very ---- way.

   (A) function..systematic
   (B) method..dutiful
   (C) purpose..diligent
   (D) end..rigid
   (E) point..perfunctory

5. During the Battle of Trafalgar, Admiral Nelson remained ---- , in full command of the situation in spite of the hysteria and panic all around him.

   (A) impassable
   (B) imperturbable
   (C) overbearing
   (D) frenetic
   (E) lackadaisical

6. Although he had spent many hours at the computer trying to solve the problem, he was the first to admit that the final solution was ---- and not the ---- of his labor.

   (A) trivial..cause
   (B) incomplete..intent
   (C) adequate..concern
   (D) schematic..fault
   (E) fortuitous..result

GO ON TO THE NEXT PAGE

8   8   8   8   8   8   8   8   8   8   8

The questions that follow the next two passages relate to the content of both, and to their relationship. The correct response may be stated outright in the passage or merely suggested.

Questions 7–19 are based on the following passages.

The following passages are excerpted from two recent essays that make an analogy between writing and sports. The author of Passage 1, whose manuscript has been rejected by his publisher, discusses the sorts of failures experienced by writers and ballplayers. The author of Passage 2 explores how his involvement in sports affected his writing career.

Passage 1

In consigning this manuscript to a desk drawer, I am comforted by the behavior of baseball players. There are *no* pitchers who do not give up home
Line runs, there are *no* batters who do not strike out.
(5) There are *no* major league pitchers or batters who have not somehow learned to survive giving up home runs and striking out. That much is obvious.

What seems to me less obvious is how these "failures" must be digested, or put to use, in the
(10) overall experience of the player. A jogger once explained to me that the nerves of the ankle are so sensitive and complex that each time a runner sets his foot down, hundreds of messages are conveyed to the runner's brain about the nature of the
(15) terrain and the requirements for weight distribution, balance, and muscle-strength. I'm certain that the ninth-inning home run that Dave Henderson hit off Donny Moore registered complexly and permanently in Moore's mind and
(20) body and that the next time Moore faced Henderson, his pitching was informed by his awful experience of October 1986. Moore's continuing baseball career depended to some extent on his converting that encounter with Henderson
(25) into something useful for his pitching. I can also imagine such an experience destroying an athlete, registering in his mind and body in such a negative way as to produce a debilitating fear.

Of the many ways in which athletes and artists
(30) are similar, one is that, unlike accountants or plumbers or insurance salesmen, to succeed at all they must perform at an extraordinary level of excellence. Another is that they must be willing to extend themselves irrationally in order to achieve
(35) that level of performance. A writer doesn't have to write all-out all the time, but he or she must be ready to write all-out any time the story requires it. Hold back and you produce what just about any literate citizen can produce, a "pretty good" piece

(40) of work. Like the cautious pitcher, the timid writer can spend a lifetime in the minor leagues.

And what more than failure—the strike out, the crucial home run given up, the manuscript criticized and rejected—is more likely to produce
(45) caution or timidity? An instinctive response to painful experience is to avoid the behavior that produced the pain. To function at the level of excellence required for survival, writers, like athletes, must go against instinct, must absorb their
(50) failures and become stronger, must endlessly repeat the behavior that produced the pain.

Passage 2

The athletic advantages of this concentration, particularly for an athlete who was making up for the absence of great natural skill, were consider-
(55) able. Concentration gave you an edge over many of your opponents, even your betters, who could not isolate themselves to that degree. For example, in football if they were ahead (or behind) by several touchdowns, if the game itself seemed to have
(60) been settled, they tended to slack off, to ease off a little, certainly to relax their own concentration. It was then that your own unwavering concentration and your own indifference to the larger point of view paid off. At the very least you could deal out
(65) surprise and discomfort to your opponents.

But it was more than that. Do you see? The ritual of physical concentration, of acute engagement in a small space while disregarding all the clamor and demands of the larger world, was the
(70) best possible lesson in precisely the kind of selfish intensity needed to create and to finish a poem, a story, or a novel. This alone mattered while all the world going on, with and without you, did not.

I was learning first in muscle, blood, and bone,
(75) not from literature and not from teachers of literature or the arts or the natural sciences, but from coaches, in particular this one coach who paid me enough attention to influence me to teach some things to myself. I was learning about art and life

GO ON TO THE NEXT PAGE

8   8   8   8   8   8   8   8   8   8   8

(80) through the abstraction of athletics in much the
same way that a soldier is, to an extent, prepared
for war by endless parade ground drill. His body
must learn to be a soldier before heart, mind, and
spirit can.

(85)   Ironically, I tend to dismiss most comparisons
of athletics to art and to "the creative process."
But only because, I think, so much that is claimed
for both is untrue. But I have come to believe—
indeed I have to believe it insofar as I believe in

(90) the validity and efficacy of art—that what comes
to us first and foremost through the body, as a
sensuous affective experience, is taken and transformed by mind and self into a thing of the spirit.
Which is only to say that what the body learns

(95) and is taught is of enormous significance—at
least until the last light of the body fails.

7. Why does the author of Passage 1 consign his manuscript to a desk drawer?

(A) To protect it from the inquisitive eyes of his
family
(B) To prevent its getting lost or disordered
(C) Because his publisher wishes to take another
look at it
(D) Because he chooses to watch a televised baseball game
(E) To set it aside as unmarketable in its current
state

8. Why is the author of Passage 1 "comforted by the
behavior of baseball players" (line 2)?

(A) He treasures the timeless rituals of America's
national pastime.
(B) He sees he is not alone in having to confront
failure and move on.
(C) He enjoys watching the frustration of the
batters who strike out.
(D) He looks at baseball from the viewpoint of a
behavioral psychologist.
(E) He welcomes any distraction from the task of
revising his novel.

9. What function in the passage is served by the discussion of the nerves in the ankle in lines 11–16?

(A) It provides a momentary digression from the
overall narrative flow.
(B) It emphasizes how strong a mental impact
Henderson's home run must have had on
Moore.
(C) It provides scientific confirmation of the
neuromuscular abilities of athletes.
(D) It illustrates that the author's interest in sports
is not limited to baseball alone.
(E) It conveys a sense of how confusing it is for
the mind to deal with so many simultaneous
messages.

10. The word "registered" in line 18 means

(A) enrolled formally
(B) expressed without words
(C) corresponded exactly
(D) made an impression
(E) qualified officially

11. The attitude of the author of Passage 1 to accountants, plumbers, and insurance salesmen (lines
30–33) can best be described as

(A) respectful
(B) cautious
(C) superior
(D) cynical
(E) hypocritical

12. In the final two paragraphs of Passage 1, the author
appears to

(A) romanticize the writer as someone heroic in his
or her accomplishments
(B) deprecate athletes for their inability to react to
experience instinctively
(C) minimize the travail that artists and athletes
endure to do their work
(D) advocate the importance of literacy to the common citizen
(E) suggest that a cautious approach would reduce
the likelihood of future failure

13. The author of Passage 2 prizes

(A) his innate athletic talent
(B) the respect of his peers
(C) his ability to focus
(D) the gift of relaxation
(E) winning at any cost

14. The word "settled" in line 60 means

(A) judged
(B) decided
(C) reconciled
(D) pacified
(E) inhabited

GO ON TO THE NEXT PAGE

8   8   8   8   8   8   8   8   8   8   8

15. What does the author mean by "indifference to the larger point of view" (lines 63 and 64)?

   (A) Inability to see the greater implications of the activity in which you were involved
   (B) Hostility to opponents coming from larger, better trained teams
   (C) Reluctance to look beyond your own immediate concerns
   (D) Refusing to care how greatly you might be hurt by your opponents
   (E) Being more concerned with the task at hand than with whether you win or lose

16. What is the function of the phrase "to an extent" in line 81?

   (A) It denies a situation.
   (B) It conveys a paradox.
   (C) It qualifies a statement.
   (D) It represents a metaphor.
   (E) It minimizes a liability.

17. The author finds it ironic that he tends to "dismiss most comparisons of athletics to art" (lines 85 and 86) because

   (A) athletics is the basis for great art
   (B) he finds comparisons generally unhelpful
   (C) he is making such a comparison
   (D) he typically is less cynical
   (E) he rejects the so-called creative process

18. The authors of both passages would agree that

   (A) the lot of the professional writer is more trying than that of the professional athlete
   (B) athletics has little to do with the actual workings of the creative process
   (C) both artists and athletes learn hard lessons in the course of mastering their art
   (D) it is important to concentrate on the things that hurt us in life
   (E) participating in sports provides a distraction from the isolation of a writer's life

19. How would the author of Passage 2 respond to the author of Passage 1's viewpoint that a failure such as giving up a key home run can destroy an athlete?

   (A) An athlete learns through his body that failure is enormously significant and affects him both physically and spiritually.
   (B) Athletes of great natural skill suffer less from the agonies of failure than less accomplished athletes do.
   (C) If an athlete plays without holding back, he will surpass athletes who are more inherently adept.
   (D) If the athlete focuses on the job at hand and not on past errors, he will continue to function successfully.
   (E) Athletes are highly sensitive performers who need to be sheltered from the clamor and demands of the larger world.

YOU MAY GO BACK AND REVIEW THIS SECTION IN THE REMAINING TIME, BUT DO NOT WORK IN ANY OTHER SECTION UNTIL TOLD TO DO SO.   **S T O P**

9 9 9 9 9 9 9

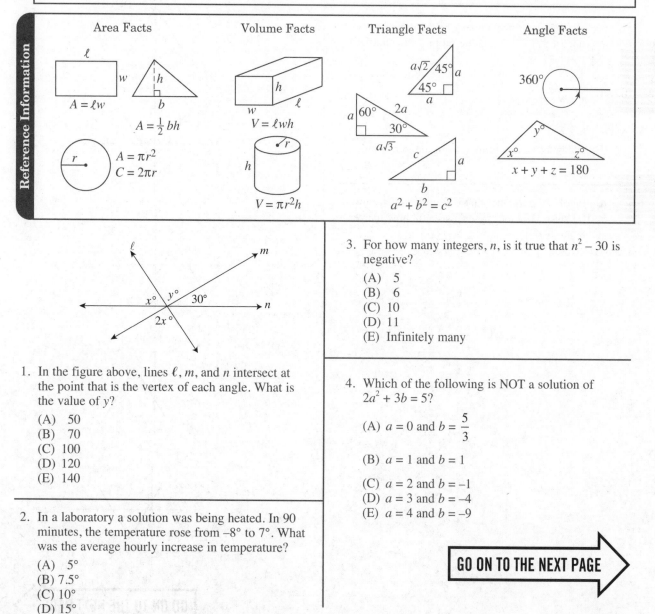

SECTION 9

Time—20 Minutes
16 Questions

For each problem in this section determine which of the five choices is correct and blacken the corresponding choice on your answer sheet. You may use any blank space on the page for your work.

Notes:

• You may use a calculator whenever you think it will be helpful.

• Only real numbers are used. No question or answer on this test involves a complex or imaginary number.

• Use the diagrams provided to help you solve the problems. Unless you see the words "<u>Note</u>: Figure not drawn to scale" under a diagram, it has been drawn as accurately as possible. Unless it is stated that a figure is three-dimensional, you may assume it lies in a plane.

• For any function, f, the domain, unless specifically restricted, is the set of all real numbers for which $f(x)$ is also a real number.

Reference Information

Area Facts

$A = \ell w$

$A = \frac{1}{2}bh$

$A = \pi r^2$
$C = 2\pi r$

Volume Facts

$V = \ell wh$

$V = \pi r^2 h$

Triangle Facts

$a^2 + b^2 = c^2$

Angle Facts

$360°$

$x + y + z = 180$

1. In the figure above, lines ℓ, m, and n intersect at the point that is the vertex of each angle. What is the value of y?

(A) 50
(B) 70
(C) 100
(D) 120
(E) 140

2. In a laboratory a solution was being heated. In 90 minutes, the temperature rose from –8° to 7°. What was the average hourly increase in temperature?

(A) 5°
(B) 7.5°
(C) 10°
(D) 15°
(E) 22.5°

3. For how many integers, n, is it true that $n^2 - 30$ is negative?

(A) 5
(B) 6
(C) 10
(D) 11
(E) Infinitely many

4. Which of the following is NOT a solution of $2a^2 + 3b = 5$?

(A) $a = 0$ and $b = \dfrac{5}{3}$

(B) $a = 1$ and $b = 1$

(C) $a = 2$ and $b = -1$
(D) $a = 3$ and $b = -4$
(E) $a = 4$ and $b = -9$

GO ON TO THE NEXT PAGE

5. What is the slope of the line that passes through $(0, 0)$ and is perpendicular to the line that passes through $(-2, 2)$ and $(3, 3)$?

   (A) −5

   (B) $-\dfrac{1}{5}$

   (C) 0

   (D) $\dfrac{1}{5}$

   (E) 5

6. If the measures of the angles of a triangle are in the ratio of 1:2:3, what is the ratio of the lengths of the sides?

   (A) 1:2:3
   (B) $1:1:\sqrt{2}$
   (C) $1:\sqrt{3}:2$
   (D) 3:4:5
   (E) It cannot be determined from the information given.

7. A googol is the number that is written as 1 followed by 100 zeros. If g represents a googol, how many digits are there in g^2?

   (A) 102
   (B) 103
   (C) 199
   (D) 201
   (E) 202

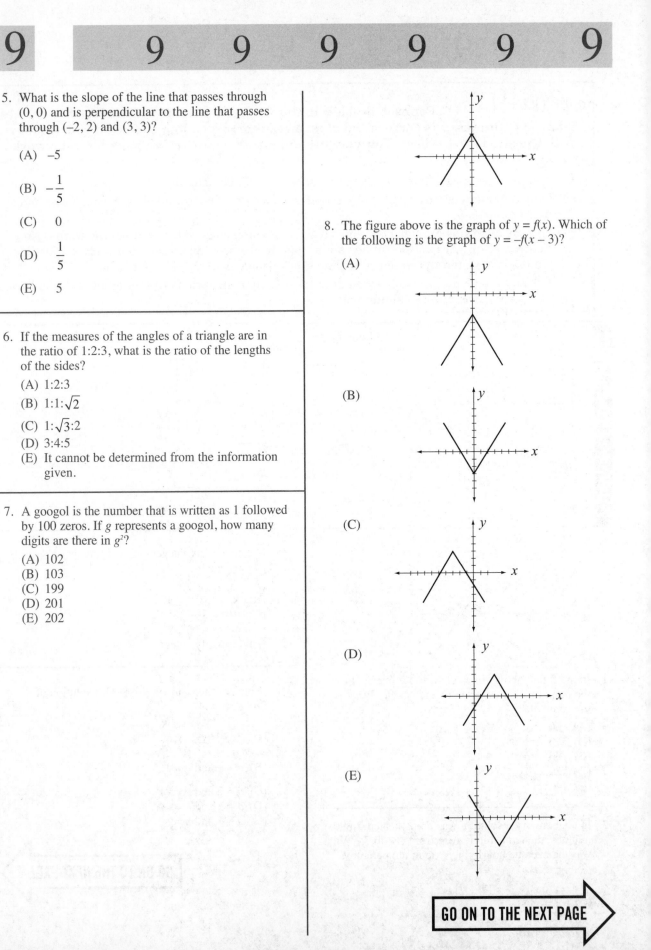

8. The figure above is the graph of $y = f(x)$. Which of the following is the graph of $y = -f(x - 3)$?

   (A)

   (B)

   (C)

   (D)

   (E)

GO ON TO THE NEXT PAGE

9   9   9   9   9   9   9

9. Which of the following expresses the area of a circle in terms of C, its circumference?

(A) $\dfrac{C^2}{4\pi}$

(B) $\dfrac{C^2}{2\pi}$

(C) $\dfrac{\sqrt{C}}{2\pi}$

(D) $\dfrac{C\pi}{4}$

(E) $\dfrac{C}{4\pi}$

10. What is the value of $\left(4^{\frac{1}{2}} \cdot 8^{\frac{1}{3}} \cdot 16^{\frac{1}{4}} \cdot 32^{\frac{1}{5}}\right)^{\frac{1}{2}}$?

(A) 2
(B) 4
(C) 8
(D) 16
(E) 64

11. If $\sqrt{x-15} - 5 = 2$ what is the value of $\sqrt{x}$?

(A) 2
(B) $\sqrt{14}$
(C) 8
(D) $\sqrt{34}$
(E) 64

12. To get to a business meeting, Joanna drove m miles in h hours, and arrived $\dfrac{1}{2}$ hour early. At what rate should she have driven to arrive exactly on time?

(A) $\dfrac{m}{2h}$

(B) $\dfrac{2m+h}{2h}$

(C) $\dfrac{2m-h}{2h}$

(D) $\dfrac{2m}{2h-1}$

(E) $\dfrac{2m}{2h+1}$

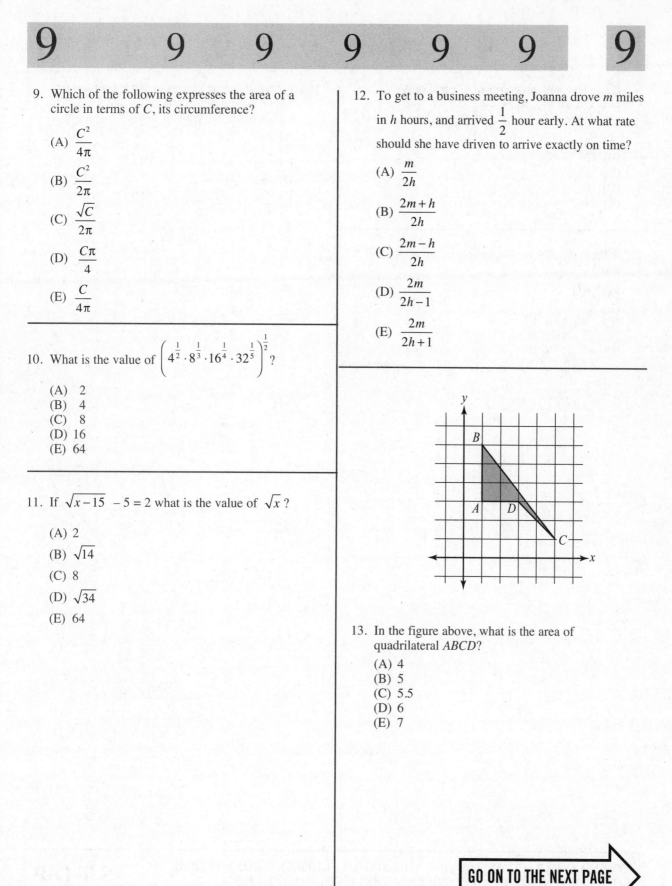

13. In the figure above, what is the area of quadrilateral $ABCD$?

(A) 4
(B) 5
(C) 5.5
(D) 6
(E) 7

GO ON TO THE NEXT PAGE ⟹

9 9 9 9 9 9 9

14. If y is inversely proportional to x and directly proportional to z, and $x = 4$ and $z = 8$ when $y = 10$, what is the value of $x + z$ when $y = 20$?

(A) 6
(B) 12
(C) 16
(D) 18
(E) 24

15. What is the average (arithmetic mean) of 3^{30}, 3^{60}, and 3^{90}?

(A) 3^{60}
(B) 3^{177}
(C) $3^{10} + 3^{20} + 3^{30}$
(D) $3^{27} + 3^{57} + 3^{87}$
(E) $3^{29} + 3^{59} + 3^{89}$

16. If a and b are the lengths of the legs of a right triangle whose hypotenuse is 10 and whose area is 20, what is the value of $(a + b)^2$?

(A) 100
(B) 120
(C) 140
(D) 180
(E) 200

YOU MAY GO BACK AND REVIEW THIS SECTION IN THE REMAINING TIME, BUT DO NOT WORK IN ANY OTHER SECTION UNTIL TOLD TO DO SO.

S T O P

10   10   10   10   10   10   10

SECTION 10	Time—10 Minutes 14 Questions	For each of the following questions, select the best answer from the choices provided and fill in the appropriate circle on the answer sheet.

Some or all parts of the following sentences are underlined. The first answer choice, (A), simply repeats the underlined part of the sentence. The other four choices present four alternative ways to phrase the underlined part. Select the answer that produces the most effective sentence, one that is clear and exact, and blacken the appropriate space on your answer sheet. In selecting your choice, be sure that it is standard written English, and that it expresses the meaning of the original sentence.

Example:

The first biography of author Eudora Welty came out in 1998 <u>and she was 89 years old at the time.</u>

(A) and she was 89 years old at the time
(B) at the time when she was 89
(C) upon becoming an 89 year old
(D) when she was 89
(E) at the age of 89 years old

Ⓐ Ⓑ Ⓒ ● Ⓔ

1. Unfortunately, soul singer Anita Baker's voice <u>has not weathered the years as well as other singers have.</u>

(A) has not weathered the years as well as other singers have
(B) had not weathered the years as well as other singers have
(C) has not been weathered by the years as well as the voices of other singers have been
(D) has not weathered the years as well as other singers' voices have
(E) has not weathered the years as good as other singers' voices have

2. <u>The mathematics teacher drew a right triangle on the blackboard, he</u> proceeded to demonstrate that we could determine the length of the longest side of the triangle if we knew the lengths of its two shorter sides.

(A) The mathematics teacher drew a right triangle on the blackboard, he
(B) The right triangle, which was drawn on the blackboard by the mathematics teacher, he
(C) After drawing a right triangle on the blackboard, the mathematics teacher
(D) A right triangle was first drawn on the blackboard by the mathematics teacher, then he
(E) Once a right triangle was drawn on the blackboard by the mathematics teacher, who then

3. An inside trader is <u>when a corporate officer who has access to "inside" or privileged information about a company's prospects uses that information</u> in buying or selling company shares.

(A) when a corporate officer who has access to "inside" or privileged information about a company's prospects uses that information
(B) when a corporate officer has access to "inside" or privileged information about a company's prospects and uses that information
(C) a corporate officer who has access to "inside" or privileged information about a company's prospects and uses that information
(D) a corporate officer who has accessed "inside" or privileged information about a company's prospects for use of that information
(E) that a corporate officer who has access to "inside" or privileged information about a company's prospects and he uses that information

GO ON TO THE NEXT PAGE

10   10   10   10   10   10   10

4. Gymnastics students perform stretching <u>exercises to develop flexibility and to become a more agile tumbler</u>.

   (A) exercises to develop flexibility and to become a more agile tumbler
   (B) exercises for the development of flexibility and to become a more agile tumbler
   (C) exercises so that they develop flexibility, becoming a more agile tumbler
   (D) exercises to develop flexibility and to become more agile tumblers
   (E) exercises because they want to develop flexibility in becoming a more agile tumbler

5. <u>Because the Ming vase is priceless plus being highly fragile,</u> it is kept safe in a sealed display case.

   (A) Because the Ming vase is priceless plus being highly fragile,
   (B) Being that the Ming vase is priceless and also it is highly fragile,
   (C) Although the Ming vase is priceless and highly fragile,
   (D) Because the Ming vase is priceless and highly fragile is why
   (E) Because the Ming vase is both priceless and highly fragile,

6. The soft, pulpy flesh of the passion fruit possesses a flavor at once tart and <u>sweet and the flavor has captivated</u> many prominent chefs, among them Alice Waters.

   (A) sweet and the flavor has captivated
   (B) sweet that has captivated
   (C) sweet that have captivated
   (D) sweet and the flavors have captivated
   (E) sweet and the favor captivates

7. Shakespeare's acting company performed in a relatively intimate setting, <u>appearing before smaller audiences than most theaters today</u>.

   (A) appearing before smaller audiences than most theaters today
   (B) they appeared before smaller audiences than most theaters today
   (C) appearing before audiences smaller than most audiences today
   (D) having appeared before smaller audiences than most theaters today
   (E) and they appeared before audiences smaller than the ones at most theaters today

8. <u>Observing the interactions of preschoolers in a playground setting, it can be seen</u> that the less adults relate to the children in their charge, the more these children relate to one another.

   (A) Observing the interactions of preschoolers in a playground setting, it can be seen
   (B) Having observed the interactions of preschoolers in a playground setting, it can be seen
   (C) If one observes the interactions of preschoolers in a playground setting, you can see
   (D) Observing the interactions of preschoolers in a playground setting, we can see
   (E) Observing the interactions of preschoolers in a playground setting can be seen

9. <u>A significant percentage of persons summoned for jury service requested a postponement, and only a few were deferred</u>.

   (A) A significant percentage of persons summoned for jury service requested a postponement, and only a few were deferred.
   (B) A significant percentage of persons, having been summoned for jury service, requested a postponement, a few were only deferred.
   (C) A significant percentage of persons summoned for jury service requested a postponement, but only a few were deferred.
   (D) After a significant percentage of persons were summoned for jury service, they requested a postponement, only a few being deferred.
   (E) Only a few were deferred, a significant percentage of persons summoned for jury service having requested a postponement.

10. <u>Far from being mercenary ambulance chasers</u>, trial lawyers perform a public service by forcing corporations to consider the potential financial cost of pollution, unsafe products, and mistreatment of workers.

   (A) Far from being mercenary ambulance chasers
   (B) Despite them being mercenary ambulance chasers
   (C) Far from them being mercenary ambulance chasers
   (D) Far from having been mercenary ambulance chasers
   (E) Further from being mercenary ambulance chasers

GO ON TO THE NEXT PAGE

10	10	10	10	10	10	10

11. *Unsafe at Any Speed* is Ralph Nader's detailed portrait of how the auto industry willfully resisted safety innovations and thus contributed to thousands of highway deaths a year.

(A) portrait of how the auto industry willfully resisted safety innovations and thus contributed to
(B) portrait of when the auto industry was willful about resisting safety innovations and thus contributing to
(C) portrait of how the auto industry fully willed themselves to resist safety innovations and thus contributed to
(D) portrait of how the auto industry willfully resisted safety innovations in order to contribute to
(E) portrait showing how the auto industry willfully resisted safety innovations, and they thus contributed to

12. In 1532, Francisco Pizarro and his troops arrived in Cuzco, took hostage the Incan king, Atahualpa, and then they demanded ransom.

(A) Atahualpa, and then they demanded ransom
(B) who was named Atahualpa, and then they demanded ransom
(C) Atahualpa, it was so they could demand ransom
(D) Atahualpa, and then there was a demand for ransom
(E) Atahualpa, and then demanded ransom

13. Although demand for cars, motorcycles, and other consumer goods are booming, the economy is growing only at roughly 4 percent a year, and the unemployment rate is about 10 percent.

(A) Although demand for cars, motorcycles, and other consumer goods are booming
(B) Because demand for cars, motorcycles, and other consumer goods are booming
(C) Although demand for cars, motorcycles, and other consumer goods is booming
(D) Although demand for cars, motorcycles, and other consumer goods have been booming
(E) Although demand of cars, motorcycles, and other consumer goods is booming

14. Samuel Sewall, who was a judge in the Salem witch trials but later repented his role and, in 1700, wrote the first attack on the American slave trade.

(A) Samuel Sewall, who was a judge in the Salem witch trials but later repented his role and, in 1700,
(B) Samuel Sewall was a judge in the Salem witch trials but who later repented his role and, in 1700,
(C) Samuel Sewall, a judge in the Salem witch trials, but later he repented his role and, in 1700,
(D) Samuel Sewall, a judge in the Salem witch trials, later repented his role and in 1700
(E) Samuel Sewall, who was a judge in the Salem witch trials but who later repented his role, and who, in 1700,

YOU MAY GO BACK AND REVIEW THIS SECTION IN THE REMAINING TIME, BUT DO NOT WORK IN ANY OTHER SECTION UNTIL TOLD TO DO SO.

STOP

Answer Key

<u>Note:</u> The letters in brackets following the Mathematical Reasoning answers refer to the sections of Chapter 9 in which you can find the information you need to answer the questions. For example, **1. C [E]** means that the answer to question 1 is C, and that the solution requires information found in Section 9-E: Averages.

Section 2   Critical Reading

1.	A	6.	A	11.	A	16.	E	21.	C
2.	D	7.	C	12.	C	17.	B	22.	C
3.	B	8.	C	13.	B	18.	D	23.	E
4.	D	9.	E	14.	C	19.	C	24.	B
5.	D	10.	B	15.	E	20.	A		

Section 3   Mathematical Reasoning

1.	C [A]	5.	C [G, K]	9.	B [G]	13.	E [G]	17.	D [D, I]
2.	C [I, J]	6.	E [I]	10.	C [E]	14.	C [G]	18.	E [R]
3.	D [A, Q]	7.	B [F]	11.	E [D, J]	15.	C [C]	19.	D [M]
4.	B [E]	8.	C [P]	12.	B [E, G]	16.	B [H, Q]	20.	E [G, H]

Section 4   Writing Skills

1.	B	8.	E	15.	B	22.	C	29.	A
2.	A	9.	C	16.	C	23.	E	30.	C
3.	C	10.	B	17.	B	24.	D	31.	B
4.	D	11.	A	18.	B	25.	C	32.	C
5.	A	12.	D	19.	A	26.	D	33.	D
6.	A	13.	C	20.	D	27.	D	34.	B
7.	D	14.	B	21.	C	28.	A	35.	C

Section 5

On this test, Section 5 was the experimental section. It could have been an extra critical reading, mathematics, or writing skills section. Remember: on the SAT you take, the experimental section may be any section from 2 to 7.

Section 6   Critical Reading

1.	E	6.	C	11.	D	16.	D	21.	E
2.	C	7.	D	12.	D	17.	D	22.	D
3.	B	8.	B	13.	C	18.	B	23.	D
4.	B	9.	C	14.	C	19.	C	24.	A
5.	C	10.	B	15.	E	20.	D		

Section 7 Mathematical Reasoning

Multiple-Choice Questions

1. **D** [A]
2. **E** [D]
3. **C** [R]
4. **D** [C, D]
5. **C** [P]
6. **C** [O]
7. **B** [E, G]
8. **A** [E]

Grid-in Questions

9. [A] — 1 5 2

10. [G] — 2 . 1

$$2.01 \le x \le 2.33$$

11. [A] — 8 1 0 0

12. [O, P] — 2 0 2

13. [J, K] — 2 8

14. [A, B] — 1 / 3 2

15. [B, D] — 1 / 8

16. [P] — 1 9

17. [O] — 8 1 9 0

18. [D, L] — 3 / 8 or . 3 7 5

Section 8   Critical Reading

1. A	5. B	9. B	13. C	17. C
2. C	6. E	10. D	14. B	18. C
3. B	7. E	11. C	15. E	19. D
4. E	8. B	12. A	16. C	

Section 9   Mathematical Reasoning

1. C [I]	5. A [N]	9. A [L]	13. A [J, K, N]
2. C [E]	6. C [D, J]	10. B [A]	14. D [D]
3. D [A, O]	7. D [A, P]	11. C [G]	15. E [A, E]
4. D [G]	8. E [R]	12. E [B, H]	16. D [J, F]

Section 10   Writing Skills

1. D	4. D	7. C	10. A	13. C
2. C	5. E	8. D	11. A	14. D
3. C	6. B	9. C	12. E	

Self-Evaluation

Now that you have completed the diagnostic test, evaluate your performance. Identify your strengths and weaknesses, and then plan a practical study program based on what you have discovered. Follow these steps to evaluate your work on the diagnostic test. (Note: You'll find the charts referred to in steps 1–5 on the next four pages.)

■ **STEP 1**   Use the answer key to check your answers for each section.

■ **STEP 2**   For each section, count the number of correct and incorrect answers (remember that you don't count omitted answers), and enter the numbers on the appropriate lines of the chart "Calculate Your Raw Score." Then do the indicated calculations to get your Critical Reading Raw Score and your Mathematical Reasoning Raw Score.

■ **STEP 3**   Consult the chart "Evaluate Your Performance" to see how well you did.

■ **STEP 4**   To pinpoint the specific areas in which you need to improve, circle the numbers of the questions that you either left blank or got wrong on the "Identify Your Weaknesses" charts. You can then see where to concentrate your efforts to get the most out of your study time. The chart for the math sections gives you page references for review and practice by skill areas. The charts for the critical reading and writing skills sections refer you to the appropriate chapters to study for each question type.

■ **STEP 5**   Wherever you had a concentration of circles, do the review and practice indicated on the charts.

Important: Remember that, in addition to evaluating your scores, you should read all of the answer explanations for questions you answered incorrectly, questions you omitted, and questions you answered correctly but found difficult. Reviewing the answer explanations will help you understand concepts and strategies, and may point out shortcuts.

Score Your Own SAT Essay

Use this table as you rate your performance on the essay-writing section of this Model Test. Circle the phrase that most accurately describes your work. Enter the numbers in the scoring chart below. Add the numbers together and divide by 6 to determine your total score. The higher your total score, the better you are likely to do on the essay section of the SAT.

   Note that on the actual SAT two readers will rate your essay; your essay score will be the sum of their two ratings and could range from 12 (highest) to 2 (lowest). Also, they will grade your essay holistically, rating it on the basis of their overall impression of its effectiveness. They will *not* analyze it piece by piece, giving separate grades for grammar, vocabulary level, and so on. Therefore, you cannot expect the score you give yourself on this Model Test to predict your eventual score on the SAT with any great degree of accuracy. Use this scoring guide instead to help you assess your writing strengths and weaknesses, so that you can decide which areas to focus on as you prepare for the SAT.

   Like most people, you may find it difficult to rate your own writing objectively. Ask a teacher or fellow student to score your essay as well. With his or her help you should gain added insights into writing your 25-minute essay.

	6	**5**	**4**	**3**	**2**	**1**
POSITION ON THE TOPIC	Clear, convincing, & insightful	Fundamentally clear & coherent	Fairly clear & coherent	Insufficiently clear	Largely unclear	Extremely unclear
ORGANIZATION OF EVIDENCE	Well organized, with strong, relevant examples	Generally well organized, with apt examples	Adequately organized, with some examples	Sketchily developed, with weak examples	Lacking focus and evidence	Unfocused and disorganized
SENTENCE STRUCTURE	Varied, appealing sentences	Reasonably varied sentences	Some variety in sentences	Little variety in sentences	Errors in sentence structure	Severe errors in sentence structure
LEVEL OF VOCABULARY	Mature & apt word choice	Competent word choice	Adequate word choice	Inappropriate or weak vocabulary	Highly limited vocabulary	Rudimentary
GRAMMAR AND USAGE	Almost entirely free of errors	Relatively free of errors	Some technical errors	Minor errors, and some major ones	Numerous major errors	Extensive severe errors
OVERALL EFFECT	Outstanding	Effective	Adequately competent	Inadequate, but shows some potential	Seriously flawed	Fundamentally deficient

Self-Scoring Chart

For each of the following categories, rate the essay from 1 (lowest) to 6 (highest)

Position on the Topic   _____

Organization of Evidence   _____

Sentence Structure   _____

Level of Vocabulary   _____

Grammar and Usage   _____

Overall Effect   _____

TOTAL   _____

(To get a score, divide the total by 6)   _____

Scoring Chart (Second Reader)

For each of the following categories, rate the essay from 1 (lowest) to 6 (highest)

Position on the Topic   _____

Organization of Evidence   _____

Sentence Structure   _____

Level of Vocabulary   _____

Grammar and Usage   _____

Overall Effect   _____

TOTAL   _____

(To get a score, divide the total by 6)   _____

Diagnostic Test

Calculate Your Raw Score
Critical Reading

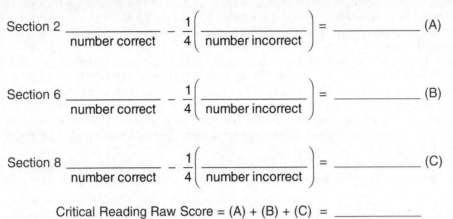

Section 2 _____ − $\frac{1}{4}$ (_____) = _____ (A)
　　　　number correct　　　number incorrect

Section 6 _____ − $\frac{1}{4}$ (_____) = _____ (B)
　　　　number correct　　　number incorrect

Section 8 _____ − $\frac{1}{4}$ (_____) = _____ (C)
　　　　number correct　　　number incorrect

Critical Reading Raw Score = (A) + (B) + (C) = _____

Mathematical Reasoning

Section 3 _____ − $\frac{1}{4}$ (_____) = _____ (D)
　　　　number correct　　　number incorrect

Section 7
Part I　_____ − $\frac{1}{4}$ (_____) = _____ (E)
(1–8)　number correct　　　number incorrect

Part II　_____　　　　　　　　　　 = _____ (F)
(9–18)　number correct

Section 9 _____ − $\frac{1}{4}$ (_____) = _____ (G)
　　　　number correct　　　number incorrect

Mathematical Reasoning Raw Score = (D) + (E) + (F) + (G) = _____

Writing Skills

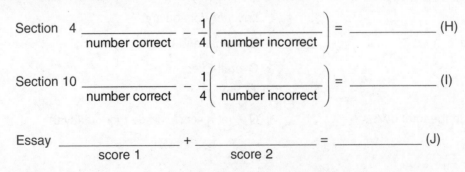

Section 4 _____ − $\frac{1}{4}$ (_____) = _____ (H)
　　　　number correct　　　number incorrect

Section 10 _____ − $\frac{1}{4}$ (_____) = _____ (I)
　　　　 number correct　　　number incorrect

Essay _____ + _____ = _____ (J)
　　　　score 1　　　　score 2

Writing Skills Raw Score = H + I (J is a separate subscore)

Evaluate Your Performance

Scaled Score	Critical Reading Raw Score	Mathematical Reasoning Raw Score	Writing Skills Raw Score
700–800	58–67	48–54	43–49
650–690	52–57	43–47	39–42
600–640	45–51	36–42	35–38
550–590	38–44	30–35	30–34
500–540	30–37	24–29	25–29
450–490	22–29	18–23	19–24
400–440	14–21	12–17	14–18
300–390	3–13	5–11	5–13
200–290	less than 3	less than 5	less than 5

Identify Your Weaknesses

Critical Reading

Question Type	Question Numbers			Chapter to Study
	Section 2	Section 6	Section 8	
Sentence Completion	1, 2, 3, 4, 5, 6, 7, 8	1, 2, 3, 4, 5	1, 2, 3, 4, 5, 6	Chapter 1
Critical Reading	9, 10, 11, 12, 13, 14, 15, 16, 17, 18, 19, 20, 21, 22, 23, 24	6, 7, 8, 9, 10, 11, 12, 13, 14, 15, 16, 17, 18, 19, 20, 21, 22, 23, 24	7, 8, 9, 10, 11, 12, 13, 14, 15, 16, 17, 18, 19	Chapter 2

Identify Your Weaknesses

Mathematical Reasoning

Section in Chapter 9		Question Numbers			Pages to Study
		Section 3	Section 7	Section 9	
A	Basic Arithmetic Concepts	1, 3	1, 9, 11, 14	3, 7, 10, 15	410–431
B	Fractions and Decimals		14, 15	12	432–449
C	Percents	15	4		450–460
D	Ratios and Proportions	11, 17	2, 4, 15, 18	6, 14	461–472
E	Averages	4, 10, 12	7, 8	2, 15	473–479
F	Polynomials	7		16	480–488
G	Equations and Inequalities	5, 9, 12, 13, 14, 20	7, 10	4, 11	489–502
H	Word Problems	2, 16, 20		12	503–513
I	Lines and Angles	2, 6, 17		1	514–524
J	Triangles	2, 11	13	6, 13, 16	525–542
K	Quadrilaterals	5	13	13	543–553
L	Circles		18	9	554–564
M	Solid Geometry	19			565–573
N	Coordinate Geometry	19		5, 13	574–588
O	Counting and Probability		6, 12, 17	3	589–600
P	Logical Reasoning	8	5, 12, 16, 18	7	601–608
Q	Data Interpretation	3, 16			609–618
R	Functions and Their Graphs	18	3	8	619–628

Identify Your Weaknesses

Writing Skills

Question Type	Question Numbers		Chapter to Study
	Section 4	Section 10	
Improving Sentences	1, 2, 3, 4, 5, 6, 7, 8, 9, 10, 11	1, 2, 3, 4, 5, 6, 7, 8, 9, 10, 11, 12, 13, 14	Chapter 6
Identifying Sentence Errors	12, 13, 14, 15, 16, 17, 18, 19, 20, 21, 22, 23, 24, 25, 26, 27, 28, 29		Chapter 6
Improving Paragraphs	30, 31, 32, 33, 34, 35		Chapter 6
Essay			Chapter 7

Answers Explained

Section 2 Critical Reading

1. A. Because lightning victims are so battered and confused, they seem like assault victims. Thus, they are often *mistaken for* victims of assault. (Cause and Effect Signal)

2. D. Anyone who has produced more than three hundred books in a single lifetime is an enormously productive or *prolific* writer. Writers are often described as prolific, but few, if any, have been as prolific as the late Dr. Asimov. Beware of Eye-Catchers: Choice A is incorrect. *Fastidious* means painstakingly careful; it has nothing to do with writing quickly. (Examples)

3. B. Time limitations would cause problems for you if you were reading a *lengthy* book. To save time, you might want to read it in an *abridged* or shortened form.
   Remember to watch for signal words that link one part of the sentence to another. The use of "because" in the opening clause is a cause signal. (Cause and Effect Signal)

4. D. Speakers wish to communicate *unambiguously* in order that there may be no *confusion* about their meaning.
   Remember to watch for signal words that link one part of the sentence to another. The presence of "and" linking two items in a pair indicates that the missing word may be a synonym or near-synonym for the other linked word. In this case, *unambiguously* is a synonym for *clearly*. Similarly, the use of "so that" in the second clause signals cause and effect. (Argument Pattern)

5. D. Lisa was normally *gregarious* or sociable. When she unexpectedly lost her job, she became quiet and *withdrawn* (distant; unsociable). Note how the signal word *Although* indicates a contrast between her normally sociable and later unsociable states. (Contrast Pattern)

6. A. Wilma Mankiller, a female, heads a major American Indian tribe. She performs her role successfully: she is "increasingly popular." By her success, she has *shattered* or exploded a myth of male supremacy. (Argument Pattern)

7. C. The commission censured or condemned the senator for doing something wrong: his expenditures of public funds were *lavish* or extravagant. He spent the public's money in an *unjustifiable*, unwarranted way. (Cause and Effect Pattern)

8. C. A stereotyped or oversimplified portrait of a slave would lead sensitive readers to express *criticism* because the issue of slavery was treated so casually. Thus, they normally would be *detractors* of the novel. However, *Huckleberry Finn* is such a fine work that even its critics acknowledge its greatness. Signal words are helpful here. "Despite" in the first clause implies a contrast, and "even" in the second clause implies that the subjects somewhat reluctantly agree that the novel is a masterpiece. (Contrast Signal)

9. E. The final sentence of the passage maintains that, contrary to expectation, the jellyfish has a sophisticated or complex genetic structure. Beware of eye-catchers. Choice B is incorrect. "Spineless" (lines 1–2) here means invertebrate, lacking a backbone or spinal column. It does not mean cowardly.

10. B. The second sentence of the passage states that the jellyfish "seems the most primitive of creatures." The last sentence of the passage, however, *contradicts* or denies that *assumption*.

11. A. The human faculty for myth is the *capacity* or ability of people to invent legends.

12. C. The fact that Raleigh is remembered more for a romantic, perhaps apocryphal, gesture than for his voyages of exploration *illustrates how legendary events outshine historical achievements in the public's mind.*

13. B. The author is writing a book about the effect of the opening of the West on the Indians living there. As a historian, he needs primary source materials—firsthand accounts of the period written by men and women living at that time. Thus, he finds the period of 1860–1890 worth mentioning because during those years the "greatest concentration of recorded experience and observation" (the bulk of original accounts) was created.

14. C. Only the white settlers looked on their intrusion into Indian territory as the opening of the West. To the Native Americans, it was an invasion. Thus, "opening" *from a Native American perspective is an inaccurate term.*

15. E. Throughout the passage the author presents and comments on the nature of the original documents that form the basis for his historical narrative. Thus, it is clear that a major concern of his is to *introduce* these "sources of almost forgotten oral history" to his readers. Choice A is incorrect. The author clearly regrets the fate of the Indians. However, he does not take this occasion to denounce or condemn the white man.

Choice B is incorrect. While the author discusses the various treaty councils, he does not evaluate or judge their effectiveness.
Choice C is incorrect. The author never touches on the current treatment of Indians.
Choice D is incorrect. The author indicates no such similarity.

16. E. Of all the thousands of published descriptions of the opening of the West, the greatest concentration or *accumulation* of accounts dates from the period of 1860 to 1890.

17. B. The author is describing a period in which Native Americans lost their land and much of their personal freedom to the same pioneers who supposedly revered the ideal of freedom. Thus, in describing the ideal of freedom revered by the pioneers as "personal freedom for those who already had it" (in other words, personal freedom for the pioneers, not the Indians), the author is being *ironic*.

18. D. You can arrive at the correct choice by the process of elimination.
Statement I is true. The passage states that the quality of the interviews depended on the interpreters' abilities. Inaccuracies could creep in because of the translators' lack of skill. Therefore, you can eliminate Choice B.
Statement II is untrue. The passage indicates that the Indians sometimes exaggerated, telling the reporters tall tales. It does not indicate that the reporters in turn overstated what they had been told. Therefore, you can eliminate Choices C and E.
Statement III is true. The passage indicates that the Indians sometimes were disinclined to speak the whole truth because they feared reprisals (retaliation) if they did. Therefore, you can eliminate choice A.
Only Choice D is left. It is the correct answer.

19. C. Brown speaks of the Indians who lived through the "doom period of their civilization," the victims of the conquest of the American West. In doing so, his tone can best be described as *elegiac*, expressing sadness about their fate and lamenting their vanished civilization.

20. A. In the fifth paragraph Brown comments upon the "graphic similes and metaphors of the natural world" found in the English translations of Indian speeches. Thus, he is impressed by their *vividness of imagery*.

21. C. Commenting about inadequate interpreters who turned eloquent Indian speeches into "flat" prose, Brown is criticizing the translations for their *pedestrian*, unimaginative quality.

22. C. Lines 73–76 state that, as the Indian leaders became more sophisticated or knowledgeable about addressing treaty councils, "they demanded the right to choose their own interpreters and recorders." Until they had become familiar with the process, *they were unaware that they had the option to demand such services*.

23. E. Brown has tried to create a narrative of the winning of the West from the victims' perspective. In asking his readers to read the book facing eastward (the way the Indians would have been looking when they first saw the whites headed west), he is asking them metaphorically *to identify* with *the Indians' viewpoint*.

24. B. In the sentence immediately preceding the one in which the phrase "equated with" appears, Brown calls the Indians "true conservationists." Such conservationists know that life is *necessarily tied to* the earth and to its resources, and that by destroying these resources, by imbalancing the equation, so to speak, "the intruders from the East" would destroy life itself.

Section 3 Mathematical Reasoning

1. C. Just quickly add up the number of miles Greg jogs each week:

$$3 + 4 + 5 + 6 + 7 + 8 + 9 = 42.$$

In 2 weeks he jogs **84** miles.

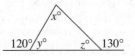

2. C. In the figure above, $x + y + z = 180$. Also, since $y = 60 \ (180 - 120)$ and $z = 50 \ (180 - 130)$, then

$$x = 180 - (50 + 60) = 180 - 110 = \mathbf{70}.$$

3. D. After an increase of 75¢, a tuna fish sandwich will cost $5.00. The only sandwiches that, after a 50¢ increase, will be more expensive than the tuna fish are the **3** that now cost *more than* $4.50.

4. B. Discard the scores of 9.2 and 9.7, and take the average of the other four scores:

$$\frac{9.4 + 9.5 + 9.6 + 9.6}{4} = \frac{38.1}{4} = \mathbf{9.525}.$$

5. C. The sum of the measures of two adjacent angles of a parallelogram is 180°. Therefore,

$$180 = 10x + 25x - 30 = 35x - 30,$$

which implies that $35x = 210$ and $x = \mathbf{6}$.

6. E. The figures below show that **all** of the choices **are possible**.

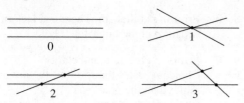

7. B. Since $a^2 - b^2 = (a - b)(a + b)$, then:

$$20 = a^2 - b^2 = (a - b)(a + b) = 10(a + b).$$

Therefore, $a + b = 2$. Adding the equations $a + b = 2$ and $a - b = 10$ gives

$$2a = 12 \Rightarrow a = 6 \Rightarrow b = -4.$$

8. C. Each year the dealer sells half of her silver, so after 1 year she owns $\left(\dfrac{1}{2}\right)1000$ ounces.

After 2 years she owns half as many ounces:

$$\left(\dfrac{1}{2}\right)\left(\dfrac{1}{2}(1000)\right) = \left(\dfrac{1}{2}\right)^2 (1000).$$

In general, after t years, she will own

$$1000\left(\dfrac{1}{2}\right)^t \text{ ounces.}$$

Since $\dfrac{1}{2} = 2^{-1}$:

$$\left(\dfrac{1}{2}\right)^t = (2^{-1})^t = 2^{-t} \text{ and } 1000\left(\dfrac{1}{2}\right)^t = \mathbf{1000 \times 2^{-t}}.$$

9. B. Since 9 is a solution of $x^2 - a = 0$, then $9^2 - a = 0 \Rightarrow 81 - a = 0 \Rightarrow a = 81$. Now solve the equation $x^4 - a = 0$.

$$x^4 - 81 = 0 \Rightarrow x^4 = 81 \Rightarrow x^2 = 9 \Rightarrow x = 3 \text{ or } -3.$$

10. C. The mode is 8, since more people earn $8 an hour than any other salary. Also, since there are 16 employees, the median is the average of the 8th and 9th items of data: $8 and $10, so the median is 9. Finally, the average of 8 and 9 is **8.5**.

11. E. If the ratio were $a{:}b{:}c$, then

$$180 = ax + bx + cx = (a + b + c)x.$$

Since in each of the choices the ratio is written in lowest terms, $a + b + c$ must be a factor of 180. This is the case in choices A through D. Only Choice E, **6:7:8**, fails: $6 + 7 + 8 = 21$, which is not a divisor of 180.

12. B. Add the two equations to get $5x + 5y = 28$.

Then dividing each term by 5, we get $x + y = \dfrac{28}{5}$. The average of x and y is

$$\dfrac{x + y}{2} = \dfrac{\dfrac{28}{5}}{2} = \dfrac{28}{10} = \mathbf{2.8}.$$

13. E. Since $W = 3$ and $2W = 3X$, then $3X = 6 \Rightarrow X = 2$. Therefore

$$3 + 7 = 2 + Y \Rightarrow Y = 10 - 2 = \mathbf{8}.$$

14. C. By definition, $W + W = X + Y \Rightarrow 2W = X + Y$; but the definition also states that $2W = 3X$, so $X = \dfrac{2}{3}W$. Therefore

$$2W = \dfrac{2}{3}W + Y \Rightarrow Y = \dfrac{4}{3}W.$$

15. C. If the ring was originally priced at $100, it was accidentally marked $40 instead of $160. The incorrect price of $40 must be increased by $120, which is 3 times, or **300%** of, the incorrect price.

16. B. John's average speed is calculated by dividing his total distance of 10 miles by the total time he spent riding his bicycle. Each tick mark on the horizontal axis of the graph represents 10 minutes. He left at 8:30 and arrived back home $1\dfrac{1}{2}$ hours later, at 10:00. However, he stopped for 10 minutes, from 9:20 to 9:30, so he was riding for only 1 hour and 20 minutes, or $\dfrac{4}{3}$ hours. Finally, $10 \div \dfrac{4}{3} = 10 \times \dfrac{3}{4} = \mathbf{7\dfrac{1}{2}}$.

17. D. Assume $AB = 3$ and $BC = 5$. The least that AC can be is 2, if A is on line $\overrightarrow{BC}$, between B and C; and the most AC can be is 8, if A is on line $\overrightarrow{BC}$, so that B is between A and C. If A is not on line $\overrightarrow{BC}$, AC can be any length between 2 and 8.

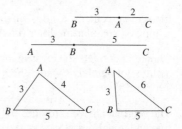

Therefore the ratio $AB{:}AC$ can be any number between 3:2 (= 1.5) and 3:8 (= 0.375). In particular, it can be 1:2 (= 0.5) and 3:8. (I and III are true.) It cannot be 1:3 (= 0.333). (II is false.) Statements **I and III only** are true.

18. E. $g(2) = f(3 \times 2) + 3 = f(6) + 3$.

 $f(6) = \sqrt{100 - 6^2} = \sqrt{100 - 36} = \sqrt{64} = 8$.

 So $g(2) = f(6) + 3 = 8 + 3 = \mathbf{11}$.

19. D. The formula for the volume of a cylinder is $V = \pi r^2 h$. Replacing r by 8 and h by π^2, we get that $V = \pi (8)^2 (\pi^2) = 64\pi^3$. If e is the edge of the cube, then the volume of the cube is e^3. So $e^3 = 64\pi^3 \Rightarrow e = \mathbf{4\pi}$.

20. E. To earn 10 points, Ellen needed to get 10 correct answers and then earn no more points on the remaining $q - 10$ questions. To earn no points on a set of questions, she had to miss 4 questions (thereby losing $4 \times \frac{1}{4} = 1$ point) for every 1 question she got right in that set. She answered $\frac{1}{5}$ of the $q - 10$ questions correctly (and $\frac{4}{5}$ of them incorrectly). The total number of correct answers was

 $$10 + \frac{q - 10}{5} = 10 + \frac{q}{5} - \frac{10}{5} = \mathbf{8 + \frac{q}{5}}.$$

 <u>Alternative solution:</u> Let c be the number of questions Ellen answered correctly, and $q - c$ the number she missed. Then her raw score is $c - \frac{1}{4}(q - c)$, which equals 10, so

 $4c - (q - c) = 40 \Rightarrow 5c - q = 40 \Rightarrow 5c = 40 + q$.

 So, $c = \frac{40 + q}{5} = \mathbf{8 + \frac{q}{5}}$.

Section 4 Writing Skills

1. B. Choice B eliminates the excessive wordiness of the original sentence without introducing any errors in diction.

2. A. As used in Choice A, the semicolon separating a pair of clauses is correct. Choices C–E introduce errors in parallel structure.

3. C. Error in agreement. *Kind* is singular and requires a singular modifier (*this*).

4. D. Choice D corrects the error in diction (*eminently*, not *imminently*) and the error in parallel structure.

5. A. The original answer provides the most effective and concise sentence.

6. A. The original sentence is correct. The singular pronoun *it* refers to the subject of the main clause, *fate* (singular).

7. D. Choices A, B, C, and E suffer from errors in the sequence of tenses.

8. E. Error in parallelism. There is a lack of parallel structure in the other four choices.

9. C. Errors in precision and clarity.
 Choice A states the result of the program rather than the goal.
 Choice B results in a sentence fragment.
 Choices D and E use the *was where* construction, which is unclear and should be avoided.

10. B. Dangling modifier. Ask yourself who revised the dissertation. Clearly, *she* (the writer) did.

11. A. Sentence is correct. *Unique* means being without a like or equal. Avoid phrases like *very unique* and *more unique* that imply there can be degrees of uniqueness.

12. D. The reflexive pronoun *myself* cannot be used as the object of the verb *frightened*. Change *myself* to *me*.

13. C. Adjective and adverb confusion. Change *regular* to *regularly*.

14. B. Error in parallelism. Change *not because of the money* to *not because he needed the money* (a clause) to parallel the clause that follows *but*.

15. B. Error in diction. Change *liable* to *likely*.

16. C. Error in subject-verb agreement. Change *is* to *are*.

17. B. Error in diction. *Latter* should not be used to refer to more than two items. Change *latter* to *last*.

18. B. Error in parallelism. Change *to aid* to *aiding*.

19. A. Adjective and adverb confusion. Change *special prepared* to *specially prepared*.

20. D. Error in tense. Change *had been* to *were*.

21. C. Error in parallelism. Change *under application* to *being applied*.

22. C. Faulty verbal. Change *satisfying* to the infinitive *to satisfy*.

23. E. Sentence is correct.

24. D. Error in pronoun-antecedent agreement. Change *they are* to *it is*.

25. C. Error in subject-verb agreement. The antecedent of *who* is *one*. Therefore, *who is* is correct.

26. D. Error in parallelism. Change *and leaving room for* to *to leave room for*.

27. D. Incomplete comparison. Compare *stories* with *stories*, not *stories* with *champion*. The sentence should read: "There are probably few comeback stories as moving as that of cycling's stalwart champion, Lance Armstrong."

28. A. Unidiomatic preposition. Replace *ability for winning* with *ability to win*.

29. A. Error in coordination and subordination. Remember: any sentence elements that are *not* underlined are by definition correct. Here, the coordinating conjunction *but* is not underlined. Coordinating conjunctions connect sentence elements that are grammatically equal. In this case, *but* should connect the main clause beginning "others restrict themselves" with another main clause. However, *while,* a subordinating conjunction, introduces a subordinate clause, not a main clause. To correct the error, delete *While* and begin the sentence *Some scientists are absorbed.*

30. C. Choice A says that the house is *in your car*, an unlikely situation.
Choice B contains an idea that the writer could not have intended.
Choice C accurately states the intended idea. It is the best answer.
Choice D, like Choice B, contains an idea that is quite absurd.
Choice E is wordy and awkwardly expressed.

31. B. All the sentences except sentence 2 contribute to the development of the essay's topic. Therefore, Choice B is the best answer.

32. C. Choice A is awkwardly expressed.
Choice B is awkward and contains the pronoun *it*, which has no specific antecedent.
Choice C is accurately expressed and is consistent with the sentences that precede and follow sentence 8. It is the best answer.
Choice D is written in a style that is different from that of the rest of the essay.
Choice E would be a good choice, but it contains a comma splice. A comma may not be used to join two independent clauses.

33. D. Choice A is quite formal and is not in keeping with the style and tone of the essay.
Choice B is close to the style and tone of the essay, but it contains the redundancy *quickly and rapidly*.
Choice C has a formal tone inconsistent with the rest of the essay.
Choice D uses the second-person pronoun and is consistent with the folksy, conversational style of the essay. It is the best answer.
Choice E uses an objective tone far different from the writing in the rest of the essay.

34. B. Choice A is only partly true. While the paragraph gives another viewpoint, the data it contains are hardly objective.
Choice B accurately states the writer's intention. It is the best answer.
Choices C, D, and E in no way describe the function of paragraph 3.

35. C. Choice A provides no particular link to the preceding paragraph.
Choice B provides a rather weak transition between paragraphs.
Choice C creates a strong bond between paragraphs by alluding to material in paragraph 3 and introducing the topic of paragraph 4. It is the best answer.
Choice D could be a good transition were it not for the error in subject-verb agreement. The subject *sounds* is plural; the verb *tells* is singular.
Choice E provides a weak transition and its writing style is not consistent with the rest of the essay.

Section 6 Critical Reading

1. E. Tiffany's works of art have survived in spite of their *fragility* (tendency to break). Remember to watch for signal words that link one part of the sentence to another. The use of "despite" in the opening phrase sets up a contrast. *Despite* signals you that Tiffany's glass works were unlikely candidates to survive for several decades.   (Contrast Signal)

2. C. A comprehensive or thorough study would not be missing *relevant* or important material. Remember to watch for signal words that link one part of the sentence to another. The use of "but" in the second clause sets up a contrast.   (Contrast Signal)

3. B. Pain is a *sensation*. Losing the ability to feel pain would leave the body *vulnerable*, defenseless, lacking its usual warnings against impending bodily harm.
Note how the second clause serves to clarify or explain what is meant by pain's being an "early warning system."   (Definition)

4. B. A *lugubrious* (exaggeratedly gloomy) manner may create laughter because it is so inappropriate in the *hilarity* (noisy gaiety) of the circus. The clown's success stems from a contrast. The missing words must be antonyms or near-antonyms. You can immediately eliminate Choices C, D, and E as nonantonym pairs. In addition, you can eliminate Choice A; *sobriety* or seriousness is an inappropriate term for describing circus life.
          (Contrast Pattern)

5. **C.** If she was *deprecatory about* her accomplishments (diminished them or saw nothing praiseworthy in them), she would be unwilling to boast about them or *flaunt* them. Note the use of "properly" to describe her unwillingness to do something. This suggests that the second missing word would have negative associations.   (Definition)

6. **C.** The author refers to Douglas in order to introduce Douglas's metaphoric description of the Everglades as the River of Grass.

7. **D.** Enduring value is value that *lasts*. The *lasting* value of the Everglades is that it provides a habitat for endangered species.

8. **B.** The author's parenthetic remark serves to *provide background on the reasons* for the scientific and governmental *concern* about the dangers of phosphorus runoff.

9. **C.** The author of Passage 1 is wholly concerned with the threat to the Everglades' fragile ecosystem. The environment is what is important to her. She mentions agricultural needs only in terms of how they have affected the River of Grass. Given her perspective, she would most likely view the author of Passage 2 as someone *inclined to overestimate the importance of the sugar industry.*

10. **B.** The author describes himself as "jarred and shocked" (lines 4 and 5). He asks himself, "What strange world was this?" His initial reaction to Mencken's prose is one of *disbelief.*
    Choice A is incorrect. Mencken rages; the narrator does not.
    Choice C is incorrect. It is unsupported by the passage.
    Choices D and E are incorrect. Again, these terms apply to Mencken, not to the narrator.

11. **D.** The narrator does *not* portray Mencken as reverent or respectful of religious belief. Instead, he says that Mencken mocks God.
    Choice A is incorrect. The narrator portrays Mencken as intrepid (brave); he wonders where Mencken gets his courage.
    Choice B is incorrect. The narrator portrays Mencken as articulate (verbally expressive); he says Mencken writes clear, clean sentences.
    Choice C is incorrect. The narrator portrays Mencken as satiric (mocking); he says Mencken makes fun of people's weaknesses.
    Choice E is incorrect. The narrator portrays Mencken as opinionated (stubborn about his

opinions; prejudiced). Mencken's book, after all, is *A Book of Prejudices.*
    Remember: when asked about specific information in the passage, spot key words in the question and scan the passage to find them (or their synonyms).

12. **D.** The mood of the book colored or *affected* the narrator's perceptions.
    Remember: when answering a vocabulary-in-context question, test each answer choice, substituting it in the sentence for the word in quotes.

13. **C.** The narrator feels a hunger for books that surges up in him. In other words, he is filled with *impatient ardor* or eagerness.
    Choice A is incorrect. The narrator has his dreams, but he is involved rather than indifferent.
    Choices B and D are incorrect. There is nothing in the lines to suggest them.
    Choice E is incorrect. The narrator is determined, but his resolve is active and eager rather than quiet.
    Remember: when asked to determine the author's attitude or tone, look for words that convey emotion or paint pictures.

14. **C.** The narrator is able to identify Mr. Gerald as an American type. He feels closer to Mr. Gerald, familiar with the limits of his life. This suggests that he smiles out of a sense of *recognition.*
    Choices A, B, D, and E are incorrect. There is nothing in the passage to suggest them.
    Remember: when asked to make inferences, base your answers on what the passage implies, not what it states directly.

15. **E.** Phrases like "of feeling something new, of being affected by something that made the look of the world different" and "filled with bookish notions" reflect the narrator's response to the new books he reads. You have here a portrait of a youth's response to his expanding intellectual horizons.
    Choice A is incorrect. The narrator is not arguing in favor of a cause; he is recounting an episode from his life.
    Choice B is incorrect. The narrator was aware of racial prejudice long before he read Mencken.
    Choice C is incorrect. The passage is not about Mencken's and Lewis's styles; it is about their effect in opening up the world to the narrator.
    Choice D is incorrect. The passage is more about the impact of art on life than about the impact of life on art.

Remember: when asked to find the main idea, be sure to check the opening and summary sentences of each paragraph.

16. **D.** The terrible robbers in the pond world are the cruel creatures that, in the course of the struggle to exist, devour their fellows.

17. **D.** Here, "catch" is used as in fishing: "a good catch of fish." Suppose you want to collect a sample of pond-dwellers. You lower a jar into the nearest pond and capture a random batch of creatures swimming by—fish, tadpoles, full-grown insects, larvae—in other words, a "mixed catch."

18. **B.** The opening paragraph states that the introduction of the *Dytiscus* larvae to the aquarium will result in a struggle for existence in which the larvae will destroy their prey. The larvae, thus, are predators (hunters of prey). This suggests that their presence would be of particular interest to naturalists studying predatory patterns at work within a closed environment such as an aquarium.

19. **C.** The author is describing how the *Dytiscus* larva looks: slim body, six legs, flat head, huge jaws. Choice A is incorrect. All the details indicate the author is describing the killer, not the victim.

20. **D.** Though the passage mentions amphibians— tadpoles—and food, it states that the tadpoles provide food for the larvae, not vice versa. The passage nowhere states that the larvae are a source of food for amphibians.
Choice A is incorrect. The passage states that the larvae secrete digestive juices; it mentions secretion in line 33.
Choice B is incorrect. The passage states that the larvae attack one another; they seize and devour their own breed (lines 53–63).
Choice C is incorrect. The passage states that the larvae are attracted to motion; prey for them "is all that moves."
Choice E is incorrect. The passage states that the larvae have ravenous appetites: their "voracity" is unique.
Remember: when asked about specific information in the passage, spot key words in the question and scan the passage to find them (or their synonyms).

21. **E.** Digesting "out of doors" refers to the larva's external conversion of food into absorbable form. Look at the sentence immediately following line 33. Break down the process step by step. The larva injects a secretion into the victim. The secretion dissolves the victim's "entire inside." That is the start of the digestive

process. It takes place inside the victim's body; in other words, *outside* the larva's body—"out of doors." Only then does the larva begin to suck up the dissolved juices of his prey.

22. **D.** Choice D is correct. You can arrive at it by the process of elimination. Statement I is true. The inside of the victim "becomes opaque" (line 42); it increases in opacity. Therefore, you can eliminate Choices B, C, and E. Statement II is also true. As the victim is drained, its body shrivels or "shrinks to a limp bundle of skin." Therefore, you can eliminate choice A. Statement III has to be untrue. The victim's head must stay on; otherwise, the dissolving interior would leak out. Only Choice D is left. It is the correct answer.

23. **D.** The author mentions rats because a rat will attack and devour other rats. He is sure rodents do this; he's not sure any other animals do so. Thus, he mentions rats and related rodents to point up an uncommon characteristic also found in Dytiscus larvae.

24. **A.** In lines 61 and 62 the author mentions some "observations of which I shall speak later." These observations deal with whether wolves try to devour other wolves. Thus, the author clearly intends to discuss the likelihood of cannibalism among wolves.
In answering questions about what may be discussed in subsequent sections of the text, pay particular attention to words that are similar in meaning to subsequent: *following*, *succeeding*, *successive*, *later*.

Section 7 Mathematical Reasoning

MULTIPLE-CHOICE QUESTIONS

1. **D.** $3|x| + 2 < 17 \Rightarrow 3|x| < 15 \Rightarrow |x| < 5$. There are **9** integers whose absolute values are less than 5: $-4, -3, -2, -1, 0, 1, 2, 3, 4$.

2. **E.** Set up a proportion:

$$\frac{1 \text{ meter}}{1 \text{ second}} = \frac{k \text{ kilometers}}{1 \text{ hour}} = \frac{1000k \text{ meters}}{60 \text{ minutes}} =$$

$$\frac{1000k \text{ meters}}{3600 \text{ seconds}} = \frac{10k \text{ meters}}{36 \text{ seconds}}$$

Cross-multiplying the first and last ratios, you get $10k = 36$, and so $k = \mathbf{3.6}$.

3. **C.** $f(-8) = (-8)^2 + \sqrt[3]{-8} = 64 + (-2) = \mathbf{62}$

4. **D.** Pick easy-to-use numbers. Assume that, in 2000, 200 boys and 100 girls earned varsity letters. Then, in 2010, there were 150 boys and 125 girls. The ratio of girls to boys was

$$125{:}150 = 5{:}6 \text{ or } \frac{\mathbf{5}}{\mathbf{6}}.$$

5. **C.** The days of the week form a repeating sequence with 7 terms in the set that repeats. The nth term is the same as the rth term, where r is the remainder when n is divided by 7. [See Section P in Chapter 9.]

$500 \div 7 = 71.428\ldots \Rightarrow$ the quotient is 71.

$71 \times 7 = 497$ and $500 - 497 = 3 \Rightarrow$ the remainder is 3.

Therefore, 500 days from Saturday will be the same day as 3 days from Saturday, namely **Tuesday**.

6. **C.** The area of rectangle $ABCD = (4)(6) = 24$.

The area of right triangle $DAB = \frac{1}{2}(4)(6) = 12$,

and the area of right triangle $ECF = \frac{1}{2}(2)(2) = 2$. Therefore, the area of quadrilateral $BDEF = 24 - 12 - 2 = 10$. Then the shaded

area is $\frac{10}{24} = \frac{5}{12}$ the area of the rectangle, and

so the required probability is $\frac{\mathbf{5}}{\mathbf{12}}$.

7. **B.** The easiest observation is that, if adding a fourth number, d, to a set doesn't change the average, then d is equal to the existing average. If you don't realize that, solve for d:

$$\frac{a+b+c+d}{4} = \frac{a+b+c}{3} \Rightarrow$$
$$3a + 3b + 3c + 3d = 4a + 4b + 4c \Rightarrow$$
$$3d = a + b + c \Rightarrow d = \frac{\mathbf{a+b+c}}{\mathbf{3}}.$$

8. **A.** If Meri earned a grade of A, she missed $(100 - A)$ points. In adjusting the grades, the teacher decided to deduct only half that number: $\frac{100 - A}{2}$, so Meri's new grade was

$$100 - \left(\frac{100 - A}{2}\right) = 100 - 50 + \frac{A}{2} = \mathbf{50} + \frac{\mathbf{A}}{\mathbf{2}}.$$

GRID-IN QUESTIONS

9. **(152)** Normally, to get 60 pencils you would need to buy 20 sets of three at 25 cents per set, a total expenditure of $20 \times 25 = 500$ cents. On sale, you could get 60 pencils by buying 12 sets of five at 29 cents per set, for a total cost of $12 \times 29 = 348$ cents. This is a savings of $500 - 348 = \mathbf{152}$ cents.

10. (any decimal between 2.01 and 2.33 or $\frac{13}{6}$)

It is given that: $\quad 1 < 3x - 5 < 2$
Add 5 to each expression: $\quad 6 < \ 3x \ < 7$

Divide each expression by 3: $\ 2 < \ x \ < \frac{7}{3}$

Grid in any decimal number or fraction

between 2 and $\frac{7}{3} = 2.33$: **2.1**, for example, or

$\frac{\mathbf{13}}{\mathbf{6}}$, which is the average of $2 = \frac{12}{6}$

and $\frac{7}{3} = \frac{14}{6}$.

11. **(8100)** $x < 10,000 \Rightarrow \sqrt{x} < \sqrt{10,000} = 100$

$\sqrt{x} < 100 \Rightarrow \dfrac{\sqrt{x}}{5} < \dfrac{100}{5} = 20$

Since $\dfrac{\sqrt{x}}{5}$ must be an even integer, the

greatest possible value of $\dfrac{\sqrt{x}}{5}$ is 18:

$\dfrac{\sqrt{x}}{5} = 18 \Rightarrow \sqrt{x} = 90 \Rightarrow x = \mathbf{8100}$.

12. **(202)** After 33 repetitions of the pattern—red, white, white, blue, blue, blue—there will be $6 \times 33 = 198$ marbles in the box, of which 99 will be blue. When these are followed by 4 more marbles (1 red, 2 whites, and 1 blue), there will be 100 blue marbles, and a total of $198 + 4 = \mathbf{202}$ marbles in all.

13. **(28)** Whether or not you can visualize (or draw) the second (large) square, you can calculate its area. The area of each of the four triangles is $\frac{1}{2}(3)(4) = 6$, for a total of 24, and the area of the 5×5 square is 25. Then, the area of the large square is $24 + 25 = 49$. Each side of the square is 7, and the perimeter is **28**.

14. $\left(\dfrac{1}{32}\right)$ $\langle\langle 3 \rangle\rangle - \langle\langle 4 \rangle\rangle = \dfrac{1}{2^{3+1}} - \dfrac{1}{2^{4+1}} = \dfrac{1}{2^4} - \dfrac{1}{2^5} = \dfrac{1}{16} - \dfrac{1}{32} = \dfrac{\mathbf{1}}{\mathbf{32}}$.

15. $\left(\dfrac{1}{8}\right)$ $\langle\langle a+3\rangle\rangle:\langle\langle a\rangle\rangle = \dfrac{1}{2^{(a+3)+1}}:\dfrac{1}{2^{a+1}} = \dfrac{1}{2^{a+4}}:\dfrac{1}{2^{a+1}} =$

$\dfrac{1}{2^{a+4}} \div \dfrac{1}{2^{a+1}} = \dfrac{1}{2^{a+4}} \times \dfrac{2^{a+1}}{1} = \dfrac{1}{2^3} = \mathbf{\dfrac{1}{8}}.$

16. (19) There are at most 14 blank cards, so at least 86 of the 100 cards have one or both of the letters A and C on them. If x is the number of cards with both letters on them, then

$$75 + 30 - x \le 86 \Rightarrow x \le 105 - 86 = \mathbf{19}.$$

This is illustrated in the Venn diagram below.

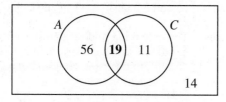

17. (8190) There are $26 \times 26 \times 9 = 6084$ PIC's with two letters and one digit, and there are $26 \times 9 \times 9 = 2106$ PIC's with one letter and two digits, for a total of $6084 + 2106 = \mathbf{8190}$.

18. $\left(\dfrac{3}{8} \text{ or } .375\right)$ If the diameter of the small white circle is d, then the diameter of the large white circle is $3d$, and the diameter of the largest circle is $d + 3d = 4d$. Then the ratio of the diameters, and hence of the radii, of the three circles is $4:3:1$. Assume the radii are 4, 3, and 1. Then the areas of the circles are 16π, 9π, and π. The sum of the areas of the white circles is 10π, the shaded region is $16\pi - 10\pi = 6\pi$, and $\dfrac{6\pi}{16\pi} = \dfrac{3}{8}$.

Section 8 Critical Reading

1. A. Voles are similar to mice; however, they are also different from them, and so may be *distinguished from* them.
    Note how the use of "although" in the opening phrase sets up the basic contrast here.
    (Contrast Signal)

2. C. Because Dr. Drew's method proved *effective*, it became a *model* for other systems.
    Remember to watch for signal words that link one part of the sentence to another. The "so...that" structure signals cause and effect.
    (Cause and Effect Signal)

3. B. The fact that the languages of the Mediterranean area were markedly (strikingly) alike eased or *facilitated* the movement of people and ideas from country to country.

Note how the specific examples in the second part of the sentence clarify the idea stated in the first part.
    (Examples)

4. E. Feeling that a job has *no point* might well lead a person to perform it in a *perfunctory* (indifferent or mechanical) manner.
    Remember: watch for signal words that link one part of the sentence to another. "Because" in the opening clause is a cause signal.
    (Cause and Effect Signal)

5. B. Nelson remained calm; he was in control in spite of the panic of battle. In other words, he was *imperturbable*, not capable of being agitated or perturbed.
    Note how the phrase "in spite of" signals the contrast between the subject's calm and the surrounding panic.
    (Contrast Signal)

6. E. Despite his hard work trying to solve the problem, the solution was not the *result* or outcome of his labor. Instead, it was *fortuitous* or accidental.
    Remember to watch for signal words that link one part of the sentence to another. The use of the "was...and not..." structure sets up a contrast. The missing words must be antonyms or near-antonyms.
    (Contrast Pattern)

7. E. The italicized introduction states that the author has had his manuscript rejected by his publisher. He is consigning or committing it to a desk drawer *to set it aside as unmarketable.*

8. B. The rejected author identifies with these baseball players, who constantly must face "failure." *He sees he is not alone in having to confront failure and move on.*

9. B. The author uses the jogger's comment to make a point about the *mental impact Henderson's home run must have had on Moore*. He reasons that, if each step a runner takes sends so many complex messages to the brain, then Henderson's ninth-inning home run must have flooded Moore's brain with messages, impressing its image indelibly in Moore's mind.

10. D. The author is talking of the impact of Henderson's home run on Moore. Registering in Moore's mind, the home run *made an impression* on him.

11. C. The author looks on himself as someone who "to succeed at all...must perform at an extraordinary level of excellence." This level of achievement, he maintains, is not demanded of accountants, plumbers, and insurance salesmen, and he seems to pride himself on belonging to a

profession that requires excellence. Thus, his attitude to members of less demanding professions can best be described as *superior*.

12. A.   The description of the writer defying his pain and extending himself irrationally to create a "masterpiece" despite the rejections of critics and publishers is a highly romantic one that elevates *the writer as someone heroic in his or her accomplishments*.

13. C.   The author of Passage 2 discusses the advantages of his ability to concentrate. Clearly, he prizes *his ability to focus* on the task at hand.

14. B.   When one football team is ahead of another by several touchdowns and there seems to be no way for the second team to catch up, the outcome of the game appears *decided* or settled.

15. E.   The "larger point of view" focuses on what to most people is the big question: the outcome of the game. The author is indifferent to this larger point of view. Concentrating on his own performance, he is *more concerned with the task at hand than with* winning or losing the game.

16. C.   Parade ground drill clearly does not entirely prepare a soldier for the reality of war. It does so only "to an extent." By using this phrase, the author *qualifies* his *statement*, making it less absolute.

17. C.   One would expect someone who dismisses or rejects most comparisons of athletics to art to avoid making such comparisons. The author, however, *is making such a comparison*. This reversal of what would have been expected is an instance of irony.

18. C.   To learn to overcome failure, to learn to give one's all in performance, to learn to focus on the work of the moment, to learn to have "the selfish intensity" that can block out the rest of the world—these are *hard lessons* that *both athletes and artists learn*.

19. D.   Throughout Passage 2, the author stresses the advantages and the power of concentration. He believes that a person who *focuses on the job at hand*, rather than dwelling on past failures, will continue to function successfully. Thus, this author is not particularly swayed by the Passage 1 author's contention that a failure such as giving up a key home run can destroy an athlete.

Section 9 Mathematical Reasoning

1. C.   Since the measure of a straight angle is $180°$, $x + y + 30 = 180$. Replacing y by $2x$, we get
$$x + 2x + 30 = 180 \Rightarrow 3x = 150.$$
So, $x = 50$ and $y = 2x = \mathbf{100}$.

2. C.   The temperature rose $8 - (-7) = 8 + 7 = 15°$ in 1.5 hours. The average hourly increase was $15° \div 1.5 = \mathbf{10°}$.

3. D.   The expression $n^2 - 30$ is negative whenever $n^2 < 30$. This is true for all integers between -5 and 5 inclusive, **11** in all (including 0).

4. D.   The only thing to do is to test each set of values to see which ones work and which one doesn't. In this case, choice D, $\boldsymbol{a = 3}$ and $\boldsymbol{b = -4}$, does not work:
$2(3)^2 + 3(-4) = 18 - 12 = 6$, not 5.
The other choices all work.

5. A.   The slope of the line, ℓ, that passes through $(-2, 2)$ and $(3, 3)$ is $\dfrac{3-2}{3-(-2)} = \dfrac{1}{5}$. The slope of any line perpendicular to ℓ is $-\dfrac{1}{\frac{1}{5}} = \mathbf{-5}$.

6. C.   For some number x, the measures of the angles are x, $2x$, and $3x$; so
$$180 = x + 2x + 3x = 6x \Rightarrow x = 30.$$
Therefore, the triangle is a 30-60-90 triangle, and the ratio of the sides is $\mathbf{1:\sqrt{3}:2}$.

7. D.   By definition, a googol is equal to 10^{100}. Therefore, $g^2 = 10^{100} \times 10^{100} = 10^{200}$, which, when it is written out, is the digit 1 followed by 200 zeros, creating an integer with **201** digits.

8. E.   The graph of $y = f(x - 3)$ is the graph of $y = f(x)$ shifted 3 units to the right, as shown in Choice D. The graph of $y = -f(x - 3)$ reflects Choice D in the x-axis, resulting in graph **E**.

9. A.   Since $C = 2\pi r$, then $r = \dfrac{C}{2\pi}$. Since the formula for the area of a circle is $A = \pi r^2$,
$$\pi r^2 = \pi\left(\frac{C}{2\pi}\right)^2 = \pi\left(\frac{C^2}{4\pi^2}\right) = \frac{C^2}{4\pi^2}.$$

10. B. $\left(4^{\frac{1}{2}} \cdot 8^{\frac{1}{3}} \cdot 16^{\frac{1}{4}} \cdot 32^{\frac{1}{5}}\right)^{\frac{1}{2}} = \left(\sqrt{4} \cdot \sqrt[3]{8} \cdot \sqrt[4]{16} \cdot \sqrt[5]{32}\right)^{\frac{1}{2}}$

$= (2 \cdot 2 \cdot 2 \cdot 2)^{\frac{1}{2}} = 16^{\frac{1}{2}} = \sqrt{16} = 4$

11. C. $\sqrt{x-15} - 5 = 2 \Rightarrow \sqrt{x-15} = 7 \Rightarrow x - 15 = 49$.

So, $x = 64 \Rightarrow \sqrt{x} = \sqrt{64} = 8$.

12. E. Joanna needed to drive the m miles in $h + \frac{1}{2}$ hours. Since $r = \frac{d}{t}$, to find her rate, you divide the distance, m, by the time, $\left(h + \frac{1}{2}\right)$:

$$\frac{m}{h + \frac{1}{2}} = \frac{2m}{2h + 1}.$$

13. A. In the figure below, the area of $\triangle BFC$ is $\frac{1}{2}(4)(5) = 10$. Then the area of the shaded quadrilateral is 10 minus the areas of square $ADEF$ [$2^2 = 4$] and triangle CDE [$\frac{1}{2}(2)(2) = 2$]: $10 - 4 - 2 = \mathbf{4}$.

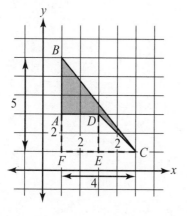

14. D. Since y is inversely proportional to x, there is a constant k such that $xy = k$. Then

$k = (4)(10) = 40$, and $40 = x(20) \Rightarrow x = 2$.

Also, since y is directly proportional to z, there is a constant m such that $\frac{y}{z} = m$.

Then $m = \frac{10}{8} = \frac{5}{4}$ and

$\frac{5}{4} = \frac{20}{z} \Rightarrow 5z = 80 \Rightarrow z = 16$,

and so

$x + z = 2 + 16 = \mathbf{18}$.

15. E. To find the average of three numbers, divide their sum by 3: $\dfrac{3^{30} + 3^{60} + 3^{90}}{3}$. To simplify this fraction, divide each term in the numerator by 3:

$$\frac{3^{30}}{3} + \frac{3^{60}}{3} + \frac{3^{90}}{3} = 3^{29} + 3^{59} + 3^{89}.$$

16. D.

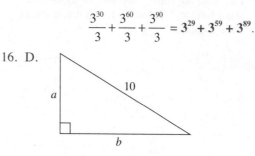

By the Pythagorean theorem,

$$a^2 + b^2 = 10^2 = 100;$$

and since the area is 20,

$$\frac{1}{2}ab = 20 \Rightarrow ab = 40, \text{ and } 2ab = 80.$$

Expand:

$$(a + b)^2 = a^2 + 2ab + b^2 = (a^2 + b^2) + 2ab.$$

Then

$$(a^2 + b^2) + 2ab = 100 + 80 = \mathbf{180}.$$

Section 10   Writing Skills

1. D. Error in logical comparison. Compare voices with voices, not voices with singers.

2. C. Run-on sentence. Choice C corrects the error by turning the initial clause ("The … blackboard") into a participial phrase ("After … blackboard") and changing the subject of the main clause from *he* to *the mathematics teacher*.

3. C. Error in usage. Do not use *when* after *is* in making a definition.

4. D. Shift in number. The subject, *students*, is plural; the subject complement should be plural as well. Change *tumbler* to *tumblers*.

5. E. Lack of parallelism. The "both … and" construction provides parallel structure.

6. B. Wordiness. Choice B makes the writer's point simply and concisely.

7. C. Error in logical comparison. Compare audiences with audiences, not with theaters.

8. D. Dangling participle. Ask yourself who is observing the preschoolers' interactions.

9. C. Error in choice of conjunction. *Many* people requested a deferment, *but* only a few received one. Use *but* rather than *and* to signal that what follows is contrary to what you might have expected.

10. A. Sentence is correct.

11. A. Sentence is correct.

12. E. Lack of parallelism. Choice E has parallel structure.

13. C. Error in subject–verb agreement. The subject, *demand*, is singular; the verb should be singular as well. Change *are* to *is*.

14. D. Sentence fragment. Choice D economically corrects the fragment.

PART THREE

TACTICS AND PRACTICE: CRITICAL READING

The Sentence Completion Question

CHAPTER 1

- Quick Overview
- Testing Tactics
- Practice Exercises
- Answer Key
- Answer Explanations

QUICK OVERVIEW

All three critical reading sections start with "fill-in-the-blank" sentence completion questions. Consider them warm-up exercises: to answer them correctly, you'll have to use both your reading comprehension and vocabulary skills. You will then be prepared for the critical reading portions of the test.

The sentence completion questions ask you to choose the best way to complete a sentence from which one or two words have been omitted. The sentences deal with the sorts of topics you've probably encountered in your general reading: ballet, banking, tarantulas, thunderstorms, paintings, plagues. However, this is *not* a test of your general knowledge, although you may feel more comfortable if you are familiar with the topic the sentence is discussing. If you're unfamiliar with the topic, don't worry about it. You should be able to answer any of the questions using what you know about how the English language works.

TIME-SAVER TIP

Here is a set of directions for the sentence completion questions that has appeared on actual SAT exams for several years. From time to time the SAT-makers come up with different sentences as examples. However, the basic directions seldom vary. Master them now. Don't waste your test time re-reading familiar directions. Spend that time answering additional questions. That's the way to boost your score!

Each sentence below has one or two blanks, each blank indicating that something has been omitted. Beneath the sentence are five lettered words or sets of words. Choose the word or set of words that best fits the meaning of the sentence as a whole.

Example:

Medieval kingdoms did not become constitutional republics overnight; on the contrary, the change was ----.

(A) unpopular   (B) unexpected
(C) advantageous   (D) sufficient
(E) gradual

Ⓐ Ⓑ Ⓒ Ⓓ ●

The phrase *on the contrary* is your key to the correct answer. It is what we call a **signal word**: it signals a contrast. *On the contrary* sets up a contrast between a hypothetical change—the change you might have assumed took place—and the actual change. Did medieval kingdoms turn into republics *overnight*? No, they did not. Instead of happening overnight, the actual change took time: it was *gradual*. The correct answer is Choice E, *gradual*.

Now that you know what to expect on sentence completion questions, work through the following tactics and learn to spot the signals that will help you fill in the blanks. Then do the practice exercises at the end of the chapter.

Testing Tactics

TACTIC

First, Read the Sentence Carefully to Get a Feel for Its Meaning.

Have you ever put together a jigsaw puzzle and wound up missing one final piece? There you are, staring at the almost complete picture. You know the shape of the missing piece. You can see where it fits. You know what its coloration must be. You know, *because you've looked hard at the incomplete picture, and you've got a sense of what's needed to make it whole.*

That's the position you're in when you're working with sentence completion questions. You have to look hard at that incomplete sentence, to read it carefully to get a sense of its drift. Once you've got a feel for the big picture, you'll be ready to come up with an answer choice that fits.

TACTIC

Before You Look at the Choices, Think of a Word That Makes Sense.

Your problem here is to find a word that best completes the sentence's thought. Before you look at the answer choices, try to come up with a word that makes logical sense in this context. Then look at all five choices supplied by the SAT-makers. If the word you thought of is one of your five choices, select it as your answer. If the word you thought of is *not* one of your five choices, look for a synonym of that word.

See how the process works in dealing with the following sentence.

> The psychologist set up the experiment to test the rat's -----; he wished to see how well the rat adjusted to the changing conditions it had to face.

Note how the part of the sentence following the semi-colon (the second clause, in technical terms) is being used to define or clarify what the psychologist is trying to test. He is trying to see how well the rat *adjusts*. What words does this suggest to you? *Flexibility*, possibly, or *adaptability*. Either of these words could complete the sentence's thought.

Here are the five answer choices given.

    (A) reflexes
    (B) communicability
    (C) stamina
    (D) sociability
    (E) adaptability

The answer clearly is *adaptability*, Choice E.

TACTIC

Look at All the Possible Answers Before You Make Your Final Choice.

You are looking for the word that *best* fits the meaning of the sentence as a whole. Don't be hasty in picking an answer. Test each answer choice, substituting it for the missing word. That way you can satisfy yourself that you have come up with the answer that best fits.

Follow this tactic as you work through the following question.

Physical laws do not, of course, in themselves force bodies to behave in a certain way, but merely ---- how, as a matter of fact, they do behave.

(A) determine
(B) preclude
(C) counteract
(D) describe
(E) commend

When you looked at the answer choices, did you find that one seemed to leap right off the page? Specifically, did Choice A, *determine*, catch your eye?

A hasty reader might easily focus on Choice A, but in this sentence *determine* doesn't really work. However, there are reasons for its appeal.

Determine often appears in a scientific context. It's a word you may have come across in class discussions of experiments: "By flying a kite during a lightning storm, Ben Franklin tried to *determine* (find out; discover) just how lightning worked."

Here, *determine* is an eye-catcher, an answer choice set up to tempt the unwary into guessing wrong. Eye-catchers are words that somehow come to mind after reading the statement. They're related in a way; they feel as if they belong in the statement, as if they're dealing with the same field.

Because you have seen *determine* previously in a scientific context, you may want to select it as your answer without thinking the sentence through. However, you *must* take time to think it through, to figure out what it is about. Here it's about physical laws (the law of gravity, for example). It says physical laws *don't* force bodies to act in a specific way. (The *law* of gravity didn't make the apple fall on Isaac Newton's head; the *force* of gravity did.)

The sentence goes on to clarify what physical laws actually do. What *do* they do? Do physical laws make discoveries about how bodies behave? No. *People* make discoveries about how bodies behave. Then people write down physical laws to describe what they have discovered. The correct answer to this question is Choice D, *describe*. Be suspicious of answer choices that come too easily.

TACTIC
4 Watch Out for Negative Words and Prefixes.

No, not, none; *non-, un-, in-*. These negative words and word parts are killers, especially in combination.

The damage to the car was insignificant.
("Don't worry about it—it's just a scratch.")
The damage to the car was not insignificant.
("Oh, no, Bart! We totaled Mom's car!")

Watch out for *not*: it's easy to overlook, but it's a key word, as the following sentence clearly illustrates.

Madison was not ---- person and thus made few public addresses; but those he made were memorable, filled with noble phrases.

(A) a reticent
(B) a stately
(C) an inspiring
(D) an introspective
(E) a communicative

What would happen if you overlooked *not* in this question? Probably you'd wind up choosing Choice A: Madison was a *reticent* (quiet; reserved) man. *For this reason* he made few public addresses.

Unfortunately, you'd have gotten things backward. The sentence isn't telling you what Madison was like. It's telling you what he was *not* like. And he was not a *communicative* person; he didn't express himself freely. However, when he did get around to expressing himself, he had valuable things to say. Choice E is the correct answer.

TACTIC

Use Your Knowledge of Context Clues to Get at the Meanings of Unfamiliar Words.

If a word used in a sentence is unfamiliar, or if an answer choice is unknown to you, look at its context in the sentence to see whether the context provides a clue to the meaning of the word. Often authors will use an unfamiliar word and then immediately define it within the same sentence.

> The ---- of Queen Elizabeth I impressed her contemporaries: she seemed to know what dignitaries and foreign leaders were thinking.
>
> (A) symbiosis
> (B) malevolence
> (C) punctiliousness
> (D) consternation
> (E) perspicacity

Looking at the five answer choices, you may feel unequipped to try to tackle the sentence at all. However, the clause that immediately follows the colon ("she seemed to know what…leaders were thinking") is there to explain and clarify that missing word. The two groups of words are juxtaposed— set beside one another—to make their relationship clear. The missing word has something to do with the queen's ability to see through those foreign leaders and practically read their thoughts.

Now that you know the missing word's general meaning, go through the answer choices to see which one makes sense. *Symbiosis* means living together cooperatively or intimately (as in "a symbiotic relationship"). It has nothing to do with being insightful or astute; you can eliminate Choice A. *Malevolence* means ill-will. The queen's ability shows her perceptiveness, not her ill-will; you can eliminate Choice B. *Punctiliousness* means carefulness about observing all the proper formalities; you can eliminate Choice C. *Consternation* means amazement or alarm. Elizabeth was clear-sighted, not confused or amazed; you can eliminate Choice D. Only Choice E is left, *perspicacity*. Elizabeth's ability to know the thoughts of foreign leaders demonstrates her acute mental vision or discernment, in other words, her perspicacity. The correct answer is Choice E.

TACTIC

Break Down Unfamiliar Words Into Recognizable Parts.

If you're having vocabulary trouble, look for familiar parts—prefixes, suffixes, and roots—in unfamiliar words.

Note that your knowledge of word parts could have helped you answer the previous question. Suppose you had been able to eliminate two of the answer choices and were trying to decide among three unfamiliar words, *symbiosis*, *punctiliousness*, and *perspicacity*. By using what you know about word parts, you still could have come up with the correct answer. Take a good look at *perspicacity*. Do you know any other words that begin with the letters *per-*? What about *pervade*, to spread through? The prefix *per-* means thoroughly or through. Next look at the letters *spic*. What other words contain those letters? Take *despicable*, for example, or *conspicuous*. A despicable person deserves to be looked down on. A conspicuous object is noticeable; it must be looked at. The root *spic* means to look at or see. Queen Elizabeth I had the ability to *see through* surfaces and perceive people's inner thoughts. In a word, she had *perspicacity*.

TACTIC

7 Watch for Signal Words That Link One Part of the Sentence to Another.

Writers use transitions to link their ideas logically. These transitions or signal words are clues that can help you figure out what the sentence actually means.

CONTRAST SIGNALS

Look for words or phrases that indicate a contrast between one idea and another. In such cases an antonym or near-antonym for another word in the sentence should be the correct answer.

Signal Words

although	in contrast	on the other hand
but	in spite of	rather than
despite	instead of	still
even though	nevertheless	yet
however	on the contrary	

See how a contrast signal works in the following easy question.

> In sharp contrast to the previous night's revelry, the wedding was ---- affair.
>
> (A) a fervent
> (B) a dignified
> (C) a chaotic
> (D) an ingenious
> (E) a jubilant

In sharp contrast signals you explicitly to look for an antonym or near-antonym of another word or idea in the sentence. The wedding, it suggests, is *different in character* from the party the night before. What was that party like? It was *revelry*: wild, noisy, even drunken partying. The wedding, therefore, was *not* wild and noisy. Instead, it was calm and formal; it was *dignified* (stately, decorous). The correct answer is Choice B, *dignified*.

SUPPORT SIGNALS

Look for words or phrases that indicate that the omitted portion of the sentence supports or continues a thought developed elsewhere in the sentence. In such cases, a synonym or near-synonym for another word in the sentence should be the correct answer.

Signal Words

additionally	furthermore
also	in addition
and	likewise
besides	moreover

See how *and* works as a support signal in the following question.

> During the Middle Ages, plague and other ---- decimated the populations of entire towns.
>
> (A) pestilences
> (B) immunizations
> (C) proclivities
> (D) indispositions
> (E) demises

The presence of *and* linking two items in a series indicates that the missing word may be a synonym or near-synonym for the other linked word. In this case, *pestilences* are, like the *plague*, deadly epidemic diseases: the medieval Black Plague was one type of pestilence. The correct answer is Choice A.

Note, by the way, that the missing word, like *plague*, must be a word with *extremely* negative associations. Therefore, you can eliminate any word with positive or neutral ones. You can even eliminate words with *mildly* negative connotations. *Immunizations* (processes giving the ability to resist a disease) have positive effects: you may dislike your flu shot, but you prefer it to coming down with the flu. You can eliminate Choice B. *Proclivities* (natural tendencies), in themselves, are neutral (you can have a proclivity for championing the rights of underdogs, or a proclivity for neatness, or a proclivity for violence); they are not *by definition* inevitably negative. Therefore, you can eliminate Choice C. Similarly, while *indispositions* (slight illnesses; minor unwillingness) are negative, they are only mildly so. You can eliminate Choice D. Choice E, *demises* (deaths) also fails to work in this context. Thus, you are left with the correct answer, Choice A.

CAUSE-AND-EFFECT SIGNALS

Look for words or phrases that indicate that one thing causes another.

Signal Words

accordingly	in order to
because	so...that
consequently	therefore
for	thus
hence	when...then

See how a cause and effect signal works in the next question.

> Tarantulas apparently have little sense of ----, for a hungry one will ignore a loudly chirping cricket placed in its cage unless the cricket happens to get in its way.
>
> (A) touch
> (B) time
> (C) hearing
> (D) self-preservation
> (E) temperature

For sets up a relationship of cause and effect. Why does the tarantula ignore the loudly chirping cricket? *Because*, it seems, the tarantula does not hear the cricket's chirps. Apparently, it has little sense of *hearing*. The correct answer is Choice C.

TACTIC

8 **Look for Words That Signal the Unexpected.**

Some words indicate that something unexpected, possibly even unwanted, exists or has occurred. These words signal a built-in contrast.

Words That Signal the Unexpected

abnormal	ironic
anomalous	odd
curious (odd)	paradoxical
illogical	surprising
incongruous	unexpected

See how such a word works in the following question.

The historian noted irony in the fact that developments considered ---- by people of that era are now viewed as having been ----.

(A) inspirational..impetuous
(B) bizarre..irrational
(C) intuitive..uncertain
(D) actual..grandiose
(E) improbable..inevitable

Before you consider the answer choices, think through the sentence. Remember, something unexpected has taken place. People of some earlier period had one idea of certain developments during that time. With hindsight, however, people today view them in an unexpected, different light. The two views actually contradict each other.

Only one answer choice presents such a mutually contradictory pair of words, Choice E. People in days gone by looked on certain developments as *improbable*, unlikely. Today we view these very developments as *inevitable*, inescapable. To a historian, such a mismatch in opinions is ironic.

TACTIC

9 In Double-Blank Sentences, Test One Blank at a Time, Not Two.

In a sentence completion question with two blanks, read through the entire sentence. Quickly decide which blank you want to work on. Then insert the appropriate word from each answer pair in that blank. Ask yourself whether this particular word makes sense in this blank. If a word makes *no* sense in the sentence, you can eliminate that answer pair.

The author portrays research psychologists not as disruptive ---- in the field of psychotherapy, but as effective ---- working ultimately toward the same ends as the psychotherapists.

(A) proponents..opponents
(B) antagonists..pundits
(C) interlocutors..surrogates
(D) meddlers..usurpers
(E) intruders..collaborators

Turn to the second part of the sentence. The research psychologists are portrayed as effective *blanks* working ultimately toward the same ends as the psychotherapists. The key phrase here is "working ultimately toward the same ends." Thus, the research psychologists are in effect collaborating with the psychotherapists to achieve a common goal. This immediately suggests that the correct answer is Choice E. Test the first word of that answer pair in the first blank. The adjective "disruptive" suggests that the first missing word is negative in tone. *Intruders* (people who rudely or inappropriately barge in) is definitely a negative term. Choice E continues to look good.

Reread the sentence with both words in place, making sure both words make sense. "The author portrays research psychologists not as disruptive intruders in the field of psychotherapy, but as effective collaborators working ultimately toward the same ends as the psychotherapists." Both words make perfect sense. The correct answer is Choice E.

Here is a second, more difficult question that you can solve using this same tactic. This time, try starting with the first word.

The author inadvertently undermined his thesis by allowing his biases to ---- his otherwise ---- scholarship.

(A) bolster..superior
(B) cloud..unfocused
(C) compromise..judicious
(D) confirm..exhaustive
(E) falsify..questionable

The author has undermined or weakened his thesis (the point he's trying to make). How has he done this? He has let his prejudices affect his work as a scholar *in a negative way*. Your first missing word must have a negative meaning; you can eliminate any answer choice whose first word has only a positive sense.

Bolster or support is wholly positive; so is *confirm*. You can eliminate Choices A and D. The three other choices need closer examination. To *cloud* someone's scholarship, obscuring or tarnishing it, would be damaging; to *falsify* scholarly work would be damaging as well. To *compromise* someone's scholarship also is damaging: if you compromise your standards, you fail to live up to the high scholarly standards expected of you. You thus endanger your scholarly reputation. (Note that this is a secondary, relatively unfamiliar meaning of *compromise*; the SAT-makers love words with multiple meanings like this.)

Now examine the context of the second missing word. Rephrase the sentence, breaking it down. The author has let his prejudices damage his scholarship, which was otherwise *good*. The second missing word must be positive in meaning.

Check out the second word of Choices B, C, and E. *Unfocused*, vague scholarly work isn't good. Neither is *questionable*, doubtful scholarship. *Judicious*, thoughtful work, however, *is* good. The correct answer is Choice C.

Remember, in double-blank sentences, the right answer must correctly fill *both* blanks. A wrong answer choice often includes one correct and one incorrect answer. Always test the second word.

Practice Exercise

Use the following practice exercise as a warm-up before you go on to the model tests. Check your answers against the answer key. For every answer you get incorrect, follow this procedure:

1. Review the unfamiliar words. Check them out in the Basic Word List in Chapter 3, or look them up in your dictionary. Again, remember that these are SAT-level words. Make use of this chance to go over what they mean.

2. Once you know the meaning of the words, see if you can spot signal words or context clues that might have helped you get the answer right. Note any word parts that you can find in the unfamiliar words.

3. Go over your guessing tactics. If you eliminated any answer choices, see whether you were correct in eliminating them. Remember, if you *can* eliminate one or two answer choices, you *should* guess. Even if you get a particular question wrong, in the long run, if you use the process of elimination correctly, you'll come out ahead of the game.

Sentence Completion Exercise

Each sentence below has one or two blanks, each blank indicating that something has been omitted. Beneath the sentence are five lettered words or sets of words. Choose the word or set of words that <u>best</u> fits the meaning of the sentence as a whole.

Example:

Although its publicity has been ----, the film itself is intelligent, well-acted, handsomely produced, and altogether ---- .

(A) tasteless..respectable
(B) extensive..moderate
(C) sophisticated..amateur
(D) risqué..crude
(E) perfect..spectacular   ● Ⓑ Ⓒ Ⓓ Ⓔ

1. The selection committee for the exhibit was amazed to see such fine work done by a mere ----.

    (A) connoisseur
    (B) artist
    (C) amateur
    (D) entrepreneur
    (E) exhibitionist

2. The teacher suspected cheating as soon as he noticed the pupil's ---- glances at his classmate's paper.

    (A) futile   (B) sporadic   (C) furtive   (D) cold
    (E) inconsequential

3. Known for his commitment to numerous worthy causes, the philanthropist deserved ---- for his ----.

    (A) recognition..folly
    (B) blame..hypocrisy
    (C) reward..modesty
    (D) admonishment..wastefulness
    (E) credit..altruism

4. Miss Watson termed Huck's behavior --- because in her opinion nothing could excuse his deliberate disregard of her commands.

    (A) devious   (B) intolerant   (C) irrevocable
    (D) indefensible   (E) boisterous

5. Either the surfing at Maui is ----, or I went there on an off day.

    (A) consistent   (B) thrilling   (C) invigorating
    (D) overrated   (E) scenic

6. Your ---- remarks spoil the effect of your speech; try not to stray from your subject.

    (A) innocuous   (B) digressive   (C) derogatory
    (D) persistent   (E) enigmatic

7. The fundraising ball turned out to be a ---- : it started late, attracted too few dancers, and lost almost a million dollars.

    (A) debacle   (B) blockbuster   (C) deluge
    (D) gala   (E) milestone

8. She was pleased by the accolades she received; like everyone else, she enjoyed being ----.

    (A) entertained   (B) praised   (C) playful
    (D) vindicated   (E) charitable

9. The stereotypical image of masculinity assumes that weeping is ---- "unmanly" behavior, and not simply a human reaction that may be ---- by either sex.

    (A) inexplicably..repented
    (B) excessively..discerned
    (C) essentially..defined
    (D) inherently..adopted
    (E) intentionally..exaggerated

10. The tapeworm is an example of ---- organism, one that lives within or on another creature, deriving some or all of its nutriment from its host.

    (A) a hospitable   (B) an exemplary
    (C) a parasitic   (D) an autonomous
    (E) a protozoan

11. There was a hint of carelessness about her appearance, as though the cut of her blouse or the fit of her slacks was a matter of ---- to her.

    (A) satisfaction   (B) aesthetics
    (C) indifference   (D) significance
    (E) controversy

12. Many educators argue that a ---- grouping of students would improve instruction because it would limit the range of student abilities in the classroom.

    (A) heterogeneous   (B) systematic
    (C) homogeneous   (D) sporadic
    (E) fragmentary

13. The younger members of the company resented the domineering and ---- manner of the office manager.

    (A) urbane   (B) prudent   (C) convivial
    (D) imperious   (E) objective

14. Bluebeard was noted for his ---- jealousy, a jealousy so extreme that it passed all reasonable bounds.

    (A) transitory   (B) rhetorical   (C) stringent
    (D) callous   (E) inordinate

15. I regret that my remarks seemed ----; I never intended to belittle you.

    (A) inadequate   (B) justified   (C) unassailable
    (D) disparaging   (E) shortsighted

16. A ---- glance pays ---- attention to details.

    (A) furtive..meticulous   (B) cursory..little
    (C) cryptic..close   (D) keen..scanty
    (E) fleeting..vigilant

17. With its elaborately carved, convoluted lines, furniture of the Baroque period was highly ---- .

    (A) functional   (B) primitive   (C) linear
    (D) spare   (E) ornate

18. His overweening pride in his accomplishments was ---- : he had accomplished little if anything at all.

    (A) unjustified   (B) innocuous   (C) systematic
    (D) rational   (E) critical

19. A ---- relationship links the rhinoceros and the oxpecker (or rhinoceros bird), for the two are mutually dependent.

    (A) monolithic   (B) superficial   (C) symbiotic
    (D) debilitating   (E) stereotypical

20. When we saw black smoke billowing from the wing of the plane, we were certain that disaster was ----.

    (A) unlikely   (B) opportune   (C) imminent
    (D) undeserved   (E) averted

21. I can vouch for his honesty; I have always found him ---- and carefully observant of the truth.

    (A) arbitrary   (B) plausible   (C) volatile
    (D) veracious   (E) innocuous

22. This well-documented history is of importance because it carefully ---- the ---- accomplishments of Native American artists who are all too little known to the public at large.

    (A) recognizes..negligible
    (B) overlooks..purported
    (C) scrutinizes..illusory
    (D) distorts..noteworthy
    (E) substantiates..considerable

23. Perhaps because he feels ---- by an excess of parental restrictions and rules, at adolescence the repressed child may break out dramatically.

    (A) nurtured   (B) appeased
    (C) confined   (D) fascinated
    (E) liberated

24. Sue felt that Jack's ---- in the face of the compelling evidence which she had presented was an example of his ---- mind.

    (A) truculence..unbiased
    (B) skepticism..open
    (C) incredulity..closed
    (D) acquiescence..keen
    (E) reluctance..impartial

25. As a girl, Emily Dickinson was ---- but also ---- : extraordinarily intense about her poetry yet exceptionally inhibited socially.

    (A) zealous..gregarious
    (B) ardent..repressed
    (C) prudent..reserved
    (D) rash..intrusive
    (E) impulsive..dedicated

26. The good night's sleep had ---- effect on the weary climber, who woke refreshed and eager to resume the ascent.

    (A) an innocuous   (B) a tonic
     (C) a minor   (D) an enervating
      (E) a detrimental

27. She is an interesting ----, an infinitely shy person who, in apparent contradiction, possesses an enormously intuitive ---- for understanding people.

    (A) aberration..disdain
    (B) caricature..talent
    (C) specimen..loathing
    (D) phenomenon..disinclination
    (E) paradox..gift

28. The coach's harsh rebuke deeply wounded the star quarterback, who had never been ---- like that before.

    (A) summoned   (B) reprimanded
     (C) stimulated   (D) placated
      (E) ignored

29. At the present time, we are suffering from ---- of stories about the war; try writing about another subject.

    (A) a calumny   (B) a dearth   (C) an insurgence
     (D) a plethora   (E) an inhibition

30. Because he was ----, he shunned human society.

    (A) a misanthrope   (B) an oligarch   (C) an anomaly
     (D) a stereotype   (E) a nonentity

31. Ernest Hemingway's prose is generally esteemed for its ---- ; as one critic puts it, Hemingway "cuts out unneeded words."

    (A) sensitivity   (B) economy   (C) gusto
     (D) breadth   (E) intricacy

32. Crows are extremely ---- : their harsh cries easily drown out the songs of neighboring birds.

    (A) fickle   (B) swarthy   (C) raucous
     (D) cordial   (E) versatile

33. After Bob had broken the punch bowl, we sensed the extent of his ---- from the way he shamefacedly avoided meeting his hostess's eye.

    (A) composure   (B) perspicacity
     (C) discomfiture   (D) forbearance
      (E) benevolence

34. Crowther maintained that the current revival was the most fatuous and ---- production of the entire theatrical season.

    (A) gripping   (B) inane   (C) prophetic
     (D) memorable   (E) salubrious

35. His olfactory sense was so highly developed that he was often called in to judge ----.

    (A) productivity   (B) colors   (C) litigation
     (D) perfume   (E) acoustics

36. Jean Georges was famous for his ---- cuisine, which brought together ingredients from many cooking traditions—Thai, Chinese, French—and combined them in innovative ways.

    (A) aesthetic   (B) clandestine
     (C) homogeneous   (D) eclectic
      (E) conventional

37. Believing that all children possess a certain natural intelligence, the headmaster exhorted the teachers to discover and ---- each student's ---- talents.

    (A) suppress..unrecognized
    (B) develop..intrinsic
    (C) redirect..specious
    (D) belittle..dormant
    (E) cultivate..gratuitous

38. Micawber's habit of spending more than he earned left him in a state of perpetual ----, but he ---- hoping to see a more affluent day.

    (A) indigence..persevered in
    (B) confusion..compromised by
    (C) enervation..retaliated by
    (D) motion..responded by
    (E) opulence..insisted on

39. The ---- of such utopian notions is reflected by the quick disintegration of the idealistic community at Brooke Farm.

    (A) timeliness   (B) creativity
     (C) impracticability   (D) effervescence
      (E) vindication

40. We were amazed that a man who had been heretofore the most ---- of public speakers could, in a single speech, electrify an audience and bring them cheering to their feet.

    (A) enthralling   (B) accomplished   (C) pedestrian
     (D) auspicious   (E) masterful

41. Despite the mixture's ---- nature, we found that by lowering its temperature in the laboratory we could dramatically reduce its tendency to vaporize.

    (A) resilient   (B) volatile   (C) homogeneous
     (D) insipid   (E) acerbic

42. Her novel published to universal acclaim, her literary gifts acknowledged by the chief figures of the Harlem Renaissance, her reputation as yet ---- by envious slights, Hurston clearly was at the ---- of her career.

    (A) undamaged..ebb   (B) untarnished..zenith
    (C) untainted..extremity   (D) blackened..mercy
    (E) unmarred..brink

43. Fitness experts claim that jogging is ----; once you begin to jog regularly, you may be unable to stop, because you are sure to love it more and more all the time.

    (A) exhausting   (B) illusive   (C) addictive
    (D) exotic   (E) overrated

44. Although newscasters often use the terms Chicano and Latino ----, students of Hispanic-American culture are profoundly aware of the ---- the two.

    (A) interchangeably..dissimilarities between
    (B) indifferently..equivalence of
    (C) deprecatingly..controversies about
    (D) unerringly..significance of
    (E) confidently..origins of

45. She maintained that the proposed legislation was ---- because it simply established an affirmative action task force without making any appropriate provision to fund such a force.

    (A) inevitable   (B) inadequate   (C) prudent
    (D) necessary   (E) beneficial

46. The faculty senate warned that, if its recommendations were to go unheeded, the differences between the administration and the teaching staff would be ---- and eventually rendered irreconcilable.

    (A) rectified   (B) exacerbated   (C) imponderable
    (D) eradicated   (E) alienated

47. Paradoxically, Helen, who had been a strict mother to her children, proved ---- mistress to her cats.

    (A) a harsh   (B) an indolent   (C) an ambivalent
    (D) a cautious   (E) a lenient

48. Famed athlete Bobby Orr was given his first pair of skates by a ---- Canadian woman who somehow "knew" he would use them to attain sporting greatness.

    (A) prosperous   (B) prescient   (C) notorious
    (D) skeptical   (E) fallible

49. The supervisor's evaluation was ---- , for she noted the employee's strong points and limitations without overly emphasizing either.

    (A) equitable   (B) laudatory   (C) practicable
    (D) slanted   (E) dogmatic

50. She has sufficient tact to ---- the ordinary crises of diplomatic life; however, even her diplomacy is insufficient to enable her to ---- the current emergency.

    (A) negotiate..comprehend
    (B) survive..exaggerate
    (C) handle..weather
    (D) ignore..transform
    (E) aggravate..resolve

Answer Key

SENTENCE COMPLETION EXERCISE

1.	C	9.	D	17.	E	25.	B	33.	C	41.	B	49.	A
2.	C	10.	C	18.	A	26.	B	34.	B	42.	B	50.	C
3.	E	11.	C	19.	C	27.	E	35.	D	43.	C		
4.	D	12.	C	20.	C	28.	B	36.	D	44.	A		
5.	D	13.	D	21.	D	29.	D	37.	B	45.	B		
6.	B	14.	E	22.	E	30.	A	38.	A	46.	B		
7.	A	15.	D	23.	C	31.	B	39.	C	47.	E		
8.	B	16.	B	24.	C	32.	C	40.	C	48.	B		

Answer Explanations

1. **(C)** The key word here is "amazed." It would not amaze a selection committee for an artist to submit fine work for their consideration. However, it might well amaze the committee to have an *amateur*, non-professional person do so.

2. **(C)** What sort of glances would make a teacher suspect a pupil was cheating? *Furtive* (sneaky; secretive) glances would.

3. **(E)** What did the philanthropist deserve for his commitment to worthy causes? He deserved *credit* for his *altruism* (unselfish concern for others).

4. **(D)** Behavior that nothing could excuse by definition is *indefensible* (unpardonable; inexcusable).

5. **(D)** The sentence implies that surfing at Maui is usually thought to be good. The speaker was disappointed when he went surfing there. Two possibilities exist: either the surfing that day was atypically poor ("I went there on an off day") or surfing at Maui is basically *overrated* (too highly valued). Note how the "either...or" structure sets up a contrast between the two clauses.

6. **(B)** The second half of the sentence advises the writer to try not to stray from his or her subject. In other words, the writer is advised to avoid making *digressive* (off-target, wandering) remarks.

7. **(A)** A fundraising event that lost almost a million dollars clearly would deserve to be described as a *debacle* (disaster; total failure).

8. **(B)** Accolades are expressions of approval. The young lady receiving these accolades enjoys being *praised*.

9. **(D)** A stereotype is an oversimplified, conventional image. According to the stereotype, "boys don't cry." This stereotype assumes that crying is *inherently* (by its very nature) not manly. It rejects the notion that crying is simply a human reaction that either sex may *adopt* (take on).

10. **(C)** By definition, an organism that lives within or on another creature, getting its nourishment from its host, is *parasitic*.

11. **(C)** Someone who does not care about her appearance would consider the look of her clothing a matter of *indifference* (little or no concern).

12. **(C)** A *homogeneous* (uniform in composition; essentially alike) class grouping by definition would limit the range of student abilities in the classroom.

13. **(D)** Subordinates would be likely to resent a domineering and *imperious* (overbearing; dictatorial) superior.

14. **(E)** Something so extreme that it passes all reasonable bounds is by definition *inordinate* (excessive).

15. **(D)** The key word here is "belittle." Although the speaker did not intend to belittle anyone, his remarks seemed *disparaging* (disrespectful; belittling).

16. **(B)** A *cursory* (superficial; passing) glance by definition pays *little* attention to details.

17. **(E)** By definition, elaborately carved furniture is *ornate* (elaborately ornamental; showy).

18. **(A)** Someone who has accomplished little or nothing does not deserve to take pride in his accomplishments; his pride is *unjustified* (unwarranted; baseless).

19. **(C)** Symbiosis is an interdependent, often mutually beneficial relationship between groups or species. Such a mutually dependent relationship is described as *symbiotic*.

20. **(C)** The appearance of the black smoke signals the passengers that disaster is *imminent* (about to occur at any moment).

21. **(D)** Someone observant of the truth is by definition *veracious* (truthful; honest).

22. **(E)** Why is this history important? It is important because it carefully *substantiates* (supports; bears

out; confirms) the *considerable* (substantial; significant) accomplishments of the Native American artists. Note the positive tone of the sentence as a whole. In the second blank, the word describing the accomplishments of the Native American artists must be positive as well.

23. **(C)** An excess of restrictions and rules most likely would make someone feel *confined* (restricted).

24. **(C)** *Incredulity* (disbelief) when faced with compelling (convincing; strongly persuasive) evidence might well be a sign of a *closed* mind, a mind not open to new arguments and ideas.

25. **(B)** Note the parallel structure in this sentence. Both halves of the sentence contrast two descriptions of the poet. The second half states she was "extraordinarily intense about her poetry," yet she was "inhibited socially." Similarly, the first half states she was *ardent* (passionate; enthusiastic), but also *repressed* (emotionally subdued) in dealing with people.

26. **(B)** By definition, *a tonic* effect is physically or mentally invigorating; it refreshes you.

27. **(E)** The key word here is "contradiction." An infinitely shy person, uncomfortable around people, who nevertheless had a strong *gift* (talent) for understanding people, would appear to be a *paradox* (contradiction).

28. **(B)** The key word here is "rebuke" (scolding; censure). The coach has rebuked the quarterback. In other words, the coach has *reprimanded* (scolded) him.

29. **(D)** The speaker suggests writing about another topic because there have been too many stories about the war. In fact, readers have been suffering from a *plethora* (overabundance; surfeit) of such tales.

30. **(A)** Someone who shuns human society is by definition *a misanthrope* (one who hates mankind).

31. **(B)** A writer who cuts out unneeded words is an economical writer, one who uses the minimum of words needed for effectiveness. Critics praise Hemingway's lean prose style for its *economy* (conciseness).

32. **(C)** Harsh cries that drown out other sounds are by definition *raucous* (grating; strident; hoarse).

33. **(C)** Bob is shamefaced (embarrassed) because he has broken his hostess's punch bowl. In avoiding meeting her eye, he shows his *discomfiture* (awkwardness; embarrassment).

34. **(B)** The key word here is "fatuous" (idiotic; silly). A fatuous theatrical production is by definition *inane* (silly; absurd).

35. **(D)** "Olfactory" means pertaining to the sense of smell. Someone with a highly developed olfactory sense would be good at judging *perfume*.

36. **(D)** Something *eclectic* is made up of elements drawn from distinctly different sources. Coming from Thai, Chinese, and French cooking traditions, Jean Georges' cuisine (style of cooking) is decidedly *eclectic*.

37. **(B)** The key concept here is the notion that children possess "a certain natural intelligence." This intelligence exists in every child: it belongs to the child by the child's very nature. It is the teacher's task to discover and *develop* such inborn, *intrinsic* talents.

38. **(A)** What is the state of someone who habitually spends more than he earns? Poverty or *indigence*. However, although Micawber was perpetually broke, he *persevered* (persisted) *in* hoping to be affluent (wealthy) some day.

39. **(C)** The idealistic community at Brooke Farm quickly disintegrated (fell apart). The rapid break-up of the community suggests the *impracticability* of such utopian notions, which are incapable of being put into practice with the means available.

40. **(C)** Why were people amazed that this speaker could electrify an audience? They were amazed because his previous speeches had been nothing to cheer about. In fact, up to then he had been the most *pedestrian* (uninspired; unexciting) of speakers.

41. **(B)** Something *volatile* by definition tends to vaporize or evaporate readily.

42. **(B)** A writer whose work was universally acclaimed or applauded and whose reputation was not yet *tarnished* (stained) would be at the *zenith* (high point) of her career.

43. **(C)** Addiction is the state of being psychologically or physically enslaved to a habit or practice. If, once you begin to jog regularly, you are unable to break the habit, then you may describe jogging as *addictive*.

44. **(A)** People who are aware of the *dissimilarities* (differences) *between* the terms Chicano and Latino would not use these terms *interchangeably* (as if one term could be used in place of the other, with no difference in meaning).

45. **(B)** Legislation that established a task force without providing any money to fund that force would clearly be *inadequate*.

46. **(B)** The warning indicates that the differences between the administration and the teaching staff will become so much worse that they will become irreconcilable (impossible to reconcile or bring into harmony). In other words, the differences will become *exacerbated* (aggravated; inflamed; worsened).

47. **(E)** The word *paradoxically* signals a contrast between the children's strict mother and the cat's *lenient* (indulgent; easy-going) owner.

48. **(B)** The quotation marks around the word "knew" suggest that the word is being used in an unusual way. The woman knew in advance or foresaw that Orr would become a great athlete. Thus, she is described as *prescient* (knowing the outcome of events before they take place).

49. **(A)** In noting both the employee's strong points and limitations in an evenhanded manner, the supervisor is being fair or *equitable*.

50. **(C)** Although she has enough diplomacy or tact to *handle* (deal with) ordinary crises, she does not have enough to *weather* (survive; get through) an extraordinary emergency.

SENTENCE COMPLETION WRAP-UP

1. First, read the sentence carefully to get a feel for its meaning.

2. Before you look at the choices, think of a word that makes sense.

3. Look at all the possible answers before you make your final choice.

4. Watch out for negative words and prefixes.

5. Use your knowledge of context clues to get at the meanings of unfamiliar words.

6. Break down unfamiliar words into recognizable parts.

7. Watch for signal words that link one part of the sentence to another.

8. Look for words that signal the unexpected.

9. In double-blank sentences, go through the answers, testing one blank at a time (and eliminating any words that don't fit).

The Critical Reading Question

- **Quick Overview**
- **Testing Tactics**
- **Practice Exercises**

- **Answer Key**
- **Answer Explanations**

QUICK OVERVIEW

Your SAT test will contain three critical reading sections (not counting any experimental critical reading part). They will most likely follow these three basic patterns.

24-Question Critical Reading Section
Questions 1–8   sentence completion
Questions 9–12   reading comprehension (2 short passages)
Questions 13–24   reading comprehension (1 long passage)

24-Question Critical Reading Section
Questions 1–5   sentence completion
Questions 6–9   reading comprehension (paired short passages)
Questions 10–24   reading comprehension (2 long passages)

19-Question Critical Reading Section
Questions 1–6   sentence completion
Questions 7–19   reading comprehension (paired long passages)

This chapter begins with basic advice about the SAT critical reading sections. TACTICS 1–7 tell you how to deal with SAT reading questions in general. TACTICS 8–14 give you the answers to the questions on the three SAT passages, plus solid hints about how to answer each type of question and short lists of key words you are sure to meet in certain question types. Finally, TACTIC 15 shows you how to deal with the long paired passages you'll face in one of the SAT's three critical reading sections.

The directions for the critical reading section on the SAT are minimal. They are:

> Each passage below is followed by questions based on its content. Answer all questions following a passage on the basis of what is <u>stated</u> or <u>implied</u> in that passage.

Testing Tactics

TACTIC

Make Use of the Introductions to Acquaint Yourself with the Text.

Almost every reading passage is preceded by an italicized introduction. Don't skip it. As you read the italicized introductory material and tackle the passage's opening sentences, try to anticipate what the passage will be about. You'll be in a better position to understand what you read.

TACTIC

Use the Line References in the Questions to Be Sure You've Gone Back to the Correct Spot in the Passage.

Most of the reading passages on the SAT tend to be long. Fortunately, the lines are numbered, and the questions often refer you to specific lines in the passage by number. It takes less time to locate a line number than to spot a word or phrase. Use the line numbers to orient yourself in the text.

TACTIC

When You Have a Choice, Tackle Passages with Familiar Subjects Before Passages with Unfamiliar Ones.

Build on what you already know and like. It's only common sense: if you know very little about botany or are uninterested in it, you are all too likely to run into trouble reading a passage about plant life.

It is hard to concentrate when you read about something that is wholly unfamiliar to you. Give yourself a break. When you have more than one reading passage in a section, start with one that interests you or that deals with a topic you know well. There is nothing wrong in skipping questions. Just remember to check the numbering of your answer sheet. You should, of course, go back to the questions you skipped if you have time.

TACTIC

In Tackling the *Short* Reading Passages, Try this Approach: First Read a Question; Then Read the Passage.

Students often ask whether it is better to read the passage first or the questions first. The answer depends on the passage, and *it depends on you*. If you are a superfast reader faced with one of the new, 100-word short reading passages, head for the questions first. As you read each question, be on the lookout for key words, either in the question itself or among the answer choices. Then run your eye down the passage, looking for those key words or their synonyms. When you locate a key word, read the relevant sentence and a couple of sentences around it to see whether you can confidently answer the question based on just that portion of the passage.

If, however, you're not a speed demon at reading, a more effective move may be to skim the whole passage and then read the questions. **Only you can decide which method works better for you.**

Here are two questions, followed by a short reading passage. Tackle the questions one at a time, each time reading the question before turning to the passage to find the correct answer.

1. In line 7, "pure" most nearly means

   (A) chaste
   (B) immaculate
   (C) guiltless
   (D) absolute
   (E) abstract

2. In line 7 ("Yes...borrowed"), the author does which of the following?

(A) denies a possibility
(B) makes a concession
(C) exaggerates a claim
(D) refutes a theory
(E) draws an inference

Now look at the passage. *Don't* read it. Just take a quick peek and skip to the instructions that follow.

> Descended from West African slaves, Georgia's Sea Islanders retain not only many African rhythms and musical instruments but also singing games more like British games than African ones. One spiraling game is "Wind up
> *Line* this borrin." Some teachers claim "borrin" is a corruption of "borrowing,"
> *(5)* and explain that penniless islanders always borrowed. The game's spiraling, happy ending shows their joy in having enough so that they no longer need to borrow. This is pure invention. Yes, islanders always borrowed. But that has nothing to do with the "borrin" in this game. The spiraling figure is the English "wind the bobbin"; the teachers' claim may sound persuasive, but it
> *(10)* just isn't true.

Here's how to tackle question 1. Look for the word *pure* in the passage. It occurs in the phrase "pure invention." Consider that phrase. What do people mean when they say a claim or statement is an invention? They mean that it is a false statement, a fabrication, a story someone made up. When they say it is *pure* invention, they are stressing that it is a complete or total fabrication. In other words, it is *absolutely* false. The correct answer is Choice D.

Now for question 2. Look at the sentence the question refers to. "Yes, islanders always borrowed." In the sentence just before, the author flatly states that the teachers' claim that *borrin* comes from *borrowing* is complete bunk ("pure invention"). The author absolutely dismisses the teachers' claim. However, she acknowledges there is some truth in what the teachers have said; islanders *have* always borrowed. In acknowledging this, she is *making a concession,* conceding that the teachers had some slight evidence supporting their claim. The correct answer is Choice B.

Note that this tactic can be a real time-saver. To find the answer to such specific, narrowly-focused questions, you don't need to read the entire passage. You need to concentrate on just a few lines of text.

TACTIC

5

In Tackling the *Long* Reading Passages, First Read the Passage; Then Read the Questions.

Longer passages require a different approach than shorter ones. If you're a fast reader, reading all the questions before you read a long passage may not save you time. In fact, it may cost you time. If you read the questions first, when you turn to the passage you will have a number of question words and phrases dancing around in your head. These phrases won't focus you; they'll distract you. You will be so involved in trying to spot the places that they occur in the passage that you'll be unable to concentrate on comprehending the passage as a whole. Why increase your anxiety and decrease your capacity to think? Instead, try tackling a long passage using the following technique.

1. Read as rapidly as you can with understanding, but do not force yourself. Do not worry about the time element. If you worry about not finishing the test, you will begin to take short cuts and miss the correct answer in your haste.

2. As you read the opening sentences, try to anticipate what the passage will be about. Who or what is the author talking about?

3. As you continue reading, notice in what part of the passage the author makes major points. In that way, even when a question does not point you to a particular line or paragraph, you should be able to head for the right section of the text *without* having to reread the entire passage. Underline key words and phrases—sparingly!

TACTIC

6   Try to Answer *All* the Questions on a Particular Passage.

Don't let yourself get bogged down on any one question; you can't afford to get stuck on one question when you have eleven more on the same passage to answer. Remember that the questions following each reading passage are *not* arranged in order of difficulty. If you are stumped by a tough reading question, do not give up and skip all the other questions on that passage. A tough question may be just one question away from an easy one. Skip the one that's got you stumped, but make a point of coming back to it later, after you've answered one or two more questions on the passage. Often, working through other questions on the same passage will provide you with information you can use to answer any questions that stumped you the first time around. If the question still stumps you, move on. It's just fine to skip an individual reading question, especially if it resembles other reading questions that you've had trouble with before.

TACTIC

7   Learn to Spot the Major Reading Question Types.

Just as it will help you to know the directions for the sentence completion questions on the SAT, it will also help you to familiarize yourself with the major types of reading questions on the test.

If you can recognize just what a given question is asking you to do, you'll be better able to tell which particular reading tactic to apply.

Here are six categories of reading questions you are sure to face.

1. **Main Idea**   Questions that test your ability to find the central thought of a passage or to judge its significance often take the following form:

The main point of the passage is to

The passage is primarily concerned with

The author's primary purpose in this passage is to

The chief theme of the passage can be best described as

Which of the following titles best describes the content of the passage?

Which of the following statements best expresses the main idea of the passage?

2. **Specific Details**   Questions that test your ability to understand what the author states *explicitly* are often worded:

According to the author

The author states all of the following EXCEPT

According to the passage, which of the following is true of the

According to the passage, the chief characteristic of the subject is

Which of the following statements is (are) best supported by the passage?

Which of the following is NOT cited in the passage as evidence of

3. **Inferences**   Questions that test your ability to go beyond the author's explicit statements and see what these statements imply may be worded:

It can be inferred from the passage that

The passage suggests that the author would support which of the following views?

The author implies that

The author apparently feels that

According to the passage, it is likely that

The passage is most likely directed toward an audience of

Which of the following statements about...can be inferred from the passage?

4. **Tone/Attitude** Questions that test your ability to sense an author's or character's emotional state often take the form:

The author's attitude to the problem can best be described as

Which of the following best describes the author's tone in the passage?

The author's tone in the passage is that of a person attempting to

The author's presentation is marked by a tone of

The passage indicates that the author experiences a feeling of

5. **Vocabulary in Context** Questions that test your ability to work out the meaning of words from their context often are worded:

As it is used in the passage, the term...can best be described as

The phrase...is used in the passage to mean that

In the passage, the word...means

The author uses the phrase...to describe

6. **Technique** Questions that test your ability to recognize a passage's method of organization or technique often are worded:

Which of the following best describes the development of this passage?

In presenting the argument, the author does all of the following EXCEPT...

The relationship between the second paragraph and the first paragraph can best be described as...

> ### TIME-SAVER TIP
>
> As you get to know these major reading question types, you will find that some question types take you longer to answer than others. (Inference questions and questions involving the word EXCEPT are particularly time-consuming.) You may also find that some question types give you more trouble than others. Make a special note of these types. If you generally get bogged down answering EXCEPT questions, these may be good ones for you to skip temporarily; plan to come back to them if you don't run out of time. Likewise, if you *always* get technique questions wrong, these may be good questions for you to skip, period. Remember, you don't have to answer every question to score high on the SAT.

TACTIC

8 When Asked to Find the Main Idea, Be Sure to Check the Opening and Summary Sentences of Each Paragraph.

The opening and closing sentences of each paragraph are key sentences for you to read. They can serve as guideposts for you, pointing out the author's main idea.

Whenever you are asked to determine a passage's main idea, *always* check each paragraph's opening and summary sentences. Typically, in each paragraph, authors provide readers with a sentence that expresses the paragraph's main idea succinctly. Although such *topic sentences* may appear anywhere in the paragraph, experienced readers customarily look for them in the opening or closing sentences.

Note that in SAT reading passages, topic sentences are sometimes implied rather than stated directly. If you cannot find a topic sentence, ask yourself these questions:

1. Whom or what is this passage about?

2. What aspect of this subject is the author talking about?

3. What is the author trying to get across about this aspect of the subject?

Read the following ethnic reading passage and apply this tactic.

> Lois Mailou Jones is one example of an answer to the charge that there are no Black or female American artists to include in art history textbooks and classes. Beginning her formal art education at the School of the Museum of
> *Line* Fine Arts in Boston, Lois Jones found herself strongly attracted to design
> (5) rather than fine arts. After teaching for a while, she went to Paris to study, on the advice of the sculptor Meta Warrick Fuller.
> It was in Paris that she first felt free to paint. Following her return to this country in 1938, Jones had an exhibit at the Vose Gallery in Boston, a major breakthrough for a Black artist at that time. Her work during this period

(10) consisted of excellent impressionist scenes of Paris. It was not until the early 1940s, after she met the Black aesthetician Alain Locke, that she began to paint works like *Mob Victim*, which explicitly dealt with her own background as a Black American. Later, in the fifties, she went often to Haiti, which had yet another influence on her style. Then a sabbatical leave in Africa again

(15) changed her imagery. Indeed, the scope of this distinguished artist's career so well spans the development of twentieth-century art that her work could be a textbook in itself.

Now look at a question on this passage. It's a good example of a main idea question.

The passage primarily focuses on the

(A) influence of Lois Jones on other artists
(B) recognition given to Lois Jones for her work
(C) experiences that influenced the work of Lois Jones
(D) obstacles that Lois Jones surmounted in her career
(E) techniques that characterize the work of Lois Jones

Look at the opening and summary sentences of the two paragraphs that make up the passage: "Lois Mailou Jones is one example of...Black or female American artists to include in art history textbooks and classes," "It was in Paris that she first felt free to paint," "Indeed, the scope of [her] career spans the development of twentieth-century art. . ." Note particularly the use of the signal word "indeed" to call your attention to the author's point. Lois Jones has had a vast range of experiences that have contributed to her work as an artist. The correct answer is Choice C.

Choice A is incorrect. The passage talks of influences on Lois Jones, not of Lois Jones's influence on others. Choice B is incorrect. The passage mentions recognition given to Jones only in passing. Choice D is incorrect. There is nothing in the passage to support it. Choice E is incorrect. The passage never deals with specific questions of craft or technique.

Certain words come up again and again in questions on a passage's purpose or main idea. Review them. It would be silly to miss an answer not because you misunderstood the passage's meaning, but because you didn't know a common question word.

Key Terms in Main Idea Questions

bolster (v.)	to support an idea or position
delineate	to outline or describe with care
depict	to represent or portray vividly
discredit	to disbelieve; to cause a loss of confidence in
document (v.)	to support by documentary evidence
elaborate (v.)	to add details to; to work out in minute detail
endorse	to support or approve
exemplify	to serve as an example of
illustrate	to clarify by the use of examples
refute	to prove to be false or incorrect
speculate	to reason, possibly on insufficient evidence

TACTIC

Familiarize Yourself with the Technical Terms Used to Describe a Passage's Organization.

Another part of understanding the author's point is understanding how the author organizes what he or she has to say. To do so, often you have to figure out how the opening sentence or paragraph is connected to the passage as a whole.

Try this question on the author's technique, based on the previous passage about Lois Mailou Jones.

Which of the following best summarizes the relationship of the first sentence to the rest of the passage?

(A) Assertion followed by supporting evidence
(B) Challenge followed by debate pro and con
(C) Prediction followed by analysis
(D) Specific instance followed by generalizations
(E) Objective reporting followed by personal reminiscences

The correct answer is Choice A. The author makes an assertion (a positive statement) about Jones's importance and then proceeds to back it up with specific details from her career.

Choice B is incorrect. There is no debate for and against the author's thesis or point about Jones; the only details given support that point. Choice C is incorrect. The author does not predict or foretell something that is going to happen; the author asserts or states positively something that is an accomplished fact. Choice D is incorrect. The author's opening general assertion is followed by specific details to support it, not the reverse. Choice E is incorrect. The author shares no personal memories or reminiscences of Jones; the writing is objective throughout.

Key Terms in Questions on Technique or Style

abstract (adj.)	theoretical; not concrete
analogy	similarity of functions or properties; likeness
antithesis	direct opposite
argumentative	presenting a logical argument
assertion	positive statement; declaration
cite	to refer to; to quote as an authority
concrete (adj.)	real; actual; not abstract
evidence	data presented as proof
explanatory	serving to explain
expository	concerned with explaining ideas, facts, etc.
generalization	simplification; general idea or principle
narrative (adj.)	relating to telling a story
persuasive	intended to convince
rhetorical	relating to the effective use of language
thesis	the central idea in a piece of writing; a point to be defended

TACTIC

10 When Asked to Choose a Title, Watch Out for Choices That Are Too Specific or Too Broad.

Someone once defined a paragraph as a group of sentences revolving around a central theme. A proper title for a paragraph, therefore, should include this central theme that each of the sentences in the paragraph is developing. It has to fit: it should be neither too broad in scope, nor too narrow; it should be specific and yet comprehensive enough to include all the essentials.

A good title for a longer passage of two or more paragraphs follows the same rules. It expresses the theme of the whole passage. It is specific, yet comprehensive. It includes the thoughts of ALL the paragraphs.

This third question on the Jones passage is a title question. Note how it resembles questions on the passage's purpose or main idea.

Which of the following is the best title for the passage?

(A) Unsung Black Artists of America
(B) A Hard Row to Hoe: The Struggles of Lois Jones
(C) Locke and Jones: Two Black Artistic Pioneers
(D) African and Haitian Influences on Lois Mailou Jones
(E) The Making of an Artist: Lois Mailou Jones

When you are trying to select the best title for a passage, watch out for words that come straight out of the passage. They may not always be your best choice. Consider Choice C. Though the author mentions Alain Locke and suggests the importance of his influence in prompting Jones to use her experiences as a black American in her art, the passage as a whole is about Jones, not about Locke and Jones. Likewise, although the passage refers to African and Haitian influences on her imagery and style, the passage is about how Jones's experiences formed her as an artist, not about the specific influences on her style. Choice D is too narrow in scope to be a good title for this text.

Choice A has the opposite problem. As a title for this passage, *Unsung Black Artists of America* is far too broad. This passage concerns itself with a particular black artist whose fame deserves to be sung.

While Choice B limits itself to Jones, it too has a flaw. The passage clearly does not dwell on Jones's struggles; instead, it focuses on influences on her artistic growth.

Of the titles suggested, Choice E is best. The passage refers to the many and varied experiences that have made Jones an important figure in the world of art. Following her progress step by step, it portrays "the making of an artist."

 TACTIC 11   **When Asked About Specific Details in a Passage, Spot Key Words in the Question and Scan the Passage to Find Them (or Their Synonyms).**

In developing the main idea of a passage, a writer will make statements to support his or her point. To answer questions about such supporting details, you *must* find a word or group of words in the passage that supports your choice of answer. The words "according to the passage" or "according to the author" should focus your attention on what the passage explicitly states. Do not be misled into choosing an answer (even one that makes good sense) if you cannot find it supported in the text.

Often detail questions ask about a particular phrase or line. The SAT generally provides numbered line references to help you locate the relevant section of the passage. Occasionally it fails to do so. In such instances, use the following technique:

1. Look for key words (nouns or verbs) in the answer choices.

2. Run your eye down the passage, looking for those key words or their synonyms. (This is called *scanning*. It is what you do when you look up someone's number in the phone book.)

3. When you find a key word or its synonym, reread the sentence to make sure the test-writer hasn't used the original wording to mislead you.

A fourth question on the Jones passage tests you on a specific detail.

> In what way did her meeting with Alain Locke affect Jones's work as an artist?
>
> (A) It inspired her to focus on French impressionist landscapes.
> (B) It influenced her to paint scenes from Black American life.
> (C) It encouraged her use of Caribbean and African imagery.
> (D) It led to a prestigious gallery showing of her paintings.
> (E) It confirmed the feasibility of her pursuing a career as an artist.

Looking at the question, what key words do you see? Does the name *Alain Locke* leap out at you? That's great. Now scan the passage, looking for that name.

Here's the sentence in which the name *Alain Locke* appears: "It was not until the early 1940s, after she met the Black aesthetician Alain Locke, that she began to paint works like *Mob Victim*, which explicitly dealt with her own background as a Black American." Locke is described as a Black aesthetician. What does this mean? Aesthetics is the branch of philosophy that studies the nature of art and makes judgments about beauty and good taste. A Black aesthetician tries to answer the question, "What is Black art?"

What effect did meeting Locke have on Jones? It caused her to re-examine the nature of her art. She had been painting scenes of Paris in the style of the French impressionists. However, she was *not* a French impressionist painter; she was a Black American painter, and after meeting Locke she began to paint works that explicitly reflected her background as a Black American. In effect, her meeting with Locke, the Black aesthetician, "influenced her to paint scenes from Black American life." The correct answer is Choice B.

Key Terms in Questions on Specific Details

aesthetic	artistic; dealing with or capable of appreciating the beautiful
allusion	an indirect reference; a casual mention
assumption	something accepted as true without proof
attribute (n.)	essential quality; characteristic
divergent	differing from another; tending to move apart
fluctuate	to shift continually; to vary irregularly
hypothetical	based on assumptions or hypotheses; supposed
incompatible	not able to exist in harmony; discordant
indicative	suggestive; pointing out (something)
inherent	firmly established by nature or habit; built-in; inborn
innate	inborn; existing from birth
innovative	novel; introducing a change; ahead of the times
misconception	mistaken idea; wrong impression
phenomenon	observable fact or occurrence; subject of scientific investigation
preclude	to make impossible; to keep from happening

TACTIC

12 When Asked to Make Inferences, Base Your Answers on What the Passage Implies, Not What It States Directly.

In *Language in Thought and Action*, S.I. Hayakawa defines an inference as "a statement about the unknown made on the basis of the known."

Inference questions require you to use your own judgment. You must not take anything directly stated by the author as an inference. Instead, you must look for clues in the passage that you can use in coming up with your own conclusion. You should choose as your answer a statement which is a logical development of the information the author has provided.

See how this tactic works as you read this fiction passage, taken from the novel *The Heart of the Matter* by Graham Greene.

> "Imagine. Forty days in the boats!" cried Mrs. Perrot. Everything over the
> river was still and blank.
> "The French behaved well this time at least," Dawson remarked.
> *Line*   "They've only brought in the dying," the doctor retorted. "They could
> (5) hardly have done less."
> Dawson exclaimed and struck at his hand. "Come inside," Mrs. Perrot said,
> "The windows are netted." The stale air was heavy with the coming rains.
> "There are some cases of fever," said the doctor, "but most are just exhaus-
> tion—the worst disease. It's what most of us die of in the end."
> (10) Mrs. Perrot turned a knob; music from the London Orpheum filtered in.
> Dawson shifted uncomfortably; the Wurlitzer organ moaned and boomed. It
> seemed to him outrageously immodest.
> Wilson came in to a welcome from Mrs. Perrot. "A surprise to see *you*,
> Major Dawson."
> (15) "Hardly, Wilson." Mr. Perrot injected. "I told you he'd be here." Dawson
> looked across at Wilson and saw him blush at Perrot's betrayal, saw too that
> his eyes gave the lie to his youth.

"Well," sneered Perrot, "any scandals from the big city?" Like a Huguenot imagining Rome, he built up a picture of frivolity, viciousness, and corruption.
(20) "We bush-folk live quietly."

Mrs. Perrot's mouth stiffened in the effort to ignore her husband in his familiar part. She pretended to listen to the old Viennese melodies.

"None," Dawson answered, watching Mrs. Perrot with pity. "People are too busy with the war."
(25) "So many files to turn over," said Perrot. "Growing rice down here would teach them what work is."

The first question based on this passage is an inference question. Note the use of the terms "suggests" and "most likely." The passage never tells you directly where the story takes place. You must put two and two together and see what you get.

The evidence in the passage suggests that the story most likely takes place

(A) on a boat during a tropical storm
(B) at a hospital during a wartime blackout
(C) in a small town in France
(D) near a rice plantation in the tropics
(E) among a group of people en route to a large Asian city

Go through the answer choices one by one. Remember that in answering inference questions you must go beyond the obvious, go beyond what the author explicitly states, to look for logical implications of what the author says.

The correct answer is Choice D, *near a rice plantation in the tropics*. Several lines in the passage suggest it: Perrot's reference to "bush-folk," people living in a tropical jungle or similar uncleared wilderness; Perrot's comment about the work involved in growing rice; the references to fever and the coming rains.

Choice A is incorrect. The people rescued have been in the boats for forty days. The story itself is not set on a boat.

Choice B is incorrect. Although the presence of a doctor and the talk of dying patients suggests a hospital and Dawson's comment implies that people elsewhere are concerned with a war, nothing in the passage suggests that it is set in a wartime blackout. The windows are not covered or blacked out to prevent light from getting out; instead, they are netted to prevent mosquitos from getting in. (Note how Dawson exclaims and swats his hand; he has just been bitten by a mosquito).

Choice C is incorrect. Although the French are mentioned, nothing suggests that the story takes place in France, a European country not noted for uncleared wilderness or tropical rains.

Choice E is incorrect. Nothing in the passage suggests these people are en route elsewhere. In addition, Wilson could not logically pretend to be surprised by Dawson's presence if they were companions on a tour.

Key Terms in Inference Questions

criterion	a standard used in judging something; a basis for comparison
excerpt	a selection from a longer work
implication	an indirect suggestion; a logical inference
imply	to suggest without stating explicitly; to mean
likelihood	probability; chance of something
plausible	appearing reasonable; apparently believable
suggestive	tending to suggest something; stimulating further thought
tentative	not definite or positive; hesitant; provisional; experimental

13 When Asked About an Attitude, Mood, or Tone, Look for Words That Convey Emotions, Express Values, or Paint Pictures.

In figuring out the attitude, mood, or tone of an author or character, take a close look at the specific language used. Is the author using adjectives to describe the subject? If so, are they words like *fragrant, tranquil, magnanimous*—words with positive connotations? Or are they words like *fetid, ruffled, stingy*—words with negative connotations?

When we speak, our tone of voice conveys our mood—frustrated, cheerful, critical, gloomy, angry. When we write, our images and descriptive phrases get our feelings across.

The second question on the Greene passage is a tone question. Note the question refers you to specific lines in which a particular character speaks. Those lines are repeated here so that you can easily refer to them.

"They've only brought in the dying," the doctor retorted. "They could hardly have done less."

"There are some cases of fever," said the doctor, "but most are just exhaustion— the worst disease. It's what most of us die of in the end."

The tone of the doctor's remarks (lines 4 and 5, 8 and 9) indicates that he is basically

(A) unselfish
(B) magnanimous
(C) indifferent
(D) rich in patience
(E) without illusions

Note the doctor's use of "only" and "hardly," words with a negative sense. The doctor is deprecating or belittling what the French have done for the sufferers from the boats, the people who are dying from the exhaustion of their forty-day journey. The doctor is *retorting*: he is replying sharply to Dawson's positive remark about the French having behaved well. The doctor has judged the French. In his eyes, they have not behaved well.

Go through the answer choices one by one to see which choice comes closest to matching your sense of the doctor's tone.

Choice A is incorrect. Nothing in the passage specifically suggests selfishness or unselfishness on his part, merely irritability.

Choice B is incorrect. The doctor sounds irritable, critical, sharp-tempered. He feels resentment for the lack of care received by the victims. He does not sound like a magnanimous, forgiving man.

Choice C is incorrect. The doctor is not indifferent or uncaring. If he did not care, he would not be so sharp in challenging Dawson's innocent remark.

Choice D is also incorrect. The doctor is quick to counter Dawson, quick to criticize the French. Impatience, not patience, distinguishes him.

The correct answer is Choice E. The doctor is without illusions. Unlike Dawson, he cannot comfort himself with the illusion that things are going well. He has no illusions about life or death: most of us, he points out unsentimentally, die of exhaustion in the end.

When you are considering questions of attitude and tone, bear in mind the nature of the SAT. It is a standardized test aimed at a wide variety of test-takers—hip-hop fans, political activists, 4-H members, computer hacks, readers of *GQ*. It is taken by Native Americans and Chinese refugees, evangelical Christians and Orthodox Jews, Buddhists and Hindus, Hispanics and blacks, New Yorkers and Nebraskans—a typically American mix.

The SAT-makers are very aware of this diversity. As members of their staff have told us, they are particularly concerned to avoid using material on the tests that might upset students (and possibly adversely affect their scores). For this reason, the goal is to be noncontroversial: to present material that won't offend *anyone*. Thus, in selecting potential reading passages, the SAT-makers tend to avoid subjects that are sensitive in favor of ones that are bland. In fact, if a passage doesn't start out bland, they revise it and cut out the spice. One SAT test, for example, includes Kenneth Clark's comment about the "sharp wits" of Romans, but cuts out his comment about their "hard heads." Another uses a passage from Mary McCarthy's prickly *Memories of a Catholic Girlhood*, but cuts out every reference to Catholic and Protestant interaction—and much of the humor, too.

How does this affect the sort of tone and attitude questions the SAT-makers ask? As you can see, the SAT-makers attempt to respect the feelings of minority group members. Thus, you can expect minority group members to be portrayed in SAT reading passages in a favorable light. If, for example, there had been an attitude question based on the Lois Mailou Jones passage, it might have been worded like this:

> The author's attitude toward the artistic achievements mentioned in the passage can best be described as one of
>
> (A) incredulity
> (B) condescension
> (C) fulsome adulation
> (D) cool indifference
> (E) hearty admiration

Hearty admiration is the only possible choice.

Key Terms in Questions on Attitude and Tone

aloof	standoffish; remote in attitude
ambivalent	of two minds; unable to decide
brusque	abrupt; curt to the point of rudeness
cautionary	conveying a warning
compassionate	sympathetic; showing pity
condescension	patronizing behavior
cynical	distrustful of the motives of others; mocking
defensive	self-justifying; constantly protecting oneself from criticism
detachment	aloofness; lack of involvement; indifference
didactic	moralizing; inclined to lecture excessively
disdain	scorn; contempt; arrogance
disparaging	belittling; disapproving
dispassionate	unbiased; objective; unemotional; calm
esteem	respect; admiration
flippant	frivolously disrespectful; lacking proper seriousness
grudging	reluctant; unwilling
hypocritical	pretending to have virtues or feelings one lacks; insincere; phony
indifference	lack of concern; lack of interest
ironic	tongue in cheek; sarcastic; contrary to what was expected
judicious	sensible; showing good judgment; prudent; wise
naïve	innocent; unsophisticated
nostalgia	sentimental yearning for the past; homesickness
objective (adj.)	impartial; unbiased; neutral
optimism	hopefulness; cheerful confidence
pedantic	narrowly focused on academic trivia; excessively bookish
pessimism	negativity; lack of hopefulness; gloom

pomposity	self-importance; excessive self-esteem
prosaic	commonplace; pedestrian; ordinary
resigned (adj.)	submissive; passively accepting the inevitable
sarcasm	cutting remarks; stinging rebuke; scorn
satirical	mocking; exposing folly to ridicule
skeptical	disbelieving; doubtful; unconvinced
trite	stale; clichéd; overused
whimsical	fanciful; capricious; unpredictable

TACTIC

When Asked to Give the Meaning of an Unfamiliar Word, Look for Nearby Context Clues.

Every student who has ever looked into a dictionary is aware that many words have more than one meaning. A common question that appears on the SAT tests your ability to determine the correct meaning of a word from its context. Sometimes the word is a common one, and you must determine its exact meaning as used by the author. At other times, the word is uncommon. You can determine its meaning by a careful examination of the text.

As always, use your knowledge of context clues and word parts (Chapter 1) to help you discover the meanings of unfamiliar words.

One question based on the Lois Mailou Jones passage asks you to determine which exact meaning of a common word is used in a particular sentence. Here is the sentence in which the word appears.

> Lois Mailou Jones is one example of an answer to the charge that there are no Black or female American artists to include in art history textbooks and classes.
>
> The word "charge" in line 1 means
>
> (A) fee
> (B) duty
> (C) onslaught
> (D) allegation
> (E) care

To answer this question, simply substitute each of the answer choices for the quoted word in its original context. Clearly, both Black and female American artists exist. Thus, the statement that there are no Black or female American artists to include in art history texts or classes is an *allegation* (unproven accusation) that our Black and female artists are not good enough to be included in the texts. Jones, however, *is* good enough. Therefore, she is an example of an answer to this false accusation or charge.

A second vocabulary question, this one based on the Greene passage, concerns an uncommon, unfamiliar word. Here is the paragraph in which the word appeared.

> "Well," sneered Perrot, "any scandals from the big city?" Like a Huguenot imagining Rome, he built up a picture of frivolity, viciousness, and corruption. "We bush-folk live quietly."
>
> A Huguenot, as used in the passage, is most likely
>
> (A) a person dying of exhaustion
> (B) a doctor angered by needless suffering
> (C) an admirer of the Roman aristocracy
> (D) a city-dweller scornful of country ways
> (E) a puritan who suspects others of immorality

What is a Huguenot? It's certainly not an everyday word. You may never have encountered the term before you read this passage. But you can figure it out. A Huguenot is someone who, when he thinks of Rome, thinks of it in terms of vice and lack of seriousness. He disapproves of it for its wickedness and frivolity. Thus, he is a puritan of sorts, a person who condemns practices that he regards as impure or corrupt. The correct answer is Choice E.

Look at the words in the immediate vicinity of the word you are defining. They will give you a sense of the meaning of the unfamiliar word.

TACTIC

15 When Dealing with Double Passages, Tackle Them One at a Time.

If the double passage section has you worried, relax. It's not that formidable, especially if you deal with it our way. Read the lines in italics introducing both passages. Then look at the two passages. Their lines will be numbered as if they were one *enormous* passage: if Passage 1 ends on line 42, Passage 2 will begin on line 43. However, they are two separate passages. Tackle them one at a time.

The questions are organized sequentially: questions about Passage 1 come before questions about Passage 2. So, do things in order. *First* read Passage 1; then jump straight to the questions and answer all those based on Passage 1. *Next* read Passage 2; then answer all the questions based on Passage 2. (The line numbers in the questions will help you spot where the questions on Passage 1 end and those on Passage 2 begin.) *Finally*, tackle the two or three questions that refer to *both* passages. Go back to both passages as needed.

Occasionally a couple of questions referring to *both* passages will precede the questions focusing on Passage 1. Do not let this minor hitch throw you. Use your common sense. You've just read the first passage. Skip the one or two questions on both passages, and head for those questions about Passage 1. Answer them. Then read Passage 2. Answer the questions on Passage 2. Finally, go back to those questions you skipped and answer them and any other questions at the end of the set that refer to both passages. Remember, however: whenever you skip from question to question, or from passage to passage, *be sure you're filling in the right ovals on your answer sheet.*

Here is an example of a double passage. Go through the questions that follow, applying the tactics you've just learned.

The following passages are excerpted from books on America's national pastime, baseball. Passage 1 is taken from an account of a particularly memorable season. Passage 2 is from a meditation on the game written in 1989 by the late literary scholar A. Bartlett Giamatti, then commissioner of baseball.

Passage 1

DiMaggio had size, power, and speed. McCarthy, his longtime manager, liked to say that DiMaggio might have stolen 60 bases a season if he had given him the green light. Stengel, his new manager, was equally impressed,
Line and when DiMaggio was on base he would point to him as an example of
(5) the perfect base runner. "Look at him," Stengel would say as DiMaggio ran out a base hit, "he's always watching the ball. He isn't watching second base. He isn't watching third base. He knows they haven't been moved. He isn't watching the ground, because he knows they haven't built a canal or a swimming pool since he was last there. He's watching the ball and the out-
(10) fielder, which is the one thing that is different on every play."
DiMaggio complemented his natural athletic ability with astonishing physical grace. He played the outfield, he ran the bases, and he batted not just effectively but with rare style. He would glide rather than run, it seemed, always smooth, always ending up where he wanted to be just when he
(15) wanted to be there. If he appeared to play effortlessly, his teammates knew otherwise. In his first season as a Yankee, Gene Woodling, who played left field, was struck by the sound of DiMaggio chasing a fly ball. He sounded

like a giant truck horse on the loose, Woodling thought, his feet thudding down hard on the grass. The great, clear noises in the open space enabled
(20) Woodling to measure the distances between them without looking.

He was the perfect Hemingway hero, for Hemingway in his novels romanticized the man who exhibited grace under pressure, who withheld any emotion lest it soil the purer statement of his deeds. DiMaggio was that kind of hero; his grace and skill were always on display, his emotions always con-
(25) cealed. This stoic grace was not achieved without a terrible price: DiMaggio was a man wound tight. He suffered from insomnia and ulcers. When he sat and watched the game he chain-smoked and drank endless cups of coffee. He was ever conscious of his obligation to play well. Late in his career, when his legs were bothering him and the Yankees had a comfortable lead in a
(30) pennant race, columnist Jimmy Cannon asked him why he played so hard— the games, after all, no longer meant so much. "Because there might be somebody out there who's never seen me play before," he answered.

Passage 2

Athletes and actors—let actors stand for the set of performing artists— share much. They share the need to make gesture as fluid and economical as
(35) possible, to make out of a welter of choices the single, precisely right one. They share the need for thousands of hours of practice in order to train the body to become the perfect, instinctive instrument to express. Both athlete and actor, out of that abundance of emotion, choice, strategy, knowledge of the terrain, mood of spectators, condition of others in the ensemble, secret
(40) awareness of injury or weakness, and as nearly an absolute *concentration* as possible so that all externalities are integrated, all distraction absorbed to the self, must be able to change the self so successfully that it changes us.

When either athlete or actor can bring all these skills to bear and focus them, then he or she will achieve that state of complete intensity and com-
(45) plete relaxation—complete coherence or integrity between what the per- former wants to do and what the performer has to do. Then, the performer is free; for then, all that has been learned, by thousands of hours of practice and discipline and by repetition of pattern, becomes natural. Then intellect is upgraded to the level of an instinct. The body follows commands that
(50) precede thinking.

When athlete and artist achieve such self-knowledge that they transform the self so that we are re-created, it is finally an exercise in power. The indi- vidual's power to dominate, on stage or field invests the whole arena around the locus of performance with his or her power. We draw from the per-
(55) former's energy, just as we scrutinize the performer's vulnerabilities, and we criticize as if we were equals (we are not) what is displayed. This is why all performers dislike or resent the audience as much as they need and enjoy it. Power flows in a mysterious circuit from performer to spectator (I assume a "live" performance) and back, and while cheers or applause are the hoped-
(60) for outcome of performing, silence or gasps are the most desired, for then the moment has occurred—then domination is complete, and as the per- former triumphs, a unity rare and inspiring results.

1. In Passage 1, Stengel is most impressed by DiMaggio's

   (A) indifference to potential dangers
   (B) tendency to overlook the bases in his haste
   (C) ability to focus on the variables
   (D) proficiency at fielding fly balls
   (E) overall swiftness and stamina

2. Stengel's comments in lines 5–10 serve chiefly to

(A) point up the stupidity of the sort of error he condemns
(B) suggest the inevitability of mistakes in running bases
(C) show it is easier to spot problems than to come up with answers
(D) answer the criticisms of DiMaggio's base running
(E) modify his earlier position on DiMaggio's ability

3. By quoting Woodling's comment on DiMaggio's running (lines 17–19), the author most likely intends to emphasize

(A) his teammates' envy of DiMaggio's natural gifts
(B) how much exertion went into DiMaggio's moves
(C) how important speed is to a baseball player
(D) Woodling's awareness of his own slowness
(E) how easily DiMaggio was able to cover territory

4. The phrase "a man wound tight" (line 26) means a man

(A) wrapped in confining bandages
(B) living in constricted quarters
(C) under intense emotional pressure
(D) who drank alcohol to excess
(E) who could throw with great force

5. In the last paragraph of Passage 1, the author acknowledges which negative aspect of DiMaggio's heroic stature?

(A) His overemphasis on physical grace
(B) His emotional romanticism
(C) The uniformity of his performance
(D) The obligation to answer the questions of reporters
(E) The burden of living up to his reputation

6. Which best describes what the author is doing in the parenthetical comment "let actors stand for the set of performing artists" (line 33)?

(A) Indicating that actors should rise out of respect for the arts
(B) Defining the way in which he is using a particular term
(C) Encouraging actors to show tolerance for their fellow artists
(D) Emphasizing that actors are superior to other performing artists
(E) Correcting a misinterpretation of the role of actors

7. The phrase "bring all these skills to bear" in line 43 is best taken to mean that the athlete

(A) comes to endure these skills
(B) carries the burden of his talent
(C) applies these skills purposefully
(D) causes himself to behave skillfully
(E) influences himself to give birth to his skills

8. To the author of Passage 2, freedom for performers depends on

(A) their subjection of the audience
(B) their willingness to depart from tradition
(C) the internalization of all they have learned
(D) their ability to interpret material independently
(E) the absence of injuries or other weaknesses

9. The author's attitude toward the concept of the equality of spectators and performers (lines 55 and 56) is one of

   (A) relative indifference
   (B) mild skepticism
   (C) explicit rejection
   (D) strong embarrassment
   (E) marked perplexity

10. Why, in lines 57 and 58, does the author of Passage 2 assume a "live" performance?

   (A) His argument assumes a mutual involvement between performer and spectator that can only occur when both are present.
   (B) He believes that televised and filmed images give a false impression of the performer's ability to the spectators.
   (C) He fears the use of "instant replay" and other broadcasting techniques will cause performers to resent spectators even more strongly.
   (D) His argument dismisses the possibility of combining live performances with filmed segments.
   (E) He prefers audiences not to have time to reflect about the performance they have just seen.

11. The author of Passage 2 would most likely react to the characterization of DiMaggio presented in lines 28–32 by pointing out that DiMaggio probably

   (A) felt some resentment of the spectator whose good opinion he supposedly sought
   (B) never achieved the degree of self-knowledge that would have transformed him
   (C) was unaware that his audience was surveying his weak points
   (D) was a purely instinctive natural athlete
   (E) was seldom criticized by his peers

12. Which of the following attributes of the ideal athlete mentioned in Passage 2 is NOT illustrated by the anecdotes about DiMaggio in Passage 1?

   (A) knowledge of the terrain
   (B) secret awareness of injury or weakness
   (C) consciousness of the condition of other teammates
   (D) ability to make gestures fluid and economical
   (E) absolute powers of concentration

13. Which of the following statements is best supported by a comparison of the two excerpts?

   (A) Both excerpts focus on the development of a specific professional athlete.
   (B) The purpose of both excerpts is to compare athletes with performing artists.
   (C) The development of ideas in both excerpts is similar.
   (D) Both excerpts examine the nature of superior athletic performance.
   (E) Both excerpts discuss athletic performance primarily in abstract terms.

DOUBLE PASSAGE ANSWER KEY

1. **C**	5. **E**	9. **C**	13. **D**
2. **A**	6. **B**	10. **A**	
3. **B**	7. **C**	11. **A**	
4. **C**	8. **C**	12. **C**	

1. **(C)** Stengel's concluding sentence indicates that DiMaggio watches "the one thing that is different on every play." In other words, DiMaggio *focuses on the variables*, the factors that change from play to play.

2. **(A)** Stengel's sarcastic comments about the mistakes DiMaggio *doesn't* make indicate just how dumb he thinks it is to look down at the ground when you should have your attention on the outfielder and the ball. Clearly, if one of his players made such an error, Stengel's response would be to say, "What's the matter, stupid? Are you afraid you're going to fall in a canal down there?"

3. **(B)** Note the context of the reference to Woodling. In the sentence immediately preceding, the author says that, if DiMaggio "appeared to play effortlessly, his teammates knew otherwise." The author then introduces a comment by Woodling, one of DiMaggio's teammates. Woodling knew a great deal of effort went into DiMaggio's playing: he describes how DiMaggio's feet pounded as he ran. Clearly, the force of DiMaggio's running is mentioned to illustrate *how much exertion went into DiMaggio's moves*.

4. **(C)** Look at the sentences following this phrase. They indicate that DiMaggio was a man *under intense emotional pressure*, one who felt so much stress that he developed ulcers and had problems getting to sleep.

5. **(E)** In the final paragraph, the author describes DiMaggio pushing himself to play hard despite his injuries. DiMaggio does so because he is trying to live up to the image his public has of him. He feels *the burden of living up to his reputation*.

6. **(B)** At this point, the questions on Passage 2 begin. In this brief aside, the author is taking a moment away from his argument to make sure the reader knows exactly who the subjects of his comparison are. He wishes to use the word *actors* to stand for or *represent* all other performers. This way every time he makes his comparison between athletes and performers he won't have to list all the various sorts of performing artists (actors, dancers, singers, acrobats, clowns) who resemble athletes in their need for physical grace, extensive rehearsal, and total concentration. Thus, in his side comment, he is *defining* how he intends to use the word *actors* throughout the discussion.

7. **(C)** The author has been describing the wide range of skills a performer utilizes in crafting an artistic or athletic performance. It is by taking these skills and *applying them purposefully* and with concentration to the task at hand that the performer achieves his or her goal.

8. **(C)** Performers are free when all they have learned becomes so natural, so internalized, that it seems instinctive. In other words, freedom depends on *the internalization* of what they have learned.

9. **(C)** The author bluntly states that we spectators are not the performers' equals. Thus, his attitude toward the concept is one of *explicit rejection*.

10. **(A)** While a spectator may feel powerfully involved with a filmed or televised image of a performer, the filmed image is unaffected by the spectator's feelings. Thus, for power to "flow in a mysterious circuit" from performer to spectator *and back,* the assumption is that both performer and spectator *must be present* in the flesh.

11. **(A)** Passage 1 indicates DiMaggio always played hard to live up to his reputation and to perform well for anyone in the stands who had never seen him play before. Clearly, he wanted the spectators to have a good opinion of him. Passage 2, however, presents a more complex picture of the relationship between the performer and his audience. On the one hand, the performer needs the audience, needs its good opinion and its applause. On the other hand, the performer also resents the audience, resents the way spectators freely point out his weaknesses and criticize his art. Thus, the author of Passage 2 might well point out that DiMaggio *felt some resentment* of the audience whom he hoped to impress with his skill.

12. **(C)** Though DiMaggio's teammates clearly were aware of *his* condition (as the Woodling anecdote illustrates), none of the anecdotes in Passage 1 indicate or even imply that DiMaggio was specifically *conscious of his teammates' condition*.

  You can answer this question by using the process of elimination. In running bases, DiMaggio never lets himself be distracted by looking at the bases or down at the ground; as Stengel says, he knows where they are. Clearly, he *knows the terrain*. You can eliminate Choice A. When DiMaggio's legs are failing him late in his career, he still pushes himself to perform well for the fan in the stands who hasn't seen him play before. In doing so, he takes into account his *secret awareness* of his legs' weakness. You can eliminate Choice B. Gliding rather than running, always smooth, never wasting a glance on inessentials, DiMaggio clearly exhibits *fluidity and economy* in his movements. You can eliminate Choice D. Running bases, DiMaggio always keeps his eye on the ball and the outfielder; he *concentrates absolutely* on them. You can eliminate Choice E. Only Choice C is left. It is the correct answer.

13. **(D)** Though one passage presents an abstract discussion of the nature of the ideal athlete and the other describes the achievements and character of a specific superior athlete, both passages *examine the nature of superior athletic performance*.

Practice Exercises

On the following pages you will find three reading exercises. Allow about 30 minutes for each group. The correct answers, as well as answer explanations, are given at the end of the chapter. Practice the testing tactics you have learned as you work. Your reading score will improve.

Exercise A

> Each of the following passages comes from a novel or short story collection that has provided reading passages on prior SATs. Use this exercise to acquaint yourself with the sort of fiction you will confront on the test and to practice answering critical reading questions based on literature.

The following passage is taken from Great Expectations *by Charles Dickens. In it, the hero, Pip, recollects a dismal period in his youth during which he for a time lost hope of ever bettering his fortunes.*

It is a most miserable thing to feel ashamed of home. There may be black ingratitude in the thing, and the punishment may be retributive and well
Line deserved; but, that it is a miserable thing, I can
(5) testify. Home had never been a very pleasant place to me, because of my sister's temper. But Joe had sanctified it and I believed in it. I had believed in the best parlor as a most elegant salon; I had believed in the front door as a mysterious portal of the Temple
(10) of State whose solemn opening was attended with a sacrifice of roast fowls; I had believed in the kitchen as a chaste though not magnificent apartment; I had believed in the forge as the glowing road to manhood. Now, it was all coarse and com-
(15) mon, and I would not have had Miss Havisham and Estella see it on any account.

Once, it had seemed to me that when I should at last roll up my shirt sleeves and go into the forge, Joe's 'prentice, I should be distinguished and happy.
(20) Now the reality was in my hold, I only felt that I was dusty with the dust of small coal, and that I had a weight upon my daily remembrance to which the anvil was a feather. There have been occasions in my later life (I suppose as in most lives) when I have
(25) felt for a time as if a thick curtain had fallen on all its interest and romance, to shut me out from any thing save dull endurance any more. Never has that curtain dropped so heavy and blank, as when my way in life lay stretched out straight before me through
(30) the newly-entered road of apprenticeship to Joe.

I remember that at a later period of my "time,"

I used to stand about the churchyard on Sunday evenings, when night was falling, comparing my own perspective with the windy marsh view, and
(35) making out some likeness between them by thinking how flat and low both were, and how on both there came an unknown way and a dark mist and then the sea. I was quite as dejected on the first working-day of my apprenticeship as in that after
(40) time; but I am glad to know that I never breathed a murmur to Joe while my indentures lasted. It is about the only thing I *am* glad to know of myself in that connection.

For, though it includes what I proceed to add,
(45) all the merit of what I proceed to add was Joe's. It was not because I was faithful, but because Joe was faithful, that I never ran away and went for a soldier or a sailor. It was not because I had a strong sense of the virtue of industry, but because
(50) Joe had a strong sense of the virtue of industry, that I worked with tolerable zeal against the grain. It is not possible to know how far the influence of any amiable honest-hearted duty-going man flies out into the world; but it is very possible to know
(55) how it has touched one's self in going by, and I know right well that any good that intermixed itself with my apprenticeship came of plain contented Joe, and not of restless aspiring discontented me.

1. The passage as a whole is best described as
   (A) an analysis of the reasons behind a change in attitude
   (B) an account of a young man's reflections on his emotional state
   (C) a description of a young man's awakening to the harsh conditions of working class life
   (D) a defense of a young man's longings for romance and glamour
   (E) a criticism of young people's ingratitude to their elders

2. It may be inferred from the passage that the young man has been apprenticed to a
   (A) cook
   (B) forger
   (C) coal miner
   (D) blacksmith
   (E) grave digger

3. In the passage, Joe is portrayed most specifically as
   (A) distinguished
   (B) virtuous
   (C) independent
   (D) homely
   (E) coarse

4. The passage suggests that the narrator's increasing discontent with his home during his apprenticeship was caused by

   (A) a new awareness on his part of how his home would appear to others
   (B) the increasing heaviness of the labor involved
   (C) the unwillingness of Joe to curb his sister's temper
   (D) the narrator's lack of an industrious character
   (E) a combination of simple ingratitude and sinfulness

5. According to the passage, the narrator gives himself a measure of credit for

   (A) working diligently despite his unhappiness
   (B) abandoning his hope of a military career
   (C) keeping his menial position secret from Miss Havisham
   (D) concealing his despondency from Joe
   (E) surrendering his childish beliefs

The following passage is excerpted from the short story "Clay" in Dubliners *by James Joyce. In this passage, tiny, unmarried Maria oversees tea for the washerwomen, all the while thinking of the treat in store for her: a night off.*

The matron had given her leave to go out as soon as the women's tea was over and Maria looked forward to her evening out. The kitchen was spick
Line and span: the cook said you could see yourself in
(5) the big copper boilers. The fire was nice and bright and on one of the side-tables were four very big barmbracks. These barmbracks seemed uncut; but if you went closer you would see that they had been cut into long thick even slices and were ready
(10) to be handed round at tea. Maria had cut them herself.
Maria was a very, very small person indeed but she had a very long nose and a very long chin. She talked a little through her nose, always soothingly: "*Yes, my dear,*" and "*No, my dear.*" She was always
(15) sent for when the women quarrelled over their tubs and always succeeded in making peace. One day the matron had said to her:
"Maria, you are a veritable peace-maker!"
And the sub-matron and two of the Board ladies
(20) had heard the compliment. And Ginger Mooney was always saying what she wouldn't do to the dummy who had charge of the irons if it wasn't for Maria. Everyone was so fond of Maria.
When the cook told her everything was ready,
(25) she went into the women's room and began to pull the big bell. In a few minutes the women began to come in by twos and threes, wiping their steaming hands in their petticoats and pulling down the sleeves of their blouses over their red steaming
(30) arms. They settled down before their huge mugs which the cook and the dummy filled up with hot tea, already mixed with milk and sugar in huge tin cans. Maria superintended the distribution of the

barmbrack and saw that every woman got her four
(35) slices. There was a great deal of laughing and joking during the meal. Lizzie Fleming said Maria was sure to get the ring and, though Fleming had said that for so many Hallow Eves, Maria had to laugh and say she didn't want any ring or man either; and
(40) when she laughed her grey-green eyes sparkled with disappointed shyness and the tip of her nose nearly met the tip of her chin. Then Ginger Mooney lifted her mug of tea and proposed Maria's health while all the other women clattered with their mugs on
(45) the table, and said she was sorry she hadn't a sup of porter to drink it in. And Maria laughed again till the tip of her nose nearly met the tip of her chin and till her minute body nearly shook itself asunder because she knew that Mooney meant well though,
(50) of course, she had the notions of a common woman.

6. The author's primary purpose in the second paragraph is to

   (A) introduce the character of a spinster
   (B) describe working conditions in a public institution
   (C) compare two women of different social classes
   (D) illustrate the value of peace-makers in society
   (E) create suspense about Maria's fate

7. The language of the passage most resembles the language of

   (A) a mystery novel
   (B) an epic
   (C) a fairy tale
   (D) institutional board reports
   (E) a sermon

8. It can be inferred from the passage that Maria would most likely view the matron as which of the following?

   (A) A political figurehead
   (B) An inept administrator
   (C) A demanding taskmaster
   (D) An intimate friend
   (E) A benevolent superior

9. We may infer from the care with which Maria has cut the barmbracks (lines 7–10) that

   (A) she fears the matron
   (B) she is in a hurry to leave
   (C) she expects the Board members for tea
   (D) it is a dangerous task
   (E) she takes pride in her work

10. It can be inferred from the passage that all the following are characteristic of Maria EXCEPT

    (A) a deferential nature
    (B) eagerness for compliments
    (C) respect for authority
    (D) dreams of matrimony
    (E) reluctance to compromise

The following passage is taken from Jane Austen's novel
Mansfield Park. *This excerpt presents Sir Thomas*
Bertram, owner of Mansfield Park, who has just joined
the members of his family.

Sir Thomas was indeed the life of the party, who
at his suggestion now seated themselves round the
fire. He had the best right to be the talker; and the
Line   delight of his sensations in being again in his own
(5)   house, in the center of his family, after such a separation, made him communicative and chatty in a
very unusual degree; and he was ready to answer
every question of his two sons almost before it was
put. All the little particulars of his proceedings and
(10)   events, his arrivals and departures, were most
promptly delivered, as he sat by Lady Bertram
and looked with heartfelt satisfaction at the faces
around him—interrupting himself more than once,
however, to remark on his good fortune in finding
(15)   them all at home—coming unexpectedly as he did
—all collected together exactly as he could have
wished, but dared not depend on.

By not one of the circle was he listened to with
such unbroken unalloyed enjoyment as by his wife,
(20)   whose feelings were so warmed by his sudden
arrival, as to place her nearer agitation than she
had been for the last twenty years. She had been
almost fluttered for a few minutes, and still remained
so sensibly animated as to put away her work, move
(25)   Pug from her side, and give all her attention and
all the rest of her sofa to her husband. She had no
anxieties for anybody to cloud *her* pleasure; her
own time had been irreproachably spent during his
absence; she had done a great deal of carpet work
(30)   and made many yards of fringe; and she would have
answered as freely for the good conduct and useful
pursuits of all the young people as for her own. It
was so agreeable to her to see him again, and hear
him talk, to have her ear amused and her whole
(35)   comprehension filled by his narratives, that she
began particularly to feel how dreadfully she must
have missed him, and how impossible it would have
been for her to bear a lengthened absence.

Mrs. Norris was by no means to be compared in
(40)   happiness to her sister. Not that *she* was incommod-
ed by many fears of Sir Thomas's disapprobation
when the present state of his house should be known,
for her judgment had been so blinded, that she could
hardly be said to show any sign of alarm; but she
(45)   was vexed by the *manner* of his return. It had left
her nothing to do. Instead of being sent for out of
the room, and seeing him first, and having to spread
the happy news through the house, Sir Thomas,
with a very reasonable dependence perhaps on the
(50)   nerves of his wife and children, had sought no confidant but the butler, and had been following him
almost instantaneously into the drawing-room. Mrs.
Norris felt herself defrauded of an office on which
she had always depended, whether his arrival or

(55)   his death were to be the thing unfolded; and was
now trying to be in a bustle without having any
thing to bustle about. Would Sir Thomas have con-
sented to eat, she might have gone to the housekeeper with troublesome directions; but Sir Thomas
(60)   resolutely declined all dinner; he would take nothing,
nothing till tea came—he would rather wait for tea.
Still Mrs. Norris was at intervals urging something
different; and in the most interesting moment of
his passage to England, when the alarm of a French
(65)   privateer was at the height, she burst through his
recital with the proposal of soup. "Sure, my dear
Sir Thomas, a basin of soup would be a much better
thing for you than tea. Do have a basin of soup."

Sir Thomas could not be provoked. "Still the
(70)   same anxiety for everybody's comfort, my dear
Mrs. Norris," was his answer. "But indeed I would
rather have nothing but tea."

11. We can infer from the opening paragraph that Sir
Thomas is customarily

(A) unwelcome at home
(B) tardy in business affairs
(C) dissatisfied with life
(D) more restrained in speech
(E) lacking in family feeling

12. The passage suggests that Sir Thomas's sudden
arrival

(A) was motivated by concern for his wife
(B) came as no surprise to Lady Bertram
(C) was timed by him to coincide with a family
        reunion
(D) was expected by the servants
(E) was received with mixed emotions

13. Which of the following titles best describes the passage?

(A) An Unexpected Return
(B) The Conversation of the Upper Class
(C) Mrs. Norris's Grievance
(D) A Romantic Reunion
(E) An Account of a Voyage Abroad

14. The author's tone in her description of Lady
Bertram's sensations (lines 20–26) is

(A) markedly scornful
(B) mildly bitter
(C) gently ironic
(D) manifestly indifferent
(E) warmly sympathetic

15. By stressing that Lady Bertram "had no anxieties for anybody to cloud *her* pleasure" (lines 26 and 27), the author primarily intends to imply that

    (A) Lady Bertram was hardhearted in ignoring the sufferings of others
    (B) it was unusual for Lady Bertram to be so unconcerned
    (C) others in the company had reason to be anxious
    (D) Sir Thomas expected his wife to be pleased to see him
    (E) Lady Bertram lived only for pleasure

16. Sir Thomas's attitude toward Mrs. Norris can best be described as one of

    (A) sharp irritation
    (B) patient forbearance
    (C) solemn disapproval
    (D) unreasoned alarm
    (E) unmixed delight

17. The office of which Mrs. Norris feels herself defrauded is most likely that of

    (A) butler
    (B) housekeeper
    (C) wife
    (D) world traveler
    (E) message-bearer

The following passage is taken from Edith Wharton's novel The Age of Innocence. *In this excerpt, the American hero has an unexpected encounter during the course of a visit to the Louvre Museum in Paris.*

    Newman promised himself to pay Mademoiselle Noemie another visit at the Louvre. He was curious about the progress of his copies, but it must be added
Line
(5) that he was still more curious about the progress of the young lady herself. He went one afternoon to the great museum, and wandered through several of the rooms in fruitless quest of her. He was bending his steps to the long hall of the Italian masters, when suddenly he found himself face to face with
(10) Valentin de Bellegarde. The young Frenchman greeted him with ardor, and assured him that he was a godsend. He himself was in the worst of humors and he wanted someone to contradict.
    "In a bad humor among all these beautiful things?"
(15) said Newman "I thought you were so fond of pictures, especially the old black ones. There are two or three here that ought to keep you in spirits."
    "Oh, today," answered Valentin, "I am not in a mood for pictures, and the more beautiful they are
(20) the less I like them. Their great staring eyes and fixed positions irritate me. I feel as if I were at some big, dull party, in a room full of people I shouldn't wish to speak to. What should I care for their beauty?

It's a bore, and, worse still, it's a reproach. I have
(25) a great many *ennuis*; I feel vicious."
    "If the Louvre has so little comfort for you, why in the world did you come here?" Newman asked.
    "That is one of my *ennuis*. I came to meet my cousin—a dreadful English cousin, a member of my
(30) mother's family—who is in Paris for a week with her husband, and who wishes me to point out the 'principal beauties.' Imagine a woman who wears a green crepe bonnet in December and has straps sticking out of the ankles of her interminable boots!
(35) My mother begged I would do something to oblige them. I have undertaken to play *valet de place* this afternoon. They were to have met me here at two o'clock, and I have been waiting for them twenty minutes. Why doesn't she arrive? She has at least
(40) a pair of feet to carry her. I don't know whether to be furious at their playing me false, or delighted to have escaped them."
    "I think in your place I would be furious," said Newman, "because they may arrive yet, and then
(45) your fury will still be of use to you. Whereas if you were delighted and they were afterwards to turn up, you might not know what to do with your delight."
    "You give me excellent advice, and I already feel better. I will be furious; I will let them go to
(50) the deuce and I myself will go with you—unless by chance you too have a rendezvous."

18. The passage indicates that Newman has gone to the Louvre in order to

    (A) meet Valentin
    (B) look at the paintings
    (C) explore Paris
    (D) keep an appointment
    (E) see Mademoiselle Noemie

19. According to the passage, Valentin is unhappy about being at the Louvre because he

    (A) hates the paintings of the Italian masters
    (B) has accidentally met Newman in the long hall
    (C) wishes to be at a party
    (D) feels that beauty should be that of nature
    (E) is supposed to guide his cousin through it

20. It can be inferred from the passage that in lines 32–39 Valentin is expressing his annoyance by

    (A) walking out of the Louvre in a fit of temper
    (B) making insulting remarks about a woman
    (C) not accepting Newman's advice
    (D) criticizing the paintings
    (E) refusing to do as his mother wishes

21. With which of the following statements would Valentin most likely agree?

    I. Clothes make the man.
    II. Blood is thicker than water.
    III. Better late than never.

    (A) I only
    (B) II only
    (C) III only
    (D) I and II only
    (E) I, II, and III

22. Newman's role in the conversation is that of

    (A) a heckler
    (B) a gossiper
    (C) a confidant
    (D) an enemy
    (E) a doubter

Exercise B

This exercise provides you with a mixture of reading passages similar in variety to what you will encounter on the SAT. Answer all questions on the basis of what is <u>stated</u> or <u>implied</u> in the passages.

The best Eskimo carvings of all ages seem to possess a powerful ability to reach across the great barriers of language and time and communicate
Line directly with us. The more we look at these carvings,
(5) the more life we perceive hidden within them. We discover subtle living forms of the animal, human, and mystical world. These arctic carvings are not the cold sculptures of a frozen world. Instead, they reveal to us the passionate feelings of a vital people
(10) well aware of all the joys, terrors, tranquility, and wildness of life around them.

Eskimo carvers are people moved by dreams. In spite of all their new contacts with the outsiders, they are still concerned with their own kind of mystical
(15) imagery. The most skillful carvers possess a bold confidence, a direct approach to their art that has a freedom unsullied by any kind of formalized training. Eskimo carvers have strong, skilled hands, used to forcing hard materials with their simple tools. Their
(20) hunting life and the northern environment invigorates them. Bad weather often imposes a special kind of leisure, giving them time in which to perfect their carvings.

They are among the last of the hunting societies
(25) that have retained some part of the keen sense of observation that we have so long forgotten. The carvers are also butchers of meat, and therefore masters in the understanding of animal anatomy. Flesh and bones and sheaths of muscle seem to move
(30) in their works. They show us how to drive the caribou, how to hold a child, how to walk cautiously

on thin ice. Through their eyes we understand the dangerous power of a polar bear. In the very best of Eskimo art we see vibrant animal and human
(35) forms that stand quietly or tensely, strongly radiating a sense of life. We can see, and even feel with our hands, the cold sleekness of seals, the hulking weight of walrus, the icy swiftness of trout, the flowing rhythm in a flight of geese. In their art we catch
(40) brief glimpses of a people who have long possessed a very different approach to the whole question of life and death.

In Eskimo art there is much evidence of humor which the carvers have in abundance. Some of the
(45) carvings are caricatures of themselves, of ourselves, and of situations, or records of ancient legends. Their laughter may be subtle, or broad and Chaucerian.

Perhaps no one can accurately define the right way or wrong way to create a carving. Each carver
(50) must follow his own way, in his own time. Technique in itself is meaningless unless it serves to express content. According to the Eskimo, the best carvings possess a sense of movement that seems to come from within the material itself, a feeling
(55) of tension, a living excitement.

1. The author is primarily concerned with

    (A) showing how Eskimo carvings achieve their effects
    (B) describing how Eskimo artists resist the influence of outsiders
    (C) discussing the significant characteristics of Eskimo art
    (D) explaining how Eskimo carvers use their strength to manipulate hard materials
    (E) interpreting the symbolism of Eskimo art

2. The author's attitude toward Eskimo art is one of

    (A) condescension
    (B) awe
    (C) admiration
    (D) regret
    (E) bewilderment

3. With which of the following statements would the author most likely agree?

    (A) Formal training may often destroy an artist's originality.
    (B) Artists should learn their craft by studying the work of experts.
    (C) The content of a work of art is insignificant.
    (D) Caricatures have no place in serious art.
    (E) Eskimo art is interesting more as an expression of a life view than as a serious art form.

4. The author gives examples of the subjects of Eskimo carvings primarily to

(A) show that they have no relevance to modern life
(B) indicate the artist's lack of imagination
(C) imply that other artists have imitated them
(D) prove that the artists' limited experience of life has been a handicap
(E) suggest the quality and variety of the work

5. According to the passage, Eskimo carvings have all the following EXCEPT

(A) wit
(B) subtlety
(C) emotional depth
(D) stylistic uniformity
(E) anatomical accuracy

Charlotte Stanhope was at this time about thirty-five years old; and, whatever may have been her faults, she had none of those which belong to old
Line young ladies. She neither dressed young, nor talked
(5) young, nor indeed looked young. She appeared to be perfectly content with her time of life, and in no way affected the graces of youth. She was a fine young woman; and had she been a man, would have been a fine young man. All that was done in the
(10) house, and was not done by servants, was done by her. She gave the orders, paid the bills, hired and dismissed the domestics, made the tea, carved the meat, and managed everything in the Stanhope household. She, and she alone, could ever induce her
(15) father to look into the state of his worldly concerns. She, and she alone, could in any degree control the absurdities of her sister. She, and she alone, prevented the whole family from falling into utter disrepute and beggary. It was by her advice that they now found
(20) themselves very unpleasantly situated in Barchester.
So far, the character of Charlotte Stanhope is not unprepossessing. But it remains to be said, that the influence which she had in her family, though it had been used to a certain extent for their worldly well-
(25) being, had not been used to their real benefit, as it might have been. She had aided her father in his indifference to his professional duties, counselling him that his livings were as much his individual property as the estates of his elder brother were the
(30) property of that worthy peer. She had for years past stifled every little rising wish for a return to England which the reverend doctor had from time to time expressed. She had encouraged her mother in her idleness in order that she herself might be mistress
(35) and manager of the Stanhope household. She had encouraged and fostered the follies of her sister, though she was always willing, and often able, to protect her from their probable result. She had done her best, and had thoroughly succeeded in spoiling
(40) her brother, and turning him loose upon the world an idle man without a profession, and without a shilling that he could call his own.

Miss Stanhope was a clever woman, able to talk on most subjects, and quite indifferent as to what
(45) the subject was. She prided herself on her freedom from English prejudice, and she might have added, from feminine delicacy. On religion she was a pure freethinker, and with much want of true affection, delighted to throw out her own views before the
(50) troubled mind of her father. To have shaken what remained of his Church of England faith would have gratified her much; but the idea of his abandoning his preferment in the church had never once present-ed itself to her mind. How could he indeed, when
(55) he had no income from any other source?

6. The passage as a whole is best characterized as

(A) a description of the members of a family
(B) a portrait of a young woman's moral and intellectual temperament
(C) an illustration of the evils of egotism
(D) an analysis of family dynamics in aristocratic society
(E) a contrast between a virtuous daughter and her disreputable family

7. The tone of the passage is best described as

(A) self-righteous and moralistic
(B) satirical and candid
(C) sympathetic and sentimental
(D) bitter and disillusioned
(E) indifferent and unfeeling

8. On the basis of the passage, which of the following statements about Dr. Stanhope can most logically be made?

(A) He is even more indolent than his wife.
(B) He resents having surrendered his authority to his daughter.
(C) He feels remorse for his professional misconduct.
(D) He has little left of his initial religious beliefs.
(E) He has disinherited his son without a shilling.

9. It can be inferred from the passage that Charlotte's mother (lines 33–35) is which of the following?

   I. An affectionate wife and mother
  II. A model of the domestic arts
 III. A woman of unassertive character

(A) I only
(B) II only
(C) III only
(D) I and III only
(E) II and III only

10. The passage suggests that Charlotte possesses all of the following characteristics EXCEPT

(A) an inappropriate flirtatiousness
(B) a lack of reverence
(C) a materialistic nature
(D) a managing disposition
(E) a touch of coarseness

The following passage on the nature of the surface of the earth is taken from a basic geology text.

Of the 197 million square miles making up the surface of the globe, 71 percent is covered by inter-connecting bodies of marine water; the Pacific Ocean
Line alone covers half the earth and averages near 14,000
(5) feet in depth. The *continents*—Eurasia, Africa, North America, South America, Australia, and Antarctica —are the portions of the *continental masses* rising above sea level. The submerged borders of the con-tinental masses are the *continental shelves,* beyond
(10) which lie the deep-sea basins.

The oceans attain their greatest depths not in their central parts, but in certain elongated furrows, or long narrow troughs, called *deeps*. These pro-found troughs have a peripheral arrangement,
(15) notably around the borders of the Pacific and Indian oceans. The position of the deeps near the continental masses suggests that the deeps, like the highest mountains, are of recent origin, since otherwise they would have been filled with waste from the
(20) lands. This suggestion is strengthened by the fact that the deeps are frequently the sites of world-shaking earthquakes. For example, the "tidal wave" that in April, 1946, caused widespread destruction along Pacific coasts resulted from a strong earth-
(25) quake on the floor of the Aleutian Deep.

The topography of the ocean floors is none too well known, since in great areas the available sound-ings are hundreds or even thousands of miles apart. However, the floor of the Atlantic is becoming fairly
(30) well known as a result of special surveys since 1920. A broad, well-defined ridge—the mid-Atlantic ridge—runs north and south between Africa and the two Americas, and numerous other major irregular-ities diversify the Atlantic floor. Closely spaced
(35) soundings show that many parts of the oceanic floors are as rugged as mountainous regions of the conti-nents. Use of the recently perfected method of echo sounding is rapidly enlarging our knowledge of submarine topography. During World War II great
(40) strides were made in mapping submarine surfaces, particularly in many parts of the vast Pacific basin.

The continents stand on the average 2870 feet— slightly more than half a mile—above sea level. North America averages 2300 feet; Europe averages
(45) only 1150 feet; and Asia, the highest of the larger continental subdivisions, averages 3200 feet. The highest point on the globe, Mount Everest in the Himalayas, is 29,000 feet above the sea; and as the greatest known depth in the sea is over 35,000 feet,
(50) the maximum *relief* (that is, the difference in altitude between the lowest and highest points) exceeds 64,000 feet, or exceeds 12 miles. The continental masses and the deep-sea basins are relief features of the first order; the deeps, ridges, and volcanic
(55) cones that diversify the sea floor, as well as the plains, plateaus, and mountains of the continents,

are relief features of the second order. The lands are unendingly subject to a complex of activities summarized in the term *erosion*, which first sculp-
(60) tures them in great detail and then tends to reduce them ultimately to sealevel. The modeling of the landscape by weather, running water, and other agents is apparent to the keenly observant eye and causes thinking people to speculate on what must
(65) be the final result of the ceaseless wearing down of the lands. Long before there was a science of geology, Shakespeare wrote "the revolution of the times makes mountains level."

11. It can be inferred from lines 1–4 that the largest ocean is the

(A) Atlantic
(B) Pacific
(C) Indian
(D) Aleutian Deep
(E) Arctic

12. According to lines 15–17, the peripheral furrows or *deeps* are found

(A) only in the Pacific and Indian oceans
(B) near earthquakes
(C) near the shore
(D) in the center of the ocean
(E) to be 14,000 feet in depth in the Pacific

13. The passage indicates that the continental masses

(A) comprise 29 percent of the earth's surface
(B) consist of six continents
(C) rise above sea level
(D) are partially underwater
(E) are relief features of the second order

14. The "revolution of the times" as used in the final sentence means

(A) the passage of years
(B) the current rebellion
(C) the science of geology
(D) the action of the ocean floor
(E) the overthrow of natural forces

15. From this passage, it can be inferred that earthquakes

(A) occur only in the peripheral furrows
(B) occur more frequently in newly formed land or sea formations
(C) are a prime cause of soil erosion
(D) will ultimately "make mountains level"
(E) are caused by the weight of water pressing on the earth's surface

The following passage is taken from the introduction to the catalog of a major exhibition of Flemish tapestries.

Tapestries are made on looms. Their distinctive weave is basically simple: the colored weft threads interface regularly with the monochrome warps, as
Line in darning or plain cloth, but as they do so, they form
(5) a design by reversing their direction when a change of color is needed. The wefts are beaten down to cover the warps completely. The result is a design or picture that is the fabric itself, not one laid upon a ground like an embroidery, a print, or brocading.
(10) The back and front of a tapestry show the same design. The weaver always follows a preexisting model, generally a drawing or painting, known as the cartoon, which in most cases he reproduces as exactly as he can. Long training is needed to become a pro-
(15) fessional tapestry weaver. It can take as much as a year to produce a yard of very finely woven tapestry.

Tapestry-woven fabrics have been made from China to Peru and from very early times to the pre- sent day, but large wall hangings in this technique,
(20) mainly of wool, are typically Northern European. Few examples predating the late fourteenth century have survived, but from about 1400 tapestries were an essential part of aristocratic life. The prince or great nobleman sent his plate and his tapestries
(25) ahead of him to furnish his castles before his arrival as he traveled through his domains; both had the same function, to display his wealth and social position. It has frequently been suggested that tapestries helped to heat stone-walled rooms, but
(30) this is a modern idea; comfort was of minor impor- tance in the Middle Ages. Tapestries were portable grandeur, instant splendor, taking the place, north of the Alps, of painted frescoes further south. They were hung without gaps between them, covering
(35) entire walls and often doors as well. Only very occa- sionally were they made as individual works of art such as altar frontals. They were usually commission- ed or bought as sets, or "chambers," and constituted the most important furnishings of any grand room,
(40) except for the display of plate, throughout the Middle Ages and the sixteenth century. Later, woven silks, ornamental wood carving, stucco decoration, and painted leather gradually replaced tapestry as ex- pensive wall coverings, until at last wallpaper was
(45) introduced in the late eighteenth century and eventually swept away almost everything else.

By the end of the eighteenth century, the "tapestry- room" [a room with every available wall surface covered with wall hangings] was no longer fashion-
(50) able: paper had replaced wall coverings of wool and silk. Tapestries, of course, were still made, but in the nineteenth century they often seem to have been produced mainly as individual works of art that astonish by their resemblance to oil paintings, tours
(55) de force woven with a remarkably large number of wefts per inch. In England during the second half of the century, William Morris attempted to reverse this trend and to bring tapestry weaving back to its true principles, those he considered to
(60) have governed it in the Middle Ages. He imitated medieval tapestries in both style and technique, using few warps to the inch, but he did not make sets; the original function for which tapestry is so admirably suited—completely covering the walls
(65) of a room and providing sumptuous surroundings for a life of pomp and splendor—could not be revived. Morris's example has been followed, though with less imitation of medieval style, by many weavers of the present century, whose coarsely
(70) woven cloths hang like single pictures and can be admired as examples of contemporary art.

16. Tapestry weaving may be characterized as which of the following?
  I.   Time-consuming
  II. Spontaneous in concept
  III. Faithful to an original

  (A) I only
  (B) III only
  (C) I and II only
  (D) I and III only
  (E) II and III only

17. The word "distinctive" in line 1 means
  (A) characteristic
  (B) stylish
  (C) discriminatory
  (D) eminent
  (E) articulate

18. Renaissance nobles carried tapestries with them to demonstrate their
  (A) piety
  (B) consequence
  (C) aesthetic judgment
  (D) need for privacy
  (E) dislike for cold

19. In contrast to nineteenth century tapestries, contemporary tapestries
  (A) are displayed in sets of panels
  (B) echo medieval themes
  (C) faithfully copy oil paintings
  (D) have a less fine weave
  (E) indicate the owner's social position

20. The primary purpose of the passage is to
  (A) explain the process of tapestry making
  (B) contrast Eastern and Western schools of tapestry
  (C) analyze the reasons for the decline in popularity of tapestries
  (D) provide a historical perspective on tapestry making
  (E) advocate a return to a more colorful way of life

Exercise C

This exercise provides you with a mixture of reading passages similar in variety to what you will encounter on the SAT. Answer all questions on the basis of what is <u>stated</u> or <u>implied</u> in the passages.

The following passage analyzes the contributions of the Mexican cowboy to American culture and to the English language.

The near-legendary history of the American West might have been quite different had the Mexican not brought cattle-raising to New Mexico and Texas.
Line The Spanish style of herding cattle on open ranges
(5) was different from the style of other Europeans, particularly the English. The American *rancho* was possible because of the lack of enough water for normal agricultural practices, and because of the easy availability of large amounts of land. This land-
(10) extensive form of cattle-raising required different techniques and brought forth the *vaquero*, the cowboy (from the Spanish *vaca*, cow) who tended the widely-scattered herds of Spanish longhorn cattle. Because of the American penchant to be consider-
(15) ed the inventors of nearly everything, the wide-open style of cattle-ranching was appropriated from the Mexican originators. As popular a folk-hero as the American cowboy is, he owes his development to the Spanish and the Mexicans, not the English.
(20) It is quite probable, as McWilliams asserts, that "with the exception of the capital required to expand the industry, there seems to have been nothing the American rancher or cowboy contributed to the development of cattle-raising in the
(25) Southwest."
Other contributions of the Mexican cowboy were: the western-style saddle with a large, ornate horn; *chaparejos*, or chaps; *lazo*, lasso; *la reata*, lariat; the cinch; the halter; the *mecate*, or horse-
(30) hair rope; chin strap for the hat; feed bag for the horse; ten-gallon hat (which comes from a mis-translation of a Spanish phrase "su sombrero galoneado" that really meant a "festooned" or "galooned" hat). Cowboy slang came from such
(35) words as: *juzgado*, hoosegow; *ranchero*, rancher; *estampida*, stampede; *calabozo*, calaboose; and *pinto* for a painted horse.
Just as the Mexican association for the protection of the rights of sheepherders gave rise to the
(40) American Sheepman's Association, the Spanish system of branding range animals and registering these brands became standard practice among Anglo stockmen. The idea of brands originated in North Africa and was brought to Spain by the Moors,
(45) along with their stocky ponies. The Mexican brands are of great antiquity, having been copied from

earlier Indian signs which include symbols of the sky—sun, moon, and stars. Hernando Cortez is said to have been the first to use a brand on the
(50) continent.

1. Which of the following would be the best title for this passage?
   (A) How to Herd Cattle
   (B) The American Cowboy: A Romantic Figure
   (C) Farming Practices in Europe and America
   (D) Hispanic Contributions to Western Ranching
   (E) Spanish Influence on American Culture

2. It can be inferred from lines 8 and 9 that American ranches developed in the West rather than the East because
   (A) more Spanish-speaking people lived in the West
   (B) there was more money available in the West
   (C) people in the East were more bound by tradition
   (D) many jobless men in the East wanted to become cowboys
   (E) there was more unsettled land available in the West

3. The author gives examples of cowboy slang (lines 34–37) in order to
   (A) arouse the reader's interest
   (B) show that he is familiar with the subject
   (C) prove that many cowboys lacked education
   (D) point out the differences between America's East and West
   (E) demonstrate how these terms originated

4. According to the author, which of the following did Mexicans contribute to ranching?
   I. Money to buy ranches
   II. Methods of handling animals
   III. Items of riding equipment
   (A) I only
   (B) II only
   (C) III only
   (D) I and II only
   (E) II and III only

5. Which of the following best describes the development of this passage?
   (A) Major points, minor points
   (B) Statement of problem, examples, proposed solution
   (C) Introduction, positive factors, negative factors
   (D) Cause, effects
   (E) Comparison, contrast

In this introduction to a pictorial survey of African art, the author describes the impact of African sculpture.

When you first saw a piece of African art, it impressed you as a unit; you did not see it as a collection of shapes or forms. This, of course, means
Line that the shapes and volumes within the sculpture
(5) itself were coordinated so successfully that the viewer was affected emotionally.

It is entirely valid to ask how, from a purely artistic point of view, this unity was achieved. And we must also inquire whether there is a recurrent
(10) pattern or rules or a plastic language and vocabulary which is responsible for the powerful communication of emotion which the best African sculpture achieves. If there is such a pattern or rules, are these rules applied consciously or instinctively to obtain
(15) so many works of such high artistic quality?

It is obvious from the study of art history that an intense and unified emotional experience, such as the Christian credo of the Byzantine or 12th or 13th century Europe, when expressed in art forms, gave
(20) great unity, coherence, and power to art. But such an integrated feeling was only the inspirational element for the artist, only the starting point of the creative act. The expression of this emotion and its realization in the work could be done only with
(25) discipline and thorough knowledge of the craft. And the African sculptor was a highly trained workman. He started his apprenticeship with a master when a child, and he learned the tribal styles and the use of the tools and the nature of woods so thoroughly
(30) that his carving became what Boas calls "motor action." He carved automatically and instinctively.

The African carver followed his rules without thinking of them; indeed, they never seem to have been formulated in words. But such rules existed,
(35) for accident and coincidence cannot explain the common plastic language of African sculpture. There is too great a consistency from one work to another. Yet, although the African, with amazing insight into art, used these rules, I am certain that he
(40) was not conscious of them. This is the great mystery of such a traditional art: talent, or the ability certain people have, without conscious effort, to follow the rules which later the analyst can discover only from the work of art which has already been created.

6. The author is primarily concerned with

(A) discussing how African sculptors achieved their effects
(B) listing the rules followed in African art
(C) relating African art to the art of 12th- or 13th-century Europe
(D) integrating emotion and realization
(E) expressing the beauty of African art

7. According to the passage, one of the outstanding features of African sculpture is

(A) its subject matter
(B) the feelings it arouses
(C) the training of the artists
(D) its strangeness
(E) its emphasis on movement

8. The word "plastic" in line 10 means

(A) synthetic
(B) linguistic
(C) consistent
(D) sculptural
(E) repetitive

9. According to the information in the passage, an African carver can be best compared to a

(A) chef following a recipe
(B) fluent speaker of English who is just beginning to study French
(C) batter who hits a homerun in his or her first baseball game
(D) concert pianist performing a well-rehearsed concerto
(E) writer who is grammatically expert but stylistically uncreative

10. Which of the following titles best summarizes the content of the passage?

(A) The Apprenticeship of the African Sculptor
(B) The History of African Sculpture
(C) How African Art Achieves Unity
(D) Analyzing African Art
(E) The Unconscious Rules of African Art

The following passages present two portraits of grandmothers. In Passage 1 Mary McCarthy shares her memories of her Catholic grandmother, who raised McCarthy and her brother after their parents' death. In Passage 2 Caroline Heilbrun tells of her Jewish grandmother, who died when Heilbrun was 10.

Passage 1

Luckily, I am writing a memoir and not a work of fiction, and therefore I do not have to account for my grandmother's unpleasing character and look
Line for the Oedipal fixation or the traumatic experience
(5) which would give her that clinical authenticity that is nowadays so desirable in portraiture. I do not know how my grandmother got the way she was; I assume, from family photographs and from the inflexibility of her habits, that she was always the
(10) same, and it seems as idle to inquire into her childhood as to ask what was ailing Iago or look for the error in toilet-training that was responsible for Lady Macbeth. My grandmother's sexual history, bristling

(15) with infant mortality in the usual style of her period, was robust and decisive: three tall, handsome sons grew up, and one attentive daughter. Her husband treated her kindly. She had money, many grand-children, and religion to sustain her. White hair,
(20) glasses, soft skin, wrinkles, needlework—all the paraphernalia of motherliness were hers; yet it was a cold, grudging, disputatious old woman who sat all day in her sunroom making tapestries from a pattern, scanning religious periodicals, and setting her iron jaw against any infraction of her ways.
(25) Combativeness was, I suppose, the dominant trait in my grandmother's nature. An aggressive churchgoer, she was quite without Christian feel ing; the mercy of the Lord Jesus had never entered her heart. Her piety was an act of war against the
(30) Protestant ascendancy. The religious magazines on her table furnished her not with food for meditation but with fresh pretexts for anger; articles attacking birth control, divorce, mixed marriages, Darwin, and secular education were her favorite reading.
(35) The teachings of the Church did not interest her, except as they were a rebuke to others; "Honor thy father and thy mother", a commandment she was no longer called upon to practice, was the one most frequently on her lips. The extermination of
(40) Protestantism, rather than spiritual perfection, was the boon she prayed for. Her mind was preoccupied with conversion; the capture of a soul for God much diverted her fancy—it made one less Protestant in the world. Foreign missions, with
(45) their overtones of good will and social service, appealed to her less strongly; it was not a *harvest* of souls that my grandmother had in mind.
This pugnacity of my grandmother's did not confine itself to sectarian enthusiasm. There was
(50) the defence of her furniture and her house against the imagined encroachments of visitors. With her, this was not the gentle and tremulous protectiveness endemic in old ladies, who fear for the safety of their possessions with a truly touching anxiety,
(55) inferring the fragility of all things from the brittle-ness of their old bones and hearing the crash of mortality in the perilous tinkling of a tea-cup. My grandmother's sentiment was more autocratic: she hated having her chairs sat in or her lawns stepped
(60) on or the water turned on in her basins, for no reason at all except pure officiousness; she even grudged the mailman his daily promenade up her sidewalk. Her home was a center of power, and she would not allow it to be derogated by easy or democratic usage.
(65) Under her jealous eye, its social properties had atrophied, and it functioned in the family structure simply as a political headquarters. The family had no friends, and entertaining was held to be a foolish and unnecessary courtesy as between blood relations.
(70) Holiday dinners fell, as a duty, on the lesser members of the organization: the daughters and daughters-in-law (converts from the false religion) offered up Baked Alaska on a platter like the head of John

(75) the Baptist, while the old people sat enthroned at the table, and only their digestive processes acknowledged, with rumbling, enigmatic salvos, the festal day.

Passage 2

My grandmother, one of Howe's sustaining women, not only ruled the household with an arm
(80) of iron, but kept a store to support them all, her blond, blue-eyed husband enjoying life rather than struggling through it. My grandmother was one of those powerful women who know that they stand between their families and an outside world filled
(85) with temptations to failure and shame. I remember her as thoroughly loving. But there can be no question that she impaired her six daughters for autonomy as thoroughly as if she had crippled them —more so. The way to security was marriage; the
(90) dread that stood in the way of this was sexual dal-liance, above all pregnancy. The horror of pregnancy in an unmarried girl is difficult, perhaps, to recap-ture now. For a Jewish girl not to be a virgin on marriage was failure. The male's rights were
(95) embodied in her lack of sexual experience, in the knowledge that he was the first, the owner.
All attempts at autonomy had to be frustrated. And of course, my grandmother's greatest weapon was her own vulnerability. She had worked hard,
(100) only her daughters knew how hard. She could not be comforted or repaid—as *my* mother would feel repaid—by a daughter's accomplishments, only by her marriage.

11. McCarthy's attitude toward her grandmother is best described as

    (A) tolerant
    (B) appreciative
    (C) indifferent
    (D) nostalgic
    (E) sardonic

12. The word "idle" in line 10 means

    (A) slothful
    (B) passive
    (C) fallow
    (D) useless
    (E) unoccupied

13. According to McCarthy, a portrait of a character in a work of modern fiction must have

    (A) photographic realism
    (B) psychological validity
    (C) sympathetic attitudes
    (D) religious qualities
    (E) historical accuracy

14. McCarthy's primary point in describing her grand-mother's physical appearance (lines 18 and 19) is best summarized by which of the following axioms?

    (A) Familiarity breeds contempt.
    (B) You can't judge a book by its cover.
    (C) One picture is worth more than ten thousand words.
    (D) There's no smoke without fire.
    (E) Blood is thicker than water.

15. By describing (in lines 52–57) the typical old woman's fear for the safety of her possessions, McCarthy emphasizes that

    (A) her grandmother feared the approach of death
    (B) old women have dangerously brittle bones
    (C) her grandmother possessed considerable wealth
    (D) her grandmother had different reasons for her actions
    (E) visitors were unwelcome in her grandmother's home

16. The word "properties" in line 65 means

    (A) belongings
    (B) aspects
    (C) holdings
    (D) titles
    (E) acreage

17. Heilbrun is critical of her grandmother primarily because

    (A) she would not allow her husband to enjoy himself
    (B) she could not accept her own vulnerability
    (C) she fostered a sense of sexual inadequacy
    (D) she discouraged her daughters' independence
    (E) she physically injured her children

18. In stating that her grandmother's greatest weapon was her own vulnerability (lines 98 and 99), Heilbrun implies that her grandmother got her way by exploiting her children's

    (A) sense of guilt
    (B) innocence of evil
    (C) feeling of indifference
    (D) abdication of responsibility
    (E) lack of experience

19. Each passage mentions which of the following as being important to the writer's grandmother?

    (A) governing the actions of others
    (B) contributing to religious organizations
    (C) protecting her children's virtue
    (D) marrying off her daughters
    (E) being surrounded by a circle of friends

20. McCarthy would most likely react to the characterization of her grandmother, like Heilbrun's grandmother, as one of the "sustaining women" (lines 78 and 79) by pointing out that

    (A) this characterization is not in good taste
    (B) the characterization fails to account for her grandmother's piety
    (C) the details of the family's social life support this characterization
    (D) her grandmother's actual conduct is not in keeping with this characterization
    (E) this characterization slightly exaggerates her grandmother's chief virtue

Answer Key

EXERCISE A

1.	**B**	6.	**A**	11.	**D**	16.	**B**	21.	**D**
2.	**D**	7.	**C**	12.	**E**	17.	**E**	22.	**C**
3.	**B**	8.	**E**	13.	**A**	18.	**E**		
4.	**A**	9.	**E**	14.	**C**	19.	**E**		
5.	**D**	10.	**E**	15.	**C**	20.	**B**		

EXERCISE B

1.	**C**	5.	**D**	9.	**C**	13.	**D**	17.	**A**
2.	**C**	6.	**B**	10.	**A**	14.	**A**	18.	**B**
3.	**A**	7.	**B**	11.	**B**	15.	**B**	19.	**D**
4.	**E**	8.	**D**	12.	**C**	16.	**D**	20.	**D**

EXERCISE C

1.	**D**	6.	**A**	11.	**E**	16.	**B**		
2.	**E**	7.	**B**	12.	**D**	17.	**D**		
3.	**E**	8.	**D**	13.	**B**	18.	**A**		
4.	**E**	9.	**D**	14.	**B**	19.	**A**		
5.	**A**	10.	**E**	15.	**D**	20.	**D**		

Answer Explanations

EXERCISE A

1. **(B)** The opening lines indicate that the narrator is *reflecting on his feelings*. Throughout the passage he uses words like "miserable," "ashamed," and "discontented" to describe his emotional state.
   Choice A is incorrect. The narrator does not analyze or dissect a change in attitude; he describes an ongoing attitude.
   Choice C is incorrect. The passage gives an example of emotional self-awareness, not of political consciousness.
   Choice D is incorrect. The narrator condemns rather than defends the longings that brought him discontentment.
   Choice E is incorrect. The narrator criticizes himself, not young people in general.

2. **(D)** The references to the forge (line 13) and the anvil (line 23) support Choice D. None of the other choices are suggested by the passage.

3. **(B)** Note the adjectives used to describe Joe: "faithful," "industrious," "kind." These are virtues, and Joe is fundamentally *virtuous*.
   Choice A is incorrect. Joe is plain and hardworking, not eminent and distinguished.
   Choice C is incorrect. The passage portrays not Joe but the narrator as desiring to be independent.
   Choice D is incorrect. It is unsupported by the passage.

Choice E is incorrect. The narrator thinks his life is coarse; he thinks Joe is virtuous.

4. **(A)** Choice A is supported by lines 15 and 16 in which the narrator states he "would not have had Miss Havisham and Estella see (his home) on any account."
   Choices B and C are incorrect. Nothing in the passage suggests either might be the case.
   Choice D is incorrect. Though the narrator may not show himself as hard-working, nothing in the passage suggests laziness led to his discontent.
   Choice E is incorrect. Nothing in the passage suggests sinfulness has prompted his discontent. In addition, although ingratitude may play a part in his discontent, shame at his background plays a far greater part.

5. **(D)** In lines 40 and 41, the narrator manages to say something good about his youthful self: "I am glad to know I never breathed a murmur to Joe." He gives himself credit for *concealing his despondency*.
   Choices A and B are incorrect. The narrator gives Joe all the credit for his having worked industriously and for his not having run away to become a soldier.
   Choices C and E are incorrect. They are unsupported by the passage.

6. **(A)** Throughout the second paragraph, the author pays particular attention to Maria's appearance, her behavior, her effect on others. If she had been *introduced* previously in the text, there would be no need to present these details about her at this point in the passage.

7. **(C)** The descriptions of the bright and shiny kitchen where you "could see yourself in the big copper boilers" and of tiny, witch-like Maria with her long nose and long chin belong to the realm of *fairy tales*.

8. **(E)** The passage mentions the matron twice: once, in the opening line, where she gives Maria permission to leave work early; once, in lines 17–18, where she pays Maria a compliment. Given this context, we can logically infer that Maria views the matron positively, finding her a *benevolent* or kindly *supervisor*.
Choices A, B, and C are incorrect. Nothing in the passage suggests Maria has a negative view of the matron.
Choice D is incorrect. Given Maria's relatively menial position, it is unlikely she and the matron would be close or intimate friends.

9. **(E)** To slice loaves so neatly and invisibly takes a great deal of care. The author specifically states that Maria has cut the loaves. Not only that, he emphasizes the importance of her having done so by placing this statement at the end of the paragraph (a key position). As the subsequent paragraphs point up, Maria is hungry for compliments. Just as she takes pride in her peacemaking, she takes pride in her ability to slice barmbracks evenly.

10. **(E)** Maria helps others to compromise or become reconciled; she herself is not necessarily unwilling to compromise.
The passage suggests that Choice A is characteristic of Maria. She speaks soothingly and respectfully. Therefore, Choice A is incorrect.
The passage suggests that Choice B is characteristic of Maria. Maria's response to Ginger Mooney's toast shows her enjoyment of being noticed in this way. Therefore, Choice B is incorrect.
The passage suggests that Choice C is characteristic of Maria. Maria's obedience to the cook and to the matron shows her respect for authority. Therefore, Choice C is incorrect.
The passage suggests that Choice D is characteristic of Maria. Maria's disappointed shyness and her forced laughter about a wedding ring and husband show that she has wistful dreams of marriage. Therefore, Choice D is incorrect.

11. **(D)** By stating that his joy at his return "made him communicative and chatty in a very unusual degree" (lines 6–7), the opening paragraph implies that Sir Thomas is usually *more restrained in speech*. Choice D is correct.
Choice A is incorrect. Nothing in the passage suggests he is usually unwelcome in his own home.
Choices B and C are incorrect. Neither is supported by the opening paragraph.
Choice E is incorrect. Sir Thomas's delight at finding his family together "exactly as he could have wished" indicates he does not lack family feeling.
Remember, when asked to make inferences, base your answers on what the passage implies, not what it states directly.

12. **(E)** The opening sentence of the second paragraph states that none of the members of his family listened to him with such "unbroken unalloyed enjoyment" as his wife did. Her enjoyment was complete and unmixed with other emotions. This suggests that others in the group face Sir Thomas's arrival not with complete pleasure but *with mixed emotions*.
Choice A is incorrect. It is unsupported by the passage.
Choice B is incorrect. Lady Bertram's fluttered or discomposed state on his arrival indicates her surprise.
Choice C is incorrect. Lines 14–15 indicate that Sir Thomas did not expect to find his whole family at home. Therefore, he had not timed his arrival to coincide with a reunion.
Choice D is incorrect. Sir Thomas has had to seek out the butler and confide the news of his arrival to him (lines 50–51). Therefore, the servants had not expected his arrival.

13. **(A)** The phrases "coming unexpectedly as he did" (line 15) and "his sudden arrival" (lines 20–21) support the idea that Sir Thomas has returned unexpectedly. Note that these key phrases are found in the closing sentence of the first paragraph and in the opening sentence of the second paragraph. Sir Thomas's unexpected return is central to the passage.
Choice B is incorrect. Although the persons talking belong to the upper classes, as a title "The Conversation of the Upper Class" is too vague.
Choice C is incorrect. Mrs. Norris's complaint or grievance (the subject of the third paragraph) is too narrow in scope to be an appropriate title for the passage as a whole.
Choice D is incorrect. Although Lady Bertram is quite pleased to have her husband home again, their reunion is placid rather than emotional or romantic.
Choice E is incorrect. Although Sir Thomas gives an account of his voyage in the first paragraph, the passage places its emphasis on the reactions of his family to his surprising return.
Remember, when asked to choose a title, watch out for choices that are too specific or too broad.

14. **(C)** Examine Lady Bertram's behavior carefully. She is not agitated (though she is "nearer agitation than she had been for the last twenty years"). She is so moved by her husband's return that she actually moves her lap dog from the sofa and makes room for her husband. Clearly, the author is making fun of Lady Bertram's idiosyncratic behavior, describing her quirky reactions in a lightly mocking, *gently ironic* way.

15. **(C)** The author italicizes the word *her* for emphasis. Lady Bertram had no worries to take away from her pleasure at Sir Thomas's return. However, she is unusual in this. The author's emphasis on her happiness *serves to suggest that others in the group have reason to be less happy about Sir Thomas's arrival*.

16. **(B)** Refusing to be provoked by Mrs. Norris's interruptions, Sir Thomas demonstrates *patient forbearance* or restraint.

Choice A is incorrect. Line 69 states that Sir Thomas "could not be provoked." Therefore, he showed no irritation.

Choice C is incorrect. Sir Thomas remarks courteously on Mrs. Norris's anxiety for everybody's comfort (lines 69–71). This implies that he in general approves rather than disapproves of her concern.

Choice D is incorrect. It is unsupported by the passage.

Choice E is incorrect. Given Mrs. Norris's interruptions of his story, it is unlikely Sir Thomas would view her with *unmixed delight*.

17. **(E)** Mrs. Norris has looked forward to spreading the news of Sir Thomas's return (or of his death!). The office she has lost is that of herald or *message-bearer*.

Choice A is incorrect. Mrs. Norris wishes to give orders to the butler, not to be the butler.

Choice B is incorrect for much the same reason.

Choice C is incorrect. Mrs. Norris is the sister of Sir Thomas's wife; the passage does not indicate that she has any desire to be his wife.

Choice D is incorrect. Mrs. Norris wishes to give news of the traveler, not to be the traveler.

18. **(E)** The first sentence of the passage states that Newman's purpose is to see Mademoiselle Noemie, to pay her another visit. Indeed, in lines 6–7, he is described as roaming "through several of the rooms in fruitless quest of her."

19. **(E)** In lines 35–36, Valentin explains that, giving in to his mother's entreaties, he has reluctantly agreed to guide his cousin through the Louvre. The prospect bores him—playing tour guide is one of his *ennuis*. He is even more bored than usual, for his cousin is late.

20. **(B)** Valentin shows what a bad mood he is in by *making insulting comments* about his cousin's poor taste in clothes, huge feet, and lack of punctuality.

Choice A is incorrect. Though Valentin's cousin is late, he has not yet stalked off in a fit of temper.

Choice C is incorrect. Valentin is quite ready to accept Newman's advice.

Choice D is incorrect. He is criticizing his English cousin's choice of clothes, not his mother's.

Choice E is incorrect. Though he is about to offer to go off with Newman, Valentin has not yet refused to do as his mother wished. Up to now, he has been a very obedient, though disgruntled, son.

21. **(D)** Use the process of elimination to answer this question.

Valentin would most likely agree with Statement I. His concern for fashionable clothing is evident from the disparaging remarks he makes about his cousin's clothes. Therefore, you can eliminate Choices B and C.

Valentin would most likely also agree with Statement II. He respects family relationships, for he has agreed to his mother's request to show the cousin around. Therefore, you can eliminate Choice A.

Valentin would probably *not* agree with Statement III. He is furious that his cousin is late. Therefore, you can eliminate Choice E.

Only Choice D is left. It is the correct answer.

22. **(C)** Valentin confides in Newman, telling the American why he is so irritated. He speaks extremely frankly, making disparaging comments about his English cousin, for he is sure that his trusted friend or *confidant* will not betray these confidences.

EXERCISE B

1. **(C)** Each paragraph discusses some important feature or *significant characteristic* of Eskimo art (its mystical quality, realistic understanding of anatomy, humor, etc.).

2. **(C)** The author's use of such terms as "powerful ability" (line 2), "masters in the understanding of animal anatomy" (line 28), and "living excitement" (line 55) indicates an *admiration* for the art.

3. **(A)** The author's comment in line 17 that Eskimo art "has a special freedom unsullied (unstained or undefiled) by any kind of formalized training" suggests that he would agree that formal training might defile or *destroy an artist's originality* and freedom of expression.

4. **(E)** Each example the author provides describes a type of Eskimo sculpture (man driving a caribou, woman holding a child, geese flying, polar bear charging) and gives the reader a sense of its *quality and variety*.

5. **(D)** Use the process of elimination to answer this question.

Choice A is incorrect. Line 43 states "there is much evidence of humor" in Eskimo art.

Choice B is incorrect. Humor in Eskimo carvings "may be subtle" (lines 46–47).

Choice C is incorrect. Eskimo carvings reveal "the passionate feelings of a vital people" (line 9); they possess *emotional depth*.

Choice E is incorrect. Eskimo sculptors are "masters in the understanding of animal anatomy" (line 28). Their works are characterized by *anatomical accuracy*.

Only Choice D is left. It is the correct answer. If "no one can accurately define the right way or wrong way to create a carving" (lines 48–49), clearly Eskimo carving lacks *stylistic uniformity*.

6. **(B)** The passage as a whole is a portrait of Charlotte Stanhope's moral and intellectual temperament or character. The opening sentence of each paragraph describes some aspect of her behavior or character which the paragraph then goes on to develop. Remember, when asked to find the main idea, be sure to check the opening and summary sentences of each paragraph.

Choice A is incorrect. While the various members of the family are described, they are described only in relationship to Charlotte.

Choice C is incorrect. Although Charlotte may well be selfish or egotistical, she does do some good for others. The passage does not illustrate the evils of egotism.

Choice D is incorrect. The passage analyzes Charlotte; it discusses the members of her family only in relationship to her.

Choice E is incorrect. While Charlotte has her virtues, the passage stresses her faults. While her family may not be described as admirable, nothing suggests that they are disreputable (not well-esteemed or well-regarded).

7. **(B)** The author presents Charlotte *candidly* and openly: her faults are not concealed. The author also presents her *satirically*: her weaknesses and those of her family are mocked or made fun of. If you find the characters in a passage foolish or pompous, the author may well be writing satirically.

Choice A is incorrect. While the author is concerned with Charlotte's moral character, he is not *moralistic* or *self-righteous*; he is describing her character, not preaching a sermon against her.

Choice C is incorrect. The author is unsympathetic to Charlotte's faults and he is not *sentimental* or emotionally excessive about her.

Choice D is incorrect. *Bitterness* is too strong a term to describe the author's tone. He has no reason to be bitter.

Choice E is incorrect. While the author's tone is not highly emotional, it is better to describe it as satiric than as *unfeeling*.

8. **(D)** Lines 50–51 mention the troubled mind of Dr. Stanhope, and state that Charlotte would have enjoyed shaking "*what remained* of his Church of England faith." The phrase "what remained" implies that little is left of Dr. Stanhope's original religious faith.

Choice A is incorrect. There is no comparison made between the two elder Stanhopes. Both are *indolent* (lazy).

Choice B is incorrect. Since only Charlotte could persuade her father to look after his affairs (lines 14 and 15), he apparently was willing to let her manage matters for him and willingly surrendered his authority.

Choice C is incorrect. There is no evidence in the passage that Dr. Stanhope feels regret or remorse.

Choice E is incorrect. While Charlotte's brother is described as moneyless (lines 41–42), there is no evidence in the passage that Dr. Stanhope has disinherited him.

9. **(C)** There is no evidence in the passage that Charlotte's mother is an affectionate wife and mother; similarly, there is no evidence that she is excellent in the "domestic arts" (making tea; managing the household—the very tasks assumed by Charlotte).

Statements I and II are incorrect. Only Statement III is correct. The sole mention of Charlotte's mother (lines 33–35) states that she was encouraged in her idleness by Charlotte. She lacks the willpower to resist Charlotte's encouragements. Thus, she shows herself to be a woman of unassertive, pliable character.

10. **(A)** The first paragraph emphasizes that Charlotte "in no way affected the graces of youth." Her manner is that of an assured mistress of a household, not a flirt.

Choice B is incorrect. Charlotte is a free-thinker (one who denies established beliefs) and thus lacks reverence or respect for religion.

Choice C is incorrect. Charlotte is concerned with her family's worldly well-being and makes her father attend to his material concerns. Thus, she has a materialistic nature.

Choice D is incorrect. Charlotte manages everything and everybody.

Choice E is incorrect. Charlotte's coarseness (vulgarity; crudeness) is implied in the reference to her "freedom...from feminine delicacy" (lines 45–47).

11. **(B)** We are told that 71 percent of the earth is covered by water and that the Pacific Ocean covers half the earth. The Pacific is obviously the largest ocean.

12. **(C)** The peripheral furrows or *deeps* are discussed in lines 13–25. We are told that these deeps are near the continental masses, and, therefore, near the shore.

13. **(D)** The last sentence of the first paragraph discusses the submerged or *underwater* portions of the continental masses.

Key Words: masses, percent, sea level, submerged, relief.

14. **(A)** Terms such as "unendingly," "ultimately," and "ceaseless" indicate that the mountains are made level over an enormous *passage of years*.

15. **(B)** The passage states that the *deeps*, the site of frequent earthquakes, are of recent origin: they were formed comparatively recently. This suggests that newly formed land and sea formations may have a greater frequency of earthquake occurrence than older, more stable formations.

Remember, when asked to make inferences, base your answers on what the passage implies, not what it states directly.

16. **(D)** Tapestry weaving is time-consuming, taking "as much as a year to produce a yard." In addition, it is faithful to the original ("The weaver always follows a preexisting model.") It is not, however, spontaneous in concept.

17. **(A)** The author mentions tapestry's distinctive or *characteristic* weave as something that distinguishes tapestry-woven materials from other fabrics (prints, brocades, etc.).

18. **(B)** By using tapestries "to display his wealth and social position," the nobleman is using them to demonstrate his *consequence* or importance.

19. **(D)** In comparison to the tightly-woven tapestries of the nineteenth century, present day wall-hangings are described as "coarsely woven cloths." Thus, they *have a less fine weave* than their predecessors.

20. **(D)** The passage explains the process of tapestry making and mentions that large wall-hangings are Western rather than Eastern in origin. Choices A and B do not reflect the passage's primary purpose. This purpose is to *provide an historical perspective on tapestry making*.

EXERCISE C

1. **(D)** The topic discussed throughout this passage is Hispanic (Spanish and Mexican) contributions to Western ranching.

2. **(E)** The first paragraph notes that ranches can develop where large amounts of land are available. It can be inferred that more unsettled land was available in the West than in the East.

3. **(E)** The use of only Mexican terms suggests that the author is using these examples of cowboy slang to demonstrate the origins of the words and prove how much Mexicans contributed.

4. **(E)** The first paragraph tells of the adoption of Mexican methods of handling animals, and the second speaks of Mexican contributions to riding equipment. The quotation at the end of the first paragraph implies that the money for the ranching industry was provided by Americans.

5. **(A)** The passage starts with the major Mexican contribution of the whole concept of ranching, goes on, in the second paragraph, to discuss lesser contributions of equipment and slang, and ends, in the third paragraph, with the relatively minor contribution of branding.

6. **(A)** Each paragraph of the passage discusses how African sculptors achieved their effects.

7. **(B)** Both the first and second paragraphs mention the emotions aroused by African sculpture.

8. **(D)** The passage discusses sculpture, so it can be inferred that "the common plastic language" means the common *sculptural* language.

9. **(D)** We are told that the African sculptor was highly trained and followed the rules without thinking about them. Similarly, a well-rehearsed pianist can perform a concerto without worrying too much about the notes. Both artists have become free to concentrate on mood or creativity.

10. **(E)** Throughout the passage, the author discusses the rules of African art. He concludes that they were unconscious.

11. **(E)** In candidly exposing her grandmother's flaws, the author exhibits a *sardonic* or scornful and sarcastic attitude.

12. **(D)** McCarthy sees as little point in speculating about her grandmother's childhood as she does in wondering about the toilet-training of a fictional character like Lady Macbeth. Such speculations are, to McCarthy's mind, idle or *useless*.

13. **(B)** The author states (somewhat ironically) that modern fictional characters must have "clinical authenticity." In other words, they must appear to be genuine or *valid* in *psychological* terms.

14. **(B)** Although the grandmother's outward appearance was soft and motherly, her essential nature was hard as nails. Clearly, you cannot judge a book (person) by its cover (outward appearance).

15. **(D)** McCarthy is building up a portrait of her grandmother as a pugnacious, autocratic person. She describes the fear old ladies have for their belongings as a very human (and understandable) reaction: aware of their own increasing fragility (and eventual death), the old ladies identify with their fragile possessions and are protective of them. McCarthy's grandmother was also protective of her belongings, but she was not the typical "gentle and tremulous" elderly woman. She was a petty tyrant and had decidedly *different reasons for her actions*.

16. **(B)** Because her grandmother was more interested in maintaining her power than in being hospitable, the social properties or *aspects* of the family home had withered and decayed till no real sociability existed.

17. **(D)** Heilbrun's central criticism is that her grandmother "impaired her six daughters for autonomy" or independence. In other words, *she discouraged her daughters' independence*.

18. **(A)** By dwelling on how hard she had worked to support her daughters and how much she would be hurt if they failed to pay her back by making good marriages, Heilbrun's grandmother exploited their *sense of guilt*.

19. **(A)** The common factor in both grandmothers' lives is their need to *govern the actions of others*. McCarthy's grandmother tyrannized everyone from the mailman to her daughters and daughters-in-law; Heilbrun's grandmother "ruled the household with an arm of iron," governing her daughters' lives.

20. **(D)** While Heilbrun's grandmother was a "sustaining woman" who provided for her family, allowing her husband to live a life of relative leisure, McCarthy's grandmother was a grudging woman, not a sustaining one. Thus, McCarthy would most likely point out that *her grandmother's actual conduct is not in keeping with this characterization*.

Build Your Vocabulary

CHAPTER 3

- **The SAT High-Frequency Word List**
- **The SAT Hot Prospects Word List**
- **The 3,500 Basic Word List**
- **Basic Word Parts**

The more you study actual SAT critical reading questions, the more you realize one thing: *the key to doing well on the critical reading portions of SAT is a strong working vocabulary of college-level words.* And the key to building that strong working vocabulary can be summed up in one word: READ.

Read widely, read deeply, read daily. If you do, your vocabulary will grow. If you don't it won't.

Reading widely, however, may not always help you remember the words you read. You may have the words in your passive vocabulary and be able to recognize them when you see them in a context and yet be unable to define them clearly or think of synonyms for them. In addition, unless you have already begun to upgrade your reading to the college level, reading widely also may not acquaint you most efficiently with college-level words.

What are college-level words? In going through the preceding two chapters, you have examined dozens of questions modeled on those in published SATs. Some of the words in these questions— *inspiring* and *communicative*—have been familiar to you; others—*pundit* and *interlocutor*—have not. Still others—*economy* and *charge*—have looked familiar, but have turned out to be defined in unexpected ways. All these words belong in your college-level vocabulary; any of them may turn up when you take the SAT.

Use the vocabulary and word parts lists in this chapter to upgrade your vocabulary to a college level. They are all excellent vocabulary building tools.

No matter how little time you have before you take the SAT, you can familiarize yourself with the sort of vocabulary you will be facing on the test. First, look over the words on our SAT High-Frequency Word List, which you'll find on the following pages. Each of these words has appeared (as answer choices or as question words) from eight to forty times on SATs published in the past two decades.

Next, look over the words on our Hot Prospects List, which appears immediately after the High-Frequency List. Though these words don't appear as often as the high-frequency words do, when they do appear, the odds are that they're *key* words in questions. As such, they deserve your special attention.

Use the flash cards in the back of this book and create others for the words you want to master. Work up memory tricks to help yourself remember them. Try using them on your parents and friends. Not only will going over these high-frequency words reassure you that you *do* know some SAT-type words, but also it may well help you on the actual day of the test. These words have turned up on recent tests; some of them may well turn up on the test you take.

The SAT High-Frequency Word List

abridge	censure	disinclination	frivolous	invert
abstemious	coercion	dismiss	frugality	ironic
abstract	commemorate	disparage	furtive	lament
abstruse	compile	disparity	garrulous	laud
accessible	complacency	disperse	glutton	lavish (ADJ)
acclaim	compliance	disputatious	gratify	lethargic
acknowledge	composure	disseminate	gratuitous	levity
adulation	comprehensive	dissent	gravity	linger
adversary	concede	divergent	gregarious	listless
adversity	conciliatory	doctrine	guile	lofty
advocate	concise	document (V)	gullible	malicious
aesthetic	concur	dogmatic	hamper (V)	marred
affable	condone	dubious	hardy	materialism
affirmation	conflagration	duplicity	haughtiness	methodical
alleviate	confound	eclectic	hedonist	meticulous
aloof	consensus	egotism	heresy	miserly
altruistic	constraint	elated	hierarchy	mitigate
ambiguous	contend	eloquence	homogeneous	morose
ambivalence	contentious	elusive	hypocritical	mundane
analogous	contract (V)	embellish	hypothetical	negate
anarchist	conviction	emulate	idiosyncrasy	nonchalance
anecdote	cordial	endorse	illusory	notoriety
animosity	corroborate	enhance	immutable	novelty
antagonism	credulity	enigma	impair	nurture
antidote	criterion	enmity	impeccable	obliterate
antiquated	cryptic	ephemeral	impede	oblivion
apathy	cursory	equivocal	implausible	obscure (V)
appease	curtail	erroneous	implement (V)	obstinate
apprehension	decorum	erudite	impudence	ominous
arbitrary	deference	esoteric	inadvertent	opaque
archaic	degradation	eulogy	inane	opportunist
arrogance	delineate	euphemism	incisive	optimist
articulate	denounce	exacerbate	incite	opulence
artifact	deplore	exalt	inclusive	orator
artisan	depravity	execute	incongruous	ostentatious
ascendancy	deprecate	exemplary	inconsequential	pacifist
ascetic	deride	exemplify	incorrigible	partisan
aspire	derivative	exhaustive	indict	peripheral
astute	despondent	exhilarating	indifferent	perpetuate
attribute (V)	detached	exonerate	indiscriminate	pervasive
augment	deterrent	expedient	induce	pessimism
austere	detrimental	expedite	inert	phenomena
authoritarian	devious	explicit	ingenious	philanthropist
autonomous	devise	exploit (V)	inherent	piety
aversion	diffuse	extol	innate	placate
belie	digression	extraneous	innocuous	ponderous
benevolent	diligence	extricate	innovation	pragmatic
bolster	diminution	exuberance	insipid	preclude
braggart	discerning	facilitate	instigate	precocious
brevity	disclose	fallacious	insularity	predator
cajole	discordant	fanaticism	integrity	predecessor
calculated	discount (V)	fastidious	intervene	presumptuous
candor	discrepancy	feasible	intimidate	pretentious
capricious	discriminating	fervor	intrepid	prevalent
censorious	disdain	flagrant	inundate	prodigal

profane	refute	rigor	submissive	transient
profound	relegate	robust	subordinate (ADJ)	trite
profusion	remorse	sage	subside	turbulence
proliferation	renounce	sanction (V)	substantiate	turmoil
prolific	repel	satirical	succinct	undermine
provincial	reprehensible	saturate	superficial	uniformity
proximity	reprimand	scanty	superfluous	unwarranted
prudent	reprove	scrupulous	surpass	usurp
qualified	repudiate	scrutinize	surreptitious	vacillate
quandary	reserve (N)	seclusion	susceptible	venerate
ramble	resigned	servile	sustain	verbose
rancor	resolution	skeptic	sycophant	vigor
ratify	resolve (N)	sluggish	taciturn	vilify
rebuttal	restraint	somber	temper (V)	vindicate
recluse	reticence	sporadic	tentative	virtuoso
recount	retract	squander	terse	volatile
rectify	reverent	stagnant	thrive	whimsical
redundant	rhetorical	static (ADJ)	tranquillity	zealot

The SAT Hot Prospects Word List

abate	complementary	fathom (V)	mirth	replete
accolade	confluence	fell (V)	misanthrope	repugnant
acquiesce	conjecture	fitful	misnomer	rescind
acrid	converge	florid	mollify	respite
acrimony	corrode	foolhardy	mosaic	resplendent
aggregate (V)	corrugated	glacial	munificent	savory
amorphous	culpable	hackneyed	nefarious	sedentary
anachronistic	debilitate	hyperbole	nuance	soporific
anomaly	debunk	iconoclastic	obdurate	spurious
antediluvian	dehydrate	ignominy	odious	spurn
antipathy	deleterious	illicit	ornate	steadfast
apocryphal	depose	impecunious	pariah	stolid
arable	desiccate	impregnable	parody	strident
ardent	diffidence	incidental	parsimony	stupefy
assiduous	dilatory	incontrovertible	paucity	supplant
assuage	discourse	indefatigable	penury	surfeit
atrophy	discrepancy	indolent	perfunctory	swagger
audacious	disquiet	ineffable	pernicious	tantamount
avarice	distend	inexorable	pitfall	tenacity
avert	dupe	insolvent	pithy	terrestrial
beguile	ebullient	insuperable	polemical	threadbare
bequeath	edify	intractable	prattle	tirade
bleak	efface	irreproachable	precarious	torpor
blighted	effervesce	jocular	profligate (ADJ)	trepidation
bombastic	elegy	labyrinth	quagmire	trifling
buttress	elicit	laconic	quell	truncate
cacophonous	elucidate	laggard	querulous	unkempt
carping	emaciated	lampoon	quiescent	unprecedented
certitude	emend	lassitude	rant	vaporize
charlatan	equanimity	lithe	rarefy	viable
circumlocution	equitable	lurid	raucous	virulent
cliché	evanescent	luxuriant	ravenous	voluble
coalesce	excerpt	meander	raze	witticism
colloquial	fallow	mercenary (ADJ)	recant	
combustible	falter	mercurial	remission	

The 3,500 Basic Word List

The 3,500 Basic Word List begins on the following page. *Do not let this list overwhelm you.* You do not need to memorize every word.

You can use this list as a sort of dictionary. When you come across an unfamiliar word in your reading and can't figure out its meaning from the context, look it up in the word list. The illustrative sentence may help make the word's meaning clear.

For each word, the following is provided:
1. The word (printed in heavy type).
2. Its part of speech (abbreviated).
3. A brief definition.
4. A sentence illustrating the word's use.
5. Whenever appropriate, related words are provided, together with their parts of speech.

The word lists are arranged in strict alphabetical order. In each word list, High-Frequency words are marked with a square bullet (■), Hot Prospects with a round one (●).

You can also use this list as a study tool if you concentrate on the High-Frequency and Hot Prospects words.

Master the words on the High-Frequency and Hot Prospects Word Lists. First, check off those words you think you know. Then, look up all the words and their definitions in the Basic Word List. Pay particular attention to the words you thought you knew. See whether any of them are defined in an unexpected way. If they are, make a special note of them. As you know from the preceding chapters, the SAT often stumps students with questions based on unfamiliar meanings of familiar-looking words.

A PLAN FOR MASTERING THE *ENTIRE* LIST

1. Allot a definite time each day for the study of a list.

2. Devote at least one hour to each list.

3. First go through the list looking at the flagged High-Frequency and Hot Prospects words and the short, simple-looking words (7 letters at most). Mark those you don't know. In studying, pay particular attention to them.

4. Go through the list again looking at the longer words. Pay particular attention to words with more than one meaning and familiar-looking words that have unusual definitions that come as a surprise to you. Study these secondary definitions.

5. List unusual words on index cards that you can shuffle and review from time to time, along with the flash cards in this book.

6. Use the illustrative sentences in the list as models and make up new sentences of your own.

Basic Word List

Word List 1   abase–adroit

abase v. lower; humiliate. Defeated, Queen Zenobia was forced to *abase* herself before the conquering Romans, who made her march in chains before the emperor in the procession celebrating his triumph. abasement, N.

abash v. embarrass. He was not at all *abashed* by her open admiration.

● **abate** v. subside; decrease, lessen. Rather than leaving immediately, they waited for the storm to *abate*. abatement, N.

abbreviate v. shorten. Because we were running out of time, the lecturer had to *abbreviate* her speech.

abdicate v. renounce; give up. When Edward VIII *abdicated* the British throne to marry the woman he loved, he surprised the entire world.

abduction N. kidnapping. The movie *Ransom* describes the attempts to rescue a multimillionaire's son after the child's *abduction* by kidnappers. abduct, v.

aberrant N. abnormal or deviant. Given the *aberrant* nature of the data, we doubted the validity of the entire experiment. also N.

abet v. aid, usually in doing something wrong; encourage. She was unwilling to *abet* him in the swindle he had planned.

abhor v. detest; hate. She *abhorred* all forms of bigotry. abhorrence, N.

abject ADJ. wretched; lacking pride. On the streets of New York the homeless live in *abject* poverty, huddling in doorways to find shelter from the wind.

abjure v. renounce upon oath. He *abjured* his allegiance to the king. abjuration, N.

abnegation N. repudiation; self-sacrifice. Though Rudolph and Duchess Flavia loved one another, their love was doomed, for she had to marry the king; their act of *abnegation* was necessary to preserve the kingdom.

abolish v. cancel; put an end to. The president of the college refused to *abolish* the physical education requirement. abolition, N.

abominable ADJ. detestable; extremely unpleasant; very bad. Mary liked John until she learned he was dating Susan; then she called him an *abominable* young man, with *abominable* taste in women.

aboriginal ADJ., N. being the first of its kind in a region; primitive; native. Her studies of the primitive art forms of the *aboriginal* Indians were widely reported in the scientific journals. aborigines, N.

abortive ADJ. unsuccessful; fruitless. Attacked by armed troops, the Chinese students had to abandon their *abortive* attempt to democratize Beijing peacefully. abort, v.

abrade v. wear away by friction; scrape; erode. Because the sharp rocks had *abraded* the skin on her legs, she dabbed iodine on the scrapes and *abrasions*.

abrasive ADJ. rubbing away; tending to grind down. Just as *abrasive* cleaning powders can wear away a shiny finish, *abrasive* remarks can wear away a listener's patience. abrade, v.

■ **abridge** v. condense or shorten. Because the publishers felt the public wanted a shorter version of *War and Peace*, they proceeded to *abridge* the novel.

abscond v. depart secretly and hide. The teller who *absconded* with the bonds went uncaptured until someone recognized him from his photograph on "America's Most Wanted."

absolute ADJ. complete; totally unlimited; certain. Although the King of Siam was an *absolute* monarch, he did not want to behead his unfaithful wife without *absolute* evidence of her infidelity.

absolve v. pardon (an offense). The father confessor *absolved* him of his sins. absolution, N.

absorb v. assimilate or incorporate; suck or drink up; wholly engage. During the nineteenth century, America *absorbed* hordes of immigrants, turning them into productive citizens. Can Huggies diapers *absorb* more liquid than Pampers can? This question does not *absorb* me; instead, it bores me. absorption, N.

abstain v. refrain; hold oneself back voluntarily from an action or practice. After considering the effect of alcohol on his athletic performance, he decided to *abstain* from drinking while he trained for the race. abstinence, N.

■ **abstemious** ADJ. sparing in eating and drinking; temperate. Concerned whether her vegetarian son's *abstemious* diet provided him with sufficient protein, the worried mother pressed food on him.

abstinence N. restraint from eating or drinking. The doctor recommended total *abstinence* from salted foods. abstain, v.

■ **abstract** ADJ. theoretical; not concrete; nonrepresentational. To him, hunger was an *abstract* concept; he had never missed a meal.

■ **abstruse** ADJ. obscure; profound; difficult to understand. Baffled by the *abstruse* philosophical texts assigned in class, Dave asked Lexy to explain Kant's *Critique of Pure Reason*.

abundant ADJ. plentiful; possessing riches or resources. At his immigration interview, Ivan listed his *abundant* reasons for coming to America: the hope of religious freedom, the prospect of employment, the promise of a more *abundant* life.

abusive ADJ. coarsely insulting; physically harmful. An *abusive* parent damages a child both mentally and physically.

abut V. border upon; adjoin. Where our estates *abut,* we must build a fence.

abysmal ADJ. bottomless. His arrogance is exceeded only by his *abysmal* ignorance.

abyss N. enormous chasm; vast bottomless pit. Darth Vader seized the evil emperor and hurled him down into the *abyss*.

academic ADJ. related to a school; not practical or directly useful. The dean's talk about reforming the college admissions system was only an *academic* discussion: we knew little, if anything, would change.

accede V. agree. If I *accede* to this demand for blackmail, I am afraid that I will be the victim of future demands.

accelerate V. move faster. In our science class, we learn how falling bodies *accelerate*.

accentuate V. emphasize; stress. If you *accentuate* the positive and eliminate the negative, you may wind up with an overoptimistic view of the world.

■ **accessible** ADJ. easy to approach; obtainable. We asked our guide whether the ruins were *accessible* on foot.

accessory N. additional object; useful but not essential thing. She bought an attractive handbag as an *accessory* for her dress. also ADJ.

■ **acclaim** V. applaud; announce with great approval. The NBC sportscasters *acclaimed* every American victory in the Olympics and decried every American defeat. also N.

acclimate V. adjust to climate. One of the difficulties of our present air age is the need of travelers to *acclimate* themselves to their new and often strange environments.

acclivity N. sharp upslope of a hill. The car would not go up the *acclivity* in high gear.

● **accolade** N. award of merit. In Hollywood, an "Oscar" is the highest *accolade*.

accommodate V. oblige or help someone; adjust or bring into harmony; adapt. Mitch always did everything possible to *accommodate* his elderly relatives, from driving them to medical appointments to helping them with paperwork. (secondary meaning)

accomplice N. partner in crime. Because he had provided the criminal with the lethal weapon, he was arrested as an *accomplice* in the murder.

accord N. agreement. She was in complete *accord* with the verdict.

accost V. approach and speak first to a person. When the two young men *accosted* me, I was frightened because I thought they were going to attack me.

accoutre V. equip. The fisherman was *accoutred* with the best that the sporting goods store could supply. accoutrements, N.

acerbity N. bitterness of speech and temper. The meeting of the United Nations General Assembly was marked with such *acerbity* that informed sources held out little hope of reaching any useful settlement of the problem. acerbic, ADJ.

acetic ADJ. vinegary. The salad had an exceedingly *acetic* flavor.

acidulous ADJ. slightly sour; sharp, caustic. James was unpopular because of his sarcastic and *acidulous* remarks.

■ **acknowledge** V. recognize; admit. Although Iris *acknowledged* that the Beatles' tunes sounded pretty dated nowadays, she still preferred them to the hip-hop songs her brothers played.

acme N. top; pinnacle. His success in this role marked the *acme* of his career as an actor.

acoustics N. science of sound; quality that makes a room easy or hard to hear in. Carnegie Hall is liked by music lovers because of its fine *acoustics*.

● **acquiesce** V. assent; agree without protesting. Although she appeared to *acquiesce* to her employer's suggestions, I could tell she had reservations about the changes he wanted made. acquiescence, N.; acquiescent, ADJ.

acquire V. obtain; get. Frederick Douglass was determined to *acquire* an education despite his master's efforts to prevent his doing so.

acquittal N. deliverance from a charge. His *acquittal* by the jury surprised those who had thought him guilty. acquit, V.

● **acrid** ADJ. sharp; bitterly pungent. The *acrid* odor of burnt gunpowder filled the room after the pistol had been fired.

● **acrimonious** ADJ. bitter in words or manner. The candidate attacked his opponent in highly *acrimonious* terms. acrimony, N.

acrophobia N. fear of heights. A born salesman, he could convince someone with a bad case of *acrophobia* to sign up for a life membership in a sky-diving club.

actuarial ADJ. calculating; pertaining to insurance statistics. According to recent *actuarial* tables, life expectancy is greater today than it was a century ago.

acuity N. sharpness. In time his youthful *acuity* of vision failed him, and he needed glasses.

acumen N. mental keenness. His business *acumen* helped him to succeed where others had failed.

acute ADJ. quickly perceptive; keen; brief and severe. The *acute* young doctor realized immediately that the gradual deterioration of her patient's once *acute* hearing was due to a chronic illness, not an *acute* one.

adage N. wise saying; proverb. There is much truth in the old *adage* about fools and their money.

adamant ADJ. hard; inflexible. Bronson played the part of a revenge-driven man, *adamant* in his determination to punish the criminals who destroyed his family. adamancy, N.

adapt V. alter; modify. Some species of animals have become extinct because they could not *adapt* to a changing environment.

addiction N. compulsive, habitual need. His *addiction* to drugs caused his friends much grief.

addle V. muddle; drive crazy; become rotten. This idiotic plan is confusing enough to *addle* anyone. addled, ADJ.

address V. direct a speech to; deal with or discuss. Due to *address* the convention in July, Brown planned to *address* the issue of low-income housing in his speech.

adept ADJ. expert at. She was *adept* at the fine art of irritating people. also N.

adhere V. stick fast. I will *adhere* to this opinion until proof that I am wrong is presented. adhesion, N.

adherent N. supporter; follower. In the wake of the scandal, the senator's one-time *adherents* quickly deserted him.

adjacent ADJ. adjoining; neighboring; close by. Philip's best friend Jason lived only four houses down the block, close but not immediately *adjacent*.

adjunct N. something added on or attached (generally nonessential or inferior). Although I don't absolutely need a second computer, I plan to buy a laptop to serve as an *adjunct* to my desktop model.

admonition N. warning. After the student protesters repeatedly rejected the dean's *admonitions*, the administration issued an ultimatum: either the students would end the demonstration at once or the campus police would arrest the demonstrators. admonish, V.

adorn V. decorate. Wall paintings and carved statues *adorned* the temple. adornment, N.

adroit ADJ. skillful. His *adroit* handling of the delicate situation pleased his employers.

Word List 2   adulation–amend

■ **adulation** N. flattery; admiration. The rock star thrived on the *adulation* of his groupies and yes men. adulate, V.

adulterate V. make impure by adding inferior or tainted substances. It is a crime to *adulterate* foods without informing the buyer; when consumers learned that Beech-Nut had *adulterated* their apple juice by mixing it with water, they protested vigorously.

advent N. arrival. Most Americans were unaware of the *advent* of the Nuclear Age until the news of Hiroshima reached them.

■ **adversary** N. opponent. The young wrestler struggled to defeat his *adversary*.

adverse ADJ. unfavorable; hostile. The recession had a highly *adverse* effect on Father's investment portfolio: he lost so much money that he could no longer afford the butler and the upstairs maid. adversity, N.

■ **adversity** N. unfavorable fortune; hardship; a calamitous event. According to the humorist Mark Twain, anyone can easily learn to endure *adversity*, as long as it is another man's.

advocacy N. support; active pleading on something's behalf. No threats could dissuade Bishop Desmond Tutu from his *advocacy* of the human rights of black South Africans.

■ **advocate** V. urge; plead for. The abolitionists *advocated* freedom for the slaves. also N.

aerie N. nest of a large bird of prey (eagle, hawk). The mother eagle swooped down on the unwitting rabbit and bore it off to her *aerie* high in the Rocky Mountains.

■ **aesthetic** ADJ. artistic; dealing with or capable of appreciation of the beautiful. The beauty of Tiffany's stained glass appealed to Esther's *aesthetic* sense. aesthete, N.

■ **affable** ADJ. easily approachable; warmly friendly. Accustomed to cold, aloof supervisors, Nicholas was amazed at how *affable* his new employer was.

affected ADJ. artificial; pretended; assumed in order to impress. His *affected* mannerisms—his "Harvard" accent, air of boredom, use of obscure foreign words—annoyed us: he acted as if he thought he was too good for his old high school friends. affectation, N.

affidavit N. written statement made under oath. The court refused to accept his statement unless he presented it in the form of an *affidavit*.

affinity N. kinship. She felt an *affinity* with all who suffered; their pains were her pains.

■ **affirmation** N. positive assertion; confirmation; solemn pledge by one who refuses to take an oath. Despite Tom's *affirmations* of innocence, Aunt Polly still suspected he had eaten the pie.

affix V. fasten; attach; add on. First the registrar had to *affix* her signature to the license; then she had to *affix* her official seal.

affliction N. state of distress; cause of suffering. Even in the midst of her *affliction*, Elizabeth tried to keep up the spirits of those around her.

affluence N. abundance; wealth. Foreigners are amazed by the *affluence* and luxury of the American way of life.

affront N. insult; offense; intentional act of disrespect. When Mrs. Proudie was not seated beside the Archdeacon at the head table, she took it as a personal *affront* and refused to speak to her hosts for a week. also V.

aftermath N. consequences; outcome; upshot. People around the world wondered what the *aftermath* of China's violent suppression of the student protests would be.

agenda N. items of business at a meeting. We had so much difficulty agreeing upon an *agenda* that there was very little time for the meeting.

agent N. means or instrument; personal representative; person acting in an official capacity. "I will be the *agent* of America's destruction," proclaimed the beady-eyed villain, whose *agent* had gotten him the role. With his face, he could never have played the part of the hero, a heroic F.B.I. *agent*.

aggrandize V. increase or intensify. The history of the past quarter century illustrates how a President may *aggrandize* his power to act aggressively in international affairs without considering the wishes of Congress.

● **aggregate** V. gather; accumulate. Before the Wall Street scandals, dealers in so-called junk bonds managed to *aggregate* great wealth in short periods of time. aggregation, N.

aggressor N. attacker. Before you punish both boys for fighting, see whether you can determine which one was the *aggressor*.

aghast ADJ. horrified. He was *aghast* at the nerve of the speaker who had insulted his host.

agility N. nimbleness. The *agility* of the acrobat amazed and thrilled the audience.

agitate V. stir up; disturb. Her fiery remarks *agitated* the already angry mob.

agnostic N. one who is skeptical of the existence or knowability of a god or any ultimate reality. *Agnostics* say we can neither prove nor disprove the existence of god; we simply just can't know. also ADJ.

alacrity N. cheerful promptness. Eager to get away to the mountains, Phil and Dave packed up their ski gear and climbed into the van with *alacrity*.

alchemy N. medieval chemistry. The changing of baser metals into gold was the goal of the students of *alchemy*. alchemist, N.

alcove N. nook; small, recessed section of a room. Though their apartment lacked a full-scale dining room, an *alcove* adjacent to the living room made an adequate breakfast nook for the young couple.

alias N. an assumed name. John Smith's *alias* was Bob Jones. also ADV.

alienate V. make hostile; separate. Her attempts to *alienate* the two friends failed because they had complete faith in each other.

alimentary ADJ. supplying nourishment. The *alimentary* canal in our bodies is so named because digestion of foods occurs there. When asked for the name of the digestive tract, Sherlock Holmes replied, "*Alimentary*, my dear Watson."

alimony N. payments made to an ex-spouse after divorce. Because Tony had supported Tina through medical school, on their divorce he asked the court to award him $500 a month in *alimony*.

allay V. calm; pacify. The crew tried to *allay* the fears of the passengers by announcing that the fire had been controlled.

allege V. state without proof. Although it is *alleged* that she has worked for the enemy, she denies the *allegation* and, legally, we can take no action against her without proof. allegation, N.

allegiance N. loyalty. Not even a term in prison could shake Lech Walesa's *allegiance* to Solidarity, the Polish trade union he had helped to found.

allegory N. story in which characters are used as symbols; fable. *Pilgrim's Progress* is an *allegory* of the temptations and victories of man's soul. allegorical, ADJ.

■ **alleviate** V. relieve. This should *alleviate* the pain; if it does not, we shall have to use stronger drugs.

alliteration N. repetition of beginning sound in poetry. "The furrow followed free" is an example of *alliteration*.

allocate V. assign. Even though the Red Cross had *allocated* a large sum for the relief of the sufferers of the disaster, many people perished.

alloy N. a mixture as of metals. *Alloys* of gold are used more frequently than the pure metal.

alloy V. mix; make less pure; lessen or moderate. Our delight at the Yankees' victory was *alloyed* by our concern for Dwight Gooden, who injured his pitching arm in the game.

allude V. refer indirectly. Try not to mention divorce in Jack's presence because he will think you are *alluding* to his marital problems with Jill.

allure V. entice; attract. *Allured* by the song of the sirens, the helmsman steered the ship toward the reef. also N.

allusion N. indirect reference. When Amanda said to the ticket scalper, "One hundred bucks? What do you want, a pound of flesh?," she was making an *allusion* to Shakespeare's *Merchant of Venice*.

aloft ADV. upward. The sailor climbed *aloft* into the rigging. To get into a loft bed, you have to climb *aloft*.

■ **aloof** ADJ. apart; reserved. Shy by nature, she remained *aloof* while all the rest conversed.

altercation N. noisy quarrel; heated dispute. In that hot-tempered household, no meal ever came to a peaceful conclusion; the inevitable *altercation* might even end in blows.

■ **altruistic** ADJ. unselfishly generous; concerned for others. In providing tutorial assistance and college scholarships for hundreds of economically disadvantaged youths, Eugene Lang performed a truly *altruistic* deed. altruism, N.

amalgamate V. combine; unite in one body. The unions will attempt to *amalgamate* their groups into one national body.

amass V. collect. The miser's aim is to *amass* and hoard as much gold as possible.

ambidextrous ADJ. capable of using either hand with equal ease. A switch-hitter in baseball should be naturally *ambidextrous*.

ambience N. environment; atmosphere. She went to the restaurant not for the food but for the *ambience*.

■ **ambiguous** ADJ. unclear or doubtful in meaning. His *ambiguous* instructions misled us; we did not know which road to take. ambiguity, N.

■ **ambivalence** N. the state of having contradictory or conflicting emotional attitudes. Torn between loving her parents one minute and hating them the next, she was confused by the *ambivalence* of her feelings. ambivalent, ADJ.

amble N. moving at an easy pace. When she first mounted the horse, she was afraid to urge the animal to go faster than a gentle *amble*. also V.

ambulatory ADJ. able to walk; not bedridden. Juan was a highly *ambulatory* patient; not only did he refuse to be confined to bed, but he insisted on riding his skateboard up and down the halls.

ameliorate V. improve. Many social workers have attempted to *ameliorate* the conditions of people living in the slums.

amenable ADJ. readily managed; willing to be led. Although the ambassador was usually *amenable* to friendly suggestions, he balked when we hinted that he should waive his diplomatic immunity and pay his parking tickets.

amend V. correct; change, generally for the better. Hoping to *amend* his condition, he left Vietnam for the United States.

Word List 3   amenities–apostate

amenities N. convenient features; courtesies. In addition to the customary *amenities* for the business traveler—fax machines, modems, a health club—the hotel offers the services of a butler versed in the social *amenities*.

amiable ADJ. agreeable; lovable; warmly friendly. In *Little Women*, Beth is the *amiable* daughter whose loving disposition endears her to all who know her.

amicable ADJ. politely friendly; not quarrelsome. Beth's sister Jo is the hot-tempered tomboy who has a hard time maintaining *amicable* relations with those around her. Jo's quarrel with her friend Laurie finally reaches an *amicable* settlement, but not because Jo turns amiable overnight.

amiss ADJ. wrong; faulty. Seeing her frown, he wondered if anything were *amiss*. also ADV.

amity N. friendship. Student exchange programs such as the Experiment in International Living were established to promote international *amity*.

amnesia N. loss of memory. Because she was suffering from *amnesia*, the police could not get the young girl to identify herself.

amnesty N. pardon. When his first child was born, the king granted *amnesty* to all in prison.

amoral ADJ. nonmoral. The *amoral* individual lacks a code of ethics; he cannot tell right from wrong. The immoral person can tell right from wrong; he chooses to do something he knows is wrong.

amorous ADJ. moved by sexual love; loving. "Love them and leave them" was the motto of the *amorous* Don Juan.

● **amorphous** ADJ. formless; lacking shape or definition. As soon as we have decided on our itinerary, we shall send you a copy; right now, our plans are still *amorphous*.

amphibian ADJ. able to live both on land and in water. Frogs are classified as *amphibian*. also N.

amphitheater N. oval building with tiers of seats. The spectators in the *amphitheater* cheered the gladiators.

ample ADJ. abundant. Bond had *ample* opportunity to escape. Why did he let us catch him?

amplify V. broaden or clarify by expanding; intensify; make stronger. Charlie Brown tried to *amplify* his remarks, but he was drowned out by jeers from the audience. Lucy was smarter: she used a loudspeaker to *amplify* her voice.

amputate V. cut off part of body; prune. Though the doctors had to *amputate* his leg to prevent the spread of cancer, the young athlete refused to let the loss of a limb keep him from participating in sports.

● **anachronistic** ADJ. having an error involving time in a story. The reference to clocks in *Julius Caesar* is *anachronistic*: clocks did not exist in Caesar's time. anachronism, N.

■ **analogous** ADJ. comparable. She called our attention to the things that had been done in an *analogous* situation and recommended that we do the same.

analogy N. similarity; parallelism. A well-known *analogy* compares the body's immune system with an army whose defending troops are the lymphocytes or white blood cells.

■ **anarchist** N. person who seeks to overturn the established government; advocate of abolishing authority. Denying she was an *anarchist*, Katya maintained she wished only to make changes in our government, not to destroy it entirely. anarchy, N.

anathema N. solemn curse; someone or something regarded as a curse. The Ayatolla Khomeini heaped *anathema* upon "the Great Satan," that is, the United States. To the Ayatolla, America and the West were *anathema*; he loathed the democratic nations, cursing them in his dying words. anathematize, V.

ancestry N. family descent. David can trace his *ancestry* as far back as the seventeenth century, when one of his *ancestors* was a court trumpeter somewhere in Germany. ancestral, ADJ.

anchor V. secure or fasten firmly; be fixed in place. We set the post in concrete to *anchor* it in place. anchorage, N.

■ **anecdote** N. short account of an amusing or interesting event. Rather than make concrete proposals for welfare reform, President Reagan told *anecdotes* about poor people who became wealthy despite their impoverished backgrounds.

anemia N. condition in which blood lacks red corpuscles. The doctor ascribes her tiredness to *anemia*. anemic, ADJ.

anesthetic N. substance that removes sensation with or without loss of consciousness. His monotonous voice acted like an *anesthetic*; his audience was soon asleep. anesthesia, N.

anguish N. acute pain; extreme suffering. Visiting the site of the explosion, the governor wept to see the *anguish* of the victims and their families.

angular ADJ. sharp-cornered; stiff in manner. Mr. Spock's features, though *angular*, were curiously attractive, in a Vulcan way.

animated ADJ. lively; spirited. Jim Carrey's facial expressions are highly *animated*: when he played Ace Ventura, he looked practically rubber-faced.

■ **animosity** N. active enmity. He incurred the *animosity* of the ruling class because he advocated limitations of their power.

animus N. hostile feeling or intent. The speaker's sarcastic comments about liberal do-gooders and elitist snobs revealed his deep-seated *animus* against his opponent.

annals N. records; history. "In this year our good King Richard died," wrote the chronicler in the kingdom's *annals*.

annex V. attach; take possession of. Mexico objected to the United States' attempts to *annex* the territory that later became the state of Texas.

annihilate V. destroy. The enemy in its revenge tried to *annihilate* the entire population.

annotate V. comment; make explanatory notes. In explanatory notes following each poem, the editor carefully *annotated* the poet's more esoteric references.

annul V. make void. The parents of the eloped couple tried to *annul* the marriage.

anoint V. consecrate. The prophet Samuel *anointed* David with oil, crowning him king of Israel.

anomalous ADJ. abnormal; irregular. He was placed in the *anomalous* position of seeming to approve procedures which he despised.

● **anomaly** N. irregularity. A bird that cannot fly is an *anomaly*.

anonymity N. state of being nameless; anonymousness. The donor of the gift asked the college not to mention him by name; the dean readily agreed to respect his *anonymity*.

anonymous ADJ. having no name. She tried to ascertain the identity of the writer of the *anonymous* letter.

■ **antagonism** N. hostility; active resistance. Barry showed his *antagonism* toward his new stepmother by ignoring her whenever she tried talking to him. antagonistic, ADJ.

antecede V. precede. The invention of the radiotelegraph *anteceded* the development of television by a quarter of a century.

antecedents N. preceding events or circumstances that influence what comes later; ancestors or early background. Susi Bechhofer's ignorance of her Jewish background had its *antecedents* in the chaos of World War II. Smuggled out of Germany and adopted by a Christian family, she knew nothing of her birth and *antecedents* until she was reunited with her family in 1989.

● **antediluvian** ADJ. antiquated; extremely ancient. Looking at his great-aunt's antique furniture, which must have been cluttering up her attic since the time of Noah's flood, the young heir exclaimed, "Heavens! How positively *antediluvian*!"

anthem N. song of praise or patriotism. Let us now all join in singing the national *anthem*.

anthology N. book of literary selections by various authors. This *anthology* of science fiction was compiled by the late Isaac Asimov. anthologize, V.

anthropocentric ADJ. regarding human beings as the center of the universe. Without considering any evidence that might challenge his *anthropocentric* viewpoint, Hector categorically maintained that dolphins could not be as intelligent as men. anthropocentrism, N.

anthropoid ADJ. manlike. The gorilla is the strongest of the *anthropoid* animals. also N.

anthropologist N. a student of the history and science of mankind. *Anthropologists* have discovered several relics of prehistoric man in this area.

anticlimax N. letdown in thought or emotion. After the fine performance in the first act, the rest of the play was an *anticlimax*. anticlimactic, ADJ.

■ **antidote** N. medicine to counteract a poison or disease. When Marge's child accidentally swallowed some cleaning fluid, the local poison control hotline instructed Marge how to administer the *antidote*.

● **antipathy** N. aversion; dislike. Tom's extreme *antipathy* for disputes keeps him from getting into arguments with his temperamental wife. Noise in any form is *antipathetic* to him. Among his other *antipathies* are honking cars, boom boxes, and heavy metal rock.

■ **antiquated** ADJ. old-fashioned; obsolete. Philip had grown so accustomed to editing his papers on word processors that he thought typewriters were too *antiquated* for him to use.

antiseptic N. substance that prevents infection. It is advisable to apply an *antiseptic* to any wound, no matter how slight or insignificant. also ADJ.

antithesis N. contrast; direct opposite of or to. This tyranny was the *antithesis* of all that he had hoped for, and he fought it with all his strength.

■ **apathy** N. lack of caring; indifference. A firm believer in democratic government, she could not understand the *apathy* of people who never bothered to vote. apathetic, ADJ.

ape V. imitate or mimic. He was suspended for a week because he had *aped* the principal in front of the whole school.

apex N. tip; summit; climax. At the *apex* of his career, the star was deluged with offers of leading roles; two years later, he was reduced to acting in mouthwash ads.

aphorism N. pithy maxim. An *aphorism* differs from an adage in that it is more philosophical or scientific. "The proper study of mankind is man" is an *aphorism*. "There's no smoke without a fire" is an adage. aphoristic, ADJ.

aplomb N. poise; assurance. Gwen's *aplomb* in handling potentially embarrassing moments was legendary around the office; when one of her clients broke a piece of her best crystal, she coolly picked up her own goblet and hurled it into the fireplace.

apocalyptic ADJ. prophetic; pertaining to revelations. The crowd jeered at the street preacher's *apocalyptic* predictions of doom. The *Apocalypse* or *Book of Revelations* of Saint John prophesies the end of the world as we know it and foretells marvels and prodigies that signal the coming doom.

● **apocryphal** ADJ. untrue; made up. To impress his friends, Tom invented *apocryphal* tales of his adventures in the big city.

apolitical ADJ. having an aversion or lack of concern for political affairs. It was hard to remain *apolitical* during the Vietnam War; even people who generally ignored public issues felt they had to take political stands.

apologist N. one who writes in defense of a cause or institution. Rather than act as an *apologist* for the current regime in Beijing and defend its brutal actions, the young diplomat decided to defect to the West.

apostate N. one who abandons his religious faith or political beliefs. Because he switched from one party to another, his former friends shunned him as an *apostate*. apostasy, N.

Word List 4   apotheosis–assurance

apotheosis N. elevation to godhood; an ideal example of something. The *apotheosis* of a Roman emperor was designed to insure his eternal greatness: people would worship at his altar forever. The hero of the musical *How to Succeed in Business…was* the *apotheosis* of yuppieness: he was the perfect upwardly-bound young man on the make.

appall V. dismay; shock. We were *appalled* by the horrifying conditions in the city's jails.

apparatus N. equipment. Firefighters use specialized *apparatus* to fight fires.

apparition N. ghost; phantom. On the castle battlements, an *apparition* materialized and spoke to Hamlet, warning him of his uncle's treachery. In *Ghostbusters*, hordes of *apparitions* materialized, only to be dematerialized by the specialized apparatus wielded by Bill Murray.

■ **appease** V. pacify or soothe; relieve. Tom and Jody tried to *appease* the crying baby by offering him one toy after another, but he would not calm down until they *appeased* his hunger by giving him a bottle.

appellation N. name; title. Macbeth was startled when the witches greeted him with an incorrect *appellation*. Why did they call him Thane of Cawdor, he wondered, when the holder of that title still lived?

append V. attach. When you *append* a bibliography to a text, you have just created an *appendix.*

application N. diligent attention. Pleased with how well Tom had whitewashed the fence, Aunt Polly praised him for his *application* to the task. apply, V. (secondary meaning)

apposite ADJ. appropriate; fitting. He was always able to find the *apposite* phrase, the correct expression for every occasion.

appraise V. estimate value of. It is difficult to *appraise* the value of old paintings; it is easier to call them priceless. appraisal, N.

appreciate V. be thankful for; increase in worth; be thoroughly conscious of. Little Orphan Annie truly *appreciated* the stocks Daddy Warbucks gave her, which *appreciated* in value considerably over the years.

apprehend V. arrest (a criminal); dread; perceive. The police will *apprehend* the culprit and convict him before long.

■ **apprehension** N. fear. His nervous glances at the passersby on the deserted street revealed his *apprehension.*

apprenticeship N. time spent as a novice learning a trade from a skilled worker. As a child, Pip had thought it would be wonderful to work as Joe's *apprentice*; now he hated his *apprenticeship* and scorned the blacksmith's trade.

apprise V. inform. When he was *apprised* of the dangerous weather conditions, he decided to postpone his trip.

approbation N. approval. She looked for some sign of *approbation* from her parents, hoping her good grades would please them.

appropriate V. acquire; take possession of for one's own use. The ranch owners *appropriated* the lands that had originally been set aside for the Indians' use.

apropos PREP. with reference to; regarding. I find your remarks *apropos* of the present situation timely and pertinent. also ADJ. and ADV.

aptitude N. fitness; talent. The counselor gave him an *aptitude* test before advising him about the career he should follow.

aquatic ADJ. pertaining to water. Paul enjoyed *aquatic* sports such as scuba diving and snorkeling.

aquiline ADJ. curved, hooked. Cartoonists exaggerated the senator's *aquiline* nose, curving it until it looked like the beak of an eagle.

● **arable** ADJ. fit for growing crops. The first settlers wrote home glowing reports of the New World, praising its vast acres of *arable* land ready for the plow.

arbiter N. a person with power to decide a dispute; judge. As an *arbiter* in labor disputes, she has won the confidence of the workers and the employers.

■ **arbitrary** ADJ. capricious; randomly chosen; tyrannical. Tom's *arbitrary* dismissal angered him; his boss had no reason to fire him. He threw an *arbitrary* assortment of clothes into his suitcase and headed off, not caring where he went.

arbitrator N. judge. Because the negotiating teams had been unable to reach a contract settlement, an outside *arbitrator* was called upon to mediate the dispute between union and management. arbitration, N.

arcade N. a covered passageway, usually lined with shops. The *arcade* was popular with shoppers because it gave them protection from the summer sun and the winter rain.

arcane ADJ. secret; mysterious; known only to the initiated. Secret brotherhoods surround themselves with *arcane* rituals and trappings to mystify outsiders. So do doctors. Consider the *arcane* terminology they use and the impression they try to give that what is *arcane* to us is obvious to them.

archaeology N. study of artifacts and relics of early mankind. The professor of *archaeology* headed an expedition to the Gobi Desert in search of ancient ruins.

■ **archaic** ADJ. antiquated. "Methinks," "thee," and "thou" are *archaic* words that are no longer part of our normal vocabulary.

archetype N. prototype; primitive pattern. The Brooklyn Bridge was the *archetype* of the many spans that now connect Manhattan with Long Island and New Jersey.

archives N. public records; place where public records are kept. These documents should be part of the *archives* so that historians may be able to evaluate them in the future.

● **ardent** ADJ. intense; passionate; zealous. Katya's *ardor* was contagious; soon all her fellow demonstrators were busily making posters and handing out flyers, inspired by her *ardent* enthusiasm for the cause. ardor, N.

arduous ADJ. hard; strenuous. Her *arduous* efforts had sapped her energy.

aria N. operatic solo. At her Metropolitan Opera audition, Marian Anderson sang an *aria* from *Norma.*

arid ADJ. dry; barren. The cactus has adapted to survive in an *arid* environment.

aristocracy N. hereditary nobility; privileged class. Americans have mixed feelings about hereditary *aristocracy*: we say all men are created equal, but we describe particularly outstanding people as natural *aristocrats*.

aromatic ADJ. fragrant. Medieval sailing vessels brought *aromatic* herbs from China to Europe.

arousal N. awakening; provocation (of a response). On *arousal*, Papa was always grumpy as a bear. The children tiptoed around the house, fearing they would *arouse* his anger by waking him up.

arraign V. charge in court; indict. After his indictment by the Grand Jury, the accused man was *arraigned* in the County Criminal Court.

array V. marshal; draw up in order. His actions were bound to *array* public sentiment against him. also N.

array V. clothe; adorn. She liked to watch her mother *array* herself in her finest clothes before going out for the evening. also N.

arrears N. being in debt. He was in *arrears* with his payments on the car.

arrest V. stop or slow down; catch someone's attention. Slipping, the trapeze artist plunged from the heights until a safety net luckily *arrested* his fall. This near-disaster *arrested* the crowd's attention.

■ **arrogance** N. pride; haughtiness. Convinced that Emma thought she was better than anyone else in the class, Ed rebuked her for her *arrogance*.

arsenal N. storage place for military equipment. People are forbidden to smoke in the *arsenal* for fear that a stray spark might set off the munitions stored there.

■ **articulate** ADJ. effective; distinct. Her *articulate* presentation of the advertising campaign impressed her employers. also V.

■ **artifact** N. object made by human beings, either handmade or mass-produced. Archaeologists debated the significance of the *artifacts* discovered in the ruins of Asia Minor but came to no conclusion about the culture they represented.

artifice N. deception; trickery. The Trojan War proved to the Greeks that cunning and *artifice* were often more effective than military might.

■ **artisan** N. manually skilled worker; craftsman, as opposed to artist. A noted *artisan*, Arturo was known for the fine craftsmanship of his inlaid cabinets.

artless ADJ. without guile; open and honest. Sophisticated and cynical, Jack could not believe Jill was as *artless* and naive as she appeared to be.

■ **ascendancy** N. controlling influence; domination. Leaders of religious cults maintain *ascendancy* over their followers by methods that can verge on brainwashing.

ascertain V. find out for certain. Please *ascertain* her present address.

■ **ascetic** ADJ. practicing self-denial; austere. The wealthy, self-indulgent young man felt oddly drawn to the strict, *ascetic* life led by members of some monastic orders. also N.

ascribe V. refer; attribute; assign. I can *ascribe* no motive for her acts.

aseptic ADJ. preventing infection; having a cleansing effect. Hospitals succeeded in lowering the mortality rate as soon as they introduced *aseptic* conditions.

ashen ADJ. ash-colored. Her face was *ashen* with fear.

asinine ADJ. stupid. "What an *asinine* comment!" said Bob contemptuously. "I've never heard such a stupid remark."

askance ADJ. with a sideways or indirect look. Looking *askance* at her questioner, she displayed her scorn.

askew ADJ. crookedly; slanted; at an angle. Judy constantly straightened the doilies on her furniture: she couldn't stand seeing them *askew*.

asperity N. sharpness (of temper). These remarks, spoken with *asperity*, stung the boys to whom they had been directed.

aspersion N. slander; slur; derogatory remark. Unscrupulous politicians practice character assassination as a political tool, casting *aspersions* on their rivals.

aspirant N. seeker after position or status. Although I am an *aspirant* for public office, I am not willing to accept the dictates of the party bosses. also ADJ.

■ **aspire** V. seek to attain; long for. Because he *aspired* to a career in professional sports, Philip enrolled in a graduate program in sports management. aspiration, N.

assail V. assault. He was *assailed* with questions after his lecture.

assay V. analyze; evaluate. When they *assayed* the ore, they found that they had discovered a very rich vein. also N.

assent V. agree; accept. It gives me great pleasure to *assent* to your request.

assert V. declare or state with confidence; put oneself forward boldly. Malcolm *asserted* that if Reese quit acting like a wimp and *asserted* himself a bit more, he'd improve his chances of getting a date. assertion, N.

assessment N. evaluation; judgment. Your high school record plays an important part in the admission committee's *assessment* of you as an applicant.

● **assiduous** ADJ. diligent. He was *assiduous*, working at this task for weeks before he felt satisfied with his results. assiduity, N.

assimilate V. absorb; cause to become homogeneous. The manner in which the United States was able to *assimilate* the hordes of immigrants during the nineteenth and early twentieth centuries will always be a source of pride to Americans. The immigrants eagerly *assimilated* new ideas and customs; they soaked them up, the way plants soak up water.

● **assuage** V. ease or lessen (pain); satisfy (hunger); soothe (anger). Jilted by Jane, Dick tried to *assuage* his heartache by indulging in ice cream. One gallon later, he had *assuaged* his appetite but not his grief.

assumption   N. something taken for granted; taking over or taking possession of. The young princess made the foolish *assumption* that the regent would not object to her *assumption* of power. assume, V.

assurance   N. promise or pledge; certainty; self-confidence. When Guthrie gave Guinness his *assurance* that rehearsals were going well, he spoke with such *assurance* that Guinness felt relieved. assure, V.

Word List 5   astral–barb

astral   ADJ. relating to the stars. She was amazed at the number of *astral* bodies the new telescope revealed.

astringent   ADJ. binding; causing contraction. The *astringent* quality of the unsweetened lemon juice made swallowing difficult. also N.

astronomical   ADJ. enormously large or extensive. The government seems willing to spend *astronomical* sums on weapons development.

■ **astute**   ADJ. wise; shrewd; keen. John Jacob Astor made *astute* investments in land, shrewdly purchasing valuable plots throughout New York City.

asunder   ADV. into parts; apart. A fierce quarrel split the partnership *asunder*: the two partners finally sundered their connections because their points of view were poles *asunder*.

asylum   N. place of refuge or shelter; protection. The refugees sought *asylum* from religious persecution in a new land.

asymmetric   ADJ. not identical on both sides of a dividing central line. Because one eyebrow was set markedly higher than the other, William's face had a particularly *asymmetric* appearance.

atavism   N. reversion to an earlier type; throwback. In his love for gardening, Martin seemed an *atavism* to his Tuscan forebears, who lavished great care on their small plots of soil.

atheistic   ADJ. denying the existence of God. His *atheistic* remarks shocked the religious worshippers.

atlas   N. a bound volume of maps, charts, or tables. Embarrassed at being unable to distinguish Slovenia from Slovakia, George W. finally consulted an *atlas*.

atone   V. make amends for; pay for. He knew no way in which he could *atone* for his brutal crime.

atrocity   N. brutal deed. In time of war, many *atrocities* are committed by invading armies.

● **atrophy**   V. waste away. After three months in a cast, your calf muscles are bound to *atrophy*; you'll need physical therapy to get back in shape. also N.

attain   V. achieve or accomplish; gain. The scarecrow sought to *attain* one goal: he wished to obtain a brain.

attentive   ADJ. alert and watchful; considerate; thoughtful. Spellbound, the *attentive* audience watched the final game of the tennis match, never taking their eyes from the ball. A cold wind sprang up; Stan's *attentive* daughter slipped a sweater over his shoulders without distracting his attention from the game.

attenuate   V. make thin; weaken. By withdrawing their forces, the generals hoped to *attenuate* the enemy lines.

attest   V. testify, bear witness. Having served as a member of the Grand Jury, I can *attest* that our system of indicting individuals is in need of improvement.

attribute   N. essential quality. His outstanding *attribute* was his kindness.

■ **attribute**   V. ascribe; explain. I *attribute* her success in science to the encouragement she received from her parents.

attrition   N. gradual decrease in numbers; reduction in the work force without firing employees; wearing away of opposition by means of harassment. In the 1960s urban churches suffered from *attrition* as members moved from the cities to the suburbs. Rather than fire staff members, church leaders followed a policy of *attrition*, allowing elderly workers to retire without replacing them.

atypical   ADJ. not normal. The child psychiatrist reassured Mrs. Keaton that playing doctor was not *atypical* behavior for a child of young Alex's age. "Yes," she replied, "but not charging for house calls!"

● **audacious**   ADJ. daring; bold. Audiences cheered as Luke Skywalker and Princess Leia made their *audacious*, death-defying leap to freedom, escaping Darth Vader's troops. audacity, N.

audit   N. examination of accounts. When the bank examiners arrived to hold their annual *audit*, they discovered the embezzlements of the chief cashier. also V.

auditory   ADJ. pertaining to the sense of hearing. Audrey suffered from *auditory* hallucinations: she thought Elvis was speaking to her from the Great Beyond.

■ **augment**   V. increase; add to. Armies *augment* their forces by calling up reinforcements; teachers *augment* their salaries by taking odd jobs.

august   ADJ. impressive; majestic. Visiting the palace at Versailles, she was impressed by the *august* surroundings in which she found herself.

auspicious   ADJ. favoring success. With favorable weather conditions, it was an *auspicious* moment to set sail. Thomas, however, had doubts about sailing: a paranoid, he became suspicious whenever conditions seemed *auspicious*.

■ **austere**   ADJ. forbiddingly stern; severely simple and unornamented. The headmaster's *austere* demeanor tended to scare off the more timid students, who never visited his study willingly. The room reflected the man, *austere* and bare, like a monk's cell, with no touches of luxury to moderate its *austerity*.

authenticate   V. confirm as genuine. After a thorough chemical analysis of the pigments and canvas, the experts were prepared to *authenticate* the painting as an original Rembrandt.

■ **authoritarian** ADJ. subordinating the individual to the state; completely dominating another's will. The leaders of the *authoritarian* regime ordered the suppression of the democratic protest movement. After years of submitting to the will of her *authoritarian* father, Elizabeth Barrett ran away from home with the poet Robert Browning.

authoritative ADJ. having the weight of authority; peremptory and dictatorial. Impressed by the young researcher's well-documented presentation, we accepted her analysis of the experiment as *authoritative*.

autocratic ADJ. having absolute, unchecked power; dictatorial. Someone accustomed to exercising authority may become *autocratic* if his or her power is unchecked. Dictators by definition are *autocrats*. Bosses who dictate behavior as well as letters can be *autocrats* too.

automaton N. robot; person performing a task mechanically. The assembly line job called for no initiative or intelligence on Homer's part; on automatic pilot, he pushed button after button like an *automaton*.

■ **autonomous** ADJ. self-governing. Although the University of California at Berkeley is just one part of the state university system, in many ways Cal Berkeley is *autonomous*, for it runs several programs that are not subject to outside control. autonomy, N.

autopsy N. examination of a dead body; post-mortem. The medical examiner ordered an *autopsy* to determine the cause of death. also V.

auxiliary ADJ. helper, additional or subsidiary. To prepare for the emergency, they built an *auxiliary* power station. also N.

avalanche N. great mass of falling snow and ice. The park ranger warned the skiers to stay on the main trails, where they would be in no danger of being buried beneath a sudden *avalanche*.

● **avarice** N. greediness for wealth. King Midas is a perfect example of *avarice*, for he was so greedy that he wished everything he touched would turn to gold.

avenge V. take vengeance for something (or on behalf of someone). Hamlet vowed he would *avenge* his father's murder and punish Claudius for his horrible crime.

aver V. assert confidently; affirm. Despite overwhelming popular skepticism about his voyage, Columbus *averred* he would succeed in finding a direct sea route to the Far East.

averse ADJ. reluctant; disinclined. The reporter was *averse* to revealing the sources of his information.

■ **aversion** N. firm dislike. Bert had an *aversion* to yuppies; Alex had an *aversion* to punks. Their mutual *aversion* was so great that they refused to speak to one another.

● **avert** V. prevent; turn away. She *averted* her eyes from the dead cat on the highway.

avid ADJ. greedy; eager for. *Avid* for pleasure, Abner partied with great *avidity*. avidity, N.

avocation N. secondary or minor occupation. His hobby proved to be so fascinating and profitable that gradually he abandoned his regular occupation and concentrated on his *avocation*.

avow V. declare openly. Lana *avowed* that she never meant to steal Debbie's boyfriend, but no one believed her *avowal* of innocence.

awe N. solemn wonder. The tourists gazed with *awe* at the tremendous expanse of the Grand Canyon.

awry ADV. crooked; wrong; amiss. Noticing that the groom's tie was slightly *awry*, the bride reached over to set it straight. A careful organizer, she hated to have anything go *awry* with her plans.

axiom N. self-evident truth requiring no proof. Before a student can begin to think along the lines of Euclidean geometry, he must accept certain principles or *axioms*.

azure ADJ. sky blue. *Azure* skies are indicative of good weather.

babble V. chatter idly. The little girl *babbled* about her doll. also N.

badger V. pester; annoy. She was forced to change her telephone number because she was *badgered* by obscene phone calls.

badinage N. teasing conversation. Her friends at work greeted the news of her engagement with cheerful *badinage*.

baffle V. frustrate; perplex. The new code *baffled* the enemy agents.

bait V. harass; tease. The school bully *baited* the smaller children, terrorizing them.

baleful ADJ. deadly; having a malign influence; ominous. The fortune teller made *baleful* predictions of terrible things to come.

balk V. foil or thwart; stop short; refuse to go on. When the warden learned that several inmates were planning to escape, he took steps to *balk* their attempt. However, he *balked* at punishing them by shackling them to the walls of their cells.

ballast N. heavy substance used to add stability or weight. The ship was listing badly to one side; it was necessary to shift the *ballast* in the hold to get her back on an even keel. also V.

balm N. something that relieves pain. Friendship is the finest *balm* for the pangs of disappointed love.

balmy ADJ. mild; fragrant. A *balmy* breeze refreshed us after the sultry blast.

banal ADJ. hackneyed; commonplace; trite; lacking originality. The hack writer's worn-out clichés made his comic sketch seem *banal*. He even resorted to the *banality* of having someone slip on a banana peel!

bandy V. discuss lightly or glibly; exchange (words) heatedly. While the president was happy to *bandy* patriotic generalizations with anyone who would listen to him, he refused to *bandy* words with unfriendly reporters at the press conference.

bane N. cause of ruin; curse. Lucy's little brother was the *bane* of her existence: his attempts to make her life miserable worked so well that she could have poisoned him with ratsbane for having such a *baneful* effect.

bantering ADJ. good-natured ridiculing. They resented his *bantering* remarks because they thought he was being sarcastic.

barb N. sharp projection from fishhook, etc.; openly cutting remark. If you were a politician, which would you prefer, being caught on the *barb* of a fishhook or being subjected to malicious verbal *barbs*? Who can blame the president if he's happier fishing than back in the capitol listening to his critics' *barbed* remarks?

Word List 6   bard–bluff

bard N. poet. The ancient *bard* Homer sang of the fall of Troy.

baroque ADJ. highly ornate. Accustomed to the severe lines of contemporary buildings, the architecture students found the flamboyance of *baroque* architecture amusing. They simply didn't go for *baroque*.

barrage N. barrier laid down by artillery fire. The company was forced to retreat through the *barrage* of heavy cannons.

barren ADJ. desolate; fruitless and unproductive; lacking. Looking out at the trackless, *barren* desert, Indiana Jones feared that his search for the missing expedition would prove *barren*.

barricade N. hastily put together defensive barrier; obstacle. Marius and his fellow students hurriedly improvised a rough *barricade* to block police access to the students' quarter. Malcolm and his brothers *barricaded* themselves in their bedroom to keep their mother from seeing the hole in the bedroom floor. also V.

barterer N. trader. The *barterer* exchanged trinkets for the natives' furs. It seemed smarter to *barter* than to pay cash.

bask V. luxuriate; take pleasure in warmth. *Basking* on the beach, she relaxed so completely that she fell asleep.

bastion N. fortress; defense. The villagers fortified the town hall, hoping this improvised *bastion* could protect them from the guerillas' raids.

bate V. let down; restrain. Until it was time to open the presents, the children had to *bate* their curiosity. bated, ADJ.

bauble N. trinket; trifle. The child was delighted with the *bauble* she had won in the grab bag.

bawdy ADJ. indecent; obscene. Jack took offense at Jill's *bawdy* remarks. What kind of young man did she think he was?

beam N. ray of light; long piece of metal or wood; course of a radio signal. V. smile radiantly. If a *beam* of light falls on you, it illuminates you; if a *beam* of iron falls on you, it eliminates you. (No one feels like *beaming* when crushed by an iron *beam*.)

beatific ADJ. giving bliss; blissful. The *beatific* smile on the child's face made us very happy.

beatitude N. blessedness; state of bliss. Growing closer to God each day, the mystic achieved a state of indescribable *beatitude*.

bedraggle V. wet thoroughly; stain with mud. We were so *bedraggled* by the severe storm that we had to change into dry clothing. bedraggled, ADJ.

beeline N. direct, quick route. As soon as the movie was over, Jim made a *beeline* for the exit.

befuddle V. confuse thoroughly. His attempts to clarify the situation succeeded only in *befuddling* her further.

beget V. father; produce; give rise to. One good turn may deserve another; it does not necessarily *beget* another.

begrudge V. resent. I *begrudge* every minute I have to spend attending meetings; they're a complete waste of time.

● **beguile** V. mislead or delude; pass time. With flattery and big talk of easy money, the con men *beguiled* Kyle into betting his allowance on the shell game. Broke, he *beguiled* himself during the long hours by playing solitaire.

behemoth N. huge creature; monstrous animal. Sportscasters nicknamed the linebacker "The *Behemoth*."

belabor V. explain or go over excessively or to a ridiculous degree; attack verbally. The debate coach warned her student not to bore the audience by *belaboring* her point.

belated ADJ. delayed. He apologized for his *belated* note of condolence to the widow of his friend and explained that he had just learned of her husband's untimely death.

beleaguer V. besiege or attack; harassed. The babysitter was surrounded by a crowd of unmanageable brats who relentlessly *beleaguered* her.

■ **belie** V. contradict; give a false impression. His coarse, hard-bitten exterior *belied* his inner sensitivity.

belittle V. disparage or depreciate; put down. Parents should not *belittle* their children's early attempts at drawing, but should encourage their efforts. Barry was a put-down artist: he was a genius at *belittling* people and making them feel small.

bellicose ADJ. warlike. His *bellicose* disposition alienated his friends.

belligerent ADJ. quarrelsome. Whenever he had too much to drink, he became *belligerent* and tried to pick fights with strangers. belligerence, N.

bemoan V. lament; express disapproval of. The widow *bemoaned* the death of her beloved husband. Although critics *bemoaned* the serious flaws in the author's novels, each year his latest book topped the best-seller list.

bemused ADJ. confused; lost in thought; preoccupied. Jill studied the garbled instructions with a *bemused* look on her face.

benediction N. blessing. The appearance of the sun after the many rainy days was like a *benediction*.

benefactor N. gift giver; patron. Scrooge later became Tiny Tim's *benefactor* and gave him gifts.

beneficial ADJ. helpful; useful. Tiny Tim's cheerful good nature had a *beneficial* influence on Scrooge's once-uncharitable disposition.

beneficiary N. person entitled to benefits or proceeds of an insurance policy or will. In Scrooge's will, he made Tiny Tim his *beneficiary*: everything he left would go to young Tim.

■ **benevolent** ADJ. generous; charitable. Mr. Fezziwig was a *benevolent* employer, who wished to make Christmas merrier for young Scrooge and his other employees.

benign ADJ. kindly; favorable; not malignant. Though her *benign* smile and gentle bearing made Miss Marple seem a sweet little old lady, in reality she was a tough-minded, shrewd observer of human nature. benignity, N.

bent ADJ.; N. determined; natural talent or inclination. *Bent* on advancing in the business world, the secretary-heroine of *Working Girl* has a true *bent* for high finance.

● **bequeath** V. leave to someone by a will; hand down. Though Maud had intended to *bequeath* the family home to her nephew, she died before changing her will. bequest, N.

berate V. scold strongly. He feared she would *berate* him for his forgetfulness.

bereavement N. state of being deprived of something valuable or beloved. His friends gathered to console him upon his sudden *bereavement*.

bereft ADJ. deprived of; lacking; desolate because of a loss. The foolish gambler soon found himself *bereft* of funds.

berserk ADV. frenzied. Angered, he went *berserk* and began to wreck the room.

beseech V. beg; plead with. The workaholic executive's wife *beseeched* him to spend more time with their son.

beset V. harass or trouble; hem in. Many vexing problems *beset* the American public school system. Sleeping Beauty's castle was *beset* on all sides by dense thickets that hid it from view.

besiege V. surround with armed forces; harass (with requests). When the bandits *besieged* the village, the villagers holed up in the town hall and prepared to withstand a long siege. Members of the new administration were *besieged* with job applications from people who had worked on the campaign.

besmirch V. soil, defile. The scandalous remarks in the newspaper *besmirch* the reputations of every member of the society.

bestial ADJ. beastlike; brutal. According to legend, the werewolf was able to abandon its human shape and take on a *bestial* form.

bestow V. give. He wished to *bestow* great honors upon the hero.

betoken V. signify; indicate. The well-equipped docks, tall piles of cargo containers, and numerous vessels being loaded all *betoken* Oakland's importance as a port.

betray V. be unfaithful; reveal (unconsciously or unwillingly). The spy *betrayed* his country by selling military secrets to the enemy. When he was taken in for questioning, the tightness of his lips *betrayed* his fear of being caught.

betroth V. become engaged to marry. The announcement that they had become *betrothed* surprised their friends who had not suspected any romance. betrothal, N.

bevy N. large group. The movie actor was surrounded by a *bevy* of starlets.

biased ADJ. slanted; prejudiced. Because the judge played golf regularly with the district attorney's father, we feared he might be *biased* in the prosecution's favor. bias, N.

bicameral ADJ. two-chambered, as a legislative body. The United States Congress is a *bicameral* body.

bicker V. quarrel. The children *bickered* morning, noon, and night, exasperating their parents.

biennial ADJ. every two years. Seeing no need to meet more frequently, the group held *biennial* meetings instead of annual ones. Plants that bear flowers *biennially* are known as *biennials*.

bigotry N. stubborn intolerance. Brought up in a democratic atmosphere, the student was shocked by the *bigotry* and narrowness expressed by several of his classmates.

bilious ADJ. suffering from indigestion; irritable. His *bilious* temperament was apparent to all who heard him rant about his difficulties.

bilk V. swindle; cheat. The con man specialized in *bilking* insurance companies.

billowing ADJ. swelling out in waves; surging. Standing over the air vent, Marilyn Monroe tried vainly to control her *billowing* skirts.

bizarre ADJ. fantastic; violently contrasting. The plot of the novel was too *bizarre* to be believed.

blanch V. bleach; whiten. Although age had *blanched* his hair, he was still vigorous and energetic.

bland ADJ. soothing or mild; agreeable. Jill tried a *bland* ointment for her sunburn. However, when Jack absent-mindedly patted her on the sunburned shoulder, she couldn't maintain a *bland* disposition.

blandishment N. flattery. Despite the salesperson's *blandishments,* the customer did not buy the outfit.

blare N. loud, harsh roar or screech; dazzling blaze of light. I don't know which is worse: the steady *blare* of a boom box deafening your ears or a sudden *blare* of flashbulbs dazzling your eyes.

blasé ADJ. bored with pleasure or dissipation. Although Beth was as thrilled with the idea of a trip to Paris as her classmates were, she tried to act super cool and *blasé*, as if she'd been abroad hundreds of times.

blasphemy N. irreverence; sacrilege; cursing. In my father's house, the Dodgers were the holiest of holies; to cheer for another team was to utter words of *blasphemy*. blasphemous, ADJ.

blatant ADJ. flagrant; conspicuously obvious; loudly offensive. To the unemployed youth from Dublin, the "No Irish Need Apply" placard in the shop window was a *blatant* mark of prejudice.

● **bleak** ADJ. cold or cheerless; unlikely to be favorable. The frigid, inhospitable Aleutian Islands are *bleak* military outposts. It's no wonder that soldiers assigned there have a *bleak* attitude toward their posting.

● **blighted** ADJ. suffering from a disease; destroyed. The extent of the *blighted* areas could be seen only when viewed from the air.

blithe ADJ. gay; joyous; carefree. Without a care in the world, Beth went her *blithe*, lighthearted way.

bloated ADJ. swollen or puffed as with water or air. Her *bloated* stomach came from drinking so much water.

bludgeon N. club; heavy-headed weapon. Attacked by Dr. Moriarty, Holmes used his walking stick as a *bludgeon* to defend himself. "Watson," he said, "I fear I may have *bludgeoned* Moriarty to death."

bluff ADJ. rough but good-natured. Jack had a *bluff* and hearty manner that belied his actual sensitivity; he never let people know how thin-skinned he really was.

bluff N. pretense (of strength); deception; high cliff. Claire thought Lord Byron's boast that he would swim the Hellespont was just a *bluff;* she was astounded when he dove from the high *bluff* into the waters below. also V.

Word List 7   blunder–canter

blunder N. error. The criminal's fatal *blunder* led to his capture. also V.

blurt V. utter impulsively. Before she could stop him, he *blurted* out the news.

bluster V. blow in heavy gusts; threaten emptily; bully. "Let the stormy winds *bluster*," cried Jack, "we'll set sail tonight." Jill let Jack *bluster*: she wasn't going anywhere, no matter what he said.

bode V. foreshadow; portend. The gloomy skies and the sulphurous odors from the mineral springs seemed to *bode* evil to those who settled in the area.

bogus ADJ. counterfeit; not authentic. The police quickly found the distributors of the *bogus* twenty-dollar bills.

bohemian ADJ. unconventional (in an artistic way). Gertrude Stein ran off to Paris to live an eccentric, *bohemian* life with her writer friends. Oakland was not *bohemian*: it was too bourgeois, too middle-class.

boisterous ADJ. violent; rough; noisy. The unruly crowd became even more *boisterous* when he tried to quiet them.

■ **bolster** V. support; reinforce. The debaters amassed file boxes full of evidence to *bolster* their arguments.

bolt N. door bar; fastening pin or screw; length of fabric. The carpenter shut the workshop door, sliding the heavy metal *bolt* into place. He sorted through his toolbox for the nuts and *bolts* and nails he would need. Before he cut into the *bolt* of canvas, he measured how much fabric he would need.

bolt V. dash or dart off; fasten (a door); gobble down. Jack was set to *bolt* out the front door, but Jill *bolted* the door. "Eat your breakfast," she said, "don't *bolt* your food."

bombardment N. attack with missiles. The enemy *bombardment* demolished the town. Members of the opposition party *bombarded* the prime minister with questions about the enemy attack.

bombastic ADJ. pompous; using inflated language. Puffed up with conceit, the orator spoke in such a *bombastic* manner that we longed to deflate him. bombast, N.

booming ADJ. deep and resonant; flourishing, thriving. "Who needs a microphone?" cried the mayor in his *booming* voice. Cheerfully he *boomed* out that, thanks to him, the city's economy was *booming*. boom, V.

boon N. blessing; benefit. The recent rains that filled our empty reservoirs were a *boon* to the whole community.

boorish ADJ. rude; insensitive. Though Mr. Collins constantly interrupted his wife, she ignored his *boorish* behavior, for she had lost hope of teaching him courtesy.

boundless ADJ. unlimited; vast. Mike's energy was *boundless*: the greater the challenge, the more vigorously he tackled the job.

bountiful ADJ. abundant; graciously generous. Thanks to the good harvest, we had a *bountiful* supply of food and we could be as *bountiful* as we liked in distributing food to the needy.

bourgeois ADJ. middle class; selfishly materialistic; dully conventional. Technically, anyone who belongs to the middle class is *bourgeois*, but, given the word's connotations, most people resent it if you call them that.

bovine ADJ. cowlike; placid and dull. Nothing excites Esther; even when she won the state lottery, she still preserved her air of *bovine* calm.

bowdlerize V. expurgate. After the film editors had *bowdlerized* the language in the script, the motion picture's rating was changed from "R" to "PG."

boycott V. refrain from buying or using. To put pressure on grape growers to stop using pesticides that harmed the farm workers' health, Cesar Chavez called for consumers to *boycott* grapes.

■ **braggart** N. boaster. Modest by nature, she was no *braggart*, preferring to let her accomplishments speak for themselves.

brandish V. wave around; flourish. Alarmed, Doctor Watson wildly *brandished* his gun until Holmes told him to put the thing away before he shot himself.

bravado N. swagger; assumed air of defiance. The *bravado* of the young criminal disappeared when he was confronted by the victims of his brutal attack.

brawn N. muscular strength; sturdiness. It takes *brawn* to become a champion weightlifter. brawny, ADJ.

brazen ADJ. insolent. Her *brazen* contempt for authority angered the officials.

breach N. breaking of contract or duty; fissure or gap. Jill sued Jack for *breach* of promise, claiming he had broken his promise to marry her. They found a *breach* in the enemy's fortifications and penetrated their lines. also V.

breadth N. width; extent. We were impressed by the *breadth* of her knowledge.

■ **brevity** N. conciseness. *Brevity* is essential when you send a telegram or cablegram; you are charged for every word.

bristling ADJ. rising like bristles; showing irritation. The dog stood there, *bristling* with anger.

brittle ADJ. easily broken; difficult. My employer's self-control was as *brittle* as an egg-shell. Her *brittle* personality made it difficult for me to get along with her.

broach V. introduce; open up. Jack did not even try to *broach* the subject of religion with his in-laws. If you *broach* a touchy subject, it may cause a breach.

brochure N. pamphlet. This *brochure* on farming was issued by the Department of Agriculture.

browbeat V. bully; intimidate. Billy resisted Ted's attempts *browbeat* him into handing over his lunch money.

browse V. graze; skim or glance at casually. "How now, brown cow, *browsing* in the green, green grass." I remember lines of verse that I came across while *browsing* through the poetry section of the local bookstore.

brunt N. main impact or shock. Tom Sawyer claimed credit for painting the fence, but the *brunt* of the work fell on others. However, he bore the *brunt* of Aunt Polly's complaints when the paint began to peel.

brusque ADJ. blunt; abrupt. Was Bruce too *brusque* when he brushed off Bob's request with a curt "Not now!"?

buccaneer N. pirate. At Disneyland the Pirates of the Caribbean sing a song about their lives as bloody *buccaneers*.

bucolic ADJ. rustic; pastoral. Filled with browsing cows and bleating sheep, the meadow was a charmingly *bucolic* sight.

buffet N. table with food set out for people to serve themselves; meal at which people help themselves to food that's been set out. Please convey the soufflé on the tray to the *buffet*. (*Buffet* rhymes with tray.)

buffet V. slap; batter; knock about. To *buffet* something is to rough it up. (*Buffet* rhymes with Muffett.) Was Miss Muffett *buffeted* by the crowd on the way to the buffet tray?

buffoonery N. clowning. In the Ace Ventura movies, Jim Carrey's *buffoonery* was hilarious: like Bozo the Clown, he's a natural *buffoon*.

bulwark N. earthwork or other strong defense; person who defends. The navy is our principal *bulwark* against invasion.

bumptious ADJ. self-assertive. His classmates called him a show-off because of his *bumptious* airs.

bungle V. mismanage; blunder. Don't botch this assignment, Bumstead; if you *bungle* the job, you're fired!

buoyant ADJ. able to float; cheerful and optimistic. When the boat capsized, her *buoyant* life jacket kept Jody afloat. Scrambling back on board, she was still in a *buoyant* mood, certain that despite the delay she'd win the race.

bureaucracy N. over-regulated administrative system marked by red tape. The Internal Revenue Service is the ultimate *bureaucracy*: taxpayers wasted so much paper filling out IRS forms that the IRS *bureaucrats* printed up a new set of rules requiring taxpayers to comply with the Paperwork Reduction Act.

burgeon V. grow forth; send out buds. In the spring, the plants that *burgeon* are a promise of the beauty that is to come.

burlesque V. give an imitation that ridicules. In *Spaceballs*, Rick Moranis *burlesques* Darth Vader of *Star Wars*, outrageously parodying Vader's stiff walk and hollow voice.

burly ADJ. husky; muscular. The *burly* mover lifted the packing crate with ease.

burnish V. make shiny by rubbing; polish. The maid *burnished* the brass fixtures until they reflected the lamplight.

bustle V. move about energetically; teem. David and the children *bustled* about the house getting in each other's way as they tried to pack for the camping trip. The whole house *bustled* with activity.

● **buttress** V. support; prop up. The attorney came up with several far-fetched arguments in a vain attempt to *buttress* his weak case. also N.

buxom ADJ. plump; full-bosomed. Fashion models are usually slim and willowy rather than *buxom*.

cabal N. small group of persons secretly united to promote their own interests. The *cabal* was defeated when their scheme was discovered.

cache N. hiding place. The detectives followed the suspect until he led them to the *cache* where he had stored his loot. He had *cached* the cash in a bag for trash: it was a hefty sum.

● **cacophonous** ADJ. discordant; inharmonious. Do the students in the orchestra enjoy the *cacophonous* sounds they make when they're tuning up? I don't know how they can stand the racket. cacophony, N.

cadaver N. corpse. In some states, it is illegal to dissect *cadavers*.

cadence N. rhythmic rise and fall (of words or sounds); beat. Marching down the road, the troops sang out, following the *cadence* set by the sergeant.

■ **cajole** V. coax; wheedle. Diane tried to *cajole* her father into letting her drive the family car. cajolery, N.

calamity N. disaster; misery. As news of the *calamity* spread, offers of relief poured in to the stricken community.

■ **calculated** ADJ. deliberately planned; likely. Lexy's choice of clothes to wear to the debate tournament was carefully *calculated*. Her conventional suit was one *calculated* to appeal to the conservative judges.

caldron N. large kettle. "Why, Mr. Crusoe," said the savage heating the giant *caldron*, "we'd love to have you for dinner!"

caliber N. ability; quality. The scholarship committee searched for students of high *caliber*, ones with the intelligence and ability to be a credit to the school.

calligraphy N. beautiful writing; excellent penmanship. As we examine ancient manuscripts, we become impressed with the *calligraphy* of the scribes.

callous ADJ. hardened; unfeeling. He had worked in the hospital for so many years that he was *callous* to the suffering in the wards. callus, N.

callow ADJ. youthful; immature; inexperienced. As a freshman, Jack was sure he was a man of the world; as a sophomore, he made fun of freshmen as *callow* youths. In both cases, his judgment showed just how *callow* he was.

calorific ADJ. heat-producing. Coal is much more *calorific* than green wood.

calumny N. malicious misrepresentation; slander. He could endure his financial failure, but he could not bear the *calumny* that his foes heaped upon him.

camaraderie N. good-fellowship. What he loved best about his job was the sense of *camaraderie* he and his co-workers shared.

cameo N. shell or jewel carved in relief; star's special appearance in a minor role in a film. Don't buy *cameos* from the street peddlers in Rome: the workmanship is wretched. Did you catch Bill Murray's *cameo* in *Little Shop of Horrors*? He was on-screen so briefly that if you blinked you missed him.

camouflage V. disguise; conceal. In order to rescue Han Solo, Princess Leia *camouflaged* herself in the helmet and cloak of a space bandit.

■ **candor** N. frankness; open honesty. Jack can carry *candor* too far: when he told Jill his honest opinion of her, she nearly slapped his face. candid, ADJ.

canine ADJ. related to dogs; dog-like. Some days the *canine* population of Berkeley seems almost to outnumber the human population.

canny ADJ. shrewd; thrifty. The *canny* Scotsman was more than a match for the swindlers.

cant N. insincere expressions of piety; jargon of thieves. Shocked by news of the minister's extramarital love affairs, the worshippers dismissed his talk about the sacredness of marriage as mere *cant*. *Cant* is a form of hypocrisy: those who can, pray; those who *cant*, pretend.

cantankerous ADJ. ill humored; irritable. Constantly complaining about his treatment and refusing to cooperate with the hospital staff, he was a *cantankerous* patient.

canter N. slow gallop. Because the racehorse had outdistanced its competition so easily, the reporter wrote that the race was won in a *canter*. also V.

Word List 8   canto–chameleon

canto N. division of a long poem. Dante's poetic masterpiece *The Divine Comedy* is divided into *cantos*.

canvass V. determine votes, etc. After *canvassing* the sentiments of his constituents, the congressman was confident that he represented the majority opinion of his district. also N.

capacious ADJ. spacious. In the *capacious* rotunda of the railroad terminal, thousands of travelers lingered while waiting for their train.

capacity N. mental or physical ability; role; ability to accommodate. Mike had the *capacity* to handle several jobs at once. In his *capacity* as president of SelecTronics he marketed an electronic dictionary with a *capacity* of 200,000 words.

capitulate V. surrender. The enemy was warned to *capitulate* or face annihilation.

■ **capricious** ADJ. unpredictable; fickle; fanciful. The storm was *capricious*: it changed course constantly. Jill was *capricious*, too: she changed boyfriends almost as often as she changed clothes. caprice, N.

caption N. title; chapter heading; text under illustration. The *captions* that accompany *The Far Side* cartoons are almost as funny as the pictures. also V.

captivate V. charm or enthrall. Bart and Lisa were *captivated* by their new nanny's winning manner.

cardinal ADJ. chief. If you want to increase your word power, the *cardinal* rule of vocabulary-building is to read.

careen V. lurch; sway from side to side. The taxicab *careened* wildly as it rounded the corner.

caricature N. exaggerated picture or description; distortion. The cartoonist's *caricature* of President Bush grossly exaggerated the size of the president's ears. also V.

carnage N. destruction of life. The film *The Killing Fields* vividly depicts the *carnage* wreaked by Pol Pot's followers in Cambodia.

carnal ADJ. fleshly. Is the public more interested in *carnal* pleasures than in spiritual matters? Compare the number of people who read *Playboy* daily to the number of those who read the Bible or Koran every day.

carnivorous ADJ. meat-eating. The lion's a *carnivorous* beast. A hunk of meat makes up his feast. A cow is not a *carnivore*. She likes the taste of grain, not gore.

● **carping** ADJ. finding fault. A *carping* critic is a nit-picker: he loves to point out flaws. If you don't like this definition, feel free to *carp*.

castigate V. criticize severely; punish. When the teacher threatened that she would *castigate* the mischievous boys if they didn't behave, they shaped up in a hurry.

casualty N. serious or fatal accident. The number of automotive *casualties* on this holiday weekend was high.

cataclysm N. violent upheaval; deluge. The Russian Revolution was a political and social *cataclysm* that overturned czarist society. cataclysmic, ADJ.

catalyst N. agent which brings about a chemical change while it remains unaffected and unchanged. Many chemical reactions cannot take place without the presence of a *catalyst*.

catapult N. slingshot; a hurling machine. Airplanes are sometimes launched from battleships by *catapults*. also V.

cataract N. great waterfall; eye abnormality. She gazed with awe at the mighty *cataract* known as Niagara Falls.

catastrophe N. calamity; disaster. The 1906 San Francisco earthquake was a *catastrophe* that destroyed most of the city. A similar earthquake striking today could have even more *catastrophic* results.

catechism N. book for religious instruction; instruction by question and answer. He taught by engaging his pupils in a *catechism* until they gave him the correct answer.

categorical ADJ. without exceptions; unqualified; absolute. Though the captain claimed he was never, never sick at sea, he finally had to qualify his *categorical* denial: he was "hardly ever" sick at sea.

cater to V. supply something desired (whether good or bad). The chef was happy to *cater to* the tastes of his highly sophisticated clientele. Critics condemned the movie industry for *catering to* the public's ever-increasing appetite for violence.

catharsis N. purging or cleansing of any passage of the body. Aristotle maintained that tragedy created a *catharsis* by purging the soul of base concepts.

catholic ADJ. broadly sympathetic; liberal. He was extremely *catholic* in his taste and read everything he could find in the library.

caucus N. private meeting of members of a party to select officers or determine policy. At the opening of Congress, the members of the Democratic Party held a *caucus* to elect the Majority Leader of the House and the Party Whip.

caulk V. make watertight by filling in cracks. Jack had to *caulk* the tiles in the shower stall to stop the leak into the basement below.

causal ADJ. implying a cause-and-effect relationship. The psychologist maintained there was a *causal* relationship between the nature of one's early childhood experiences and one's adult personality. causality, N.

caustic ADJ. burning; sarcastically biting. The critic's *caustic* comments angered the actors, who resented his cutting remarks.

cavalcade N. procession; parade. As described by Chaucer, the *cavalcade* of Canterbury pilgrims was a motley group.

cavalier ADJ. offhand or casual; haughty. The disguised prince resented the *cavalier* way in which the palace guards treated him. How dared they handle a member of the royal family so unceremoniously!

cavil V. make frivolous objections. It's fine when you make sensible criticisms, but it really bugs me when you *cavil* about unimportant details. also N.

cede V. yield (title, territory) to; surrender formally. Eventually the descendants of England's Henry II were forced to *cede* their French territories to the King of France.

celebrated ADJ. famous; well-known. Thanks to their race to break Roger Maris's home-run record, Sammy Sosa and Mark McGwire are two of America's most *celebrated* baseball players. celebrity, N.

celerity N. speed; rapidity. Hamlet resented his mother's *celerity* in remarrying within a month after his father's death.

celestial ADJ. heavenly; relating to the sky. Pointing his primitive telescope at the heavens, Galileo explored the *celestial* mysteries.

celibate ADJ. unmarried; abstaining from sexual intercourse. Though Havelock Ellis wrote extensively about sexual practices, recent studies maintain he was *celibate* throughout his life. celibacy, N.

censor N. overseer of morals; person who reads to eliminate inappropriate remarks. Soldiers dislike having their mail read by a *censor* but understand the need for this precaution. also V.

■ **censorious** ADJ. critical. *Censorious* people delight in casting blame.

■ **censure** V. blame; criticize. The senator was *censured* for behavior inappropriate to a member of Congress. also N.

centrifugal ADJ. radiating; departing from the center. Many automatic drying machines remove excess moisture from clothing by *centrifugal* force.

centripetal ADJ. tending toward the center. Does *centripetal* force or the force of gravity bring orbiting bodies to the earth's surface?

cerebral ADJ. pertaining to the brain or intellect. The heroes of *Dumb and Dumber* were poorly equipped for *cerebral* pursuits.

cerebration N. thought. Mathematics problems sometimes require much *cerebration*.

ceremonious ADJ. marked by formality. Ordinary dress would be inappropriate at so *ceremonious* an affair.

● **certitude** N. certainty. Though there was no *certitude* of his getting the job, Lou thought he had a good chance of doing so.

cessation N. stoppage. The airline's employees threatened a *cessation* of all work if management failed to meet their demands. cease, V.

cession N. yielding to another; ceding. The *cession* of Alaska to the United States is discussed in this chapter.

chafe V. warm by rubbing; make sore (by rubbing). Chilled, he *chafed* his hands before the fire. The collar of his school uniform *chafed* Tom's neck, but not as much the school's strict rules *chafed* his spirit. also N.

chaff N. worthless products of an endeavor. When you separate the wheat from the *chaff,* be sure you throw out the *chaff.*

chaffing ADJ. bantering; joking. Sometimes Chad's flippant, *chaffing* remarks annoy us. Still, Chad's *chaffing* keeps us laughing. also N.

chagrin N. vexation (caused by humiliation or injured pride); disappointment. Embarrassed by his parents' shabby, working-class appearance, Doug felt their visit to his school would bring him nothing but *chagrin*. Someone filled with *chagrin* doesn't grin: he's too mortified.

chameleon N. lizard that changes color in different situations. Like the *chameleon,* he assumed the political thinking of every group he met.

Word List 9   champion–coincidence

champion V. support militantly. Martin Luther King, Jr., won the Nobel Peace Prize because he *championed* the oppressed in their struggle for equality.

chaotic ADJ. in utter disorder. He tried to bring order into the *chaotic* state of affairs. chaos, N.

charisma N. divine gift; great popular charm or appeal of a political leader Political commentators have deplored the importance of a candidate's *charisma* in these days of television campaigning.

● **charlatan** N. quack; pretender to knowledge. When they realized that the Wizard didn't know how to get them back to Kansas, Dorothy and her companions were indignant that they'd been duped by a *charlatan*.

chary ADJ. cautious; sparing or restrained about giving. A prudent, thrifty, New Englander, DeWitt was as *chary* of investing money in junk bonds as he was *chary* of paying people unnecessary compliments.

chasm N. abyss. Looking down from the Cliffs of Doom, Frodo and his companions could not see the bottom of the *chasm*.

chaste ADJ. pure; virginal; modest. To ensure that his bride would stay *chaste* while he was off to the wars, the crusader had her fitted out with a *chastity* belt. chastity, N.

chasten V. discipline; punish in order to correct. Whom God loves, God *chastens*.

chastise V. punish. "Spare the rod and spoil the child" was Miss Watson's motto: she relished whipping Huck with a birch rod to *chastise* him.

chauvinist N. blindly devoted patriot. A *chauvinist* cannot recognize any faults in his country, no matter how flagrant they may be. Likewise, a male *chauvinist* cannot recognize his bias in favor of his own sex, no matter how flagrant that may be. chauvinistic, ADJ.

check V. stop motion; curb or restrain. Thrusting out her arm, Grandma *checked* Bobby's lunge at his sister. "Young man," she said, "you'd better *check* your temper." (secondary meaning)

checkered ADJ. marked by changes in fortune. During his *checkered* career he had lived in palatial mansions and in dreary boardinghouses.

cherubic ADJ. angelic; innocent-looking. With her cheerful smile and rosy cheeks, she was a particularly *cherubic* child.

chicanery N. trickery; deception. Those sneaky lawyers misrepresented what occurred, made up all sorts of implausible alternative scenarios to confuse the jurors, and in general depended on *chicanery* to win the case.

chide V. scold. Grandma began to *chide* Steven for his lying.

chimerical ADJ. fantastically improbable; highly unrealistic; imaginative. As everyone expected, Ted's *chimerical* scheme to make a fortune by raising ermines in his back yard proved a dismal failure.

chisel N. wedgelike tool for cutting. With his hammer and *chisel*, the sculptor chipped away at the block of marble.

chisel V. swindle or cheat; cut with a chisel. That crook *chiseled* me out of a hundred dollars when he sold me that "marble" statue he'd *chiseled* out of some cheap hunk of rock.

chivalrous ADJ. courteous; faithful; brave. *Chivalrous* behavior involves noble words and good deeds.

choleric ADJ. hot-tempered. His flushed, angry face indicated a *choleric* nature.

choreography N. art of representing dances in written symbols; arrangement of dances. Merce Cunningham uses a computer in designing *choreography*: a software program allows him to compose sequences of possible moves and immediately view them on-screen.

chronic ADJ. long established as a disease. The doctors were finally able to attribute his *chronic* headaches and nausea to traces of formaldehyde gas in his apartment.

chronicle V. report; record (in chronological order). The gossip columnist was paid to *chronicle* the latest escapades of the socially prominent celebrities. also N.

churlish ADJ. boorish; rude. Dismayed by his *churlish* manners at the party, the girls vowed never to invite him again.

cipher N. secret code. Lacking his code book, the spy was unable to decode the message sent to him in *cipher*.

cipher N. nonentity; worthless person or thing. She claimed her ex-husband was a total *cipher* and wondered why she had ever married him.

circuitous ADJ. roundabout. To avoid the traffic congestion on the main highways, she took a *circuitous* route. circuit, N.

● **circumlocution** N. indirect or roundabout expression. He was afraid to call a spade a spade and resorted to *circumlocutions* to avoid direct reference to his subject.

circumscribe V. limit; confine. School regulations *circumscribed* Elle's social life: she hated having to follow rules that limited her activities.

circumspect ADJ. prudent; cautious. Investigating before acting, she tried always to be *circumspect*.

circumvent V. outwit; baffle. In order to *circumvent* the enemy, we will make two preliminary attacks in other sections before starting our major campaign.

cite V. quote; command. She could *cite* passages in the Bible from memory. citation, N.

civil ADJ. having to do with citizens or the state; courteous and polite. Although Internal Revenue Service agents are *civil* servants, they are not always *civil* to suspected tax cheats.

clairvoyant ADJ., N. having foresight; fortuneteller. Cassandra's *clairvoyant* warning was not heeded by the Trojans. clairvoyance, N.

clamber V. climb by crawling. She *clambered* over the wall.

clamor N. noise. The *clamor* of the children at play outside made it impossible for her to take a nap. also V.

clandestine ADJ. secret. After avoiding their chaperon, the lovers had a *clandestine* meeting.

clangor N. loud, resounding noise. The blacksmith was accustomed to the *clangor* of hammers on steel.

clasp N. fastening device; firm grip. When the *clasp* on Judy's bracelet broke, Fred repaired it, bending the hook back into shape. He then helped her slip on the bracelet, holding it firm in the sure *clasp* of his hand.

cleave V. split or sever; cling to; remain faithful to. With her heavy cleaver, Julia Child can *cleave* a whole roast duck in two. Soaked through, the soldier tugged at the uniform that *cleaved* annoyingly to his body. He would *cleave* to his post, come rain or shine.

cleft N. split. Trying for a fresh handhold, the mountain-climber grasped the edge of a *cleft* in the sheer rockface. also ADJ.

clemency N. disposition to be lenient; mildness, as of the weather. The lawyer was pleased when the case was sent to Judge Smith's chambers because Smith was noted for her *clemency* toward first offenders.

clench V. close tightly; grasp. "Open wide," said the dentist, but Clint *clenched* his teeth even more tightly than before.

● **cliché** N. phrase dulled in meaning by repetition. High school compositions are often marred by such *clichés* as "strong as an ox."

clientele N. body of customers. The rock club attracted a young, stylish *clientele*.

climactic ADJ. relating to the highest point. When he reached the *climactic* portions of the book, he could not stop reading. climax, N.

clime N. region; climate. His doctor advised him to move to a milder *clime*.

clip N. section of filmed material. Phil's job at Fox Sports involved selecting *clips* of the day's sporting highlights for later broadcast. also V.

clique N. small exclusive group. Fitzgerald wished that he belonged to the *clique* of popular athletes and big men on campus who seemed to run Princeton's social life.

cloister N. monastery or convent. The nuns lived a secluded life in the *cloister*.

clout N. great influence (especially political or social). Gatsby wondered whether he had enough *clout* to be admitted to the exclusive club.

cloying ADJ. distasteful (because excessive); excessively sweet or sentimental. Disliking the *cloying* sweetness of standard wedding cakes, Jody and Tom chose to have homemade carrot cake at the reception. cloy, V.

clump N. cluster or close group (of bushes, trees); mass; sound of heavy treading. Hiding behind the *clump* of bushes, the fugitives waited for the heavy *clump* of the soldiers' feet to fade away.

coagulate V. thicken; congeal; clot. Even after you remove the pudding from the burner, it will continue to *coagulate* as it stands; therefore, do not overcook the pudding, lest it become too thick.

● **coalesce** V. combine; fuse. The brooks *coalesce* into one large river. When minor political parties *coalesce*, their *coalescence* may create a major coalition.

coalition N. partnership; league; union. The Rainbow *Coalition* united people of all races in a common cause.

coddle V. to treat gently. Don't *coddle* the children so much; they need a taste of discipline.

codify V. arrange (laws, rules) as a code; classify. We need to take the varying rules and regulations of the different health agencies and *codify* them into a national health code.

■ **coercion** N. use of force to get someone to obey. The inquisitors used both physical and psychological *coercion* to force Joan of Arc to deny that her visions were sent by God. coerce, V.

cogent ADJ. convincing. It was inevitable that David chose to go to Harvard: he had several *cogent* reasons for doing so, including a full-tuition scholarship. Katya argued her case with such *cogency* that the jury had to decide in favor of her client.

cogitate V. think over. *Cogitate* on this problem; the solution will come.

cognate ADJ. related linguistically: allied by blood: similar or akin in nature. The English word "mother" is *cognate* to the Latin word "mater," whose influence is visible in the words "maternal" and "maternity." also N.

cognitive ADJ. having to do with knowing or perceiving; related to the mental processes. Though Jack was emotionally immature, his *cognitive* development was admirable; he was very advanced intellectually.

cognizance N. knowledge. During the election campaign, the two candidates were kept in full *cognizance* of the international situation.

cohere V. stick together. Solids have a greater tendency to *cohere* than liquids.

cohesion N. tendency to keep together. A firm believer in the maxim "Divide and conquer," the evil emperor, by means of lies and trickery, sought to disrupt the *cohesion* of the federation of free nations.

coiffure N. hairstyle. You can make a statement with your choice of *coiffure*: in the sixties many African-Americans affirmed their racial heritage by wearing their hair in Afros.

coin V. make coins; invent or fabricate. Mints *coin* good money; counterfeiters *coin* fakes. Slanderers *coin* nasty rumors; writers *coin* words. A neologism is an expression that's been newly-*coined*.

coincidence N. two or more things occurring at the same time by chance. Was it just a *coincidence* that John and she had chanced to meet at the market for three days running, or was he deliberately trying to seek her out? coincidental, ADJ.

Word List 10   collaborate–congenital

collaborate   v. work together. Two writers *collaborated* in preparing this book.

collage   N. work of art put together from fragments. Scraps of cloth, paper doilies, and old photographs all went into her *collage*.

collate   v. examine in order to verify authenticity; arrange in order. They *collated* the newly found manuscripts to determine their age.

collateral   N. security given for loan. The sum you wish to borrow is so large that it must be secured by *collateral*.

● **colloquial**   ADJ. pertaining to conversational or common speech. Some of the new, less formal reading passages on the SAT have a *colloquial* tone that is intended to make them more appealing to students.

collusion   N. conspiring in a fraudulent scheme. The swindlers were found guilty of *collusion*.

colossal   ADJ. huge. Radio City Music Hall has a *colossal* stage.

comatose   ADJ. in a coma; extremely sleepy. The long-winded orator soon had his audience in a *comatose* state.

● **combustible**   ADJ. easily burned. After the recent outbreak of fires in private homes, the fire commissioner ordered that all *combustible* materials be kept in safe containers. also N.

comely   ADJ. attractive; agreeable. I would rather have a poor and *comely* wife than a rich and homely one.

comeuppance   N. rebuke; deserts. After his earlier rudeness, we were delighted to see him get his *comeuppance*.

commandeer   v. to draft for military purposes; to take for public use. The policeman *commandeered* the first car that approached and ordered the driver to go to the nearest hospital.

■ **commemorate**   v. honor the memory of. The statue of the Minute Man *commemorates* the valiant soldiers who fought in the Revolutionary War.

commensurate   ADJ. equal in extent. Your reward will be *commensurate* with your effort.

commiserate   v. feel or express pity or sympathy for. Her friends *commiserated* with the widow.

commodious   ADJ. spacious and comfortable. After sleeping in small roadside cabins, they found their hotel suite *commodious*.

communal   ADJ. held in common; of a group of people. When they were divorced, they had trouble dividing their *communal* property.

compact   N. agreement; contract. The signers of the Mayflower *Compact* were establishing a form of government.

compact   ADJ. tightly packed; firm; brief. His short, *compact* body was better suited to wrestling than to basketball.

comparable   ADJ. similar. People whose jobs are *comparable* in difficulty should receive *comparable* pay.

compatible   ADJ. harmonious; in harmony with. They were *compatible* neighbors, never quarreling over unimportant matters. compatibility, N.

compelling   ADJ. overpowering; irresistible in effect. The prosecutor presented a well-reasoned case, but the defense attorney's *compelling* arguments for leniency won over the jury.

compensatory   ADJ. making up for; repaying. Can a *compensatory* education program make up for the inadequate schooling he received in earlier years?

■ **compile**   v. assemble; gather; accumulate. We planned to *compile* a list of the words most frequently used on SAT examinations.

■ **complacency**   N. self-satisfaction; smugness. Full of *complacency* about his latest victories, he looked smugly at the row of trophies on his mantelpiece. complacent, ADJ.

complaisant   ADJ. trying to please; obliging. Always ready to accede to his noble patron's wishes, Mr. Collins was a *complaisant*, even obsequious, character.

complement   v. complete; consummate; make perfect. The waiter recommended a glass of port to *complement* the cheese. also N.

● **complementary**   ADJ. serving to complete something. John and Lisa's skills are *complementary*: he's good at following a daily routine, while she's great at improvising and handling emergencies. Together they make a great team.

■ **compliance**   N. readiness to yield; conformity in fulfilling requirements. Bullheaded Bill was not noted for easy *compliance* with the demands of others. As an architect, however, Bill recognized that his design for the new school had to be in *compliance* with the local building code.

compliant   ADJ. yielding. Because Joel usually gave in and went along with whatever his friends desired, his mother worried that he might be too *compliant*.

complicity   N. participation; involvement. You cannot keep your *complicity* in this affair secret very long; you would be wise to admit your involvement immediately.

component   N. element; ingredient. I wish all the *components* of my stereo system were working at the same time.

■ **composure**   N. mental calmness. Even the latest work crisis failed to shake her *composure*.

compound   v. combine; constitute; pay interest; increase. The makers of the popular cold remedy *compounded* a nasal decongestant with an antihistamine. also N.

■ **comprehensive**   ADJ. thorough; inclusive. This book provides a *comprehensive* review of verbal and math skills for the SAT.

compress   v. close; squeeze; contract. She *compressed* the package under her arm.

comprise   v. include; consist of. If the District of Columbia were to be granted statehood, the United States of America would *comprise* fifty-one states, not just fifty.

compromise   v. adjust or settle by making mutual concessions; endanger the interests or reputation of. Sometimes the presence of a neutral third party can help adversaries *compromise* their differences. Unfortunately, you're not neutral; therefore, your presence here *compromises* our chances of reaching an agreement. also N.

compunction N. remorse. The judge was especially severe in his sentencing because he felt that the criminal had shown no *compunction* for his heinous crime.

compute V. reckon; calculate. He failed to *compute* the interest, so his bank balance was not accurate. computation, N.

concave ADJ. hollow. The back-packers found partial shelter from the storm by huddling against the *concave* wall of the cliff.

■ **concede** V. admit; yield. Despite all the evidence Monica had assembled, Mark refused to *concede* that she was right.

conceit N. vanity or self-love; whimsical idea; extravagant metaphor. Although Jack was smug and puffed up with *conceit*, he was an entertaining companion, always expressing himself in amusing *conceits* and witty turns of phrase.

concentric ADJ. having a common center. The target was made of *concentric* circles.

conception N. beginning; forming of an idea. At the first *conception* of the work, he was consulted. conceive, V.

concerted ADJ. mutually agreed on; done together. All the Girl Scouts made a *concerted* effort to raise funds for their annual outing. When the movie star appeared, his fans let out a *concerted* sigh.

concession N. an act of yielding. Before they could reach an agreement, both sides had to make certain *concessions*.

■ **conciliatory** ADJ. reconciling; soothing. She was still angry despite his *conciliatory* words. conciliate, V.

■ **concise** ADJ. brief and compact. When you define a new word, be *concise*: the shorter the definition, the easier it is to remember.

conclusive ADJ. decisive; ending all debate. When the stolen books turned up in John's locker, we finally had *conclusive* evidence of the identity of the mysterious thief.

concoct V. prepare by combining; make up in concert. How did the inventive chef ever *concoct* such a strange dish? concoction, N.

concomitant N. that which accompanies. Culture is not always a *concomitant* of wealth. also ADJ.

concord N. harmony; agreement between people or things. Watching Tweedledum and Tweedledee battle, Alice wondered at their lack of *concord*.

■ **concur** V. agree. Did you *concur* with the decision of the court or did you find it unfair?

concurrent ADJ. happening at the same time. In America, the colonists were resisting the demands of the mother country; at the *concurrent* moment in France, the middle class was sowing the seeds of rebellion.

condemn V. censure; sentence; force or limit to a particular state. In *My Cousin Vinnie*, Vinnie's fiancée *condemned* Vinnie for mishandling his cousin Tony's defense. If Vinnie didn't do a better job defending Tony, the judge would *condemn* Tony to death, and Vinnie would be *condemned* to cleaning toilets for a living.

condense V. make more compact or dense; shorten or abridge; reduce into a denser form. If you squeeze a slice of Wonder Bread, taking out the extra air, you can *condense* it into a pellet the size of a sugar cube. If you cut out the unnecessary words from your essay, you can *condense* it to a paragraph. As the bathroom cooled down, the steam from the shower *condensed* into droplets of water.

condescend V. act conscious of descending to a lower level; patronize. Though Jill had been a star softball player in college, when she played a pickup game at the park she never *condescended* to her less experienced teammates. condescension, N.

condiments N. seasonings; spices. The chef seasoned the dish with so much garlic that we could hardly taste the other *condiments*.

condole V. express sympathetic sorrow. His friends gathered to *condole* with him over his loss. condolence, N.

■ **condone** V. overlook; forgive; give tacit approval; excuse. Unlike Widow Douglass, who *condoned* Huck's minor offenses, Miss Watson did nothing but scold.

conducive ADJ. contributive; tending to. Rest and proper diet are *conducive* to good health.

confidant N. trusted friend. He had no *confidants* with whom he could discuss his problems at home.

confine V. shut in; restrict. The terrorists had *confined* their prisoner in a small room. However, they had not chained him to the wall or done anything else to *confine* his movements further. confinement, N.

confirm V. corroborate; verify; support. I have several witnesses who will *confirm* my account of what happened.

confiscate V. seize; commandeer. The army *confiscated* all available supplies of uranium.

■ **conflagration** N. great fire. In the *conflagration* that followed the 1906 earthquake, much of San Francisco was destroyed.

● **confluence** N. flowing together; crowd. They built the city at the *confluence* of two rivers.

conformity N. harmony; agreement. In *conformity* with our rules and regulations, I am calling a meeting of our organization.

■ **confound** V. confuse; puzzle. No mystery could *confound* Sherlock Holmes for long.

confrontation N. act of facing someone or something; encounter, often hostile. Morris hoped to avoid any *confrontations* with his ex-wife, but he kept on running into her at the health club. How would you like to *confront* someone who can bench press 200 pounds? confront, V., confrontational, ADJ.

congeal V. freeze; coagulate. His blood *congealed* in his veins as he saw the dread monster rush toward him.

congenial ADJ. pleasant; friendly. My father loved to go out for a meal with *congenial* companions.

congenital ADJ. existing at birth. Were you born stupid, or did you just turn out this way? In other words, is your idiocy *congenital* or acquired? Doctors are able to cure some *congenital* deformities such as cleft palates by performing operations on infants.

Word List 11 conglomeration–countermand

conglomeration N. mass of material sticking together. In such a *conglomeration* of miscellaneous statistics, it was impossible to find a single area of analysis.

congruent ADJ. in agreement; corresponding. In formulating a hypothesis, we must keep it *congruent* with what we know of the real world; it cannot disagree with our experience.

● **conjecture** V. surmise; guess. Although there was no official count, the organizers *conjectured* that more than 10,000 marchers took part in the March for Peace. also N.

conjugal ADJ. pertaining to marriage. Their dreams of *conjugal* bliss were shattered as soon as their temperaments clashed.

conjure V. summon a devil; practice magic; imagine or invent. Sorcerers *conjure* devils to appear. Magicians *conjure* white rabbits out of hats. Political candidates *conjure* up images of reformed cities and a world at peace.

connivance N. assistance; pretense of ignorance of something wrong; permission to offend. With the *connivance* of his friends, he plotted to embarrass the teacher. connive, V.

connoisseur N. person competent to act as a judge of art, etc.; a lover of an art. She had developed into a *connoisseur* of fine china.

connotation N. suggested or implied meaning of an expression. Foreigners frequently are unaware of the *connotations* of the words they use.

connubial ADJ. pertaining to marriage or the matrimonial state. In his telegram, he wished the newlyweds a lifetime of *connubial* bliss.

conscientious ADJ. scrupulous; careful. A *conscientious* editor, she checked every definition for its accuracy.

consecrate V. dedicate; sanctify. We shall *consecrate* our lives to this noble purpose.

■ **consensus** N. general agreement. Every time the garden club members had nearly reached a *consensus* about what to plant, Mistress Mary, quite contrary, disagreed.

consequential ADJ. pompous; important; self-important. Convinced of his own importance, the actor strutted about the dressing room with a *consequential* air.

conservatory N. school of the fine arts (especially music or drama). A gifted violinist, Marya was selected to study at the *conservatory*.

consign V. deliver officially; entrust; set apart. The court *consigned* the child to her paternal grandmother's care. consignment, N.

consistency N. absence of contradictions; dependability; uniformity; degree of thickness. Holmes judged puddings and explanations on their *consistency:* he liked his puddings without lumps and his explanations without improbabilities.

console V. lessen sadness or disappointment; give comfort. When her father died, Marius did his best to *console* Cosette.

consolidation N. unification; process of becoming firmer or stronger. The recent *consolidation* of several small airlines into one major company has left observers of the industry wondering whether room still exists for the "little guy" in aviation. consolidate, V.

consonance N. harmony; agreement. Her agitation seemed out of *consonance* with her usual calm.

consort V. associate with. We frequently judge people by the company with whom they *consort*.

consort N. husband or wife. The search for a *consort* for the young Queen Victoria ended happily.

conspicuous ADJ. easily seen; noticeable; striking. Janet was *conspicuous* both for her red hair and for her height.

conspiracy N. treacherous plot. Brutus and Cassius joined in the *conspiracy* to kill Julius Caesar. conspire, V.

constituent N. supporter. The congressman received hundreds of letters from angry *constituents* after the Equal Rights Amendment failed to pass.

■ **constraint** N. compulsion; repression of feelings. There was a feeling of *constraint* in the room because no one dared to criticize the speaker. constrain, V.

construe V. explain; interpret. If I *construe* your remarks correctly, you disagree with the theory already advanced.

consummate ADJ. complete. I have never seen anyone who makes as many stupid errors as you do; what a *consummate* idiot you are! also V.

contagion N. infection. Fearing *contagion,* they took great steps to prevent the spread of the disease.

contaminate V. pollute. The sewage system of the city so *contaminated* the water that swimming was forbidden.

contemporary N. person belonging to the same period. Though Charlotte Brontë and George Eliot were *contemporaries,* the two novelists depicted their Victorian world in markedly different ways. also ADJ.

contempt N. scorn; disdain. The heavyweight boxer looked on ordinary people with *contempt,* scorning them as weaklings who couldn't hurt a fly. We thought it was *contemptible* of him to be *contemptuous* of people for being weak.

■ **contend** V. struggle; compete; assert earnestly. Sociologist Harry Edwards *contends* that young black athletes are exploited by some college recruiters.

contention N. claim; thesis. It is our *contention* that, if you follow our tactics, you will boost your score on the SAT. contend, V.

■ **contentious** ADJ. quarrelsome. Disagreeing violently with the referees' ruling, the coach became so *contentious* that they threw him out of the game.

contest V. dispute. The defeated candidate attempted to *contest* the election results.

context N. writings preceding and following the passage quoted. Because these lines are taken out of *context*, they do not convey the message the author intended.

contiguous ADJ. adjacent to; touching upon. The two countries are *contiguous* for a few miles; then they are separated by the gulf.

continence N. self-restraint; sexual chastity. At the convent, Connie vowed to lead a life of *continence*. The question was, could Connie be content with always being *continent*?

contingent ADJ. dependent on; conditional. Caroline's father informed her that any raise in her allowance was *contingent* on the quality of her final grades. contingency, N.

contingent N. group that makes up part of a gathering. The New York *contingent* of delegates at the Democratic National Convention was a boisterous, sometimes rowdy lot.

contortions N. twistings; distortions. As the effects of the opiate wore away, the *contortions* of the patient became more violent and demonstrated how much pain she was enduring.

contraband N. ADJ. illegal trade; smuggling. The Coast Guard tries to prevent traffic in *contraband* goods.

■ **contract** V. compress or shrink; make a pledge; catch a disease. Warm metal expands; cold metal *contracts*.

contravene V. contradict; oppose; infringe on or transgress. Mr. Barrett did not expect his frail daughter Elizabeth to *contravene* his will by eloping with Robert Browning.

contrite ADJ. penitent. Her *contrite* tears did not influence the judge when he imposed sentence. contrition, N.

contrived ADJ. forced; artificial; not spontaneous. Feeling ill at ease with his new in-laws, James made a few *contrived* attempts at conversation and then retreated into silence.

controvert V. oppose with arguments; attempt to refute; contradict. The witness's testimony was so clear and her reputation for honesty so well-established that the defense attorney decided it was wiser to make no attempt to *controvert* what she said.

conundrum N. riddle. During the long car ride, she invented *conundrums* to entertain the children.

convene V. assemble. Because much needed legislation had to be enacted, the governor ordered the legislature to *convene* in special session by January 15.

convention N. social or moral custom; established practice. Flying in the face of *convention*, George Sand shocked society by taking lovers and wearing men's clothes.

conventional ADJ. ordinary; typical. His *conventional* upbringing left him wholly unprepared for his wife's eccentric family.

● **converge** V. approach; tend to meet; come together. African-American men from all over the United States con-

verged on Washington to take part in the historic Million Men march.

conversant ADJ. familiar with. The lawyer is *conversant* with all the evidence.

converse N. opposite. The inevitable *converse* of peace is not war but annihilation.

converse V. chat; talk informally. Eva was all ears while Lulu and Lola *conversed*. Wasn't it rude of her to eavesdrop on their *conversation*? conversation, N.

convert N. one who has adopted a different religion or opinion. On his trip to Japan, though the President spoke at length about the virtues of American automobiles, he made few *converts* to his beliefs. also V.

convex ADJ. curving outward. He polished the *convex* lens of his telescope.

conveyance N. vehicle; transfer. During the transit strike, commuters used various kinds of *conveyances*.

■ **conviction** N. judgment that someone is guilty of a crime; strongly held belief. Even her *conviction* for murder did not shake Peter's *conviction* that Harriet was innocent of the crime.

convivial ADJ. festive; gay; characterized by joviality. The *convivial* celebrators of the victory sang their college songs.

convoke V. call together. Congress was *convoked* at the outbreak of the emergency. convocation, N.

convoluted ADJ. coiled around; involved; intricate. The new tax regulations are so *convoluted* that even accountants have trouble following their twists and turns.

copious ADJ. plentiful. She had *copious* reasons for rejecting the proposal.

coquette N. flirt. Because she refused to give him an answer to his proposal of marriage, he called her a *coquette*. also V.

■ **cordial** ADJ. gracious; heartfelt. Our hosts greeted us at the airport with a *cordial* welcome and a hearty hug.

cordon N. extended line of men or fortifications to prevent access or egress. The police *cordon* was so tight that the criminals could not leave the area. also V.

cornucopia N. horn overflowing with fruit and grain; symbol of abundance. The encyclopedia salesman claimed the new edition was a veritable *cornucopia* of information, an inexhaustible source of knowledge for the entire family.

corollary N. consequence; accompaniment. Brotherly love is a complex emotion, with sibling rivalry its natural *corollary*.

coronation N. ceremony of crowning a queen or king. When the witches told Macbeth he would be king, they failed to warn him he would lose his crown soon after his *coronation*.

corporeal ADJ. bodily; material. The doctor had no patience with spiritual matters: his job was to attend to his patients' *corporeal* problems, not to minister to their souls.

corpulent ADJ. very fat. The *corpulent* man resolved to reduce. corpulence, N.

correlation N. mutual relationship. He sought to determine the *correlation* that existed between ability in algebra and ability to interpret reading exercises. correlate, V., N.

■ **corroborate** V. confirm; support. Though Huck was quite willing to *corroborate* Tom's story, Aunt Polly knew better than to believe either of them.

● **corrode** V. destroy by chemical action. The girders supporting the bridge *corroded* so gradually that no one suspected any danger until the bridge suddenly collapsed. corrosion, N.

corrosive ADJ. eating away by chemicals or disease. Stainless steel is able to withstand the effects of *corrosive* chemicals. corrode, V.

● **corrugated** ADJ. wrinkled; ridged. She wished she could smooth away the wrinkles from his *corrugated* brow.

cosmic ADJ. pertaining to the universe; vast. *Cosmic* rays derive their name from the fact that they bombard the earth's atmosphere from outer space. cosmos, N.

cosmopolitan ADJ. sophisticated. Her years in the capitol had transformed her into a *cosmopolitan* young woman highly aware of international affairs.

coterie N. group that meets socially; select circle. After his book had been published, he was invited to join the literary *coterie* that lunched daily at the hotel.

countenance V. approve; tolerate. He refused to *countenance* such rude behavior on their part.

countenance N. face. When Jose saw his newborn daughter, a proud smile spread across his *countenance*.

countermand V. cancel; revoke. The general *countermanded* the orders issued in his absence.

Word List 12   counterpart–decelerate

counterpart N. a thing that completes another; things very much alike. Night and day are *counterparts*, complementing one another.

coup N. highly successful action or sudden attack. As the news of his *coup* spread throughout Wall Street, his fellow brokers dropped by to congratulate him.

couple V. join; unite. The Flying Karamazovs *couple* expert juggling and amateur joking in their nightclub act.

courier N. messenger. The publisher sent a special *courier* to pick up the manuscript.

covenant N. agreement. We must comply with the terms of the *covenant*.

covert ADJ. secret; hidden; implied. Investigations of the Central Intelligence Agency and other secret service networks reveal that such *covert* operations can get out of control.

covetous ADJ. avaricious; eagerly desirous of. The child was *covetous* by nature and wanted to take the toys belonging to his classmates. covet, V.

cow V. terrorize; intimidate. The little boy was so *cowed* by the hulking bully that he gave up his lunch money without a word of protest.

cower V. shrink quivering, as from fear. The frightened child *cowered* in the corner of the room.

coy ADJ. shy; modest; coquettish. Reluctant to commit herself so early in the game, Kay was *coy* in her answers to Ken's offer.

cozen V. cheat; hoodwink; swindle. He was the kind of individual who would *cozen* his friends in a cheap card game but remain eminently ethical in all business dealings.

crabbed ADJ. sour; peevish. The *crabbed* old man was avoided by the children because he scolded them when they made noise.

craftiness N. slyness; trickiness. In many Native American legends, the coyote is the clever trickster, the embodiment of *craftiness*. crafty, N.

crass ADJ. very unrefined; grossly insensible. The film critic deplored the *crass* commercialism of movie-makers who abandon artistic standards in order to make a quick buck.

craven ADJ. cowardly. Lillian's *craven* refusal to join the protest was criticized by her comrades, who had expected her to be brave enough to stand up for her beliefs.

credence N. belief. Do not place any *credence* in his promises.

credibility N. believability. Because the candidate had made some pretty unbelievable promises, we began to question the *credibility* of everything she said.

credo N. creed. I believe we may best describe his *credo* by saying that it approximates the Golden Rule.

■ **credulity** N. belief on slight evidence; gullibility; naivete. Con artists take advantage of the *credulity* of inexperienced investors to swindle them out of their savings. credulous, ADJ.

creed N. system of religious or ethical belief. Any loyal American's *creed* must emphasize love of democracy.

crescendo N. increase in the volume or intensity, as in a musical passage; climax. The music suddenly shifted its mood, dramatically switching from a muted, contemplative passage to a *crescendo* with blaring trumpets and clashing cymbals.

crest N. highest point of a hill; foamy top of a wave. Fleeing the tidal wave, the islanders scrambled to reach the *crest* of Mount Lucinda. With relief, they watched the *crest* of the wave break well below their vantage point.

crestfallen ADJ. dejected; dispirited. We were surprised at his reaction to the failure of his project; instead of being *crestfallen*, he was busily engaged in planning new activities.

cringe V. shrink back, as if in fear. The dog *cringed*, expecting a blow.

■ **criterion** N. standard used in judging. What *criterion* did you use when you selected this essay as the prizewinner? criteria, PL.

crop V. cut off unwanted parts of a photograph; graze. With care, David *cropped* the picture until its edges neatly framed the flock of sheep *cropping* the grass.

crotchety ADJ. eccentric; whimsical. Although he was reputed to be a *crotchety* old gentleman, I found his ideas substantially sound and sensible.

crux N. crucial point. This is the *crux* of the entire problem: everything centers on its being resolved.

crypt N. secret recess or vault, usually used for burial. Until recently, only bodies of rulers and leading statesmen were interred in this *crypt*.

■ **cryptic** ADJ. mysterious; hidden; secret. Thoroughly baffled by Holmes's *cryptic* remarks, Watson wondered whether Holmes was intentionally concealing his thoughts about the crime.

cubicle N. small compartment partitioned off; small bed-chamber. Hoping to personalize their workspace, the staff members decorated their tiny identical *cubicles* in markedly individual ways.

cuisine N. style of cooking. French *cuisine* is noted for its use of sauces and wines.

culinary ADJ. relating to cooking. Many chefs attribute their *culinary* skill to the wise use of spices.

cull V. pick out; reject. Every month the farmer *culls* the nonlaying hens from his flock and sells them to the local butcher. also N.

culminate V. attain the highest point; climax. George Bush's years of service to the Republican Party *culminated* in his being chosen as the Republican candidate for the presidency. His subsequent inauguration as President of the United States marked the *culmination* of his political career.

● **culpable** ADJ. deserving blame. Corrupt politicians who condone the activities of the gamblers are equally *culpable*.

cumbersome ADJ. heavy; hard to manage. He was burdened down with *cumbersome* parcels.

cumulative ADJ. growing by addition. Vocabulary building is a *cumulative* process: as you go through your flash cards, you will add new words to your vocabulary, one by one.

cupidity N. greed. The defeated people could not satisfy the *cupidity* of the conquerors, who demanded excessive tribute.

curator N. superintendent; manager. The members of the board of trustees of the museum expected the new *curator* to plan events and exhibitions that would make the museum more popular.

curmudgeon N. churlish, miserly individual. Although he was regarded by many as a *curmudgeon*, a few of us were aware of the many kindnesses and acts of charity that he secretly performed.

cursive ADJ. flowing, running. In normal writing we run our letters together in *cursive* form; in printing, we separate the letters.

■ **cursory** ADJ. casual; hastily done. Because a *cursory* examination of the ruins indicates the possibility of arson, we believe the insurance agency should undertake a more extensive investigation of the fire's cause.

■ **curtail** V. shorten; reduce. When Herb asked Diane for a date, she said she was really sorry she couldn't go out with him, but her dad had ordered her to *curtail* her social life.

cynical ADJ. skeptical or distrustful of human motives. *Cynical* from birth, Sidney was suspicious whenever anyone gave him a gift "with no strings attached." cynic, N.

cynosure N. the object of general attention. As soon as the movie star entered the room, she became the *cynosure* of all eyes.

dabble V. work at in a non-serious fashion; splash around. The amateur painter *dabbled* at art, but seldom produced a finished piece. The children *dabbled* their hands in the bird bath, splashing one another gleefully.

dais N. raised platform for guests of honor. When he approached the *dais*, he was greeted by cheers from the people who had come to honor him.

dank ADJ. damp. The walls of the dungeon were *dank* and slimy.

dapper ADJ. neat and trim. In "The Odd Couple" TV show, Tony Randall played Felix Unger, an excessively *dapper* soul who could not stand to have a hair out of place.

dappled ADJ. spotted. The sunlight filtering through the screens created a *dappled* effect on the wall.

daub V. smear (as with paint). From the way he *daubed* his paint on the canvas, I could tell he knew nothing of oils. also N.

daunt V. intimidate; frighten. "Boast all you like of your prowess. Mere words cannot *daunt* me," the hero answered the villain.

dauntless ADJ. bold. Despite the dangerous nature of the undertaking, the *dauntless* soldier volunteered for the assignment.

dawdle V. loiter; waste time. We have to meet a deadline so don't *dawdle*; just get down to work.

deadlock N. standstill; stalemate. Because negotiations had reached a *deadlock*, some of the delegates had begun to mutter about breaking off the talks. also V.

deadpan ADJ. wooden; impersonal. We wanted to see how long he could maintain his *deadpan* expression.

dearth N. scarcity. The *dearth* of skilled labor compelled the employers to open trade schools.

debacle N. sudden downfall; complete disaster. In the *Airplane* movies, every flight turns into a *debacle*, with passengers and crew members collapsing, engines falling apart, and carry-on baggage popping out of the overhead bins.

debase V. reduce in quality or value; lower in esteem; degrade. In *The King and I*, Anna refuses to kneel down and prostrate herself before the king, for she feels that to do so would *debase* her position, and she will not submit to such *debasement*.

debauch V. corrupt; seduce from virtue. Did Socrates' teachings lead the young men of Athens to be virtuous citizens, or did they *debauch* the young men, causing them to question the customs of their fathers? Clearly, Socrates' philosophical talks were nothing like the wild *debauchery* of the toga parties in *Animal House*.

● **debilitate** V. weaken; enfeeble. Michael's severe bout of the flu *debilitated* him so much that he was too tired to go to work for a week.

debonair ADJ. friendly; aiming to please. The *debonair* youth was liked by all who met him, because of his cheerful and obliging manner.

debris N. rubble. A full year after the earthquake in Mexico City, they were still carting away the *debris*.

● **debunk** V. expose as false, exaggerated, worthless, etc; ridicule. Pointing out that he consistently had voted against strengthening anti-pollution legislation, reporters *debunked* the candidate's claim that he was a fervent environmentalist.

debutante N. young woman making formal entrance into society. As a *debutante,* she was often mentioned in the society columns of the newspapers.

decadence N. decay. The moral *decadence* of the people was reflected in the lewd literature of the period.

decapitate V. behead. They did not hang Lady Jane Grey; they *decapitated* her. "Off with her head!" cried the Duchess, eager to *decapitate* poor Alice.

decelerate V. slow down. Seeing the emergency blinkers in the road ahead, he *decelerated* quickly.

Word List 13 deciduous–derivative

deciduous ADJ. falling off as of leaves. The oak is a *deciduous* tree; in winter it looks quite bare.

decimate V. kill, usually one out of ten. We do more to *decimate* our population in automobile accidents than we do in war.

decipher V. interpret secret code. Lacking his code book, the spy was unable to *decipher* the scrambled message sent to him from the KGB.

declivity N. downward slope. The children loved to ski down the *declivity.*

decolleté ADJ. having a low-necked dress. Current fashion decrees that evening gowns be *decolleté* this season; bare shoulders are again the vogue.

decomposition N. decay. Despite the body's advanced state of *decomposition,* the police were able to identify the murdered man.

■ **decorum** N. propriety; orderliness and good taste in manners. Even the best-mannered students have trouble behaving with *decorum* on the last day of school. decorous, ADJ.

decoy N. lure or bait. The wild ducks were not fooled by the *decoy.* also V.

decrepit ADJ. worn out by age. The *decrepit* car blocked traffic on the highway. decrepitude, N.

decry V. express strong disapproval of; disparage. The founder of the Children's Defense Fund, Marian Wright Edelman, strongly *decries* the lack of financial and moral support for children in America today.

deducible ADJ. derived by reasoning. If we accept your premise, your conclusions are easily *deducible.*

deface V. mar; disfigure. If you *deface* a library book, you will have to pay a hefty fine.

defame V. harm someone's reputation; malign; slander. If you try to *defame* my good name, my lawyers will see you in court. If rival candidates persist in *defaming* one another, the voters may conclude that all politicians are crooks. defamation, N.

default N. failure to act. When the visiting team failed to show up for the big game, they lost the game by *default.* When Jack failed to make the payments on his Jaguar, the dealership took back the car because he had *defaulted* on his debt.

defeatist ADJ. attitude of one who is ready to accept defeat as a natural outcome. If you maintain your *defeatist* attitude, you will never succeed. also N.

defection N. desertion. The children, who had made him an idol, were hurt most by his *defection* from our cause.

defer V. delay till later; exempt temporarily. In wartime, some young men immediately volunteer to serve; others *defer* making plans until they hear from their draft boards. During the Vietnam War, many young men, hoping to be *deferred*, requested student *deferments*.

defer V. give in respectfully; submit. When it comes to making decisions about purchasing software, we must *defer* to Michael, our computer guru; he gets the final word. Michael, however, can *defer* these questions to no one; only he can decide.

■ **deference** N. courteous regard for another's wish. In *deference* to the minister's request, please do not take photographs during the wedding service.

defiance N. refusal to yield; resistance. When John reached the "terrible two's," he responded to every parental request with howls of *defiance.* defy, V.

defile V. pollute; profane. The hoodlums *defiled* the church with their scurrilous writing.

definitive ADJ. final; complete. Carl Sandburg's *Abraham Lincoln* may be regarded as the *definitive* work on the life of the Great Emancipator.

deflect V. turn aside. His life was saved when his cigarette case *deflected* the bullet.

defray V. pay the costs of. Her employer offered to *defray* the costs of her postgraduate education.

deft ADJ. neat; skillful. The *deft* waiter uncorked the champagne without spilling a drop.

defunct ADJ. dead; no longer in use or existence. The lawyers sought to examine the books of the *defunct* corporation.

defuse V. remove the fuse of a bomb; reduce or eliminate a threat. Police negotiators are trained to *defuse* dangerous situations by avoiding confrontational language and behavior.

degenerate V. become worse; deteriorate. As the fight dragged on, the champion's style *degenerated* until he could barely keep on his feet.

■ **degradation** N. humiliation; debasement; degeneration. Some secretaries object to fetching the boss a cup of coffee because they resent the *degradation* of being made to do such lowly tasks. degrade, v.

● **dehydrate** v. remove water from; dry out. Running under a hot sun quickly *dehydrates* the body; joggers soon learn to carry water bottles and to drink from them frequently.

deify v. turn into a god; idolize. Admire Elvis Presley all you want; just don't *deify* him.

deign v. condescend; stoop. The celebrated fashion designer would not *deign* to speak to a mere seamstress; his overburdened assistant had to convey the master's wishes to the lowly workers assembling his great designs.

delectable ADJ. delightful; delicious. We thanked our host for a most *delectable* meal.

delete v. erase; strike out. Less is more: if you *delete* this paragraph, your whole essay will have greater appeal.

● **deleterious** ADJ. harmful. If you believe that smoking is *deleterious* to your health (and the Surgeon General certainly does), then quit!

deliberate v. consider; ponder. Offered the new job, she asked for time to *deliberate* before she told them her decision.

■ **delineate** v. portray; depict; sketch. Using only a few descriptive phrases, Austen *delineates* the character of Mr. Collins so well that we can predict his every move. delineation, N.

delirium N. mental disorder marked by confusion. In his *delirium*, the drunkard saw pink panthers and talking pigs. Perhaps he wasn't *delirious*: he might just have wandered into a movie.

delude v. deceive. His mistress may have *deluded* herself into believing that he would leave his wife and marry her.

deluge N. flood; rush. When we advertised the position, we received a *deluge* of applications.

delusion N. false belief; hallucination. Don suffers from *delusions* of grandeur: he thinks he's a world-famous author when he's published just one paperback book.

delve v. dig; investigate. *Delving* into old books and manuscripts is part of a researcher's job.

demagogue N. person who appeals to people's prejudice; false leader of people. He was accused of being a *demagogue* because he made promises that aroused futile hopes in his listeners.

demean v. degrade; humiliate. Standing on his dignity, he refused to *demean* himself by replying to the offensive letter. If you truly believed in the dignity of labor, you would not think it would *demean* you to work as a janitor.

demeanor N. behavior; bearing. His sober *demeanor* quieted the noisy revelers.

demented ADJ. insane. Doctor Demento was a lunatic radio personality who liked to act as if he were truly *demented*. If you're *demented*, your mental state is out of whack; in other words, you're wacky.

demise N. death. Upon the *demise* of the dictator, a bitter dispute about succession to power developed.

demolition N. destruction. One of the major aims of the air force was the complete *demolition* of all means of transportation by bombing of rail lines and terminals. demolish, v.

demoniac ADJ. fiendish. The Spanish Inquisition devised many *demoniac* means of torture. demon, N.

demur v. object (because of doubts, scruples); hesitate. When offered a post on the board of directors, David *demurred*: he had scruples about taking on the job because he was unsure he could handle it in addition to his other responsibilities.

demure ADJ. grave; serious; coy. She was *demure* and reserved, a nice modest girl whom any young man would be proud to take home to his mother.

demystify v. clarify; free from mystery or obscurity. Helpful doctors *demystify* medical procedures by describing them in everyday language, explaining that a myringotomy, for example, is an operation involving making a small hole in one's eardrum.

denigrate v. blacken. All attempts to *denigrate* the character of our late president have failed; the people still love him and cherish his memory.

denizen N. inhabitant or resident; regular visitor. In *The Untouchables*, Eliot Ness fights Al Capone and the other *denizens* of Chicago's underworld. Ness's fight against corruption was the talk of all the *denizens* of the local bars.

denotation N. meaning; distinguishing by name. A dictionary will always give us the *denotation* of a word; frequently, it will also give us the connotations. denote, v.

denouement N. outcome; final development of the plot of a play. The play was childishly written; the *denouement* was obvious to sophisticated theatergoers as early as the middle of the first act.

■ **denounce** v. condemn; criticize. The reform candidate *denounced* the corrupt city officers for having betrayed the public's trust. denunciation, N.

depict v. portray. In this sensational exposé, the author *depicts* Beatle John Lennon as a drug-crazed neurotic. Do you question the accuracy of this *depiction* of Lennon?

deplete v. reduce; exhaust. We must wait until we *deplete* our present inventory before we order replacements.

■ **deplore** v. regret; disapprove of. Although I *deplore* the vulgarity of your language, I defend your right to express yourself freely.

deploy v. spread out [troops] in an extended though shallow battle line. The general ordered the battalion to *deploy* in order to meet the enemy offensive.

● **depose** v. dethrone; remove from office. The army attempted to *depose* the king and set up a military government.

deposition N. testimony under oath. He made his *deposition* in the judge's chamber.

■ **depravity** N. extreme corruption; wickedness. The *depravity* of Caligula's behavior came to sicken even those who had willingly participated in his earlier, comparatively innocent orgies.

■ **deprecate** v. express disapproval of; protest against; belittle. A firm believer in old-fashioned courtesy, Miss Post *deprecated* the modern tendency to address new acquaintances by their first names. deprecatory, ADJ.

depreciate v. lessen in value. If you neglect this property, it will *depreciate*.

depredation N. plundering. After the *depredations* of the invaders, the people were penniless.

derange v. make insane; disarrange. Hamlet's cruel rejection *deranged* poor Ophelia; in her madness, she drowned herself.

derelict ADJ. abandoned; negligent. The *derelict* craft was a menace to navigation. Whoever abandoned it in the middle of the harbor was *derelict* in living up to his responsibilities as a boat owner. also N.

■ **deride** v. ridicule; make fun of. The critics *derided* his pretentious dialogue and refused to consider his play seriously. derision, N.

■ **derivative** ADJ. unoriginal; derived from another source. Although her early poetry was clearly *derivative* in nature, the critics thought she had promise and eventually would find her own voice.

Word List 14 derogatory–disgruntle

derogatory ADJ. expressing a low opinion. I resent your *derogatory* remarks.

descant v. discuss fully. He was willing to *descant* upon any topic of conversation, even when he knew very little about the subject under discussion. also N.

descry v. catch sight of. In the distance, we could barely *descry* the enemy vessels.

desecrate v. profane; violate the sanctity of. Shattering the altar and trampling the holy objects underfoot, the invaders *desecrated* the sanctuary.

● **desiccate** v. dry up. A tour of this smokehouse will give you an idea of how the pioneers used to *desiccate* food in order to preserve it.

desolate ADJ. unpopulated. After six months in the crowded, bustling metropolis, David was so sick of people that he was ready to head for the most *desolate* patch of wilderness he could find.

desolate v. rob of joy; lay waste to; forsake. The bandits *desolated* the countryside, burning farms and carrying off the harvest.

despise v. look on with scorn; regard as worthless or distasteful. Mr. Bond, I *despise* spies; I look down on them as mean, *despicable*, honorless men, whom I would wipe from the face of the earth with as little concern as I would scrape dog droppings from the bottom of my shoe.

despoil v. strip of valuables; rob. Seeking plunder, the raiders *despoiled* the village, carrying off any valuables they found.

■ **despondent** ADJ. depressed; gloomy. To the dismay of his parents, William became seriously *despondent* after he broke up with Jan; they despaired of finding a cure for his gloom. despondency, N.

despot N. tyrant; harsh, authoritarian ruler. How could a benevolent king turn overnight into a *despot*?

destitute ADJ. extremely poor. Because they had no health insurance, the father's costly illness left the family *destitute*.

desultory ADJ. aimless; haphazard; digressing at random. In prison Malcolm X set himself the task of reading straight through the dictionary; to him, reading was purposeful, not *desultory*.

■ **detached** ADJ. emotionally removed; calm and objective; physically unconnected. A psychoanalyst must maintain a *detached* point of view and stay uninvolved with his or her patients' personal lives. To a child growing up in an apartment or a row house, to live in a *detached* house was an unattainable dream.

detergent N. cleansing agent. Many new *detergents* have replaced soap.

determination N. resolve; measurement or calculation; decision. Nothing could shake his *determination* that his children would get the best education that money could buy. Thanks to my pocket calculator, my *determination* of the answer to the problem took only seconds of my time.

■ **deterrent** N. something that discourages; hindrance. Does the threat of capital punishment serve as a *deterrent* to potential killers? deter, v.

detraction N. slandering; aspersion. He is offended by your frequent *detractions* of his ability as a leader.

■ **detrimental** ADJ. harmful; damaging. The candidate's acceptance of major financial contributions from a well-known racist ultimately proved *detrimental* to his campaign, for he lost the backing of many of his early grassroots supporters. detriment, N.

deviate v. turn away from (a principle, norm); depart; diverge. Richard never *deviated* from his daily routine: every day he set off for work at eight o'clock, had his sack lunch (peanut butter on whole wheat) at 12:15, and headed home at the stroke of five.

■ **devious** ADJ. roundabout; erratic; not straightforward. The Joker's plan was so *devious* that it was only with great difficulty we could follow its shifts and dodges.

■ **devise** v. think up; invent; plan. How clever he must be to have *devised* such a devious plan! What ingenious inventions might he have *devised* if he had turned his mind to science and not to crime.

devoid ADJ. lacking. You may think her mind is a total void, but she's actually not *devoid* of intelligence. She just sounds like an airhead.

devotee N. enthusiastic follower. A *devotee* of the opera, he bought season tickets every year.

devout ADJ. pious. The *devout* man prayed daily.

dexterous ADJ. skillful. The magician was so *dexterous* that we could not follow him as he performed his tricks.

diabolical ADJ. devilish. "What a fiend I am, to devise such a *diabolical* scheme to destroy Gotham City," chortled the Joker gleefully.

diagnosis N. art of identifying a disease; analysis of a condition. In medical school Margaret developed her skill at *diagnosis*, learning how to read volumes from a rapid pulse or a hacking cough. diagnose, V.; diagnostic, ADJ.

dialectical ADJ. relating to the art of debate; mutual or reciprocal. The debate coach's students grew to develop great forensic and *dialectical* skill. Teaching, however, is inherently a *dialectical* situation: the coach learned at least as much from her students as they learned from her. dialectics, N.

diaphanous ADJ. sheer; transparent. Through the *diaphanous* curtains, the burglar could clearly see the large jewelry box on the dressing table.

diatribe N. bitter scolding; invective. During the lengthy *diatribe* delivered by his opponent he remained calm and self-controlled.

dichotomy N. split; branching into two parts (especially contradictory ones). Willie didn't know how to resolve the *dichotomy* between his ambition to go to college and his childhood longing to run away and join the circus. Then he heard about Ringling Brothers Circus College, and he knew he'd found the perfect school.

dictum N. authoritative and weighty statement; saying; maxim. University administrations still follow the old *dictum* of "Publish or perish." They don't care how good a teacher you are; if you don't publish enough papers, you're out of a job.

didactic ADJ. teaching; instructional. Pope's lengthy poem *An Essay on Man* is too *didactic* for my taste: I dislike it when poets turn preachy and moralize.

differentiate V. distinguish; perceive a difference between. Tweedledum and Tweedledee were like two peas in a pod; not even Mother Tweedle could *differentiate* the one from the other.

● **diffidence** N. shyness. You must overcome your *diffidence* if you intend to become a salesperson.

■ **diffuse** ADJ. wordy; rambling; spread out (like a gas). If you pay authors by the word, you tempt them to produce *diffuse* manuscripts rather than brief ones. diffusion, N.

■ **digression** N. wandering away from the subject. Nobody minded when Professor Renoir's lectures wandered away from their official theme; his *digressions* were always more fascinating than the topic of the day. digress, V.

dilapidated ADJ. ruined because of neglect. The *dilapidated* old building needed far more work than just a new coat of paint. dilapidation, N.

dilate V. expand. In the dark, the pupils of your eyes *dilate*.

● **dilatory** ADJ. delaying. If you are *dilatory* in paying bills, your credit rating may suffer.

dilemma N. problem; choice of two unsatisfactory alternatives. In this *dilemma*, he knew no one to whom he could turn for advice.

dilettante N. aimless follower of the arts; amateur; dabbler. He was not serious in his painting; he was rather a *dilettante*.

■ **diligence** N. steadiness of effort; persistent hard work. Her employers were greatly impressed by her *diligence* and offered her a partnership in the firm. diligent, ADJ.

dilute V. make less concentrated; reduce in strength. She preferred to *dilute* her coffee with milk.

■ **diminution** N. lessening; reduction in size. Old Jack was as sharp at eighty as he had been at fifty; increasing age led to no *diminution* of his mental acuity.

din N. continued loud noise. The *din* of the jackhammers outside the classroom window drowned out the lecturer's voice. also V.

dingy ADJ. dull; not fresh; cheerless. Refusing to be depressed by her *dingy* studio apartment, Bea spent the weekend polishing the floors and windows and hanging bright posters on the walls.

dint N. means; effort. By *dint* of much hard work, the volunteers were able to place the raging forest fire under control.

dire ADJ. disastrous. People ignored her *dire* predictions of an approaching depression.

dirge N. lament with music. The funeral *dirge* stirred us to tears.

disabuse V. correct a false impression; undeceive. I will attempt to *disabuse* you of your impression of my client's guilt; I know he is innocent.

disaffected ADJ. disloyal. Once the most loyal of Gorbachev's supporters, Sheverdnaze found himself becoming increasingly *disaffected*.

disapprobation N. disapproval; condemnation. The conservative father viewed his daughter's radical boyfriend with *disapprobation*.

disarray N. a disorderly or untidy state. After the New Year's party, the once orderly house was in total *disarray*.

disavowal N. denial; disclaiming. His *disavowal* of his part in the conspiracy was not believed by the jury. disavow, V.

disband V. dissolve; disperse. The chess club *disbanded* after its disastrous initial season.

disburse V. pay out. When you *disburse* money on the company's behalf, be sure to get a receipt.

discernible ADJ. distinguishable; perceivable. The ships in the harbor were not *discernible* in the fog. discern, V.

■ **discerning** ADJ. mentally quick and observant; having insight. Though no genius, the star was sufficiently *discerning* to tell her true friends from the countless phonies who flattered her.

disclaim V. disown; renounce claim to. If I grant you this privilege, will you *disclaim* all other rights?

■ **disclose** v. reveal. Although competitors offered him bribes, he refused to *disclose* any information about his company's forthcoming product. disclosure, N.

discombobulated ADJ. confused; discomposed. The novice square dancer became so *discombobulated* that he wandered into the wrong set.

discomfit v. put to rout; defeat; disconcert. This ruse will *discomfit* the enemy. discomfiture, N. discomfited, ADJ.

discomposure N. agitation; loss of poise. Perpetually poised, Agent 007 never exhibited a moment's *discomposure*.

disconcert v. confuse; upset; embarrass. The lawyer was *disconcerted* by the evidence produced by her adversary.

disconsolate ADJ. sad. The death of his wife left him *disconsolate.*

discord N. conflict; lack of harmony. Watching Tweedledum battle Tweedledee, Alice wondered what had caused this pointless *discord.*

■ **discordant** ADJ. not harmonious; conflicting. Nothing is quite so *discordant* as the sound of a junior high school orchestra tuning up.

■ **discount** v. disregard; dismiss. Be prepared to *discount* what he has to say about his ex-wife.

● **discourse** N. formal discussion; conversation. The young Plato was drawn to the Agora to hear the philosophical *discourse* of Socrates and his followers. also v.

discredit v. defame; destroy confidence in; disbelieve. The campaign was highly negative in tone; each candidate tried to *discredit* the other.

● **discrepancy** N. lack of consistency; difference. The police noticed some *discrepancies* in his description of the crime and did not believe him.

discrete ADJ. separate; unconnected. The universe is composed of *discrete* bodies.

discretion N. prudence; ability to adjust actions to circumstances. Use your *discretion* in this matter and do not discuss it with anyone. discreet, ADJ.

■ **discriminating** ADJ. able to see differences; prejudiced. A superb interpreter of Picasso, she was sufficiently *discriminating* to judge the most complex works of modern art. (secondary meaning) discrimination, N.

discursive ADJ. digressing; rambling. As the lecturer wandered from topic to topic, we wondered what if any point there was to his *discursive* remarks.

■ **disdain** v. view with scorn or contempt. In the film *Funny Face*, the bookish heroine *disdained* fashion models for their lack of intellectual interests. also N.

disembark v. go ashore; unload cargo from a ship. Before the passengers could *disembark*, they had to pick up their passports from the ship's purser.

disenfranchise v. deprive of a civil right. The imposition of the poll tax effectively *disenfranchised* poor Southern blacks, who lost their right to vote.

disengage v. uncouple; separate; disconnect. A standard movie routine involves the hero's desperate attempt to *disengage* a railroad car from a moving train.

disfigure v. mar in beauty; spoil. An ugly frown *disfigured* his normally pleasant face.

disgorge v. surrender something; eject; vomit. Unwilling to *disgorge* the cash he had stolen from the pension fund, the embezzler tried to run away.

disgruntle v. make discontented. The passengers were *disgruntled* by the numerous delays.

Word List 15   dishearten–duplicity

dishearten v. discourage; cause to lose courage or hope. His failure to pass the bar exam *disheartened* him.

disheveled ADJ. untidy. Your *disheveled* appearance will hurt your chances in this interview.

■ **disinclination** N. unwillingness. Some mornings I feel a great *disinclination* to get out of bed.

disingenuous ADJ. lacking genuine candor; insincere. Now that we know the mayor and his wife are engaged in a bitter divorce fight, we find their earlier remarks regretting their lack of time together remarkably *disingenuous.*

disinter v. dig up; unearth. They *disinterred* the body and held an autopsy.

disinterested ADJ. unprejudiced. Given the judge's political ambitions and the lawyers' financial interest in the case, the only *disinterested* person in the courtroom may have been the court reporter.

disjointed ADJ. disconnected. His remarks were so *disjointed* that we could not follow his reasoning.

dislodge v. remove (forcibly). Thrusting her fist up under the choking man's lower ribs, Margaret used the Heimlich maneuver to *dislodge* the food caught in his throat.

dismantle v. take apart. When the show closed, they *dismantled* the scenery before storing it.

dismay v. discourage; frighten. The huge amount of work she had left to do *dismayed* her. also N.

dismember v. cut into small parts. When the Austrian Empire was *dismembered*, several new countries were established.

■ **dismiss** v. put away from consideration; reject. Believing in John's love for her, she *dismissed* the notion that he might be unfaithful. (secondary meaning)

■ **disparage** v. belittle. A doting mother, Emma was more likely to praise her son's crude attempts at art than to *disparage* them.

disparate ADJ. basically different; unrelated. Unfortunately, Tony and Tina have *disparate* notions of marriage: Tony sees it as a carefree extended love affair, while Tina sees it as a solemn commitment to build a family and a home.

■ **disparity** N. difference; condition of inequality. Their *disparity* in rank made no difference at all to the prince and Cinderella.

dispassionate ADJ. calm; impartial. Known in the company for his cool judgment, Bill could impartially examine the causes of a problem, giving a *dispassionate* analysis of what had gone wrong, and go on to suggest how to correct the mess.

dispatch N. speediness; prompt execution; message sent with all due speed. Young Napoleon defeated the enemy with all possible *dispatch;* he then sent a *dispatch* to headquarters informing his commander of the great victory. also V.

dispel V. scatter; drive away; cause to vanish. The bright sunlight eventually *dispelled* the morning mist.

■ **disperse** V. scatter. The police fired tear gas into the crowd to *disperse* the protesters. dispersion, N.

dispirited ADJ. lacking in spirit. The coach used all the tricks at his command to buoy up the enthusiasm of his team, which had become *dispirited* at the loss of the star player.

■ **disputatious** ADJ. argumentative; fond of arguing. Convinced he knew more than his lawyers, Alan was a *disputatious* client, ready to argue about the best way to conduct the case. disputant, N.

disquiet V. make uneasy or anxious. Holmes's absence for a day, slightly *disquieted* Watson; after a week with no word, however, Watson's uneasiness about his missing friend had grown into a deep fear for his safety. disquietude, N.

dissection N. analysis; cutting apart in order to examine. The *dissection* of frogs in the laboratory is particularly unpleasant to some students.

dissemble V. disguise; pretend. Even though John tried to *dissemble* his motive for taking modern dance, we all knew he was there not to dance but to meet girls.

■ **disseminate** V. distribute; spread; scatter (like seeds). By their use of the Internet, propagandists have been able to *disseminate* their pet doctrines to new audiences around the globe.

■ **dissent** V. disagree. In the recent Supreme Court decision, Justice O'Connor *dissented* from the majority opinion. also N.

dissertation N. formal essay. In order to earn a graduate degree from many of our universities, a candidate is frequently required to prepare a *dissertation* on some scholarly subject.

dissident ADJ. dissenting; rebellious. In the purge that followed the student demonstrations at Tiananmen Square, the government hunted down the *dissident* students and their supporters. also N.

dissimulate V. pretend; conceal by feigning. Although the governor tried to *dissimulate* his feelings about the opposing candidate, we all knew he despised his rival.

dissipate V. squander; waste; scatter. He is a fine artist, but I fear he may *dissipate* his gifts if he keeps wasting his time playing games.

dissolute ADJ. loose in morals. The *dissolute* life led by the ancient Romans is indeed shocking.

dissolution N. breaking of a union; decay; termination. Which caused King Lear more suffering: the *dissolution* of his kingdom into warring factions, or the *dissolution* of his aged, failing body?

dissonance N. discord. Composer Charles Ives often used *dissonance*—clashing or unresolved chords—for special effects in his musical works.

dissuade V. persuade not to do; discourage. Since Tom could not *dissuade* Huck from running away from home, he decided to run away with him. dissuasion, N.

distant ADJ. reserved or aloof; cold in manner. His *distant* greeting made me feel unwelcome from the start. (secondary meaning)

● **distend** V. expand; swell out. I can tell when he is under stress by the way the veins *distend* on his forehead.

distill V. extract the essence; purify; refine. A moonshiner *distills* mash into whiskey; an epigrammatist *distills* thoughts into quips.

distinction N. honor; contrast; discrimination. A holder of the Medal of Honor, George served with great *distinction* in World War II. He made a *distinction*, however, between World War II and Vietnam, which he considered an immoral conflict.

distort V. twist out of shape. It is difficult to believe the newspaper accounts of the riots because of the way some reporters *distort* and exaggerate the actual events. distortion, N.

distraught ADJ. upset; distracted by anxiety. The *distraught* parents frantically searched the ravine for their lost child.

diurnal ADJ. daily. A farmer cannot neglect his *diurnal* tasks at any time; cows, for example, must be milked regularly.

diva N. operatic singer; prima donna. Although world famous as a *diva,* she did not indulge in fits of temperament.

diverge V. vary; go in different directions from the same point. The spokes of the wheel *diverge* from the hub.

■ **divergent** ADJ. differing; deviating. Since graduating from medical school, the two doctors have taken *divergent* paths, one going on to become a nationally prominent surgeon, the other dedicating himself to a small family practice in his home town. divergence, N.

diverse ADJ. differing in some characteristics; various. The professor suggested *diverse* ways of approaching the assignment and recommended that we choose one of them. diversity, N.

diversion N. act of turning aside; pastime. After studying for several hours, he needed a *diversion* from work. divert, V.

diversity N. variety; dissimilitude. The *diversity* of colleges in this country indicates that many levels of ability are being cared for.

divest V. strip; deprive. He was *divested* of his power to act and could no longer govern. divestiture, N.

divine V. perceive intuitively; foresee the future. Nothing infuriated Tom more than Aunt Polly's ability to *divine* when he was telling the truth.

divulge V. reveal. No lover of gossip, Charlotte would never *divulge* anything that a friend told her in confidence.

docile ADJ. obedient; easily managed. As *docile* as he seems today, that old lion was once a ferocious, snarling beast. docility, N.

doctrinaire ADJ. unable to compromise about points of doctrine; dogmatic; unyielding. Weng had hoped that the student-led democracy movement might bring about change in China, but the repressive response of the *doctrinaire* hard-liners crushed his dreams of democracy.

■ **doctrine** N. teachings, in general; particular principle (religious, legal, etc.) taught. He was so committed to the *doctrines* of his faith that he was unable to evaluate them impartially.

■ **document** V. provide written evidence. She kept all the receipts from her business trip in order to *document* her expenses for the firm. also N.

dogged ADJ. determined; stubborn. *Les Miserables* tells of Inspector Javert's long, *dogged* pursuit of the criminal Jean Valjean.

doggerel N. poor verse. Although we find occasional snatches of genuine poetry in her work, most of her writing is mere *doggerel*.

■ **dogmatic** ADJ. opinionated; arbitrary; doctrinal. We tried to discourage Doug from being so *dogmatic*, but never could convince him that his opinions might be wrong.

doldrums N. blues; listlessness; slack period. Once the excitement of meeting her deadline was over, she found herself in the *doldrums*.

doleful ADJ. sorrowful. He found the *doleful* lamentations of the bereaved family emotionally disturbing and he left as quickly as he could.

dolt N. stupid person. The heroes of *Dumb and Dumber* are, as the title suggests, a classic pair of *dolts*.

domicile N. home. Although his legal *domicile* was in New York City, his work kept him away from his residence for many years. also v.

domineer V. rule over tyrannically. Students prefer teachers who guide, not ones who *domineer*.

don V. put on. When Clark Kent has to *don* his Superman outfit, he changes clothes in a convenient phone booth.

doodle V. scribble or draw aimlessly; waste time. Art's teachers scolded him when he *doodled* all over the margins of his papers.

dormant ADJ. sleeping; lethargic; latent. At fifty her long-*dormant* ambition to write flared up once more; within a year she had completed the first of her great historical novels.

dossier N. file of documents on a subject. Ordered by J. Edgar Hoover to investigate the senator, the FBI compiled a complete *dossier* on him.

dote V. be excessively fond of; show signs of mental decline. Not only grandmothers bore you with stories about their brilliant grandchildren; grandfathers *dote* on the little rascals, too. Poor old Alf clearly *doted*: the senile old *dotard* was past it; in fact, he was in his *dotage*.

douse V. plunge into water; drench; extinguish. They *doused* each other with hoses and water balloons.

dowdy ADJ. slovenly; untidy. She tried to change her *dowdy* image by buying a new fashionable wardrobe.

downcast ADJ. disheartened; sad. Cheerful and optimistic by nature, Beth was never *downcast* despite the difficulties she faced.

drab ADJ. dull; lacking color; cheerless. The Dutch woman's *drab* winter coat contrasted with the distinctive, colorful native costume she wore beneath it.

draconian ADJ. extremely severe. When the principal canceled the senior prom because some seniors had been late to school that week, we thought the *draconian* punishment was far too harsh for such a minor violation of the rules.

dregs N. sediment; worthless residue. David poured the wine carefully to avoid stirring up the *dregs*.

drivel N. nonsense; foolishness. Why do I have to spend my days listening to such idiotic *drivel*? *Drivel* is related to *dribble*: think of a dribbling, *driveling* idiot.

droll ADJ. queer and amusing. He was a popular guest because his *droll* anecdotes were always entertaining.

drone N. idle person; male bee. Content to let his wife support him, the would-be writer was in reality nothing but a *drone*.

drone V. talk dully; buzz or murmur like a bee. On a gorgeous day, who wants to be stuck in a classroom listening to the teacher *drone*?

dross N. waste matter; worthless impurities. Many methods have been devised to separate the valuable metal from the *dross*.

drudgery N. menial work. Cinderella's fairy godmother rescued her from a life of *drudgery*.

■ **dubious** ADJ. questionable; filled with doubt. Many critics of the SAT contend the test is of *dubious* worth. Jay claimed he could get a perfect 2400 on the new SAT, but Ellen was *dubious*: she knew he hadn't cracked a book in three years.

ductile ADJ. malleable; flexible; pliable. Copper is an extremely *ductile* material: you can stretch it into the thinnest of wires, bend it, even wind it into loops.

dulcet ADJ. sweet sounding. The *dulcet* sounds of the birds at dawn were soon drowned out by the roar of traffic passing our motel.

dumbfound V. astonish. Egbert's perfect 2400 on his SAT exam *dumbfounded* his classmates, who had always found him to be perfectly dumb.

● **dupe** N. someone easily fooled. While the gullible Watson often was made a *dupe* by unscrupulous parties, Sherlock Holmes was far more difficult to fool. also v.

■ **duplicity** N. double-dealing; hypocrisy. When Tanya learned that Mark had been two-timing her, she was furious at his *duplicity*.

Word List 16   duration–encroachment

duration   N. length of time something lasts. Because she wanted the children to make a good impression on the dinner guests, Mother promised them a treat if they'd behave for the *duration* of the meal.

duress   N. forcible restraint, especially unlawfully. The hostages were held under *duress* until the prisoners' demands were met.

dutiful   ADJ. respectful; obedient. When Mother told Billy to kiss Great-Aunt Hattie, the boy obediently gave the old woman a *dutiful* peck on her cheek.

dwarf   V. cause to seem small. The giant redwoods and high cliffs *dwarfed* the elegant Ahwahnee Hotel, making it appear a modest lodge rather than an imposing hostelry.

dwindle   V. shrink; reduce. The food in the life boat gradually *dwindled* away to nothing; in the end, they ate the ship's cook.

dynamic   ADJ. energetic; vigorously active. The *dynamic* aerobics instructor kept her students on the run; she was a little *dynamo*.

earthy   ADJ. unrefined; coarse. His *earthy* remarks often embarrassed the women in his audience.

ebb   V. recede; lessen. Sitting on the beach, Mrs. Dalloway watched the tide *ebb*: the waters receded, drawing away from her as she sat there all alone. also N.

● **ebullient**   ADJ. showing excitement; overflowing with enthusiasm. Amy's *ebullient* nature could not be repressed; she was always bubbling over with excitement. ebullience, N.

eccentric   ADJ. irregular; odd; whimsical; bizarre. The comet veered dangerously close to the earth in its *eccentric* orbit. People came up with some *eccentric* ideas for dealing with the emergency: someone even suggested tieing a knot in the comet's tail!

eccentricity   N. oddity; idiosyncrasy. Some of his friends tried to account for his rudeness to strangers as the *eccentricity* of genius.

ecclesiastic   ADJ. pertaining to the church. The minister donned his *ecclesiastic* garb and walked to the pulpit. also N.

■ **eclectic**   ADJ. composed of elements drawn from disparate sources. His style of interior decoration was *eclectic*: bits and pieces of furnishings from widely divergent periods, strikingly juxtaposed to create a unique decor. eclecticism, N.

eclipse   V. darken; extinguish; surpass. The new stock market high *eclipsed* the previous record set in 1995.

ecologist   N. a person concerned with the interrelationship between living organisms and their environment. The *ecologist* was concerned that the new dam would upset the natural balance of the creatures living in Glen Canyon.

economy   N. efficiency or conciseness in using something. Reading the epigrams of Pope, I admire the *economy* of his verse: in few words he conveys worlds of meaning. (secondary meaning)

ecstasy   N. rapture; joy; any overpowering emotion. When Allison received her long-hoped-for letter of acceptance from Harvard, she was in *ecstasy*. ecstatic, ADJ.

edict   N. decree (especially issued by a sovereign); official command. The emperor issued an *edict* decreeing that everyone should come see him model his magnificent new clothes.

● **edify**   V. instruct; correct morally. Although his purpose was to *edify* and not to entertain his audience, many of his listeners were amused rather than enlightened.

eerie   ADJ. weird. In that *eerie* setting, it was easy to believe in ghosts and other supernatural beings.

● **efface**   V. rub out. The coin had been handled so many times that its date had been *effaced*.

effectual   ADJ. able to produce a desired effect; valid. Medical researchers are concerned because of the development of drug-resistant strains of bacteria; many once useful antibiotics are no longer *effectual* in curing bacterial infections.

● **effervescence**   N. inner excitement or exuberance; bubbling from fermentation or carbonation. Nothing depressed Sue for long; her natural *effervescence* soon reasserted itself. Soda that loses its *effervescence* goes flat. effervescent, ADJ. effervesce, V.

effete   ADJ. lacking vigor; worn out; sterile. Is the Democratic Party still a vital political force, or is it an *effete*, powerless faction, wedded to outmoded liberal policies?

efficacy   N. power to produce desired effect. The *efficacy* of this drug depends on the regularity of the dosage. efficacious, ADJ.

effrontery   N. shameless boldness. She had the *effrontery* to insult the guest.

effusive   ADJ. pouring forth; gushing. Her *effusive* manner of greeting her friends finally began to irritate them. effusion, N.

egoism   N. excessive interest in one's self; belief that one should be interested in one's self rather than in others. His *egoism* prevented him from seeing the needs of his colleagues.

■ **egotistical**   ADJ. excessively self-centered; self-important; conceited. Typical *egotistical* remark: "But enough of this chit-chat about you and your little problems. Let's talk about what's really important: *Me!*"

egregious   ADJ. notorious; conspicuously bad or shocking. She was an *egregious* liar; we all knew better than to believe a word she said. Ed's housekeeping was *egregious*: he let his dirty dishes pile up so long that they were stuck together with last week's food.

egress   N. exit. Barnum's sign "To the *Egress*" fooled many people who thought they were going to see an animal and instead found themselves in the street.

ejaculation   N. exclamation. He could not repress an *ejaculation* of surprise when he heard the news.

elaboration   N. addition of details; intricacy. Tell what happened simply, without any *elaboration*. elaborate, V.

■ **elated** ADJ. overjoyed; in high spirits. Grinning from ear to ear, Bonnie Blair was clearly *elated* by her fifth Olympic gold medal. elation, N.

● **elegy** N. poem or song expressing lamentation. On the death of Edward King, Milton composed the *elegy* "Lycidas." elegiacal, ADJ.

● **elicit** V. draw out by discussion. The detectives tried to *elicit* where he had hidden his loot.

elixir N. cure-all; something invigorating. The news of her chance to go abroad acted on her like an *elixir*.

ellipsis N. omission of words from a text. Sometimes an *ellipsis* can lead to a dangling modifier, as in the sentence "Once dressed, you should refrigerate the potato salad."

elliptical ADJ. oval; ambiguous, either purposely or because key words have left out. An *elliptical* billiard ball wobbles because it is not perfectly round; an *elliptical* remark baffles because it is not perfectly clear.

■ **eloquence** N. expressiveness; persuasive speech. The crowds were stirred by Martin Luther King's *eloquence*. eloquent, ADJ.

● **elucidate** V. explain; enlighten. He was called upon to *elucidate* the disputed points in his article.

■ **elusive** ADJ. evasive; baffling; hard to grasp. Trying to pin down exactly when the contractors would be finished remodeling the house, Nancy was frustrated by their *elusive* replies. elude, V.

● **emaciated** ADJ. thin and wasted. Many severe illnesses leave their victims so *emaciated* that they must gain back their lost weight before they can fully recover.

emanate V. issue forth. A strong odor of sulphur *emanated* from the spring.

emancipate V. set free. At first, the attempts of the Abolitionists to *emancipate* the slaves were unpopular in New England as well as in the South.

embargo N. ban on commerce or other activity. As a result of the *embargo*, trade with the colonies was at a standstill.

embark V. commence; go on board a boat or airplane; begin a journey. In devoting herself to the study of gorillas, Dian Fossey *embarked* on a course of action that was to cost her her life.

embed V. enclose; place in something. Tales of actual historical figures like King Alfred have become *embedded* in legends.

■ **embellish** V. adorn; ornament. The costume designer *embellished* the leading lady's ball gown with yards and yards of ribbon and lace.

embezzlement N. stealing. The bank teller confessed his *embezzlement* of the funds.

embody V. personify; make concrete; incorporate. Cheering on his rival Mark McGwire's efforts to break Roger Maris's home run record, Sammy Sosa *embodied* the spirit of true sportsmanship.

embrace V. hug; adopt or espouse; accept readily; encircle; include. Clasping Maid Marian in his arms, Robin Hood *embraced* her lovingly. In joining the outlaws in Sherwood Forest, she had openly *embraced* their cause.

embroider V. decorate with needlework; ornament with fancy or fictitious details. For her mother's birthday, Beth *embroidered* a lovely design on a handkerchief. When asked what made her late getting home, Jo *embroidered* her account with tales of runaway horses and rescuing people from a ditch. embroidery, N.

embroil V. throw into confusion; involve in strife; entangle. He became *embroiled* in the heated discussion when he tried to arbitrate the dispute.

embryonic ADJ. undeveloped; rudimentary. The CEO reminisced about the good old days when the computer industry was still in its *embryonic* stage and start-up companies were founded in family garages.

● **emend** V. correct; correct by a critic. The critic *emended* the book by selecting the passages which he thought most appropriate to the text.

emendation N. correction of errors; improvement. Please initial all the *emendations* you have made in this contract.

eminent ADJ. high; lofty. After his appointment to this *eminent* position, he seldom had time for his former friends.

emissary N. agent; messenger. The secretary of state was sent as the president's special *emissary* to the conference on disarmament.

empathy N. ability to identify with another's feelings, ideas, etc. What made Ann such a fine counselor was her *empathy*, her ability to put herself in her client's place and feel his emotions as if they were her own. empathize, V.

empirical ADJ. based on experience. He distrusted hunches and intuitive flashes; he placed his reliance entirely on *empirical* data.

■ **emulate** V. imitate; rival. In a brief essay, describe a person you admire, someone whose virtues you would like to *emulate*.

enamored ADJ. in love. Narcissus became *enamored* of his own beauty.

encipher V. encode; convert a message into code. One of Bond's first lessons was how to *encipher* the messages he sent to Miss Moneypenny so that none of his other lady friends could decipher them.

enclave N. territory enclosed within an alien land. The Vatican is an independent *enclave* in Italy.

encomium N. high praise; eulogy. Uneasy with the *encomiums* expressed by his supporters, Tolkien felt unworthy of such high praise.

encompass V. surround. A moat, or deep water-filled trench, *encompassed* the castle, protecting it from attack.

encroachment N. gradual intrusion. The *encroachment* of the factories upon the neighborhood lowered the value of the real estate.

Word List 17 encumber–etymology

encumber v. burden. Some people *encumber* themselves with too much luggage when they take short trips.

endearment N. fond statement. Your gifts and *endearments* cannot make me forget your earlier insolence.

endemic ADJ. prevailing among a specific group of people or in a specific area or country. This disease is *endemic* in this part of the world; more than 80 percent of the population are at one time or another affected by it.

■ **endorse** v. approve; support. Everyone waited to see which one of the rival candidates for the city council the mayor would *endorse*. (secondary meaning) endorsement, N.

enduring ADJ. lasting; surviving. Keats believed in the *enduring* power of great art, which would outlast its creators' brief lives.

energize v. invigorate; make forceful and active. Rather than exhausting Maggie, dancing *energized* her.

enervate v. weaken. She was slow to recover from her illness; even a short walk to the window would *enervate* her.

enfranchise v. to admit to the rights of citizenship (especially the right to vote). Although Blacks were *enfranchised* shortly after the Civil War, women did not receive the right to vote until 1920.

engage v. attract; hire; pledge oneself; confront. "Your case has *engaged* my interest, my lord," said Holmes. "You may *engage* my services."

engaging ADJ. charming; attractive. Everyone liked Nancy's pleasant manners and *engaging* personality.

engender v. cause; produce. To receive praise for real accomplishments *engenders* self-confidence in a child.

engross v. occupy fully. John was so *engrossed* in his studies that he did not hear his mother call.

■ **enhance** v. increase; improve. You can *enhance* your chances of being admitted to the college of your choice by learning to write well; an excellent essay can *enhance* any application.

■ **enigma** N. puzzle; mystery. "What *do* women want?" asked Dr. Sigmund Freud. Their behavior was an *enigma* to him. enigmatic, ADJ.

■ **enmity** N. ill will; hatred. At Camp David, President Carter labored to bring an end to the *enmity* that prevented the peaceful coexistence of Egypt and Israel.

ennui N. boredom. The monotonous routine of hospital life induced a feeling of *ennui* that made him moody and irritable.

enormity N. hugeness (in a bad sense). He did not realize the *enormity* of his crime until he saw what suffering he had caused.

enrapture v. please intensely. The audience was *enraptured* by the freshness of the voices and the excellent orchestration.

ensconce v. settle comfortably. Now that their children were *ensconced* safely in the private school, the jet-setting parents decided to leave for Europe.

ensemble N. group of (supporting) players; organic unity; costume. As a dancer with the Oakland Ballet, Benjamin enjoyed being part of the *ensemble*. Having acted with one another for well over a decade, the cast members have developed a true sense of *ensemble*: they work together seamlessly. Mitzi wore a charming two-piece *ensemble* designed by Donna Karan.

entail v. require; necessitate; involve. Building a college-level vocabulary will *entail* some work on your part.

enterprising ADJ. full of initiative. By coming up with fresh ways to market the company's products, Mike proved himself to be an *enterprising* businessman.

enthrall v. capture; enslave. From the moment he saw her picture, he was *enthralled* by her beauty.

entice v. lure; attract; tempt. She always tried to *entice* her baby brother into mischief.

entitlement N. right to claim something; right to benefits. While Bill was *entitled* to use a company car while he worked for the firm, the company's lawyers questioned his *entitlement* to the vehicle once he'd quit his job.

entity N. real being. As soon as the Charter was adopted, the United Nations became an *entity* and had to be considered as a factor in world diplomacy.

entourage N. group of attendants; retinue. Surrounded by the members of his *entourage*, the mayor hurried into city hall, shouting a brusque "No comment!" to the reporters lining the steps.

entrance v. put under a spell; carry away with emotion. Shafts of sunlight on a wall could *entrance* her and leave her spellbound.

entreat v. plead; ask earnestly. She *entreated* her father to let her stay out till midnight.

entrepreneur N. businessman; contractor. Opponents of our present tax program argue that it discourages *entrepreneurs* from trying new fields of business activity.

enumerate v. list; mention one by one. Huck hung his head in shame as Miss Watson *enumerated* his many flaws.

enunciate v. speak distinctly. Stop mumbling! How will people understand you if you do not *enunciate*?

eon N. long period of time; an age. It has taken *eons* for our civilization to develop.

■ **ephemeral** ADJ. short-lived; fleeting. The mayfly is an *ephemeral* creature: its adult life lasts little more than a day.

epic N. long heroic poem, or similar work of art. Kurosawa's film *Seven Samurai* is an *epic* portraying the struggle of seven warriors to destroy a band of robbers. also ADJ.

epicure N. connoisseur of food and drink. *Epicures* frequent this restaurant because it features exotic wines and dishes. epicurean, ADJ.

epigram N. witty thought or saying, usually short. Poor Richard's *epigrams* made Benjamin Franklin famous.

epilogue N. short speech at conclusion of dramatic work. The audience was so disappointed in the play that many did not remain to hear the *epilogue*.

episodic ADJ. loosely connected; divided into incidents. Though he tried to follow the plot of *Gravity's Rainbow*, John found the novel too *episodic*; he enjoyed individual passages, but had trouble following the work as a whole.

epistolary ADJ. consisting of letters. Mark Harris's *Wake Up, Stupid!* is a modern *epistolary* novel that uses letters, telegrams, and newspaper clippings to tell the hero's story. The movie *You've Got Mail* tells a story using e-mail; does that make it an *e-pistolary* movie? epistle, N.

epitaph N. inscription in memory of a dead person. In his will, he dictated the *epitaph* he wanted placed on his tombstone.

epithet N. word or phrase characteristically used to describe a person or thing. So many kings of France were named Charles that you could tell them apart only by their *epithets*: Charles the Wise was someone far different from Charles the Fat.

epitome N. perfect example or embodiment. Singing "I am the very model of a modern Major-General," in *The Pirates of Penzance*, Major-General Stanley proclaimed himself the *epitome* of an officer and a gentleman.

epoch N. period of time. The glacial *epoch* lasted for thousands of years.

equable ADJ. tranquil; steady; uniform. After the hot summers and cold winters of New England, he found the climate of the West Indies *equable* and pleasant.

● **equanimity** N. calmness of temperament; composure. Even the inevitable strains of caring for an ailing mother did not disturb Bea's *equanimity*.

equilibrium N. balance. After the divorce, he needed some time to regain his *equilibrium*.

equinox N. period of equal days and nights; the beginning of Spring and Autumn. The vernal *equinox* is usually marked by heavy rainstorms.

● **equitable** ADJ. fair; impartial. I am seeking an *equitable* solution to this dispute, one that will be fair and acceptable to both sides.

equity N. fairness; justice. Our courts guarantee *equity* to all.

■ **equivocal** ADJ. ambiguous; intentionally misleading. Rejecting the candidate's *equivocal* comments on tax reform, the reporters pressed him to state clearly where he stood on the issue. equivocate, V.

equivocate V. lie; mislead; attempt to conceal the truth. No matter how bad the news is, give it to us straight. Above all, don't *equivocate*.

erode V. eat away. The limestone was *eroded* by the dripping water until only a thin shell remained. erosion, N.

erotic ADJ. arousing sexual desire; pertaining to sexual love. Films with significant *erotic* content are rated R; pornographic films are rated X.

erratic ADJ. odd; unpredictable. Investors become anxious when the stock market appears *erratic*.

■ **erroneous** ADJ. mistaken; wrong. I thought my answer was correct, but it was *erroneous*.

■ **erudite** ADJ. learned; scholarly. Unlike much scholarly writing, Huizinga's prose was entertaining as well as *erudite*, lively as well as learned.

escapade N. prank; flighty conduct. The headmaster could not regard this latest *escapade* as a boyish joke and expelled the young man.

escapism N. avoiding reality by diverting oneself with amusements. Before you criticize her constant reading as mere *escapism*, note how greatly her vocabulary has improved since she began spending her days buried in books.

eschew V. avoid. Hoping to present himself to his girlfriend as a totally reformed character, he tried to *eschew* all the vices, especially chewing tobacco and drinking bathtub gin.

■ **esoteric** ADJ. hard to understand; known only to the chosen few. *The New Yorker* short stories often include *esoteric* allusions to obscure people and events: the implication is, if you are in the in-crowd, you'll get the reference; if you come from Cleveland, you won't.

espionage N. spying. In order to maintain its power, the government developed a system of *espionage* that penetrated every household.

espouse V. adopt; support. She was always ready to *espouse* a worthy cause.

esteem V. respect; value. Jill *esteemed* Jack's taste in music, but she deplored his taste in clothes.

estranged ADJ. separated; alienated. The *estranged* wife sought a divorce. estrangement, N.

ethereal ADJ. light; heavenly; unusually refined. In Shakespeare's *The Tempest*, the spirit Ariel is an *ethereal* creature, too airy and unearthly for our mortal world.

ethnic ADJ. relating to races. Intolerance between *ethnic* groups is deplorable and usually is based on lack of information.

ethos N. underlying character of a culture, group, etc. Seeing how tenderly ordinary Spaniards treated her small daughter made author Barbara Kingsolver aware of how greatly children were valued in the Spanish *ethos*.

etymology N. study of word parts. A knowledge of *etymology* can help you on many English tests: if you know what the roots and prefixes mean, you can determine the meanings of unfamiliar words.

Word List 18 eulogy–faculty

■ **eulogy** N. expression of praise, often on the occasion of someone's death. Instead of delivering a spoken *eulogy* at Genny's memorial service, Jeff sang a song he had written in her honor.

■ **euphemism** N. mild expression in place of an unpleasant one. The expression "he passed away" is a *euphemism* for "he died."

euphonious ADJ. pleasing in sound. *Euphonious* even when spoken, the Italian language is particularly pleasing to the ear when sung. euphony. N.

euphoria N. feeling of great happiness and well-being (sometimes exaggerated). Delighted with her SAT scores, sure that the university would accept her, Allison was filled with *euphoria*. euphoric, ADJ.

● **evanescent** ADJ. fleeting; vanishing. Brandon's satisfaction in his new job was *evanescent*, for he immediately began to notice its many drawbacks. evanescence, N.

evasive ADJ. not frank; eluding. Your *evasive* answers convinced the judge that you were withholding important evidence. evade, V.

evenhanded ADJ. impartial; fair. Do men and women receive *evenhanded* treatment from their teachers, or, as recent studies suggest, do teachers pay more attention to male students than to females?

evince V. show clearly. When he tried to answer the questions, he *evinced* his ignorance of the subject matter.

evocative ADJ. tending to call up (emotions, memories). Scent can be remarkably *evocative*: the aroma of pipe tobacco *evokes* the memory of my father; a whiff of talcum powder calls up images of my daughter as a child.

■ **exacerbate** V. worsen; embitter. The latest bombing *exacerbated* England's already existing bitterness against the IRA, causing the prime minister to break off the peace talks abruptly.

exacting ADJ. extremely demanding. Cleaning the ceiling of the Sistine Chapel was an *exacting* task, one that demanded extremely meticulous care on the part of the restorers. exaction, N.

■ **exalt** V. raise in rank or dignity; praise. The actor Alec Guinness was *exalted* to the rank of knighthood by the queen.

exasperate V. vex. Johnny often *exasperates* his mother with his pranks.

exceptionable ADJ. objectionable. Do you find the punk rock band Green Day a highly *exceptionable*, thoroughly distasteful group, or do you think they are exceptionally talented performers?

● **excerpt** N. selected passage (written or musical). The cinematic equivalent of an *excerpt* from a novel is a clip from a film. also V.

excise V. cut away; cut out. When you *excise* the dead and dying limbs of a tree, you not only improve its appearance but also enhance its chances of bearing fruit. excision. N.

exclaim V. cry out suddenly. "Watson! Behind you!" Holmes *exclaimed*, seeing the assassin hurl himself on his friend.

excoriate V. scold with biting harshness; strip the skin off. Seeing the holes in Bill's new pants, his mother furiously *excoriated* him for ruining his good clothes. The tight, starched collar chafed and *excoriated* his neck, rubbing it raw.

exculpate V. clear from blame. He was *exculpated* of the crime when the real criminal confessed.

execrable ADJ. very bad. The anecdote was in such *execrable* taste that it revolted the audience.

■ **execute** V. put into effect; carry out. The choreographer wanted to see how well she could *execute* a pirouette. (secondary meaning) execution, N.

exegesis N. explanation; interpretation, especially of a biblical text. The minister based her sermon on her *exegesis* of a difficult passage from the book of Job. exegetical, ADJ.

■ **exemplary** ADJ. serving as a model; outstanding. At commencement the dean praised Ellen for her *exemplary* behavior as class president.

■ **exemplify** V. serve as an example of; embody. For a generation of balletgoers, Rudolf Nureyev *exemplified* the ideal of masculine grace.

exempt ADJ. not subject to a duty, obligation. Because of his flat feet, Foster was *exempt* from serving in the armed forces. also V.

exertion N. effort; expenditure of much physical work. The *exertion* spent in unscrewing the rusty bolt left her exhausted.

■ **exhaustive** ADJ. thorough; comprehensive. We have made an *exhaustive* study of all published SAT tests and are happy to share our research with you.

■ **exhilarating** ADJ. invigorating and refreshing; cheering. Though some of the hikers found tramping through the snow tiring, Jeffrey found the walk on the cold, crisp day *exhilarating*.

exhort V. urge. The evangelist *exhorted* all the sinners in his audience to repent. exhortation, N.

exhume V. dig out of the ground; remove from the grave. Could evidence that might identify the serial killer have been buried with his victim? To answer this question, the police asked the authorities for permission to *exhume* the victim's body.

exigency N. urgent situation. In this *exigency*, we must look for aid from our allies.

exodus N. departure. The *exodus* from the hot and stuffy city was particularly noticeable on Friday evenings.

■ **exonerate** V. acquit; exculpate. The defense team feverishly sought fresh evidence that might *exonerate* their client.

exorbitant ADJ. excessive. The people grumbled at his *exorbitant* prices but paid them because he had a monopoly.

exorcise V. drive out evil spirits. By incantation and prayer, the medicine man sought to *exorcise* the evil spirits which had taken possession of the young warrior.

exotic ADJ. not native; strange. Because of his *exotic* headdress, he was followed in the streets by small children who laughed at his strange appearance.

expansive ADJ. outgoing and sociable; broad and extensive; able to increase in size. Mr. Fezziwig was in an *expansive* humor, cheerfully urging his guests to join in the Christmas feast. Looking down on his *expansive* paunch, he sighed: if his belly *expanded* any further, he'd need an *expansive* waistline for his pants.

expatriate N. exile; someone who has withdrawn from his native land. Henry James was an American *expatriate* who settled in England.

■ **expedient** ADJ. suitable; practical; politic. A pragmatic politician, he was guided by what was *expedient* rather than by what was ethical. expediency, N.

■ **expedite** V. hasten. Because we are on a tight schedule, we hope you will be able to *expedite* the delivery of our order. The more *expeditious* your response is, the happier we'll be.

expenditure N. payment or expense; output. When you are operating on an expense account, you must keep receipts for all your *expenditures*. If you don't save your receipts, you won't get repaid without the *expenditure* of a lot of energy arguing with the firm's accountants.

expertise N. specialized knowledge; expert skill. Although she was knowledgeable in a number of fields, she was hired for her particular *expertise* in computer programming.

expiate V. make amends for (a sin). Jean Valjean tried to *expiate* his crimes by performing acts of charity.

expletive N. interjection; profane oath. The sergeant's remarks were filled with *expletives* that offended the new recruits.

explicate V. explain; interpret; clarify. Harry Levin *explicated* James Joyce's often bewildering novels with such clarity that even *Finnegan's Wake* seemed comprehensible to his students.

■ **explicit** ADJ. totally clear; definite; outspoken. Don't just hint around that you're dissatisfied: be *explicit* about what's bugging you.

exploit N. deed or action, particularly a brave deed. Raoul Wallenberg was noted for his *exploits* in rescuing Jews from Hitler's forces.

■ **exploit** V. make use of, sometimes unjustly. Cesar Chavez fought attempts to *exploit* migrant farmworkers in California. exploitation, N. exploitative, ADJ.

expository ADJ. explanatory; serving to explain. The manual that came with my VCR was no masterpiece of *expository* prose: its explanations were so garbled that I couldn't even figure out how to rewind a tape. exposition, N.

exposure N. risk, particularly of being exposed to disease or to the elements; unmasking; act of laying something open. *Exposure* to sun and wind had dried out her hair and weathered her face. She looked so changed that she no longer feared *exposure* as the notorious Irene Adler, one-time antagonist of Sherlock Holmes.

expropriate V. take possession of. He questioned the government's right to *expropriate* his land to create a wildlife preserve.

expunge V. cancel; remove. If you behave, I will *expunge* this notation from your record.

expurgate V. clean; remove offensive parts of a book. The editors felt that certain passages in the book had to be *expurgated* before it could be used in the classroom.

extant ADJ. still in existence. Although the book is out of print, some copies are still *extant*. Unfortunately, all of them are in libraries or private collections; none are for sale.

extent N. degree; magnitude; scope. What is the *extent* of the patient's injuries? If they are not too *extensive*, we can treat him on an outpatient basis.

extenuate V. weaken; mitigate. It is easier for us to *extenuate* our own shortcomings than those of others.

■ **extol** V. praise; glorify. The president *extolled* the astronauts, calling them the pioneers of the Space Age.

extort V. wring from; get money by threats, etc. The blackmailer *extorted* money from his victim.

extradition N. surrender of prisoner by one state to another. The lawyers opposed the *extradition* of their client on the grounds that for more than five years he had been a model citizen.

■ **extraneous** ADJ. not essential; superfluous. No wonder Ted can't think straight! His mind is so cluttered up with *extraneous* trivia, he can't concentrate on the essentials.

extrapolation N. projection; conjecture. Based on their *extrapolation* from the results of the primaries on Super Tuesday, the networks predicted that Bob Dole would be the Republican candidate for the presidency. extrapolate, V.

■ **extricate** V. free; disentangle. Icebreakers were needed to *extricate* the trapped whales from the icy floes that closed them in.

extrinsic ADJ. external; not essential; extraneous. A critically acclaimed *extrinsic* feature of the Chrysler Building is its ornate spire. The judge would not admit the testimony, ruling that it was *extrinsic* to the matter at hand.

extrovert N. person interested mostly in external objects and actions. A good salesman is usually an *extrovert*, who likes to mingle with people.

extrude V. force or push out. Much pressure is required to *extrude* these plastics.

■ **exuberance** N. overflowing abundance; joyful enthusiasm; flamboyance; lavishness. I was bowled over by the *exuberance* of Amy's welcome. What an enthusiastic greeting!

exude V. discharge; give forth. We get maple syrup from the sap that *exudes* from the trees in early spring. exudation, N.

exult V. rejoice. We *exulted* when our team won the victory.

fabricate V. build; lie. If we *fabricate* the buildings in this project out of standardized sections, we can reduce construction costs considerably. Because of Jack's tendency to *fabricate*, Jill had trouble believing a word he said.

facade N. front (of building); superficial or false appearance. The ornate *facade* of the church was often photographed by tourists, who never bothered to walk around the building to view its other sides. Susan seemed super-confident, but that was just a *facade* she put on to hide her insecurity.

facet N. small plane surface (of a gem); a side. The stonecutter decided to improve the rough diamond by providing it with several *facets*.

facetious ADJ. joking (often inappropriately); humorous. I'm serious about this project; I don't need any *facetious*, smart-alecky cracks about do-gooder little rich girls.

facile ADJ. easily accomplished; ready or fluent; superficial. Words came easily to Jonathan: he was a *facile* speaker and prided himself on being ready to make a speech at a moment's notice.

■ **facilitate** V. help bring about; make less difficult. Rest and proper nourishment should *facilitate* the patient's recovery.

facsimile N. copy. Many museums sell *facsimiles* of the works of art on display.

faction N. party; clique; dissension. The quarrels and bickering of the two small *factions* within the club disturbed the majority of the members.

faculty N. mental or bodily powers; teaching staff. As he grew old, Professor Twiggly feared he might lose his *faculties* and become unfit to teach. However, he had tenure: whether or not he was in full possession of his *faculties*, the school couldn't kick him off the *faculty*.

Word List 19   fallacious–flinch

■ **fallacious** ADJ. false; misleading. Paradoxically, *fallacious* reasoning does not always yield erroneous results: even though your logic may be faulty, the answer you get may nevertheless be correct. fallacy, N.

fallible ADJ. liable to err. I know I am *fallible,* but I feel confident that I am right this time.

● **fallow** ADJ. plowed but not sowed; uncultivated. Farmers have learned that it is advisable to permit land to lie *fallow* every few years.

● **falter** V. hesitate. When told to dive off the high board, she did not *falter*, but proceeded at once.

■ **fanaticism** N. excessive zeal; extreme devotion to a belief or cause. When Islamic fundamentalists demanded the death of Salman Rushdie because his novel questioned their faith, world opinion condemned them for their *fanaticism*.

fancy N. notion; whim; inclination. Martin took a *fancy* to paint his toenails purple. Assuming he would outgrow such *fanciful* behavior, his parents ignored his *fancy* feet. also ADJ.

fanfare N. call by bugles or trumpets. The exposition was opened with a *fanfare* of trumpets and the firing of cannon.

farce N. broad comedy; mockery. Nothing went right; the entire interview degenerated into a *farce*. farcical, ADJ.

■ **fastidious** ADJ. difficult to please; squeamish. Bobby was such a *fastidious* eater that he would eat a sandwich only if his mother first cut off every scrap of crust.

fatalism N. belief that events are determined by forces beyond one's control. With *fatalism,* he accepted the hardships that beset him. fatalistic, ADJ.

● **fathom** V. comprehend; investigate. I find his motives impossible to *fathom*; in fact, I'm totally clueless about what goes on in his mind.

fatuous ADJ. foolish; inane. He is far too intelligent to utter such *fatuous* remarks.

fauna N. animals of a period or region. The scientist could visualize the *fauna* of the period by examining the skeletal remains and the fossils.

fawning ADJ. courting favor by cringing and flattering. She was constantly surrounded by a group of *fawning* admirers who hoped to win some favor. fawn, V.

faze V. disconcert; dismay. No crisis could *faze* the resourceful hotel manager.

■ **feasible** ADJ. practical. Is it *feasible* to build a new stadium for the Yankees on New York's West Side? Without additional funding, the project is clearly unrealistic.

fecundity N. fertility; fruitfulness. The *fecundity* of his mind is illustrated by the many vivid images in his poems.

feign V. pretend. Bobby *feigned* illness, hoping that his mother would let him stay home from school.

feint N. trick; shift; sham blow. The boxer was fooled by his opponent's *feint* and dropped his guard. also V.

felicitous ADJ. apt; suitably expressed; well chosen. He was famous for his *felicitous* remarks and was called upon to serve as master-of-ceremonies at many a banquet. felicity, N.

felicity N. happiness; appropriateness (of a remark, choice, etc.). She wrote a note to the newlyweds wishing them great *felicity* in their wedded life.

fell ADJ. cruel; deadly. Newspaper reports of the SARS epidemic told of the tragic spread of the *fell* disease.

● **fell** V. cut or knock down; bring down (with a missile). Crying "Timber!" Paul Bunyan *felled* the mighty redwood tree. Robin Hood loosed his arrow and *felled* the king's deer.

felon N. person convicted of a grave crime. A convicted *felon* loses the right to vote.

feral ADJ. not domestic; wild. Abandoned by their owners, dogs may revert to their *feral* state, roaming the woods in packs.

ferment N. agitation; commotion. With the breakup of the Soviet Union, much of Eastern Europe was in a state of *ferment*.

ferret V. drive or hunt out of hiding. She *ferreted* out their secret.

fervent ADJ. ardent; hot. She felt that the *fervent* praise was excessive and somewhat undeserved.

fervid ADJ. ardent. Her *fervid* enthusiasm inspired all of us to undertake the dangerous mission.

■ **fervor** N. glowing ardor; intensity of feeling. At the protest rally, the students cheered the strikers and booed the dean with equal *fervor*.

fester V. rankle; produce irritation or resentment. Joe's insult *festered* in Anne's mind for days, and made her too angry to speak to him.

festive ADJ. joyous; celebratory. Their wedding in the park was a *festive* occasion.

fetid ADJ. malodorous. The neglected wound became *fetid*.

fetter V. shackle. The prisoner was *fettered* to the wall.

fiasco N. total failure. Tanya's attempt to look sophisticated by taking up smoking was a *fiasco*: she lit the filter, choked when she tried to inhale, and burned a hole in her boyfriend's couch.

fickle ADJ. changeable; faithless. As soon as Romeo saw Juliet, he forgot all about his old girlfriend Rosaline. Was Romeo *fickle*?

fictitious ADJ. imaginary. Although this book purports to be a biography of George Washington, many of the incidents are *fictitious*.

fidelity N. loyalty. Iago wickedly manipulates Othello, arousing his jealousy and causing him to question his wife's *fidelity*.

figment N. invention; imaginary thing. Was he hearing real voices in the night, or were they just a *figment* of his imagination?

figurative ADJ. not literal, but metaphorical; using a figure of speech. "To lose one's marbles" is a *figurative* expression; if you're told that Jack has lost his marbles, no one expects you to rush out to buy him a replacement set.

filament N. fine thread or fiber; threadlike structure within a lightbulb. A ray of sunlight illuminated the *filaments* of the spider web, turning the web into a net of gold.

filch V. steal. The boys *filched* apples from the fruit stand.

filial ADJ. pertaining to a son or daughter. Many children forget their *filial* obligations and disregard the wishes of their parents.

filibuster V. to block legislation by making long speeches. Even though we disapproved of Senator Foghorn's political goals, we were impressed by his ability to *filibuster* endlessly to keep an issue from coming to a vote.

finale N. conclusion. It is not until we reach the *finale* of this play that we can understand the author's message.

finesse N. delicate skill. The *finesse* and adroitness with which the surgeon wielded her scalpel impressed all the observers in the operating room.

finicky ADJ. too particular; fussy. The little girl was *finicky* about her food, leaving over anything that wasn't to her taste.

firebrand N. hothead: troublemaker. The police tried to keep track of all the local *firebrands* when the President came to town.

fissure N. crevice. The mountain climbers secured footholds in tiny *fissures* in the rock.

● **fitful** ADJ. spasmodic; intermittent. After several *fitful* attempts, he decided to postpone the start of the project until he felt more energetic.

flabbergasted ADJ. astounded; astonished; overcome with surprise. In the film *Flubber,* the hero invents a remarkable substance whose amazing properties leave his coworkers *flabbergasted.* flabbergast, V.

flaccid ADJ. flabby. His sedentary life had left him with *flaccid* muscles.

flag V. droop; grow feeble. When the opposing hockey team scored its third goal only minutes into the first quarter, the home team's spirits *flagged.* flagging, ADJ.

■ **flagrant** ADJ. conspicuously wicked; blatant; outrageous. The governor's appointment of his brother-in-law to the State Supreme Court was a *flagrant* violation of the state laws against nepotism (favoritism based on kinship).

flair N. talent. She has an uncanny *flair* for discovering new artists before the public has become aware of their existence.

flamboyant ADJ. ornate. Modern architecture has discarded the *flamboyant* trimming on buildings and emphasizes simplicity of line.

flaunt V. display ostentatiously. Mae West saw nothing wrong with showing off her considerable physical charms, saying, "Honey, if you've got it, *flaunt* it!"

fleck V. spot. Her cheeks, *flecked* with tears, were testimony to the hours of weeping.

fledgling ADJ. inexperienced. The folk dance club set up an apprentice program to allow *fledgling* dance callers a chance to polish their skills. also N.

fleece N. wool coat of a sheep. They shear sheep of their *fleece,* which they then comb into separate strands of wool.

fleece V. rob; plunder. The tricksters *fleeced* him of his inheritance.

flick N. light stroke as with a whip. The horse needed no encouragement; one *flick* of the whip was all the jockey had to apply to get the animal to run at top speed.

flinch V. hesitate, shrink. He did not *flinch* in the face of danger but fought back bravely.

Word List 20 flippant–gaffe

flippant ADJ. lacking proper seriousness. When Mark told Mona he loved her, she dismissed his earnest declaration with a *flippant* "Oh, you say that to all the girls!" flippancy, N.

flit V. fly; dart lightly; pass swiftly by. Like a bee *flitting* from flower to flower, Rose *flitted* from one boyfriend to the next.

flora N. plants of a region or era. Because she was a botanist, she spent most of her time studying the *flora* of the desert.

● **florid** ADJ. ruddy; reddish; flowery. If you go to Florida and get a sunburn, your complexion will look *florid*. If your postcards about the trip praise Florida in flowery words, your prose sounds *florid*.

flounder V. struggle and thrash about; proceed clumsily or falter. Up to his knees in the bog, Floyd *floundered* about, trying to regain his footing. Bewildered by the new software, Flo *floundered* until Jan showed her how to get started.

flourish V. grow well; prosper; decorate with ornaments. The orange trees *flourished* in the sun.

flout V. reject; mock. The headstrong youth *flouted* all authority; he refused to be curbed.

fluctuate V. waver; shift. The water pressure in our shower *fluctuates* wildly; you start rinsing yourself off with a trickle, and, two minutes later, a blast of water nearly knocks you down.

fluency N. smoothness of speech. He spoke French with *fluency* and ease.

fluke N. unlikely occurrence; stroke of fortune. When Douglas defeated Tyson for the heavyweight championship, some sportscasters dismissed his victory as a *fluke*.

fluster V. confuse. The teacher's sudden question *flustered* him and he stammered his reply.

flux N. flowing; series of changes. While conditions are in such a state of *flux*, I do not wish to commit myself too deeply in this affair.

fodder N. coarse food for cattle, horses, etc. One of Nancy's chores at the ranch was to put fresh supplies of *fodder* in the horses' stalls.

foible N. weakness; slight fault. We can overlook the *foibles* of our friends; no one is perfect.

foil N. contrast. In *Star Wars*, dark, evil Darth Vader is a perfect *foil* for fair-haired, naive Luke Skywalker.

foil V. defeat; frustrate. In the end, Skywalker is able to *foil* Vader's diabolical schemes.

foment V. stir up; instigate. Cheryl's archenemy Heather spread some nasty rumors that *fomented* trouble in the club. Do you think Cheryl's foe meant to *foment* such discord?

• **foolhardy** ADJ. rash. Don't be *foolhardy*. Get the advice of experienced people before undertaking this venture.

fop N. dandy; man excessively concerned with his clothes. People who dismissed young Mizrahi as a *fop* felt chagrined when he turned into one of the top fashion designers of his day. foppish, ADJ.

forbearance N. patience. Be patient with John. Treat him with *forbearance*: he is still weak from his illness.

forebears N. ancestors. Reverence for one's *forebears* (sometimes referred to as ancestor worship) plays an important part in many Oriental cultures.

foreboding N. premonition of evil. Suspecting no conspiracies against him, Caesar gently ridiculed his wife's *forebodings* about the Ides of March.

forensic ADJ. suitable to debate or courts of law. In her best *forensic* manner, the lawyer addressed the jury. forensics, N.

foreshadow V. give an indication beforehand; portend; prefigure. In retrospect, political analysts realized that Yeltsin's defiance of the attempted coup *foreshadowed* his emergence as the dominant figure of the new Russian republic.

foresight N. ability to foresee future happenings; prudence. A wise investor, she had the *foresight* to buy land just before the current real estate boom.

forestall V. prevent by taking action in advance. By setting up a prenuptial agreement, the prospective bride and groom hoped to *forestall* any potential arguments about money in the event of a divorce.

forgo V. give up; do without. Determined to lose weight for the summer, Ida decided to *forgo* dessert until she could fit into a size eight again.

forlorn ADJ. sad and lonely; wretched. Deserted by her big sisters and her friends, the *forlorn* child sat sadly on the steps awaiting their return.

formality N. ceremonious quality; something done just for form's sake. The president received the visiting heads of state with due *formality*: flags waving, honor guards standing at attention, anthems sounding at full blast. Signing this petition is a mere *formality*; it does not obligate you in any way.

formidable ADJ. inspiring fear or apprehension; difficult; awe-inspiring. In the film *Meet the Parents*, the hero is understandably nervous around his fiancee's father, a *formidable* CIA agent.

forsake V. desert; abandon; renounce. No one expected Foster to *forsake* his wife and children and run off with another woman.

forswear V. renounce; abandon. The captured knight could escape death only if he agreed to *forswear* Christianity and embrace Islam as the one true faith.

forte N. strong point or special talent. I am not eager to play this rather serious role, for my *forte* is comedy.

forthright ADJ. outspoken; straightforward; frank. Never afraid to call a spade a spade, she was perhaps too *forthright* to be a successful party politician.

fortitude N. bravery; courage. He was awarded the medal for his *fortitude* in the battle.

fortuitous ADJ. accidental; by chance. Though he pretended their encounter was *fortuitous*, he'd actually been hanging around her usual haunts for the past two weeks, hoping she'd turn up.

forum N. place of assembly to discuss public concerns; meeting for discussion. The film opens with a shot of the ancient *Forum* in Rome, where several senators are discussing the strange new sect known as Christians. At the end of the movie, its director presided over a *forum* examining new fashions in filmmaking.

foster V. rear; encourage. According to the legend, Romulus and Remus were *fostered* by a she-wolf who raised the abandoned infants with her own cubs. also ADJ.

founder V. fail completely; sink. After hitting the submerged iceberg, the *Titanic* started taking in water rapidly and soon *foundered*.

founder N. person who establishes (an organization, business). Among those drowned when the *Titanic* sank was the *founder* of the Abraham & Straus department store.

fracas N. brawl, melee. The military police stopped the *fracas* in the bar and arrested the belligerents.

fractious ADJ. unruly; disobedient; irritable. Bucking and kicking, the *fractious* horse unseated its rider.

frail ADJ. weak. The delicate child seemed too *frail* to lift the heavy carton. frailty, N.

franchise N. right granted by authority; right to vote; business licensed to sell a product in a particular territory. The city issued a *franchise* to the company to operate surface transit lines on the streets for ninety-nine years. For most of American history women lacked the right to vote: not until the early twentieth century was the *franchise* granted to women. Stan owns a Carvel's ice cream *franchise* in Chinatown.

frantic ADJ. wild. At the time of the collision, many people became *frantic* with fear.

fraternize V. associate in a friendly way. After the game, the members of the two teams *fraternized* as cheerfully as if they had never been rivals.

fraudulent ADJ. cheating; deceitful. The government seeks to prevent *fraudulent* and misleading advertising.

fraught ADJ. filled. Since this enterprise is *fraught* with danger, I will ask for volunteers who are willing to assume the risks.

fray N. brawl. The three musketeers were in the thick of the *fray*.

frenetic ADJ. frenzied; frantic. His *frenetic* activities convinced us that he had no organized plan of operation.

frenzied ADJ. madly excited. As soon as they smelled smoke, the *frenzied* animals milled about in their cages.

fret V. to be annoyed or vexed. To *fret* over your poor grades is foolish; instead, decide to work harder in the future.

friction N. clash in opinion; rubbing against. At this time when harmony is essential, we cannot afford to have any *friction* in our group.

frigid ADJ. intensely cold. Alaska is in the *frigid* zone.

■ **frivolous** ADJ. lacking in seriousness; self-indulgently carefree; relatively unimportant. Though Nancy enjoyed Bill's *frivolous*, lighthearted companionship, she sometimes wondered whether he could ever be serious. frivolity, N.

frolicsome ADJ. prankish; gay. The *frolicsome* puppy tried to lick the face of its master.

■ **frugality** N. thrift; economy. In economically hard times, anyone who doesn't learn to practice *frugality* risks bankruptcy. frugal, ADJ.

fruition N. bearing of fruit; fulfillment; realization. After years of saving and scrimping, her dream of owning her own home finally came to *fruition*.

frustrate V. thwart; defeat. Constant partisan bickering *frustrated* the governor's efforts to convince the legislature to approve his proposed budget.

fugitive ADJ. fleeting or transitory; roving. The film brought a few *fugitive* images to her mind, but on the whole it made no lasting impression upon her.

fulcrum N. support on which a lever rests. If we use this stone as a *fulcrum* and the crowbar as a lever, we may be able to move this boulder.

fulsome ADJ. disgustingly excessive. Disgusted by her fans' *fulsome* admiration, the movie star retreated from the public, crying, "I want to be alone!"

fundamental V. basic; primary; essential. The committee discussed all sorts of side issues without ever getting down to addressing the *fundamental* problem.

furlough N. leave of absence; vacation granted a soldier or civil servant. Dreaming of her loved ones back in the States, the young soldier could hardly wait for her upcoming *furlough*.

furor N. frenzy; great excitement. The story of her embezzlement of the funds created a *furor* on the Stock Exchange.

■ **furtive** ADJ. stealthy; sneaky. Noticing the *furtive* glance the customer gave the diamond bracelet on the counter, the jeweler wondered whether he had a potential shoplifter on his hands.

fusion N. union; blending; synthesis. So-called rockabilly music represents a *fusion* of country music and blues that became rock and roll.

futile ADJ. useless; hopeless; ineffectual. It is *futile* for me to try to get any work done around here while the telephone is ringing every thirty seconds. futility, N.

gadfly N. animal-biting fly; an irritating person. Like a *gadfly*, he irritated all the guests at the hotel; within forty-eight hours, everyone regarded him as an annoying busybody.

gaffe N. social blunder. According to Miss Manners, to call your husband by your lover's name is worse than a mere *gaffe*; it is a tactical mistake.

Word List 21   gainsay–gory

gainsay V. deny. Even though it reflected badly upon him, he was too honest to *gainsay* the truth of the report.

gait N. manner of walking or running; speed. The lame man walked with an uneven *gait*.

galaxy N. large, isolated system of stars, such as the Milky Way; any collection of brilliant personalities. Science fiction stories speculate about the possible existence of life in other *galaxies*. The deaths of such famous actors as John Candy and George Burns tells us that the *galaxy* of Hollywood superstars is rapidly disappearing.

gale N. windstorm; gust of wind; emotional outburst (laughter, tears). The Weather Channel warned viewers about a rising *gale*, with winds of up to sixty miles per hour.

gall N. bitterness; nerve. The knowledge of his failure filled him with *gall*.

gall V. annoy; chafe. Their taunts *galled* him.

galvanize V. stimulate by shock; stir up; revitalize. News that the prince was almost at their door *galvanized* the ugly stepsisters into a frenzy of combing and primping.

gambit N. opening in chess in which a piece is sacrificed. The player was afraid to accept his opponent's *gambit* because he feared a trap which as yet he could not see.

gambol V. skip; leap playfully. Watching the children *gambol* in the park, Betty marveled at their youthful energy and spirit.

gamely ADV. bravely; with spirit. Because he had fought *gamely* against a much superior boxer, the crowd gave him a standing ovation when he left the arena.

gamut N. entire range. In a classic put-down of actress Katharine Hepburn, the critic Dorothy Parker wrote that the actress ran the *gamut* of emotion from A to B.

gape V. open widely; stare open-mouthed. The huge pit *gaped* before him; if he stumbled, he would fall in. Slack-jawed in wonder, Huck *gaped* at the huge stalactites hanging down from the ceiling of the limestone cavern.

garbled ADJ. mixed up; jumbled; distorted. A favorite party game involves passing a whispered message from one person to another until, by the time it reaches the last player, the message is totally *garbled*.

gargantuan ADJ. huge; enormous. The *gargantuan* wrestler was terrified of mice.

garish ADJ. over-bright in color; gaudy. She wore a gaudy rhinestone necklace with an excessively *garish* gold lamé dress.

garner V. gather; store up. In her long career as an actress, Katharine Hepburn *garnered* many awards, including the coveted Oscar.

garnish V. decorate. The chef *garnished* the boiled potatoes with a sprinkling of parsley. also N.

■ **garrulous** ADJ. loquacious; wordy; talkative. My Uncle Henry is the most *garrulous* person in Cayuga County: he can outtalk anyone I know. garrulity, N.

gauche ADJ. clumsy; coarse and uncouth. Compared to the sophisticated young ladies in their elegant gowns, tomboyish Jo felt *gauche* and out of place.

gaudy ADJ. flashy; showy. The newest Trump skyscraper is typically *gaudy*, covered in gilded panels that gleam in the sun.

gaunt ADJ. lean and angular; barren. His once round face looked surprisingly *gaunt* after he had lost weight.

gavel N. hammerlike tool; mallet. "Sold!" cried the auctioneer, banging her *gavel* on the table to indicate she'd accepted the final bid.

gawk V. stare foolishly; look in open-mouthed awe. The country boy *gawked* at the skyscrapers and neon lights of the big city.

genealogy N. record of descent; lineage. He was proud of his *genealogy* and constantly referred to the achievements of his ancestors.

generality N. vague statement. This report is filled with *generalities*; be more specific in your statements.

generate V. cause; produce; create. In his first days in office, President Clinton managed to *generate* a new mood of optimism; we just hoped he could *generate* some new jobs.

generic ADJ. characteristic of an entire class or species. Sue knew so many computer programmers who spent their spare time playing fantasy games that she began to think that playing Dungeons & Dragons was a *generic* trait.

genesis N. beginning; origin. Tracing the *genesis* of a family is the theme of *Roots*.

geniality N. cheerfulness; kindliness; sympathy. This restaurant is famous and popular because of the *geniality* of the proprietor who tries to make everyone happy.

genre N. particular variety of art or literature. Both a short story writer and a poet, Langston Hughes proved himself equally skilled in either *genre*.

genteel ADJ. well-bred; elegant. We are looking for a man with a *genteel* appearance who can inspire confidence by his cultivated manner.

gentility N. those of gentle birth; refinement. Her family was proud of its *gentility* and elegance.

gentry N. people of standing; class of people just below nobility. The local *gentry* did not welcome the visits of the summer tourists and tried to ignore their presence in the community.

germane ADJ. pertinent; bearing upon the case at hand. The judge refused to allow the testimony to be heard by the jury because it was not *germane* to the case.

germinal ADJ. pertaining to a germ; creative. Such an idea is *germinal;* I am certain that it will influence thinkers and philosophers for many generations.

germinate V. cause to sprout; sprout. After the seeds *germinate* and develop their permanent leaves, the plants may be removed from the cold frames and transplanted to the garden.

gesticulation N. motion; gesture. We were still too far off to make out what Mother was shouting, but from her animated *gesticulations* we could tell she wanted us to hurry home instantly.

ghastly ADJ. horrible. The murdered man was a *ghastly* sight.

gibberish N. nonsense; babbling. Did you hear that fool boy spouting *gibberish* about monsters from outer space? gibber, V.

gibe V. mock; taunt; scoff at. The ugly stepsisters constantly *gibed* at Cinderella, taunting her about her ragged clothes.

gingerly ADV. very carefully. To separate egg whites, first crack the egg *gingerly*.

girth N. distance around something; circumference. It took an extra-large cummerbund to fit around Andrew Carnegie's considerable *girth*.

gist N. essence. She was asked to give the *gist* of the essay in two sentences.

● **glacial** ADJ. like a glacier; extremely cold. Never a warm person, when offended John could seem positively *glacial*.

glaring ADJ. highly conspicuous; harshly bright. *Glaring* spelling or grammatical errors in your resumé will unfavorably impress potential employers.

glaze V. cover with a thin and shiny surface. The freezing rain *glazed* the streets and made driving hazardous. also N.

glib ADJ. fluent; facile; slick. Keeping up a steady patter to entertain his customers, the kitchen gadget salesman was a *glib* speaker, never at a loss for a word.

glimmer V. shine erratically; twinkle. In the darkness of the cavern, the glowworms hanging from the cavern roof *glimmered* like distant stars.

gloat V. express evil satisfaction; view malevolently. As you *gloat* over your ill-gotten wealth, do you think of the many victims you have defrauded?

glossary N. brief explanation of words used in the text. I have found the *glossary* in this book very useful; it has eliminated many trips to the dictionary.

gloss over V. explain away. No matter how hard he tried to talk around the issue, President Bush could not *gloss over* the fact that he had raised taxes after all.

glossy ADJ. smooth and shining. I want this photograph printed on *glossy* paper, not matte.

glower V. scowl. The angry boy *glowered* at his father.

glut V. overstock; fill to excess. The many manufacturers *glutted* the market and could not find purchasers for the excess articles they had produced. also N.

■ **glutton** N. someone who eats too much. When Mother saw that Bobby had eaten all the cookies, she called him a little *glutton*. gluttonous, ADJ.

gnarled ADJ. twisted. The weather-beaten old sailor was as *gnarled* and bent as an old oak tree.

gnome N. dwarf; underground spirit. In medieval mythology, *gnomes* were the special guardians and inhabitants of subterranean mines.

goad V. urge on; spur; incite. Mother was afraid that Ben's wild friends would *goad* him into doing something that would get him into trouble with the law. also N.

gorge N. small, steep-walled canyon. The white-water rafting guide warned us about the rapids farther downstream, where the river cut through a narrow *gorge*.

gorge V. stuff oneself. The gluttonous guest *gorged* himself with food as though he had not eaten for days.

gory ADJ. bloody. The audience shuddered as they listened to the details of the *gory* massacre.

Word List 22   gouge–hiatus

gouge V. tear out. In that fight, all the rules were forgotten; the adversaries bit, kicked, and tried to *gouge* each other's eyes out.

gourmet N. connoisseur of food and drink. The *gourmet* stated that this was the best onion soup she had ever tasted.

graduated ADJ. arranged by degrees (of height, difficulty, etc.). Margaret loved her *graduated* set of Russian hollow wooden dolls; she spent hours happily putting the smaller dolls into their larger counterparts.

graft N. piece of transplanted tissue; portion of plant inserted in another plant. After the fire, Greg required skin *grafts* to replace the badly damaged areas on his forearms. also V.

grandeur N. impressiveness; stateliness; majesty. No matter how often he hiked through the mountains, David never failed to be struck by the *grandeur* of the Sierra Nevada range.

grandiloquent ADJ. pompous; bombastic; using high-sounding language. The politician could never speak simply; she was always *grandiloquent*.

grandiose ADJ. pretentious; high-flown; ridiculously exaggerated; impressive. The aged matinee idol still had *grandiose* notions of his supposed importance in the theatrical world.

granulate V. form into grains. Sugar that has been *granulated* dissolves more readily than lump sugar. granule, N.

graphic ADJ. pertaining to the art of delineating; vividly described. The description of the winter storm was so *graphic* that you could almost feel the hailstones.

grapple V. wrestle; come to grips with. He *grappled* with the burglar and overpowered him.

grate V. make a harsh noise; have an unpleasant effect; shred. The screams of the quarreling children *grated* on her nerves.

■ **gratify** V. please. Lori's parents were *gratified* by her successful performance on the SAT.

gratis ADJ. free. The company offered to give one package *gratis* to every purchaser of one of their products. also ADJ.

■ **gratuitous** ADJ. given freely; unwarranted; uncalled for. Quit making *gratuitous* comments about my driving; no one asked you for your opinion.

■ **gravity** N. seriousness. We could tell we were in serious trouble from the *gravity* of the principal's expression. (secondary meaning) grave, ADJ.

■ **gregarious** ADJ. sociable. Typically, partygoers are *gregarious*; hermits are not.

grievance N. cause of complaint. When her supervisor ignored her complaint, she took her *grievance* to the union.

grill V. question severely. In violation of the Miranda law, the police *grilled* the suspect for several hours before reading him his rights. (secondary meaning)

grimace N. a facial distortion to show feeling such as pain, disgust, etc. Even though he remained silent, his *grimace* indicated his displeasure. also V.

grisly ADJ. ghastly. She shuddered at the *grisly* sight.

grouse V. complain; fuss. Students traditionally *grouse* about the abysmal quality of "mystery meat" and similar dormitory food.

grotesque ADJ. fantastic; comically hideous. On Halloween people enjoy wearing *grotesque* costumes.

grovel V. crawl or creep on ground; remain prostrate. Mr. Wickfield was never harsh to his employees; he could not understand why Uriah would always cringe and *grovel* as if he expected a beating.

grudging ADJ. unwilling; reluctant; stingy. We received only *grudging* support from the mayor despite his earlier promises of aid.

gruel V. liquid food made by boiling oatmeal, etc., in milk or water. Our daily allotment of *gruel* made the meal not only monotonous but also unpalatable.

grueling ADJ. exhausting. The marathon is a *grueling* race.

gruesome ADJ. grisly; horrible. His face was the stuff of nightmares: all the children in the audience screamed when Freddy Kruger's *gruesome* countenance was flashed on the screen.

gruff ADJ. rough-mannered. Although he was blunt and *gruff* with most people, he was always gentle with children.

■ **guile** N. deceit; duplicity; wiliness; cunning. Iago uses considerable *guile* to trick Othello into believing that Desdemona has been unfaithful.

guileless ADJ. without deceit. He is naive, simple, and *guileless;* he cannot be guilty of fraud.

guise N. appearance; costume. In the *guise* of a plumber, the detective investigated the murder case.

■ **gullible** ADJ. easily deceived. Overly *gullible* people have only themselves to blame if they fall for con artists repeatedly. As the saying goes, "Fool me once, shame on you. Fool me twice, shame on *me.*"

gustatory ADJ. affecting the sense of taste. The Thai restaurant offered an unusual *gustatory* experience for those used to a bland cuisine.

gusto N. enjoyment; enthusiasm. He accepted the assignment with such *gusto* that I feel he would have been satisfied with a smaller salary.

gusty ADJ. windy. The *gusty* weather made sailing precarious.

● **hackneyed** ADJ. commonplace; trite. When the reviewer criticized the movie for its *hackneyed* plot, we agreed; we had seen similar stories hundreds of times before.

haggard ADJ. wasted away; gaunt. After his long illness, he was pale and *haggard.*

haggle V. argue about prices. I prefer to shop in a store that has a one-price policy because, whenever I *haggle* with a shopkeeper, I am never certain that I paid a fair price for the articles I purchased.

hallowed ADJ. blessed; consecrated. Although the dead girl's parents had never been active churchgoers, they insisted that their daughter be buried in *hallowed* ground.

hallucination N. delusion. I think you were frightened by a *hallucination* you created in your own mind.

halting ADJ. hesitant; faltering. Novice extemporaneous speakers often talk in a *halting* fashion as they grope for the right words.

■ **hamper** V. obstruct. The new mother didn't realize how much the effort of caring for an infant would *hamper* her ability to keep an immaculate house.

haphazard ADJ. random; unsystematic; aimless. In place of a systematic family policy, America has a *haphazard* patchwork of institutions and programs created in response to immediate crises.

harangue N. noisy speech. In her lengthy *harangue,* the principal berated the offenders. also V.

harass V. to annoy by repeated attacks. When he could not pay his bills as quickly as he had promised, he was *harassed* by his creditors.

harbinger N. forerunner. The crocus is an early *harbinger* of spring.

harbor V. provide a refuge for; hide. The church *harbored* illegal aliens who were political refugees.

■ **hardy** ADJ. sturdy; robust; able to stand inclement weather. We asked the gardening expert to recommend particularly *hardy* plants that could withstand our harsh New England winters.

harrowing ADJ. agonizing; distressing; traumatic. At first the former prisoner did not wish to discuss his *harrowing* months of captivity as a political hostage.

■ **haughtiness** N. pride; arrogance. When she realized that Darcy believed himself too good to dance with his inferiors, Elizabeth took great offense at his *haughtiness.*

hazardous ADJ. dangerous. Your occupation is too *hazardous* for insurance companies to consider your application.

hazy ADJ. slightly obscure. In *hazy* weather, you cannot see the top of this mountain.

headlong ADJ. hasty; rash. The slave seized the unexpected chance to make a *headlong* dash across the border to freedom.

headstrong ADJ. stubborn; willful; unyielding. Because she refused to marry the man her parents had chosen for her, everyone scolded Minna and called her a foolish, *headstrong* girl.

heckler N. person who harasses others. The *heckler* kept interrupting the speaker with rude remarks. heckle, V.

■ **hedonist** N. one who believes that pleasure is the sole aim in life. A thoroughgoing *hedonist,* he considered only his own pleasure and ignored any claims others had on his money or time.

heed V. pay attention to; consider. We hope you *heed* our advice and get a good night's sleep before the test. also N.

heedless ADJ. not noticing; disregarding. He drove on, *heedless* of the danger warnings placed at the side of the road.

heinous ADJ. atrocious; hatefully bad. Hitler's *heinous* crimes will never be forgotten.

herbivorous ADJ. grain-eating. Some *herbivorous* animals have two stomachs for digesting their food.

■ **heresy** N. opinion contrary to popular belief; opinion contrary to accepted religion. Galileo's assertion that the earth moved around the sun directly contradicted the religious teachings of his day; as a result, he was tried for *heresy.* heretic, N.

hermetic ADJ. sealed by fusion so as to be airtight. After you sterilize the bandages, place them in a container and seal it with a *hermetic* seal to protect them from contamination by airborne bacteria.

hermitage N. home of a hermit. Even in his remote *hermitage* he could not escape completely from the world.

heterodox ADJ. unorthodox; unconventional. To those who upheld the belief that the earth did not move, Galileo's theory that the earth circled the sun was disturbingly *heterodox*.

heterogeneous ADJ. dissimilar; mixed. This year's entering class is a remarkably *heterogeneous* body: it includes students from forty different states and twenty-six foreign countries, some the children of billionaires, others the offspring of welfare families. heterogeneity, N.

heyday N. time of greatest success; prime. In their *heyday*, the San Francisco Forty-Niners won the Super Bowl two years running.

hiatus N. gap; interruption in duration or continuity; pause. During the summer *hiatus*, many students try to earn enough money to pay their tuition for the next school year.

Word List 23   hibernal–imbibe

hibernal ADJ. wintry. Bears prepare for their long *hibernal* sleep by overeating.

hibernate V. sleep throughout the winter. Bears are one of the many species of animals that *hibernate*. hibernation, N.

■ **hierarchy** N. arrangement by rank or standing; authoritarian body divided into ranks. To be low man on the totem pole is to have an inferior place in the *hierarchy*.

hilarity N. boisterous mirth. No longer able to contain their *hilarity*, they broke into great guffaws and whoops of laughter.

hindrance N. block; obstacle. Stalled cars along the highway are a *hindrance* to traffic that tow trucks should remove without delay. hinder, V.

histrionic ADJ. theatrical. He was proud of his *histrionic* ability and wanted to play the role of Hamlet. histrionics, N.

hoard V. stockpile; accumulate for future use. Whenever there are rumors of a food shortage, many people are tempted to *hoard* food. also N.

hoary ADJ. white with age. Old Father Time was *hoary* and wrinkled with age.

hoax N. trick; deception; fraud. In the case of Piltdown man, a scientific forgery managed to fool the experts for nearly half a century, when the *hoax* was finally unmasked. also V.

hodgepodge N. jumble; mixture of ill-suited elements. The reviewer roundly condemned the play as a *hodgepodge* of random and purposeless encounters carried out by a cast lacking any uniformity of accent or style.

homage N. honor; tribute. In her speech she tried to pay *homage* to a great man.

■ **homogeneous** ADJ. of the same kind. Because the student body at Elite Prep was so *homogeneous*, Sara and James decided to send their daughter to a school that offered greater cultural diversity. homogenize, V.

hone V. sharpen. To make shaving easier, he *honed* his razor with great care.

hoodwink V. deceive; delude. Having been *hoodwinked* once by the fast-talking salesman, he was extremely cautious when he went to purchase a used car.

horde N. crowd. Just before Christmas the stores are filled with *hordes* of shoppers.

horticultural ADJ. pertaining to cultivation of gardens. When he bought his house, he began to look for flowers and decorative shrubs, and began to read books dealing with *horticultural* matters.

host N. great number; person entertaining guests; animal or plant from which a parasite gets its nourishment. You must attend to a *host* of details if you wish to succeed as *host* of a formal dinner party. Leeches are parasites that cling to their *hosts* and drink their *hosts*' blood.

hostility N. unfriendliness; hatred. A child who has been the sole object of his parents' affection often feels *hostility* toward a new baby in the family, resenting the newcomer who has taken his place.

hovel N. shack; small, wretched house. He wondered how poor people could stand living in such a *hovel*.

hover V. hang about; wait nearby. The police helicopter *hovered* above the accident.

hue N. color; aspect. The aviary contained birds of every possible *hue*.

hulking ADJ. massive; bulky; great in size. Despite his *hulking* build, the heavyweight boxing champion was surprisingly light on his feet. hulk, N.

humane ADJ. marked by kindness or consideration. It is ironic that the *Humane* Society sometimes must show its compassion toward mistreated animals by killing them to put them out of their misery.

humdrum ADJ. dull; monotonous. After his years of adventure, he could not settle down to a *humdrum* existence.

humid ADJ. damp. Oakland's *humid* climate aggravated Richard's asthma, so he decided to move to a drier area.

humility N. humbleness of spirit. Despite his fame as a Nobel Prize winner, Bishop Tutu spoke with a *humility* and lack of self-importance that immediately won over his listeners.

hurtle V. crash; rush. The runaway train *hurtled* toward disaster.

husband V. use sparingly; conserve; save. Marathon runners must *husband* their energy so that they can keep going for the entire distance.

hybrid N. mongrel; mixed breed. Mendel's formula explains the appearance of *hybrids* and pure species in breeding. also ADJ.

hydrophobia N. rabies; fear of water. A dog that bites a human being must be observed for symptoms of *hydrophobia*.

hyperbole N. exaggeration; overstatement. As far as I'm concerned, Apple's claims about the new computer are pure *hyperbole*: no machine is that good!

hypercritical ADJ. excessively exacting. You are *hypercritical* in your demands for perfection; we all make mistakes.

hypochondriac N. person unduly worried about his health; worrier without cause about illness. The doctor prescribed chocolate pills for his patient who was a *hypochondriac*.

■ **hypocritical** ADJ. pretending to be virtuous; deceiving. It was *hypocritical* of Martha to say nice things about my poetry to me and then make fun of my verses behind my back. hypocrisy, N.

■ **hypothetical** ADJ. based on assumptions or hypotheses; supposed. Suppose you are accepted by Harvard, Stanford, and Brown. Which one would you choose to attend? Remember, this is only a *hypothetical* situation. hypothesis, N.

icon N. religious image; idol. The *icons* on the walls of the church were painted in the 13th century.

● **iconoclastic** ADJ. attacking cherished traditions. Deeply *iconoclastic*, Jean Genet deliberately set out to shock conventional theatergoers with his radical plays.

ideology N. system of ideas of a group. For people who had grown up believing in the communist *ideology*, it was hard to adjust to capitalism.

idiom N. expression whose meaning as a whole differs from the meanings of its individual words; distinctive style. The phrase "to lose one's marbles" is an *idiom*: if I say that Joe's lost his marbles, I'm not asking you to find some for him. I'm telling you *idiomatically* that he's crazy.

■ **idiosyncrasy** N. individual trait, usually odd in nature; eccentricity. One of Richard Nixon's little *idiosyncrasies* was his liking for ketchup on cottage cheese. One of Hannibal Lecter's little *idiosyncrasies* was his liking for human flesh. idiosyncratic, ADJ.

idolatry N. worship of idols; excessive admiration. Such *idolatry* of singers of country music is typical of the excessive enthusiasm of youth.

ignite V. kindle; light. When Desi crooned, "Baby, light my fire," literal-minded Lucy looked around for some paper to *ignite*.

ignoble ADJ. unworthy; base in nature; not noble. Sir Galahad was so pure in heart that he could never stoop to perform an *ignoble* deed.

● **ignominy** N. deep disgrace; shame or dishonor. To lose the Ping-Pong match to a trained chimpanzee! How could Rollo stand the *ignominy* of his defeat? ignominious, ADJ.

● **illicit** ADJ. illegal. The defense attorney maintained that his client had never performed any *illicit* action.

illimitable ADJ. infinite. Man, having explored the far corners of the earth, is now reaching out into *illimitable* space.

illuminate V. brighten; clear up or make understandable; enlighten. Just as a lamp can *illuminate* a dark room, a perceptive comment can *illuminate* a knotty problem.

illusion N. misleading vision. It is easy to create an optical *illusion* in which lines of equal length appear different.

■ **illusory** ADJ. deceptive; not real. Unfortunately, the costs of running the lemonade stand were so high that Tom's profits proved *illusory*.

imbalance N. lack of balance or symmetry; disproportion. To correct racial *imbalance* in the schools, school boards have bussed black children into white neighborhoods and white children into black ones.

imbibe V. drink in. The dry soil *imbibed* the rain quickly.

Word List 24 immaculate–incessant

immaculate ADJ. spotless; flawless; absolutely clean. Ken and Jessica were wonderful tenants and left the apartment in *immaculate* condition when they moved out.

imminent ADJ. near at hand; impending. Rosa was such a last-minute worker that she could never start writing a paper till the deadline was *imminent*.

immobility N. state of being unable to move. Peter's fear of snakes shocked him into *immobility*; then the use of his limbs returned to him, and he bolted from the room.

immune ADJ. resistant to; free or exempt from. Fortunately, Florence had contracted chicken pox as a child and was *immune* to it when her baby broke out in spots.

■ **immutable** ADJ. unchangeable. All things change over time; nothing is *immutable*.

■ **impair** V. injure; hurt. Drinking alcohol can *impair* your ability to drive safely; if you're going to drink, don't drive.

impale V. pierce. He was *impaled* by the spear hurled by his adversary.

impalpable ADJ. imperceptible; intangible. The ash is so fine that it is *impalpable* to the touch but it can be seen as a fine layer covering the window ledge.

impart V. reveal or tell; grant. Polly begged Grandma to *impart* her recipe for rugeleh, but her grandmother wouldn't say a word.

impartial ADJ. not biased; fair. Knowing she could not be *impartial* about her own child, Jo refused to judge any match in which Billy was competing.

impassable ADJ. not able to be traveled or crossed. A giant redwood had fallen across the highway, blocking all four lanes: the road was *impassable*.

impasse N. predicament from which there is no escape; deadlock. The negotiators reported they had reached an *impasse* in their talks and had little hope of resolving the deadlock swiftly.

impassive ADJ. without feeling; imperturbable; stoical. Refusing to let the enemy see how deeply shaken he was by his capture, the prisoner kept his face *impassive*.

impeach V. charge with crime in office; indict. The angry congressman wanted to *impeach* the president for his misdeeds.

■ **impeccable** ADJ. faultless. The uncrowned queen of the fashion industry, Diana was acclaimed for her *impeccable* taste.

● **impecunious** ADJ. without money. Though Scrooge claimed he was too *impecunious* to give alms, he easily could have afforded to be charitable.

■ **impede** V. hinder; block; delay. A series of accidents *impeded* the launching of the space shuttle.

impediment N. hindrance; stumbling-block. She had a speech *impediment* that prevented her speaking clearly.

impel V. drive or force onward. A strong feeling of urgency *impelled* her; if she failed to finish the project right then, she knew that she would never get it done.

impenetrable ADJ. not able to be pierced or · entered; beyond understanding. How could the murderer have gotten into the locked room? To Watson, the mystery, like the room, was *impenetrable*.

impending ADJ. nearing; approaching. The entire country was saddened by the news of his *impending* death.

impenitent ADJ. not repentant. We could see from his tough guy attitude that he was *impenitent*.

imperative ADJ. absolutely necessary; critically important. It is *imperative* that you be extremely agreeable to Great-Aunt Maud when she comes to tea: otherwise she might not leave you that million dollars in her will. also N.

imperceptible ADJ. unnoticeable; undetectable. Fortunately, the stain on the blouse was *imperceptible* after the blouse had gone through the wash.

imperial ADJ. like an emperor; related to an empire. When hotel owner Leona Helmsley appeared in ads as Queen Leona standing guard over the Palace Hotel, her critics mocked her *imperial* fancies.

imperious ADJ. domineering; haughty. Jane rather liked a man to be masterful, but Mr. Rochester seemed so bent on getting his own way that he was actually *imperious*!

impermeable ADJ. impervious; not permitting passage through its substance. Sue chose a raincoat made of Gore-Tex because the material is *impermeable* to liquids.

impertinent ADJ. insolent; rude. His neighbors' *impertinent* curiosity about his lack of dates angered Ted. It was downright rude of them to ask him such personal questions.

imperturbable ADJ. calm; placid; composed. In the midst of the battle, the Duke of Wellington remained *imperturbable* and in full command of the situation despite the hysteria and panic all around him. imperturbability, N.

impervious ADJ. impenetrable; incapable of being damaged or distressed. The carpet salesman told Simone that his most expensive brand of floor covering was warranted to be *impervious* to ordinary wear and tear. Having read so many negative reviews of his acting, the movie star had learned to ignore them, and was now *impervious* to criticism.

impetuous ADJ. violent; hasty; rash. "Leap before you look" was the motto suggested by one particularly *impetuous* young man.

impetus N. incentive; stimulus; moving force. A new federal highway program would create jobs and give added *impetus* to our economic recovery.

impiety N. irreverence; lack of respect for God. When members of the youth group draped the church in toilet paper one Halloween, the minister reprimanded them for their *impiety*. impious, ADJ.

impinge V. infringe; touch; collide with. How could they be married without *impinging* on one another's freedom?

implacable ADJ. incapable of being pacified. Madame Defarge was the *implacable* enemy of the Evremonde family.

■ **implausible** ADJ. unlikely; unbelievable. Though her alibi seemed *implausible,* it in fact turned out to be true.

■ **implement** V. put into effect; supply with tools. The mayor was unwilling to *implement* the plan until she was sure it had the governor's backing. also N.

implicate V. incriminate; show to be involved. Here's the deal: if you agree to take the witness stand and *implicate* your partners in crime, the prosecution will recommend that the judge go easy in sentencing you.

implication N. something hinted at or suggested. When Miss Watson said she hadn't seen her purse since the last time Jim was in the house, the *implication* was that she suspected Jim had taken it. imply, V.

implicit ADJ. understood but not stated. Jack never told Jill he adored her; he believed his love was *implicit* in his actions.

implore V. beg. He *implored* her to give him a second chance.

imply V. suggest a meaning not expressed; signify. When Aunt Millie said, "My! That's a big piece of pie, young man!" was she *implying* that Bobby was being a glutton in helping himself to such a huge piece?

imponderable ADJ. not able to be determined precisely. Psychology is not a precise science; far too many *imponderable* factors play a part in determining human behavior.

import N. importance; meaning. To Miss Manners, proper etiquette was a matter of great *import*. Because Tom knew so little about medical matters, it took a while for the full *import* of the doctor's words to sink in.

importunate ADJ. urging; demanding. He tried to hide from his *importunate* creditors until his allowance arrived.

importune V. beg persistently. Democratic and Republican phone solicitors *importuned* her for contributions so frequently that she decided to give nothing to either party.

impostor N. someone who assumes a false identity. "This man is no doctor! He is a fraud!" cried Holmes, exposing the *impostor*.

impotent ADJ. weak; ineffective. Although he wished to break the nicotine habit, he found himself *impotent* to resist the craving for a cigarette.

impoverished ADJ. poor. The loss of their farm left the family *impoverished* and without hope.

● **impregnable** ADJ. invulnerable. Until the development of the airplane as a military weapon, the fort was considered *impregnable*.

impromptu ADJ. without previous preparation; off the cuff; on the spur of the moment. The judges were amazed that she could make such a thorough, well-supported presentation in an *impromptu* speech.

impropriety N. improperness; unsuitableness. Because of the *impropriety* of the punk rocker's slashed T-shirt and jeans, the management refused to admit him to the hotel's very formal dining room.

improvident ADJ. thriftless. He was constantly being warned to mend his *improvident* ways and begin to "save for a rainy day." improvidence, N.

improvise V. compose on the spur of the moment. She would sit at the piano and *improvise* for hours on themes from Bach and Handel.

imprudent ADJ. lacking caution; injudicious. It is *imprudent* to exercise vigorously and become overheated when you are unwell.

■ **impudence** N. impertinence; insolence. Kissed on the cheek by a perfect stranger, Lady Catherine exclaimed, "Of all the nerve! Young man, I should have you horse-whipped for your *impudence*."

impugn V. dispute or contradict (often in an insulting way); challenge; gainsay. Our treasurer was furious when the finance committee's report *impugned* the accuracy of his financial records and recommended that he should take bonehead math.

impunity N. freedom from punishment or harm. A 98-pound weakling can't attack a beachfront bully with *impunity*: the poor, puny guy is sure to get mashed.

imputation N. accusation; charge; reproach. Paradoxically, the guiltier he was of the offense with which he was charged, the more he resented the *imputation*.

■ **inadvertently** ADV. unintentionally; by oversight; carelessly. Judy's great fear was that she might *inadvertently* omit a question on the exam and mismark her whole answer sheet.

inalienable ADJ. not to be taken away; nontransferable. The Declaration of Independence asserts that all people possess certain *inalienable* human rights that no powers on earth can take away.

■ **inane** ADJ. silly; senseless. There's no point to what you're saying. Why are you bothering to make such *inane* remarks?

inanimate ADJ. lifeless. She was asked to identify the still and *inanimate* body.

inarticulate ADJ. speechless; producing indistinct speech. He became *inarticulate* with rage and uttered sounds without meaning.

inaugurate V. start; initiate; install in office. The airline decided to *inaugurate* its new route to the Far East with a special reduced fare offer. inaugural, ADJ.

incandescent ADJ. strikingly bright; shining with intense heat. If you leave on an *incandescent* light bulb, it quickly grows too hot to touch.

incantation N. singing or chanting of magic spells; magical formula. Uttering *incantations* to make the brew more potent, the witch doctor stirred the liquid in the caldron.

incapacitate V. disable. During the winter, many people were *incapacitated* by respiratory ailments.

incarcerate V. imprison. The civil rights workers were willing to be arrested and even *incarcerated* if by their imprisonment they could serve the cause.

incarnation N. act of assuming a human body and human nature. The *incarnation* of Jesus Christ is a basic tenet of Christian theology.

incense V. enrage; infuriate. Cruelty to defenseless animals *incensed* Kit: the very idea brought tears of anger to her eyes.

incentive N. spur; motive. Mike's strong desire to outshine his big sister was all the *incentive* he needed to do well in school.

inception N. start; beginning. She was involved with the project from its *inception*.

incessant ADJ. uninterrupted; unceasing. In a famous TV commercial, the frogs' *incessant* croaking goes on and on until eventually it turns into a single word: "Bud-weis-er."

Word List 25   inchoate–ingenious

inchoate ADJ. recently begun; rudimentary; elementary. Before the Creation, the world was an *inchoate* mass.

incidence N. rate of occurrence; particular occurrence. Health professionals expressed great concern over the high *incidence* of infant mortality in major urban areas.

● **incidental** ADJ. not essential; minor. The scholarship covered his major expenses at college and some of his *incidental* expenses as well.

incipient ADJ. beginning; in an early stage. I will go to sleep early for I want to break an *incipient* cold.

■ **incisive** ADJ. cutting; sharp. His *incisive* remarks made us see the fallacy in our plans.

■ **incite** V. arouse to action; goad; motivate; induce to exist. In a fiery speech, Mario *incited* his fellow students to go out on strike to protest the university's anti-affirmative action stand.

inclement ADJ. stormy; unkind. In *inclement* weather, I like to curl up on the sofa with a good book and listen to the storm blowing outside.

incline N. slope; slant. The architect recommended that the nursing home's ramp be rebuilt because its *incline* was too steep for wheelchairs.

inclined ADJ. tending or leaning toward; bent. Though I am *inclined* to be skeptical, the witness's manner *inclines* me to believe his story. also V.

■ **inclusive** ADJ. tending to include all. The comedian turned down the invitation to join the Players' Club, saying any club that would let him in was too *inclusive* for him.

incoherence N. unintelligibility; lack of logic or relevance. "This essay makes no sense at all," commented the teacher, giving it an F because of its *incoherence*.

incompatible ADJ. inharmonious. The married couple argued incessantly and finally decided to separate because they were *incompatible*. incompatibility, N.

■ **incongruous** ADJ. not fitting; absurd. Dave saw nothing *incongruous* about wearing sneakers with his tuxedo; he couldn't understand why his date took one look at him and started to laugh. incongruity, N.

■ **inconsequential** ADJ. insignificant; unimportant. Brushing off Ali's apologies for having broken the wineglass, Tamara said, "Don't worry about it; it's *inconsequential.*"

inconsistency N. state of being self-contradictory; lack of uniformity or steadiness. How are lawyers different from agricultural inspectors? While lawyers check *inconsistencies* in witnesses' statements, agricultural inspectors check *inconsistencies* in Grade A eggs. inconsistent, ADJ.

incontinent ADJ. lacking self-restraint; licentious. His *incontinent* behavior off stage so shocked many people that they refused to attend the plays and movies in which he appeared.

● **incontrovertible** ADJ. indisputable; not open to question. Unless you find the evidence against my client absolutely *incontrovertible*, you must declare her not guilty of this charge.

incorporate V. introduce something into a larger whole; combine; unite. Breaking with precedent, President Truman ordered the military to *incorporate* blacks into every branch of the armed services. also ADJ.

incorporeal ADJ. lacking a material body; insubstantial. While Casper the friendly ghost is an *incorporeal* being, nevertheless he and his fellow ghosts make quite an impact on the physical world.

■ **incorrigible** ADJ. not correctable. Though Widow Douglass hoped to reform Huck, Miss Watson called him *incorrigible* and said he would come to no good end.

incredulous ADJ. withholding belief; skeptical. When Jack claimed he hadn't eaten the jelly doughnut, Jill took an *incredulous* look at his smeared face and laughed. incredulity, N.

increment N. increase. The new contract calls for a 10 percent *increment* in salary for each employee for the next two years.

incriminate V. accuse. The evidence gathered against the racketeers *incriminates* some high public officials as well.

incubate V. hatch; scheme. Because our supply of electricity has been cut off, we shall have to rely on the hens to *incubate* these eggs.

inculcate V. teach; instill. In an effort to *inculcate* religious devotion, the officials ordered that the school day begin with the singing of a hymn.

incumbent ADJ. obligatory; currently holding an office. It is *incumbent* upon all *incumbent* elected officials to keep accurate records of expenses incurred in office. also N.

incur V. bring upon oneself. His parents refused to pay any future debts he might *incur*.

incursion N. temporary invasion. The nightly *incursions* and hit-and-run raids of our neighbors across the border tried the patience of the country to the point where we decided to retaliate in force.

● **indefatigable** ADJ. tireless. Although the effort of taking out the garbage tired Wayne out for the entire morning, when it came to partying, he was *indefatigable*.

indelible ADJ. not able to be erased. The *indelible* ink left a permanent mark on my shirt. Young Bill Clinton's meeting with President Kennedy made an *indelible* impression on the youth.

indentation N. notch; deep recess. You can tell one tree from another by examining their leaves and noting the differences in the *indentations* along the edges of the leaves. indent, V.

indenture V. bind as servant or apprentice to master. Many immigrants could come to America only after they had *indentured* themselves for several years. also N.

indeterminate ADJ. uncertain; not clearly fixed; indefinite. That interest rates shall rise appears certain; when they will do so, however, remains *indeterminate*.

indicative ADJ. suggestive; implying. A lack of appetite may be *indicative* of a major mental or physical disorder.

indices N. PL. signs; indications. Many college admissions officers believe that SAT scores and high school grades are the best *indices* of a student's potential to succeed in college. N. SG. index.

■ **indict** V. charge. The district attorney didn't want to *indict* the suspect until she was sure she had a strong enough case to convince a jury. indictment, N.

■ **indifferent** ADJ. unmoved or unconcerned by; mediocre. Because Ann felt no desire to marry, she was *indifferent* to Carl's constant proposals. Not only was she *indifferent* to him personally, but she felt that, given his general silliness, he would make an *indifferent* husband.

indigenous ADJ. native. Cigarettes are made of tobacco, a plant *indigenous* to the New World.

indigent ADJ. poor; destitute. Someone who is truly *indigent* can't even afford to buy a pack of cigarettes. [Don't mix up *indigent* and *indigenous*. See previous sentence.]

indignation N. anger at an injustice. He felt *indignation* at the ill-treatment of helpless animals.

indignity N. offensive or insulting treatment. Although he seemed to accept cheerfully the *indignities* heaped upon him, he was inwardly very angry.

indiscretion N. lack of tactfulness or sound judgment. Terrified that the least *indiscretion* could jeopardize his political career, the novice politician never uttered an unguarded word. indiscreet, ADJ.

■ **indiscriminate** ADJ. choosing at random; confused. She disapproved of her son's *indiscriminate* television viewing and decided to restrict him to educational programs.

indisputable ADJ. too certain to be disputed. In the face of these *indisputable* statements, I withdraw my complaint.

indissoluble ADJ. permanent. The *indissoluble* bonds of marriage are all too often being dissolved.

indoctrinate V. instruct in a doctrine or ideology. Cuban-Americans resisted sending Elian Gonzalez back to Cuba because he would be *indoctrinated* there with Communist principles.

● **indolent** ADJ. lazy. Couch potatoes lead an *indolent* life lying back on their Lazyboy recliners watching TV. indolence, N.

indomitable ADJ. unconquerable; unyielding. Focusing on her game despite all her personal problems, tennis champion Steffi Graf proved she had an *indomitable* will to win.

indubitable ADJ. unable to be doubted; unquestionable. Auditioning for the chorus line, Molly was an *indubitable* hit: the director fired the leading lady and hired Molly in her place!

■ **induce** V. persuade; bring about. After the quarrel, Tina said nothing could *induce* her to talk to Tony again. inducement, N.

indulgent ADJ. humoring; yielding; lenient. Jay's mom was excessively *indulgent*: she bought him every Nintendo cartridge and video game on the market. She *indulged* Jay so much, she spoiled him rotten.

industrious ADJ. diligent; hard-working. Look busy when the boss walks by your desk; it never hurts to appear *industrious*. industry, N.

inebriated ADJ. habitually intoxicated; drunk. Abe was *inebriated* more often than he was sober. Because of his *inebriety*, he was discharged from his job as a bus driver.

● **ineffable** ADJ. unutterable; cannot be expressed in speech. Looking down at her newborn daughter, Ruth felt such *ineffable* joy that, for the first time in her adult life, she had no words to convey what was in her heart.

ineffectual ADJ. not effective; weak. Because the candidate failed to get across his message to the public, his campaign was *ineffectual*.

inefficacious ADJ. not effective; unable to produce a desired result. All Lois's coaxing and urging was *inefficacious*: Clark still refused to join her and Superman for dinner. inefficacy, N.

inept ADJ. lacking skill; unsuited; incompetent. The *inept* glovemaker was all thumbs.

inequity N. unfairness. In demanding equal pay for equal work, women protest the basic *inequity* of a system that gives greater financial rewards to men.

■ **inert** ADJ. inactive; lacking power to move. "Get up, you lazybones," she cried to her husband, who lay in bed *inert*. inertia, N.

inevitable ADJ. unavoidable. Though death and taxes are both supposedly *inevitable*, some people avoid paying taxes for years.

● **inexorable** ADJ. relentless; unyielding; implacable. After listening to the pleas for clemency, the judge was *inexorable* and gave the convicted man the maximum punishment allowed by law.

infallible ADJ. unerring. Jane refused to believe the pope was *infallible*, reasoning, "All human beings are capable of error. The pope is a human being. Therefore, the pope is capable of error."

infamous ADJ. notoriously bad. Charles Manson and Jeffrey Dahmer are both *infamous* killers.

infantile ADJ. childish. When will he outgrow such *infantile* behavior?

infer V. deduce; conclude. From the students' glazed looks, it was easy for me to *infer* that they were bored out of their minds. inference, N.

infernal ADJ. pertaining to hell; devilish. Batman was baffled: he could think of no way to hinder the Joker's *infernal* scheme to destroy the city.

infidel N. unbeliever. The Saracens made war against the *infidels*.

infiltrate V. pass into or through; penetrate (an organization) sneakily. In order to be able to *infiltrate* enemy lines at night without being seen, the scouts darkened their faces and wore black coveralls. infiltrator, N.

infinitesimal ADJ. exceedingly small; so small as to be almost nonexistent. Making sure everyone was aware she was on an extremely strict diet, Melanie said she would have only an *infinitesimal* sliver of pie.

infirmity N. weakness. Her greatest *infirmity* was lack of willpower.

inflated ADJ. exaggerated; pompous; enlarged (with air or gas). His claims about the new product were *inflated*; it did not work as well as he had promised.

influx N. flowing into. The *influx* of refugees into the country has taxed the relief agencies severely.

informal ADJ. absence of ceremony; casual. The English teacher preferred *informal* discussions to prepared lectures.

infraction N. violation (of a rule or regulation); breach. When Dennis Rodman butted heads with that referee, he committed a clear *infraction* of NBA rules.

infuriate V. enrage; anger. Her big brother's teasing always *infuriated* Margaret; no matter how hard she tried to keep her temper, he always got her goat.

infusion N. act of introducing or instilling a quality; liquid solution. The rookie quarterback brought an *infusion* of new life and vigor to the tired team. infuse, V.

■ **ingenious** ADJ. clever; resourceful. Kit admired the *ingenious* way that her computer keyboard opened up to reveal the built-in CD-ROM below. ingenuity, N.

Word List 26   ingenue–invigorate

ingenue N. an artless girl; an actress who plays such parts. Although she was forty, she still insisted that she be cast as an *ingenue* and refused to play more mature roles.

ingenuous ADJ. naive and trusting; young; unsophisticated. The woodsman had not realized how *ingenuous* Little Red Riding Hood was until he heard that she had gone off for a walk in the woods with the Big Bad Wolf.

ingrained ADJ. deeply established; firmly rooted. Try as they would, the missionaries were unable to uproot the *ingrained* superstitions of the natives.

ingrate N. ungrateful person. That *ingrate* Bob sneered at the tie I gave him.

ingratiate V. make an effort to become popular with. In *All About Eve,* the heroine, an aspiring actress, wages a clever campaign to *ingratiate* herself with Margo Channing, an established star.

■ **inherent** ADJ. firmly established by nature or habit. Katya's *inherent* love of justice caused her to champion anyone she considered treated unfairly by society.

inhibit V. restrain; retard or prevent. Only two things *inhibited* him from taking a punch at Mike Tyson: Tyson's left hook, and Tyson's right jab. The protective undercoating on my car *inhibits* the formation of rust.

inimical ADJ. unfriendly; hostile; harmful; detrimental. I've always been friendly to Martha. Why is she so *inimical* to me?

inimitable ADJ. matchless; not able to be imitated. We admire Auden for his *inimitable* use of language; he is one of a kind.

iniquitous ADJ. wicked; immoral; unrighteous. Whether or not King Richard III was responsible for the murder of the two young princes in the Tower, it was an *iniquitous* deed. iniquity, N.

initiate V. begin; originate; receive into a group. The college is about to *initiate* a program in reducing math anxiety among students.

injurious ADJ. harmful. Smoking cigarettes can be *injurious* to your health.

inkling N. hint. This came as a complete surprise to me as I did not have the slightest *inkling* of your plans.

■ **innate** ADJ. inborn. Mozart's parents soon recognized young Wolfgang's *innate* talent for music.

■ **innocuous** ADJ. harmless. An occasional glass of wine with dinner is relatively *innocuous* and should have no ill effect on you.

■ **innovation** N. change; introduction of something new. Although Richard liked to keep up with all the latest technological *innovations*, he didn't always abandon tried and true techniques in favor of something new. innovate, V.

innovative ADJ. novel; introducing a change. The establishment of our SAT computer data base has enabled us to come up with some *innovative* tactics for doing well on the SAT.

innuendo N. hint; insinuation. I can defend myself against direct accusations; *innuendos* and oblique attacks on my character are what trouble me.

inopportune ADJ. untimely; poorly chosen. A rock concert is an *inopportune* setting for a quiet conversation.

inordinate ADJ. unrestrained; excessive. She had an *inordinate* fondness for candy, eating two or three boxes in a single day.

inquisitor N. questioner (especially harsh); investigator. Fearing being grilled ruthlessly by the secret police, Masha faced her *inquisitors* with trepidation.

insalubrious ADJ. unwholesome; not healthful. The mosquito-ridden swamp was an *insalubrious* place, a breeding ground for malarial contagion.

insatiable ADJ. not easily satisfied; unquenchable; greedy. David's appetite for oysters was *insatiable*: he could easily eat four dozen at a single sitting.

inscrutable ADJ. impenetrable; not readily understood; mysterious. Experienced poker players try to keep their expressions *inscrutable*, hiding their reactions to the cards behind a so-called "poker face."

insensible ADJ. unconscious; unresponsive. Sherry and I are very different; at times when I would be covered with embarrassment, she seems *insensible* to shame.

insidious ADJ. treacherous; stealthy; sly. The fifth column is *insidious* because it works secretly within our territory for our defeat.

insightful ADJ. discerning; perceptive. Sol thought he was very *insightful* about human behavior, but he was actually clueless as to why people acted the way they did.

insinuate V. hint; imply; creep in. When you said I looked robust, did you mean to *insinuate* that I'm getting fat?

■ **insipid** ADJ. lacking in flavor; dull. Flat prose and flat ginger ale are equally *insipid*: both lack sparkle.

insolence N. impudent disrespect; haughtiness. How dare you treat me so rudely! The manager will hear of your *insolence*. insolent, ADJ.

● **insolvent** ADJ. bankrupt; unable to repay one's debts. Although young Lord Widgeon was *insolvent*, he had no fear of being thrown into debtors' prison, for he was sure that if his creditors pressed him for payment his wealthy parents would repay what he owed. insolvency, N.

■ **instigate** V. urge; start; provoke. Rumors of police corruption led the mayor to *instigate* an investigation into the department's activities.

insubordination N. disobedience; rebelliousness. At the slightest hint of *insubordination* from the sailors of the *Bounty*, Captain Bligh had them flogged; finally, they mutinied.

insubstantial ADJ. lacking substance; insignificant; frail. His hopes for a career in acting proved *insubstantial*; no one would cast him, even in an *insubstantial* role.

■ **insularity** N. narrow-mindedness; isolation. The *insularity* of the islanders manifested itself in their suspicion of anything foreign. insular, ADJ.

insulated ADJ. set apart; isolated. A well-to-do bachelor, James spent his money freely, *insulated* from the cares of his friends, who had families to support.

● **insuperable** ADJ. insurmountable; unbeatable. Though the odds against their survival seemed *insuperable*, the Apollo 13 astronauts reached earth safely.

insurgent ADJ. rebellious. Because the *insurgent* forces had occupied the capital and had gained control of the railway lines, several of the war correspondents covering the uprising predicted a rebel victory.

insurmountable ADJ. overwhelming; unbeatable; insuperable. Faced by almost *insurmountable* obstacles, the members of the underground maintained their courage and will to resist.

insurrection N. rebellion; uprising. In retrospect, given how badly the British treated the American colonists, the eventual *insurrection* seems inevitable.

intangible ADJ. not able to be perceived by touch; vague. Though the financial benefits of his Oxford post were meager,

Lewis was drawn to it by its *intangible* rewards: prestige, intellectual freedom, the fellowship of his peers.

integral ADJ. complete; necessary for completeness. Physical education is an *integral* part of our curriculum; a sound mind and a sound body are complementary.

integrate V. make whole; combine; make into one unit. We hope to *integrate* the French, Spanish, and Italian programs into a combined Romance languages department.

■ **integrity** N. uprightness; wholeness. Lincoln, whose personal *integrity* has inspired millions, fought a civil war to maintain the *integrity* of the Republic, that these United States might remain undivided for all time.

intellect N. higher mental powers. If you wish to develop your *intellect*, read the great books.

intelligentsia N. the intelligent and educated classes [often used derogatorily]. She preferred discussions about sports and politics to the literary conversations of the *intelligentsia*.

intemperate ADJ. immoderate; excessive; extreme. In a temper, Tony refused to tone down his *intemperate* remarks.

interim N. meantime. The company will not consider our proposal until next week; in the *interim*, let us proceed as we have in the past.

interloper N. intruder; unwanted meddler. The merchant thought of his competitors as *interlopers* who were stealing away his trade.

interminable ADJ. endless. Although his speech lasted for only twenty minutes, it seemed *interminable* to his bored audience.

intermittent ADJ. periodic; on and off. The outdoor wedding reception had to be moved indoors to avoid the *intermittent* showers that fell on and off all afternoon.

interrogate V. question closely; cross-examine. Knowing that the Nazis would *interrogate* him about his background, the secret agent invented a cover story that would help him meet their questions.

■ **intervene** V. come between. When two close friends get into a fight, be careful if you try to *intervene*; they may join forces to gang up on you.

intimacy N. closeness, often affectionate; privacy; familiarity. In a moment of rare *intimacy*, the mayor allowed the reporters a glimpse of his personal feelings about his family. intimate, ADJ.

intimate V. hint; suggest. Was Dick *intimating* that Jane had bad breath when he asked if she'd like a breath mint?

■ **intimidate** V. frighten. I'll learn karate and then those big bullies won't be able to *intimidate* me any more.

● **intractable** ADJ. unruly; stubborn; unyielding. Charlie Brown's friend Pigpen was *intractable*: he absolutely refused to take a bath.

intransigence N. refusal of any compromise; stubbornness. The negotiating team had not expected such *intransigence* from the striking workers, who rejected any hint of a compromise. intransigent, ADJ.

■ **intrepid** ADJ. fearless. For her *intrepid* conduct nursing the wounded during the war, Florence Nightingale was honored by Queen Victoria.

intricate ADJ. complex; knotty; tangled. Philip spent many hours designing mazes so *intricate* that none of his classmates could solve them. intricacy, N.

intrinsic ADJ. essential; inherent; built-in. Although my grandmother's china has little *intrinsic* value, I shall always cherish it for the memories it evokes.

introspective ADJ. looking within oneself. Though young Francis of Assisi led a wild and worldly life, even then he had *introspective* moments during which he examined his soul.

introvert N. one who is introspective; inclined to think more about oneself. Uncommunicative by nature and disinclined to look outside himself, he was a classic *introvert*.

intrude V. trespass; enter as an uninvited person. She hesitated to *intrude* on their conversation.

intuition N. immediate insight; power of knowing without reasoning. Even though Tony denied that anything was wrong, Tina trusted her *intuition* that something was bothering him. intuitive, ADJ.

■ **inundate** V. overwhelm; flood; submerge. This semester I am *inundated* with work: You should see the piles of paperwork flooding my desk. Until the great dam was built, the waters of the Nile used to *inundate* the river valley like clockwork every year.

inured ADJ. accustomed; hardened. She became *inured* to the Alaskan cold.

invalidate V. weaken; destroy. The relatives who received little or nothing sought to *invalidate* the will by claiming that the deceased had not been in his right mind when he had signed the document.

invasive ADJ. tending to spread aggressively; intrusive. Giving up our war with the *invasive* blackberry vines that had taken over the back yard, we covered the lawn with concrete. invade, V.

invective N. abuse. He had expected criticism but not the *invective* that greeted his proposal. inveigh, V.

inveigle V. entice; persuade; wheedle. Flattering Adam about his good taste in food, Eve *inveigled* him into taking a bite of her apple pie.

inverse ADJ. opposite. There is an *inverse* ratio between the strength of light and its distance.

■ **invert** V. turn upside down or inside out. When he *inverted* his body in a handstand, he felt the blood rush to his head.

inveterate ADJ. deep-rooted; habitual. An *inveterate* smoker, Bob cannot seem to break the habit, no matter how hard he tries.

invidious ADJ. designed to create ill will or envy. We disregarded her *invidious* remarks because we realized how jealous she was.

invigorate V. energize; stimulate. A quick dip in the pool *invigorated* Meg, and with renewed energy she got back to work.

Word List 27   invincible–laggard

invincible   ADJ. unconquerable. Superman is *invincible*.

inviolable   ADJ. secure from corruption, attack, or violation; unassailable. Batman considered his oath to keep the people of Gotham City safe *inviolable*: nothing on earth could make him break this promise.

invocation   N. prayer for help; calling upon as a reference or support. The service of Morning Prayer opens with an *invocation* during which we ask God to hear our prayers.

invoke   V. call upon; ask for. She *invoked* her advisor's aid in filling out her financial aid forms.

invulnerable   ADJ. incapable of injury. Achilles was *invulnerable* except in his heel.

iota   N. very small quantity. She hadn't an *iota* of common sense.

irascible   ADJ. irritable; easily angered. Miss Minchin's *irascible* temper intimidated the younger schoolgirls, who feared she'd burst into a rage at any moment.

irate   ADJ. angry. When John's mother found out he had overdrawn his checking account for the third month in a row, she was so *irate* she could scarcely speak to him.

ire   N. anger. The waiter tried unsuccessfully to placate the *ire* of the diner who had found a cockroach in her soup.

iridescent   ADJ. exhibiting rainbowlike colors. She admired the *iridescent* hues of the oil that floated on the surface of the water.

irksome   ADJ. annoying; tedious. He found working on the assembly line *irksome* because of the monotony of the operation he had to perform. irk, V.

■ **ironic**   ADJ. resulting in an unexpected and contrary outcome. It is *ironic* that his success came when he least wanted it.

irony   N. hidden sarcasm or satire; use of words that seem to mean the opposite of what they actually mean. Gradually his listeners began to realize that the excessive praise he was lavishing on his opponent was actually *irony*; he was in fact ridiculing the poor fool.

irrational   ADJ. illogical; lacking reason; insane. Many people have such an *irrational* fear of snakes that they panic at the sight of a harmless garter snake.

irreconcilable   ADJ. incompatible; not able to be resolved. Because the separated couple were *irreconcilable*, the marriage counselor recommended a divorce.

irrefutable   ADJ. indisputable; incontrovertible; undeniable. No matter how hard I tried to find a good comeback for her argument, I couldn't think of one: her logic was *irrefutable*.

irrelevant   ADJ. not applicable; unrelated. No matter how *irrelevant* the patient's mumblings may seem, they give us some indications of what he has on his mind.

irremediable   ADJ. incurable; uncorrectable. The error she made was *irremediable*; she could see no way to repair it.

irreparable   ADJ. not able to be corrected or repaired. Your apology cannot atone for the *irreparable* damage you have done to her reputation.

irrepressible   ADJ. unable to be restrained or held back. My friend Kitty's curiosity was *irrepressible*: she poked her nose into everybody's business and just laughed when I warned her that curiosity killed the cat.

● **irreproachable**   ADJ. blameless; impeccable. Homer's conduct at the office party was *irreproachable*; even Marge didn't have anything bad to say about how he behaved.

irresolute   ADJ. uncertain how to act; weak. Once you have made your decision, don't waver; a leader should never appear *irresolute*.

irretrievable   ADJ. impossible to recover or regain; irreparable. The left fielder tried to retrieve the ball, but it flew over the fence, bounced off a wall, and fell into the sewer: it was *irretrievable*.

irreverence   N. lack of proper respect. Some audience members were amused by the *irreverence* of the comedian's jokes about the Pope; others felt offended by his lack of respect for their faith. irreverent, ADJ.

irrevocable   ADJ. unalterable; irreversible. As Sue dropped the "Dear John" letter into the mailbox, she suddenly had second thoughts and wanted to take it back, but she could not: her action was *irrevocable*.

itinerant   ADJ. wandering; traveling. He was an *itinerant* peddler and traveled through Pennsylvania and Virginia selling his wares. also N.

itinerary   N. plan of a trip. Disliking sudden changes in plans when she traveled abroad, Ethel refused to make any alterations in her *itinerary*.

jabber   V. chatter rapidly or unintelligibly. Why does the fellow insist on *jabbering* away in French when I can't understand a word he says?

jaded   ADJ. fatigued; surfeited. He looked for exotic foods to stimulate his *jaded* appetite.

jargon   N. language used by a special group; technical terminology; gibberish. The computer salesmen at the store used a *jargon* of their own that we simply couldn't follow; we had no idea what they were jabbering about.

jaundiced   ADJ. prejudiced (envious, hostile or resentful); yellowed. Because Sue disliked Carolyn, she looked at Carolyn's paintings with a *jaundiced* eye, calling them formless smears. Newborn infants afflicted with *jaundice* look slightly yellow: they have *jaundiced* skin.

jaunt   N. trip; short journey. He took a quick *jaunt* to Atlantic City.

jaunty   ADJ. lighthearted; animated; easy and carefree. In *An American in Paris*, Gene Kelly sang and danced his way through "I Got Rhythm" in a properly *jaunty* style.

jeopardize   V. endanger; imperil; put at risk. You can't give me a D in chemistry: you'll *jeopardize* my chances of getting into M.I.T. jeopardy, N.

jettison V. throw overboard. In order to enable the ship to ride safely through the storm, the captain had to *jettison* much of his cargo.

jingoist N. extremely aggressive and militant patriot; warlike chauvinist. Always bellowing "America first!," the congressman was such a *jingoist* you could almost hear the sabers rattling as he marched down the halls. jingoism, N.

jocose ADJ. given to joking. The salesman was so *jocose* that many of his customers suggested that he become a "stand-up" comic.

● **jocular** ADJ. said or done in jest. Although Bill knew the boss hated jokes, he couldn't resist making one *jocular* remark.

jollity N. gaiety; cheerfulness. The festive Christmas dinner was a merry one, and old and young alike joined in the general *jollity*.

jostle V. shove; bump. In the subway he was *jostled* by the crowds.

jovial ADJ. good-natured; merry. A frown seemed out of place on his invariably *jovial* face.

jubilation N. rejoicing. There was great *jubilation* when the armistice was announced. jubilant, ADJ.

judicious ADJ. sound in judgment; wise. At a key moment in his life, he made a *judicious* investment that was the foundation of his later wealth.

juncture N. crisis; joining point. At this critical *juncture,* let us think carefully before determining the course we shall follow.

junta N. group of men joined in political intrigue; cabal. As soon as he learned of its existence, the dictator ordered the execution of all of the members of the *junta*.

jurisprudence N. science of law. He was more a student of *jurisprudence* than a practitioner of the law.

justification N. good or just reason; defense; excuse. The jury found him guilty of the more serious charge because they could see no possible *justification* for his actions.

kernel N. central or vital part; whole seed (as of corn). "Watson, buried within this tissue of lies there is a *kernel* of truth; when I find it, the mystery will be solved."

killjoy N. grouch; spoilsport. At breakfast we had all been enjoying our bacon and eggs until that *killjoy* John started talking about how bad animal fats were for our health.

kindle V. start a fire; inspire. One of the first things Ben learned in the Boy Scouts was how to *kindle* a fire by rubbing two dry sticks together. Her teacher's praise for her poetry *kindled* a spark of hope inside Maya.

kindred ADJ. related; belonging to the same family. Tom Sawyer and Huck Finn were *kindred* spirits, born mischief makers who were always up to some new tomfoolery.

kinetic ADJ. producing motion. Designers of the electric automobile find that their greatest obstacle lies in the development of light and efficient storage batteries, the source of the *kinetic* energy needed to propel the vehicle.

kleptomaniac N. person who has a compulsive desire to steal. They discovered that the wealthy customer was a *kleptomaniac* when they caught her stealing some cheap trinkets.

knave N. untrustworthy person; rogue; scoundrel. Any politician nicknamed Tricky Dick clearly has the reputation of a *knave*. knavery, N.

knit V. contract into wrinkles; grow together. Whenever David worries, his brow *knits* in a frown. When he broke his leg, he sat around the house all day waiting for the bones to *knit*.

knotty ADJ. intricate; difficult; tangled. What to Watson had been a *knotty* problem, to Sherlock Holmes was simplicity itself.

kudos N. honor; glory; praise. The singer complacently received *kudos* from his entourage on his performance.

laborious ADJ. demanding much work or care; tedious. In putting together his dictionary of the English language, Doctor Johnson undertook a *laborious* task.

● **labyrinth** N. maze. Hiding from Indian Joe, Tom and Becky soon lost themselves in the *labyrinth* of secret underground caves. labyrinthine, ADJ.

laceration N. torn, ragged wound. The stock car driver needed stitches to close up the *lacerations* he received in the car crash.

lachrymose ADJ. producing tears. His voice has a *lachrymose* quality more appropriate to a funeral than a class reunion.

lackadaisical ADJ. lacking purpose or zest; halfhearted; languid. Because Gatsby had his mind more on his love life than on his finances, he did a very *lackadaisical* job of managing his money.

lackluster ADJ. dull. We were disappointed by the *lackluster* performance.

● **laconic** ADJ. brief and to the point. Many of the characters portrayed by Clint Eastwood are *laconic* types: strong men of few words.

● **laggard** ADJ. slow; sluggish. The sailor had been taught not to be *laggard* in carrying out orders. also N. lag, N., V.

Word List 28 lament–lout

■ **lament** V. grieve; express sorrow. Even advocates of the war *lamented* the loss of so many lives in combat. also N. lamentation, N.

● **lampoon** V. ridicule. This article *lampoons* the pretensions of some movie moguls. also N.

languid ADJ. weary; sluggish; listless. Her siege of illness left her *languid* and pallid.

languish V. lose animation; lose strength. Left at Miss Minchin's school for girls while her father went off to war, Sarah Crewe refused to *languish*; instead, she hid her grief and actively befriended her less fortunate classmates.

languor N. lassitude; depression. His friends tried to overcome the *languor* into which he had fallen by taking him to parties and to the theater.

lap V. take in food or drink with one's tongue; splash gently. The kitten neatly *lapped* up her milk. The waves softly *lapped* against the pier.

larceny N. theft. Because of the prisoner's record, the district attorney refused to reduce the charge from grand *larceny* to petty *larceny*.

largess N. generous gift. Lady Bountiful distributed *largess* to the poor.

● **lassitude** N. languor; weariness. After a massage and a long soak in the hot tub, I gave in to my growing *lassitude* and lay down for a nap.

latent ADJ. potential but undeveloped; dormant; hidden. Polaroid pictures are popular at parties, because you can see the *latent* photographic image gradually appear before your eyes.

lateral ADJ. coming from the side. In order to get good plant growth, the gardener must pinch off all *lateral* shoots.

latitude N. freedom from narrow limitations. I think you have permitted your son too much *latitude* in this matter.

■ **laud** V. praise. The NFL *lauded* Boomer Esiason's efforts to raise money to combat cystic fibrosis. laudable, laudatory, ADJ.

■ **lavish** ADJ. generous; openhanded; extravagant; wasteful. Her wealthy suitors wooed her with lavish gifts. also V.

lax ADJ. careless. We dislike restaurants where the service is *lax* and inattentive.

leaven V. cause to rise or grow lighter; enliven. As bread dough is *leavened*, it puffs up, expanding in volume.

lecherous ADJ. lustful; impure in thought and deed. The villain of the play, a *lecherous* old banker, lusted after the poor farmer's beautiful daughter.

leery ADJ. suspicious; cautious. Don't eat the sushi at this restaurant; I'm a bit *leery* about how fresh the raw fish is.

legacy N. a gift made by a will. Part of my *legacy* from my parents is an album of family photographs.

legend N. explanatory list of symbols on a map. The *legend* at the bottom of the map made it clear which symbols stood for rest areas along the highway and which stood for public camp sites. (secondary meaning)

legerdemain N. sleight of hand. The magician demonstrated his renowned *legerdemain*.

leniency N. mildness; permissiveness. Considering the gravity of the offense, we were surprised by the *leniency* of the sentence.

lethal ADJ. deadly. It is unwise to leave *lethal* weapons where children may find them.

■ **lethargic** ADJ. drowsy; dull. The stuffy room made her *lethargic*: she felt as if she was about to nod off.

■ **levity** N. lack of seriousness; lightness. Stop giggling and wriggling around in the pew: such *levity* is improper in church.

levy V. impose (a fine); collect (a payment). Crying "No taxation without representation," the colonists demonstrated against England's power to *levy* taxes.

lewd ADJ. lustful. They found his *lewd* stories objectionable.

lexicographer N. compiler of a dictionary. The new dictionary is the work of many *lexicographers* who spent years compiling and editing the work.

lexicon N. dictionary. I cannot find this word in any *lexicon* in the library.

liability N. drawback; debts. Her lack of an extensive vocabulary was a *liability* that she was eventually able to overcome.

liaison N. contact keeping parts of an organization in communication; go-between; secret love affair. As the *liaison* between the American and British forces during World War II, the colonel had to ease tensions between the leaders of the two armies. Romeo's romantic *liaison* with Juliet ended in tragedy.

libel N. defamatory statement; act of writing something that smears a person's character. If Batman wrote that the Joker was a dirty, rotten, mass-murdering criminal, could the Joker sue Batman for *libel*?

liberator N. one who sets free. Simon Bolivar, who led the South American colonies in their rebellion against Spanish rule, is known as the great *liberator*. liberate, V.

licentious ADJ. amoral; lewd and lascivious; unrestrained. Unscrupulously seducing the daughter of his host, Don Juan felt no qualms about the immorality of his *licentious* behavior.

lilliputian ADJ. extremely small. Tiny and delicate, the model was built on a *lilliputian* scale. also N.

limber ADJ. flexible. Hours of ballet classes kept him *limber*.

limerick N. humorous short verse. The *limerick* form is the best; its meter is pure anapest. A *limerick's* fun for most everyone, and the word may occur on your test.

limpid ADJ. clear; transparent; lucid. We could see swarms of colorful tropical fish in the *limpid* waters of the peaceful cove.

linchpin N. something that holds or links various parts together. The *linchpin* in the district attorney's case was a photograph showing the defendant shaking hands with the hired killer.

lineage N. descent; ancestry. He traced his *lineage* back to Mayflower days.

■ **linger** V. loiter or dawdle; continue or persist. Hoping to see Juliet pass by, Romeo *lingered* outside the Capulet house for hours. Though Mother made stuffed cabbage on Monday, the smell *lingered* around the house for days.

linguistic ADJ. pertaining to language. Exposed to most modern European languages in childhood, she grew up to be a *linguistic* prodigy.

liniment N. ointment; lotion; salve. The trainer carefully applied the *liniment* to the quarterback's bruise, gently rubbing it into the skin.

lionize V. treat as a celebrity. She enjoyed being *lionized* and adored by the public.

liquidate V. settle accounts; clear up. He was able to *liquidate* all his debts in a short period of time.

list V. tilt; lean over. That flagpole should be absolutely vertical; instead, it *lists* to one side. (secondary meaning)

■ **listless** ADJ. lacking in spirit or energy. We had expected him to be full of enthusiasm and were surprised by his *listless* attitude.

● **lithe** ADJ. flexible; supple. Her figure was *lithe* and willowy.

litigation N. lawsuit. Try to settle this without involving any lawyers; I do not want to become bogged down in *litigation*. litigant, N.

livid ADJ. lead-colored; black and blue; enraged. His face was so *livid* with rage that we were afraid that he might have an attack of apoplexy.

loath ADJ. reluctant; disinclined. Fearing for their son's safety, the overprotective parents were *loath* to let him go on the class trip.

loathe V. detest. Booing and hissing, the audience showed how much they *loathed* the wicked villain.

■ **lofty** ADJ. very high. Though Barbara Jordan's fellow students used to tease her about her *lofty* ambitions, she rose to hold one of the highest positions in the land.

log N. record of a voyage or flight; record of day to day activities. "Flogged two seamen today for insubordination" wrote Captain Bligh in the *Bounty's log*. To see how much work I've accomplished recently, just take a look at the number of new files listed on my computer *log*.

loiter V. hang around; linger. The policeman told him not to *loiter* in the alley.

loll V. lounge about. They *lolled* around in their chairs watching television.

longevity N. long life. When he reached ninety, the old man was proud of his *longevity*.

loom V. appear or take shape (usually in an enlarged or distorted form). The shadow of the gallows *loomed* threateningly above the small boy.

lope V. gallop slowly. As the horses *loped* along, we had an opportunity to admire the ever-changing scenery.

loquacious ADJ. talkative. Though our daughter barely says a word to us these days, put a phone in her hand and see how *loquacious* she can be: our phone bills are out of sight! loquacity, N.

lout N. clumsy person. That awkward *lout* dropped my priceless vase!

Word List 29 lucid–maul

lucid ADJ. easily understood; clear; intelligible. Ellen makes an excellent teacher: her explanations of technical points are *lucid* enough for a child to grasp.

lucrative ADJ. profitable. He turned his hobby into a *lucrative* profession.

ludicrous ADJ. ridiculous; laughable; absurd. Gwen tried to keep a straight face, but Bill's suggestion was so *ludicrous* that she finally had to laugh.

lugubrious ADJ. mournful. Gloomy Gus walked around town with a *lugubrious* expression on his face.

lull N. moment of calm. Not wanting to get wet, they waited under the awning for a *lull* in the rain.

lull V. soothe; cause one to relax one's guard; subside. The mother's gentle song *lulled* the child to sleep. Malcolm tried to come up with a plausible story to *lull* his mother's suspicions, but she didn't believe a word he said.

lumber V. move heavily or clumsily. Still somewhat torpid after its long hibernation, the bear *lumbered* through the woods.

luminary N. celebrity; dignitary. A leading light of the American stage, Ethel Barrymore was a theatrical *luminary* whose name lives on.

luminous ADJ. shining; issuing light. The sun is a *luminous* body.

lummox N. big, clumsy, often stupid person. Because he was highly overweight and looked ungainly, John Candy often was cast as a slow-witted *lummox*.

lunge V. quickly dive forward; thrust. The wide receiver *lunged* forward to grab the football. With his sword, Dartagnan *lunged* at his adversary.

● **lurid** ADJ. wild; sensational; graphic; gruesome. Do the *lurid* cover stories in the *Enquirer* actually attract people to buy that trashy tabloid?

lurk V. stealthily lie in waiting; slink; exist unperceived. "Who knows what evil *lurks* in the hearts of men? The Shadow knows."

luscious ADJ. pleasing to taste or smell. The ripe peach was *luscious*.

luster N. shine; gloss. The soft *luster* of the silk in the dim light was pleasing.

lustrous ADJ. shining. Her large and *lustrous* eyes lent a touch of beauty to an otherwise plain face.

● **luxuriant** ADJ. abundant; rich and splendid; fertile. Lady Godiva was completely covered by her *luxuriant* hair.

machinations N. evil schemes or plots. Fortunately, Batman saw through the wily *machinations* of the Riddler and saved Gotham City from destruction by the forces of evil.

madrigal N. pastoral song. His program of folk songs included several *madrigals* which he sang to the accompaniment of a lute.

maelstrom N. whirlpool. The canoe was tossed about in the *maelstrom*.

magnanimous ADJ. generous; great-hearted. Philanthropists by definition are *magnanimous*; misers, by definition, are not. Cordelia was too *magnanimous* to resent her father's unkindness to her; instead, she generously forgave him. magnanimity, N.

magnate N. person of prominence or influence. Growing up in Pittsburgh, Annie Dillard was surrounded by the mansions of the great steel and coal *magnates* who set their mark on that city.

magnitude N. greatness; extent. It is difficult to comprehend the *magnitude* of his crime.

maim V. mutilate; injure. The hospital could not take care of all who had been wounded or *maimed* in the railroad accident.

maladroit ADJ. clumsy; bungling. "Oh! My stupid tongue!" exclaimed Jane, embarrassed at having said anything so *maladroit*.

malady N. illness. A mysterious *malady* swept the country, filling doctors' offices with feverish, purple-spotted patients.

malaise N. uneasiness; vague feeling of ill health. Feeling slightly queasy before going onstage, Carol realized that this touch of *malaise* was merely stage fright.

malapropism N. comic misuse of a word. When Mrs. Malaprop accuses Lydia of being "as headstrong as an allegory on the banks of the Nile," she confuses "allegory" and "alligator" in a typical *malapropism*.

malcontent N. person dissatisfied with existing state of affairs. One of the few *malcontents* in Congress, he constantly voiced his objections to the presidential program. also ADJ.

malediction N. curse. When the magic mirror revealed that Snow White was still alive, the wicked queen cried out in rage and uttered dreadful *maledictions*.

malefactor N. evildoer; criminal. Mighty Mouse will save the day, hunting down *malefactors* and rescuing innocent mice from peril.

malevolent ADJ. wishing evil. Iago is a *malevolent* villain who takes pleasure in ruining Othello.

malfeasance N. wrongdoing. The authorities did not discover the campaign manager's *malfeasance* until after he had spent most of the money he had embezzled.

■ **malicious** ADJ. hateful; spiteful. Jealous of Cinderella's beauty, her *malicious* stepsisters expressed their spite by forcing her to do menial tasks. malice, N.

malign V. speak evil of; bad-mouth; defame. Putting her hands over her ears, Rose refused to listen to Betty *malign* her friend Susan.

malignant ADJ. injurious; tending to cause death; aggressively malevolent. Though many tumors are benign, some are *malignant*, growing out of control and endangering the life of the patient.

malingerer N. one who feigns illness to escape duty. The captain ordered the sergeant to punish all *malingerers* and force them to work. malinger, V.

malleable ADJ. capable of being shaped by pounding; impressionable. Gold is a *malleable* metal, easily shaped into bracelets and rings. Fagin hoped Oliver was a *malleable* lad, easily shaped into a thief.

malodorous ADJ. foul-smelling. The compost heap was most *malodorous* in summer.

mammal N. a vertebrate animal whose female suckles its young. Many people regard the whale as a fish and do not realize that it is a *mammal*.

mammoth ADJ. gigantic; enormous. To try to memorize every word on this vocabulary list would be a *mammoth* undertaking; take on projects that are more manageable in size.

mandate N. order; charge. In his inaugural address, the president stated that he had a *mandate* from the people to seek an end to social evils such as poverty. also V.

mandatory ADJ. obligatory; compulsory. It is *mandatory* that, before graduation, all students must pass the swimming test.

maniacal ADJ. raging mad; insane. Though Mr. Rochester had locked his mad wife in the attic, he could still hear her *maniacal* laughter echoing throughout the house.

manifest ADJ. evident; visible; obvious. Digby's embarrassment when he met Madonna was *manifest*: his ears turned bright pink, he kept scuffing one shoe in the dirt, and he couldn't look her in the eye.

manifesto N. declaration; statement of policy. The *Communist Manifesto* by Marx and Engels proclaimed the principles of modern communism.

manipulate V. operate with one's hands; control or play upon (people, forces, etc.) artfully. Jim Henson understood how to *manipulate* the Muppets. Madonna understands how to *manipulate* men (and publicity).

mannered ADJ. affected; not natural. Attempting to copy the style of his wealthy neighbors, Gatsby adopted a *mannered*, artificial way of speech.

marital ADJ. pertaining to marriage. After the publication of her book of *marital* advice, she was often consulted by married couples on the verge of divorce.

marked ADJ. noticeable or pronounced; targeted for vengeance. He walked with a *marked* limp, a souvenir of an old I.R.A. attack. As British ambassador, he knew he was a *marked* man, for he knew the Irish Republican Army wanted him dead.

■ **marred** ADJ. damaged; disfigured. She had to refinish the *marred* surface of the table. mar, V.

marshal V. put in order. At a debate tournament, extemporaneous speakers have only a minute or two to *marshal* their thoughts before they address their audience.

marsupial N. one of a family of mammals that nurse their offspring in a pouch. The most common *marsupial* in North America is the opossum.

martial ADJ. warlike. The sound of *martial* music inspired the young cadet with dreams of military glory.

martinet N. strict disciplinarian. No talking at meals! No mingling with the servants! Miss Minchin was a *martinet* who insisted that the schoolgirls in her charge observe each regulation to the letter.

martyr N. one who voluntarily suffers death for his or her religion or cause; great sufferer. By burning her at the stake, the English made Joan of Arc a *martyr* for her faith. Mother played the *martyr* by staying home cleaning the house while the rest of the family went off to the beach.

masochist N. person who enjoys his own pain. The *masochist* begs, "Hit me." The sadist smiles and says, "I won't."

material ADJ. made of physical matter; unspiritual; important. Probing the mysteries of this *material* world has always fascinated physicist George Whitesides. Reporters nicknamed Madonna the *Material* Girl because, despite her name, she seemed wholly uninterested in spiritual values. Lexy's active participation made a *material* difference to the success of the fund-raiser.

■ **materialism** N. preoccupation with physical comforts and things. By its nature, *materialism* is opposed to idealism, for where the materialist emphasizes the needs of the body, the idealist emphasizes the needs of the soul.

maternal ADJ. motherly. Many animals display *maternal* instincts only while their offspring are young and helpless.

matriarch N. woman who rules a family or larger social group. The *matriarch* ruled her gypsy tribe with a firm hand.

matriculate V. enroll (in college or graduate school). Incoming students formally *matriculate* at our college in a special ceremony during which they sign the official register of students.

matrix N. point of origin; array of numbers or algebraic symbols; mold or die. Some historians claim the Nile Valley was the *matrix* of Western civilization.

maudlin ADJ. effusively sentimental. Whenever a particularly *maudlin* tearjerker was playing at the movies, Marvin would embarrass himself by weeping copiously.

maul V. handle roughly. The rock star was *mauled* by his over-excited fans.

Word List 30   maverick–misrepresent

maverick N. rebel; nonconformist. To the masculine literary establishment, George Sand with her insistence on wearing trousers and smoking cigars was clearly a *maverick* who fought her proper womanly role.

mawkish ADJ. mushy and gushy; icky-sticky sentimental; maudlin. Whenever Gigi and her boyfriend would sigh and get all lovey-dovey, her little brother would shout, "Yuck!" protesting their *mawkish* behavior.

maxim N. proverb; a truth pithily stated. Aesop's story of the hare and the tortoise illustrates the *maxim* "Slow and steady wins the race."

meager ADJ. scanty; inadequate. Still hungry after his *meager* serving of porridge, Oliver Twist asked for a second helping.

● **meander** V. wind or turn in its course. Needing to stay close to a source of water, he followed every twist and turn of the stream as it *meandered* through the countryside.

meddlesome ADJ. interfering. He felt his marriage was suffering because of his *meddlesome* mother-in-law.

mediate V. settle a dispute through the services of an outsider. King Solomon was asked to *mediate* a dispute between two women, each of whom claimed to be the mother of the same child.

mediocre ADJ. ordinary; commonplace. We were disappointed because he gave a rather *mediocre* performance in this role.

meditation N. reflection; thought. She reached her decision only after much *meditation*.

medley N. mixture. To avoid boring dancers by playing any one tune for too long, bands may combine three or four tunes into a *medley*.

meek ADJ. quiet and obedient; spiritless. Can Lois Lane see through Superman's disguise and spot the superhero hiding behind the guise of *meek*, timorous Clark Kent? Mr. Barrett never expected his *meek* daughter would dare to defy him by eloping with her suitor.

melancholy ADJ. gloomy; morose; blue. To Eugene, stuck in his small town, a train whistle was a *melancholy* sound, for it made him think of all the places he would never get to see.

mellifluous ADJ. sweetly or smoothly flowing; melodious. Italian is a *mellifluous* language, especially suited to being sung.

membrane N. thin soft sheet of animal or vegetable tissue. Each individual section of an orange is covered with a thin, transparent *membrane*. membranous, ADJ.

memento N. token; reminder. Take this book as a *memento* of your visit.

menagerie N. collection of wild animals. Whenever the children run wild around the house, Mom shouts, "Calm down! I'm not running a *menagerie*!"

mendacious ADJ. lying; habitually dishonest. Distrusting Huck from the start, Miss Watson assumed he was *mendacious* and refused to believe a word he said.

mendicant N. beggar. "O noble sir, give alms to the poor," cried Aladdin, playing the *mendicant*.

menial ADJ. suitable for servants; lowly; mean. Her wicked stepmother forced Cinderella to do *menial* tasks around the house while her ugly stepsisters lolled around painting their toenails.

mentor N. teacher. During this very trying period, she could not have had a better *mentor*, for the teacher was sympathetic and understanding.

● **mercenary** ADJ. interested in money or gain. Andy's every act was prompted by *mercenary* motives: his first question was always "What's in it for me?"

● **mercurial** ADJ. capricious; changing; fickle. Quick as quicksilver to change, he was *mercurial* in nature and therefore unreliable.

merger N. combination (of two business corporations). When the firm's president married the director of financial planning, the office joke was that it wasn't a marriage, it was a *merger*.

mesmerize V. hypnotize. The incessant drone seemed to *mesmerize* him and place him in a trance.

metallurgical ADJ. pertaining to the art of removing metals from ores. During the course of his *metallurgical* research, the scientist developed a steel alloy of tremendous strength.

metamorphosis N. change of form; major transformation. The *metamorphosis* of caterpillar to butterfly is typical of many such changes in animal life. metamorphose, V.

metaphor N. implied comparison. "He soared like an eagle" is an example of a simile; "He is an eagle in flight," a *metaphor*.

metaphysical ADJ. pertaining to speculative philosophy. The modern poets have gone back to the fanciful poems of the *metaphysical* poets of the seventeenth century for many of their images. metaphysics, N.

■ **methodical** ADJ. systematic. An accountant must be *methodical* and maintain order among his financial records.

■ **meticulous** ADJ. excessively careful; painstaking; scrupulous. Martha Stewart was a *meticulous* housekeeper, fussing about each and every detail that went into making up her perfect home.

metropolis N. large city. Every evening the terminal is filled with thousands of commuters going from this *metropolis* to their homes in the suburbs.

mettle N. courage; spirit. When challenged by the other horses in the race, the thoroughbred proved its *mettle* by its determination to hold the lead.

miasma N. swamp gas; heavy, vaporous atmosphere, often emanating from decaying matter; pervasive corrupting influence. The smog hung over Victorian London like a dark cloud; noisome, reeking of decay, it was a visible *miasma*.

microcosm N. small world; the world in miniature. The small village community that Jane Austen depicts serves as a *microcosm* of English society in her time, for in this small world we see all the social classes meeting and mingling.

migrant ADJ. changing its habitat; wandering. *Migrant* workers return to the Central Valley each year at harvest time. also N.

migratory ADJ. wandering. The return of the *migratory* birds to the northern sections of this country is a harbinger of spring. migrate, V.

milieu N. environment; means of expression. Surrounded by smooth preppies and arty bohemians, the country boy from Smalltown, USA, felt out of his *milieu*. Although he has produced excellent oil paintings and lithographs, his proper *milieu* is watercolor.

militant ADJ. combative; bellicose. Although at this time he was advocating a policy of neutrality, one could usually find him adopting a more *militant* attitude. also N.

mimicry N. imitation. Her gift for *mimicry* was so great that her friends said that she should be in the theater.

mincing ADJ. affectedly dainty. Yum-Yum walked across the stage with *mincing* steps.

minuscule ADJ. extremely small. Why should I involve myself with a project with so *minuscule* a chance for success?

minute ADJ. extremely small. The twins resembled one another closely; only *minute* differences set them apart.

minutiae N. petty details. She would have liked to ignore the *minutiae* of daily living.

mirage N. unreal reflection; optical illusion. The lost prospector was fooled by a *mirage* in the desert.

mire V. entangle; stick in swampy ground. Their rear wheels became *mired* in mud. also N.

● **mirth** N. merriment; laughter. Sober Malvolio found Sir Toby's *mirth* improper.

● **misanthrope** N. one who hates mankind. In *Gulliver's Travels*, Swift portrays an image of humanity as vile, degraded beasts; for this reason, various critics consider him a *misanthrope*.

misapprehension N. error; misunderstanding. To avoid *misapprehension*, I am going to ask all of you to repeat the instructions I have given.

miscellany N. mixture of writings on various subjects. This is an interesting *miscellany* of nineteenth-century prose and poetry.

mischance N. ill luck. By *mischance*, he lost his week's salary.

misconception N. mistaken idea. "Sir, you are suffering from a *misconception*. I do not wish to marry you in the least!"

misconstrue V. interpret incorrectly; misjudge. She took the passage seriously rather than humorously because she *misconstrued* the author's ironic tone.

misdemeanor N. minor crime. The culprit pleaded guilty to a *misdemeanor* rather than face trial for a felony.

■ **miserly** ADJ. stingy; mean. Transformed by his vision on Christmas Eve, mean old Scrooge ceased being *miserly* and became a generous, kind old man.

misgivings N. doubts. Hamlet described his *misgivings* to Horatio but decided to fence with Laertes despite his foreboding of evil.

mishap N. accident. With a little care you could have avoided this *mishap*.

● **misnomer** N. wrong name; incorrect designation. His tyrannical conduct proved to all that his nickname, King Eric the Just, was a *misnomer*.

misrepresent V. give a false or incorrect impression, often deliberately; serve unsatisfactorily as a representative. In his job application, Milton *misrepresented* his academic background; he was fired when his employers discovered the truth. The reformers accused Senator Gunbucks of *misrepresenting* his constituents and claimed he took bribes from the NRA.

Word List 31 missile–natty

missile N. object to be thrown or projected. After carefully folding his book report into a paper airplane, Beavis threw the *missile* across the classroom at Butthead. Rocket scientists are building guided *missiles*; Beavis and Butthead can barely make unguided ones.

missive N. letter. The ambassador received a *missive* from the secretary of state.

mite N. very small object or creature; small coin. Gnats are annoying *mites* that sting.

■ **mitigate** V. appease; moderate. Nothing Jason did could *mitigate* Medea's anger; she refused to forgive him for betraying her.

mnemonic ADJ. pertaining to memory. He used *mnemonic* tricks to master new words.

mobile ADJ. movable; not fixed. The *mobile* blood bank operated by the Red Cross visited our neighborhood today. mobility, N.

mock V. ridicule; imitate, often in derision. It is unkind to *mock* anyone; it is stupid to *mock* anyone significantly bigger than you. mockery, N.

mode N. prevailing style; manner; way of doing something. The rock star had to have her hair done in the latest *mode*: frizzed, with occasional moussed spikes for variety. Henry plans to adopt a simpler *mode* of life: he is going to become a mushroom hunter and live off the land.

modicum N. limited quantity. Although his story is based on a *modicum* of truth, most of the events he describes are fictitious.

modulate V. tone down in intensity; regulate; change from one key to another. Always singing at the top of her lungs, the budding Brunhilde never learned to *modulate* her voice.

molecule N. the smallest particle (one or more atoms) of a substance, having all the properties of that substance. In chemistry, we study how atoms and *molecules* react to form new substances.

● **mollify** V. soothe. The airline customer service representative tried to *mollify* the angry passenger by offering her a seat in first class.

molten ADJ. melted. The city of Pompeii was destroyed by volcanic ash rather than by *molten* lava flowing from Mount Vesuvius.

momentous ADJ. very important. When Marie and Pierre Curie discovered radium, they had no idea of the *momentous* impact their discovery would have upon society.

momentum N. quantity of motion of a moving body; impetus. The car lost *momentum* as it tried to ascend the steep hill.

monarchy N. government under a single ruler. Though England today is a *monarchy*, there is some question whether it will be one in twenty years, given the present discontent at the prospect of Prince Charles as king.

monastic ADJ. related to monks or monasteries; removed from worldly concerns. Withdrawing from the world, Thomas Merton joined a contemplative religious order and adopted the *monastic* life.

monetary ADJ. pertaining to money. Jane held the family purse strings: she made all *monetary* decisions affecting the household.

monochromatic ADJ. having only one color. Most people who are color blind actually can distinguish several colors; some, however, have a truly *monochromatic* view of a world all in shades of gray.

monolithic ADJ. solidly uniform; unyielding. Knowing the importance of appearing resolute, the patriots sought to present a *monolithic* front.

monosyllabic ADJ. having only one syllable. No matter what he was asked, the taciturn New Englander answered with a *monosyllabic* "Yep" or "Nope." monosyllable, N.

monotony N. sameness leading to boredom. What could be more deadly dull than the *monotony* of punching numbers into a computer hour after hour?

montage N. photographic composition combining elements from different sources. In one early *montage*, Beauchamp brought together pictures of broken mannequins and newspaper clippings about the Vietnam War.

monumental ADJ. massive. Writing a dictionary is a *monumental* task.

moodiness N. fits of depression or gloom. Her recurrent *moodiness* left her feeling as if she had fallen into a black hole.

moratorium N. legal delay of payment. If we declare a *moratorium* and delay collection of debts for six months, I am sure the farmers will be able to meet their bills.

morbid ADJ. given to unwholesome thought; moody; characteristic of disease. People who come to disaster sites just to peer at the grisly wreckage are indulging their *morbid* curiosity.

mores N. conventions; moral standards; customs. In America, Benazir Bhutto dressed as Western women did; in Pakistan, however, she followed the *mores* of her people, dressing in traditional veil and robes.

moribund ADJ. dying. Hearst took a *moribund*, failing weekly newspaper and transformed it into one of the liveliest, most profitable daily papers around.

■ **morose** ADJ. ill-humored; sullen; melancholy. Forced to take early retirement, Bill acted *morose* for months; then, all of a sudden, he shook off his sullen mood and was his usual cheerful self.

mortician N. undertaker. The *mortician* prepared the corpse for burial.

mortify V. humiliate; punish the flesh. She was so *mortified* by her blunder that she ran to her room in tears.

● **mosaic** N. picture made of colorful small inlaid tiles. The mayor compared the city to a beautiful *mosaic* made up of people of every race and religion on earth.

mote N. small speck. The tiniest *mote* in the eye is very painful.

motif N. theme. This simple *motif* runs throughout the entire score.

motley ADJ. multi-colored; mixed. The jester wore a *motley* tunic, red and green and blue and gold all patched together haphazardly. Captain Ahab had gathered a *motley* crew to sail the vessel: old sea dogs and runaway boys, pillars of the church and drunkards, even a tattooed islander who terrified the rest of the crew.

mottled ADJ. blotched in coloring; spotted. When old Falstaff blushed, his face was *mottled* with embarrassment, all pink and purple and red.

muddle V. confuse; mix up. His thoughts were *muddled* and chaotic. also N.

muggy ADJ. warm and damp. August in New York City is often *muggy*.

multifaceted ADJ. having many aspects. A *multifaceted* composer, Roger Davidson has recorded original pieces that range from ragtime tangos to choral masses.

multifarious ADJ. varied; greatly diversified. A career woman and mother, she was constantly busy with the *multifarious* activities of her daily life.

multiform ADJ. having many forms. Snowflakes are *multiform* but always hexagonal.

multilingual ADJ. having many languages. Because Switzerland is surrounded by France, Germany, Italy, and Austria, many Swiss people are *multilingual*.

multiplicity N. state of being numerous. He was appalled by the *multiplicity* of details he had to complete before setting out on his mission.

■ **mundane** ADJ. worldly as opposed to spiritual; everyday. Uninterested in philosophical or spiritual discussions, Tom talked only of *mundane* matters such as the daily weather forecast or the latest basketball results.

● **munificent** ADJ. very generous. Shamelessly fawning over a particularly generous donor, the dean kept on referring to her as "our *munificent* benefactor." munificence, N.

mural N. wall painting. The walls of the Chicano Community Center are covered with *murals* painted in the style of Diego Rivera, the great Mexican artist.

murky ADJ. dark and gloomy; thick with fog; vague. The *murky* depths of the swamp were so dark that one couldn't tell the vines and branches from the snakes.

muse V. ponder. For a moment he *mused* about the beauty of the scene, but his thoughts soon changed as he recalled his own personal problems. also N.

mushroom V. expand or grow rapidly. Between 1990 and 1999, the population of Silicon Valley *mushroomed*; with the rapidly increasing demand for housing, home prices skyrocketed as well.

musky ADJ. having the odor of musk. She left a trace of *musky* perfume behind her.

muster V. gather; assemble. Washington *mustered* his forces at Trenton. also N.

musty ADJ. stale; spoiled by age. The attic was dark and *musty*.

mutability N. ability to change in form; fickleness. Going from rags to riches, and then back to rags again, the bankrupt financier was a victim of the *mutability* of fortune.

muted ADJ. silent; muffled; toned down. Thanks to the thick, sound-absorbing walls of the cathedral, only *muted* traffic noise reached the worshippers within.

mutinous ADJ. unruly; rebellious. The captain had to use force to quiet his *mutinous* crew. mutiny, N.

myopic ADJ. nearsighted; lacking foresight. Stumbling into doors despite the coke bottle lenses on his glasses, the nearsighted Mr. Magoo is markedly *myopic*. In playing all summer long and ignoring to store up food for winter, the grasshopper in Aesop's fable was *myopic* as well.

myriad N. very large number. *Myriads* of mosquitoes from the swamps invaded our village every twilight. also ADJ.

mystify V. bewilder purposely. When doctors speak in medical jargon, they often *mystify* their patients, who have little knowledge of medical terminology.

nadir N. lowest point. Although few people realized it, the Dow-Jones averages had reached their *nadir* and would soon begin an upward surge.

naiveté N. quality of being unsophisticated; simplicity; artlessness; gullibility. Touched by the *naiveté* of sweet, convent-trained Cosette, Marius pledges himself to protect her innocence. naive, ADJ.

narcissist N. conceited person; someone in love with his own image. A *narcissist* is her own best friend.

narrative ADJ. related to telling a story. A born teller of tales, Tillie Olsen used her impressive *narrative* skills to advantage in her story "I Stand Here Ironing." narrate, V.

nascent ADJ. incipient; coming into being. If we could identify these revolutionary movements in their *nascent* state, we would be able to eliminate serious trouble in later years.

natty ADJ. neatly or smartly dressed. Priding himself on being a *natty* dresser, the gangster Bugsy Siegel collected a wardrobe of imported suits and ties.

Word List 32 nauseate–obsessive

nauseate V. cause to become sick; fill with disgust. The foul smells began to *nauseate* him.

nautical ADJ. pertaining to ships or navigation. The Maritime Museum contains many models of clipper ships, logbooks, anchors and many other items of a *nautical* nature.

navigable ADJ. wide and deep enough to allow ships to pass through; able to be steered. So much sand had built up at the bottom of the canal that the waterway was barely *navigable*.

nebulous ADJ. vague; hazy; cloudy. Phil and Dave tried to come up with a clear, intelligible business plan, not some hazy, *nebulous* proposal.

necromancy N. black magic; dealings with the dead. The evil sorceror performed feats of *necromancy*, calling on the spirits of the dead to tell the future.

● **nefarious** ADJ. very wicked. The villain's crimes, though various, were one and all *nefarious*.

■ **negate** V. cancel out; nullify; deny. A sudden surge of adrenalin can *negate* the effects of fatigue: there's nothing like a good shock to wake you up.

negligence N. neglect; failure to take reasonable care. Tommy failed to put back the cover on the well after he fetched his pail of water; because of his *negligence*, Kitty fell in.

negligible ADJ. so small, trifling, or unimportant that it may be easily disregarded. Because the damage to his car had been *negligible*, Michael decided he wouldn't bother to report the matter to his insurance company.

nemesis N. someone seeking revenge. Abandoned at sea in a small boat, the vengeful Captain Bligh vowed to be the *nemesis* of Fletcher Christian and his fellow mutineers.

neologism N. new or newly coined word or phrase. As we invent new techniques and professions, we must also invent *neologisms* such as "microcomputer" and "astronaut" to describe them.

neophyte N. recent convert; beginner. This mountain slope contains slides that will challenge experts as well as *neophytes*.

nepotism N. favoritism (to a relative). John left his position with the company because he felt that advancement was based on *nepotism* rather than ability.

nettle V. annoy; vex. Do not let him *nettle* you with his sarcastic remarks.

neutral ADJ. impartial; not supporting one side over another. Reluctant to get mixed up in someone else's quarrel, Bobby tried to remain *neutral,* but eventually he had to take sides.

nicety N. subtlety; precision; minute distinction; fine point. This word list provides illustrative sentences for each entry word; it cannot, however, explain all the *niceties* of current English usage.

nihilist N. one who believes traditional beliefs to be groundless and existence meaningless; absolute skeptic; revolutionary terrorist. In his final days, Hitler revealed himself a power-mad *nihilist*, ready to annihilate all of Western Europe, even to destroy Germany itself, in order that his will might prevail. The root of the word *nihilist* is *nihil*, Latin for *nothing*. nihilism, N.

nip V. stop something's growth or development; snip off; bite; make numb with cold. The twins were plotting mischief, but Mother intervened and *nipped* that plan in the bud. The gardener *nipped* off a lovely rose and gave it to me. Last week a guard dog *nipped* the postman in the leg; this week the extreme chill *nipped* his fingers till he could barely hold the mail.

nirvana N. in Buddhist teachings, the ideal state in which the individual loses himself in the attainment of an impersonal beatitude. Despite his desire to achieve *nirvana*, the young Buddhist found that even the buzzing of a fly could distract him from his meditation.

nocturnal ADJ. done at night. Mr. Jones obtained a watchdog to prevent the *nocturnal* raids on his chicken coops.

noisome ADJ. foul-smelling; unwholesome. The *noisome* atmosphere downwind of the oil refinery not only stank, it damaged the lungs of everyone living in the area.

nomadic ADJ. wandering. Several *nomadic* tribes of Indians would hunt in this area each year.

nomenclature N. terminology; system of names. Sharon found Latin word parts useful in translating medical *nomenclature*: when her son had to have a bilateral myringotomy, she figured out that he just needed a hole in each of his eardrums to end the earaches he had.

nominal ADJ. in name only; trifling. He offered to drive her to the airport for only a *nominal* fee.

■ **nonchalance** N. indifference; lack of concern; composure. Cool, calm, and collected under fire, James Bond shows remarkable *nonchalance* in the face of danger.

noncommittal ADJ. neutral; unpledged; undecided. We were annoyed by his *noncommittal* reply for we had been led to expect definite assurances of his approval.

nondescript ADJ. undistinctive; ordinary. The private detective was a short, *nondescript* fellow with no outstanding features, the sort of person one would never notice in a crowd.

nonentity N. person of no importance; nonexistence. Because the two older princes dismissed their youngest brother as a *nonentity*, they did not realize that he was quietly plotting to seize the throne.

nonplus V. bring to halt by confusion; perplex. Jack's uncharacteristic rudeness *nonplussed* Jill, leaving her uncertain how to react.

nostalgia N. homesickness; longing for the past. My grandfather seldom spoke of life in the old country; he had little patience with *nostalgia*. nostalgic, ADJ.

notable ADJ. conspicuous; important; distinguished. Normally *notable* for his calm in the kitchen, today the head cook was shaking, for the *notable* chef Julia Child was coming to dinner.

■ **notoriety** N. disrepute; ill fame. To the starlet, any publicity was good publicity: if she couldn't have a good reputation, she'd settle for *notoriety*. notorious, ADJ.

■ **novelty** N. something new; newness. The computer is no longer a *novelty* at work; every desk in our office has one. novel, ADJ.

novice N. beginner. Even a *novice* at working with computers can install voice recognition software by following the easy steps outlined in the user's manual.

noxious ADJ. harmful. We must trace the source of these *noxious* gases before they asphyxiate us.

● **nuance** N. shade of difference in meaning or color; subtle distinction. Jody gazed at the Monet landscape for an hour, appreciating every subtle *nuance* of color in the painting.

nullify V. to make invalid. Once the contract was *nullified,* it no longer had any legal force.

nuptial ADJ. related to marriage. Reluctant to be married in a traditional setting, they decided to hold their *nuptial* ceremony at the carousel in Golden Gate Park.

■ **nurture** V. nourish; educate; foster. The Head Start program attempts to *nurture* pre-kindergarten children so that they will do well when they enter public school. also N.

nutrient N. nourishing substance. As a budding nutritionist, Kim has learned to design diets that contain foods rich in important basic *nutrients*.

oaf N. stupid, awkward person. "Watch what you're doing, you clumsy *oaf*!" Bill shouted at the waiter who had drenched him with iced coffee.

● **obdurate**   ADJ. stubborn. He was *obdurate* in his refusal to listen to our complaints.

obese   ADJ. fat. It is advisable that *obese* people try to lose weight.

obfuscate   V. confuse; muddle; cause confusion; make needlessly complex. Was the president's spokesman trying to clarify the hidden weapons mystery, or was he trying to *obfuscate* the issue so the voters would never figure out what had gone on?

obituary   ADJ. death notice. I first learned of her death when I read the *obituary* column in the newspaper. also N.

objective   ADJ. not influenced by emotions; fair. Even though he was her son, she tried to be *objective* about his behavior.

objective   N. goal; aim. A degree in medicine was her ultimate *objective*.

obligatory   ADJ. binding; required. It is *obligatory* that books borrowed from the library be returned within two weeks.

oblique   ADJ. indirect; slanting (deviating from the perpendicular or from a straight line). Casting a quick, *oblique* glance at the reviewing stand, the sergeant ordered the company to march "*Oblique* Right."

■ **obliterate**   V. destroy completely. The tidal wave *obliterated* several island villages.

■ **oblivion**   N. obscurity; forgetfulness. After a decade of popularity, Hurston's works had fallen into *oblivion*; no one bothered to read them anymore.

oblivious   ADJ. inattentive or unmindful; wholly absorbed. Deep in her book, Nancy was *oblivious* to the noisy squabbles of her brother and his friends.

obnoxious   ADJ. offensive; objectionable. A sneak and a tattletale, Sid was an *obnoxious* little brat.

obscure   ADJ. dark; vague; unclear. Even after I read the poem a fourth time, its meaning was still *obscure*. obscurity, N.

■ **obscure**   V. darken; make unclear. At times he seemed purposely to *obscure* his meaning, preferring mystery to clarity.

obsequious   ADJ. slavishly attentive; servile; sycophantic. Helen liked to be served by people who behaved as if they respected themselves; nothing irritated her more than an excessively *obsequious* waiter or a fawning salesclerk.

obsessive   ADJ. related to thinking about something constantly; preoccupying. Ballet, which had been a hobby, began to dominate his life: his love of dancing became *obsessive*. obsession, N.

Word List 33   obsolete–pacifist

obsolete   ADJ. no longer useful; outmoded; antiquated. The invention of the pocket calculator made the slide rule used by generations of engineers *obsolete*.

■ **obstinate**   ADJ. stubborn; hard to control or treat. We tried to persuade him to give up smoking, but he was *obstinate* and refused to change. Blackberry stickers are the most

obstinate weeds I know: once established in a yard, they're extremely hard to root out. obstinacy, N.

obstreperous   ADJ. boisterous; noisy. What do you do when an *obstreperous* horde of drunken policemen goes carousing through your hotel, crashing into potted plants and singing vulgar songs?

obtrude   V. push (oneself or one's ideas) forward or intrude; butt in; stick out or extrude. Because Fanny was reluctant to *obtrude* her opinions about child-raising upon her daughter-in-law, she kept a close watch on her tongue. obtrusive, ADJ.

obtuse   ADJ. blunt; stupid. Because Mr. Collins was too *obtuse* to take a hint, Elizabeth finally had to tell him that she wouldn't marry him if he were the last man on earth.

obviate   V. prevent; make unnecessary. In the twentieth century, people believed electronic communications would *obviate* the need for hard copy; they envisioned a paperless society.

● **odious**   ADJ. hateful; vile. Cinderella's ugly stepsisters had the *odious* habit of popping their zits in public.

odium   N. strong dislike or contempt; hatefulness; disrepute. Unable to bear the *odium* attached to their family name, the killer's parents changed their name and moved away from their hometown.

odorous   ADJ. having an odor. This variety of hybrid tea rose is more *odorous* than the one you have in your garden.

odyssey   N. long, eventful journey. The refugee's journey from Cambodia was a terrifying *odyssey*.

offensive   ADJ. attacking; insulting; distasteful. Getting into street brawls is no minor matter for professional boxers, who are required by law to restrict their *offensive* impulses to the ring.

offhand   ADJ. casual; done without prior thought. Expecting to be treated with due propriety by her hosts, Great-Aunt Maud was offended by their *offhand* manner.

officious   ADJ. meddlesome; excessively pushy in offering one's services. Judy wanted to look over the new computer models on her own, but the *officious* salesman kept on butting in with "helpful" advice until she was ready to walk out of the store.

ogle   V. look at amorously; make eyes at. At the coffee house, Walter was too shy to *ogle* the pretty girls openly; instead, he peeked out at them from behind a rubber plant.

olfactory   ADJ. concerning the sense of smell. A wine taster must have a discriminating palate and a keen *olfactory* sense, for a good wine appeals both to the taste buds and to the nose.

oligarchy   N. government by a privileged few. One small clique ran the student council: what had been intended as a democratic governing body had turned into an *oligarchy*.

■ **ominous**   ADJ. threatening. Those clouds are *ominous*; they suggest a severe storm is on the way.

omnipotent   ADJ. all-powerful. Under Stalin, the Soviet government seemed *omnipotent*: no one dared defy the all-powerful State.

omnipresent ADJ. universally present; ubiquitous. The Beatles are a major musical force, whose influence is *omnipresent* in all contemporary popular music.

omniscient ADJ. all-knowing. I may not be *omniscient*, but I know a bit more than you do, young man!

omnivorous ADJ. eating both plant and animal food; devouring everything. Some animals, including man, are *omnivorous* and eat both meat and vegetables; others are either carnivorous or herbivorous.

onerous ADJ. burdensome. He asked for an assistant because his work load was too *onerous*.

onset N. beginning; attack. Caught unprepared by the sudden *onset* of the storm, we rushed around the house closing windows and bringing the garden furniture into shelter. Caught unprepared by the enemy *onset*, the troops scrambled to take shelter.

onus N. burden; responsibility. The emperor was spared the *onus* of signing the surrender papers; instead, he relegated the assignment to his generals.

opalescent ADJ. iridescent; lustrous. The oil slick on the water had an *opalescent*, rainbow-like sheen.

■ **opaque** ADJ. dark; not transparent. The *opaque* window shade kept the sunlight out of the room. opacity, N.

opiate N. medicine to induce sleep or deaden pain; something that relieves emotions or causes inaction. To say that religion is the *opiate* of the people is to condemn religion as a drug that keeps the people quiet and submissive to those in power.

opportune ADJ. timely; well-chosen. Sally looked at her father struggling to balance his checkbook; clearly this would not be an *opportune* moment to ask him for a raise in her allowance.

■ **opportunist** N. individual who sacrifices principles for expediency by taking advantage of circumstances. Joe is such an *opportunist* that he tripled the price of bottled water at his store as soon as the earthquake struck. Because it can break water pipes, an earthquake is, to most people, a disaster; to Joe, it was an *opportunity*.

■ **optimist** N. person who looks on the good side. The pessimist says the glass is half-empty; the *optimist* says it is half-full.

optimum ADJ. most favorable. If you wait for the *optimum* moment to act, you may never begin your project. also N.

optional ADJ. not obligatory; left to one's choice. Most colleges require applicants to submit SAT scores; at some colleges, however, submitting SAT scores is *optional*.

■ **opulence** N. extreme wealth; luxuriousness; abundance. The glitter and *opulence* of the ballroom took Cinderella's breath away. opulent, ADJ.

opus N. work. Although many critics hailed his Fifth Symphony as his greatest work, he did not regard it as his major *opus*.

oracular ADJ. prophetic; uttered as if with divine authority; mysterious or ambiguous. Like many others who sought divine guidance from the *oracle* at Delphi, Oedipus could not understand the enigmatic *oracular* warning he received.

■ **orator** N. public speaker. The abolitionist Frederick Douglass was a brilliant *orator* whose speeches brought home to his audience the evils of slavery.

ordain V. decree or command; grant holy orders; predestine. The king *ordained* that no foreigner should be allowed to enter the city. The Bishop of Michigan *ordained* David a deacon in the Episcopal Church. The young lovers felt that fate had *ordained* their meeting.

ordeal N. severe trial or affliction. June was so painfully shy that it was an *ordeal* for her to speak up when the teacher called on her in class.

ordinance N. decree. Passing a red light is a violation of a city *ordinance*.

ordination N. ceremony making someone a minister. At the young priest's *ordination*, the members of the congregation presented him with a set of vestments. ordain, V.

orgy N. wild, drunken revelry; unrestrained indulgence in a tendency. The Roman emperor's *orgies* were far wilder than the toga party in the movie *Animal House*. When her income tax refund check finally arrived, Sally indulged in an *orgy* of shopping.

orient V. get one's bearings; adjust. Philip spent his first day in Denver *orienting* himself to the city.

orientation N. act of finding oneself in society. Freshman *orientation* provides the incoming students with an opportunity to learn about their new environment and their place in it.

● **ornate** ADJ. excessively or elaborately decorated. With its elaborately carved, convoluted lines, furniture of the Baroque period was highly *ornate*.

ornithology N. study of birds. Audubon's studies of American birds greatly influenced the course of *ornithology*.

orthodox ADJ. traditional; conservative in belief. Faced with a problem, he preferred to take an *orthodox* approach rather than shock anyone. orthodoxy, N.

oscillate V. vibrate pendulumlike; waver. It is interesting to note how public opinion *oscillates* between the extremes of optimism and pessimism.

ossify V. change or harden into bone. When he called his opponent a "bonehead," he implied that his adversary's brain had *ossified* to the point that he was incapable of clear thinking.

ostensible ADJ. apparent; professed; pretended. Although the *ostensible* purpose of this expedition is to discover new lands, we are really interested in finding new markets for our products.

■ **ostentatious** ADJ. showy; pretentious; trying to attract attention. Donald Trump's latest casino in Atlantic City is the most *ostentatious* gambling palace in the East: it easily outglitters its competitors. ostentation, N.

ostracize V. exclude from public favor; ban. As soon as the newspapers carried the story of his connection with the criminals, his friends began to *ostracize* him. ostracism, N.

oust V. expel; drive out. The world wondered if Aquino would be able to *oust* Marcos from office. ouster, N.

outlandish ADJ. bizarre; peculiar; unconventional. The eccentric professor who engages in markedly *outlandish* behavior is a stock figure in novels with an academic setting.

outmoded ADJ. no longer stylish; old-fashioned. Unconcerned about keeping in style, Lenore was perfectly happy to wear *outmoded* clothes as long as they were clean and unfrayed.

outskirts N. fringes; outer borders. We lived, not in central London, but in one of those peripheral suburbs that spring up on the *outskirts* of a great city.

outspoken ADJ. candid; blunt. The candidate was too *outspoken* to be a successful politician; he had not yet learned to weigh his words carefully.

outstrip V. surpass; outdo. Jesse Owens easily *outstripped* his white competitors to win the gold medal at the Olympic Games.

outwit V. outsmart; trick. By disguising himself as an old woman, Holmes was able to *outwit* his pursuers and escape capture.

ovation N. enthusiastic applause. When the popular tenor Placido Domingo came on stage in the first act of *La Boheme*, he was greeted by a tremendous *ovation*.

overbearing ADJ. bossy and arrogant; decisively important. Certain of her own importance, and of the unimportance of everyone else, Lady Bracknell was intolerably *overbearing* in her manner. "In choosing a husband," she said, "good birth is of *overbearing* importance; compared to that, neither wealth nor talent signifies."

overt ADJ. open to view. According to the United States Constitution, a person must commit an *overt* act before he may be tried for treason.

overwrought ADJ. extremely agitated; hysterical. When Kate heard the news of the sudden tragedy, she became too *overwrought* to work and had to leave the office early.

■ **pacifist** N. one opposed to force; antimilitarist. During the war, though the *pacifists* refused to bear arms, they nevertheless served in the front lines as ambulance drivers and medical corpsmen.

Word List 34 pacify–peccadillo

pacify V. soothe; make calm or quiet; subdue. Dentists criticize the practice of giving fussy children sweets to *pacify* them.

pact N. agreement; treaty. Tweedledum and Tweedledee made a *pact* not to quarrel anymore.

paean N. song of praise or joy. *Paeans* celebrating the victory filled the air.

painstaking ADJ. showing hard work; taking great care. The new high-frequency word list is the result of *painstaking* efforts on the part of our research staff.

palatable ADJ. agreeable; pleasing to the taste. Neither Jack's underbaked opinions nor his overcooked casseroles were *palatable* to Jill.

palette N. flat surface on which painter mixes pigments; range of colors commonly used by a particular artist. The artist's apprentices had the messy job of cleaning his brushes and *palette*. Through chromatic analysis, the forgers were able to match all the colors in Monet's *palette*.

pall V. grow tiresome. The study of word lists can eventually *pall* and put one to sleep.

palliate V. lessen the violence of (a disease); alleviate; moderate intensity; gloss over with excuses. Not content merely to *palliate* the patient's sores and cankers, the researcher sought a means of wiping out the disease. palliative, ADJ.

pallid ADJ. pale; wan. Because his job required that he work at night and sleep during the day, he had an exceptionally *pallid* complexion.

palpable ADJ. tangible; easily perceptible; unmistakable. The patient's enlarged spleen was *palpable*: even the first year medical student could feel it.

palpitate V. throb; flutter. As he became excited, his heart began to *palpitate* more and more erratically.

paltry ADJ. insignificant; petty; trifling. One hundred dollars for a genuine imitation Rolex watch! Lady, this is a *paltry* sum to pay for such a high-class piece of jewelry.

pan V. criticize harshly. Hoping for a rave review of his new show, the playwright was miserable when the critics *panned* it unanimously.

panacea N. cure-all; remedy for all diseases. The rich youth cynically declared that the *panacea* for all speeding tickets was a big enough bribe.

panache N. flair; flamboyance. Many performers imitate Noel Coward, but few have his *panache* and sense of style.

pandemic ADJ. widespread; affecting the majority of people. They feared the AIDS epidemic would soon reach *pandemic* proportions.

pandemonium N. wild tumult. When the ships collided in the harbor, *pandemonium* broke out among the passengers.

pander V. cater to the low desires of others. The reviewer accused the makers of *Lethal Weapon* of *pandering* to the masses' taste for violence.

panegyric N. formal praise. Blushing at all the praise heaped upon him by the speakers, the modest hero said, "I don't deserve such *panegyrics*."

panoramic ADJ. related to an unobstructed and comprehensive view. From Inspiration Point we had a magnificent *panoramic* view of the Marin headlands and San Francisco Bay. panorama, N.

pantomime N. acting without dialogue. Artists in *pantomime* need no words to communicate with their audience; their only language is gesture. also V.

parable N. short, simple story teaching a moral. Let us apply to our own conduct the lesson that this *parable* teaches.

paradigm N. model; example; pattern. Pavlov's experiment in which he trains a dog to salivate on hearing a bell is a *paradigm* of the conditioned-response experiment in behavioral psychology. Barron's *How to Prepare for College Entrance Examinations* was a *paradigm* for all the SAT-prep books that followed.

paradox N. something apparently contradictory in nature; statement that looks false but is actually correct. Richard presents a bit of a *paradox*, for he is a card-carrying member of both the National Rifle Association and the relatively pacifist American Civil Liberties Union.

paragon N. model of perfection. Her fellow students disliked Lavinia because Miss Minchin always pointed her out as a *paragon* of virtue.

parallelism N. state of being parallel; similarity. Although the twins were separated at birth and grew up in different adoptive families, a striking *parallelism* exists between their lives.

parameter N. boundary; limiting factor; distinguishing characteristic. According to feminist Andrea Dworkin, men have defined the *parameters* of every subject; now women must redefine the limits of each field.

paramount ADJ. foremost in importance; supreme. Proper nutrition and hygiene are of *paramount* importance in adolescent development and growth.

paranoia N. psychosis marked by delusions of grandeur or persecution. Suffering from *paranoia*, Don claimed everyone was out to get him; ironically, his claim was accurate: even *paranoids* have enemies.

paraphernalia N. equipment; odds and ends. His desk was cluttered with paper, pen, ink, dictionary and other *paraphernalia* of the writing craft.

paraphrase V. restate a passage in one's own words while retaining thought of author. In 250 words or less, *paraphrase* this article. also N.

parasite N. animal or plant living on another; toady; sycophant. The tapeworm is an example of the kind of *parasite* that may infest the human body.

parched ADJ. extremely dry; very thirsty. The *parched* desert landscape seemed hostile to life.

● **pariah** N. social outcast. If everyone ostracized singer Mariah Carey, would she then be Mariah the *pariah*?

parity N. equality in status or amount; close resemblance. Unfortunately, some doubt exists whether women's salaries will ever achieve *parity* with men's.

parochial ADJ. narrow in outlook; provincial; related to parishes. Although Jane Austen sets her novels in small rural communities, her concerns are universal, not *parochial*.

● **parody** N. humorous imitation; spoof; takeoff; travesty. The show *Forbidden Broadway* presents *parodies* spoofing the year's new productions playing on Broadway.

paroxysm N. fit or attack of pain, laughter, rage. When he heard of his son's misdeeds, he was seized by a *paroxysm* of rage.

parry V. ward off a blow; deflect. Unwilling to injure his opponent in such a pointless clash, Dartagnan simply tried to *parry* his rival's thrusts. What fun it was to watch Katharine Hepburn and Spencer Tracy *parry* each other's verbal thrusts in their classic screwball comedies!

● **parsimony** N. stinginess; excessive frugality. Furious because her father wouldn't let her buy out the clothing store, Annie accused him of *parsimony*.

partial ADJ. incomplete; having a liking for something. In this issue we have published only a *partial* list of contributors because we lack space to acknowledge everyone. I am extremely *partial* to chocolate eclairs.

partiality N. inclination; bias. As a judge, not only must I be unbiased, but I must also avoid any evidence of *partiality* when I award the prize.

■ **partisan** ADJ. one-sided; prejudiced; committed to a party. On certain issues of principle, she refused to take a *partisan* stand, but let her conscience be her guide. Rather than joining forces to solve our nation's problems, the Democrats and Republicans spend their time on *partisan* struggles. also N.

partition V. divide into parts. Before their second daughter was born, Jason and Lizzie decided each child needed a room of her own, and so they *partitioned* a large bedroom into two small but separate rooms. also N.

passive ADJ. not active; acted upon. Mahatma Gandhi urged his followers to pursue a program of *passive* resistance as he felt that it was more effective than violence and acts of terrorism.

passport N. legal document identifying the bearer as a citizen of a country and allowing him or her to travel abroad. In arranging your first trip abroad, be sure to allow yourself enough time to apply for and receive your *passport*: you won't be allowed to travel without one.

pastiche N. piece of writing or music made up of borrowed bits and pieces; hodgepodge. Her essay was a *pastiche* of fragments of articles she had found on the Internet.

pastoral ADJ. rural; simple and peaceful; idyllic; related to shepherds. Tired of the stress of life in the city, Dana dreamed of moving to the country and enjoying a simple *pastoral* life.

patent ADJ. open for the public to read; obvious. It was *patent* to everyone that the witness spoke the truth. also N.

pathetic ADJ. causing sadness, compassion, pity; touching. Everyone in the auditorium was weeping by the time he finished his *pathetic* tale about the orphaned boy.

pathological ADJ. related to the study of disease; diseased or markedly abnormal. Jerome's *pathological* fear of germs led him to wash his hands a hundred times a day. pathology, N.

pathos N. tender sorrow; pity; quality in art or literature that produces these feelings. The quiet tone of *pathos* that ran through the novel never degenerated into the maudlin or the overly sentimental.

patina N. green crust on old bronze works; tone slowly taken by varnished painting. Judging by the *patina* on this bronze statue, we can conclude that this is the work of a medieval artist.

patriarch N. father and ruler of a family or tribe. In many primitive tribes, the leader and lawmaker was the *patriarch*.

patrician ADJ. noble; aristocratic. We greatly admired her well-bred, *patrician* elegance. also N.

patronize V. support; act superior toward; be a customer of. Penniless artists hope to find some wealthy art-lover who will *patronize* them. If some condescending wine steward *patronized* me because he saw I knew nothing about fine wine, I'd refuse to *patronize* his restaurant.

● **paucity** N. scarcity. They closed the restaurant because the *paucity* of customers made it uneconomical to operate.

pauper N. very poor person. Though Widow Brown was living on a reduced income, she was by no means a *pauper*.

peccadillo N. slight offense. When Peter Piper picked a peck of Polly Potter's pickles, did Pete commit a major crime or just a *peccadillo*?

Word List 35 pecuniary–philanderer

pecuniary ADJ. pertaining to money. Seldom earning enough to cover their expenses, folk dance teachers work because they love dancing, not because they expect any *pecuniary* reward.

pedagogy N. teaching; art of education. Though Maria Montessori gained fame for her innovations in *pedagogy*, it took years before her teaching techniques were common practice in American schools.

pedantic ADJ. showing off learning; bookish. Leavening his decisions with humorous, down-to-earth anecdotes, Judge Walker was not at all the *pedantic* legal scholar. pedant, pedantry, N.

pedestrian ADJ. ordinary; unimaginative. Unintentionally boring, he wrote page after page of *pedestrian* prose.

peerless ADJ. having no equal; incomparable. The reigning operatic tenor of his generation, to his admirers Luciano Pavarotti was *peerless*: no one could compare with him.

pejorative ADJ. negative in connotation; having a belittling effect. Instead of criticizing Schwarzenegger's policies, the Democrats made *pejorative* comments about his character.

pellucid ADJ. transparent; limpid; easy to understand. After reading these stodgy philosophers, I find Bertrand Russell's *pellucid* style very enjoyable.

penchant N. strong inclination; liking. Dave has a *penchant* for taking risks: one semester he went steady with three girls, two of whom were stars on the school karate team.

penitent ADJ. repentant. When he realized the enormity of his crime, he became remorseful and *penitent*. also N.

pensive ADJ. dreamily thoughtful; thoughtful with a hint of sadness; contemplative. The *pensive* lover gazed at the portrait of his beloved and deeply sighed.

● **penury** N. severe poverty; stinginess. When his pension fund failed, George feared he would end his days in *penury*. He became such a penny pincher that he turned into a closefisted, *penurious* miser.

perceptive ADJ. insightful; aware; wise. Although Maud was a generally *perceptive* critic, she had her blind spots: she could never see flaws in the work of her friends.

percussion ADJ. striking one object against another sharply. The drum is a *percussion* instrument. also N.

perdition N. damnation; complete ruin. Praying for salvation, young Steven Daedalus feared he was damned to eternal *perdition*.

peregrination N. journey. Auntie Mame was a world traveler whose *peregrinations* took her from Tiajuana to Timbuctoo.

peremptory ADJ. demanding and leaving no choice. From Jack's *peremptory* knock on the door, Jill could tell he would not give up until she let him in.

perennial N. something that is continuing or recurrent. These plants are hardy *perennials* and will bloom for many years. also ADJ.

perfidious ADJ. treacherous; disloyal. When Caesar realized that Brutus had betrayed him, he reproached his *perfidious* friend. perfidy, N.

perforate V. pierce; put a hole through. Before you can open the aspirin bottle, you must first *perforate* the plastic safety seal that covers the cap.

● **perfunctory** ADJ. superficial; not thorough; lacking interest, care, or enthusiasm. The auditor's *perfunctory* inspection of the books overlooked many errors. Giving the tabletop only a *perfunctory* swipe with her dust cloth, Betty promised herself she'd clean it more thoroughly tomorrow.

perimeter N. outer boundary. To find the *perimeter* of any quadrilateral, we add the lengths of the four sides.

■ **peripheral** ADJ. marginal; outer. We lived, not in central London, but in one of those *peripheral* suburbs that spring up on the outskirts of a great city. periphery, N.

perjury N. false testimony while under oath. Rather than lie under oath and perhaps be indicted for *perjury*, the witness chose to take the Fifth Amendment, refusing to answer any questions on the grounds that he might incriminate himself.

permeable ADJ. penetrable; porous; allowing liquids or gas to pass through. If your jogging clothes weren't made out of *permeable* fabric, you'd drown in your own perspiration (figuratively speaking).

permeate V. pass through; spread. The odor of frying onions *permeated* the air.

● **pernicious** ADJ. very destructive. Crack cocaine has had a *pernicious* effect on urban society: it has destroyed families, turned children into drug dealers, and increased the spread of violent crimes.

perpetrate V. commit an offense. Only an insane person could *perpetrate* such a horrible crime.

perpetual ADJ. everlasting. Ponce de Leon hoped to find the legendary fountain of *perpetual* youth.

■ **perpetuate** V. make something last; preserve from extinction. Some critics attack *The Adventures of Huckleberry Finn* because they believe Twain's book *perpetuates* a false image of Blacks in this country.

perquisite N. any gain above stipulated salary. The *perquisites* attached to this job make it even more attractive than the salary indicates.

persevere V. persist; endure; strive. Despite the church's threats to excommunicate him for heresy, Galileo *persevered* in his belief that the earth moved around the sun.

persona N. public personality or facade. Offstage the comedian was a sullen, irritable grumbler, a far cry from his ever-cheerful adopted stage *persona*.

personable ADJ. attractive. Though not as strikingly handsome as a movie star, James was nonetheless a *personable* young man.

perspicacious ADJ. having insight; penetrating; astute. "Absolutely brilliant, Holmes!" cried Watson, as Holmes made yet another *perspicacious* deduction. perspicacity, N.

pert ADJ. impertinent; forward. The matron in charge of the orphanage thought Annie was *pert* and disrespectful.

pertinacious ADJ. stubborn; persistent. He is bound to succeed because his *pertinacious* nature will not permit him to quit.

pertinent ADJ. to the point; relevant. Virginia Woolf's words on women's rights are as *pertinent* today as they were when she wrote them nearly a century ago.

perturb V. disturb greatly. The thought that electricity might be leaking out of the empty lightbulb sockets *perturbed* my aunt so much that at night she crept about the house screwing fresh bulbs in the vacant spots. perturbation, N.

peruse V. read with care. After the conflagration that burned down her house, Joan closely *perused* her home insurance policy to discover exactly what benefits her coverage provided her. perusal, N.

■ **pervasive** ADJ. pervading; spread throughout every part. Despite airing them for several hours, Martha could not rid her clothes of the *pervasive* odor of mothballs that clung to them. pervade, V.

perverse ADJ. stubbornly wrongheaded; wicked and perverted. When Jack was in a *perverse* mood, he would do the opposite of whatever Jill asked him. When Hannibal Lecter was in a *perverse* mood, he ate the flesh of his victims. Jack acted out of *perversity*. Hannibal's act proved his *perversion*.

■ **pessimism** N. belief that life is basically bad or evil; gloominess. Considering how well you have done in the course so far, you have no real reason for such *pessimism* about your final grade.

petrify V. turn to stone. His sudden, unexpected appearance shocked her into immobility: she was *petrified*.

petty ADJ. trivial; unimportant; very small. She had no major complaints to make about his work, only a few *petty* quibbles that were almost too minor to state.

petulant ADJ. touchy; peevish. If you'd had hardly any sleep for three nights and people kept phoning and waking you up, you'd sound pretty *petulant*, too.

■ **phenomena** N. observable facts; subjects of scientific investigation. We kept careful records of the *phenomena* we noted in the course of these experiments.

philanderer N. faithless lover; flirt. Swearing he had never so much as looked at another woman, Ralph assured Alice he was no *philanderer*.

Word List 36　philanthropist–precedent

■ **philanthropist** N. lover of mankind; doer of good. In his role as *philanthropist* and public benefactor, John D. Rockefeller, Sr., donated millions to charity; as an individual, however, he was a tight-fisted old man.

philistine N. narrow-minded person, uncultured and exclusively interested in material gain. A *philistine* knows the price of everything, but the value of nothing.

phlegmatic ADJ. calm; not easily disturbed. The nurse was a cheerful but *phlegmatic* person, unexcited in the face of sudden emergencies.

phobia N. morbid fear. Her fear of flying was more than mere nervousness; it was a real *phobia*.

phoenix N. symbol of immortality or rebirth. Like the legendary *phoenix* rising from its ashes, the city of San Francisco rose again after its destruction during the 1906 earthquake.

phylum N. major class of plants; primary branch of animal kingdom; division. In sorting out her hundreds of packets of seeds, Katya decided to file them by *phylum*.

physiological ADJ. pertaining to the science of the function of living organisms. To understand this disease fully, we must examine not only its *physiological* aspects but also its psychological elements.

picaresque ADJ. pertaining to rogues in literature. *Tom Jones* has been hailed as one of the best *picaresque* novels in the English language.

piecemeal ADV. one piece at a time; gradually. Tolstoy's *War and Peace* is too huge to finish in one sitting; I'll have to read it *piecemeal*.

pied ADJ. variegated; multicolored. The *Pied* Piper of Hamelin got his name from the multicolored clothing he wore.

■ **piety** N. religious devotion; godliness. The nuns in the convent were noted for their *piety;* they spent their days in worship and prayer. pious, ADJ.

pigment N. coloring matter. Van Gogh mixed various *pigments* with linseed oil to create his paints.

pillage V. plunder. The enemy *pillaged* the quiet village and left it in ruins.

pine V. languish, decline; long for, yearn. Though she tried to be happy living with Clara in the city, Heidi *pined* for the mountains and for her gruff but loving grandfather.

pinnacle N. peak. We could see the morning sunlight illuminate the *pinnacle* while the rest of the mountain lay in shadow.

pious ADJ. devout; religious. The challenge for church people today is how to be *pious* in the best sense, that is, to be devout without becoming hypocritical or sanctimonious. piety, N.

piquant ADJ. pleasantly tart-tasting; stimulating. The *piquant* sauce added to our enjoyment of the meal. piquancy, N.

pique N. irritation; resentment. She showed her *pique* at her loss by refusing to appear with the other contestants at the end of the competition. also v.

pique V. provoke or arouse; annoy. "I know something *you* don't know," said Lucy, trying to *pique* Ethel's interest.

● **pitfall** N. hidden danger; concealed trap. Her parents warned young Sophie against the many *pitfalls* that lay in wait for her in the dangerous big city.

● **pithy** ADJ. concise; meaningful; substantial; meaty. While other girls might have gone on and on about how uncool Elton was, Liz summed it up in one *pithy* remark: "He's bogus!"

pittance N. a small allowance or wage. He could not live on the *pittance* he received as a pension and had to look for an additional source of revenue.

pivotal ADJ. crucial; key; vital. The new "smart weapons" technology played a *pivotal* role in the quick resolution of the war with Iraq.

■ **placate** V. pacify; conciliate. The store manager tried to *placate* the angry customer, offering to replace the damaged merchandise or to give back her money right away.

placebo N. harmless substance prescribed as a dummy pill. In a controlled experiment, fifty volunteers were given aspirin tablets; the control group received only *placebos*.

placid ADJ. peaceful; calm. Looking at the storm-tossed waters of the lake, Bob wondered how people had ever come to call it Lake *Placid*.

plagiarize V. steal another's ideas and pass them off as one's own. The teacher could tell that the student had *plagiarized* parts of his essay; she could recognize whole paragraphs straight from *Barron's Book Notes*. plagiarism, N.

plaintive ADJ. mournful. The dove has a *plaintive* and melancholy call.

plasticity N. ability to be molded. When clay dries out, it loses its *plasticity* and becomes less malleable.

platitude N. trite remark; commonplace statement. In giving advice to his son, old Polonius expressed himself only in *platitudes*; every word out of his mouth was a commonplace.

plaudit N. enthusiastically worded approval; round of applause. The theatrical company reprinted the *plaudits* of the critics in its advertisements. plauditory, ADJ.

plausible ADJ. having a show of truth but open to doubt; specious. Your mother made you stay home from school because she needed you to program the VCR? I'm sorry, you'll have to come up with a more *plausible* excuse than that.

plenitude N. abundance; completeness. Looking in the pantry, we admired the *plenitude* of fruits and pickles we had preserved during the summer.

plethora N. excess; overabundance. She offered a *plethora* of excuses for her shortcomings.

pliable ADJ. flexible; yielding; adaptable. In remodeling the bathroom, we have replaced all the old, rigid lead pipes with new, *pliable* copper tubing.

pliant ADJ. flexible; easily influenced. Pinocchio's disposition was *pliant*; he was like putty in his tempters' hands.

plight N. condition, state (especially a bad state or condition); predicament. Many people feel that the federal government should do more to alleviate the *plight* of the homeless. Loggers, unmoved by the *plight* of the spotted owl, plan to continue logging whether or not they ruin the owl's habitat.

plumage N. feathers of a bird. Bird watchers identify different species of bird by their characteristic songs and distinctive *plumage*.

plumb ADJ. checking perpendicularity; vertical. Before hanging wallpaper it is advisable to drop a *plumb* line from the ceiling as a guide. also N. and v.

plumb V. examine critically in order to understand; measure depth (by sounding). Try as he would, Watson could never fully *plumb* the depths of Holmes's thought processes.

plummet V. fall sharply. Stock prices *plummeted* as Wall Street reacted to the crisis in the economy.

plutocracy N. society ruled by the wealthy. From the way the government caters to the rich, you might think our society is a *plutocracy* rather than a democracy.

podium N. pedestal; raised platform. The audience applauded as the conductor made his way to the *podium*.

poignancy N. quality of being deeply moving; keenness of emotion. Watching the tearful reunion of the long-separated mother and child, the social worker was touched by the *poignancy* of the scene. poignant, ADJ.

polarize V. split into opposite extremes or camps. The abortion issue has *polarized* the country into pro-choice and anti-abortion camps. polarization, N.

● **polemical** ADJ. aggressive in verbal attack; disputatious. Lexy was a master of *polemical* rhetoric; she should have worn a T-shirt with the slogan "Born to Debate."

politic ADJ. expedient; prudent; well advised. Even though he was disappointed by the size of the bonus he was offered, he did not think it *politic* to refuse it.

polygamist N. one who has more than one spouse at a time. He was arrested as a *polygamist* when his two wives filed complaints about him.

polyglot ADJ. speaking several languages. New York City is a *polyglot* community because of the thousands of immigrants who settle there.

pomposity N. self-important behavior; acting like a stuffed shirt. Although the commencement speaker had some good things to say, we had to laugh at his *pomposity* and general air of parading his own dignity. pompous, ADJ.

■ **ponderous** ADJ. weighty; unwieldy. His humor lacked the light touch; his jokes were always *ponderous*.

pontifical ADJ. pertaining to a bishop or pope; pompous or pretentious. From his earliest days at the seminary, John seemed destined for a high *pontifical* office. However, he sounded so pompous when he *pontificated* that he never was chosen *pontiff* after all.

pore V. study industriously; ponder; scrutinize. Determined to become a physician, Beth spent hours *poring* over her anatomy text.

porous ADJ. full of pores; like a sieve. Dancers like to wear *porous* clothing because it allows the ready passage of water and air.

portend V. foretell; presage. The king did not know what these omens might *portend* and asked his soothsayers to interpret them.

portent N. sign; omen; forewarning. He regarded the black cloud as a *portent* of evil.

portly ADJ. stately; stout. The overweight gentleman was referred to as *portly* by the polite salesclerk.

poseur N. person who pretends to be sophisticated, elegant, etc., to impress others. Some thought Salvador Dali was a brilliant painter; others dismissed him as a *poseur*.

posterity N. descendants; future generations. We hope to leave a better world to *posterity*.

posthumous ADJ. after death (as of child born after father's death or book published after author's death). The critics ignored his works during his lifetime; it was only after the *posthumous* publication of his last novel that they recognized his great talent.

postulate N. essential premise; underlying assumption. The basic *postulate* of democracy, set forth in the Declaration of Independence, is that all men are created equal.

potable ADJ. suitable for drinking. The recent drought in the Middle Atlantic states has emphasized the need for extensive research in ways of making sea water *potable*. also N.

potent ADJ. powerful; persuasive; greatly influential. Looking at the expiration date on the cough syrup bottle, we wondered whether the medication would still be *potent*. potency, N.

potentate N. monarch; sovereign. The *potentate* spent more time at Monte Carlo than he did at home on his throne.

potential ADJ. expressing possibility; latent. The cello teacher viewed every new pupil as a *potential* Yo-Yo Ma. also N.

potion N. dose (of liquid). Tristan and Isolde drink a love *potion* in the first act of the opera.

practicable ADJ. feasible. The board of directors decided that the plan was *practicable* and agreed to undertake the project.

practical ADJ. based on experience; useful. He was a *practical* man, opposed to theory.

practitioner N. someone engaged in a profession (law, medicine). In need of a hip replacement, Carl sought a *practitioner* with considerable experience performing this particular surgery.

■ **pragmatic** ADJ. practical (as opposed to idealistic); concerned with the practical worth or impact of something. This coming trip to France should provide me with a *pragmatic* test of the value of my conversational French class.

pragmatist N. practical person. No *pragmatist* enjoys becoming involved in a game he can never win.

prank N. mischievous trick. Is tipping over garbage cans on Halloween merely a childish *prank*, or is it vandalism?

prate V. speak foolishly; boast idly. Despite Elizabeth's obvious disinclination for the topic, Mr. Collins *prated* on and on about his wonderful prospects as a husband, thanks to his noble patron, Lady Catherine de Burgh.

● **prattle** V. babble. Baby John *prattled* on and on about the cats and his ball and the Cookie Monster.

preamble N. introductory statement. In the *Preamble* to the Constitution, the purpose of the document is set forth.

● **precarious** ADJ. uncertain; risky. Saying the stock would be a *precarious* investment, the broker advised her client against purchasing it.

precedent N. something preceding in time that may be used as an authority or guide for future action. If I buy you a car for your sixteenth birthday, your brothers will want me to buy them cars when they turn sixteen, too; I can't afford to set such an expensive *precedent*. The law professor asked Jill to state which famous case served as a *precedent* for the court's decision in *Brown II*.

Word List 37 precept–propitiate

precept N. practical rule guiding conduct. "Love thy neighbor as thyself" is a worthwhile *precept*.

precinct N. district or division of a city. Ed McBain's detective novels set in the 87th *precinct* provide an exciting picture of police work.

precipice N. cliff; dangerous position. Suddenly Indiana Jones found himself dangling from the edge of a *precipice*.

precipitate ADJ. rash; premature; hasty; sudden. Though I was angry enough to resign on the spot, I had enough sense to keep myself from quitting a job in such a *precipitate* fashion.

precipitate V. throw headlong; hasten. The removal of American political support appears to have *precipitated* the downfall of the Marcos regime.

precipitous ADJ. steep; overhasty. This hill is difficult to climb because it is so *precipitous*; one slip, and our descent will be *precipitous* as well.

précis N. concise summing up of main points. Before making her presentation at the conference, Ellen wrote up a neat *précis* of the major elements she would cover.

precise ADJ. exact. If you don't give me *precise* directions and a map, I'll never find your place.

■ **preclude** V. make impossible; eliminate. The fact that the band was already booked to play in Hollywood on New Year's Eve *precluded* their accepting the New Year's Eve gig in London they were offered.

■ **precocious** ADJ. advanced in development. Listening to the grown-up way the child discussed serious topics, we couldn't help remarking how *precocious* she was. precocity, N.

precursor N. forerunner. Though Gray and Burns share many traits with the Romantic poets who followed them, most critics consider them *precursors* of the Romantic Movement, not true Romantics.

■ **predator** N. creature that seizes and devours another animal; person who robs or exploits others. Not just cats, but a wide variety of *predators*—owls, hawks, weasels, foxes—catch mice for dinner. A carnivore is by definition *predatory*, for he *preys* on weaker creatures.

■ **predecessor** N. former occupant of a post. I hope I can live up to the fine example set by my late *predecessor* in this office.

predetermine V. predestine; settle or decide beforehand; influence markedly. Romeo and Juliet believed that Fate had *predetermined* their meeting. Bea gathered estimates from caterers, florists, and stationers so that she could *predetermine* the costs of holding a catered buffet. Philip's love of athletics *predetermined* his choice of a career in sports marketing.

predicament N. tricky or dangerous situation; dilemma. Tied to the railroad tracks by the villain, Pauline strained against her bonds. How would she escape from this terrible *predicament*?

predilection N. partiality; preference. Although Ogden Nash wrote all sorts of poetry over the years, he had a definite *predilection* for limericks.

predispose V. give an inclination toward; make susceptible to. Oleg's love of dressing up his big sister's Barbie doll may have *predisposed* him to become a fashion designer. Genetic influences apparently *predispose* people to certain forms of cancer.

preeminent ADJ. outstanding; superior. The king traveled to Boston because he wanted the *preeminent* surgeon in the field to perform the operation.

preempt V. head off; forestall by acting first; appropriate for oneself; supplant. Hoping to *preempt* any attempts by the opposition to make educational reform a hot political issue, the candidate set out her own plan to revitalize the public schools. preemptive, ADJ.

preen V. make oneself tidy in appearance; feel self-satisfaction. As Kitty *preened* before the mirror, carefully smoothing her shining hair, she couldn't help *preening* over how pretty she looked.

prehensile ADJ. capable of grasping or holding. Monkeys use not only their arms and legs but also their *prehensile* tails in traveling through the trees.

prelate N. church dignitary. The archbishop of Moscow and other high-ranking *prelates* visited the Russian Orthodox seminary.

prelude N. introduction; forerunner. I am afraid that this border raid is the *prelude* to more serious attacks.

premeditate V. plan in advance. She had *premeditated* the murder for months, reading about common poisons and buying weed killer that contained arsenic.

premise N. assumption; postulate. Based on the *premise* that there's no fool like an old fool, P. T. Barnum hired a ninety-year-old clown for his circus.

premonition N. forewarning. In horror movies, the hero often has a *premonition* of danger, yet he foolishly ignores it.

preposterous ADJ. absurd; ridiculous. When he tried to downplay his youthful experiments with marijuana by saying he hadn't inhaled, we all thought, "What a *preposterous* excuse!"

prerogative N. privilege; unquestionable right. The president cannot levy taxes; that is the *prerogative* of the legislative branch of government.

presage V. foretell. The vultures flying overhead *presaged* the discovery of the corpse in the desert.

prescience N. ability to foretell the future. Given the current wave of Japan-bashing, it does not take *prescience* for me to foresee problems in our future trade relations with Japan.

presentiment N. feeling something will happen; anticipatory fear; premonition. Saying goodbye at the airport, Jack had a sudden *presentiment* that this was the last time he would see Jill.

prestige N. impression produced by achievements or reputation. Many students want to go to Harvard College not for the education offered but for the *prestige* of Harvard's name.

■ **presumptuous** ADJ. overconfident; impertinently bold; taking liberties. Matilda thought it was somewhat *presumptuous* of the young man to have addressed her without first having been introduced. Perhaps manners were freer here in the New World.

■ **pretentious** ADJ. ostentatious; pompous; making unjustified claims; overly ambitious. None of the other prize winners are wearing their medals; isn't it a bit *pretentious* of you to wear yours?

preternatural ADJ. beyond what is normal in nature. Malcolm's mother's total ability to tell when he was lying struck him as almost *preternatural*.

pretext N. excuse. He looked for a good *pretext* to get out of paying a visit to his aunt.

prevail V. induce; triumph over. He tried to *prevail* on her to type his essay for him.

■ **prevalent** ADJ. widespread; generally accepted. A radical committed to social change, Reed had no patience with the conservative views *prevalent* in the America of his day.

prevaricate V. lie. Some people believe that to *prevaricate* in a good cause is justifiable and regard such a statement as a "white lie."

prey N. target of a hunt; victim. In *Stalking the Wild Asparagus*, Euell Gibbons has as his *prey* not wild beasts but wild plants. also V.

prim ADJ. very precise and formal; exceedingly proper. Never having worked as a governess before, Jane thought it best to assume a very *prim* and proper manner so that her charges would not take liberties with her.

primordial ADJ. existing at the beginning (of time); rudimentary. The Neanderthal Man is one of our *primordial* ancestors.

primp V. groom oneself with care; adorn oneself. The groom stood by idly while his nervous bride-to-be *primped* one last time before the mirror.

pristine ADJ. characteristic of earlier times; primitive; unspoiled. This area has been preserved in all its *pristine* wildness.

privation N. hardship; want. In his youth, he knew hunger and *privation*.

probe V. explore with tools. The surgeon *probed* the wound for foreign matter before suturing it. also N.

problematic ADJ. doubtful; unsettled; questionable; perplexing. Given the way building costs have exceeded estimates for the job, whether the arena will ever be completed is *problematic*.

proclivity N. inclination; natural tendency. Watching the two-year-old voluntarily put away his toys, I was amazed by his *proclivity* for neatness.

procrastinate V. postpone; delay or put off. Looking at four years of receipts and checks he still had to sort through, Bob was truly sorry he had *procrastinated* for so long and not finished filing his taxes long ago.

prod V. poke; stir up; urge. If you *prod* him hard enough, he'll eventually clean his room.

■ **prodigal** ADJ. wasteful; reckless with money. Don't be so *prodigal* spending my money; when you've earned some money yourself, you can waste it as much as you want! also N.

prodigious ADJ. marvelous; enormous. Watching the champion weight lifter heave the weighty barbell to shoulder height and then boost it overhead, we marveled at his *prodigious* strength.

prodigy N. marvel; highly gifted child. Menuhin *was a prodigy*, performing wonders on his violin when he was barely eight years old.

■ **profane** V. violate; desecrate; treat unworthily. The members of the mysterious Far Eastern cult sought to kill the British explorer because he had *profaned* the sanctity of their holy goblet by using it as an ashtray. also ADJ.

● **profligate** ADJ. dissipated; wasteful; wildly immoral. Although surrounded by wild and *profligate* companions, she nevertheless managed to retain some sense of decency.

■ **profound** ADJ. deep; not superficial; complete. Freud's remarkable insights into human behavior caused his fellow scientists to honor him as a *profound* thinker. profundity, N.

■ **profusion** N. overabundance; lavish expenditure; excess. Freddy was so overwhelmed by the *profusion* of choices on the menu that he knocked over his wine glass and soaked his host. He made *profuse* apologies to his host, the waiter, the bus boy, the people at the next table, and the attendant handing out paper towels.

progenitor N. ancestor. The Roth family, whose *progenitors* emigrated from Germany early in the nineteenth century, settled in Peru, Illinois.

progeny N. children; offspring. He was proud of his *progeny* in general, but regarded George as the most promising of all his children.

prognosis N. forecasted course of a disease; prediction. If the doctor's *prognosis* is correct, the patient will be in a coma for at least twenty-four hours.

projectile N. missile. Man has always hurled *projectiles* at his enemy, whether in the form of stones or of highly explosive shells.

proletarian N. member of the working class; blue collar person. "Workers of the world, unite! You have nothing to lose but your chains" is addressed to *proletarians*, not preppies. So is *Blue Collar Holler*. proletariat, N.

■ **proliferation** N. rapid growth; spread; multiplication. Times of economic hardship inevitably encourage the *proliferation* of countless get-rich-quick schemes. proliferate, V.

■ **prolific** ADJ. abundantly fruitful. My editors must assume I'm a *prolific* writer: they expect me to revise six books this year!

prolixity N. tedious wordiness; verbosity. A writer who suffers from *prolixity* tells his readers everything they *never* wanted to know about his subject (or were too bored to ask). prolix, ADJ.

prologue N. introduction (to a poem or play). In the *prologue* to *Romeo and Juliet*, Shakespeare introduces the audience to the feud between the Montagues and the Capulets.

prolong V. make longer; draw out; lengthen. In their determination to discover ways to *prolong* human life, doctors fail to take into account that longer lives are not always happier ones.

prominent ADJ. conspicuous; notable; sticking out. Have you ever noticed that Prince Charles's *prominent* ears make him look like the big-eared character in *Mad* comics?

promiscuous ADJ. mixed indiscriminately; haphazard; irregular, particularly sexually. In the opera *La Bohème*, we get a picture of the *promiscuous* life led by the young artists of Paris.

promote V. help to flourish; advance in rank; publicize. Founder of the Children's Defense Fund, Marian Wright Edelman ceaselessly *promotes* the welfare of young people everywhere.

prompt v. cause; provoke; provide a cue for an actor. Whatever *prompted* you to ask for such a big piece of cake when you're on a diet?

promulgate v. proclaim a doctrine or law; make known by official publication. When Moses came down from the mountaintop all set to *promulgate* God's commandments, he freaked out on discovering his followers worshipping a golden calf.

prone ADJ. inclined to; prostrate. She was *prone* to sudden fits of anger during which she would lie *prone* on the floor, screaming and kicking her heels.

propagate v. multiply; spread. Since bacteria *propagate* more quickly in unsanitary environments, it is important to keep hospital rooms clean.

propellants N. substances that propel or drive forward. The development of our missile program has forced our scientists to seek more powerful *propellants.*

propensity N. natural inclination. Convinced of his own talent, Sol has an unfortunate *propensity* to belittle the talents of others.

prophetic ADJ. foretelling the future. I have no magical *prophetic* powers; when I predict what will happen, I base my predictions on common sense. prophesy, v.

propinquity N. nearness; kinship. Their relationship could not be explained as being based on mere *propinquity;* they were more than relatives, they were true friends.

propitiate v. appease. The natives offered sacrifices to *propitiate* the gods.

Word List 38 propitious–quarry

propitious ADJ. favorable; fortunate; advantageous. Chloe consulted her horoscope to see whether Tuesday would be a *propitious* day to dump her boyfriend.

proponent N. supporter; backer; opposite of opponent. In the Senate, *proponents* of the universal health care measure lobbied to gain additional support for the controversial legislation.

propound v. put forth for analysis. In your discussion, you have *propounded* several questions; let us consider each one separately.

propriety N. fitness; correct conduct. Miss Manners counsels her readers so that they may behave with due *propriety* in any social situation and not embarrass themselves.

propulsive ADJ. driving forward. The jet plane has a greater *propulsive* power than the engine-driven plane.

prosaic ADJ. dull and unimaginative; matter-of-fact; factual. Though the ad writers came up with an original way to publicize the product, the head office rejected it for a more *prosaic*, ordinary slogan.

proscribe v. ostracize; banish; outlaw. Antony, Octavius, and Lepidus *proscribed* all those who had conspired against Julius Caesar.

proselytize v. convert to a religion or belief. In these interfaith meetings, there must be no attempt to *proselytize; we* must respect all points of view.

prosperity N. good fortune; financial success; physical well-being. Promising to stay together "for richer, for poorer," the newlyweds vowed to be true to one another in *prosperity* and hardship alike.

prostrate v. stretch out full on ground. He *prostrated* himself before the idol. also ADJ.

protean ADJ. versatile; able to take on many shapes. A remarkably *protean* actor, Alec Guinness could take on any role.

protégé N. person receiving protection and support from a patron. Born with an independent spirit, Cyrano de Bergerac refused to be a *protégé* of Cardinal Richelieu.

protocol N. diplomatic etiquette. We must run this state dinner according to *protocol* if we are to avoid offending any of our guests.

prototype N. original work used as a model by others. The National Air and Space Museum displays the Wright brothers' first plane, the *prototype* of all the American aircraft that came after.

protract v. prolong. Seeking to delay the union members' vote, the management team tried to *protract* the negotiations endlessly.

protrude v. stick out. His fingers *protruded* from the holes in his gloves. protrusion, N.

protuberance N. protrusion; bulge. A ganglionic cyst is a fluid-filled tumor that develops near a joint membrane or tendon sheath, and that bulges beneath the skin, forming a *protuberance.*

provident ADJ. displaying foresight; thrifty; preparing for emergencies. In his usual *provident* manner, he had insured himself against this type of loss.

■ **provincial** ADJ. pertaining to a province; limited in outlook; unsophisticated. As *provincial* governor, Sir Henry administered the Queen's law in his remote corner of Canada. Caught up in local problems, out of touch with London news, he became sadly *provincial.*

provisional ADJ. tentative. Kim's acceptance as an American Express card holder was *provisional:* before issuing her a card, American Express wanted to check her employment record and credit history.

provocative ADJ. arousing anger or interest; annoying. In a typically *provocative* act, the bully kicked sand into the weaker man's face. provocation, N.; provoke, v.

prowess N. extraordinary ability; military bravery. Performing triple axels and double lutzes at the age of six, the young figure skater was world famous for her *prowess* on the ice.

■ **proximity** N. nearness. Blind people sometimes develop a compensatory ability to sense the *proximity* of objects around them.

proxy N. authorized agent. Please act as my *proxy* and vote for this slate of candidates in my absence.

prude N. excessively modest person. The X-rated film was definitely not for *prudes.* prudish, ADJ.

■ **prudent** ADJ. cautious; careful. A miser hoards money not because he is *prudent* but because he is greedy. prudence, N.

prune V. cut away; trim. With the help of her editor, she was able to *prune* her overlong manuscript into publishable form.

prurient ADJ. having or causing lustful thoughts and desires. Aroused by his *prurient* impulses, the dirty old man leered at the sweet young thing and offered to give her a sample of his "prowess."

pseudonym N. pen name. Samuel Clemens' *pseudonym* was Mark Twain.

psyche N. soul; mind. It is difficult to delve into the *psyche* of a human being.

puerile ADJ. childish; immature. Throwing tantrums! You should have outgrown such *puerile* behavior years ago.

pugilist N. boxer. The famous *pugilist* Cassius Clay changed his name to Muhammed Ali.

pugnacity N. combativeness; disposition to fight. "Put up your dukes!" he cried, making a fist to show his *pugnacity*. pugnacious, ADJ.

pulchritude N. beauty; comeliness. I do not envy the judges who have to select this year's Miss America from this collection of female *pulchritude*.

pulverize V. crush or grind into dust. Before sprinkling the dried herbs into the stew, Michael first *pulverized* them into a fine powder.

pummel V. beat or pound with fists. Swinging wildly, Pam *pummeled* her brother around the head and shoulders.

punctilious ADJ. laying stress on niceties of conduct or form; minutely attentive to fine points (perhaps too much so). Percy is *punctilious* about observing the rules of etiquette whenever Miss Manners invites him to stay. punctiliousness, N.

pundit N. authority on a subject; learned person; expert. Some authors who write about the SAT as if they are *pundits* actually know very little about the test.

pungent ADJ. stinging; sharp in taste or smell; caustic. The *pungent* odor of ripe Limburger cheese appealed to Simone but made Stanley gag.

punitive ADJ. punishing. He asked for *punitive* measures against the offender.

puny ADJ. insignificant; tiny; weak. Our *puny* efforts to stop the flood were futile.

purchase N. firm grasp or footing. The mountaineer struggled to get a proper *purchase* on the slippery rock. (secondary meaning)

purge V. remove or get rid of something unwanted; free from blame or guilt; cleanse or purify. When the Communist government *purged* the party to get rid of members suspected of capitalist sympathies, they sent the disloyal members to labor camps in Siberia.

purported ADJ. alleged; claimed; reputed or rumored. The *purported* Satanists sacrificing live roosters in the park turned out to be a party of Shriners holding a chicken barbecue.

purse V. pucker; contract into wrinkles. Miss Watson *pursed* her lips to show her disapproval of Huck's bedraggled appearance.

purveyor N. furnisher of foodstuffs; caterer. As *purveyor* of rare wines and viands, he traveled through France and Italy every year in search of new products to sell.

pusillanimous ADJ. cowardly; fainthearted. In *The Wizard of Oz*, Dorothy's friend the Cowardly Lion wishes he were brave and not *pusillanimous*.

putrid ADJ. foul; rotten; decayed. When we removed the bandage, we could tell from the *putrid* smell that the wound had turned gangrenous. putrescence, N.

quack N. charlatan; impostor. Don't let that *quack* fool you with his extravagant claims; he can't cure you.

quadruped N. four-footed animal. Most mammals are *quadrupeds*.

quaff V. drink with relish. As we *quaffed* our ale, we listened to the lively songs of the students in the tavern.

● **quagmire** N. soft, wet, boggy land; complex or dangerous situation from which it is difficult to free oneself. Up to her knees in mud, Myra wondered how on earth she was going to extricate herself from this *quagmire*.

quail V. cower; lose heart. The Cowardly Lion was afraid that he would *quail* in the face of danger.

quaint ADJ. odd; old-fashioned; picturesque. Her *quaint* clothes and old-fashioned language marked her as an eccentric.

■ **qualified** ADJ. limited; restricted. Unable to give the candidate full support, the mayor gave him only a *qualified* endorsement. (secondary meaning)

qualms N. misgivings; uneasy fears, especially about matters of conscience. I have no *qualms* about giving this assignment to Helen; I know she will handle it admirably.

■ **quandary** N. dilemma. When both Harvard and Stanford accepted Laura, she was in a *quandary* as to which school she should attend.

quarantine N. isolation of person or ship to prevent spread of infection. We will have to place this house under *quarantine* until we determine the exact nature of the disease. also V.

quarry N. victim; object of a hunt. The police closed in on their *quarry*.

quarry V. dig into. They *quarried* blocks of marble out of the hillside. also N.

Word List 39 queasy–recurrent

queasy ADJ. easily nauseated; squeamish. Remember that great chase movie, the one with the carsick passenger? That's right: *Queasy Rider*!

● **quell** V. extinguish; put down; quiet. Miss Minchin's demeanor was so stern and forbidding that she could *quell* any unrest among her students with one intimidating glance.

quench V. douse or extinguish; assuage or satisfy. No matter how much water the hiker drank, she could not *quench* her thirst.

● **querulous** ADJ. fretful; whining. Even the most agreeable toddlers can begin to act *querulous* if they miss their nap.

query N. inquiry; question. In her column "Ask Beth," the columnist invites young readers to send her their *queries* about life and love.

quibble N. minor objection or complaint. Aside from a few hundred teensy-weensy *quibbles* about the set, the script, the actors, the director, the costumes, the lighting, and the props, the hypercritical critic loved the play. also V.

● **quiescent** ADJ. at rest; dormant; temporarily inactive. After the massive eruption, fear of Mount Etna was great; people did not return to cultivate the rich hillside lands until the volcano had been *quiescent* for a full two years. quiescence, N.

quietude N. tranquility. He was impressed by the air of *quietude* and peace that pervaded the valley.

quintessence N. purest and highest embodiment. Gandhi maintained that to befriend someone who regards himself as your enemy is the *quintessence* of true religion.

quip N. taunt. You are unpopular because you are too free with your *quips* and sarcastic comments. also V.

quirk N. startling twist; caprice. By a *quirk* of fate, he found himself working for the man whom he had discharged years before.

quiver V. tremble; shake. The bird dog's nose twitched and his whiskers *quivered* as he strained eagerly against the leash. also N.

quiver N. case for arrows. Robin Hood reached back and plucked one last arrow from his *quiver*. (secondary meaning)

quixotic ADJ. idealistic but impractical. Constantly coming up with *quixotic*, unworkable schemes to save the world, Simon has his heart in the right place, but his head somewhere in the clouds.

quizzical ADJ. teasing; bantering; mocking; curious. When the skinny teenager tripped over his own feet stepping into the bullpen, Coach raised one *quizzical* eyebrow, shook his head, and said, "Okay, kid. You're here, let's see what you've got."

quorum N. number of members necessary to conduct a meeting. The senator asked for a roll call to determine whether a *quorum* was present.

rabid ADJ. like a fanatic; furious. He was a *rabid* follower of the Dodgers and watched them play whenever he could go to the ballpark.

raconteur N. storyteller. My father was a gifted *raconteur* with an unlimited supply of anecdotes.

rail V. scold; rant. You may *rail* at him all you want; you will never change him.

raiment N. clothing. "How can I go to the ball?" asked Cinderella. "I have no *raiment* fit to wear."

rally V. call up or summon (forces, vital powers, etc.); revive or recuperate. Washington quickly *rallied* his troops to fight off the British attack. The patient had been sinking throughout the night, but at dawn she *rallied* and made a complete recovery.

■ **ramble** V. wander aimlessly (physically or mentally). Listening to the teacher *ramble*, Judy wondered whether he'd ever get to his point.

ramification N. branching out; subdivision. We must examine all the *ramifications* of this problem.

ramify V. divide into branches or subdivisions. When the plant begins to *ramify*, it is advisable to nip off most of the new branches.

ramp N. slope; inclined plane. The house was built with *ramps* instead of stairs in order to enable the man in the wheelchair to move easily from room to room and floor to floor.

rampant ADJ. growing in profusion; unrestrained. The *rampant* weeds in the garden choked the flowers until they died.

ramshackle ADJ. rickety; falling apart. The boys propped up the *ramshackle* clubhouse with a couple of boards.

rancid ADJ. having the odor of stale fat. The *rancid* odor filling the ship's galley nauseated the crew.

■ **rancor** N. bitterness; hatred. Thirty years after the war, she could not let go of the past but was still consumed with *rancor* against the foe.

random ADJ. without definite purpose, plan, or aim; haphazard. Although the sponsor of the raffle claimed all winners were chosen at *random*, people had their suspicions when the grand prize went to the sponsor's brother-in-law.

rankle V. irritate; fester. The memory of having been jilted *rankled* him for years.

● **rant** V. rave; talk excitedly; scold; make a grandiloquent speech. When he heard that I'd totaled the family car, Dad began to *rant* at me like a complete madman.

rapacious ADJ. excessively greedy; predatory. The *rapacious* brigands stripped the villagers of all their possessions. rapacity, N.

rapport N. emotional closeness; harmony. In team teaching, it is important that all teachers in the group have good *rapport* with one another.

rapt ADJ. absorbed; enchanted. Caught up in the wonder of the storyteller's tale, the *rapt* listeners sat motionless, hanging on his every word.

rarefied ADJ. made less dense [of a gas]. The mountain climbers had difficulty breathing in the *rarefied* atmosphere. rarefy, V.

raspy ADJ. grating; harsh. The sergeant's *raspy* voice grated on the recruits' ears.

■ **ratify** V. approve formally; confirm; verify. Party leaders doubted that they had enough votes in both houses of Congress to *ratify* the constitutional amendment.

ratiocination   N. reasoning; act of drawing conclusions from premises. While Watson was a man of average intelligence, Holmes was a genius, whose gift for *ratiocination* made him a superb detective.

rationale   N. fundamental reason or justification; grounds for an action. Her need to have someplace to hang her earring collection was Dora's *rationale* for piercing fifteen holes in each ear.

rationalize   V. give a plausible reason for an action in place of a true, less admirable one; offer an excuse. When David told gabby Gabrielle he couldn't give her a ride to the dance because he had no room in the car, he was *rationalizing*; actually, he couldn't stand being cooped up in a car with anyone who talked as much as she did.

● **raucous**   ADJ. harsh and shrill; disorderly and boisterous. The *raucous* crowd of New Year's Eve revelers got progressively noisier as midnight drew near.

rave   N. overwhelmingly favorable review. Though critic John Simon seldom has a good word to say about most contemporary plays, his review of *All in the Timing* was a total *rave*.

ravel   V. fall apart into tangles; unravel or untwist; entangle. A single thread pulled loose, and the entire scarf started to *ravel*.

● **ravenous**   ADJ. extremely hungry. The *ravenous* dog upset several garbage pails in its search for food.

● **raze**   V. destroy completely. Spelling is important: to raise a building is to put it up; to *raze* a building is to tear it down.

reactionary   ADJ. recoiling from progress; politically ultra-conservative. Opposing the use of English in worship services, *reactionary* forces in the church fought to reinstate the mass in Latin.

realm   N. kingdom; field or sphere. In the animal *realm*, the lion is the king of beasts.

reaper   N. one who harvests grain. Death, the Grim *Reaper*, cuts down mortal men and women, just as a farmer cuts down the ripened grain. reap, V.

rebuff   V. snub; beat back. She *rebuffed* his invitation so smoothly that he did not realize he had been snubbed. also N.

rebuke   V. scold harshly; criticize severely. No matter how sharply Miss Watson *rebuked* Huck for his misconduct, he never talked back but just stood there like a stump. also N.

■ **rebuttal**   N. refutation; response with contrary evidence. The defense lawyer confidently listened to the prosecutor sum up his case, sure that she could answer his arguments in her *rebuttal*.

recalcitrant   ADJ. obstinately stubborn; determined to resist authority; unruly. Which animal do you think is more *recalcitrant*, a pig or a mule?

● **recant**   V. disclaim or disavow; retract a previous statement; openly confess error. Those who can, keep true to their faith; those who can't, *recant*. Hoping to make Joan of Arc *recant* her sworn testimony, her English captors tried to convince her that her visions had been sent to her by the Devil.

recapitulate   V. summarize. Let us *recapitulate* what has been said thus far before going ahead.

recast   V. reconstruct (a sentence, story, etc.); fashion again. Let me *recast* this sentence in terms your feeble brain can grasp: in words of one syllable, you are a fool.

receptive   ADJ. quick or willing to receive ideas, suggestions, etc. Adventure-loving Huck Finn proved a *receptive* audience for Tom's tales of buried treasure and piracy.

recession   N. withdrawal; retreat; time of low economic activity. The slow *recession* of the flood waters created problems for the crews working to restore power to the area. recede, V.

recidivism   N. habitual return to crime. Prison reformers in the United States are disturbed by the high rate of *recidivism*; the number of men serving second and third terms in prison indicates the failure of prisons to rehabilitate the inmates.

recipient   N. receiver. Although he had been the *recipient* of many favors, he was not grateful to his benefactor.

reciprocal   ADJ. mutual; exchangeable; interacting. The two nations signed a *reciprocal* trade agreement.

reciprocate   V. repay in kind. If they attack us, we shall be compelled to *reciprocate* and bomb their territory. reciprocity, N.

■ **recluse**   N. hermit; loner. Disappointed in love, Miss Emily became a *recluse*; she shut herself away in her empty mansion and refused to see another living soul. reclusive, ADJ.

reconcile   V. correct inconsistencies; become friendly after a quarrel. Each month when we try to *reconcile* our checkbook with the bank statement, we quarrel. However, despite these monthly lovers' quarrels, we always manage to *reconcile*.

reconnaissance   N. survey of enemy by soldiers; reconnoitering. If you encounter any enemy soldiers during your *reconnaissance,* capture them for questioning.

■ **recount**   V. narrate or tell; count over again. A born storyteller, my father loved to *recount* anecdotes about his early years in New York.

recourse   N. resorting to help when in trouble. The boy's only *recourse* was to appeal to his father for aid.

recrimination   N. countercharges. Loud and angry *recriminations* were her answer to his accusations.

■ **rectify**   V. set right; correct. You had better send a check to *rectify* your account before American Express cancels your credit card.

rectitude   N. uprightness; moral virtue; correctness of judgment. The Eagle Scout was a model of *rectitude*.

recumbent   ADJ. reclining; lying down completely or in part. The command "AT EASE" does not permit you to take a *recumbent* position.

recuperate   V. recover. The doctors were worried because the patient did not *recuperate* as rapidly as they had expected.

recurrent   ADJ. occurring again and again. Richard's *recurrent* asthma attacks disturbed us and we consulted a physician.

Word List 40 redolent–rescind

redolent ADJ. fragrant; odorous; suggestive of an odor. Even though it is February, the air is *redolent* of spring.

redoubtable ADJ. formidable; causing fear. During the Cold War period, neighboring countries tried not to offend the Russians because they could be *redoubtable* foes.

redress N. remedy; compensation. Do you mean to tell me that I can get no *redress* for my injuries? also V.

■ **redundant** ADJ. superfluous; repetitious; excessively wordy. The bottle of wine I brought to Bob's was certainly *redundant*: how was I to know Bob owned a winery? In your essay, you repeat several points unnecessarily; try to be less *redundant* in the future. redundancy, N.

reek V. emit (odor). The room *reeked* of stale tobacco smoke. also N.

refraction N. bending of a ray of light. When you look at a stick inserted in water, it looks bent because of the *refraction* of the light by the water.

refractory ADJ. stubborn; unmanageable. Though his jockey whipped him, the *refractory* horse stubbornly refused to enter the starting gate.

refrain V. abstain from; resist. N. chorus. Whenever he heard a song with a lively chorus, Sol could never *refrain* from joining in on the *refrain*.

refurbish V. renovate; make bright by polishing. The furniture in the lobby was worn, the paint faded; clearly, it was time to *refurbish* the lobby.

■ **refute** V. disprove. The defense called several respectable witnesses who were able to *refute* the false testimony of the prosecution's sole witness. refutation, N.

regal ADJ. royal. Prince Albert had a *regal* manner.

regale V. entertain. John *regaled* us with tales of his adventures in Africa.

regeneration N. renewal or restoration (of a bodily part); spiritual rebirth. Hoping for insights into healing human injuries, biologists study the process of *regeneration* in lizards that regrow lost tails.

regime N. method or system of government. When the French mention the Old *Regime,* they refer to the government existing before the revolution.

regimen N. prescribed diet and habits. I doubt whether the results warrant our living under such a strict *regimen.*

rehabilitate V. restore to proper condition. We must *rehabilitate* those whom we send to prison.

reimburse V. repay. Let me know what you have spent and I will *reimburse* you.

reiterate V. repeat. He *reiterated* the warning to make sure everyone understood it.

rejoinder N. retort; comeback; reply. When someone has been rude to me, I find it particularly satisfying to come up with a quick *rejoinder.*

rejuvenate V. make young again. The charlatan claimed that his elixir would *rejuvenate* the aged and weary.

■ **relegate** V. banish to an inferior position; delegate; assign. After Ralph dropped his second tray of drinks that week, the manager swiftly *relegated* him to a minor post cleaning up behind the bar.

relent V. give in. When her stern father would not *relent* and allow her to marry Robert Browning, Elizabeth Barrett eloped with her suitor. relentless, ADJ.

relevant ADJ. pertinent; referring to the case in hand. How *relevant* Virginia Woolf's essays are to women writers today! It's as if Woolf in the 1930s foresaw our current literary struggles. relevancy, N.

relic N. surviving remnant; memento. Egypt's Department of Antiquities prohibits tourists from taking mummies and other ancient *relics* out of the country. Mike keeps his photos of his trip to Egypt in a box with other *relics* of his travels.

relinquish V. give up something with reluctance; yield. Denise never realized how hard it would be for her to *relinquish* her newborn son to the care of his adoptive parents. Once you get used to fringe benefits like expense account meals and a company car, it's very hard to *relinquish* them.

relish V. savor; enjoy. Watching Peter enthusiastically chow down, I thought, "Now there's a man who *relishes* a good dinner!" also N.

remediable ADJ. reparable. Let us be grateful that the damage is *remediable*.

remedial ADJ. curative; corrective. Because he was a slow reader, he decided to take a course in *remedial* reading.

reminiscence N. recollection. Her *reminiscences* of her experiences are so fascinating that she ought to write a book.

remiss ADJ. negligent. The guard was accused of being *remiss* in his duty when the prisoner escaped.

● **remission** N. temporary moderation of disease symptoms; cancellation of a debt; forgiveness or pardon. Though the senator had been treated for cancer, his symptoms were in *remission*, and he was considered fit enough to handle the strains of a presidential race.

remnant N. remainder. I suggest that you wait until the store places the *remnants* of these goods on sale.

remonstrance N. protest; objection. The authorities were deaf to the pastor's *remonstrances* about the lack of police protection in the area. remonstrate, V.

■ **remorse** N. guilt; self-reproach. The murderer felt no *remorse* for his crime.

remunerative ADJ. compensating; rewarding. I find my new work so *remunerative* that I may not return to my previous employment. remuneration, N.

rend V. split; tear apart. In his grief, he tried to *rend* his garments. rent, N.

render V. deliver; provide; represent. He *rendered* aid to the needy and indigent.

rendition N. translation; artistic interpretation of a song, etc. The audience cheered enthusiastically as she completed her *rendition* of the aria.

renegade N. deserter; traitor. Because he had abandoned his post and joined forces with the Indians, his fellow officers considered the hero of *Dances with Wolves* a *renegade*. also ADJ.

renege V. deny; go back on. He *reneged* on paying off his debt.

■ **renounce** V. abandon; disown; repudiate. Even though she knew she would be burned at the stake as a witch, Joan of Arc refused to *renounce* her belief that her voices came from God. renunciation, N.

renovate V. restore to good condition; renew. We *renovated* our kitchen, replacing the old cabinets and countertop and installing new appliances.

renown N. fame. For many years an unheralded researcher, Barbara McClintock gained international *renown* when she won the Nobel Prize in Physiology and Medicine. renowned, ADJ.

rent N. rip; split. Kit did an excellent job of mending the *rent* in the lining of her coat.

reparable ADJ. capable of being repaired. Fortunately, the damage to our car was *reparable*, and after two weeks in the shop it looks brand new.

reparation N. amends; compensation. At the peace conference, the defeated country promised to pay *reparations* to the victors.

repast N. meal; feast; banquet. The caterers prepared a delicious *repast* for Fred and Judy's wedding day.

repeal V. revoke; annul. What would the effect on our society be if we decriminalized drug use by *repealing* the laws against the possession and sale of narcotics?

■ **repel** V. drive away; disgust. At first, the Beast's ferocious appearance *repelled* Beauty, but she came to love the tender heart hidden behind that beastly exterior.

repellent ADJ. driving away; unattractive. Mosquitoes find the odor so *repellent* that they leave any spot where this liquid has been sprayed. also N.

repercussion N. result or impact (of an event, etc.); rebound; reverberation. The brothers' quarrel had serious *repercussions*, for it led to their estrangement.

repertoire N. list of works of music, drama, etc., a performer is prepared to present. The opera company decided to include *Madame Butterfly* in its *repertoire* for the following season.

replenish V. fill up again. Before she could take another backpacking trip, Carla had to *replenish* her stock of freeze-dried foods.

● **replete** ADJ. filled to the brim or to the point of being stuffed; abundantly supplied. The movie star's memoir was *replete* with juicy details about the love life of half of Hollywood.

replica N. copy. Are you going to hang this *replica* of the Declaration of Independence in the classroom or in the auditorium?

replicate V. reproduce; duplicate. Because he had always wanted a palace, Donald decided to *replicate* the Taj Mahal in miniature on his estate.

repository N. storehouse. Libraries are *repositories* of the world's best thoughts.

■ **reprehensible** ADJ. deserving blame. Shocked by the viciousness of the bombing, politicians of every party uniformly condemned the terrorists' *reprehensible* deed.

repress V. restrain; crush; oppress. Anne's parents tried to curb her impetuosity without *repressing* her boundless high spirits.

reprieve N. temporary stay. During the twenty-four-hour *reprieve*, the lawyers sought to make the stay of execution permanent. also V.

■ **reprimand** V. reprove severely; rebuke. Every time Ermengarde made a mistake in class, she was afraid that Miss Minchin would *reprimand* her and tell her father how badly she was doing in school. also N.

reprisal N. retaliation. I am confident that we are ready for any *reprisals* the enemy may undertake.

reprise N. musical repetition; repeat performance; recurrent action. We enjoyed the soprano's solo in Act I so much that we were delighted by its *reprise* in the finale.

reproach V. express disapproval or disappointment. He never could do anything wrong without imagining how the look on his mother's face would *reproach* him afterwards. reproachful, ADJ.

reprobate N. person hardened in sin, devoid of a sense of decency. I cannot understand why he has so many admirers if he is the *reprobate* you say he is.

■ **reprove** V. censure; rebuke. Though Aunt Bea at times had to *reprove* Opie for inattention in church, she believed he was at heart a God-fearing lad.

■ **repudiate** V. disown; disavow. On separating from Tony, Tina announced that she would *repudiate* all debts incurred by her soon-to-be ex-husband.

● **repugnant** ADJ. loathsome; hateful. Whereas some people like earthworms, others find them *repugnant* and view them with disgust.

repulsion N. distaste; act of driving back. Hating bloodshed, she viewed war with *repulsion*. Even defensive battles distressed her, for the *repulsion* of enemy forces is never accomplished bloodlessly.

reputable ADJ. respectable. If you want to buy antiques, look for a *reputable* dealer; far too many dealers today pass off fakes as genuine antiques.

reputed ADJ. supposed. Though he is the *reputed* father of the child, no one can be sure. repute, N.

requisite N. necessary requirement. Many colleges state that a student must offer three years of a language as a *requisite* for admission.

requite V. repay; revenge. The wretch *requited* his benefactors by betraying them.

● **rescind** V. cancel. Because of the public outcry against the new taxes, the senator proposed a bill to *rescind* the unpopular financial measure.

Word List 41   resentment–sacrosanct

resentment   N. indignation; bitterness; displeasure. Not wanting to appear a sore loser, Bill tried to hide his *resentment* of Barry's success.

■ **reserve**   N. self-control; formal but distant manner. Although some girls were attracted by Mark's air of *reserve,* Judy was put off by it, for she felt his aloofness indicated a lack of openness. reserved, ADJ.

residue   N. remainder; balance. In his will, he requested that after payment of debts, taxes, and funeral expenses, the *residue* be given to his wife. residual, ADJ.

■ **resigned**   ADJ. accepting one's fate; unresisting; patiently submissive. *Resigned* to his downtrodden existence, Bob Cratchit was too meek to protest Scrooge's bullying. resignation, N.

resilient   ADJ. elastic; having the power of springing back. Highly *resilient,* steel makes excellent bedsprings. resilience, N.

■ **resolution**   N. determination; resolve. Nothing could shake his *resolution* that his children would get the best education that money could buy. resolute, ADJ.

■ **resolve**   N. determination; firmness of purpose. How dare you question my *resolve* to take up sky-diving! Of course I haven't changed my mind!

resolve   V. decide; settle; solve. Holmes *resolved* to travel to Bohemia to *resolve* the dispute between Irene Adler and the king.

resonant   ADJ. echoing; resounding; deep and full in sound. The deep, *resonant* voice of the actor James Earl Jones makes him particularly effective when he appears on stage.

respiration   N. breathing; exhalation. The doctor found that the patient's years of smoking had adversely affected both his lung capacity and his rate of *respiration.*

● **respite**   N. interval of relief; time for rest; delay in punishment. After working nonstop on this project for three straight months, I need a *respite!* For David, the two weeks vacationing in New Zealand were a delightful *respite* from the pressures of his job.

● **resplendent**   ADJ. dazzling; glorious; brilliant. While all the adults were commenting how glorious the emperor looked in his *resplendent* new clothes, one little boy was heard to say, "But he's naked!"

responsiveness   N. state of reacting readily to appeals, orders, etc. The audience cheered and applauded, delighting the performers by its *responsiveness.*

restitution   N. reparation; indemnification. He offered to make *restitution* for the window broken by his son.

restive   ADJ. restlessly impatient; obstinately resisting control. Waiting impatiently in line to see Santa Claus, even the best-behaved children grow *restive* and start to fidget.

■ **restraint**   N. moderation or self-control; controlling force; restriction. Control yourself, young lady! Show some *restraint!*

resumption   N. taking up again; recommencement. During summer break, Don had not realized how much he missed university life; at the *resumption* of classes, however, he felt marked excitement and pleasure. resume, V.

resurge   V. rise again; flow to and fro. It was startling to see the spirit of nationalism *resurge* as the Soviet Union disintegrated into a loose federation of ethnic and national groups. resurgence, N.

retain   V. keep; employ. Fighting to *retain* his seat in Congress, Senator Foghorn *retained* a new manager to head his reelection campaign.

retaliation   N. repayment in kind (usually for bad treatment). Because everyone knew the Princeton Band had stolen Brown's mascot, the whole Princeton student body expected some sort of *retaliation* from Brown. retaliate, V.

retentive   ADJ. able to retain or keep; able to remember. Priding herself on her *retentive* memory, she claimed she never forgot a face.

■ **reticence**   N. reserve; uncommunicativeness; inclination to silence. Fearing his competitors might get advance word about his plans from talkative staff members, Hughes preferred *reticence* from his employees to loquacity. reticent, ADJ.

retinue   N. following; attendants. The queen's *retinue* followed her down the aisle.

retiring   ADJ. modest; shy. Given Susan's *retiring* personality, no one expected her to take up public speaking; surprisingly enough, she became a star of the school debate team.

retort   N. quick sharp reply. Even when it was advisable for her to keep her mouth shut, she was always ready with a quick *retort.* also V.

■ **retract**   V. withdraw; take back. When I saw how Fred and his fraternity brothers had trashed the frat house, I decided to *retract* my offer to let them use our summer cottage for the weekend. retraction, N.

retrench   V. cut down; economize. In order to be able to afford to send their children to college, they would have to *retrench.* retrenchment, N.

retribution   N. vengeance; compensation; punishment for offenses. The evangelist maintained that an angry deity would exact *retribution* from the sinners.

retrieve   V. recover; find and bring in. The dog was intelligent and quickly learned to *retrieve* the game killed by the hunter.

retroactive   ADJ. taking effect before its enactment (as a law) or imposition (as a tax). Because the new pension law was *retroactive* to the first of the year, even though Martha had retired in February she was eligible for the pension.

retrograde   V. go backwards; degenerate. instead of advancing, our civilization seems to have *retrograded* in ethics and culture. also ADJ.

retrospective   ADJ. looking back on the past. The Museum of Graphic Arts is holding a *retrospective* showing of the paintings of Michael Whelan over the past two decades.

revelry   N. boisterous merrymaking. New Year's Eve is a night of *revelry*

■ **reverent** ADJ. respectful; worshipful. Though I bow my head in church and recite the prayers, sometimes I don't feel properly *reverent*. revere, V.

reverie N. daydream; musing. He was awakened from his *reverie* by the teacher's question.

revert V. relapse; backslide; turn back to. Most of the time Andy seemed sensitive and mature, but occasionally he would *revert* to his smart-alecky, macho, adolescent self.

revile V. attack with abusive language; vilify. Though most of his contemporaries *reviled* Captain Kidd as a notorious, bloody-handed pirate, some of his fellow merchant-captains believed him innocent of his alleged crimes.

revoke V. cancel; retract. Repeat offenders who continue to drive under the influence of alcohol face having their driver's licenses permanently *revoked*.

revulsion N. sudden violent change of feeling; reaction. Many people in this country who admired dictatorships underwent a *revulsion* when they realized what Hitler and Mussolini were trying to do.

rhapsodize V. to speak or write in an exaggeratedly enthusiastic manner. She greatly enjoyed her Hawaiian vacation and *rhapsodized* about it for weeks.

rhetoric N. art of effective communication; insincere language. All writers, by necessity, must be skilled in *rhetoric*.

■ **rhetorical** ADJ. pertaining to effective communication; insincere in language. To win his audience, the speaker used every *rhetorical* trick in the book.

ribald ADJ. wanton; profane. He sang a *ribald* song that offended many of the more prudish listeners.

riddle V. pierce with holes; permeate or spread throughout. With his machine gun, Tracy *riddled* the car with bullets till it looked like a slice of Swiss cheese. During the proofreaders' strike, the newspaper was *riddled* with typos.

rife ADJ. abundant; current. Discontent was *rife* among the early settlers, who had not foreseen the harshness of life in the New World.

rift N. opening; break. The plane was lost in the stormy sky until the pilot saw the city through a *rift* in the clouds.

rig V. fix or manipulate. The ward boss was able to *rig* the election by bribing people to stuff the ballot boxes with ballots marked in his candidate's favor.

rigid ADJ. stiff and unyielding; strict; hard and unbending. By living with a man to whom she was not married, George Eliot broke Victorian society's most *rigid* rule of respectable behavior.

■ **rigor** N. severity. Many settlers could not stand the *rigors* of the New England winters.

rigorous ADJ. severe; harsh; demanding; exact. Disliked by his superiors, the officer candidate in *An Officer and a Gentleman* endured an extremely *rigorous* training program.

rile V. vex; irritate; muddy. Red had a hair-trigger temper: he was an easy man to *rile*.

riveting ADJ. absorbing; engrossing. The reviewer described Byatt's novel *Possession* as a *riveting* tale, one so absorbing that he had finished it in a single night.

■ **robust** ADJ. vigorous; strong. After pumping iron and taking karate for six months, the little old lady was so *robust* that she could break a plank with her fist.

roil V. to make liquids murky by stirring up sediment. Be careful when you pour not to *roil* the wine; if you stir up the sediment you'll destroy the flavor.

roster N. list. They print the *roster* of players in the season's program.

rote N. repetition. He recited the passage by *rote* and gave no indication he understood what he was saying.

rotundity N. roundness; sonorousness of speech. Short, squat, and round as a bowling ball, he was the very model of *rotundity*.

rousing ADJ. lively; stirring. "And now, let's have a *rousing* welcome for TV's own Roseanne Barr, who'll lead us in a *rousing* rendition of 'The Star-Spangled Banner.'"

rout V. stampede; drive out. The reinforcements were able to *rout* the enemy. also N.

rubble N. broken fragments. Ten years after World War II, some of the *rubble* left by enemy bombings could still be seen.

ruddy ADJ. reddish; healthy-looking. Santa Claus's *ruddy* cheeks nicely complement Rudolph the Reindeer's bright red nose.

rudimentary ADJ. not developed; elementary; crude. Although my grandmother's English vocabulary was limited to a few *rudimentary* phrases, she always could make herself understood.

rue V. regret; lament; mourn. Tina *rued* the night she met Tony and wondered how she ever fell for such a jerk. rueful, ADJ.

ruffian N. bully; scoundrel. The *ruffians* threw stones at the police.

ruminate V. chew over and over (mentally, or, like cows, physically); mull over; ponder. Unable to digest quickly the baffling events of the day, Reuben *ruminated* about them till four in the morning.

rummage V. ransack; thoroughly search. When we *rummaged* through the trunks in the attic, we found many souvenirs of our childhood days. also N.

ruse N. trick; stratagem. You will not be able to fool your friends with such an obvious *ruse*.

rustic ADJ. pertaining to country people; uncouth. The backwoodsman looked out of place in his *rustic* attire.

ruthless ADJ. pitiless; cruel. Captain Hook was a dangerous, *ruthless* villain who would stop at nothing to destroy Peter Pan.

saboteur N. one who commits sabotage; destroyer of property. Members of the Resistance acted as *saboteurs*, blowing up train lines to prevent supplies from reaching the Nazi army.

saccharine ADJ. cloyingly sweet. She tried to ingratiate herself, speaking sweetly and smiling a *saccharine* smile.

sacrilegious ADJ. desecrating; profane. His stealing of the altar cloth was a very *sacrilegious* act.

sacrosanct ADJ. most sacred; inviolable. The brash insurance salesman invaded the *sacrosanct* privacy of the office of the president of the company.

Word List 42   sadistic–sentinel

sadistic ADJ. inclined to cruelty. If we are to improve conditions in this prison, we must first get rid of the *sadistic* warden.

saga N. Scandinavian myth; any legend. This is a *saga* of the sea and the men who risk their lives on it.

sagacious ADJ. perceptive; shrewd; having insight. My father was a *sagacious* judge of character: he could spot a phony a mile away. sagacity, N.

■ **sage** N. person celebrated for wisdom. Hearing tales of a mysterious Master of All Knowledge who lived in the hills of Tibet, Sandy was possessed with a burning desire to consult the legendary *sage*. also ADJ.

salacious ADJ. lascivious; lustful. Chaucer's monk is not pious but *salacious*, a teller of lewd tales and ribald jests.

salient ADJ. protruding; strikingly conspicuous; jumping. Good readers quickly grasp the *salient* and significant points of a passage; indeed, the ideas almost leap out at them, demanding their attention.

salubrious ADJ. promoting good health; healthful. The health resort advertised the *salubrious* properties of the waters of its famous hot springs.

salutary ADJ. tending to improve; beneficial; wholesome. The punishment had a *salutary* effect on the boy, as he became a model student.

salvage V. rescue from loss. All attempts to *salvage* the wrecked ship failed. also N.

salvo N. discharge of firearms; military salute. The boom of the enemy's opening *salvo* made the petrified private jump.

sanctimonious ADJ. falsely holy; feigning piety. Mark Twain mocked pious hypocrites, calling one a *sanctimonious* old iceberg who looked like he was waiting for a vacancy in the Trinity.

■ **sanction** V. approve; ratify. Nothing will convince me to *sanction* the engagement of my daughter to such a worthless young man.

sanctuary N. refuge; shelter; shrine; holy place. The tiny attic was Helen's *sanctuary* to which she fled when she had to get away from the rest of her family.

sanguine ADJ. cheerful; hopeful. Let's not be too *sanguine* about the outcome of the election; we may still lose.

sap V. diminish; undermine. The element kryptonite has an unhealthy effect on Superman: it *saps* his strength.

sarcasm N. scornful remarks; stinging rebuke. Though Ralph pretended to ignore the mocking comments of his supposed friends, their *sarcasm* wounded him deeply.

sardonic ADJ. cynically mocking; sarcastic. Dorothy Parker's wry couplet, "Men seldom make passes at girls who wear glasses," epitomizes her *sardonic* wit.

sartorial ADJ. pertaining to tailors. *GQ Magazine* provides *sartorial* advice for the not-so-well-dressed man.

sate V. satisfy to the full; cloy. Its hunger *sated,* the lion dozed.

satellite N. small body revolving around a larger one. During the first few years of the Space Age, hundreds of *satellites* were launched by Russia and the United States.

satiate V. satisfy fully. Having stuffed themselves until they were *satiated*, the guests were so full they were ready for a nap.

satire N. form of literature in which irony, sarcasm, and ridicule are employed to attack vice and folly. *Gulliver's Travels*, which is regarded by many as a tale for children, is actually a bitter *satire* attacking man's folly.

■ **satirical** ADJ. mocking. The humor of cartoonist Gary Trudeau often is *satirical;* through the comments of the Doonesbury characters, Trudeau ridicules political corruption and folly.

■ **saturate** V. soak thoroughly. *Saturate* your sponge with water until it can't hold any more.

saturnine ADJ. gloomy. Do not be misled by his *saturnine* countenance; he is not as gloomy as he looks.

saunter V. stroll slowly. As we *sauntered* through the park, we stopped frequently to admire the spring flowers.

savant N. learned scholar. Despite all her academic honors, Dr. Diamond disliked being classed as a *savant:* considering herself a simple researcher, she refused to describe herself in such grandiose terms.

savor V. enjoy; have a distinctive flavor, smell, or quality. Relishing his triumph, the actor especially *savored* the chagrin of the critics who had predicted his failure.

● **savory** ADJ. tasty; pleasing, attractive, or agreeable. Julia Child's recipes enable amateur chefs to create *savory* delicacies for their guests.

scad N. a great quantity. Refusing Dave's offer to lend him a shirt, Phil replied, "No, thanks, I've got *scads* of clothes."

scale V. climb up; ascend. In order to locate a book on the top shelf of the stacks, Lee had to *scale* an exceptionally rickety ladder.

scamp N. rascal. Despite his mischievous behavior, Malcolm was such an engaging *scamp* that his mother almost lacked the heart to punish him.

■ **scanty** ADJ. meager; insufficient. Thinking his helping of food was *scanty*, Oliver Twist asked for more.

scapegoat N. someone who bears the blame for others. After the *Challenger* disaster, NASA searched for *scapegoats* on whom they could cast the blame.

scavenge V. hunt through discarded materials for usable items; search, especially for food. If you need car parts that the dealers no longer stock, try *scavenging* for odd bits and pieces at the auto wreckers' yards. scavenger, N.

scenario N. plot outline; screenplay; opera libretto. Scaramouche startled the other actors in the commedia troupe when he suddenly departed from their customary *scenario* and began to improvise.

schematic ADJ. relating to an outline or diagram; using a system of symbols. In working out the solution to this logic puzzle, you may find it helpful to construct a simple *schematic* diagram outlining the order of events.

schism N. division; split. His reforms led to a *schism* in the church and the establishment of a new sect opposing the old order.

scintillate V. sparkle; flash. I enjoy her dinner parties because the food is excellent and the conversation *scintillates*.

scoff V. mock; ridicule. He *scoffed* at dentists until he had his first toothache.

scourge N. cause of widespread devastation; severe punishment; whip. Abraham Lincoln wrote, "Fondly do we hope, fervently do we pray, that this mighty *scourge* of war speedily may pass away." also V.

scruple V. fret about; hesitate, for ethical reasons. Fearing that her husband had become involved in an affair, she did not *scruple* to read his diary. also N.

■ **scrupulous** ADJ. conscientious; extremely thorough. Though Alfred is *scrupulous* in fulfilling his duties at work, he is less conscientious about his obligations to his family and friends.

■ **scrutinize** V. examine closely and critically. Searching for flaws, the sergeant *scrutinized* every detail of the private's uniform.

scuffle V. struggle confusedly; move off in a confused hurry. The twins briefly *scuffled*, wrestling to see which of them would get the toy. When their big brother yelled, "Let go of my Gameboy!" they *scuffled* off down the hall.

scurrilous ADJ. vulgar; coarse; foul-mouthed; obscene. Politicians often face *scurrilous* attacks from angry constituents.

scurry V. move briskly. The White Rabbit had to *scurry* to get to his appointment on time.

scurvy ADJ. despicable; contemptible. Peter Pan sneered at Captain Hook and his *scurvy* crew.

scuttle V. scurry; run with short, rapid steps. The bug *scuttled* rapidly across the floor.

scuttle V. sink. The sailors decided to *scuttle* their vessel rather than surrender it to the enemy.

seamy ADJ. sordid; unwholesome. In *The Godfather*, Michael Corleone is unwilling to expose his wife and children to the *seamy* side of his life as the son of a Mafia don.

sear V. char or burn; brand. Accidentally brushing against the hot grill, she *seared* her hand badly.

seasoned ADJ. experienced. Though pleased with her new batch of rookies, the basketball coach wished she had a few more *seasoned* players on the team.

secession N. withdrawal. The *secession* of the Southern states provided Lincoln with his first major problem after his inauguration. secede, V.

■ **seclusion** N. isolation; solitude. One moment she loved crowds; the next, she sought *seclusion*. seclude, V.

secrete V. hide away; produce and release a substance into an organism. The pack rat *secretes* odds and ends in its nest; the pancreas *secretes* insulin in the islets of Langerhans.

sect N. separate religious body; faction. As university chaplain, she sought to address universal religious issues and not limit herself to concerns of any one *sect*.

sectarian ADJ. relating to a religious faction or subgroup; narrow-minded; limited. Far from being broad-minded, the religious leader was intolerant of new ideas, paying attention only to purely *sectarian* interests. sect. N.

secular ADJ. worldly; not pertaining to church matters; temporal. The church leaders decided not to interfere in *secular* matters.

sedate ADJ. calm and composed; dignified. To calm the agitated pony, we teamed him with a *sedate* mare who easily accepted the harness.

● **sedentary** ADJ. requiring sitting. Sitting all day at the computer, Sharon grew to resent the *sedentary* nature of her job.

sedition N. resistance to authority; insubordination. His words, though not treasonous in themselves, were calculated to arouse thoughts of *sedition*.

sedulous ADJ. diligent; hardworking. After weeks of patient and *sedulous* labor, we completed our detailed analysis of every published SAT examination.

seedy ADJ. run-down; decrepit; disreputable. I would rather stay in dormitory lodgings in a decent youth hostel than have a room of my own in a *seedy* downtown hotel.

seemly ADJ. proper; appropriate. Lady Bracknell did not think it was *seemly* for Ernest to lack a proper family: no baby abandoned on a doorstep could grow up to be a fit match for *her* daughter.

seep V. ooze; trickle. During the rainstorm, water *seeped* through the crack in the basement wall and damaged the floor boards. seepage, N.

seethe V. be disturbed; boil. The nation was *seething* with discontent as the noblemen continued their arrogant ways.

seismic ADJ. pertaining to earthquakes. The Richter scale is a measurement of *seismic* disturbances.

seminary N. school for training future ministers; academy for young women. Sure of his priestly vocation, Terrence planned to pursue his theological training at the local Roman Catholic *seminary*.

sensual ADJ. devoted to the pleasures of the senses; carnal; voluptuous. Giving in to his *sensual* appetites, he sampled the carnal delights of the fleshpots.

sententious ADJ. terse; concise; aphoristic. After reading so many redundant speeches, I find his *sententious* style particularly pleasing.

sentinel N. sentry; lookout. Though camped in enemy territory, Bledsoe ignored the elementary precaution of posting *sentinels* around the encampment.

Word List 43 sequester–solvent

sequester V. isolate; retire from public life; segregate; seclude. Banished from his kingdom, the wizard Prospero *sequestered* himself on a desert island. To prevent the jurors from hearing news broadcasts about the case, the judge decided to *sequester* the jury.

serendipity N. gift for finding valuable or desirable things by accident; accidental good fortune or luck. Many scientific discoveries are a matter of *serendipity*: Newton was not sitting under a tree thinking about gravity when the apple dropped on his head.

serenity N. calmness; placidity. The sound of air raid sirens pierced the *serenity* of the quiet village of Pearl Harbor.

serpentine ADJ. winding; twisting. The car swerved at every curve in the *serpentine* road.

■ **servile** ADJ. slavish; cringing. Constantly fawning on his employer, humble Uriah Heap was a *servile* creature.

servitude N. slavery; compulsory labor. Born a slave, Frederick Douglass resented his life of *servitude* and plotted to escape to the North.

sever V. cut; separate. The released prisoner wanted to begin a new life and *sever* all connections with his criminal past. Dr. Guillotin invented a machine that could neatly *sever* an aristocratic head from its equally aristocratic body. Unfortunately, he couldn't collect any *severance* pay. severance, N.

severity N. harshness; intensity; sternness; austerity. The *severity* of Jane's migraine attack was so great that she took to her bed for a week.

shackle V. chain; fetter. In a chain gang, convicts are *shackled* together to prevent their escape. also N.

sham V. pretend. He *shammed* sickness to get out of going to school. also N.

shambles N. wreck; mess. After the hurricane, the Carolina coast was a *shambles*. After the New Year's Eve party, the apartment was a *shambles*.

shard N. fragment, generally of pottery. The archaeologist assigned several students the task of reassembling earthenware vessels from the *shards* he had brought back from the expedition.

shear V. cut or clip (hair, fleece); strip of something. You may not care to cut a sheep's hair, but Sarah *shears* sheep for Little Bo Peep.

sheathe V. place into a case. As soon as he recognized the approaching men, he *sheathed* his dagger and hailed them as friends.

sheer ADJ. very thin or transparent; very steep; absolute. Wearing nothing but an almost *sheer* robe, Delilah draped herself against the *sheer* temple wall. Beholding her, Samson was overcome by her *sheer* beauty. Then she sheared his hair.

shimmer V. glimmer intermittently. The moonlight *shimmered* on the water as the moon broke through the clouds for a moment. also N.

shirk V. avoid (responsibility, work, etc.); malinger. Brian has a strong sense of duty; he would never *shirk* any responsibility.

shoddy ADJ. inferior; trashy; cheap. Grumbling, "They don't make things the way they used to," Grandpa complained about the *shoddy* workmanship nowadays.

shrewd ADJ. clever; astute. A *shrewd* investor, he took clever advantage of the fluctuations of the stock market.

shroud V. hide from view; wrap for burial. Fog *shrouded* Dracula's castle, hiding the ruined tower beneath sheets of mist.

shun V. keep away from. Cherishing his solitude, the recluse *shunned* the company of other human beings.

shyster N. lawyer using questionable methods. On *L.A. Law*, Brackman was horrified to learn that his newly-discovered half brother was nothing but a cheap *shyster*.

sibling N. brother or sister. We may not enjoy being *siblings*, but we cannot forget that we still belong to the same family.

simile N. comparison of one thing with another, using the word *like* or *as*. "My love is like a red, red rose" is a *simile*.

simper V. smirk; smile affectedly. Complimented on her appearance, Stella self-consciously *simpered*.

simplistic ADJ. oversimplified. Though Jack's solution dealt adequately with one aspect of the problem, it was *simplistic* in failing to consider various complications that might arise.

simulate V. feign. He *simulated* insanity in order to avoid punishment for his crime.

sinecure N. well-paid position with little responsibility. My job is no *sinecure*; I work long hours and have much responsibility.

sinewy ADJ. tough; strong and firm. The steak was too *sinewy* to chew.

singular ADJ. unique; extraordinary; odd. Though the young man tried to understand Father William's *singular* behavior, he still found it odd that the old man incessantly stood on his head. singularity, N.

sinister ADJ. evil; conveying a sense of ill omen. Aware of the Penguin's *sinister* purpose, Batman wondered how he could save Gotham City from the ravages of his evil enemy.

sinuous ADJ. winding; bending in and out; not morally honest. The snake moved in a *sinuous* manner.

■ **skeptic** N. doubter; person who suspends judgment until the evidence supporting a point of view has been examined. I am a *skeptic* about the new health plan; I want some proof that it can work. skepticism, N.

skimp V. provide scantily; live very economically. They were forced to *skimp* on necessities in order to make their limited supplies last the winter.

skinflint N. stingy person; miser. Scrooge was an ungenerous old *skinflint* until he reformed his ways and became a notable philanthropist.

skirmish N. minor fight. Custer's troops expected they might run into a *skirmish* or two on maneuvers; they did not expect to face a major battle. also V.

skulk V. move furtively and secretly. He *skulked* through the less fashionable sections of the city in order to avoid meeting any of his former friends.

slacken V. slow up; loosen. As they passed the finish line, the runners *slackened* their pace.

slake V. quench; sate. When we reached the oasis, we were able to *slake* our thirst.

slander N. defamation; utterance of false and malicious statements. Considering the negative comments politicians make about each other, it's a wonder that more of them aren't sued for *slander*. also V.

slapdash ADJ. haphazard; careless; sloppy. From the number of typos and misspellings I've found in it, it's clear that Mario proofread the report in a remarkably *slapdash* fashion.

sleeper N. something originally of little value or importance that in time becomes very valuable. Unnoticed by the critics at its publication, the eventual Pulitzer Prize winner was a classic *sleeper*.

sleight N. dexterity. The magician amazed the audience with his *sleight* of hand.

slight N. insult to one's dignity; snub. Hypersensitive and ready to take offense at any discourtesy, Bertha was always on the lookout for real or imaginary *slights*. also V.

slipshod ADJ. untidy or slovenly; shabby. As a master craftsman, the carpenter prided himself on not doing *slipshod* work.

slither V. slip or slide. During the recent ice storm, many people *slithered* down this hill as they walked to the station.

slothful ADJ. lazy. Lying idly on the sofa while others worked, Reggie denied he was *slothful*: "I just supervise better lying down."

slough V. cast off. Each spring, the snake *sloughs* off its skin.

slovenly ADJ. untidy; careless in work habits. Unshaven, sitting around in his bathrobe all afternoon, Gus didn't seem to care about the *slovenly* appearance he presented. The dark ring around the bathtub and the spider webs hanging from the beams proved what a *slovenly* housekeeper she was.

sluggard N. lazy person. Someone who leaps happily out of bed first thing in the morning and cheerfully sets off to work is no *sluggard*.

■ **sluggish** ADJ. slow; lazy; lethargic. After two nights without sleep, she felt *sluggish* and incapable of exertion.

slur V. speak indistinctly; mumble. When Sol has too much to drink, he starts to *slur* his words: "Washamatter? Cansh you undershtand what I shay?"

slur N. insult to one's character or reputation; slander. Polls revealed that the front-runner's standing had been badly damaged by the *slurs* and innuendoes circulated by his opponent's staff. also V. (secondary meaning)

smirk N. conceited smile. Wipe that *smirk* off your face! also V.

smolder V. burn without flame; be liable to break out at any moment. The rags *smoldered* for hours before they burst into flame.

snicker N. half-stifled laugh. The boy could not suppress a *snicker* when the teacher sat on the tack. also V.

snivel V. run at the nose; snuffle; whine. Don't you come *sniveling* to me complaining about your big brother.

sobriety N. moderation (especially regarding indulgence in alcohol); seriousness. Neither falling-down drunks nor stand-up comics are noted for *sobriety*. sober, ADJ.

sodden ADJ. soaked; dull, as if from drink. He set his *sodden* overcoat near the radiator to dry.

sojourn N. temporary stay. After his *sojourn* in Florida, he began to long for the colder climate of his native New England home.

solace N. comfort in trouble. I hope you will find *solace* in the thought that all of us share your loss.

solecism N. construction that is flagrantly incorrect grammatically. I must give this paper a failing mark because it contains many *solecisms*.

solemnity N. seriousness; gravity. The minister was concerned that nothing should disturb the *solemnity* of the marriage service. solemn, ADJ.

solicit V. request earnestly; seek. Knowing she needed to have a solid majority for the budget to pass, the mayor telephoned all the members of the city council to *solicit* their votes.

solicitous ADJ. worried; concerned. Dora was delicate, David knew, and he was very *solicitous* about her health during her pregnancy.

soliloquy N. talking to oneself. Dramatists use the *soliloquy* as a device to reveal a character's innermost thoughts and emotions.

solitude N. state of being alone; seclusion. Much depends on how much you like your own company. What to one person seems fearful isolation to another is blessed *solitude*.

soluble ADJ. able to be dissolved; able to be explained. Sugar is *soluble* in water; put a sugar cube in water and it will quickly dissolve.

solvent ADJ. able to pay all debts. By dint of very frugal living, he was finally able to become *solvent* and avoid bankruptcy proceedings.

solvent N. substance that dissolves another. Dip a cube of sugar into a cup of water; note how the water acts as a *solvent*, causing the cube to break down.

Word List 44 somber–sublime

■ **somber** ADJ. gloomy; depressing; dark; drab. From the doctor's grim expression, I could tell he had *somber* news. Dull brown and charcoal gray are pretty *somber* colors; can't you wear something bright?

somnolent ADJ. half asleep. The heavy meal and the over-heated room made us all *somnolent* and indifferent to the speaker.

sonorous ADJ. resonant. His *sonorous* voice resounded through the hall.

sophisticated ADJ. worldly-wise and urbane; complex. When Sophie makes wisecracks, she thinks she sounds *sophisticated*, but instead she sounds sophomoric. A few years ago the new IBM laptop with the butterfly keyboard and the built-in quadspeed fax modem seemed the height of computer *sophistication*.

sophistry N. seemingly plausible but fallacious reasoning. Instead of advancing valid arguments, he tried to over-whelm his audience with a flood of *sophistries*.

sophomoric ADJ. immature; half-baked, like a sophomore. Even if you're only a freshman, it's no compliment to be told your humor is *sophomoric*. The humor in *Dumb and Dumber* is *sophomoric* at best.

● **soporific** ADJ. sleep-causing; marked by sleepiness. Pro-fessor Pringle's lectures were so *soporific* that even he fell asleep in class. also N.

sordid ADJ. vile; filthy; wretched; mean. Talk show hosts seem willing to discuss any topic, no matter how *sordid* and disgusting it may be.

sovereign ADJ. efficacious; supreme or paramount; self-governing. Professor Pennywhistle claimed his panacea was a *sovereign* cure for all chronic complaints. In medicine the *sovereign* task of the doctor is to do no harm. Rebelling against the mother country, the onetime colony now pro-claimed itself a *sovereign* state. also N.

sparse ADJ. not thick; thinly scattered; scanty. No matter how carefully Albert combed his hair to make it look as full as possible, it still looked *sparse*.

spartan ADJ. avoiding luxury and comfort; sternly disci-plined. Looking over the bare, unheated room, with its hard cot, he wondered what he was doing in such *spartan* quar-ters. Only his *spartan* sense of duty kept him at his post.

spasmodic ADJ. fitful; periodic. The *spasmodic* coughing in the auditorium annoyed the performers.

spat N. squabble; minor dispute. What had started out as a mere *spat* escalated into a full-blown argument.

spate N. sudden flood or strong outburst; a large number or amount. After the *spate* of angry words that came pouring out of him, Mary was sure they would never be reconciled.

spatial ADJ. relating to space. NASA is engaged in an ongoing program of *spatial* exploration. Certain exercises test your sense of *spatial* relations by asking you to identify two views of an object seen from different points in space.

spawn V. lay eggs. Fish ladders had to be built in the dams to assist the salmon returning to *spawn* in their native streams. also N.

specious ADJ. seemingly reasonable but incorrect; mis-leading (often intentionally). To claim that, because houses and birds both have wings, both can fly, is extremely *spe-cious* reasoning.

spectrum N. colored band produced when beam of light passes through a prism. The visible portion of the *spectrum* includes red at one end and violet at the other.

spendthrift N. someone who wastes money. Easy access to credit encourages people to turn into *spendthrifts* who shop till they drop.

sphinx-like ADJ. enigmatic; mysterious. The Mona Lisa's *sphinx-like* expression has intrigued and mystified art lovers for centuries.

splice V. fasten together; unite. Before you *splice* two strips of tape together, be sure to line them up evenly. also N.

spontaneity N. lack of premeditation; naturalness; freedom from constraint. When Anne and Amy met, Amy impulsively hugged her new colleague, but Anne drew back, unpre-pared for such *spontaneity*. The cast over-rehearsed the play so much that the eventual performance lacked any *spontaneity*. spontaneous, ADJ.

■ **sporadic** ADJ. occurring irregularly. Although you can still hear *sporadic* outbursts of laughter and singing outside, the big Halloween parade has passed; the party's over till next year.

sportive ADJ. playful. Half man, half goat, the mischievous, *sportive* fauns gamboled on the green.

spry ADJ. vigorously active; nimble. She was eighty years old, yet still *spry* and alert.

● **spurious** ADJ. false; counterfeit; forged; illogical. The antique dealer hero of Jonathan Gash's mystery novels gives the reader tips on how to tell *spurious* antiques from the real thing. Natasha's claim to be the lost heir of the Romanoffs was *spurious*: the only thing Russian about her was the vodka she drank!

● **spurn** V. reject; scorn. The heroine *spurned* the villain's advances.

squabble N. minor quarrel; bickering. Children invariably get involved in petty *squabbles*; wise parents know when to inter-fere and when to let the children work things out on their own.

squalor N. filth; degradation; dirty, neglected state. Rusted, broken-down cars in its yard, trash piled up on the porch, tar paper peeling from the roof, the shack was the picture of *squalor*. squalid, ADJ.

■ **squander** V. waste. If you *squander* your allowance on candy and comic books, you won't have any money left to buy the new box of crayons you want.

squat ADJ. stocky; short and thick. Tolkien's hobbits are somewhat *squat*, sturdy little creatures, fond of good ale, good music, and good mushrooms.

staccato ADJ. played in an abrupt manner; marked by abrupt sharp sound. His *staccato* speech reminded one of the sound of a machine gun.

■ **stagnant** ADJ. motionless; stale; dull. Mosquitoes commonly breed in ponds of *stagnant* water. Mike's career was *stagnant*; it wasn't going anywhere, and neither was he! stagnate, V.

staid ADJ. sober; sedate. The wild parties at the fraternity house appealed to the jocks and slackers, but appalled the more *staid* and serious students on campus.

stalemate N. deadlock. Negotiations between the union and the employers have reached a *stalemate*; neither side is willing to budge from previously stated positions.

stalwart ADJ. strong and vigorous; unwaveringly dependable. We thought the congressman was a *stalwart* Republican until he voted against President Bush's Medicare reform bill. also N.

stamina N. strength; staying power. I doubt that she has the *stamina* to run the full distance of the marathon race.

stanch V. check flow of blood. It is imperative that we *stanch* the gushing wound before we attend to the other injuries.

stanza N. division of a poem. Do you know the last *stanza* of "The Star-Spangled Banner"?

■ **static** ADJ. unchanging; lacking development. Why watch chess on TV? I like watching a game with action, not something *static* where nothing seems to be going on.

statute N. law enacted by the legislature. The *statute* of limitations sets the limits on how long you have to take legal action in specific cases.

● **steadfast** ADJ. loyal; unswerving. Penelope was *steadfast* in her affections, faithfully waiting for Ulysses to return from his wanderings.

stealth N. slyness; sneakiness; secretiveness. Fearing detection by the sentries on duty, the scout inched his way toward the enemy camp with great *stealth*.

steep V. soak; saturate. Be sure to *steep* the fabric in the dyebath for the full time prescribed.

stellar ADJ. pertaining to the stars. He was the *stellar* attraction of the entire performance.

stem V. check the flow. The paramedic used a tourniquet to *stem* the bleeding from the slashed artery.

stem from V. arise from. Milton's problems in school *stemmed from* his poor study habits.

stereotype N. fixed and unvarying representation; standardized mental picture, often reflecting prejudice. Critics object to the character of Jim in *The Adventures of Huckleberry Finn* because he seems to reflect the *stereotype* of the happy, ignorant slave.

stifle V. suppress; extinguish; inhibit. Halfway through the boring lecture, Laura gave up trying to *stifle* her yawns.

stigma N. token of disgrace; brand. I do not attach any *stigma* to the fact that you were accused of this crime; the fact that you were acquitted clears you completely.

stigmatize V. brand; mark as wicked. I do not want to *stigmatize* this young offender for life by sending her to prison.

stilted ADJ. bombastic; inflated. His *stilted* rhetoric did not impress the college audience; they were immune to bombastic utterances.

stint N. supply; allotted amount; assigned portion of work. He performed his daily *stint* cheerfully and willingly. also V.

stint V. be thrifty; set limits. "Spare no expense," the bride's father said, refusing to *stint* on the wedding arrangements.

stipend N. pay for services. There is a nominal *stipend* for this position.

stipulate V. make express conditions; specify. Before agreeing to reduce American military forces in Europe, the president *stipulated* that NATO inspection teams be allowed to inspect Soviet bases.

stodgy ADJ. stuffy; boringly conservative. For a young person, Winston seems remarkably *stodgy*: you'd expect someone his age to show a little more life.

stoic ADJ. impassive; unmoved by joy or grief. I wasn't particularly *stoic* when I had my flu shot; I squealed like a stuck pig. also N.

stoke V. stir up a fire; feed plentifully. As a Scout Marisa learned how to light a fire, how to *stoke* it if it started to die down, and how to extinguish it completely.

● **stolid** ADJ. unruffled; impassive; dull. Marianne wanted a romantic, passionate suitor like Willoughby, not a *stolid*, unimaginative one like Colonel Brandon.

stratagem N. deceptive scheme. Though Wellington's forces seemed in full retreat, in reality their withdrawal was a *stratagem* intended to lure the enemy away from its sheltered position.

stratify V. divide into classes; be arranged into strata. As the economic gap between the rich and the poor increased, Roman society grew increasingly *stratified*.

stratum N. layer of earth's surface; layer of society. Neither an elitist nor a reverse snob, Mitch had friends from every social *stratum*.

strew V. spread randomly; sprinkle; scatter. Preceding the bride to the altar, the flower girl will *strew* rose petals along the aisle.

stricture N. restriction; adverse criticism. Huck regularly disobeyed Miss Watson's rules and *strictures* upon his behavior: he wouldn't wear shoes, no matter what she said.

● **strident** ADJ. loud and harsh; insistent. Whenever Sue became angry, she tried not to raise her voice; she had no desire to appear *strident*.

stringent ADJ. severe; rigid; constricted. Fearing the rapid spread of the SARS virus, the Canadian government imposed *stringent* quarantine measures.

strut N. pompous walk; swagger. Looking at his self-important *strut* as he swaggered about the parade ground, I could tell Colonel Blimp thought highly of himself. also V.

strut N. supporting bar. The engineer calculated that the *strut* supporting the rafter needed to be reinforced. (secondary meaning)

studied ADJ. not spontaneous; deliberate; thoughtful. Given Jill's previous slights, Jack felt that the omission of his name from the guest list was a *studied* insult.

stultify V. cause to appear or become stupid or inconsistent; frustrate or hinder. His long hours in the blacking factory left young Dickens numb and incurious, as if the menial labor had *stultified* his brain.

● **stupefy** V. make numb; stun; amaze. Disapproving of drugs in general, Laura refused to take sleeping pills or any other medicine that might *stupefy* her. stupefaction, N.

stupor N. state of apathy; daze; lack of awareness. The paramedics shook the unconscious man but could not rouse him from his *stupor*.

stymie V. present an obstacle; stump. The detective was *stymied* by the contradictory evidence in the robbery investigation. also N.

suavity N. urbanity; polish. The elegant actor is particularly good in roles that require *suavity* and sophistication.

subdued ADJ. less intense; quieter. Bob liked the *subdued* lighting at the restaurant because he thought it was romantic. I just thought it was dimly lit.

subjective ADJ. occurring or taking place within the subject; unreal. Your analysis is highly *subjective;* you have permitted your emotions and your opinions to color your thinking.

subjugate V. conquer; bring under control. Alexander the Great conquered most of the known world of his time, first *subjugating* the Persians under Darius, then defeating the armies of India's King Porus.

sublime ADJ. exalted or noble and uplifting; utter. Lucy was in awe of Desi's *sublime* musicianship, while he was in awe of her *sublime* naiveté.

Word List 45   subliminal–tantamount

subliminal ADJ. below conscious awareness. The pulse of the music began to work on the crowd in a *subliminal* way: they rocked to the rhythm unconsciously.

■ **submissive** ADJ. yielding; timid. When he refused to permit Elizabeth to marry her poet, Mr. Barrett expected her to be properly *submissive;* instead, she eloped!

■ **subordinate** ADJ. occupying a lower rank; inferior; submissive. Bishop Proudie's wife expected all the *subordinate* clergy to behave with great deference to the wife of their superior.

suborn V. persuade to act unlawfully (especially to commit perjury). In *The Godfather*, the mobsters used bribery and threats to *suborn* the witnesses against Don Michael Corleone.

subpoena N. writ summoning a witness to appear. The prosecutor's office was ready to serve a *subpoena* on the reluctant witness. also V.

subsequent ADJ. following; later. In *subsequent* lessons, we shall take up more difficult problems.

subservient ADJ. behaving like a slave; servile; obsequious. He was proud and dignified; he refused to be *subservient* to anyone.

■ **subside** V. settle down; descend; grow quiet. The doctor assured us that the fever would eventually *subside*.

subsidiary N. something secondary in importance or subordinate; auxiliary. The Turner Broadcasting System is a wholly owned *subsidiary* of AOL Time Warner. First deal with the critical issues, then with the *subsidiary* ones. also ADJ.

subsidy N. direct financial aid by government, etc. Without this *subsidy,* American ship operators would not be able to compete in world markets.

subsistence N. means needed to support life; existence. Farming those barren, depleted fields, he raised barely enough food for his family's *subsistence*.

substantial ADJ. ample; solid; in essentials. The generous scholarship represented a *substantial* sum of money.

■ **substantiate** V. establish by evidence; verify; support. These endorsements from satisfied customers *substantiate* our claim that Barron's *How to Prepare for the SAT* is the best SAT-prep book on the market.

substantive ADJ. real, as opposed to imaginary; essential; solidly based; substantial. Bishop Tutu received the Nobel Peace Prize in recognition of his *substantive* contributions to the peace movement in South Africa.

subterfuge N. deceitful stratagem; trick; pretense. Hiding from his pursuers, the fugitive used every *subterfuge* he could think of to get them off his track.

subtlety N. perceptiveness; ingenuity; delicacy. Never obvious, she expressed herself with such *subtlety* that her remarks went right over the heads of most of her audience. subtle, ADJ.

subversive ADJ. tending to overthrow; destructive. At first glance, the notion that styrofoam cups may actually be more ecologically sound than paper cups strikes most environmentalists as *subversive*.

■ **succinct** ADJ. brief; terse; compact. Don't bore your audience with excess verbiage: be *succinct*.

succor V. aid; assist; comfort. If you believe that con man has come here to *succor* you in your hour of need, you're an even bigger sucker than I thought. also N.

succulent ADJ. juicy; full of richness. To some people, Florida citrus fruits are more *succulent* than those from California. also N.

succumb V. yield; give in; die. I *succumb* to temptation whenever I see chocolate.

suffragist N. advocate of voting rights (for women). In recognition of her efforts to win the vote for women, Congress authorized coining a silver dollar honoring the *suffragist* Susan B. Anthony

sully V. tarnish; soil. He felt that it was beneath his dignity to *sully* his hands in such menial labor.

sultry ADJ. sweltering. He could not adjust himself to the *sultry* climate of the tropics.

summation N. act of finding the total; summary. In his *summation*, the lawyer emphasized the testimony given by the two witnesses.

summit N. utmost height or pinnacle; highest point (of a mountain, etc.) The *summit* of the amateur mountain climber's aspirations was someday to reach the *summit* of Mount Everest.

sumptuous ADJ. lavish; rich. I cannot recall when I have had such a *sumptuous* Thanksgiving feast.

sunder V. separate; part. Northern and southern Ireland are politically and religiously *sundered*.

supercilious ADJ. arrogant; condescending; patronizing. The *supercilious* headwaiter sneered at customers whom he thought did not fit in at a restaurant catering to an ultra-fashionable crowd.

■ **superficial** ADJ. trivial; shallow. Since your report gave only a *superficial* analysis of the problem, I cannot give you more than a passing grade.

■ **superfluous** ADJ. unnecessary; excessive; overabundant. Betsy lacked the heart to tell June that the wedding present she brought was *superfluous*; she and Bob had already received five toasters. Please try not to include so many *superfluous* details in your report; just give me the facts. superfluity, N.

superimpose V. place over something else. The filmmakers *superimposed* the credits over the movie's opening scene.

supersede V. cause to be set aside; replace; make obsolete. The new bulk mailing postal regulation *supersedes* the old one. If you continue to follow the old regulation, your bulk mailing will be returned to you.

● **supplant** V. replace; usurp. Bolingbroke, later to be known as King Henry IV, fought to *supplant* his cousin, Richard III, as King of England.

supple ADJ. flexible; pliant. Years of yoga exercises made Grace's body *supple*.

supplicate V. petition humbly; pray to grant a favor. We *supplicate* Your Majesty to grant him amnesty.

supposition N. hypothesis; the act of supposing. I based my decision to confide in him on the *supposition* that he would be discreet. suppose, V.

suppress V. stifle; overwhelm; subdue; inhibit. Too polite to laugh in anyone's face, Roy did his best to *suppress* his amusement at Ed's inane remark.

● **surfeit** V. satiate; stuff; indulge to excess in anything. Every Thanksgiving we are *surfeited* with an overabundance of holiday treats. also N.

surly ADJ. rude; cross. Because of his *surly* attitude, many people avoided his company.

surmise V. suspect; guess; imagine. I *surmise* that Suzanne will be late for this meeting; I've never known her to be on time. also N.

surmount V. overcome. Could Helen Keller, blind and deaf since childhood, *surmount* her physical disabilities and lead a productive life?

■ **surpass** V. exceed. Her SAT scores *surpassed* our expectations.

■ **surreptitious** ADJ. secret; furtive; sneaky; hidden. Hoping to discover where his mom had hidden the Christmas presents, Timmy took a *surreptitious* peek into the master bedroom closet.

surrogate N. substitute. For a fatherless child, a male teacher may become a father *surrogate*.

surveillance N. watching; guarding. The FBI kept the house under constant *surveillance* in the hope of capturing all the criminals at one time.

■ **susceptible** ADJ. impressionable; easily influenced; having little resistance, as to a disease; receptive to. Said the patent medicine man to his very *susceptible* customer: "Buy this new miracle drug, and you will no longer be *susceptible* to the common cold."

■ **sustain** V. experience; support; nourish. He *sustained* such a severe injury that the doctors feared he would be unable to work to *sustain* his growing family.

sustenance N. means of support, food, nourishment. In the tropics, the natives find *sustenance* easy to obtain, due to all the fruit trees.

swagger V. behave arrogantly or pompously; strut or walk proudly. The conquering hero didn't simply stride down the street; he *swaggered*. also N.

swarm N. dense moving crowd; large group of honeybees. At the height of the city hall scandals, a constant *swarm* of reporters followed the mayor everywhere. also V.

swarthy ADJ. dark; dusky. Despite the stereotypes, not all Italians are *swarthy*; many are fair and blond.

swathe V. wrap around; bandage. When I visited him in the hospital, I found him *swathed* in bandages.

swelter V. be oppressed by heat. I am going to buy an air conditioning unit for my apartment as I do not intend to *swelter* through another hot and humid summer.

swerve V. deviate; turn aside sharply. The car *swerved* wildly as the driver struggled to regain control of the wheel.

swindler N. cheat. She was gullible and trusting, an easy victim for the first *swindler* who came along.

sybarite N. lover of luxury. Rich people are not always *sybarites;* some of them have little taste for a life of luxury.

● **sycophant** N. servile flatterer; bootlicker; yes man. Fed up with the toadies and flunkies who made up his entourage, the star cried, "Get out, all of you! I'm sick of *sycophants*!" sycophancy, N.

symbiosis N. interdependent relationship (between groups, species), often mutually beneficial. Both the crocodile bird and the crocodile derive benefit from their *symbiosis*: pecking away at food particles embedded in the crocodile's teeth, the bird receives nourishment; the crocodile, meanwhile, receives proper dental hygiene. symbiotic, ADJ.

symmetry N. arrangement of parts so that balance is obtained; congruity. Something lopsided by definition lacks *symmetry*.

synoptic ADJ. providing a general overview; summary. The professor turned to the latest issue of *Dissertation Abstracts* for a *synoptic* account of what was new in the field. synopsis, N.

synthesis N. combining parts into a whole. Now that we have succeeded in isolating this drug, our next problem is to plan its *synthesis* in the laboratory. synthesize, V.

table V. set aside a resolution or proposal for future consideration. Because we seem unable to agree on this issue at the moment, let us *table* the motion for now and come back to it at a later date.

tacit ADJ. understood; not put into words. We have a *tacit* agreement based on only a handshake.

■ **taciturn** ADJ. habitually silent; talking little. The stereotypical cowboy is a *taciturn* soul, answering lengthy questions with "Yep" or "Nope."

tactile ADJ. pertaining to the organs or sense of touch. His callused hands had lost their *tactile* sensitivity.

taint V. contaminate; cause to lose purity; modify with a trace of something bad. One speck of dirt on your utensils may contain enough germs to *taint* an entire batch of preserves.

talisman N. charm to bring good luck and avert misfortune. Joe believed the carved pendant he found in Vietnam served him as a *talisman* and brought him safely through the war.

tangential ADJ. peripheral; only slightly connected; digressing. Despite Clark's attempts to distract her with *tangential* remarks, Lois kept on coming back to her main question: why couldn't he come out to dinner with Superman and her?

tangible ADJ. able to be touched; real; palpable. Although Tom did not own a house, he had several *tangible* assets—a car, a television, a PC—that he could sell if he needed cash.

tantalize V. tease; torture with disappointment. Tom *tantalized* his younger brother, holding the ball just too high for Jimmy to reach.

● **tantamount** ADJ. equivalent in effect or value. Because so few Southern blacks could afford to pay the poll tax, the imposition of this tax on prospective voters was *tantamount* to disenfranchisement for black voters.

Word List 46   tantrum–tonic

tantrum N. fit of petulance; caprice. The child learned that he could have almost anything if he had a *tantrum*.

tarry V. delay; dawdle. We can't *tarry* if we want to get to the airport on time.

taut ADJ. tight; ready. The captain maintained that he ran a *taut* ship.

tautological ADJ. needlessly repetitious. In the sentence "It was visible to the eye," the phrase "to the eye" is *tautological*.

tautology N. unnecessary repetition. "Joyful happiness" is an illustration of *tautology*.

tawdry ADJ. cheap and gaudy. He won a few *tawdry* trinkets in Coney Island.

tedious ADJ. boring; tiring. The repetitious nature of work on the assembly line made Martin's job very *tedious*. tedium, N.

temerity N. boldness; rashness. Do you have the *temerity* to argue with me?

■ **temper** V. moderate; tone down or restrain; toughen (steel). Not even her supervisor's grumpiness could *temper* Nancy's enthusiasm for her new job.

temperament N. characteristic frame of mind; disposition; emotional excess. Although the twins look alike, they differ markedly in *temperament*: Todd is calm, but Rod is excitable.

temperate ADJ. restrained; self-controlled; moderate in respect to temperature. Try to be *temperate* in your eating this holiday season; if you control your appetite, you won't gain too much weight.

tempestuous ADJ. stormy; impassioned; violent. Racket-throwing tennis star John McEnroe was famed for his displays of *tempestuous* temperament.

tempo N. speed of music. I find the band's *tempo* too slow for such a lively dance.

temporal ADJ. not lasting forever; limited by time; secular. At one time in our history, *temporal* rulers assumed that they had been given their thrones by divine right.

temporize V. act evasively to gain time; avoid committing oneself. Ordered by King John to drive Robin Hood out of Sherwood Forest, the sheriff *temporized*, hoping to put off any confrontation with the outlaw band.

tenacious ADJ. holding fast. I had to struggle to break his *tenacious* hold on my arm.

● **tenacity** N. firmness; persistence. Jean Valjean could not believe the *tenacity* of Inspector Javert. Here all Valjean had done was to steal a loaf of bread, and the inspector had pursued him doggedly for twenty years!

tendentious ADJ. having an aim; biased; designed to further a cause. The editorials in this periodical are *tendentious* rather than truth-seeking.

tender V. offer; extend. Although no formal charges had been made against him, in the wake of the recent scandal the mayor felt he should *tender* his resignation.

tenet N. doctrine; dogma. The agnostic did not accept the *tenets* of their faith.

tensile ADJ. capable of being stretched. Mountain climbers must know the *tensile* strength of their ropes.

■ **tentative** ADJ. hesitant; not fully worked out or developed; experimental; not definite or positive. Unsure of his welcome at the Christmas party, Scrooge took a *tentative* step into his nephew's drawing room.

tenuous ADJ. thin; rare; slim. The allegiance of our allies is based on such *tenuous* ties that we have little hope they will remain loyal.

tenure N. holding of an office; time during which such an office is held. A special recall election put a sudden end to Gray Davis's *tenure* in office as governor of California.

tepid   ADJ. lukewarm. To avoid scalding the baby, make sure the bath water is *tepid*, not hot.

termination   N. end. Though the time for *termination* of the project was near, we still had a lot of work to finish before we shut up shop. terminate, V.

terminology   N. terms used in a science or art. In talking to patients, doctors should either avoid medical *terminology* altogether or take time to explain the technical terms they use.

● **terrestrial**   ADJ. earthly (as opposed to celestial); pertaining to the land. In many science fiction films, alien invaders from outer space plan to destroy all *terrestrial* life.

■ **terse**   ADJ. concise; abrupt; pithy. There is a fine line between speech that is *terse* and to the point and speech that is too abrupt.

testy   ADJ. irritable; short-tempered. My advice is to avoid discussing this problem with him today as he is rather *testy* and may shout at you.

tether   V. tie with a rope. Before we went to sleep, we *tethered* the horses to prevent their wandering off during the night.

thematic   ADJ. relating to a unifying motif or idea. Those who think of *Moby Dick* as a simple adventure story about whaling miss its underlying *thematic* import.

theocracy   N. government run by religious leaders. Though some Pilgrims aboard the *Mayflower* favored the establishment of a *theocracy* in New England, many of their fellow voyagers preferred a nonreligious form of government.

theoretical   ADJ. not practical or applied; hypothetical. Bob was better at applied engineering and computer programming than he was at *theoretical* physics and math. While I can still think of some *theoretical* objections to your plan, you've convinced me of its basic soundness.

therapeutic   ADJ. curative. Now better known for its racetrack, Saratoga Springs first gained attention for the *therapeutic* qualities of its famous "healing waters." therapy, N.

thermal   ADJ. pertaining to heat. On cold, wintry days, Jack dresses for warmth, putting on his *thermal* underwear. also N.

thespian   ADJ. pertaining to drama. Her success in the school play convinced her she was destined for a *thespian* career. also N.

● **threadbare**   ADJ. worn through till the threads show; shabby and poor. The poor adjunct professor hid the *threadbare* spots on his jacket by sewing leather patches on his sleeves.

thrifty   ADJ. careful about money; economical. A *thrifty* shopper compares prices before making major purchases.

■ **thrive**   V. prosper; flourish. Despite the impact of the recession on the restaurant trade, Philip's cafe *thrived*.

throes   N. violent anguish. The *throes* of despair can be as devastating as the spasms accompanying physical pain.

throng   N. crowd. *Throngs* of shoppers jammed the aisles. also V.

thwart   V. prevent; frustrate; oppose and defeat. Batman searched for a way to *thwart* the Joker's evil plan to destroy Gotham City.

tightwad   N. excessively frugal person; miser. Jill called Jack a *tightwad* because he never picked up the check.

timidity   N. lack of self-confidence or courage. If you are to succeed as a salesman, you must first lose your *timidity* and fear of failure.

timorous   ADJ. fearful; demonstrating fear. His *timorous* manner betrayed the fear he felt at the moment.

● **tirade**   N. extended scolding; denunciation; harangue. The cigar smoker went into a bitter *tirade*, denouncing the anti-smoking forces that had succeeded in banning smoking from most planes and restaurants.

titanic   ADJ. gigantic. *Titanic* waves beat against the majestic S.S. *Titanic*, driving it against the concealed iceberg.

title   N. right or claim to possession; mark of rank; name (of a book, film, etc.). Though the penniless Duke of Ragwort no longer held *title* to the family estate, he still retained his *title* as head of one of England's oldest families.

titter   N. nervous laugh. Her aunt's constant *titter* nearly drove her mad. also V.

titular   ADJ. nominal holding of title without obligations. Although he was the *titular* head of the company, the real decisions were made by his general manager.

toady   N. servile flatterer; yes man. Never tell the boss anything he doesn't wish to hear: he doesn't want an independent adviser, he just wants a *toady*. also V.

tome   N. large volume. He spent much time in the libraries poring over ancient *tomes*.

tonic   ADJ. invigorating; refreshing. The tart homemade ginger ale had a *tonic* effect on Kit: she perked right up. also N.

Word List 47   topography–ubiquitous

topography   N. physical features of a region. Before the generals gave the order to attack, they ordered a complete study of the *topography* of the region.

● **torpor**   N. lethargy; sluggishness; dormancy. Throughout the winter, nothing aroused the bear from his *torpor*: he would not emerge from hibernation until spring. torpid, ADJ.

torrent   N. rushing stream; flood. Day after day of heavy rain saturated the hillside until the water ran downhill in *torrents*. torrential, ADJ.

torrid   ADJ. passionate; hot or scorching. Harlequin Romances publish *torrid* tales of love affairs, some set in *torrid* climates.

tortuous   ADJ. winding; full of curves. Because this road is so *tortuous*, it is unwise to go faster than twenty miles an hour on it.

totter   V. move unsteadily; sway, as if about to fall. On unsteady feet, the drunk *tottered* down the hill to the nearest bar.

touchstone   N. stone used to test the fineness of gold alloys; criterion. What *touchstone* can be used to measure the character of a person?

touchy ADJ. sensitive; irascible. Do not mention his bald spot; he's very *touchy* about it.

tout V. publicize; praise excessively. I lost confidence in my broker after he *touted* some junk bonds to me that turned out to be a bad investment.

toxic ADJ. poisonous. We must seek an antidote for whatever *toxic* substance he has eaten. toxicity, N.

tract N. region of land (often imprecisely described); pamphlet. The king granted William Penn a *tract* of land in the New World. Penn then printed a *tract* in which he encouraged settlers to join his colony.

tractable ADJ. docile; easily managed. Although Susan seemed a *tractable* young woman, she had a stubborn streak of independence that occasionally led her to defy the powers-that-be when she felt they were in the wrong.

traduce V. expose to slander. His opponents tried to *traduce* the candidate's reputation by spreading rumors about his past.

trajectory N. path taken by a projectile. The police tried to locate the spot from which the assassin had fired the fatal shot by tracing the *trajectory* of the bullet.

■ **tranquillity** N. calmness; peace. After the commotion and excitement of the city, I appreciate the *tranquillity* of these fields and forests.

transcendent ADJ. surpassing; exceeding ordinary limits; superior. For the amateur chef, dining at the four-star restaurant was a *transcendent* experience: the meal surpassed his wildest dreams.

transcribe V. copy. When you *transcribe* your notes, please send a copy to Mr. Smith and keep the original for our files. transcription, N.

transgression N. violation of a law; sin. Although Widow Douglass was willing to overlook Huck's *transgressions*, Miss Watson refused to forgive and forget.

■ **transient** ADJ. momentary; temporary; staying for a short time. Lexy's joy at finding the perfect Christmas gift for Phil was *transient*; she still had to find presents for the cousins and Uncle Bob. Located near the airport, this hotel caters to a largely *transient* trade. transience, N.

transition N. going from one state of action to another. During the period of *transition* from oil heat to gas heat, the furnace will have to be shut off.

transitory ADJ. impermanent; fleeting. Fame is *transitory*: today's rising star is all too soon tomorrow's washed-up has-been. transitoriness, N.

translucent ADJ. partly transparent. We could not recognize the people in the next room because of the *translucent* curtains that separated us.

transmute V. change; convert to something different. He was unable to *transmute* his dreams into actualities.

transparent ADJ. easily detected; permitting light to pass through freely. John's pride in his son is *transparent*; no one who sees the two of them together can miss it.

transport N. strong emotion. Margo was a creature of extremes, at one moment in *transports* of joy over a vivid sunset, at another moment in *transports* of grief over a dying bird. also V. (secondary meaning)

trappings N. outward decorations; ornaments. He loved the *trappings* of success: the limousines, the stock options, the company jet.

traumatic ADJ. pertaining to an injury caused by violence. In his nightmares, he kept on recalling the *traumatic* experience of being wounded in battle.

travail N. painful physical or mental labor; drudgery; torment. Like every other high school student she knew, Sherry hated the yearlong *travail* of cramming for the SAT. also V.

traverse V. go through or across. When you *traverse* this field, be careful of the bull.

travesty N. harshly distorted imitation; parody; debased likeness. Phillips's translation of *Don Quixote* is so inadequate and clumsy that it seems a *travesty* of the original.

treacly ADJ. sticky sweet; cloyingly sentimental. Irritatingly cheerful, always looking on the bright side, Pollyanna speaks nothing but *treacly* sentimentalities. treacle, N.

treatise N. article treating a subject systematically and thoroughly. He is preparing a *treatise* on the Elizabethan playwrights for his graduate degree.

trek N. travel; journey. The tribe made their *trek* farther north that summer in search of game. also V.

tremor N. trembling; slight quiver. She had a nervous *tremor* in her right hand.

tremulous ADJ. trembling; wavering. She was *tremulous* more from excitement than from fear.

trenchant ADJ. forceful and vigorous; cutting. With his *trenchant* wit, Rich cuts straight to the heart of the matter, panning a truly dreadful play.

● **trepidation** N. fear; nervous apprehension. As she entered the office of the dean of admissions, Sharon felt some *trepidation* about how she would do in her interview.

trespass V. unlawfully enter the boundaries of someone else's property. The wicked baron flogged any poacher who *trespassed* on his private hunting grounds. also N.

tribute N. tax levied by a ruler; mark of respect. The colonists refused to pay *tribute* to a foreign despot.

● **trifling** ADJ. trivial; unimportant. Why bother going to see a doctor for such a *trifling*, everyday cold?

trigger V. set off. John is touchy today; say one word wrong and you'll *trigger* an explosion.

■ **trite** ADJ. hackneyed; commonplace. The *trite* and predictable situations in many television programs turn off many viewers, who, in turn, turn off their sets.

trivial ADJ. unimportant; trifling. Too many magazines ignore newsworthy subjects and feature *trivial* affairs. trivia, N.

trough N. container for feeding farm animals; lowest point (of a wave, business cycle, etc.) The hungry pigs struggled to get at the fresh swill in the *trough*. The surfer rode her board, coasting along in the *trough* between two waves.

truculence N. aggressiveness; ferocity. Tynan's reviews were noted for their caustic attacks and general tone of *truculence*. truculent, ADJ.

truism N. self-evident truth. Many a *truism* is summed up in a proverb; for example, "Marry in haste, repent at leisure."

● **truncate** V. cut the top off. The top of a cone that has been *truncated* in a plane parallel to its base is a circle.

tumult N. commotion; riot; noise. She could not make herself heard over the *tumult* of the mob.

turbid ADJ. muddy; having the sediment disturbed. The water was *turbid* after the children had waded through it.

■ **turbulence** N. state of violent agitation. Warned of approaching *turbulence* in the atmosphere, the pilot told the passengers to fasten their seat belts.

turgid ADJ. swollen; distended. The *turgid* river threatened to overflow the levees and flood the countryside.

■ **turmoil** N. great commotion and confusion. Lydia running off with a soldier! Mother fainting at the news! The Bennet household was in *turmoil*.

turncoat N. traitor. The British considered Benedict Arnold a loyalist; the Americans considered him a *turncoat*.

turpitude N. depravity. A visitor may be denied admittance to this country if she has been guilty of moral *turpitude*.

tutelage N. guardianship; training. Under the *tutelage* of such masters of the instrument, she made rapid progress as a virtuoso.

tycoon N. wealthy leader. John D. Rockefeller was a prominent *tycoon*.

typhoon N. tropical hurricane or cyclone. If you liked *Twister*, you'll love *Typhoon*!

tyranny N. oppression; cruel government. Frederick Douglass fought against the *tyranny* of slavery throughout his life.

tyro N. beginner; novice. For a mere *tyro*, you have produced some wonderfully expert results.

ubiquitous ADJ. being everywhere; omnipresent. That Christmas "The Little Drummer Boy" seemed *ubiquitous*; David heard the tune everywhere.

Word List 48   ulterior–vehement

ulterior ADJ. unstated; hidden; more remote. Suspicious of altruistic gestures, he looked for an *ulterior* motive behind every charitable deed.

ultimate ADJ. final; not susceptible to further analysis. Scientists are searching for *ultimate* truths.

unaccountable ADJ. inexplicable; unreasonable or mysterious. I have taken an *unaccountable* dislike to my doctor: "I do not love thee, Doctor Fell. The reason why, I cannot tell."

unanimity N. complete agreement. We were surprised by the *unanimity* with which members of both parties accepted our proposals. unanimous, ADJ.

unassailable ADJ. not subject to question; not open to attack. Penelope's virtue was *unassailable*; while she waited for her husband to come back from the war, no other man had a chance.

unassuming ADJ. modest. He is so *unassuming* that some people fail to realize how great a man he really is.

unbridled ADJ. violent. She had a sudden fit of *unbridled* rage.

uncanny ADJ. strange; mysterious. You have the *uncanny* knack of reading my innermost thoughts.

unconscionable ADJ. unscrupulous; excessive. She found the loan shark's demands *unconscionable* and impossible to meet.

uncouth ADJ. outlandish; clumsy; boorish. Most biographers portray Lincoln as an *uncouth* and ungainly young man.

unctuous ADJ. oily; bland; insincerely suave. Uriah Heep disguised his nefarious actions by *unctuous* protestations of his "humility."

underlying ADJ. fundamental; lying below. The *underlying* cause of the student riot was not the strict curfew rule but the moldy cafeteria food. Miss Marple seems a sweet little old lady at first, but there's an iron will *underlying* that soft and fluffy facade.

■ **undermine** V. weaken; sap. The recent corruption scandals have *undermined* many people's faith in the city government. The recent torrential rains have washed away much of the cliffside; the deluge threatens to *undermine* the pillars supporting several houses at the edge of the cliff.

underscore V. emphasize. Addressing the jogging class, Kim *underscored* the importance to runners of good nutrition.

undulating ADJ. moving with a wavelike motion. The Hilo Hula Festival was an *undulating* sea of grass skirts.

unearth V. dig up. When they *unearthed* the city, the archeologists found many relics of an ancient civilization.

unequivocal ADJ. plain; obvious; unmistakable. My answer to your proposal is an *unequivocal* and absolute "No."

unerringly ADJ. infallibly. My teacher *unerringly* pounced on the one typographical error in my essay.

unfathomable ADJ. incomprehensible; impenetrable. Unable to get to the bottom of the mystery, Watson declared it was *unfathomable*.

unfetter V. liberate; free from chains. Chained to the wall for months on end, the hostage despaired that he would ever be *unfettered*.

ungainly ADJ. awkward; clumsy; unwieldy. "If you want to know whether Nick's an *ungainly* dancer, check out my bruised feet," said Nora. Anyone who has ever tried to carry a bass fiddle knows it's an *ungainly* instrument.

■ **uniformity** N. sameness; monotony. At *Persons* magazine, we strive for *uniformity* of style; as a result, all our writers wind up sounding exactly alike.

unimpeachable ADJ. blameless and exemplary. Her conduct in office was *unimpeachable* and her record is spotless.

uninhibited ADJ. unrepressed. The congregation was shocked by her *uninhibited* laughter during the sermon.

unintimidating ADJ. unfrightening. Though Phil had expected to feel overawed when he met Steve Young, he found the famous quarterback friendly and *unintimidating*.

unique ADJ. without an equal; single in kind. You have the *unique* distinction of being the only student whom I have had to fail in this course.

universal ADJ. characterizing or affecting all; present everywhere. At first, no one shared Christopher's opinions; his theory that the world was round was met with *universal* disdain.

● **unkempt** ADJ. disheveled; uncared for in appearance. Jeremy hated his neighbor's *unkempt* lawn: he thought its neglected appearance had a detrimental effect on neighborhood property values.

unmitigated ADJ. unrelieved or immoderate; absolute. After four days of *unmitigated* heat, I was ready to collapse from heat prostration. The congresswoman's husband was an *unmitigated* jerk: not only did he abandon her, he took her campaign funds, too!

unobtrusive ADJ. inconspicuous; not blatant. Reluctant to attract notice, the governess took a chair in a far corner of the room and tried to be as *unobtrusive* as possible.

unpalatable ADJ. distasteful; disagreeable. "I refuse to swallow your conclusion," said she, finding his logic *unpalatable*.

● **unprecedented** ADJ. novel; unparalleled. For a first novel, Margaret Mitchell's novel *Gone with the Wind* was an *unprecedented* success.

unprepossessing ADJ. unattractive. During adolescence many attractive young people somehow acquire the false notion that their appearance is *unprepossessing*.

unravel V. disentangle; solve. With equal ease Miss Marple *unraveled* tangled balls of yarn and baffling murder mysteries.

unrequited ADJ. not reciprocated. Suffering the pangs of *unrequited* love, Olivia rebukes Cesario for his hardheartedness.

unruly ADJ. disobedient; lawless. The only way to curb this *unruly* mob is to use tear gas.

unscathed ADJ. unharmed. They prayed he would come back from the war *unscathed*.

unseemly ADJ. unbecoming; indecent; in poor taste. When he put whoopie cushions on all the seats in the funeral parlor, his conduct was most *unseemly*.

unsightly ADJ. ugly. Although James was an experienced emergency room nurse, he occasionally became queasy when faced with a particularly *unsightly* injury.

unstinting ADJ. giving generously; not holding back. The dean praised the donor of the new science building for her *unstinting* generosity.

untenable ADJ. indefensible; not able to be maintained. Wayne is so contrary that, the more *untenable* a position is, the harder he'll try to defend it.

■ **unwarranted** ADJ. unjustified; groundless; undeserved. Your assumption that I would accept your proposal is *unwarranted*, sir; I do not want to marry you at all. We could not understand Martin's *unwarranted* rudeness to his mother's guests.

unwieldy ADJ. awkward; cumbersome; unmanageable. The large carton was so *unwieldy* that the movers had trouble getting it up the stairs.

unwitting ADJ. unintentional; not knowing. She was the *unwitting* tool of the swindlers.

upbraid V. severely scold; reprimand. Not only did Miss Minchin *upbraid* Ermengarde for her disobedience, but she hung her up by her braids from a coat rack in the classroom.

uproarious ADJ. marked by commotion; extremely funny; very noisy. The *uproarious* comedy hit *Ace Ventura: Pet Detective* starred Jim Carrey, whose comic mugging provoked gales of *uproarious* laughter from audiences coast to coast.

upshot N. outcome. The *upshot* of the rematch was that the former champion proved that he still possessed all the skills of his youth.

urbane ADJ. suave; refined; elegant. The courtier was *urbane* and sophisticated. urbanity, N.

■ **usurp** V. seize another's power or rank. The revolution ended when the victorious rebel general succeeded in his attempt to *usurp* the throne.

utopia N. ideal place, state, or society. Fed up with this imperfect universe, Don would have liked to run off to Shangri-la or some other imaginary *utopia*. utopian, ADJ.

■ **vacillate** V. waver; fluctuate. Uncertain which suitor she ought to marry, the princess *vacillated*, saying now one, now the other. The big boss likes his people to be decisive: when he asks you for your opinion, whatever you do, don't *vacillate*. vacillation, N.

vacuous ADJ. empty; inane. The *vacuous* remarks of the politician annoyed the audience, who had hoped to hear more than empty platitudes.

vagabond N. wanderer; tramp. In summer, college students wander the roads of Europe like carefree *vagabonds*. also ADJ.

vagrant N. a homeless wanderer. Because he was a stranger in town with no visible means of support, Martin feared he would be jailed as a *vagrant*. vagrancy, N.

valedictory ADJ. pertaining to farewell. I found the *valedictory* address too long; leave-taking should be brief.

valid ADJ. logically convincing; sound; legally acceptable. You're going to have to come up with a better argument if you want to convince me that your reasoning is *valid*.

validate V. confirm; ratify. I will not publish my findings until I *validate* my results.

valor N. bravery. He received the Medal of Honor for his *valor* in battle.

vanguard N. advance guard of a military force; forefront of a movement. When no enemy was in sight, the Duke of Plaza Toro marched in the *vanguard* of his troops, but once the bullets flew above, he headed for the rear.

vantage N. position giving an advantage. They fired upon the enemy from behind trees, walls and any other point of *vantage* they could find.

vapid ADJ. dull and unimaginative; insipid and flavorless. "*Bor*-ing!" said Jessica, as she suffered through yet another *vapid* lecture about Dead White Male Poets.

● **vaporize** V. turn into vapor (steam, gas, fog, etc.). "Zap!" went Super Mario's atomic ray gun as he *vaporized* another deadly foe.

variegated ADJ. many-colored. Without her glasses, Gretchen saw the fields of tulips as a *variegated* blur.

veer V. change in direction. After what seemed an eternity, the wind *veered* to the east and the storm abated.

vehement ADJ. forceful; intensely emotional; with marked vigor. Alfred became so *vehement* in describing what was wrong with the Internal Revenue Service that he began jumping up and down and frothing at the mouth. vehemence, N.

Word List 49   velocity–vogue

velocity N. speed. The train went by at considerable *velocity*.

venal ADJ. capable of being bribed. The *venal* policeman cheerfully accepted the bribe offered him by the speeding motorist whom he had stopped.

vendetta N. blood feud. Hoping to stop the street warfare disrupting his city, the Duke ordered the Capulet and Montague families to end their bitter *vendetta*.

veneer N. thin layer; cover. Casual acquaintances were deceived by his *veneer* of sophistication and failed to recognize his fundamental shallowness.

venerable ADJ. deserving high respect. We do not mean to be disrespectful when we refuse to follow the advice of our *venerable* leader.

■ **venerate** V. revere. In Tibet today, the common people still *venerate* their traditional spiritual leader, the Dalai Lama.

venial ADJ. forgivable; trivial. When Jean Valjean stole a loaf of bread to feed his starving sister, he committed a *venial* offense.

venom N. poison; hatred. Bitten by a rattlesnake on his ankle, the cowboy contortionist curled up like a pretzel and sucked the *venom* out of the wound.

vent N. a small opening; outlet. The wine did not flow because the air *vent* in the barrel was clogged.

vent V. express; utter. The angry teacher *vented* his wrath on his class.

ventriloquist N. someone who can make his or her voice seem to come from another person or thing. In the classic movie *Dead of Night*, the *ventriloquist* is possessed by his wooden dummy, which torments its master, driving him to madness and murder.

venturesome ADJ. bold. A group of *venturesome* women were the first to scale Mt. Annapurna.

veracity N. truthfulness. Asserting his *veracity*, young George Washington proclaimed, "Father, I cannot tell a lie!"

verbalize V. put into words. I know you don't like to talk about these things, but please try to *verbalize* your feelings.

verbatim ADV. word for word. Blessed with a retentive memory, he could repeat lengthy messages *verbatim*. also ADJ.

verbiage N. pompous array of words. After we had waded through all the *verbiage,* we discovered that the writer had said very little.

■ **verbose** ADJ. wordy. Someone mute can't talk; someone *verbose* can hardly stop talking.

verge N. border; edge. Madame Curie knew she was on the *verge* of discovering the secrets of radioactive elements. also V.

verisimilitude N. appearance of truth; likelihood. Critics praised her for the *verisimilitude* of her performance as Lady Macbeth. She was completely believable.

verity N. quality of being true; lasting truth or principle. Did you question the *verity* of Kato Kaelin's testimony about what he heard the night Nicole Brown Simpson was slain? To the skeptic, everything was relative: there were no eternal *verities* in which one could believe.

vernacular N. living language; natural style. Cut out those old-fashioned thee's and thou's and write in the *vernacular*. also ADJ.

versatile ADJ. having many talents; capable of working in many fields. She was a *versatile* athlete, earning varsity letters in basketball, hockey, and track.

vertex N. summit. Let us drop a perpendicular line from the *vertex* of the triangle to the base.

vertigo N. severe dizziness. When you test potential airplane pilots for susceptibility to spells of *vertigo*, be sure to hand out air-sickness bags.

verve N. energy in expressing ideas, especially artistically; liveliness. In his rhymes, Seuss writes with such *verve* and good humor that adults as well as children delight in the adventures of *The Cat in the Hat*.

vestige N. trace; remains. We discovered *vestiges* of early Indian life in the cave. vestigial, ADJ.

vex N. annoy; distress. Please try not to *vex* your mother; she is doing the best she can.

● **viable** ADJ. practical or workable; capable of maintaining life. That idea won't work. Let me see whether I can come up with a *viable* alternative.

vicarious ADJ. acting as a substitute; done by a deputy. Though Violet was too meek to talk back to anybody, she got a *vicarious* kick out of Rita's sharp retorts.

vicissitude N. change of fortune. Humbled by life's *vicissitudes*, the last emperor of China worked as a lowly gardener in the palace over which he had once ruled.

vie V. contend; compete. Politicians *vie* with one another, competing for donations and votes.

vigilance N. watchfulness. Eternal *vigilance* is the price of liberty.

vignette N. picture; short literary sketch. The *New Yorker* published her latest *vignette*.

■ **vigor** N. active strength. Although he was over seventy years old, Jack had the *vigor* of a man in his prime. vigorous, ADJ.

■ **vilify** V. slander. Waging a highly negative campaign, the candidate attempted to *vilify* his opponent's reputation. vilification, N.

■ **vindicate** V. clear from blame; exonerate; justify or support. The lawyer's goal was to *vindicate* her client and prove him innocent on all charges. The critics' extremely favorable reviews *vindicate* my opinion that *The Madness of King George* is a brilliant movie.

vindictive ADJ. out for revenge; malicious. I think it's unworthy of Martha to be so *vindictive*; she shouldn't stoop to such petty acts of revenge.

viper N. poisonous snake. The habitat of the horned *viper,* a particularly venomous snake, is in sandy regions like the Sahara or the Sinai peninsula.

virile ADJ. manly. I do not accept the premise that a man proves he's *virile* by being belligerent.

virtual ADJ. in essence; for practical purposes. She is a *virtual* financial wizard when it comes to money matters.

virtue N. goodness, moral excellence; good quality. *Virtue* carried to extremes can turn into vice: humility, for example, can degenerate into servility and spinelessness.

■ **virtuoso** N. highly skilled artist. The promising young cellist Yo-Yo Ma grew into a *virtuoso* whose performances thrilled audiences throughout the world. virtuosity, N.

● **virulent** ADJ. extremely poisonous; hostile; bitter. Laid up with a *virulent* case of measles, Vera blamed her doctors because her recovery took so long. In fact, she became quite *virulent* on the subject of the quality of modern medical care.

virus N. disease communicator. The doctors are looking for a specific medicine to control this *virus*.

visceral ADJ. felt in one's inner organs. She disliked the *visceral* sensations she had whenever she rode the roller coaster.

viscous ADJ. sticky; gluey. Melted tar is a *viscous* substance. viscosity, N.

visionary ADJ. produced by imagination; fanciful; mystical. She was given to *visionary* schemes that never materialized. also N.

vital ADJ. vibrant and lively; critical; living, breathing. The *vital,* highly energetic first aid instructor stressed that it was *vital* in examining accident victims to note their *vital* signs.

vitriolic ADJ. corrosive; sarcastic. Oil of *vitriol,* or sulfuric acid, leaves scars on the flesh; *vitriolic* criticism leaves scars on the soul.

vituperative ADJ. abusive; scolding. He became more *vituperative* as he realized that we were not going to grant him his wish.

vivacious ADJ. animated; lively. She had always been *vivacious* and sparkling.

vociferous ADJ. clamorous; noisy. The crowd grew *vociferous* in its anger and threatened to take the law into its own hands.

vogue N. popular fashion. Jeans are the *vogue* on college campuses.

Word List 50   volatile–zephyr

■ **volatile** ADJ. changeable; explosive; evaporating rapidly. The political climate today is extremely *volatile*: no one can predict what the electorate will do next. Maria Callas's temper was extremely *volatile*: the only thing you could predict was that she was sure to blow up. Acetone is an extremely *volatile* liquid: it evaporates instantly.

volition N. act of making a conscious choice. She selected this dress of her own *volition*.

● **voluble** ADJ. fluent; glib; talkative. The excessively *voluble* speaker suffers from logorrhea: he runs off at the mouth a lot!

voluminous ADJ. bulky; large. A caftan is a *voluminous* garment; most people wearing one look as if they're draped in a small tent.

voluptuous ADJ. suggesting sensual delights; sensuously pleasing. Renoir's paintings of nude women accent his subjects' rosy-tinted flesh and full, *voluptuous* figures.

voracious ADJ. ravenous. The wolf is a *voracious* animal, its hunger never satisfied.

vortex N. whirlwind; whirlpool; center of turbulence; predicament into which one is inexorably plunged. Sucked into the *vortex* of the tornado, Dorothy and Toto were carried from Kansas to Oz.

vouchsafe V. grant; choose to give in reply; permit. Occasionally the rock star would drift out onto the balcony and *vouchsafe* the crowd below a glimpse of her celebrated features. The professor *vouchsafed* not a word to the students' questions about what would be covered on the test.

voyeur N. Peeping Tom. Nancy called her brother a *voyeur* when she caught him aiming his binoculars at an upstairs window of the house of the newlyweds next door.

vulnerable ADJ. susceptible to wounds. His opponents could not harm Achilles, who was *vulnerable* only in his heel.

waffle V. speak equivocally about an issue. When asked directly about the governor's involvement in the savings and loan scandal, the press secretary *waffled*, talking all around the issue.

waft V. moved gently by wind or waves. Daydreaming, he gazed at the leaves that *wafted* past his window.

waggish ADJ. mischievous; humorous; tricky. He was a prankster who, unfortunately, often overlooked the damage he could cause with his *waggish* tricks. wag, N.

waif N. homeless child or animal. Although he already had eight cats, he could not resist adopting yet another feline *waif.*

waive V. give up a claim or right voluntarily; refrain from enforcing; postpone considering. Although, technically, prospective students had to live in Piedmont to attend high school there, occasionally the school *waived* the residence requirement in order to enroll promising athletes.

wake N. trail of ship or other object through water; path of something that has gone before. The *wake* of the swan gliding through the water glistened in the moonlight. Reporters and photographers converged on South Carolina in the *wake* of the hurricane that devastated much of the eastern seaboard.

wallow V. roll in; indulge in; become helpless. The hippopotamus loves to *wallow* in the mud.

wan ADJ. having a pale or sickly color; pallid. The convalescent looked frail and *wan*, her skin almost as white as the sheets on her sickbed.

wane V. decrease in size or strength; draw gradually to an end. The verb *wax*, which means to grow in size, is an antonym for *wane*. As it burns, does a wax candle *wane*?

wanton ADJ. unrestrained; willfully malicious; unchaste. Pointing to the stack of bills, Sheldon criticized Sarah for her *wanton* expenditures. In response, Sarah accused Sheldon of making an unfounded, *wanton* attack.

warble V. sing; babble. Every morning the birds *warbled* outside her window. also N.

warrant V. justify; authorize. Before the judge issues the injunction, you must convince her this action is *warranted.*

warranty N. guarantee; assurance by seller. The purchaser of this automobile is protected by the manufacturer's *warranty* that the company will replace any defective part for five years or 50,000 miles.

wary ADJ. very cautious. The spies grew *wary* as they approached the sentry.

wastrel N. profligate. His neighbors denounced him as a *wastrel* who had dissipated his inheritance.

watershed N. crucial dividing point. The invention of the personal computer proved a historic *watershed,* for it opened the way to today's Information Age.

wax V. increase; grow. With proper handling, his fortunes *waxed* and he became rich.

waylay V. ambush; lie in wait. They agreed to *waylay* their victim as he passed through the dark alley going home.

wean V. accustom a baby to not nurse; give up a cherished activity. He decided he would *wean* himself away from eating junk food and stick to fruits and vegetables.

weather V. endure the effects of weather or other forces. Reporters wondered whether Governor Gray Davis would *weather* his latest political challenge and remain in office, or whether he would be California's first governor to be recalled.

welter N. turmoil; bewildering jumble. The existing *welter* of overlapping federal and state programs cries out for immediate reform.

wheedle V. cajole; coax; deceive by flattery. She knows she can *wheedle* almost anything she wants from her father.

whet V. sharpen; stimulate. The odors from the kitchen are *whetting* my appetite; I will be ravenous by the time the meal is served.

whiff N. puff or gust (of air, scent, etc.); hint. The slightest *whiff* of Old Spice cologne brought memories of George to her mind.

■ **whimsical** ADJ. capricious; fanciful. In *Mrs. Doubtfire*, the hero is a playful, *whimsical* man who takes a notion to dress up as a woman so that he can look after his children, who are in the custody of his ex-wife. whimsy, N.

willful ADJ. intentional; headstrong. Donald had planned to kill his wife for months; clearly, her death was a case of deliberate, *willful* murder, not a crime of passion committed by a hasty, *willful* youth unable to foresee the consequences of his deeds.

wily ADJ. cunning; artful. If coyotes are supposed to be such sneaky, *wily* creatures, how does Road Runner always manage to outwit Wile E. Coyote?

wince V. shrink back; flinch. The screech of the chalk on the blackboard made her *wince.*

windfall N. unexpected lucky event. This huge tax refund is quite a *windfall.*

winnow V. sift; separate good parts from bad. This test will *winnow* out the students who study from those who don't bother.

winsome ADJ. agreeable; gracious; engaging. By her *winsome* manner, she made herself liked by everyone who met her.

wispy ADJ. thin; slight; barely discernible. Worried about preserving his few *wispy* tufts of hair, Walter carefully massaged his scalp and applied hair restorer every night.

wistful ADJ. vaguely longing; sadly thoughtful. With a last *wistful* glance at the happy couples dancing in the hall, Sue headed back to her room to study for her exam.

withdrawn ADJ. introverted; remote. Rebuffed by his colleagues, the initially outgoing young researcher became increasingly *withdrawn.*

wither V. shrivel; decay. Cut flowers are beautiful for a day, but all too soon they *wither.*

withhold V. refuse to give; hold back. The tenants decided to *withhold* a portion of the rent until the landlord kept his promise to renovate the building.

withstand V. stand up against; successfully resist. If you can *withstand* all the peer pressure in high school to cut classes and goof off, you should survive college just fine.

witless ADJ. foolish; idiotic. If Beavis is a half-wit, then Butthead is totally *witless.*

● **witticism** N. witty saying; wisecrack. I don't mean any criticism, but that last *witticism* totally hurt my feelings.

wizardry N. sorcery; magic. Merlin the Magician amazed the knights with his *wizardry.*

woe N. deep, inconsolable grief; affliction; suffering. Pale and wan with grief, Wanda was bowed down beneath the burden of her *woes.*

worldly ADJ. engrossed in matters of this earth; not spiritual. You must leave your *worldly* goods behind you when you go to meet your Maker.

wrath N. anger; fury. She turned to him, full of *wrath,* and said, "What makes you think I'll accept lower pay for this job than you get?"

wrench V. pull; strain; twist. She *wrenched* free of her attacker and landed a powerful kick to his kneecap.

writhe V. twist in coils; contort in pain. In *Dances with Snakes*, the snake dancer wriggled sinuously as her boa constrictor *writhed* around her torso.

wry ADJ. twisted; with a humorous twist. We enjoy Dorothy Parker's verse for its *wry* wit.

xenophobia N. fear or hatred of foreigners. *Xenophobia* is directed against foreign people, not necessarily against foreign products: even *xenophobes* patronize Chinese restaurants and buy Japanese TVs.

yen N. longing; urge. She had a *yen* to get away and live on her own for a while.

yield V. give in; surrender. The wounded knight refused to *yield* to his foe.

yield N. amount produced; crop; income on investment. An experienced farmer can estimate the annual *yield* of his acres with surprising accuracy. also V.

yoke V. join together, unite. I don't wish to be *yoked* to him in marriage, as if we were cattle pulling a plow. also N.

yore N. time past. He dreamed of the elegant homes of *yore,* but gave no thought to their inelegant plumbing.

zany ADJ. crazy; comic. I can watch the Marx brothers' *zany* antics for hours.

zeal N. eager enthusiasm. Katya's *zeal* was contagious; soon all her fellow students were busily making posters, inspired by her ardent enthusiasm for the cause. zealous, ADJ.

■ **zealot** N. fanatic; person who shows excessive zeal. Though Glenn was devout, he was no *zealot*; he never tried to force his beliefs on his friends.

zenith N. point directly overhead in the sky; summit. When the sun was at its *zenith,* the glare was not as strong as at sunrise and sunset.

zephyr N. gentle breeze; west wind. When these *zephyrs* blow, it is good to be in an open boat under a full sail.

Basic Word Parts

In addition to reviewing the SAT High-Frequency Word List, what other quick vocabulary-building tactics can you follow when you face an SAT deadline?

One good approach is to learn how to build up (and tear apart) words. You know that words are made up of other words: the *room* in which you *store* things is the *storeroom;* the person whose job is to *keep* the *books* is the *bookkeeper.*

Just as words are made up of other words, words are also made up of word parts: prefixes, suffixes, and roots. If you know your basic word parts, you can figure out the meanings of thousands of unfamiliar words.

POWER UP YOUR PERFORMANCE!

Don't let big words throw you. Build your vocabulary with prefixes, suffixes, and roots.

Learn 30 key word parts and unlock 10,000 words.

Learn 50 key word parts and unlock 100,000 words!

COMMON PREFIXES

Prefixes are syllables that precede the root or stem of a word and change or refine its meaning.

Prefix	Meaning	Illustration
ab, abs	from, away from	*abduct* lead away, kidnap *abjure* renounce *abject* degraded, cast down
ad, ac, af, ag, an, ap, ar, as, at	to, forward	*adit* entrance *adjure* request earnestly *admit* allow entrance *accord* agreement, harmony *affliction* distress *aggregation* collection *annexation* add to *apparition* ghost *arraignment* indictment *assumption* arrogance, the taking for granted *attendance* presence, the persons present
ambi	both	*ambidextrous* skilled with both hands *ambiguous* of double meaning *ambivalent* having two conflicting emotions
an, a	without	*anarchy* lack of government *anemia* lack of blood *amoral* without moral sense

Prefix	Meaning	Illustration
ante	before	*antecedent* preceding event or word *antediluvian* ancient (before the flood) *ante-nuptial* before the wedding
anti	against, opposite	*antipathy* hatred *antiseptic* against infection *antithetical* exactly opposite
arch	chief, first	*archetype* original *archbishop* chief bishop *archeology* study of first or ancient times
be	over, thoroughly	*bedaub* smear over *befuddle* confuse thoroughly *beguile* deceive, charm thoroughly
bi	two	*bicameral* composed of two houses (Congress) *biennial* every two years *bicycle* two-wheeled vehicle
cata	down	*catastrophe* disaster *cataract* waterfall *catapult* hurl (throw down)
circum	around	*circumnavigate* sail around (the globe) *circumspect* cautious (looking around) *circumscribe* limit (place a circle around)
com, co, col, con, cor	with, together	*combine* merge with *commerce* trade with *communicate* correspond with *coeditor* joint editor *collateral* subordinate, connected *conference* meeting *corroborate* confirm
contra, contro	against	*contravene* conflict with *controversy* dispute
de	down, away	*debase* lower in value *decadence* deterioration *decant* pour off
demi	partly, half	*demigod* partly divine being
di	two	*dichotomy* division into two parts *dilemma* choice between two bad alternatives
dia	across	*diagonal* across a figure *diameter* distance across a circle *diagram* outline drawing
dis, dif	not, apart	*discord* lack of harmony *differ* disagree (carry apart) *disparity* condition of inequality; difference

Prefix	Meaning	Illustration
dys	faulty, bad	*dyslexia* faulty ability to read *dyspepsia* indigestion
ex, e	out	*expel* drive out *extirpate* root out *eject* throw out
extra, extro	beyond, outside	*extracurricular* beyond the curriculum *extraterritorial* beyond a nation's bounds *extrovert* person interested chiefly in external objects and actions
hyper	above; excessively	*hyperbole* exaggeration *hyperventilate* breathe at an excessive rate
hypo	beneath; lower	*hypoglycemia* low blood sugar
in, il, im, ir	not	*inefficient* not efficient *inarticulate* not clear or distinct *illegible* not readable *impeccable* not capable of sinning; flawless *irrevocable* not able to be called back
in, il, im, ir	in, on, upon	*invite* call in *illustration* something that makes clear *impression* effect upon mind or feelings *irradiate* shine upon
inter	between, among	*intervene* come between *international* between nations *interjection* a statement thrown in
intra, intro	within	*intramural* within a school *introvert* person who turns within himself
macro	large, long	*macrobiotic* tending to prolong life *macrocosm* the great world (the entire universe)
mega	great, million	*megalomania* delusions of grandeur *megaton* explosive force of a million tons of TNT
meta	involving change	*metamorphosis* change of form
micro	small	*microcosm* miniature universe *microbe* minute organism *microscopic* extremely small
mis	bad, improper	*misdemeanor* minor crime; bad conduct *mischance* unfortunate accident *misnomer* wrong name
mis	hatred	*misanthrope* person who hates mankind *misogynist* woman-hater

Prefix	Meaning	Illustration
mono	one	*monarchy* government by one ruler *monotheism* belief in one god
multi	many	*multifarious* having many parts *multitudinous* numerous
neo	new	*neologism* newly coined word *neophyte* beginner; novice
non	not	*noncommittal* undecided *nonentity* person of no importance
ob, oc, of, op	against	*obloquy* infamy; disgrace *obtrude* push into prominence *occlude* close; block out *offend* insult *opponent* someone who struggles against; foe
olig	few	*oligarchy* government by a few
pan	all, every	*panacea* cure-all *panorama* unobstructed view in all directions
para	beyond, related	*parallel* similar *paraphrase* restate; translate
per	through, completely	*permeable* allowing passage through *pervade* spread throughout
peri	around, near	*perimeter* outer boundary *periphery* edge *periphrastic* stated in a roundabout way
poly	many	*polygamist* person with several spouses *polyglot* speaking several languages
post	after	*postpone* delay *posterity* generations that follow *posthumous* after death
pre	before	*preamble* introductory statement *prefix* word part placed before a root/stem *premonition* forewarning
prim	first	*primordial* existing at the dawn of time *primogeniture* state of being the first born
pro	forward, in favor of	*propulsive* driving forward *proponent* supporter
proto	first	*prototype* first of its kind
pseudo	false	*pseudonym* pen name

Prefix	Meaning	Illustration
re	again, back	*reiterate* repeat *reimburse* pay back
retro	backward	*retrospect* looking back *retroactive* effective as of a past date
se	away, aside	*secede* withdraw *seclude* shut away *seduce* lead astray
semi	half, partly	*semiannual* every six months *semiconscious* partly conscious
sub, suc, suf, sug, **sup, sus**	under, less	*subway* underground road *subjugate* bring under control *succumb* yield; cease to resist *suffuse* spread through *suggest* hint *suppress* put down by force *suspend* delay
super, sur	over, above	*supernatural* above natural things *supervise* oversee *surtax* additional tax
syn, sym, syl, sys	with, together	*synchronize* time together *synthesize* combine together *sympathize* pity; identify with *syllogism* explanation of how ideas relate *system* network
tele	far	*telemetry* measurement from a distance *telegraphic* communicated over a distance
trans	across	*transport* carry across *transpose* reverse, move across
ultra	beyond, excessive	*ultramodern* excessively modern *ultracritical* exceedingly critical
un	not	*unfeigned* not pretended; real *unkempt* not combed; disheveled *unwitting* not knowing; unintentional
under	below	*undergird* strengthen underneath *underling* someone inferior
uni	one	*unison* oneness of pitch; complete accord *unicycle* one-wheeled vehicle
vice	in place of	*vicarious* acting as a substitute *viceroy* governor acting in place of a king
with	away, against	*withhold* hold back; keep *withstand* stand up against; resist

COMMON ROOTS AND STEMS

Roots are basic word elements that have been carried over into English. *Stems* are variations of roots brought about by changes in declension or conjugation.

Root or Stem	Meaning	Illustration
ac, acr	sharp	*acrimonious* bitter; caustic *acerbity* bitterness of temper *acidulate* to make somewhat acid or sour
aev, ev	age, era	*primeval* of the first age *coeval* of the same age or era *medieval* or *mediaeval* of the middle ages
ag, act	do	*act* deed *agent* doer
agog	leader	*demagogue* false leader of people *pedagogue* teacher (leader of children)
agri, agrari	field	*agrarian* one who works in the field *agriculture* cultivation of fields *peregrination* wandering (through fields)
ali	another	*alias* assumed (another) name *alienate* estrange (turn away from another)
alt	high	*altitude* height *altimeter* instrument for measuring height
alter	other	*altruistic* unselfish, considering others *alter ego* a second self
am	love	*amorous* loving, especially sexually *amity* friendship *amicable* friendly
anim	mind, soul	*animadvert* cast criticism upon *unanimous* of one mind *magnanimity* greatness of mind or spirit
ann, enn	year	*annuity* yearly remittance *biennial* every two years *perennial* present all year; persisting for several years
anthrop	man	*anthropology* study of man *misanthrope* hater of mankind *philanthropy* love of mankind; charity
apt	fit	*aptitude* skill *adapt* make suitable or fit

Root or Stem	Meaning	Illustration
aqua	water	*aqueduct* passageway for conducting water *aquatic* living in water *aqua fortis* nitric acid (strong water)
arch	ruler, first	*archaeology* study of antiquities (study of first things) *monarch* sole ruler *anarchy* lack of government
aster	star	*astronomy* study of the stars *asterisk* star-like type character (*) *disaster* catastrophe (contrary star)
aud, audit	hear	*audible* able to be heard *auditorium* place where people may be heard *audience* hearers
auto	self	*autocracy* rule by one person (self) *automobile* vehicle that moves by itself *autobiography* story of one's own life
belli	war	*bellicose* inclined to fight *belligerent* inclined to wage war *rebellious* resisting authority
ben, bon	good	*benefactor* one who does good deeds *benevolence* charity (wishing good) *bonus* something extra above regular pay
biblio	book	*bibliography* list of books *bibliophile* lover of books *Bible* The Book
bio	life	*biography* writing about a person's life *biology* study of living things *biochemist* student of the chemistry of living things
breve	short	*brevity* briefness *abbreviate* shorten *breviloquent* marked by brevity of speech
cad, cas	to fall	*decadent* deteriorating *cadence* intonation, musical movement *cascade* waterfall
cap, capt, cept, cip	to take	*capture* seize *participate* take part *precept* wise saying (originally a command)
capit, capt	head	*decapitate* remove (cut off) someone's head *captain* chief
carn	flesh	*carnivorous* flesh-eating *carnage* destruction of life *carnal* fleshly

Root or Stem	Meaning	Illustration
ced, cess	to yield, to go	*recede* go back, withdraw *antecedent* that which goes before *process* go forward
celer	swift	*celerity* swiftness *decelerate* reduce swiftness *accelerate* increase swiftness
cent	one hundred	*century* one hundred years *centennial* hundredth anniversary *centipede* many-footed, wingless animal
chron	time	*chronology* timetable of events *anachronism* a thing out of time sequence *chronicle* register events in order of time
cid, cis	to cut, to kill	*incision* a cut (surgical) *homicide* killing of a man *fratricide* killing of a brother
cit, citat	to call, to start	*incite* stir up, start up *excite* stir up *recitation* a recalling (or repeating) aloud
civi	citizen	*civilization* society of citizens, culture *civilian* member of community *civil* courteous
clam, clamat	to cry out	*clamorous* loud *declamation* speech *acclamation* shouted approval
claud, claus, clos,clud	to close	*claustrophobia* fear of close places *enclose* close in *conclude* finish
cognosc, cognit	to learn	*agnostic* lacking knowledge, skeptical *incognito* traveling under assumed name *cognition* knowledge
compl	to fill	*complete* filled out *complement* that which completes something *comply* fulfill
cord	heart	*accord* agreement (from the heart) *cordial* friendly *discord* lack of harmony
corpor	body	*incorporate* organize into a body *corporeal* pertaining to the body, fleshly *corpse* dead body
cred, credit	to believe	*incredulous* not believing, skeptical *credulity* gullibility *credence* belief

Root or Stem	Meaning	Illustration
cur	to care	*curator* person who has the care of something *sinecure* position without responsibility *secure* safe
curr, curs	to run	*excursion* journey *cursory* brief *precursor* forerunner
da, dat	to give	*data* facts, statistics *mandate* command *date* given time
deb, debit	to owe	*debt* something owed *indebtedness* debt *debenture* bond
dem	people	*democracy* rule of the people *demagogue* (false) leader of the people *epidemic* widespread (among the people)
derm	skin	*epidermis* skin *pachyderm* thick-skinned quadruped *dermatology* study of skin and its disorders
di, diurn	day	*diary* a daily record of activities, feelings, etc. *diurnal* pertaining to daytime
dic, dict	to say	*abdicate* renounce *diction* speech *verdict* statement of jury
doc, doct	to teach	*docile* obedient; easily taught *document* something that provides evidence *doctor* learned person (originally, teacher)
domin	to rule	*dominate* have power over *domain* land under rule *dominant* prevailing
duc, duct	to lead	*viaduct* arched roadway *aqueduct* artificial waterway
dynam	power, strength	*dynamic* powerful *dynamite* powerful explosive *dynamo* engine making electrical power
ego	I	*egoist* person who is self-interested *egotist* selfish person *egocentric* revolving about self
erg, urg	work	*energy* power *ergatocracy* rule of the workers *metallurgy* science and technology of metals

Root or Stem	Meaning	Illustration
err	to wander	*error* mistake *erratic* not reliable, wandering *knight-errant* wandering knight
eu	good, well, beautiful	*eupeptic* having good digestion *eulogize* praise *euphemism* substitution of pleasant way of saying something blunt
fac, fic, fec, fect	to make, to do	*factory* place where things are made *fiction* manufactured story *affect* cause to change
fall, fals	to deceive	*fallacious* misleading *infallible* not prone to error, perfect *falsify* lie
fer, lat	to bring, to bear	*transfer* bring from one place to another *translate* bring from one language to another *conifer* bearing cones, as pine trees
fid	belief, faith	*infidel* nonbeliever, heathen *confidence* assurance, belief
fin	end, limit	*confine* keep within limits *finite* having definite limits
flect, flex	bend	*flexible* able to bend *deflect* bend away, turn aside
fort	luck, chance	*fortuitous* accidental, occurring by chance *fortunate* lucky
fort	strong	*fortitude* strength, firmness of mind *fortification* strengthening *fortress* stronghold
frag, fract	break	*fragile* easily broken *infraction* breaking of a rule *fractious* unruly, tending to break rules
fug	flee	*fugitive* someone who flees *refuge* shelter, home for someone fleeing
fus	pour	*effusive* gushing, pouring out *diffuse* widespread (poured in many directions)
gam	marriage	*monogamy* marriage to one person *bigamy* marriage to two people at the same time *polygamy* having many wives or husbands at the same time
gen, gener	class, race	*genus* group of animals with similar traits *generic* characteristic of a class *gender* class organized by sex

Root or Stem	Meaning	Illustration
grad, gress	go, step	*digress* go astray (from the main point) *regress* go backwards *gradual* step by step, by degrees
graph, gram	writing	*epigram* pithy statement *telegram* instantaneous message over great distance *stenography* shorthand (writing narrowly)
greg	flock, herd	*gregarious* tending to group together as in a herd *aggregate* group, total *egregious* conspicuously bad; shocking
helio	sun	*heliotrope* flower that faces the sun *heliograph* instrument that uses the sun's rays to send signals
it, itiner	journey, road	*exit* way out *itinerary* plan of journey
jac, jact, jec	to throw	*projectile* missile; something thrown forward *trajectory* path taken by thrown object *ejaculatory* casting or throwing out
jur, jurat	to swear	*perjure* testify falsely *jury* group of men and women sworn to seek the truth *adjuration* solemn urging
labor, laborat	to work	*laboratory* place where work is done *collaborate* work together with others *laborious* difficult
leg, lect, lig	to choose, to read	*election* choice *legible* able to be read *eligible* able to be selected
leg	law	*legislature* law-making body *legitimate* lawful *legal* lawful
liber, libr	book	*library* collection of books *libretto* the "book" of a musical play *libel* slander (originally found in a little book)
liber	free	*liberation* the fact of setting free *liberal* generous (giving freely); tolerant
log	word, study	*entomology* study of insects *etymology* study of word parts and derivations *monologue* speech by one person
loqu, locut	to talk	*soliloquy* speech by one individual *loquacious* talkative *elocution* speech

Root or Stem	Meaning	Illustration
luc	light	*elucidate* enlighten *lucid* clear *translucent* allowing some light to pass through
magn	great	*magnify* enlarge *magnanimity* generosity, greatness of soul *magnitude* greatness, extent
mal	bad	*malevolent* wishing evil *malediction* curse *malefactor* evil-doer
man	hand	*manufacture* create (make by hand) *manuscript* written by hand *emancipate* free (let go from the hand)
mar	sea	*maritime* connected with seafaring *submarine* undersea craft *mariner* seaman
mater, matr	mother	*maternal* pertaining to motherhood *matriarch* female ruler of a family, group, or state *matrilineal* descended on the mother's side
mit, miss	to send	*missile* projectile *dismiss* send away *transmit* send across
mob, mot, mov	move	*mobilize* cause to move *motility* ability to move *immovable* not able to be moved
mon, monit	to warn	*admonish* warn *premonition* foreboding *monitor* watcher (warner)
mori, mort	to die	*mortuary* funeral parlor *moribund* dying *immortal* not dying
morph	shape, form	*amorphous* formless, lacking shape *metamorphosis* change of shape *anthropomorphic* in the shape of man
mut	change	*immutable* not able to be changed *mutate* undergo a great change *mutability* changeableness, inconstancy
nat	born	*innate* from birth *prenatal* before birth *nativity* birth
nav	ship	*navigate* sail a ship *circumnavigate* sail around the world *naval* pertaining to ships

Root or Stem	Meaning	Illustration
neg	deny	*negation* denial *renege* deny, go back on one's word *renegade* turncoat, traitor
nomen	name	*nomenclature* act of naming, terminology *nominal* in name only (as opposed to actual) *cognomen* surname, distinguishing nickname
nov	new	*novice* beginner *renovate* make new again *novelty* newness
omni	all	*omniscient* all knowing *omnipotent* all powerful *omnivorous* eating everything
oper	to work	*operate* work *cooperation* working together
pac	peace	*pacify* make peaceful *pacific* peaceful *pacifist* person opposed to war
pass	feel	*dispassionate* free of emotion *impassioned* emotion-filled *impassive* showing no feeling
pater, patr	father	*patriotism* love of one's country (fatherland) *patriarch* male ruler of a family, group, or state *paternity* fatherhood
path	disease, feeling	*pathology* study of diseased tissue *apathetic* lacking feeling; indifferent *antipathy* hostile feeling
ped, pod	foot	*impediment* stumbling-block; hindrance *tripod* three-footed stand *quadruped* four-footed animal
ped	child	*pedagogue* teacher of children *pediatrician* children's doctor
pel, puls	to drive	*compulsion* a forcing to do *repel* drive back *expel* drive out, banish
pet, petit	to seek	*petition* request *appetite* craving, desire *compete* vie with others
phil	love	*philanthropist* benefactor, lover of humanity *Anglophile* lover of everything English *philanderer* one involved in brief love affairs

Root or Stem	Meaning	Illustration
pon, posit	to place	*postpone* place after *positive* definite, unquestioned (definitely placed)
port, portat	to carry	*portable* able to be carried *transport* carry across *export* carry out (of country)
poten	able, powerful	*omnipotent* all-powerful *potentate* powerful person *impotent* powerless
psych	mind	*psychology* study of the mind *psychosis* mental disorder *psychopath* mentally ill person
put, putat	to trim, to calculate	*putative* supposed (calculated) *computation* calculation *amputate* cut off
quer, ques, quir, quis	to ask	*inquiry* investigation *inquisitive* questioning *query* question
reg, rect	rule	*regicide* murder of a ruler *regent* ruler *insurrection* rebellion; overthrow of a ruler
rid, ris	to laugh	*derision* scorn *risibility* inclination to laughter *ridiculous* deserving to be laughed at
rog, rogat	to ask	*interrogate* question *prerogative* privilege
rupt	to break	*interrupt* break into *bankrupt* insolvent *rupture* a break
sacr	holy	*sacred* holy *sacrilegious* impious, violating something holy *sacrament* religious act
sci	to know	*science* knowledge *omniscient* knowing all *conscious* aware
scop	watch, see	*periscope* device for seeing around corners *microscope* device for seeing small objects
scrib, script	to write	*transcribe* make a written copy *script* written text *circumscribe* write around, limit
sect	cut	*dissect* cut apart *bisect* cut into two pieces

Root or Stem	Meaning	Illustration
sed, sess	to sit	*sedentary* inactive (sitting) *session* meeting
sent, sens	to think, to feel	*consent* agree *resent* show indignation *sensitive* showing feeling
sequi, secut, seque	to follow	*consecutive* following in order *sequence* arrangement *sequel* that which follows *non sequitur* something that does not follow logically
solv, solut	to loosen	*absolve* free from blame *dissolute* morally lax *absolute* complete (not loosened)
somn	sleep	*insomnia* inability to sleep *somnolent* sleepy *somnambulist* sleepwalker
soph	wisdom	*philosopher* lover of wisdom *sophisticated* worldly wise
spec, spect	to look at	*spectator* observer *aspect* appearance *circumspect* cautious (looking around)
spir	breathe	*respiratory* pertaining to breathing *spirited* full of life (breath)
string, strict	bind	*stringent* strict *constrict* become tight *stricture* limit, something that restrains
stru, struct	build	*constructive* helping to build *construe* analyze (how something is built)
tang, tact, ting	to touch	*tangent* touching *contact* touching with, meeting *contingent* depending upon
tempor	time	*contemporary* at same time *extemporaneous* impromptu *temporize* delay
ten, tent	to hold	*tenable* able to be held *tenure* holding of office *retentive* holding; having a good memory
term	end	*interminable* endless *terminate* end
terr	land	*terrestrial* pertaining to earth *subterranean* underground

Root or Stem	Meaning	Illustration
therm	heat	*thermostat* instrument that regulates heat *diathermy* sending heat through body tissues
tors, tort	twist	*distort* twist out of true shape or meaning *torsion* act of twisting *tortuous* twisting
tract	drag, pull	*distract* pull (one's attention) away *intractable* stubborn, unable to be dragged *attraction* pull, drawing quality
trud, trus	push, shove	*intrude* push one's way in *protrusion* something sticking out
urb	city	*urban* pertaining to a city *urbane* polished, sophisticated (pertaining to a city dweller) *suburban* outside of a city
vac	empty	*vacuous* lacking content, empty-headed *evacuate* compel to empty an area
vad, vas	go	*invade* enter in a hostile fashion *evasive* not frank; eluding
veni, vent, ven	to come	*intervene* come between *prevent* stop *convention* meeting
ver	true	*veracious* truthful *verify* check the truth *verisimilitude* appearance of truth
verb	word	*verbose* wordy *verbiage* excessive use of words *verbatim* word for word
vers, vert	turn	*vertigo* turning dizzy *revert* turn back (to an earlier state) *diversion* something causing one to turn aside
via	way	*deviation* departure from the way *viaduct* roadway (arched) *trivial* trifling (small talk at crossroads)
vid, vis	to see	*vision* sight *evidence* things seen *vista* view
vinc, vict, vanq	to conquer	*invincible* unconquerable *victory* winning *vanquish* defeat

Root or Stem	Meaning	Illustration
viv, vit	alive	*vivisection* operating on living animals *vivacious* full of life *vitality* liveliness
voc, vocat	to call	*avocation* calling, minor occupation *provocation* calling or rousing the anger of *invocation* calling in prayer
vol	wish	*malevolent* wishing someone ill *voluntary* of one's own will
volv, volut	to roll	*revolve* roll around *evolve* roll out, develop *convolution* coiled state

COMMON SUFFIXES

Suffixes are syllables that are added to a word. Occasionally, they change the meaning of the word; more frequently, they serve to change the grammatical form of the word (noun to adjective, adjective to noun, noun to verb).

Suffix	Meaning	Illustration
able, ible	capable of (adjective suffix)	*portable* able to be carried *interminable* not able to be limited *legible* able to be read
ac, ic	like, pertaining to (adjective suffix)	*cardiac* pertaining to the heart *aquatic* pertaining to the water *dramatic* pertaining to the drama
acious, icious	full of (adjective suffix)	*audacious* full of daring *perspicacious* full of mental perception *avaricious* full of greed
al	pertaining to (adjective or noun suffix)	*maniacal* insane *final* pertaining to the end *logical* pertaining to logic
ant, ent	full of (adjective or noun suffix)	*eloquent* pertaining to fluid, effective speech *suppliant* pleader (person full of requests) *verdant* green
ary	like, connected with (adjective or noun suffix)	*dictionary* book connected with words *honorary* with honor *luminary* celestial body
ate	to make (verb suffix)	*consecrate* to make holy *enervate* to make weary *mitigate* to make less severe
ation	that which is (noun suffix)	*exasperation* irritation *irritation* annoyance
cy	state of being (noun suffix)	*democracy* government ruled by the people *obstinacy* stubbornness *accuracy* correctness
eer, er, or	person who (noun suffix)	*mutineer* person who rebels *lecher* person who lusts *censor* person who deletes improper remarks
escent	becoming (adjective suffix)	*evanescent* tending to vanish *pubescent* arriving at puberty
fic	making, doing (adjective suffix)	*terrific* arousing great fear *soporific* causing sleep

Suffix	Meaning	Illustration
fy	to make (verb suffix)	*magnify* enlarge *petrify* turn to stone *beautify* make beautiful
iferous	producing, bearing (adjective suffix)	*pestiferous* carrying disease *vociferous* bearing a loud voice
il, ile	pertaining to, capable of (adjective suffix)	*puerile* pertaining to a boy or child *ductile* capable of being hammered or drawn *civil* polite
ism	doctrine, belief (noun suffix)	*monotheism* belief in one god *fanaticism* excessive zeal; extreme belief
ist	dealer, doer (noun suffix)	*fascist* one who believes in a fascist state *realist* one who is realistic *artist* one who deals with art
ity	state of being (noun suffix)	*annuity* yearly grant *credulity* state of being unduly willing to believe *sagacity* wisdom
ive	like (adjective suffix)	*expensive* costly *quantitative* concerned with quantity *effusive* gushing
ize, ise	make (verb suffix)	*victimize* make a victim of *rationalize* make rational *harmonize* make harmonious *enfranchise* make free or set free
oid	resembling, like (adjective suffix)	*ovoid* like an egg *anthropoid* resembling man *spheroid* resembling a sphere
ose	full of (adjective suffix)	*verbose* full of words *lachrymose* full of tears
osis	condition (noun suffix)	*psychosis* diseased mental condition *neurosis* nervous condition *hypnosis* condition of induced sleep
ous	full of (adjective suffix)	*nauseous* full of nausea *ludicrous* foolish
tude	state of (noun suffix)	*fortitude* state of strength *beatitude* state of blessedness *certitude* state of sureness

PART THREE

TACTICS AND PRACTICE: WRITING SKILLS

Grammar, Plain and Fanciful[1]

- **Sentences**
- **Subject**
- **Predicate**
- **Verbs**

Plain grammar gives us the horrors. Our eyes glaze over when we read "Nouns are words that name or designate persons, places, things, states, or qualities." Nevertheless, we need to have some understanding of grammar to survive the writing sections on the SAT. That brings us to fanciful grammar, the rules of grammar illustrated in ways to keep both the reader and the writer awake.

First, we need to be sure we understand what a sentence is. A sentence consists of at least two parts: a subject or topic (the someone or something we are talking about) and a predicate or comment (what we are saying about that someone or something). It may have other parts, but these two are essential.

Let's look at a few sentences.

The witch is bending over the cauldron.

The witch bending over the cauldron is a student.

The cauldron bubbled.

The pot overflowed.

She was scalded.

Her long, thin, elegant fingers writhed with the agony of her burns.

The professor of herbology concocted a healing salve.

The witch's blistered digits twitched as the infirmarian slathered dollops of ointment on the irritated skin.

In each of the sentences above, the complete subject appears in **boldface.** Within each complete subject, there is a simple subject, the heart of the matter, a noun or pronoun.

---

[1]With thanks and/or apologies to J. K. Rowling, J. R. R. Tolkien, C. S. Lewis, William Butler Yeats, Diana Wynne Jones, Homer (the Great), Homer (the Simpson), and of course the ever-popular Anon.

In each of the sentences below, the simple subject appears in **boldface** also.

The **wizard** wavered.

The **troll** pounced.

It bounced off the bannister.

The **incantations** chanted by the enchanter were consistently off-key.

A **spoonful** of sugar makes the elixir go down.

(*Wizard, troll, incantations,* and *spoonful* all are nouns. *It* is a pronoun, of course.)

Now let's look at the predicate, the comment about the subject.

The witch **is bending over the cauldron.**

Berenice and Benedick **hid under the cloak of invisibility.**

The professor of herbology **concocted a healing salve.**

The troll **pounced.**

The mandrake **began to scream.**

In each of the sentences above, the part in **boldface** is the complete predicate, or everything the sentence has to say about its subject. Just as within each complete subject lies a simple subject, within each complete predicate lies a simple predicate, or verb. The simple predicate (the verb) appears in **boldface** in each of the sentences below.

The witch **is bending** over the cauldron.

The mandrake **began** to scream.

Berenice and Benedick **hid** under the cloak of invisibility.

The troll **pounced.**

The subject usually precedes the predicate. However, exceptions do occur.

Over the parapets and into the sky flew **a silver and gold Rolls Royce.**

There were **twenty-nine would-be wizards** practicing their potions.

Simple subjects can be compound (that means you're talking about more than one someone or something). A compound subject consists of at least two subjects, linked by *and, or,* or *nor.* These subjects have something in common: they may or may not enjoy doing things together, but they do share the same verb.

A witch and **an apprentice** are bending over the cauldron.

Berenice or **Benedick** lurked beneath the balustrade.

Either **the lion** or **the witch** escaped from the wardrobe.

The Greeks and **the Trojans** ran down to the sea higgledy-piggledy.

Neither **the mandrake** nor **the mummy** enjoyed being dug up.

Simple predicates can be compound as well (that means the schizophrenic subject gets to do more than one thing at a time). A compound predicate consists of at least two verbs—linked by *and, or, nor, yet,* or *but*—that have a common subject.

The cauldron **bubbled** and **overflowed.**

Her long, thin, elegant fingers **writhed** with the agony of her burns or **flexed** in evidence of her dexterity.

The glum troll neither **bustled** nor **bounced.**

I **will arise** and **go** now, and **go** to Innisfree.

The Greeks and the Trojans **ran** down to the sea higgledy-piggledy yet never **got** their armor wet.

The walrus **wept** but **ate** the oysters, every one.

Completing this discussion of the basic sentence pattern and completing the predicate as well is the complement. The complement is the part of the predicate that lets us know just what (or whom) the verb has been up to. It completes the verb. Often it answers the question "What?"

Witches want. (This could be an existential comment on the nature of witches, but it's simply an incomplete predicate.)

What do witches want?

Witches want **equal rites.**

Witches want **some enchanted evenings.**

Witches want **a chicken in every cauldron.**

Witches want **not to be hassled by wizards.**

Witches want **to sit down for a spell.**

Now we know. The complement clues us in, satisfying our curiosity as it helps the verb tell its tale. Complements come in several guises. There is the direct object. Direct objects are directly affected by the actions of verbs. They are like punching bags: they feel the effect of the blow.

In the following examples, the direct object is <u>underlined</u>.

The troll holds **several <u>captives</u>.**

The troll holds **his <u>tongue</u> with difficulty.**

The troll holds **<u>him</u> in a headlock.**

The troll holds **<u>her</u> in shackles and suspense.**

Some verbs may have both a direct object and an indirect object. Examples include *assign, award, bake, bring, buy, furnish, give, grant, issue, lend, mail, offer, present, sell, send, ship, show,* and *take.* These verbs raise a fresh question: *To whom* or *for whom* (*to what* or *for what*) is the subject performing this action? The indirect object is the person (or place or thing) to whom or for whom the subject performs the action.

The troll sends his compliments.
[The subject is *troll*; the verb, *sends*; the direct object, *compliments*.]

To whom does the troll send his compliments?
The troll sends the **chef** his compliments.
[The indirect object is *chef*.]

The owl bought new sails.
[The subject is *owl*; the verb, *bought*; the direct object, *sails*.]

For what did the owl buy new sails?
The owl bought the pea-green **boat** new sails.
[The indirect object is *boat*.]

The Greeks showed no mercy.
[The subject is *Greeks*; the verb, *showed*; the direct object, *mercy*.]

To whom (or to what) did the Greeks show no mercy?
The Greeks showed the **Trojans** no mercy.
The Greeks showed **Troy** no mercy.

Yet another form of complement is the subject (or subjective) complement. Just as transitive verbs[2] by definition must have direct objects to be complete, linking verbs (*be, become, feel, look, seem, smell, sound, taste,* etc.) must hook up with a noun, adjective, or pronoun to avoid going through an identity crisis.

The troll is. (Yet another existential comment on the "is-ness" of trolls? No, just an example of a linking verb looking for its missing link.)

The troll is *what?*

The troll is a born **storyteller.** [The noun *storyteller,* the subject complement, identifies or explains *troll,* the subject.]

The troll is *what?*

The troll is so **droll.** [The adjective *droll,* meaning whimsically humorous, describes or qualifies *troll.*]

Only certain verbs take subject complements: *to be,* in all its forms (*am, are, is, was, were,* etc.); sensory verbs (*feel, look, smell, sound, taste*); and other state of being verbs (*appear, become, grow, prove, remain, seem, stay, turn*).

Imogen looks a **fright.**

The potion proved **palatable.** In other words, it tasted **good.**

The troll grows **bold,** but Sybilla remains **cold.**

Our final group of complements consists of the object (or objective) complements. These tagalongs follow the direct object, identifying it or qualifying it. We find them in the vicinity of such verbs as *appoint, call, consider, designate, elect, find, label, make, name, nominate, render,* and *term.*

The walrus found the oysters. [The subject is *walrus;* the verb, *found;* the direct object, *oysters.*]

The walrus found the oysters **yummy.** [Direct object is *oysters.* Object complement is *yummy.*]

Sybilla considers the troll an uncouth **brute.** [Direct object is *troll.* Object complement is *brute.* Sybilla is not being very complimentary about the troll.]

Sybilla's scorn makes the troll **melancholy.** In fact, it renders him downright **glum.**

On this note, we leave the basic sentence. In the following chapter we, together with the troll, the walrus, and several junior witches, will explore some common problems in grammar and usage that are likely to turn up on the SAT.

---

[2]A transitive verb *must* have a direct object to complete its meaning. For example, take the verb *hate.* It's a typical transitive verb: without a direct object it feels incomplete. Only a refugee from a bad horror movie would wander around proclaiming, "I hate, I hate...." The subject hates *something.* "I hate spinach." "I hate Donald Trump." "I hate MTV."

Verbs that do not have direct objects are called intransitive verbs. These verbs tell you all you need to know about the subject. No direct objects needed at all. Think of the seven dwarfs. Doc *blusters.* Grumpy *frowns.* Bashful *stammers.* Sleepy *dozes* and *snores.* Happy *chuckles.* Sneezy...you guessed it. Linking verbs (forms of *be, seem, feel,* etc., that relate the subject to the subject complement) are by definition intransitive verbs.

Some verbs can be transitive in one sentence and intransitive in another:

"Auntie Em," cried Dorothy, "I *missed* you so much!" (Transitive)

"Oops!" said the knife-thrower. "I *missed.*" (Intransitive)

Do not worry about these labels. What's important is that you understand how the words are being used.

Verbs That Can Take Direct Objects

Examples: catch, diaper, drink, empty, expel, hit, kiss

Catch the ball.
       _
         DIRECT OBJECT

(The direct object tells **what** or **whom** is caught.)

Verbs That Can Take Both Direct and Indirect Objects

Examples: bring, give, lend, mail, sell, show, take

Bring Barney the book.
    /   _
INDIRECT OBJECT   DIRECT OBJECT

(The direct object tells **what** or **whom** is brought. The indirect object tells **to what** or **to whom** the object is brought.)

Verbs That Can Take Subject Complements

Examples: appear, be, become, feel, look, seem, sound

I feel confident.
_   /
SUBJECT   SUBJECT COMPLEMENT

(The subject complement tells **how** the subject feels.)

Verbs That Can Take Object Complements

Examples: appoint, consider, drive, find, make

Grammar drives me crazy.
           /   _
         OBJECT   OBJECT COMPLEMENT

(The object complement tells **how** the object is affected.)

Common Problems in Grammar and Usage

- **Common Problems in Grammar**
- **Problems with Agreement**
- **Problems with Case**
- **Problems Involving Modifiers**
- **Common Problems in Usage**
- **Picking Proper Prepositions**

COMMON PROBLEMS IN GRAMMAR

Sentence Fragments

What is a sentence fragment? A sentence fragment is a broken chunk of sentence in need of fixing. The poor fractured thing can't stand alone. In this section, we'll look at some broken sentences and fix them, too.

Here are the fragments. Let's examine them one at a time.

When the troll bounced off the bannister.

Muttering over the cauldron.

To harvest mandrakes nocturnally.

In our preparation of the purple potion.

Or lurk beneath the balustrade.

Say the first sentence fragment aloud: "When the troll bounced off the bannister." Say it again. Do you feel as if something is missing? Do the words trigger questions in your mind? "What?" "What happened?" That's great. You are reacting to a dependent clause—a clause preceded by a subordinating conjunction, in this case, the conjunction *when*—that is being treated as if it were a sentence. But it isn't.

Here are a couple of ways to correct this fragment. You can simply chop off the subordinating conjunction *when*, leaving yourself with a simple sentence:

The troll bounced off the bannister.

You can also provide the dependent clause with an independent clause to lean on:

When the troll bounced off the bannister, **he bowled over the professor of herbology.**

The little wizards laughed to see such sport when the troll bounced off the bannister.

Now for the second fragment, "Muttering over the cauldron." Again, something feels incomplete. This is a phrase, either a participial phrase (a group of related words that functions as an adjective or adverb) or a gerund phrase (a verb form ending in –*ing* that functions as a noun). These labels do not matter. What matters is that you fix the fragment. It needs a subject; it also needs a complete verb. Here's the simplest way to repair it.

The witch is muttering over the cauldron.

You've added a subject (*The witch*) and added *is* to complete the verb (*is muttering*).

Here's another:

Muttering over the cauldron **is a bad habit that good witches should avoid.**

You've used *Muttering over the cauldron* as the subject and added a predicate.

Here's a third:

Muttering over the cauldron, **the witch failed to enunciate the incantation clearly.**

You've used *Muttering over the cauldron* as an adjective, modifying the sentence's subject, *witch*.

The third fragment again has several fixes. You can turn the infinitive phrase "To harvest mandrakes nocturnally" into a command:

Harvest mandrakes nocturnally! (The professor of herbology does not recommend that you harvest them by day.)

You can provide a simple subject and complete the verb:

We will harvest mandrakes nocturnally.

You can treat "To harvest mandrakes nocturnally" as the subject of your sentence and add a predicate:

To harvest mandrakes nocturnally **is a task that only a fearless junior wizard would undertake.**

You can also keep "To harvest mandrakes nocturnally" as an infinitive phrase and attach it to an independent clause:

To harvest mandrakes nocturnally, **you must wait for a completely moonless night.**

The next to last sentence fragment, "In our preparation of the purple potion," is a prepositional phrase.

To fix it, you can provide a simple subject and create a verb:

We prepared the purple potion.

You can assume an implicit subject (*you*) and turn it into a command:

Prepare the purple potion!

You can also attach it to an independent clause:

We miscalculated the proportions in our preparation of the purple potion.

The final sentence fragment, "Or lurk beneath the balustrade," is part of a compound predicate. Take away the initial *Or* and you have a command:

Lurk beneath the balustrade!

Provide a simple subject and you have a straightforward declarative sentence:

Orcs lurk beneath the balustrade.

Combine the fragment with the other part or parts of the compound predicate, and you have a complete sentence:

Orcs slink around the cellarage or lurk beneath the balustrade.

Here is a question involving a sentence fragment. See whether you can select the correct answer.

> Some parts of the following sentence are underlined. The first answer choice, (A), simply repeats the underlined part of the sentence. The other four choices present four alternative ways to phrase the underlined part. Select the answer that produces the most effective sentence, one that is clear and exact. In selecting your choice, be sure that it is standard written English, and that it expresses the meaning of the original sentence.
>
> Example:
>
> J. K. Rowling, a British novelist, whose fame as an innovator in the field of fantasy may come to equal that of J. R. R. Tolkien.
>
> (A) J. K. Rowling, a British novelist, whose fame as an innovator
> (B) A British novelist who is famous as an innovator, J. K. Rowling
> (C) J. K. Rowling, who is a British novelist and whose fame as an innovator
> (D) J. K. Rowling is a British novelist whose fame as an innovator
> (E) A British novelist, J. K. Rowling, who is a famous innovator

Did you spot that the original sentence was missing its verb? The sentence's subject is J. K. Rowling. She *is* a British novelist. That is the core of the sentence. Everything else in the sentence simply serves to clarify what kind of novelist Rowling is. She is a novelist whose fame may come to equal Tolkien's fame. The correct answer is Choice D.

Try this second question, also involving a sentence fragment.

> The new vacation resort, featuring tropical gardens and man-made lagoons, and overlooks a magnificent white sand beach.
>
> (A) resort, featuring tropical gardens and man-made lagoons, and overlooks a magnificent white sand beach
> (B) resort overlooks a magnificent white sand beach, it features tropical gardens and man-made lagoons
> (C) resort, featuring tropical gardens and man-made lagoons and overlooking a magnificent white sand beach
> (D) resort, featuring tropical gardens and man-made lagoons, overlooks a magnificent white sand beach
> (E) resort to feature tropical gardens and man-made lagoons and to overlook a magnificent white sand beach

What makes this a sentence fragment? Note the presence of *and* just before the verb *overlooks*. The presence of *and* immediately before a verb is a sign of a compound predicate, as in the sentence "The cauldron bubbled and overflowed." (*Definition*: A compound predicate consists of at least two verbs, linked by *and*, *or*, *nor*, *yet*, or *but*, that have a common subject.) But there is only one verb here, not two.

How can you fix this fragment? You can rewrite the sentence, substituting the verb *features* for the participle *featuring* so that the sentence has two verbs:

The new vacation resort **features** tropical gardens and man-made lagoons and **overlooks** a magnificent white sand beach.

Or, you can simply take away the *and*. The sentence then would read:

The new vacation resort, featuring tropical gardens and man-made lagoons, **overlooks** a magnificent white sand beach.

This sentence is grammatically complete. It has a subject, *resort*, and a verb, *overlooks*. The bit between the commas ("featuring...lagoons") simply describes the subject. (It's called a participial phrase.) The correct answer is Choice D.

The Run-On Sentence

The run-on sentence is a criminal connection operating under several aliases: the *comma fault sentence*, the *comma splice sentence*, the *fused sentence*. Fortunately, there's no need for you to learn the grammar teachers' names for these flawed sentences. You just need to know they are flawed.

Here are two run-on sentences. It's easy to spot the comma fault or comma splice: it's the one containing the comma.

> EXAMPLE 1: The wizards tasted the potion, they found the mixture tasty.

> EXAMPLE 2: The troll is very hungry I think he is going to pounce.

The *comma splice* or *comma fault* sentence is a sentence in which two independent, self-supporting clauses are improperly connected by a comma. Clearly, the two are in need of a separation if not a divorce. Example 1 above illustrates a comma splice or comma fault. The *fused sentence* (Example 2) consists of two sentences that run together without benefit of any punctuation at all. Such sentences are definitely *not* PG (Properly Grammatical).

You can correct run-on sentences in at least four different ways.

1. Use a period, not a comma, at the end of the first independent clause. Begin the second independent clause with a capital letter.

   The wizards tasted the potion. They found the mixture tasty.

   The troll is very hungry. I think he is going to pounce.

2. Connect the two independent clauses by using a coordinating conjunction.

   The wizards tasted the potion, and they found the mixture tasty.

   The troll is very hungry, so I think he is going to pounce.

3. Insert a semicolon between two main clauses that are not already connected by a coordinating conjunction.

   The wizards tasted the potion; they found the mixture tasty.

   The troll is very hungry; I think he is going to pounce.

4. Use a subordinating conjunction to indicate that one of the independent clauses is dependent on the other.

   When the wizards tasted the potion, they found the mixture tasty.

   Because the troll is very hungry, I think he is going to pounce.

Here is a question involving a run-on sentence. See whether you can select the correct answer.

> Some parts of the following sentence are underlined. The first answer choice, (A), simply repeats the underlined part of the sentence. The other four choices present four alternative ways to phrase the underlined part. Select the answer that produces the most effective sentence, one that is clear and exact. In selecting your choice, be sure that it is standard written English, and that it expresses the meaning of the original sentence.
>
> Example:
>
> Many students work after school and on weekends, consequently they do not have much time for doing their homework.
>
> (A) weekends, consequently they do not have
> (B) weekends, they do not have
> (C) weekends, as a consequence they do not have
> (D) weekends, therefore they do not have
> (E) weekends; consequently, they do not have

What makes this a run-on sentence? There are two main clauses here, separated by a comma. The rule is, use a comma between main clauses only when they are linked by a coordinating conjunction (*and, but, for, or, nor, so, yet*). There's no coordinating conjunction here, so you know the sentence as it stands is wrong. The main clauses here are linked by *consequently*, which is what grammar teachers call a conjunctive adverb. A rule also covers conjunctive adverbs. That rule is, use a semicolon before a conjunctive adverb set between two main clauses. Only one answer choice uses a semicolon before *consequently*: the correct answer, Choice E.

PROBLEMS WITH AGREEMENT
Subject–Verb Agreement

The verb and its subject must get along; otherwise, things turn nasty. The rule is that a verb and its subject must agree in person and number. A singular verb must have a singular subject; a plural verb must have a plural subject.

Here are some singular subjects, properly agreeing with their singular verbs:

I conjure	You lurk	She undulates
I am conjuring	You are lurking	He is ogling
I have conjured	You have lurked	It has levitated

Here are the corresponding plural subjects with their plural verbs:

We pirouette	You pillage	They sulk
We are pirouetting	You are pillaging	They are sulking
We have pirouetted	You have pillaged	They have sulked

Normally, it's simple to match a singular subject with an appropriate singular verb, or a plural subject with a plural verb. However, problems can arise, especially when phrases or parenthetical expressions separate the subject from the verb. Even the rudest intrusion is no reason for the subject and the verb to disagree.

SUBJECT–VERB AGREEMENT

Is the subject singular, or is it plural? Sometimes it's hard to tell.

It's hard to tell when *lots* of words come between the subject and the verb, separating them.

> The cost of test prep books, flash cards, and SAT tutoring sessions make DVD prices seem cheap.

What's the subject? *Cost*. (It's what you're talking about.)

What's the verb? *Make*.

Here's how to check whether things agree. *First*, cross out everything in between the subject and the verb.

The cost ~~of test prep books, flash cards, and SAT tutoring sessions~~ make DVD prices seem cheap.

Next, read aloud what's left.

The cost make DVD prices seem cheap.

Does that sound right to you? No. The subject, *cost*, is singular; the verb should be singular also. **The cost *makes* DVD prices seem cheap.**

Note how the following singular subjects agree with their singular verbs.

A **cluster** of grapes **was** hanging just out of the fox's reach.

The **elixir** in these bottles **is** brewed from honey and rue.

The **dexterity** of her long, thin, elegant fingers **has** improved immeasurably since she began playing the vielle.

The **cabin** of clay and wattles **was** built by William Butler Yeats.

Parenthetical expressions are introduced by *as well as*, *with*, *along with*, *together with*, *in addition to*, *no less than*, *rather than, like*, and similar phrases. Although they come between the subject and the verb, they do not interfere with the subject and verb's agreement.

The **owl** together with the pussycat **has** gone to sea in a beautiful pea-green boat.

The **walrus** with the carpenter **is** eating all the oysters.

Dorothy along with the lion, the scarecrow, the woodman, and her little dog Toto **is** following the yellow brick road.

Berenice as well as Benedick **was** hidden under the cloak.

The Trojan **horse,** including the Greek soldiers hidden within it, **was** hauled through the gates of Troy.

Henbane, rather than hellebore or rue, **is** the secret ingredient in this potion.

Henbane, in addition to hops, **gives** the potion a real kick.

I, like the mandrake, **am** ready to scream.

Likewise, if a clause comes between the subject and its verb, it should not cause them to disagree. A singular subject still takes a singular verb.

The **troll** who lurched along the corridors **was** looking for the loo.

The **phoenix** that arose from the ashes **has** scattered cinders everywhere.

The **way** you're wrestling those alligators **is** causing them some distress.

A compound subject (two or more nouns or pronouns connected by *and*) traditionally takes a plural verb.

The walrus and the carpenter were strolling on the strand.

"The King and I," said Alice, "are on our way to tea."

However, there are exceptions. If the compound subject refers to a single person or thing, don't worry that it is made up of multiple nouns. Simply regard it as singular and follow it with a singular verb.

The Lion, the Witch, and the Wardrobe, written by C.S. Lewis, is an admirable tale.

The Eagle and Child is a pub in Oxford where Lewis and Tolkien regularly sampled the admirable ale.

Green eggs and ham was our family's favorite breakfast every St. Patrick's Day.

The King and I is a musical comedy.

Frodo's guide and betrayer literally bites the hand that feeds him. (Both *guide* and *betrayer* refer to the same creature, Gollum.)

(Note that the title of a work of art—a novel, poem, painting, play, opera, ballet, statue—*always* takes a singular verb, even if the title contains a plural subject. *The Burghers of Calais* is a statue by Rodin. The burgers of Burger King are whoppers.)

Some words are inherently singular. In American English, collective nouns like *team, community, jury, swarm, entourage,* and so on are customarily treated as singular.

The croquet <u>team</u> <u>is</u> playing brilliantly, don't you think?

The <u>community</u> of swamp dwellers <u>has</u> elected Pogo president.

The <u>jury</u> <u>was</u> convinced that Alice should be decapitated.

A <u>swarm</u> of bees <u>is</u> dive-bombing Willie Yeats.

My <u>entourage</u> of sycophants <u>fawns</u> on me in a most satisfying fashion.

However, when a collective noun is used to refer to *individual members* of a group, it is considered a plural noun.

The <u>jury</u> <u>were</u> unable to reach a verdict. (The individual jurors could not come to a decision.)

I hate it when my <u>entourage</u> of sycophants <u>compete</u> with one another for my attention. (This sentence is technically correct. However, it calls excessive attention to its correctness. In real life, you'd want to rewrite it. Here's one possible revision: I hate it when my hangers-on compete with one another for my attention.)

Sometimes the article used with a collective noun is a clue to whether the verb is singular or plural. The expressions *the number* and *the variety* generally are regarded as singular and take a singular verb. The expressions *a number* and *a variety* generally are regarded as plural and take a plural verb.

<u>The number</u> of angels able to dance on the head of a pin <u>is limited</u> by Fire Department regulations.

<u>A number</u> of angels able to dance on the head of a pin <u>have been booked</u> to perform at Radio City Music Hall.

<u>The variety</u> of potions concocted by the junior wizards <u>is</u> indescribable.

<u>A variety</u> of noises in the night <u>have alarmed</u> the palace guard. (Has Imogen been serenading Peregrine again?)

Some nouns look plural but refer to something singular. These nouns take singular verbs. Consider *billiards, checkers,* and *dominoes* (the game, not the pieces). Each is an individual game. What about *astrophysics, economics, ethics, linguistics, mathematics, politics, statistics* (the field as a whole, not any specific figures), and *thermodynamics?* Each is an individual discipline or organized body of knowledge. What about *measles, mumps,* and *rickets?* Each is an individual disease. Other camouflaged singular nouns are *customs* (as in baggage inspections at borders), *molasses, news,* and *summons.*

While <u>dominoes</u> <u>is</u> Dominick's favorite pastime, <u>billiards</u> <u>is</u> Benedick's.

The <u>molasses</u> in the potion <u>disguises</u> the taste of garlic and hellebore.

<u>Rickets</u> <u>is</u> endemic in trolls because of their inadequate exposure to sunlight. (Trolls who get adequate exposure to sunlight suffer instead from petrification.)

This <u>summons</u> to a midnight assignation <u>was</u> from Sybilla, not from Berenice.

Some plural nouns actually name single things that are made of two connected parts: *eyeglasses, knickers, pliers, scissors, sunglasses, tights, tongs, trousers, tweezers.* Don't let this confuse you. Just match them up with plural verbs.

Imogen's <u>knickers</u> <u>are</u> in a twist.

Peregrine's <u>sunglasses</u> <u>are</u> in the Lost and Found.

Watch out, however, when these plural nouns crop up in the phrase "a pair of...." The *scissors are* on the escritoire, but a *pair* of scissors *is* on the writing desk.

Watch out, also, when a sentence begins with *here* or *there*. In such cases, the subject of the verb *follows* the verb in the sentence.

There <u>are</u> many <u>angels</u> dancing on the head of this pin. [*Angels* is the subject of the verb *are*.]

Here <u>is</u> the <u>pellet</u> with the poison. [*Pellet* is the subject of the verb *is*.]

In the wizard's library there <u>exist</u> many unusual spelling <u>books</u>. [*Books* is the subject of the verb *exist*.]

Somewhere over the rainbow there <u>lies</u> the <u>land</u> of Oz. [*Land* is the subject of the verb *lies*.]

Likewise, watch out for sentences whose word order is inverted, so that the verb precedes the subject. In such cases, your mission is to find the actual subject.

Among the greatest treasures of all the realms <u>is</u> the <u>cloak</u> of invisibility.

Beyond the reckoning of man <u>are</u> the <u>workings</u> of a wizard's mind.

(An even greater mystery to men <u>are</u> the <u>workings</u> of a woman's mind....)

SUBJECT–VERB AGREEMENT

Is the subject singular, or is it plural? Sometimes it's hard to tell.

It's hard to tell when the subject follows the verb.

In front of the main library, an impressive building that faces Fifth Avenue, stands two marble lions.

What's the subject? *Two marble lions.* (They're what you're talking about.)

Where's the subject? At the end of the sentence, *after* the verb.

What's the verb? *Stands.*

Here's how to check whether things agree. *First*, reverse the subject and verb, so that they're in the normal order.

Two marble lions stands.

Next, read that aloud. Does that sound right to you? No. The subject, *lions*, is plural; the verb should be plural also. One marble lion *stands*; two marble lions *stand*.

Finally, substitute the correct verb form in the original sentence.

In front of the main library, an impressive building that faces Fifth Avenue, stand two marble lions.

Here is a question involving subject–verb agreement.

The following sentence may contain an error in grammar, usage, choice of words, or idioms. Either there is just one error in a sentence or the sentence is correct. Some words or phrases are underlined and lettered; everything else in the sentence is correct.

If an underlined word or phrase is incorrect, choose that letter; if the sentence is correct, select <u>No error</u>.

Example:

<u>Proficiency</u> in mathematics and language skills <u>are</u> <u>tested</u> in third grade
      A   B   C
and eighth grade <u>as well as</u> in high school. <u>No error</u>
                  D   E

Do not let yourself be fooled by nouns or pronouns that come between the subject and the verb. The subject of this sentence is *not* the plural noun *skills*. It is the singular noun, *proficiency*. The verb should be singular as well. The answer containing the subject–verb agreement error is Choice B. To correct the error, substitute *is* for *are*.

Pronoun–Verb Agreement

Watch out for errors in agreement between pronouns and verbs. (A pronoun is *not* a noun that has lost its amateur standing. Instead, it's a last-minute substitute, called upon to stand in for a noun that's overworked.) You already know the basic pronouns: *I, you, he, she, it, we, they* and their various forms. Here is an additional bunch of singular pronouns that, when used as subjects, typically team up with singular verbs.

Each of the songs Imogen sang was off-key. (Was that why her knickers were in a twist?)

Either of the potions packs a punch.

Neither of the orcs packs a lunch. (But, then, neither of the orcs is a vegetarian).

Someone in my entourage has been nibbling my chocolates.

Does anyone who is anyone go to Innisfree nowadays?

Everything is up to date in Kansas City.

Somebody loves Imogen; she wonders who.

Nobody loves the troll. (At least, no one admits to loving the troll. Everybody is much too shy.)

Does everyone really love Raymond?

Exception: Although singular subjects linked by *either...or* or *neither...nor* typically team up with singular verbs, a different rule applies when one subject is singular and one is plural. In such cases, proximity matters: the verb agrees with the subject nearest to it. (This rule also holds true when singular and plural subjects are linked by the correlative conjunctions *not only...but also* and *not...but.*)

Either the troll or the orcs have broken the balustrade.

Either the hobbits or the elf has hidden the wizard's pipe.

Neither the junior witches nor the professor of herbology has come up with a cure for warts.

Neither Dorothy nor her three companions were happy about carrying Toto everywhere.

Not only the oysters but also the walrus was eager to go for a stroll.

Not only Berenice but also Benedick and the troll have hidden under the cloak of invisibility.

Oddly enough, not the carpenter but the oysters were consumed by a desire to go for a stroll.

Not the elves but the dwarf enjoys messing about in caves.

The words *few, many,* and *several* are plural; they take a plural verb.

Many are cold, but few are frozen.

Several are decidedly lukewarm.

Here is a question involving pronoun–verb agreement.

> The following sentence may contain an error in grammar, usage, choice of words, or idioms. Either there is just one error in a sentence or the sentence is correct. Some words or phrases are underlined and lettered; everything else in the sentence is correct.
>
> If an underlined word or phrase is incorrect, choose that letter; if the sentence is correct, select <u>No error</u>.
>
> Example:
>
> <u>Neither</u> the President nor the members of his Cabinet <u>was</u> <u>happy with</u>
>   A   B   C
>
> the reporter's account of dissension <u>within</u> their ranks. <u>No error</u>
>   D   E

Here we have one subject that is singular (*President*) and one that is plural (*members*). In such cases, the verb agrees with the subject nearest to it. *Members* is plural; therefore, the verb should be plural as well. Substitute *were* for *was*. The correct answer is Choice B.

Pronoun–Antecedent Agreement

A pronoun must agree with its antecedent in person, number, and gender. (The antecedent is the noun or pronoun to which the pronoun refers, or possibly defers.) Such a degree of agreement is unlikely, but in grammar (almost) all things are possible.

> The munchkins welcomed <u>Dorothy</u> as <u>she</u> arrived in Munchkinland. (The antecedent *Dorothy* is a third person singular feminine noun; *she* is the third person singular feminine pronoun.)

Sometimes the antecedent is an indefinite singular pronoun: *any, anybody, anyone, each, either, every, everybody, everyone, neither, nobody, no one, somebody,* or *someone.* If so, the pronoun should be singular.

> <u>Neither</u> of the twins is wearing <u>his</u> propeller beanie.

> <u>Each</u> of the bronco-busters was assigned <u>his or her</u> own horse.

> <u>Anybody</u> with any sense would refrain from serenading <u>his</u> inamorata on television.

When the antecedent is compound (two or more nouns or pronouns connected by *and*), the pronoun should be plural.

> <u>The walrus</u> and <u>the carpenter</u> relished <u>their</u> outing with the oysters.

> <u>The walrus</u> always takes salt in <u>his</u> tea.

> <u>Christopher Robin</u> and <u>I</u> always have honey in <u>ours</u>.

> <u>You</u> and <u>your nasty little dog</u> will get <u>yours</u> someday!

When the antecedent is part of an *either...or* or *neither...nor* statement, the pronoun will find it most politic to agree with the nearer antecedent.

> Either Sybilla or <u>Berenice</u> always has the troll on <u>her</u> mind. (Actually, they both do, but in different ways.)

> [Given the *either...or* construction, you need to check which antecedent is nearer to the pronoun. The ever-feminine, highly singular *Berenice* is; therefore, the correct pronoun is *her* rather than *their.*]

> Neither the professor of herbology nor the junior <u>wizards</u> have finished digging up <u>their</u> mandrake roots. [*Wizards* is closer to *their.*]

> Neither the hobbits nor the <u>wizard</u> has eaten all <u>his</u> mushrooms. [*Wizard* is closer to *his.*]

Here is a question involving pronoun–antecedent agreement.

> The following sentence may contain an error in grammar, usage, choice of words, or idioms. Either there is just one error in a sentence or the sentence is correct. Some words or phrases are underlined and lettered; everything else in the sentence is correct.
>
> If an underlined word or phrase is incorrect, choose that letter; if the sentence is correct, select No error.
>
> Example:
>
> Admirers of the vocal ensemble *Chanticleer* have come to wonder over the
>   ————————A————————
>
> years whether the group, known for their mastery of Gregorian chant, might
>   ——B——
>
> have abandoned its roots in early music to explore new musical paths. No error
>   —C——   ——D——   ——E——

The error here is in Choice B. The sentence is talking about a group. Is the group known for *their* mastery or for *its* mastery? *Group* is a collective noun. In American English collective nouns are usually treated as singular and take singular pronouns. Is that the case here? Yes. How can you be sure? Later in the sentence, a second pronoun appears: *its*. This pronoun refers back to the same noun: *group*. *Its* is *not* underlined. Therefore, by definition, the singular pronoun must be correct.

In solving error identification questions, remember that anything *not* underlined in the sentence is correct.

PROBLEMS WITH CASE

Now to get down to cases. In the English language, there are three: nominative (sometimes called subjective), possessive, and objective. Cases are special forms of words that signal how these words function in sentences. Most nouns, many indefinite pronouns, and a couple of personal pronouns reveal little about themselves: they have special case forms only for the possessive case (*Berenice's* cauldron, the *potion's* pungency, *its* flavor, *your* tastebuds, *anyone's* guess, *nobody's* sweetheart). Several pronouns, however, reveal much more, as the following chart demonstrates.

Case Study

Nominative	Possessive	Objective
I	my/mine	me
we	our/ours	us
you	your/yours	you
he	his/his	him
she	her/hers	her
it	its/its	it
they	their/theirs	them
who	whose/whose	whom

The Nominative Case: *I, we, he, she, it, they, you, who*

The nominative case signals that the pronoun involved is functioning as the subject of a verb or as a subject complement.

> Ludovic and *I* purloined the Grey Poupon. [subject of verb]

> The only contestants still tossing gnomes were Berenice and *he*. [subject complement]

> The eventual winners—*he and she*—each received a keg of ale. [As used here, *he* and *she* are appositives—nouns or pronouns set beside another noun or noun substitute to explain or identify it. Here, they identify the subject, *winners*.]

> Sir Bedivere unhorsed the knight *who* had debagged Sir Caradoc. [subject in clause]

The Possessive Case: *mine, ours, his, hers, theirs, yours*; *my, our, his, her, its, their, your, whose*

The possessive case signals ownership. Two-year-olds have an inherent understanding of the possessive: *Mine!*

> Drink to me only with *thine* eyes, and I will pledge with *mine*.

> Please remember that the walrus takes only salt in *his* tea, while Christopher Robin and I prefer honey in *ours*, and the Duchess enjoys a drop of Drambuie in *hers*.

> Ludovic put henbane in *whose* tea?

The possessive case also serves to indicate that a quality belongs to or is characteristic of someone or something.

> Her long, thin, elegant fingers once again demonstrated *their* dexterity.

> The troll rebounded at Berenice but failed to shake *her* composure.

A noun or pronoun immediately preceding a gerund (that is, a verbal that ends in *-ing* and acts like a noun) is in the possessive case.

> The *troll's* bouncing into the bannister creates problems for passersby on the staircase. [*Troll's* immediately precedes the gerund *bouncing*.]

> The troll would enjoy *his* bouncing more if Sybilla rather than Berenice caught him on the rebound. [*His* immediately precedes the gerund *bouncing*.]

The Objective Case

Traditionally, the objective case indicates that a noun or pronoun receives whatever action is taking place. A pronoun in the objective case can serve as a direct object of a transitive verb, as an indirect object, as an object of a preposition, or, oddly enough, as the subject or object of an infinitive.

> Berenice bounced *him* off the bannister again. [direct object]

> The walrus gave *them* no chance to refuse his invitation to go for a stroll. [indirect object]

> William Yeats, by *whom* the small cabin was built, was a better poet than carpenter. [object of preposition within a clause]

> Peregrine expected *her* to serenade *him*. [subject and object of the infinitive *to serenade*.]

Be careful to use objective pronouns as objects of prepositions.

> Everyone loves Raymond *except* Berenice and *me*.

> Between you and *me,* I'm becoming suspicious of Sybilla and *him*.

Here are a couple of questions with problems involving case.

> The following sentences may contain an error in grammar, usage, choice of words, or idioms. Either there is just one error in a sentence or the sentence is correct. Some words or phrases are underlined and lettered; everything else in the sentence is correct.
>
> If an underlined word or phrase is incorrect, choose that letter; if the sentence is correct, select No error.
>
> Example:
>
> All of the flood victims except Lloyd and I have decided to accept the
>   A   B   C
>
> settlement proposed by the insurance company. No error
>   D   E

The object of the preposition *except* should be in the objective case. Change *I* to *me*. The error in the sentence is Choice A.

> Because the other jurors and her differed in their interpretation of the judge's
>   A   B   C   D
> instructions, they asked for a clarification. No error
>   E

Here we have a compound subject. The subject of the initial clause ("Because...instructions") should be in the nominative case. Change *her* to *she*. The correct answer is Choice B.

Many confusions about case involve compound subjects ("the other jurors and she") or compound objects of prepositions ("except Lloyd and me"). If you are having trouble recognizing which form of a pronoun to use, try reversing the noun-pronoun word order, or even dropping the noun. For example, instead of saying "Because the other jurors and her differed," try saying "Because her and the other jurors differed." Or simply say, "Because her differed." Does the pronoun sound odd to you? It should. When that happens, check whether the pronoun is in the right case.

PROBLEMS INVOLVING MODIFIERS

Unclear Placement of Modifiers

Location, location, location. In general, adjectives, adverbs, adjective phrases, adverbial phrases, adjective clauses, and adverbial clauses need to be close to the word they modify. If these modifiers are separated from the word they modify, confusion may set in.

Some specific rules to apply:

1 Place the adverbs *only, almost, even, ever, just, merely,* and *scarcely* right next to the word they modify.

   Ambiguous: The walrus *almost* ate all the oysters. (Did he just chew them up and spit them out without swallowing?)

   Clear: The walrus ate *almost* all the oysters. (He left a few for the carpenter.)

   Ambiguous: This elephant *only* costs peanuts.

   Clear: *Only* this elephant costs peanuts. (The other elephants are traded for papayas and pomegranates.)

   Clear: This elephant costs *only* peanuts. (What a cheap price for such a princely pachyderm!)

2 Place phrases close to the word they modify.

Unclear: The advertisement stated that a used cauldron was wanted by an elderly witch *with stubby legs*. (Obviously, the advertisement was not written to reveal the lady's physical oddity.)

Clear: The advertisement stated that a used cauldron *with stubby legs* was wanted by an elderly witch.

3 Place adjective clauses near the words they modify.

Misplaced: The owl and the pussycat bought a wedding ring from the pig *which cost one shilling*.

Clear: The owl and the pussycat bought a wedding ring *which cost one shilling* from the pig.

4 Words that may modify either a preceding or following word are called *squinting modifiers*. (They look both ways at once; no wonder they're walleyed.) To correct the ambiguity, move the modifier so that its relationship to one word is clear.

Squinting: Peregrine said that if Imogen refused to quit caterwauling beneath his balcony *in two minutes* he would send for the troll.

Clear: Peregrine said that he would send for the troll if Imogen refused to quit caterwauling beneath his balcony *in two minutes*.

Clear: Peregrine said that he would send for the troll *in two minutes* if Imogen refused to quit caterwauling beneath his balcony.

Squinting: The oysters agreed *on Sunday* to go for a stroll with the walrus.

Clear: *On Sunday*, the oysters agreed to go for a stroll with the walrus.

Clear: The oysters agreed to go for a stroll with the walrus *on Sunday*.

Dangling Modifiers

When modifying phrases or clauses precede the main clause of a sentence, position is everything. These modifiers should come directly before the subject of the main clause and should clearly refer to that subject. If the modifiers foolishly hang out in the wrong part of the sentence, they may wind up dangling there making no sense at all.

To correct a dangling modifier, rearrange the words of the sentence to bring together the subject and its wayward modifier. You may need to add a few words to the sentence to clarify its meaning.

Dangling Participle: Walking down the Yellow Brick Road, the Castle of Great Oz was seen. (Did you ever see a castle walking? Well, I didn't.)

Corrected: Walking down the Yellow Brick Road, Dorothy and her companions saw the Castle of Great Oz. (The participle *walking* immediately precedes the subject of the main clause *Dorothy and her companions*.)

In the preceding example, the participial phrase comes at the beginning of the sentence. In the example below, the participial phrase follows the sentence base.

Dangling Participle: The time passed very enjoyably, singing songs and romping with Toto. (Who's that romping with Toto?)

Corrected: They passed the time very enjoyably, singing songs and romping with Toto.

Watch out for dangling phrases containing gerunds or infinitives.

Dangling Phrase Containing Gerund: Upon hearing the report that a troll had been found in the cellars, the building was cleared. (Again, ask yourself who heard the report. Even though the building was a school for wizards, its walls did *not* have ears.)

Corrected: Upon hearing the report that a troll had been found in the cellars, the headmaster cleared the building.

Dangling Phrase Containing Infinitive: Unable to defeat the Trojans in open battle, a trick was resorted to by the Greeks.

Corrected: Unable to defeat the Trojans in open battle, the Greeks resorted to a trick.

Be careful when you create elliptical constructions (ones in which some words are implied rather than explicitly stated) that you don't cut out so many words that you wind up with a dangling elliptical adverb clause.

Dangling Elliptical Construction: *When presented with the potion*, not one drop was drunk.

Corrected: *When presented with the potion, nobody* drank a drop.

Corrected: *When they were presented with the potion*, not one drop was drunk.

Yet Another Dangling Elliptical Construction: *Although only a small dog*, Dorothy found Toto a big responsibility.

Corrected: *Although Toto was only a small dog*, Dorothy found him a big responsibility.

Here are a couple of questions involving misplaced modifiers:

> Some parts of the following sentences are underlined. The first answer choice, (A), simply repeats the underlined part of the sentence. The other four choices present four alternative ways to phrase the underlined part. Select the answer that produces the most effective sentence, one that is clear and exact. In selecting your choice, be sure that it is standard written English, and that it expresses the meaning of the original sentence.
>
> Example:
>
> Returning to Harvard after three decades, the campus seemed much less cheery to Sharon than it had been when she was studying there.
>
> (A) Returning to Harvard after three decades, the campus seemed much less cheery to Sharon
> (B) After Sharon returned to Harvard in three decades, it seemed a much less cheery campus to her
> (C) Having returned to Harvard after three decades, it seemed a much less cheery campus to Sharon
> (D) When Sharon returned to Harvard after three decades, she thought the campus much less cheery
> (E) Sharon returned to Harvard after three decades, and then she thought the campus much less cheery

Did you recognize that the original sentence contains a dangling modifier? Clearly, the campus did not return to Harvard; Sharon returned to Harvard. By replacing the participial phrase with a subordinate clause ("When...decades") and by making *she* the subject of the sentence, Choice D corrects the error in the original sentence.

Try this second question, also involving a dangling modifier.

> Having drafted the museum floor plan with exceptional care, that the planning commission rejected his design upset the architect greatly.
>
> (A) that the planning commission rejected his design upset the architect greatly
> (B) the planning commission's rejection of his design caused the architect a great upset
> (C) the architect found the planning commission's rejection of his design greatly upsetting
> (D) the architect was greatly upset about the planning commission rejecting his design
> (E) the architect's upset at the planning commission's rejection of his design was great.

Again, ask yourself who drafted the museum floor plan. Clearly, it was the architect. *Architect,* therefore, must be the sentence's subject. The correct answer must be either Choice C or Choice D. Choice D, however, introduces a fresh error. The phrase "rejecting his design" is a gerund. As a rule, you should use the possessive case before a gerund: to be correct, the sentence would have to read "the architect was greatly upset about the planning <u>commission's</u> rejecting his design." Choice D, therefore, is incorrect. The correct answer is Choice C.

COMMON PROBLEMS IN USAGE
Words Often Misused or Confused

Errors in *diction*—that is, choice of words—frequently crop up on the Writing Section of the SAT. Here are some of the most common diction errors to watch for:

accept/except. These two words are often confused. *Accept* means to take or receive; to give a favorable response to something; to regard as proper. *Except*, when used as a verb, means to preclude or exclude. (*Except* may also be used as a preposition or a conjunction.)

 Benedick will *accept* the gnome-tossing award on Berenice's behalf.

 The necromancer's deeds were so nefarious that he was *excepted* from the general pardon. In other words, they pardoned everyone *except* him.

affect/effect. *Affect*, used as a verb, means to influence or impress, and to feign or assume. *Effect*, used as a verb, means to cause or bring about.

 When Berenice bounced the troll against the balustrade, she *effected* a major change in his behavior.

 The blow *affected* him conspicuously, denting his skull and his complacency.

 To cover her embarrassment about the brawl, Berenice *affected* an air of nonchalance.

Effect and *affect* are also used as nouns. *Effect* as a noun means result, purpose, or influence. *Affect*, a much less common noun, is a psychological term referring to an observed emotional response.

 Did being bounced against the balustrade have a beneficial *effect* on the troll?

 The troll's *affect* was flat. So was his skull.

aggravate. *Aggravate* means to worsen or exacerbate. Do not use it as a synonym for *annoy* or *irritate*.

 The orc will *aggravate* his condition if he tries to toss any gnomes so soon after his operation.

 The professor of herbology was *irritated* [not *aggravated*] by the mandrakes' screams.

ain't. *Ain't* is nonstandard. Avoid it.

already/all ready. These expressions are frequently confused. *Already* means previously; *all ready* means completely prepared.

 The mandrakes have *already* been dug up.

 Now the mandrakes are *all ready* to be replanted.

alright. Use *all right* instead of the misspelling *alright*. (Is that *all right* with you?)

altogether/all together. *All together* means as a group. *Altogether* means entirely, completely.

 The walrus waited until the oysters were *all together* on the beach before he ate them.

 There was *altogether* too much sand in those oysters.

among/between. Use *among* when you are discussing more than two persons or things; *between*, when you are limiting yourself to only two persons or things.

> The oysters were divided *among* the walrus, the carpenter, and the troll.

> The relationship *between* Berenice and Benedick has always been a bit kinky.

amount/number. Use *amount* when you are referring to mass, bulk, or quantity. Use *number* when the quantity can be counted.

> We were amazed by the *amount* of henbane the troll could eat without getting sick.

> We were amazed by the *number* of hens the troll could eat without getting sick.

and etc. The *and* is unnecessary. Cut it.

being as/being that. These phrases are nonstandard; avoid them. Use *since* or *because*.

beside/besides. These words are often confused. *Beside* is always a preposition. It means "next to" or, sometimes, "apart from." Watch out for possible ambiguities or ambiguous possibilities. "No one was seated at the Round Table *beside* Sir Bedivere" has two possible meanings.

> No one was seated at the Round Table *beside* Sir Bedivere. [There were empty seats on either side of Bedivere; however, Sir Kay, Sir Gawain, and Sir Galahad were sitting across from him on the other side of the table.]

> No one was seated at the Round Table *beside* Sir Bedivere. [Poor Bedivere was all alone.]

Besides, when used as a preposition, means "in addition to" or "other than."

> *Besides* oysters, the walrus and the carpenter have eaten countless cockles and mussels and clams.

> Who will go to the bear-baiting *besides* Berenice and Benedick?

Besides also is used as an adverb. At such times, it means moreover or also.

> The troll broke the balustrade—and the newel post *besides*.

between. See *among*.

but what. Avoid this phrase. Use *that* instead.

> Wrong: Imogen could not believe *but what* Peregrine would overlook their assignation.

> Better: Imogen could not believe *that* Peregrine would overlook their assignation.

can't hardly/can't scarcely. You have just encountered the dreaded double negative. (I *can hardly* believe anyone writes that way, can you?) Use *can hardly* or *can scarcely*.

conscious/conscience. Do not confuse these words. *Conscious*, an adjective, means aware and alert; it also means deliberate.

> Don't talk to Berenice before she's had her morning cup of coffee; she isn't really *conscious* until she has some caffeine in her system.

> When Ludovic laced the professor's potion with strychnine, was he making a *conscious* attempt to kill the prof?

Conscience, a noun, means one's sense of right and wrong.

> Don't bother appealing to the orc's *conscience*: he has none.

could of. This phrase is nonstandard. Substitute *could have*.

different from/different than. Current usage accepts both forms; however, a Google check indicates that *different from* is the more popular usage.

effect. See *affect*.

farther/further. Some writers use the adverb *farther* when discussing physical or spatial distances; *further*, when discussing quantities. Most use them interchangeably. The adjective *further* is a synonym for *additional*.

Benedick has given up gnome-tossing contests because Berenice always tosses her gnomes yards *farther* than Benedick can toss his. [adverb]

This elixir is *further* enriched by abundant infusions of henbane and hellebore. [adverb]

Stay tuned for *further* announcements of the latest results in today's gnome-tossing state finals. [adjective]

fewer/less. Use *fewer* with things that you can count (one hippogriff, two hippogriffs...); *less*, with things that you cannot count but can measure in other ways.

"There are *fewer* oysters on the beach today than yesterday, I fear. How sad!" said the carpenter, and brushed away a tear.

Berenice should pay *less* attention to troll tossing and more to divination and elementary herbology.

former/latter. Use *former* and *latter* only when you discuss two items. (*Former* refers to the first item in a series of two; *latter*, to the second.) When you discuss a series of three or more items, use *first* and *last*.

Who was madder, the March Hare or the Hatter? Was it the *former*, or was it the *latter* (the Hatter)?

Though the spoon, the knife, and the fork each asked the dish to elope, everyone knows the dish ran away with the *first*.

further. See *farther*.

had of/had have. These phrases are nonstandard. Substitute *had*.

Do Not Write: If Benedick had of [nonstandard] tossed the gnome a foot farther, he could of [also nonstandard] won the contest.

Write: If Benedick *had* tossed the gnome a foot farther, he *could have* won the contest.

hanged/hung. Both words are the past participle of the verb *hang*. However, in writing formal English, use *hanged* when you are discussing someone's execution; use *hung* when you are talking about the suspension of an object.

Ludovic objected to being *hanged* at dawn, saying he wouldn't get up that early for anybody's execution, much less his own.

The stockings were *hung* from the chimney with care.

hardly/scarcely. These words are sufficiently negative on their own that you don't need any extra negatives (like *not, nothing,* or *without*) to get your point across. In fact, if you do add that extra *not* or *nothing,* you've perpetrated the dreaded double negative.

Do Not Write: The walrus couldn't hardly eat another bite.

Write: The walrus *could hardly* eat another bite.

Do Not Write: Compared to the walrus, the carpenter ate hardly nothing.

Write: Compared to the walrus, the carpenter ate *hardly anything* (or anyone).

Do Not Write: The troll pounced without scarcely a moment's hesitation.

Write: The troll pounced *with scarcely* a moment's hesitation.

imply/infer. People often use these words interchangeably to mean hint at or suggest. However, *imply* and *infer* have precise meanings that you need to tell apart. *Imply* means to suggest something without coming right out and saying it. *Infer* means to draw a conclusion, basing it on some sort of evidence.

> When Auntie Em said, "My! That's a big piece of pie, young lady," did she mean to *imply* that Dorothy was being a glutton in taking such a huge slice?

> Dorothy *inferred* from Auntie Em's comment that she'd better not ask for a second piece.

> Imogen *inferred* from the fresh dent in the troll's skull that Berenice had been bouncing him off the balustrade again.

in back of. Avoid this expression. Use *behind* instead.

incredible/incredulous. *Incredible* means unbelievable, too improbable to be believed. *Incredulous* means doubtful or skeptical, unwilling to believe.

> When Ludovic saw Berenice juggling three trolls in the air, he was amazed at her *incredible* strength.

> Do you believe all this jabber about Berenice's strength, or are you *incredulous?*

irregardless. This nonstandard usage particularly irritates graders. Use *regardless* instead.

kind of/sort of. In writing formal prose, avoid using these phrases adverbially (that is, with the meaning of *somewhat* or *to a degree*, as in "kind of bashful" or "sort of infatuated.") Use words like *quite*, *rather*, or *somewhat* instead.

> Informal: Dorothy was kind of annoyed by the wizard's obfuscations.

> Approved: Dorothy was *quite* annoyed by the wizard's obfuscations.

kind of a/sort of a. In writing formal prose, cut out the *a*.

> Do Not Write: Sybilla seldom brews this kind of a potion.

> Write: Sybilla seldom brews this *kind of* potion.

last/latter. See *former.*

later/latter. Use *later* when you're talking about time (you'll do it sooner or later). Use *latter* when you're talking about the second one of a group of two (not the former—that comes first—but the latter).

> Every night Imogen stays up *later* and *later* serenading Peregrine.

> Berenice tossed both the troll and a gnome. The *latter* bounced farther.

lay/lie. *Lay,* a transitive verb, means to put or place. *Lie,* an intransitive verb, means to rest or recline. One way to tell whether to use *lay (laying, laid)* or *lie (lying, lay, lain)* is to examine the sentence. If the verb has an object, use the correct form of *lay.* If the verb has no object, use *lie.*

> Toto, *lie* down and roll over!

> Toto *lay* down on the floor. [*Lay* is past tense of *lie.*]

> Auntie Em, Toto's just *lying* there. He's not rolling over!

> How long *has* he *lain* there, Dorothy? Maybe he's taking a nap. [The verb has no object. *Has lain* is the present perfect tense of *lie.*]

> Berenice, please *lay* the troll down gently. [Object is *troll.*]

> Instead of *laying* the troll down, Berenice bounced him off the bannister.

> Ludovic *laid* the loot on the escritoire. [Object is *loot. Laid* is past tense of *lay.*]

learn/teach. *Learn* means to get knowledge; *teach* means to instruct, to give knowledge or information. Don't confuse the two.

> Incorrect: I'll learn you, you stupid troll!
>
> Correct: I'll *teach* you, you obtuse orc!

leave/let. *Leave* primarily means to depart; *let,* to permit. Don't confuse them. (*Leave,* when followed by an object and an infinitive or a participial phrase, as in "Leave him to do his worst" or "Leave it to Beaver," has other meanings. Consult an unabridged dictionary.)

> Incorrect: Leave me go, Berenice.
>
> Correct: *Let* me go, Berenice. Please *let* me leave.

less. See *fewer.*

liable to/likely to. *Likely to* refers simply to probability. When speaking informally, people are likely to use *liable to* in place of *likely to.* However, in formal writing, *liable to* conveys a sense of possible harm or misfortune.

> Informal: The owl and the pussycat are liable to go for a sail. [This is a simple statement of probability. More formally, you would write "The owl and the pussycat are likely to go for a sail."]
>
> Preferable: The beautiful but leaky pea-green boat is *liable to* sink. [This conveys a sense of likely danger.]

lie. See *lay.*

loose/lose. These are not synonyms. *Loose* is primarily an adjective meaning free or inexact or not firmly fastened ("a *loose* prisoner," "a *loose* translation," "a *loose* tooth.") As a verb, *loose* means to set free or let fly.

> *Loose* the elephants!
>
> The elf *loosed* his arrows at the orcs.

Lose is always a verb.

> If the elf *loses* any more arrows in the bushes, he won't have any left to loose at the orcs.
>
> Hey, baby, *lose* the sidekick, and you and I can have a good time.

me and. Unacceptable as part of a compound subject.

> Nonstandard: Me and Berenice can beat any three trolls in the house.
>
> Preferred: Berenice *and I* can beat any three trolls in the house. (Actually, Berenice can beat them perfectly well without any help from me.)

number. See *amount.*

of. Don't write *of* in place of *have* in the expressions *could have, would have, should have, must have,* and so on.

off of. In formal writing, the *of* is superfluous. Cut it.

> Incorrect: The troll bounced off of the bannister.
>
> Correct: The troll bounced *off* the bannister.

principal/principle. Do not confuse the adjective *principal,* meaning chief, with the noun *principle,* a rule or law.

> Berenice's *principal principle* (that is, her chief rule of conduct) is "The bigger they are, the harder they bounce."

In a few cases, *principal* is used as a noun: the *principal* of a loan (the main sum you borrowed); the *principal* in a transaction (the chief person involved in the deal); the *principal* of a school (originally the head teacher). Don't worry about these instances. If you can substitute the word *rule* for the noun in your sentence, then the word you want is *principle*.

raise/rise. Do not confuse the verb *raise (raised, raising)* with *rise (rose, risen, rising)*. *Raise* means to increase, to lift up, to collect, or to nurture. It is transitive (it takes an object). *Rise* means to ascend, to get up, or to grow. It is intransitive (no objects need apply).

Incorrect:	They are rising the portcullis.
Correct:	They are *raising* the portcullis. [The object is portcullis, a most heavy object indeed.]
Incorrect:	The sun raised over the battlements.
Correct:	The sun *rose* over the battlements.

real. This word is an adjective meaning genuine or concrete. Do not use it as an adverb meaning very or extremely.

Too Informal:	This is a real weird list of illustrative sentences.
Preferable:	This is a *really* weird list of illustrative sentences.
Even Better:	This is an *extremely* weird list of illustrative sentences.

the reason is because. This expression is ungrammatical. If you decide to use the phrase *the reason is*, follow it with a concise statement of the reason, not with a *because* clause.

Incorrect:	*The reason* the oysters failed to answer *is because* the walrus and the carpenter had eaten every one.
Correct But Wordy:	*The reason* the oysters failed to answer *is that* the walrus and the carpenter had eaten every one.
Correct & Concise:	The oysters failed to answer *because* the walrus and the carpenter had eaten every one.

same. Lawyers and writers of commercial documents sometimes use *same* as a pronoun. In writing essays, use the pronouns *it, them, this, that* in its place.

Incorrect:	I have received your billet-doux and will answer same once my messenger owl returns home.
Correct:	I have received your billet-doux and will answer *it* once my messenger owl returns home.

scarcely. See *hardly*.

sort of. See *kind of*.

teach. See *learn*.

try and. Avoid this phrase. Use *try to* in its place.

Incorrect:	We must try and destroy the Ring of the Enemy.
Correct:	We must *try to* destroy the Ring of the Enemy.

unique. The adjective *unique* describes something that is the only one of its kind. Don't qualify this adjective by *more, most, less, least, slightly,* or *a little bit*. It's just as illogical to label something a little bit unique as it is to describe someone as a little bit pregnant.

Incorrect:	Only the One Ring has the power to rule elves, dwarfs, and mortal men. It is most unique.
Correct:	Only the One Ring has the power to rule elves, dwarfs, and mortal men. It is *unique*.

PICKING PROPER PREPOSITIONS

Occasionally, you may get back papers from your teachers with certain expressions labeled "unidiomatic." Often these errors involve prepositions. When you are in doubt about what preposition to use after a particular word, look up that word in an unabridged dictionary. Meanwhile, look over the list below to see which preposition customarily accompanies the following words.

accede to

Sybilla graciously *acceded to* Peregrine's request to compose a villanelle.

according to

According to Abelard, Esperanto is the language of love.

accuse of

Berenice vociferously *accused* the troll *of* borrowing her leotard.

addicted to

The professor of herbology is reputedly *addicted to* comfrey tea.

adhere to

Muttering the conjunction spell under his breath, the wizard *adhered* the brigand *to* the bottom of the balcony.

adverse to

Imogen is *adverse to* Peregrine's writing verse to other women.

afflict with

The wizard *afflicted* the brigand *with* borborygmus and boils.

agree on (come to terms)

The owl and the pussycat could not *agree on* what color to repaint their pea-green boat.

agree with (suit; be similar to; be consistent with)

Burping miserably, the carpenter confessed that a diet of oysters did not *agree with* him.

agreeable to

The troll found tiddlywinks an occupation most *agreeable to* his tastes.

amazement at

Imagine Imogen's *amazement at* discovering the brigand dangling from the bottom of the balcony!

amenable to

Excessively *amenable to* persuasion, Imogen is the archetypal girl who can't say no.

appetite for

The walrus had an insatiable *appetite for* oysters.

appreciation of

The troll's *appreciation of* the fine points of pillaging was sadly limited.

aside from

The professor of potions had run out of ingredients, *aside from* a few sprigs of dried hellebore.

associate with

Dorothy's Auntie Em warned her not to *associate with* lions and tigers and bears.

blame for, blame on

Orcs never *blame* themselves *for* ravaging the environment; instead, they *blame* the damage *on* the trolls.

capable of

Who knows what vile and abhorrent deeds trolls are *capable of?*

chary of

Snow White was insufficiently *chary of* accepting apples from strange old women.

compatible with

Is Peregrine *compatible with* Imogen? I doubt it!

comply with

Sybilla was reluctant to *comply with* the troll's incessant importuning.

conform to (occasionally **conform with**)

Apprentice wizards are expected to obey their masters and *conform to* proper wizardly practices.

conversant with

Anyone *conversant with* trolls' table manners knows better than to invite one to tea.

desire for

Even Sybilla's *desire for* new experiences could not tempt her to elope with the troll.

desirous of

Being *desirous of* a salad for dinner, Gargantua cut some heads of lettuce as large as walnut trees.

desist from

If the troll does not *desist from* importuning Sybilla, she's going to sic Berenice on him.

die of

When Homer's belching drowned out her saxophone solo, Lisa nearly *died of* embarrassment.

different from

In what way is Tweedledum *different from* Tweedledee? I thought they were exactly alike.

disagree with

Hellebore *disagreed with* the pygmy, causing his stomach to rumble. (The pygmy had borborygmi.)

disdain for

The immaculate elves were too polite to show their *disdain for* the unkempt orcs.

enamored of

The troll is *enamored of* Sybilla, who in turn is *enamored of* Benedick.

indulge in

Berenice *indulges in* the curious hobby of tossing trolls.

inferior to

The orcs' perfunctory grooming was *inferior to* the elves' more meticulous toilette.

oblivious to

Imogen is *oblivious to* Peregrine's flaws and all too aware of his perfection.

partial to

The walrus is extremely *partial to* oysters; he likes them too much for their own good.

peculiar to

A total aversion to sunlight is a condition *peculiar to* vampires and trolls.

preoccupation with

The troll could not comprehend Sybilla's *preoccupation with* Benedick.

prevent from

There is nothing we can do to *prevent* Berenice *from* bouncing the troll off the balustrade. We'll have to catch him on the rebound.

prior to

Prior to eating the oysters, the walrus and the carpenter took them for a stroll.

prone to

Imogen is *prone to* infatuations. Just ask Peregrine.

separate from

No wicked witch could *separate* Dorothy *from* her little dog Toto.

tamper with

Do not *tamper with* the purple potion.

weary of

Will Berenice ever *weary of* bouncing the troll off the balustrade?

willing to

I'm *willing to* bet that she won't.

THE VAGARIES OF VERBS

Verbs are the shape-shifters of the English language. They change their forms to indicate **person** (*who* is acting), **number** (*how many* are acting), **tense** (*when* the action is happening), **voice** (whether something is acting, as in being *active*, or is being acted upon, or *passive*), and **mood**.

Mood is the best. What's your mood? Do you feel like ordering someone around?

"Lurk!" you command. That's the *imperative* mood.

"Please lurk," you request. The mood's still imperative, but polite.

Then there's the *indicative* mood. If you're making a simple statement, indicating or pointing out something, or asking a straightforward question, you're using the indicative mood.

"The troll is lurking in the bushes."

"What do you think he wants?"

Finally, there's the *subjunctive* mood. You use the subjunctive when things are a bit iffy:

(statement contrary to fact)
"If I *were* the troll, I *would head* for the hills now." (Why should the troll head for the hills? Berenice is about to pounce.)

(recommendation)
"When I find the troll, I will suggest that he *hide*."

Some verbs are *regular*: when they shift into the past tense, they do it in the standard way by adding *-ed* or *-d*.

The troll lurk**ed**.

Berenice pounce**d**.

Others, however, are *irregular*: when they form the past tense, they either change in unusual ways (*think* becomes *thought*), or they don't change at all (*put* stays the same).

Here is a list of irregular verbs, showing the correct forms for the present tense, past tense, and past participle. Many you know already, but some will be unfamiliar to you. Don't let their shifts in form fool you when you run into them on the SAT.

Irregular Verbs

Present Tense	Past Tense	Past Participle
arise	arose	arisen
awake	awaked, awoke	awaked, awoke
bear	bore	borne
beat	beat	beaten
befall	befell	befallen
begin	began	begun
bend	bent	bent
bid (command)	bade	bidden
bid (command)	bid	bid
bind	bound	bound
blow	blew	blown
break	broke	broken
bring	brought	brought
broadcast	broadcast, broadcasted	broadcast, broadcasted
build	built	built
burst	burst	bust
buy	bought	bought
cast	cast	cast
catch	caught	caught
choose	chose	chosen
cling	clung	clung
come	came	come
creep	crept	crept
deal	dealt	dealt
dive	dived, dove	dived
do	did	done
draw	drew	drawn
drink	drank	drunk
drive	drove	driven
eat	ate	eaten
fall	fell	fallen
feed	fed	fed
feel	felt	felt
fight	fought	fought
find	found	found
flee	fled	fled
fling	flung	flung
fly	flew	flown
forebear	forbore	forborne
forbid	forbade	forbidden
forget	forgot	forgotten, forgot
forgive	forgave	forgiven

Present Tense	Past Tense	Past Participle
forsake	forsook	forsaken
freeze	froze	frozen
get	got	got, gotten
give	gave	given
go	went	gone
grow	grew	grown
hang*	hung, hanged*	hung, hanged*
have	had	had
hit	hit	hit
hold	held	held
kneel	knelt, kneeled	knelt
know	knew	known
lay	laid	laid
lead	led	led
leave	left	left
lend	lent	lent
lie	lay	lain
lose	lost	lost
make	made	made
meet	met	met
put	put	put
read	read	read
ring	rang	rung
rise	rose	risen
run	ran	run
see	saw	seen
seek	sought	sought
sell	sold	sold
send	sent	sent
set	set	set
shine	shone	shone
shrink	shrank, shrunk	shrunk, shrunken
sing	sang	sung
sink	sank	sunk
slay	slew	slain
sit	sat	sat
sleep	slept	slept
slide	slid	slid
sling	slung	slung
slink	slunk	slunk
speak	spoke	spoken
spring	sprang, sprung	sprung

*See the list of Words Often Misused or Confused, page 286.

Present Tense	Past Tense	Past Participle
steal	stole	stolen
stick	stuck	stuck
sting	stung	stung
stride	strode	stridden
strike	struck	struck
swear	swore	sworn
sweat	sweat, sweated	sweated
sweep	swept	swept
swim	swam	swum
swing	swung	swung
take	took	taken
teach	taught	taught
tear	tore	torn
telecast	telecast, telecasted	telecast, telecasted
tell	told	told
think	thought	thought
thrive, thrived	throve, thriven	throve, thriven
throw	threw	thrown
wake	waked, woke	waked, woken
wear	wore	worn
weep	wept	wept
win	won	won
wind	wound	wound
work	worked, wrought	worked, wrought
wring	wrung	wrung
write	wrote	written

The Writing Skills Questions

- **Identifying Sentence Errors**
- **Improving Sentences**
- **Improving Paragraphs**

- **Common Grammar and Usage Errors**

The questions in the writing skills sections test your ability to recognize clear, correct standard written English, the kind of writing your college professors will expect on the papers you write for them. You'll be expected to know basic grammar, such as subject-verb agreement, pronoun-antecedent agreement, correct verb tense, correct sentence structure, and correct diction. You'll need to know how to recognize a dangling participle and how to spot when two parts of a sentence are not clearly connected. You'll also need to know when a paragraph is (or isn't) properly developed and organized.

IDENTIFYING SENTENCE ERRORS

There are three different kinds of questions on the writing skills sections of the SAT: identifying sentence errors, improving sentences, and improving paragraphs. Almost half of them are identifying sentence errors questions in which you have to find an error in the underlined section of a sentence. You do not have to correct the sentence or explain what is wrong. Here are the directions.

The sentences in this section may contain errors in grammar, usage, choice of words, or idioms. Either there is just one error in a sentence or the sentence is correct. Some words or phrases are underlined and lettered; everything else in the sentence is correct.

If an underlined word or phrase is incorrect, choose that letter; if the sentence is correct, select <u>No error</u>. Then blacken the appropriate space on your answer sheet.

Example:

The region has a climate <u>so severe that</u> plants <u>growing there</u> rarely
 A B

had been more than twelve inches <u>high.</u> <u>No error</u>
 C D E

(A) (B) ● (D) (E)

Testing Tactics

TACTIC

1 Remember that the error, if there is one, must be in the underlined part of the sentence.

You don't have to worry about making improvements that could be made in the rest of the sentence. For example, if you have a sentence in which the subject is plural and the verb is singular, you could call either one the error. But if only the verb is underlined, the error for that sentence is the verb.

See how the first tactic works in dealing with the following sentence.

> If one follows the <u>discipline of</u> Hatha Yoga, <u>you know</u> the critical
>   A   B
>
> importance of physical purification <u>to render</u> the body <u>fit for</u> the practice
>   C   D
>
> of higher meditation. <u>No error</u>
>   E

What's wrong with the sentence above? The writer makes an abrupt, unnecessary shift in person, switching from the pronoun *one* ("one follows") to the pronoun *you* ("you know"). There are two ways to fix this sentence. You can rewrite it like this:

> If you follow the discipline of Hatha Yoga, you know the critical importance of physical purification to render the body fit for the practice of higher meditation.

You can also rewrite it like this:

> If one follows the discipline of Hatha Yoga, one knows the critical importance of physical purification to render the body fit for the practice of higher meditation.

However, your job is *not* to rewrite the sentence. Your job is simply to spot the error, and that error *must be in an underlined part.* You know the shift in person is incorrect. That means the error is Choice B.

In answering error identification questions, focus on the underlined portions of the sentence. Don't waste your time thinking of other ways to make the sentence work.

TACTIC

2 Use your ear for the language.

Remember, you don't have to name the error, or be able to explain why it is wrong. All you have to do is recognize that something *is* wrong. On the early, easy questions in the set, if a word or phrase sounds wrong to you, it probably is, even if you don't know why.

See if your ear helps you with this question.

> <u>In my history class</u> I learned <u>why</u> the American colonies <u>opposed the British,</u>
>   A   B   C
>
> how they organized the militia, and <u>the work of the Continental Congress</u> .
>   D
>
> <u>No error</u>
>   E

The last part of this sentence probably sounds funny to you—awkward, strange, wooden. You may not know exactly what it is, but something sounds wrong here. If you followed your instincts and chose Choice D as the error, you would be right. The error is a lack of parallel structure. The sentence is listing three things you learned, and they should all be in the same form. Your ear expects the pattern to be the same. Since the first two items listed are clauses, the third should be too: "In my history class I learned why the American colonies opposed the British, how they organized the militia, and how the Continental Congress worked."

TACTIC

3 Look first for the most common errors.

Most of the sentences will have errors. If you are having trouble finding mistakes, check for some of the more common ones: subject–verb agreement, pronoun–antecedent problems, misuse of adjectives and adverbs, dangling modifiers. But look for errors only in the underlined parts of the sentence.

> Marilyn and I ran as fast as we could, but we missed our train, which
>   A   B   C
> made us late for work. No error
>   D   E

Imagine that you have this sentence, and you can't see what is wrong with it. Start at the beginning and check each answer choice. *I* is part of the subject, so it is the right case: after all, you wouldn't say "Me ran fast." *Fast* can be an adverb, so it is being used correctly here. *Which* is a pronoun, and needs a noun for its antecedent. The only available noun is *train*, but that doesn't make sense (the train didn't make us late—*missing* the train made us late). So there is your error, Choice C.

TACTIC

4 Remember that not every sentence contains an error.

Ten to twenty percent of the time, the sentence is correct as it stands. Do not get so caught up in hunting for errors that you start seeing errors that aren't there. If no obvious errors strike your eye and the sentence sounds natural to your ear, go with Choice E: No error.

IMPROVING SENTENCES

The most numerous questions in the two writing skills sections involve spotting the form of a sentence that works best. In these improving sentence questions, you will be presented with five different versions of the same sentence; you must choose the best one. Here are the directions:

> Some or all parts of the following sentences are underlined. The first answer choice, (A), simply repeats the underlined part of the sentence. The other four choices present four alternative ways to phrase the underlined part. Select the answer that produces the most effective sentence, one that is clear and exact, and blacken the appropriate space on your answer sheet. In selecting your choice, be sure that it is standard written English, and that it expresses the meaning of the original sentence.
>
> Example:
>
> The first biography of author Eudora Welty came out in 1998 and she was 89 years old at the time.
>
> (A) and she was 89 years old at the time
> (B) at the time when she was 89
> (C) upon becoming an 89 year old
> (D) when she was 89
> (E) at the age of 89 years old
>
>   Ⓐ Ⓑ Ⓒ ● Ⓔ

Testing Tactics

TACTIC

1

If you spot an error in the underlined section, eliminate any answer that also contains that error.

If something in the underlined section of a sentence correction question strikes you as an obvious error, you can immediately ignore any answer choices that also contain the error. Remember, you still don't have to be able to explain what is wrong. You just need to pick something that sounds correct. If the error you found in the underlined section is absent from more than one of the answer choices, look over those choices again to see if they add any new errors.

> Being as I had studied for the test with a tutor, I was confident.
>
> (A) Being as I had studied for the test
> (B) Being as I studied for the test
> (C) Since I studied for the test
> (D) Since I had studied for the test
> (E) Because I studied for the test

Since you immediately recognize that *Being as* is not acceptable as a conjunction in standard written English, you can eliminate choices A and B right away. But you also know that both *Since* and *Because* are perfectly acceptable conjunctions, so you have to look more closely at Choices C, D, and E. The only other changes these choices make are in the tense of the verb. Since the studying occurred before the taking of the test, the past perfect tense, *had studied*, is correct, so the answer is Choice D. Even if you hadn't known that, you could have figured it out. Since *Because* and *Since* are both acceptable conjunctions, and since Choices C and E both use the same verb, *studied,* in the simple past tense, those two choices must be wrong. Otherwise, they would both be right, and the SAT doesn't have questions with two right answers.

TACTIC

2

If you don't spot the error in the underlined section, look for changes in the answer choices.

Sometimes it's hard to spot what's wrong with the underlined section in a sentence correction question. When that happens, turn to the answer choices. Find the changes in the answers. The changes will tell you what kind of error is being tested. When you substitute the answer choices in the original sentence, ask yourself which of these choices makes the sentence seem clearest to you. That may well be the correct answer choice.

> Even the play's most minor characters work together with extraordinary skill, their interplay creates a moving theatrical experience.
>
> (A) their interplay creates a moving theatrical experience
> (B) a moving theatrical experience is created by their interplay
> (C) and their interplay creates a moving theatrical experience
> (D) and a moving theatrical experience being the creation of their interplay
> (E) with their interplay they create a moving theatrical experience

Look at the underlined section of the sentence. Nothing seems wrong with it. It could stand on its own as an independent sentence: *Their interplay creates a moving theatrical experience.* Choices B and E are similar to it, for both could stand as independent sentences. Choices C and D, however, are not independent sentences; both begin with the linking word *and.* The error needing correction here is the common comma splice, in which two sentences are carelessly linked with only a comma. Choice C corrects this error in the simplest way possible, adding the word *and* to tie these sentences together.

TACTIC

Make sure that all parts of the sentence are logically connected.

Not all parts of a sentence are created equal. Some parts should be subordinated to the rest, connected with subordinating conjunctions or relative pronouns, not just added on with *and*. Overuse of *and* frequently makes sentences sound babyish. Compare "We had dinner at the Hard Rock Cafe, and we went to a concert" with "After we had dinner at the Hard Rock Cafe, we went to a concert."

The rock star always had enthusiastic fans <u>and they loved him</u>.

(A) and they loved him
(B) and they loving him
(C) what loved him
(D) who loved him
(E) which loved him

The original version of this sentence doesn't have any grammatical errors, but it is a poor sentence because it doesn't connect its two clauses logically. The second clause ("and they loved him") is merely adding information about the fans, so it should be turned into an adjective clause, introduced by a relative pronoun. Choices D and E both seem to fit, but you know that *which* should never be used to refer to people, so Choice D is obviously the correct answer.

TACTIC

Make sure that all parts of a sentence given in a series are similar in form.

If they are not, the sentence suffers from a lack of parallel structure. The sentence "I'm taking classes in algebra, history, and how to speak French" lacks parallel structure. *Algebra* and *history* are nouns, names of subjects. The third subject should also be a noun: *conversational French*.

In this chapter we'll analyze both types of questions, <u>suggest useful techniques for tackling them, providing some sample items for you to try</u>.

(A) suggest useful techniques for tackling them, providing some sample items for you to try
(B) suggest useful techniques for tackling them, providing some sample items which you can try
(C) suggest useful tactics for tackling them, and provide some sample items for you to try
(D) and suggest useful techniques for tackling them by providing some sample items for you to try
(E) having suggested useful techniques for tackling them and provided some sample items for you to try

To answer questions like this correctly, you must pay particular attention to what the sentence means. You must first decide whether *analyzing, suggesting,* and *providing* are logically equal in importance here. Since they are—all are activities that "we" will do—they should be given equal emphasis. Only Choice C provides the proper parallel structure.

5   Pay particular attention to the shorter answer choices.

(This tactic also applies to certain paragraph correction questions.) Good prose is economical. Often the correct answer choice will be the shortest, most direct way of making a point. If you spot no grammatical errors or errors in logic in a concise answer choice, it may well be right.

> The turning point in the battle of Waterloo probably was <u>Blucher, who was arriving</u> in time to save the day.
>
> (A) Blucher, who was arriving
> (B) Blucher, in that he arrived
> (C) Blucher's arrival
> (D) when Blucher was arriving
> (E) that Blucher had arrived

Which answer choice uses the fewest words? Choice C, *Blucher's arrival.* It also happens to be the right answer.

Choice C is both concise in style and correct in grammar. Look back at the original sentence. Strip it of its modifiers, and what is left? "The turning point . . . was Blucher." A turning point is not a person; it is a *thing.* The turning point in the battle was not Blucher, but Blucher's *action,* the thing he did. The correct answer is Choice C, *Blucher's arrival.* Pay particular attention to such concise answer choices. If a concise choice sounds natural when you substitute it for the original underlined phrase, it's a reasonable guess.

IMPROVING PARAGRAPHS

In the improving paragraph questions, you will confront a flawed student essay followed by six questions. In some cases, you must select the answer choice that best rewrites and combines portions of two separate sentences. In others, you must decide where in the essay a sentence best fits. In still others, you must choose what sort of additional information would most strengthen the writer's argument. Here are the directions.

The passage below is the unedited draft of a student's essay. Parts of the essay need to be rewritten to make the meaning clearer and more precise. Read the essay carefully.

The essay is followed by six questions about changes that might improve all or part of the organization, development, sentence structure, use of language, appropriateness to the audience, or use of standard written English. In each case, choose the answer that most clearly and effectively expresses the student's intended meaning. Indicate your choice by blackening the corresponding space on the answer sheet.

---

[1] Nowadays the average cost of a new home in San Francisco is over $500,000. [2] For this reason it is not surprising that people are talking about a cheaper new type of home called a Glidehouse. [3] The Glidehouse is a type of factory-built housing. [4] It was designed by a young woman architect named Michelle Kaufmann. [5] Michelle was disgusted by having to pay $600,000 for a fixer-upper. [6] So she designed a kind of a modular house with walls that glide.

Sentences 3, 4, and 5 (reproduced below) could best be written in which of the following ways?

> *The Glidehouse is a type of factory-built housing. It was designed by a young woman architect named Michelle Kaufmann. Michelle was disgusted by having to pay $600,000 for a fixer-upper.*

(A) (Exactly as shown above)

(B) The Glidehouse typifies factory-built housing. A young woman architect named Michelle Kaufmann designed it, having been disgusted at having to pay $600,000 for a fixer-upper.

(C) The Glidehouse is a type of factory-built home, it was a young woman architect named Michelle Kaufmann who designed it because she resented having to pay $600,000 for a fixer-upper.

(D) An example of housing that has been built in a factory, the Glidehouse was the design of a young woman architect named Michelle Kaufmann whom having to pay $600,000 for a fixer-upper resented.

(E) The Glidehouse, a factory-built home, was designed by the architect Michelle Kaufmann, who resented having to pay $600,000 for a fixer-upper.

In the original essay, sentences 3, 4, and 5 are wordy and rely heavily on passive voice constructions. Read aloud, they sound choppy. Choice E combines these three simple sentences into a single sentence that is both coherent and grammatically correct.

Testing Tactics

TACTIC 1

First read the passage; then read the questions.

Whether you choose to skim the student essay quickly or to read it closely, you need to have a reasonable idea of what the student author is trying to say before you set out to correct this rough first draft.

TACTIC 2

First tackle the questions that ask you to improve individual sentences; then tackle the ones that ask you to strengthen the passage as a whole.

In the sentence correction questions, you've just been weeding out ineffective sentences and selecting effective ones. Here you're doing more of the same. It generally takes less time to spot an effective sentence than it does to figure out a way to strengthen an argument or link up two paragraphs.

TACTIC 3

Consider whether the addition of signal words or phrases— transitions—would strengthen the passage or particular sentences within it.

If the essay is trying to contrast two ideas, it might benefit from the addition of a contrast signal.

Contrast Signals: *although, despite, however, in contrast, nevertheless, on the contrary, on the other hand.*

If one portion of the essay is trying to support or continue a thought developed elsewhere in the passage, it might benefit from the addition of a support signal.

Support Signals: *additionally, furthermore, in addition, likewise, moreover.*

If the essay is trying to indicate that one thing causes another, it might benefit from the addition of a cause-and-effect signal.

Cause-and-Effect Signals: *accordingly, as a result of, because, consequently, hence, therefore, thus.*

Pay particular attention to answer choices that contain such signal words.

TACTIC

4

When you tackle the questions, *go back to the passage* to verify each answer choice.

See whether your revised version of a particular sentence sounds right in its context. Ask yourself whether your choice follows naturally from the sentence before.

COMMON GRAMMAR AND USAGE ERRORS

Some errors are more common than others in this section. Here are a dozen that appear frequently on the examination. Watch out for them when you do the practice exercises and when you take the SAT.

The Run-On Sentence

> *Mary's party was very exciting, it lasted until 2 A.M.*
> *It is raining today, I need a raincoat.*

You may also have heard this error called a comma splice. It can be corrected by making two sentences instead of one:

> *Mary's party was very exciting. It lasted until 2 A.M.*

or by using a semicolon in place of the comma:

> *Mary's party was very exciting; it lasted until 2 A.M.*

or by proper compounding:

> *Mary's party was very exciting and lasted until 2 A.M.*

You can also correct this error with proper subordination. The second example above could be corrected:

> *Since it is raining today, I need a raincoat.*

> *It is raining today, so I need a raincoat.*

The Sentence Fragment

> *Since John was talking during the entire class, making it impossible for anyone to concentrate.*

This is the opposite of the first error. Instead of too much in one sentence, here you have too little. Do not be misled by the length of the fragment. It must have a main clause before it can be a complete sentence. All you have in this example is the cause. You still need a result. For example, the sentence could be corrected:

> *Since John was talking during the entire class, making it impossible for anyone to concentrate, the teacher made him stay after school.*

Error in the Case of a Noun or Pronoun

Between you and I, this test is not really very difficult.

Case problems usually involve personal pronouns, which are in the nominative case (*I, he, she, we, they, who*) when they are used as subjects or predicate nominatives, and in the objective case (*me, him, her, us, them, whom*) when they are used as direct objects, indirect objects, and objects of prepositions. In this example, if you realize that *between* is a preposition, you know that *I* should be changed to the objective *me* because it is the object of a preposition.

Error in Subject–Verb Agreement

Harvard College, along with several other Ivy League schools, are sending students to the conference.

Phrases starting with *along with* or *as well as* or *in addition to* that are placed in between the subject and the verb do not affect the verb. The subject of this sentence is *Harvard College,* so the verb should be *is sending.*

There is three bears living in that house.

Sentences that begin with *there* almost always have the subject after the verb. The subject of this sentence is *bears,* so the verb should be *are.*

Error in Pronoun–Number Agreement

Every one of the girls on the team is trying to do their best.

Every pronoun must have a specific noun or noun substitute for an antecedent, and it must agree with that antecedent in number (singular or plural). In this example, *their* refers to *one* and must be singular:

Every one of the girls on the team is trying to do her best.

Error in the Tense or Form of a Verb

After the sun set behind the mountain, a cool breeze sprang up and brought relief from the heat.

Make sure the verbs in a sentence appear in the proper sequence of tenses, so that it is clear what happened when. Since, according to the sentence, the breeze did not appear until after the sun had finished setting, the setting belongs in the past perfect tense:

After the sun had set behind the mountain, a cool breeze sprang up and brought relief from the heat.

Error in Logical Comparison

I can go to California or Florida. I wonder which is best.

When you are comparing only two things, you should use the comparative form of the adjective, not the superlative:

I wonder which is better.

Comparisons must also be complete and logical.

The rooms on the second floor are larger than the first floor.

It would be a strange building that had rooms larger than an entire floor. Logically, this sentence should be corrected to:

The rooms on the second floor are larger than those on the first floor.

Adjective and Adverb Confusion

She did good on the test.

They felt badly about leaving their friends.

These are the two most common ways that adjectives and adverbs are misused. In the first example, when you are talking about how someone did, you want the adverb *well*, not the adjective *good*:

She did well on the test.

In the second example, after a linking verb like *feel* you want a predicate adjective to describe the subject:

They felt bad about leaving their friends.

Error in Modification and Word Order

Reaching for the book, the ladder slipped out from under him.

A participial phrase at the beginning of the sentence should describe the subject of the sentence. Since it doesn't make sense to think of a ladder reaching for a book, this participle is left dangling with nothing to modify. The sentence needs some rewriting:

When he reached for the book, the ladder slipped out from under him.

Error in Parallelism

In his book on winter sports, the author discusses ice-skating, skiing, hockey, and how to fish in an ice-covered lake.

Logically, equal and similar ideas belong in similar form. This shows that they are equal. In this sentence, the author discusses four sports, and all four should be presented the same way:

In his book on winter sports, the author discusses ice skating, skiing, hockey, and fishing in an ice-covered lake.

Error in Diction or Idiom

The affects of the storm could be seen everywhere.

Your ear for the language will help you handle these errors, especially if you are accustomed to reading standard English. These questions test you on words that are frequently misused, on levels of usage (informal versus formal), and on standard English idioms. In this example, the verb *affect,* meaning "to influence," has been confused with the noun *effect,* meaning "result."

The effects of the storm could be seen everywhere.

The exercises that follow will give you practice in answering the three types of questions you'll find on the Identifying Sentence Errors questions, Improving Sentence questions, and Improving Paragraph questions. When you have completed each exercise, check your answers against the answer key. Then, read the answer explanations for any questions you either answered incorrectly or omitted.

Practice Exercises

The sentences in this section may contain errors in grammar, usage, choice of words, or idioms. Either there is just one error in a sentence or the sentence is correct. Some words or phrases are underlined and lettered; everything else in the sentence is correct.

If an underlined word or phrase is incorrect, choose that letter; if the sentence is correct, select <u>No error</u>. Then blacken the appropriate space on your answer sheet.

Example:

The region has a climate <u>so severe that</u> plants
                          A
<u>growing there</u> rarely <u>had been</u> more than twelve
      B   C
inches <u>high</u>. <u>No error</u>
       D   E

Ⓐ Ⓑ ● Ⓓ Ⓔ

1. We were <u>already</u> <u>to leave for</u> the amusement park
              A   B
   when John's car <u>broke down</u>; we <u>were forced</u> to
                        C   D
   postpone our outing. <u>No error</u>
                          E

2. <u>By order of</u> the Student Council, the <u>wearing of</u>
       A   B
   slacks by <u>we</u> girls in school <u>has been permitted</u>.
              C   D
   <u>No error</u>
    E

3. <u>Each</u> one of the dogs in the show <u>require</u> a
    A   B
   special <u>kind of</u> diet. <u>No error</u>
   C   D   E

4. The major difficulty <u>confronting</u> the authorities
                          A
   <u>was</u> the reluctance of the people <u>to talk</u>; they had
    B   C
   been warned not <u>to say nothing</u> to the police.
                      D
   <u>No error</u>
    E

5. If I <u>were</u> you, I would never permit <u>him</u>
         A   B
   <u>to take part</u> in such an <u>exhausting and painful</u>
        C   D
   activity. <u>No error</u>
              E

6. Stanford White, <u>who</u> is one of America's
                    A
   <u>most notable</u> architects, <u>have designed</u> many famous
        B   C
   buildings, <u>among them</u> the original Madison Square
                  D
   Garden. <u>No error</u>
            E

7. The notion <u>of allowing</u> the <u>institution of</u> slavery
                  A   B
   <u>to continue</u> to exist in a democratic society had no
        C
   appeal to either the violent followers of John Brown
   <u>nor</u> the peaceful disciples of Sojourner Truth.
    D
   <u>No error</u>
    E

8. Some students <u>prefer</u> watching videos to <u>textbooks</u>
                    A   B
   because they feel <u>uncomfortable with</u> the
                          C
   presentation <u>of</u> information in a non-oral form.
                 D
   <u>No error</u>
    E

9. There was so much conversation <u>in back of</u> me
    A   B
   <u>that</u> I <u>couldn't</u> hear the actors on the stage.
    C   D
   <u>No error</u>
    E

10. This book is <u>too</u> elementary; it can <u>help</u> neither
                  A   B
    you <u>nor</u> <u>I</u>. <u>No error</u>
         C   D   E

11. In a way <u>we</u> may say <u>that</u> we <u>have reached</u> the
            A   B   C

    <u>end of</u> the Industrial Revolution. <u>No error</u>
       D   E

12. <u>Although</u> the books are <u>altogether</u> on the shelf,
        A   B

    <u>they</u> are not arranged in <u>any kind of</u> order.
      C   D

    <u>No error</u>
       E

13. The <u>reason for</u> my <u>prolonged absence</u> from
          A   B

    class <u>was</u> <u>because</u> I was ill for three weeks.
         C   D

    <u>No error</u>
       E

14. <u>According to</u> researchers, the weapons and work
        A

    implements <u>used</u> by Cro-Magnon hunters appear
              B

    <u>being</u> <u>actually quite</u> "modern." <u>No error</u>
       C   D   E

15. Since we were caught <u>completely unawares</u>, the
                      A

    <u>affect</u> of Ms. Rivera's remarks <u>was startling</u>; some
      B   C

    were shocked, <u>but</u> others were angry. <u>No error</u>
              D   E

16. The committee <u>had intended</u> both <u>you and I</u> to speak
               A   B

    at the assembly; <u>however</u>, <u>only</u> one of us will be
                  C   D

    able to talk. <u>No error</u>
               E

17. The existence of rundown "welfare hotels"

    <u>in which</u> homeless families <u>reside</u> at enormous
      A   B

    <u>cost</u> to the taxpayer provides a shameful
      C

    <u>commentary of</u> America's commitment to house
         D

    the poor. <u>No error</u>
           E

18. We have heard that the <u>principal</u> has decided
                     A

    <u>whom</u> the prize winners <u>will be</u> <u>and</u> will
      B   C   D

    announce the names in the assembly today.

    <u>No error</u>
       E

19. As soon as the sun <u>had rose</u> <u>over</u> the mountains,
              A   B   C

    the valley became <u>unbearably hot</u> and stifling.
                   D

    <u>No error</u>
       E

20. <u>They</u> are both <u>excellent books</u>, but this one <u>is</u>
      A   B   C

    <u>best</u>. <u>No error</u>
      D   E

21. Although the news <u>had come</u> as a surprise <u>to all</u>
                 A   B

    in the room, both Jane and Oprah tried to do

    <u>her</u> work <u>as though</u> nothing had happened.
      C   D

    <u>No error</u>
       E

22. <u>Even</u> well-known fashion designers have difficulty
      A

    staying on top <u>from one season to another</u>
                    B

    because of <u>changeable moods</u> and needs in the
           C   D

    marketplace. <u>No error</u>
              E

23. Arms control has been <u>under discussion</u> for
                    A

    decades with the former Soviet Union, <u>but</u> solutions
                              B

    <u>are still</u> <u>alluding</u> the major powers. <u>No error</u>
      C   D   E

24. Perhaps sports enthusiasts are realizing <u>that</u>
                                               A

    jogging is <u>not easy on</u> joints and tendons, for
                    B

    the <u>latest</u> fad <u>is being walking.</u> <u>No error</u>
          C   D   E

25. Technological advances <u>can cause</u> factual data to
                              A

    become obsolete within a <u>short time;</u> <u>yet,</u> students
                                 B   C

    should concentrate on <u>reasoning skills,</u> not facts.
                              D

    <u>No error</u>
       E

26. If anyone cares <u>to join</u> me in this campaign, <u>either</u>
    A   B   C

    now or in the near future, <u>they</u> will be welcomed
                                  D

    gratefully. <u>No error</u>
                   E

27. The poems <u>with which</u> he occasionally
                   A

    <u>desired to regale</u> the fashionable world were
           B

    <u>invariably bad</u>—stereotyped, bombastic, and
          C

    even ludicrous. <u>No error</u>
         D   E

28. <u>Ever since</u> the <u>quality of</u> teacher education came
       A   B

    under public scrutiny, suggestions for <u>upgrading</u> the
                                               C

    profession <u>are abounding.</u> <u>No error</u>
                   D   E

29. <u>Because</u> the door was locked and bolted, the police
       A

    <u>were forced</u> to <u>break</u> into the apartment <u>through</u> the
        B   C   D

    bedroom window. <u>No error</u>
                        E

30. I <u>will</u> <u>always</u> remember <u>you</u> <u>standing by</u> me
       A   B   C   D

    offering me encouragement. <u>No error</u>
                                   E

31. With special training, capuchin monkeys

    <u>can enable</u> quadriplegics <u>as well as</u> other
        A   B

    handicapped individuals <u>to become</u>
                               C

    <u>increasingly independent</u> . <u>No error</u>
            D   E

32. <u>Contrary to</u> what had previously been reported, the
       A

    conditions <u>governing</u> the truce between Libya and
                  B

    Chad <u>arranged by</u> the United Nations <u>has</u> not yet
            C   D

    been revealed. <u>No error</u>
                      E

33. Avid readers generally either admire <u>or</u> dislike
                                          A

    Ernest Hemingway's journalistic <u>style of</u> writing;
                                        B

    few have no opinion <u>of him.</u> <u>No error</u>
         C   D   E

34. In 1986, the nuclear disaster at Chernobyl

    <u>has aroused</u> intense speculation <u>about</u> the
        A   B

    long-term <u>effects of</u> radiation that continued for
                  C

    <u>the better part of</u> a year. <u>No error</u>
           D   E

35. Howard Hughes, <u>who</u> <u>became</u> the subject of bizarre
                      A   B

    rumors <u>as a result of</u> his extreme reclusiveness,
                C

    was well-known as an aviator, industrialist, and

    <u>in producing motion pictures</u> . <u>No error</u>
            D   E

Some or all parts of the following sentences are underlined. The first answer choice, (A), simply repeats the underlined part of the sentence. The other four choices present four alternative ways to phrase the underlined part. Select the answer that produces the most effective sentence, one that is clear and exact, and blacken the appropriate space on your answer sheet. In selecting your choice, be sure that it is standard written English, and that it expresses the meaning of the original sentence.

Example:

The first biography of author Eudora Welty came out in 1998 and she was 89 years old at the time.

(A) and she was 89 years old at the time
(B) at the time when she was 89
(C) upon becoming an 89 year old
(D) when she was 89
(E) at the age of 89 years old

Ⓐ Ⓑ Ⓒ ● Ⓔ

36. The child is neither encouraged to be critical or to examine all the evidence before forming an opinion.

(A) neither encouraged to be critical or to examine
(B) neither encouraged to be critical nor to examine
(C) either encouraged to be critical or to examine
(D) encouraged either to be critical nor to examine
(E) not encouraged either to be critical or to examine

37. The process by which the community influence the actions of its members is known as social control.

(A) influence the actions of its members
(B) influences the actions of its members
(C) had influenced the actions of its members
(D) influences the actions of their members
(E) will influence the actions of its members

38. Play being recognized as an important factor improving mental and physical health and thereby reducing human misery and poverty.

(A) Play being recognized as
(B) By recognizing play as
(C) Their recognizing play as
(D) Recognition of it being
(E) Play is recognized as

39. To be sure, there would be scarcely any time left over for other things if school children would have been expected to have considered all sides of every matter, on which they hold opinions.

(A) would have been expected to have considered
(B) should have been expected to have considered
(C) were expected to consider
(D) will be expected to have considered
(E) were expected to be considered

40. Using it wisely, leisure promotes health, efficiency and happiness.

(A) Using it wisely
(B) If it is used wisely
(C) Having used it wisely
(D) Because of its wise use
(E) Because of usefulness

41. In giving expression to the play instincts of the human race, new vigor and effectiveness are afforded by recreation to the body and to the mind.

(A) new vigor and effectiveness are afforded by recreation to the body and to the mind
(B) recreation affords new vigor and effectiveness to the body and to the mind
(C) there are afforded new vigor and effectiveness to the body and to the mind
(D) by recreation the body and the mind are afforded new vigor and effectiveness
(E) to the body and to the mind afford new vigor and effectiveness to themselves by recreation

42. Depending on skillful suggestion, argument is seldom used in advertising.

(A) Depending on skillful suggestion, argument is seldom used in advertising.
(B) Argument is seldom used in advertising, which depends instead on skillful suggestion.
(C) Skillful suggestion is depended on by advertisers instead of argument.
(D) Suggestion, which is more skillful, is used in place of argument by advertisers.
(E) Instead of suggestion, depending on argument is used by skillful advertisers.

43. When this war is over, no nation will either be isolated in war or peace.

(A) either be isolated in war or peace
(B) be either isolated in war or peace
(C) be isolated in neither war nor peace
(D) be isolated either in war or in peace
(E) be isolated neither in war or peace

44. Thanks to the prevailing westerly winds, dust <u>blowing east from the drought-stricken plains</u> travels halfway across the continent to fall on the cities of the East Coast.

    (A) blowing east from the drought-stricken plains
    (B) that, blowing east from the drought-stricken plains,
    (C) from the drought-stricken plains and blows east
    (D) that is from the drought-stricken plains blowing east
    (E) blowing east that is from the plains that are drought-stricken

45. Americans are learning that their concept of a research worker <u>toiling alone in a laboratory and who discovers miraculous cures</u> has been highly idealized and glamorized.

    (A) toiling alone in a laboratory and who discovers miraculous cures
    (B) toiling alone in a laboratory and discovers miraculous cures
    (C) toiling alone in a laboratory to discover miraculous cures
    (D) who toil alone in the laboratory and discover miraculous cures
    (E) has toiled alone hoping to discover miraculous cures

46. However many mistakes have been made in our past, the tradition of America, <u>not only the champion of freedom but also fair play</u>, still lives among millions who can see light and hope scarcely anywhere else.

    (A) not only the champion of freedom but also fair play
    (B) the champion of not only freedom but also of fair play
    (C) the champion not only of freedom but also of fair play
    (D) not only the champion but also freedom and fair play
    (E) not the champion of freedom only, but also fair play

47. <u>Examining the principal movements sweeping through the world, it can be seen</u> that they are being accelerated by the war.

    (A) Examining the principal movements sweeping through the world, it can be seen
    (B) Having examined the principal movements sweeping through the world, it can be seen
    (C) Examining the principal movements sweeping through the world can be seen
    (D) Examining the principal movements sweeping through the world, we can see
    (E) It can be seen examining the principal movements sweeping through the world

48. <u>The FCC is broadening its view on what constitutes indecent programming</u>, radio stations are taking a closer look at their broadcasters' materials.

    (A) The FCC is broadening its view on what constitutes indecent programming
    (B) The FCC, broadening its view on what constitutes indecent programming, has caused
    (C) The FCC is broadening its view on what constitutes indecent programming, as a result
    (D) Since the FCC is broadening its view on what constitutes indecent programming
    (E) The FCC, having broadened its view on what constitutes indecent programming

49. As district attorney, Elizabeth Holtzman not only had the responsibility of supervising a staff of dedicated young lawyers <u>but she had the task of maintaining good relations with the police also</u>.

    (A) but she had the task of maintaining good relations with the police also
    (B) but she also had the task of maintaining good relations with the police
    (C) but also had the task of maintaining good relations with the police
    (D) but she had the task to maintain good relations with the police also
    (E) but also she had the task to maintain good relations with the police

50. Many politicians are now trying to take uncontroversial positions on <u>issues; the purpose being to allow them to appeal</u> to as wide a segment of the voting population as possible.

    (A) issues; the purpose being to allow them to appeal
    (B) issues in order to appeal
    (C) issues, the purpose is to allow them to appeal
    (D) issues and the purpose is to allow them to appeal
    (E) issues; that was allowing them to appeal

The passage below is the unedited draft of a student's essay. Parts of the essay need to be rewritten to make the meaning clearer and more precise. Read the essay carefully.

The essay is followed by six questions about changes that might improve all or part of the organization, development, sentence structure, use of language, appropriateness to the audience, or use of standard written English. In each case, choose the answer that most clearly and effectively expresses the student's intended meaning. Indicate your choice by blackening the corresponding space on the answer sheet.

[1] Throughout history, people have speculated about the future. [2] Will it be a utopia? they wondered. [3] Will injustice and poverty be eliminated? [4] Will people accept ethnic diversity, learning to live in peace? [5] Will the world be clean and unpolluted? [6] Or will technology aid us in creating a trap for ourselves we cannot escape, for example such as the world in 1984? [7] At the start of each new century, these questions are in the back of our minds.

[8] Science fiction often portrays the future as a technological Garden of Eden. [9] With interactive computers, TVs and robots at our command, we barely need to lift a finger to go to school, to work, to go shopping, and education is also easy and convenient. [10] Yet, the problems of the real twentieth century seem to point in another direction. [11] The environment, far from improving, keeps deteriorating. [12] Wars and other civil conflicts breakout regularly. [13] The world's population is growing out of control. [14] The majority of people on earth live in poverty. [15] Many of them are starving. [16] Illiteracy is a problem in most poor countries. [17] Diseases and malnourishment is very common. [18] Rich countries like the U.S.A. don't have the resources to help the "have-not" countries.

[19] Instead, think instead of all the silly inventions such as tablets you put in your toilet tank to make the water blue, or electric toothbrushes. [20] More money is spent on space and defense than on education and health care. [21] Advancements in agriculture can produce enough food to feed the whole country, yet people in the U.S. are starving.

[22] Although the USSR is gone, the nuclear threat continues from small countries like Iraq. [23] Until the world puts its priorities straight, we can't look for a bright future in the twenty-first century, despite the rosy picture painted for us by the science fiction writers.

51. In the context of paragraph 1, which of the following is the best revision of sentence 6?

   (A) Or will technology create a trap for ourselves from which we cannot escape, for example the world in *1984*?
   (B) Or will technology aid people in creating a trap for themselves that they cannot escape; for example, the world in *1984*?
   (C) Or will technology create a trap from which there is no escape, as it did in the world in *1984*?
   (D) Or will technology trap us in an inescapable world, for example, it did so in the world of *1984*?
   (E) Perhaps technology will aid people in creating a trap for themselves from which they cannot escape, just as they did it in the world of *1984*.

52. With regard to the essay as a whole, which of the following best describes the writer's intention in paragraph 1?

   (A) To announce the purpose of the essay
   (B) To compare two ideas discussed later in the essay
   (C) To take a position on the essay's main issue
   (D) To reveal the organization of the essay
   (E) To raise questions that will be answered in the essay

53. Which of the following is the best revision of the underlined segment of sentence 9 below?

   [9] With interactive computers, TVs and robots at our command, we barely need to lift a finger to go to school, to work, to go shopping, and education is also easy and convenient.

   (A) and to go shopping, while education is also easy and convenient
   (B) to go shopping, and getting an education is also easy and convenient
   (C) to go shopping as well as educating ourselves are all easy and convenient
   (D) to shop, and an easy and convenient education
   (E) to shop, and to get an easy and convenient education

54. Which of the following is the most effective way to combine sentences 14, 15, 16, and 17?

    (A) The majority of people on earth are living in poverty and are starving, with illiteracy, and disease and being malnourished are also a common problems.
    (B) Common problems for the majority of people on earth are poverty, illiteracy, diseases, malnourishment, and many are illiterate.
    (C) The majority of people on earth are poor, starving, sick, malnourished and illiterate.
    (D) Common among the poor majority on earth is poverty, starvation, disease, malnourishment, and illiteracy.
    (E) The majority of the earth's people living in poverty with starvation, disease, malnourishment and illiteracy a constant threat.

55. In the context of the sentences that precede and follow sentence 19, which of the following is the most effective revision of sentence 19?

    (A) Instead they are devoting resources on silly inventions such as tablets to make toilet tank water blue or electric toothbrushes.
    (B) Instead, they waste their resources on producing silly inventions like electric toothbrushes and tablets for bluing toilet tank water.
    (C) Think of all the silly inventions: tablets you put in your toilet tank to make the water blue and electric toothbrushes.
    (D) Instead, tablets you put in your toilet tank to make the water blue or electric toothbrushes are examples of useless products on the market today.
    (E) Instead of spending on useful things, think of all the silly inventions such as tablets you put in your toilet tank to make the water blue or electric toothbrushes.

56. Which of the following revisions would most improve the overall coherence of the essay?

    (A) Move sentence 7 to paragraph 2
    (B) Move sentence 10 to paragraph 1
    (C) Move sentence 22 to paragraph 2
    (D) Delete sentence 8
    (E) Delete sentence 23

Answer Key

1.	**A**	13.	**D**	25.	**C**	37.	**B**	49.	**C**
2.	**C**	14.	**C**	26.	**D**	38.	**E**	50.	**B**
3.	**B**	15.	**B**	27.	**E**	39.	**C**	51.	**C**
4.	**D**	16.	**B**	28.	**D**	40.	**B**	52.	**E**
5.	**E**	17.	**D**	29.	**E**	41.	**B**	53.	**E**
6.	**C**	18.	**B**	30.	**C**	42.	**B**	54.	**C**
7.	**D**	19.	**B**	31.	**E**	43.	**D**	55.	**B**
8.	**B**	20.	**D**	32.	**D**	44.	**A**	56.	**C**
9.	**B**	21.	**C**	33.	**D**	45.	**C**		
10.	**D**	22.	**E**	34.	**A**	46.	**C**		
11.	**E**	23.	**D**	35.	**D**	47.	**D**		
12.	**B**	24.	**D**	36.	**E**	48.	**D**		

Answer Explanations

1. **(A)** Error in diction. Should be *all ready*. *All ready* means the group is ready; *already* means prior to a given time, previously.

2. **(C)** Error in pronoun case. Should be *us*. The expression *us girls* is the object of the preposition *by*.

3. **(B)** Error in subject–verb agreement. Should be *requires*. Verb should agree with the subject (*each one*).

4. **(D)** Should be *to say anything*. *Not to say nothing* is a double negative.

5. **(E)** Sentence is correct.

6. **(C)** Error in subject–verb agreement. Since the subject is Stanford White (singular), change *have designed* to *has designed*.

7. **(D)** Error in use of correlatives. Change *nor* to *or*. The correct form of the correlative pairs *either* with *or*.

8. **(B)** Error in parallel structure. Change *textbooks* to *reading textbooks*. To have parallel structure, the linked sentence elements must share the same grammatical form.

9. **(B)** Error in diction. Change *in back of* to *behind*.

10. **(D)** Error in pronoun case. Should be *me*. Pronoun is the object of the verb *can help*.

11. **(E)** Sentence is correct.

12. **(B)** Error in diction. Should be *all together*. *All together* means in a group; *altogether* means entirely.

13. **(D)** Improper use of *because*. Change to *that* (*The reason . . . was that . . . .*).

14. **(C)** Incorrect verbal. Change the participle *being* to the infinitive *to be*.

15. **(B)** Error in diction. Change *affect* (a verb meaning to influence or pretend) to *effect* (a noun meaning result).

16. **(B)** Error in pronoun case. Should be *me*. Subjects of infinitives are in the objective case.

17. **(D)** Error in idiom. Change *commentary of* to *commentary on*.

18. **(B)** Error in pronoun case. Should be *who*. The pronoun is the predicate complement of *will be* and is in the nominative case.

19. **(B)** Should be *had risen*. The past participle of the verb *to rise* is *risen*.

20. **(D)** Error in comparison of modifiers. Should be *better*. Do not use the superlative when comparing two things.

21. **(C)** Error in pronoun–number agreement. Should be *their* instead of *her*. The antecedent of the pronoun is *Jane and Oprah* (plural).

22. **(E)** Sentence is correct.

23. **(D)** Error in diction. Change *alluding* (meaning to refer indirectly) to *eluding* (meaning to evade).

24. **(D)** Confusion of verb and gerund (verbal noun). Change *is being walking* to *is walking*.

25. **(C)** Error in coordination and subordination. Change *yet* to *therefore* or another similar connector to clarify the connection between the clauses.

26. **(D)** Error in pronoun–number agreement. Should be *he or she*. The antecedent of the pronoun is *anyone* (singular).

27. **(E)** Sentence is correct.

28. **(D)** Error in sequence of tenses. Change *are abounding* to *have abounded*. The present perfect tense talks about an action that occurs at one time, but is seen in relation to another time.

29. **(E)** Sentence is correct.

30. **(C)** Error in pronoun case. Should be *your*. The pronoun modifying a gerund (verbal noun) should be in the possessive case.

31. **(E)** Sentence is correct.

32. **(D)** Error in subject–verb agreement. Since the subject is *conditions* (plural), change *has* to *have*.

33. **(D)** Error in pronoun. Since the sentence speaks about Hemingway's style rather than about Hemingway, the phrase should read *of it,* not *of him*.

34. **(A)** Error in sequence of tenses. Change *has aroused* to *aroused*. The present perfect tense (*has aroused*) is used for indefinite time. In this sentence, the time is defined as *the better part of a year*.

35. **(D)** Lack of parallel structure. Change *in producing motion pictures* to *motion picture producer*.

36. **(E)** This question involves two aspects of correct English. *Neither* should be followed by *nor; either* by *or*. Choices A and D are, therefore, incorrect. The words *neither . . . nor* and *either . . . or* should be placed before the two items being discussed—*to be critical* and *to examine*. Choice E meets both requirements.

37. **(B)** This question tests agreement. Errors in subject–verb agreement and pronoun–number agreement are both involved. *Community* (singular) needs a singular verb, *influences*. Also, the pronoun that refers to *community* should be singular (*its*).

38. **(E)** Error in following conventions. This is an incomplete sentence or fragment. The sentence needs a verb to establish a principal clause. Choice E provides the verb (*is recognized*) and presents the only complete sentence in the group.

39. **(C)** *Would have been expected* is incorrect as a verb in a clause introduced by the conjunction *if*. *Had been expected* or *were expected* is preferable. *To have considered* does not follow correct sequence of tense and should be changed to *to consider*.

40. **(B)** Error in modification and word order. One way of correcting a dangling participle is to change the participial phrase to a clause. Choices B and D substitute clauses for the phrase. However, Choice D changes the meaning of the sentence. Choice B is correct.

41. **(B)** Error in modification and word order. As it stands, the sentence contains a dangling modifier. This is corrected by making *recreation* the subject of the sentence, in the process switching from the passive to the active voice. Choice E also provides a subject for the sentence; however, the meaning of the sentence is changed in Choice E.

42. **(B)** Error in modification and word order. As presented, the sentence contains a dangling participle, *depending*. Choice B corrects this error. The other choices change the emphasis presented by the author.

43. **(D)** Error in word order. *Either . . . or* should precede the two choices offered (*in war* and *in peace*).

44. **(A)** Sentence is correct.

45. **(C)** Error in parallelism. In the underlined phrase, you will find two modifiers of *worker-toiling* and *who discovers*. The first is a participial phrase and the second a clause. This results in an error in parallel structure. Choice B also has an error in parallel structure. Choice C corrects this by eliminating one of the modifiers of *worker*. Choice D corrects the error in parallel structure but introduces an error in agreement between subject and verb—*who* (singular) and *toil* (plural). Choice E changes the tense and also the meaning of the original sentence.

46. **(C)** Error in parallelism. Parallel structure requires that *not only* and *but also* immediately precede the words they limit.

47. **(D)** Error in modification and word order. Choices A, B, and E are incorrect because of the dangling participle. Choice C is incoherent. Choice D correctly eliminates the dangling participle by introducing the subject *we*.

48. **(D)** Error in comma splice. The punctuation in Choices A and C creates a run-on sentence. Choices B and E are both ungrammatical. Choice D corrects the run-on sentence by changing the beginning clause into the adverb clause that starts with the subordinating conjunction *since*.

49. **(C)** Error in parallelism. Since the words *not only* immediately precede the verb in the first half of the sentence, the words *but also* should immediately

precede the verb in the second half. This error in parallel structure is corrected in choice C.

50. **(B)** Error in coordination and subordination. The punctuation in Choices A, C, D, and E creates an incomplete sentence or fragment. Choice B corrects the error by linking the elements with *in order to*.

51. **(C)** Choice A is awkward and shifts the pronoun usage in the paragraph from third to first person. Choice B is awkward and contains a semicolon error. A semicolon is used to separate two independent clauses. The material after the semicolon is a sentence fragment. Choice C is succinctly and accurately expressed. It is the best answer. Choice D contains a comma splice between *world* and *for*. A comma may not be used to join two independent clauses. Choice E is awkwardly expressed and contains the pronoun *it*, which lacks a clear referent.

52. **(E)** Choice A indirectly describes the purpose of paragraph 1 but does not identify the writer's main intention. Choices B, C, and D fail to describe the writer's main intention. Choice E accurately describes the writer's main intention. It is the best answer.

53. **(E)** Choice A is grammatically correct but cumbersome. Choice B contains an error in parallel construction. The clause that begins *and getting* is not grammatically parallel to the previous items on the list. Choice C contains a mixed construction. The first and last parts of the sentence are grammatically unrelated. Choice D contains faulty parallel structure. Choice E is correct and accurately expressed. It is the best answer.

54. **(C)** Choice A is wordy and awkwardly expressed. Choice B contains an error in parallel structure. The clause *and many are illiterate* is not grammatically parallel to the previous items on the list of problems. Choice C is concise and accurately expressed. It is the best answer. Choice D is concise, but it contains an error in subject–verb agreement. The subject is *poverty, starvation . . . etc.*, which requires a plural verb; the verb *is* is singular. Choice E is a sentence fragment; it has no main verb.

55. **(B)** Choice A contains an error in idiom. The standard phrase is *devoting to*, not *devoting on*. Choice B ties sentence 19 to the previous sentence and is accurately expressed. It is the best answer. Choice C fails to improve the coherence of the paragraph. Choice D is unrelated to the context of the paragraph. Choice E is insufficiently related to the context of the paragraph.

56. **(C)** Choice A should stay put because it provides a transition between the questions in paragraph 1 and the beginning of paragraph 2. Choice B is a pivotal sentence in paragraph 2 and should not be moved. Choice C fits the topics of paragraph 2, therefore, sentence 22 should be moved to paragraph 2. Choice C is the best answer. Choice D is needed as an introductory sentence in paragraph 2. It should not be deleted. Choice E provides the essay with a meaningful conclusion and should not be deleted.

CHAPTER 7

Writing a 25-Minute Essay

- **Scoring Overview**
- **Facts About the SAT Essay**
- **How to Write an Essay in 25 Minutes**

- **Testing Tactics**
- **Resources to Help You Become a Better Writer**
- **Scoring the Essay**

In this chapter you will find basic guidelines for writing an essay, plus tips on dealing with the pressures inherent in writing a timed essay on an unfamiliar topic. You'll also become acquainted with a host of resources that will help you develop your essay-writing skills.

SCORING OVERVIEW

First, a few words about how your SAT essay will be scored, and about what the readers expect of you. Two readers will grade your essay in about two minutes, reading it very quickly to judge it as a whole. (The College Board calls this process *holistic scoring.*) Each reader will assign your essay a score of 1 to 6, with 6 the highest possible score. If both readers give your essay a 4, your combined score will be 8. If one reader gives your essay a 3 and the other assigns it a 4, your combined score will be 7. If the two readers seriously disagree about your score—for example, if one reader considers your essay a 3 and the other judges it a 5—a third reader will look over your essay and determine your score.

A word of warning: *It is possible to receive no credit for your essay.* The test directions state you *must* write on the assigned topic. An essay on any other topic is unacceptable. If you write on another topic, you will receive a score of zero.

Scored sample essays appear at the end of this chapter.

Both your essay subscore (that is, your combined score of 2 to 12) and your multiple-choice writing subscore will go into making up your eventual writing skills score, with the essay subscore counting as one-third of your total writing score.

FACTS ABOUT THE SAT ESSAY

Before we take you, minute by minute, through writing a 25-minute essay, here are some facts about the essay writing section on the SAT.

1. It will be the first section on your test.

2. It will consist of a 4-page student response sheet.

3. Page 1 is your sign-in sheet. It tells you to:

   - get ready to plan and write an essay in 25 minutes
   - use the blank space at the bottom of page 2 for outlining and jotting notes
   - use the lined pages (pages 3 and 4) for writing your essay
   - use pencil
   - be careful not to run out of space
   - be careful to write or print neatly
   - be careful to write on the assigned topic

   DO NOT WRITE ON ANOTHER TOPIC. AN ESSAY ON ANOTHER TOPIC IS UNACCEPTABLE.

4. Page 2 is your essay prompt. It presents you with a quote and gives you an assignment to

   - think about the quote
   - answer a question about the quote by writing an essay
   - support your viewpoint with evidence, that is, with examples and reasons
   - use examples from your reading, schoolwork, or personal experience

5. Pages 3 and 4 are where you write your essay.

Frequently Asked Questions—Deciphering the Directions

1. Is it better to print or to write in cursive?

   ☐ print   ☐ cursive   ☐ whatever is more legible

2. Should I skip lines, double-spacing my essay, or should I write on every line?

   ☐ single space   ☐ double space   ☐ it does not matter

3. Should I make extra-wide margins, so that my essay looks longer?

   ☐ yes   ☐ no   ☐ it does not matter

4. Will the length of my essay affect my score?

   ☐ yes   ☐ no

5. Should I write in pen or pencil?

   ☐ pen   ☐ pencil   ☐ it does not matter

6. Will the readers give me any credit for the outline and notes I write on page 2?

   ☐ yes   ☐ no   ☐ I don't know

7. Should I prepare a standard essay in advance and tweak it to make it fit the topic?

   ☐ yes   ☐ no   ☐ I don't know

8. Is it better to use personal examples or to use examples from books and magazines?

   ☐ personal examples   ☐ books and magazines   ☐ it does not matter

Answers to Frequently Asked Questions

1. *Whatever is more legible.* Neatness counts. As long as printing or writing in cursive doesn't slow you down, write in whichever style is easier to read. *Legibility really matters.* Remember, what the graders see is a scanned copy of your essay, not the original paper. If your handwriting is sloppy or if you cross out every other word, your essay is going to be hard to read. Scanning will only make things worse. Write as neatly and clearly as you can.

2. *Single space.* Don't take the chance of running out of room. Write on every line.

3. *No.* You won't fool the readers into thinking you've written more than you actually have.

4. *Yes.* According to a 2005 analysis of graded sample SAT essays by Dr. Les Perelman of MIT, the longer the essay, the higher the score. As you practice writing essays and when you take your test, go for length as well as legibility.

5. *Pencil.* You get no credit if you write in pen.

6. *No.* The readers will read only what you've written on the lined pages of your student response sheet.

7. *No.* You *must* write on the assigned topic. If you write on any other topic, you will get a score of zero. Don't assume you can memorize a standard essay and then tweak or fiddle with it to make it fit the assignment. Focus on *this* assignment, *this* essay prompt. Answer the question that you have been asked.

8. *It does not matter.* As long as the examples you choose support the position you take, they can come from your personal experience, from your observations of others, from your reading, your coursework, your browsing on the Internet. Quotes from Shakespeare and references to nano-technology may look impressive, but if they don't further your argument, they are worthless. A good example is *appropriate* to your argument: it helps you make your point.

Now that you're clued in on the basics of the essay-writing section, here's how to deal with it on the day of the test.

HOW TO WRITE AN ESSAY IN 25 MINUTES
Minute One—Analyze

Look at the essay question or prompt. What is it asking you to do? Is it prompting you to explain the reasons for an opinion of yours? Is it prompting you to take a stand on a particular issue? If you are being asked to argue for or against something, you may have an immediate gut reaction to what you're being asked. Pay attention to how you feel. If your immediate reaction is "Of course!" or "Never!" ask yourself why you feel that way. See whether you can spot any key word or short phrase in the prompt that triggers your reaction. For example, consider the following essay prompt:

> "If we rest, we rust." This statement is certainly true; inactivity and lack of exertion over time can cause our skills to deteriorate through disuse. In fact, people who have ceased practicing an activity for a long period and who attempt to take it up again frequently are thwarted in doing so because of the decline of their skills.

Do you think that rest has a detrimental effect on us and that we must keep active to avoid losing our edge? Plan and write an essay in which you explain your position on this issue. You may use examples from history, literature, popular culture, current events, or personal experience to support your position.

What key words trigger your reaction? *Rest* and *rust*.

Minute Two—Brainstorm

Write down the key words you spotted in the prompt. Circle them. Now write down all the words and phrases that you associate with these key words. What words come to your mind, for example, when you think of *rest*?

Neutral words like *sleep, inactivity, motionlessness*?

Negative words like *idleness, laziness, indolence*?

Positive words like *relaxing, tranquil, trouble free*?

Even if you have never thought that there might be a connection between resting and rusting, you have some mental associations with these ideas. By brainstorming, or clustering, as this process is sometimes called, you get in touch with these associations, call up the wealth of ideas you already have, and forget any worries you may have had about having nothing to say.

Note, by the way, in the illustration that follows, the many other words and phrases that branch off from the key words *rest* and *rust*. When you brainstorm, your mind leads you in innumerable directions, hinting at the whole range of what you already know about the subject at hand. If you feel like it, draw lines and arrows linking the various words and phrases to your two key words. Don't worry about setting these words and phrases in any particular order. Just play with them, jotting them down and doodling around them—a sense of where you are going will emerge.

You have plenty to say. You have gut reactions to all sorts of questions. Trust yourself. Let the brainstorming process tap the knowledge and feelings that lie within you.

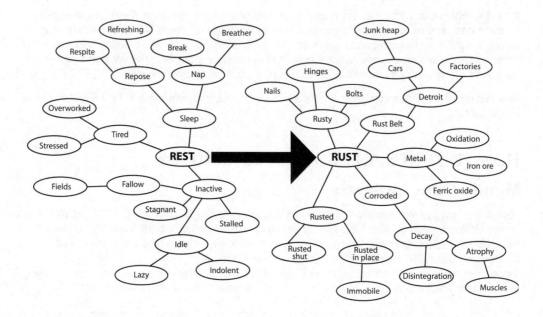

Minute Three—Take a Stand

After you have been brainstorming for a bit, something inside you is going to say, "Now—now I know what I'm going to write." Trust that inner sense. You know where you are going—now put it into words.

Look over your "map" or record of your mental associations and see what patterns have emerged. Just what is it that you have to say? Are you *for* the idea that if we rest, we rust? Are you *against* the idea? What you are doing is coming up with a statement of your position—words to express your initial gut reaction—a *thesis sentence* for your essay.

T<small>HESIS</small> 1: I believe that, if we rest, we rust, because inactivity and lack of exertion lead to loss of vitality and to decay.

T<small>HESIS</small> 2: I believe that, if we rest, we do not rust, because our times of rest enable us to restore our mental and physical energy and to gain perspective on our lives.

Here are two preliminary thesis sentences, one for, one against. Note how their main clauses start: *I believe that*. Cut out that preliminary song and dance. In your thesis sentence, simply take a stand:

If we rest, we do not rust: our times of rest enable us to restore our mental and physical energy and to gain perspective on our lives.

The examiners want to see whether you can express your ideas clearly. Make your point clear to them from the start.

In a sense, the test-makers give you your introduction. All you have to do is take the prompt and rephrase it, putting it into your own words. This does not take much work. Remember, your job is to prove your writing competence, not to demonstrate your literary style. You do not need to open your essay with a quotation (The philosopher Blaise Pascal warns us, "Our nature consists in motion; complete rest is death.") or with a statement designed to startle your reader ("Sleep is for sissies."). You simply need to take a stand. In doing so, however, you must exercise some caution: you must limit your thesis to something you can handle in a few hundred words.

The one problem with brainstorming is that you may wind up feeling that you have too much to say. Your job is not to write everything you possibly can about the topic. It is to write one or two pages and make a single clear point. Avoid starting with open-ended statements like "Keeping active is important" or "Everybody needs rest." These are weak thesis statements—they are too broad to help you focus on the topic and too vague to show why you hold the opinion that you have. In writing your thesis statement, limit yourself. State your point—and be ready to support it with reasons.

Minute Four—Outline

Now take a minute to organize what you are going to say in outline form. In a sense, your thesis sentence sets up everything else you have to say. If you have a clear thesis, the essay almost writes itself.

Your goal is to produce a four- or five-paragraph essay consisting of a brief introduction, two or three solid paragraphs presenting examples that support your thesis, and a conclusion that restates your thesis. This is what such an essay looks like:

INTRODUCTION

THESIS SENTENCE: State your point (often last sentence of opening paragraph)
Summary of Essay: Present your supporting examples (2–3 sentences)

EXAMPLE PARAGRAPH 1

TOPIC SENTENCE: State the main idea of this paragraph. Show how it relates to your thesis.
Development of Example: Provide specific facts about the first example. Show how this example supports your argument. Be as detailed as possible: cite names, places, events. (3–5 sentences)

EXAMPLE PARAGRAPH 2

TOPIC SENTENCE: State the main idea of this paragraph. Show how it relates to your thesis. (Use transition words to connect this paragraph to the previous example paragraph.)
Development of Example: Provide specific facts about the second example. Show how this example supports your argument. Be as detailed as possible: cite names, places, events. (3–5 sentences)

EXAMPLE PARAGRAPH 3 (OPTIONAL)

Write a third paragraph <u>only</u> if you have enough time left to wrap up your essay.

TOPIC SENTENCE: State the main idea of this paragraph. Show how it relates to your thesis. (Use transition words to connect this paragraph to the previous example paragraph.)
Development of Example: Provide specific facts about the third example. Show how this example supports your argument. Be as detailed as possible: cite names, places, events. (3–5 sentences)

> **CONCLUSION**
>
> RECAP: Summarize your argument, restating your main points (1 sentence)
> Expansion of Your Position: Consider the broader implications of your argument.
> Place your discussion within a larger context.

See how each of the thesis sentences just discussed sets up the essay, in each case requiring a slightly different outline.

OUTLINE 1

I. Introduction—State your overall thesis

If we rest, we rust: inactivity and lack of exertion get in the way of progress and lead to the loss of vitality and to decay.

II. State the point of your first supporting paragraph.

We have to keep moving to keep up with others and to avoid falling behind. This is as true for industries as for individuals.

Examples:
A. United States auto industry's decline: GM vs. Honda
B. Outmoded technology: pay phones, cassettes

III. State the point of your second supporting paragraph.

We have to keep active to prevent our skills from going bad.

Examples:
A. Loss of memory with age
B. Muscles atrophy from disuse

IV. Conclusion—Restate your thesis

> **GOOD EXAMPLES**
>
> • Detailed—names, dates, places, events
> • Varied—personal, literary, historical, contemporary

OUTLINE 2

I. Introduction—State your thesis

If we rest, we do not rust: our times of rest enable us to restore our mental and physical energy and to gain perspective on our lives.

II. State the point of your first supporting paragraph.

We need times of rest to restore us mentally and physically.

Examples:
A. Sleep deprivation lowers IQ
B. New work hour limits for hospital residents
C. Exercise programs build in rest days

III. State the point of your second supporting paragraph.

Rest allows us to develop perspective and to set goals.

A. Caught up in rat race
B. My brother's gap year, when he decided what he wanted to do in life

IV. Conclusion—Restate your thesis

> ## ORGANIZING YOUR EXAMPLES: ONE TACTIC TO TRY
>
> Start with the personal: catch your reader's attention with a personal example, something uniquely your own. Make it vivid and concrete.
>
> Move on to the general: take your second example from history or literature or current events.
>
> Be sure to develop your examples thoroughly. Two carefully thought-out, detailed examples will impress your readers more than a hodgepodge of oversimplified examples will.

Minutes Five to Seventeen—Write

You have 12 minutes to begin writing your essay. You have your opening, your outline, and your conclusion all in mind. Devote this time to putting down your thoughts, writing as much as you legibly can. Try to write neatly, but don't worry so much about neatness that you wind up clenching your pencil for dear life. There is no problem if you occasionally cross something out or erase.

> **NEATNESS COUNTS!**
>
> Is your handwriting hard to read? If your printing is more legible than your cursive, go ahead and print.

Minute Eighteen—Perform a Reality Check

You have been writing for 12 minutes straight. Take a moment to see how far you have gotten in your outline. If you've written your introduction and have barely finished your first supporting paragraph, now's the time for you to abandon the idea of writing a five- or six-paragraph essay. Instead, whip through the second supporting paragraph and start on your conclusion. You need to allow yourself enough time both to come up with a good ending and to look over your essay before you turn it in.

Minutes Nineteen to Twenty-Two—Wrap Things Up

Finish the supporting paragraph you've been working on, and bring your essay to a close. You'll be able to fine-tune your essay in just a moment.

Minute Twenty-Three—Read and React

Expert writers often test their work by reading it aloud. In the exam room, you cannot read out loud. However, when you read your essay silently, take your time and listen with your inner ear to how it sounds. Read to get a sense of your essay's logic and of its rhythm. Does one sentence flow smoothly into the next? Would they flow more smoothly if you were to add a transition word or phrase (*therefore, however, nevertheless, in contrast, similarly*)? Do the sentences follow a logical order? Is any key idea or example missing? Does any sentence seem out of place? How would things sound if you cut out that awkward sentence or inserted that transition word?

Take a moment to act on your response to hearing your essay. If it sounded to you as if a transition word was needed, insert it. If it sounded to you as if a sentence should be cut, delete it. Trust your inner ear, but do not attempt to do too much. You know your basic outline for the essay is good. You have neither the need nor the time to attempt a total revision.

> **TAKE TIME FOR TRANSITIONS**
>
> Transition words are signposts that show your readers the direction your argument is going. They are cues that help your readers figure out how your ideas fit together logically. Graders like them if you use them well.

Minute Twenty-Four—Proofread

Think of yourself as an editor. You need to have an eye for errors that damage your text. Take a minute to look over your essay for problems in spelling and grammar. From your English classes, you should have an idea of particular words and grammatical constructions that have given you trouble in the past—sentence fragments, or phrases like "everybody except my teacher and I." See whether you can spot any of these words or constructions in your essay. Correct those errors that you find.

SHOW WHAT YOU KNOW, NOT WHAT YOU DON'T KNOW.

Don't risk misusing a word just to show off. You get no points for using big words incorrectly.

Minute Twenty-Five—Reword, Reread, Relax

Look over the vocabulary used in your essay. In your concern to get your thoughts on paper, have you limited yourself to an over-simple vocabulary? Have you used one word over and over again, never substituting a synonym? Try upgrading your vocabulary judiciously. Replace one word or phrase in the essay with a synonym—*deteriorating* in place of *going bad* in the sentence "We have to keep active to prevent our skills from going bad," for example. Substitute a somewhat more specific adjective or adverb for a vague one—*insignificant* in place of *not important*; *extremely* busy in place of *really* busy. Again, do not attempt to do too much. Change only one or two words. Replace them with stronger, college-level words, *words whose meanings you are sure you know.*

Look over the changes in the paragraph below to see how the student writer replaced a couple of easy words with more complex ones *whose meanings she knew:*

> Helen Hayes takes a firm stand against ~~laziness~~ indolence when she says, "If we rest, we rust." Though ~~laziness~~ indolence is commonly considered a sin at worst, and a waste at best, our negative attitude toward rest is ~~not good~~ detrimental. Rest is critical to progress because it enables us to function well and it helps us to set appropriate goals.

Now that you've looked over your essay like an editor, give yourself one final opportunity to hear your words again. Reread the composition to yourself, making sure that the changes you have made have not harmed the flow of your text.

You have just completed a basic four- or five-paragraph essay. Now it is time to regroup your forces and relax before you go on to the next section of the test. Take a deep breath. At this point, you have earned a break.

Skill-Building Exercise: Generating Good Examples

For each prompt below, come up with one personal example and one "impersonal" example (an example from literature, history, or contemporary life).

1. Essay Prompt

> *Progress is not an illusion; it happens, but it is slow and invariably disappointing.*
>
> George Orwell

Is progress necessarily slow and invariably disappointing? Plan and write an essay in which you explain your position on this issue. You may use examples from history, literature, popular culture, current events, or personal experience to support your position.

Personal Example   Learning to play an instrument _____

(Fill in your example) _____

Impersonal Example   Equal opportunity for women and minorities _____

(Fill in your example) _____

2. Essay Prompt

   The harder the conflict, the more glorious the triumph. What we obtain too cheap, we esteem too lightly.

   Thomas Paine

   Do we most value the things that are difficult to attain? Plan and write an essay in which you explain your position on this issue. You may use examples from history, literature, popular culture, current events, or personal experience to support your position.

   Personal Example   Winning a medal in gymnastics

   (Fill in your example) _____

   Impersonal Example   Frederick Douglass learned to read despite his master

   (Fill in your example) _____

3. Essay Prompt

   We can succeed only by concert. It is not "Can any of us imagine better?" but "Can we all do better?"

   Abraham Lincoln

   Can we achieve success only through collective effort rather than as individuals? Plan and write an essay in which you explain your position on this issue. You may use examples from history, literature, popular culture, current events, or personal experience to support your position.

   Personal Example   My rehab after the accident

   (Fill in your example) _____

   Impersonal Example   China's great leap forward

   (Fill in your example) _____

4. Essay Prompt

   Success is somebody else's failure.

   Ursula Le Guin

   When somebody wins, does someone else invariably have to lose? Can there be no "win–win" situations? Plan and write an essay in which you explain your position on this issue. You may use examples from history, literature, popular culture, current events, or personal experience to support your position.

   Personal Example   Winning the lead in the school play

   (Fill in your example) _____

   Impersonal Example   United States westward expansion and treatment of Native Americans

   (Fill in your example) _____

Testing Tactics

Keep Careful Track of Your Time.

Doing so is especially necessary on the essay section. Writing an essay on an unfamiliar subject is pressure enough. You don't need the added pressure that you'll feel if you lose track of the time and discover you have only 60 seconds left to write the two final paragraphs that are critical to your argument.

Pace Yourself: Keep to Your Essay-Writing Plan.

You have only 25 minutes. Allow yourself 3 to 4 minutes for prewriting. Read the essay topic or prompt with care. If you haven't a clue where to begin, jot down words and ideas that pop into your mind when you look at the prompt (brainstorming). Generate questions about the topic until you come up with a point you want to make. Briefly outline what you plan to say. Then devote the remaining 18 plus minutes to writing your essay, reserving 2 or 3 minutes at the end to clean up your draft.

Write As Much As You Can Within the Allotted Time.

On the SAT, longer essays have tended to receive higher scores than shorter ones. Be clear, be coherent, but don't kill yourself trying to be concise.

Don't Forget to State Your Conclusion.

It's all too easy to get so caught up in writing your essay that you run out of time before you can come to a conclusion. Nail that conclusion! If you don't, your readers are bound to notice that your concluding paragraph is missing.

Remember That You Don't Have to Write a
Perfect Essay to Earn a High Score.

The readers are instructed to overlook false starts ("beginning stutters," some readers call them) and incomplete conclusions in determining your score. With only 2 minutes to read your essay, they don't have time to check your facts. It's all too easy to psych yourself out about the essay-writing assignment and wind up so blocked that you can barely write a paragraph, much less a fully-developed essay. Relax. Loosen your grip on your pen. Shake out your fingers if that helps. Your job is to turn out a promising first draft in 25 minutes, not to create a finished work of prose.

Write As Legibly As You Possibly Can.

Neatness helps. If your printing is neater than your cursive and you can print rapidly, by all means print. Keep within the margins on the page. The easier you make the readers' job, the more well-disposed they will be toward your essay.

Follow Traditional Essay-Writing Conventions.

Make a point of showing the readers you know the "right" way to set up an essay. Indent each new paragraph clearly. Use transitions—signal words and phrases, such as "consequently" and "for this reason"—to indicate your progress from idea to idea.

Don't Alter Your Essay Capriciously.

Change what you have written only if you have a solid reason for doing so. If you have time to read over your paper and spot a grammatical error or a spelling mistake, by all means correct it, making sure your correction is legible. However, try to avoid making major alterations in your text. Last-minute changes can create more problems than they solve. You may run out of time and wind up with a muddle instead of a coherent argument. Or, in your haste to finish your revision, you may scribble sentences that not even a cryptologist could decipher.

Upgrade Your Vocabulary Judiciously.

Top-scoring essays typically include a sprinkling of "college-level" words. (See our High-Frequency Word List in Chapter 3.) The readers like your using big words, words like *theoretical* and *allusion*, but **only if you use them correctly**. Don't try to bluff: it's too risky. If you have a minute or two to spare and are absolutely sure of the meaning of a college-level word that you can substitute for a simple one, go for it. But use your judgment.

Don't Second-Guess Yourself.

Once you have finished writing your essay, let it go. You have been concentrating on a single topic for almost half an hour, and you may find it difficult to refocus on a set of multiple-choice questions when you are still worrying about your essay. Avoid the temptation to criticize yourself for those grammatical and spelling errors you may have made or to brood over all the clever arguments you *might* have made. Take a deep breath, loosen up your shoulders, and move on.

RESOURCES TO HELP YOU BECOME A BETTER WRITER

Recommended Sources of Practice Essay Topics

To practice brainstorming and outlining, you need a good supply of potential essay topics. One excellent source is an Internet Quote of the Day.

Great Web Sites for Quotes

www.BrainyQuote.com/quotes/topics.html

http://www.saidwhat.co.uk/research

www.quotationspage.com/qotd.html

http://www.bartleby.com/quotations/

Good Books of Quotations

The Harper Book of Quotations Revised Edition, Robert I. Fitzhenry

Peter's Quotations: Ideas for Our Times, Laurence J. Peter

Recommended Books on Writing

The Elements of Style, Strunk and White (Strunk's original *Elements of Style*, without E. B. White's revisions and added chapter, is available on the Web at *www.bartleby.com/141/*)

The Careful Writer, Theodore M. Bernstein

The Practical Stylist, Sheridan Baker

On Writing Well, William K. Zinsser

Line by Line: How to Edit Your Own Writing, Claire Kehrwald Cook

A Dictionary of Modern English Usage, H. W. Fowler (Fowler's classic *The King's English* is available on the Web at *www.bartleby.com/116/*)

Additional Sources of Writing Help

You learn to write by writing and rewriting, preferably with lots of feedback from your teachers and classmates. If you are not getting enough opportunities to write in high school, create fresh opportunities for yourself.

Find writing help through after-school tutorials, public library programs, etc.

Join your high school forensics team, and consider specializing in impromptu debate.

Set up writing cooperatives with your fellow students and practice critiquing one another's drafts.

Volunteer as a reporter for your local neighborhood newspaper.

Keep a folder of your old book reports and compositions, and review it periodically to see whether you are still making the same old mistakes.

Find writing help through the Internet. Potentially useful web sites are:

http://homeworktips.about.com/od/essaywriting/a/fiveparagraph.htm

http://writingcenter.gmu.edu/
The George Mason University Writing Center site contains useful material on grammar, punctuation, and the writing process.

http://rwc.hunter.cuny.edu/reading-writing/on-line.html
The Hunter College Writing Center site is a source of handouts on grammar and mechanics, the writing demands of different disciplines, and the writing process in general.

www.lynchburg.edu/writcntr/guide/
The Lynchburg College Writing Center provides online guides to grammar and to general writing techniques.

www.nutsandboltsguide.com
Author Michael Harvey offers extracts from his reader-friendly *Nuts and Bolts of College Writing*.

www.powa.org
The Paradigm Online Writing Assistant provides advice on writing and revising various types of essays.

www.scholastic.com/writewit/index.htm
The Scholastic site features an excellent section, Writing with Writers, offering workshops on writing news articles, speeches, and book reviews.

www.teenwriting.about.com
In addition to providing advice on the writing process and on fine-tuning your grammar, the Teenwriting Forum enables teens to discuss writing problems and critique one another's poetry and prose.

SCORING THE ESSAY

What characteristics distinguish essays at the various scoring levels? Here's what the test makers say:

Scoring Level 6

Essays on this level demonstrate a clear command of writing and thinking skills, despite the occasional, infrequent minor error. Characteristics of essays on this level include:

1. intelligent, convincing development of a position on the issue
2. selection of relevant examples and other evidence to support its position
3. smooth, well-orchestrated progression from idea to idea
4. use of varied sentence types and appropriate vocabulary
5. freedom from most technical flaws (mistakes in grammar, usage, diction)

These essays are *insightful*.

Scoring Level 5

Essays on this level exhibit a generally dependable command of writing and thinking skills, despite some mistakes along the way. Characteristics of essays on this level include:

1. proficient, coherent development of a position on the issue
2. selection of basically relevant evidence to support its position
3. relatively well-ordered progression from idea to idea
4. reasonably varied sentence structure
5. relative freedom from technical flaws

These essays are *effective*.

Scoring Level 4

Essays on this level exhibit a generally adequate command of writing and thinking skills, although they are typically inconsistent in quality. Characteristics of essays on this level include:

1. workmanlike development of a position on the issue
2. selection of reasonably appropriate evidence to support its position
3. acceptable progression from idea to idea
4. somewhat varied sentence structure
5. some flaws in mechanics, usage, and grammar

These essays are *competent*.

Scoring Level 3

Essays on this level exhibit an insufficient command of writing and thinking skills, although they do show some signs of developing proficiency. Characteristics of essays on this level include:

1. sketchy development of a position on the issue
2. selection of weak or inappropriate evidence to support its position
3. erratic progression from idea to idea
4. somewhat limited vocabulary
5. inadequately varied sentence structure
6. multiple flaws in mechanics, usage, and grammar

These essays are *inadequate*.

Scoring Level 2

Essays on this level exhibit a quite flawed command of writing and thinking skills. Characteristics of essays on this level include:

1. limited development of a position on the issue
2. selection of weak or inappropriate evidence to support its position
3. tendency toward incoherence
4. highly limited vocabulary
5. numerous problems with sentence structure
6. errors in mechanics, usage, and grammar serious enough to interfere with the reader's comprehension

These essays are *seriously flawed*.

Scoring Level 1

Essays on this level exhibit an acutely flawed command of writing and thinking skills. Characteristics of an essay on this level include:

1. absence of evidence to support a point of view
2. lack of a position on the issue
3. absence of focus and organization
4. rudimentary vocabulary
5. severe problems with sentence structure
6. extensive flaws in mechanics, usage, and grammar severe enough to block the reader's comprehension.

These essays are *fundamentally deficient*.

SAMPLE SCORED ESSAYS

Look over the following scored sample essays to see the characteristic strengths and weaknesses of compositions on each of the six scoring levels. These essays are all based on the following question.

> *The harder the conflict, the more glorious the triumph. What we obtain too cheap, we esteem too lightly.*
> —Thomas Paine

ASSIGNMENT: Do we most value the things that are difficult to attain? Plan and write an essay in which you explain your position on this issue. You may use examples from history, literature, popular culture, current events, or personal experience to support your position.

SAMPLE ESSAY U—SCORE 6

Those who have overcome great adversity in life can take satisfaction from Thomas Paine's assertion, "The harder the conflict, the more glorious the triumph." For people truly to appreciate their victories, they must be able to contrast these victories with the hardships they have undergone. To value their good fortune, they must suffer ill fortune as well.

In Charlotte Bronte's *Jane Eyre*, the theme of overcoming adversity occurs again and again. At each stage of Jane's life she struggles to overcome adversity and, succeeding, values her victory against the odds. In the novel's opening chapters, the orphaned Jane is at the mercy of her wealthy, uncaring Aunt Reed and her bullying cousin John. When she is sent away to Lowood School, she is overjoyed, because she is free from their cruelties. Yet Jane soon finds that her life at Lowood School is not as idylic as she had hoped it would be. Though she finds a friend in Helen Burns, Jane and the other students face adversity in the form of Mr. Brocklehurst, the headmaster, who deprives the girls of proper clothing and nourishment and spends school funds on his own family. Only after an epidemic hits the school, killing Helen, do the authorities step in to remove Mr. Brocklehurst and restore the school.

Jane survives this adversity and grows up to become a teacher at Lowood School. Facing a dull existence, she desires new experiences and accepts a position as governness at an

SAMPLE ESSAY U—SCORE 6 (CONTINUED)

estate owned by a man named Rochester. She wins his love and they are to be married when she discovers on their wedding day that he is already married to a madwoman, Bertha Mason, whom he cannot divorce. Jane is torn between her love for Rochester and her conscience. She struggles with herself and wins a hard victory: she runs away from Rochester, and, penniless and ill, lives on the streets until she is taken in by the Rivers family. Once again, she has survived adversity, and she rejoices as she regains her peace of mind and begins to do good works teaching in the local charity school.

Jane has survived, and in time she wins her greatest victory. St. John Rivers urges Jane to join him in missionary work in India and offers to marry her. Still loving Rochester, she does not wish to marry Rivers; however, she feels drawn to a life of service as a missionary. She struggles with herself, and one night she mysteriously hears Rochester's voice calling her name. Jane immediately hurries back to Rochester's estate and finds it has been burned to the ground by Bertha Mason, who died in the fire. Rochester also has suffered adversity: trying to save Bertha and the servant from the flames, he has lost his eyesight and one of his hands and needs Jane's help to keep him from giving in to despair. This is Jane's greatest victory and Rochester's as well, for they marry and live happily. Having struggled with their consciences and fought temptation, they value all the more their glorious victory.

SAMPLE ESSAY V—SCORE 5

When Thomas Paine wrote "The harder the conflict, the more glorious the triumph," he was writing in a time of war. The American colonies were still struggling to win their independance against the English. It was a hard and bloody conflict that pitted brother against brother. Paine wrote to inspire his fellow countrymen to persist in the fight. He promised them they would value their freedom even more because it had been so hard to attain. Paine's words inspired the people then and they can inspire us today.

Today Americans are fighting a terrible war, a war against terrorism. This war has taken reservists from jobs and families to face danger and death in the Middle East. These soldiers have been doing their job fighting our country's battles. They have been walking in harm's way. By fighting hard against the evils of terrorism and to bring democracy to the Middle East they are demonstrating to the world that "the harder the conflict, the more glorious the triumph."

In addition to our soldiers overseas today, the civil rights workers who protested in the South during the fifties and sixties also fought a great fight and won glorious victories. Students sat in at lunch counters and marched to integrate all-white schools. They faced fire hoses and police dogs singing "We shall overcome" and showed they were willing to fight and die for the principle of equal rights and equal opportunity. Freedom riders came to the South; some of them even died there. They paid with their lives so that others might be free. Without their attempts to break down the barriers, injustice and racial prejudice might still prevale.

Many times people who are engaged in a great conflict may feel like giving up, but our soldiers today and the civil rights workers of yesterday teach us a different lesson. The most important fights to fight are the hardest ones, the ones that cost some people everything they have. Only by fighting such a hard fight will you truly value your victory. That was true in Thomas Paine's time and in Martin Luther King's time and in our time today.

SAMPLE ESSAY W—SCORE 4

I partly agree with Thomas Paine's idea that "The harder the conflict, the more glorious the triumph." When you struggle hard for something, you can appreciate it more than if ~~you~~ it comes to you easily, however you can also decide it wasn't worth the fight. There are times when keeping on fighting is the best thing to do, while other times giving up the fight makes the most sence. You need to choose whether or not to keep fighting depending on what the situation is.

In ordinary life young people face many conflicts, especially when they have to decide about education and careers. There are many colleges in the ~~world~~ United States where the students have to fight hard to get accepted. They also can cost a lot of money. There are in addition many ~~care~~ careers that take hard work and persistence before you can get a good job. An example of this is medicine, where people who want to become doctors have to pass course after course just to get into medical school and

SAMPLE ESSAY W—SCORE 4 (CONTINUED)

then have to complete medical school and pass their boards before they can practice medicine. Another example of struggling hard to get an education was in the south during the civil rights movement when black people fought to integrate the schools.

Many people today still have to fight to get a good education or a job. One ~~example~~ problem is outsourcing. Outsourcing is when American jobs go to peoples overseas, for example in India. The American people who lose their jobs are struggling to get new ones, but sometime there are no new jobs in their home town or they have to find a job in a different field. This is also true for young people just coming out of college. The struggle is hard but the reward is great.

Just as Thomas Paine wrote in his quote, "the harder the conflict, the more glorious the triumph." It costs a lot of money and effort to get a good education. It takes a lot of searching to find a good job. But when you get that job or the degree, you will know how special it can be.

SAMPLE ESSAY X—SCORE 3

People often think that they would like an easy life. They think conflict and fighting are always bad. However it seems when they have to fight for what they want they are happier with what they get.

The phrase "easy come, easy go" shows how people do not value things they can get easily. They have low esteem. At least some struggle is necessary in making the victories feel more meaningfull. There are some fights that are too hard to win and then no one is happy, but if someone can fight and win they are better off.

Some conflicts are simply too much to handle, for various reasons. Often times a fight cannot be won because one side is too strong. Conflicts can bring out the best in people, they can bring out the worst in people too. There is just no way of avoiding conflicts, so if you have to fight do your best to win and let yourself feel good about the victory.

SAMPLE ESSAY Y—SCORE 2

Fighting a hard conflict is a difficult thing. There are always wars and no one can predicts which side is going to win. If you look back at all the wars the United States has gotten in to over the years, many have ended up with a withdrawl and not a victory. In some cases the goverment tells the public that it is a victory but that is not necesarly true. They only tell the public about the fights they win or sometimes they make it sound like they won even if they have not. To feel realy victorious about a conflict you have to actually win it. Thomas Paine once said "The harder the conflict, the more glorious the triumph. What we obtain too cheaply, we esteem too lightly." But it is realy cheap to pretend to win a victory.

SAMPLE ESSAY Z—SCORE 1

THomas Pain conce said "The harder the conflict, the more glorious the triumph" If a conflict is hard it is not all bad because when u win you are happier then befor. A hard conflict can be very bad dangerous for a community and its people. When things are bad the people can be discouraged phcysologicly and even give up. Many times they need to fight hard and things get better they will have a triumph.

PART THREE

TACTICS AND PRACTICE: MATHEMATICS

Introduction to the Math Sections

PART THREE consists of this Introduction and two extremely important chapters. Chapter 8 presents several important strategies that can be used on any mathematics questions that appear on the SAT. Chapter 9 contains a complete review of all the mathematics you need to know in order to do well on the SAT, as well as hundreds of sample problems patterned on actual test questions.

FIVE TYPES OF TACTICS

Five different types of tactics are discussed in this book.

1. In Part One you learned many basic tactics used by all good test-takers; for example, read each question carefully, pace yourself, don't get bogged down on any one question, guess whenever you can eliminate choices, and never waste time reading the directions. These tactics apply to all sections of the SAT: critical reading, mathematics, and writing.

2. In Chapters 1 and 2 you learned the important tactics needed for handling the questions in the critical reading sections.

3. In Chapters 4, 5, and 6 you learned tactics for handling the three different types of writing skills questions, and in Chapter 7 you learned strategies for writing a good essay.

4. In Chapter 8 you will find all of the tactics that apply to the mathematics sections of the SAT. Specific strategies are presented to deal with each type of multiple-choice and grid-in question found on the SAT.

5. In Chapter 9 you will learn or review all of the mathematics that is needed for the SAT, and you will master the tactics and key facts that apply to each of the different mathematical topics.

Using these tactics will enable you to answer more quickly many problems that you already know how to do. The greatest value of these tactics, however, is that they will allow you to answer correctly, or make educated guesses on, problems that you *do not know how to do*.

WHEN TO STUDY CHAPTER 9

How much time you initially devote to Chapter 9 should depend on how good your math skills are. If you are an excellent student who consistently earns A's in math, you can initially skip the instructional parts of Chapter 9. If, however, while doing the model tests in Part Four, you find that you keep making mistakes on certain types of problems (averages, percentages, geometry, etc.) or if you are spending too much time on them, you should then study the appropriate sections of Chapter 9. Even if your math skills are excellent, and you don't need the review, you should do the sample questions in those sections; they are an excellent source of additional SAT questions. If you know that your math skills are not very good, it is advisable to review the material in Chapter 9, including working out the problems, *before* tackling the model tests in Part Four.

No matter how good you are in math, *you should carefully read and do the sample problems in Chapter 8*. For many of these problems, two solutions are given: the most direct mathematical solution and a solution using one or more of the special tactics taught in these chapters.

AN IMPORTANT SYMBOL

Throughout the book, the symbol "$\Rightarrow$" is used to indicate that one step in the solution of a problem follows *immediately* from the preceding one, and that no explanation is necessary. You should read:

$$2x = 12 \Rightarrow x = 6$$

as $2x = 12$ *implies* (or *which implies*) that $x = 6$, or, *since* $2x = 12$, then $x = 6$.

Here is a sample solution, using $\Rightarrow$, to the following problem:

What is the value of $3x^2 - 7$ when $x = -5$?

$$x = -5 \Rightarrow x^2 = (-5)^2 = 25 \Rightarrow 3x^2 = 3(25) = 75 \Rightarrow$$
$$3x^2 - 7 = 75 - 7 = \mathbf{68}.$$

When the reason for a step is not obvious, $\Rightarrow$ is not used: rather, an explanation is given, often including a reference to a KEY FACT from Chapter 9. In many solutions, some steps are explained, while others are linked by the $\Rightarrow$ symbol, as in the following example:

EXAMPLE

In the diagram at the right, if $w = 30$, what is z?

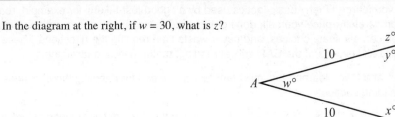

- By KEY FACT J1, $w + x + y = 180$.
- Since $\triangle ABC$ is isosceles, $x = y$ [KEY FACT J5].
- Therefore, $w + 2y = 180 \Rightarrow 30 + 2y = 180 \Rightarrow 2y = 150 \Rightarrow y = 75$.
- Finally, since $y + z = 180$ [KEY FACT I3], $75 + z = 180 \Rightarrow z = \mathbf{105}$.

SEVEN IMPORTANT HEADINGS

In Chapters 8 and 9, you will see seven headings that will appear either in the text or in the margins. They will indicate valuable information and will help to guide you as you study this book. Here is a brief explanation of each heading.

- A useful strategy for attacking a certain type of problem. Some TACTICS give you advice on how to handle multiple-choice questions, regardless of the subject matter. Others point out ways to handle specific subject matter, such as finding averages or solving equations, regardless of the type of problem.

-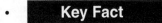

    An important mathematical fact that you should commit to memory because it comes up often on the SAT.

- > **REFERENCE FACT**
  >
  > A basic mathematical fact that is included in the "Reference Information" that appears on the first page of every math section.

- > **Helpful Hint**
  >
  > A useful idea that will help you solve a problem more easily or avoid a pitfall.

- **CAUTION:** A warning of a potential danger. Often a CAUTION points out a common error or a source of careless mistakes.

- *Calculator Shortcut*

  A method of using your calculator, even when it is unnecessary, to help you get an answer faster than you otherwise might. Often this heading will signal an unusual or nonstandard way of using your calculator that you might not think of.

- **CALCULATOR HINT**

  Often, a way of using your calculator to get an answer that you could get more quickly without the calculator if you only knew how. CALCULATOR HINTS allow you to use your calculator to get answers to questions you would otherwise have to omit or guess at.

USE OF THE CALCULATOR

Before doing any of the work in Part Three and the model tests in Part Four, you should reread the short discussion in Part One on the use of calculators on the SAT. As you do the sample problems in this book, always have available the calculator you intend to take to the SAT, and use it whenever you think it will be helpful. Throughout the rest of the book, whenever the use of a calculator is recommended, the icon has been placed next to the example or question. Remember: no problem *requires* the use of a calculator, but there are several for which it is helpful.

Because students' mathematical knowledge and arithmetic skills vary considerably, the decision as to when to use a calculator is highly subjective. Consider the following rather easy problem. Would you use a calculator?

What is the average (arithmetic mean) of 301, 303, and 305?

Let's analyze the four possibilities:

1. Some students would use their calculators twice: first to add, $301 + 303 + 305 = 909$, and then to divide, $909 \div 3 = 303$.

2. Others would use their calculators just once: to add the numbers; these students would then divide mentally.

3. Others would not use their calculators at all, because they could add the three numbers mentally faster than they could on a calculator. (Just say to yourself: 300, 300, and 300 is 900; and 1 + 3 + 5 is 9 more.)

4. Finally, others would do no calculations whatsoever. They would realize that the average of any three consecutive odd integers is the middle one: 301, **303**, 305.

> **Helpful Hint**
>
> In general, you should do very little arithmetic longhand. If you can't do a calculation mentally, use your calculator. In particular, avoid long division and multiplication in which the factors have two or more digits. If you know that $13^2 = 169$, terrific; if not, it's better to use your calculator than to multiply with paper and pencil.

NOTE: The more the calculator was used, the *longer* it took to solve the problem. Use your calculator only when it will really save you time or if you think you will make a mistake without it.

MEMORIZE IMPORTANT FACTS AND DIRECTIONS

Immediately preceding the multiple-choice questions, you will see the following set of instructions.

> **For each problem in this section, determine which of the five choices is correct and blacken the corresponding choice on your answer sheet. You may use any blank space on the page for your work.**
>
> ### Notes:
> - You may use a calculator whenever you think it will be helpful.
> - Use the diagrams provided to help you solve the problems. Unless you see the words "<u>Note</u>: Figure not drawn to scale" under a diagram, it has been drawn as accurately as possible. Unless it is stated that a figure is three-dimensional, you may assume it lies in a plane.

Immediately preceding the grid-in questions, you will see the following set of instructions.

Directions for Student-Produced Response Questions (Grid-ins)

For each of these questions, first solve the problem, and then enter your answer on the grid provided on the answer sheet. The instructions for entering your answers are as follows:
- First, write your answer in the boxes at the top of the grid.
- Second, grid your answer in the columns below the boxes.
- Use the fraction bar in the first row or the decimal point in the second row to enter fractions and decimal answers.

- Grid only one space in each column.
- Entering the answer in the boxes is recommended as an aid in gridding, but is not required.
- The machine scoring your exam can read only what you grid, so you **must grid in your answers correctly to get credit.**
- If a question has more than one correct answer, grid in only one of these answers.
- The grid does not have a minus sign, so **no answer can be negative.**
- A mixed number *must* be converted to an improper fraction or a decimal before it is gridded. Enter $1\frac{1}{4}$ as 5/4 or 1.25; the machine will interpret 1 1/4 as $\frac{11}{4}$ and mark it wrong.
- **All decimals must be entered as accurately as possible.** Here are the three acceptable ways of gridding

$$\frac{3}{11} = 0.272727...$$

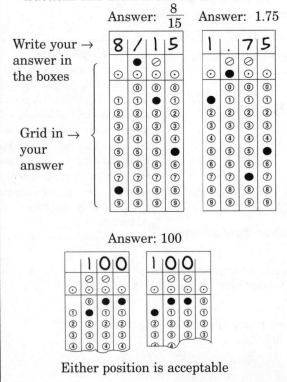

Answer: $\frac{8}{15}$ Answer: 1.75

Write your → answer in the boxes

Grid in → your answer

Answer: 100

Either position is acceptable

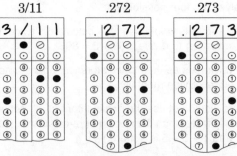

3/11   .272   .273

- Note that rounding to .273 is acceptable, because you are using the full grid, but you would receive **no credit** for .3 or .27, because these answers are less accurate.

On the first page of every mathematics section of the SAT, a box labeled "Reference Information" contains several basic math facts and formulas. In each math section of every model test in this book, you will find the exact same information.

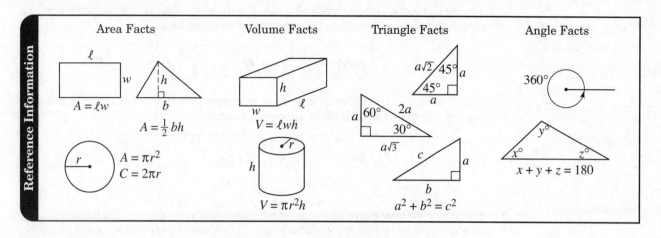

The College Board's official guide, *SAT Preparation Booklet*, offers the following tip:

> **The test does not require you to memorize formulas.** Commonly used formulas are provided in the test booklet at the beginning of each mathematical section.

If you interpret this to mean "Don't bother memorizing the formulas provided," this is terrible advice. It may be reassuring to know that, if you should forget a basic geometry fact, you can look it up in the box headed "Reference Information," but you should decide right now that you will never have to do that. During the test, you don't want to spend any precious time looking up facts that you can learn now. All of these "commonly used formulas" and other important facts are presented in Chapter 9. As you learn and review these facts, you should commit them to memory.

Helpful Hint

As you prepare for this test, memorize the directions for each section. *When you take the SAT, do not waste even one second reading directions.*

ENTERING YOUR ANSWERS ON THE ANSWER SHEET

Indicate your answers to math multiple-choice questions on your answer sheet exactly as you do for critical reading and writing skills questions. Once you determine which answer choice you believe is correct, blacken the corresponding oval on the answer sheet. For grid-in questions the situation is a little more complicated.

The answer sheet for the section containing grid-in questions will have one blank grid for each question. Each one will look exactly like the grid on the left, below. After solving a problem, the first step is to write the answer in the four boxes at the top of the grid. You then blacken the appropriate oval under each box. For example, if your answer to a question is 2450, you write 2450 at the top of the grid, one digit in each box, and then in each column blacken the oval that contains the number you wrote at the top of the column. (See the grid on the right, below.) This is not difficult; but there are some special rules concerning grid-in questions, so let's go over them before you practice gridding-in some numbers.

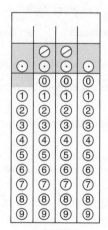
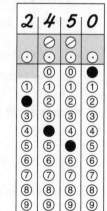

1. The only symbols that appear in the grid are the digits 0 to 9, a decimal point, and a slash (/), used to write fractions. Keep in mind that, since there is no negative sign, *the answer to every grid-in question is a positive number or zero*.

2. Be aware that you will receive credit for a correct answer no matter where you grid it. For example, the answer 17 could be gridded in any of three positions:

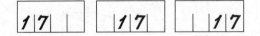

Neverthelesss, try to consistently *write all your answers* the way numbers are usually displayed—*to the right, with blank spaces at the left*.

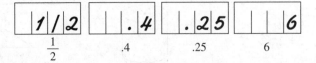

$\frac{1}{2}$ .4 .25 6

3. ***Never round off your answers***. If a decimal answer will fit in the grid and you round it off, your answer will be marked wrong. For example, if the answer is .148 and you correctly round it off to the nearest hundredth and enter .15, you will receive *no credit*. If a decimal answer will not fit in the grid, enter a decimal point in the first column, followed by the first three digits. For example, if your answer is 0.454545..., enter it as .454. You would receive credit if you rounded it to .455, but don't. You might occasionally make a mistake in rounding, whereas you'll *never* make a mistake if you just copy the first three digits. *Note:* If the correct answer has more than two decimal digits, *you must use all four columns of the grid*. You will receive *no credit* for .4 or .5 or .45. (These answers are not accurate enough.)

4. ***Never write a 0 before the decimal point***. The first column of the grid doesn't even have a 0 in it. If the correct answer is 0.3333..., you must grid it as .333. You can't grid 0.33, and 0.3 is not accurate enough.

5. ***Never reduce fractions***.

   • If your answer is a fraction that will fit in the grid, such as $\frac{2}{3}$ or $\frac{4}{18}$ or $\frac{6}{34}$, *just enter it*. Don't waste time reducing it or converting it to a decimal.

   • If your answer is a fraction that won't fit in the grid, do not attempt to reduce it; use your calculator to *convert it to a decimal*. For example, $\frac{24}{65}$ won't fit in a grid—it would require five spaces: 2 4 / 6 5. Don't waste even a few seconds trying to reduce it; just divide on your calculator, and enter .369.

   Unlike $\frac{24}{65}$, the fraction $\frac{24}{64}$ can be reduced—to $\frac{12}{32}$, which doesn't help, or to $\frac{6}{16}$ or $\frac{3}{8}$, either of which could be entered. *Don't do it!* Reducing a fraction takes time, and you might make a mistake. You won't make a mistake if you just use your calculator: $24 \div 64 = .375$.

6. ***Be aware that you can never enter a mixed number***. If your answer is $2\frac{1}{2}$, you *cannot* leave a space and enter your answer as 2 1/2. Also, if you enter $2\,1\,/\,2$, the machine will read it as $\frac{21}{2}$ and mark it wrong. You must enter $2\frac{1}{2}$ as the improper fraction $\frac{5}{2}$ or as the decimal 2.5.

7. Since full credit is given for any equivalent answer, use these guidelines to **enter your answer in the simplest way**. If your answer is $\frac{6}{9}$, you should enter 6/9. (However, credit would be given for any of the following: 2/3, 4/6, 8/12, .666, .667.)

8. Sometimes grid-in questions have more than one correct answer. On these questions, **grid in only one of the acceptable answers**. For example, if a question asked for a positive number less than 100 that was divisible by both 5 and 7, you could enter *either* 35 *or* 70, but not both. Similarly, if a question asked for a number between $\frac{3}{7}$ and $\frac{5}{9}$, you could

   enter any *one* of more than 100 possibilities: fractions such as $\frac{1}{2}$ and $\frac{4}{9}$ or *any* decimal between .429 and .554—.43 or .499 or .52, for example.

9. **Keep in mind that there is no penalty for a wrong answer to a grid-in question**. Therefore, you might as well guess, even if you have no idea what to do. As you will see shortly, there are some strategies for making intelligent guesses.

10. Be sure to **grid every answer very carefully**. The computer does not read what you have written in the boxes; it reads only the answer in the grid. If the correct answer to a question is 100 and you write 100 in the boxes, but accidentally grid in 200, you get *no* credit.

11. If you know that the answer to a question is 100, can you just grid it in and not bother writing it on top? Yes, you will get full credit, and so some SAT guides recommend that you don't waste time writing the answer. This is terrible advice. Instead, **write each answer in the boxes**. It takes less than 2 seconds per answer to do this, and it definitely cuts down on careless errors in gridding. More important, if you go back to check your work, it is much easier to read what's in the boxes on top than what's in the grid.

12. Be aware that the smallest number that can be gridded is 0; the largest is 9999. No number greater than 100 can have a decimal point. The largest number less than 100 that can be gridded is 99.9; the smallest number greater than 100 that can be gridded is 101.

Practice in Gridding-in Numbers

Now, check your understanding of these guidelines. Use the empty numbered grids that follow to show how you would enter these answers.

1.   123

2. $\dfrac{7}{11}$

3. $2\dfrac{3}{4}$

4. $\dfrac{8}{30}$

5.   1.1111...

6.   0

7. $\dfrac{48}{80}$

8. $\dfrac{83}{100}$

9. $\dfrac{19}{15}$

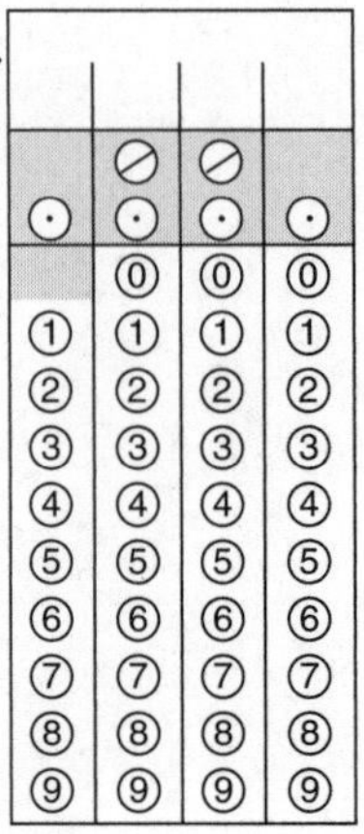

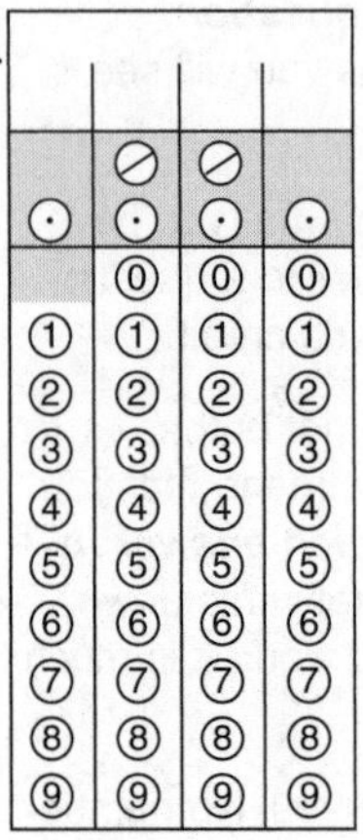

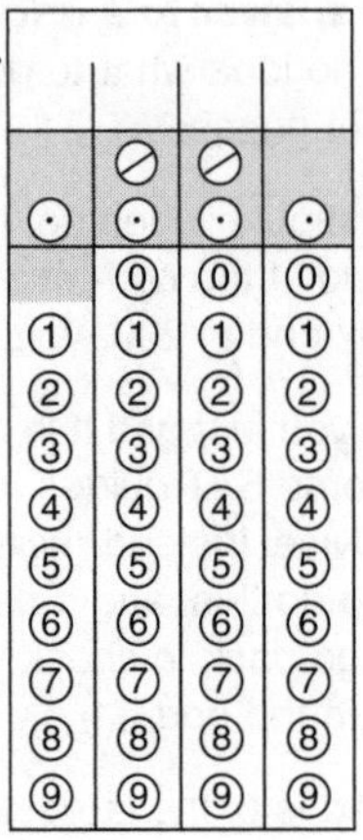

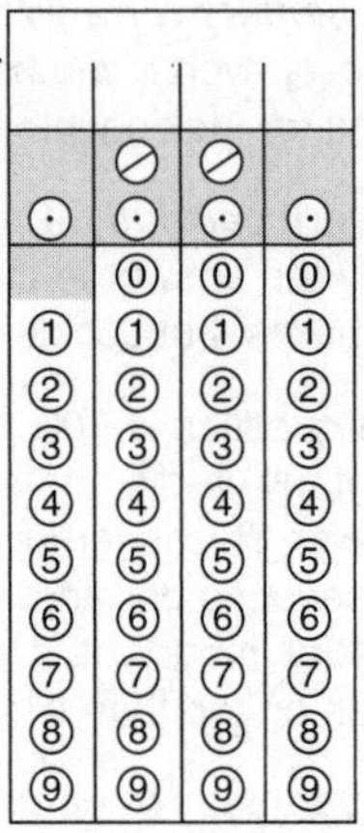

10. $3\dfrac{5}{18}$

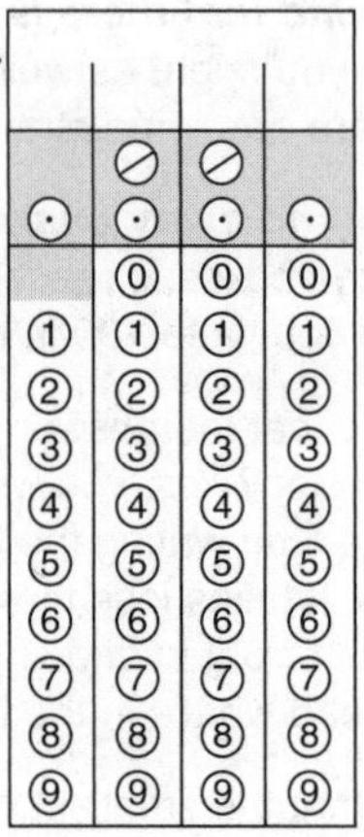

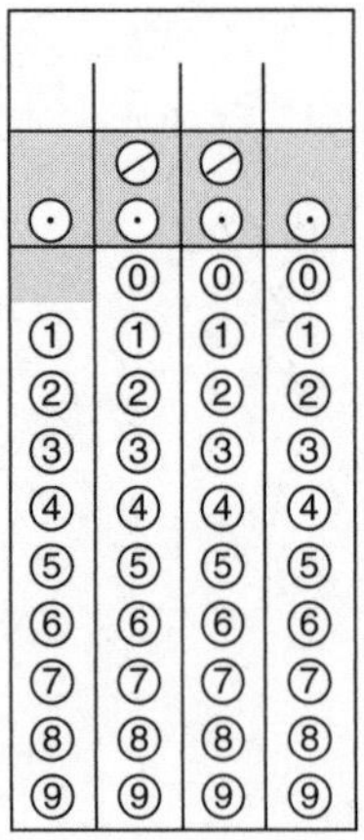

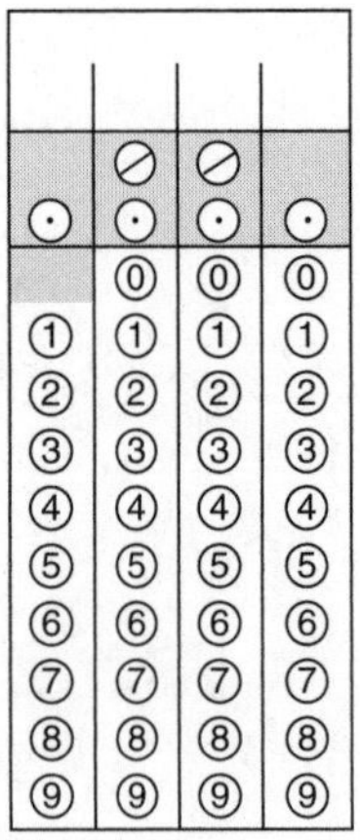

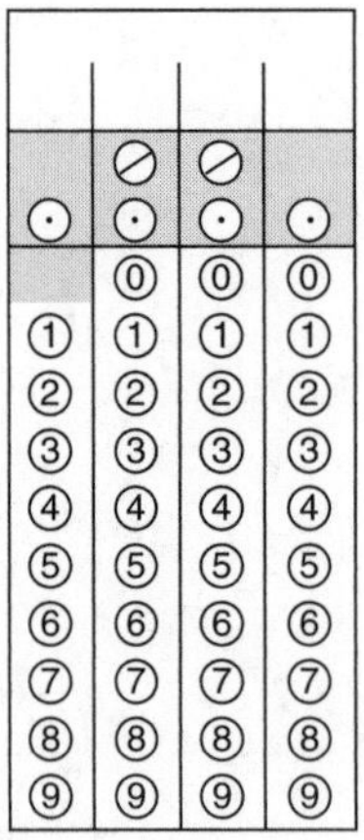

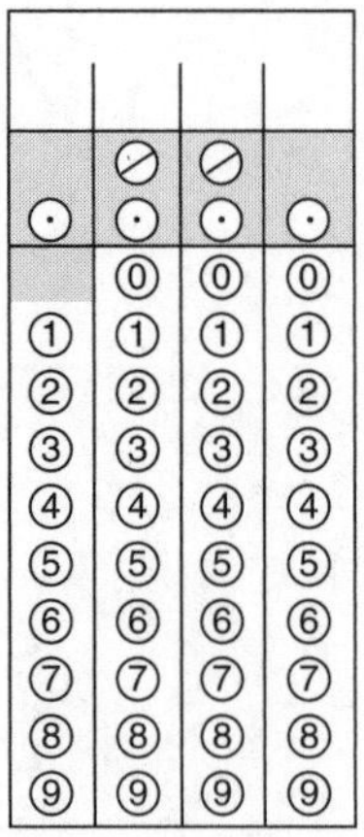

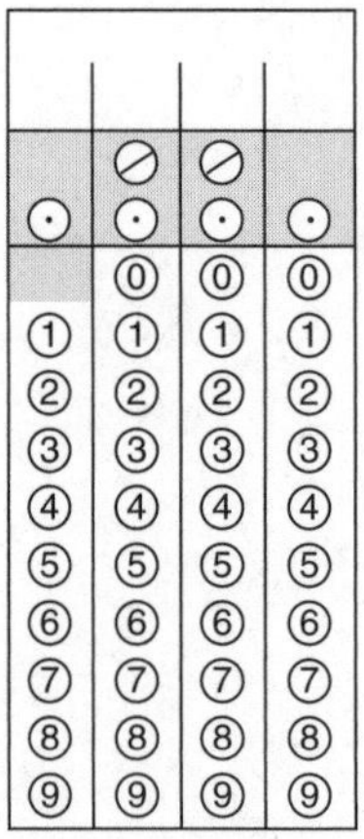

Solutions. Each grid shows the recommended answer. Other acceptable answers, if any, are written below each grid.

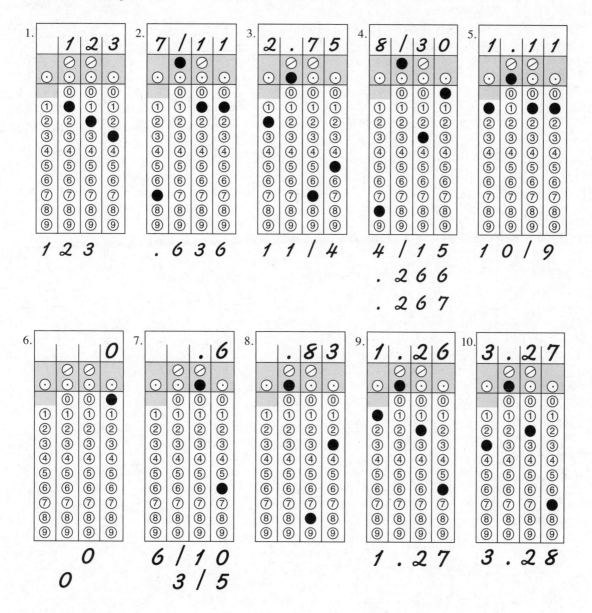

1. 1 2 3

   123

2. 7 / 1 1

   . 6 3 6

3. 2 . 7 5

   1 1 / 4

4. 8 / 3 0

   4 / 1 5
   . 2 6 6
   . 2 6 7

5. 1 . 1 1

   1 0 / 9

6. 0

   0
   0

7. . 6

   6 / 1 0
   3 / 5

8. . 8 3

9. 1 . 2 6

   1 . 2 7

10. 3 . 2 7

    3 . 2 8

If you missed even one of these, go back and reread the rules for gridding. *You never want to have a correct answer and get no credit because you didn't grid it properly.* Whenever you practice grid-in problems, actually grid in the answers. Make sure you understand all of these rules *now*. When you actually take the SAT, don't even look at the instructions for gridding.

Math Strategies and Tactics

Most of the questions in the mathematics sections of the SAT are multiple-choice questions. Immediately preceding each set of multiple-choice questions you will see the following directions:

> In this section *solve each problem*, using any available space on the page for scratchwork. *Then* decide which is the best of the choices given and fill in the corresponding oval on the answer sheet. (Emphasis added.)

The directions are very simple. Basically, they tell you to ignore, at first, the fact that these are multiple-choice questions. Just *solve each problem*, and *then* look at the five choices to see which one is best. As you will learn in this chapter, however, that is not always the best strategy.

In this chapter you will learn all of the important strategies you need to help you answer these multiple-choice questions. As a bonus, almost every one of these tactics can also be used on the grid-in questions. However, as invaluable as these tactics are, use them only when you need them.

The first four tactics deal with the best ways of handling diagrams.

TACTIC 1.　　**Draw a diagram.**
TACTIC 2.　　**If a diagram has been drawn to scale, trust it.**
TACTIC 3.　　**If a diagram has not been drawn to scale, redraw it.**
TACTIC 4.　　**Add a line to a diagram.**

To implement these tactics, you need to be able to draw line segments and angles accurately, and also to be able to look at segments and angles and accurately estimate their measures. Let's look at three variations of the same problem.

> a. If the diagonal of a rectangle is twice as long as the shorter side, what is the degree measure of the angle the diagonal makes with the longer side?

> b. In the rectangle at the right, what is the value of *x*?

> c. In the rectangle at the right, what is the value of *x*?

Note: Figure not drawn to scale

> **NOTE**
>
> If you know how to solve a problem and are confident that you can do so accurately and reasonably quickly, JUST DO IT!

For the moment, let's ignore the correct mathematical way to solve this problem. You should be able to look at the diagram in (b) and "see" that *x* is about 30, *certainly* between 25 and 35. In (a), however, you aren't given a diagram, and in (c) the diagram is useless because it hasn't been drawn to scale. In each of these cases, you should be able to draw a diagram that looks just like the one in (b); then you can look at *your* diagram and "see" that the measure of the angle in question is about 30°.

If this were a multiple-choice question, and the choices were as follows:

(A) 15   (B) 30   (C) 45   (D) 60   (E) 75

you would, of course, choose **30 (B)**. If the choices were

(A) 20   (B) 25   (C) 30   (D) 35   (E) 40

you would be a little less confident, but you should still choose **30**, here (**C**).

If this were a grid-in problem, you would be much less certain of your answer, but should surely bubble in 30, rather than guess a "strange" number such as 28 or 31.

By the way, *x* is *exactly* 30. A right triangle in which one leg is half the hypotenuse must be a 30-60-90 triangle, and that leg is opposite the 30° angle [see KEY FACT J11].

But how can you know the value of *x* just by looking at the diagram in (b)? In this section, you will learn not only how to look at *any* angle and know its measure within 5 or 10°, but also how to draw any angle with the same accuracy. You will also learn how to draw line segments of the correct lengths, so that your diagrams won't be as bad as the one in (c). Do you see what is wrong with that diagram? The diagonal is *labeled* 4 and one of the sides is *labeled* 2, but the diagonal, *as drawn*, isn't nearly twice as long as the side.

Consider the following example:

EXAMPLE 1

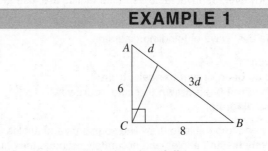

In the figure above, what is the value of *d*?

(A) 2
(B) 2.5
(C) 3
(D) 3.5
(E) 4

Solution. Since there is no note indicating that the diagram has not been drawn to scale, you can trust it [see TACTIC 2].

• Clearly, *d* is less than *AC*, which is 6; but all five choices are less than 6, so that doesn't help.
• Actually, it looks as though *d* is less than *half* of *AC*, or 3.
• Assume it is, and eliminate choices C, D, and E.

You could now guess between choices A and B; but if you measure, you'll *know* which is right. However, there's a problem—on the SAT, you are *not* allowed to use a ruler, a compass, or a protractor. Then how can you measure anything? *Use the back of your answer sheet!* Here are two ways to do this, with the procedures illustrated below.

1. Turn your answer sheet over, place one corner of it on point *A*, and with your pencil make a small mark to indicate length *d*. Now use this "ruler" to measure *AC*. Put a dot on *AC d* units from *A*; slide the answer sheet, mark off a second segment of length *d*, and do this once more. The third mark is well past *C*, so 3*d* is more than 6; that is, *d* > 2. Eliminate A.

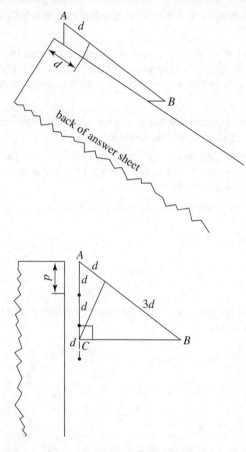

2. On the back of your answer sheet, measure *AC* and *BC* from the same point. The distance between them is 2. Compare 2 to *d*; *d* is longer. Eliminate A.

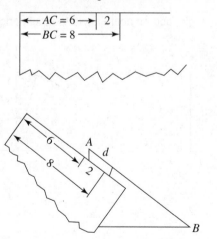

• The answer is **2.5 (B)**.

Finally, erase the dot or mark you made on the back of your answer sheet, so it won't confuse you if you need to make a new "ruler" for another question. Also, there should be no stray pencil marks anywhere on the answer sheet when you hand it in.

To answer this question without TACTIC 2, use the Pythagorean theorem to obtain $AB = 10$ (or recognize that this is a 6-8-10 right triangle) and then solve the equation: $d + 3d = 10 \Rightarrow d = \mathbf{2.5}$.

To take full advantage of TACTICS 1, 2, and 3, you need to be able to measure angles as well as line segments. Fortunately, this is very easy. In fact, you should be able to *look* at any angle and know its measure within 5–10°, and be able to *draw* any angle accurately within 10°. Let's see how.

First, you should easily recognize a 90° angle and can probably draw one freehand, or you can always just trace the corner of your answer sheet.

Second, to draw a 45° angle, just bisect a 90° angle. Again, you can probably do this freehand. If not, or to be more accurate, draw a right angle, mark off the same distance on each side, draw a square, and then draw in the diagonal.

Third, to draw other acute angles, just divide the two 45° angles in the above diagram with as many lines as are necessary.

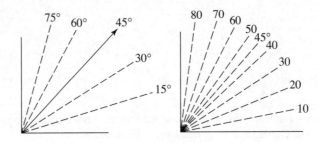

Finally, to draw an obtuse angle, add an acute angle to a right angle.

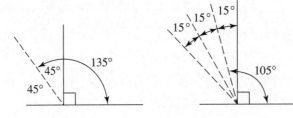

Now, to estimate the measure of a given angle, just draw in some lines.

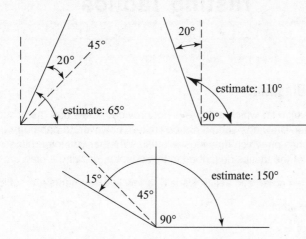

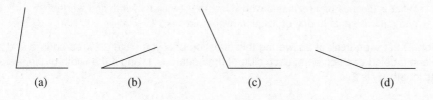

To test yourself, find the measure of each angle shown below. The answers follow.

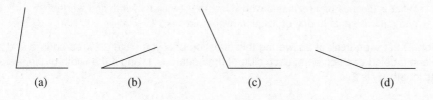

(a)   (b)   (c)   (d)

Answers: (a) 80° (b) 20° (c) 115° (d) 160°.
Did you come within 10° on each one?

Testing Tactics

TACTIC

1 Draw a Diagram.

On any geometry question for which a figure is not provided, draw one (as accurately as possible) in your test booklet. Drawings should not be limited, however, to geometry questions; there are many other questions on which drawings will help. Whether you intend to solve a problem directly or to use one of the tactics described in this chapter, drawing a diagram is the first step.

A good drawing requires no artistic ability. Usually, a few line segments are sufficient.

Let's consider some examples.

EXAMPLE 2

What is the area of a rectangle whose length is twice its width and whose perimeter is equal to that of a square whose area is 1?

Solution. Don't even think of answering this question until you have drawn a square and a rectangle and labeled each of them: each side of the square is 1; and if the width of the rectangle is w, its length (ℓ) is $2w$.

Now, write the required equation and solve it:

$$6w = 4 \Rightarrow w = \frac{4}{6} = \frac{2}{3} \Rightarrow 2w = \frac{4}{3}.$$

The area of the rectangle $= \ell w = \left(\frac{4}{3}\right)\left(\frac{2}{3}\right) = \frac{8}{9}.$

EXAMPLE 3

A jar contains 10 red marbles and 30 green ones. How many red marbles must be added to the jar so that 60% of the marbles will be red?

Solution. Draw a diagram and label it. From the diagram it is clear that there are now $40 + x$ marbles in the jar, of which $10 + x$ are red. Since you want the fraction of red marbles to be

60% $\left(= \frac{3}{5}\right)$, you have $\dfrac{10+x}{40+x} = \dfrac{3}{5}.$

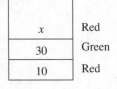

Cross-multiplying gives:

$$5(10 + x) = 3(40 + x) \Rightarrow$$

$$50 + 5x = 120 + 3x \Rightarrow 2x = 70 \Rightarrow x = \mathbf{35}.$$

Of course, you could have set up the equation and solved it without the diagram, but the drawing makes the solution easier and you are less likely to make a careless mistake.

EXAMPLE 4

The diagonal of square II is equal to the perimeter of square I. The area of square II is how many times the area of square I?

(A) 2

(B) $2\sqrt{2}$

(C) 4

(D) $4\sqrt{2}$

(E) 8

It is certainly possible to answer this question without drawing a diagram, but don't. Get in the habit of *always* drawing a diagram for a geometry problem. Often a good drawing will lead you to the correct solution; other times, as you will see here, it prevents you from making a careless error or it allows you to get the right answer *even if you don't know how to solve the problem.*

Solution. Draw a small square (square I), and next to it mark off a line segment equal in length to the perimeter of the square (4 times the side of the square). Then draw a second square (square II) whose diagonal is equal to the length of the line segment.

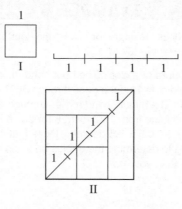

You can see how much larger square II is. In fact, if you draw four squares the size of square I inside square II, you can see that the answer to this question is certainly much more than 4, so eliminate choices A, B, and C. Then, if you don't know how to proceed, just guess between D and E. In fact, $4\sqrt{2} \approx 5.6$, and even that is too small, so you should choose **8 (E)**, the correct answer.

Mathematical Solution. If the side of square I is 1, its perimeter is 4. Then the diagonal of square II is 4. Now use the formula $A = \frac{1}{2}d^2$ (KEY FACT K8) to find that the area of square II is $\frac{1}{2}(4)^2 = \frac{1}{2}(16) = 8$, whereas the area of square I is 1.

EXAMPLE 5

Tony drove 8 miles west, 6 miles north, 3 miles east, and 6 more miles north. How far was Tony from his starting place?

(A) 13

(B) 17

(C) 19

(D) 21

(E) 23

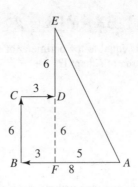

Solution. Draw a diagram. Now, extend line segment $\overline{ED}$ until it intersects $\overline{AB}$ at F [see TACTIC 4]. Then, $\triangle AFE$ is a right triangle whose legs are 5 and 12 and, therefore, whose hypotenuse is **13 (A)**.

[If you drew the diagram accurately, you could get the right answer by measuring!]

EXAMPLE 6

By how many degrees does the angle formed by the hour hand and the minute hand of a clock increase from 1:27 to 1:28?

Solution. Draw a simple picture of a clock. The hour hand makes a complete revolution, 360°, once every 12 hours. Therefore, in 1 hour it goes through 360° ÷ 12 = 30°, and in 1 minute it advances through 30° ÷ 60 = 0.5°. The minute hand moves through 30° every 5 minutes and 6° each 1 minute. Therefore, in the minute from 1:27 to 1:28 (or any other minute), the *difference* between the hands increases by 6 − 0.5 = **5.5** degrees. [Note that it was not necessary, and would have been more time-consuming to determine the angles between the hands at 1:27 and 1:28 (See TACTIC 10: Don't do more than you have to).]

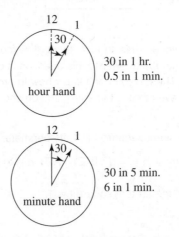

If a Diagram Is Drawn to Scale, Trust It, and Use Your Eyes.

Remember that every diagram that appears on the SAT has been drawn as accurately as possible *unless* you see "Note: Figure not drawn to scale" written below it.

For figures that are drawn to scale, the following are true: line segments that appear to be the same length *are* the same length; if an angle clearly looks obtuse, it *is* obtuse; and if one angle appears larger than another, you may assume that it *is* larger.

Try Examples 7 and 8, which have diagrams that have been drawn to scale. Both of these examples would be classified as hard questions. On an actual SAT, questions of comparable difficulty would be answered correctly by at most 20–35% of the students taking the exam. After you master TACTIC 2, you should have no trouble with problems like these.

EXAMPLE 7

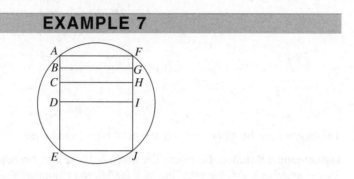

In the figure above, $\overline{EF}$, not shown, is a diagonal of rectangle *AFJE* and a diameter of the circle. *D* is the midpoint of $\overline{AE}$, *C* is the midpoint of $\overline{AD}$, and *B* is the midpoint of $\overline{AC}$.

If *AE* is 8 and the radius of the circle is 5, what is the area of rectangle *BGHC*?

(A) 4
(B) 6
(C) 8
(D) 12
(E) 24

Solution. Since there is no note indicating that the diagram has not been drawn to scale, you can trust it.

- The area of rectangle *BGHC* is the product of its width, *BC*, and its length, *BG*.
- $AE = 8 \Rightarrow AD = 4 \Rightarrow AC = 2 \Rightarrow BC = 1$.
- $\overline{BG}$ *appears* to be longer than $\overline{AD}$, which is 4, and shorter than $\overline{AE}$, which is 8. Therefore, *BG* *is* more than 4 and *is* less than 8.
- Then, the area of *BGHC* is more than $1 \times 4 = 4$ and less than $1 \times 8 = 8$.
- The only choice between 4 and 8 is **6**. The answer is **B**.

Note that you never used the fact that the radius of the circle is 5, information that is necessary to actually *solve* the problem. You were able to answer this question *merely by looking at the diagram*. Were you just lucky? What if the five choices had been 4, 5, 6, 7, and 8, so that there were three choices between 4 and 8, not just one? Well, you could have eliminated 4 and 8 and guessed, or you could have looked at the diagram even more closely. *BG appears* to be about the same length as *CE*, which is 6. If *BG is* 6, then the area of *BGHC is* exactly 6. How can you be sure? Measure the lengths!

On the answer sheet make two small pencil marks to indicate length *BG*:

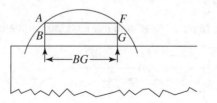

Now, use that length to measure *CE*:

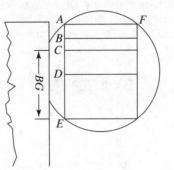

The lengths *are* the same. *BG is* 6; the area *is* 6. It's not a guess after all.

Mathematical Solution. Diameter $\overline{EF}$, which is 10, is also the hypotenuse of right triangle *EAF*. Since leg $\overline{AE}$ is 8, $\overline{AF}$, the other leg, is 6 (either you recognize this as a 6-8-10 triangle, or you use the Pythagorean theorem). Since *BG = AF*, *BG* is 6, and the area *is* **6**.

If Example 7 had been a grid-in problem instead of a multiple-choice question, you could have used TACTIC 2 in exactly the same way, but you would have been less sure of your answer. If, based on a diagram, you know that the area of a rectangle is about 6 or the measure of an angle is about 30°, you can almost always pick the correct choice, but on a grid-in you can't be certain that the area isn't 6.2 or the angle 31°. Nevertheless, if you can't solve a problem directly, you should always grid in a "simple" number that is consistent with the diagram.

EXAMPLE 8

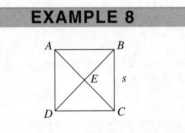

In the figure above, square *ABCD* has been divided into four triangles by its diagonals. If the perimeter of each triangle is 1, what is the perimeter of the square?

(A) $\dfrac{4}{3}$

(B) 2

(C) 3

(D) $4(\sqrt{2}+1)$

(E) $\dfrac{4}{\sqrt{2}+1}$

Solution Using TACTIC 2. Make a "ruler" and mark off the perimeter of △*BEC*; label that 1.

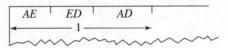

Now, mark off the perimeter of square *ABCD*.

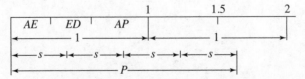

It should be clear that P is much less than 2 (eliminate B and C), but more than 1.5 (eliminate A). The answer must be D or E. If it is obvious to you that choice D is greater than 4, eliminate it and choose **E**; otherwise, use your calculator to evaluate choice D (9.66) and choice E (1.65).

Mathematical Solution. Let s be a side of the square. Then, since $\triangle BEC$ is a 45-45-90 right

triangle, BE and EC are each $\dfrac{s}{\sqrt{2}} = \dfrac{s}{\sqrt{2}} \cdot \dfrac{\sqrt{2}}{\sqrt{2}} = \dfrac{s\sqrt{2}}{2}$. Therefore, the perimeter of $\triangle BEC$ is

$\dfrac{s\sqrt{2}}{2} + \dfrac{s\sqrt{2}}{2} + s$, which equals 1. Now solving for s:

$$1 = \frac{s\sqrt{2}}{2} + \frac{s\sqrt{2}}{2} + s = s\sqrt{2} + s$$

$$1 = s(\sqrt{2} + 1)$$

$$s = \frac{1}{\sqrt{2} + 1}$$

Finally, $P = 4s = \dfrac{4}{\sqrt{2} + 1}$. Even if you could do this (and most students can't), it is far easier to use TACTIC 2.

Remember that the goal of this book is to help you get credit (i) for *all* the problems you know how to do, and (ii), by using the TACTICS, for *many* that you don't know how to do. Example 8 is typical. Most students omit it because it is too hard. *You*, however, can now answer it correctly, even though you may not be able to solve it directly.

EXAMPLE 9

In the figure to the right, what is the value of x?

(A) 55
(B) 95
(C) 125
(D) 135
(E) 145

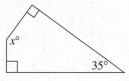

EXAMPLE 10

In the figure to the right, what is the value of $x - y$?

(A) −30
(B) −15
(C)   0
(D) 15
(E) 30

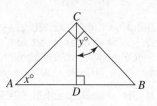

Solution 9 Using TACTIC 2. Since the diagram is drawn to scale, trust it. Look at *x*: it appears to be *about* 90 + 50 = 140. In this case, using TACTIC 2 did not get you the exact answer. It only enabled you to narrow down the choices to (D) or (E). At this point you would guess—unless, of course, you know the following mathematical solution.

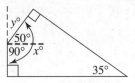

Mathematical Solution 9. The sum of the measures of the four angles in *any* quadrilateral is 360° (KEY FACT K1). Then

$$360 = 90 + 90 + 35 + x = 215 + x \Rightarrow$$
$$x = 360 - 215 = \textbf{145 (E)}.$$

Solution 10 Using TACTIC 2. In the diagram, *x* and *y* look about the same, so assume they are. Certainly, neither one is 30° or even 15° greater than the other. Therefore, $x - y = \textbf{0 (C)}$.

Mathematical Solution 10. The sums of the measures of the three angles in triangles *ABC* and *CBD* are equal (they are both 180°). Then

$$90 + m\angle B + x = 90 + m\angle B + y \Rightarrow x = y \Rightarrow x - y = \textbf{0 (C)}.$$

Now try Examples 11–13, in which the diagrams are drawn to scale, and you need to find the measures of angles. Even if you know that you can solve these problems directly, practice TACTIC 2 and estimate the answers. The correct mathematical solutions without using this tactic are also given.

EXAMPLE 11

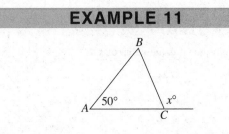

If, in the figure at the right, *AB* = *AC*, what is the value of *x*?

(A) 135
(B) 125
(C) 115
(D) 65
(E) 50

Solution Using TACTIC 2. *Ignore all the information in the question.* Just "measure" *x*. Draw *DC* perpendicular to *AB*, and let *EC* divide right angle *DCA* into two 45° angles, ∠*DCE* and ∠*ACE*. Now, ∠*DCB* is about half of ∠*DCE*, say 20–25°. Therefore, your estimate for *x* should be about 110 (90 + 20) or 115 (90 + 25). Choose **C**.

Mathematical Solution. Since △*ABC* is isosceles, with *AB* = *AC*, the other two angles in the triangle, ∠*B* and ∠*C*, each measure 65°. Therefore,

$$x + 65 = 180 \Rightarrow x = \textbf{115}.$$

EXAMPLE 12

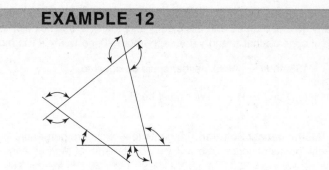

In the figure above, what is the sum of the measures of all of the marked angles?

(A) 360°
(B) 540°
(C) 720°
(D) 900°
(E) 1080°

Solution Using TACTIC 2. Make your best estimate of each angle, and add up the values. The five choices are so far apart that, even if you're off by 15° or more on some of the angles, you'll get the right answer. The sum of the estimates shown below is 690°, so the correct answer *must* be **720° (C)**.

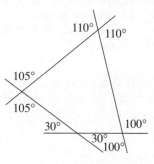

Mathematical Solution. Each of the eight marked angles is an exterior angle of the quadrilateral. If we take one angle from each pair, their sum is 360° (KEY FACT K3); so, taking both angles at each vertex, we find that the sum of the measures is 360° + 360° = **720°**.

EXAMPLE 13

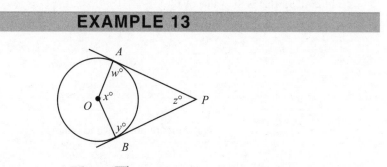

In the diagram above, rays $\overrightarrow{PA}$ and $\overrightarrow{PB}$ are tangent to circle O. Which of the following is equal to z?

(A) x
(B) $180 - x$
(C) $w + x + y$
(D) $\dfrac{w + x + y}{2}$
(E) $\dfrac{w + x + y}{3}$

Solution Using TACTIC 2. The diagram is drawn to scale, so trust it. In the figure, x is clearly greater than 90 and z is clearly less than 90, so choices A and C are surely wrong. Also, it appears that w and y are each about 90, so $w + x + y$ is more than 270. Since $\dfrac{270}{2} = 135$ and $\dfrac{270}{3} = 90$, neither could be equal to z.

Eliminate D and E. The answer must be **B**.

Mathematical Solution. Tangents to a circle are perpendicular to the radii drawn to the points of contact, so $w = y = 90$. The sum of the four angles in a quadrilateral is 360°, so $w + x + y + z = 360$. Then $90 + x + 90 + z = 360 \Rightarrow x + z = 180 \Rightarrow z = \mathbf{180 - x}$ **(B)**.

TACTIC

3 **If a Diagram Is _Not_ Drawn to Scale, Redraw It to Scale, and Then Use Your Eyes.**

For figures that have not been drawn to scale, you can make _no_ assumptions. Lines that look parallel may not be; an angle that appears to be obtuse may, in fact, be acute; two line segments may have the same length even though one looks twice as long as the other.

Helpful Hint

In order to redraw a diagram to scale, you first have to ask yourself, "What is wrong with the original diagram?" If an angle is marked 45°, but in the figure it looks like a 75° angle, redraw it. If two line segments appear to be parallel, but you have not been told that they are, redraw them so that they are clearly _not_ parallel. If two segments appear to have the same length, but one is marked 5 and the other 10, redraw them so that the second segment is twice as long as the first.

In the examples illustrating TACTIC 2, all of the diagrams were drawn to scale and could be used to advantage. When diagrams have not been drawn to scale, you must be much more careful. TACTIC 3 tells you to redraw the diagram _as accurately as possible_, based on the information you are given, and then to apply the technique of TACTIC 2.

CAUTION: Redrawing a diagram, even roughly, takes time. Do this only when you do not see an easy direct solution to the problem.

EXAMPLE 14

In $\triangle ACB$, what is the value of x?

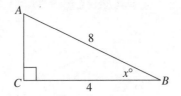

Note: Figure not drawn to scale

(A) 75
(B) 60
(C) 45
(D) 30
(E) 15

Solution. In what way is this figure not drawn to scale? $AB = 8$ and $BC = 4$, but in the figure $\overline{AB}$ is *not* twice as long as $\overline{BC}$. Redraw the triangle so that $\overline{AB}$ *is* twice as long as $\overline{BC}$.

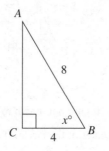

Now, just look: x is about **60 (B)**.

In fact, x is exactly 60. If the hypotenuse of a right triangle is twice the length of one of the legs, the triangle is a 30-60-90 triangle, and the angle formed by the hypotenuse and that leg is 60° (see Section 9-J).

EXAMPLE 15

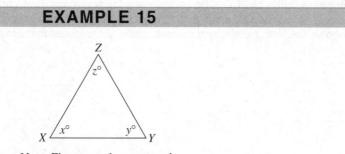

Note: Figure not drawn to scale

In $\triangle XYZ$ at the right, if $XY < YZ < ZX$, then which of the following *must* be true?

(A) $x < 60$
(B) $z < 60$
(C) $y < z$
(D) $x < z$
(E) $y < x$

Solution. As drawn, the diagram is useless. The triangle looks like an equilateral triangle, even though the question states that $XY < YZ < ZX$. Redraw the figure so that the condition is satisfied (that is, $\overline{ZX}$ is clearly the longest side and $\overline{XY}$ the shortest).

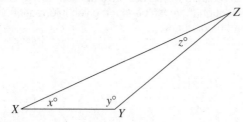

From the redrawn figure, it is clear that y is the largest angle, so eliminate choices C and E. Also, since $z < x$, eliminate D as well. Both x and z appear to be less than 60, but only one answer can be correct. Since $z < x$, if only one of these angles is less than 60, it must be z. Therefore, **$z < 60$ (B)** must be true.

EXAMPLE 16

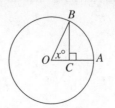

<u>Note</u>: Figure not drawn to scale

In the figure above, *O* is the center of the circle. If *OA* = 4 and *BC* = 2, what is the value of *x*?

(A) 15
(B) 25
(C) 30
(D) 45
(E) 60

Solution Using TACTIC 3. Do you see why the figure isn't drawn to scale? $\overline{BC}$, which is 2, looks almost as long as $\overline{OA}$, which is 4. Redraw the diagram, making sure that $\overline{BC}$ is only one-half as long as $\overline{OA}$. With the diagram drawn to scale, you can see that *x* is approximately **30 (C)**.

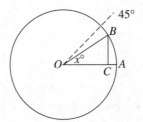

Mathematical Solution. Since $\overline{OB}$ is a radius, it has the same length as radius $\overline{OA}$, which is 4. Then $\triangle BCO$ is a right triangle in which the hypotenuse is twice as long as one leg. This can occur *only* in a 30-60-90 triangle, and the angle opposite that leg measures 30°. Therefore, *x* = **30**.

TACTIC

4   Add a Line to a Diagram.

Occasionally, after staring at a diagram, you still have no idea how to solve the problem to which it applies. It looks as though there isn't enough given information. In this case, it often helps to draw another line in the diagram.

EXAMPLE 17

In the figure to the right, Q is a point on the circle whose center is O and whose radius is r, and $OPQR$ is a rectangle. What is the length of diagonal $\overline{PR}$?

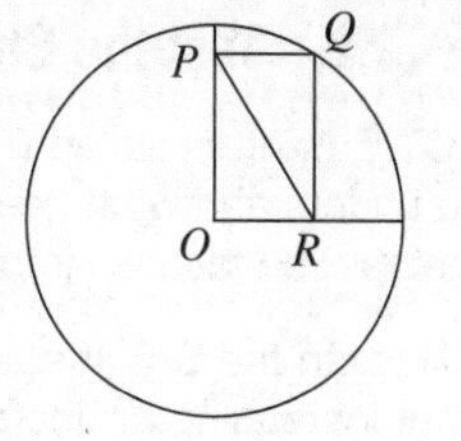

(A) r

(B) r^2

(C) $\dfrac{r^2}{\pi}$

(D) $\dfrac{r\sqrt{2}}{\pi}$

(E) It cannot be determined from the information given.

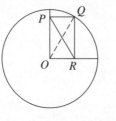

Solution. If, after staring at the diagram and thinking about rectangles, circles, and the Pythagorean theorem, you're still lost, don't give up. Ask yourself, "Can I add another line to this diagram?" As soon as you think to draw in $\overline{OQ}$, the other diagonal, the problem becomes easy: the two diagonals are congruent, and, since $\overline{OQ}$ is a radius, $OQ = PR = \boldsymbol{r}$ **(A)**.

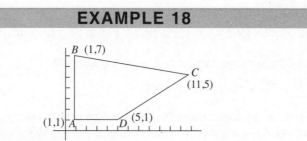

Note that you could also have made a "ruler" and seen that $\overline{PR}$ is equal to r.

EXAMPLE 18

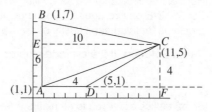

What is the area of quadrilateral $ABCD$?

Solution. Since the quadrilateral is irregular, you don't know any formula to get the answer. However, if you draw in $\overline{AC}$, you will divide $ABCD$ into two triangles, each of whose areas can be determined. If you then draw in $\overline{CE}$ and $\overline{CF}$, the heights of the

two triangles, you see that the area of $\triangle ACD$ is

$\dfrac{1}{2}(4)(4) = 8$, and the area of $\triangle BAC$ is $\dfrac{1}{2}(6)(10) = 30$.
Then the area of $ABCD$ is $30 + 8 = \mathbf{38}$.

Note that this problem could also have been solved by drawing in lines to create rectangle $ABEF$, and subtracting the areas of $\triangle BEC$ and $\triangle CFD$ from the area of the rectangle.

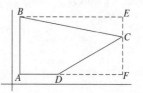

TACTIC

5 Test the Choices, Starting with C.

TACTIC 5, often called *backsolving*, is useful when you are asked to solve for an unknown and you understand what needs to be done to answer the question, but you want to avoid doing the algebra. The idea is simple: test the various choices to see which one is correct.

NOTE: On the SAT the answers to virtually all numerical multiple-choice questions are listed in either increasing or decreasing order. Consequently, C is the middle value; and in applying TACTIC 5, *you should always start with C*. For example, assume that choices A, B, C, D, and E are given in increasing order. Try C. If it works, you've found the answer. If C doesn't work, you should now know whether you need to test a larger number or a smaller one, and that informa- tion permits you to eliminate two more choices. If C is too small, you need a larger number, so A and B are out; if C is too large, you can eliminate D and E, which are even larger.

Example 19 illustrates the proper use of TACTIC 5.

EXAMPLE 19

If the average (arithmetic mean) of 2, 7, and x is 12, what is the value of x?

(A)   9
(B) 12
(C) 21
(D) 27
(E) 36

Solution. Use TACTIC 5. Test choice C: $x = 21$.

- Is the average of 2, 7, and 21 equal to 12?
- No: $\dfrac{2+7+21}{3} = \dfrac{30}{3} = 10$, which is *too small.*
- Eliminate C; also, since, for the average to be 12, x must be *greater* than 21, eliminate A and B.
- Try choice D: $x = \mathbf{27}$. Is the average of 2, 7, and 27 equal to 12?
- Yes: $\dfrac{2+7+27}{3} = \dfrac{36}{3} = \mathbf{12}$. The answer is **D**.

Every problem that can be solved using TACTIC 5 can be solved directly, often in less time. Therefore, we stress: *if you are confident that you can solve a problem quickly and accurately, just do so.*

Here is the direct method for solving Example 19, which is *faster* than backsolving. (See Section 9-E on averages.) If you know this method, you should use it and save TACTIC 5 for problems that you can't easily solve directly.

Direct Solution. If the average of three numbers is 12, their sum is 36. Then

$$2 + 7 + x = 36 \Rightarrow 9 + x = 36 \Rightarrow x = \mathbf{27}.$$

Some tactics allow you to eliminate a few choices so that you can make an educated guess. On problems where TACTIC 5 can be used, it *always* leads you to the right answer. The only reason not to use it on a particular problem is that you can easily solve the problem directly.

Now try applying TACTIC 5 to Examples 20 and 21.

EXAMPLE 20

If the sum of five consecutive even integers is 740, what is the largest of these integers?

(A) 156
(B) 152
(C) 146
(D) 144
(E) 142

Solution. Use TACTIC 5. Test choice C: 146.

- If 146 is the largest of the five integers, the integers are 146, 144, 142, 140, and 138. Quickly add them on your calculator. The sum is 710.
- Since 710 is too small, eliminate C, D, and E.
- If you noticed that the amount by which 710 is too small is 30, you should realize that each of the five numbers needs to be increased by 6; therefore, the largest is **152 (B)**.
- If you didn't notice, just try 152, and see that it works.

This solution is easy, and it avoids having to set up and solve the required equation:

$$n + (n + 2) + (n + 4) + (n + 6) + (n + 8) = 740.$$

EXAMPLE 21

A competition offers a total of $250,000 in prize money to be shared by the top three contestants. If the money is to be divided among them in the ratio of 1:3:6, what is the value of the largest prize?

(A) $ 25,000
(B) $ 75,000
(C) $100,000
(D) $125,000
(E) $150,000

Solution. Use TACTIC 5. Test choice C: $100,000.

- If the largest prize is $100,000, the second largest is $50,000 (they are in the ratio of 6:3 = 2:1). The third prize is much less than $50,000, so all three add up to less than $200,000.
- Eliminate A, B, and C; and, since $100,000 is *way* too small, try E, not D.
- Test choice E. The prizes are **$150,000**, $75,000, and $25,000 (one-third of $75,000). Their total *is* $250,000. The answer is **E**.

Again, TACTIC 5 lets you avoid the algebra if you can't do it or just don't want to. Here is the correct solution. By TACTIC D1 the three prizes are x, $3x$, and $6x$. Therefore,

$$x + 3x + 6x = \$250{,}000 \Rightarrow 10x = \$250{,}000.$$

So, $x = \$25{,}000$ and $6x = \mathbf{\$150{,}000}$.

EXAMPLE 22

If $2\sqrt{2x+1}+5=8$, then $x=$

(A) $-\dfrac{1}{8}$

(B) 0

(C) $\dfrac{5}{8}$

(D) 1

(E) $\dfrac{9}{8}$

 Solution. Since plugging in 0 is much easier than plugging in $\dfrac{5}{8}$, start with B. If $x = 0$, the left-hand side of the equation is $2\sqrt{1}+5$, which is equal to 7 and so is too small. Eliminate

A and B, and try something bigger. Preferring whole numbers to fractions, try choice D. If $x = 1$, then $2\sqrt{2(1)+1}+5=2\sqrt{3}+5\approx 8.46$.

Since that's too big, eliminate D and E. The answer must be **C** $\dfrac{5}{8}$.

Again, remember: no matter what the choices are, backsolve *only* if you can't easily do the algebra. Some students would do this problem directly:

$$2\sqrt{2x+1}+5=8 \Rightarrow 2\sqrt{2x+1}=3 \Rightarrow \sqrt{2x+1}=\dfrac{3}{2}.$$

So, $2x+1=\left(\dfrac{3}{2}\right)^2=\dfrac{9}{4} \Rightarrow 2x=\dfrac{5}{4} \Rightarrow x=\dfrac{5}{8}.$

Helpful Hint

Don't start with C if some other choice is much easier to work with. If you start with B and it is too small, you may be able to eliminate only two choices (A and B), instead of three, but you will save time if plugging in choice C would be messy.

---

and save backsolving for an even harder problem. You have to determine which method is better for you.

For some multiple-choice questions on the SAT, you *have to* test the various choices. On these problems you are not really backsolving (there is nothing to solve!); rather you are testing whether a particular choice satisfies a given condition.

Examples 23 and 24 are two such problems. In Example 23, you are asked for the *largest* integer that satisfies a certain condition. Usually, some of the smaller integers offered as choices also satisfy the condition, but your job is to find the largest one.

EXAMPLE 23

What is the largest integer, n, such that $\dfrac{112}{2^n}$ is an integer?

(A) 1
(B) 2
(C) 3
(D) 4
(E) 5

Solution. Since you want the *largest* value of n for which $\dfrac{112}{2^n}$ is an integer, start by testing 5, choice E, the largest of the choices.

- Is $\dfrac{112}{2^5}$ an integer? No: $\dfrac{112}{2^5} = \dfrac{112}{32} = 3.5$.

Eliminate E and try D.

- Is $\dfrac{112}{2^4}$ an integer? Yes: $2^4 = 16$, and $\dfrac{112}{16} = 7$.

- The answer is **4 (D)**.

It doesn't matter whether any of the smaller choices works (you need the *largest*), although in this case they *all* do.

Surprisingly, on a problem that asks for the *smallest* number satisfying a property, you should also start with E, because the choices for these problems are usually given in decreasing order.

It is also better to start with E on questions such as Example 24, in which you are asked "which of the following...?" The right answer is *rarely* one of the first choices.

Sometimes a question asks which of the five choices satisfies a certain condition. Usually, in this situation there is no way to answer the question directly. Rather, you must look at the choices and test each of them until you find one that works. At that point, stop—none of the other choices could be correct. There is no particular order in which to test the choices, but it makes sense to test the easier ones first. For example, it is usually easier to test whole numbers than fractions and positive numbers than negative ones.

EXAMPLE 24

Which of the following is NOT equivalent to $\dfrac{3}{5}$?

(A) $\dfrac{24}{40}$

(B) 60%

(C) 0.6

(D) $\dfrac{3}{7} \times \dfrac{7}{5}$

(E) $\dfrac{3}{7} \div \dfrac{7}{5}$

Solution. Here, you have to test each of the choices until you find one that satisfies the condition that it is *not* equal to $\dfrac{3}{5}$. If, as you glance at the choices to see if any would be easier to test than the others, you happen to notice that $60\% = 0.6$, then you can immediately eliminate choices B and C, since it is impossible that both are correct.

- Test choice A. Reduce $\dfrac{24}{40}$ by dividing the numerator and denominator by 8: $\dfrac{24}{40} = \dfrac{3}{5}$.

- Test choice D. $\dfrac{3}{7} \times \dfrac{7}{5} = \dfrac{3}{5}$.

- You now know that **E** must be the correct answer. In fact, $\dfrac{3}{7} \div \dfrac{7}{5} = \dfrac{3}{7} \times \dfrac{5}{7} = \dfrac{15}{49} \neq \dfrac{3}{5}$.

If you think of a grid-in problem as a multiple-choice question in which the choices accidentally got erased, you can still use TACTIC 5. To test choices, you just have to make them up. Let's illustrate by looking again at Examples 19 and 20, except that now the choices are missing.

EXAMPLE 19

If the average (arithmetic mean) of 2, 7, and *x* is 12, what is the value of *x*?

Instead of starting with choice C, you have to pick a starting number. Any number will do, but when the numbers in the problem are 2, 7, and 12, it's more likely that *x* is 10 or 20 than 100 or 1000.

Solution. You could start with 10; but if you immediately realize that the average of 2, 7, and 10 is less than 10 (so it can't be 12), you'll try a bigger number, say 20. The average of 2, 7, and 20 is

$$\frac{2+7+20}{3} = \frac{29}{3} = 9\frac{2}{3},$$

which is too small. Try *x* = 30:

$$\frac{2+7+30}{3} = \frac{39}{3} = 13,$$

just a bit too big. Since 12 is closer to 13 than it is to $9\frac{2}{3}$, your next choice should be closer to 30 than 20, surely more than 25. Your third try might well be **27**, which works.

EXAMPLE 20

If the sum of five consecutive even integers is 740, what is the largest of these integers?

Solution. You can start with any number. If you realize that the sum of five numbers, each of which is near 100, is about 500, and that the sum of five numbers, each of which is near 200, is about 1000, you will immediately start with a number in between, say 150:

$$150 + 148 + 146 + 144 + 142 = 730.$$

Since 730 is too small but extremely close, try a number just slightly larger than 150, say **152**, which works.

TACTIC

Replace Variables with Numbers.

Mastery of TACTIC 6 is critical for anyone developing good test-taking skills. This tactic can be used whenever the five choices in a multiple-choice math question involve the variables in the question. There are three steps:

1. Replace each variable with an easy-to-use number.

2. Solve the problem using those numbers.

3. Evaluate each of the five choices with the numbers you picked to see which choice is equal to the answer you obtained.

Examples 25 and 26 illustrate the proper use of TACTIC 6.

EXAMPLE 25

If a is equal to b multiplied by c, which of the following is equal to b divided by c?

(A) $\dfrac{a}{bc}$

(B) $\dfrac{ab}{c}$

(C) $\dfrac{a}{c}$

(D) $\dfrac{a}{c^2}$

(E) $\dfrac{a}{bc^2}$

Solution.

• Pick three easy-to-use numbers that satisfy $a = bc$: for example, $a = 6$, $b = 2$, $c = 3$.

• Solve the problem with these numbers: $b \div c = \dfrac{b}{c} = \dfrac{2}{3}$.

• Check each of the five choices to see which one is equal to $\dfrac{2}{3}$:

(A) $\dfrac{a}{bc} = \dfrac{6}{(2)(3)} = 1$: NO.   (B) $\dfrac{ab}{c} = \dfrac{(6)(3)}{\overset{3}{\underset{1}{\cancel{3}}}} = 6$: NO.

(C) $\dfrac{a}{c} = \dfrac{6}{3} = 2$: NO.   (D) $\dfrac{a}{c^2} = \dfrac{6}{3^2} = \dfrac{6}{9} = \dfrac{2}{3}$: YES!

Still check (E): $\dfrac{a}{bc^2} = \dfrac{6}{2(3^2)} = \dfrac{6}{18} = \dfrac{1}{3}$: NO.

• The answer is **D**.

EXAMPLE 26

If the sum of four consecutive odd integers is s, then, in terms of s, what is the greatest of these integers?

(A) $\dfrac{s-12}{4}$

(B) $\dfrac{s-6}{4}$

(C) $\dfrac{s+6}{4}$

(D) $\dfrac{s+12}{4}$

(E) $\dfrac{s+16}{4}$

Solution.

- Pick four easy-to-use consecutive odd integers: say, 1, 3, 5, 7. Then *s*, their sum, is 16.
- Solve the problem with these numbers: the greatest of these integers is 7.
- When *s* = 16, the five choices are $\dfrac{s-12}{4} = \dfrac{4}{4}$, $\dfrac{s-6}{4} = \dfrac{10}{4}$, $\dfrac{s+6}{4} = \dfrac{22}{4}$, $\dfrac{\boldsymbol{s+12}}{4} = \dfrac{28}{4}$,

$\dfrac{s+16}{4} = \dfrac{32}{4}$.

- Only $\dfrac{28}{4}$, choice **D**, is equal to 7.

Of course, Examples 25 and 26 can be solved without using TACTIC 6 *if your algebra skills are good*. Here are the solutions.

Solution 25. $a = bc \Rightarrow b = \dfrac{a}{c} \Rightarrow b \div c = \dfrac{a}{c} \div c = \dfrac{\boldsymbol{a}}{\boldsymbol{c^2}}$.

Solution 26. Let *n*, *n* + 2, *n* + 4, and *n* + 6 be four consecutive odd integers, and let *s* be their sum. Then:

$$s = n + (n+2) + (n+4) + (n+6) = 4n + 12.$$

Therefore:

$$n = \frac{s-12}{4} \Rightarrow n + 6 = \frac{s-12}{4} + 6 = \frac{s-12}{4} + \frac{24}{4} = \frac{\boldsymbol{s+12}}{\boldsymbol{4}}.$$

The important point is that, if you are uncomfortable with the correct algebraic solution, you don't have to omit these questions. You can use TACTIC 6 and *always* get the right answer. Of course, even if you can do the algebra, you should use TACTIC 6 if you think you can solve the problem faster or will be less likely to make a mistake. With the proper use of the tactics in this chapter, you can correctly answer many problems that you may not know how to solve mathematically.

Examples 27 and 28 are somewhat different. You are asked to reason through word problems involving only variables. Most students find problems like these mind-boggling. Here, the use of TACTIC 6 is essential; without it, Example 27 is difficult and Example 28 is nearly impossible. TACTIC 6 is not easy to master, but with practice you will catch on.

Helpful Hint

Replace the variables with numbers that are easy to use, not necessarily ones that make sense. *It is perfectly OK to ignore reality.* A school can have five students, apples can cost $10 each, trains can go 5 miles per hour or 1000 miles per hour—it doesn't matter.

EXAMPLE 27

If a school cafeteria needs *c* cans of soup each week for each student, and if there are *s* students in the school, for how many weeks will *x* cans of soup last?

(A) $\dfrac{cx}{s}$

(B) $\dfrac{xs}{c}$

(C) $\dfrac{s}{cx}$

(D) $\dfrac{x}{cs}$

(E) csx

Solution.

- Replace c, s, and x with three easy-to-use numbers. If a school cafeteria needs 2 cans of soup each week for each student, and if there are 5 students in the school, how many weeks will 20 cans of soup last?
- Since the cafeteria needs $2 \times 5 = 10$ cans of soup per week, 20 cans will last for 2 weeks.
- Which of the choices equals 2 when $c = 2$, $s = 5$, and $x = 20$?
- The five choices become: $\dfrac{cx}{s} = 8$, $\dfrac{xs}{c} = 50$, $\dfrac{s}{cx} = \dfrac{1}{8}$, $\dfrac{x}{cs} = 2$, $csx = 200$.

The answer is **D**.

EXAMPLE 28

If p painters can paint h houses in 4 days, how many houses can 6 painters, working at the same rate, paint in 2 days?

(A) $\dfrac{h}{3p}$

(B) $\dfrac{3hp}{4}$

(C) $\dfrac{hp}{12}$

(D) $\dfrac{3h}{p}$

(E) $\dfrac{3p}{h}$

Solution.

- Pick two easy-to-use numbers, say $p = 1$ and $h = 1$. Then 1 painter can paint 1 house in 4 days.
- Then, 6 painters can paint 6 houses in 4 days, and so in 2 days 6 painters can paint 3 houses.

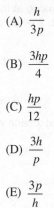

Painters	Houses	Days
1	1	4
6	6	4
6	3	2

- Evaluate the five choices when $p = 1$ and $h = 1$, and find the choice that equals 3:

(A) $\dfrac{h}{3p} = \dfrac{1}{3(1)} = \dfrac{1}{3}$: NO.

(B) $\dfrac{3hp}{4} = \dfrac{3(1)(1)}{4} = \dfrac{3}{4}$: NO.

(C) $\dfrac{hp}{12} = \dfrac{(1)(1)}{12} = \dfrac{1}{12}$: NO.

(D) $\dfrac{3h}{p} = \dfrac{3(1)}{1} = 3$: YES.

(E) $\dfrac{3p}{h} = \dfrac{3(1)}{1} = 3$: YES.

- Eliminate A, B, and C. But both D and E are 3. *What now*?
- Change *one* of the numbers, and test only D and E. Suppose that 1 painter could paint 100 houses, instead of just 1, in 4 days. Then 6 painters could paint lots of houses—certainly many more than 3.
- Of D and E, which will be *bigger* if you replace *h* by 100 instead of 1? In D, the numerator, and hence the whole fraction, which is $\frac{3h}{p}$, will be much bigger. In E, the denominator will be larger and the value of the fraction smaller.
- The answer is **D**.

Example 28 illustrates that replacing a variable by 1 is *not* a good idea in this type of problem. The reason is that multiplying by 1 and dividing by 1 give the same result: $3x$ and $\frac{3}{x}$ are each equal to 3 when $x = 1$. It is also *not* a good idea to use the same number for different variables: $\frac{3a}{b}$ and $\frac{3b}{a}$ are each equal to 3 when *a* and *b* are equal.

A good choice in Example 28 would be to let $p = 6$ and $h = 4$. Example 28 would then read, "If 6 painters can paint 4 houses in 4 days, how many houses can 6 painters, working at the same rate, paint in 2 days?" The answer is obviously 2, and only choice **D** is equal to 2 when $p = 6$ and $h = 4$.

Even though Examples 27 and 28 are much more abstract than Examples 25 and 26, they too can be solved directly and more quickly *if* you can manipulate the variables.

Algebraic Solution 27. If each week the school needs *c* cans for each of the *s* students, then it will need *cs* cans per week. Dividing *cs* into *x* gives the number of weeks that *x* cans will last: $\frac{x}{cs}$.

Algebraic Solution 28. Since 1 painter can do $\frac{1}{p}$ times the amount of work of *p* painters, if *p* painters can paint *h* houses in 4 days, then 1 painter can paint $\frac{h}{p}$ houses in 4 days.

In 1 day he can paint $\frac{1}{4}$ times the number of houses he can paint in 4 days; so, in 1 day, 1 painter can paint $\frac{1}{4} \times \frac{h}{p} = \frac{h}{4p}$ houses. Of course, in 1 day, 6 painters can paint 6 times as many houses: $\frac{6h}{4p}$. Finally, in 2 days these painters can paint twice as many houses: $2\left(\frac{6h}{4p}\right) = \frac{12h}{4p} = \frac{3h}{p}$. Even if you could carefully reason this out, why would you want to?

Now, practice TACTIC 6 on the following problems.

EXAMPLE 29

Nadia will be *x* years old *y* years from now. How old was she *z* years ago?

(A) $x + y + z$
(B) $x + y - z$
(C) $x - y - z$
(D) $y - x - z$
(E) $z - y - x$

EXAMPLE 30

If $a = b + \dfrac{1}{2}$, $b = 2c + \dfrac{1}{2}$, and $c = 3d + \dfrac{1}{2}$, which of the following is an expression for d in terms of a?

(A) $\dfrac{a-2}{6}$

(B) $\dfrac{2a-3}{6}$

(C) $\dfrac{2a-3}{12}$

(D) $\dfrac{3a-2}{18}$

(E) $\dfrac{4a-3}{24}$

EXAMPLE 31

Anne drove for h hours at a constant rate of r miles per hour. How many miles did she go during the final 20 minutes of her drive?

(A) $20r$

(B) $\dfrac{hr}{3}$

(C) $3rh$

(D) $\dfrac{hr}{20}$

(E) $\dfrac{r}{3}$

Solution 29. Assume Nadia will be 10 in 2 years. How old was she 3 years ago? If she will be 10 in 2 years, she is 8 now and 3 years ago was 5. Which of the choices equals 5 when $x = 10$, $y = 2$, and $z = 3$? Only $x - y - z$ **(C)**.

Solution 30. Let $d = 1$. Then $c = 3\dfrac{1}{2}$, $b = 7\dfrac{1}{2}$, and $a = 8$. Which of the choices equals 1 when

$a = 8$? Only $\dfrac{a-2}{6}$ **(A)**.

Solution 31. If Anne drove at 60 miles per hour for 2 hours, how far did she go in the last 20 minutes?

Since 20 minutes is $\dfrac{1}{3}$ of an hour, she went $20 \left(\dfrac{1}{3} \text{ of } 60 \right)$ miles.

Only $\dfrac{r}{3}$ **(E)** = 20 when $r = 60$ and $h = 2$.

Notice that h is irrelevant. Whether Anne had been driving for 2 hours or 20 hours, the distance she covered in her last 20 minutes would be the same.

TACTIC

7 Choose an Appropriate Number.

TACTIC 7 is similar to TACTIC 6 in that you pick a convenient number. However, here no variable is given in the problem. TACTIC 7 is especially useful in problems involving fractions, ratios, and percents.

EXAMPLE 32

At Central High School each student studies exactly one foreign language. Three-fifths of the students take Spanish, and one-fourth of the remaining students take Italian. If all of the others take French, what <u>percent</u> of the students take French?

(A) 10
(B) 15
(C) 20
(D) 25
(E) 30

> **Helpful Hint**
> In problems involving fractions, the best number to use is the least common denominator of all the fractions. In problems involving percents, the easiest number to use is 100. (See Sections 9-B and 9-C.)

Solution. The least common denominator of $\frac{3}{5}$ and $\frac{1}{4}$ is 20, so assume that there are 20 students at Central High. (Remember that the number you choose doesn't have to be realistic.) Then the number of students taking Spanish is 12 $\left(\frac{3}{5} \text{ of } 20 \right)$. Of the remaining 8 students, 2 $\left(\frac{1}{4} \text{ of } 8 \right)$ take Italian. The other 6 take French. Finally, 6 is **30%** of 20. The answer is **E**.

EXAMPLE 33

From 2003 to 2004 the number of boys in the school chess club decreased by 20%, and the number of girls in the club increased by 20%. The ratio of girls to boys in the club in 2004 was how many times the ratio of girls to boys in the club in 2003?

(A) $\frac{2}{3}$

(B) $\frac{4}{5}$

(C) 1

(D) $\frac{5}{4}$

(E) $\frac{3}{2}$

Solution. This problem involves percents, so try to use 100. Assume that in 2003 there were 100 boys and 100 girls in the club. Since 20% of 100 is 20, in 2004 there were 120 girls (a 20% increase) and 80 boys (a 20% decrease). See the following chart:

Year	Number of Girls	Number of Boys	Ratio of Girls to Boys
2003	100	100	$\dfrac{100}{100} = 1$
2004	120	80	$\dfrac{120}{80} = \dfrac{3}{2}$

The chart shows that the 2003 ratio of 1 was multiplied by $\dfrac{3}{2}$. The answer is **E**.

Here are two more problems where TACTIC 7 is useful.

EXAMPLE 34

In a particular triathlon the athletes cover $\dfrac{1}{24}$ of the total distance by swimming, $\dfrac{1}{3}$ of it by running, and the rest by bike. What is the ratio of the distance covered by bike to the distance covered by running?

(A) 15:1
(B) 15:8
(C) 8:5
(D) 5:8
(E) 8:15

EXAMPLE 35

From 2002 to 2003 the sales of a book decreased by 80%. If the sales in 2004 were the same as in 2002, by what percent did they increase from 2003 to 2004?

(A) 80%
(B) 100%
(C) 120%
(D) 400%
(E) 500%

Solution 34. The least common denominator of the two fractions is 24, so assume that the total distance is 24 miles. Then, the athletes swim for 1 mile and run for 8 $\left(\dfrac{1}{3} \text{ of } 24 \right)$ miles. The remaining 15 miles they cover by bike. Therefore, the required ratio is **15:8 (B)**.

Solution 35. Use TACTIC 7, and assume that 100 copies were sold in 2002 (and 2004). Sales dropped by 80 (80% of 100) to 20 in 2003 and then increased by 80, from 20 back to 100, in 2004. The percent increase was

$$\frac{\text{actual increase}}{\text{original amount}} \times 100\% = \frac{80}{20} \times 100\% = \textbf{400\% (D)}.$$

Eliminate Absurd Choices, and Guess.

When you have no idea how to solve a problem, eliminate all the absurd choices and *guess* from among the remaining ones.

In Part One, you read that only very infrequently should you omit a problem that you have time to work on. During the course of an SAT, you will probably find at least a few multiple-choice questions that you have no idea how to solve. *Do not omit these questions!* Often two or three of the answers are absurd. Eliminate them and *guess*. Occasionally, four of the choices are absurd. When this occurs, your answer is no longer a guess.

What makes a choice absurd? Lots of things. Even if you don't know how to solve a problem, even with very hard ones, you may realize that:

- the answer must be positive, but some of the choices are negative;
- the answer must be even, but some of the choices are odd;
- the answer must be less than 100, but some choices exceed 100;
- a ratio must be less than 1, but some choices are greater than or equal to 1.

Let's look at several examples. In a few of them the information given is intentionally insufficient to solve the problem, but you will still be able to determine that some of the answers are absurd. In each case the "solution" provided will indicate which choices you should have eliminated. At that point you would simply guess. [See Part One for a complete discussion of guessing.] Remember: on the SAT when you have to guess, don't agonize. Just make your choice and then move on.

EXAMPLE 36

A region inside a semicircle of radius r is shaded. What is the area of the shaded region?

(A) $\frac{1}{4}\pi r^2$

(B) $\frac{1}{3}\pi r^2$

(C) $\frac{1}{2}\pi r^2$

(D) $\frac{2}{3}\pi r^2$

(E) $\frac{3}{4}\pi r^2$

Solution. You may have no idea how to find the area of the shaded region, but you should know that, since the area of a circle is πr^2, the area of a semicircle is $\frac{1}{2}\pi r^2$. Therefore, the area of the shaded region must be *less than* $\frac{1}{2}\pi r^2$, so eliminate C, D, and E. On an actual problem that includes a diagram, if the diagram is drawn to scale, you may be able to make an educated guess between A and B. If not, just choose one or the other.

EXAMPLE 37

The average of 5, 10, 15, and *x* is 20. What is *x*?

(A) 0
(B) 20
(C) 25
(D) 45
(E) 50

Solution. If the average of four numbers is 20, and three of them are less than 20, the other one must be greater than 20. Eliminate A and B and guess. If you further realize that, since 5 and 10 are *a lot* less than 20, *x* will probably be *a lot* more than 20, you can eliminate C, as well. Then guess either D or E.

EXAMPLE 38

If 25% of 220 equals 5.5% of *w*, what is *w*?

(A)   10
(B)   55
(C)   100
(D)   110
(E) 1000

Solution. Since 5.5% of *w* equals 25% of 220, which is surely greater than 5.5% of 220, *w* must be *greater* than 220. Eliminate A, B, C, and D. The answer *must* be **E**!

Example 38 illustrates an important point. *Even if you know how to solve a problem*, if you immediately see that four of the five choices are absurd, just pick the remaining choice and move on.

EXAMPLE 39

A prize of $27,000 is to be divided in some ratio among three people. What is the largest share?

(A) $18,900
(B) $13,500
(C) $ 8100
(D) $ 5400
(E) $ 2700

Solution. If the prize were divided equally, each share would be worth $9000. If it is divided unequally, the largest share is surely *more than* $9000, so eliminate C, D, and E. In an actual question, you would be told what the ratio is, and that information should enable you to eliminate A or B. If not, you would just guess.

EXAMPLE 40

A jar contains only red and blue marbles. The ratio of the number of red marbles to the number of blue marbles is 5:3. What percent of the marbles are blue?

(A) 37.5%
(B) 50%
(C) 60%
(D) 62.5%
(E) 80%

Solution. Since there are 5 red marbles for every 3 blue ones, there are fewer blue ones than red ones. Therefore, *fewer than half* (50%) of the marbles are blue. Eliminate B, C, D, and E. The answer is **A**.

EXAMPLE 41

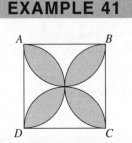

In the figure above, four semicircles are drawn, each centered at the midpoint of one of the sides of square *ABCD*. Each of the four shaded "petals" is the intersection of two of the semicircles. If *AB* = 4, what is the total area of the shaded region?

(A) 8π
(B) $32 - 8\pi$
(C) $16 - 8\pi$
(D) $8\pi - 32$
(E) $8\pi - 16$

Solution. The diagram is drawn to scale. Therefore, you can trust it in making your estimate (TACTIC 2).

• Since the shaded area *appears* to take up a little more than half of the square, it does.
• The area of the square is 16, so the area of the shaded region must be *about* 9.
   • *Using your calculator*, but only when you need it, check each choice. Since π is slightly more than 3, 8π (which appears in each choice) is somewhat more than 24, approximately 25.

• (A) $8\pi \approx 25$. More than the whole square: *way* too big.
• (B) $32 - 8\pi \approx 7$. Too small.
• (C) $16 - 8\pi$ is negative. Clearly impossible!
• (D) $8\pi - 32$ is also negative.
• (E) **$8\pi - 16$** ≈ 25 – 16 = 9. Finally! The answer is **E**.

Note: Three of the choices are absurd: A is more than the area of the entire square, and C and D are negative and so can be eliminated immediately. No matter what your estimate was, at worst you had to guess between two choices.

Now use TACTIC 8 on each of the following problems. Even if you know how to solve them, don't. Practice this technique, and see how many choices you can eliminate *without* actually solving.

EXAMPLE 42

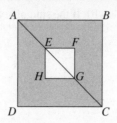

In the figure above, diagonal $\overline{EG}$ of square $EFGH$ is one-half of diagonal $\overline{AD}$ of square $ABCD$. What is the ratio of the area of the shaded region to the area of $ABCD$?

(A) $\sqrt{2}:1$

(B) $3:4$

(C) $\sqrt{2}:2$

(D) $1:2$

(E) $1:2\sqrt{2}$

EXAMPLE 43

Jim receives a commission of 25¢ for every $20.00 worth of merchandise he sells. What percent is his commission?

(A) $1\frac{1}{4}\%$

(B) $2\frac{1}{2}\%$

(C) 5%

(D) 25%

(E) 125%

EXAMPLE 44

From 1990 to 2000, Michael's weight increased by 25%. If his weight was W kilograms in 2000, what was it in 1990?

(A) $1.75W$
(B) $1.25W$
(C) $1.20W$
(D) $.80W$
(E) $.75W$

EXAMPLE 45

The average of 10 numbers is –10. If the sum of six of them is 100, what is the average of the other four?

(A) –100
(B) –50
(C) 0
(D) 50
(E) 100

EXAMPLE 46

What is 3% of 4%?

(A) 0.07%
(B) 0.12%
(C) 1.2%
(D) 7%
(E) 12%

EXAMPLE 47

If $f(x) = 4x^2 + 2x^4$, what is the value of $f(-2)$?

(A) –48
(B) –32
(C) 0
(D) 48
(E) 320

Solution 42. Obviously, the shaded region is smaller than square *ABCD*, so the ratio must be less than 1. Eliminate A ($\sqrt{2} > 1.4$). Also, from the diagram, it is clear that the shaded region is more than half of square *ABCD*, so the ratio is greater than 0.5. Eliminate D and E. Since 3:4 = 0.75 and $\sqrt{2}$:2 $\approx$ 0.71, B and C are too close to tell, just by looking, which is right, so guess. The answer is **B**.

Solution 43. Clearly, a commission of 25¢ on $20 is quite small. Eliminate D and E, and guess one of the small percents. If you realize that 1% of $20 is 20¢, then you know the answer is a little more than 1%, and you should guess A (maybe B, but definitely not C). The answer is **A**.

Solution 44. Since Michael's weight increased, his weight in 1990 was *less than W*. Eliminate A, B, and C and guess. The answer is **D**.

Solution 45. Since the average of all 10 numbers is negative, so is their sum. However, the sum of the first six is positive, so the sum (and the average) of the others must be negative. Eliminate C, D, and E. The answer is **B**.

Solution 46. Since 3% of a number is just a small part of it, 3% of 4% must be *much less* than 4%. Eliminate D and E, and probably C. The answer is **B**.

Solution 47. Any nonzero number raised to an even power is positive, so $4x^2 + 2x^4$ is positive. Eliminate A, B, and C. If you can't evaluate $f(-2)$, guess between D and E. If you have a hunch that E is too big, choose D. The answer is **D**.

TACTIC

9 Subtract to Find Shaded Regions.

Whenever part of a figure is white and part is shaded, the straightforward way to find the area of the shaded portion is to find the area of the entire figure and then subtract from it the area of the white region. Of course, if you are asked for the area of the white region, you can, instead, subtract the shaded area from the total area. Occasionally, you may see an easy way to calculate the shaded area directly, but usually you should subtract.

EXAMPLE 48

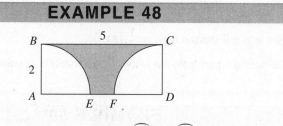

In the figure above, *ABCD* is a rectangle, and $\overset{\frown}{BE}$ and $\overset{\frown}{CF}$ are arcs of circles centered at *A* and *D*. What is the area of the shaded region?

(A) $10 - \pi$
(B) $2(5 - \pi)$
(C) $2(5 - 2\pi)$
(D) $6 + 2\pi$
(E) $5(2 - \pi)$

Solution. The entire region is a 2×5 rectangle whose area is 10. Since each white region is a quarter-circle of radius 2, the combined area of these regions is that of a semicircle of radius 2: $\frac{1}{2}\pi(2)^2 = 2\pi$. Therefore, the area of the shaded region is $10 - 2\pi = \mathbf{2(5 - \pi)}$ **(B)**.

EXAMPLE 49

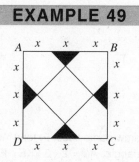

In the figure above, each side of square *ABCD* is divided into three equal parts. If a point is chosen at random inside the square, what is the probability it will be in the shaded region?

(A) $\dfrac{1}{9}$

(B) $\dfrac{1}{8}$

(C) $\dfrac{1}{6}$

(D) $\dfrac{1}{4}$

(E) $\dfrac{1}{3}$

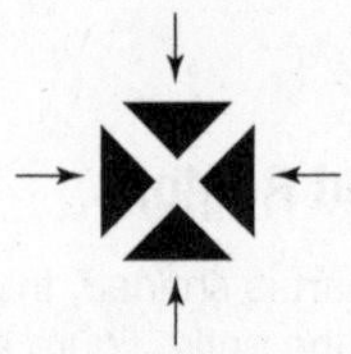

Solution. Since the answer doesn't depend on the value of *x* (the *probability* will be the same no matter what *x* is), let *x* = 1. Then the area of the whole square is $3^2 = 9$. The area of each shaded triangle or of all the white sections can be calculated, but there's an easier way: notice that, if you slide the four shaded triangles together, they form a square of side 1. Therefore, the total shaded area is 1, and so the shaded area is $\frac{1}{9}$ of the total area and the probability that the chosen point is in the shaded area is $\frac{1}{9}$ **(A)**.

The idea of subtracting a part from the whole works with line segments as well as areas.

EXAMPLE 50

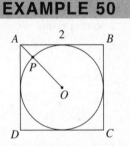

In the figure above, the circle with center *O* is inscribed in square *ABCD*. Line segment $\overline{AO}$ intersects the circle at *P*. What is the length of $\overline{AP}$?

(A) 1

(B) $2 - \sqrt{2}$

(C) $1 - \dfrac{\sqrt{2}}{2}$

(D) $2\sqrt{2} - 2$

(E) $\sqrt{2} - 1$

Solution. First use TACTIC 4 and draw some lines. Extend $\overline{AO}$ to form diagonal $\overline{AC}$. Then, since △*ADC* is an isosceles right triangle, $AC = 2\sqrt{2}$ (KEY FACT J8) and *AO* is half of that, or $\sqrt{2}$. Then draw in diameter $\overline{EF}$ parallel to $\overline{AD}$. Since the diameter is 2 (*EF* = *AD* = 2), the radius is 1. Finally, subtract: $AP = AO - PO = \sqrt{2} - 1$ **(E)**.

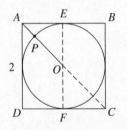

Note: If you don't realize which lines to add and/or you can't reason a question like this one out, *do not* omit it. You can still use TACTIC 2: trust the diagram. Since $AB = 2$, then $AE = 1$, and AP is clearly less than 0.5.

 With your calculator evaluate each choice. A, B, and D are all greater than 0.5. Eliminate them, and guess either C or E.

TACTIC 10   Don't Do More Than You Have To.

In Example 6 on page 360, you were asked, "By how many degrees does the angle formed by the hour hand and the minute hand of a clock increase from 1:27 to 1:28?" If you look at the solution, you will see that we didn't have to calculate either angle. This is a common situation. *Look for shortcuts.* Since a problem can often be solved in more than one way, you should always look for the easiest method. Consider the following examples.

EXAMPLE 51

If $5(3x - 7) = 20$, what is $3x - 8$?

It's not difficult to solve for *x*:

$$5(3x - 7) = 20 \Rightarrow 15x - 35 = 20 \Rightarrow 15x = 55 \Rightarrow$$
$$x = \frac{55}{15} = \frac{11}{3}.$$

But it's too much work. Besides, once you find that $x = \frac{11}{3}$, you still have to multiply to get $3x$:

$3\left(\frac{11}{3}\right) = 11$, and then subtract to get $3x - 8$: $11 - 8 = \mathbf{3}$.

Solution. The key is to recognize that you don't need *x*. Finding $3x - 7$ is easy (just divide the original equation by 5), and $3x - 8$ is just 1 less:

$$5(3x - 7) = 20 \Rightarrow 3x - 7 = 4 \Rightarrow 3x - 8 = \mathbf{3}.$$

EXAMPLE 52

If $7x + 3y = 17$ and $3x + 7y = 19$, what is the average (arithmetic mean) of *x* and *y*?

The obvious way to do this is to first find *x* and *y* by solving the two equations simultaneously and then to take their average. If you are familiar with this method, try it now, before reading further. If you work carefully, you should find that $x = \frac{31}{20}$ and $y = \frac{41}{20}$, and their average is

$\dfrac{\frac{31}{20} + \frac{41}{20}}{2} = \dfrac{9}{5}$ or **1.8**. This method is not too difficult; but it is quite time-consuming, and no

problem on the SAT requires you to do so much work.

Look for a shortcut. Is there a way to find the average without first finding *x* and *y*? Absolutely! Here's the best way to do this.

Solution. Add the two equations:

$$7x + 3y = 17$$
$$+\ 3x + 7y = 19$$
$$\overline{10x + 10y = 36}$$

Divide each side by 10:

$$x + y = 3.6$$

Calculate the average:

$$\frac{x+y}{2} = \frac{3.6}{2} = \textbf{1.8}$$

When you learn TACTIC 17, you will see that adding two equations, as was done here, is the standard way to attack problems such as this on the SAT.

TACTIC

11   Pay Attention to Units.

Often the answer to a question must be in units different from those used in the given data. As you read the question, <u>underline</u> exactly what you are being asked. Do the examiners want hours or minutes or seconds, dollars or cents, feet or inches, meters or centimeters? On multiple-choice questions an answer with the wrong units is almost always one of the choices.

EXAMPLE 53

At a speed of 48 miles per hour, how many minutes will be required to drive 32 miles?

(A) $\frac{2}{3}$

(B) $\frac{3}{2}$

(C) 40

(D) 45

(E) 2400

Solution. This is a relatively easy question. Just be attentive. Since $\frac{32}{48} = \frac{2}{3}$, it will take $\frac{2}{3}$

of an *hour* to drive 32 miles. Choice A is $\frac{2}{3}$; but that is *not* the correct answer because you

are asked how many *minutes* will be required. (Did you underline the word "minutes" in the

question?) The correct answer is $\frac{2}{3}(60) = \textbf{40 (C)}$.

Note that you could have been asked how many *seconds* would be needed, in which case the answer would be 40(60) = 2400 (E).

EXAMPLE 54

The wholesale price of potatoes is usually 3 pounds for $1.79. How much money, in cents, did a restaurant save when it was able to purchase 600 pounds of potatoes at 2 pounds for $1.15?

Solution. For 600 pounds the restaurant would normally have to buy 200 3-pound bags for $200 \times \$1.79 = \$358$. On sale, it bought 300 2-pound bags for $300 \times \$1.15 = \$345$. Therefore, the restaurant saved 13 dollars. *Do not* grid in 13. If you underline the word "cents" you won't forget to convert the units: 13 dollars is **1300** cents.

TACTIC

12 Use Your Calculator.

You already know that you can use a calculator on the SAT. (See Part One for a complete discussion of calculator usage.) The main reason to use a calculator is that it enables you to do arithmetic more quickly and more accurately than you can by hand on *problems that you know how to solve*. (For instance, in Example 54, you should use your calculator to multiply 200×1.79.) The purpose of TACTIC 12 is to show you how to use your calculator to get the right answer to *questions that you do not know how to solve or you cannot solve*.

EXAMPLE 55

If $x^2 = 2$, what is the value of $\left(x + \dfrac{1}{x}\right)\left(x - \dfrac{1}{x}\right)$?

(A) 1

(B) 1.5

(C) $1 + \sqrt{2}$

(D) $2 + \sqrt{2}$

(E) $1.5 + 2\sqrt{2}$

Solution. The College Board would consider this a hard question, and most students would either omit it or, worse, miss it. The best approach is to realize that $\left(x + \dfrac{1}{x}\right)\left(x - \dfrac{1}{x}\right)$ is a product of the form

$$(a + b)(a - b) = a^2 - b^2.$$

Therefore:

$$\left(x + \frac{1}{x}\right)\left(x - \frac{1}{x}\right) = x^2 - \frac{1}{x^2} = 2 - \frac{1}{2} = \textbf{1.5 (B)}.$$

If you didn't see this solution, you could still solve the problem by writing $x = \sqrt{2}$ and then trying to multiply and simplify $\left(\sqrt{2} + \dfrac{1}{\sqrt{2}}\right)\left(\sqrt{2} - \dfrac{1}{\sqrt{2}}\right)$. It is likely, however, that you would make a mistake somewhere along the way.

The better method is to *use your calculator*. $\sqrt{2} \approx 1.414$ and $\dfrac{1}{\sqrt{2}} \approx 0.707$, so

$$\left(\sqrt{2} + \frac{1}{\sqrt{2}}\right)\left(\sqrt{2} - \frac{1}{\sqrt{2}}\right) \approx (1.414 + 0.707)(1.414 - 0.707) = (2.121)(0.707) = 1.499547.$$

Clearly, choose **1.5**, the small difference being due to the rounding off of $\sqrt{2}$ as 1.414.

If this were a grid-in question, you should *not* grid in 1.49, since you know that that's only an approximation. Rather, you should guess a simple number near 1.499, such as 1.5. In fact, if you don't round off, and just use the value your calculator gives for $\sqrt{2}$ (1.414213562, say), you will probably get 1.5 exactly (although you may get 1.49999999 or 1.50000001).

EXAMPLE 56

If a and b are positive numbers, with $a^3 = 3$ and $a^5 = 12b^2$, what is the ratio of a to b?

Solution. This is another difficult question that most students would omit or miss. If you think to divide the second equation by the first, however, the problem is not too bad:

$$\frac{a^5}{a^3} = \frac{12b^2}{3} = 4b^2 \quad \text{and} \quad \frac{a^5}{a^3} = a^2.$$

Then

$$a^2 = 4b^2 \Rightarrow \frac{a^2}{b^2} = 4 \Rightarrow \frac{a}{b} = \mathbf{2}.$$

If you don't see this, you can still solve the problem with your *scientific* calculator:

$$a = \sqrt[3]{3} \approx 1.44225 \Rightarrow a^5 \approx 6.24026 \Rightarrow b^2 = \frac{6.24026}{12} \approx 0.52 \Rightarrow b \approx \sqrt{0.52} \approx 0.7211.$$

So, $\frac{a}{b} \approx \frac{1.44225}{0.7211} = 2.00007$.

Grid in 2.

EXAMPLE 57

What is the value of $\dfrac{1+\dfrac{7}{5}}{1-\dfrac{5}{7}}$?

Solution. There are two straightforward ways to do this: (i) multiply the numerator and denominator by 35, the LCM of 5 and 7, and (ii) simplify and divide:

(i) $\dfrac{35\left(1+\dfrac{7}{5}\right)}{35\left(1-\dfrac{5}{7}\right)} = \dfrac{35+49}{35-25} = \dfrac{84}{10} = \mathbf{8.4}$.

(ii) $\dfrac{1+\dfrac{7}{5}}{1-\dfrac{5}{7}} = \dfrac{\dfrac{12}{5}}{\dfrac{2}{7}} = \dfrac{\cancel{12}^{6}}{5} \times \dfrac{7}{\cancel{2}_{1}} = \dfrac{42}{5} = \mathbf{8.4}$.

However, if you don't like working with fractions, you can easily do the arithmetic on *any* calculator. Be sure you know how *your* calculator works. Be sure that when you evaluate the given complex fraction you get 8.4.

If this had been a multiple-choice question, the five choices would probably have been fractions, in which case the correct answer would be $\dfrac{42}{5}$. If you had solved this with your calculator, you would then have had to use the calculator to determine which of the fractions offered as choices was equal to 8.4.

13   Know When *Not* to Use Your Calculator.

Don't get into the habit of using your calculator on every problem involving arithmetic. Since many problems can be solved more easily and faster without a calculator, learn to use your calculator only when you need it (see Part One).

EXAMPLE 58

John had $150. He used 85% of it to pay his electric bill and 5% of it on a gift for his mother. How much did he have left?

Solution. Many students would use their calculators on each step of this problem.

Electric bill:	$150 × .85 = $127.50
Gift for mother:	$150 × .05 = $7.50
Total spent:	$127.50 + $7.50 = $135
Amount left:	$150 − $135 = **$15**

Good test-takers would have proceeded as follows, finishing the problem in less time than it takes to calculate the first percent: John used 90% of his money, so he had 10% left; and 10% of $150 is **$15**.

14   Systematically Make Lists.

When a question asks "how many," often the best strategy is to make a list of all the possibilities. It is important that you make the list in a *systematic* fashion so that you don't inadvertently leave something out. Often, shortly after starting the list, you can see a pattern developing and can figure out how many more entries there will be without writing them all down.

Even if the question does not specifically ask "how many," you may need to count some items to answer it; in this case, as well, the best plan may be to make a list.

Listing things systematically means writing them in numerical order (if the entries are numbers) or in alphabetical order (if the entries are letters). If the answer to "how many" is a small number (as in Example 59), just list all possibilities. If the answer is a large number (as in Example 60), start the list and write enough entries to enable you to see a pattern.

EXAMPLE 59

The product of three positive integers is 300. If one of them is 5, what is the least possible value of the sum of the other two?

Solution. Since one of the integers is 5, the product of the other two is 60 (5 × 60 = 300). Systematically, list all possible pairs, (*a*, *b*), of positive integers whose product is 60, and check their sums. First, let *a* =1, then 2, and so on.

a	*b*	*a + b*
1	60	61
2	30	32
3	20	23
4	15	19
5	12	17
6	10	16

The answer is **16**.

EXAMPLE 60

A palindrome is a number, such as 93539, that reads the same forward and backward. How many palindromes are there between 100 and 1000?

Solution. First, write down
the numbers in the 100's   101, 111, 121, 131, 141,
that end in 1:   151, 161, 171, 181, 191

Now write the numbers   202, 212, 222, 232, 242,
beginning and ending in 2:   252, 262, 272, 282, 292

By now you should see the pattern: there are 10 numbers beginning with 1, and 10 beginning with 2, and there will be 10 beginning with 3, 4, ..., 9 for a total of $9 \times 10 = $ **90** palindromes.

EXAMPLE 61

In how many ways can Al, Bob, Charlie, Dan, and Ed stand in a line if Bob must be first and either Charlie or Dan must be last?

Solution. Represent the five boys as A, B, C, D, and E. Placing Charlie last, you see that the order is B __ __ __ C. Systematically fill in the blanks with A, D, and E. Write all the three-letter "words" you can in alphabetical order so you don't accidentally skip one.

```
A D E
A E D
D A E
D E A
E A D
E D A
```

There are 6 possibilities when C is last. Clearly, there will be 6 more when D is last. Therefore, there are **12** ways in all to satisfy the conditions of the problem.

See Section O in Chapter 9 for additional examples and for another method of solving these problems using the counting principle.

15 Trust All Grids, Graphs, and Charts.

Figures that show the grid lines of a graph are *always* accurate, whether or not the coordinates of the points are given. For example, in the figure below, you can determine each of the following:

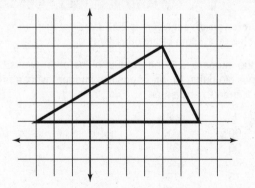

• the lengths of all three sides of the triangle;
• the perimeter of the triangle;
• the area of the triangle;
• the slope of each line segment.

EXAMPLE 62

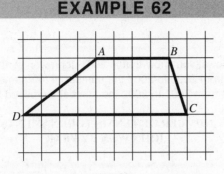

In the grid above, what is the area of quadrilateral *ABCD*?

(A) 19.5
(B) 21
(C) 25.5
(D) 27
(E) 34

Solution. $\overline{AB}$ and $\overline{CD}$ are parallel (they're both horizontal), so *ABCD* is a trapezoid. If you know that the formula for the area of a trapezoid is $A = \frac{1}{2}(b_1 + b_2)h$, use it. By counting boxes, you see that

$$b_1 = CD = 9, \ b_2 = AB = 4, \text{ and } h = 3.$$

Therefore, the area is $\frac{1}{2}(9+4)(3) = $ **19.5 (A)**.

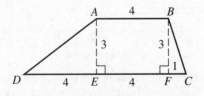

If you don't know the formula, use $\overline{AE}$ and $\overline{BF}$ to divide *ABCD* into a rectangle *(ABFE)* and two right triangles *(AED* and *BFC)*. Their areas are 12, 6, and 1.5, respectively, for a total area of **19.5**.

For sample problems using grids, see Section 9-N on coordinate geometry.

SAT problems that use any kind of charts or graphs are *always* drawn accurately and can be trusted. For example, suppose that you are told that each of the 1000 students at Central High School studies exactly one foreign language. Then, from the circle graph that follows, you may conclude that fewer than half of the students study Spanish, but more students study Spanish than any other language; that approximately 250 students study French; that fewer students study German than any other language; and that approximately the same number of students are studying Latin and Italian.

FOREIGN LANGUAGES STUDIED BY
1000 STUDENTS AT CENTRAL HIGH SCHOOL

From the bar graph that follows, you know that in 2001 John won exactly three tournaments, and you can calculate that from 2000 to 2001 the number of tournaments he won decreased by 50% (from 6 to 3), whereas from 2001 to 2002 the number increased by 300% (from 3 to 12).

NUMBER OF TENNIS TOURNAMENTS
JOHN WON BY YEAR

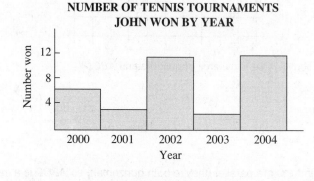

EXAMPLE 63

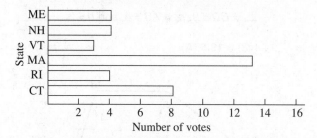

The chart above depicts the number of electoral votes assigned to each of the six New England states. What is the average (arithmetic mean) number of electoral votes, to the <u>nearest tenth</u>, assigned to these states?

(A) 4.0
(B) 5.7
(C) 6.0
(D) 6.5
(E) 6.7

Solution. Since you can trust the chart to be accurate, the total number of electoral votes for the six states is

$$4 + 4 + 3 + 13 + 4 + 8 = 36$$

and the average is 36 ÷ 6 = **6 (C)**.

Several different types of questions concerning bar graphs, circle graphs, line graphs, and various charts and tables can be found in Section 9-Q.

TACTIC
16

Read the Definitions of Strange Symbols Very Carefully.

On almost every SAT a few questions use symbols, such as ⊕, □, ☺, ✷, and ✚, that you have never before seen in a mathematics problem. How can you answer such a question? Don't panic! It's easy; you are always told exactly what the symbol means! All you have to do is follow the directions carefully.

EXAMPLE 64

For any numbers a and b, a ☺ b is defined as a ☺ $b = \dfrac{a+b}{a-b}$. What is the value of 25 ☺ 15?

Solution. The definition of "☺" tells you that, whenever two numbers surround a "happy face," you are to form a fraction in which the numerator is the sum of the numbers and the denominator is their difference. Here, 25 ☺ 15 is the fraction whose numerator is 25 + 15 = 40 and whose denominator is 25 − 15 = 10: $\dfrac{40}{10} = $ **4**.

Sometimes the same symbol is used in two (or even three) questions. In these cases, the first question is easy and involves only numbers; the second is a bit harder and usually contains variables.

Examples 65–67 refer to the following definition.

For any numbers x and y, let $x * y$ be defined as $x * y = xy - (x + y)$.

Follow the directions given in the definition and try to answer Examples 65–67 before reading the solutions.

EXAMPLE 65

What is the value of $-2 * 3$?

(A) −11
(B) −7
(C)   0
(D)   6
(E)   7

EXAMPLE 66

For what value of x does $x * 5 = x * 10$?

(A) −5
(B) −1
(C)   0
(D)   1
(E)   5

EXAMPLE 67

How many positive numbers are solutions of the equation $y * y = y$?

(A) None
(B) 1
(C) 2
(D) 3
(E) More than 3

Solution 65.

$$-2 * 3 = (-2)(3) - (-2 + 3) = -6 - (1) = -7 \text{ (B)}.$$

Solution 66. Since $x * 5 = x * 10$

$$5x - (5 + x) = 10x - (10 + x)$$
$$5x - 5 - x = 10x - 10 - x$$
$$4x - 5 = 9x - 10$$
$$5x = 5 \Rightarrow x = 1 \text{ (D)}.$$

Solution 67.

$$y * y = y \Rightarrow y^2 - 2y = y \Rightarrow y^2 - 3y = 0.$$

So, $y(y - 3) = 0 \Rightarrow y = 0$ or $y = 3$.

There is only **1** positive solution, 3 **(D)**.

EXAMPLE 68

For any real numbers c and d, $c ⌘ d$ is defined to be $c^d + d^c$. What is the value of $1 ⌘ (2 ⌘ 3)$?

Solution. Remember the correct order of operations: always do first what's in the parentheses (see Section 9-A).

$$2 ⌘ 3 = 2^3 + 3^2 = 8 + 9 = 17$$

and

$$1 ⌘ 17 = 1^{17} + 17^1 = 1 + 17 = 18.$$

Grid-in **18**.

TACTIC

Add Equations.

When a question involves two equations that do not have exponents, either add the equations or subtract them. If there are three or more equations, add them.

Helpful Hint
Very often, answering a question that involves two or more equations does *not* require you to solve the equations. Remember TACTIC 10: Do not do any more than is necessary.

EXAMPLE 69

If $3x + 5y = 14$ and $x - y = 6$, what is the average of x and y?

(A) 0
(B) 2.5
(C) 3
(D) 3.5
(E) 5

Solution. Add the equations:

$$3x + 5y = 14$$
$$+ \quad x - y = 6$$
$$\overline{4x + 4y = 20}$$

Divide each side by 4:

$$x + y = 5$$

The average of x and y is their sum divided by 2: $\dfrac{x+y}{2} = \dfrac{5}{2} = \mathbf{2.5}$

The answer is **B**.

Note that you *could have* actually solved for x and y [$x = 5.5$, $y = -0.5$], and then taken their average. However, that would have been time-consuming and unnecessary.

Here are two more problems involving two or more equations.

EXAMPLE 70

If $a - b + c = 7$ and $a + b - c = 11$, which of the following statements MUST be true?

  I. a is positive
 II. $b > c$
III. $bc < 0$

(A) None
(B) I only
(C) II only
(D) III only
(E) I and II only

EXAMPLE 71

If $a - b = 1$, $b - c = 2$, and $c - a = d$, what is the value of d?

(A) -3
(B) -1
(C) 1
(D) 3
(E) It cannot be determined from the information given.

Solution 70. Start by adding the two equations:

$$a - b + c = 7$$
$$+ a + b - c = 11$$
$$\overline{2a = 18}$$

Therefore, $a = 9$. (I is true.)

Replace a by 9 in each equation to obtain two new equations:

$9 - b + c = 7 \Rightarrow -b + c = -2$
and
$9 + b - c = 11 \Rightarrow b - c = 2$

Since $b - c = 2$, then $b > c$. (II is true.)

As long as $b = c + 2$, however, there are no restrictions on b *and* c: if $b = 2$ and $c = 0$, $bc = 0$. (III is false.)

The answer is **E**.

Solution 71. Add the three equations:

$$a - b = 1$$
$$b - c = 2$$
$$+ c - a = d$$
$$\overline{0 = 3 + d \Rightarrow d = \mathbf{-3}}$$

The answer is **A**.

Practice Exercises

Multiple-Choice Questions

1. In 1995, Diana read 10 English books and 7 French books. In 1996, she read twice as many French books as English books. If 60% of the books that she read during the 2 years were French, how many English and French books did she read in 1996?

   (A) 16
   (B) 26
   (C) 32
   (D) 39
   (E) 48

2. In the figure below, if the radius of circle O is 10, what is the length of diagonal $\overline{AC}$ of rectangle $OABC$?

   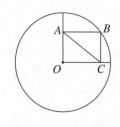

   (A) $\sqrt{2}$
   (B) $\sqrt{10}$
   (C) $5\sqrt{2}$
   (D) 10
   (E) $10\sqrt{2}$

3. In the figure below, vertex Q of square $OPQR$ is on a circle with center O. If the area of the square is 8, what is the area of the circle?

   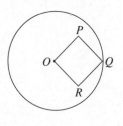

   (A) 8π
   (B) $8\pi\sqrt{2}$
   (C) 16π
   (D) 32π
   (E) 64π

4. In the figure below, $\overline{AB}$ and $\overline{AC}$ are two chords in a circle of radius 5. What is the sum of the lengths of the two chords?

   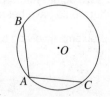

   <u>Note</u>: Figure not drawn to scale

   (A) 10
   (B) 15
   (C) 5π
   (D) 10π
   (E) It cannot be determined from the information given.

5. In the figure below, $ABCD$ is a square and AED is an equilateral triangle. If $AB = 2$, what is the area of the shaded region?

   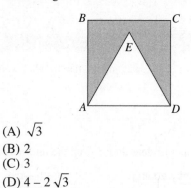

   (A) $\sqrt{3}$
   (B) 2
   (C) 3
   (D) $4 - 2\sqrt{3}$
   (E) $4 - \sqrt{3}$

6. If $5x + 13 = 31$, what is the value of $\sqrt{5x + 31}$?

   (A) $\sqrt{13}$
   (B) $\sqrt{\dfrac{173}{5}}$
   (C) 7
   (D) 13
   (E) 169

7. At Nat's Nuts a $2\frac{1}{4}$-pound bag of pistachio nuts costs \$6.00. At this rate, what is the cost, in cents, of a bag weighing 9 ounces?
(<u>Note</u>: 1 pound = 16 ounces)

   (A)   1.5
   (B)   24
   (C)   150
   (D) 1350
   (E) 2400

8. If $12a + 3b = 1$ and $7b - 2a = 9$, what is the average (arithmetic mean) of a and b?

   (A) 0.1
   (B) 0.5
   (C) 1
   (D) 2.5
   (E) 5

9. Jessica has 4 times as many books as John and 5 times as many as Karen. If Karen has more than 40 books, what is the least number of books that Jessica can have?

   (A) 240
   (B) 220
   (C) 210
   (D) 205
   (E) 200

Questions 10 and 11 refer to the following definition.

For any numbers a and b, $a \bigstar b = \dfrac{a}{b} + \dfrac{b}{a}$.

10. Which of the following is equal to $(1 \bigstar 2) \bigstar 3$?

    (A) $1 \bigstar 6$
    (B) $2 \bigstar 3$
    (C) $3 \bigstar 4$
    (D) $4 \bigstar 5$
    (E) $5 \bigstar 6$

11. For how many ordered pairs of positive integers (x, y) is $x \bigstar y = 2$?

    (A) None
    (B) 1
    (C) 2
    (D) 3
    (E) More than 3

12. What is the largest integer, n, that satisfies the inequality $n^2 + 8n - 3 < n^2 + 7n + 8$?

    (A)   0
    (B)   5
    (C)   7
    (D) 10
    (E) 11

13. If $a < b$ and c is the sum of a and b, which of the following is the positive difference between a and b?

    (A) $2a - c$
    (B) $2b - c$
    (C) $c - 2b$
    (D) $c - a + b$
    (E) $c - a - b$

14. If w widgets cost c cents, how many widgets can you get for d dollars?

    (A) $\dfrac{100dw}{c}$

    (B) $\dfrac{dw}{100c}$

    (C) $100cdw$

    (D) $\dfrac{dw}{c}$

    (E) cdw

15. If 120% of a is equal to 80% of b, which of the following is equal to $a + b$?

    (A) $1.5a$
    (B) $2a$
    (C) $2.5a$
    (D) $3a$
    (E) $5a$

16. In the figure at the right, $WXYZ$ is a square whose sides are 12. AB, CD, EF, and GH are each 8, and are the diameters of the four semicircles. What is the area of the shaded region?

    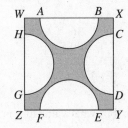

    (A) $144 - 128\pi$
    (B) $144 - 64\pi$
    (C) $144 - 32\pi$
    (D) $144 - 16\pi$
    (E) 16π

17. Which of the following numbers can be expressed as the product of three different integers greater than 1?

    I. 25
    II. 36
    III. 45

    (A) I only
    (B) II only
    (C) III only
    (D) II and III only
    (E) I, II, and III

18. What is the average of $4y + 3$ and $2y - 1$?

    (A) $3y + 1$
    (B) $3y + 2$
    (C) $3y + 4$
    (D) $y + 1$
    (E) $y + 2$

19. If x and y are integers such that $x^3 = y^2$, which of the following CANNOT be the value of y?

    (A) -1
    (B) 1
    (C) 8
    (D) 16
    (E) 27

20. What is a divided by $a\%$ of a?

    (A) $\dfrac{a}{100}$

    (B) $\dfrac{100}{a}$

    (C) $\dfrac{a^2}{100}$

    (D) $\dfrac{100}{a^2}$

    (E) $100a$

21. If an object is moving at a speed of 36 kilometers per hour, how many meters does it travel in 1 second?

    (A) 10
    (B) 36
    (C) 100
    (D) 360
    (E) 1000

22. For what value of x is $8^{2x-4} = 16^x$?

    (A) 2
    (B) 3
    (C) 4
    (D) 6
    (E) 8

23. On a certain Russian-American committee, $\dfrac{2}{3}$ of the members are men, and $\dfrac{3}{8}$ of the men are Americans. If $\dfrac{3}{5}$ of the committee members are Russians, what fraction of the members are American women?

    (A) $\dfrac{3}{20}$

    (B) $\dfrac{11}{60}$

    (C) $\dfrac{1}{4}$

    (D) $\dfrac{2}{5}$

    (E) $\dfrac{5}{12}$

24. If m is a positive integer, which of the following could be true?

    I. m^2 is a prime number.
    II. $\sqrt{m}$ is a prime number.
    III. $m^2 = \sqrt{m}$

    (A) I only
    (B) II only
    (C) III only
    (D) II and III only
    (E) I, II, and III

25. If $x\%$ of y is 10, what is y?

    (A) $\dfrac{10}{x}$

    (B) $\dfrac{100}{x}$

    (C) $\dfrac{1000}{x}$

    (D) $\dfrac{x}{100}$

    (E) $\dfrac{x}{10}$

Grid-in Questions

26. In writing all of the integers from 1 to 300, how many times is the digit 1 used?

29. At a certain university, $\frac{1}{4}$ of the applicants failed to meet minimum standards and were rejected immediately. Of those who met the standards, $\frac{2}{5}$ were accepted. If 1200 applicants were accepted, how many applied?

27. If $a + 2b = 14$ and $5a + 4b = 16$, what is the average (arithmetic mean) of a and b?

30. How many integers between 1 and 1000 are the product of two consecutive integers?

28. In the figure below, the area of circle O is 12. What is the area of the shaded sector?

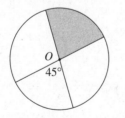

<u>Note</u>: Figure not drawn to scale

Answer Key

1.	**E**	6.	**C**	11.	**E**	16.	**C**	21.	**A**
2.	**D**	7.	**C**	12.	**D**	17.	**B**	22.	**D**
3.	**C**	8.	**B**	13.	**B**	18.	**A**	23.	**A**
4.	**E**	9.	**B**	14.	**A**	19.	**D**	24.	**D**
5.	**E**	10.	**E**	15.	**C**	20.	**B**	25.	**C**

26. `1 6 0`

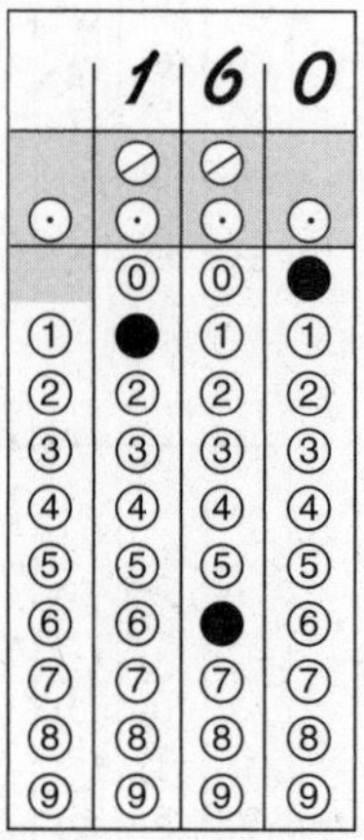

27. `5 / 2` or `2 . 5`

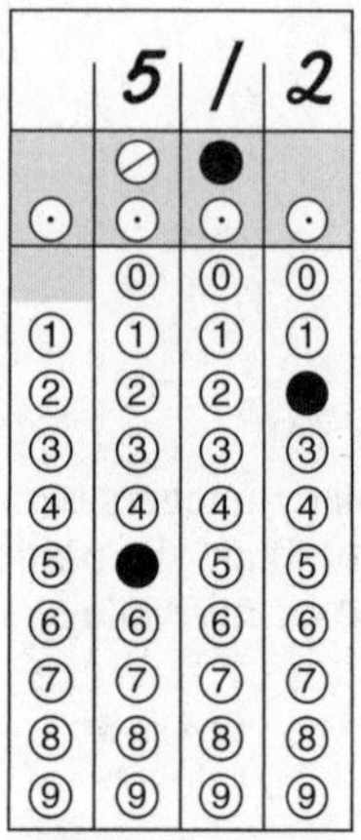

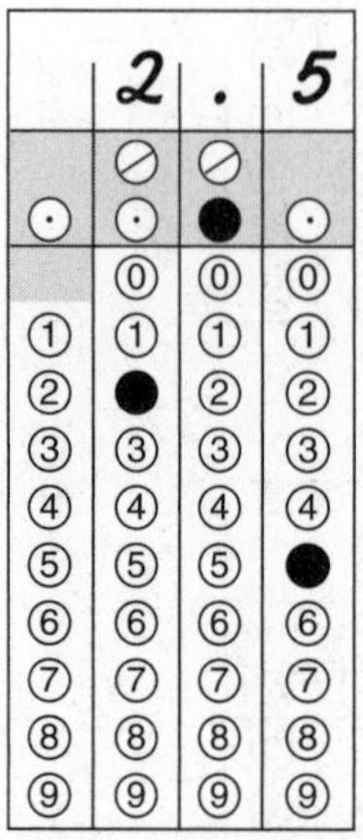

28. `1 2 / 8` or `3 / 2` or `1 . 5`

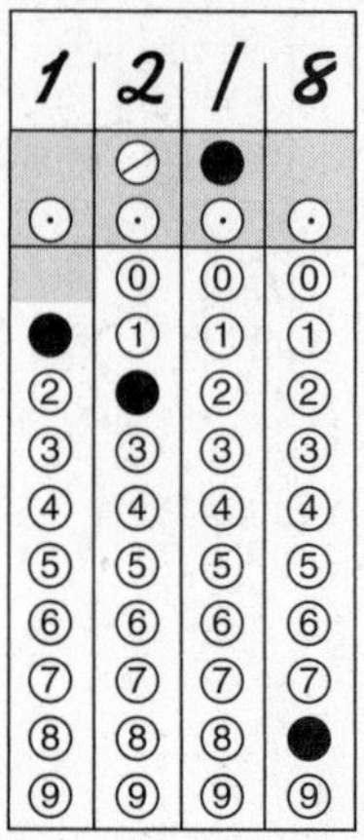

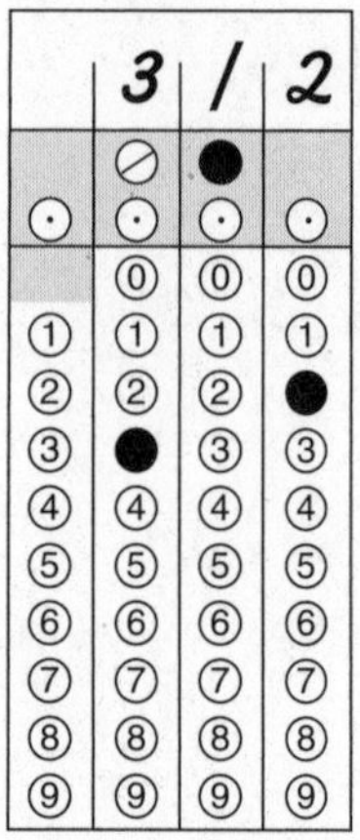

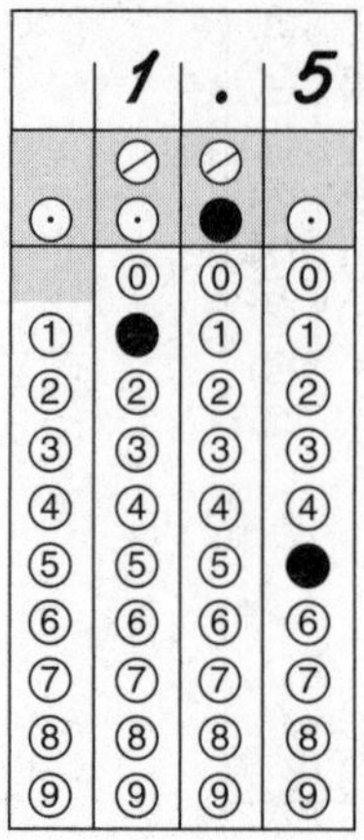

29. `4 0 0 0`

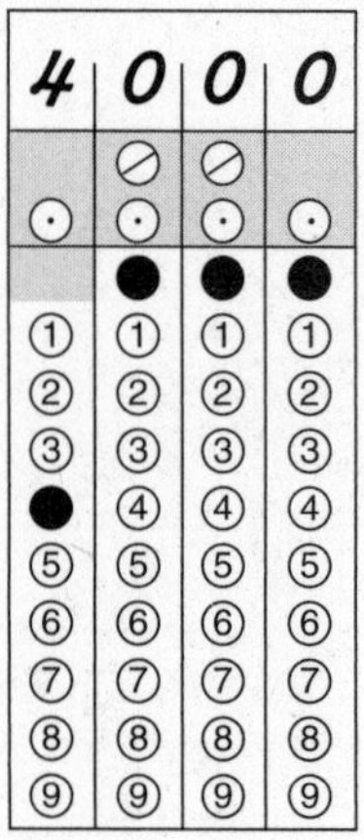

30. `3 1`

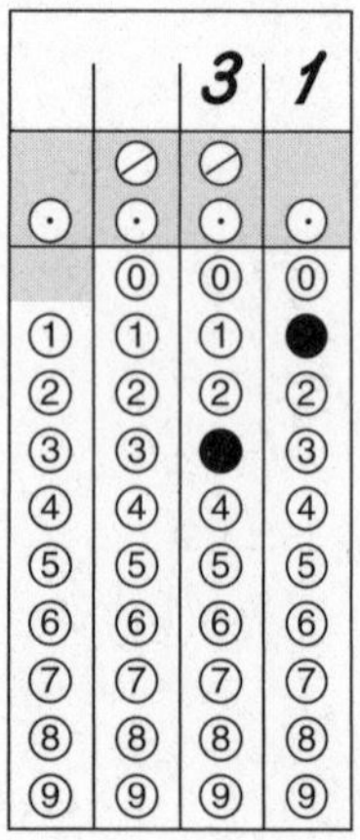

Answer Explanations

Note: For many problems, an alternative solution, indicated by two asterisks (**), follows the first solution. In this case, one of the solutions is the direct mathematical one and the other is based on one of the tactics discussed in this chapter.

1. E. Use TACTIC 1: draw a diagram representing a pile of books or a bookshelf.

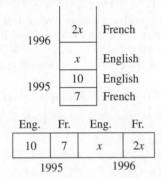

	Eng.	Fr.	Eng.	Fr.
	10	7	x	$2x$
		1995		1996

In the 2 years the number of French books Diana read was $7 + 2x$, and the total number of books was $17 + 3x$. Then 60% or

$$\frac{3}{5} = \frac{7+2x}{17+3x}.$$ To solve, cross-multiply:

$$35 + 10x = 51 + 9x \Rightarrow x = 16.$$

In 1996, Diana read 16 English books and 32 French books, a total of **48** books.

2. D. Even if you can't solve this problem, don't omit it. Use TACTIC 2: trust the diagram. $\overline{AC}$ is clearly longer than $\overline{OC}$, and very close to radius $\overline{OE}$ (measure them).

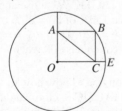

Therefore, AC must be about 10. Either by inspection or with your calculator, check the choices. They are approximately as follows:

(A) $\sqrt{2} = 1.4$ (B) $\sqrt{10} = 3.1$

(C) $5\sqrt{2} = 7$ (D) 10 (E) $10\sqrt{2} = 14$.

The answer must be **10**.

The answer *is* **10. The two diagonals are equal, and diagonal $\overline{OB}$ is a radius.

3. C. As in question 2, if you get stuck trying to answer this, use TACTIC 2: look at the diagram.

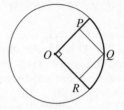

Square *OPQR*, whose area is 8, takes up most of the quarter circle, so the area of the quarter circle is certainly between 11 and 14. The area of the whole circle is 4 times as great: between 44 and 56. Check the choices. They are approximately as follows:
(A) $8\pi = 25$ (B) $8\pi\sqrt{2} = 36$ (C) $16\pi = 50$
(D) $32\pi = 100$ (E) $64\pi = 200$.
The answer is clearly **16π**.
Use TACTIC 4: draw in line segment $\overline{OQ}$. Since the area of the square is 8, each side is $\sqrt{8}$, and diagonal $\overline{OQ}$ is $\sqrt{8} \cdot \sqrt{2} = \sqrt{16} = 4$. But $\overline{OQ}$ is also a radius, so the area of the circle is $\pi(4)^2 = $ **16π.

4. E. Use TACTIC 3. Since the diagram has not been drawn to scale, you are free to redraw it. $\overline{AB}$ and $\overline{AC}$ could each be very short, in which case the sum of their lengths could surely be less than 5. Therefore, none of choices A, B, C, and D could be the answer. The sum **cannot be determined from the information given**.

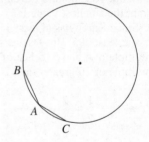

5. E. Use TACTIC 9: subtract to find the shaded area. The area of square *ABCD* is 4. The area of $\triangle AED$ is $\frac{2^2\sqrt{3}}{4} = \frac{4\sqrt{3}}{4} = \sqrt{3}$ (see Section 9-J). Then the area of the shaded region is **$4 - \sqrt{3}$**.

Use TACTIC 2: trust the diagram. The area of the square is 4 and the shaded area appears to take up more than half of the square. So the area should be more than 2 but definitely less than 3. Only choice E ($4 - \sqrt{3}$**) works.

6. C.   Use TACTIC 10: don't do more than you have to. In particular, don't solve for x. Here $5x + 13 = 31 \Rightarrow 5x = 18$.
So, $\sqrt{5x + 31} = \sqrt{18 + 31} = \sqrt{49} = \mathbf{7}$.

7. C.   This is a relatively simple ratio, but use TACTIC 11 and make sure you get the units right. You need to know that there are 100 cents in a dollar and 16 ounces in a pound.

$$\frac{price}{weight} : \frac{6 \text{ dollars}}{2.25 \text{ pounds}} = \frac{600 \text{ cents}}{36 \text{ ounces}} = \frac{x \text{ cents}}{9 \text{ ounces}}.$$

Now cross-multiply and solve:
$36x = 5400 \Rightarrow x = \mathbf{150}$.

8. B.   Use TACTIC 17, and add the two equations to get

$$10a + 10b = 10 \Rightarrow a + b = 1 \Rightarrow$$

$$\frac{a+b}{2} = \frac{1}{2} = \mathbf{0.5}.$$

Remember TACTIC 10: don't do more than you have to. In particular, do *not* solve for a and b.

9. B.   Use TACTIC 5: backsolve. Since you want the least number, start with the smallest answer, E. If Jessica had 200 books, Karen would have 40; but Karen has more than 40, so 200 is too small. Neither 205 (D) nor 210 (C), is a multiple of 4, so John wouldn't have a whole number of books. Finally, **220** works. (So does 240, but you shouldn't even test it since you want the smallest value.)
Since Karen has at least 41 books, Jessica has at least 205. But Jessica's total must be a multiple of 4 and 5, hence of 20. The smallest multiple of 20 greater than 205 is **220.

10. E. $(1 \star 2) = \dfrac{1}{2} + \dfrac{2}{1} = 2\dfrac{1}{2} = \dfrac{5}{2}$.

Then $(1 \star 2) \star 3 = \dfrac{5}{2} \star 3 =$

$\dfrac{\frac{5}{2}}{3} + \dfrac{3}{\frac{5}{2}} = \dfrac{5}{6} + \dfrac{6}{5} = 5 \star 6$.

11. E. $x \star y = \dfrac{x}{y} + \dfrac{y}{x} = \dfrac{x^2 + y^2}{xy}$.

So, $x \star y = 2 \Rightarrow \dfrac{x^2 + y^2}{xy} = 2 \Rightarrow$

$x^2 + y^2 = 2xy \Rightarrow x^2 - 2xy + y^2 = 0$.
So, $(x - y)^2 = 0 \Rightarrow x - y = 0 \Rightarrow x = y$.

So $(1, 1), (2, 2), (3, 3), (4, 4), \ldots$ are all ordered pairs of positive integers that satisfy the given condition.

12. D.   Use TACTIC 5: backsolve (using your calculator). Test the choices, starting with E (since you want the largest value):

$$11^2 + 8(11) - 3 = 121 + 88 - 3 = 206,$$

and

$$11^2 + 7(11) + 8 = 121 + 77 + 8 = 206.$$
The two sides are equal. When $n = \mathbf{10}$, however, the left-hand side is smaller:
$100 + 80 - 3 = 177$ and $100 + 70 + 8 = 178$.
** $n^2 + 8n - 3 < n^2 + 7n + 8 \Rightarrow n < 11$.

13. B.   Use TACTIC 6. Pick simple values for a, b, and c. Let $a = 1$, $b = 2$, and $c = 3$. Then $b - a = 1$. Only choice B, $\mathbf{2b - c}$, is equal to 1 when $b = 2$ and $c = 3$.
** $c = a + b \Rightarrow a = c - b$.
So, $b - a = b - (c - b) = \mathbf{2b - c}$.

14. A.   Use TACTIC 6: replace variables with numbers. If 2 widgets cost 10 cents, then widgets cost 5 cents each; and for 3 dollars, you can get 60 widgets. Which of the choices equals 60 when $w = 2$, $c = 10$, and $d = 3$?

Only $\dfrac{100dw}{c}$.

**Convert d dollars to $100d$ cents, and set the
ratios equal: $\dfrac{\text{widgets}}{\text{cents}} = \dfrac{w}{c} = \dfrac{x}{100d}$.

Multiply both sides by $100d$: $x = \dfrac{100dw}{c}$.

15. C.   Use TACTIC 7: choose appropriate numbers. Since 120% of 80 = 80% of 120, let $a = 80$ and $b = 120$. Then $a + b = 200$. Which of the choices equals 200 when $a = 80$? Only $\mathbf{2.5a}$.

16. C.   If you don't know how to solve this, you must use TACTIC 8: eliminate the absurd choices and guess. Which choices are absurd? Certainly, A and B, both of which are negative. Also, using your calculator, you can see that choice D is about 94, which is much more than half the area of the square, and so is much too large. Guess between C (about 43) and E (about 50). If you remember that the way to find shaded areas is to subtract, guess C: $\mathbf{144 - 32\pi}$, the answer choice with a minus sign.
**The area of the square is $12^2 = 144$. The area of each semicircle is 8π, one-half the area of a circle of radius 4. Together the areas of the semicircles total 32π, and the area of the shaded region is $\mathbf{144 - 32\pi}$.

17. **B.** Treat the number in each of the three Roman numeral choices as a separate true/false question.

    - Could 25 be expressed as the product of three different integers greater than 1? No, 25 has only two positive factors greater than 1 (5 and 25), and so clearly cannot be the product of three different positive factors. (I is false.)
    - Could 36 be expressed as the product of three different positive factors? Yes, $36 = 2 \times 3 \times 6$. (**II** is true.)
    - Could 45 be expressed as the product of three different integers greater than 1? No, the factors of 45 that are greater than 1 are 3, 5, 9, 15, and 45; no three of them have a product equal to 45. (III is false.)

    Only II is true.

18. **A.** To find the average, add the two quantities and divide by 2:

    $$\frac{(4y+3)+(2y-1)}{2} = \frac{6y+2}{2} = 3y+1.$$

    Use TACTIC 6. Let $y = 1$. Then $4y + 3 = 7$ and $2y - 1 = 1$. The average of 7 and 1 is $\frac{7+1}{2} = 4$. Of the five choices, only **3y + 1** is equal to 4 when $y = 1$.

19. **D.** Use TACTIC 5: test the choices. When there is no advantage to starting with any particular choice, start with E. Could $y = 27$? Is there an integer x such that $x^3 = 27^2 = 729$? Use your calculator to evaluate $\sqrt[3]{729}$ or test some numbers: $10^3 = 1000$ — too large; $9^3 = 729$ works. Try choice D: 16. Is there an integer x such that $x^3 = 16^2 = 256$? No: $5^3 = 125$, $6^3 = 216$, so 5 and 6 are too small; but $7^3 = 343$, which is too large. Alternatively, use your calculator to see that $\sqrt[3]{256}$ is not an integer. The answer is **16**.

20. **B.** $a \div (a\% \text{ of } a) = a \div \left(\frac{a}{100} \times a\right) = a \div \left(\frac{a^2}{100}\right) = a \times \frac{100}{a^2} = \frac{\mathbf{100}}{\mathbf{a}}.$

    Use TACTICS 6 and 7: replace a by a number; use 100 since the problem involves percents.

    $$100 \div (100\% \text{ of } 100) = 100 \div 100 = 1.$$

    Test each choice; which one equals 1 when $a = 100$?

    A and B: $\frac{100}{100} = 1$.

    Eliminate C, D, and E; and test A and B with another value, 50, for a:

    $$50 \div (50\% \text{ of } 50) = 50 \div (25) = 2.$$

    Now, only $\frac{\mathbf{100}}{\mathbf{a}}$ works: $\frac{100}{50} = 2$.

21. **A.** Set up a ratio:

    $$\frac{\text{distance}}{\text{time}} = \frac{36 \text{ kilometers}}{1 \text{ hour}} =$$

    $$\frac{36,000 \text{ meters}}{60 \text{ minutes}} = \frac{36,000 \text{ meters}}{3600 \text{ seconds}}$$

    $$= \mathbf{10} \text{ meters/second}.$$

    Use TACTIC 5: Test choices, starting with C:

    100 meters/second = 6000 meters/minute = 360,000 meters/hour = 360 kilometers/hour.

    Not only is that result too big, but it is too big by a factor of 10. The answer is **10**.

22. **D.** Use TACTIC 5: backsolve, using your calculator. Let $x = 4$: then $8^{2(4)-4} = 8^4 = 4096$, whereas $16^4 = 65,536$. Eliminate A, B, and C, and try a larger value. Let $x = 6$: then

    $$8^{2(6)-4} = 8^8 = 16,777,216$$

    and

    $$16^6 = 16,777,216.$$

    $8^{2x-4} = 16^x \Rightarrow (2^3)^{2x-4} = (2^4)^x$. Then $3(2x - 4) = 4x \Rightarrow 6x - 12 = 4x$ and so $2x = 12 \Rightarrow x = \mathbf{6}$.

23. **A.** Use TACTIC 7: choose appropriate numbers. The LCM of all the denominators is 120, so assume that the committee has 120 members. Then there are $\frac{2}{3} \times 120 = 80$ men and 40 women. Of the 80 men, 30 $\left(\frac{3}{8} \times 80\right)$ are Americans. Since there are 72 $\left(\frac{3}{5} \times 120\right)$ Russians, there are $120 - 72 = 48$ Americans, of whom 30 are men, so the other 18 are women.

Finally, the fraction of American women is

$\dfrac{18}{120} = \dfrac{3}{20}$, as illustrated in the Venn diagram below.

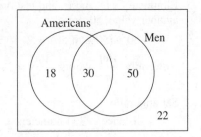

24. **D.** Check each statement separately.

- Could m^2 be a prime number? No, 1 is not a prime, and for any integer $m > 1$, m^2 is not a prime since it has at least three factors: 1, m, and m^2. (I is false.)

- Could $\sqrt{m}$ be a prime number? Yes, if $m = 4$, then $\sqrt{m} = \sqrt{4} = 2$, which is a prime. (II is true.)

- Could $m^2 = \sqrt{m}$? Yes, if $m = 1$, then $m^2 = \sqrt{m}$, since both are equal to 1. (III is true.)
  II and III only are true.

25. **C.** Use TACTICS 6 and 7. Since 100% of 10 is 10, let $x = 100$ and $y = 10$. When $x = 100$, choices C and E are each 10. Eliminate A, B, and D, and try some other numbers: 50% of 20 is 10.

Of C and E, only $\dfrac{1000}{x} = 20$ when $x = 50$.

26. **(160)** Use TACTIC 14. Systematically list the numbers that contain the digit 1, writing as many as you need to see the pattern. Between 1 and 99 the digit 1 is used 10 times as the units digit (1, 11, 21, …, 91) and 10 times as the tens digit (10, 11, 12, …, 19) for a total of 20 times. From 200 to 299, there are 20 more times (the same 20 but preceded by 2). Finally, from 100 to 199 there are 20 more plus 100 numbers where the digit 1 is used in the hundreds place. The total is
$20 + 20 + 20 + 100 = \mathbf{160}$.

27. $\left(\dfrac{5}{2}\text{ or } 2.5\right)$ Use TACTIC 10: don't do more than is necessary. You don't need to solve this system of equations; you don't need to know the values of a and b, only their average. Use TACTIC 17. Add the two equations:

$6a + 6b = 30 \Rightarrow a + b = 5.$

Then, $\dfrac{a+b}{2} = \dfrac{5}{2}$ or **2.5**.

28. $\left(\dfrac{12}{8}\text{ or }\dfrac{3}{2}\text{ or }1.5\right)$ The shaded sector is $\dfrac{45}{360} = \dfrac{1}{8}$

of the circle, so its area is $\dfrac{1}{8}$ of 12: $\dfrac{\mathbf{12}}{\mathbf{8}}$ or $\dfrac{\mathbf{3}}{\mathbf{2}}$

or **1.5**. (Note that, since $\dfrac{12}{8}$ fits in the grid, it is not necessary to reduce it or to convert it to a decimal. See Chapter 8.)
**If you didn't see that, use TACTIC 3 and redraw the figure to scale by making the angle as close as possible to 45°. It is now clear that the sector is $\dfrac{1}{8}$ of the circle (or very close to it).

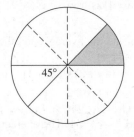

29. **(4000)** Use TACTIC 7: choose an appropriate number. The LCD of $\dfrac{1}{4}$ and $\dfrac{2}{5}$ is 20, so *assume* that there were 20 applicants. Then $\dfrac{1}{4}(20) = 5$ failed to meet the minimum standards. Of the remaining 15 applicants, $\dfrac{2}{5}$, or 6, were accepted, so 6 of every 20 applicants were accepted. Set up a proportion:

$$\dfrac{6}{20} = \dfrac{1200}{x} \Rightarrow 6x = 24{,}000 \Rightarrow x = \mathbf{4000}.$$

30. **(31)** Use TACTIC 14. List the integers systematically: $1 \times 2, 2 \times 3, \ldots, 24 \times 25, \ldots$. You don't have to multiply and list the products (2, 6, 12, … , 600, …); you just have to know when to stop. The largest product less than 1000 is $31 \times 32 = 992$, so there are **31** integers.

Reviewing Mathematics

This chapter provides a comprehensive review of all of the mathematics that you need to know for the SAT. Let's start by saying what you *don't* need to know. The SAT is *not* a test in high school mathematics. There are *no* questions on trigonometry, logarithms, complex numbers, exponential functions, geometric transformations, parabolas, ellipses, hyperbolas, truth tables, combinations and permutations, or standard deviation. You will *not* have to graph a straight line, use the quadratic formula, know the equation of a circle, write a geometry proof, do a compass and straightedge construction, prove a trig identity, or solve a complicated word problem. What *do* you need to know?

About 85 percent of the test questions are divided approximately evenly among topics in arithmetic, elementary algebra, and the fundamentals of geometry. The remaining 15 percent of the questions represent a few basic miscellaneous topics, such as probability and counting, interpretation of data, functions, and logical reasoning. Surprisingly, a lot of the mathematics that you need to know for the SAT you learned before you left middle school or junior high school. There are some questions on elementary algebra, basic geometry, and concepts of functions—material that you have learned in high school—but not very many.

Why, then, if no advanced mathematics is on the SAT, do so many students find some of the questions difficult? The answer is that the College Board considers the SAT to be "a test of general reasoning abilities." It attempts to use basic concepts of arithmetic, algebra, and geometry as a method of testing your ability to think logically. The Board is not testing whether you know how to calculate an average, find the area of a circle, use the Pythagorean theorem, or read a bar graph. *It assumes you can.* In fact, because the Board is not even interested in testing your memory, many of the formulas you will need are listed at the beginning of each math section. In other words, the College Board's objective is to use your familiarity with numbers and geometric figures as a way of testing your *logical thinking skills.*

Since, to do well on the SAT, you must know basic arithmetic, algebra, and geometry, this chapter reviews *everything* you need to know. But that's not enough. You have to be able to use these concepts in ways that may be unfamiliar to you. That's where the tactics and strategies from Chapter 8 come in.

This chapter is divided into 18 sections, numbered 9-A through 9-R. Each section deals with a different topic, and in it you are given the basic definitions, key facts, and tactics that you need to solve SAT-type questions on that topic. The especially important facts, which are referenced in the solutions to sample problems and to the Model Tests in Part Four, are labeled KEY FACTS and are numbered. Following each KEY FACT are one or more sample SAT-type questions that use that fact. Also included in some sections are test-taking tactics specific to the topics discussed.

Basically, Chapter 9 is broken down as follows:

- Topics in Arithmetic   Sections A–E
- Topics in Algebra   Sections F–H
- Topics in Geometry   Sections I–N
- Miscellaneous Topics   Sections O–R

No topic, however, really belongs to only one category. Average problems are discussed in the arithmetic sections, but on the SAT you need to be able also to take the average of algebraic expressions and the average of the measures of the angles of a triangle. Most algebra problems involve arithmetic, as well; on many geometry problems you need to use algebra; and several of the problems in the miscellaneous topics sections require a knowledge of arithmetic and/or algebra.

At the end of each section is a set of exercises that consists of a variety of multiple-choice and grid-in questions, similar to actual SAT questions, that utilize the concepts covered in the section. You should use whichever TACTICS and KEY FACTS from that section that you think are appropriate. If you've mastered the material in the section, you should be able to answer most of the questions. If you get stuck, you can use the various strategies you learned in Chapter 8; but then you should carefully read the solutions that are provided, so that you understand the correct mathematical way to answer the question. In the solutions some references are made to the TACTICS from Chapter 8, but the major emphasis here is on doing the mathematics properly.

Finally, one small disclaimer is appropriate. This is not a mathematics textbook—it is a *review* of the essential facts that you need to know to do well on the SAT. Undoubtedly, you have already learned most, if not all, of them. If, however, you find some topics with which you are unfamiliar or on which you need more information, get a copy of Barron's *Arithmetic the Easy Way*, *Algebra the Easy Way*, and/or *Geometry the Easy Way*. For additional practice on SAT-type questions, see Barron's *Math Workbook for the NEW SAT*.

ARITHMETIC

To do well on the SAT, you need to feel comfortable with most topics of basic arithmetic. The first five sections of Chapter 9 provide you with a review of basic arithmetic concepts; fractions and decimals; percents; ratios and proportions; and averages. Because you will have a calculator with you at the test, you will not have to do long division, multiply three-digit numbers, or perform any other tedious calculations by hand. If you use a calculator with fraction capability, you can even avoid finding least common denominators and reducing fractions.

The solutions to more than one-third of the mathematics questions on the SAT depend on your knowing the KEY FACTS in these sections. Be sure to review them all.

9-A Basic Arithmetic Concepts

A *set* is a collection of "things" that have been grouped together in some way. Those "things" are called the *elements* or *members* of the set, and we say that the "thing" is in the set. For example:

- If *A* is the set of former presidents of the United States, then John Adams *is an element of A*.

- If *B* is the set of vowels in the English alphabet, then *i is a member of B*.

- If *C* is the set of prime numbers, then 17 *is in C*.

The symbol for "is an element (or member) of" is ∈, so we can write "$17 \in C$."

The *union* of two sets, *X* and *Y*, is the set consisting of all the elements that are in *X* or in *Y* or in both. Note that this definition includes the elements that are in *X and Y*. The union is represented as $X \cup Y$. Therefore, $a \in X \cup Y$ if and only if $a \in X$ or $a \in Y$.

The *intersection* of two sets, *X* and *Y*, is the set consisting only of the elements that are in both *X* and *Y*. The intersection is represented as $X \cap Y$. Therefore, $b \in X \cap Y$ if and only if $b \in X$ and $b \in Y$.

In describing a set of numbers, we usually list the elements inside a pair of braces. For example, let *X* be the set of prime numbers less than 10, and let *Y* be the set of odd positive integers less than 10.

$$X = \{2, 3, 5, 7\} \qquad\qquad Y = \{1, 3, 5, 7, 9\}$$

$$X \cup Y = \{1, 2, 3, 5, 7, 9\}$$

$$X \cap Y = \{3, 5, 7\}$$

The **solution set** of an equation is the set of all numbers that satisfy the equation.

EXAMPLE 1

If A is the solution set of the equation $x^2 - 4 = 0$ and B is the solution set of the equation $x^2 - 3x + 2 = 0$, how many elements are in the union of the two sets?

Solution. Solving each equation (see Section 9-G if you need to review how to solve a quadratic equation), you get $A = \{-2, 2\}$ and $B = \{1, 2\}$. Therefore, $A \cup B = \{-2, 1, 2\}$. There are **3** elements in the union.

Let's start our review of arithmetic by discussing the most important sets of numbers and their properties. On the SAT the word *number* always means "real number," a number that can be represented by a point on the number line.

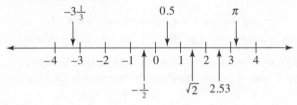

Signed Numbers

The numbers to the right of 0 on the number line are called **positive**, and those to the left of 0 are **negative**. Negative numbers must be written with a *negative sign* (–2); positive numbers can be written with a *plus sign* (+2) but are usually written without it (2). All numbers can be called **signed numbers**.

Key Fact A1

For any number a, exactly one of the following is true:

     • a **is negative.**   • $a = 0$.   • a **is positive.**

The **absolute value** of a number a, denoted as $|a|$, is the distance between a and 0 on the number line. Since 3 is 3 units to the right of 0 on the number line and –3 is 3 units to the left of 0, both have absolute values of 3:

     • $|3| = 3$ • $|-3| = 3$

EXAMPLE 2

What is the value of $\big|\,|3| - |-5|\,\big|$?

(A) –8
(B) –2
(C) 0
(D) 2
(E) 8

Solution. $\big|\,|3| - |-5|\,\big| = |3 - 5| = |-2| = 2$ **(D)**.

Key Fact A2

For any number *a* and positive number *b*:

- |*a*| = *b* ⇒ *a* = *b* or *a* = −*b*.
- |*a*| < *b* ⇒ −*b* < *a* < *b*.
- |*a*| > *b* ⇒ *a* < −*b* or *a* > *b*.

EXAMPLE 3

How many integers satisfy the inequality |*x*| < π?

- (A) 0
- (B) 3
- (C) 4
- (D) 7
- (E) More than 7

Solution. By KEY FACT A2,

$$|x| < \pi \Rightarrow -\pi < x < \pi \Rightarrow -3.14 < x < 3.14.$$

There are **7** integers that satisfy this inequality: −3, −2, −1, 0, 1, 2, 3. Choice **D** is correct.

Arithmetic is basically concerned with the addition, subtraction, multiplication, and division of numbers. Column 3 of the table below shows the terms used to describe the results of these operations.

Operation	Symbol	Result	Example	
Addition	+	*Sum*	16 is the sum of 12 and 4.	16 = 12 + 4
Subtraction	−	*Difference*	8 is the difference of 12 and 4.	8 = 12 − 4
Multiplication*	×	*Product*	48 is the product of 12 and 4.	48 = 12 × 4
Division	÷	*Quotient*	3 is the quotient of 12 and 4.	3 = 12 ÷ 4

*Multiplication can be indicated also by a dot, parentheses, or the juxtaposition of symbols without any sign: $2^2 \cdot 2^4$, 3(4), 3(*x* + 2), 3*a*, 4*abc*.

Given any two numbers *a* and *b*, you can *always* find their sum, difference, product, and quotient (with a calculator, if necessary), except that we can *never divide by zero:*

- 0 ÷ 7 = 0   • 7 ÷ 0 is meaningless.

EXAMPLE 4

What is the sum of the product and the quotient of 7 and 7?

Solution. Product: 7 × 7 = 49. Quotient: 7 ÷ 7 = 1. Sum: 49 + 1 = **50**.

Key Fact A3

For any number *a*: *a* × 0 = 0. Conversely, if the product of two or more numbers is 0, *at least one* of them must be 0.
- If *ab* = 0, then *a* = 0 or *b* = 0.
- If *xyz* = 0, then *x* = 0 or *y* = 0 or *z* = 0.

EXAMPLE 5

What is the product of all the integers from –3 to 6?

Solution. Before reaching for your calculator, think. You are asked for the product of 10 numbers, one of which is 0. Then, by KEY FACT A3, the product is **0**.

Key Fact A4

The product and the quotient of two positive numbers or two negative numbers are positive; the product and the quotient of a positive number and a negative number are negative.

×	+	−
+	+	−
−	−	+

÷	+	−
+	+	−
−	−	+

$6 \times 3 = 18$ $6 \times (-3) = -18$ $(-6) \times 3 = -18$ $(-6) \times (-3) = 18$
$6 \div 3 = 2$ $6 \div (-3) = -2$ $(-6) \div 3 = -2$ $(-6) \div (-3) = 2$

To determine whether a product of more than two numbers is positive or negative, count the number of negative factors.

Key Fact A5

• **The product of an *even* number of negative factors is positive.**
• **The product of an *odd* number of negative factors is negative.**

EXAMPLE 6

If the product of 10 numbers is positive, what is the greatest number of them that could be negative?

(A) 0
(B) 1
(C) 5
(D) 9
(E) 10

Solution. Since by KEY FACT A5, the product of 10 negative numbers is positive, all **10** of the numbers could be negative **(E)**.

Key Fact A6

The *reciprocal* of any nonzero number a is $\dfrac{1}{a}$.

The product of any number and its reciprocal is 1: $a\left(\dfrac{1}{a}\right) = 1$.

Key Fact A7

• **The sum of two positive numbers is positive.**
• **The sum of two negative numbers is negative.**
• **To find the sum of a positive and a negative number, find the difference of their absolute values and use the sign of the number with the larger absolute value.**

$$6 + 2 = 8 \qquad (-6) + (-2) = -8$$

To calculate either $6 + (-2)$ or $(-6) + 2$, take the difference, $6 - 2 = 4$, and use the sign of the number whose absolute value is 6:

$$6 + (-2) = 4 \qquad (-6) + 2 = -4$$

Key Fact A8

The sum of any number and its opposite is 0: $a + (-a) = 0$.

Many properties of arithmetic depend on the relationships between subtraction and addition and between division and multiplication. Subtracting a number is the same as adding its opposite, and dividing by a number is the same as multiplying by its reciprocal.

$$a - b = a + (-b) \qquad a \div b = a \left(\frac{1}{b} \right)$$

Many problems involving subtraction and division can be simplified by changing them to addition and multiplication problems, respectively.

Key Fact A9

To subtract signed numbers, change the problem to an addition problem by changing the sign of what is being subtracted, and then use KEY FACT A7.

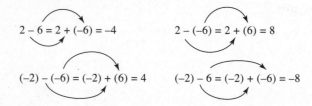

$$2 - 6 = 2 + (-6) = -4 \qquad 2 - (-6) = 2 + (6) = 8$$

$$(-2) - (-6) = (-2) + (6) = 4 \qquad (-2) - 6 = (-2) + (-6) = -8$$

In each case, the minus sign was changed to a plus sign, and either the 6 was changed to –6 or the –6 was changed to 6.

CALCULATOR HINT

All arithmetic involving signed numbers can be accomplished on *any* calculator, but not all calculators handle negative numbers in the same way. Be sure you know how to enter negative numbers and how to use them on *your* calculator.

Integers

The *integers* are   {... , –4, –3, –2, –1, 0, 1, 2, 3, 4, ...}.

The *positive integers* are   {1, 2, 3, 4, 5, ...}.

The *negative integers* are   {..., –5, –4, –3, –2, –1}.

Note: The integer 0 is neither positive nor negative. Therefore, if an SAT question asks how many positive numbers have a certain property, and the only numbers with that property are –2, –1, 0, 1, and 2, the answer is 2.

Consecutive integers are two or more integers, written in sequence, each of which is 1 more than the preceding integer. For example:

$$22, 23 \quad 6, 7, 8, 9 \quad -2, -1, 0, 1 \quad n, n+1, n+2, n+3$$

EXAMPLE 7

If the sum of three consecutive integers is less than 75, what is the greatest possible value of the smallest of the three integers?

Solution. Let the numbers be n, $n+1$, and $n+2$. Then

$$n + (n+1) + (n+2) = 3n + 3 \Rightarrow 3n + 3 < 75 \Rightarrow 3n < 72 \Rightarrow n < 24.$$

The most n can be is **23**. (See Section 9-G for help in solving inequalities like this one.)

Of course, you don't *need* to do the algebra (see Chapter 8, TACTIC 7). Try three consecutive integers near 25, say 24, 25, 26. Their sum is 75, which is *slightly* too big (the sum needs to be *less* than 75), so the numbers must be **23**, 24, 25.

> **CAUTION:** Never assume that *number* means *integer*: 3 is the only integer between 2 and 4, but there are infinitely many numbers between 2 and 4, including 2.5, 3.99, $\dfrac{10}{3}$, π, and $\sqrt{10}$.

EXAMPLE 8

If $2 < x < 4$ and $3 < y < 7$, what is the largest integer value of $x + y$?

Solution. If x and y are integers, the largest value is $3 + 6 = 9$. However, although $x + y$ is to be an integer, neither x nor y must be. If $x = 3.8$ and $y = 6.2$, then $x + y = $ **10**.

The sum, the difference, and the product of two integers are *always* integers; the quotient of two integers may be, but is not necessarily, an integer. The quotient $23 \div 10$ can be expressed as $\dfrac{23}{10}$ or $2\dfrac{3}{10}$ or 2.3. If the quotient is to be an integer, we can also say that the quotient is 2 and there is a ***remainder*** of 3.

The way we express the answer depends on the question. For example, if \$23 are to be divided among 10 people, each one will get \$2.30 (2.3 dollars); but if 23 books are to be divided among 10 people, each one will get 2 books and 3 will be left over (the remainder).

 Calculator Shortcut

The standard way to find quotients and remainders is to use long division; but on the SAT, you *never* do long division: you use your calculator. To find the remainder when 100 is divided by 7, divide on your calculator: $100 \div 7 = 14.285714....$ This tells you that the quotient is 14. (Ignore everything to the right of the decimal point.) To find the remainder, multiply: $14 \times 7 = 98$, and then subtract: $100 - 98 = $ **2**.

EXAMPLE 9

If a is the remainder when 999 is divided by 7, and b is the remainder when 777 is divided by 9, what is the remainder when a is divided by b?

Solution.

$999 \div 7 = 142.714...;\ 7 \times 142 = 994;\ 999 - 994 = 5 = a.$

$777 \div 9 = 86.333...;\ 9 \times 86 = 774;\ 777 - 774 = 3 = b.$

Finally, when 5 is divided by 3, the quotient is 1 and the remainder is **2**.

EXAMPLE 10

How many positive integers less than 100 have a remainder of 3 when divided by 7?

Solution. To have a remainder of 3 when divided by 7, an integer must be 3 more than a multiple of 7. For example, when 73 is divided by 7, the quotient is 10 and the remainder is 3: $73 = 10 \times 7 + 3$. Just take the multiples of 7 and add 3:

$$\underline{0} \times 7 + 3 = 3; \qquad \underline{1} \times 7 + 3 = 10; \qquad \underline{2} \times 7 + 3 = 17; ... ; \underline{13} \times 7 + 3 = 94$$

There are **14** positive integers less than 100 that have a remainder of 3 when divided by 7.

If a and b are integers, the following four terms are synonymous:

a is a ***divisor*** of b.	a is a ***factor*** of b.
b is ***divisible*** by a.	b is a ***multiple*** of a.

All these statements mean that, when b is divided by a, there is no remainder (or, more precisely, the remainder is 0). For example:

3 is a divisor of 12.	3 is a factor of 12.
12 is divisible by 3.	12 is a multiple of 3.

Key Fact A10

Every integer has a finite set of factors (or divisors) and an infinite set of multiples.

The factors of 12:   −12, −6, −4, −3, −2, −1, 1, 2, 3, 4, 6, 12

The multiples of 12:   ... , −48, −36, −24, −12, 0, 12, 24, 36, 48, ...

Helpful Hint
Memorize the list of the ten smallest primes.

The only positive divisor of 1 is 1. Every other positive integer has at least two positive divisors: 1 and itself, and possibly many more. For example, 6 is divisible by 1 and 6, as well as by 2 and 3; whereas 7 is divisible only by 1 and 7. Positive integers, such as 7, that have exactly two positive divisors are called ***prime numbers*** or ***primes***. Here are the first several primes:

2, 3, 5, 7, 11, 13, 17, 19, 23, 29

Memorize this list—it will come in handy. Note that 1 is *not* a prime.

Key Fact A11

CAUTION

1 is *not* a prime.

Every integer greater than 1 that is not a prime can be written as a product of primes.

To find the prime factorization of any integer, find any two factors: if they're both primes, you are done; if not, factor them. Continue until each factor has been written in terms of primes.

A useful method is to make a *factor tree*.

For example, here are the prime factorizations of 108 and 240:

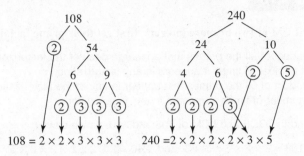

$$108 = 2 \times 2 \times 3 \times 3 \times 3 \qquad 240 = 2 \times 2 \times 2 \times 2 \times 3 \times 5$$

EXAMPLE 11

For any positive integer a, let $\lceil a \rfloor$ denote the smallest prime factor of a. Which of the following is equal to $\lceil 35 \rfloor$?

(A) $\lceil 10 \rfloor$

(B) $\lceil 15 \rfloor$

(C) $\lceil 45 \rfloor$

(D) $\lceil 55 \rfloor$

(E) $\lceil 75 \rfloor$

Solution. Check the first few primes; 35 is not divisible by 2 or 3, but is divisible by 5, so 5 is the *smallest* prime factor of 35, and $\lceil 35 \rfloor = 5$. Now check the five choices: $\lceil 10 \rfloor = 2$, and $\lceil 15 \rfloor$, $\lceil 45 \rfloor$, and $\lceil 75 \rfloor$ are all equal to 3. Only $\lceil \mathbf{55} \rfloor = 5$. The answer is **D**.

The **least common multiple (LCM)** of two or more integers is the smallest positive integer that is a multiple of each of them. For example, the LCM of 6 and 10 is 30. Infinitely many positive integers are multiples of both 6 and 10, including 60, 90, 180, 600, 6000, and 66,000,000, but 30 is the smallest one.

The **greatest common factor (GCF)** or **greatest common divisor (GCD)** of two or more integers is the largest integer that is a factor of each of them. For example, the only positive integers that are factors of both 6 and 10 are 1 and 2, so the GCF of 6 and 10 is 2. For small numbers, you can often find the GCF and LCM by inspection. For larger numbers, KEY FACTS A12 and A13 are useful.

Key Fact A12

The product of the GCF and LCM of two numbers is equal to the product of the two numbers.

Helpful Hint

It is usually easier to find the GCF than the LCM. For example, you may see immediately that the GCF of 36 and 48 is 12. You can then use KEY FACT A12 to find the LCM: since $GCF \times LCM = 36 \times 48$:

$$LCM = \frac{\overset{3}{\cancel{36}} \times 48}{\underset{1}{\cancel{12}}} = 3 \times 48 = 144.$$

Key Fact A13

To find the GCF or LCM of two or more integers, first get their prime factorizations.

- The GCF is the product of all the primes that appear in each of the factorizations, using each prime the smallest number of times it appears in any factorization.
- The LCM is the product of all the primes that appear in any of the factorizations, using each prime the largest number of times it appears in any factorization.

For example, let's find the GCF and LCM of 108 and 240. As we saw:

$$108 = 2 \times 2 \times 3 \times 3 \times 3 \quad \text{and} \quad 240 = 2 \times 2 \times 2 \times 2 \times 3 \times 5.$$

- **GCF**. The primes that appear in both factorizations are 2 and 3. Since 2 appears twice in the factorization of 108 and 4 times in the factorization of 240, we take it twice; 3 appears 3 times in the factorization of 108, but only once in the factorization of 240, so we take it just once. The GCF = $2 \times 2 \times 3 =$ **12**.
- **LCM**. We take one of the factorizations and add to it any primes from the other that are not yet listed. We'll start with $2 \times 2 \times 3 \times 3 \times 3$ (108) and look at the primes from 240. There are four 2's; we already wrote two 2's, so we need two more; there is a 3, but we already have that; there is a 5, which we need. The LCM = $(2 \times 2 \times 3 \times 3 \times 3) \times (2 \times 2 \times 5) = 108 \times 20 =$ **2160**.

EXAMPLE 12

What is the smallest number that is divisible by both 34 and 35?

Solution. You are being asked for the LCM of 34 and 35.

By KEY FACT A12, the LCM = $\dfrac{34 \times 35}{\text{GCF}}$. The GCF, however, is 1 since no number greater than 1 divides evenly into both 34 and 35. The LCM is $34 \times 35 =$ **1190**.

The *even numbers* are all the multiples of 2: $\{..., -4, -2, 0, 2, 4, 6, ...\}$.

The *odd numbers* are all the integers not divisible by 2: $\{..., -5, -3, -1, 1, 3, 5, ...\}$.

Note:
- The terms *odd* and *even* apply only to integers.
- Every integer (positive, negative, or 0) is either odd or even.
- 0 is an even integer; it is a multiple of 2 ($0 = 0 \times 2$).
- 0 is a multiple of *every* integer ($0 = 0 \times n$).
- 2 is the only even prime number.

> **NOTE**
> - The GCF of two consecutive integers is 1.
> - The GCF of two consecutive even integers is 2.

Key Fact A14

The tables below summarize three important facts:

1. **If two integers are both even or both odd, their sum and difference are even.**

2. **If one integer is even and the other odd, their sum and difference are odd.**

3. **The product of two integers is even unless both of them are odd.**

+ and −	even	odd		×	even	odd
even	even	odd		even	even	even
odd	odd	even		odd	even	odd

Exponents and Roots

Repeated addition of the same number is indicated by multiplication:

$$17 + 17 + 17 + 17 + 17 + 17 + 17 = 7 \times 17.$$

Repeated multiplication of the same number is indicated by an exponent:

$$17 \times 17 \times 17 \times 17 \times 17 \times 17 \times 17 = 17^7.$$

In the expression 17^7, 17 is called the **base** and 7 is the **exponent**.

On the SAT, most of the exponents you will encounter are positive integers; these are defined in KEY FACT A15. Occasionally you may see an exponent that is zero or negative or is a fraction; these exponents are defined later in KEY FACT A20.

Key Fact A15

For any number b: $b^1 = b$.

For any number b and integer $n > 1$: $b^n = b \times b \times \cdots \times b$, where b is used as a factor n times.

(i) $2^5 \times 2^3 = (2 \times 2 \times 2 \times 2 \times 2) \times (2 \times 2 \times 2) = 2^8 = 2^{5+3}$.

(ii) $\dfrac{2^5}{2^3} = \dfrac{2 \times 2 \times 2 \times 2 \times 2}{2 \times 2 \times 2} = 2 \times 2 = 2^2 = 2^{5-3}$.

(iii) $(2^2)^3 = (2 \times 2)^3 = (2 \times 2) \times (2 \times 2) \times (2 \times 2) = 2^6 = 2^{2 \times 3}$.

(iv) $2^3 \times 7^3 = (2 \times 2 \times 2) \times (7 \times 7 \times 7) = (2 \times 7)(2 \times 7)(2 \times 7) = (\mathbf{2 \times 7})^3$.

(v) $\dfrac{2^3}{7^3} = \dfrac{2 \times 2 \times 2}{7 \times 7 \times 7} = \dfrac{2}{7} \times \dfrac{2}{7} \times \dfrac{2}{7} = \left(\dfrac{2}{7}\right)^3$.

These five examples illustrate the five important laws of exponents given in KEY FACT A16.

Key Fact A16

Helpful Hint
Memorize these laws of exponents; they are very useful.

For any numbers b and c and positive integers m and n:

(i) $b^m b^n = b^{m+n}$ (ii) $\dfrac{b^m}{b^n} = b^{m-n}$ (iii) $(b^m)^n = b^{mn}$ (iv) $b^m c^m = (bc)^m$ (v) $\dfrac{b^m}{c^m} = \left(\dfrac{b}{c}\right)^m$

CAUTION: In (i) and (ii) the bases are the same, and in (iv) the exponents are the same. None of these rules applies to expressions such as $2^5 \times 3^4$, in which both the bases and the exponents are different.

EXAMPLE 13

If $2^x = 32$, what is x^2?

Helpful Hint
Write out the first ten powers of 2 and memorize them.

Solution. To solve $2^x = 32$, just count (and keep track of) how many 2's you need to multiply to get 32: $2 \times 2 \times 2 \times 2 \times 2 = 32$, so $x = 5$ and $x^2 = \mathbf{25}$.

EXAMPLE 14

If $3^a \times 3^b = 3^{100}$, what is the average (arithmetic mean) of a and b?

Solution. Since $3^a \times 3^b = 3^{a+b}$, you can see that

$$a + b = 100 \Rightarrow \frac{a+b}{2} = \mathbf{50}.$$

The next KEY FACT is an immediate consequence of KEY FACTS A4 and A5.

Key Fact A17

For any positive integer n:

(i) $\mathbf{0^n = 0}$.

(ii) **If a is positive, a^n is positive.**

(iii) **If a is negative, a^n is positive if n is even, and negative if n is odd.**

EXAMPLE 15

Which of the following statements is (are) true?

I. $-2^{10} > 0$

II. $-(-2)^{10} > 0$

III. $2^{10} - (-2)^{10} > 0$

(A) None
(B) I only
(C) III only
(D) I and III only
(E) I, II, and III

Solution.

Since 2^{10} is positive, -2^{10} is negative. (I is false.)

Since $(-2)^{10}$ is positive, $-(-2)^{10}$ is negative. (II is false.)

Since $(-2)^{10} = 2^{10}$, $2^{10} - (-2)^{10} = 0$. (III is false.)

None of the statements is true. Choice **A** is correct.

Squares and Square Roots

The exponent that appears most often on the SAT is 2. It is used to form the square of a number, as in πr^2 (the area of a circle), $a^2 + b^2 = c^2$ (the Pythagorean theorem), or $x^2 - y^2$ (the difference of two squares). Therefore, it is helpful to recognize the **perfect squares**, numbers that are the squares of integers. The squares of the integers from 0 to 15 are as follows:

x	0	1	2	3	4	5	6	7
x^2	0	1	4	9	16	25	36	49

x	8	9	10	11	12	13	14	15
x^2	64	81	100	121	144	169	196	225

There are two numbers that satisfy the equation $x^2 = 9$: $x = 3$ and $x = -3$. The positive number, 3, is called the **square root** of 9 and is denoted by the symbol $\sqrt{9}$.

Clearly, each perfect square has a square root: $\sqrt{0} = 0$, $\sqrt{36} = 6$, $\sqrt{81} = 9$, and $\sqrt{144} = 12$. It is an important fact, however, that *every* positive number has a square root.

Key Fact A18

For any positive number a, there is a positive number b that satisfies the equation $b^2 = a$. That number is called the square root of a, and we write $b = \sqrt{a}$.

Therefore, for any positive number a: $\sqrt{a} \times \sqrt{a} = (\sqrt{a})^2 = a$.

The only difference between $\sqrt{9}$ and $\sqrt{10}$ is that the first square root is an integer, while the second one isn't. Since 10 is a little more than 9, we should expect that $\sqrt{10}$ is a little more than $\sqrt{9}$, which is 3. In fact, $(3.1)^2 = 9.61$, which is close to 10; and $(3.16)^2 = 9.9856$, which is very close to 10, so $\sqrt{10} \approx 3.16$. Square roots of integers that aren't perfect squares can be approximated as accurately as we wish, and by pressing the $\sqrt{}$ key on our calculators we can get much more accuracy than is needed for the SAT. Actually, most answers involving square roots use the square root symbol.

EXAMPLE 16

What is the circumference of a circle whose area is 10π?

(A) 5π
(B) 10π
(C) $\pi\sqrt{10}$
(D) $2\pi\sqrt{10}$
(E) $\pi\sqrt{20}$

Solution. See Section 9-L for the formulas for the area and circumference of a circle. Since the area of a circle is given by the formula $A = \pi r^2$, then

$$\pi r^2 = 10\pi \Rightarrow r^2 = 10 \Rightarrow r = \sqrt{10}.$$

Since the circumference is given by the formula $C = 2\pi r$, then $C = \mathbf{2\pi\sqrt{10}}$ **(D)**.

Key Fact A19

For any positive numbers a and b:

$$\sqrt{ab} = \sqrt{a} \times \sqrt{b} \quad \text{and} \quad \sqrt{\frac{a}{b}} = \frac{\sqrt{a}}{\sqrt{b}}.$$

CAUTION: $\sqrt{a+b} \neq \sqrt{a} + \sqrt{b}$.

For example: $5 = \sqrt{25} = \sqrt{9+16} \neq \sqrt{9} + \sqrt{16} = 3 + 4 = 7$.

CAUTION: Although it is always true that $(\sqrt{a})^2 = a$, $\sqrt{a^2} = a$ is *not* true if a is negative:

$$\sqrt{(-5)^2} = \sqrt{25} = 5, \text{ } not -5.$$

In the same way that we write $b = \sqrt{a}$ to indicate that $a^2 = b$, we write

$\qquad b = \sqrt[3]{a}$ to indicate that $b^3 = a$,

and

$\qquad b = \sqrt[4]{a}$ to indicate that $b^4 = a$.

For example,

$\qquad \sqrt[3]{64} = 4$ because $4^3 = 64$,

and

$\qquad \sqrt[4]{16} = 2$ because $2^4 = 16$.

So far, the only exponents we have considered have been positive integers. We now expand our definition to include other numbers as exponents.

Key Fact A20

• **For any real number $a \neq 0$: $a^0 = 1$.**

• **For any real number $a \neq 0$: $a^{-n} = \dfrac{1}{a^n}$.**

• **For any *positive* number a and positive integer n: $a^{\frac{1}{n}} = \sqrt[n]{a}$.**

Here are some examples to illustrate the definitions in KEY FACT A20:

$$4^0 = 1, \quad 4^{-3} = \frac{1}{4^3} = \frac{1}{64}, \quad 4^{\frac{1}{2}} = \sqrt{4} = 2,$$

$$8^0 = 1, \quad 8^{-1} = \frac{1}{8^1} = \frac{1}{8}, \quad 8^{\frac{1}{3}} = \sqrt[3]{8} = 2.$$

Key Fact A21

The laws of exponents given in KEY FACT A16 are true for *any* exponents, not just positive integers.

For example:

(i) $\quad 2^{-4} \times 2^4 = 2^{-4+4} = 2^0 = 1$

(ii) $\quad \dfrac{2^3}{2^5} = 2^{3-5} = 2^{-2} = \dfrac{1}{2^2} = \dfrac{1}{4}$

(iii) $\quad \left(2^{-6}\right)^{\frac{1}{2}} = 2^{(-6)\frac{1}{2}} = 2^{-3} = \dfrac{1}{2^3} = \dfrac{1}{8}$

(iv) $\quad \left(2^3\right)^{\frac{1}{6}} = 2^{\frac{3}{6}} = 2^{\frac{1}{2}} = \sqrt{2}$

(v) $\quad 2^{\frac{3}{4}} = 2^{3\left(\frac{1}{4}\right)} = \left(2^3\right)^{\frac{1}{4}} = 8^{\frac{1}{4}} = \sqrt[4]{8}$

> **REMEMBER**
>
> *All* exponents satisfy the basic laws of exponents.

EXAMPLE 17

What is the value of $5^{\frac{1}{5}} \times 5^{\frac{2}{5}} \times 5^{\frac{3}{5}} \times 5^{\frac{4}{5}}$?

Solution. $5^{\frac{1}{5}} \times 5^{\frac{2}{5}} \times 5^{\frac{3}{5}} \times 5^{\frac{4}{5}} = 5^{\left(\frac{1}{5}+\frac{2}{5}+\frac{3}{5}+\frac{4}{5}\right)} = 5^{\frac{10}{5}} = 5^2 = \mathbf{25}$.

PEMDAS

When a calculation requires performing more than one operation, it is important to carry the operations out in the correct order. For decades students have memorized the sentence "Please Excuse My Dear Aunt Sally," or just the acronym, PEMDAS, to remember the proper order of operations. The letters stand for:

- Parentheses: first do whatever appears in parentheses, following PEMDAS within the parentheses also if necessary.
- Exponents: next evaluate all terms with exponents.
- Multiplication and Division: then do all multiplications and divisions *in order from left to right*— do *not* multiply first and then divide.
- Addition and Subtraction: finally, do all additions and subtractions *in order from left to right*— do *not* add first and then subtract.

Here are some worked-out examples.

1. $12 + 3 \times 2 = 12 + 6 = 18$ [Multiply before you add.]
   $(12 + 3) \times 2 = 15 \times 2 = 30$ [First add in the parentheses.]

2. $12 \div 3 \times 2 = 4 \times 2 = 8$ [Just go from left to right.]
   $12 \div (3 \times 2) = 12 \div 6 = 2$ [Multiply first.]

3. $5 \times 2^3 = 5 \times 8 = 40$ [Do the exponent first.]
   $(5 \times 2)^3 = 10^3 = 1000$ [Multiply first.]

4. $4 + 4 \div (2 + 6) = 4 + 4 \div 8 = 4 + .5 = 4.5$
   [Do parentheses first, then division.]

5. $100 - 2^2(3 + 4 \times 5) = 100 - 2^2(23) = 100 - 4(23) = 100 - 92 = 8$
   [Do parentheses first (using PEMDAS), then the exponent, then multiplication.]

***Calculator
Shortcut***

Almost every scientific and graphing calculator automatically follows PEMDAS. Test each of these calculations on *your* calculator. Be sure you know whether or not you need to use parentheses or to put anything in memory as you proceed.

There is one situation when you shouldn't start with what's in the parentheses. Consider the following two examples.

(i) What is the value of $7(100 - 1)$?
   Using PEMDAS, you would write $7(100 - 1) = 7(99)$; and then, multiplying on your calculator, you would get **693**. But you can do the arithmetic more quickly in your head if you think of it this way: $7(100 - 1) = 700 - 7 = 693$.

(ii) What is the value of $(77 + 49) \div 7$?
   If you followed the rules of PEMDAS, you would first add: $77 + 49 = 126$, and then divide: $126 \div 7 = \mathbf{18}$. This is definitely more difficult and time-consuming than mentally calculating $\frac{77}{7} + \frac{49}{7} = 11 + 7 = 18$.

Both of these examples illustrate the very important distributive law.

For any real numbers *a*, *b*, and *c*:

- $a(b + c) = ab + ac$,
- $a(b - c) = ab - ac$;

and, if $a \neq 0$,

- $\dfrac{b + c}{a} = \dfrac{b}{a} + \dfrac{c}{a}$,
- $\dfrac{b - c}{a} = \dfrac{b}{a} - \dfrac{c}{a}$.

Helpful Hint

Many students use the distributive law with multiplication but forget about it with division. Don't make that mistake.

EXAMPLE 18

If $a = 3(x - 7)$ and $b = 3x - 7$, what is the value of $a - b$?

(A) −28
(B) −14
(C) 0
(D) $3x - 14$
(E) $3x + 7$

Solution. $a - b = 3(x - 7) - (3x - 7) = 3x - 21 - 3x + 7 = -21 + 7 = \mathbf{-14}$ **(B)**.

EXAMPLE 19

What is the average (arithmetic mean) of 3^{10}, 3^{20}, and 3^{30}?

(A) 60
(B) 3^{20}
(C) 3^{30}
(D) 3^{60}
(E) $3^9 + 3^{19} + 3^{29}$

Solution. $\dfrac{3^{10} + 3^{20} + 3^{30}}{3} = \dfrac{3^{10}}{3} + \dfrac{3^{20}}{3} + \dfrac{3^{30}}{3} = \dfrac{3^{10}}{3^1} + \dfrac{3^{20}}{3^1} + \dfrac{3^{30}}{3^1} = \mathbf{3^9 + 3^{19} + 3^{29}}$ **(E)**.

NOTE

The proper use of the distributive law is essential in the algebra review in Section 9-F.

Inequalities

The number *a* is ***greater than*** the number *b*, denoted as $a > b$, if *a* is to the right of *b* on the number line. Similarly, *a* is ***less than*** *b*, denoted as $a < b$, if *a* is to the left of *b* on the number line. Therefore, if *a* is positive, $a > 0$; and if *a* is negative, $a < 0$. Clearly, if $a > b$, then $b < a$.

KEY FACT A23 gives an important alternative way to describe *greater than* and *less than*.

Key Fact A23

- **For any numbers *a* and *b*: $a > b$ means that $a - b$ is positive.**
- **For any numbers *a* and *b*: $a < b$ means that $a - b$ is negative.**

Key Fact A24

For any numbers *a* and *b*, exactly one of the following is true:

$$a > b \quad \text{or} \quad a = b \quad \text{or} \quad a < b.$$

The symbol $\geq$ means **greater than or equal to** and the symbol $''$ means **less than or equal to**. The statement "$x \geq 5$" means that x can be 5 or any number greater than 5; the statement "$x \leq 5$" means that x can be 5 or any number less than 5.

The statement "$2 < x < 5$" is an abbreviation for the statement "$2 < x$ and $x < 5$." It means that x is a number between 2 and 5 (greater than 2 and less than 5).

KEY FACTS A25 and A26 give some important information about inequalities that you need to know for the SAT.

Key Fact A25   The Arithmetic of Inequalities

- **Adding a number to an inequality or subtracting a number from the inequality preserves the inequality.**

  If $a < b$, then $a + c < b + c$ and $a - c < b - c$.
  $3 < 7 \Rightarrow 3 + 100 < 7 + 100 \quad (103 < 107)$
  $3 < 7 \Rightarrow 3 - 100 < 7 - 100 \quad (-97 < -93)$

- **Adding inequalities in the same direction preserves them.**

  If $a < b$ and $c < d$, then $a + c < b + d$.
  $3 < 7$ and $5 < 10 \Rightarrow 3 + 5 < 7 + 10 \quad (8 < 17)$

- **Multiplying or dividing an inequality by a positive number preserves the inequality.**

  If $a < b$, and c is positive, then $ac < bc$ and $\dfrac{a}{c} < \dfrac{b}{c}$.
  $3 < 7 \Rightarrow 3 \times 100 < 7 \times 100 \quad (300 < 700)$
  $3 < 7 \Rightarrow 3 \div 100 < 7 \div 100 \quad \left(\dfrac{3}{100} < \dfrac{7}{100} \right)$

- **Multiplying or dividing an inequality by a negative number reverses the inequality.**

  If $a < b$, and c is negative, then $ac > bc$ and $\dfrac{a}{c} > \dfrac{b}{c}$.
  $3 < 7 \Rightarrow 3 \times (-100) > 7 \times (-100) \quad (-300 > -700)$
  $3 < 7 \Rightarrow 3 \div (-100) > 7 \div (-100) \quad \left(-\dfrac{3}{100} > -\dfrac{7}{100} \right)$

- **Taking negatives reverses an inequality.**

  If $a < b$, then $-a > -b$, and if $a > b$, then $-a < -b$.
  $3 < 7 \Rightarrow -3 > -7$, and $7 > 3 \Rightarrow -7 < -3$.

- **If two numbers are each positive or each negative, taking reciprocals reverses an inequality.**

  If a and b are both positive or both negative and $a < b$,
  then $\dfrac{1}{a} > \dfrac{1}{b}$.

  $3 < 7 \Rightarrow \dfrac{1}{3} > \dfrac{1}{7}$ and $-7 < -3 \Rightarrow \dfrac{1}{-7} > \dfrac{1}{-3}$

Helpful Hint

Be sure you understand KEY FACT A25; it is very useful. Also, review the important properties listed in KEY FACTS A26–A28. These properties come up frequently on the SAT.

Key Fact A26 Important Inequalities for Numbers Between 0 and 1

- If $0 < x < 1$, and a is positive, then $xa < a$.
  For example, $0.85 \times 19 < 19$.

- If $0 < x < 1$, and m and n are integers with $m > n > 1$, then $x^m < x^n < x$.

  For example, $\left(\dfrac{1}{2}\right)^5 < \left(\dfrac{1}{2}\right)^2 < \dfrac{1}{2}$.

- If $0 < x < 1$, then $\sqrt{x} > x$.

  For example, $\sqrt{\dfrac{3}{4}} > \dfrac{3}{4}$.

- If $0 < x < 1$, then $\dfrac{1}{x} > x$. In fact, $\dfrac{1}{x} > 1$.

  For example, $\dfrac{1}{0.2} > 1 > 0.2$.

Key Fact A27 Properties of Zero

- **0 is the only number that is neither positive nor negative.**
- **0 is smaller than every positive number and greater than every negative number.**
- **0 is an even integer.**
- **0 is a multiple of every integer.**
- **For every number a: $a + 0 = a$ and $a - 0 = a$.**
- **For every number a: $a \times 0 = 0$.**
- **For every integer n: $0^n = 0$.**
- **For every number a (including 0): $a \div 0$ and $\dfrac{a}{0}$ are *meaningless expressions*.**

  (They are *undefined*.)

- **For every number a other than 0: $0 \div a = \dfrac{0}{a} = 0$.**

- **0 is the only number that is equal to its opposite: $0 = -0$.**
- **If the product of two or more numbers is 0, at least one of the numbers is 0.**

Key Fact A28 Properties of 1

- **For any number a: $1 \times a = a$ and $\dfrac{a}{1} = a$.**
- **For any integer n: $1^n = 1$.**
- **1 is a divisor of every integer.**
- **1 is the smallest positive integer.**
- **1 is an odd integer.**
- **1 is the only integer with only one divisor. It is not a prime.**

Exercises on Basic Arithmetic Concepts

Multiple-Choice Questions

1. For how many positive integers, a, is it true that $a^2 \le 2a$?

   (A) None
   (B) 1
   (C) 2
   (D) 4
   (E) More than 4

2. If $0 < a < b < 1$, which of the following is (are) true?

   I. $a - b$ is negative.

   II. $\dfrac{1}{ab}$ is positive.

   III. $\dfrac{1}{b} - \dfrac{1}{a}$ is positive.

   (A) I only
   (B) II only
   (C) III only
   (D) I and II only
   (E) I, II, and III

3. If a and b are negative, and c is positive, which of the following is (are) true?

   I. $a - b < a - c$

   II. if $a < b$, then $\dfrac{a}{c} < \dfrac{b}{c}$.

   III. $\dfrac{1}{b} < \dfrac{1}{c}$

   (A) I only
   (B) II only
   (C) III only
   (D) II and III only
   (E) I, II, and III

4. At 3:00 A.M. the temperature was 13° below zero. By noon it had risen to 32°. What was the average hourly increase in temperature?

   (A) $\left(\dfrac{19}{9}\right)^\circ$

   (B) $\left(\dfrac{19}{6}\right)^\circ$

   (C) 5°
   (D) 7.5°
   (E) 45°

5. If $(7^a)(7^b) = \dfrac{7^c}{7^d}$, what is d in terms of a, b, and c?

   (A) $\dfrac{c}{ab}$

   (B) $c - a - b$

   (C) $a + b - c$

   (D) $c - ab$

   (E) $\dfrac{c}{a+b}$

6. If p and q are primes greater than 2, which of the following *must* be true?

   I. $p + q$ is even.
   II. pq is odd.
   III. $p^2 - q^2$ is even.

   (A) I only
   (B) II only
   (C) I and II only
   (D) I and III only
   (E) I, II, and III

Questions 7 and 8 refer to the following definition.

For any positive integer n, $\tau(n)$ represents the number of positive divisors of n.

7. Which of the following is (are) true?

   I. $\tau(5) = \tau(7)$

   II. $\tau(5) \cdot \tau(7) = \tau(35)$

   III. $\tau(5) + \tau(7) = \tau(12)$

   (A) I only
   (B) II only
   (C) I and II only
   (D) I and III only
   (E) I, II, and III

8. What is the value of $\tau(\tau(\tau(12)))$?

   (A) 1
   (B) 2
   (C) 3
   (D) 4
   (E) 6

9. Which of the following is equal to $(7^8 \times 7^9)^{10}$?

    (A) 7^{27}
    (B) 7^{82}
    (C) 7^{170}
    (D) 49^{170}
    (E) 49^{720}

10. If $x \, \textbf{\textcircled{$\ast$}} \, y$ represents the number of integers greater than x and less than y, what is the value of

    $-\pi \, \textbf{\textcircled{$\ast$}} \, \sqrt{2}$?

    (A) 2
    (B) 3
    (C) 4
    (D) 5
    (E) 6

11. If $0 < x < 1$, which of the following lists the numbers in increasing order?

    (A) $\sqrt{x}, x, x^2$

    (B) $x^2, x, \sqrt{x}$

    (C) $x^2, \sqrt{x}, x$

    (D) $x, x^2, \sqrt{x}$

    (E) $x, \sqrt{x}, x^2$

Grid-in Questions

12. At Ben's Butcher Shop 99 pounds of chopped meat is being divided into packages each weighing 2.5 pounds. How many pounds of meat are left when there isn't enough to make another whole package?

13. Maria has two electronic beepers. One of them beeps every 4 seconds; the other beeps every 9 seconds. If they are turned on at exactly the same time, how many times during the next hour will both beepers beep at the same time?

14. If $-7 \le x \le 7$ and $0 \le y \le 12$, what is the greatest possible value of $y - x$?

15. If x is an integer less than 1000 that has a remainder of 1 when it is divided by 2, 3, 4, 5, 6, or 7, what is one possible value of x?

16. What is the value of $2^4 \div 2^{-4}$?

17. What is the value of
$|(-2 - 3) - (2 - 3)|$?

18. For any integer, a, greater than
1, let $\uparrow a \downarrow$ be the greatest prime
factor of a. What is $\uparrow 132 \downarrow$?

19. If the product of four consecutive integers is equal to one of
the integers, what is the largest
possible value of one of the
integers?

20. If x and y are positive integers,
and $(13^x)^y = 13^{13}$, what is the
average (arithmetic mean) of x
and y?

Answer Key

1. **C**   4. **C**   7. **C**   10. **D**
2. **D**   5. **B**   8. **C**   11. **B**
3. **D**   6. **E**   9. **C**

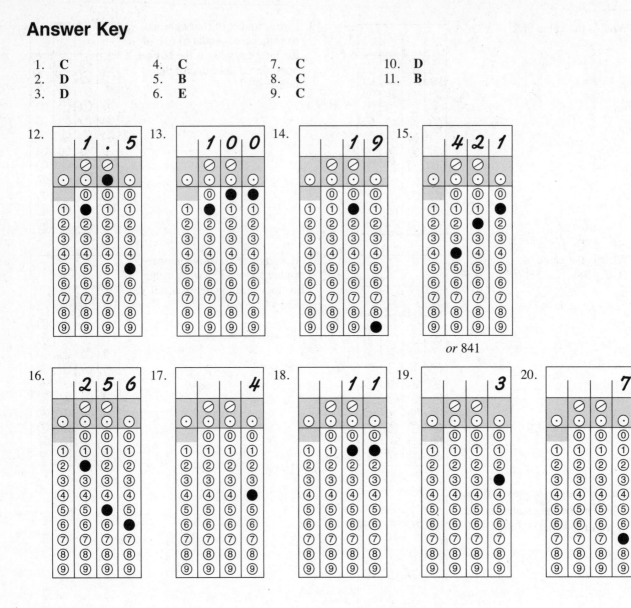

15. *or* 841

Answer Explanations

1. **C.** Since a is positive, divide both sides of the given inequality by a: $a^2 \leq 2a \Rightarrow a \leq 2 \Rightarrow a = 1$ or 2. There are two positive integers that satisfy the given inequality.

2. **D.**
   - Since $a < b$, $a - b$ is negative. (I is true.)
   - Since a and b are positive, so is their product, ab; and the reciprocal of a positive number is positive. (II is true.)
   - $\dfrac{1}{b} - \dfrac{1}{a} = \dfrac{a-b}{ab}$. Since the numerator, $a - b$, is negative and the denominator, ab, is positive, the value of the fraction is negative. (III is false.)

3. **D.**
   - Since b is negative and c is positive,
     $$b < c \Rightarrow -b > -c \Rightarrow a - b > a - c.$$
     (I is false.)
   - Since c is positive, dividing by c preserves the inequality. (II is true.)
   - Since b is negative, $\dfrac{1}{b}$ is negative, and so is less than $\dfrac{1}{c}$, which is positive. (III is true.)

4. **C.** In the 9 hours from 3:00 A.M. to noon, the temperature rose $32 - (-13) = 32 + 13 = 45°$. Therefore, the average hourly increase was $45 \div 9 = 5°$.

5. **B.** $(7^a)(7^b) = 7^{a+b}$, and $\dfrac{7^c}{7^d} = 7^{c-d}$. Therefore:
   $$a + b = c - d \Rightarrow a + b + d = c \Rightarrow$$
   $$d = c - a - b.$$

6. **E.** All primes greater than 2 are odd, so p and q are odd, and $p + q$ is even. (I is true.) The product of two odd numbers is odd. (II is true.) Since p and q are odd, so are their squares, and so the difference of the squares is even. (III is true.)

7. **C.** Since 5 and 7 have two positive factors each, $\tau(5) = \tau(7)$. (I is true.) Since 35 has four divisors (1, 5, 7, and 35) and $\tau(5) \cdot \tau(7) = 2 \times 2 = 4$, II is true. The value of $\tau(12)$ is 6, which is *not* equal to $2 + 2$. (III is false.)

8. **C.** $\tau(\tau(\tau(12))) = \tau(\tau(6)) = \tau(4) = 3.$

9. **C.** First, multiply inside the parentheses: $7^8 \times 7^9 = 7^{17}$; then raise to the 10th power: $(7^{17})^{10} = 7^{170}$.

10. **D.** There are five integers ($1, 0, -1, -2, -3$) that are greater than -3.14 ($-\pi$) and less than 1.41 ($\sqrt{2}$).

11. **B.** For any number, x, between 0 and 1: $x^2 < x$ and $x < \sqrt{x}$.

12. **(1.5)** Divide: $99 \div 2.5 = 39.6$. The butchers can make 39 packages, weighing a total of $39 \times 2.5 = 97.5$ pounds, and have $99 - 97.5 = 1.5$ pounds of meat left over.

13. **(100)** Since 36 is the LCM of 4 and 9, the beepers will beep together every 36 seconds. One hour = 60 minutes = 3600 seconds, and so the simultaneous beeping will occur 100 times.

14. **(19)** To make $y - x$ as large as possible, let y be as large as possible (12), and subtract the smallest amount possible ($x = -7$): $12 - (-7) = 19$.

15. **(421 or 841)** The LCM of 2, 3, 4, 5, 6, 7 is 420, so 420 is divisible by each of these integers, and there will be a remainder of 1 when 421 is divided by any of them. One more than any multiple of 420 will also work.

16. **(256)** $2^4 \div 2^{-4} = \dfrac{2^4}{2^{-4}} = 2^{4-(-4)} = 2^{4+4} = 2^8 = 256.$

17. **(4)** $|(-2 - 3) - (2 - 3)| = |(-5) - (-1)| = |-5 + 1| = |-4| = 4.$

18. **(11)** The easiest way to find the greatest prime factor of 132 is to find its prime factorization: $132 = 2 \times 2 \times 3 \times 11$, so 11 is the greatest prime factor.

19. **(3)** If all four integers were negative, their product would be positive, and so could not equal one of them. If all four integers were positive, their product would be much greater than any of them (even $1 \times 2 \times 3 \times 4 = 24$). Therefore, the integers must include 0, in which case their product *is* 0. The largest set of four consecutive integers that includes 0 is 0, 1, 2, 3.

20. **(7)** Since $13^{13} = (13^x)^y = 13^{xy}$, then $xy = 13$. The only positive integers whose product is 13 are 1 and 13. Their average is
    $$\frac{1 + 13}{2} = 7.$$

9-B Fractions and Decimals

Several questions on the SAT involve fractions and/or decimals. In this section we will review all of the important facts on these topics that you need to know for the SAT. Even if you are using a calculator with fraction capabilities, it is essential that you review all of this material thoroughly.

When a whole is *divided* into *n* equal parts, each part is called *one-nth* of the whole, written as $\frac{1}{n}$. For example, if a pizza is cut (*divided*) into eight equal slices, each slice is one-eighth $\left(\frac{1}{8}\right)$ of the pizza; a day is *divided* into 24 equal hours, so an hour is one-twenty-fourth $\left(\frac{1}{24}\right)$ of a day; and an inch is one-twelfth $\left(\frac{1}{12}\right)$ of a foot.

- If Sam slept for 5 hours, he slept for five-twenty-fourths $\left(\frac{5}{24}\right)$ of a day.

- If Tom bought eight slices of pizza, he bought eight-eighths $\left(\frac{8}{8}\right)$ of a pie.

- If Joe's shelf is 30 inches long, it measures thirty-twelfths $\left(\frac{30}{12}\right)$ of a foot.

Numbers such as $\frac{5}{24}$, $\frac{8}{8}$, and $\frac{30}{12}$, in which one integer is written over a second integer, are called **fractions**. The center line is the fraction bar. The number above the bar is called the **numerator**, and the number below the bar is the **denominator**.

> **CAUTION:** The denominator of a fraction can *never* be 0.

- A fraction such as $\frac{5}{24}$, in which the numerator is less than the denominator, is called a **proper fraction**. Its value is less than 1.
- A fraction such as $\frac{30}{12}$, in which the numerator is more than the denominator, is called an **improper fraction**. Its value is greater than 1.
- A fraction such as $\frac{8}{8}$, in which the numerator and denominator are the same, is also an **improper fraction**, but it is equal to 1.

It is useful to think of the fraction bar as a symbol for division. If three pizzas are divided equally among eight people, each person gets $\frac{3}{8}$ of a pizza. If you actually use your calculator to divide 3 by 8, you get $\frac{3}{8} = 0.375$.

Key Fact B1

Every fraction, proper or improper, can be expressed in decimal form (or as a whole number) by dividing the numerator by the denominator. For example:

$$\frac{3}{10} = 0.3 \qquad \frac{3}{4} = 0.75 \qquad \frac{5}{8} = 0.625 \qquad \frac{3}{16} = 0.1875$$

$$\frac{8}{8} = 1 \qquad \frac{11}{8} = 1.375 \qquad \frac{48}{16} = 3 \qquad \frac{100}{8} = 12.5$$

Note: Any number beginning with a decimal point can be written with a 0 to the left of the decimal point. In fact, some calculators will express 3 ÷ 8 as .375, whereas others will print 0.375.

Unlike the examples above, when most fractions are converted to decimals, the division does not terminate after two, three, or four decimal places; rather it goes on forever with some set of digits repeating itself.

Calculator Shortcut

On the SAT, *never* do long division to convert a fraction to a decimal. Use your calculator.

$$\frac{2}{3} = 0.666666... \quad \frac{3}{11} = 0.272727... \quad \frac{5}{12} = 0.416666... \quad \frac{17}{15} = 1.133333...$$

On the SAT, *you do not need to be concerned with this repetition.* On grid-in problems you just enter as much of the number as will fit in the grid; and on multiple-choice questions, all numbers written as decimals terminate.

Although on the SAT you will have occasion to convert fractions to decimals (by dividing), you will not have to convert decimals to fractions.

Comparing Fractions and Decimals

Key Fact B2

To compare two decimals, follow these rules:

- **Whichever number has the greater number to the left of the decimal point is greater: since 11 > 9, 11.001 > 9.896; and since 1 > 0, 1.234 > 0.8. (Recall that, if a decimal has no number to the left of the decimal point, you may assume that a 0 is there, so 1.234 > .8).**
- **If the numbers to the left of the decimal point are equal (or if there are no numbers to the left of the decimal point), proceed as follows:**

  1. **If the numbers do not have the same number of digits to the right of the decimal point, add zeros at the end of the shorter one until the numbers of digits are equal.**

  2. **Now, compare the numbers, *ignoring* the decimal point itself.**

For example, to compare 1.83 and 1.823, add 0 at the end of 1.83, forming 1.830. Now, *thinking of them as whole numbers*, compare the numbers, ignoring the decimal point:

$$1830 > 1823 \Rightarrow 1.830 > 1.823.$$

Key Fact B3

To compare two fractions, use your calculator to convert them to decimals. Then apply KEY FACT B2. This *always* works.

For example, to compare $\frac{1}{3}$ and $\frac{3}{8}$, write $\frac{1}{3} = 0.3333...$ and $\frac{3}{8} = 0.375$.

Since $0.375 > 0.333$, $\frac{3}{8} > \frac{1}{3}$.

CALCULATOR HINT

You can always use your calculator to compare two numbers: fractions, decimals, or integers. By KEY FACT A21, $a > b$ means $a - b$ is positive, and $a < b$ means $a - b$ is negative. Therefore, to compare two numbers, just subtract them. For example,

$$1.83 - 1.823 = .007 \Rightarrow 1.83 > 1.823,$$
$$.2139 - .239 = -.0251 \Rightarrow .2139 < .239,$$
$$\frac{1}{3} - \frac{3}{8} = -\frac{1}{24} \Rightarrow \frac{1}{3} < \frac{3}{8},$$
$$-6 - (-7) = 1 \Rightarrow -6 > -7.$$

Key Fact B4

When comparing fractions, there are three situations in which it is faster *not* to use your calculator to convert fractions to decimals (although, of course, that will work).

1. The fractions have the same positive denominator. Then the fraction with the larger numerator is greater. Just as $9 are more than $7, and 9 books are more than 7 books, 9 tenths is more than 7 tenths: $\dfrac{9}{10} > \dfrac{7}{10}$.

2. The fractions have the same numerator. Then, if the denominators are positive, the fraction with the smaller denominator is greater. If you divide a cake into five equal pieces, each piece is larger than a piece you would get if you divided the cake into 10 equal pieces: $\dfrac{1}{5} > \dfrac{1}{10}$, and similarly $\dfrac{3}{5} > \dfrac{3}{10}$.

3. The fractions are so familiar or easy to work with that you already know the answer. For example, $\dfrac{3}{4} > \dfrac{1}{5}$ and $\dfrac{11}{20} > \dfrac{1}{2}$.

Key Fact B5

KEY FACTS B2, B3, and B4 apply to *positive* decimals and fractions. Clearly, any positive number is greater than any negative number. For negative decimals and fractions, use KEY FACT A25, which states that, if $a > b$, then $-a < -b$.

$$\frac{1}{2} > \frac{1}{5} \Rightarrow -\frac{1}{2} < -\frac{1}{5} \quad \text{and} \quad .83 > .829 \Rightarrow -.83 < -.829$$

EXAMPLE 1

Which of the following lists the fractions $\dfrac{2}{3}$, $\dfrac{5}{8}$, $\dfrac{7}{11}$, and $\dfrac{13}{20}$ in order from least to greatest?

(A) $\dfrac{2}{3}, \dfrac{5}{8}, \dfrac{7}{11}, \dfrac{13}{20}$

(B) $\dfrac{5}{8}, \dfrac{7}{11}, \dfrac{13}{20}, \dfrac{2}{3}$

(C) $\dfrac{5}{8}, \dfrac{13}{20}, \dfrac{7}{11}, \dfrac{2}{3}$

(D) $\dfrac{13}{20}, \dfrac{7}{11}, \dfrac{5}{8}, \dfrac{2}{3}$

(E) $\dfrac{7}{11}, \dfrac{13}{20}, \dfrac{2}{3}, \dfrac{5}{8}$

Solution. On your calculator convert each fraction to a decimal, writing down the first few decimal places:

$$\frac{2}{3} = 0.666, \quad \frac{5}{8} = 0.625, \quad \frac{7}{11} = 0.636, \quad \text{and} \quad \frac{13}{20} = 0.65.$$

It is now easy to order the decimals:

$$0.625 < 0.636 < 0.650 < 0.666.$$

The answer is $\frac{5}{8}, \frac{7}{11}, \frac{13}{20}, \frac{2}{3}$ **(B)**.

Equivalent Fractions

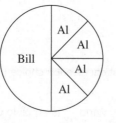

If Bill and Al shared a pizza, and Bill ate $\frac{1}{2}$ and Al ate $\frac{4}{8}$, they had exactly the same amount

of the pizza. We express this idea by saying that $\frac{1}{2}$ and $\frac{4}{8}$ are ***equivalent fractions***: that is, they have the exact same value.

Note: If you multiply both the numerator and the denominator of $\frac{1}{2}$ by 4, you get $\frac{4}{8}$; and if

you divide both the numerator and the denominator of $\frac{4}{8}$ by 4, you get $\frac{1}{2}$.

This illustrates the next KEY FACT.

Key Fact B6

Two fractions are equivalent if multiplying or dividing both the numerator and the denominator of the first fraction *by the same number* gives the second fraction.

Consider the following two cases.

1. Are $\frac{3}{8}$ and $\frac{45}{120}$ equivalent? There is a number that, when multiplied

   by 3 gives 45, and there is a number that, when multiplied by 8, gives 120. By KEY FACT B6, if these numbers are the same, the fractions are equivalent. They *are* the same number: $3 \times 15 = 45$ and $8 \times 15 = 120$.

2. Are $\frac{2}{3}$ and $\frac{28}{45}$ equivalent? Since $2 \times 14 = 28$, but $3 \times 14 \neq 45$, the

   fractions are *not* equivalent. Alternatively, $28 \div 14 = 2$, but $45 \div 14 \neq 3$.

Calculator Shortcut

To determine whether two fractions are equivalent, convert them to decimals by dividing. For the fractions to be equivalent, the two quotients must be the same.

EXAMPLE 2

Which of the following is NOT equivalent to $\dfrac{15}{24}$?

(A) $\dfrac{45}{72}$

(B) $\dfrac{60}{96}$

(C) $\dfrac{180}{288}$

(D) $\dfrac{5}{8}$

(E) $\dfrac{3}{5}$

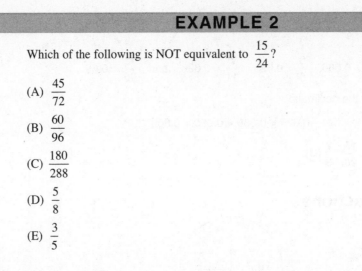 **Solution.** Since $\dfrac{15}{24} = 0.625$, just check each choice until you find the one that is NOT

equal to 0.625. Each of $\dfrac{45}{72}$, $\dfrac{60}{96}$, $\dfrac{180}{288}$, and $\dfrac{5}{8}$ is equal to 0.625. Only $\dfrac{3}{5}$ **(E)** does not equal

0.625 $\left(\dfrac{3}{5} = 0.6\right)$.

A fraction is in ***lowest terms*** if no positive integer greater than 1 is a factor of both the numerator

and the denominator. For example, $\dfrac{9}{20}$ is in lowest terms, since no integer greater than 1 is a

factor of both 9 and 20; but $\dfrac{9}{24}$ is not in lowest terms, since 3 is a factor of both 9 and 24.

Key Fact B7

Every fraction can be *reduced* to lowest terms by dividing the numerator and the denominator by their greatest common factor (GCF). If the GCF is 1, the fraction is already in lowest terms.

EXAMPLE 3

For any positive integer n, $n!$ means the product of all the integers from 1 to n.

What is the value of $\dfrac{6!}{8!}$?

(A) $\dfrac{1}{56}$

(B) $\dfrac{1}{48}$

(C) $\dfrac{1}{8}$

(D) $\dfrac{1}{4}$

(E) $\dfrac{3}{4}$

Solution. Assume that you don't see the easy way to do this. On your calculator quickly multiply or use the ! key:

$$6! = 1 \cdot 2 \cdot 3 \cdot 4 \cdot 5 \cdot 6 = 720,$$
$$8! = 1 \cdot 2 \cdot 3 \cdot 4 \cdot 5 \cdot 6 \cdot 7 \cdot 8 = 40,320.$$

You are now faced with reducing $\dfrac{720}{40,320}$. Don't do it; just use your calculator to divide:

$\dfrac{720}{40,320} = 0.0178...$, and now test the choices, starting with C.

$\dfrac{1}{8} = 0.125$, which is too large. Eliminate C as well as D and E, which are even larger, and try

A or B. In fact, $\dfrac{1}{56} = 0.0178....$ Choice **A** is correct. Here's the easy solution:

$$\frac{6!}{8!} = \frac{\overset{1}{\cancel{6 \times 5 \times 4 \times 3 \times 2 \times 1}}}{8 \times 7 \times \underset{1}{\cancel{6 \times 5 \times 4 \times 3 \times 2 \times 1}}} = \frac{1}{8 \times 7} = \frac{1}{\mathbf{56}}.$$

This solution takes only a few seconds, but the calculator solution is simple enough and can surely be done in less than a minute.

Arithmetic Operations with Decimals

On the SAT, *all* decimal arithmetic (including whole numbers) that you can't easily do in your head should be done on your calculator. This shortcut saves time and avoids careless errors. If you know that $12 \times 12 = 144$ and that $1.2 \times 1.2 = 1.44$, fine; but if you're not sure, use your calculator rather than your pencil. You should even use your calculator to multiply 0.2×0.2 if there's any chance that you would get 0.4 instead of 0.04 as the answer.

You should *not* have to use your calculator to multiply or divide any decimal number by a power of 10, because multiplying and dividing by 10 or 100 or 1000 is a calcuation you should be able to do easily in your head.

> **Helpful Hint**
> Any whole number can be treated as a decimal: $7 = 7.0$.

Key Fact B8

To multiply any decimal or whole number by a power of 10, move the decimal point as many places to the right as there are 0's in the power of 10, filling in with 0's if necessary.

$$1.35 \times 10 = 13.5 \qquad 1.35 \times 100 = 135$$

$$1.35 \times 1000 = 1350$$

$$23 \times 10 = 230 \qquad 23 \times 100 = 2300$$

$$23 \times 1,000,000 = 23,000,000$$

Key Fact B9

To divide any decimal or whole number by a power of 10, move the decimal point as many places to the left as there are 0's in the power of 10, filling in with 0's if necessary.

$$67.8 \div 10 = 6.78 \quad 67.8 \div 100 = 0.678$$
$$1 \qquad\qquad 2$$

$$67.8 \div 1000 = 0.0678$$
$$3$$

$$14 \div 10 = 1.4 \quad 14 \div 100 = 0.14$$
$$1 \qquad\qquad 2$$

$$14 \div 1,000,000 = 0.000014$$
$$6$$

On the SAT, you *never* have to round off decimal answers. On grid-ins just enter the number, putting in as many digits after the decimal point as fit. For example, enter 3.125 as $\boxed{3}\boxed{.}\boxed{1}\boxed{2}$ and .1488 as $\boxed{.}\boxed{1}\boxed{4}\boxed{8}$. However, you do have to know how to round off, because *occasionally* there is a question about that procedure.

Key Fact B10

To *round off* a decimal number to any place, follow these rules, which are fully explained with examples in the table below.

- Keep all of the digits to the left of the specified place.
- In that place, keep the digit if the next digit is < 5, and increase that digit by 1 if the next digit is ≥ 5. (*Note:* 9 increased by 1 is 10: put down the 0 and carry the 1.)
- If there are still digits to the left of the decimal point, change them to 0's and eliminate the decimal point and everything that follows it.
- If you are at or beyond the decimal point, stop: don't write any more digits.

For example, here is how to round off 3815.296 to any place.

Round to the Nearest:	Procedure	Answer
thousand	The digit in the thousands place is 3; since the next digit (8) is ≥ 5, increase the 3 to a 4; fill in the 3 places to the left of the decimal point with 0's.	4000
hundred	The digit in the hundreds place is 8; keep everything to the left of it, and keep the 8 since the next digit (1) is < 5; fill in 0's to the left of the decimal point.	3800
ten	The digit in the tens place is 1; keep everything to the left of it, and increase the 1 to a 2 since the next digit (5) is ≥ 5; fill in 0's to the left of the decimal point.	3820
one	The digit in the ones place is 5; keep everything to the left of it, and keep the 5 since the next digit (2) is < 5; there are no more places to the left of the decimal point, so stop.	3815
tenth	The digit in the tenths place is 2; keep everything to the left of it, and increase the 2 to a 3 since the next digit (9) is ≥ 5; you are beyond the decimal point, so stop.	3815.3
hundredth	The digit in the hundredths place is 9; keep everything to the left of it, and, since the next digit (6) is ≥ 5, increase the 9 to a 10; put down the 0 and carry a 1 into the tenths place: 0.29 becomes 0.30; since you are beyond the decimal point, stop.	3815.30

EXAMPLE 4

When 423,890 is rounded off to the nearest thousand, how many digits will be changed?

(A) 0
(B) 1
(C) 2
(D) 3
(E) 4

Solution. When 423,890 is rounded off to the nearest thousand, **3** digits are changed: 424,000 **(D)**.

Arithmetic Operations with Fractions

Key Fact B11

To multiply two fractions, multiply their numerators and multiply their denominators.

$$\frac{3}{5} \times \frac{4}{7} = \frac{3 \times 4}{5 \times 7} = \frac{12}{35}$$

Key Fact B12

To multiply a fraction by any other number, write that number as a fraction whose denominator is 1.

$$\frac{3}{5} \times 7 = \frac{3}{5} \times \frac{7}{1} = \frac{21}{5} \qquad \frac{3}{4} \times \pi = \frac{3}{4} \times \frac{\pi}{1} = \frac{3\pi}{4}$$

TACTIC

B1

Before multiplying fractions, reduce. You may reduce by dividing any numerator and any denominator by a common factor.

EXAMPLE 5

Express the product $\frac{3}{4} \times \frac{8}{9} \times \frac{15}{16}$ in lowest terms.

Solution. If you just multiply the numerators and denominators (with a calculator, of course), you get $\frac{360}{576}$, which is a nuisance to reduce. Also, dividing on your calculator won't help, since your answer is supposed to be a fraction in lowest terms. It is better to use TACTIC B1 and reduce first:

$$\frac{\overset{1}{\cancel{3}}}{4} \times \frac{\overset{1}{\cancel{8}}}{\underset{3}{\cancel{9}}} \times \frac{\overset{5}{\cancel{15}}}{\underset{2}{\cancel{16}}} = \frac{1 \times 1 \times 5}{4 \times 1 \times 2} = \frac{5}{8}.$$

TACTIC

B2

When a problem requires you to find a fraction *of* a number, multiply.

EXAMPLE 6

If $\dfrac{4}{7}$ of the 350 sophomores at Adams High School are girls, and $\dfrac{7}{8}$ of the girls

play on a team, how many sophomore girls do NOT play on a team?

 Solution. There are $\dfrac{4}{7} \times 350 = 200$ sophomore girls.

Of these, $\dfrac{7}{8} \times 200 = 175$ play on a team. Then, $200 - 175 = \mathbf{25}$ do not play on a team.

How should you multiply $\dfrac{4}{7} \times 350$? If you can do this mentally, you should:

$$\dfrac{4}{\overset{}{\underset{1}{7}}} \times \overset{50}{\cancel{350}} = 200.$$

The next step, however, requires you to multiply $\dfrac{7}{8}$ by 200, and more likely than not you don't

immediately see that 200 divided by 8 is 25 or that 7 times 25 equals 175:

$$\dfrac{7}{\overset{}{\underset{1}{8}}} \times \overset{25}{\cancel{200}} = 175.$$

For any step that you can't do instantly, you should use your calculator:

$$(4 \div 7) \times 350 \times (7 \div 8) = 175.$$

CALCULATOR HINT

If you are going to use your calculator on a problem, don't bother reducing anything. Given

the choice of multiplying $\dfrac{48}{128} \times 80$ or $\dfrac{3}{8} \times 80$, you would prefer the second option, but

for *your calculator* the first one is just as easy.

The ***reciprocal*** of any nonzero number, *x*, is the number $\dfrac{1}{x}$. The reciprocal of the fraction $\dfrac{a}{b}$

is the fraction $\dfrac{b}{a}$.

Key Fact B13

To divide any number by a fraction, multiply the number by the reciprocal of the fraction.

$$20 \div \dfrac{2}{3} = \dfrac{\overset{10}{\cancel{20}}}{1} \times \dfrac{3}{\underset{1}{\cancel{2}}} = 30 \qquad \dfrac{3}{5} \div \dfrac{2}{3} = \dfrac{3}{5} \times \dfrac{3}{2} = \dfrac{9}{10}$$

$$\sqrt{2} \div \dfrac{2}{3} = \dfrac{\sqrt{2}}{1} \times \dfrac{3}{2} = \dfrac{3\sqrt{2}}{2}$$

EXAMPLE 7

In the meat department of a supermarket, 100 pounds of chopped meat was

divided into packages, each of which weighed $\frac{4}{7}$ pound. How many packages were there?

Solution. $100 \div \frac{4}{7} = \frac{\overset{25}{\cancel{100}}}{1} \times \frac{7}{\cancel{4}_1} = \textbf{175}$.

Key Fact B14

To add or subtract fractions with the same denominator, add or subtract the numerators and keep the denominator.

$$\frac{4}{9}+\frac{1}{9}=\frac{5}{9} \quad \text{and} \quad \frac{4}{9}-\frac{1}{9}=\frac{3}{9}=\frac{1}{3}.$$

To add or subtract fractions with different denominators, first rewrite the fractions as equivalent fractions with the same denominator.

$$\frac{1}{6}+\frac{3}{4}=\frac{2}{12}+\frac{9}{12}=\frac{11}{12}.$$

Note: The *easiest* denominator to find is the product of the denominators ($6 \times 4 = 24$, in this example), but the *best* denominator to use is the *least common denominator*, which is the least common multiple (LCM) of the denominators (12 in this case). Using the least common denominator minimizes the amount of reducing that is necessary to express the answer in lowest terms.

Key Fact B15

If $\frac{a}{b}$ is the fraction of the whole that satisfies some property, then $1 - \frac{a}{b}$ is the fraction

of the whole that does *not* satisfy it.

EXAMPLE 8

In a jar, $\frac{1}{2}$ of the marbles are red, $\frac{1}{4}$ are white, and $\frac{1}{5}$ are blue. What fraction

of the marbles are neither red, white, nor blue?

Solution. The red, white, and blue marbles constitute

$$\frac{1}{2}+\frac{1}{4}+\frac{1}{5}=\frac{10}{20}+\frac{5}{20}+\frac{4}{20}=\frac{19}{20}.$$

of the total, so

$$1-\frac{19}{20}=\frac{20}{20}-\frac{19}{20}=\frac{1}{20}$$

of the marbles are neither red, white, nor blue.

EXAMPLE 9

Ali ate $\frac{1}{3}$ of a cake and Jason ate $\frac{1}{4}$ of it. What fraction of the cake was still uneaten?

EXAMPLE 10

Ali ate $\frac{1}{3}$ of a cake and Jason ate $\frac{1}{4}$ of what was left. What fraction of the cake was still uneaten?

CAUTION: Be sure to read questions carefully. In Example 9, Jason ate $\frac{1}{4}$ of the cake. In Example 10, however, he ate only $\frac{1}{4}$ of the $\frac{2}{3}$ that was left after Ali had her piece. He ate

$$\frac{1}{\cancel{4}_2} \times \frac{\cancel{2}^1}{3} = \frac{1}{6}$$

of the cake.

Solution 9. $\frac{1}{3} + \frac{1}{4} = \frac{4}{12} + \frac{3}{12} = \frac{7}{12}$ of the cake was eaten, and $1 - \frac{7}{12} = \frac{5}{12}$ was uneaten.

Solution 10. $\frac{1}{3} + \frac{1}{6} = \frac{2}{6} + \frac{1}{6} = \frac{3}{6} = \frac{1}{2}$ of the cake was eaten, and the other $\frac{1}{2}$ was uneaten.

Arithmetic Operations with Mixed Numbers

A *mixed number* is a number, such as $3\frac{1}{2}$, that consists of an integer followed by a fraction.

The mixed number is an abbreviation for the *sum* of the integer and the fraction; so $3\frac{1}{2}$ is an abbreviation for $3 + \frac{1}{2}$.

Every mixed number can be written as an improper fraction, and every improper fraction can be written as a mixed number:

$$3\frac{1}{2} = 3 + \frac{1}{2} = \frac{3}{1} + \frac{1}{2} = \frac{6}{2} + \frac{1}{2} = \frac{7}{2} \quad \text{and} \quad \frac{7}{2} = \frac{6}{2} + \frac{1}{2} = 3 + \frac{1}{2} = 3\frac{1}{2}.$$

Key Fact B16

To write a mixed number as an improper fraction, or an improper fraction as a mixed number, follow these rules:

1. To write a mixed number $\left(3\frac{1}{2}\right)$ as an improper fraction, multiply the whole number (3) by the denominator (2), add the numerator (1), and write the sum over the denominator (2):

$$\frac{3 \times 2 + 1}{2} = \frac{7}{2}.$$

2. To write an improper fraction $\left(\dfrac{7}{2}\right)$ as a mixed number, divide the numerator by the denominator; the quotient (3) is the whole number.

Place the remainder (1) over the denominator to form the fractional part $\left(\dfrac{1}{2}\right)$: $3\dfrac{1}{2}$.

> **CAUTION:** You can *never* grid in a mixed number. You must change it to an improper fraction or a decimal.

Key Fact B17

To add mixed numbers, add the integers and also add the fractions.

$$5\frac{1}{4} + 3\frac{2}{3} = (5+3) + \left(\frac{1}{4}+\frac{2}{3}\right) = 8 + \left(\frac{3}{12}+\frac{8}{12}\right) = 8 + \frac{11}{12} = 8\frac{11}{12}$$

$$5\frac{3}{4} + 3\frac{2}{3} = (5+3) + \left(\frac{3}{4}+\frac{2}{3}\right) = 8 + \left(\frac{9}{12}+\frac{8}{12}\right) =$$

$$8 + \frac{17}{12} = 8 + 1\frac{5}{12} = 8 + 1 + \frac{5}{12} = 9\frac{5}{12}$$

Helpful Hint

Understanding the procedures in Key Facts B17, B18, and B19 will help you avoid careless mistakes. However, any arithmetic that you can't do in your head, you should do on your calculator.

Key Fact B18

To subtract mixed numbers, subtract the integers and also subtract the fractions. If, however, the fraction in the second number is greater than the fraction in the first number, you first have to borrow 1 from the integer part.

For example, since $\dfrac{2}{3} > \dfrac{1}{4}$, you can't subtract $5\dfrac{1}{4} - 3\dfrac{2}{3}$ until you borrow 1 from the 5:

$$5\frac{1}{4} = 5 + \frac{1}{4} = (4+1) + \frac{1}{4} = 4 + \left(1+\frac{1}{4}\right) = 4 + \frac{5}{4}.$$

Now, you have

$$5\frac{1}{4} - 3\frac{2}{3} = 4\frac{5}{4} - 3\frac{2}{3} = (4-3) + \left(\frac{5}{4}-\frac{2}{3}\right) = 1 + \left(\frac{15}{12}-\frac{8}{12}\right) = 1\frac{7}{12}.$$

Key Fact B19

To multiply or divide mixed numbers, change them to improper fractions.

$$1\frac{2}{3} \times 3\frac{1}{4} = \frac{5}{3} \times \frac{13}{4} = \frac{65}{12} = 5\frac{5}{12}.$$

> **CAUTION:** Be aware that $3\left(5\dfrac{1}{2}\right)$ is *not* $15\dfrac{1}{2}$; rather:
>
> $$3\left(5\frac{1}{2}\right) = 3\left(5+\frac{1}{2}\right) = 15 + \frac{3}{2} = 15 + 1\frac{1}{2} = 16\frac{1}{2}.$$

Complex Fractions

A *complex fraction* is a fraction, such as $\dfrac{1+\dfrac{1}{6}}{2-\dfrac{3}{4}}$, that has one or more fractions in its numerator or denominator or both.

Key Fact B20

There are two ways to simplify a complex fraction:

1. Multiply *every* term in the numerator and denominator by the least common multiple of all the denominators that appear in the fraction.

2. Simplify the numerator and the denominator, and divide.

To simplify $\dfrac{1+\dfrac{1}{6}}{2-\dfrac{3}{4}}$, multiply each term by 12, the LCM of 6 and 4:

Calculator Shortcut

Remember that, on the SAT, if you ever get stuck on a fraction problem, you can always convert the fractions to decimals and do all the work on your calculator.

$$\frac{12(1)+\cancel{12}\left(\dfrac{1}{\cancel{6}}\right)^{2}}{12(2)-\cancel{12}\left(\dfrac{3}{\cancel{4}}\right)^{1}}=\frac{12+2}{24-9}=\frac{14}{15},$$

or write

$$\frac{1+\dfrac{1}{6}}{2-\dfrac{3}{4}}=\frac{\dfrac{7}{6}}{\dfrac{5}{4}}=\frac{7}{\cancel{6}_{3}}\times\frac{\cancel{4}^{2}}{5}=\frac{14}{15}.$$

Exercises on Fractions and Decimals

Multiple-Choice Questions

1. A French class has 12 boys and 18 girls. Boys are what fraction of the class?

   (A) $\dfrac{2}{5}$

   (B) $\dfrac{3}{5}$

   (C) $\dfrac{2}{3}$

   (D) $\dfrac{3}{4}$

   (E) $\dfrac{3}{2}$

2. For how many integers, a, between 30 and 40 is it true that $\dfrac{5}{a}$, $\dfrac{8}{a}$, and $\dfrac{13}{a}$ are all in lowest terms?

   (A) 1
   (B) 2
   (C) 3
   (D) 4
   (E) 5

3. $\dfrac{1}{4}$ is the average (arithmetic mean) of $\dfrac{1}{5}$ and what number?

   (A) $\dfrac{1}{20}$

   (B) $\dfrac{3}{10}$

   (C) $\dfrac{1}{3}$

   (D) $\dfrac{9}{20}$

   (E) $\dfrac{9}{40}$

4. If $\dfrac{3}{11}$ of a number is 22, what is $\dfrac{6}{11}$ of that number?

   (A) 6
   (B) 11
   (C) 12
   (D) 33
   (E) 44

5. What fractional part of a week is 98 hours?

   (A) $\dfrac{7}{24}$

   (B) $\dfrac{24}{98}$

   (C) $\dfrac{1}{2}$

   (D) $\dfrac{4}{7}$

   (E) $\dfrac{7}{12}$

6. $\dfrac{5}{8}$ of 24 is equal to $\dfrac{15}{7}$ of what number?

   (A) 7
   (B) 8
   (C) 15

   (D) $\dfrac{7}{225}$

   (E) $\dfrac{225}{7}$

7. Which of the following is less than $\dfrac{5}{9}$?

   (A) $\dfrac{5}{8}$

   (B) $\dfrac{21}{36}$

   (C) $\dfrac{25}{45}$

   (D) $\dfrac{55}{100}$

   (E) .565

8. Which of the following is (are) greater than x when $x = \dfrac{9}{11}$?

  I. $\dfrac{1}{x}$

  II. $\dfrac{x+1}{x}$

  III. $\dfrac{x+1}{x-1}$

  (A) I only
  (B) I and II only
  (C) I and III only
  (D) II and III only
  (E) I, II, and III

9. Which of the following statements is true?

  (A) $\dfrac{3}{8} < \dfrac{4}{11} < \dfrac{5}{13}$

  (B) $\dfrac{4}{11} < \dfrac{3}{8} < \dfrac{5}{13}$

  (C) $\dfrac{5}{13} < \dfrac{4}{11} < \dfrac{3}{8}$

  (D) $\dfrac{4}{11} < \dfrac{5}{13} < \dfrac{3}{8}$

  (E) $\dfrac{3}{8} < \dfrac{5}{13} < \dfrac{4}{11}$

10. If $a = 0.99$, which of the following is (are) less than a?

  I. $\sqrt{a}$

  II. a^2

  III. $\dfrac{1}{a}$

  (A) None
  (B) I only
  (C) II only
  (D) III only
  (E) II and III only

11. For the final step in a calculation, Paul accidentally divided by 1000 instead of multiplying by 1000. What should he do to his answer to correct it?

  (A) Multiply it by 1000.
  (B) Multiply it by 100,000.
  (C) Multiply it by 1,000,000.
  (D) Square it.
  (E) Double it.

Grid-in Questions

12. One day at Central High School, $\dfrac{1}{12}$ of the students were absent, and $\dfrac{1}{5}$ of those present went on a field trip. If the number of students staying in school was 704, how many students are enrolled at Central High?

13. What is a possible value of x if $\dfrac{3}{5} < \dfrac{1}{x} < \dfrac{7}{9}$?

14. If $7a = 3$ and $3b = 7$, what is the value of $\dfrac{a}{b}$?

15. If $A = \{1, 2, 3\}$, $B = \{2, 3, 4\}$, and C is the set consisting of all the fractions whose numerators are in A and whose denominators are in B, what is the product of all of the numbers in C?

Answer Key

1. **A**   3. **B**   5. **E**   7. **D**   9. **B**   11. **C**
2. **C**   4. **E**   6. **A**   8. **B**   10. **C**

12. **9 6 0**

13. **1 . 5 0**

$1.28 < x < 1.67$

14. **9 / 4 9** or **. 1 8 3**

15. **1 / 6 4** or **. 0 1 5**

Answer Explanations

1. **A.** The class has 30 students, of whom 12 are boys. The boys make up $\frac{12}{30} = \frac{2}{5}$ of the class.

2. **C.** If a is even, then $\frac{8}{a}$ is *not* in lowest terms, since both a and 8 are divisible by 2. The only possibilities are 31, 33, 35, 37, and 39, but $\frac{5}{35} = \frac{1}{7}$ and $\frac{13}{39} = \frac{1}{3}$, so only 31, 33, and 37 (that is, 3 integers) remain.

3. **B.** The average of $\frac{1}{5}$ and another number, x, is

$$\frac{\frac{1}{5} + x}{2} = \frac{1}{4}.$$

Multiplying both sides by 2 yields

$$\frac{1}{5} + x = \frac{1}{2} \Rightarrow x = \frac{1}{2} - \frac{1}{5} = \frac{5}{10} - \frac{2}{10} = \frac{3}{10}.$$

4. **E.** Don't bother writing an equation for this one; just think. You know that $\frac{3}{11}$ of the number is 22, and $\frac{6}{11}$ of a number is twice as much as $\frac{3}{11}$ of it: $2 \times 22 = 44$.

5. **E.** There are 24 hours in a day and 7 days in a week, so there are $24 \times 7 = 168$ hours in a week: $\frac{98}{168} = \frac{7}{12}$.

6. **A.** If x is the number,

$$\frac{15}{7}x = \frac{5}{\overset{}{\underset{1}{8}}} \times \overset{3}{24} = 15.$$

Then, $\frac{15}{7}x = 15$, which means (dividing by 15) that $\frac{1}{7}x = 1$, so $x = 7$.

7. **D.** Use your calculator: $\frac{5}{9} = 0.5555555....$ Choice C is also equal to $0.555555...$; choices A, B, and E are all greater; only $\frac{55}{100} = 0.55$ is less.

8. **B.**
   - The reciprocal of a number less than 1 is greater than 1. (I is true).
   - $\frac{x+1}{x} = 1 + \frac{1}{x}$, which is greater than 1. (II is true).
   - When $x = \frac{9}{11}$, $x + 1$ is positive, whereas $x - 1$ is negative. Then $\frac{x+1}{x-1}$ is negative, and hence less than 1. (III is false.)

9. **B.** Use your calculator to convert each fraction to a decimal:

$$\frac{4}{11} = 0.3636..., \quad \frac{3}{8} = 0.375, \quad \frac{5}{13} = 0.3846....$$

This is the correct order.

10. **C.**
    - Since $a < 1$, then $\sqrt{a} > a$. (I is false.)
    - Since $a < 1$, then $a^2 < a$. (II is true.)
    - The reciprocal of a number less than 1 is greater than 1. (III is false.)

11. **C.** Multiplying the incorrect answer by 1000 would undo the final division Paul made—the point at which he should have multiplied by 1000. Then, to correct his error, he would have to multiply again by 1000. In all, he should multiply by $1000 \times 1000 = 1,000,000$.

12. **(960)** If s is the number of students enrolled, $\frac{1}{12}s$ is the number who were absent, and $\frac{11}{12}s$ is the number who were present. Since $\frac{1}{5}$ of those present went on a field trip, $\frac{4}{5}$ of them stayed in school. Therefore,

$$704 = \frac{\overset{1}{4}}{5} \times \frac{11}{\underset{3}{12}}s = \frac{11}{15}$$

$$s = 704 \div \frac{11}{15} = 704 \times \frac{15}{11} = 960.$$

13. $(1.28 < x < 1.67)$ Since $\frac{3}{5} = .6$ and $\frac{7}{9} = .777...,$

$\frac{1}{x}$ can be any number between .6 and .777.

If $\frac{1}{x} = .7 = \frac{7}{10}$, then $x = \frac{10}{7}$ or 1.42;

if $\frac{1}{x} = .75 = \frac{3}{4}$, then $x = \frac{4}{3}$ or 1.33;

and so on.

15. $\left(\frac{1}{64} \text{ or } .015 \right)$ Nine fractions are formed:

$\frac{1}{3}, \frac{1}{4}, \frac{2}{2}, \frac{2}{3}, \frac{2}{4}, \frac{3}{2}, \frac{3}{3}, \frac{3}{4}$.

When you multiply, the three 2's and the three 3's in the numerators cancel with the three 2's and three 3's in the denominators. Then, the numerator is 1 and the denominator is

$4 \times 4 \times 4 = 64$. Grid in $\frac{1}{64}$ or .015.

14. $\left(\frac{9}{49} \text{ or } .183 \right)$ Since $7a = 3$ and $3b = 7$, then

$a = \frac{3}{7}$ and $b = \frac{7}{3}$. So

$$\frac{a}{b} = \frac{3}{7} \div \frac{7}{3} = \frac{3}{7} \times \frac{3}{7} = \frac{9}{49} \text{ or } .183.$$

9-C Percents

Helpful Hint
A percent is just a fraction whose denominator is 100:

$$x\% = \frac{x}{100}.$$

The word **percent** means "hundredth." The symbol "%" is used to express the word *percent*. For example, "17 percent" means "17 hundredths" and can be written with a % symbol, as a fraction, or as a decimal:

$$17\% = \frac{17}{100} = 0.17.$$

Key Fact C1

To convert a percent to a decimal, or a percent to a fraction, follow these rules:

1. To convert a percent to a decimal, drop the % symbol and move the decimal point two places to the left, adding 0's if necessary. (Remember: it is assumed that there is a decimal point to the right of any whole number.)

2. To convert a percent to a fraction, drop the % symbol, write the number over 100, and reduce.

$$25\% = 0.25 = \frac{25}{100} = \frac{1}{4} \qquad 100\% = 1.00 = \frac{100}{100}$$

$$12.5\% = 0.125 = \frac{12.5}{100} = \frac{125}{1000} = \frac{1}{8}$$

$$1\% = 0.01 = \frac{1}{100} \qquad \frac{1}{2}\% = 0.5\% = 0.005 = \frac{.5}{100} = \frac{1}{200}$$

$$250\% = 2.50 = \frac{250}{100} = \frac{5}{2}$$

Key Fact C2

To convert a decimal to a percent, or a fraction to a percent, follow these rules:

1. To convert a decimal to a percent, move the decimal point two places to the right, adding 0's if necessary, and add the % symbol.

2. To convert a fraction to a percent, first convert the fraction to a decimal, then do step 1.

$$0.375 = 37.5\% \quad 0.3 = 30\% \quad 1.25 = 125\% \quad 10 = 1000\%$$

$$\frac{3}{4} = 0.75 = 75\% \qquad \frac{1}{3} = 0.33333... = 33.333...\% = 33\frac{1}{3}\%$$

$$\frac{1}{5} = 0.2 = 20\%$$

You should be familiar with the following basic conversions:

$\frac{1}{2} = 50\%$	$\frac{1}{10} = 10\%$	$\frac{6}{10} = \frac{3}{5} = 60\%$
$\frac{1}{3} = 33\frac{1}{3}\%$	$\frac{2}{10} = \frac{1}{5} = 20\%$	$\frac{7}{10} = 70\%$
$\frac{2}{3} = 66\frac{2}{3}\%$	$\frac{3}{10} = 30\%$	$\frac{8}{10} = \frac{4}{5} = 80\%$
$\frac{1}{4} = 25\%$	$\frac{4}{10} = \frac{2}{5} = 40\%$	$\frac{9}{10} = 90\%$
$\frac{3}{4} = 75\%$	$\frac{5}{10} = \frac{1}{2} = 50\%$	$\frac{10}{10} = 1 = 100\%$

Knowing these conversions can help you to solve many problems more quickly. For example, the fastest way to find 25% of 32 is to know that 25% = $\frac{1}{4}$, and that $\frac{1}{4}$ of 32 is 8, *not* to use your calculator.

It is important to keep in mind, however, that *any* problem involving percents can be done on your calculator: to find 25% of 32, write 25% as a decimal and multiply: $32 \times .25 = 8$.

Here is another example of mental math being much faster than calculator math. Since 10% = $\frac{1}{10}$, to take 10% of a number, just divide by 10 by moving the decimal point one place to the left: 10% of 60 is 6. Also, since 5% is half of 10%, then 5% of 60 is 3 (half of 6); and since 30% is 3 times 10%, then 30% of 60 is 18 (3×6).

Practice this shortcut, because improving your ability to do mental math will add valuable points to your score on the SAT.

Solving Percent Problems

Now, consider these three questions:

(i) What is 45% of 200?
(ii) 90 is 45% of what number?
(iii) 90 is what percent of 200?

Each question can be answered easily by using your calculator, but you must first set the question up properly so that you know what to multiply or divide. In each case, there is one unknown; call it *x*. Now, just translate each sentence, replacing "is" by "=" and the unknown by *x*.

(i) $x = 45\%$ of $200 \Rightarrow x = 0.45 \times 200 = 90$.
(ii) $90 = 45\%$ of $x \Rightarrow 90 = 0.45x \Rightarrow x = 90 \div 0.45 = 200$.

(iii) $90 = x\%$ of $200 \Rightarrow 90 = \dfrac{x}{\underset{1}{100}}(\overset{2}{200}) \Rightarrow x = 45$.

Many students have been taught to answer questions such as these by writing this proportion:

$$\frac{is}{of} = \frac{percent}{100}$$

To use this method, think of *is, of,* and *percent* as variables. In each percent problem you are given two variables and asked to find the third, which you label *x*. Of course, you then solve the equation by cross-multiplying.

For example, the three problems solved above could be handled as follows:

(i) <u>What is</u> 45% of 200? (Let *x* = the *is* number.)

$$\frac{x}{200} = \frac{45}{100} \Rightarrow 100x = 45(200) = 9000 \Rightarrow x = 90$$

(ii) 90 is 45% <u>of what number</u>? (Let *x* = the *of* number.)

$$\frac{90}{x} = \frac{45}{100} \Rightarrow 9000 = 45x \Rightarrow x = 200$$

(iii) 90 is <u>what %</u> of 200? (Let *x* = the *percent*.)

$$\frac{90}{200} = \frac{x}{100} \Rightarrow 200x = 9000 \Rightarrow x = 45$$

EXAMPLE 1

Brian gave 20% of his baseball cards to Scott and 15% to Adam. If he still had 520 cards, how many did he have originally?

 Solution. Originally, Brian had 100% of the cards (all of them). After he gave away 35% of them, he had 100% − 35% = 65% of them left. Then 520 is 65% of what number?

$$520 = .65x \Rightarrow x = 520 \div .65 = \mathbf{800}$$

EXAMPLE 2

After Michael gave 110 baseball cards to Sally and 75 to Heidi, he had 315 left. What percent of his cards did Michael give away?

 Solution. Michael gave away a total of 185 cards and had 315 left. Therefore, he started with 185 + 315 = 500 cards. Then 185 is what percent of 500?

$$185 = \frac{x}{\cancel{100}_{1}}(\cancel{500}^{5}) \Rightarrow 5x = 185 \Rightarrow x = 185 \div 5 = \mathbf{37}$$

Michael gave away 37% of his cards.

Since *percent* means "hundredth," the easiest number to use in any percent problem is 100:

$$a\% \text{ of } 100 = \frac{a}{100}(100) = a.$$

Key Fact C3

For any positive number *a*: *a*% of 100 is *a*.

For example, 11.2% of 100 is 11.2; 500% of 100 is 500; and $\frac{1}{2}\%$ of 100 = $\frac{1}{2}$.

TACTIC

C1

In any problem involving percents, use the number 100.

EXAMPLE 3

In 1970 the populations of town A and town B were the same. From 1970 to 1980, however, the population of town A increased by 60% while the population of town B decreased by 60%. In 1980, the population of town B was what percent of the population of town A?

(A) 25%
(B) 36%
(C) 40%
(D) 60%
(E) 120%

Solution. In your math class, you would let *x* be the population of town A in 1970 and then proceed to set up an algebra problem. *Don't do that on the SAT.* Assume that the populations of both towns were 100 in 1970. Then, since 60% of 100 is 60, in 1980 the populations were 100 + 60 = 160 (town A) and 100 − 60 = 40 (town B). Then, in 1980, town B's population was $\frac{40}{160} = \frac{1}{4} = \mathbf{25\%}$ of town A's. Choice **A** is correct.

Since $a\%$ of b is $\dfrac{a}{100}(b) = \dfrac{ab}{100}$, and $b\%$ of a is $\dfrac{b}{100}(a) = \dfrac{ba}{100}$, KEY FACT C4 follows.

Key Fact C4

For any positive numbers a and b: $a\%$ of $b = b\%$ of a.

Percent Increase and Decrease

Helpful Hint
Be sure to learn
KEY FACT C5. It
is very important.

Key Fact C5

The *percent increase* of a quantity is $\dfrac{\text{actual increase}}{\text{original amount}} \times 100\%$.

The *percent decrease* of a quantity is $\dfrac{\text{actual decrease}}{\text{original amount}} \times 100\%$.

For example:

• If the price of a DVD player rises from $80 to $100, the actual increase is $20, and the percent increase is

$$\frac{\overset{1}{\cancel{20}}}{\underset{4}{\cancel{80}}} \times 100\% = \frac{1}{4} \times 100\% = 25\%.$$

• If a $100 DVD player is on sale for $80, the actual decrease in price is $20, and the percent decrease is

$$\frac{20}{\underset{1}{\cancel{100}}} \times \overset{1}{\cancel{100}}\% = 20\%.$$

Note that the percent increase in going from 80 to 100 is not the same as the percent decrease in going from 100 to 80.

Key Fact C6

If $a < b$, the percent increase in going from a to b is *always* greater than the percent decrease in going from b to a.

Key Fact C7

• To increase a number by $k\%$, multiply it by $(1 + k\%)$.
• To decrease a number by $k\%$, multiply it by $(1 - k\%)$.

For example:

• The value of a $1600 investment after a 25% increase is $1600(1 + 25\%) = \$1600(1.25) = \$2000$.
• If the investment then loses 25% of its value, it is worth $2000(1 - 25\%) = \$2000(.75) = \$1500$.

Note that, after a 25% increase followed by a 25% decrease, the value is $1500, $100 less than the original amount.

EXAMPLE 4

From 2003 to 2004, the number of applicants to a college increased 15% to 5060. How many applicants were there in 2003?

(A) 759
(B) 4301
(C) 4400
(D) 5819
(E) 5953

Solution. The number of applicants in 2003 was 5060 ÷ 1.15 = **4400 (C)**.

<u>Note</u>: Some students find percent problems like Example 4 to be harder than other types. Now, you should be able to solve them correctly. If, however, you get stuck on a problem like this on the SAT, you still should answer it. In Example 4, since the number of applicants increased from 2003 to 2004, the number in 2003 was clearly fewer than 5060, so eliminate D and E. Also, 759 (A) is much too small, leaving only B and C as reasonable choices. Therefore, do not omit the question—guess. This situation, in which some of the choices are absurd, is commonplace on the SAT. (See TACTIC 8.)

> **CAUTION:** Percents over 100%, which come up most often on questions involving percent increases, are confusing for many students. Be sure you understand that 100% of a particular number is that number, 200% of a number is 2 times the number, and 1000% of a number is 10 times the number. For example, if the value of an investment rises from $1000 to $5000, the investment is now worth 5 times, or 500%, as much as it was originally; but there has been only a *400%* increase in value:
>
> $$\frac{\text{actual increase}}{\text{original amount}} \times 100\% = \frac{4000}{1000} \times 100\% = 4 \times 100\% = 400\%.$$

Calculator Shortcut

If a number is the result of increasing another number by $k\%$, then, to find the original number, divide by $(1 + k\%)$. Also, if a number is the result of decreasing another number by $k\%$, then to find the original number, divide it by $(1 - k\%)$.

EXAMPLE 5

The population of a town doubled every 10 years from 1960 to 1990. What was the percent increase in population during this time?

Solution. The population doubled 3 times from, say, 100 to 200 to 400 to 800. Therefore, the population in 1990 was 8 times the population in 1960, but this was an increase of 700 people, or **700%**.

Exercises on Percents

Multiple-Choice Questions

1. Charlie bought a $60 radio on sale at 5% off. How much did he pay, including 5% sales tax?

    (A) $54.15
    (B) $57.00
    (C) $57.75
    (D) $59.85
    (E) $60.00

2. If a is a positive number, 400% of a is what percent of $400a$?

    (A) 0.01
    (B) 0.1
    (C) 1
    (D) 10
    (E) 100

3. What percent of 50 is b?

    (A) $\dfrac{b}{50}$

    (B) $\dfrac{b}{2}$

    (C) $\dfrac{50}{b}$

    (D) $\dfrac{2}{b}$

    (E) $2b$

4. At Harry's Discount Hardware everything is sold for 20% less than the price marked. If Harry buys tool kits for $80, what price should he mark them if he wants to make a 20% profit on his cost?

    (A) $96
    (B) $100
    (C) $112
    (D) $120
    (E) $125

5. 9 is $\dfrac{1}{3}$% of what number?

    (A) 0.03
    (B) .27
    (C) 3
    (D) 300
    (E) 2700

6. Mr. Howard was planning on depositing a certain amount of money each month into a college fund for his children. He then decided not to make any contributions during June and July. To make the same annual contribution that he had originally planned, by what percent should he increase his monthly deposits?

    (A) $16\dfrac{2}{3}$%

    (B) 20%

    (C) 25%

    (D) $33\dfrac{1}{3}$%

    (E) It cannot be determined from the information given.

7. During his second week on the job, Jason earned $110. This represented a 25% increase over his earnings of the previous week. How much did he earn during his first week of work?

    (A) $82.50
    (B) $85.00
    (C) $88.00
    (D) $137.50
    (E) $146.67

8. What is 10% of 20% of 30%?

    (A) 0.006%
    (B) 0.6%
    (C) 6%
    (D) 60%
    (E) 6000%

9. If 1 micron = 10,000 angstroms, then 100 angstroms is what percent of 10 microns?

    (A) 0.0001%
    (B) 0.001%
    (C) 0.01%
    (D) 0.1%
    (E) 1%

10. On a test consisting of 80 questions, Marie answered 75% of the first 60 questions correctly. What percent of the other 20 questions did she need to answer correctly for her grade on the entire exam to be 80%?

    (A) 85%
    (B) 87.5%
    (C) 90%
    (D) 95%
    (E) 100%

Grid-in Questions

11. A jar contains 2000 marbles. If 61.5% of them are red, 27.2% of them are white, and 10% of them are blue, how many are neither red, white, nor blue?

12. If 25 students took an exam and 4 of them failed, what percent of them passed?

13. There are twice as many girls as boys in an English class. If 30% of the girls and 45% of the boys have already handed in their book reports, what percent of the students have not yet handed in their reports?

14. During a sale a clerk was putting a new price tag on each item. On one radio, he accidentally raised the price by 15% instead of lowering the price by 15%. As a result the price on the tag was $45 too high. What was the original price, in dollars, of the radio?

15. If a person has an income of $100,000, what percent of his income does he pay in federal income tax if the tax rate is as given below?

    15% of the first $30,000
    of income,

    28% of the next $30,000
    of income, and

    31% of all income in excess
    of $60,000.

16. The price of a can of soup was increased by 20%. How many cans can be purchased for the amount of money that used to buy 300 cans?

17. An art dealer bought a painting for $1000 and later sold it for $10,000. By what percent did the value of the painting increase?

18. Jar B has 20% more marbles than jar A. What percent of the marbles in jar B have to be moved to jar A, in order that the number of marbles in each jar will be the same?

19. Wendy drew a square. She then erased it and drew a second square whose sides were 3 times the sides of the first square. The area of the second square is k% greater than the area of the first square. What is k?

20. In a large jar full of jelly beans, 30% of them are red, and 40% of the red jelly beans are cherry. If 25% of the non-cherry-flavored red jelly beans are raspberry, what percent of all the jelly beans are either cherry or raspberry?

Answer Key

1. **D**
2. **C**
3. **E**
4. **D**
5. **E**
6. **B**
7. **C**
8. **B**
9. **D**
10. **D**

11. 26

12. 84

13. 65

14. 150

15. 25.3

16. 250

17. 900

18. 8.33 or 25/3

19. 800

20. 16.5

Answer Explanations

1. D. Since 5% of 60 is 3, Charlie saved $3, and thus paid $57 for the radio. He then had to pay 5% sales tax on the $57: $.05 \times 57 = 2.85$, so the total cost was $57 + $2.85 = $59.85.

2. C. 400% of $a = 4a$, which is 1% of $400a$.

3. E. If b is x% of 50, then

$$\frac{b}{50} = \frac{x}{100} \Rightarrow 100b = 50x \Rightarrow x = 2b.$$

4. D. Since 20% of 80 is 16, Harry wants to get $96 for each tool kit he sells. What price should the tool kits be marked so that, after a 20% discount, the customer will pay $96? If x represents the marked price, then

$$0.80x = \$96 \Rightarrow x = \$96 \div .80 = \$120.$$

5. E. $9 = \dfrac{\frac{1}{3}}{100}x = \dfrac{1}{300}x \Rightarrow x = 9 \times 300 = 2700.$

6. B. Assume that Mr. Howard was going to contribute $100 each month, for an annual total of $1200. Having decided not to contribute for 2 months, he would have to contribute the $1200 in 10 monthly deposits of $120 each. This is an increase of $20, and a percent increase of

$$\frac{\text{actual increase}}{\text{original amount}} = \frac{20}{100} = 20\%.$$

7. C. To find Jason's earnings during his first week, divide his earnings of the second week by 1.25: $110 \div 1.25 = $88.
   **If you let x represent Jason's earnings during the first week, then

$$x + 0.25x = 110 \Rightarrow 1.25x = 110,$$

and so, as above, $x = 110 \div 1.25 = 88.$

8. B. 10% of 20% of 30% = $.10 \times .20 \times .30 = 0.006 = 0.6\%.$

9. D. 1 micron = 10,000 angstroms $\Rightarrow$ 10 microns = 100,000 angstroms; then, dividing both sides by 1000 gives

$$100 \text{ angstroms} = \frac{1}{1000} (10 \text{ microns}); \text{ and}$$

$$\frac{1}{1000} = 0.001 = 0.1\%.$$

10. D. To earn 80% on the entire exam, Marie needs to correctly answer 64 questions (80% of 80). So far, she has answered 45 questions correctly (75% of 60). Therefore, on the last 20 questions she needs $64 - 45 = 19$ correct

answers; and $\dfrac{19}{20} = 95\%.$

11. (26) Since $61.5 + 27.2 + 10 = 98.7$, then 98.7% of the marbles are red, white, or blue, and the other $100\% - 98.7\% = 1.3\%$ are some other colors. Therefore:

$$1.3\% \text{ of } 2000 = 0.013 \times 2000 = 26.$$

12. (84) If 4 of the 25 students failed, then the other 21 students passed, and $\dfrac{21}{25} = 0.84 = 84\%.$

13. (65) Assume that there are 100 boys and 200 girls in the class. Then, 45 boys (45% of 100) and 60 girls (30% of 200) have handed in their reports. Then, 105 of the 300 students have handed in the reports, and $300 - 105 = 195$ have not. What percent of 300 is 195?

$$\frac{195}{300} = 0.65 = 65\%.$$

14. (150) If p represents the original price, the radio was priced at $1.15p$ instead of $.85p$. Since this was a $45 difference:

$$45 = 1.15p - .85p = 0.30p \Rightarrow$$
$$p = 45 \div .30 = 150.$$

15. (25.3) A person with a $100,000 income would pay 15% of $30,000 plus 28% of $30,000 plus 31% of $40,000:

$$(.15 \times 30,000) + (.28 \times 30,000) +$$
$$(.31 \times 40,000) = 4,500 + 8,400 + 12,400 = 25,300$$

and 25,300 is 25.3% of 100,000.

16. (250) Assume that a can of soup used to cost $1 and that it now costs $1.20 (20% more). Then 300 cans of soup used to cost $300. How many cans costing $1.20 each can be bought for $300?

$$300 \div 1.20 = 250.$$

17. (900) The increase in the value of the painting was $9000, and

$$\text{percent increase} = \frac{\text{actual increase}}{\text{original cost}} \times 100\% =$$

$$\frac{9000}{1000} \times 100\% = 900\%.$$

18. $\left(8.33 \text{ or } \dfrac{25}{3}\right)$ Assume that there are 100 marbles in jar A and 120 in jar B. You may already see that, if 10 marbles are moved, each jar will contain 110. If not, let x be the number of marbles to be moved, and solve the equation:

$$120 - x = 100 + x \Rightarrow 20 = 2x \Rightarrow x = 10.$$

Finally, 10 is what percent of 120?

$$\frac{10}{120} = \frac{1}{12} = 8\frac{1}{3}\%.$$

19. (800) Assume that the sides of the first square were 1 inch long, so that the area was 1 square inch. Then, the sides of the second square were 3 inches long, and its area was 9 square inches, an increase of 8 square inches or 800%.

20. (16.5) Since 40% of the red jelly beans are cherry, 60% of the red jelly beans are not cherry. Also, 25% of 60% is 15%, so 15% of the red jelly beans are raspberry and 40% are cherry, for a total of 55%. Therefore, the raspberry and cherry jelly beans constitute 55% of the 30% of the jelly beans that are red. Finally, 55% of 30% is 16.5%.

9-D Ratios and Proportions

A ***ratio*** is a fraction that compares two quantities that are measured in the *same* units. One quantity is the numerator of the fraction, and the other quantity is the denominator.

For example, if there are 4 boys and 16 girls on the debate team, the ratio of the number of boys to the number of girls on the team is 4 to 16, or $\frac{4}{16}$, often written as 4:16. Since a ratio is a fraction, it can be reduced or converted to a decimal or a percent. The following are different ways to express the same ratio:

$$4 \text{ to } 16, \quad 4{:}16, \quad \frac{4}{16} \qquad\qquad 2 \text{ to } 8, \quad 2{:}8, \quad \frac{2}{8}$$

$$1 \text{ to } 4, \quad 1{:}4, \quad \frac{1}{4} \qquad\qquad 0.25, \quad 25\%$$

> **CAUTION:** Saying that the ratio of boys to girls on the team is 1:4 does *not* mean that $\frac{1}{4}$ of the team members are boys. It means that, for each boy on the team there are 4 girls, so, of every 5 members of the team, 4 are girls and 1 is a boy. Boys, therefore, make up $\frac{1}{5}$ of the team, and girls $\frac{4}{5}$.

Helpful Hint
Remember that ratios can *always* be written as fractions.

Key Fact D1

If a set of objects is divided into two groups in the ratio of $a{:}b$, then the first group contains $\frac{a}{a+b}$ of the objects and the second group contains $\frac{b}{a+b}$ of the objects.

EXAMPLE 1

Last year, the ratio of the number of math tests John passed to the number of math tests he failed was 7:3. What percent of his math tests did John pass?

Solution. John passed $\dfrac{7}{7+3} = \dfrac{7}{10}$ = **70%** of his math tests.

EXAMPLE 2

If 45% of the students at a college are male, what is the ratio of male students to female students?

Reminder: In problems involving percents, the best number to use is 100.

Solution. Assume that there are 100 students. Then, 45 of them are male, and 55 of them (100 – 45) are female.

The ratio of males to females is $\dfrac{45}{55} = \dfrac{9}{11}$.

If we know how many boys and girls there are in a club, then, clearly, we know not only the ratio of boys to girls, but also several other ratios. For example, if the club has 7 boys and 3 girls, the ratio of boys to girls is $\frac{7}{3}$, the ratio of girls to boys is $\frac{3}{7}$, the ratio of boys to members is $\frac{7}{10}$, the ratio of members to girls is $\frac{10}{3}$, and so on.

However, if we know a ratio, we *cannot* determine from that fact alone how many objects there are. For example, if a jar contains only red and blue marbles, and if the ratio of red marbles to blue marbles is 3:5, there *may be* 3 red marbles and 5 blue marbles, but *not necessarily*. There may be 300 red marbles and 500 blue ones, since the ratio 300:500 reduces to 3:5. In the same way, all of the following are possibilities for the distribution of the marbles:

Red	6	12	33	51	150	3000	*3x*
Blue	10	20	55	85	250	5000	*5x*

The important thing to observe is that the number of red marbles can be *any* multiple of 3, as long as the number of blue marbles is the *same* multiple of 5.

Key Fact D2

If two numbers are in the ratio of *a:b*, then, for some number *x*, the first number is *ax* and the second number is *bx*. If the ratio is in lowest terms, and if the quantities must be integers, then *x* is also an integer.

TACTIC

In any ratio problem, write the letter *x* after each number and use some given information to solve for *x*.

EXAMPLE 3

If the ratio of boys to girls at a school picnic is 5:3, which of the following CANNOT be the number of children at the picnic?

(A) 24
(B) 40
(C) 96
(D) 150
(E) 720

Solution. If 5*x* and 3*x* are the number of boys and the number of girls, respectively, at the picnic, then the number of children present is 5*x* + 3*x* = 8*x*. Therefore, the number of children must be a multiple of 8. Only **150 (D)** is not divisible by 8.

Note: Assume that the ratio of the number of pounds of cole slaw to the number of pounds of potato salad consumed at the school picnic was 5:3. Then, it is possible that a total of exactly 150 pounds of these foods was eaten: 93.75 pounds of cole slaw and 56.25 pounds of potato salad. In Example 3, however, 150 isn't a possible answer because there has to be a *whole number* of boys and girls.

EXAMPLE 4

The measures of the two acute angles of a right triangle are in the ratio of 5:13. What is the measure of the larger acute angle?

Solution. Let the measure of the smaller angle be 5*x* and the measure of the larger angle be 13*x*. Since the sum of the measures of the two acute angles of a right triangle is 90° (KEY FACT J3):

$$5x + 13x = 90 \Rightarrow 18x = 90 \Rightarrow x = 5.$$

Therefore, the measure of the larger angle is $13 \times 5 =$ **65°**.

Ratios can be extended to three or four or more terms. For example, we can say that the ratio of freshmen to sophomores to juniors to seniors in the school band is 6:8:5:8, which means that for every 6 freshmen in the band there are 8 sophomores, 5 juniors, and 8 seniors.

Note: TACTIC D1 applies to extended ratios, as well.

EXAMPLE 5

Frannie's Frozen Yogurt sells three flavors: vanilla, chocolate, and coffee. One day, Frannie sold 240 cones, and the ratio of vanilla to chocolate to coffee was 8:17:15. How many chocolate cones were sold that day?

Solution. Let $8x$, $17x$, and $15x$ be the number of vanilla, of chocolate, and of coffee cones sold, respectively. Then:

$$8x + 17x + 15x = 240 \Rightarrow 40x = 240 \Rightarrow x = 6.$$

The number of chocolate cones sold was $17 \times 6 =$ **102**.

Key Fact D3

KEY FACT D1 applies to extended ratios, as well. If a set of objects is divided into three groups in the ratio $a{:}b{:}c$, then the first group contains $\dfrac{a}{a+b+c}$ of the objects, the second $\dfrac{b}{a+b+c}$, and the third $\dfrac{c}{a+b+c}$.

EXAMPLE 6

If the ratio of vanilla to chocolate to coffee cones sold at Frannie's was 8:17:15 on a particular day, what percent of the cones sold were chocolate?

Solution. Chocolate cones made up $\dfrac{17}{8+17+15} = \dfrac{17}{40} =$ **42.5%** of the total.

A jar contains a number of red (R), white (W), and blue (B) marbles. Suppose that R:W = 2:3 and W:B = 3:5. Then, for every 2 red marbles, there are 3 white ones, and for those 3 white ones, there are 5 blue ones. Then, R:B = 2:5, and we can form the extended ratio R:W:B = 2:3:5.

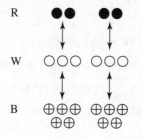

If the ratios were R:W = 2:3 and W:B = 4:5, however, we couldn't combine them as easily. From the diagram below, we see that for every 8 reds there are 15 blues, so R:B = 8:15.

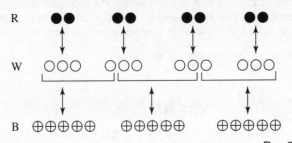

To see this without drawing a picture, we write the ratios as fractions: $\dfrac{R}{W} = \dfrac{2}{3}$ and $\dfrac{W}{B} = \dfrac{4}{5}$.

Then, we multiply the fractions:

$$\frac{R}{\cancel{W}} \times \frac{\cancel{W}}{B} = \frac{2}{3} \times \frac{4}{5} = \frac{8}{15}, \quad \text{so} \quad \frac{R}{B} = \frac{8}{15}.$$

Not only does this give us R:B = 8:15, but also, if we multiply both W numbers, $3 \times 4 = 12$, we can write the extended ratio: R:W:B = 8:12:15.

EXAMPLE 7

Jar A and jar B each contain 70 marbles, all of which are red, white, or blue.

In jar A, R:W = 2:3 and W:B = 3:5.
In jar B, R:W = 2:3 and W:B = 4:5.

What is the total number of white marbles in the two jars?

Solution. From the discussion immediately preceding this example, in jar A the extended ratio R:W:B is 2:3:5, which implies that the white marbles constitute $\dfrac{3}{2+3+5} = \dfrac{3}{10}$ of the total:

$$\frac{3}{\cancel{10}} \times \cancel{70} = 21.$$

In jar B the extended ratio R:W:B is 8:12:15, so the white marbles are $\dfrac{12}{8+12+15} = \dfrac{12}{35}$ of the total:

$$\frac{12}{\cancel{35}} \times \cancel{70}^{2} = 24.$$

Finally, there is a total of 21 + 24 = **45** white marbles.

A **proportion** is an equation that states that two ratios are equivalent. Since ratios are just fractions, any equation, such as $\dfrac{4}{6} = \dfrac{10}{15}$, in which each side is a single fraction is a proportion. Usually the proportions encountered on the SAT involve one or more variables.

TACTIC

D2

Solve proportions by cross-multiplying: if $\dfrac{a}{b} = \dfrac{c}{d}$, then $ad = bc$.

Several problems on the SAT can be solved by setting up proportions. These problems are usually quite easy and are among the first few in a section.

EXAMPLE 8

If $\dfrac{3}{7} = \dfrac{x}{84}$, what is the value of x?

Solution. Cross-multiply: $3(84) = 7x \Rightarrow 252 = 7x \Rightarrow x = \mathbf{36}$.

EXAMPLE 9

If $\dfrac{x+2}{17} = \dfrac{x}{16}$, what is the value of $\dfrac{x+6}{19}$?

Solution. Cross-multiply: $16(x + 2) = 17x \Rightarrow 16x + 32 = 17x \Rightarrow x = 32$, so

$$\frac{x+6}{19} = \frac{32+6}{19} = \frac{38}{19} = \mathbf{2}.$$

EXAMPLE 10

A state law requires that on any field trip the ratio of the number of chaperones to the number of students must be at least 1:12. If 100 students are going on a field trip, what is the minimum number of chaperones required?

Solution. Let x represent the number of chaperones required, and set up a proportion:

$$\frac{\text{number of chaperones}}{\text{number of students}} = \frac{1}{12} = \frac{x}{100}.$$

Cross-multiply: $100 = 12x \Rightarrow x = 8.33$. This, of course, is *not* the answer since, clearly, the number of chaperones must be a whole number. Since x is greater than 8, you know that 8 chaperones will not be enough. The answer is **9**.

A *rate* is a fraction that compares two quantities that are measured in *different* units. The word *per* often appears in rate problems: miles per hour, dollars per week, cents per ounce, children per classroom, and so on.

TACTIC

D3

Set rate problems up just like ratio problems. Then, solve the proportions by cross-multiplying.

EXAMPLE 11

Sharon read 24 pages of her book in 15 minutes. At this rate, how many pages can she read in 40 minutes?

Solution. Handle this rate problem exactly like a ratio problem. Set up a proportion and cross-multiply:

$$\frac{\text{pages}}{\text{minutes}} = \frac{24}{15} = \frac{x}{40} \Rightarrow 15x = 40 \times 24 = 960 \Rightarrow x = \mathbf{64}.$$

When the denominator in the given rate is 1 unit (1 minute, 1 mile, 1 dollar), the problem can be solved by a single division or multiplication. Consider Examples 12 and 13.

EXAMPLE 12

If Jack types at the rate of 35 words per minute, how long will he take to type 987 words?

EXAMPLE 13

If Jack types at the rate of 35 words per minute, how many words can he type in 85 minutes?

To solve, set up the proportions and cross-multiply.

Solution 12. $\dfrac{\text{words typed}}{\text{minutes}} = \dfrac{35}{1} = \dfrac{987}{x} \Rightarrow 35x = 987 \Rightarrow x = \dfrac{987}{35} = \textbf{28.2}$ minutes.

Solution 13. $\dfrac{\text{words typed}}{\text{minutes}} = \dfrac{35}{1} = \dfrac{x}{85} \Rightarrow x = 35 \times 85 = \textbf{2975}$ words.

Notice that, in Example 12, all that was done was to divide 987 by 35, and in Example 13, 35 was multiplied by 85. If you realize that, you don't have to introduce *x* and set up a proportion. You must know, however, whether to multiply or divide. If you're not absolutely positive which is correct, write the proportion; then you can't go wrong.

CAUTION: In rate problems it is essential that the units in both fractions be the same.

EXAMPLE 14

If three apples cost 50¢, how many apples can you buy for $20?

Solution. You have to set up a proportion, but it is *not* $\dfrac{3}{50} = \dfrac{x}{20}$. In the first fraction, the

denominator represents *cents*, whereas in the second fraction, the denominator represents *dollars*. The units must be the same. You can change 50 cents to 0.5 dollar, or you can change 20 dollars to 2000 cents:

$$\frac{3}{50} = \frac{x}{2000} \Rightarrow 50x = 6000 \Rightarrow x = \textbf{120} \text{ apples.}$$

On the SAT, many rate problems involve only variables. These problems are handled in exactly the same way.

EXAMPLE 15

If *a* apples cost *c* cents, how many apples can be bought for *d* dollars?

(A) $100acd$

(B) $\dfrac{100d}{ac}$

(C) $\dfrac{ad}{100c}$

(D) $\dfrac{c}{100ad}$

(E) $\dfrac{100ad}{c}$

Solution. First change *d* dollars to 100*d* cents; then set up the proportion and cross-multiply:

$$\frac{\text{apples}}{\text{cents}} = \frac{a}{c} = \frac{x}{100d} \Rightarrow 100ad = cx \Rightarrow x = \frac{100ad}{c} \textbf{ (E)}.$$

Every SAT has one or two questions like Example 15, and most students find them very difficult. Be sure to do all the exercises at the end of this section, but also see TACTIC 6 in Chapter 8 for another way to handle these problems.

Notice that in rate problems, as one quantity increases or decreases, so does the other. If you are driving at 45 miles per hour, the more hours you drive, the further you go; if you drive fewer miles, less time is required.

Rate problems are examples of ***direct variation.*** We say that one variable is ***directly proportional*** to a second variable if their quotient is a constant. If *y* is directly proportional to *x*, there is a constant *k*, such that $\frac{y}{x} = k$.

When two quantities vary directly, as one quantity increases (or decreases), so does the other. The constant is the rate of increase or decrease. In Example 11, the number of pages Sharon reads varies directly with the number of minutes she reads. Sharon's rate of reading is 1.6 pages per minute.

The quotient $\frac{\text{pages}}{\text{minutes}}$ is constant: $\frac{24}{15} = 1.6$ and $\frac{64}{40} = 1.6$.

EXAMPLE 16

If *p* is directly proportional to *q*, and if *q* = 12 when *p* = 8, then what is the value of *p* when *q* = 15?

Solution. Since *p* and *q* are directly proportional, the quoteint $\frac{p}{q}$ is a constant, so $\frac{8}{12} = \frac{p}{15}$.

Cross-multiply:

$$12p = 8 \times 15 = 120 \Rightarrow p = \textbf{10}.$$

In some problems, however, as one quantity increases, the other decreases. These problems *cannot* be solved by setting up a proportion. Consider Examples 17 and 18, which look similar but must be handled differently.

EXAMPLE 17

A hospital needs 150 pills to treat 6 patients for a week. How many pills does it need to treat 10 patients for a week?

EXAMPLE 18

A hospital has enough pills on hand to treat 10 patients for 14 days. How long will the pills last if there are 35 patients?

Solution 17. Example 16 is a standard rate problem. The more patients there are, the more pills are needed.

The *ratio* or *quotient* remains constant:

$$\frac{150}{6} = \frac{x}{10} \Rightarrow 6x = 1500 = x = \textbf{250}.$$

In Example 18, the situation is different. With more patients, the supply of pills will last for a shorter period of time; if there were fewer patients, the supply would last longer. It is not the ratio that remains constant; it is the *product*.

Solution 18. We are told that the hospital has enough pills to last for $10 \times 14 = 140$ patient-days:

$$140 \text{ patient-days} = (10 \text{ patients}) \times (14 \text{ days}).$$
$$140 \text{ patient-days} = (20 \text{ patients}) \times (7 \text{ days}).$$
$$140 \text{ patient-days} = (70 \text{ patients}) \times (2 \text{ days}).$$

To solve Example 18, write:

$$140 \text{ patient-days} = (35 \text{ patients}) \times (d \text{ days}) \Rightarrow d = \frac{140}{35} = \mathbf{4}.$$

Helpful Hint
Be sure you understand the definitions of direct variation and indirect variation.

Problems like this one are examples of ***inverse variation***. We say that one variable is ***inversely proportional*** to a second variable if their product is a constant. If y is inversely proportional to x, there is a constant k such that $xy = k$.

EXAMPLE 19

If p is inversely proportional to q^2, and if $q = 2$ when $p = 6$, what is the value of p when $q = 6$?

Solution. Since p and q^2 are inversely proportional, the product pq^2 is a constant, so

$$6 \times 2^2 = p \times 6^2 \Rightarrow 24 = 36p \Rightarrow p = \frac{24}{36} = \frac{\mathbf{2}}{\mathbf{3}}.$$

In Example 18, the number of patients varies inversely with the number of days that the supply of pills lasts. The product, patients $\times$ days, is constant. Notice that, as the number of patients increases from 10 to 20 to 70, the number of days the supply of pills lasts decreases, from 14 to 7 to 2.

EXAMPLE 20

If 15 workers can paint a certain number of houses in 24 days, how many days will 40 workers take, working at the same rate, to do the same job?

Solution. Clearly, the more workers there are, the less time will be required. This is an example of inverse variation, so multiply. The job takes:

$$(15 \text{ workers}) \times (24 \text{ days}) = 360 \text{ worker-days}.$$

Then $(40 \text{ workers}) \times (d \text{ days}) = 360$ worker-days.

$$40d = 360 \Rightarrow d = \mathbf{9}.$$

This job will take **9** days.

Exercises on Ratios and Proportions

Multiple-Choice Questions

1. If $\frac{2}{3}$ of the workers in an office are nonsmokers, what is the ratio of smokers to nonsmokers?

   (A) 2:5
   (B) 1:2
   (C) 3:5
   (D) 2:3
   (E) 3:2

2. If 80% of the applicants to a program were rejected, what is the ratio of the number accepted to the number rejected?

   (A) $\frac{1}{5}$

   (B) $\frac{1}{4}$

   (C) $\frac{2}{5}$

   (D) $\frac{4}{5}$

   (E) $\frac{4}{1}$

3. The measures of the three angles in a triangle are in the ratio 1:1:2. Which of the following *must* be true?

   I. The triangle is isosceles.
   II. The triangle is a right triangle.
   III. The triangle is equilateral.

   (A) None
   (B) I only
   (C) II only
   (D) I and II only
   (E) I and III only

4. What is the ratio of the circumference of a circle to its radius?

   (A) 1

   (B) $\frac{\pi}{2}$

   (C) $\sqrt{\pi}$

   (D) π

   (E) 2π

5. If $a{:}b = 3{:}5$ and $a{:}c = 5{:}7$, what is the value of $b{:}c$?

   (A) 3:7
   (B) 21:35
   (C) 21:25
   (D) 25:21
   (E) 7:3

6. In the diagram below, $b{:}a = 7{:}2$. What is $b - a$?

   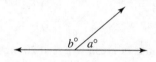

   (A) 20
   (B) 70
   (C) 100
   (D) 110
   (E) 160

7. If x is a positive number and $\frac{x}{3} = \frac{12}{x}$, then $x =$

   (A) 3
   (B) 4
   (C) 6
   (D) 12
   (E) 36

8. A snail can move i inches in m minutes. At this rate, how many feet can it move in h hours?

   (A) $\dfrac{5hi}{m}$

   (B) $\dfrac{60hi}{m}$

   (C) $\dfrac{hi}{12m}$

   (D) $\dfrac{5m}{hi}$

   (E) $5him$

9. Barbra can grade t tests in $\dfrac{1}{x}$ hours. At this rate, how many tests can she grade in x hours?

   (A) tx

   (B) tx^2

   (C) $\dfrac{1}{t}$

   (D) $\dfrac{x}{t}$

   (E) $\dfrac{1}{tx}$

10. If 500 pounds of mush will feed 20 pigs for a week, for how many days will 200 pounds of mush feed 14 pigs?

    (A) 4
    (B) 5
    (C) 6
    (D) 7
    (E) 8

Grid-in Questions

11. John can read 72 pages per hour. At this rate, how many pages can he read in 72 minutes?

12. If $3a = 2b$ and $3b = 5c$, what is the ratio of a to c?

13. If $\dfrac{3x-1}{25} = \dfrac{x+5}{11}$, what is the value of x?

14. Three associates agreed to split the profit of an investment in the ratio of 2:5:8. If the profit was $3000, what is the difference between the largest share and the smallest?

15. If y is inversely proportional to x, and $y = 8$ when $x = 4$, what is the value of y when $x = 5$?

Answer Key

1. **B**	3. **D**	5. **D**	7. **C**	9. **B**
2. **B**	4. **E**	6. **C**	8. **A**	10. **A**

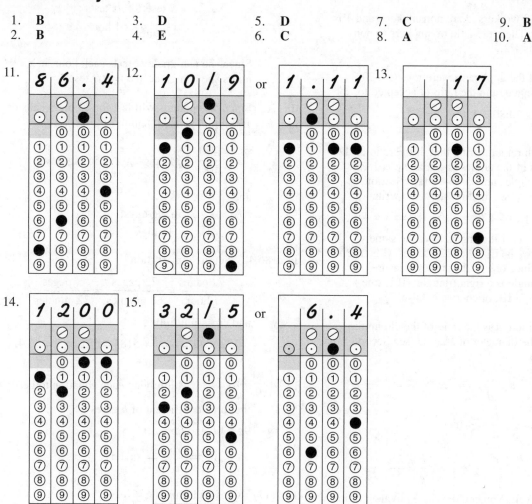

Answer Explanations

1. **B.** Of every 3 workers, 2 are nonsmokers, and 1 is a smoker. Then, the ratio of smokers to non-smokers is 1:2.

2. **B.** If 80% of the applicants were rejected, 20% were accepted, and the ratio of accepted to rejected is $20:80 = 1:4 = \dfrac{1}{4}$.

3. **D.** It is worth remembering that, if the ratio of the measures of the angles of a triangle is 1:1:2, then the angles are 45-45-90 (see Section 9-J). Otherwise, the first step is to write

   $$x + x + 2x = 180 \Rightarrow 4x = 180 \Rightarrow x = 45.$$

   - Since two of the angles have the same measure, the triangle is isosceles. (I is true.)
   - Also, since one of the angles measures 90°, the triangle is a right triangle. (II is true.)
   - Statement III, of course, is false.

4. **E.** By definition, π is the ratio of the circumference to the diameter of a circle (see Section 12-L), so

   $$\pi = \frac{C}{d} = \frac{C}{2r} \Rightarrow 2\pi = \frac{C}{r}.$$

5. **D.** Since $\dfrac{a}{b} = \dfrac{3}{5}$, $\dfrac{b}{a} = \dfrac{5}{3}$, then

   $$\frac{b}{\cancel{a}} \times \frac{\cancel{a}}{c} = \frac{5}{3} \times \frac{5}{7} \Rightarrow \frac{b}{c} = \frac{25}{21}.$$

   Alternatively, you could write equivalent ratios with the same value for a:

   $a:b = 3:5 = 15:25$ and $a:c = 5:7 = 15:21$.

   Then, when $a = 15$, $b = 25$ and $c = 21$.

6. **C.** Let $b = 7x$ and $a = 2x$. Then

   $$7x + 2x = 180 \Rightarrow 9x = 180 \Rightarrow x = 20 \Rightarrow$$
   $$b = 140 \text{ and } a = 40 \Rightarrow$$
   $$b - a = 140 - 40 = 100.$$

7. **C.** To solve a proportion, cross-multiply:

   $$\frac{x}{3} = \frac{12}{x} \Rightarrow x^2 = 36 \Rightarrow x = 6.$$

8. **A.** Set up the proportion, keeping track of units:

   $$\frac{x \text{ feet}}{h \text{ hours}} = \frac{12x \text{ inches}}{60h \text{ minutes}} = \frac{i \text{ inches}}{m \text{ minutes}} \Rightarrow$$
   $$\frac{x}{5h} = \frac{i}{m} \Rightarrow x = \frac{5hi}{m}.$$

9. **B.** Barbra grades at the rate of

   $$\frac{t \text{ tests}}{\dfrac{1}{x} \text{ hours}} = \frac{tx \text{ tests}}{1 \text{ hour}}.$$

   Since she can grade tx tests each hour, in x hours she can grade $x(tx) = tx^2$ tests.

10. **A.** Since 500 pounds will last for 20 pig-weeks or 140 pig-days, 200 pounds will last for

    $$\frac{200}{\cancel{500}} \times 140 \text{ pig-days} = 56 \text{ pig-days},$$

    and

    $$\frac{56 \text{ pig-days}}{14 \text{ pigs}} = 4 \text{ days}.$$

11. **(86.4)** Set up a proportion:

    $$\frac{72 \text{ pages}}{1 \text{ hour}} = \frac{72 \text{ pages}}{60 \text{ minutes}} = \frac{x \text{ pages}}{72 \text{ minutes}}$$

    and cross-multiply:

    $$72 \times 72 = 60x \Rightarrow 5184 = 60x \Rightarrow x = 86.4.$$

12. $\left(\dfrac{10}{9} \text{ or } 1.11 \right)$ Multiplying each equation to get the same coefficient of b gives

    $9a = 6b$ and $6b = 10c \Rightarrow$

    $$9a = 10c \Rightarrow \frac{a}{c} = \frac{10}{9} \text{ or } 1.11.$$

13. **(17)** Cross-multiplying gives

    $$11(3x - 1) = 25(x + 5) \Rightarrow$$
    $$33x - 11 = 25x + 125 \Rightarrow$$
    $$8x = 136 \Rightarrow x = 17.$$

14. **(1200)** The shares are $2x$, $5x$, and $8x$, and their sum is 3000:

    $$2x + 5x + 8x = 3000 \Rightarrow 15x = 3000 \Rightarrow x = 200,$$

    so $8x - 2x = 6x = 1200$.

15. $\left(\dfrac{32}{5} \text{ or } 6.4 \right)$ If y is inversely proportional to x, there is a constant k such that $xy = k$, so $k = (8)(4) = 32$. Thus

    $$32 = 5y, \text{ and } y = \frac{32}{5} \text{ or } 6.4.$$

9-E Averages

The *average* of a set of *n* numbers is the sum of those numbers divided by *n*:

$$\text{average} = \frac{\text{sum of the } n \text{ numbers}}{n}$$

or simply

$$A = \frac{\text{sum}}{n}.$$

If you took three math tests so far this year and your grades were 80, 90, and 76, to calculate your average, you would add the three grades and divide by 3:

$$\frac{80 + 90 + 76}{3} = \frac{246}{3} = 82.$$

The technical name for average is "arithmetic mean," and on the SAT those words always appear in parentheses—for example, "What is the average (arithmetic mean) of 80, 90, and 76?"

Very often on the SAT, you are not asked to find an average; rather, you are given the average of a set of numbers and asked to provide some other information. The key to solving all of these problems is to first find the sum of the numbers. Since $A = \frac{\text{sum}}{n}$, multiplying both sides by *n* yields this equation: sum = *nA*.

> **Helpful Hint**
> On the SAT you can ignore the words "arithmetic mean." They simply mean "average."

TACTIC

E1

If you know the average, *A*, of a set of *n* numbers, multiply *A* by *n* to get their sum.

> **Helpful Hint**
> Most SAT problems involving averages can be solved using TACTIC 1.

EXAMPLE 1

One day a delivery-truck driver picked up 25 packages whose average (arithmetic mean) weight was 14.2 pounds. What was the total weight, in pounds, of all the packages?

 Solution. Use TACTIC E1: 25 × 14.2 = **355**.

NOTE: You do not know how much any individual package weighed or how many packages weighed more or less than 14.2 pounds. All you know is the total weight.

EXAMPLE 2

John took five English tests during the first marking period, and his average (arithmetic mean) was 85. If his average after the first three tests was 83, what was the average of his fourth and fifth tests?

(A) 83
(B) 85
(C) 87
(D) 88
(E) 90

 Solution.

• Use TACTIC E1: On his five tests John earned 5 × 85 = 425 points.
• Use TACTIC E1 again: On the first three tests he earned 3 × 83 = 249 points.

• Subtract: On his last two tests he earned 425 − 249 = 176 points.

• Calculate his average on his last two tests: $\dfrac{176}{2}$ = **88 (D)**.

NOTE: You cannot determine John's grade on even one of the five tests.

Key Fact E1

If all the numbers in a set are the same, then that number is the average.

Key Fact E2

If the numbers in a set are not all the same, then the average must be greater than the smallest number and less than the largest number. Equivalently, at least one of the numbers is less than the average and at least one is greater.

If Mary's test grades are 85, 85, 85, and 85, her average is 85. If Bob's test grades are 76, 83, 88, and 88, his average must be greater than 76 and less than 88. What can we conclude if, after taking five tests, Ellen's average is 90? We know that she earned exactly 5 × 90 = 450 points, and that either she got 90 on every test or at least one grade was less than 90 and at least one was over 90. Here are a few of the thousands of possibilities for Ellen's grades:

(a) 90, 90, 90, 90, 90
(b) 80, 90, 90, 90, 100
(c) 83, 84, 87, 97, 99
(d) 77, 88, 93, 95, 97
(e) 50, 100, 100, 100, 100

Key Fact E3

Assume that the average of a set of numbers is A. If a number, x, is added to the set and a new average is calculated, then the new average will be less than, equal to, or greater than A, depending on whether x is less than, equal to, or greater than A, respectively.

EXAMPLE 3

Let n be an integer greater than 1, let a = the average (arithmetic mean) of the integers from 1 to n, and let b = the average of the integers from 0 to n. Which of the following could be true?

I. $a = b$

II. $a < b$

III. $a > b$

(A) I only
(B) II only
(C) III only
(D) II and III only
(E) I, II, and III

Solution 1. Since a is the average of the integers from 1 to n, a is surely greater than 1. You are told that b is the average of those same n numbers and 0. Since the extra number, 0, is less than a, b must be less than a. Only Statement **III (C)** is true.

Solution 2. Clearly, the sum of the $n + 1$ integers from 0 to n is the same as the sum of the n integers from 1 to n. Since that sum is positive, dividing by $n + 1$ yields a smaller quotient than dividing by n (KEY FACT B4).

If in Example 3 $n = 12$, then you could calculate each average as follows:

$$0 + 1 + 2 + 3 + 4 + 5 + \mathbf{6} + 7 + 8 + 9 + 10 + 11 + 12 = 78 \text{ and } \frac{78}{13} = 6;$$

$$1 + 2 + 3 + 4 + 5 + \mathbf{6} + \mathbf{7} + 8 + 9 + 10 + 11 + 12 = 78 \text{ and } \frac{78}{12} = 6.5.$$

Notice that the average of the 13 *consecutive* integers 0, 1,...,12 is the *middle integer*, **6**, and the average of the 12 *consecutive* integers 1, 2,...,12 is the *average of the two middle integers*, **6** and **7**. This is a special case of KEY FACT E4.

Key Fact E4

Whenever n numbers form an arithmetic sequence (one in which the difference between any two consecutive terms is the same): (i) if n is odd, the average of the numbers is the middle term in the sequence; and (ii) if n is even, the average of the numbers is the average of the two middle terms.

For example, in the arithmetic sequence 6, 9, 12, 15, 18, the average is the middle number, 12; and in the sequence 10, 20, 30, 40, 50, 60, the average is 35, the average of the two middle numbers—30 and 40.

EXAMPLE 4

On Thursday, 20 of the 25 students in a chemistry class took a test, and their average (arithmetic mean) was 80. On Friday, the other 5 students took the test, and their average (arithmetic mean) was 90. What was the average for the entire class?

(A) 80
(B) 82
(C) 84
(D) 85
(E) 88

Solution. The class average is calculated by dividing the sum of all 25 test grades by 25.

- The first 20 students earned a total of: $20 \times 80 = 1600$ points
- The other 5 students earned a total of: $5 \times 90 = 450$ points
- Add: altogether the class earned: $1600 + 450 = 2050$ points

- Calculate the class average: $\dfrac{2050}{25} = 82$ **(B)**.

Helpful Hint

Without doing any calculations, you should immediately realize that, since the grade of 80 is being given more weight than the grade of 90, the average will be closer to 80 than to 90—certainly *less than 85*.

Notice that the answer to Example 4 is *not* 85, which is the average of 80 and 90. The averages of 80 and 90 were earned by different numbers of students, and so the two averages must be given different weights in the calculation. For this reason, 82 is called a ***weighted average***.

Key Fact E5

To calculate the weighted average of a set of numbers, multiply each number in the set by the number of times it appears, add all the products, and divide by the total number of numbers in the set.

The solution to Example 4 should look like this:

$$\frac{20(80)+5(90)}{25}=\frac{1600+450}{25}=\frac{2050}{25}=82.$$

Problems involving *average speed* will be discussed in Section 9-H, but we mention them briefly here because they are closely related to problems on weighted averages.

EXAMPLE 5

For the first 3 hours of her trip, Susan drove at 50 miles per hour. Then, because of construction delays, she drove at only 40 miles per hour for the next 2 hours. What was her average speed, in miles per hour, for the entire trip?

Solution. This is just a weighted average:

$$\frac{3(50)+2(40)}{5}=\frac{150+80}{5}=\frac{230}{5}=\mathbf{46}.$$

Note that in each of the above fractions the numerator is the total distance traveled and the denominator the total time the trip took. This is *always* the way to find an average speed. Consider the following slight variation of Example 5.

EXAMPLE 5A

For the first 100 miles of her trip, Susan drove at 50 miles per hour. Then, because of construction delays, she drove at only 40 miles per hour for the next 120 miles. What was her average speed, in miles per hour, for the entire trip?

Solution. This is not a *weighted* average. Here you immediately know the total distance: 220 miles. To get the total time, find the time for each portion and add: the first 100 miles took 100 ÷ 50 = 2 hours, and the next 120 miles took 120 ÷ 40 = 3 hours. The average speed was $\frac{220}{5}$ = **44** miles per hour.

Notice that in Example 5, since Susan spent more time traveling at 50 than at 40 miles per hour, her average speed was closer to 50; in Example 5a, however, she spent more time driving at 40 than at 50 miles per hour, so her average speed was closer to 40.

Two other terms associated with averages are ***median*** and ***mode***.

• In a set of *n* numbers arranged in increasing order, the ***median*** is the middle number (if *n* is odd), or the average of the two middle numbers (if *n* is even).
• In any set of numbers, the ***mode*** is the number that appears most often.

EXAMPLE 6

During a 10-day period, Olga received the following number of phone calls each day: 2, 3, 9, 3, 5, 7, 7, 10, 7, 6. What is the average (arithmetic mean) of the median and mode of this set of data?

Solution. The first step is to write the data in increasing order: 2, 3, 3, 5, 6, 7, 7, 7, 9, 10.

• The median is 6.5, the average of the middle two numbers.
• The mode is 7, the number that appears more often than any other.
• The average of the median and the mode is $\frac{6.5+7}{2}$ = **6.75**.

Exercises on Averages

Multiple-Choice Questions

1. Justin's average (arithmetic mean) on four tests is 80. What grade does he need on his fifth test to raise his average to 84?

   (A) 82
   (B) 84
   (C) 92
   (D) 96
   (E) 100

2. Judy's average (arithmetic mean) on four tests is 80. Assuming she can earn no more than 100 on any test, what is the least she can earn on her fifth test and still have a chance for an 85 average after seven tests?

   (A) 60
   (B) 70
   (C) 75
   (D) 80
   (E) 85

3. Adam's average (arithmetic mean) on four tests is 80. Which of the following CANNOT be the number of tests on which he earned exactly 80 points?

   (A) 0
   (B) 1
   (C) 2
   (D) 3
   (E) 4

4. If $a + b = 3(c + d)$, which of the following is the average (arithmetic mean) of a, b, c, and d?

   (A) $\dfrac{c+d}{4}$

   (B) $\dfrac{3(c+d)}{8}$

   (C) $\dfrac{c+d}{2}$

   (D) $\dfrac{3(c+d)}{4}$

   (E) $c + d$

5. If the average (arithmetic mean) of $5, 6, 7$, and w is 8, what is the value of w?

   (A) 8
   (B) 12
   (C) 14
   (D) 16
   (E) 24

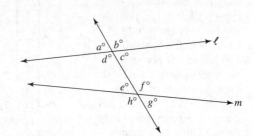

6. In the diagram above, lines ℓ and m are *not* parallel. If A represents the average (arithmetic mean) of the measures of all eight angles, which of the following is true?

   (A) $A = 45°$
   (B) $45° < A < 90°$
   (C) $A = 90°$
   (D) $90° < A < 180°$
   (E) It cannot be determined from the information given.

7. What is the average (arithmetic mean) of 2^{10} and 2^{20}?

   (A) 2^{15}
   (B) $2^5 + 2^{10}$
   (C) $2^9 + 2^{19}$
   (D) 2^{29}
   (E) 30

8. Let M be the median, and m the mode, of the following set of numbers: $10, 70, 20, 40, 70, 90$. What is the average (arithmetic mean) of M and m?

   (A) 50
   (B) 55
   (C) 60
   (D) 62.5
   (E) 65

9. Which of the following is the average (arithmetic mean) of $x^2 - 10, 30 - x^2$, and $6x + 10$?

   (A) $2x + 10$
   (B) $2x + 30$
   (C) $3x + 15$
   (D) $2x^2 + 6x + 30$
   (E) $6x + 10$

Grid-in Questions

10. The average (arithmetic mean)
weight of the students in the
French Club is 150 pounds,
and the average weight of the
students in the Spanish Club is
130 pounds. If no one is a
member of both clubs, if the
average weight of all the
students is 142 pounds, and if
there are 30 members in the
French Club, how many
members are there in the
Spanish Club?

11. If $10a + 10b = 35$, what is the
average (arithmetic mean) of a
and b?

12. What is the average (arithmetic
mean) of the measures of the
five angles in a pentagon?

Answer Key

1.	E	3.	D	5.	C	7.	C	9.	A
2.	C	4.	E	6.	C	8.	D		

10. **20**   11. **1.75** or **7/4**   12. **108**

Answer Explanations

1. **E.** Use TACTIC E1. For Justin's average on five tests to be 84, he needs a total of $5 \times 84 = 420$ points. So far, he has earned $4 \times 80 = 320$ points. Therefore, he needs a grade of 100 points on the fifth test.

2. **C.** Use TACTIC E1. So far, Judy has earned 320 points. She can survive a low grade on test 5 if she gets the maximum possible on both the sixth and seventh tests. Assume she gets two 100's. Then her total for tests 1, 2, 3, 4, 6, and 7 will be 520. For her seven-test average to be 85, she needs a total of $7 \times 85 = 595$ points. Therefore, she needs at least $595 - 520 = 75$ points.

3. **D.** Adam could not have earned exactly 80 on three tests. If he did, his average for those three tests would clearly be 80; and since adding the fourth score didn't change his average, KEY FACT E3 tells us that his fourth score must also be 80. Therefore, it is *not* possible for him to have earned exactly 80 on each of three tests.
   Alternative solution. Could Adam have earned a total of 320 points with:

0 grade of 80?	Easily; for example, 20, 100, 100, 100 or 60, 70, 90, 100.
1 grade of 80?	Lots of ways; 80, 40, 100, 100, for instance.
2 grades of 80?	Yes; 80, 80, 60, 100, for instance.
4 grades of 80?	Sure: 80, 80, 80, 80.
3 grades of 80?	No! If $80 + 80 + 80 + x = 320$, then $x = 80$, as well.

4. **E.** Calculate the average:
   $$\frac{a+b+c+d}{4} = \frac{3(c+d)+c+d}{4} = \frac{3c+3d+c+d}{4} = \frac{4c+4d}{4} = c+d$$

5. **C.** Use TACTIC E1. The sum of the four numbers is $4 \times 8 = 32$. Then
   $$5+6+7+w = 32 \Rightarrow$$
   $$18 + w = 32 \Rightarrow w = 14.$$

6. **C.** $a+b+c+d = 360$ and $w+x+y+z = 360$ (see Section 9-I); so the sum of the measures of all eight angles is $360° + 360° = 720°$, and their average, A, is $720° \div 8 = 90°$.

7. **C.** The average of 2^{10} and 2^{20} is
   $$\frac{2^{10}+2^{20}}{2} = \frac{2^{10}}{2}+\frac{2^{20}}{2} = 2^9 + 2^{19}.$$
   (See Section 9-A if you had trouble with the exponents.)
   Alternative solution. Use your calculator and estimate: 2^{10} is about 1000 and 2^{20} is about 1,000,000. Their average is about 500,000. None of the wrong choices is even close.

8. **D.** Arrange the numbers in increasing order: 10, 20, 40, 70, 70, 90. The median, M, is the average of the middle two numbers: $\frac{40+70}{2} = 55$; the mode, m, is 70, the number that appears most frequently. The average of M and m, therefore, is the average of 55 and 70, which is 62.5.

9. **A.** Find the sum of the three expressions, and divide by 3:
   $$(x^2 - 10) + (30 - x^2) + (6x + 10) = 6x + 30$$
   and $\dfrac{6x+30}{3} = 2x + 10$.

   Alternative solution. If you get bogged down in the algebra, use TACTIC 6 from Chapter 8. Choose an easy number for x: 1, for example. Then, the three numbers become -9, 29, and 16, whose average is 12. Only A has a value of 12 when $x = 1$. This is also an easy way to check your answer, if you use the first solution.

10. **(20)** Let x = number of students in the Spanish Club, and write the weighted average:
    $$142 = \frac{30(150) + x(130)}{30 + x}$$
    Cross-multiply:
    $$142(30 + x) = 30(150) + 130x \Rightarrow$$
    $$4260 + 142x = 4500 + 130x \Rightarrow$$
    $$12x = 240 \Rightarrow x = 20.$$

11. **(1.75 or $\frac{7}{4}$)** Since $10a + 10b = 35$, dividing both sides of the equation by 10 gives $a + b = 3.5$. Therefore, the average of a and b is
    $$3.5 \div 2 = 1.75 \text{ or } \frac{7}{4}.$$

12. **(108)** The average of the measures of the five angles is the sum of their measures divided by 5. The sum is $(5 - 2) \times 180 = 3 \times 180 = 540$ (see Section 9-K), so their average is $540 \div 5 = 108$.

ALGEBRA

For the SAT you need to know only a small part of the algebra normally taught in high school. Sections 9-F, 9-G, and 9-H review only the albegraic topics that you need for the SAT.

9-F Polynomials

Even though the terms *monomial*, *binomial*, *trinomial*, and *polynomial* are not used on the SAT, you must be able to work with simple polynomials, and the use of these terms will make it easy to discuss the important concepts.

A **monomial** is any number or variable or product of numbers and variables. Each of the following is a monomial:

$$3 \quad -4 \quad x \quad y \quad 3x \quad -4xyz \quad 5x^3 \quad 1.5xy^2 \quad a^3b^4$$

The number that appears in front of the variable or variables in a monomial is called the **coefficient**. The coefficient of $5x^3$ is 5. If there is no number, the coefficient is 1 or –1, because x means $1x$ and $-ab^2$ means $-1ab^2$.

On the SAT, you are often asked to evaluate a monomial for specific values of the variables.

EXAMPLE 1

What is the value of $-3a^2b$ when $a = -4$ and $b = 0.5$?

Solution. Rewrite the expression, replacing the letters a and b by the numbers –4 and 0.5, respectively. Make sure to write each number in parentheses. Then evaluate: $-3(-4)^2(0.5) = -3(16)(0.5) = \mathbf{-24}$.

> **CAUTION:** Be sure you follow PEMDAS: handle exponents before the other operations. In Example 1, you *cannot* multiply –4 by –3, get 12, and then square 12.

A **polynomial** is a monomial or the sum of two or more monomials. Each monomial that makes up the polynomial is called a **term** of the polynomial. Each of the following is a polynomial:

$$2x^2 \quad 2x^2 + 3 \quad 3x^2 - 7 \quad x^2 + 5x - 1$$
$$a^2b + b^2a \quad x^2 - y^2 \quad w^2 - 2w + 1$$

The first polynomial in the above list is a monomial; the second, third, fifth, and sixth polynomials are called **binomials** because each has two terms; the fourth and seventh polynomials are called **trinomials** because each has three terms. Two terms are called **like terms** if they have exactly the same variables and exponents; they can differ only in their coefficients: $5a^2b$ and $-3a^2b$ are like terms, whereas a^2b and b^2a are not.

The polynomial $3x^2 + 4x + 5x + 2x^2 + x - 7$ has six terms, but some of them are like terms and can be combined:

$$3x^2 + 2x^2 = 5x^2 \quad \text{and} \quad 4x + 5x + x = 10x.$$

Therefore, the original polynomial is equivalent to the trinomial $5x^2 + 10x - 7$.

Key Fact F1

The only terms of a polynomial that can be combined are like terms.

Key Fact F2

To add two polynomials, first enclose each one in parentheses and put a plus sign between them; then erase the parentheses and combine like terms.

Helpful Hint

To add, subtract, multiply, and divide polynomials, use the usual laws of arithmetic. To avoid careless errors, write each polynomial in parentheses before performing any arithmetic operations.

EXAMPLE 2

What is the sum of $5x^2 + 10x - 7$ and $3x^2 - 4x + 2$?

Solution. $(5x^2 + 10x - 7) + (3x^2 - 4x + 2)$
$= 5x^2 + 10x - 7 + 3x^2 - 4x + 2$
$= (5x^2 + 3x^2) + (10x - 4x) + (-7 + 2)$
$= \mathbf{8x^2 + 6x - 5}$.

Key Fact F3

To subtract two polynomials, enclose each one in parentheses, change the minus sign between them to a plus sign, and change the sign of every term in the second parentheses. Then use KEY FACT F2 to add them: erase the parentheses and combine like terms.

CAUTION: Make sure you get the order right in a subtraction problem.

EXAMPLE 3

Subtract $3x^2 - 4x + 2$ from $5x^2 + 10x - 7$.

Solution. Be careful. Start with the second polynomial and subtract the first:

$$(5x^2 + 10x - 7) - (3x^2 - 4x + 2) =$$
$$(5x^2 + 10x - 7) + (-3x^2 + 4x - 2) = \mathbf{2x^2 + 14x - 9}.$$

EXAMPLE 4

What is the average (arithmetic mean) of $5x^2 + 10x - 7$, $3x^2 - 4x + 2$, and $4x^2 + 2$?

Solution. As in any average problem, add and divide:

$$(5x^2 + 10x - 7) + (3x^2 - 4x + 2) + (4x^2 + 2) = 12x^2 + 6x - 3,$$

and by the distributive law (KEY FACT A22):

$$\frac{12x^2 + 6x - 3}{3} = \mathbf{4x^2 + 2x - 1}.$$

Key Fact F4

To multiply monomials, first multiply their coefficients, and then multiply their variables by adding the exponents (see Section 9-A).

EXAMPLE 5

What is the product of $3xy^2z^3$ and $-2x^2y$?

Solution. $(3xy^2z^3)(-2x^2y) = 3(-2)(x)(x^2)(y^2)(y)(z^3) = -6x^3y^3z^3$.

All other polynomials are multiplied by using the distributive law.

Key Fact F5

To multiply a monomial by any polynomial, just multiply each term of the polynomial by the monomial.

EXAMPLE 6

What is the product of $2a$ and $3a^2 - 6ab + b^2$?

Solution. $2a(3a^2 - 6ab + b^2) = 6a^3 - 12a^2b + 2ab^2$.

On the SAT, the only other polynomials that you may be asked to multiply are two binomials.

Key Fact F6

To multiply two binomials, use the so-called FOIL method, which is really nothing more than the distributive law. Multiply each term in the first parentheses by each term in the second parentheses and simplify by combining terms, if possible.

$$(2x - 7)(3x + 2) = (2x)(3x) + (2x)(2) + (-7)(3x) + (-7)(2) =$$

First terms   Outer terms   Inner terms   Last terms

$$6x^2 + 4x - 21x - 14 = 6x^2 - 17x - 14.$$

EXAMPLE 7

What is the value of $(x - 2)(x + 3) - (x - 4)(x + 5)$?

Solution. First, multiply both pairs of binomials:

$$(x - 2)(x + 3) = x^2 + 3x - 2x - 6 = x^2 + x - 6$$
$$(x - 4)(x + 5) = x^2 + 5x - 4x - 20 = x^2 + x - 20$$

Now, subtract: $(x^2 + x - 6) - (x^2 + x - 20) = x^2 + x - 6 - x^2 - x + 20 = $ **14**.

Key Fact F7

Helpful Hint
If you memorize the products in KEY FACT F7, you won't have to multiply the binomials out each time you need them.

The three most important binomial products on the SAT are these:

- $(x - y)(x + y) = x^2 + xy - yx - y^2 = x^2 - y^2$
- $(x - y)^2 = (x - y)(x - y) = x^2 - xy - yx + y^2 = x^2 - 2xy + y^2$
- $(x + y)^2 = (x + y)(x + y) = x^2 + xy + yx + y^2 = x^2 + 2xy + y^2$

EXAMPLE 8

If $a - b = 17.5$ and $a + b = 10$, what is the value of $a^2 - b^2$?

Solution. Section 9-G reviews the methods used to solve such a pair of equations; but even if you know how to solve them, *you should not do so here.* You don't need to know the values of a and b to answer this question. The moment you see $a^2 - b^2$, you should think $(a - b)(a + b)$. Then:

$$a^2 - b^2 = (a - b)(a + b) = (17.5)(10) = \mathbf{175}.$$

EXAMPLE 9

If $x^2 + y^2 = 36$ and $(x + y)^2 = 64$, what is the value of xy?

Solution. Here, $64 = (x + y)^2 = x^2 + 2xy + y^2 = x^2 + y^2 + 2xy = 36 + 2xy$. Therefore:

$$2xy = 64 - 36 = 28 \Rightarrow xy = \mathbf{14}.$$

On the SAT, the only division of polynomials you will have to do is to divide a polynomial by a monomial. You will *not* have to do long division of polynomials.

Key Fact F8

To divide a polynomial by a monomial, use the distributive law. Then simplify each term by reducing the fraction formed by the coefficients to lowest terms and applying the laws of exponents.

EXAMPLE 10

What is the quotient when $32a^2b + 12ab^3c$ is divided by $8ab$?

Solution. By the distributive law,

$$\frac{32a^2b + 12ab^3c}{8ab} = \frac{32a^2b}{8ab} + \frac{12ab^3c}{8ab}.$$

Now reduce each fraction: $\mathbf{4a + \dfrac{3}{2}b^2c}$.

On the SAT, the most important way to use the three formulas in KEY FACT F7 is to recognize them in reverse. In other words, whenever you see $x^2 - y^2$, you should realize that it can be rewritten as $(x - y)(x + y)$. This process, which is the reverse of multiplication, is called ***factoring***.

EXAMPLE 11

If $x^2 - y^2 = 14$ and $x - y = 7$, what is the value of $x + y$?

Solution. Since $x^2 - y^2 = (x - y)(x + y)$, you have

$$14 = 7(x + y) \Rightarrow x + y = 2.$$

Note that you could solve for x and y ($x = 4.5$, $y = -2.5$) and then add; but you shouldn't because this method takes much more time.

To ***factor*** a polynomial, you must find other polynomials whose product is the original polynomial. For example, since $2x(3x - 5) = 6x^2 - 10x$, then $2x$ and $3x - 5$ are each factors of $6x^2 - 10x$; and since $(a - b)(a + b) = a^2 - b^2$, then $(a - b)$ and $(a + b)$ are factors of $a^2 - b^2$.

On the SAT, you will have to do almost no factoring. Occasionally, an SAT will have a question which requires you to solve a very simple quadratic equation such as $x^2 - x - 6 = 0$. Often you can solve it by inspection since the roots will be two small integers. At worst you will have to factor:

$$x^2 - x - 6 = 0 \Rightarrow (x - 3)(x + 2) = 0 \Rightarrow x - 3 = 0 \text{ or } x + 2 = 0 \Rightarrow x = 3 \text{ or } x = -2.$$

A typical SAT may also have one question that requires you to simplify an algebraic expression. In that case, you will probably have to do some simple factoring.

Key Fact F9

To factor a polynomial, the first step is *always* to use the distributive property to remove the greatest common factor of all the terms.

For example:

$$6xy + 8yz = 2y(3x + 4z) \qquad \text{and} \qquad x^3 + x^2 + x = x(x^2 + x + 1)$$

Key Fact F10

To factor a trinomial use trial and error to find the binomials whose product is the given trinomial.

For example:

$$x^2 + 4x + 4 = (x + 2)(x + 2) \text{ (see KEY FACT F7)}.$$
$$x^2 - 3x - 10 = (x - 5)(x + 2).$$
$$2x^2 + 18x + 16 = 2(x^2 + 9x + 8) = 2(x + 8)(x + 1).$$

EXAMPLE 12

Which of the following is equivalent to $\dfrac{3x^2 - 12}{x^2 - 4x + 4}$?

(A) 3

(B) $\dfrac{3(x + 2)}{x - 2}$

(C) $\dfrac{3(x + 4)}{x - 4}$

(D) $\dfrac{3x + 2}{x - 2}$

(E) $\dfrac{6}{4x - 4}$

Solution.

$$\frac{3x^2 - 12}{x^2 - 4x + 4} = \frac{3(x^2 - 4)}{(x - 2)(x - 2)} = \frac{3(x - 2)(x + 2)}{(x - 2)(x - 2)} = \frac{3(x + 2)}{x - 2} \textbf{ (B)}.$$

In Example 12, when $x = 3$, the value of $\frac{3x^2 - 12}{x^2 - 4x + 4}$ is

$$\frac{3(3)^2 - 12}{3^2 - 4(3) + 4} = \frac{27 - 12}{9 - 12 + 4} = \frac{15}{1} = 15.$$

Only choice B is 15 when $x = 3$: $\frac{3(3+2)}{3-2} = \frac{3(5)}{1} = 15$.

Note that this method does not depend on the choice of *x*. You can verify, for example, that, if $x = 5$, the original expression and the correct answer are both equal to 7.

Helpful Hint

If you ever get stuck trying to simplify an algebraic expression, just plug in a number and test the answers.

Although the coefficient of any term in a polynomial can be a fraction, such as $\frac{2}{3}x^2 - \frac{1}{2}x$, the variable itself cannot be in the denominator. An expression such as $\frac{3+x}{x^2}$, which has a variable in the denominator, is called an ***algebraic fraction***. Fortunately, you should have no trouble with algebraic fractions since they are handled just like regular fractions. The rules that you reviewed in Section 9-B for adding, subtracting, multiplying, and dividing fractions apply also to algebraic fractions.

EXAMPLE 13

What is the sum of the reciprocals of x^2 and y^2?

Solution. To add $\frac{1}{x^2} + \frac{1}{y^2}$, you need a common denominator, which is x^2y^2.

Multiply the numerator and denominator of $\frac{1}{x^2}$ by y^2 and the numerator and denominator of $\frac{1}{y^2}$ by x^2:

$$\frac{1}{x^2} + \frac{1}{y^2} = \frac{y^2}{x^2y^2} + \frac{x^2}{x^2y^2} = \mathbf{\frac{x^2 + y^2}{x^2y^2}}.$$

Exercises on Polynomials

Multiple-Choice Questions

1. If $a^2 - b^2 = 21$ and $a^2 + b^2 = 29$, which of the following could be the value of ab?

   I. -10

   II. $5\sqrt{2}$

   III. 10

   (A) I only
   (B) II only
   (C) III only
   (D) I and III only
   (E) II and III only

2. What is the average (arithmetic mean) of $x^2 + 2x - 3$, $3x^2 - 2x - 3$, and $30 - 4x^2$?

   (A) $\dfrac{8x^2 + 4x + 24}{3}$

   (B) $\dfrac{8x^2 + 24}{3}$

   (C) $\dfrac{24 - 4x}{3}$

   (D) -12

   (E) 8

3. If $a^2 + b^2 = 4$ and $(a - b)^2 = 2$, what is the value of ab?

   (A) 1
   (B) $\sqrt{2}$
   (C) 2
   (D) 3
   (E) 4

4. If $\dfrac{1}{a} + \dfrac{1}{b} = \dfrac{1}{c}$ and $ab = c$, what is the average (arithmetic mean) of a and b?

   (A) 0

   (B) $\dfrac{1}{2}$

   (C) 1

   (D) $\dfrac{c}{2}$

   (E) $\dfrac{a + b}{2c}$

5. If $x \neq 2$ and $x \neq -2$, which of the following is equivalent to $\dfrac{x^3 + 3x^2 - 10x}{2x^2 - 8}$?

   (A) $\dfrac{x(x - 5)}{2(x - 2)}$

   (B) $\dfrac{x(x + 5)}{2(x + 2)}$

   (C) $\dfrac{x(x - 5)}{2(x + 2)}$

   (D) $\dfrac{x(x + 5)}{2(x - 2)}$

   (E) $\dfrac{x^2 + 5}{(2x + 4)}$

Grid-in Questions

6. What is the value of $\dfrac{a^2 - b^2}{a - b}$ when $a = 17.9$ and $b = 19.7$?

7. If $x^2 - y^2 = 28$ and $x - y = 8$, what is the average (arithmetic mean) of x and y?

8. What is the value of
   $(2x + 3)(x + 6) - (2x - 5)(x + 10)$?

9. What is the value of
   $x^2 + 12x + 36$ when $x = 64$?

10. If $\left(\dfrac{1}{a} + a\right)^2 = 100$, what is
    the value of $\dfrac{1}{a^2} + a^2$?

Answer Key

1. **D**   2. **E**   3. **A**   4. **B**   5. **B**

6. `3 7 . 6`   7. `1 . 7 5`   8. `6 8`   9. `4 9 0 0`   10. `9 8`

Answer Explanations

1. D.   Add the two equations:

$$2a^2 = 50 \Rightarrow a^2 = 25 \Rightarrow b^2 = 4.$$

Then, $a = 5$ or -5 and $b = 2$ or -2. The only possibilities for the product ab are -10 and 10. (Only I and III are true.)

2. E.   To find the average, take the sum of the three polynomials and then divide by 3. The sum is

$$(x^2 + 2x - 3) + (3x^2 - 2x - 3) + (30 - 4x^2) = 24,$$

and $24 \div 3 = 8$.

3. A.   Start by squaring $a - b$:

$$(a - b)^2 = a^2 - 2ab + b^2. \text{ Then}$$

$$2 = 4 - 2ab \Rightarrow 2ab = 2 \Rightarrow ab = 1.$$

4. B. $$\frac{1}{c} = \frac{1}{a} + \frac{1}{b} = \frac{a+b}{ab} = \frac{a+b}{c} \Rightarrow$$

$$1 = a + b \Rightarrow \frac{a+b}{2} = \frac{1}{2}.$$

5. B. $$\frac{x^3 + 3x^2 - 10x}{2x^2 - 8} = \frac{x(x^2 + 3x - 10)}{2(x^2 - 4)} =$$

$$\frac{x(x+5)(x-2)}{2(x+2)(x-2)} = \frac{x(x+5)}{2(x+2)}.$$

6. (37.6) $$\frac{a^2 - b^2}{a - b} = \frac{(a-b)(a+b)}{a-b} = a + b =$$

$$17.9 + 19.7 = 37.6.$$

7. (1.75)   Since $x^2 - y^2 = (x - y)(x + y)$, we have:

$$28 = (x - y)(x + y) = 8(x + y) \Rightarrow$$
$$x + y = 28 \div 8 = 3.5.$$

Finally, the average of x and y is

$$\frac{x+y}{2} = \frac{3.5}{2} = 1.75.$$

8. (68)   First, multiply out both pairs of binomials:

$$(2x + 3)(x + 6) = 2x^2 + 15x + 18$$
and $$(2x - 5)(x + 10) = 2x^2 + 15x - 50.$$

Now subtract:

$$(2x^2 + 15x + 18) - (2x^2 + 15x - 50) =$$
$$18 - (-50) = 68.$$

Alternative solution. Note that, since this is a grid-in question, the answer must be a (positive) number. All of the x's must cancel out. Therefore, the answer will be the same no matter what x is, so pick a simple value for x. If $x = 0$: $(3)(6) - (-5)(10) = 18 - (-50) = 68$; if $x = 4$: $(11)(10) - (3)(14) = 110 - 42 = 68$.

9. (4900)   Of course, you can do this problem on your calculator; but you can do it quicker if you recognize that $x^2 + 12x + 36 = (x + 6)^2$. The value is $(64 + 6)^2 = 70^2 = 4900$.

10. (98) $$100 = \left(\frac{1}{a} + a\right)^2 = \frac{1}{a^2} + 2 + a^2$$

$$\Rightarrow \frac{1}{a^2} + a^2 = 98.$$

9-G Solving Equations and Inequalities

The most important thing to remember when solving an *equation* is that you can manipulate the equation in any way, as long as *you do the same thing to both sides*. For example, you may always add the same number to each side, subtract the same number from each side, multiply or divide each side by the same number (except 0), square each side, take the square root of each side (if the quantities are positive), or take the reciprocal of each side. These comments apply to inequalities, as well, but here you must be very careful because some procedures, such as multiplying or dividing by a negative number and taking reciprocals, reverse inequalities (see KEY FACT A25).

Equations and inequalities that have only one variable and no exponents can be solved using the simple six-step method outlined in the solution of Example 1.

EXAMPLE 1

If $\frac{1}{2}x + 3(x - 2) = 2(x + 1) + 1$, what is the value of x?

Solution. Follow the steps outlined in the following table.

Step	What to Do	Example 1
1	Get rid of fractions and decimals by multiplying both sides by the lowest common denominator (LCD).	Multiply each term by 2: $x + 6(x - 2) = 4(x + 1) + 2$.
2	Get rid of all parentheses by using the distributive law.	$x + 6x - 12 = 4x + 4 + 2$.
3	Combine like terms on each side.	$7x - 12 = 4x + 6$.
4	By adding or subtracting, get all the variables on one side.	Subtract $4x$ from each side: $3x - 12 = 6$.
5	By adding or subtracting, get all the plain numbers on the other side.	Add 12 to each side: $3x = 18$.
6	Divide both sides by the coefficient of the variable.*	Divide both sides by 3: $x = \mathbf{6}$.

*If you start with an inequality and in Step 6 you divide by a negative number, remember to reverse the inequality (see KEY FACT A25).

Example 1 is actually much harder than any equation on the SAT, because it requires all six steps. On the SAT that never happens. Think of the six steps as a list of questions that must be answered. Ask whether each step is necessary. If it is, do it; if it isn't, move on to the next one.

Let's look at Example 2, which does not require all six steps.

EXAMPLE 2

For what real number n is it true that $3(n - 20) = n$?

(A) −10
(B) 0
(C) 10
(D) 20
(E) 30

Solution. Do each of the six steps necessary.

Step	Question	Yes/No	What to Do
1	Are there any fractions or decimals?	No	
2	Are there any parentheses?	Yes	Get rid of them: $3n - 60 = n$.
3	Are there any like terms to combine?	No	
4	Are there variables on both sides?	Yes	Subtract n from each side: $2n - 60 = 0$.
5	Is there a plain number on the same side as the variable?	Yes	Add 60 to each side: $2n = 60$.
6	Does the variable have a coefficient?	Yes	Divide both sides by 2: $n = \mathbf{30}$.

TACTIC

G1

Memorize the six steps *in order*, and use this method whenever you have to solve this type of equation or inequality.

EXAMPLE 3

Three brothers divided a prize as follows. The oldest received $\dfrac{2}{5}$, the middle brother received $\dfrac{1}{3}$, and the youngest received the remaining $120. What was the value, in dollars, of the prize?

Solution. If x represents the value of the prize, then

$$\frac{2}{5}x + \frac{1}{3}x + 120 = x.$$

Solve this equation using the six-step method.

Step	Question	Yes/No	What to Do
1	Are there any fractions or decimals?	Yes	Get rid of them: multiply by 15.* $15\left(\dfrac{2}{5}x\right) + 15\left(\dfrac{1}{3}x\right) + 15(120) = 15(x)$. $6x + 5x + 1800 = 15x$.
2	Are there any parentheses?	No	
3	Are there any like terms to combine?	Yes	Combine them: $11x + 1800 = 15x$.
4	Are there variables on both sides?	Yes	Subtract $11x$ from each side: $1800 = 4x$.
5	Is there a plain number on the same side as the variable?	No	
6	Does the variable have a coefficient?	Yes	Divide both sides by 4: $x = \mathbf{450}$.

*Multiply by 15 since it is the LCM of the two denominators, 3 and 5.

Sometimes on the SAT, you are given an equation with several variables and asked to solve for one of them in terms of the others.

TACTIC

When you have to solve for one variable in terms of the others, treat all of the others as if they were numbers, and apply the six-step method.

EXAMPLE 4

If $a = 3b - c$, what is the value of b in terms of a and c?

Solution. To solve for b, treat a and c as numbers and use the six-step method with b as the variable.

Step	Question	Yes/No	What to Do
1	Are there any fractions or decimals?	No	
2	Are there any parentheses?	No	
3	Are there any like terms to combine?	No	
4	Are there variables on both sides?	No	Remember: the only variable is b.
5	Is there a plain number on the same side as the variable?	Yes	Remember: you're considering c as a number, and it is on the same side as b, the variable. Add c to both sides: $a + c = 3b$.
6	Does the variable have a coefficient?	Yes	Divide both sides by 3: $b = \dfrac{a+c}{3}$.

Sometimes when solving equations, you may see a shortcut. For example, to solve $7(w - 3) = 42$, you can save time if you start by dividing both sides by 7, getting $w - 3 = 6$, rather than using the distributive law to eliminate the parentheses. Similarly, if you have to solve a proportion such as $\dfrac{x}{7} = \dfrac{3}{5}$, it is easier to cross-multiply, getting $5x = 21$, than to multiply both sides by 35 to get rid of the fractions (although that's exactly what cross-multiplying accomplishes). Other shortcuts will be illustrated in the problems at the end of the section. If you spot such a shortcut, use it; but if you don't, be assured that the six-step method *always* works.

EXAMPLE 5

If $x - 4 = 11$, what is the value of $x - 8$?

(A) –15
(B) –7
(C) –1
(D) 7
(E) 15

Solution. Going immediately to Step 5, add 4 to each side of the equation: $x = 15$. But this is *not* the answer. You need the value, not of x, but of $x - 8$: $15 - 8 = \textbf{7 (D)}$.

Helpful Hint

In applying the six-step method, you shouldn't actually write out the table, as was done in Examples 1–4, since it would be too time-consuming. Instead, use the method as a guideline and mentally go through each step, doing whichever ones are required.

As in Example 5, on the SAT you are often asked to solve for something other than the simple variable. In Example 5, you could have been asked for the value of x^2, $x + 4$, $(x - 4)^2$, and so on.

TACTIC

G3   As you read each question on the SAT, circle in your test booklet what you are looking for. Then you will always be sure to answer the question that is asked.

Occasionally on the SAT, you will have to solve an equation such as $3\sqrt{x} - 1 = 5$, which involves a radical. Proceed normally, treating the radical as the variable and using whichever of the six steps are necessary until you have a radical equal to a number. Then raise each side to the same power. For example, if the radical is a square root, square both sides; if the radical is a cube root, cube both sides.

EXAMPLE 6

If $3\sqrt{x} - 1 = 5$, then $x =$

Solution.

- Add 1 to each side: $3\sqrt{x} = 6$.

- Divide each side by 3: $\sqrt{x} = 2$.

- Now square each side: $\left(\sqrt{x}\right)^2 = 2^2 \Rightarrow x = \mathbf{4}$.

EXAMPLE 7

If $4\left(\sqrt{x} + 1\right) = \sqrt{x} + 25$, then $x =$

Solution.

- Get rid of the parentheses: $4\sqrt{x} + 4 = \sqrt{x} + 25$.

- Subtract $\sqrt{x}$ from each side: $3\sqrt{x} + 4 = 25$.

- Subtract 4 from each side: $3\sqrt{x} = 21$.

- Divide each side by 3: $\sqrt{x} = 7$.

- Square each side: $x = 7^2 = \mathbf{49}$.

EXAMPLE 8

If $\sqrt[3]{x} - 4 = 1$, then $x =$

Solution.

- Add 4 to each side: $\sqrt[3]{x} = 5$.

- Cube each side: $\left(\sqrt[3]{x}\right)^3 = 5^3 \Rightarrow x = \mathbf{125}$.

EXAMPLE 9

If $2x - 5 = 98$, what is the value of $2x + 5$?

Solution. First, circle what you are asked for (the value of $2x + 5$), and then look at the question carefully. The best approach is to observe that $2x + 5$ is 10 more than $2x - 5$, so the answer is **108** (10 more than 98). Next best would be to do only one step of the six-step method, and add 5 to both sides: $2x = 103$. Now, again add 5 to both sides: $2x + 5 = 103 + 5 = 108$. The *worst* method would be to divide $2x = 103$ by 2, get $x = 51.5$, and then use that value to calculate $2x + 5$.

Helpful Hint
Very often, solving the given equation is *not* the quickest way to answer a question.

EXAMPLE 10

If w is an integer, and the average (arithmetic mean) of 3, 4, and w is less than 10, what is the greatest possible value of w?

Solution.

- Set up the inequality: $\dfrac{3+4+w}{3} < 10$.
- Get rid of fractions: $3 + 4 + w < 30$.
- Combine like terms: $7 + w < 30$.
- Subtract 7 from both sides: $w < 23$.

Since w is an integer, the most it can be is **22**.

Consider the following variation of Example 10.

EXAMPLE 10A

Assume that this is a grid-in question.

If the average (arithmetic mean) of 3, 4, and w is less than 10, what is the greatest possible value of w that can be entered in the grid?

Solution. Just as in Example 10, you get $w < 23$. The largest number less than 23 that can be entered in a grid is **22.9**.

The six-step method works also when there are variables in denominators.

EXAMPLE 11

For what value of x is $\dfrac{4}{x} + \dfrac{3}{5} = \dfrac{10}{x}$?

Solution. Multiply each side by the LCD, $5x$:

$$5x\left(\frac{4}{x}\right) + 5x\left(\frac{3}{5}\right) = 5x\left(\frac{10}{x}\right) \Rightarrow 20 + 3x = 50.$$

Now solve normally:

$$20 + 3x = 50 \Rightarrow 3x = 30 \Rightarrow x = \mathbf{10}.$$

EXAMPLE 12

If x is positive, and $y = 5x^2 + 3$, which of the following is an expression for x in terms of y?

(A) $\sqrt{\dfrac{y}{5} - 3}$

(B) $\sqrt{\dfrac{y-3}{5}}$

(C) $\dfrac{\sqrt{y-3}}{5}$

(D) $\dfrac{\sqrt{y}-3}{5}$

(E) $\dfrac{\sqrt{y}-\sqrt{3}}{5}$

Solution. The six-step method works only when there are no exponents. So, treat x^2 as a single variable, and use the method as far as you can:

$$y = 5x^2 + 3 \Rightarrow y - 3 = 5x^2 \Rightarrow \frac{y-3}{5} = x^2.$$

Now take the square root of each side: $x = \sqrt{\dfrac{y-3}{5}}$ **(B)**.

> **CAUTION:** Doing the same thing to each *side* of an equation does *not* mean doing the same thing to each *term* of the equation. Study Examples 13 and 14 carefully.

EXAMPLE 13

If $\dfrac{1}{a} = \dfrac{1}{b} + \dfrac{1}{c}$, what is a in terms of b and c?

Note: You *cannot* just take the reciprocal of each term; the answer is *not* $a = b + c$. Here are two solutions.

Solution 1. First add the fractions on the right-hand side:

$$\frac{1}{a} = \frac{1}{b} + \frac{1}{c} = \frac{b+c}{bc}.$$

Now, take the reciprocal of *each side*: $a = \dfrac{bc}{b+c}$.

Solution 2. Use the six-step method. Multiply each term by abc, the LCD:

$$abc\left(\frac{1}{a}\right) = abc\left(\frac{1}{b}\right) + abc\left(\frac{1}{c}\right) \Rightarrow bc = ac + ab = a(c+b) \Rightarrow a = \frac{bc}{c+b}.$$

EXAMPLE 14

If $a > 0$ and $a^2 + b^2 = c^2$, what is a in terms of b and c?

Note: You *cannot* take the square root of each term and write $a + b = c$.

Solution. $a^2 + b^2 = c^2 \Rightarrow a^2 = c^2 - b^2$. Now, take the square root of *each side*:

$$a = \sqrt{a^2} = \sqrt{c^2 - b^2}.$$

EXAMPLE 15

If $a = b(c + d)$, what is d in terms of a, b, and c?

(A) $\dfrac{a}{b} - c$

(B) $a - bc$

(C) $\dfrac{a}{bc}$

(D) $\dfrac{a}{bc} - b$

(E) $\dfrac{a - c}{b}$

Solution. Use the six-step method:

$$a = b(c + d) \Rightarrow a = bc + bd \Rightarrow a - bc = bd \Rightarrow d = \frac{a - bc}{b}.$$

Now what? This answer isn't one of the choices. It is, however, *equivalent* to one of the choices. Use the distributive law to divide a by b and bc by b:

$$\frac{a - bc}{b} = \frac{a}{b} - \frac{bc}{b} = \frac{a}{b} - c \text{ (A)}.$$

There are a few other types of equations that you may need to solve on the SAT. Fortunately, they are quite easy. You probably will not have to solve a quadratic equation, one in which the variable is raised to the second power. If you do, however, you will not need the quadratic formula, and you will probably not have to factor. Here are two examples.

Helpful Hint
On a multiple-choice question, if your answer is not among the five choices, check to see whether it is *equivalent* to one of the choices.

EXAMPLE 16

If x is a positive number and $x^2 + 4 = 125$, what is the value of x?

Solution. When there is an x^2-term, but no x-term, just take the square root:

$$x^2 + 4 = 125 \Rightarrow x^2 = 121 \Rightarrow x = \sqrt{121} = \mathbf{11}.$$

If the equation had been $x^2 + 9 = 125$, the solution would have been $x = \sqrt{116}$. Since $116 = 4 \times 29$, this can be reduced to $\sqrt{4} \times \sqrt{29} = 2\sqrt{29}$.

Calculator Shortcut

If you can easily simplify a square root, that's great; but on the SAT, you never have to. The answers to grid-in problems don't involve square roots, and if the answer to a multiple-choice question turns out to be $\sqrt{116}$, you can use your calculator to see which of the five choices is equal to 10.77.

EXAMPLE 17

What is the largest value of x that satisfies the equation $2x^2 - 3x = 0$?

Solution. When an equation has an x^2-term and an x-term but no constant term, solve by factoring out the x and using the fact that, if the product of two numbers is 0, one of them must be 0 (KEY FACT A3):

$$2x^2 - 3x = 0 \Rightarrow x(2x - 3) = 0.$$
$$\text{So, } x = 0 \text{ or } 2x - 3 = 0 \Rightarrow$$
$$x = 0 \text{ or } 2x = 3 \Rightarrow$$
$$x = 0 \text{ or } x = 1.5.$$

The largest value is **1.5**.

In another type of equation that occasionally appears on the SAT, the variable is in the exponent. Equations of this type can often be solved by inspection.

EXAMPLE 18

If $2^{x+3} = 32$, what is the value of 3^{x+2}?

Solution. How many 2's do you have to multiply together to get 32? If you don't know that the answer is 5, just multiply and keep track. Count the 2's on your fingers as you say to yourself, "2 times 2 is 4, times 2 is 8, times 2 is 16, times 2 is 32." Then

$$2^{x+3} = 32 = 2^5 \Rightarrow x + 3 = 5 \Rightarrow x = 2.$$

Therefore, $x + 2 = 4$, and $3^{x+2} = 3^4 = 3 \times 3 \times 3 \times 3 = \mathbf{81}$.

Occasionally, both sides of an equation have variables in the exponents. In that case, it is necessary to write both exponentials with the same base.

EXAMPLE 19

If $4^{w+3} = 8^{w-1}$, what is the value of w?

Solution. Since it is necessary to have the same base on each side of the equation, write $4 = 2^2$ and $8 = 2^3$. Then

$$4^{w+3} = (2^2)^{w+3} = 2^{2(w+3)} = 2^{2w+6}$$

and

$$8^{w-1} = (2^3)^{w-1} = 2^{3(w-1)} = 2^{3w-3}.$$

Therefore, $2^{2w+6} = 2^{3w-3} \Rightarrow 2w + 6 = 3w - 3 \Rightarrow w = \mathbf{9}$.

Systems of Linear Equations

The equations $x + y = 10$ and $x - y = 2$ each have lots of solutions (infinitely many, in fact). Some of them are given in the following tables.

$x + y = 10$

x	5	**6**	4	1	1.2	10	20
y	5	**4**	6	9	8.8	0	-10
$x + y$	10	10	10	10	10	10	10

$x - y = 2$							
x	5	**6**	2	0	2.5	19	40
y	3	**4**	0	−2	.5	17	38
$x - y$	2	2	2	2	2	2	2

However, only one pair of numbers, $x = 6$ and $y = 4$, satisfies both equations simultaneously: $6 + 4 = 10$ and $6 - 4 = 2$. These numbers, then, are the only solution of the **system of equations** $\begin{cases} x + y = 10 \\ x - y = 2 \end{cases}$.

A system of equations is a set of two or more equations involving two or more variables. To solve such a system, you must find, for all of the variables, values that will make each equation true. In an algebra course you learn several ways to solve systems of equations. On the SAT, the most useful way is to add or subtract (usually add) the equations. Examples 20 and 21 demonstrate this method, and Example 22 shows one other way to handle some systems of equations.

TACTIC

To solve a system of equations, add or subtract them. If there are more than two equations, add them.

EXAMPLE 20

If the sum of two numbers is 10 and their difference is 2, what is their product?

Solution. Letting x and y represent the two numbers, write two equations and then add them:

$$\begin{array}{r} x + y = 10 \\ + \ x - y = 2 \\ \hline 2x \quad\ = 12 \Rightarrow x = 6. \end{array}$$

Replacing x by 6 in $x + y = 10$ yields $y = 4$. The product of the two numbers is **24**.

EXAMPLE 21

If $3a + 5b = 10$ and $5a + 3b = 30$, what is the average (arithmetic mean) of a and b?

(A) 2.5
(B) 4
(C) 5
(D) 20
(E) It cannot be determined from the information given.

Solution. Add the two equations:

$$\begin{array}{r} 3a + 5b = 10 \\ + \ 5a + 3b = 30 \\ \hline 8a + 8b = 40 \end{array}$$

Divide both sides by 8: $a + b = 5$

The average of a and b is: $\dfrac{a+b}{2} = \dfrac{5}{2} =$ **2.5 (A)**

Note: It is not only unnecessary but also foolish to first solve for a and b ($a = 7.5$ and $b = -2.5$).

> **Helpful Hint**
>
> On the SAT, most problems involving systems of equations do *not* require you to solve the systems. These problems usually ask for something other than the value of each variable. Read the questions very carefully, circle what you need, and do not do more than is required.

For additional examples of the proper use of TACTIC G4, see the examples following TACTIC 17 in Chapter 8.

Occasionally on the SAT, it is as easy, or easier, to solve a system of equations by substitution.

If one of the equations in a system of equations consists of a single variable equal to some expression, substitute that expression for the variable in the other equation.

EXAMPLE 22

If $x + y = 10$ and $y = x - 2$, what is the value of xy?

Solution. This is essentially the same problem as Example 20. However, since here the second equation states that a single variable (y) is equal to some expression ($x - 2$), substitution is a better method than adding. Replace y by $x - 2$ in the first equation: $x + y = 10$ becomes $x + (x - 2) = 10$. Then

$$2x - 2 = 10 \Rightarrow 2x = 12 \Rightarrow x = 6.$$

To find the value of y, replace x by 6 in either of the original equations:

$$6 + y = 10 \Rightarrow y = 4 \text{ or } y = 6 - 2 = 4.$$

Finally, $xy = (6)(4) = \mathbf{24}$.

Exercises on Solving Equations and Inequalities

Multiple-Choice Questions

1. If $4x + 12 = 36$, what is the value of $x + 3$?

   (A) 3
   (B) 6
   (C) 9
   (D) 12
   (E) 18

2. If $4x + 13 = 7 - 2x$, what is the value of x?

   (A) $-\dfrac{10}{3}$

   (B) -3

   (C) -1

   (D) 1

   (E) $\dfrac{10}{3}$

3. If $ax - b = c - dx$, what is the value of x in terms of a, b, c, and d?

   (A) $\dfrac{b+c}{a+d}$

   (B) $\dfrac{c-b}{a-d}$

   (C) $\dfrac{b+c-d}{a}$

   (D) $\dfrac{c-b}{a+d}$

   (E) $\dfrac{c}{b} - \dfrac{d}{a}$

4. If $\dfrac{1}{3}x + \dfrac{1}{6}x + \dfrac{1}{9}x = 33$, what is the value of x?

   (A) 3
   (B) 18
   (C) 27
   (D) 54
   (E) 72

5. If $17 - 2\sqrt{x} = 14$, what is the value of x?

   (A) $\dfrac{9}{4}$

   (B) $\dfrac{29}{4}$

   (C) 36
   (D) 196
   (E) There is no value of x that satisfies the equation.

6. If $32^{a+b} = 16^{a+2b}$, then $a =$

   (A) b
   (B) $2b$
   (C) $3b$
   (D) $b + 2$
   (E) $b - 2$

7. If the average (arithmetic mean) of $3a$ and $4b$ is less than 50, and a is twice b, what is the largest integer value of a?

   (A) 9
   (B) 10
   (C) 11
   (D) 19
   (E) 20

8. If $\dfrac{1}{a-b} = 5$, then $a =$

   (A) $b + 5$

   (B) $b - 5$

   (C) $b + \dfrac{1}{5}$

   (D) $b - \dfrac{1}{5}$

   (E) $\dfrac{1-5b}{5}$

9. If $x = 3a + 7$ and $y = 9a^2$, what is y in terms of x?

(A) $(x - 7)^2$

(B) $3(x - 7)^2$

(C) $\dfrac{(x - 7)^2}{3}$

(D) $\dfrac{(x + 7)^2}{3}$

(E) $(x + 7)^2$

10. Which of the following is a solution of $3|x + 1| - 5 = -2$?

(A) -2
(B) 1
(C) $\dfrac{4}{3}$
(D) 2
(E) The equation has no solution.

Grid-in Questions

11. If $x - 4 = 9$, what is the value of $x^2 - 4$?

12. If $7x + 10 = 44$, what is the value of $7x - 10$?

13. If $3x - 4 = 9$, what is the value of $(3x - 4)^2$?

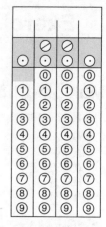

14. If $x^{-3} = \dfrac{1}{4x}$, what is one possible value of x?

15. If $x^2 + 3 < 4$ and $2x^2 + 3 > 4$, what is one possible value of x?

Answer Key

1. **C**	3. **A**	5. **A**	7. **D**	9. **A**
2. **C**	4. **D**	6. **C**	8. **C**	10. **A**

11. **165**

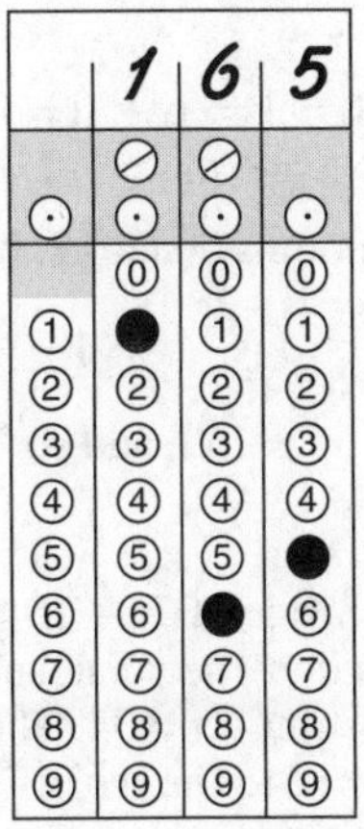

12. **24**

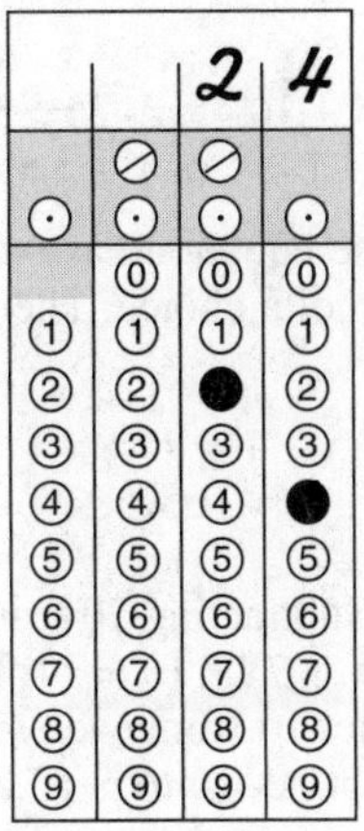

13. **81**

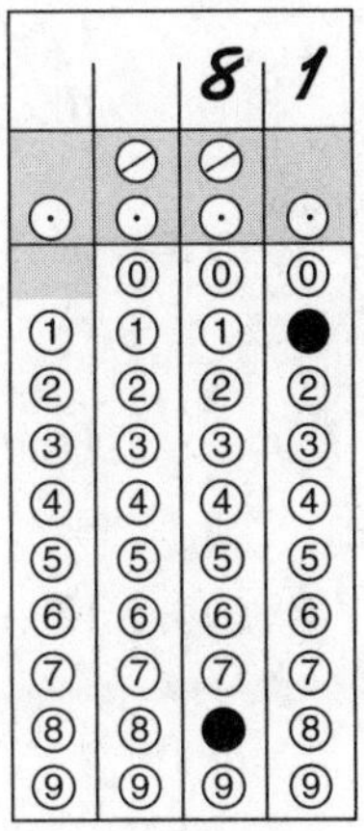

14. **2**

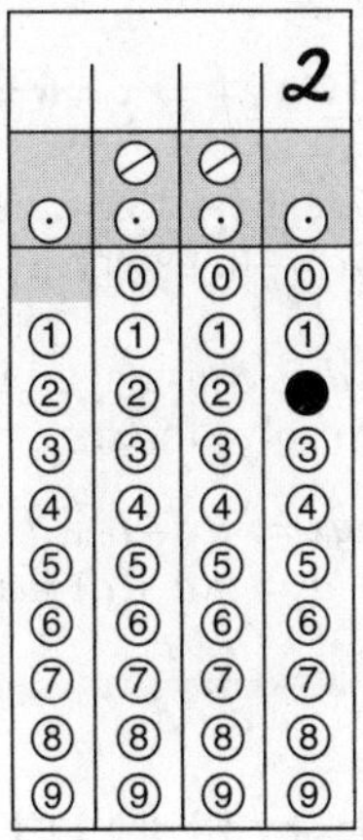

15. **.75**

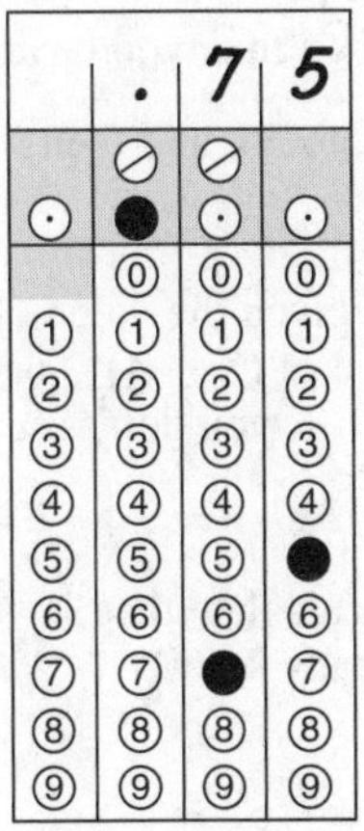

$.707 < x < 1$

Answer Explanations

1. **C.** The easiest method is to recognize that $x + 3$ is $\frac{1}{4}$ of $4x + 12$, and, therefore, equals $\frac{1}{4}$ of 36, which is 9. If you don't see that, solve normally:

   $$4x + 12 = 36 \Rightarrow 4x = 24 \Rightarrow x = 6 \Rightarrow x + 3 = 9.$$

2. **C.** Add $2x$ to each side: $6x + 13 = 7$. Subtract 13 from each side: $6x = -6$. Divide by 6: $x = -1$.

3. **A.** Treat a, b, c, and d as constants, and use the six-step method to solve for x:

   $$ax - b = c - dx \Rightarrow ax - b + dx = c \Rightarrow$$
   $$ax + dx = c + b \Rightarrow x(a + d) = b + c \Rightarrow$$
   $$x = \frac{b + c}{a + d}.$$

4. **D.** Multiply both sides by 18, the LCD:

   $$18\left(\frac{1}{3}x + \frac{1}{6}x + \frac{1}{9}x\right) = 18(33) \Rightarrow$$
   $$6x + 3x + 2x = 594 \Rightarrow 11x = 594 \Rightarrow x = 54.$$

   Mentally, it's easier not to multiply 18×33; leave it in that form and divide by 11:

   $$\frac{18 \times \overset{3}{\cancel{33}}}{\underset{1}{\cancel{11}}} = 18 \times 3 = 54.$$ Since you have a calculator, however, you might as well use it.

5. **A.** $17 - 2\sqrt{x} = 14 \Rightarrow -2\sqrt{x} = -3 \Rightarrow 2\sqrt{x} = 3 \Rightarrow \sqrt{x} = \frac{3}{2} \Rightarrow x = \frac{9}{4}.$

6. **C.** $32^{a+b} = (2^5)^{a+b} = 2^{5a+5b}$, and $16^{a+2b} = (2^4)^{a+2b} = 2^{4a+8b}$. Therefore:

   $$5a + 5b = 4a + 8b \Rightarrow a + 5b = 8b \Rightarrow a = 3b.$$

7. **D.** Since $a = 2b$, then $2a = 4b$. Therefore, the average of $3a$ and $4b$ is the average of $3a$ and $2a$, which is $2.5a$. Therefore, $2.5a < 50 \Rightarrow a < 20$, so the largest integer value of a is 19.

8. **C.** Take the reciprocal of each side:

   $$a - b = \frac{1}{5}, \text{ so } a = b + \frac{1}{5}.$$

9. **A.** If $x = 3a + 7$, then $x - 7 = 3a$ and $a = \frac{x - 7}{3}$. Therefore

   $$y = 9a^2 = 9\left(\frac{x-7}{3}\right)^2 = \overset{1}{\cancel{9}}\frac{(x-7)^2}{\underset{1}{\cancel{3^2}}} = (x-7)^2.$$

10. **A.** $3|x + 1| - 5 = -2 \Rightarrow 3|x + 1| = 3 \Rightarrow |x + 1| = 1 \Rightarrow x + 1 = 1$ or $x + 1 = -1 \Rightarrow x = 0$ or $x = -2$.

    The equation has two solutions, 0 and -2, but 0 is not a choice. The answer is -2.

11. **(165)** $x - 4 = 9 \Rightarrow x = 13 \Rightarrow x^2 = 169$, and so $x^2 - 4 = 165$.

12. **(24)** Subtracting 20 from each side of $7x + 10 = 44$ gives $7x - 10 = 24$. If you don't see that, subtract 10 from each side, getting $7x = 34$. Then subtract 10 to get $7x - 10 = 24$. The worst alternative is to divide both sides of $7x = 34$ by 7 to get $x = \frac{34}{7}$; then you have to multiply by 7 to get back to 34, and then subtract 10.

13. **(81)** Be alert. Since you are given the value of $3x - 4$, and want the value of $(3x - 4)^2$, just square both sides: $9^2 = 81$. If you don't see that, you'll waste time solving $3x - 4 = 9$ $\left(x = \frac{13}{3}\right)$, only to use that value to calculate that $3x - 4$ is equal to 9, which you aready knew.

14. **(2)** $x^{-3} = \frac{1}{4x} \Rightarrow 4x(x^{-3}) = 1 \Rightarrow 4x^{-2} = 1$. So,

    $$x^{-2} = \frac{1}{4} \Rightarrow \frac{1}{x^2} = \frac{1}{4} \Rightarrow x^2 = 4 \Rightarrow x = 2 \text{ or } x = -2.$$

    Since -2 cannot be entered in a grid, the only acceptable solution is 2.

15. **(.707 < x < 1)** $x^2 + 3 < 4 \Rightarrow x^2 < 1$, and $2x^2 + 3 > 4 \Rightarrow 2x^2 > 1 \Rightarrow x^2 > .5$. Grid in any number between $\sqrt{.5} \approx .707$ and 1.

9-H Word Problems

A typical SAT has several word problems, covering almost every math topic for which you are responsible. In this chapter you have already seen word problems on consecutive integers in Section 9-A, fractions and percents in Sections 9-B and 9-C, ratios and proportions in Section 9-D, and averages in Section 9-E. Later in this chapter you will see word problems involving circles, triangles, and other geometric figures. A few of these problems can be solved just with arithmetic, but most of them require basic algebra.

To solve word problems algebraically, you must treat algebra as a foreign language and learn to translate "word for word" from English into algebra, just as you would from English into French or Spanish or any other foreign language. When translating into algebra, you use some letter (often x) to represent the unknown quantity you are trying to determine. It is this translation process that causes difficulty for some students. Once the translation is completed, solving is easy using the techniques already reviewed.

Consider the pairs of typical SAT questions in Examples 1 and 2. The first ones in each pair (1a and 2a) would be considered easy, whereas the second ones (1b and 2b) would be considered harder.

EXAMPLE 1A

What is 4% of 4% of 40,000?

EXAMPLE 1B

In a lottery, 4% of the tickets printed can be redeemed for prizes, and 4% of those tickets have values in excess of $100. If the state prints 40,000 tickets, how many of them can be redeemed for more than $100?

EXAMPLE 2A

If $x + 7 = 2(x - 8)$, what is the value of x?

EXAMPLE 2B

In 7 years Erin will be twice as old as she was 8 years ago. How old is Erin now?

Once you translate the words into arithmetic expressions or algebraic equations, Examples 1a and 1b and 2a and 2b are clearly identical. The problem that many students have is doing the translation. It really isn't very difficult, and you'll learn how. First, though, look over the following English-to-algebra "dictionary."

English Words	Mathematical Meaning	Symbol
Is, was, will be, had, has, will have, is equal to, is the same as	Equals	=
Plus, more than, sum, increased by, added to, exceeds, received, got, older than, farther than, greater than	Addition	+
Minus, fewer, less than, difference, decreased by, subtracted from, younger than, gave, lost	Subtraction	−
Times, of, product, multiplied by	Multiplication	×
Divided by, quotient, per, for	Division	$\div$, $\dfrac{a}{b}$
More than, greater than	Inequality	>
At least	Inequality	≥
Fewer than, less than	Inequality	<
At most	Inequality	≤
What, how many, etc.	Unknown quantity	x (or some other variable)

Let's use this "dictionary" to translate some phrases and sentences.

1. The <u>sum</u> of 5 and some number <u>is</u> 13. $5 + x = 13$

2. John <u>was</u> 2 years <u>younger than</u> Sam. $J = S - 2$

3. Bill has <u>at most</u> $100. $B \le 100$

4. The <u>product</u> of 2 and a number <u>exceeds</u> that number by 5 (is 5 more than). $2n = n + 5$

In translating a statement, you first must decide what quantity the variable will represent. Often, this is obvious. Other times there is more than one possibility.

Let's translate and solve the two examples at the beginning of this section, and then look at a few new ones.

EXAMPLE 1B

In a lottery, 4% of the tickets printed can be redeemed for prizes, and 4% of those tickets have values in excess of $100. If the state prints 40,000 tickets, how many of them can be redeemed for more than $100?

Solution. Let x be the number of tickets worth more than $100. Then

$$x = 4\% \text{ of } 4\% \text{ of } 40{,}000 = 0.04 \times 0.04 \times 40{,}000 = \mathbf{64},$$

which is also the solution to Example 1a.

EXAMPLE 2B

In 7 years Erin will be twice as old as she was 8 years ago. How old is Erin now?

Solution. Let *x* be Erin's age now; 8 years ago she was *x* – 8 and 7 years from now she will be *x* + 7. Then,

$$x + 7 = 2(x - 8),$$

and

$x + 7 = 2(x - 8) \Rightarrow x + 7 = 2x - 16 \Rightarrow 7 = x - 16 \Rightarrow x = \textbf{23}$, which is also the solution to Example 2a.

EXAMPLE 3

The product of 2 and 8 more than a certain number is 10 times that number. What is the number?

Solution. Let *x* represent the unknown number. Then

$$2(8 + x) = 10x,$$

and

$$2(8 + x) = 10x \Rightarrow 16 + 2x = 10x \Rightarrow 8x = 16 \Rightarrow x = \textbf{2}.$$

EXAMPLE 4

If the sum of three consecutive integers is 20 more than the middle integer, what is the smallest of the three?

Solution. Let *n* represent the smallest of the three integers. Then

$$n + (n + 1) + (n + 2) = 20 + (n + 1),$$

and

$$n + n + 1 + n + 2 = 20 + n + 1 \Rightarrow 3n + 3 = 21 + n \Rightarrow 2n + 3 = 21 \Rightarrow 2n = 18 \Rightarrow n = \textbf{9}.$$

(The integers are 9, 10, and 11.)

Most algebraic word problems on the SAT are not very difficult. If, after studying this section, you still get stuck on a question, don't despair. Use the tactics that you learned in Chapter 8. In each of Examples 3 and 4, if you had been given choices, you could have backsolved; and if the questions had been grid-ins, you could have used trial and error (effectively, backsolving by making up your own choices). Here's how.

Alternative Solution to Example 3. Pick a starting number and test (using your calculator, if necessary).

Try 10: 8 + 10 = 18 and 2 × 18 = 36, but 10 × 10 = 100, which is *much too big*.

Try 5:   8 + 5 = 13 and 2 × 13 = 26, but 10 × 5 = 50, which is *still too big*.

Try 2:   8 + 2 = 10 and 2 × 10 = 20, and 10 × 2 = 20. That's it.

Alternative Solution to Example 4. You need three consecutive integers whose sum is 20 more than the middle one. Obviously, 1, 2, 3 and 5, 6, 7 are too small; neither one even adds up to 20.

Try 10, 11, 12: 10 + 11 + 12 = 33, which is 22 more than 11—a bit too much.

Try 9, 10, 11: 9 + 10 + 11 = 30, which *is* 20 more than 10.

Of course, if you can do the algebra, that's usually the best way, to handle these problems. On grid-ins you might have to backsolve with several numbers before zooming in on the correct answer; also, if the correct answer was a fraction, such as $\frac{13}{5}$, you might never find it. In the rest of this section, the proper ways to set up and solve various word problems are stressed.

> **Helpful Hint**
> In all word problems on the SAT, remember to circle what you're looking for. Don't answer the wrong question!

Age Problems

In problems involving ages, remember that "years ago" means you need to subtract, and "years from now" means you need to add.

EXAMPLE 5

In 1980, Judy was 3 times as old as Adam, but in 1984 she was only twice as old as he was. How old was Adam in 1990?

(A) 4
(B) 8
(C) 12
(D) 14
(E) 16

Solution. Let *x* be Adam's age in 1980, and fill in the table below.

Year	Judy	Adam
1980	$3x$	x
1984	$3x + 4$	$x + 4$

Helpful Hint
It is often very useful to organize the data from a word problem in a table.

Now translate: Judy's age in 1984 was twice Adam's age in 1984:

$$3x + 4 = 2(x + 4)$$
$$3x + 4 = 2x + 8 \Rightarrow x + 4 = 8 \Rightarrow x = 4.$$

Adam was 4 in 1980. However, 4 is *not* the answer to this question. Did you remember to circle what you're looking for? The question *could have* asked for Adam's age in 1980 (choice A) or 1984 (choice B) or Judy's age in any year whatsoever (choice C is 1980, and choice E is 1984); but it didn't. It asked for *Adam's age in 1990*. Since he was 4 in 1980, then 10 years later, in 1990, he was **14 (D)**.

Distance Problems

All distance problems involve one of three variations of the same formula:

$$\text{distance} = \text{rate} \times \text{time} \qquad \text{rate} = \frac{\text{distance}}{\text{time}} \qquad \text{time} = \frac{\text{distance}}{\text{rate}}$$

These are usually abbreviated as $d = rt$, $r = \dfrac{d}{t}$, and $t = \dfrac{d}{r}$.

EXAMPLE 6

How much longer, in <u>seconds</u>, is required to drive 1 mile at 40 miles per hour than at 60 miles per hour?

Solution. The time to drive 1 mile at 40 miles per hour is given by

$$t = \frac{1 \text{ mile}}{40 \text{ miles per hour}} = \frac{1}{40} \text{ hour} = \frac{1}{40} \times \overset{3}{\cancel{60}} \text{ minutes} = \frac{3}{2} \text{ minutes} = 1\frac{1}{2} \text{ minutes.}$$

The time to drive 1 mile at 60 miles per hour is given by

$$t = \frac{1 \text{ mile}}{60 \text{ miles per hour}} = \frac{1}{60} \text{ hour} = 1 \text{ minute}.$$

The difference is $\frac{1}{2}$ minute = **30** seconds.

Note that this solution used the time formula given but required only arithmetic, not algebra. Example 7 requires an algebraic solution.

EXAMPLE 7

Mark drove to a meeting at 60 miles per hour. Returning over the same route, he encountered heavy traffic, and was able to drive at only 40 miles per hour. If the return trip took 1 hour longer, how many miles did he drive each way?

(A)   2
(B)   3
(C)   5
(D) 120
(E) 240

Solution. Let x represent the number of hours Mark took to go, and make a table.

	Rate	Time	Distance
Going	60	x	$60x$
Returning	40	$x + 1$	$40(x + 1)$

Since Mark drove the same distance going and returning:

$$60x = 40(x + 1) \Rightarrow 60x = 40x + 40 \Rightarrow 20x = 40 \Rightarrow x = 2.$$

Now be sure to answer the correct question. Choices A, B, and C are the times, in hours, for going, returning, and the round trip; choices D and E are the distances each way and round-trip. You could have been asked for any of the five. If you circled what you're looking for, you won't make a careless mistake. Mark drove **120** miles each way, and so the correct answer is **D**.

The d in the formula $d = rt$ stands for distance, but it could represent any type of work that is performed at a certain rate, r, for a certain amount of time, t. Example 7 need not be about distance. Instead of driving 120 miles at 60 miles per hour for 2 hours, Mark could have read 120 pages at a rate of 60 pages per hour for 2 hours, or planted 120 flowers at the rate of 60 flowers per hour for 2 hours, or typed 120 words at a rate of 60 words per minute for 2 minutes.

This section concludes with a miscellaneous collection of word problems of the type that you may find on the SAT. Some of them are similar to problems already discussed in preceding sections.

EXAMPLE 8

At 8:00 P.M., the hostess of the party remarked that only $\frac{1}{4}$ of her guests had arrived so far, but that, as soon as 10 more showed up, $\frac{1}{3}$ of the guests would be there. How many people were invited?

Solution. Let *x* represent the number of people invited. First, translate the first sentence of the problem into algebra: $\frac{1}{4}x + 10 = \frac{1}{3}x$. Then, use the six-step method of Section 9-G to solve the equation.

Multiply each term by 12: $3x + 120 = 4x$.

Subtract 3*x* from each side: *x* = **120**.

EXAMPLE 9

In a family of three, the father weighed 5 times as much as the child, and the mother weighed $\frac{3}{4}$ as much as the father. If the three of them weighed a total of 390 pounds, how much did the mother weigh?

Helpful Hint

You often have a choice as to what you will let the variable represent. Don't necessarily have it represent what you're looking for; rather, choose what will make the problem easiest to solve.

In this problem it is easier to let *x* represent the weight of the child, and 5*x* the weight of the father, than to let *x* represent the weight of the father, and $\frac{1}{5}x$ the weight of the child. The worst choice would be to let *x* represent the weight of the mother; in that case, since the mother's weight is $\frac{3}{4}$ that of the father's, his weight would be $\frac{4}{3}$ of hers.

Solution. Let *x* = weight of the child; then 5*x* = weight of the father, and $\frac{3}{4}(5x)$ = weight of the mother. Since their combined weight is 390:

$$x + 5x + \frac{15}{4}x = 390.$$

Multiply by 4 to get rid of the fraction:

$$4x + 20x + 15x = 1560.$$

Combine like terms and then divide:

$$39x = 1560 \Rightarrow x = 40.$$

The child weighed 40 pounds, the father weighed $5 \times 40 = 200$ pounds, and the mother weighed $\frac{3}{4}(200) = $ **150 pounds**.

EXAMPLE 10

A teacher wrote three consecutive odd integers on the board. She then multiplied the first by 2, the second by 3, and the third by 4. Finally, she added all six numbers and got a sum of 400. What was the smallest number she wrote?

Solution. Let *n* be the first odd integer she wrote. Since the difference between any two consecutive odd integers is 2 (3, 5, 7, 9, etc.), the next consecutive odd integer is *n* + 2 and the third is *n* + 4. The required equation is

$$n + (n + 2) + (n + 4) + 2n + 3(n + 2) + 4(n + 4) = 400.$$

Simplifying gives

$$n + n + 2 + n + 4 + 2n + 3n + 6 + 4n + 16 = 400 \Rightarrow$$
$$12n + 28 = 400 \Rightarrow 12n = 372 \Rightarrow n = 31.$$

Exercises on Word Problems

Multiple-Choice Questions

1. In the afternoon, Judy read 100 pages at the rate of 60 pages per hour; in the evening, when she was tired, she read another 100 pages at the rate of 40 pages per hour. In pages per hour, what was her average rate of reading for the day?

   (A) 45
   (B) 48
   (C) 50
   (D) 52
   (E) 55

2. If the sum of five consecutive integers is S, what is the largest of those integers in terms of S?

   (A) $\dfrac{S-10}{5}$

   (B) $\dfrac{S+4}{4}$

   (C) $\dfrac{S+5}{4}$

   (D) $\dfrac{S-5}{2}$

   (E) $\dfrac{S+10}{5}$

3. A jar contains only red, white, and blue marbles. The number of red marbles is $\dfrac{4}{5}$ the number of white ones, and the number of white ones is $\dfrac{3}{4}$ the number of blue ones. If there are 470 marbles in all, how many of them are blue?

   (A) 120
   (B) 135
   (C) 150
   (D) 184
   (E) 200

4. As a fund-raiser, the Key Club was selling two types of candy: lollipops at 40 cents each and chocolate bars at 75 cents each. On Monday, the members sold 150 candies and raised 74 dollars. How many lollipops did they sell?

   (A) 75
   (B) 90
   (C) 96
   (D) 110
   (E) 120

5. On a certain project the only grades awarded were 75 and 100. If 85 students completed the project and the average of their grades was 85, how many earned 100?

   (A) 34
   (B) 40
   (C) 45
   (D) 51
   (E) 60

6. Aaron has 3 times as much money as Josh. If Aaron gives Josh $50, Josh will then have 3 times as much money as Aaron. How much money do the two of them have together?

   (A) $ 75
   (B) $100
   (C) $125
   (D) $150
   (E) $200

7. If $\dfrac{1}{2}x$ years ago Jason was 12, and $\dfrac{1}{2}x$ years from now he will be $2x$ years old, how old will he be $3x$ years from now?

   (A) 18
   (B) 24
   (C) 30
   (D) 54
   (E) His age cannot be determined from the information given.

8. Two printing presses working together can complete a job in 2.5 hours. Working alone, press A can do the job in 10 hours. How many hours will press B take to do the job by itself?

   (A) $3\dfrac{1}{3}$

   (B) 4

   (C) 5

   (D) $6\dfrac{1}{4}$

   (E) $7\dfrac{1}{2}$

9. Henry drove 100 miles to visit a friend. If he had driven 8 miles per hour faster than he did, he would have arrived in $\frac{5}{6}$ of the time he actually took. How many <u>minutes</u> did the trip take?

(A) 100
(B) 120
(C) 125
(D) 144
(E) 150

10. Since 1950, when Martin graduated from high school, he has gained 2 pounds every year. In 1980 he was 40% heavier than in 1950. What percent of his 1995 weight was his 1980 weight?

(A) 80
(B) 85
(C) 87.5
(D) 90
(E) 95

Grid-in Questions

11. What is the greater of two numbers whose product is 900, if the sum of the two numbers exceeds their difference by 30?

12. The number of shells in Fred's collection is 80% of the number in Phil's collection. If Phil has 80 more shells than Fred, how many do they have altogether?

13. Karen played a game several times. She received $5 every time she won and had to pay $2 every time she lost. If the ratio of the number of times she won to the number of times she lost was 3:2, and if she won a total of $66, how many times did she play this game?

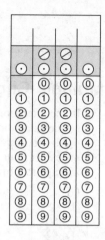

14. Each of the 10 players on the basketball team shot 100 free throws, and the average number of baskets made was 75. When the highest and lowest scores were eliminated, the average number of baskets for the remaining 8 players was 79. What is the smallest number of baskets anyone could have made?

15. In an office there was a small cash box. One day Ann took half of the money plus $1 more. Then Dan took half of the remaining money plus $1 more. Stan then took the remaining $11. How many dollars were originally in the box?

Answer Key

1. **B**	3. **E**	5. **A**	7. **D**	9. **E**	
2. **E**	4. **D**	6. **B**	8. **A**	10. **C**	

11. **6 0**

12. **7 2 0**

13. **3 0**

14. **1 8**

15. **5 0**

Answer Explanations

1. **B.** Judy's average rate of reading is determined by dividing the total number of pages she read (200) by the total amount of time she spent reading. In the afternoon she read for $\frac{100}{60} = \frac{5}{3}$ hours, and in the evening for $\frac{100}{40} = \frac{5}{2}$ hours, for a total time of

$$\frac{5}{3} + \frac{5}{2} = \frac{10}{6} + \frac{15}{6} = \frac{25}{6} \text{ hours.}$$

Her average rate was

$$200 \div \frac{25}{6} = \overset{8}{200} \times \frac{6}{\underset{1}{25}} = 48 \text{ pages per hour.}$$

2. **E.** Let the five consecutive integers be $n, n+1, n+2, n+3, n+4$. Then:

$$S = n + n + 1 + n + 2 + n + 3 + n + 4 =$$
$$5n + 10 \Rightarrow 5n = S - 10 \Rightarrow n = \frac{S-10}{5}.$$

Choice A, $\frac{S-10}{5}$, is the *smallest* of the integers; the *largest* is

$$n + 4 = \frac{S-10}{5} + 4 = \frac{S-10}{5} + \frac{20}{5} = \frac{S+10}{5}.$$

3. **E.** If there are b blue marbles, there are $\frac{3}{4}b$ white ones, and $\frac{4}{5}\left(\frac{3}{4}b\right) = \frac{3}{5}b$ red ones. Then,

$$470 = b + \frac{3}{4}b + \frac{3}{5}b = b\left(1 + \frac{3}{4} + \frac{3}{5}\right) = \frac{47}{20}b,$$

so $b = 470 \div \frac{47}{20} = \overset{10}{470} \times \frac{20}{\underset{1}{47}} = 200.$

4. **D.** If x represents the number of chocolate bars sold, then the number of lollipops sold is $150 - x$. You must use the same units, so you can write 75 cents as 0.75 dollar or 74 dollars as 7400 cents. Avoid the decimals: x chocolates sold for $75x$ cents and $(150 - x)$ lollipops sold for $40(150 - x)$ cents. Therefore:

$$7400 = 75x + 40(150 - x) =$$
$$75x + 6000 - 40x = 6000 + 35x \Rightarrow$$
$$1400 = 35x \Rightarrow x = 40,$$

and $150 - 40 = 110$.

5. **A.** Let x represent the number of students earning 100; then $85 - x$ is the number of students earning 75. Then:

$$85 = \frac{100x + 75(85 - x)}{85} =$$
$$\frac{100x + 6375 - 75x}{85} = \frac{25x - 6375}{85} \Rightarrow$$
$$7225 = 25x - 6375 \Rightarrow 850 = 25x \Rightarrow x = 34.$$

6. **B.**

	Josh	Aaron
At the beginning	x	$3x$
After the gift	$x + 50$	$3x - 50$

After the gift, Josh will have 3 times as much money as Aaron:

$$x + 50 = 3(3x - 50) \Rightarrow x + 50 = 9x - 150.$$

So, $8x = 200 \Rightarrow x = 25$.

Therefore, Josh has $25 and Aaron has $75, for a total of $100.

7. **D.** Since $\frac{1}{2}x$ years ago Jason was 12, he is now $12 + \frac{1}{2}x$; and $\frac{1}{2}x$ years from now, he will be $12 + \frac{1}{2}x + \frac{1}{2}x = 12 + x$. At that time he will be $2x$ years old, so $12 + x = 2x \Rightarrow x = 12$. Thus, he is now $12 + 6 = 18$, and $3x$, or 36, years from now he will be $18 + 36 = 54$.

8. **A.** Let x represent the number of hours press B would take working alone.

	Press A Alone	Press B Alone	Together
Part of job that can be completed in 1 hour	$\frac{1}{10}$	$\frac{1}{x}$	$\frac{1}{2.5}$
Part of job that can be completed in 2.5 hours	$\frac{2.5}{10}$	$\frac{2.5}{x}$	1

- Write the equation: $\frac{2.5}{10} + \frac{2.5}{x} = 1$
- Multiply each term by $10x$: $2.5x + 25 = 10x$
- Subtract $2.5x$ from each side: $25 = 7.5x$
- Divide each side by 7.5: $x = 3\frac{1}{3}$ hours

9. E. Let t represent the time, in hours, and r the rate, in miles per hour, that Henry drove. Then

$$t = \frac{100}{r} \quad \text{and} \quad \frac{5}{6}t = \frac{100}{r+8}.$$

Multiply the second equation by $\frac{6}{5}$:

$$\frac{\cancel{6}}{\cancel{5}}\left(\frac{\cancel{5}}{\cancel{6}}t\right) = \frac{6}{5}\left(\frac{100}{r+8}\right) \Rightarrow t = \frac{600}{5r+40}, \quad \text{so}$$

$$\frac{100}{r} = \frac{600}{5r+40}.$$

Cross-multiply:

$$500r + 4000 = 600r \Rightarrow 100r = 4000 \Rightarrow r = 40.$$

Henry drove at 40 miles per hour, and the trip took $100 \div 40 = 2.5$ hours $= 150$ minutes. (Had he driven at 48 miles per hour, the trip would have taken 125 minutes.)

10. C. Let x represent Martin's weight in 1950. By 1980, he had gained 60 pounds (2 pounds per year for 30 years) and was 40% heavier:

$$60 = 0.40x \Rightarrow x = 60 \div 0.4 = 150.$$

In 1980, he weighed 210 pounds, and 15 years later, in 1995, he weighed 240:

$$\frac{21\cancel{0}}{24\cancel{0}} = \frac{7}{8} = 87.5\%.$$

11. (60) Let x be the greater and y the smaller of the two numbers; then

$$(x + y) = 30 + (x - y) \Rightarrow y = 30 - y \Rightarrow$$
$$2y = 30 \Rightarrow y = 15;$$

and, since $xy = 900$, $x = 900 \div 15 = 60$.

12. (720) If x represents the number of shells in Phil's collection, then Fred has $.80x$ shells. Since Phil has 80 more shells than Fred:

$$x = .80x + 80 \Rightarrow .20x = 80.$$

So, $x = 80 \div .20 = 400$.
Then Phil has 400 shells and Fred has $(.80) \times 400 = 320$ shells: a total of 720 shells.

13. (30) Use TACTIC D1: write the letter x after each number in the ratio. Karen won $3x$ times and lost $2x$ times, and thus played a total of $5x$ games. Since she got $5 every time she won, she received $5(3x) = \$15x$. Also, since she paid \$2 for each loss, she paid out $\$2(2x) = \$4x$. Therefore, her net winnings were $\$15x - \$4x = \$11x$, which you are told was \$66. Then, $11x = 66 \Rightarrow x = 6$, and so $5x = 30$.

14. (18) Since the average for all 10 players was 75, the total number of baskets made was $10 \times 75 = 750$. Also, since 8 of the players had an average of 79, they made a total of $8 \times 79 = 632$ baskets. The other 2 players, therefore, made $750 - 632 = 118$ baskets. The most baskets that the player with the highest number could have made was 100, so the player with the lowest number had to have made at least 18.

15. (50) You can avoid some messy algebra by working backwards. Put back the \$11 Stan took; then put back the extra \$1 that Dan took. There is now \$12, which means that, when Dan took his half, he took \$12. Put that back. Now there is \$24 in the box. Put back the extra \$1 that Ann took. The box now has \$25, so before Ann took her half, there was \$50. *Algebraic solution*. Assume that there were originally x dollars in the box. Ann took $\frac{1}{2}x + 1$, leaving $\frac{1}{2}x - 1$. Dan then took $\frac{1}{2}$ of that plus \$1 more; he took

$$\frac{1}{2}\left(\frac{1}{2}x - 1\right) + 1 = \frac{1}{4}x - \frac{1}{2} + 1 = \frac{1}{4}x + \frac{1}{2}.$$

Then Stan took \$11. Since together they took all x dollars:

$$x = \left(\frac{1}{2}x + 1\right) + \left(\frac{1}{4}x + \frac{1}{2}\right) + 11 = \frac{3}{4}x + 12\frac{1}{2}.$$

Therefore, $12\frac{1}{2} = \frac{1}{4}x \Rightarrow x = 50$.

GEOMETRY

Although about 30% of the math questions on the SAT involve geometry, you need to know only a relatively small number of facts—far less than you would learn in a geometry course—and, of course, you need provide no proofs. The next six sections review all of the geometry that you need to know to do well on the SAT. Also, the material is presented exactly as it appears on the SAT, using the same vocabulary and notation, which may be slightly different from the terminology you have used in your math classes. There are plenty of sample multiple-choice and grid-in problems for you to solve, and they will show you exactly how these topics are treated on the SAT.

9-I Lines and Angles

On the SAT, lines are usually referred to by lowercase letters, typically ℓ, m, and n. If P and Q are any points on line ℓ, we can also refer to ℓ as PQ. In general, we have the following notations:

- PQ represents the **line** that goes through P and Q:

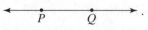

- PQ represents a **ray**; it consists of point P and all the points on PQ that are on the same side of P as Q:

- $\overline{PQ}$ represents a **line segment** (often referred to simply as a **segment**); it consists of points P and Q and all the points on PQ that are between them:

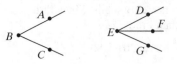

- PQ represents the **length** of segment $\overline{PQ}$.

> **NOTE**
>
> $\overline{AB} \cong \overline{PQ}$ means *exactly* the same thing as $AB = PQ$.

If $\overline{AB}$ and $\overline{PQ}$ have the same length, we say that $\overline{AB}$ and $\overline{PQ}$ are **congruent,** and write $\overline{AB} \cong \overline{PQ}$. We can also write $AB = PQ$.

An **angle** is formed by the intersection of two line segments, rays, or lines. The point of intersection is called the **vertex**.

An angle can be named by three points: a point on one side, the vertex, and a point on the other side. When there is no possible ambiguity, the angle can be named just by its vertex. For example, in the diagram below we can refer to the angle on the left as $\angle B$ or $\angle ABC$. To talk about $\angle E$, on the right, however, would be ambiguous; $\angle E$ might mean $\angle DEF$ or $\angle FEG$ or $\angle DEG$.

> **NOTE**
>
> $\angle A \cong \angle B$ means *exactly* the same thing as m$\angle A =$ m$\angle B$.

On the SAT, angles are always measured in degrees. The degree measure of $\angle ABC$ is represented by m$\angle ABC$. If $\angle P$ and $\angle Q$ have the same measure, we say that they are congruent and write $\angle P \cong \angle Q$. In the diagram below, $\angle A$ and $\angle B$ at the left are right angles. Therefore, m$\angle A = 90$ and m$\angle B = 90$, so m$\angle A =$ m$\angle B$ and $\angle A \cong \angle B$. In equilateral triangle PQR, at the right, m$\angle P =$ m$\angle Q =$ m$\angle R = 60$, and $\angle P \cong \angle Q \cong \angle R$.

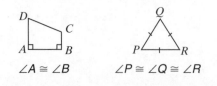

$\angle A \cong \angle B$ $\angle P \cong \angle Q \cong \angle R$

Key Fact I1

Angles are classified according to their degree measures.

• An *acute* angle measures less than 90°.
• A *right* angle measures 90°.
• An *obtuse* angle measures more than 90° but less than 180°.
• A *straight* angle measures 180°.

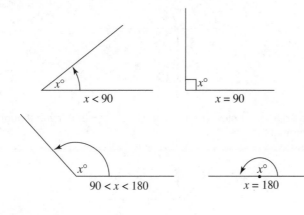

Key Fact I2

If two or more angles form a straight angle, the sum of their measures is 180°.

KEY FACT I2 is one of the facts provided in the "Reference Information" at the beginning of each math section.

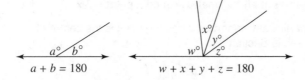

EXAMPLE 1

In the figure below, R, S, and T are all on line ℓ. What is the average (arithmetic mean) of a, b, c, d, and e?

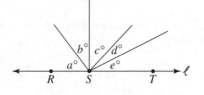
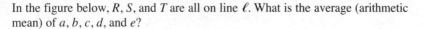

Solution. Since ∠*RST* is a straight angle, by KEY FACT I2, the sum of *a*, *b*, *c*, *d*, and *e* is 180, and so their average is $\frac{180}{5}$ = **36**.

In the figure below, since $a + b + c + d = 180$ and $e + f + g = 180$,
$a + b + c + d + e + f + g = 180 + 180 = 360$.

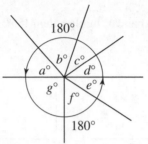

It is also true that in the diagram below $u + v + w + x + y + z = 360$, even though none of the angles forms a straight angle.

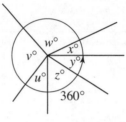

Key Fact I3

The sum of the measures of all the angles around a point is 360°.

NOTE: This fact is particularly important when the point is the center of a circle, as will be seen in Section 9-L.

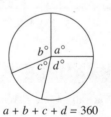

$a + b + c + d = 360$

When two lines intersect, four angles are formed. The two angles in each pair of opposite angles are called ***vertical angles***.

NOTE

KEY FACT I4 means that if ∠*A* and ∠*B* are vertical angles, then m∠*A* = m∠*B*.

Key Fact I4

Vertical angles are congruent.

EXAMPLE 2

In the figure below, what is the value of *a*?

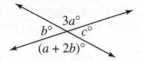

Solution. Because vertical angles are congruent:

$$a + 2b = 3a \Rightarrow 2b = 2a \Rightarrow a = b.$$

For the same reason, *b* = *c*. Therefore, *a*, *b*, and *c* are all equal. Replace each *b* and *c* in the figure with *a*, and add:

$$a + a + 3a + a + 2a = 360 \Rightarrow 8a = 360 \Rightarrow a = \mathbf{45}.$$

Consider these vertical angles:

By KEY FACT I4, *a* = *c* and *b* = *d*.

By KEY FACT I2, *a* + *b* = 180, *b* + *c* = 180, *c* + *d* = 180, and *a* + *d* = 180.

It follows that, if any of the four angles is a right angle, all the angles are right angles.

EXAMPLE 3

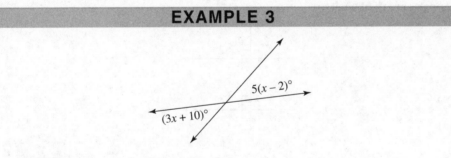

In the figure above, what is the value of *x*?

(A) 6
(B) 8
(C) 10
(D) 20
(E) 40

Solution. Since vertical angles are congruent:

$$3x + 10 = 5(x - 2) \Rightarrow 3x + 10 = 5x - 10 \Rightarrow 3x + 20 = 5x \Rightarrow 20 = 2x \Rightarrow x = \mathbf{10 \ (C)}.$$

In the figures below, line ℓ divides ∠*ABC* into two congruent angles, and line *k* divides line segment $\overline{DE}$ into two congruent segments. Line ℓ is said to **bisect** the angle, and line *k* **bisects** the line segment. Point *M* is called the **midpoint** of segment $\overline{DE}$.

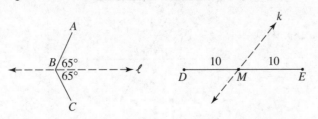

EXAMPLE 4

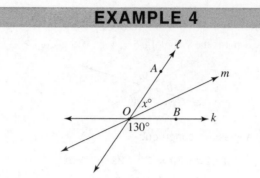

In the figure above, lines k, ℓ, and m intersect at O. If line m bisects $\angle AOB$, what is the value of x?

Solution. Here, m$\angle AOB$ + 130 = 180 ⇒ m$\angle AOB$ = 50; and since $\angle AOB$ is bisected, **x = 25**.

Two lines that intersect to form right angles are said to be ***perpendicular***.

Two lines that never intersect are said to be ***parallel***. Consequently, parallel lines form no angles. However, if a third line, called a ***transversal***, intersects a pair of parallel lines, eight angles are formed, and the relationships among these angles are very important.

Key Fact I5

If a pair of parallel lines is cut by a transversal that is perpendicular to the parallel lines, all eight angles are right angles.

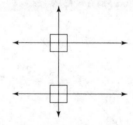

Key Fact I6

If a pair of parallel lines is cut by a transversal that is *not* perpendicular to the parallel lines:

• **Four of the angles are acute, and four are obtuse.**
• **All four acute angles are congruent:** $a = c = e = g$.
• **All four obtuse angles are congruent:** $b = d = f = h$.
• **The sum of any acute angle and any obtuse angle is 180°:**
  for example, $d + e = 180$, $c + f = 180$, $b + g = 180$, ...

Key Fact I7

If a pair of lines that are not parallel is cut by a transversal, *none* of the statements listed in KEY FACT I6 is true.

Key Fact I8

If a line is perpendicular to each of a pair of lines, then these lines are parallel.

EXAMPLE 5

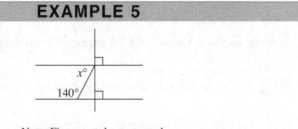

Note: Figure not drawn to scale

What is the value of x in the figure above?

(A) 40
(B) 50
(C) 90
(D) 140
(E) It cannot be determined from the information given.

Solution. Despite the fact that the figure has not been drawn to scale, the little squares assure you that the vertical line is perpendicular to both of the horizontal ones, so these lines are parallel. Therefore, the sum of the 140° obtuse angle and the acute angle marked $x°$ is 180°: $x + 140 = 180 \Rightarrow x = $ **40 (A)**.

NOTE: If the two little squares indicating right angles were not in the figure, the answer would be E: "It cannot be determined from the information given." You are not told that the two lines that look parallel are actually parallel; and since the figure is not drawn to scale, you certainly cannot make that assumption. If the lines are not parallel, then $140 + x$ is *not* 180, and x cannot be determined.

EXAMPLE 6

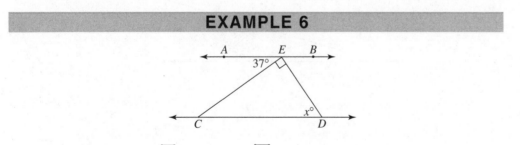

In the figure above, $\overleftrightarrow{AB}$ is parallel to $\overleftrightarrow{CD}$. What is the value of x?

Solution. Let *y* be the measure of ∠*BED*. Then by KEY FACT 12:

$$37 + 90 + y = 180 \Rightarrow 127 + y = 180 \Rightarrow y = 53.$$

Since $\overleftrightarrow{AB}$ is parallel to $\overleftrightarrow{CD}$ by KEY FACT 16, $x = y \Rightarrow x = \mathbf{53}$.

EXAMPLE 7

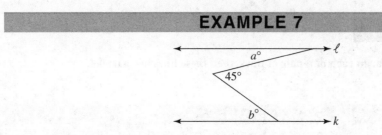

In the figure above, lines ℓ and *k* are parallel. What is the value of *a + b*?

(A) 45
(B) 60
(C) 90
(D) 135
(E) It cannot be determined from the information given.

Solution. If you were asked for the value of either *a* or *b*, the answer would be E—neither one can be determined; but if you are clever, you can find the value of *a + b*. Draw a line parallel to ℓ and *k* through the vertex of the angle. Then, looking at the top two lines, you see that *a = x*, and looking at the bottom two lines, you have *b = y*. Therefore, *a + b = x + y =* **45 (A)**.

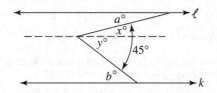

Alternative solution. Draw a different line and use a fact from Section 9-J on triangles. Extend one of the line segments to form a triangle. Since ℓ and *k* are parallel, the measure of the bottom angle in the triangle equals *a*. Now, use the fact that the sum of the measures of the three angles in a triangle is 180° or, even easier, that the given 45° angle is an exterior angle, and so is equal to the sum of *a* and *b*.

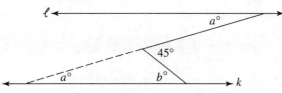

Exercises on Lines and Angles

Multiple-Choice Questions

1. In the figure below, what is the value of b?

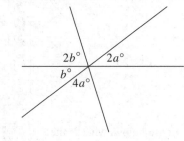

    (A) 9
    (B) 18
    (C) 27
    (D) 36
    (E) 45

2. In the figure below, what is the value of x if $y{:}x = 3{:}2$?

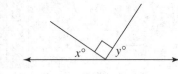

    (A) 18
    (B) 27
    (C) 36
    (D) 45
    (E) 54

3. What is the measure of the angle formed by the minute and hour hands of a clock at 1:50?

    (A) 90°
    (B) 95°
    (C) 105°
    (D) 115°
    (E) 120°

4. Concerning the figure below, if $a = b$, which of the following statements *must* be true?

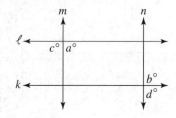

Note: Figure not drawn to scale

  I. $c = d$.
 II. ℓ and k are parallel.
III. m and ℓ are perpendicular.

    (A) None
    (B) I only
    (C) I and II only
    (D) I and III only
    (E) I, II, and III

5. In the figure below, B and C lie on line n, m bisects $\angle AOC$, and ℓ bisects $\angle AOB$. What is the measure of $\angle DOE$?

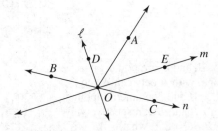

Note: Figure not drawn to scale

    (A) 75°
    (B) 90°
    (C) 105°
    (D) 120°
    (E) It cannot be determined from the information given.

Grid-in Questions

6. In the figure below, what is the value of $\dfrac{b+a}{b-a}$?

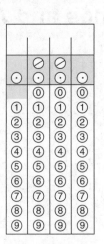

7. In the figure below, $a{:}b = 3{:}5$ and $c{:}b = 2{:}1$. What is the measure of the largest angle?

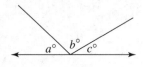

Note: Figure not drawn to scale

8. A, B, and C are points on a line, with B between A and C. Let M and N be the midpoints of $\overline{AB}$ and $\overline{BC}$, respectively. If $AB{:}BC = 3{:}1$, what is $AB{:}MN$?

9. In the figure below, lines k and ℓ are parallel. What is the value of $y - x$?

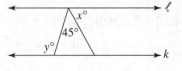

10. In the figure below, what is the average (arithmetic mean) of the measures of the five angles?

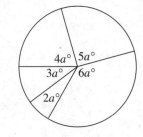

Answer Key

1. **D**   2. **C**   3. **D**   4. **B**   5. **B**

6. | | | *1* | *1* |
7. | | *1* | *0* | *0* |
8. | | *3* | / | *2* | or | *1* | . | *5* |
9. | | | *4* | *5* |
10. | | | *7* | *2* |

Answer Explanations

1. **D.** Since vertical angles are congruent, the measures of the two unmarked angles are $2b°$ and $4a°$. Also, since the sum of all six angles is $360°$:

$$360 = 4a + 2b + 2a + 4a + 2b + b = 10a + 5b.$$

Note that since the angles labeled a and $2b$ are vertical angles, $b = 2a$, and so $5b = 10a$. Hence:

$$360 = 10a + 5b = 10a + 10a = 20a \Rightarrow$$
$$a = 18 \Rightarrow b = 36.$$

2. **C.** Since $x + y + 90 = 180$, then $x + y = 90$. Also, since $y{:}x = 3{:}2$, then $y = 3t$ and $x = 2t$. Therefore:

$$3t + 2t = 90 \Rightarrow 5t = 90 \Rightarrow$$
$$t = 18 \Rightarrow x = 2(18) = 36.$$

3. **D.** For problems such as this, always draw a diagram. The measure of each of the 12 central angles from one number to the next on the clock is $30°$. At 1:50 the minute hand is pointing at 10, and the hour hand has gone $\dfrac{50}{60} = \dfrac{5}{6}$ of the way from 1 to 2. Then, from 10 to 1 on the clock is $90°$, and from 1 to the hour hand is $\dfrac{5}{6}(30°) = 25°$, for a total of $90° + 25° = 115°$.

4. **B.** No conclusion can be drawn about the lines; they could form any angles whatsoever. (II and III are both false.) Statement I is true: $c = 180 - a = 180 - b = d$.

5. **B.** Let $x = \dfrac{1}{2}\mathrm{m}\angle AOC$, and $y = \dfrac{1}{2}\mathrm{m}\angle AOB$. Then,

$$x + y = \dfrac{1}{2}\mathrm{m}\angle AOC + \dfrac{1}{2}\mathrm{m}\angle AOB =$$

$$\dfrac{1}{2}(\mathrm{m}\angle AOC + \mathrm{m}\angle AOB) =$$

$$\dfrac{1}{2}(180°) = 90°.$$

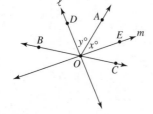

6. **(11)** From the diagram, you see that $6a = 180$, which implies that $a = 30$, and that $5b = 180$, which implies that $b = 36$. Therefore:

$$\frac{b+a}{b-a} = \frac{36+30}{36-30} = \frac{66}{6} = 11.$$

7. **(100)** Since $a{:}b = 3{:}5$, then for some number x, $a = 3x$ and $b = 5x$; and since $c{:}b = 2{:}1$, then $c = 2b = 10x$. Then:

$$3x + 5x + 10x = 180 \Rightarrow 18x = 180.$$

So, $x = 10$ and $c = 10x = 10(10) = 100$.

8. $\left(\dfrac{3}{2} \text{ or } 1.5\right)$ If a diagram is not provided on a geometry question, draw one. Since

$AB{:}BC = 3{:}1$, let $AB = 3$ and $BC = 1$.

From the figure above, you can see that

$$AB{:}MN = \frac{3}{2} = 1.5.$$

9. **(45)** Since lines ℓ and k are parallel, the angle marked y in the given diagram and the sum of the angles marked x and 45 are equal: $y = x + 45 \Rightarrow y - x = 45$.

10. **(72)** The markings in the five angles are irrelevant. The sum of the measures of these angles is $360°$, and $360 \div 5 = 72$. If you calculated the measure of each angle, you should have gotten 36, 54, 72, 90, and 108; but you would have wasted time.

9-J Triangles

More geometry questions on the SAT pertain to triangles than to any other topic. To answer these questions correctly, you need to know several important facts about the angles and sides of triangles. The KEY FACTS in this section are extremely useful. Read them carefully, a few times if necessary, and *make sure you learn them all.*

Key Fact J1

In any triangle, the sum of the measures of the three angles is 180°.

REFERENCE FACT

KEY FACT J1 is one of the facts provided in the "Reference Information" at the beginning of each math section.

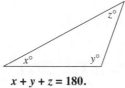

$$x + y + z = 180.$$

Figure 1 illustrates KEY FACT J1 for five different triangles, which will be discussed below.

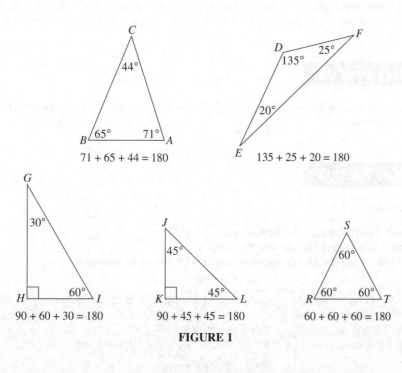

$71 + 65 + 44 = 180$

$135 + 25 + 20 = 180$

$90 + 60 + 30 = 180$

$90 + 45 + 45 = 180$

$60 + 60 + 60 = 180$

FIGURE 1

EXAMPLE 1

In the figure below, what is the value of *x*?

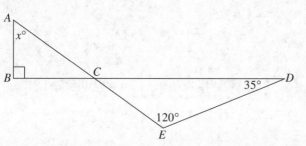

Solution. Use KEY FACT J1 twice: first, for △*CDE* and then for △*ABC*.

- m∠*DCE* + 120 + 35 = 180 ⟹ m∠*DCE* + 155 = 180 ⟹ m∠*DCE* = 25.
- Since vertical angles are congruent, m∠*ACB* = 25 (see KEY FACT I4).
- x + 90 + 25 = 180 ⟹ x + 115 = 180 ⟹ x = **65**.

EXAMPLE 2

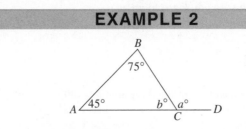

In the figure above, what is the value of *a*?

Solution. First find the value of *b*:

$$180 = 45 + 75 + b = 120 + b \Rightarrow b = 60.$$

Then, $a + b = 180 \Rightarrow a = 180 - b = 180 - 60 = \mathbf{120}$.

In Example 2, ∠*BCD*, which is formed by one side of △*ABC* and the extension of another side, is called an *exterior angle*. Note that, to find *a*, you did not have to first find *b*; you could just have added the other two angles: *a* = 75 + 45 = 120. This is a useful fact to remember.

Key Fact J2

The measure of an exterior angle of a triangle is equal to the sum of the measures of the two opposite interior angles.

Key Fact J3

In any triangle:

- the longest side is opposite the largest angle;
- the shortest side is opposite the smallest angle;
- sides with the same length are opposite angles with the same measure.

CAUTION: In KEY FACT J3 the condition "in any triangle" is crucial. If the angles are not in the same triangle, none of the conclusions holds. For example, in Figure 2 below *AB*, and *DE* are *not* equal even though each is opposite a 90° angle; and in Figure 3, *QS* is not the longest side even though it is opposite the largest angle.

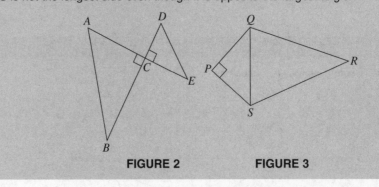

FIGURE 2   **FIGURE 3**

Consider triangles *ABC*, *JKL*, and *RST* in Figure 1 on page 525.

- In △*ABC*: $\overline{BC}$ is the longest side since it is opposite ∠*A*, the largest angle (71°). Similarly, $\overline{AB}$ is the shortest side since it is opposite ∠*C*, the smallest angle (44°). Therefore, *AB* < *AC* < *BC*.
- In △*JKL*: Angles *J* and *L* have the same measure (45°), so *JK* = *KL*.
- In △*RST*: Since all three angles have the same measure (60°), all three sides have the same length: *RS* = *ST* = *TR*.

EXAMPLE 3

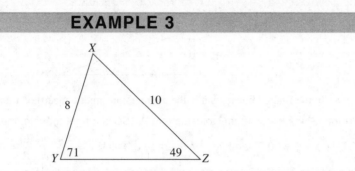

In the figure above, which of the following statements concerning the length of side $\overline{YZ}$ is true?

(A) *YZ* < 8
(B) *YZ* = 8
(C) 8 < *YZ* < 10
(D) *YZ* = 10
(E) *YZ* > 10

Solution.

- By KEY FACT J1, m∠*X* + 71 + 49 = 180 ⟹ m∠*X* = 60.
- Then *Y* is the largest angle, *Z* is the smallest, and *X* is in between.
- Therefore, by KEY FACT J3: *XY* < *YZ* < *XZ* ⟹ 8 < *YZ* < 10.
- The answer is **C**.

Classification of Triangles

Name	Lengths of Sides	Measures of Angles	Examples from Figure 1
Scalene	all 3 different	all 3 different	*ABC, DEF, GHI*
Isosceles	2 the same	2 the same	*JKL*
Equilateral	all 3 the same	all 3 the same	*RST*

Acute triangles are triangles such as *ABC* and *RST*, in which all three angles are acute. An acute triangle can be scalene, isosceles, or equilateral.

Obtuse triangles are triangles such as *DEF*, in which one angle is obtuse and two are acute. An obtuse triangle can be scalene or isosceles.

Right triangles are triangles such as *GHI* and *JKL*, which have one right angle and two acute ones. A right triangle can be scalene or isosceles. The side opposite the 90° angle is called the **hypotenuse**, and by KEY FACT J3 it is the longest side. The other two sides are called the **legs**.

If *x* and *y* are the measures of the acute angles of a right triangle, then by KEY FACT J1: 90 + *x* + *y* = 180, and so *x* + *y* = 90.

Key Fact J4

In any right triangle, the sum of the measures of the two acute angles is 90°.

EXAMPLE 4

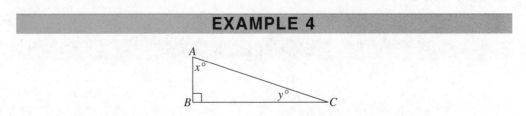

In the figure above, what is the average (arithmetic mean) of *x* and *y*?

Solution. Since the diagram indicates that △*ABC* is a right triangle, then, by KEY

FACT J4, *x* + *y* = 90. Therefore, the average of *x* and *y* = $\dfrac{x+y}{2} = \dfrac{90}{2} =$ **45**.

The most important facts concerning right triangles are the **Pythagorean theorem** and its converse, which are given in KEY FACT J5 and repeated as the first line of KEY FACT J6.

Key Fact J5

Let *a*, *b*, and *c* be the sides of △*ABC*, with $a \le b \le c$.

- If △*ABC* is a right triangle, $a^2 + b^2 = c^2$;
- If $a^2 + b^2 = c^2$, then △*ABC* is a right triangle.

REFERENCE FACT

The Pythagorean theorem is one of the facts provided in the "Reference Information" at the beginning of each math section.

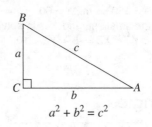

$$a^2 + b^2 = c^2$$

Key Fact J6

Let *a*, *b*, and *c* be the sides of △*ABC*, with $a \le b \le c$.

- $a^2 + b^2 = c^2$ if and only if ∠*C* is a right angle.
- $a^2 + b^2 < c^2$ if and only if ∠*C* is obtuse.
- $a^2 + b^2 > c^2$ if and only if ∠*C* is acute.

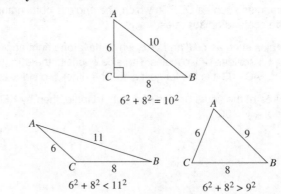

$$6^2 + 8^2 = 10^2$$

$$6^2 + 8^2 < 11^2 \qquad 6^2 + 8^2 > 9^2$$

EXAMPLE 5

Which of the following CANNOT be the lengths of the sides of a right triangle?

(A) 3, 4, 5

(B) 1, 1, $\sqrt{2}$

(C) 1, $\sqrt{3}$, 2

(D) $\sqrt{3}$, $\sqrt{4}$, $\sqrt{5}$

(E) 30, 40, 50

Solution. Just check the choices.

- (A): $3^2 + 4^2 = 9 + 16 = 25 = 5^2$ These *are* the lengths of the sides of a right triangle.
- (B): $1^2 + 1^2 = 1 + 1 = 2 = (\sqrt{2})^2$ These *are* the lengths of the sides of a right triangle.
- (C): $1^2 + (\sqrt{3})^2 = 1 + 3 = 4 = 2^2$ These *are* the lengths of the sides of a right triangle.
- (D): $(\sqrt{3})^2 + (\sqrt{4})^2 = 3 + 4 = 7 \neq (\sqrt{5})^2$ These *are not* the lengths of the sides of a right triangle.

Stop. The answer is **D**. There is no need to check choice E—but if you did, you would find that 30, 40, 50 *are* the lengths of the sides of a right triangle.

Below are the right triangles that appear most often on the SAT. You should recognize them immediately whenever they come up in questions. Carefully study each one, and memorize KEY FACTS J7–J11.

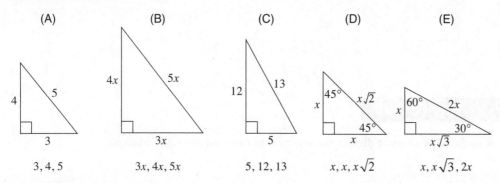

On the SAT, the most common right triangles whose sides are integers are the 3-4-5 triangle (A) and its multiples (B).

Key Fact J7

For any positive number x, there is a right triangle whose sides are $3x$, $4x$, $5x$.

For example:

$x = 1$	3, 4, 5		$x = 5$	15, 20, 25
$x = 2$	6, 8, 10		$x = 10$	30, 40, 50
$x = 3$	9, 12, 15		$x = 50$	150, 200, 250
$x = 4$	12, 16, 20		$x = 100$	300, 400, 500

NOTE: KEY FACT J6 applies even if x is not an integer. For example:

         $x = 0.5$ 1.5, 2, 2.5 $x = \pi$ 3π, 4π, 5π

The only other right triangle with integer sides that you should recognize immediately is the one whose sides are 5, 12, 13 (C).

Let *x* = length of each leg, and *h* = length of the hypotenuse, of an isosceles right triangle (D). By the Pythagorean theorem,

$$x^2 + x^2 = h^2 \Rightarrow 2x^2 = h^2 \Rightarrow h = \sqrt{2x^2} = x\sqrt{2}.$$

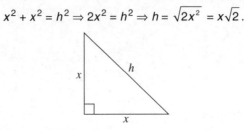

Key Fact J8

In a 45-45-90 right triangle, the sides are x, x, and $x\sqrt{2}$. Therefore:

• **By multiplying the length of a leg by $\sqrt{2}$, you get the hypotenuse.**

• **By dividing the hypotenuse by $\sqrt{2}$, you get the length of each leg.**

REFERENCE FACT

KEY FACT J8 is one of the facts provided in the "Reference Information" at the beginning of each math section.

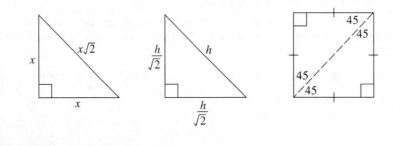

Key Fact J9

The diagonal of a square divides the square into two isosceles right triangles.

The last important right triangle is the one whose angles measure 30°, 60°, and 90°.

Key Fact J10

An altitude divides an equilateral triangle into two 30-60-90 right triangles.

Let 2*x* be the length of each side of equilateral triangle *ABC*, in which altitude $\overline{AD}$ is drawn.

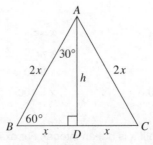

Then △*ADB* is a 30-60-90 right triangle, and its sides are *x*, 2*x*, and *h*. By the Pythagorean theorem, $x^2 + h^2 = (2x)^2 = 4x^2 \Rightarrow h^2 = 3x^2 \Rightarrow h = \sqrt{3x^2} = x\sqrt{3}.$

Key Fact J11

REFERENCE FACT

KEY FACT J11 is one of the facts provided in the "Reference Information" at the beginning of each math section.

In a 30-60-90 right triangle the sides are x, $x\sqrt{3}$, and $2x$.

If you know the length of the shorter leg (x):

• multiply it by $\sqrt{3}$ to get the length of the longer leg;
• multiply it by 2 to get the length of the hypotenuse.

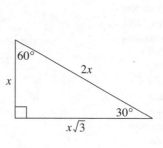

If you know the length of the longer leg (a):

• divide it by $\sqrt{3}$ to get the length of the shorter leg;
• multiply the shorter leg by 2 to get the length of the hypotenuse.

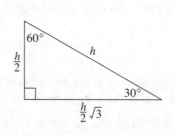

If you know the length of the hypotenuse (h):

• divide it by 2 to get the length of the shorter leg;
• multiply the shorter leg by $\sqrt{3}$ to get the length of the longer leg.

EXAMPLE 6

What is the area of a square whose diagonal is 10?

(A) 20
(B) 40
(C) 50
(D) 100
(E) 200

Solution. Draw a diagonal in a square of side s, creating a 45-45-90 right triangle. By KEY FACT J8:

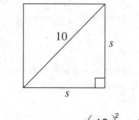

$$s = \frac{10}{\sqrt{2}} \quad \text{and} \quad A = s^2 = \left(\frac{10}{\sqrt{2}}\right)^2 = \frac{100}{2} = \mathbf{50}.$$

The answer is **C**.

[KEY FACT K8 gives the formula for the area of a square based on this example: $A = \dfrac{d^2}{2}$, where d is the length of a diagonal.]

EXAMPLE 7

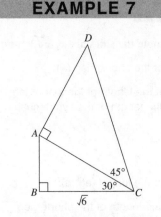

Helpful Hint

If you know some elementary trigonometry, you could use the sine, cosine, and tangent ratios to solve questions involving 30-60-90 triangles and 45-45-90 triangles. But YOU SHOULDN'T. Rather, you should use KEY FACTS J8 and J11. You should know these facts by heart; but in case you forget, they are given to you in the Reference Information on the first page of each math section.

In the diagram above, if $BC = \sqrt{6}$, what is the value of CD?

Solution. $\triangle ABC$ and $\triangle DAC$ are 30-60-90 and 45-45-90 right triangles, respectively. Use KEY FACTS J11 and J8.

• Divide $\overline{BC}$, the length of the longer leg, by $\sqrt{3}$ to get $\overline{AB}$, the length of the shorter leg:

$$\frac{\sqrt{6}}{\sqrt{3}} = \sqrt{2}.$$

• Multiply $\overline{AB}$ by 2 to get the length of the hypotenuse: $AC = 2\sqrt{2}$.
• Since $\overline{AC}$ is also a leg of isosceles right triangle DAC, to get the length of hypotenuse $\overline{CD}$,

multiply AC by $\sqrt{2}$: $CD = 2\sqrt{2} \times \sqrt{2} = 2 \times (\sqrt{2})(\sqrt{2}) = 2 \times 2 = \mathbf{4}$.

Key Fact J12 Triangle Inequality

The sum of the lengths of any two sides of a triangle is greater than the length of the third side.

The best way to remember this is to see that, in $\triangle ABC$, $x + y$, the length of the path from A to C through B, is greater than z, the length of the direct path from A to C.

Helpful Hint

Almost every SAT has at least one question whose solution requires you to use the triangle inequality. Be sure you know KEY FACTS J12 and J13.

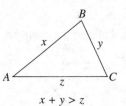

$x + y > z$

NOTE: If you subtract x from each side of $x + y > z$, you see that $z - x < y$.

Key Fact J13

The difference between the lengths of any two sides of a triangle is less than the length of the third side.

EXAMPLE 8

If the lengths of two sides of a triangle are 6 and 7, which of the following could be the length of the third side?

   I. 1
  II. 5
 III. 15

(A) None
(B) I only
(C) II only
(D) I and II only
(E) I, II, and III

> **NOTE**
>
> If *a* and *b* are the lengths of two sides of a triangle with *a* > *b*, then any number greater than *a* − *b* and less than *a* + *b* could be the length of the third side.

Solution. Use KEY FACTS J12 and J13.

• The length of the third side must be *less* than 6 + 7 = 13. (III is false.)
• The length of the third side must be *greater* than 7 − 6 = 1. (I is false.)
• *Any* number between 1 and 13 could be the length of the third side. (II is true.)

The answer is **C**.

The following diagram illustrates several triangles two of whose sides have lengths of 6 and 7.

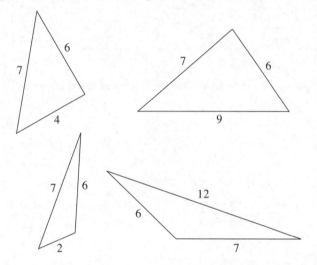

On the SAT, two other terms that appear regularly in triangle problems are **perimeter** and **area** (see Section 9-K).

EXAMPLE 9

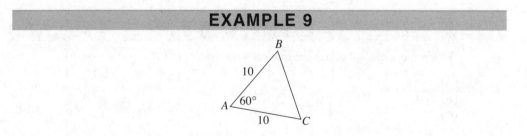

In the figure above, what is the perimeter of △*ABC*?

Solution. First, use KEY FACTS J3 and J1 to find the measures of the angles.

- Since $AB = AC$, $m\angle B = m\angle C$. Represent each measure by x.
- Then, $x + x + 60 = 180 \Rightarrow 2x = 120 \Rightarrow x = 60$.
- Since the measure of each angle of $\triangle ABC$ is 60°, the triangle is equilateral.
- Then, $BC = 10$, and the perimeter is 10 + 10 + 10 = **30**.

Key Fact J14

The area of a triangle is given by $A = \frac{1}{2}bh$, where b = base and h = height.

REFERENCE FACT

KEY FACT J14 is one of the facts provided in the "Reference Information" at the beginning of each math section.

NOTE:

1. *Any* side of the triangle can be taken as the base.
2. The height is a line segment drawn perpendicular to the base from the opposite vertex.
3. In a right triangle, either leg can be the base and the other the height.

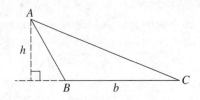

4. The height may be outside the triangle. [See the figure above.]

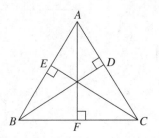

In the figure above:

- If $\overline{AC}$ is the base, $\overline{BD}$ is the height.
- If $\overline{AB}$ is the base, $\overline{CE}$ is the height.
- If $\overline{BC}$ is the base, $\overline{AF}$ is the height.

EXAMPLE 10

What is the area of an equilateral triangle whose sides are 10?

(A) 30
(B) $25\sqrt{3}$
(C) 50
(D) $50\sqrt{3}$
(E) 100

Solution. Draw an equilateral triangle and one of its altitudes.

- By KEY FACT J10, △*ADB* is a 30-60-90 right triangle.
- By KEY FACT J11, *BD* = 5 and *AD* = $5\sqrt{3}$.
- The area of △*ABC* = $\frac{1}{2}$(10)($5\sqrt{3}$) = **$25\sqrt{3}$ (B)**.

Replacing 10 by *s* in Example 10 yields a very useful result.

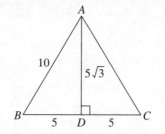

Key Fact J15

If *A* represents the area of an equilateral triangle with side *s*, then $A = \dfrac{s^2\sqrt{3}}{4}$.

Two triangles, such as I and II in the figure below, that have the same shape, but not necessarily the same size, are said to be **similar**.

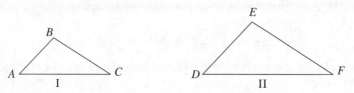

KEY FACT J16 makes this intuitive definition mathematically precise.

Key Fact J16

Two triangles are *similar* provided that the following two conditions are satisfied.

1. The three angles in the first triangle are congruent to the three angles in the second triangle.

$$m\angle A = m\angle D, \quad m\angle B = m\angle E, \quad m\angle C = m\angle F.$$

2. The lengths of the corresponding sides of the two triangles are in proportion:

$$\frac{AB}{DE} = \frac{BC}{EF} = \frac{AC}{DF}.$$

NOTE: Corresponding sides are sides opposite angles of the same measure.

An important theorem in geometry states that, if condition 1 in KEY FACT J16 is satisfied, then condition 2 is automatically satisfied. Therefore, to show that two triangles are similar, it is sufficient to show that their angles have the same measure. Furthermore, if the measures of two angles of one triangle are equal to the measures of two angles of a second triangle, then the measures of the third angles are also equal. This is summarized in KEY FACT J17.

Key Fact J17

If the measures of two angles of one triangle are equal to the measures of two angles of a second triangle, the triangles are similar.

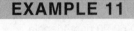

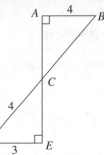

In the diagram above, what is *BC*?

Solution. Since vertical angles are congruent, m∠*ECD* = m∠*ACB*. Also, m∠*A* = m∠*E* since both ∠*A* and ∠*E* are right angles. Then the measures of two angles of △*CAB* are equal to the measures of two angles of △*CED*, and by KEY FACT J17, the two triangles are similar. Finally, by KEY FACT J16, corresponding sides are in proportion. Therefore:

$$\frac{DE}{AB} = \frac{DC}{BC} \Rightarrow \frac{3}{4} = \frac{4}{BC} \Rightarrow 3(BC) = 16 \Rightarrow BC = \frac{16}{3}.$$

If two triangles are similar, the common ratio of their corresponding sides is called the ***ratio of similitude***.

Key Fact J18

If two triangles are similar, and if *k* is the ratio of similitude, then:

- **The ratio of all the linear measurements of the triangles is *k*.**
- **The ratio of the areas of the triangles is k^2.**

In the figure below, △*ABC* and △*PQR* are similar with m∠*C* = m∠*R*.

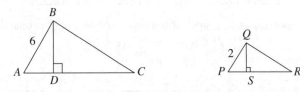

Then $\overline{AB}$ and $\overline{PQ}$ are corresponding sides, and the ratio of similitude is $\frac{6}{2} = 3$.

Therefore,

- All the sides are in the ratio of 3:1:

$$BC = \mathbf{3} \times QR, \qquad AC = \mathbf{3} \times PR.$$

- The altitudes are in the ratio of 3:1:

$$BD = \mathbf{3} \times QS.$$

- The perimeters are in the ratio of 3:1:

$$\text{Perimeter of } \triangle ABC = \mathbf{3} \times (\text{perimeter of } \triangle PQR).$$

- The areas are in the ratio of 9:1:

$$\text{Area of } \triangle ABC = \mathbf{9} \times (\text{area of } \triangle PQR).$$

Exercises on Triangles

Multiple-Choice Questions

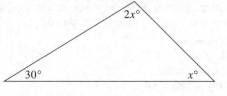

1. In the triangle above, what is the value of x?

    (A) 20
    (B) 30
    (C) 40
    (D) 50
    (E) 60

2. What is the area of an equilateral triangle whose altitude is 6?

    (A) 18

    (B) $12\sqrt{3}$

    (C) $18\sqrt{3}$

    (D) 36

    (E) $24\sqrt{3}$

3. Two sides of a right triangle are 12 and 13. Which of the following could be the length of the third side?

    I. 5
    II. 11

    III. $\sqrt{313}$

    (A) I only
    (B) II only
    (C) I and II only
    (D) I and III only
    (E) I, II, and III

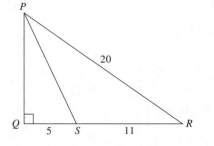

4. What is the value of PS in the triangle above?

    (A) $5\sqrt{2}$
    (B) 10
    (C) 11
    (D) 13
    (E) $12\sqrt{2}$

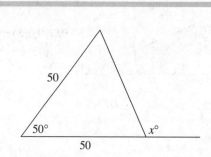

5. What is the value of x in the figure above?

    (A) 80
    (B) 100
    (C) 115
    (D) 120
    (E) 130

6. What is the smallest integer, x, for which x, $x + 5$, and $2x - 15$ can be the lengths of the sides of a triangle?

    (A) 8
    (B) 9
    (C) 10
    (D) 11
    (E) 12

Questions 7 and 8 refer to the following figure.

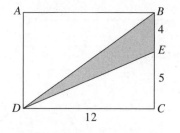

$ABCD$ is a rectangle.

7. What is the area of $\triangle BED$?

    (A) 12
    (B) 24
    (C) 36
    (D) 48
    (E) 60

8. What is the perimeter of $\triangle BED$?

    (A) $19 + 5\sqrt{2}$
    (B) 28
    (C) $17 + \sqrt{185}$
    (D) 32
    (E) 36

Questions 9 and 10 refer to the following figure.

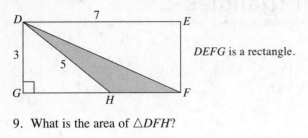

DEFG is a rectangle.

9. What is the area of △*DFH*?

(A) 3
(B) 4.5
(C) 6
(D) 7.5
(E) 10

10. What is the perimeter of △*DFH*?

(A) $8 + \sqrt{41}$
(B) $8 + \sqrt{58}$
(C) 16
(D) 17
(E) 18

Questions 11 and 12 refer to the following figure.

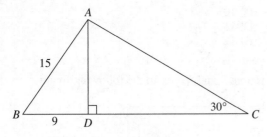

11. What is the perimeter of △*ABC*?

(A) 48
(B) $48 + 12\sqrt{2}$
(C) $48 + 12\sqrt{3}$
(D) 72
(E) It cannot be determined from the information given.

12. What is the area of △*ABC*?

(A) 108
(B) $54 + 72\sqrt{2}$
(C) $54 + 72\sqrt{3}$
(D) 198
(E) It cannot be determined from the information given.

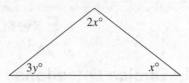

13. Which of the following expresses a true relationship between *x* and *y* in the figure above?

(A) $y = 60 - x$
(B) $y = x$
(C) $x + y = 90$
(D) $y = 180 - 3x$
(E) $x = 90 - 3y$

Questions 14 and 15 refer to the following figure, in which rectangle *ABCD* is divided into two 30-60-90 triangles, a 45-45-90 triangle, and shaded triangle *ABF*.

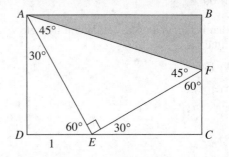

14. What is the perimeter of shaded triangle *ABF*?

(A) $\sqrt{2} + 2\sqrt{3}$
(B) $1 + \sqrt{2} + \sqrt{3}$
(C) $2 + \sqrt{2} + \sqrt{3}$
(D) $2 + 2\sqrt{2} + \sqrt{3}$
(E) $2\sqrt{2} + 2\sqrt{3}$

15. What is the area of shaded triangle *ABF*?

(A) $\dfrac{\sqrt{3}}{2}$
(B) 1
(C) $\dfrac{2\sqrt{3}}{3}$
(D) $\dfrac{\sqrt{3}+1}{2}$
(E) $\sqrt{2}(\sqrt{3}+1)$

Grid-in Questions

16. If the difference between the measures of the two smaller angles of a right triangle is 20°, what is the measure, in degrees, of the smallest angle?

Questions 17 and 18 refer to the figure below.

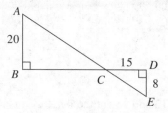

17. What is the perimeter of △ABC?

18. What is the area of △ABC?

19. Reanna and Jason each drew a triangle. Both triangles have sides of length 10 and 20, and the length of the third side of each triangle is an integer. What is the greatest possible difference between the perimeters of the two triangles?

20. If the measures of the angles of a triangle are in the ratio of 1:2:3, and if the perimeter of the triangle is $30 + 10\sqrt{3}$, what is the length of the smallest side?

Answer Key

1.	**D**	4.	**D**	7.	**B**	10.	**B**	13.	**A**
2.	**B**	5.	**C**	8.	**D**	11.	**C**	14.	**E**
3.	**D**	6.	**D**	9.	**B**	12.	**C**	15.	**B**

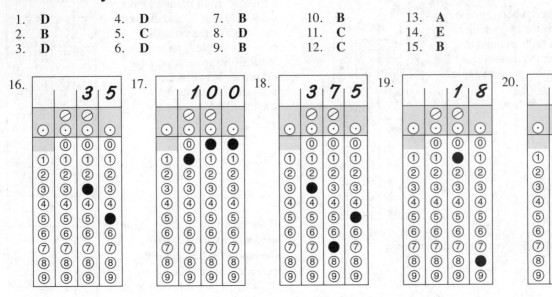

16. `3 5` 17. `1 0 0` 18. `3 7 5` 19. `1 8` 20. `1 0`

Answer Explanations

1. **D.** $x + 2x + 30 = 180 \Rightarrow 3x + 30 = 180 \Rightarrow$ $3x = 150 \Rightarrow x = 50$.

2. **B.** Sketch and label equilateral triangle ABC, and draw in altitude $\overline{AD}$, whose length is given as 6.

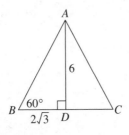

   By KEY FACT J11:

   $$BD = \frac{6}{\sqrt{3}} = \frac{6}{\sqrt{3}} \cdot \frac{\sqrt{3}}{\sqrt{3}} = \frac{6\sqrt{3}}{3} = 2\sqrt{3},$$

   Since $\overline{BD}$ is one-half the base of the triangle, the area is $2\sqrt{3} \times 6 = 12\sqrt{3}$.

3. **D.** If the triangle were not required to be right, by KEY FACTS J11 and J12 *any* number greater than 1 and less than 25 could be the length of the third side. For a right triangle, however, there are only *two* possibilities.
   - If 13 is the hypotenuse and one of the legs is 12, then the other leg is 5. (I is true.) (If you didn't recognize the 5-12-13 triangle, use the Pythagorean theorem: $12^2 + x^2 = 13^2$, and solve.)

   - If 12 and 13 are the lengths of the two legs, then use the Pythagorean theorem to find the length of the hypotenuse:

     $$12^2 + 13^2 = c^2 \Rightarrow c^2 = 144 + 169 = 313.$$

     So, $c = \sqrt{313}$.

     (III is true.)
     Since $11^2 + 12^2 \neq 13^2$, an 11-12-13 triangle is not a *right* triangle. (II is false.)

4. **D.** Use the Pythagorean theorem twice, unless you recognize the common right triangles in this figure (*which you should*). Since $PR = 20$ and $QR = 16$, $\triangle PQR$ is a $3x$-$4x$-$5x$ right triangle with $x = 4$. Then $PQ = 12$, and $\triangle PQS$ is a right triangle whose legs are 5 and 12. The hypotenuse, PS, therefore, is 13. [If you had difficulty with this question, review the material, but in the meantime remember TACTIC 2: trust the diagram. $\overline{PS}$ is longer than $\overline{SR}$, so you can eliminate A, B, and C, and $\overline{PS}$ is clearly shorter than $\overline{QR}$, so eliminate E.]

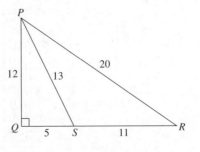

5. C. Label the other angles:

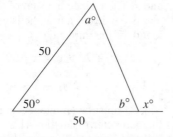
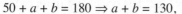

$$50 + a + b = 180 \Rightarrow a + b = 130,$$

and since the triangle is isosceles, $a = b$. Therefore, a and b are each 65, and $x = 180 - 65 = 115$.

6. D. In a triangle the sum of the lengths of any two sides must be greater than the third side. For $x + (x + 5)$ to be greater than $2x - 15$, $2x + 5$ must be greater than $2x - 15$; but that's always true. For $x + (2x - 15)$ to be greater than $x + 5$, $3x - 15$ must be greater than $x + 5$; but $3x - 15 > x + 5$ is true only if $2x > 20$, which means $x > 10$. The smallest integer value of x is 11.

7. B. You *could* calculate the area of the rectangle and subtract the areas of the two white right triangles, but don't. If $\overline{BE}$ is the base of $\triangle BED$, $\overline{DC}$ is the height.

The area is $\frac{1}{2}(BE)(DC) = \frac{1}{2}(4)(12) = 24$.

8. D. Since both $\overline{BD}$ and $\overline{ED}$ are the hypotenuses of right triangles, their lengths can be calculated by the Pythagorean theorem, but again these are triangles you should recognize: the sides of $\triangle DCE$ are 5-12-13, and those of $\triangle BAD$ are 9-12-15 ($3x$-$4x$-$5x$, with $x = 3$). Therefore, the perimeter of $\triangle BED$ is $4 + 13 + 15 = 32$.

9. B. Since $\triangle DGH$ is a right triangle, whose hypotenuse is 5 and one of whose legs is 3, the other leg, GH, is 4. Since $GF = DE = 7$, $HF = 3$. Now, $\triangle DFH$ has a base of 3 (HF) and a height of 3 (DG), and its area is

$\frac{1}{2}(3)(3) = 4.5$.

10. B. For $\triangle DFH$, you already have that $DH = 5$ and $HF = 3$; you need only find DF, which is the hypotenuse of $\triangle DEF$. By the Pythagorean theorem,

$$3^2 + 7^2 = (DF)^2 \Rightarrow (DF)^2 = 9 + 49 = 58.$$
So, $DF = \sqrt{58}$.

The perimeter is $3 + 5 + \sqrt{58} = 8 + \sqrt{58}$.

11. C. Triangle ADB is a right triangle whose hypotenuse is 15 and one of whose legs is 9, so this is a $3x$-$4x$-$5x$ triangle with $x = 3$, and $AD = 12$. Now $\triangle ADC$ is a 30-60-90 triangle, whose shorter leg is 12. Hypotenuse AC is 24, and leg CD is $12\sqrt{3}$, so the perimeter is

$$24 + 15 + 9 + 12\sqrt{3} = 48 + 12\sqrt{3}.$$

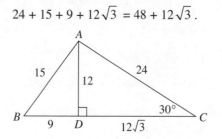

12. C. From the solution to Exercise 11, you have the base ($9 + 12\sqrt{3}$) and the height (12) of $\triangle ABC$. Then, the area is

$\frac{1}{2}(12)(9 + 12\sqrt{3}) = 54 + 72\sqrt{3}$.

13. A. $x + 2x + 3y = 180 \Rightarrow 3x + 3y = 180 \Rightarrow$

$x + y = 60 \Rightarrow y = 60 - x$.

14. E.

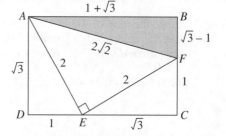

You are given enough information to determine the sides of all the triangles. Both 30-60-90 triangles have sides 1, $\sqrt{3}$, 2; and the 45-45-90 triangle has sides 2, 2, $2\sqrt{2}$. Also,

$AB = CD = 1 + \sqrt{3}$, and

$BF = AD - CF = \sqrt{3} - 1$.

Then, the perimeter of the shaded triangle is

$1 + \sqrt{3} + \sqrt{3} - 1 + 2\sqrt{2} = 2\sqrt{2} + 2\sqrt{3}$.

15. B. The area of $\triangle ABF = \frac{1}{2}(\sqrt{3} + 1)(\sqrt{3} - 1) =$

$\frac{1}{2}(3 - 1) = \frac{1}{2}(2) = 1$.

16. (35)

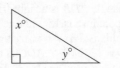

- Draw a diagram and label it. Let x be the measure of the larger angle and y be the measure of the smaller angle. Then,

$$x + y = 90$$
$$\underline{+\ x - y = 20}$$

- Add the equations: $2x = 110$

Then $x = 55$, and $y = 90 - 55 = 35$.

17. (100) By the Pythagorean theorem,
$8^2 + 15^2 = (CE)^2 \Rightarrow$
$(CE)^2 = 64 + 225 = 289.$

So, $CE = \sqrt{289} = 17.$
Then the perimeter of $\triangle CDE$ is
$8 + 15 + 17 = 40.$
Triangles ABC and CDE are similar (each has a 90° angle, and the vertical angles at C are congruent). The ratio of similitude is $\dfrac{20}{8} = 2.5,$

so the perimeter of $\triangle ABC$ is $2.5 \times 40 = 100.$

18. (375) The area of $\triangle CDE = \dfrac{1}{2}(8)(15) = 60.$

Since the ratio of similitude for the two triangles (as calculated in Solution 17) is 2.5, the area of $\triangle ABC$ is $(2.5)^2$ times the area of $\triangle CDE$:
$(2.5)^2 \times 60 = 6.25 \times 60 = 375.$

19. (18) Assume a triangle has sides of length 10, 20, and x. Then, since the sum of the lengths of any two sides of a triangle is greater than the length of the third side,

$$10 + 20 > x \Rightarrow x < 30$$
$$\text{and}$$
$$x + 10 > 20 \Rightarrow x > 10$$

Since x must be an integer, $11 \le x \le 29$, and the perimeter P satisfies $41 \le P \le 59$. The greatest possible difference then between the two perimeters is $59 - 41 = 18$.

20. (10) If the measures of the angles are in the ratio of 1:2:3, then:

$$x + 2x + 3x = 180 \Rightarrow 6x = 180 \Rightarrow x = 30.$$

The triangle is a 30-60-90 right triangle, and the sides are a, $2a$, and $a\sqrt{3}$. The perimeter therefore is $3a + a\sqrt{3} = a(3 + \sqrt{3})$, so

$$a(3 + \sqrt{3}) = 30 + 10\sqrt{3} = 10(3 + \sqrt{3}).$$

So, $a = 10$.

9-K Quadrilaterals and Other Polygons

A *polygon* is a closed geometric figure made up of line segments. The line segments are called *sides*, and the endpoints of the line segments are called *vertices* (each one is a *vertex*). Line segments inside the polygon drawn from one vertex to another are called *diagonals*.

The simplest polygons, which have three sides, are the triangles, which you studied in Section 9-J. A polygon with four sides is called a *quadrilateral*. There are special names (such as *pentagon* and *hexagon*) for polygons with more than four sides, but you do not need to know any of them for the SAT.

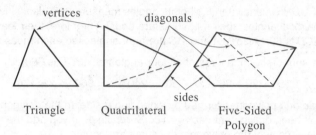

Triangle   Quadrilateral   Five-Sided Polygon

This section will present a few facts about polygons in general and then review the key facts you need to know about three special quadrilaterals.

Every quadrilateral has two diagonals. If you draw in either one, you will divide the quadrilateral into two triangles.

Since the sum of the measures of the three angles in each of the triangles is 180°, the sum of the measures of the angles in the quadrilateral is 360°.

Key Fact K1

In any quadrilateral, the sum of the measures of the four angles is 360°.

In exactly the same way as shown above, any polygon can be divided into triangles by drawing in all of the diagonals emanating from one vertex.

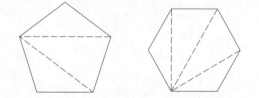

Notice that a five-sided polygon is divided into three triangles, and a six-sided polygon is divided into four triangles. In general, an *n*-sided polygon is divided into $(n - 2)$ triangles, which leads to KEY FACT K2.

Key Fact K2

The sum of the measures of the *n* angles in a polygon with *n* sides is $(n - 2) \times 180°$.

EXAMPLE 1

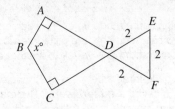

In the figure above, what is the value of *x*?

Solution. Since △*DEF* is equilateral, all of its angles measure 60°; also, since the two angles at vertex D are vertical angles, their measures are equal. Therefore, the measure of ∠*D* in quadrilateral *ABCD* is 60°. Also, ∠*A* and ∠*C* are right angles, so each measures 90°.

Finally, since the sum of the measures of all four angles of *ABCD* is 360°:

$$60 + 90 + 90 + x = 360 \Rightarrow 240 + x = 360 \Rightarrow x = \textbf{120}.$$

An ***exterior angle*** of a polygon is formed by extending a side. In the polygons below, one exterior angle has been drawn in at each vertex. Surprisingly, if you add the measures of all of the exterior angles in any of the polygons, the sums are equal.

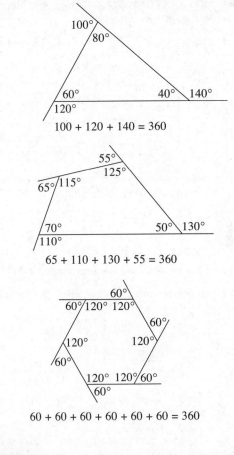

Key Fact K3

In any polygon, the sum of the measures of the exterior angles, taking one at each vertex, is 360°.

EXAMPLE 2

A 10-sided polygon is drawn in which each angle has the same measure. What is the measure, in degrees, of each angle?

Solution 1. By KEY FACT K2, the sum of the degree measures of the 10 angles is (10 − 2) × 180 = 8 × 180 = 1440. Then, each angle is 1440 ÷ 10 = **144**.

Solution 2. By KEY FACT K3, the sum of the degree measures of the 10 exterior angles is 360, so each one is 36. Therefore, the degree measure of each interior angle is 180 − 36 = **144**.

A ***parallelogram*** is a quadrilateral in which both pairs of opposite sides are parallel.

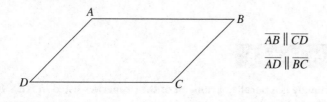

$\overline{AB} \parallel \overline{CD}$

$\overline{AD} \parallel \overline{BC}$

Key Fact K4

Parallelograms have the following properties:

- **Opposite sides are congruent: $AB = CD$ and $AD = BC$.**
- **Opposite angles are congruent: $a = c$ and $b = d$.**
- **Consecutive angles add up to 180°: $a + b = 180$, $b + c = 180$, $c + d = 180$, and $a + d = 180$.**
- **The two diagonals bisect each other: $AE = EC$ and $BE = ED$.**
- **A diagonal divides the parallelogram into two triangles that have exactly the same size and shape. (The triangles are congruent.)**

EXAMPLE 3

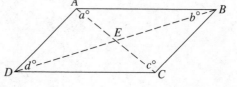

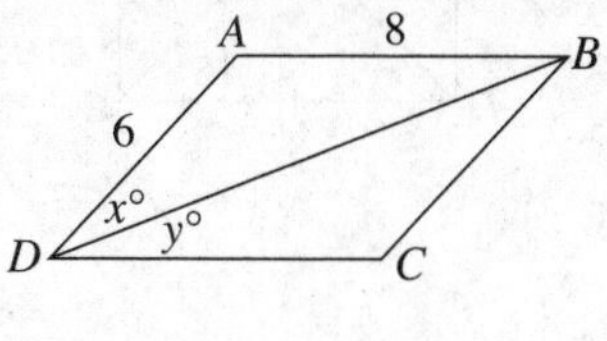

In the figure above, *ABCD* is a parallelogram. Which of the following statements *must* be true?

(A) $x < y$
(B) $x = y$
(C) $x > y$
(D) $x + y < 90$
(E) $x + y > 90$

Solution. Since $\overline{AB}$ and $\overline{CD}$ are parallel line segments cut by transversal $\overline{BD}$, m∠ABD = y. In △ABD, AB > AD, so by KEY FACT J3 the measure of the angle opposite $\overline{AB}$ is greater than the measure of the angle opposite $\overline{AD}$. Therefore, **$x > y$ (C)**.

A ***rectangle*** is a parallelogram in which all four angles are right angles. Two adjacent sides of a rectangle are usually called the ***length*** (ℓ) and the ***width*** (w). Note that the length is not necessarily greater than the width.

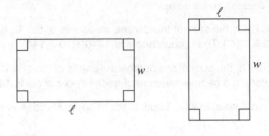

Key Fact K5

Since a rectangle is a parallelogram, all of the properties listed in **KEY FACT K4** hold for rectangles. In addition:

- The measure of each angle in a rectangle is **90°**.
- The diagonals of a rectangle are congruent: $\overline{AC} \cong \overline{BD}$.

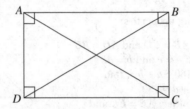

A ***square*** is a rectangle in which all four sides have the same length.

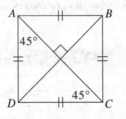

Key Fact K6

Since a square is a rectangle, all of the properties listed in **KEY FACTS K4** and **K5** hold for squares. In addition:

- All four sides have the same length.
- Each diagonal divides the square into two 45-45-90 right triangles.
- The diagonals are perpendicular to each other: $\overline{AC} \perp \overline{BD}$.

EXAMPLE 4

What is the length of each side of a square if its diagonals are 10?

Solution. Draw a diagram. In square *ABCD*, diagonal $\overline{AC}$ is the hypotenuse of a 45-45-90 right triangle, and side $\overline{AB}$ is a leg of that triangle. By KEY FACT J7,

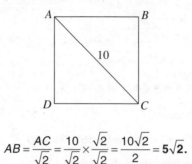

$$AB = \frac{AC}{\sqrt{2}} = \frac{10}{\sqrt{2}} \times \frac{\sqrt{2}}{\sqrt{2}} = \frac{10\sqrt{2}}{2} = \mathbf{5\sqrt{2}}.$$

The **perimeter** (P) of any polygon is the sum of the lengths of all of its sides. The only polygons for which we have formulas for the perimeter are the rectangle and the square.

Key Fact K7

In a rectangle, $P = 2(\ell + w)$; in a square, $P = 4s$.

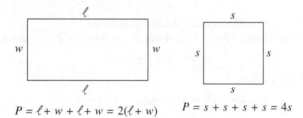

$$P = \ell + w + \ell + w = 2(\ell + w) \qquad P = s + s + s + s = 4s$$

EXAMPLE 5

The length of a rectangle is twice its width. If the perimeter of the rectangle is the same as the perimeter of a square of side 6, what is the square of the length of a diagonal of the rectangle?

Solution. Don't do anything until you have drawn diagrams.

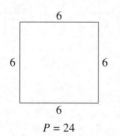

$$P = 24$$

Since the perimeter of the square is 24, the perimeter of the rectangle is also 24. Then

$$2(\ell + w) = 24 \Rightarrow \ell + w = 12.$$

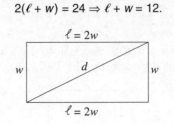

But $\ell = 2w$, so

$$2w + w = 3w = 12 \Rightarrow w = 4 \text{ (and } \ell = 8).$$

Finally, use the Pythagorean theorem:

$$d^2 = 4^2 + 8^2 = 16 + 64 = \mathbf{80}.$$

In Section 9-J you reviewed the formula for the *area* of a triangle. The only other polygons for which you need to know area formulas are the parallelogram, rectangle, and square.

- Parallelogram: Since the area of each of the two triangles formed by drawing a diagonal in a parallelogram is $\frac{1}{2} bh$, the area of the parallelogram is twice as great:

$$A = \frac{1}{2} bh + \frac{1}{2} bh = bh.$$

- Rectangle: In a rectangle the same formula holds, but it is usually written as

$$A = \ell w,$$

using the terms *length* and *width* instead of *base* and *height*.
- Square: In a square the length and width are equal; we label each of them s (side), and write

$$A = s \times s = s^2.$$

If d is the diagonal of a square,

$$d = s\sqrt{2} \Rightarrow d^2 = 2s^2 \Rightarrow s^2 = \frac{1}{2} d^2.$$

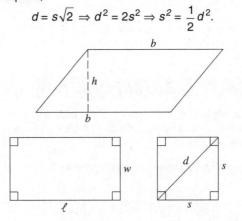

Key Fact K8

Here are the area formulas you need to know:

- For a parallelogram: $A = bh$.
- For a rectangle: $A = \ell w$.
- For a square: $A = s^2$ or $A = \dfrac{1}{2}d^2$.

EXAMPLE 6

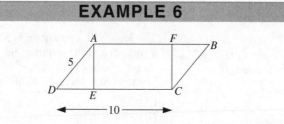

In the figure above, the area of parallelogram *ABCD* is 40. What is the area of rectangle *AFCE*?

(A) 20
(B) 24
(C) 28
(D) 32
(E) 36

Solution. Since the base, *CD*, is 10 and the area is 40, the height, *AE*, must be 4. Then △*AED* must be a 3-4-5 right triangle with *DE* = 3, which implies that *EC* = 7. The area of the rectangle is $7 \times 4 = $ **28 (C)**.

Exercises on Quadrilaterals and Other Polygons

Multiple-Choice Questions

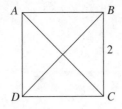

1. In the figure above, the two diagonals divide square *ABCD* into four small triangles. What is the sum of the perimeters of those triangles?

   (A) $2 + 2\sqrt{2}$

   (B) $8 + 4\sqrt{2}$

   (C) $8 + 8\sqrt{2}$

   (D) 16

   (E) 24

2. If the length of a rectangle is 4 times its width, and if its area is 144, what is its perimeter?

   (A) 6
   (B) 24
   (C) 30
   (D) 60
   (E) 96

3. If the angles of a five-sided polygon are in the ratio of 2:3:3:5:5, what is the degree measure of the smallest angle?

   (A) 20
   (B) 40
   (C) 60
   (D) 80
   (E) 90

Questions 4 and 5 refer to a rectangle in which the length of each diagonal is 12, and one of the angles formed by the diagonal and a side measures 30°.

4. What is the area of the rectangle?

   (A) 18
   (B) 72
   (C) $18\sqrt{3}$

   (D) $36\sqrt{3}$

   (E) $36\sqrt{2}$

5. What is the perimeter of the rectangle?

   (A) 18
   (B) 24
   (C) $12 + 12\sqrt{3}$

   (D) $18 + 6\sqrt{3}$

   (E) $24\sqrt{2}$

6. The length of a rectangle is 5 more than the side of a square, and the width of the rectangle is 5 less than the side of the square. If the area of the square is 45, what is the area of the rectangle?

   (A) 20
   (B) 25
   (C) 45
   (D) 50
   (E) 70

Questions 7 and 8 refer to the following figure, in which *M*, *N*, *O*, and *P* are the midpoints of the sides of rectangle *ABCD*.

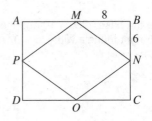

7. What is the perimeter of quadrilateral *MNOP*?

   (A) 24
   (B) 32
   (C) 40
   (D) 48
   (E) 60

8. What is the area of quadrilateral *MNOP*?

   (A) 48
   (B) 60
   (C) 72
   (D) 96
   (E) 108

Questions 9 and 10 refer to the following figure, in which *M* and *N* are midpoints of two of the sides of square *ABCD*.

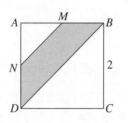

9. What is the perimeter of the shaded region?

   (A) 3
   (B) $2 + 3\sqrt{2}$
   (C) $3 + 2\sqrt{2}$
   (D) 5
   (E) 8

10. What is the area of the shaded region?

   (A) 1.5
   (B) 1.75
   (C) 3
   (D) $2\sqrt{2}$
   (E) $3\sqrt{2}$

Grid-in Questions

11. In the figure below, *ABCD* is a parallelogram. What is the value of $y - z$?

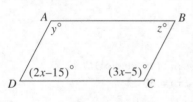

12. In the figure below, what is the sum of the degree measures of all of the marked angles?

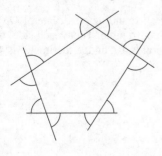

13. If, in the figures below, the area of rectangle *ABCD* is 100, what is the area of rectangle *EFGH*?

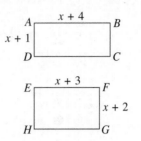

14. How many sides does a polygon have if the measure of each interior angle is 8 times the degree measure of each exterior angle?

15. In quadrilateral *WXYZ*, the measure of $\angle Z$ is 10 more than twice the average of the measures of the other three angles. What is the measure, in degrees, of $\angle Z$?

Answer Key

1.	**C**	3.	**C**	5.	**C**	7.	**C**	9.	**B**
2.	**D**	4.	**D**	6.	**A**	8.	**D**	10.	**A**

11. 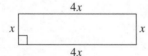 5 0 12. 7 2 0 13. 1 0 2 14. 1 8 15. 1 5 0

Answer Explanations

1. **C.** Each of the four small triangles is a 45-45-90 right triangle whose hypotenuse is 2. Therefore, each leg is $\frac{2}{\sqrt{2}} = \sqrt{2}$. The perimeter of each small triangle is $2 + 2\sqrt{2}$, and the sum of the perimeters is 4 times as great: $8 + 8\sqrt{2}$.

2. **D.** Draw a diagram and label it.

Since the area is 144, then

$$144 = 4x^2 \Rightarrow x^2 = 36 \Rightarrow x = 6.$$

The width is 6, the length is 24, and the perimeter is 60.

3. **C.** The sum of the degree measures of the angles of a five-sided polygon is $(5 - 2) \times 180 = 3 \times 180 = 540$. Then:

$$540 = 2x + 3x + 3x + 5x + 5x = 18x.$$

So, $x = 540 \div 18 = 30$.

The degree measure of the smallest angle is $2x$: $2 \times 30 = 60$.

4. **D.** Draw a diagram and label it. Since $\triangle BCD$ is a 30-60-90 right triangle, BC is 6 (half the hypotenuse) and CD is $6\sqrt{3}$.

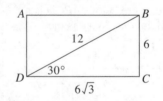

Then the area of rectangle $ABCD$ is $\ell w = 6(6\sqrt{3}) = 36\sqrt{3}$.

5. **C.** The perimeter of the rectangle is $2(\ell + w) = 2(6 + 6\sqrt{3}) = 12 + 12\sqrt{3}$.

6. **A.** Let x represent the side of the square. Then the dimensions of the rectangle are $(x + 5)$ and $(x - 5)$, and its area is $(x + 5)(x - 5) = x^2 - 25$. Since 45 is the area of the square, $x^2 = 45$, and so $x^2 - 25 = 20$.

7. **C.** Each triangle surrounding quadrilateral *MNOP* is a 6-8-10 right triangle. Then, each side of the quadrilateral is 10, and its perimeter is 40.

8. D. The area of each of the triangles is $\frac{1}{2}(6)(8) =$ 24, so together the four triangles have an area of 96. The area of the rectangle is $16 \times 12 = 192$. Therefore, the area of quadrilateral *MNOP* is $192 - 96 = 96$.
NOTE: Joining the midpoints of the four sides of any quadrilateral creates a parallelogram whose area is one-half the area of the original quadrilateral.

9. B. Since *M* and *N* are midpoints of sides of length 2, *AM*, *MB*, *AN*, and *ND* are each equal to 1. Also, $MN = \sqrt{2}$, since it's the hypotenuse of an isosceles right triangle whose legs are 1; and $BD = 2\sqrt{2}$, since it's the hypotenuse of an isosceles right triangle whose legs are 2. Then, the perimeter of the shaded region is $1 + \sqrt{2} + 1 + 2\sqrt{2} = 2 + 3\sqrt{2}$.

10. A. The area of $\triangle ABD = \frac{1}{2}(2)(2) = 2$, and the area of $\triangle AMN = \frac{1}{2}(1)(1) = 0.5$. The area of the shaded region is $2 - 0.5 = 1.5$.

11. (50) The sum of the degree measures of two consecutive angles of a parallelogram is 180, so
$$180 = (3x - 5) + (2x - 15) = 5x - 20.$$
So, $5x = 200 \Rightarrow x = 40$.
Since opposite angles of a parallelogram are equal, $y = 3x - 5 = 115$ and $z = 2x - 15 = 65$. Then $y - z = 50$.

12. (720) Each of the 10 marked angles is an exterior angle of the pentagon. If you take one angle at each vertex, the sum of the degree measures of those five angles is 360; the sum of the degree measures of the other five is also 360: $360 + 360 = 720$.

13. (102) The area of rectangle $ABCD = (x + 1)(x + 4) = x^2 + 5x + 4$. The area of rectangle $EFGH = (x + 2)(x + 3) = x^2 + 5x + 6$, which is exactly 2 more than the area of rectangle *ABCD*: $100 + 2 = 102$.

14. (18) The sum of the degree measures of an interior and exterior angle is 180, so 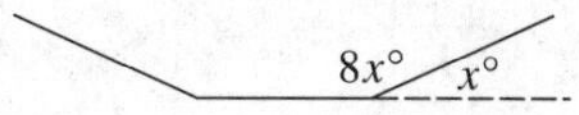
$$180 = 8x + x = 9x \Rightarrow x = 20.$$
Since the sum of the degree measures of all the exterior angles of a polygon is 360, there are $360 \div 20 = 18$ angles and, of course, 18 sides.

15. (150) Let *W*, *X*, *Y*, and *Z* represent the degree measures of the four angles. Since
$$W + X + Y + Z = 360,$$
then
$$W + X + Y = 360 - Z.$$
Also:
$$Z = 10 + 2\left(\frac{W+X+Y}{3}\right) = 10 + 2\left(\frac{360-Z}{3}\right).$$
Then:
$$Z = 10 + \frac{2}{3}(360) - \frac{2}{3}Z = 10 + 240 - \frac{2}{3}Z$$
$$\Rightarrow \frac{5}{3}Z = 250 \Rightarrow Z = 150.$$

9-L Circles

A *circle* consists of all the points that are the same distance from one fixed point, called the *center*. That distance is called the *radius* of the circle. The figure at the right is a circle of radius 1 unit whose center is at point *O*. *A*, *B*, *C*, *D*, and *E*, which are each 1 unit from *O*, are all

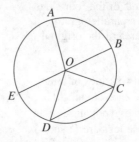

points on circle *O*. The word *radius* is also used to represent any of the line segments joining the center and a point on the circle. The plural of *radius* is *radii*. In circle *O*, above, $\overline{OA}$, $\overline{OB}$, $\overline{OC}$, $\overline{OD}$, and $\overline{OE}$ are all radii. If a circle has radius *r*, each of the radii is *r* units long.

Key Fact L1

Any triangle, such as $\triangle COD$ in the figure above, formed by connecting the endpoints of two radii is isosceles.

EXAMPLE 1

If *P* and *Q* are points on circle *O*, what is the value of *x*?

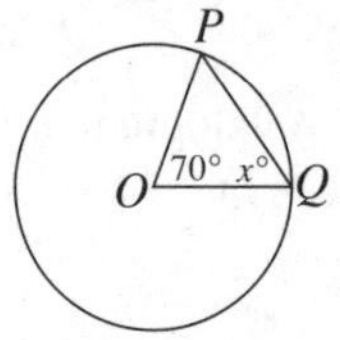

Solution. Since $\overline{OP} \cong \overline{OQ}$ (each is a radius of the circle), $\triangle POQ$ is isosceles. Then $\angle P$ and $\angle Q$ are congruent, so

$$70 + x + x = 180 \Rightarrow 2x = 110 \Rightarrow x = \mathbf{55}.$$

A line segment, such as $\overline{BE}$ in circle *O* at the beginning of this section, whose endpoints are on a circle and that passes through the center is called a *diameter*. Since $\overline{BE}$ is made up of two radii, $\overline{OB}$ and $\overline{OE}$, a diameter is twice as long as a radius.

Key Fact L2

If *d* is the diameter and *r* the radius of a circle, then *d* = 2*r*.

Key Fact L3

A diameter is the longest line segment that can be drawn in a circle.

The total length around a circle, from *A* to *B* to *C* to *D* to *E* and back to *A* in the circle at the beginning of this section, is called the ***circumference*** of the circle. In every circle the ratio of the circumference to the diameter is exactly the same and is denoted by the symbol π (the Greek letter pi).

Key Fact L4

For every circle:

$$\pi = \frac{\text{circumference}}{\text{diameter}} = \frac{C}{d} \quad \text{or} \quad C = \pi d \quad \text{or} \quad C = 2\pi r.$$

Key Fact L5

The value of π is *approximately* 3.14.

REFERENCE FACT

The formula for the circumference of a circle is one of the facts provided in the "Reference Information" at the beginning of each math section.

CALCULATOR HINT

On almost every question on the SAT that involves circles, you are expected to leave your answer in terms of π, so don't multiply by 3.14 unless you must. If you need an approximation—to test a choice, for example—then use your calculator. If you have a scientific calculator, use the π key. This not only is faster and more accurate than punching in 3.14, but also avoids careless mistakes in entering.

EXAMPLE 2

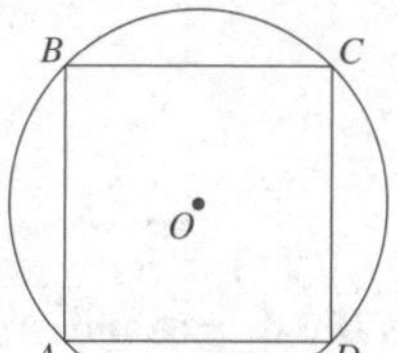

In the figure above, square *ABCD* is inscribed in circle *O*. If the area of the square is 50, what is the circumference of the circle?

(A) $\pi\sqrt{50}$
(B) 10π
(C) 25π
(D) 50π
(E) 100π

Solution. Since the area of square *ABCD* is 50, the length of each side is $\sqrt{50}$. Diagonal $\overline{AC}$ divides the square into two isosceles right triangles whose legs are $\sqrt{50}$ and whose hypotenuse is $\overline{AC}$. So, $\overline{AC} = \left(\sqrt{50}\right)\left(\sqrt{2}\right) = \sqrt{100} = 10$. But since $\overline{AC}$ is also a diameter of circle *O*, the circumference is $\pi d = \mathbf{10\pi}$ **(B)**.

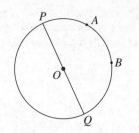

An *arc* consists of two points on a circle and all the points between them. If two points, such as *P* and *Q* in circle *O*, are the endpoints of a diameter, they divide the circle into two arcs called *semicircles*. On the SAT, *arc AB* always refers to the small arc joining *A* and *B*. To refer to the large arc going from *A* to *B* through *P* and *Q*, we would say *arc APB* or *arc AQB*.

An angle whose vertex is at the center of a circle is called a ***central angle***.

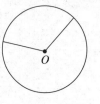

Key Fact L6

The degree measure of a complete circle is 360.

Key Fact L7

The degree measure of an arc equals the degree measure of the central angle that intercepts it.

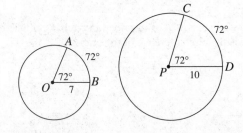

> **CAUTION:** Degree measure is *not* a measure of length. In the circles above, arc *AB* and arc *CD* each measure 72°, even though arc *CD* is much longer.

How long *is* arc *CD*? Since the radius of circle *P* is 10, its circumference is 20π [2πr = 2π(10) = 20π]. Since there are 360° in a circle, arc *CD* is $\frac{72}{360}$, or $\frac{1}{5}$, of the circumference: $\frac{1}{5}(20\pi) = 4\pi$.

Key Fact L8

The formula for the area of a circle of radius r is $A = \pi r^2$.

The area of circle P in Key Fact L7 is $\pi(10)^2 = 100\pi$ square units.

The area of sector CPD is $\dfrac{1}{5}$ of the area of the circle: $\dfrac{1}{5}(100\pi) = 20\pi$.

REFERENCE FACT

KEY FACT L8 is one of the facts provided in the "Reference Information" at the beginning of each math section.

Key Fact L9

If an arc measures $x°$, the length of the arc is $\dfrac{x}{360}(2\pi r)$; and the area of the sector formed by the arc and two radii is $\dfrac{x}{360}(\pi r^2)$.

Examples 3 and 4 refer to the circle below.

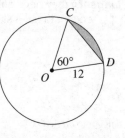

EXAMPLE 3

What is the area of the shaded region?

(A) $144\pi - 144\sqrt{3}$

(B) $144\pi - 36\sqrt{3}$

(C) $144\pi - 72$

(D) $24\pi - 36\sqrt{3}$

(E) $24\pi - 72$

Solution. The area of the shaded region is equal to the area of sector COD minus the area of $\triangle COD$. The area of the circle is $\pi(12)^2 = 144\pi$. Since $\dfrac{60}{360} = \dfrac{1}{6}$, the area of sector COD is $\dfrac{1}{6}(144\pi) = 24\pi$. Since m$\angle O = 60$, m$\angle C +$ m$\angle D = 120$; but $\triangle COD$ is isosceles, so $\angle C = \angle D$.

Therefore, each measures $60°$, and the triangle is equilateral. Finally, by KEY FACT J15,

$$\text{area of } \triangle COD = \frac{12^2\sqrt{3}}{4} = \frac{144\sqrt{3}}{4} = 36\sqrt{3},$$

so the area of the shaded region is **$24\pi - 36\sqrt{3}$ (D)**.

EXAMPLE 4

What is the perimeter of the shaded region?

(A) $12 + 4\pi$
(B) $12 + 12\pi$
(C) $12 + 24\pi$
(D) $12\sqrt{2} + 4\pi$
(E) $12\sqrt{2} + 24\pi$

Solution. Since $\triangle COD$ is equilateral, $CD = 12$. Since

$$\text{circumference of circle} = 2\pi(12) = 24\pi \Rightarrow$$

$$\text{arc } CD = \frac{1}{6}(24\pi) = 4\pi,$$

the perimeter is **12 + 4π (A)**.

A line and a circle or two circles are ***tangent*** if they have only one point of intersection. A circle is ***inscribed*** in a triangle or square if it is tangent to each side. A polygon is ***inscribed*** in a circle if each vertex is on the circle.

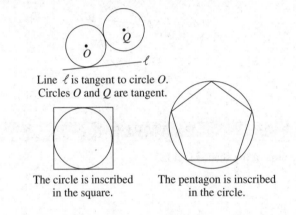

Line ℓ is tangent to circle O.
Circles O and Q are tangent.

The circle is inscribed
in the square.

The pentagon is inscribed
in the circle.

EXAMPLE 5

A is the center of a circle whose radius is 10, and B is the center of a circle whose diameter is 10. If these two circles are tangent to one another, what is the area of the circle whose diameter is $\overline{AB}$?

(A) 30π
(B) 56.25π
(C) 100π
(D) 225π
(E) 400π

Solution. Draw a diagram. Since the diameter of circle B is 10, its radius is 5. Then the diameter, $\overline{AB}$, of the dotted circle is 15, its radius is 7.5, and its area is $\pi(7.5)^2 = $ **56.25π (B)**. (Note that you should use your calculator to square 7.5 but not to multiply by π.)

Helpful Hint

On multiple-choice questions involving circles, the choices are almost always in terms of π, so you shouldn't multiply anything by 3.14.

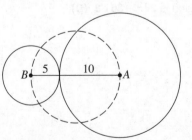

EXAMPLE 6

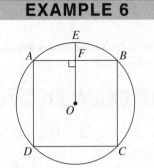

In the figure above, square *ABCD* is inscribed in a circle whose center is *O* and whose radius is 4. If $\overline{EO} \perp \overline{AB}$ at *F*, what is the length of $\overline{EF}$?

(A) 2

(B) $\sqrt{2}$

(C) $2\sqrt{2}$

(D) $4 - \sqrt{2}$

(E) $4 - 2\sqrt{2}$

Solution. Draw diagonal $\overline{AC}$. Then, $\triangle AFO$ is a 45-45-90 right triangle. Since hypotenuse *AO* is a radius, its length is 4; and by KEY FACT J8:

$$OF = \frac{4}{\sqrt{2}} = \frac{4}{\sqrt{2}} \times \frac{\sqrt{2}}{\sqrt{2}} = 2\sqrt{2}.$$

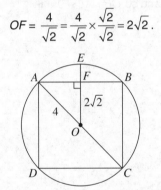

EO = 4 since it is also a radius. Then

$$EF = EO - OF = \mathbf{4 - 2\sqrt{2}} \textbf{ (E)}.$$

In the figure below, line ℓ is tangent to circle *O* at point *P*.

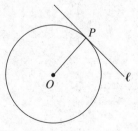

An important theorem in geometry states that radius $\overline{OP}$ is perpendicular to ℓ.

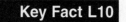

Key Fact L10

A line tangent to a circle is perpendicular to the radius drawn to the point of contact.

EXAMPLE 7

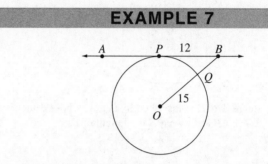

Helpful Hint
You don't have to take the time to use the Pythagorean theorem if you recognize this as a multiple of a 3-4-5 triangle.

In the figure above, $\overrightarrow{AB}$ is tangent to circle O at point P. If $OB = 15$ and $PB = 12$, what is QB?

Solution. Draw in radius $\overline{OP}$, creating $\triangle OPB$. By KEY FACT L10, $\overline{OP} \perp \overline{AB}$, so $\triangle OPB$ is a right triangle. Then, by the Pythagorean theorem,

$$OP^2 + PB^2 = OB^2 \Rightarrow OP^2 + 144 = 225.$$
$$\text{So, } OP^2 = 81 \Rightarrow OP = 9.$$

Since all radii are equal, $OQ = 9$ and so $QB = 15 - 9 = \mathbf{6}$.

Exercises on Circles

Multiple-Choice Questions

1. What is the circumference of a circle whose area is 100π?

    (A) 10
    (B) 20
    (C) 10π
    (D) 20π
    (E) 25π

2. What is the area of a circle whose circumference is π?

    (A) $\dfrac{\pi}{4}$

    (B) $\dfrac{\pi}{2}$

    (C) π
    (D) 2π
    (E) 4π

3. What is the area of a circle that is inscribed in a square of area 2?

    (A) $\dfrac{\pi}{4}$

    (B) $\dfrac{\pi}{2}$

    (C) π

    (D) $\pi\sqrt{2}$

    (E) 2π

4. A square of area 2 is inscribed in a circle. What is the area of the circle?

    (A) $\dfrac{\pi}{4}$

    (B) $\dfrac{\pi}{2}$

    (C) π

    (D) $\pi\sqrt{2}$

    (E) 2π

Questions 5 and 6 refer to the following figure.

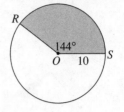

5. What is the length of arc *RS*?

    (A) 8
    (B) 20
    (C) 8π
    (D) 20π
    (E) 40π

6. What is the area of the shaded sector?

    (A) 8
    (B) 20
    (C) 8π
    (D) 20π
    (E) 40π

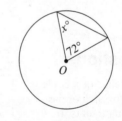

7. In the figure above, what is the value of *x*?

    (A) 30
    (B) 36
    (C) 45
    (D) 54
    (E) 60

8. If *A* is the area and *C* the circumference of a circle, which of the following is an expression for *A* in terms of *C*?

    (A) $\dfrac{C^2}{4\pi}$

    (B) $\dfrac{C^2}{4\pi^2}$

    (C) $2C\sqrt{\pi}$

    (D) $2C^2\sqrt{\pi}$

    (E) $\dfrac{C^2\sqrt{\pi}}{4}$

9. What is the area of a circle whose radius is the diagonal of a square whose area is 4?

   (A) 2π
   (B) $2\pi\sqrt{2}$
   (C) 4π
   (D) 8π
   (E) 16π

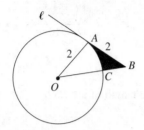

10. In the figure above, ℓ is tangent to circle O at A, and $OA = AB = 2$. What is the area of the shaded region?

   (A) $\dfrac{1}{2}\pi$

   (B) $4 - \dfrac{1}{2}\pi$

   (C) $2 - \dfrac{1}{2}\pi$

   (D) $2 - \pi$

   (E) $4 - 4\pi$

Grid-in Questions

11. The circumference of a circle is $a\pi$ units, and the area of the circle is $b\pi$ square units. If $a = b$, what is the radius of the circle?

12. A 9×12 rectangle is inscribed in a circle. What is the radius of the circle?

13. In the figure below, the ratio of the length of arc AB to the circumference of the circle is 2 to 15. What is the value of y?

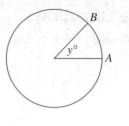

14. If the area of the shaded region is $k\pi$, what is the value of k?

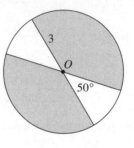

15. If line ℓ is tangent to circle O at point P, if B is a point on ℓ such that $PB = 8$, and if $OB = 10$, what is the radius of the circle?

Answer Key

1.	**D**	3.	**B**	5.	**C**
2.	**A**	4.	**C**	6.	**E**

7.	**D**	9.	**D**
8.	**A**	10.	**C**

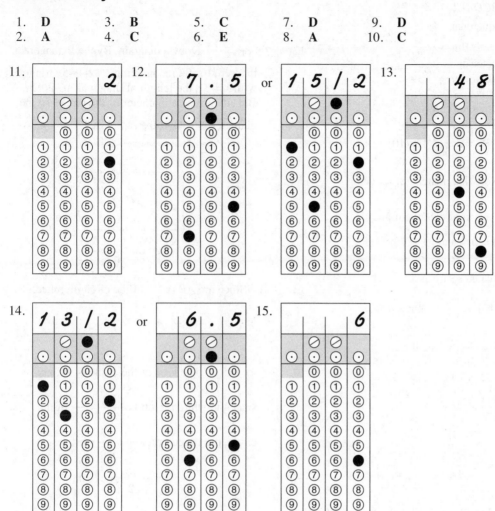

Answer Explanations

1. D. $A = \pi r^2 = 100\pi \Rightarrow r^2 = 100 \Rightarrow r = 10$.
   $C = 2\pi r = 2\pi(10) = 20\pi$.

2. A. $C = 2\pi r = \pi \Rightarrow 2r = 1 \Rightarrow r = \dfrac{1}{2}$.

   $A = \pi r^2 = \pi\left(\dfrac{1}{2}\right)^2 = \dfrac{1}{4}\pi = \dfrac{\pi}{4}$.

3. B. Draw a diagram. Since the area of square $ABCD$ is 2, $AD = \sqrt{2}$.

   Then, diameter $EF = \sqrt{2}$

   and radius $OE = \dfrac{\sqrt{2}}{2}$, so

   area $= \pi\left(\dfrac{\sqrt{2}}{2}\right)^2 = \dfrac{2}{4}\pi = \dfrac{\pi}{2}$.

4. **C.** Draw a diagram. Since the area of square $ABCD$ is 2, $AD = \sqrt{2}$. Then diagonal $BD = \sqrt{2} \times \sqrt{2} = 2$. But $\overline{BD}$ is also a diameter of the circle, so the diameter is 2 and the radius is 1. Therefore, the area is $\pi(1)^2 = \pi$.

5. **C.** The length of arc $RS = \left(\dfrac{144}{360}\right)2\pi(10) =$

   $\left(\dfrac{2}{5}\right)20\pi = 8\pi$. [Note that, instead of reducing

   $\dfrac{144}{360}$, you should use your calculator and

   divide: $144 \div 360 = 0.4$, and $(0.4)(20\pi) = 8\pi$.]

6. **E.** The area of the shaded sector is
   $$\left(\dfrac{144}{360}\right)\pi(10)^2 = \left(\dfrac{2}{5}\right)100\pi = 40\pi.$$

7. **D.** The triangle is isosceles, so the third (unmarked) angle is also x:
   $180 = 72 + 2x \Rightarrow 2x = 108 \Rightarrow x = 54$.

8. **A.** $C = 2\pi r \Rightarrow r = \dfrac{C}{2\pi}$.

   Since $A = \pi r^2, A = \pi\left(\dfrac{C}{2\pi}\right)^2 = \pi\left(\dfrac{C^2}{4\pi^2}\right) = \dfrac{C^2}{4\pi}$.

9. **D.** If the area of the square is 4, each side is 2, and the length of a diagonal is $2\sqrt{2}$. The area of a circle whose radius is $2\sqrt{2}$ is $\pi(2\sqrt{2})^2 = 8\pi$.

10. **C.** Since ℓ is tangent to circle O at A, $\overline{OA} \perp \ell$ and $\triangle OAB$ is an isosceles right triangle. Then $m\angle O = 45$.
    The area of the shaded region is the area of $\triangle OAB$ minus the area of sector OAC.

    The area of $\triangle OAB$ is $\dfrac{1}{2}(2)(2) = 2$. Since the

    area of the circle is $\pi(2^2) = 4\pi$, the area of

    sector OAC is $\dfrac{45}{360} = \dfrac{1}{8}$ of 4π, or $\dfrac{1}{2}\pi$.

    Finally, the area of the shaded region is $2 - \dfrac{1}{2}\pi$.

11. **(2)** Since $a = b$, then $C = a\pi = b\pi = A$, so
    $$2\pi r = \pi r^2 \Rightarrow 2r = r^2 \Rightarrow r = 2.$$

12. $\left(7.5 \text{ or } \dfrac{15}{2}\right)$ Draw a diagram. By the Pythagorean theorem (or by recognizing a $3x$-$4x$-$5x$ triangle with $x = 3$), the length of diagonal $\overline{AC}$ is 15. But $\overline{AC}$ is also a diameter of the circle, so the diameter is 15 and the radius is 7.5 or $\dfrac{15}{2}$.

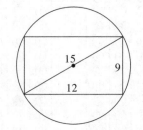

13. **(48)** Since arc AB is $\dfrac{2}{15}$ of the circumference,

    y is $\dfrac{2}{15} \times 360 = 48$.

14. $\left(\dfrac{13}{2} \text{ or } 6.5\right)$ The area of the circle is 9π; and

    since the white region is $\dfrac{100}{360} = \dfrac{5}{18}$ of the

    circle, the shaded region is $\dfrac{13}{18}$ of it:

    $$\dfrac{13}{18} \times 9\pi = \dfrac{13}{2}\pi \text{ or } 6.5\pi.$$

15. **(6)** Draw a diagram and label it.

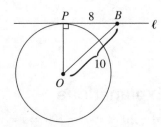

Since radius $\overline{OP}$ is perpendicular to ℓ, $\triangle OPB$ is a right triangle.
By the Pythagorean theorem,
$$OP^2 + 8^2 = 10^2 \Rightarrow OP^2 + 64 = 100.$$
So, $OP^2 = 36 \Rightarrow OP = 6$.

(Of course, you should save time by recognizing a 6-8-10 right triangle.)

9-M Solid Geometry

There is very little solid geometry on the SAT. Basically, all you need to know are the formulas for the volumes and surface areas of rectangular solids (including cubes) and cylinders.

A **rectangular solid** or **box** is a solid formed by six rectangles, called **faces**. The sides of the rectangles are called **edges**. As shown in the diagram that follows, the edges are the **length**, **width**, and **height**.

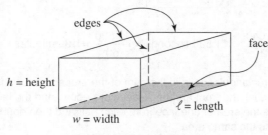

RECTANGULAR SOLID

A **cube** is a rectangular solid in which the length, width, and height are equal, so that all the edges are the same length.

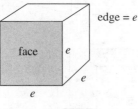

CUBE

The **volume** of a solid, which is the amount of space it occupies, is measured in **cubic units**. One cubic unit is the amount of space occupied by a cube all of whose edges are 1 unit long. In the figure above, if the length of each edge of the cube is 1 inch, the area of each face is 1 square inch, and the volume of the cube is 1 cubic inch.

Key Fact M1

The formula for the volume of a rectangular solid is $V = \ell wh$.

In a cube, all the edges are equal. Therefore, if e is the length of an edge, the formula for the volume is $V = e^3$.

EXAMPLE 1

The base of a rectangular tank is 2 feet wide and 4 feet long; the height of the tank is 20 inches. If water is pouring into the tank at the rate of 2 cubic inches per second, how many <u>hours</u> will be required to fill the tank?

Solution. Draw a diagram. Change all the units to inches (2 feet = 24 inches and 4 feet = 48 inches). Then the volume of the tank is 24 × 48 × 20 = 23,040 cubic inches. At 2 cubic inches per second:

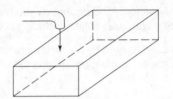

 required time = $\dfrac{23,040}{2}$ = 11,520 seconds = $\dfrac{11,520}{60}$ = 192 minutes = $\dfrac{192}{60}$ = **3.2** hours.

The ***surface area*** of a rectangular solid is the sum of the areas of the six faces. Since the top and bottom faces are equal, the front and back faces are equal, and the left and right faces are equal, you can calculate the area of one face from each pair and then double the sum. In a cube, each of the six faces has the same area.

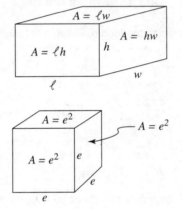

Key Fact M2

The formula for the surface area of a rectangular solid is $A = 2(\ell w + \ell h + wh)$. The formula for the surface area of a cube is $A = 6e^2$.

EXAMPLE 2

The volume of a cube is v cubic yards, and its surface area is a square feet. If $v = a$, what is the length, in <u>inches</u>, of each edge?

Solution. Draw a diagram. If *e* is the length of the edge in yards, then 3*e* is the length in feet, and 36*e* is the length in inches.

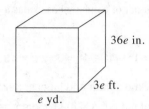

Therefore, $v = e^3$ and $a = 6(3e)^2 = 6(9e^2) = 54e^2$.
Since $v = a$, $e^3 = 54e^2 \Rightarrow e = 54$; the length of each edge is 36(54) = **1944** inches.

A **diagonal** of a box is a line segment joining a vertex on the top of the box to the opposite vertex on the bottom. A box has four diagonals, all the same length. In the box below they are line segments $\overline{AG}$, $\overline{BH}$, $\overline{CE}$, and $\overline{DF}$.

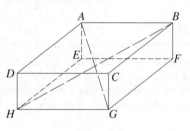

Key Fact M3

A diagonal of a box is the longest line segment that can be drawn between two points on the box.

Key Fact M4

If the dimensions of a box are ℓ, w, and h, and if d is the length of a diagonal, then $d^2 = \ell^2 + w^2 + h^2$.

For example, in the box below:

$$d^2 = 3^2 + 4^2 + 12^2 = 9 + 16 + 144 = 169 \Rightarrow d = 13.$$

This formula is really just an extended Pythagorean theorem. $\overline{EG}$ is the diagonal of rectangular base *EFGH*. Since the sides of the base are 3 and 4, *EG* is 5. Now, $\triangle CGE$ is a right triangle whose legs are 12 and 5, so diagonal $\overline{CE}$ is 13. (The only reason not to use the Pythagorean theorem is that these triangles are so familiar.)

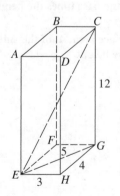

EXAMPLE 3

What is the length of a diagonal of a cube whose sides are 1?

Solution. Use the formula:

$$d^2 = 1^2 + 1^2 + 1^2 = 3 \Rightarrow d = \sqrt{3}.$$

Without the formula you would draw a diagram and label it. Since the base is a 1 × 1 square, its diagonal is $\sqrt{2}$. Then the diagonal of the cube is the hypotenuse of a right triangle whose legs are 1 and $\sqrt{2}$, so

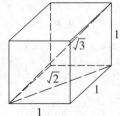

$$d^2 = 1^2 + (\sqrt{2})^2 = 1 + 2 = 3, \quad \text{and} \quad d = \sqrt{3}.$$

A *cylinder* is similar to a rectangular solid except that the base is a circle instead of a rectangle. The volume of a cylinder is the area of its circular base (πr^2) times its height (h). The surface area of a cylinder depends on whether you are envisioning a tube, such as a straw, without a top or bottom, or a can, which has both a top and a bottom.

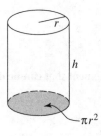

Key Fact M5

- The volume, V, of a cylinder whose circular base has radius r and whose height is h is the area of the base times the height:

$$V = \pi r^2 h.$$

- The surface area, A, of the side of the cylinder is the circumference of the circular base times the height:

$$A = 2\pi rh.$$

REFERENCE FACT

The formula for the volume of a cylinder is one of the facts provided in the "Reference Information" at the beginning of each math section.

EXAMPLE 4

The volume of a cube and the volume of a cylinder are equal. If the edge of the cube and the radius of the cylinder are each 6, which of the following is the best approximation of the height of the cube?

(A) 1
(B) 2
(C) 3
(D) 6
(E) 12

Solution. The volume of the cube is $6^3 = 216$. The volume of the cylinder is $\pi(6^2)h = 36\pi h$. Then

$$216 = 36\pi h \Rightarrow \pi h = 6 \Rightarrow h = \frac{6}{\pi}.$$

Since π is approximately 3, h is approximately **2 (B)**.

You now know the only formulas you will need. Any other solid geometry questions that may appear on the SAT will require you to visualize a situation and reason it out, rather than to apply a formula.

EXAMPLE 5

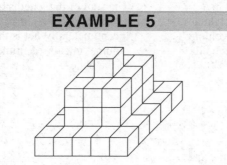

How many small blocks are needed to construct the tower in the figure above?

Solution. You need to "see" the answer. The top level consists of 1 block, the second and third levels consist of 9 blocks each, and the bottom layer consists of 25 blocks. The total is $1 + 9 + 9 + 25 = $ **44**.

Exercises on Solid Geometry

Multiple-Choice Questions

1. What is the volume of a cube whose surface area is 150?

    (A)   25
    (B)   100
    (C)   125
    (D)   1000
    (E) 15,625

2. What is the surface area of a cube whose volume is 64?

    (A)   16
    (B)   64
    (C)   96
    (D) 128
    (E) 384

3. A solid metal cube of side 3 inches is placed in a rectangular tank whose length, width, and height are 3, 4, and 5 inches, respectively. What is the volume, in cubic units, of water that the tank can now hold?

    (A) 20
    (B) 27
    (C) 33
    (D) 48
    (E) 60

4. The height, h, of a cylinder is equal to the edge of a cube. If the cylinder and the cube have the same volume, what is the radius of the cylinder?

    (A) $\dfrac{h}{\sqrt{\pi}}$

    (B) $h\sqrt{\pi}$

    (C) $\dfrac{\sqrt{\pi}}{h}$

    (D) $\dfrac{h^2}{\pi}$

    (E) πh^2

5. If the height of a cylinder is 4 times its circumference, what is the volume of the cylinder in terms of its circumference, C?

    (A) $\dfrac{C^3}{\pi}$

    (B) $\dfrac{2C^3}{\pi}$

    (C) $\dfrac{2C^2}{\pi^2}$

    (D) $\dfrac{\pi C^2}{4}$

    (E) $4\pi C^3$

Grid-in Questions

6. The sum of the lengths of all the edges of a cube is 6 centimeters. What is the volume, in cubic centimeters, of the cube?

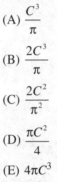

7. A 5-foot-long cylindrical pipe has an inner diameter of 6 feet and an outer diameter of 8 feet. If the total surface area (inside and out, including the ends) is $k\pi$, what is the value of k?

8. What is the number of cubic inches in 1 cubic foot?

9. A rectangular tank has a base that is 10 centimeters by 5 centimeters and a height of 20 centimeters. If the tank is half full of water, by how many centimeters will the water level rise if 325 cubic centimeters are poured into the tank?

10. Three identical balls fit snugly into a cylindrical can: the radius of the spheres equals the radius of the can, and the balls just touch the bottom and the top of the can. If the formula for the volume of a sphere is $V = \frac{4}{3}\pi r^3$, what fraction of the volume of the can is taken up by the balls?

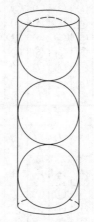

Answer Key

1. **C**   2. **C**   3. **C**   4. **A**   5. **A**

6. $1/8$ or $.125$ 7. 84 8. 1728

9. 6.5 10. $2/3$ or $.666$ or $.667$

Answer Explanations

1. **C.** Since the surface area is 150, each of the six faces of the cube is a square whose area is $150 \div 6 = 25$. Then, each edge is 5, and the volume is $5^3 = 125$.

2. **C.** Since the volume of the cube is 64, then $e^3 = 64 \Rightarrow e = 4$. The surface area is $6e^2 = 6 \times 16 = 96$.

3. **C.** The volume of the tank is $3 \times 4 \times 5 = 60$ cubic units, but the solid cube is taking up $3^3 = 27$ cubic units. Therefore, the tank can hold $60 - 27 = 33$ cubic units of water.

4. **A.** Since the volumes are equal, $\pi r^2 h = e^3 = h^3$. Therefore,

$$\pi r^2 = h^2 \Rightarrow r^2 = \frac{h^2}{\pi} \Rightarrow r = \frac{h}{\sqrt{\pi}}.$$

5. **A.** Since $V = \pi r^2 h$, you need to express r and h in terms of C. It is given that $h = 4C$; and since $C = 2\pi r$, then $r = \dfrac{C}{2\pi}$. Therefore,

$$V = \pi \left(\frac{C}{2\pi}\right)^2 (4C) = \pi \left(\frac{C^2}{4\pi^2}\right)(4C) = \frac{C^3}{\pi}.$$

6. $\left(\dfrac{1}{8} \text{ or } .125\right)$ Since a cube has 12 edges:

$$12e = 6 \Rightarrow e = \frac{1}{2}.$$

Therefore: $V = e^3 = \left(\dfrac{1}{2}\right)^3 = \dfrac{1}{8}$ or $.125$.

7. (84) Draw a diagram and label it. Since the surface of a cylinder is given by $A = 2\pi rh$, the area of the exterior is $2\pi(4)(5) = 40\pi$, and the area of the interior is $2\pi(3)(5) = 30\pi$. The area of *each* shaded end is the area of the outer circle minus the area of the inner circle: $16\pi - 9\pi = 7\pi$, so

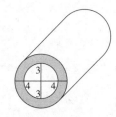

total surface area =
$40\pi + 30\pi + 7\pi + 7\pi = 84\pi \Rightarrow k = 84.$

8. (1728) The volume of a cube whose edges are 1 foot can be expressed in either of two ways:

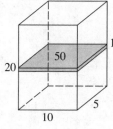

$$(1 \text{ foot})^3 = 1 \text{ cubic foot} \quad \text{or}$$
$$(12 \text{ inches})^3 = 1728 \text{ cubic inches}.$$

9. (6.5) Draw a diagram. Since the area of the base is $5 \times 10 = 50$ square centimeters, each 1 centimeter of depth has a volume of 50 cubic centimeters. Therefore, 325 cubic centimeters will raise the water level $325 \div 50 = 6.5$ centimeters. (Note that the fact that the tank was half full was not used, except to be sure that the tank didn't overflow. Since the tank was half full, the water was 10 centimeters deep, and the water level could rise by 6.5 centimeters. Had the tank been three-fourths full, the water would have been 15 centimeters deep, and the extra water would have caused the level to rise 5 centimeters, filling the tank; the rest of the water would have spilled out.)

10. $\left(\dfrac{2}{3} \text{ or } .666 \text{ or } .667\right)$ To avoid using r, assume that the radii of the spheres and the can are 1. Then the volume of each ball is $\dfrac{4}{3}\pi(1)^3 = \dfrac{4}{3}\pi$, and the total volume of the three balls is

$$3\left(\frac{4}{3}\pi\right) = 4\pi.$$ Since the volume of the can is $\pi(1)^2(6) = 6\pi$, the balls take up $\dfrac{4\pi}{6\pi} = \dfrac{2}{3}$ of the can. Grid in $\dfrac{2}{3}$ or $.666$ or $.667$.

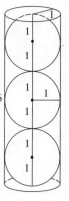

9-N Coordinate Geometry

The coordinate plane is formed by two perpendicular number lines called the **x-axis** and **y-axis**, which intersect at the **origin**. The axes divide the plane into four **quadrants**, labeled, in counterclockwise order, I, II, III, and IV.

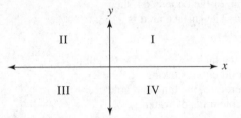

Each point in the plane is assigned two numbers, an **x-coordinate** and a **y-coordinate**, which are written as an ordered pair, **(x, y)**.

- Points to the right of the y-axis have positive x-coordinates, and those to the left have negative x-coordinates.
- Points above the x-axis have positive y-coordinates, and those below it have negative y-coordinates.
- If a point is on the x-axis, its y-coordinate is 0.
- If a point is on the y-axis, its x-coordinate is 0.

For example, point *A* in the figure below is labeled (2, 3), since it is 2 units to the right of the y-axis and 3 units above the x-axis. Similarly, point *B*(–3, –5) is in Quadrant III, 3 units to the left of the y-axis and 5 units below the x-axis.

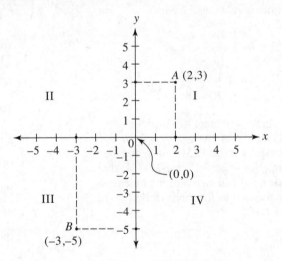

EXAMPLE 1

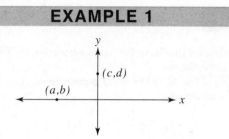

In the figure above, all of the following are equal EXCEPT

(A) *ab*
(B) *ac*
(C) *ad*
(D) *bc*
(E) *bd*

Solution. Since (a, b) lies on the *x*-axis, $b = 0$. Since (c, d) lies on the *y*-axis, $c = 0$. Each of the choices is equal to 0 except *ad* **(C)**.

EXAMPLE 2

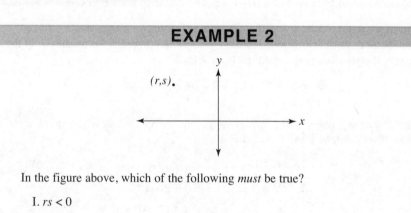

In the figure above, which of the following *must* be true?

   I. $rs < 0$

   II. $r < s$

   III. $r + s = 0$

(A) None
(B) I only
(C) II only
(D) I and II only
(E) I, II, and III

Solution. Since (r, s) is in Quadrant II, *r* is negative and *s* is positive. Then $rs < 0$ (I is true) and $r < s$ (II is true). Although $r + s$ could be equal to 0, it does not have to equal 0 (III is false). **Only I and II** must be true **(D)**.

Often a question requires you to calculate the distance between two points. This task is easiest when the points lie on the same horizontal or vertical line.

Key Fact N1

- **All the points on a horizontal line have the same *y*-coordinate. To find the distance between them, subtract their *x*-coordinates.**
- **All the points on a vertical line have the same *x*-coordinate. To find the distance between them, subtract their *y*-coordinates.**

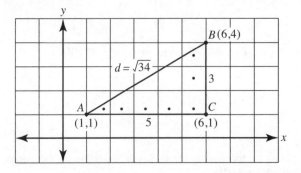

In the graph, the distance from *A* to *C* is 6 − 1 = 5. The distance from *B* to *C* is 4 − 1 = 3.

It is a little harder, but not much, to find the distance between two points that are not on the same horizontal or vertical line; just use the Pythagorean theorem. For example, in the preceding graph, if *d* represents the distance from *A* to *B*,

$$d^2 = 5^2 + 3^2 = 25 + 9 = 34 \Rightarrow d = \sqrt{34}.$$

CAUTION: You *cannot* count boxes unless the points are on the same horizontal or vertical line. The distance between *A* and *B* is 5, not 4.

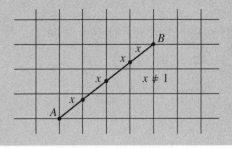

Key Fact N2

The distance, *d*, between two points, $A(x_1, y_1)$ and $B(x_2, y_2)$, can be calculated using the distance formula:

$$d = \sqrt{(x_2 - x_1)^2 + (y_2 - y_1)^2}.$$

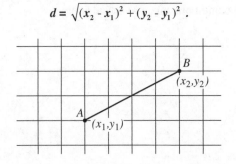

The distance formula is nothing more than the Pythagorean theorem, so you never need to use it. You can always create a right triangle by drawing a horizontal line through one of the points and a vertical line through the other, and then use the Pythagorean theorem. For example, to find the distance between $A(1, 1)$ and $B(5, 4)$, create a right triangle by drawing a horizonal line through A and a vertical line through B.

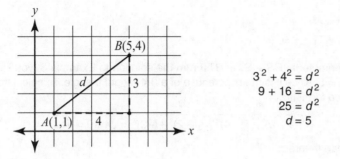

$$3^2 + 4^2 = d^2$$
$$9 + 16 = d^2$$
$$25 = d^2$$
$$d = 5$$

Examples 3 and 4 refer to the triangle in the following figure.

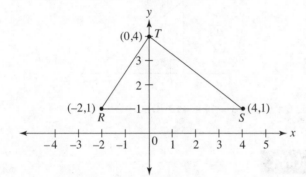

EXAMPLE 3

What is the area of $\triangle RST$?

(A) 6
(B) 9
(C) 12
(D) 15
(E) 18

Solution. $R(-2, 1)$ and $S(4, 1)$ lie on the same horizontal line, so $RS = 4 - (-2) = 6$. Let that be the base of the triangle. Then the height is the distance along the vertical line from T to RS: $4 - 1 = 3$. The area is $\frac{1}{2}(6)(3) = $ **9 (B)**.

EXAMPLE 4

What is the perimeter of △*RST*?

(A) 13
(B) 14
(C) 16
(D) $11 + \sqrt{13}$
(E) $11 + \sqrt{61}$

Solution. The perimeter is *RS* + *ST* + *RT*. From the solution to Example 3, you know that *RS* = 6. Also, *ST* = 5, since it is the hypotenuse of a 3-4-5 right triangle. To calculate *RT*, use either the distance formula:

$$\sqrt{(-2-0)^2 + (1-4)^2} = \sqrt{(-2)^2 + (-3)^2} = \sqrt{4+9} = \sqrt{13}$$

or the Pythagorean theorem:

$$RT^2 = 2^2 + 3^2 = 4 + 9 = 13 \Rightarrow RT = \sqrt{13}.$$

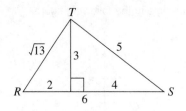

Then the perimeter is $6 + 5 + \sqrt{13} = \mathbf{11 + \sqrt{13}}$ **(D)**.

Key Fact N3

If *P* (x_1, y_1) and *Q* (x_2, y_2) are any two points, then the midpoint, *M*, of segment $\overline{PQ}$ is the point whose coordinates are $\left(\dfrac{x_1 + x_2}{2}, \dfrac{y_1 + y_2}{2} \right)$.

EXAMPLE 5

A $(2, -3)$ and *B* $(8, 5)$ are the endpoints of a diameter of a circle. What are the coordinates of the center of the circle?

(A) $(3, 1)$
(B) $(3, 4)$
(C) $(5, 1)$
(D) $(5, 4)$
(E) $(10, 2)$

Solution. The center of a circle is the midpoint of any diameter. Therefore, the coordinates are $\left(\dfrac{2+8}{2}, \dfrac{-3+5}{2} \right) = \left(\dfrac{10}{2}, \dfrac{2}{2} \right) = \mathbf{(5, 1)}$ **(C)**.

The *slope* of a line is a number that indicates how steep the line is.

Key Fact N4

• Vertical lines *do not have slopes*.
• To find the slope of any other line, proceed as follows:

1. Choose any two points, $A(x_1, y_1)$ and $B(x_2, y_2)$, on the line.

2. Take the differences of the y-coordinates, $y_2 - y_1$, and the x-coordinates, $x_2 - x_1$.

3. Divide: slope = $\dfrac{y_2 - y_1}{x_2 - x_1}$.

We will illustrate the next KEY FACT by using this formula to calculate the slopes of RS, RT, and ST from Example 3: $R(-2, 1)$, $S(4, 1)$, $T(0, 4)$.

Key Fact N5

• The slope of any horizontal line is 0:

$$\text{slope of } \overline{RS} = \frac{1-1}{4-(-2)} = \frac{0}{6} = 0.$$

• The slope of any line that goes up as you move from left to right is positive:

$$\text{slope of } \overline{RT} = \frac{4-1}{0-(-2)} = \frac{3}{2}.$$

• The slope of any line that goes down as you move from left to right is negative:

$$\text{slope of } \overline{ST} = \frac{1-4}{4-0} = -\frac{3}{4}.$$

EXAMPLE 6

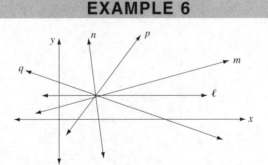

In the figure above, which line has the greatest slope?

(A) ℓ
(B) m
(C) n
(D) p
(E) q

Solution. Since the slope of line ℓ is 0 and the slopes of lines n and q are negative, eliminate choices A, C, and E. Lines m and p have positive slopes, but line p is steeper. **(D)**

The next key fact concerns the relationships between the slopes of parallel and perpendicular lines.

Key Fact N6

- **If two nonvertical lines are parallel, their slopes are equal.**
- **If two nonvertical lines are perpendicular, the product of their slopes is –1.**

If the product of two numbers, *r* and *s*, is –1, then

$$rs = -1 \Rightarrow r = -\frac{1}{s}.$$

Therefore, another way to express the second part of KEY FACT N6 is to say that, **if two nonvertical lines are perpendicular, the slope of one is the negative reciprocal of the slope of the other.**

EXAMPLE 7

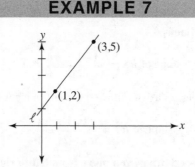

In the figure above, line ℓ passes through points (1, 2) and (3, 5). Line *m* (not shown) is perpendicular to ℓ. What is the slope of line *m*?

(A) $-\dfrac{3}{2}$

(B) $-\dfrac{2}{3}$

(C) 0

(D) $\dfrac{2}{3}$

(E) $\dfrac{3}{2}$

Solution. First use the slope formula to calculate the slope of line ℓ: $\dfrac{5-2}{3-1} = \dfrac{3}{2}$.

Then the slope of line *m* is the negative reciprocal of $\dfrac{3}{2}$, which is $-\dfrac{2}{3}$ **(B)**.

Note that you can see from the diagram in Example 7 that the slope of ℓ is positive. If you sketch any line perpendicular to ℓ, you can see that its slope is negative. So immediately you know the answer must be A or B.

Every line that is drawn in the coordinate plane has an equation. All the points on a horizontal line have the same *y*-coordinate. For example, in the following figure, horizontal line ℓ passes through (–3, 3), (0, 3), (2, 3), (5, 3), and (10, 3).

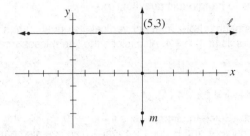

The equation of line ℓ is $y = 3$.

Similarly, every point on vertical line m has an x-coordinate equal to 5, and the equation of m is $x = 5$.

Every other line in the coordinate plane has an equation that can be written in the form $y = mx + b$, where m is the slope of the line and b is the **y-intercept**—the y-coordinate of the point where the line crosses the y-axis. These facts are summarized in KEY FACT N7.

Key Fact N7

- **For any real number a: $x = a$ is the equation of the vertical line that crosses the x-axis at $(a, 0)$.**
- **For any real number b: $y = b$ is the equation of the horizontal line that crosses the y-axis at $(0, b)$.**
- **For any real numbers b and m: $y = mx + b$ is the equation of the line that crosses the y-axis at $(0, b)$ and whose slope is m.**

On the SAT, you won't have to graph a line, but you may have to recognize the graph of a line. In a multiple-choice question, you may be given the graph of a line and asked which of the five choices is the equation of that line; or you may be given the equation of a line and asked which of the five choices is the correct graph.

EXAMPLE 8

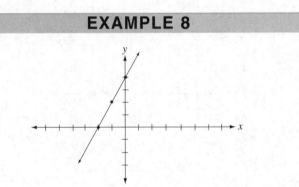

Which of the following is the equation of the line in the figure above?

(A) $y = 2x + 4$

(B) $y = \dfrac{1}{2}x + 4$

(C) $y = 2x - 2$

(D) $y = \dfrac{1}{2}x - 4$

(E) $y = 4x + 2$

There are two different ways to handle this question.

Solution 1. Since the line is neither horizontal nor vertical, its equation has the form $y = mx + b$. Since the line crosses the *y*-axis at 4, $b = 4$. Also, since the line passes through (–2, 0) and (0, 4), its slope is $\dfrac{4-0}{0-(-2)} = \dfrac{4}{2} = 2$.

So $m = 2$, and the equation is **$y = 2x + 4$ (A)**.

Solution 2. Test some points. Since the line passes through (0, 4), $y = 4$ when $x = 0$. Plug in 0 for *x* in the five choices; only in A and B does *y* equal 4. The line also passes through (–2, 0), so when $x = -2$, $y = 0$.

Replace *x* by –2 in choices A and B.

- $2(-2) + 4 = -4 + 4 = 0$, so A works.

- $\dfrac{1}{2}(-2) + 4 = -1 + 4 = 3$, so B does not work.

EXAMPLE 9

Which of the following is the graph of the line whose equation is $3y = 2x + 6$?

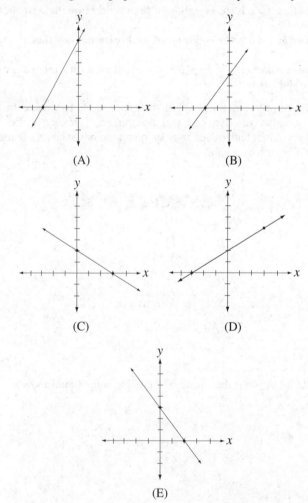

Solution 1. Express $3y = 2x + 6$ in standard form by dividing each term by 3: $y = \dfrac{2}{3}x + 2$. From this equation you see that the *y*-intercept is 2. Eliminate choices A, B, and E. Since the slope $\dfrac{2}{3}$ is positive, eliminate C. The answer must be **D**.

Solution 2. Test some points.

- When $x = 0$, $3y = 2(0) + 6 = 6 \Rightarrow y = 2$, so (0, 2) is a point on the graph.
- When $x = 3$, $3y = 2(3) + 6 = 12 \Rightarrow y = 4$, so (3, 4) is on the graph.

Only choice **D** passes through both (0, 2) and (3, 4).

Exercises on Coordinate Geometry

Multiple-Choice Questions

1. If $A(-1, 1)$ and $B(3, -1)$ are the endpoints of one side of square $ABCD$, what is the area of the square?

   (A) 12
   (B) 16
   (C) 20
   (D) 25
   (E) 36

2. If $P(2, 1)$ and $Q(8, 1)$ are two of the vertices of a rectangle, which of the following *cannot* be another of the vertices?

   (A) $(2, 8)$
   (B) $(8, 2)$
   (C) $(2, -8)$
   (D) $(-2, 8)$
   (E) $(8, 8)$

3. A circle whose center is at $(6,8)$ passes through the origin. Which of the following points is NOT on the circle?

   (A) $(12, 0)$
   (B) $(6, -2)$
   (C) $(16, 8)$
   (D) $(-2, 12)$
   (E) $(-4, 8)$

4. What is the slope of the line that passes through (a, b) and $\left(\dfrac{1}{a}, b\right)$?

   (A) 0

   (B) $\dfrac{1}{b}$

   (C) $\dfrac{1 - a^2}{a}$

   (D) $\dfrac{a^2 - 1}{a}$

   (E) Undefined

5. If $c \neq 0$ and the slope of the line passing through $(-c, c)$ and $(3c, a)$ is 1, which of the following is an expression for a in terms of c?

   (A) $-3c$

   (B) $-\dfrac{c}{3}$

   (C) $2c$
   (D) $3c$
   (E) $5c$

6. What is the slope of the line that passes through $(3, 2)$ and is parallel to the line that passes through $(-2, 3)$ and $(2, -3)$?

   (A) $-\dfrac{3}{2}$

   (B) $-\dfrac{2}{3}$

   (C) $\dfrac{2}{3}$

   (D) 1

   (E) $\dfrac{3}{2}$

7. What is the slope of the line that passes through $(3, 2)$ and is perpendicular to the line that passes through $(-2, 3)$ and $(2, -3)$?

   (A) $-\dfrac{3}{2}$

   (B) $-\dfrac{2}{3}$

   (C) $\dfrac{2}{3}$

   (D) 1

   (E) $\dfrac{3}{2}$

8. What is the equation of the line that passes through $(4, -4)$ and $(4, 4)$?

   (A) $x = 4$
   (B) $y = 4$
   (C) $y = 4x$
   (D) $y = 4x + 4$
   (E) $y = 4x - 4$

9. Line ℓ is tangent to a circle whose center is at (3, 2). If the point of tangency is (6, 6), what is the slope of line ℓ?

(A) $-\dfrac{4}{3}$

(B) $-\dfrac{3}{4}$

(C) 0

(D) $\dfrac{3}{4}$

(E) $\dfrac{4}{3}$

10. What is the equation of the line that crosses the *y*-axis at (0, 5) and crosses the *x*-axis at (5, 0)?

(A) $x = 5$
(B) $y = 5$
(C) $y = x + 5$
(D) $y = x - 5$
(E) $y = -x + 5$

Grid-in Questions

11. If the coordinates of △*RST* are *R*(0, 0), *S*(7, 0), and *T*(2, 5), what is the sum of the slopes of the three sides of the triangle?

12. If the area of circle *O* below is *k*π, what is the value of *k*?

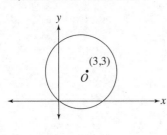

Questions 13 and 14 concern parallelogram *JKLM*, whose coordinates are *J*(−5, 2), *K*(−2, 6), *L*(5, 6), *M*(2, 2).

13. What is the area of parallelogram *JKLM*?

14. What is the perimeter of parallelogram *JKLM*?

15. What is the area of quadrilateral *ABCD*?

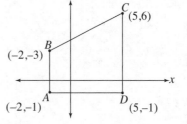

Answer Key

1. **C**   3. **D**   5. **E**   7. **C**   9. **B**
2. **D**   4. **A**   6. **A**   8. **A**   10. **E**

11. **1.5**

12. **18**

13. **28**

14. **24**

15. **38.5** or **77/2**

Answer Explanations

1. **C.** The area of square *ABCD* is s^2, where $s = AB$. To calculate s, use the distance formula:

$$s = \sqrt{(3-(-1))^2 + (-1-1)^2} = \sqrt{4^2 + (-2)^2} = \sqrt{16+4} = \sqrt{20}.$$

Then $s^2 = 20$.

2. **D.** Draw a diagram. Any point whose *x*-coordinate is 2 or 8 could be another vertex. Of the choices, only $(-2, 8)$ is *not* possible.

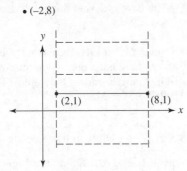

3. **D.** Draw a diagram. The radius of the circle is 10 (since it's the hypotenuse of a 6-8-10 right triangle). Which of the choices is (are) 10 units from $(6, 8)$?

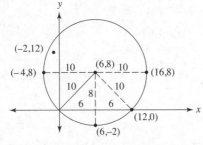

 • First, check the easy ones; E: $(-4, 8)$ and C: $(16, 8)$ are 10 units to the left and right of $(6, 8)$, and B: $(6, -2)$ is 10 units below.
 • Check A: $(12, 0)$, which works, and D: $(-2, 12)$, which doesn't.
 The answer is **D**.

4. **A.** The formula for the slope is $\dfrac{y_2 - y_1}{x_2 - x_1}$; but before using it, look at the question again. Since the *y*-coordinates are equal, the numerator, and thus the fraction, equals 0.

5. **E.** The slope is equal to

$$\frac{y_2 - y_1}{x_2 - x_1} = \frac{a - c}{3c - (-c)} = \frac{a-c}{4c} = 1.$$

So, $a - c = 4c \Rightarrow a = 5c$.

6. **A.** Use TACTIC 1: draw a diagram. Quickly sketch the line through $(-2, 3)$ and $(2, -3)$ and the line parallel to it that goes through $(3, 2)$.

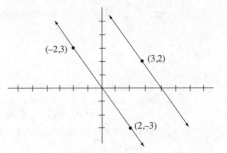

Clearly, the slopes of both lines are negative. The answer must be A or B. By KEY FACT N4, the slope of the line through $(-2, 3)$ and $(2, -3)$ is

$$\frac{-3-3}{2-(-2)} = \frac{-6}{4} = -\frac{3}{2}.$$

By KEY FACT N6, nonvertical parallel lines have equal slopes, so the answer is $-\dfrac{3}{2}$. Note that it is irrelevant that the second line passes through $(3, 2)$.

7. **C.** By KEY FACT N4, the slope of the line through $(-2, 3)$ and $(2, -3)$ is

$$\frac{-3-3}{2-(-2)} = \frac{-6}{4} = -\frac{3}{2}.$$

By KEY FACT N6, if two nonvertical lines are perpendicular, the product of their slopes is -1. Then, if m is the slope of the perpendicular line,

$$-\frac{3}{2}m = -1 \Rightarrow -3m = -2 \Rightarrow m = \frac{2}{3}.$$

As in Exercise 6, it is irrelevant that the line passes through $(3, 2)$.

8. **A.** A quick sketch shows that the line that passes through $(4, -4)$ and $(4, 4)$ is vertical. Then, by KEY FACT N7, its equation is $x = 4$.

9. **B.** Draw a rough sketch.

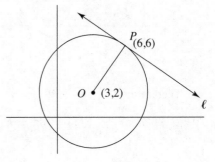

Line segment $\overline{OP}$, joining $(3, 2)$ and $(6, -6)$ is a radius and so, by KEY FACT L10, is perpendicular to line ℓ. The slope of $\overline{OP}$ is $\dfrac{6-2}{6-3} = \dfrac{4}{3}$. Therefore, the slope of ℓ is $-\dfrac{3}{4}$.

10. **E.** Since the line is neither horizontal nor vertical, its equation has the form $y = mx + b$. Since it crosses the y-axis at $(0, 5)$, $b = 5$. Since it passes through $(0, 5)$ and $(5, 0)$, its slope is $\dfrac{0-5}{5-0} = \dfrac{-5}{5} = -1$ and its equation is

$$y = -1x + 5 \text{ or } y = -x + 5.$$

11. **(1.5)** Sketch the triangle, and then calculate the slopes. Since $\overline{RS}$ is horizontal, its slope is 0.

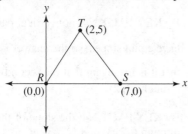

The slope of $\overline{RT} = \dfrac{5-0}{2-0} = 2.5$.

The slope of $\overline{ST} = \dfrac{5-0}{2-7} = \dfrac{5}{-5} = -1$.
Now add: $0 + 2.5 + (-1) = 1.5$.

12. **(18)** Since the line segment joining $(3, 3)$ and $(0, 0)$ is a radius of the circle, the radius equals $3\sqrt{2}$.

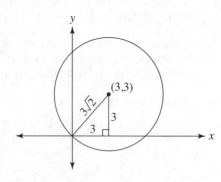

Therefore,

$$\text{area} = \pi\left(3\sqrt{2}\right)^2 = 18\pi \Rightarrow k = 18.$$

Here is the diagram for solutions 13 and 14.

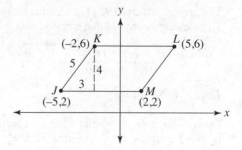

13. **(28)** The base is 7, and the height is 4. The area is $7 \times 4 = 28$.

14. **(24)** Sides $\overline{JM}$ and $\overline{KL}$ are each 7. Also, sides $\overline{JK}$ and $\overline{LM}$ are each the hypotenuse of a 3-4-5 right triangle, and so they are 5. The perimeter is $2(7 + 5) = 24$.

15. $\left(38.5 \text{ or } \dfrac{77}{2}\right)$ Draw in line segment $\overline{BE}$, dividing quadrilateral $ABCD$ into rectangle $ABED$ and $\triangle BEC$.
The area of the rectangle is $4 \times 7 = 28$, and the area of the triangle is $\dfrac{1}{2}(7)(3) = 10.5$.
The total area is 38.5 or $\dfrac{77}{2}$.

MISCELLANEOUS TOPICS

9-O Counting and Probability

Some questions on the SAT begin, "How many ... ." In these problems you are being asked to count something: how many apples can Maria buy, how many dollars did Jose spend, how many pages did Elizabeth read, how many numbers satisfy a certain property, or how many ways are there to complete a particular task. Sometimes these problems can be handled by simple arithmetic. Other times it helps to use TACTIC 14 and systematically make a list. Occasionally it helps to know the counting principle and other strategies that will be reviewed in this section.

Counting

USING ARITHMETIC TO COUNT

Examples 1–3 require only arithmetic. Be careful, though; they are not the same.

EXAMPLE 1

John bought some apples. If he entered the store with $113 and left with $109, how much did the apples cost?

EXAMPLE 2

Kim was selling tickets for the school play. One day she sold tickets numbered 109 through 113. How many tickets did she sell that day?

EXAMPLE 3

John is the 109th person in a line, and Kim is the 113th person. How many people are there between John and Kim?

Solutions 1–3. It may seem that each of these examples requires a simple subtraction: $113 - 109 = 4$. In Example 1, John did spend **$4** on apples. In Example 2, however, Kim sold **5** tickets; and in Example 3, only **3** people are on line between John and Kim! Assume that John went into the store with 113 one-dollar bills, numbered 1 through 113; he spent the 4 dollars numbered 113, 112, 111, and 110, and still had the dollars numbered 1 through 109; Kim sold the 5 tickets numbered 109, 110, 111, 112, and 113; and between John and Kim the 110th, 111th, and 112th persons—3 people—were on line.

- In Example 1, you just need to subtract: $113 - 109 = 4$.
- In Example 2, you need to subtract *and then add 1*: $113 - 109 + 1 = 4 + 1 = 5$.
- In Example 3, you need to subtract and then *subtract 1 more*: $113 - 109 - 1 = 3$.

Although Example 1 is too easy for the SAT, questions such as Examples 2 and 3 appear frequently, because they're not as obvious and they require that little extra thought. *When do you have to add or subtract 1?*

The issue is whether or not the first and last numbers are included. In Example 1, John spent dollar number 113, but he still had dollar 109 when he left the store. In Example 2, Kim sold both ticket number 109 and ticket 113. In Example 3, neither Kim (the 113th person) nor John (the 109th person) should be counted.

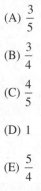

Key Fact O1

To count how many integers there are between two integers, follow these rules:

• **If exactly one of the endpoints is included: subtract.**
• **If both endpoints are included: subtract and then add 1.**
• **If neither endpoint is included: subtract and then subtract 1 more.**

EXAMPLE 4

From 1:09 to 1:13, Elaine read pages 109 through 113 in her English book. What was her rate of reading, in pages per minute?

(A) $\dfrac{3}{5}$

(B) $\dfrac{3}{4}$

(C) $\dfrac{4}{5}$

(D) 1

(E) $\dfrac{5}{4}$

Solution. Since Elaine read both pages 109 and 113, she read 113 − 109 + 1 = 5 pages. She started reading during the minute that started at 1:09 (and ended at 1:10). Since she stopped reading at 1:13, she did not read during the minute that began at 1:13 (and ended at 1:14), so she read for 1:13 − 1:09 = 4 minutes. She read at the rate of $\dfrac{5}{4}$ pages per minute (**E**).

SYSTEMATICALLY MAKING A LIST

When the numbers in a problem are small, it is often better to systematically list all of the possibilities than to risk making an error in arithmetic. In Example 4, rather than even thinking about whether or not to add 1 or subtract 1 after subtracting the numbers of pages, you could have just quickly jotted down the pages Elaine read (109, 110, 111, 112, 113), and then counted them.

EXAMPLE 5

Blair has 4 paintings in the basement. She is going to bring up 2 of them and hang 1 in her den and 1 in her bedroom. In how many ways can she choose which paintings go in each room?

(A) 4
(B) 6
(C) 12
(D) 16
(E) 24

Solution. Label the paintings 1, 2, 3, and 4, write B for bedroom and D for den, and make a list.

B-D	B-D	B-D	B-D
1-2	2-2	3-1	4-1
1-3	2-3	3-2	4-2
1-4	2-4	3-4	4-3

There are **12** ways to choose **(C)**.

For additional examples of systematically making lists, see TACTIC 14 in Chapter 8.

In Example 5, making a list was feasible, but if Blair had 10 paintings and needed to hang 4 of them, it would be impossible to list all the different ways of hanging them. In such cases you need the *counting principle*.

USING THE COUNTING PRINCIPLE

Key Fact O2

If two jobs need to be completed and there are *m* ways to do the first job and *n* ways to do the second job, then there are *m* × *n* ways to do one job followed by the other. This principle can be extended to any number of jobs.

In Example 5, the first job was to pick 1 of the 4 paintings and hang it in the bedroom. That could be done in 4 ways. The second job was to pick a second painting to hang in the den. That job could be accomplished by choosing any of the remaining 3 paintings. There are $4 \times 3 = 12$ ways to hang the 2 paintings.

Now, assume there are 10 paintings to be hung in 4 rooms. The first job is to choose 1 of the 10 paintings for the bedroom. The second job is to choose 1 of the 9 remaining paintings to hang in the den. The third job is to choose 1 of the 8 remaining paintings for, say, the living room. Finally, the fourth job is to pick 1 of the 7 remaining paintings for the dining room. These 4 jobs can be completed in $10 \times 9 \times 8 \times 7 = 5040$ ways.

EXAMPLE 6

How many integers are there between 100 and 1000 all of whose digits are odd?

Solution. You're looking for three-digit numbers, such as 135, 711, 353, and 999, in which all three digits are odd. Note that you are *not* required to use three different digits. Although you certainly wouldn't want to list all of the possibilities, you could count them by listing some of them and seeing whether a pattern develops. In the 100's there are 5 numbers that begin with 11: 111, 113, 115, 117, 119. Similarly, there are 5 numbers that begin with 13: 131, 133, 135, 137, 139; 5 numbers that begin with 15, 5 that begin with 17, and 5 that begin with 19, for a total of $5 \times 5 = 25$ in the 100's. In the same way there are 25 in the 300's, 25 in the 500's, 25 in the 700's, and 25 in the 900's, for a grand total of $5 \times 25 = 125$. You can actually do this calculation in less time than it takes to read this paragraph.

The best way to solve Example 6, however, is to use the counting principle. Think of writing a three-digit number as three jobs that need to be done. The first job is to select one of the five odd digits and use it as the digit in the hundreds place. The second job is to select one of the five odd digits to be the digit that goes in the tens place. Finally, the third job is to select one of the five odd digits to be the digit in the units place. Each of these jobs can be done in 5 ways, so the total number of ways is $5 \times 5 \times 5 = 125$.

USING VENN DIAGRAMS

A **Venn diagram** is a figure with two or three overlapping circles, usually enclosed in a rectangle, that is used to solve certain counting problems. To illustrate, assume that a school has 100 seniors. The following Venn diagram, which divides the rectangle into four regions, shows the distribution of those students in the band and the orchestra.

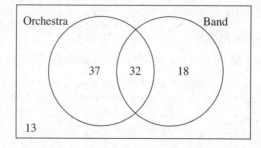

The 32 written in the part of the diagram where the two circles overlap represents the 32 seniors who are in both band and orchestra. The 18 written in the circle on the right represents the 18 seniors who are in the band but not in the orchestra, while the 37 written in the left circle represents the 37 seniors who are in the orchestra but not in the band. Finally, the 13 written in the rectangle outside the circles represents the 13 seniors who are in neither band nor orchestra. The numbers in all four regions must add up to the total number of seniors: $32 + 18 + 37 + 13 = 100$.

Note that there are 50 seniors in the band—32 who are also in the orchestra and 18 who are not in the orchestra. Similarly, there are $32 + 37 = 69$ seniors in the orchestra. Be careful: the 50 names on the band roster and the 69 names on the orchestra roster add up to 119 names—more than the number of seniors. The reason is that 32 names are on both lists and so have been counted twice. The number of seniors who are in band or orchestra is only $119 - 32 = 87$. Those 87, together with the 13 who are in neither band nor orchestra, make up the total of 100.

Although no problem on an SAT *requires* the use of a Venn diagram, occasionally there will be a problem that you will be able to solve more easily if you draw a Venn diagram, as in Example 7.

EXAMPLE 7

Of the 410 students at Kennedy High School, 240 study Spanish and 180 study French. If 25 students study neither language, how many students study both?

Solution. Draw a Venn diagram. Let *x* represent the number of students who study both languages, and write *x* in the part of the diagram where the two circles overlap.

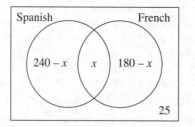

Then the number who study only Spanish is $240 - x$, and the number who study only French is $180 - x$. The number who study at least one of the languages is $410 - 25 = 385$, so

$$385 = (240 - x) + x + (180 - x) = 420 - x.$$

So, $x = 420 - 385 = $ **35** who study both.

Probability

The ***probability*** that an ***event*** will occur is a number between 0 and 1, usually written as a fraction, that indicates how likely it is that the event will happen. For example, for the spinner at the right, there are 4 possible outcomes: it is equally likely that the spinner will stop in any of the four regions. There is 1 chance in 4 that it will stop in the region marked 2, so we say that

the probability of spinning a 2 is one-fourth and write $P(2) = \dfrac{1}{4}$. Since 2 is the only even number

on the spinner, we could also say $P(\text{even}) = \dfrac{1}{4}$. Also, there are 3 chances in 4 that the spinner

will land in a region with an odd number in it, so $P(\text{odd}) = \dfrac{3}{4}$.

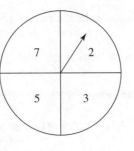

Key Fact O3

If *E* is any event, the probability that *E* will occur is given by

$$P(E) = \frac{\textbf{number of favorable outcomes}}{\textbf{total number of possible outcomes}},$$

assuming that all of the possible outcomes are equally likely.

In the preceding example, each of the four regions is the same size, so it is equally likely that the spinner will land on the 2, 3, 5, or 7. Therefore:

$$P(\text{odd}) = \frac{\text{number of ways of getting an odd number}}{\text{total number of possible outcomes}} = \frac{3}{4}.$$

Note that the probability of *not* getting an odd number is 1 minus the probability of getting an odd number:

$$1 - \frac{3}{4} = \frac{1}{4}.$$

Let's look at some other probabilities associated with spinning this spinner once:

$P(\text{number} > 10) =$

$\dfrac{\text{number of ways of getting a number} > 10}{\text{total number of possible outcomes}} = \dfrac{0}{4} = 0.$

$P(\text{prime number}) =$

$\dfrac{\text{number of ways of getting a prime number}}{\text{total number of possible outcomes}} = \dfrac{4}{4} = 1.$

$P(\text{number} < 4) =$

$\dfrac{\text{number of ways of getting a number} < 4}{\text{total number of possible outcomes}} = \dfrac{2}{4} = \dfrac{1}{2}.$

NOTE

Although probabilities are defined as fractions, they can also be written as decimals or percents.

Key Fact O4

Let E be an event, and let $P(E)$ be the probability that it will occur.

• If E is **impossible** (such as getting a number greater than 10 in the spinner example), **$P(E) = 0$.**
• If it is **certain** that E will occur (such as getting a prime number in the spinner example), **$P(E) = 1$.**
• In all cases, **$0 \le P(E) \le 1$.**
• The probability that event E will *not* occur is **$1 - P(E)$.**
• If two or more events constitute all the outcomes, the sum of their probabilities is 1.

   [For example, $P(\text{even}) + P(\text{odd}) = \dfrac{1}{4} + \dfrac{3}{4} = 1.$]

• The more likely it is that an event will occur, the higher (the closer to 1) its probability is; the less likely it is that an event will occur, the lower (the closer to 0) its probability is.

Even though probability is defined as a fraction, probabilities can also be written as decimals or percents.

Instead of writing $P(E) = \dfrac{1}{2}$, you can write

$$P(E) = .50 \text{ or } P(E) = 50\%.$$

EXAMPLE 8

In 2003, Thanksgiving was on Thursday, November 27, and there are 30 days in November. If one day in November 2003 was chosen at random for a concert, what is the probability that the concert was on a weekend (Saturday or Sunday)?

There are two ways to answer this: either quickly draw a calendar, or reason out the solution.

Solution 1. Make a blank calendar and put 27 in the Thursday column:

S	M	T	W	Th	F	S
				27		

Now just go forward and backward from 27. Enter 28, 29, 30 and then 26, 25, 24, … 1.

S	M	T	W	Th	F	S
						1
2	3	4	5	6	7	8
9	10	11	12	13	14	15
16	17	18	19	20	21	22
23	24	25	26	27	28	29
30						

Finally, count (or circle) the Saturdays and Sundays. There are 5 of each for a total of 10, so the probability is $\dfrac{10}{30} = \dfrac{1}{3}$.

Solution 2. Since the 27th was a Thursday, the 28th, 29th, and 30th were Friday, Saturday, and Sunday, respectively. Repeatedly subtracting 7, you see that the Saturdays were on November 29, 22, 15, 8, 1 and the Sundays were on November 30, 23, 16, 9, 2 for a total of 10 weekend days. Then $\frac{10}{30} = \frac{1}{3}$.

EXAMPLE 9

An integer between 100 and 999, inclusive, is chosen at random. What is the probability that all the digits of the number are odd?

Solution. By KEY FACT O1, since both endpoints are included, there are 999 – 100 + 1 = 900 integers between 100 and 999. In Example 6, you saw that there are 125 three-digit numbers all of whose digits are odd. Therefore, the probability is

$$\frac{\text{number of favorable outcomes}}{\text{total number of possible outcomes}} = \frac{125}{900} = \frac{5}{36} \approx .138$$

Occasionally, on an SAT there will be a question that relates probability and geometry. The next KEY FACT will help you deal with that type of question.

Key Fact O5

If a point is chosen at random inside a geometrical figure, the probability that the chosen point lies in a particular region is:

$$\frac{\text{area of that region}}{\text{area of the whole figure}}.$$

EXAMPLE 10

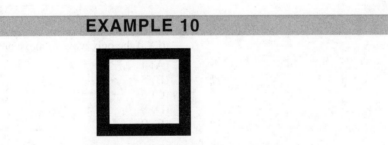

In the figure above, a white square whose sides are 4 has been pasted on a black square whose sides are 5. If a point is chosen at random from the large square, what is the probability that the point is in the black area?

Solution. The area of the large square is $5^2 = 25$, and the area of the white square is $4^2 = 16$. Therefore, the area of the black region is 25 – 16 = 9, and the probability that the chosen point is in the black area is $\frac{9}{25}$.

Exercises on Counting and Probability

Multiple-Choice Questions

1. A cafeteria has a lunch special, consisting of soup or salad, a sandwich, coffee or tea, and a dessert. If the menu lists 3 soups, 2 salads, 8 sandwiches, and 7 desserts, how many different lunches can you choose? (**NOTE:** Two lunches are different if they differ in any aspect.)

    (A) 22
    (B) 280
    (C) 336
    (D) 560
    (E) 672

2. Dwight Eisenhower was born on October 14, 1890, and died on March 28, 1969. What was his age, in years, at the time of his death?

    (A) 77
    (B) 78
    (C) 79
    (D) 80
    (E) 81

3. There are 27 students in Mr. White's homeroom. What is the probability that at least 3 of them have their birthdays in the same month?

    (A) 0

    (B) $\dfrac{3}{27}$

    (C) $\dfrac{3}{12}$

    (D) $\dfrac{1}{2}$

    (E) 1

4. A jar has 5 marbles, 1 of each of the colors red, white, blue, green, and yellow. If 4 marbles are removed from the jar, what is the probability that the yellow marble was removed?

    (A) $\dfrac{1}{20}$

    (B) $\dfrac{1}{5}$

    (C) $\dfrac{1}{4}$

    (D) $\dfrac{4}{5}$

    (E) $\dfrac{5}{4}$

5. Let A be the set of primes less than 6, and B be the set of positive odd numbers less than 6. How many different sums of the form $a + b$ are possible if a is in A and b is in B?

    (A) 6
    (B) 7
    (C) 8
    (D) 9
    (E) 10

6. A printer that can print 1 page in 5 seconds shuts down for 3 minutes to cool off after every hour of operation. How many minutes will the printer take to print 3600 pages?

    (A)   300
    (B)   312
    (C)   315
    (D) 18,000
    (E) 18,897

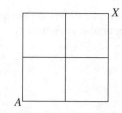

7. In the figure above, how many paths are there from A to X if the only ways to move are up and to the right?

    (A) 4
    (B) 5
    (C) 6
    (D) 8
    (E) 9

8. A jar contains 20 marbles: 4 red, 6 white, and 10 blue. If you remove 1 marble at a time, randomly, what is the minimum number that you must remove to be certain that you have at least 2 marbles of each color?

    (A) 6
    (B) 10
    (C) 12
    (D) 16
    (E) 18

9. At the audition for the school play, n people tried out. If k people went before Judy, who went before Liz, and m people went after Liz, how many people tried out between Judy and Liz?

    (A) $n - m - k - 2$
    (B) $n - m - k - 1$
    (C) $n - m - k$
    (D) $n - m - k + 1$
    (E) $n - m - k + 2$

Note: Figure not drawn to scale

10. In the figure above, each of the small circles has a radius of 2 and the large circle has a radius of 6. If a point is chosen at random inside the large circle, what is the probability that the point lies in the shaded region?

(A) $\dfrac{7}{9}$

(B) $\dfrac{2}{3}$

(C) $\dfrac{5}{4}$

(D) $\dfrac{1}{3}$

(E) $\dfrac{2}{9}$

Grid-in Questions

11. There are 100 people on a line. Andy is the 37th person, and Ali is the 67th person. If a person on line is chosen at random, what is the probability that the person is standing between Andy and Ali?

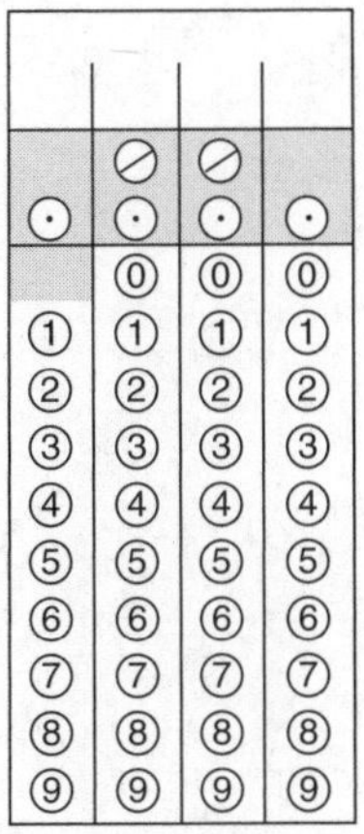

12. How many four-digit numbers have only even digits?

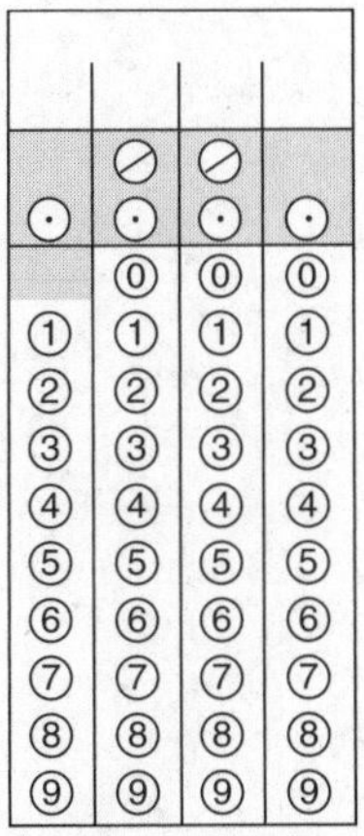

13. How many ways are there to rearrange the letters in the word *elation*, if the first and last letter must each be a vowel?

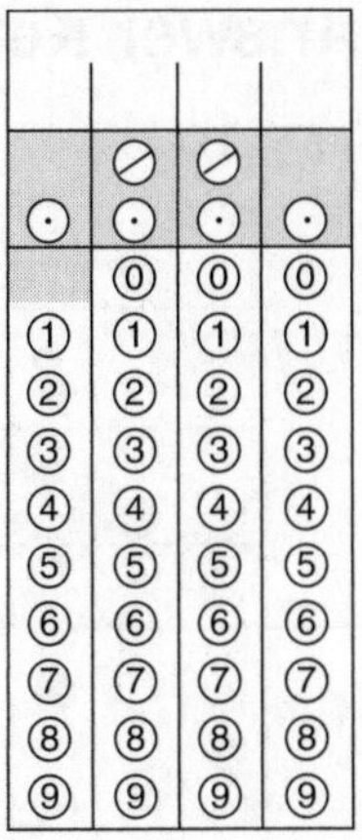

Questions 14 and 15 refer to the following diagram. *A* is the set of positive integers less than 20; *B* is the set of positive integers that contain the digit 7; and *C* is the set of primes.

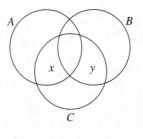

14. How many numbers are members of the region labeled *x*?

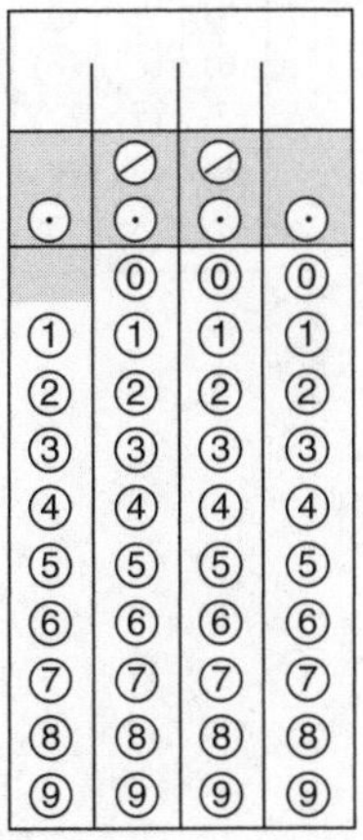

15. What is one number less than 50 that is a member of the region labeled *y*?

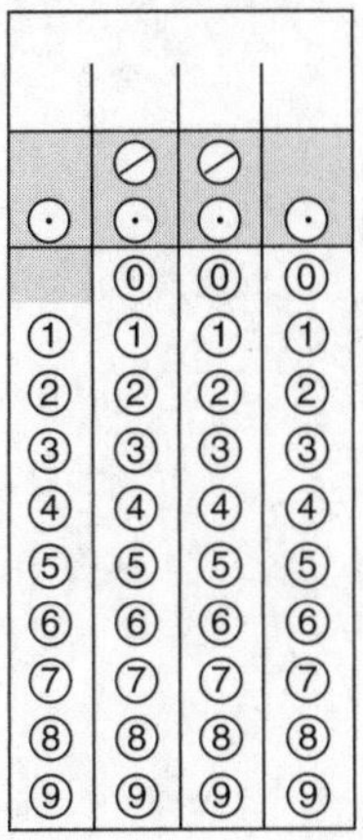

Answer Key

1. **D**   3. **E**   5. **B**   7. **C**   9. **A**
2. **B**   4. **D**   6. **B**   8. **E**   10. **A**

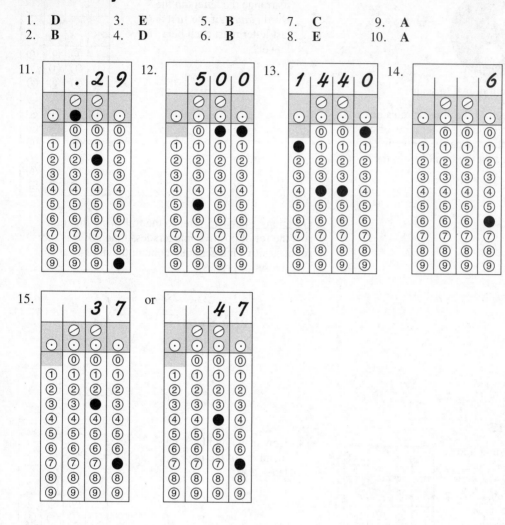

Answer Explanations

1. D. You can choose your first course (soup or salad) in 5 ways, your beverage in 2 ways, your sandwich in 8 ways, and your dessert in 7 ways. The counting principle says to multiply: $5 \times 2 \times 8 \times 7 = 560$. (Note that, if you got soup *and* a salad, then, instead of 5 choices for the first course, there would have been $2 \times 3 = 6$ choices for the first two courses.)

2. B. President Eisenhower's last birthday was in October 1968. His age at death was $1968 - 1890 = 78$ years.

3. E. If there were no month in which at least 3 students had a birthday, then each month would have the birthdays of at most 2 students. But that's not possible; even if there were 2 birthdays in January, 2 in February, ..., and 2 in December, only 24 students would be accounted for. It is guaranteed that, with more than 24 students, at least 1 month will have 3 or more birthdays. The probability is 1.

4. D. It is equally likely that any 1 of the 5 marbles will be the one that is not removed. Therefore, the probability that the yellow marble is left is $\frac{1}{5}$, and the probability that it is removed is $\frac{4}{5}$.

5. B. $A = \{2, 3, 5\}$ and $B = \{1, 3, 5\}$. Any of the 3 numbers in A could be added to any of the 3 numbers in B, so 9 sums could be formed. However, there could be some duplication. List the sums systematically; first add 1 to each number in A, then 3, and then 5: 3, 4, 6; 5, $\cancel{6}$, 10; 7, 8, $\cancel{10}$. There are 7 *different* sums.

6. B. Use the given information to find the rate of pages per hour.

$$\frac{1 \text{ page}}{5 \text{ seconds}} = \frac{12 \text{ pages}}{1 \text{ minute}} = \frac{720 \text{ pages}}{1 \text{ hour}},$$

so 3600 pages will take $3600 \div 720 = 5$ hours, or 300 minutes, of printing time. There will also be 12 minutes (4×3 minutes) when the printer is shut down to cool off, for a total of 312 minutes. Note that there are 5 printing periods and 4 cooling-off periods.

7. C. Either label all the vertices and systematically list the possibilities, or systematically trace the diagram. If you start by going from A to B, there are 3 paths: you can get up to the top by BC, EF, or HX, and once there must proceed to the right. Similarly, there are 3 paths if you start by going right from A to D. In all, there are 6 paths from A to X.

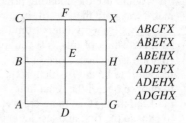

ABCFX
ABEFX
ABEHX
ADEFX
ADEHX
ADGHX

8. E. In a problem like this one, the easiest thing to do is to see what could go wrong in your attempt to get 2 marbles of each color. If you were really unlucky, you might remove 10 blue ones in a row, followed by all 6 white ones. At that point you would have 16 marbles, and you still wouldn't have even 1 red. The next 2 marbles, however, must both be red. The answer is 18.

9. A. It may help to draw a line and label it. Since k people went before Judy, she was number $k + 1$ to try out; and since m people went after Liz, she was number $n - m$ to try out. Then, the number of people to try out between Judy and Liz was

$$(n - m) - (k + 1) - 1 = n - m - k - 2.$$

10. A. Since the formula for the area of a circle is πr^2, the area of each small circle is $\pi(2^2) = 4\pi$. Then the total white area is 8π. The area of the large circle is $\pi(6^2) = 36\pi$. Therefore, the area of the shaded region is $36\pi - 8\pi = 28\pi$, and the probability that a point chosen at random lies in that shaded region is $\frac{28\pi}{36\pi} = \frac{7}{9}$.

11. (.29) There are $67 - 37 - 1 = 29$ people between Andy and Ali. The probability that the person chosen is standing between them is $\frac{29}{100} = .29$.

12. (500)   The easiest way to answer this question is to use the counting principle. The first digit can be chosen in any of 4 ways (2, 4, 6, 8), whereas the second, third, and fourth digits can be chosen in any of 5 ways (0, 2, 4, 6, 8). Therefore, the total number of four-digit numbers with only even digits is $4 \times 5 \times 5 \times 5 = 500$.

13. (1440)   Again, use the counting principle. How many ways are there to fill in seven blanks, _ _ _ _ _ _ _, with letters from the word *elation*? Think of this as seven jobs to do. The first job is to choose one of the 4 vowels in the word to be the first letter; the second job is to choose one of the remaining 3 vowels to be the last letter. Thus, there are $4 \times 3 = 12$ ways to choose the first and last letters. Since there are no other restrictions, the five other jobs are to place the remaining 5 letters in the five remaining blanks. There are 5 choices for the first blank, 4 for the next, then 3, then 2, and finally 1. There are $12 \times 5 \times 4 \times 3 \times 2 \times 1 = 1440$ arrangements.

14. (6)   In the diagram, the region labeled *x* contains all of the primes less than 20 that do not contain the digit 7. They are 2, 3, 5, 11, 13, 19—6 numbers in all.

15. (37 or 47)   Region *y* consists of primes that contain the digit 7 and are greater than 20.

9-P Logical Reasoning

All of the questions on the SAT (even the critical reading ones) require some logical reasoning. In fact, the official name of the test is the "SAT Reasoning Test." However, there are often a few questions on the mathematics sections of the SAT that do not fit into any of the standard mathematics topics. They require "logical reasoning" as opposed to knowledge of a particular fact from arithmetic, algebra, or geometry. Some of the problems don't even involve numbers or geometric figures. This section and the exercises that follow it present a variety of examples to illustrate the kinds of "logic" questions that you may encounter.

Alphanumeric Problems

An *alphanumeric problem* is an arithmetic problem in which some or all of the digits have been replaced by letters, and it is your job to determine what numbers the letters represent. The easiest way to explain this is to work out a few examples.

EXAMPLE 1

In the correctly worked out addition problem at the right, each letter represents a different digit. What is the value of A?

$$\begin{array}{r} AB \\ + AB \\ \hline BCC \end{array}$$

Solution. Since the two-digit number AB is less than 100, $AB + AB < 200$, implying that BCC is a number between 100 and 199. No matter what, B must be 1. Replace *each B* in the problem with 1.

The addition now looks like this:

$$\begin{array}{r} A1 \\ + A1 \\ \hline 1CC \end{array}$$

Since $1 + 1 = 2$, rewrite the problem again, replacing each C with 2:

$$\begin{array}{r} A1 \\ + A1 \\ \hline 122 \end{array}$$

Finally, since $A + A = 12$, then $A = $ **6**.

Key Fact P1

If the sum of two two-digit numbers is a three-digit number, the first digit of the sum is 1. Similarly, if the sum of two three-digit numbers is a four-digit number, the first digit of the sum is 1.

EXAMPLE 2

In the correctly worked out multiplication problem at the right, each letter represents a different digit. What is the value of $A + B + C + D$?

$$\begin{array}{r} ABA \\ \times\ A \\ \hline CBD5 \end{array}$$

Solution. The first step in the multiplication is to multiply $A \times A$. Since 5 is the only digit whose square ends in 5, A must be 5, so replace *each* A with 5.

The problem now looks like this:

$$\begin{array}{r} 5B5 \\ \times\ 5 \\ \hline CBD5 \end{array}$$

Since $5 \times 500 = 2500$ and $5 \times 600 = 3000$, the product $CBC5$ is somewhere between. Therefore, $C = 2$ and $B \geq 5$. Rewrite the problem again, replacing C with 2:

$$\begin{array}{r} 5B5 \\ \times\ 5 \\ \hline 2BD5 \end{array}$$

Since A is 5, B isn't 5, so B is at least 6. Notice that the second digit of $5B5$ and the second digit of $2BD5$ are the same. But $5 \times 5\underline{6}5 = 2\underline{8}25$; $5 \times 5\underline{7}5 = 2\underline{8}75$; and $5 \times 5\underline{8}5 = 2\underline{9}25$, none of which works.

Try $5 \times 5\underline{9}5 = 2\underline{9}75$, which does.

$$\begin{array}{r} 595 \\ \times\ 5 \\ \hline 2975 \end{array}$$

Then $B = 9$ and $D = 7$:

$$A + B + C + D = 5 + 9 + 2 + 7 = \mathbf{23}.$$

Example 2 is harder than most alphanumerics on an SAT because you have to find the values of all four letters, but the reasoning for each step is exactly what you must be able to do. If the solution wasn't completely clear, go back and reread it.

Sequences

A *sequence* is just a list of numbers separated by commas. It can be finite, such as 1, 3, 5, 7, 9; or it can be infinite, such as 5, 10, 15, 20, 25, ... Each number in the list is called a *term* of the sequence. The terms of a sequence don't have to follow any pattern or rule, but on the SAT they always do. The most common type of sequence question presents you with a rule for finding the terms of a sequence, and then asks you for a particular term.

TACTIC

P1

Never answer a question involving a sequence without writing out at least the first five terms.

EXAMPLE 3

A sequence is formed as follows: the first term is 3, and every other term is 4 more than the term that precedes it. What is the 100th term?

Solution. The sequence begins 3, 7, 11, 15, 19, 23 (7 is 4 more than 3, 11 is 4 more than 7, etc.). Clearly, you could continue writing out the terms, and if the question asked for the 10th term, that would be the easiest thing to do. You are not, however, going to write out 100 terms. What you need now is a little imagination or inspiration. How else can you describe the terms of this sequence? The terms are just 1 less than the corresponding multiples of 4 (4, 8, 12, 16, 20, 24 ...): 7, which is the *2*nd term, is 1 less than 2×4; 19, which is the *5*th term, is 1 less than 5×4. Now you have the solution. The *100*th term is 1 less than 100×4: $400 - 1 = \mathbf{399}$.

In Examples 4–6, the sequences S_n are formed as follows:

For any positive integer n: the first term of the sequence S_n is n, and every term after the first is 1 more than twice the preceding term.

EXAMPLE 4

What is the value of the smallest term of S_5 that is greater than 100?

Solution. Sequence S_5 proceeds as follows: 5, 11, 23, 47, 95, 191, ..., so the smallest term greater than 100 is **191**.

EXAMPLE 5

What is the units digit of the 500th term of S_9?

Solution. Of course, you're not going to write out 500 terms of any sequence, but you *always* write out the first five: 9, 19, 39, 79, 159, ...

There's no question about it: the units digit of *every* term is **9**.

EXAMPLE 6

If one of the first 10 terms of S_{1000} is chosen at random, what is the probability that it is odd?

Solution. For any integer m whatsoever, $2m$ is even and $2m + 1$ is odd. The first term of S_{1000} is 1000, but every other term is odd. The probability is $\dfrac{9}{10}$.

Two types of sequences that occasionally appear on the SAT are ***arithmetic sequences*** and ***geometric sequences.***

An ***arithmetic sequence*** is a sequence such as the one in Example 3, in which the difference between any two consecutive terms is the same. In Example 3 that difference was 4. An easy way to find the nth term of such a sequence is to start with the first term and add the common difference $n - 1$ times. In Example 3, the sixth term is 23, which can be obtained by taking the first term, 3, and adding the common difference, 4, five times: $3 + 5(4) = 23$. In the same way, the 100th term is $3 + 99(4) = 3 + 396 = 399$.

Key Fact P2

If $a_1, a_2, a_3, \ldots$ is an arithmetic sequence whose common difference is d, then $a_n = a_1 + (n - 1)\, d$.

A ***geometric sequence*** is a sequence in which the ratio between any two consecutive terms is the same. For example, the sequence, 2, 10, 50, 250, 1250, ... is a geometric sequence: the ratios $\dfrac{10}{2}, \dfrac{50}{10}, \dfrac{250}{50}$ are all equal to 5.

An easy way to find the nth term of a geometric sequence is to start with the first term and multiply it by the common ratio $n - 1$ times. For example, in the sequence 2, 10, 50, 250, 1250, ... the fourth term is 250, which can be obtained by taking the first term, 2, and multiplying it by the common ratio, 5, three times: $2 \times 5 \times 5 \times 5 = 2 \times 5^3 = 2 \times 125 = 250$. In the same way, the 100th term is 2×5^{99}.

Key Fact P3

If $a_1, a_2, a_3, \ldots$ is a geometric sequence whose common ratio is r, then $a_n = a_1\, (r)^{n-1}$.

Consider the following three sequences:

(i) 1, 7, 13, 19, 25, 31, …

(ii) 6, 3, $\dfrac{3}{2}$, $\dfrac{3}{4}$, $\dfrac{3}{8}$, $\dfrac{3}{16}$, …

(iii) 1, 2, 3, 5, 8, 13, …

Sequence (i) is an arithmetic sequence in which the common difference is 6. A reasonable SAT question would be: What is the 75th term of this sequence? By KEY FACT P2, the answer is $1 + 74(6) = 1 + 444 = 445$. This could be a multiple-choice or a grid-in question.

Sequence (ii) is a geometric sequence in which the common ratio is $\dfrac{1}{2}$. A reasonable SAT question would be: What is the 75th term of this sequence? By KEY FACT P3, the answer is $6 \times \left(\dfrac{1}{2}\right)^{74}$. This could only be a multiple-choice question because there is no way to grid in such an answer. It is likely that one of the answer choices would, in fact, be $6 \times \left(\dfrac{1}{2}\right)^{74}$. But since

$$6 \times \left(\dfrac{1}{2}\right)^{74} = 6 \times \dfrac{1}{2} \times \left(\dfrac{1}{2}\right)^{73} = 3 \times \left(\dfrac{1}{2}\right)^{73},$$

the correct answer choice could also be $3 \times \left(\dfrac{1}{2}\right)^{73}$.

Sequence (iii) is neither an arithmetic sequence nor a geometric sequence: there is no common difference $(13 - 8 \neq 8 - 5)$, and there is no common ratio $\left(\dfrac{13}{8} \neq \dfrac{8}{5}\right)$.

Therefore, you have no formula for evaluating the nth term of this sequence, and it would *not* be reasonable to ask for the 75th term. If you were told that the rule for the sequence is that each term is the sum of the two preceding terms $(3 = 1 + 2, 5 = 2 + 3, 8 = 3 + 5, …)$, then it would be reasonable to ask: What is the smallest term in this sequence that is greater than 100? The answer is 144, which you could get just by calculating five more terms. 1, 2, 3, 5, 8, 13, 21, 34, 55, 89, 144.

In some sequences the terms repeat in a cyclical pattern.

TACTIC

When k numbers form a repeating sequence, to find the nth number, divide n by k and take the remainder r. The rth term and the nth term are the same.

Examples 7 and 8 refer to the infinite sequence 1, 4, 2, 8, 5, 7, 1, 4, 2, 8, 5, 7, … , in which the six digits 1, 4, 2, 8, 5, and 7 keep repeating in that order.

EXAMPLE 7

What is the 500th term of the sequence?

Solution. When 500 is divided by 6, the quotient is 83 $(6 \times 83 = 498)$ and the remainder is 2. Therefore, the first 498 terms are just the numbers 1, 4, 2, 8, 5, 7 repeated 83 times. The 498th term is the 83rd 7 in the sequence. Then the pattern repeats again: the 499th term is 1, and the 500th term is **4**.

In this example, notice that the 500th term is the same as the 2nd term. This occurs because 2 is the remainder when 500 is divided by 6.

EXAMPLE 8

What is the sum of the 800th through the 805th terms of the sequence?

Solution. Don't waste time determining what the 800th term is. Any six consecutive terms of the sequence consist, in some order, of exactly the same six numbers: 1, 4, 2, 8, 5, and 7. Their sum is **27**.

Patterns

Some SAT questions are based on repeating patterns. These are very similar to repeating sequences, except that the terms don't have to be numbers.

EXAMPLE 9

In order to divide the campers at a camp into six teams (the reds, whites, blues, greens, yellows, and browns), the director had all the campers form a line. Then, starting with the first person, each camper on line called out a color, repeating this pattern: red, white, blue, green, yellow, brown, red, white, blue, green, yellow, brown, ... What color was called out by the 500th camper?

(A) Red
(B) White
(C) Green
(D) Yellow
(E) Brown

Solution. This is exactly the same as Example 9. When 500 is divided by 6, the quotient is 83 and the remainder is 2. Then, by TACTIC P2, the 500th camper called out the same color as the 2nd camper: **white (B)**.

EXAMPLE 10

Last year Elaine's birthday was on Friday. If Susan's birthday was 150 days after Elaine's, how many Sundays were there between Elaine's birthday and Susan's birthday?

Solution. The 7 days of the week repeat in cyclical pattern. Using TACTIC P2, divide 150 by 7, getting a quotient of 21 and a remainder of 3. Thus, the 150th day after Elaine's birthday was Monday, the same as the 3rd day after her birthday. During the 21 full weeks between Elaine's and Susan's birthdays, there were 21 Sundays, and there was 1 more during the last 3 days, for a total of **22**.

Exercises on Logical Reasoning

Multiple-Choice Questions

1. In the correctly worked out addition problem at the right, each letter represents a different digit. What is the value of *A*?

   $$\begin{array}{r} 3A \\ + A3 \\ \hline BBC \end{array}$$

   (A) 5
   (B) 6
   (C) 7
   (D) 8
   (E) 9

2. In the United States, Thanksgiving is celebrated on the fourth Thursday in November. Which of the following statements is (are) true?

   I. Thanksgiving is always the last Thursday in November.
   II. Thanksgiving is never celebrated on November 22.
   III. Thanksgiving cannot be celebrated on the same date 2 years in a row.

   (A) None
   (B) I only
   (C) II only
   (D) III only
   (E) I and III only

3. A gum-ball dispenser is filled with exactly 1000 pieces of gum. The gum balls always come out in the following order: 1 red, 2 blue, 3 green, 4 yellow, and 5 white. After the fifth white, the pattern repeats, starting with 1 red, and so on. What is the color of the last gum ball to come out of the machine?

   (A) Red
   (B) Blue
   (C) Green
   (D) Yellow
   (E) White

4. The Declaration of Independence was signed in July 1776. What month and year was it 500 months later?

   (A) March 1817
   (B) August 1817
   (C) November 1817
   (D) March 1818
   (E) May 1818

5. In the correctly worked out multiplication problem at the right, each letter represents a different digit. What is the value of $A + B + C$?

   $$\begin{array}{r} AB \\ \times\ 3 \\ \hline CBB \end{array}$$

   (A) 12
   (B) 15
   (C) 18
   (D) 21
   (E) 27

6. If a population that is initially 100 triples every year, which of the following is an expression for the size of the population after *t* months?

   (A) 100×3^t

   (B) 100×12^{3t}

   (C) $100 \times 3^{\frac{t}{12}}$

   (D) $100 \times 3^{\frac{12}{t}}$

   (E) 100×3^{12t}

Grid-in Questions

7. In the correctly worked out addition problem below, each letter represents a different digit. What is the number *CBA*?

   $$\begin{array}{r} 3A \\ 4A \\ + AA \\ \hline CBA \end{array}$$

8. Three children guessed the number of jelly beans in a jar. The guesses were 98, 137, and 164. None of the guesses was correct. One guess was off by 12, another by 27, and the third by 39. How many jelly beans were in the jar?

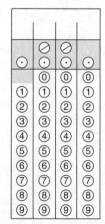

9. The pointer on the dial below moves 3 numbers clockwise every minute. If it starts at 1, what number will it be pointing to in exactly 1 hour?

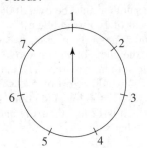

10. A sequence is formed by choosing a number, x, to be the first term. Every term after the first is y more than the preceding term. If the 8th term is 19 and the 12th term is 29, what is xy?

Answer Key

1. **C**   3. **D**   5. **B**
2. **D**   4. **D**   6. **C**

7. **1 3 5**

8. **1 2 5**

9. **6**

10. **3 . 7 5**   or   **1 5 / 4**

Answer Explanations

1. **C.** By KEY FACT P1, $B = 1$, so the sum looks like this:

$$\begin{array}{r} 3A \\ + A3 \\ \hline 11C \end{array}$$

   If $A \le 6$, then the $A + 3$ in each column will be a one-digit number, so A is at least 7. In fact, 7 works.

$$\begin{array}{r} 37 \\ + 73 \\ \hline 110 \end{array}$$

2. **D.** If November 1 is a Thursday, then so are November 8, 15, 22, and 29. Therefore, Thanksgiving could fall on November 22 (II is false); and if it does, it is not the last Thursday in November (I is false). Assume that one year Thanksgiving falls on Thursday, November X. Then exactly 52 weeks (or $7 \times 52 = 364$ days) later it will again be Thursday, but it won't be November X, because November X comes 365 (or 366) days after the preceding November X (III is true).

3. **D.** Since the pattern repeats itself after every 15 gum balls, divide 1000 by 15. The quotient is 66, and the remainder is 10. Therefore, the 1000th gum ball is the same color as the 10th, which is yellow.

4. **D.** The 12 months of the year form a repeating sequence.
   $500 \div 12 = 41.666\ldots$ and $41 \times 12 = 492$. Therefore, exactly 41 years (or 492 months) after July 1776 it will be July in the year $1776 + 41 = 1817$.
   Since $500 - 492 = 8$, 500 months after July 1776 is 8 months after July 1817, which is March 1818.

5. **B.** Since $AB < 100$, 3 times AB is less than $3 \times 100 = 300$, so C is 1 or 2. Since 3 times B ends in B, B is either 0 or 5. It can't be 0 because neither 100 nor 200 is a multiple of 3: so $B = 5$.

$$\begin{array}{r} AB \\ \times \ 3 \\ \hline CBB \end{array}$$

   The simplest thing to do now is test whether 155 or 255 is a multiple of 3: 155 isn't, but $255 = 3 \times 85$. Then $C = 2$ and $A = 8$. Finally, $A + B + C = 8 + 5 + 2 = 15$.

$$\begin{array}{r} A5 \\ \times \ 3 \\ \hline C55 \end{array}$$

6. **C.** Since t months is $\dfrac{t}{12}$ years, the population triples $\dfrac{t}{12}$ times. After t months, the population will be $100 \times 3^{\frac{t}{12}}$.

7. **(135)** A can't be 0, and the only other digit A that, multiplied by 3, ends in A is 5 ($3 \times 5 = 15$). $A = 5$, and $CBA = 35 + 45 + 55 = 135$.

$$\begin{array}{r} 3A \\ 4A \\ + AA \\ \hline CBA \end{array}$$

8. **(125)** There are lots of ways to reason this out. Here is one. The number must be over 100; otherwise the guess of 164 would be off by more than 64, and none of the guesses was that far wrong, Thus, the guess of 98 was too low. If it was 12 too low, there would be 110 jelly beans, but then 164 would be off by 54, which isn't right. If 98 was 27 too low, the number would be 125, which is 12 less than 137 and 39 less than 164. That's it.

9. **(6)** To see the pattern develop, write out the locations of the pointer for the first few minutes. Advancing 3 numbers per minute, it goes from $1 \to 4 \to 7 \to 3 \to 6 \to 2 \to 5 \to 1$; and when it is back to 1, the whole cycle repeats. To know where the pointer will be in 60 minutes, divide 60 by 7. Since the quotient is 8 and the remainder is 4, after 60 minutes the pointer will be pointing to the same number it pointed to after 4 minutes. Be careful. That number is not 3; it's 6. After 1 minute the pointer is at 4, after 2 minutes it's at 7, and so on.
   Alternative solution. Since the pointer advances 3 numbers per minute, it advances $3 \times 60 = 180$ minutes per hour. Dividing 180 by 7 gives a quotient of 25 and a remainder of 5, so the pointer makes 25 complete cycles and then advances 5 more numbers, from 1 to 6.

10. $\left(3.75 \text{ or } \dfrac{15}{4} \right)$ Each term is y more than the preceding term; therefore, the 9th term is $19 + y$, the 10th term is $19 + y + y = 19 + 2y$, the 11th term is $19 + 2y + y = 19 + 3y$, and the 12th term is $19 + 3y + y = 19 + 4y$. But the 12th term is 29, so
    $$29 = 19 + 4y \Rightarrow 10 = 4y \Rightarrow y = 2.5.$$
    You could now count backward from the 8th term to the 1st term, subtracting 2.5 each time. Instead, note that, to get from the 1st to the 8th term, it was necessary to add 2.5 seven times. Therefore:
    $$x + (7 \times 2.5) = 19 \Rightarrow x + 17.5 = 19 \Rightarrow x = 1.5.$$
    Finally,
    $$xy = 1.5 \times 2.5 = 3.75 \text{ or } \frac{15}{4}.$$

9-Q Interpretation of Data

Typically, the SAT has a few questions that require you to interpret and/or manipulate the data that appear in some type of table or graph. The graphs will be no more complicated, and probably will be simpler, than the ones that you usually see in newspapers and magazines or in your science or social studies textbooks.

Sometimes you are asked two questions based on the same set of data. In this case, the first question is usually quite easy, requiring only that you *read* the information in the table or graph. The second question is usually a little more challenging and may ask you to *interpret* the data, or *manipulate* them, or *make a prediction* based on them.

The data can be presented in the columns of a table or displayed graphically. The graphs that appear most often are bar graphs, line graphs, circle graphs, and scatter-plot diagrams. This section illustrates each of these and gives examples of the types of questions that may be asked.

Although the second hint is good advice on *all* SAT questions, it is particularly important on table and graph problems because there is so much information that can be used, and so many different questions can be asked.

Let's start by looking at a *line graph*. A line graph indicates how one or more quantities change over time. The horizontal axis is usually marked off in units of time; the units on the vertical axis can represent almost any type of numerical data: dollars, weights, exam grades, number of people, and so on.

Here is a typical line graph:

> **Helpful Hint**
> Before even reading the questions based on a graph or table, take 10 or 15 seconds to look it over. Make sure you understand the information that is being displayed and the units of the quantities involved.

> **Helpful Hint**
> After looking over the entire graph, read the first question. Be clear about what is being asked, and circle it in your test booklet. Answer the questions based only on the information provided in the graph.

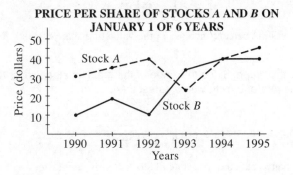

PRICE PER SHARE OF STOCKS *A* AND *B* ON JANUARY 1 OF 6 YEARS

Before reading even one of the questions based on the above graph, you should have acquired *at least* the following information:

(i) The graph gives the values of two different stocks.
(ii) The graph covers the period from January 1, 1990, to January 1, 1995.
(iii) During that time, both stocks rose in value.

There are literally dozens of questions that could be asked about the data in this graph. The next seven examples are typical of the types of questions that appear on the SAT.

EXAMPLE 1

What is the difference, in dollars, between the highest and lowest values of a share of stock *A*?

Solution. The lowest value of stock *A* was $25 (in 1993); the highest value was $40 (in 1995). The difference is **$15**.

EXAMPLE 2

On January 1 of what year was the difference in the values of a share of stock *A* and a share of stock *B* the greatest?

Solution. Just look at the graph. The difference was clearly the greatest in **1992**. (Note that you don't have to calculate what the difference was.)

EXAMPLE 3

On January 1 of what year was the ratio of the value of a share of stock *A* to the value of a share of stock *B* the greatest?

Solution. From 1993 to 1995 the values of the two stocks were fairly close, so those years are not candidates. In 1992 the ratio was 40:10 or 4:1 or 4. In 1991 the ratio was 35:20 or 7:4 or 1.75. In 1990 the ratio was 30:10 or 3:1 or 3. The ratio was greatest in **1990**.

EXAMPLE 4

In what year was the percent increase in the value of a share of stock *B* the greatest?

Solution. Just look at the graph. Since the slope of the graph is steepest in **1992** (between 1/1/92 and 1/1/93), the rate of growth was greatest then.

EXAMPLE 5

During how many years did the value of stock *B* grow at a faster rate than that of stock *A*?

Solution. Again, look at the slopes.

- In 1990, *B* rose more sharply than *A*. (✓)
- In 1991, *B* fell while *A* rose.
- In 1992, *B* rose while *A* fell. (✓)
- In 1993, *A* rose more sharply than *B*.
- In 1994, *A* rose; *B* stayed the same.

B grew at a faster rate during **2** years.

EXAMPLE 6

What was the average yearly increase in the value of a share of stock *A* from 1990 to 1995?

Solution. Over the 5-year period from January 1, 1990, to January 1, 1995, the value of a share of stock *A* rose from \$30 to \$45, an increase of \$15. The average yearly increase was \$15 ÷ 5 years or **\$3** per year.

EXAMPLE 7

If from 1995 to 2000 the value of each stock increased at the same rate as it did from 1990 to 1995, what would be the ratio of the value of a share of stock *B* to the value of a share of stock *A*?

Solution. From 1990 to 1995, the value of stock *A* increased by 50% (from \$30 to \$45) and the value of stock *B* quadrupled (from \$10 to \$40). At the same rates, stock *A* would have grown from \$45 to \$67.50 in the years 1995–2000, while stock *B* would have grown from \$40 to \$160. The ratio of the value of a share of stock *B* to the value of a share of stock *A* would have been 160 to 67.5, or approximately **2.37**.

To answer these seven questions, most (but not all) of the data contained in the graph was used. On the SAT, if you had two questions based on that line graph, you can see that there would be many items of information you would not use.

The same information that was given in the preceding line graph, could have been presented in a *table* or in a *bar graph*.

> **Helpful Hint**
> On data interpretation questions ignore the extraneous information you are given. Zero in on exactly what you need.

PRICE PER SHARE OF STOCKS *A* AND *B* ON JANUARY 1 OF 6 YEARS

Stock	Prices (dollars)					
	1990	1991	1992	1993	1994	1995
Stock *A*	30	35	40	25	40	45
Stock *B*	10	20	15	35	40	40

PRICE PER SHARE OF STOCKS *A* AND *B* ON JANUARY 1 OF 6 YEARS

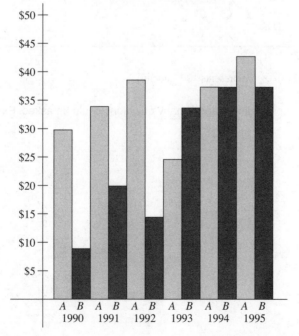

In a bar graph, the taller the bar, the greater is the value of the quantity. Bar graphs can also be drawn horizontally; in that case the longer the bar, the greater is the quantity. You will see examples of each type in the exercises at the end of this section, in the model tests, and, of course, on the SAT.

The following bar graph shows the numbers of students taking courses in the various foreign languages offered at a state college.

**NUMBERS OF STUDENTS ENROLLED IN
LANGUAGE COURSES AT STATE COLLEGE IN 2004**

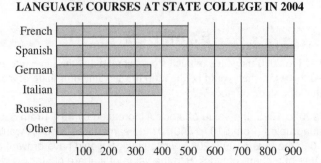

In a slight variation of the horizontal bar graph, the bars are replaced by a string of icons, or symbols. For example, the graph below, in which each picture of a person represents 100 students, conveys the same information as does the preceding bar graph.

**NUMBERS OF STUDENTS ENROLLED IN
LANGUAGE COURSES AT STATE COLLEGE IN 2004**

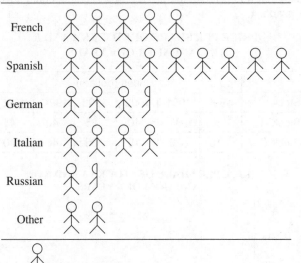

Each ⚊ represents 100 students.

From either of the two preceding graphs, many questions could be asked. Examples 8–10 illustrate a few types.

EXAMPLE 8

What is the total number of students enrolled in language classes?

Solution. Just read the graph and add: **2500**.

EXAMPLE 9

If the "Other" category includes five languages, what is the average (arithmetic mean) number of students studying each language offered at the college?

Solution. There are 2500 students divided among 10 languages (the 5 listed plus the 5 in the "Other" category): 2500 ÷ 10 = **250**.

EXAMPLE 10

If the number of students studying Italian next year is the same as the number taking Spanish this year, by what percent will the number of students taking Italian increase?

Solution. The number of students taking Italian will increase by 500 from 400 to 900. This represents a $\dfrac{500}{400} \times 100\% =$ **125%** increase.

A ***circle graph*** is another way to present data pictorially. In a circle graph, which is sometimes called a ***pie chart***, the circle is divided into sectors, with the size of each sector exactly proportional to the quantity it represents.

For example, the information included in the preceding bar graph is presented in the following circle graph.

**NUMBERS OF STUDENTS ENROLLED IN
LANGUAGE COURSES AT STATE COLLEGE IN 2004**

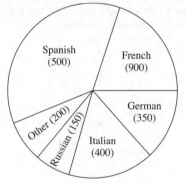

Usually on the SAT, in each sector of the circle is noted the number of degrees of its central angle or the percent of the total data it contains. For example, in the circle graph above, since 500 of the 2500 language students at State College are studying French, the sector representing French is exactly $\dfrac{1}{5}$ of the circle. On the SAT this sector would also be marked either $72°$ $\left(\dfrac{1}{5} \text{ of } 360°\right)$ or 20% $\left(\dfrac{1}{5} \text{ of } 100\%\right)$. The SAT graph would look like one of the graphs on the next page.

**DISTRIBUTION OF THE 2500 STUDENTS
ENROLLED IN LANGUAGE COURSES**

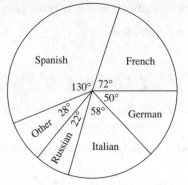

**DISTRIBUTION OF THE 2500 STUDENTS
ENROLLED IN LANGUAGE COURSES**

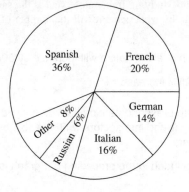

Very often on the SAT, some data are omitted from a circle graph, and it is your job to determine the missing item. Examples 11 and 12 are based on the following circle graph, which
shows the distribution of marbles by color in a large jar.

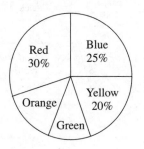

EXAMPLE 11

If the jar contains 1200 marbles and there are twice as many orange marbles as there are green, how many green marbles are there?

Solution. Since the red, blue, and yellow marbles constitute 75% of the total (30% + 25% + 20%), the orange and green ones combined account for 25% of the total: 25% of 1200 = 300. Then, since the ratio of orange marbles to green ones is 2:1, there are 200 orange marbles and **100** green ones.

EXAMPLE 12

Assume that the jar contains 1200 marbles, and that all of the red ones are removed and replaced by an equal number of marbles, all of which are blue or yellow. If the ratio of blue to yellow marbles remains the same, how many additional yellow marbles are there?

Solution. Since 30% of 1200 is 360, the 360 red marbles were replaced by 360 blue and

yellow ones. To maintain the current blue to yellow ratio of 25 to 20, or 5 to 4, $\frac{5}{9}$ of the new

marbles would be blue and $\frac{4}{9}$ would be yellow: $\frac{4}{9}$ of 360 = **160**.

Exercises on Interpretation of Data

Multiple-Choice Questions

Questions 1–3 refer to the following graph.

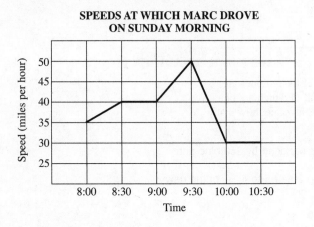

**SPEEDS AT WHICH MARC DROVE
ON SUNDAY MORNING**

1. For what percent of the time was Marc driving at 40 miles per hour or faster?

   (A) 20
   (B) 25
   (C) $33\frac{1}{3}$
   (D) 40
   (E) 50

2. How far, in miles, did Marc drive between 8:30 and 9:00?

   (A) 0
   (B) 20
   (C) 30
   (D) 40
   (E) It cannot be determined from the information given.

3. What was Marc's average speed, in miles per hour, between 8:30 and 9:30?

   (A) 40
   (B) $41\frac{2}{3}$
   (C) 42.5
   (D) 45
   (E) It cannot be determined from the information given.

Questions 4–6 refer to the following graph.

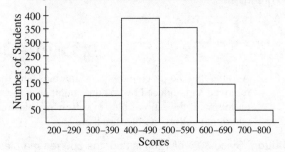

**CRITICAL READING SAT SCORES OF ALL THE
JUNIORS AT CENTRAL HIGH SCHOOL**

4. How many juniors at Central High School took the SAT?

   (A) 1000
   (B) 1100
   (C) 1200
   (D) 1250
   (E) 1300

5. What percent of the juniors had Critical Reading SAT scores of less than 600?

   (A) $95\frac{5}{11}$
   (B) $83\frac{1}{3}$
   (C) $81\frac{9}{11}$
   (D) 80
   (E) It cannot be determined from the information given.

6. How many juniors had Critical Reading SAT scores between 450 and 550?

   (A) 360
   (B) 375
   (C) 525
   (D) 750
   (E) It cannot be determined from the information given.

Questions 7 and 8 refer to the following graph.

2010 SMITH FAMILY HOUSEHOLD BUDGET

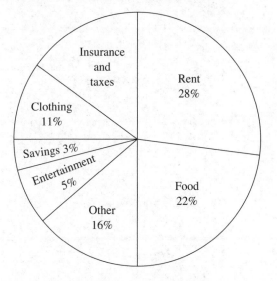

7. If the Smiths' income in 2010 was $40,000, how much more did they spend on insurance and taxes than they did on clothing?

(A) $1600
(B) $2000
(C) $3200
(D) $4400
(E) $6000

8. What is the degree measure of the central angle of the sector representing insurance and taxes?

(A) 45
(B) 54
(C) 60
(D) 72
(E) 90

Grid-in Questions

Questions 9 and 10 refer to the following graph.

DISTRIBUTION OF GRADES OF 500 STUDENTS ON THE FINAL EXAM IN MATH

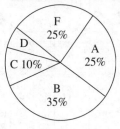

9. How many students earned a grade of D?

10. What percent of the students who failed the exam would have had to pass it, in order for the percent of students passing the exam to be at least 85%?

Answer Key

1. **E**	3. **C**	5. **C**	7. **A**
2. **B**	4. **B**	6. **E**	8. **B**

9. 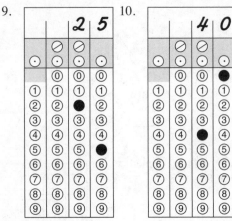   10.

Answer Explanations

1. **E.** Of the $2\frac{1}{2}$ hours (from 8:00 until 10:30) that Marc was driving, he was going 40 miles per hour or faster for $1\frac{1}{4}$ hours (from 8:30 until 9:45). Therefore, he was driving at 40 miles per hour or faster 50% of the time.

2. **B.** During the half hour between 8:30 and 9:00, Marc was driving at a constant rate of 40 miles per hour, so he drove $\frac{1}{2} \times 40 = 20$ miles.

3. **C.** From the graph it is clear that, from 9:00 to 9:30, Marc's speed increased steadily from 40 to 50 miles per hour and that his average speed was 45 miles per hour. From 8:30 to 9:00 his average speed was clearly 40 miles per hour. Then, for the entire hour, he averaged $\frac{40 + 45}{2} = 42.5$ miles per hour.

4. **B.** Just read the graph carefully, and add the numbers of juniors who had scores in each range:

$$50 + 100 + 400 + 350 + 150 + 50 = 1100.$$

5. **C.** Of the 1100 students, 900 had scores less than 600, and $\frac{900}{1100} = 81\frac{9}{11}\%$.

6. **E.** There is no way of knowing. It is possible, though very unlikely, that all of the scores between 400 and 590 were between 400 and 420 or 570 and 590, and that no one scored between 450 and 550. Undoubtedly, some did, but you can't tell how many.

7. **A.** The total percent for the six categories for which percents are given is

$$28 + 22 + 16 + 5 + 3 + 11 = 85,$$

so the percent of their income that the Smiths spend on insurance and taxes is 15%. Since they spend 11% on clothing, the difference between the two categories is 4%. Finally, 4% of $40,000 is $1600.

8. **B.** Since insurance and taxes take up 15% of the Smiths' income (see solution 7), the sector representing insurance and taxes must be 15% of the circle. The degree measure of the central angle for this sector is 15% of 360 = 54.

9. **(25)** Since 25% + 35% + 10% + 25% = 95% of the students earned grades of A, B, C, or F, 5% earned grades of D: 5% of 500 = 25.

10. **(40)** For the passing rate to have been at least 85%, no more than 75 students (15% of 500) could have failed. Of the 125 students (25% of 500) who actually failed, 50 of them would have had to pass: 50 of 125 is 40%.

9-R Functions and Their Graphs

You have undoubtedly studied functions many times in your math classes. However, most of what you learned about functions is *not* tested on the SAT. This section reviews the basic facts about functions and their graphs that you do need for the SAT.

As used on the SAT, a **function** is a rule that assigns to each number in one set a number in another set. The function is usually designated by the letter *f*, although other letters such as *g* and *h* are sometimes used. The numbers in the first set are labeled *x*, and the number in the second set to which *x* is assigned by the function is designated by the letter *y* or by *f*(*x*).

For example, we can write $y = f(x) = 2x + 3$. This function assigns, to each real number *x*, the number $2x + 3$.

The number assigned to 5 is $2(5) + 3 = 10 + 3 = 13$, and the number assigned to –5 is $2(-5) + 3 = -10 + 3 = -7$.

To express these facts, we write

$$f(5) = 13 \text{ and } f(-5) = -7.$$

The proper way to think of the function $f(x) = 2x + 3$ is that *f* takes *anything* and assigns to it 2 times *that thing* plus 3:

$$f(anything) = 2(that\ thing) + 3.$$

- $f(100) = 2(100) + 3 = 203$
- $f(0) = 2(0) + 3 = 0 + 3 = 3$
- $f(a) = 2a + 3$
- $f(a + b) = 2(a + b) + 3$
- $f(x^2) = 2x^2 + 3$
- $f(2x^2 + 3) = 2(2x^2 + 3) + 3 = 4x^2 + 9$
- $f(f(x)) = 2(f(x)) + 3 = 2(2x + 3) + 3 = 4x + 6 + 3 = 4x + 9$

EXAMPLE 1

If $f(x) = x^2 + 2x$, what is $f(3) + f(-3)$?

Solution. $f(3) = 3^2 + 2(3) = 9 + 6 = 15,$

$f(-3) = (-3)^2 + 2(-3) = 9 - 6 = 3.$

Then $f(3) + f(-3) = \mathbf{15 + 3 = 18}.$

EXAMPLE 2

If $f(x) = x^2 + 2x$, what is $f(x + 2)$?

(A) $x^2 + 2x + 4$
(B) $x^2 + 2x + 8$
(C) $x^2 + 6x + 4$
(D) $x^2 + 6x + 8$
(E) $x^3 + 4x^2 + 4x$

Solution. $f(x + 2) = (x + 2)^2 + 2(x + 2) = (x^2 + 4x + 4) + (2x + 4) = \mathbf{x^2 + 6x + 8\ (D)}.$

Sometimes on the SAT, you are asked a question that tests both your understanding of what a function is and your ability to do some basic algebra. The following example does just that.

EXAMPLE 3

If $f(x) = 3x + 3$, for what value of a is it true that $3f(a) = f(2a)$?

(A) −3
(B) −2
(C)   0
(D)   2
(E)   3

Solution. $3f(a) = 3(3a + 3) = 9a + 9,$

$f(2a) = 3(2a) + 3 = 6a + 3.$

Therefore, $9a + 9 = 6a + 3 \Rightarrow 3a = -6 \Rightarrow a = -2$ **(B)**.

The **graph** of a function, *f*, is a certain set of points in the coordinate plane. Point (a, b) is on the graph of *f* if and only if $b = f(a)$. For example, the graph of $f(x) = 2x + 3$ consists of all points (x, y) such that $y = 2x + 3$. Since $f(5) = 13$ and $f(-5) = -7$, then $(5, 13)$ and $(-5, -7)$ are both points on the graph of $f(x) = 2x + 3$. In Section 9-N, you saw that the graph of $y = 2x + 3$ is a line whose slope is 2 and whose *y*-intercept is 3.

On the SAT you may have to know whether a certain point is on the graph of a given function, but you won't have to actually graph the function.

EXAMPLE 4

Which of the following is NOT a point on the graph of
$f(x) = x^2 + \dfrac{4}{x^2}$?

(A) $(1, 5)$
(B) $(-1, 5)$
(C) $(2, 5)$
(D) $(-2, -5)$
(E) $(4, 16.25)$

Solution.

Test each answer choice until you find one that does NOT work.

- $f(1) = 1^2 + \dfrac{4}{1^2} = 1 + 4 = 5$. So, $(1, 5)$ *is* a point on the graph.

- $f(-1) = (-1)^2 + \dfrac{4}{(-1)^2} = 1 + 4 = 5$. So, $(-1, 5)$ *is* a point on the graph.

- $f(2) = 2^2 + \dfrac{4}{2^2} = 4 + 1 = 5$. So, $(2, 5)$ *is* a point on the graph.

- $f(-2) = (-2)^2 + \dfrac{4}{(-2)^2} = 4 + 1 = 5 \neq -5$. So, $(-2, 5)$ is a point on the graph, but **(−2, −5)** is NOT.

The answer is choice **D**.

EXAMPLE 5

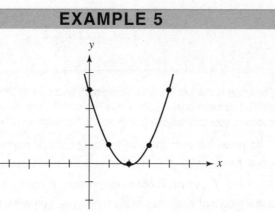

Which of the following could be the equation of the graph shown in the figure above?

(A) $y = -2x + 4$
(B) $y = 2x + 4$
(C) $y = x^2$
(D) $y = 2x^2 - 4$
(E) $y = x^2 - 4x + 4$

Solution. Since the graph passes through $(2, 0)$, $x = 2$ and $y = 0$ must satisfy the equation. Test each of the five choices in order.

- (A) Does $0 = -2(2) + 4$?   Yes
- (B) Does $0 = 2(2) + 4$?   No
- (C) Does $0 = 2^2$?   No
- (D) Does $0 = 2(2^2) - 4$?   No
- (E) Does $0 = 2^2 - 4(2) + 4$?   Yes

The answer is A or E. To break the tie, try another point on the graph, say $(0, 4)$ and test choices A and E.

- (A) Does $4 = -2(0) + 4$?   Yes
- (E) Does $4 = (0)^2 - 4(0) + 4$?   Yes

Unfortunately, that didn't help. Try one more, point $(1, 1)$.

- (A) Does $1 = -2(1) + 4$?   No
- (E) Does $1 = 1^2 - 4(1) + 4$?   Yes

The answer is $y = \boldsymbol{x^2 - 4x + 4}$ **(E)**.

You can think of a function as a machine. A washing machine performs a function. It cleans clothes: dirty clothes go in and clean clothes come out. In the same way you can think of $f(x) = 2x + 3$ as a machine. When 5 goes in, 13 comes out; when -5 goes in, -7 comes out.

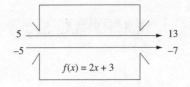

$$f(x) = 2x + 3$$

The *domain* of a function is the set of all real numbers that can go into the machine without causing a problem. The domain of $f(x) = 2x + 3$ is the set of all real numbers, because, for any real number whatsoever, you can double it and add 3. No number will cause the machine to jam.

If $f(x) = \sqrt{2x+3}$, however, the domain is not the set of all real numbers. Although 5 is in the domain of *f*, because $f(5) = \sqrt{2(5)+3} = \sqrt{13}$, –5 is not in the domain of *f*. The reason is that $\sqrt{2(-5)+3} = \sqrt{-10+3} = \sqrt{-7}$, which is not a real number. If you try to evaluate $\sqrt{2(-5)+3}$ on your calculator (a machine that evaluates many functions), you will get an error message.

Since the domain of a function is the set of all real numbers except those that cause problems, you need to know what can cause a problem. Many things can be troublesome, but for the SAT you need to know about only two of them.

Key Fact R1

A number *x* is *not* in the domain of $y = f(x)$ if evaluating $f(x)$ would require you to divide by 0 or to take the square root of a negative number.

EXAMPLE 6

Which of the following numbers is NOT in the domain of $f(x) = \sqrt{4-x}$?

(A) –6
(B) –4
(C)   0
(D)   4
(E)   6

Solution. Since you cannot take the square root of a negative number, the domain of $f(x) = \sqrt{4-x}$ is the set of all real numbers *x* such that $4 - x \geq 0 \Rightarrow 4 \geq x$. Only **6**, **E** is not in the domain.

Note that 4 is in the domain of $f(x) = \sqrt{4-x}$ because $f(4) = \sqrt{4-4} = \sqrt{0} = 0$. But 4 is *not* in the domain of $g(x) = \dfrac{1}{\sqrt{4-x}}$ because $\dfrac{1}{\sqrt{4-4}} = \dfrac{1}{\sqrt{0}} = \dfrac{1}{0}$, which is undefined. Remember, you can *never* divide by 0.

Again, if a function is thought of as a machine, the *range* of a function is the set of all real numbers that can come out of the machine. Recall that, if $f(x) = 2x + 3$, then $f(5) = 13$ and $f(-5) = -7$, so 13 and –7 are both in the range of $f(x)$. In general, it is much harder to find the range of a function than to find its domain, but you will usually be able to test whether a particular number is in the range.

EXAMPLE 7

Which of the following is NOT in the range of $f(x) = x^2 - 3$?

(A) 6
(B) 1
(C) 0
(D) –1
(E) –6

Solution. Since for any real number x, $x^2 \geq 0$, then $x^2 - 3 \geq -3$. Therefore, **–6 (E)** is not in the range of $f(x)$.

Note that in the solution to Example 6 you do not have to test each of the choices, but you can. To test whether 6 is in the range of $f(x)$, see whether there is a number x such that $f(x) = 6$: $x^2 - 3 = 6 \Rightarrow x^2 = 9 \Rightarrow x = 3$ or $x = -3$.

Then $f(3) = 6$, and 6 is in the range. Similarly, $f(2) = 1$, $f(\sqrt{3}) = 0$, and $f(\sqrt{2}) = -1$, so 1, 0, and –1 are also in the range. If you test –6, you see that $f(x) = -6 \Rightarrow x^2 - 3 = -6 \Rightarrow x^2 = -3$.

But there is no real number whose square is –3. Nothing that can go into the machine will cause –6 to come out.

On the SAT, questions such as Examples 5 and 6 above may be phrased without using the words "domain" and "range." For example, Example 5 may be expressed as follows:

> The function $f(x) = \sqrt{4 - x}$ is defined for each of the following numbers EXCEPT
>
> (A) –6
> (B) –4
> (C) 0
> (D) 4
> (E) 6

Similarly, Example 7 may be expressed as follows:

> For the function $f(x) = x^2 - 3$, which of the following numbers may NOT be the value of $f(x)$?
>
> (A) 6
> (B) 1
> (C) 0
> (D) –1
> (E) –6

On the SAT you take, it is likely that there will be one question that shows you a graph and asks you which of five other graphs is related to the original one in a certain way. To answer such a question, you can either test points or use the five facts listed in the following KEY FACT.

Key Fact R2

If $f(x)$ is a function and r is a positive number:

1. The graph of $y = f(x) + r$ is obtained by shifting the graph of $y = f(x)$ UP r units.

2. The graph of $y = f(x) - r$ is obtained by shifting the graph of $y = f(x)$ DOWN r units.

3. The graph of $y = f(x + r)$ is obtained by shifting the graph of $y = f(x)$ r units to the LEFT.

4. The graph of $y = f(x - r)$ is obtained by shifting the graph of $y = f(x)$ r units to the RIGHT.

5. The graph of $y = -f(x)$ is obtained by reflecting the graph of $y = f(x)$ in the x-axis.

Each part of KEY FACT R2 is illustrated below.

Figure (a) is the graph of the absolute-value function: $y = f(x) = |x|$. Figures (b)–(f) are transformations of the original graph.

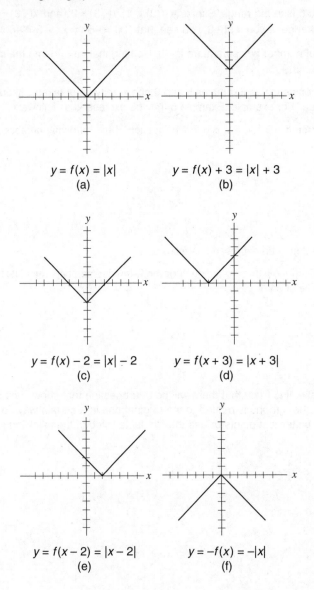

$y = f(x) = |x|$
(a)

$y = f(x) + 3 = |x| + 3$
(b)

$y = f(x) - 2 = |x| - 2$
(c)

$y = f(x + 3) = |x + 3|$
(d)

$y = f(x - 2) = |x - 2|$
(e)

$y = -f(x) = -|x|$
(f)

EXAMPLE 8

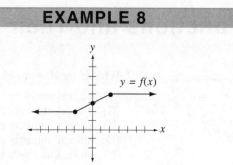

If the figure above is the graph of $y = f(x)$, which of the following is the graph of $y = f(x + 2)$?

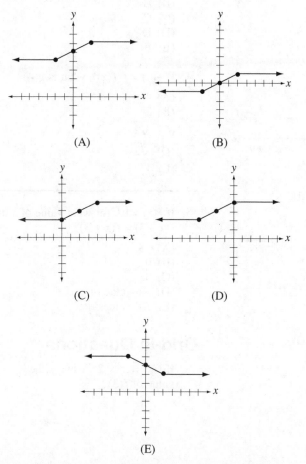

(A) (B)

(C) (D)

(E)

Solution 1. Since (0, 3) is a point on the graph of $y = f(x)$, $f(0) = 3$. Then $3 = f(0) = f(-2 + 2)$ and so $(-2, 3)$ is a point on the graph of $y = f(x + 2)$. Only choice **D** passes through $(-2, 3)$. Note that, if two or three of the graphs passed through $(-2, 3)$, you would test those graphs with a second point, say $(2, 4)$.

Solution 2. By KEY FACT R2, the graph of $y = f(x + 2)$ results from shifting the graph of $y = f(x)$ 2 units to the left. Only choice **D** is 2 units to the left of the graph in question.

Exercises on Functions and Their Graphs

Multiple-Choice Questions

Questions 1–4 concern the function $y = f(x) = \sqrt{x}$, whose graph is shown below. Choices (A)–(E) are graphs of functions that are somehow related to $f(x)$.

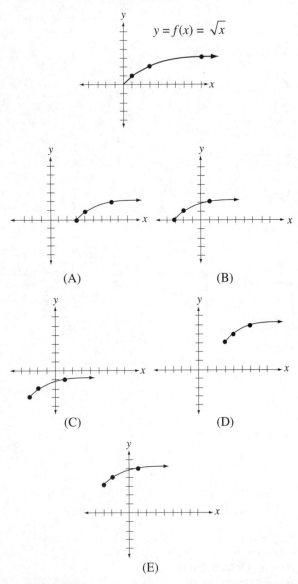

(A)

(B)

(C)

(D)

(E)

1. Which of the graphs is the graph of $y = f(x - 3)$?

   (A) A
   (B) B
   (C) C
   (D) D
   (E) E

2. What is the domain of the function $y = f(x - 3)$?

   (A) All real numbers
   (B) All real numbers except 3
   (C) All real numbers greater than 3
   (D) All real numbers greater than or equal to 3
   (E) All real numbers less than 3

3. Which of the graphs is the graph of $y = f(x + 3) + 3$?

   (A) A
   (B) B
   (C) C
   (D) D
   (E) E

4. If $g(x) = f(f(x))$, what is $g(4)$?

   (A) 4
   (B) 2
   (C) $\sqrt{2}$
   (D) $\sqrt{2}$
   (E) 1

5. If $f(x) = |x|$, for what value of x does $f(x - 3) = f(x + 3)$?

   (A) –3
   (B) 0
   (C) 3
   (D) No value of x
   (E) All values of x

Grid-in Questions

6. If $f(x) = x^2 - 2^x$, what is the value of $f(3)$?

7. What is the smallest integer
   that is NOT in the domain
   of $f(x) = \sqrt{\pi - x}$?

9. How many positive integers are
   in the range of $f(x)$?

<u>Questions 8 and 9</u> concern the function $f(x) = 8 - 2x^2$.

8. How many integers satisfy the
   condition that $f(x)$ is positive?

10. If $f(x) = x + 5$, for what value
    of x does $f(4x) = f(x + 4)$?

Answer Key

1. **A** 2. **D** 3. **E** 4. **C** 5. **B**

6. **1**   7. **4**   8. **3**   9. **8**

10.

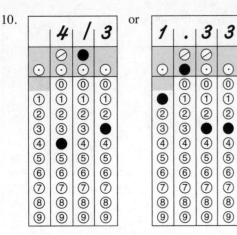

Answer Explanations

1. **A.** The graph of $y = f(x - 3)$ is the result of shifting the given graph 3 units to the right.

2. **D.** The domain of $y = f(x - 3) = \sqrt{x - 3}$ is the set of all real numbers such that $x - 3 \geq 0$. So, the domain consists of all real numbers greater than or equal to 3.

3. **E.** To get the graph of $y = f(x + 3)$, you need to shift the original graph 3 units to the left (this is graph (B)). Then, to get the graph of $y = f(x + 3) + 3$, shift graph (B) 3 units up, yielding graph (E).

4. **C.** $g(4) = f(f(4)) = \sqrt{f(4)} = \sqrt{\sqrt{4}} = \sqrt{2}$.

5. **B.** If $|x - 3| = |x + 3|$, then either $x - 3 = x + 3$, which is impossible, or
$x - 3 = -(x + 3) \Rightarrow x - 3 = -x - 3$.
Then $x = -x$, and so $x = 0$.

6. **(1)** $f(3) = 3^2 - 2^3 = 9 - 8 = 1$.

7. **(4)** Since you can't take the square root of a negative number, the domain of $f(x)$ consists of every real number, x, such that $\pi - x \geq 0$. The numbers that are *not* in the domain of $f(x)$ satisfy the inequality $\pi - x < 0 \Rightarrow \pi < x$. The smallest integer greater than π is 4.

8. **(3)** $f(x)$ is positive $\Rightarrow f(x) > 0 \Rightarrow 8 - 2x^2 > 0$.
So, $8 > 2x^2$ and, therefore, $4 > x^2$.
The only integers whose squares are less than 4 are $-1, 0$, and 1; there are 3 of them. Note that $f(2)$ and $f(-2)$ are both 0, which is not positive.

9. **(8)** Since x^2, and hence $2x^2$, must be greater than or equal to 0, the maximum value of $f(x)$ is 8. This means that 8 is the largest number in the range of $f(x)$. In fact, every number less than or equal to 8 is in the range. There are 8 positive integers in the range: $1, 2, 3, 4, 5, 6, 7, 8$. For example, $f(0) = 8, f(1) = 6$,
$f(\sqrt{2}) = 4$, and $f(\sqrt{2}) = 1$.

10. **($\frac{4}{3}$ or 1.33)** If $f(x) = x + 5$, then $f(4x) = 4x + 5$ and $f(x + 4) = (x + 4) + 5 = x + 9$.
Then
$$4x + 5 = x + 9 \Rightarrow 3x = 4 \Rightarrow x = \frac{4}{3} \text{ or } 1.33.$$

PART FOUR

TEST YOURSELF

Five Model SAT Tests

- 5 Model Tests
- Answer Keys
- Self-Evaluations
- Answer Explanations

Y ou are now about to take a major step in preparing yourself to handle an actual SAT. Before you are 5 Model Tests patterned after current published SATs. Up to now, you've concentrated on specific areas and on general testing techniques. You've mastered tactics and answered practice questions. Now you have a chance to test yourself—thoroughly, repeatedly—before you walk in that test center door.

These 5 Model Tests resemble the actual SAT in format, in difficulty, and in content. When you take them, take them as if they *were* the actual SAT.

BUILD YOUR STAMINA

Don't start and then stop and take time out for a soda or for an important phone call. To do well on the SAT, you have to focus on the test, and nothing but the test, for hours at a time. Many high school students have never had to sit through a 4-hour examination before they take their first SAT. To survive such a long exam takes *stamina*, and, as marathon runners know, the only way to build stamina is to put in the necessary time during practice sessions.

REFINE YOUR SKILLS

You know how to maximize your score by tackling easy questions first and by eliminating wrong answers whenever you can. Put these skills into practice. If you find yourself spending too much time on any one question, make an educated guess and move on. Remember to check frequently to make sure you are indicating your answers in the right spots. This is a great chance for you to get these skills down pat.

SPOT YOUR WEAK POINTS

Do you need a bit more drill in a particular area? After you take each test, consult the self-evaluation section and the answer explanations for that test to pinpoint any areas that need work. *Don't just evaluate your scores.* Build your skills. Read the answer explanations for each question you answered incorrectly, each question you omitted, and each question you answered correctly but found hard. The answer explanation section is tailor-made to help you. You'll find reminders of tactics, definitions of terms, explanations of why the correct answer works. You'll even find an occasional shortcut or two and an explanation of why an incorrect answer didn't work.

Use the answer explanation section to help you spot specific types of questions that you want to review. Suppose, for example, you've omitted answering several reading questions on a test. Going through the answer explanations, you find that all of these questions are of the Inference type. You know right then that you can boost your score by mastering the specific skill needed to deal with inferences.

TAKE A DEEP BREATH—AND SMILE!

It's hard to stay calm when those around you are tense, and you're bound to run into some pretty tense people when you take the SAT. (Not everyone works through this book, unfortunately.) So you may experience a slight case of "exam nerves" on the big day. Don't worry about it.

1. Being keyed up for an examination isn't always bad: you may outdo yourself because you are so worked up.
2. Total panic is unlikely to set in: you know too much.

You know you can handle a 3¾-hour test.

You know you can handle the sorts of questions you'll find on the SAT.

You know you can omit several questions and *still* score high. Answer correctly only 50–60% of the questions, omitting others, and you'll get a better than average score (and hundreds of solid, well-known colleges are out there right now, looking for serious students with just that kind of score). Answer more than that correctly and you should wind up with a superior score.

MAKE YOUR PRACTICE PAY—APPROXIMATE THE TEST

1. Whenever possible, complete an entire Model Test at one sitting.
2. Use a clock or timer.
3. Allow *precisely* 25 minutes for each of Sections 1 through 7, 20 minutes for each of Sections 8 and 9, and 10 minutes for Section 10. (If you finish any section in less than the allotted time, review your answers or go back to a question you omitted.)
4. After each section, give yourself a 1-minute break, and take 10-minute breaks after Sections 3 and 7.
5. Allow no talking in the test room.
6. Work rapidly without wasting time.

Answer Sheet—Test 1

Section 1   **ESSAY**

Test 1

Essay (continued)

If a section has fewer questions than answer spaces, leave the extra spaces blank.

Remove answer sheet by cutting on dotted line

Section 2

1 (A) (B) (C) (D) (E)	8 (A) (B) (C) (D) (E)	15 (A) (B) (C) (D) (E)	22 (A) (B) (C) (D) (E)	29 (A) (B) (C) (D) (E)
2 (A) (B) (C) (D) (E)	9 (A) (B) (C) (D) (E)	16 (A) (B) (C) (D) (E)	23 (A) (B) (C) (D) (E)	30 (A) (B) (C) (D) (E)
3 (A) (B) (C) (D) (E)	10 (A) (B) (C) (D) (E)	17 (A) (B) (C) (D) (E)	24 (A) (B) (C) (D) (E)	31 (A) (B) (C) (D) (E)
4 (A) (B) (C) (D) (E)	11 (A) (B) (C) (D) (E)	18 (A) (B) (C) (D) (E)	25 (A) (B) (C) (D) (E)	32 (A) (B) (C) (D) (E)
5 (A) (B) (C) (D) (E)	12 (A) (B) (C) (D) (E)	19 (A) (B) (C) (D) (E)	26 (A) (B) (C) (D) (E)	33 (A) (B) (C) (D) (E)
6 (A) (B) (C) (D) (E)	13 (A) (B) (C) (D) (E)	20 (A) (B) (C) (D) (E)	27 (A) (B) (C) (D) (E)	34 (A) (B) (C) (D) (E)
7 (A) (B) (C) (D) (E)	14 (A) (B) (C) (D) (E)	21 (A) (B) (C) (D) (E)	28 (A) (B) (C) (D) (E)	35 (A) (B) (C) (D) (E)

Section 3

1 (A) (B) (C) (D) (E)	8 (A) (B) (C) (D) (E)	15 (A) (B) (C) (D) (E)	22 (A) (B) (C) (D) (E)	29 (A) (B) (C) (D) (E)
2 (A) (B) (C) (D) (E)	9 (A) (B) (C) (D) (E)	16 (A) (B) (C) (D) (E)	23 (A) (B) (C) (D) (E)	30 (A) (B) (C) (D) (E)
3 (A) (B) (C) (D) (E)	10 (A) (B) (C) (D) (E)	17 (A) (B) (C) (D) (E)	24 (A) (B) (C) (D) (E)	31 (A) (B) (C) (D) (E)
4 (A) (B) (C) (D) (E)	11 (A) (B) (C) (D) (E)	18 (A) (B) (C) (D) (E)	25 (A) (B) (C) (D) (E)	32 (A) (B) (C) (D) (E)
5 (A) (B) (C) (D) (E)	12 (A) (B) (C) (D) (E)	19 (A) (B) (C) (D) (E)	26 (A) (B) (C) (D) (E)	33 (A) (B) (C) (D) (E)
6 (A) (B) (C) (D) (E)	13 (A) (B) (C) (D) (E)	20 (A) (B) (C) (D) (E)	27 (A) (B) (C) (D) (E)	34 (A) (B) (C) (D) (E)
7 (A) (B) (C) (D) (E)	14 (A) (B) (C) (D) (E)	21 (A) (B) (C) (D) (E)	28 (A) (B) (C) (D) (E)	35 (A) (B) (C) (D) (E)

Section 4

1 (A) (B) (C) (D) (E)	8 (A) (B) (C) (D) (E)	15 (A) (B) (C) (D) (E)	22 (A) (B) (C) (D) (E)	29 (A) (B) (C) (D) (E)
2 (A) (B) (C) (D) (E)	9 (A) (B) (C) (D) (E)	16 (A) (B) (C) (D) (E)	23 (A) (B) (C) (D) (E)	30 (A) (B) (C) (D) (E)
3 (A) (B) (C) (D) (E)	10 (A) (B) (C) (D) (E)	17 (A) (B) (C) (D) (E)	24 (A) (B) (C) (D) (E)	31 (A) (B) (C) (D) (E)
4 (A) (B) (C) (D) (E)	11 (A) (B) (C) (D) (E)	18 (A) (B) (C) (D) (E)	25 (A) (B) (C) (D) (E)	32 (A) (B) (C) (D) (E)
5 (A) (B) (C) (D) (E)	12 (A) (B) (C) (D) (E)	19 (A) (B) (C) (D) (E)	26 (A) (B) (C) (D) (E)	33 (A) (B) (C) (D) (E)
6 (A) (B) (C) (D) (E)	13 (A) (B) (C) (D) (E)	20 (A) (B) (C) (D) (E)	27 (A) (B) (C) (D) (E)	34 (A) (B) (C) (D) (E)
7 (A) (B) (C) (D) (E)	14 (A) (B) (C) (D) (E)	21 (A) (B) (C) (D) (E)	28 (A) (B) (C) (D) (E)	35 (A) (B) (C) (D) (E)

Section 6

1 (A) (B) (C) (D) (E)	8 (A) (B) (C) (D) (E)	15 (A) (B) (C) (D) (E)	22 (A) (B) (C) (D) (E)	29 (A) (B) (C) (D) (E)
2 (A) (B) (C) (D) (E)	9 (A) (B) (C) (D) (E)	16 (A) (B) (C) (D) (E)	23 (A) (B) (C) (D) (E)	30 (A) (B) (C) (D) (E)
3 (A) (B) (C) (D) (E)	10 (A) (B) (C) (D) (E)	17 (A) (B) (C) (D) (E)	24 (A) (B) (C) (D) (E)	31 (A) (B) (C) (D) (E)
4 (A) (B) (C) (D) (E)	11 (A) (B) (C) (D) (E)	18 (A) (B) (C) (D) (E)	25 (A) (B) (C) (D) (E)	32 (A) (B) (C) (D) (E)
5 (A) (B) (C) (D) (E)	12 (A) (B) (C) (D) (E)	19 (A) (B) (C) (D) (E)	26 (A) (B) (C) (D) (E)	33 (A) (B) (C) (D) (E)
6 (A) (B) (C) (D) (E)	13 (A) (B) (C) (D) (E)	20 (A) (B) (C) (D) (E)	27 (A) (B) (C) (D) (E)	34 (A) (B) (C) (D) (E)
7 (A) (B) (C) (D) (E)	14 (A) (B) (C) (D) (E)	21 (A) (B) (C) (D) (E)	28 (A) (B) (C) (D) (E)	35 (A) (B) (C) (D) (E)

Section 7

1 Ⓐ Ⓑ Ⓒ Ⓓ Ⓔ   3 Ⓐ Ⓑ Ⓒ Ⓓ Ⓔ   5 Ⓐ Ⓑ Ⓒ Ⓓ Ⓔ   7 Ⓐ Ⓑ Ⓒ Ⓓ Ⓔ
2 Ⓐ Ⓑ Ⓒ Ⓓ Ⓔ   4 Ⓐ Ⓑ Ⓒ Ⓓ Ⓔ   6 Ⓐ Ⓑ Ⓒ Ⓓ Ⓔ   8 Ⓐ Ⓑ Ⓒ Ⓓ Ⓔ

9 | 10 | 11 | 12 | 13

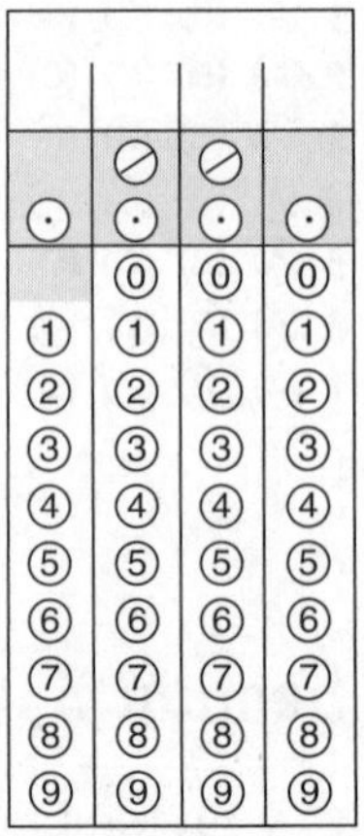

14 | 15 | 16 | 17 | 18

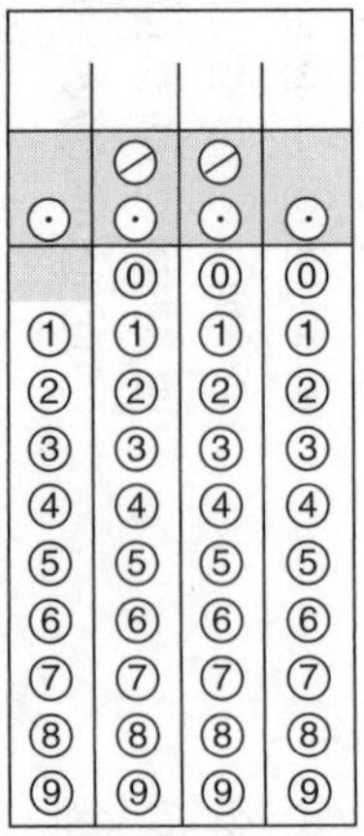

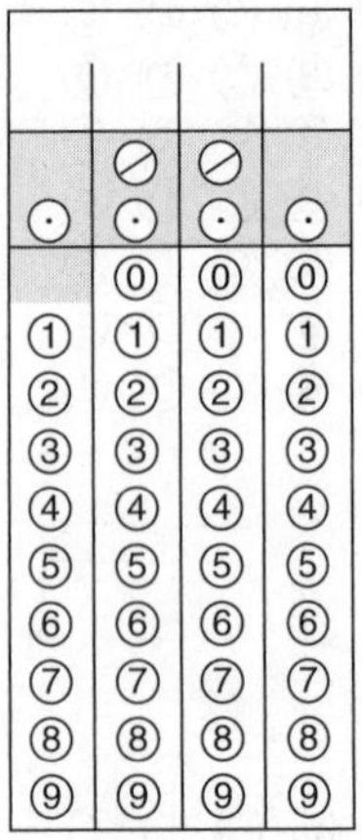

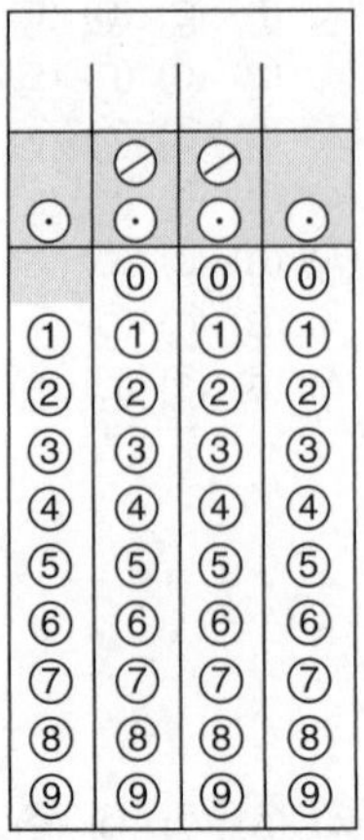

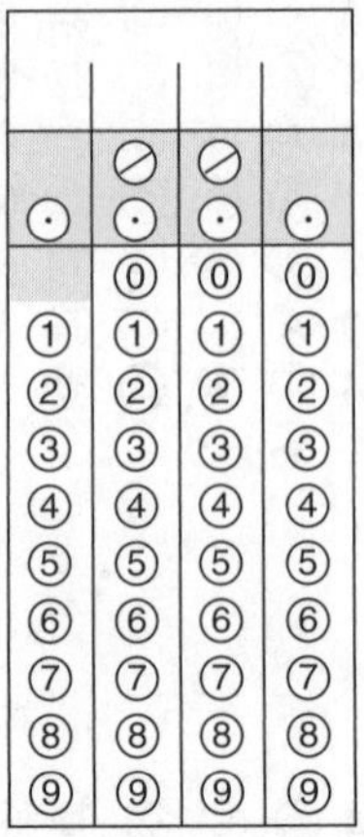

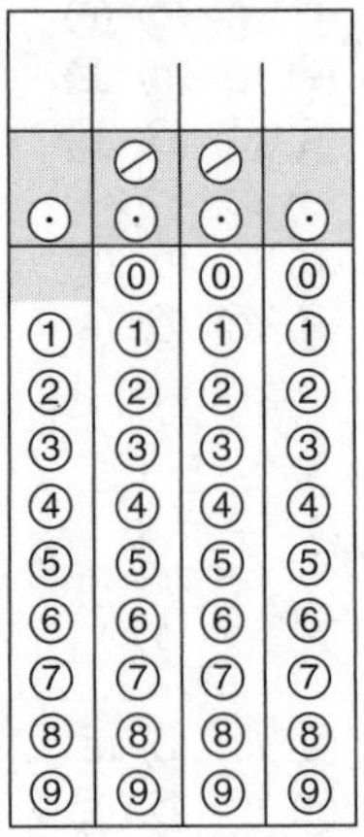

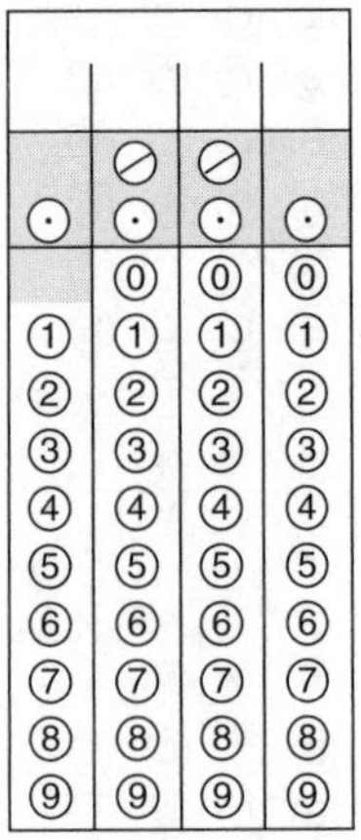

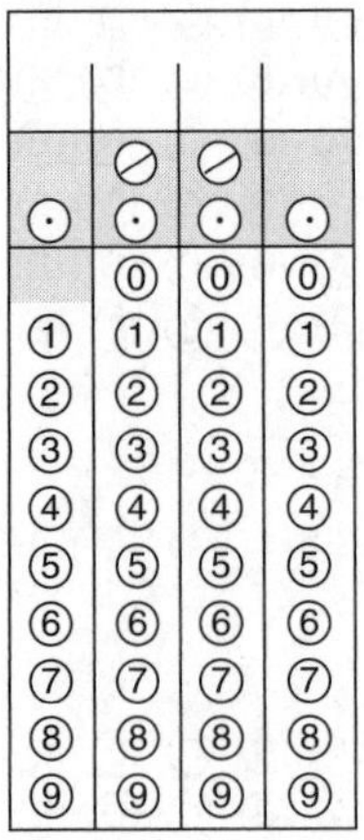

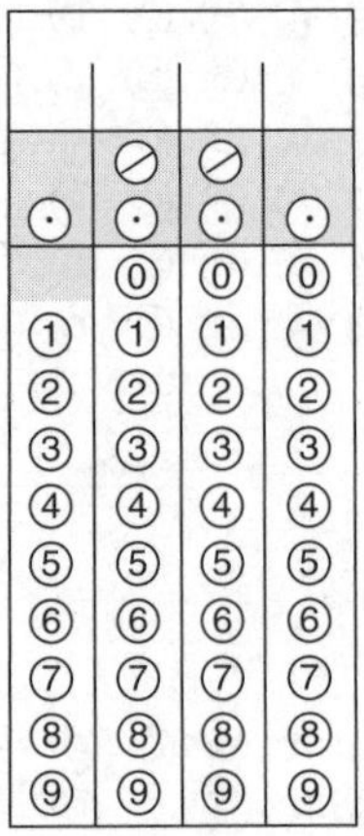

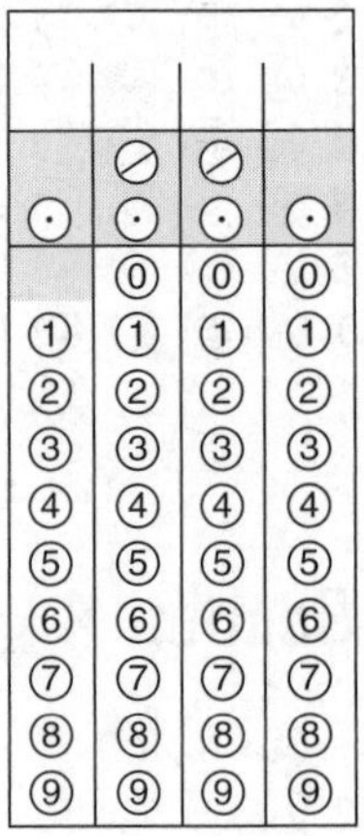

(Grid-in answer boxes numbered 9–18, each with fraction bars, decimal points, and bubbles numbered 0–9)

Section 8

1 Ⓐ Ⓑ Ⓒ Ⓓ Ⓔ   5 Ⓐ Ⓑ Ⓒ Ⓓ Ⓔ   9 Ⓐ Ⓑ Ⓒ Ⓓ Ⓔ   13 Ⓐ Ⓑ Ⓒ Ⓓ Ⓔ   17 Ⓐ Ⓑ Ⓒ Ⓓ Ⓔ
2 Ⓐ Ⓑ Ⓒ Ⓓ Ⓔ   6 Ⓐ Ⓑ Ⓒ Ⓓ Ⓔ   10 Ⓐ Ⓑ Ⓒ Ⓓ Ⓔ   14 Ⓐ Ⓑ Ⓒ Ⓓ Ⓔ   18 Ⓐ Ⓑ Ⓒ Ⓓ Ⓔ
3 Ⓐ Ⓑ Ⓒ Ⓓ Ⓔ   7 Ⓐ Ⓑ Ⓒ Ⓓ Ⓔ   11 Ⓐ Ⓑ Ⓒ Ⓓ Ⓔ   15 Ⓐ Ⓑ Ⓒ Ⓓ Ⓔ   19 Ⓐ Ⓑ Ⓒ Ⓓ Ⓔ
4 Ⓐ Ⓑ Ⓒ Ⓓ Ⓔ   8 Ⓐ Ⓑ Ⓒ Ⓓ Ⓔ   12 Ⓐ Ⓑ Ⓒ Ⓓ Ⓔ   16 Ⓐ Ⓑ Ⓒ Ⓓ Ⓔ   20 Ⓐ Ⓑ Ⓒ Ⓓ Ⓔ

Section 9

1 Ⓐ Ⓑ Ⓒ Ⓓ Ⓔ   5 Ⓐ Ⓑ Ⓒ Ⓓ Ⓔ   9 Ⓐ Ⓑ Ⓒ Ⓓ Ⓔ   13 Ⓐ Ⓑ Ⓒ Ⓓ Ⓔ   17 Ⓐ Ⓑ Ⓒ Ⓓ Ⓔ
2 Ⓐ Ⓑ Ⓒ Ⓓ Ⓔ   6 Ⓐ Ⓑ Ⓒ Ⓓ Ⓔ   10 Ⓐ Ⓑ Ⓒ Ⓓ Ⓔ   14 Ⓐ Ⓑ Ⓒ Ⓓ Ⓔ   18 Ⓐ Ⓑ Ⓒ Ⓓ Ⓔ
3 Ⓐ Ⓑ Ⓒ Ⓓ Ⓔ   7 Ⓐ Ⓑ Ⓒ Ⓓ Ⓔ   11 Ⓐ Ⓑ Ⓒ Ⓓ Ⓔ   15 Ⓐ Ⓑ Ⓒ Ⓓ Ⓔ   19 Ⓐ Ⓑ Ⓒ Ⓓ Ⓔ
4 Ⓐ Ⓑ Ⓒ Ⓓ Ⓔ   8 Ⓐ Ⓑ Ⓒ Ⓓ Ⓔ   12 Ⓐ Ⓑ Ⓒ Ⓓ Ⓔ   16 Ⓐ Ⓑ Ⓒ Ⓓ Ⓔ   20 Ⓐ Ⓑ Ⓒ Ⓓ Ⓔ

Section 10

1 Ⓐ Ⓑ Ⓒ Ⓓ Ⓔ   5 Ⓐ Ⓑ Ⓒ Ⓓ Ⓔ   9 Ⓐ Ⓑ Ⓒ Ⓓ Ⓔ   13 Ⓐ Ⓑ Ⓒ Ⓓ Ⓔ   17 Ⓐ Ⓑ Ⓒ Ⓓ Ⓔ
2 Ⓐ Ⓑ Ⓒ Ⓓ Ⓔ   6 Ⓐ Ⓑ Ⓒ Ⓓ Ⓔ   10 Ⓐ Ⓑ Ⓒ Ⓓ Ⓔ   14 Ⓐ Ⓑ Ⓒ Ⓓ Ⓔ   18 Ⓐ Ⓑ Ⓒ Ⓓ Ⓔ
3 Ⓐ Ⓑ Ⓒ Ⓓ Ⓔ   7 Ⓐ Ⓑ Ⓒ Ⓓ Ⓔ   11 Ⓐ Ⓑ Ⓒ Ⓓ Ⓔ   15 Ⓐ Ⓑ Ⓒ Ⓓ Ⓔ   19 Ⓐ Ⓑ Ⓒ Ⓓ Ⓔ
4 Ⓐ Ⓑ Ⓒ Ⓓ Ⓔ   8 Ⓐ Ⓑ Ⓒ Ⓓ Ⓔ   12 Ⓐ Ⓑ Ⓒ Ⓓ Ⓔ   16 Ⓐ Ⓑ Ⓒ Ⓓ Ⓔ   20 Ⓐ Ⓑ Ⓒ Ⓓ Ⓔ

Test 1

SECTION 1   **Time—25 Minutes**   **ESSAY**

The excerpt appearing below makes a point about a particular topic. Read the passage carefully, and think about the assignment that follows.

The novelist John Hersey wrote, "Learning starts with failure;
the first failure is the beginning of education."

ASSIGNMENT: What are your thoughts on the idea that failure is necessary for education to take place? Compose an essay in which you express your views on this topic. Your essay may support, refute, or qualify the views expressed in the excerpt. What you write, however, must be relevant to the topic under discussion. Additionally, you must support your viewpoint, indicating your reasoning and providing examples based on your studies and/or experience.

2 2 2 2 2 2 2 2 2 2 2

SECTION 2   **Time—25 Minutes**   Select the best answer to each of the following questions; then
             24 Questions   blacken the appropriate space on your answer sheet.

Each of the following sentences contains one or two blanks; each blank indicates that a word or set of words has been left out. Below the sentence are five words or phrases, lettered A through E. Select the word or set of words that best completes the sentence.

Example:

Fame is ----; today's rising star is all too soon tomorrow's washed-up has-been.

(A) rewarding   (B) gradual
(C) essential   (D) spontaneous
 (E) transitory

Ⓐ Ⓑ Ⓒ Ⓓ ●

---

1. Although he is ---- about the problems that still confront blacks in ballet, Mitchell nevertheless is optimistic about the future, especially that of his own dance company.

   (A) hopeful   (B) uninformed   (C) abstract
    (D) realistic   (E) unconcerned

2. Despite all its ---- , a term of enlistment in the Peace Corps can be both stirring and satisfying to a college graduate still undecided on a career.

   (A) rewards   (B) incongruity   (C) prestige
    (D) seclusion   (E) frustrations

3. Although he had numerous films to his credit and a reputation for technical ---- , the moviemaker lacked originality; all his films were sadly ---- of the work of others.

   (A) skill..independent
   (B) ability..unconscious
   (C) expertise..derivative
   (D) competence..contradictory
   (E) blunders..enamored

4. John Gielgud crowned a distinguished career of playing Shakespearean roles by giving a performance that was ---- .

   (A) mediocre
   (B) outmoded
   (C) superficial
   (D) unsurpassable
   (E) insipid

5. Those interested in learning more about how genetics applies to trees will have to ---- the excellent technical journals where most of the pertinent material is ---- .

   (A) subscribe to..ignored
   (B) suffer through..located
   (C) rely on..unrepresented
   (D) resort to..found
   (E) see through..published

6. Rent control restrictions on small apartment owners may unfortunately ---- rather than alleviate housing problems.

   (A) resolve   (B) diminish   (C) castigate
    (D) minimize   (E) exacerbate

7. In the light of Dickens's description of the lively, even ---- dance parties of his time, Sharp's approach to country dancing may seem too formal, suggesting more ---- than is necessary.

   (A) sophisticated..expertise
   (B) rowdy..decorum
   (C) prudish..propriety
   (D) lewd..ribaldry
   (E) enjoyable..vitality

8. The heretofore peaceful natives, seeking ---- the treachery of their supposed allies, became, ---- according to their perspective, embittered and vindictive.

   (A) acquiescence in..understandably
   (B) magnanimity towards..logically
   (C) evidence of..impartially
   (D) retribution for..justifiably
   (E) exoneration of..ironically

GO ON TO THE NEXT PAGE

2 2 2 2 2 2 2 2 2 2 2 **2**

Read each of the passages below, and then answer the questions that follow the passage. The correct response may be stated outright or merely suggested in the passage.

Questions 9 and 10 are based on the following passage.

On the playgrounds of Brooklyn, basketball is more religious rite than sport. Its devotees are on the court ten hours a day, six days a week.
Line Seventeen- and eighteen-year-olds have rheuma-
(5) toid knees from the constant pounding of their feet on the asphalt. They play through the afternoon heat with little more to fuel them than a can of soda, and they play at night in the dim illumination of nearby streetlights. They play even in
(10) the dead of winter, banging away at the netless rims, hoping for salvation in the form of a contract with the NBA.

9. The facilities for playing basketball available to the seventeen- and eighteen-year-olds described in the passage can best be characterized as

(A) professional
(B) sheltered
(C) rudimentary
(D) well designed
(E) seldom accessible

10. The "salvation" mentioned in the final sentence most likely refers to

(A) a realistic expectation of athletic success
(B) the potential for excellence that exists in all players
(C) formal promises made to amateur athletes by the NBA
(D) the ideal of sportsmanship exemplified by professional athletes
(E) a deliverance from poverty through professional sports

Questions 11 and 12 are based on the following passage.

This excerpt from Mark Twain's Roughing It *describes an animal Twain encountered during his travels in the West.*

The coyote is a long, slim, sick and sorry-looking skeleton, with a gray wolf-skin stretched over it, a tolerably bushy tail that forever sags down, a
Line furtive and evil eye, and a long, sharp face, with
(5) slightly lifted lip and exposed teeth. He has a general slinking expression all over. The coyote is a living, breathing allegory of Want. He is *always* hungry. He is always poor, out of luck, and friendless. The meanest creatures despise him, and even
(10) the fleas would desert him for a velocipede.

11. The passage above can best be characterized as an example of

(A) scientific analysis
(B) nostalgic anecdote
(C) humorous exaggeration
(D) objective reportage
(E) lyrical description

12. The word "meanest" (line 9) most nearly means

(A) most ordinary
(B) most stingy
(C) most ashamed
(D) most effective
(E) most contemptible

GO ON TO THE NEXT PAGE

2 2 2 2 2 2 2 2 2 2 2

Questions 13–24 are based on the following passage.

The following excerpt is taken from "Life on the Rocks: the Galapagos" by writer Annie Dillard. Like Charles Darwin, originator of the theory of evolution, Dillard visited the Galapagos Islands in the Pacific. In this passage she muses on the islands, on Darwin, and on the evolutionary process.

Charles Darwin came to the Galapagos in 1835, on the *Beagle*; he was twenty-six. He threw the marine iguanas as far as he could into the
Line water; he rode the tortoises and sampled their
(5) meat. He noticed that the tortoises' carapaces varied wildly from island to island; so also did the forms of various mockingbirds. He made collections. Nine years later he wrote in a letter, "I am almost convinced (quite contrary to the opinion I
(10) started with) that species are not (it is like confessing a murder) immutable." In 1859 he published *On the Origin of Species*, and in 1871 *The Descent of Man*. It is fashionable now to disparage Darwin's originality; not even the surliest of
(15) his detractors, however, faults his painstaking methods or denies his impact.

It all began in the Galapagos, with these finches. The finches in the Galapagos are called Darwin's finches; they are everywhere in the
(20) islands, sparrowlike, and almost identical but for their differing beaks. At first Darwin scarcely noticed their importance. But by 1839, when he revised his journal of the *Beagle* voyage, he added a key sentence about the finches' beaks:
(25) "Seeing this gradation and diversity of structure in one small, intimately related group of birds, one might really fancy that from an original paucity of birds in this archipelago, one species had been taken and modified for different ends."
(30) And so it was.

The finches come when called. I don't know why it works, but it does. Scientists in the Galapagos have passed down the call: you say pssssssh psssssh pssssssh psssssh until you run out
(35) of breath; then you say it again until the island runs out of birds. You stand on a flat of sand by a shallow lagoon rimmed in mangrove thickets and call the birds right out of the sky. It works anywhere, from island to island.
(40) Once, on the island of James, I was standing propped against a leafless *palo santo* tree on a semiarid inland slope, when the naturalist called the birds.

From other leafless *palo santo* trees flew the
(45) yellow warblers, speckling the air with bright bounced sun. Gray mockingbirds came running. And from the green prickly pear cactus, from the thorny acacias, sere grasses, bracken and manzanilla, from the loose black lava, the bare dust,
(50) the fern-hung mouths of caverns or the tops of sunlit logs—came the finches. They fell in from every direction like colored bits in a turning kaleidoscope. They circled and homed to a vortex, like a whirlwind of chips, like draining water. The tree
(55) on which I leaned was the vortex. A dry series of puffs hit my cheeks. Then a rough pulse from the tree's thin trunk met my palm and rang up my arm—and another, and another. The tree trunk agitated against my hand like a captured cricket: I
(60) looked up. The lighting birds were rocking the tree. It was an appearing act: before there were barren branches; now there were birds like leaves.

Darwin's finches are not brightly colored; they are black, gray, brown, or faintly olive. Their
(65) names are even duller: the large ground finch, the medium ground finch, the small ground finch; the large insectivorous tree finch; the vegetarian tree finch; the cactus ground finch, and so forth. But the beaks are interesting, and the beaks' origins
(70) even more so.

Some finches wield chunky parrot beaks modified for cracking seeds. Some have slender warbler beaks, short for nabbing insects, long for probing plants. One sports the long chisel beak of
(75) a woodpecker; it bores wood for insect grubs and often uses a twig or cactus spine as a pickle fork when the grub won't dislodge. They have all evolved, fanwise, from one bird.

The finches evolved in isolation. So did every-
(80) thing else on earth. With the finches, you can see how it happened. The Galapagos islands are near enough to the mainland that some strays could hazard there; they are far enough away that those strays could evolve in isolation from parent
(85) species. And the separate islands are near enough to each other for further dispersal, further isolation, and the eventual reassembling of distinct species. (In other words, finches blew to the Galapagos, blew to various islands, evolved into
(90) differing species, and blew back together again.) The tree finches and the ground finches, the woodpecker finch and the warbler finch, veered into being on isolated rocks. The witless green sea shaped those beaks as surely as it shaped the
(95) beaches. Now on the finches in the *palo santo* tree you see adaptive radiation's results, a fluorescent spray of horn. It is as though an archipelago were an arpeggio, a rapid series of distinct but related notes. If the Galapagos had been one uni-
(100) fied island, there would be one dull note, one super-dull finch.

GO ON TO THE NEXT PAGE

2 2 2 2 2 2 2 2 2 2 2

13. Dillard's initial portrayal of Darwin (lines 1–5) conveys primarily a sense of his

    (A) methodical research
    (B) instant commitment
    (C) youthful playfulness
    (D) lack of original thought
    (E) steadiness of purpose

14. From lines 8–11 one can conclude that Darwin originally viewed species as

    (A) unchanging   (B) original   (C) ambiguous
    (D) evolutionary   (E) indistinguishable

15. In the phrase "It all began in the Galapagos" (line 17), "It" refers to the origins of

    (A) sentient life
    (B) distinct species of creatures
    (C) Darwin's theory of evolution
    (D) controlled experimentation
    (E) Darwin's interest in nature

16. The word "ends" in line 29 means

    (A) borders   (B) extremities   (C) limits
    (D) purposes   (E) deaths

17. The use of the phrase "run out" two times (lines 32–36) emphasizes the

    (A) waste of energy involved
    (B) difference between the actions of humans and birds
    (C) impatience of the naturalists calling the birds
    (D) nervousness of the author in strange situations
    (E) overwhelming response of the birds

18. The word "lighting" in line 60 means

    (A) illuminating
    (B) landing
    (C) shining
    (D) weightless
    (E) flapping

19. The pulse that Dillard feels (lines 56–58) is most likely

    (A) the agitated beating of her heart
    (B) the rhythm of the birds' touching down
    (C) the leaping of crickets against the tree
    (D) a painful throbbing in her arm
    (E) the wind of the birds' passing

20. Dillard's description of the finches (lines 71–75) serves chiefly to

    (A) contrast their overall drabness with their variety in one specific aspect
    (B) illustrate the predominance of tree finches over ground finches
    (C) emphasize the use of memorable names to distinguish different species
    (D) convey a sense of the possibilities for further evolution in the finch family
    (E) distinguish them from the warblers and mockingbirds found in the islands

21. Lines 71–78 suggest that the finches' beaks evolved in ways that

    (A) mimicked a fanlike shape
    (B) protected the birds from attack
    (C) captured Darwin's interest
    (D) enhanced the birds' attractiveness
    (E) enabled them to reach nourishment

22. The word "hazard" in line 83 means

    (A) venture
    (B) speculate
    (C) be imperiled
    (D) run aground
    (E) develop

23. The "fluorescent spray of horn" referred to by the author in lines 96 and 97 is most likely

    (A) a series of musical notes
    (B) a flock of birds
    (C) the birds' shiny beaks
    (D) branches of the *palo santo* tree
    (E) a primitive musical instrument

24. In the final paragraph, the author does all of the following EXCEPT

    (A) restate an assertion
    (B) make a comparison
    (C) define a term
    (D) refute an argument
    (E) describe a sequence of events

YOU MAY GO BACK AND REVIEW THIS SECTION IN THE REMAINING TIME, BUT DO NOT WORK IN ANY OTHER SECTION UNTIL TOLD TO DO SO.

S T O P

3   3 3 3 3 3 3 3 3 3 3   3

SECTION 3

Time—25 Minutes
20 Questions

For each problem in this section determine which of the five choices is correct and blacken the corresponding choice on your answer sheet. You may use any blank space on the page for your work.

Notes:

- You may use a calculator whenever you think it will be helpful.
- Only real numbers are used. No question or answer on this test involves a complex or imaginary number.
- Use the diagrams provided to help you solve the problems. Unless you see the words "Note: Figure not drawn to scale" under a diagram, it has been drawn as accurately as possible. Unless it is stated that a figure is three-dimensional, you may assume it lies in a plane.
- For any function f, the domain, unless specifically restricted, is the set of all real numbers for which $f(x)$ is also a real number.

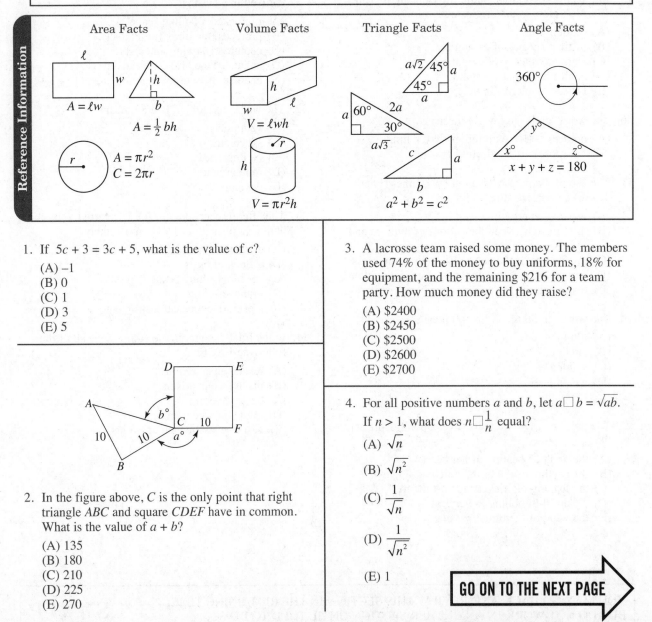

Reference Information

Area Facts

$A = \ell w$

$A = \frac{1}{2} bh$

$A = \pi r^2$
$C = 2\pi r$

Volume Facts

$V = \ell wh$

$V = \pi r^2 h$

Triangle Facts

$a^2 + b^2 = c^2$

Angle Facts

$x + y + z = 180$

1. If $5c + 3 = 3c + 5$, what is the value of c?

(A) –1
(B) 0
(C) 1
(D) 3
(E) 5

2. In the figure above, C is the only point that right triangle ABC and square $CDEF$ have in common. What is the value of $a + b$?

(A) 135
(B) 180
(C) 210
(D) 225
(E) 270

3. A lacrosse team raised some money. The members used 74% of the money to buy uniforms, 18% for equipment, and the remaining $216 for a team party. How much money did they raise?

(A) $2400
(B) $2450
(C) $2500
(D) $2600
(E) $2700

4. For all positive numbers a and b, let $a \square b = \sqrt{ab}$. If $n > 1$, what does $n \square \frac{1}{n}$ equal?

(A) $\sqrt{n}$

(B) $\sqrt{n^2}$

(C) $\dfrac{1}{\sqrt{n}}$

(D) $\dfrac{1}{\sqrt{n^2}}$

(E) 1

GO ON TO THE NEXT PAGE

3   3 3 3 3 3 3 3 3 3 3   3

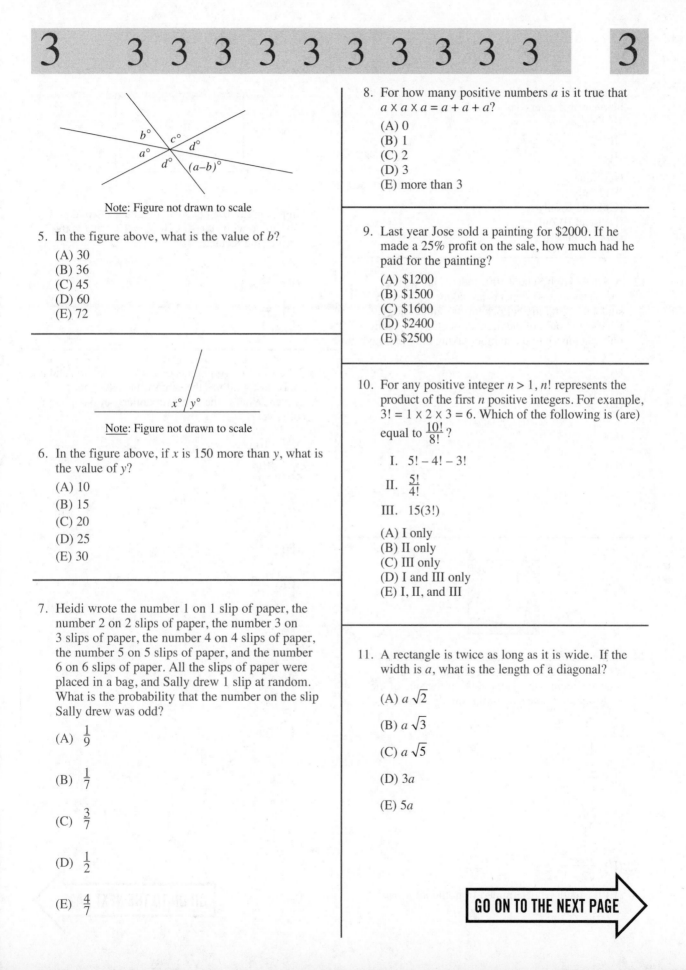

Note: Figure not drawn to scale

5. In the figure above, what is the value of b?

(A) 30
(B) 36
(C) 45
(D) 60
(E) 72

Note: Figure not drawn to scale

6. In the figure above, if x is 150 more than y, what is the value of y?

(A) 10
(B) 15
(C) 20
(D) 25
(E) 30

7. Heidi wrote the number 1 on 1 slip of paper, the number 2 on 2 slips of paper, the number 3 on 3 slips of paper, the number 4 on 4 slips of paper, the number 5 on 5 slips of paper, and the number 6 on 6 slips of paper. All the slips of paper were placed in a bag, and Sally drew 1 slip at random. What is the probability that the number on the slip Sally drew was odd?

(A) $\dfrac{1}{9}$

(B) $\dfrac{1}{7}$

(C) $\dfrac{3}{7}$

(D) $\dfrac{1}{2}$

(E) $\dfrac{4}{7}$

8. For how many positive numbers a is it true that $a \times a \times a = a + a + a$?

(A) 0
(B) 1
(C) 2
(D) 3
(E) more than 3

9. Last year Jose sold a painting for $2000. If he made a 25% profit on the sale, how much had he paid for the painting?

(A) $1200
(B) $1500
(C) $1600
(D) $2400
(E) $2500

10. For any positive integer $n > 1$, $n!$ represents the product of the first n positive integers. For example, $3! = 1 \times 2 \times 3 = 6$. Which of the following is (are) equal to $\dfrac{10!}{8!}$?

I. $5! - 4! - 3!$

II. $\dfrac{5!}{4!}$

III. $15(3!)$

(A) I only
(B) II only
(C) III only
(D) I and III only
(E) I, II, and III

11. A rectangle is twice as long as it is wide. If the width is a, what is the length of a diagonal?

(A) $a\sqrt{2}$

(B) $a\sqrt{3}$

(C) $a\sqrt{5}$

(D) $3a$

(E) $5a$

GO ON TO THE NEXT PAGE

12. If $abc = 1$, which of the following could be the number of integers among a, b, and c?

   I. 1
  II. 2
 III. 3

(A) None
(B) I only
(C) I and II only
(D) I and III only
(E) I, II, and III

13. At Essex High School 100 students are taking chemistry and 80 students are taking biology. If 20 students are taking both chemistry and biology, what is the ratio of the number of students taking only chemistry to the number taking only biology?

(A) $\dfrac{3}{4}$

(B) $\dfrac{4}{5}$

(C) $\dfrac{1}{1}$

(D) $\dfrac{5}{4}$

(E) $\dfrac{4}{3}$

14. In the figure above, a small square is drawn inside a large square. If the shaded area and the white area are equal, what is the ratio of the side of the large square to the side of the small square?

(A) $\dfrac{\sqrt{2}}{1}$

(B) $\dfrac{2}{1}$

(C) $\dfrac{2\sqrt{2}}{1}$

(D) $\dfrac{2}{\sqrt{2}-1}$

(E) It cannot be determined from the information given.

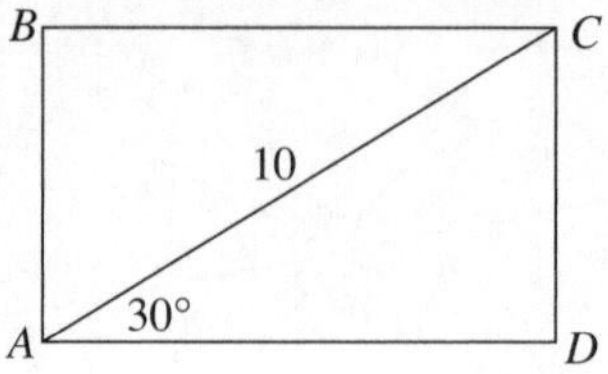

15. In rectangle $ABCD$ above, diagonal $\overline{AC}$ makes a 30° angle with side $\overline{AD}$. If $AC = 10$, what is the area of the rectangle?

(A) $25\sqrt{2}$

(B) $25\sqrt{3}$
(C) 48
(D) 50
(E) 100

16. The value of 10 pounds of gold is d dollars, and a pound of gold has the same value as p pounds of silver. What is the value, in dollars, of one pound of silver?

(A) $\dfrac{d}{10p}$

(B) $\dfrac{10p}{d}$

(C) $\dfrac{dp}{10}$

(D) $\dfrac{p}{10d}$

(E) $\dfrac{10d}{p}$

GO ON TO THE NEXT PAGE

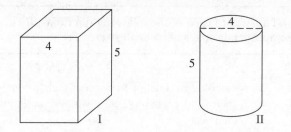

I

II

17. Of the figures above, container I is a rectangular solid whose base is a square 4 inches on a side, and container II is a cylinder whose base is a circle of diameter 4 inches. The height of each container is 5 inches. How much more water, in cubic inches, will container I hold than container II?

(A) $4(4 - \pi)$
(B) $20(4 - \pi)$
(C) $80(\pi - 1)$
(D) $80(1 - \pi)$
(E) It cannot be determined from the information given.

18. The number of cells growing in a particular Petri dish doubles every 30 minutes. If at 8:00 A.M. there were 60 cells in the dish, how many were there at noon of the same day?

(A) 60×2^{-8}
(B) 60×2^{-4}
(C) 60×2^{4}
(D) 60×4^{4}
(E) 60×4^{8}

19. The distance between Ali's house and college is exactly 135 miles. If she drove $\frac{2}{3}$ of the distance in 135 minutes, what was her average speed, in miles per hour?

(A) 40
(B) 45
(C) 60
(D) 67.5
(E) 75

20. The average (arithmetic mean) weight of five students is 150.4 pounds. If no student weighs less than 130 pounds and if no two students' weights are within 5 pounds of each other, what is the most, in pounds, that any one of the students can weigh?

(A) 172
(B) 192
(C) 202
(D) 232
(E) 242

YOU MAY GO BACK AND REVIEW THIS SECTION IN THE REMAINING TIME, BUT DO NOT WORK IN ANY OTHER SECTION UNTIL TOLD TO DO SO.

S T O P

4 | 4 4 4 4 4 4 4 4 4 4 | 4

SECTION 4 | Time—25 Minutes 35 Questions | Select the best answer to each of the following questions; then blacken the appropriate space on your answer sheet.

Some or all parts of the following sentences are underlined. The first answer choice, (A), simply repeats the underlined part of the sentence. The other four choices present four alternative ways to phrase the underlined part. Select the answer that produces the most effective sentence, one that is clear and exact, and blacken the appropriate space on your answer sheet. In selecting your choice, be sure that it is standard written English, and that it expresses the meaning of the original sentence.

Example:
The first biography of author Eudora Welty came out in 1998 and she was 89 years old at the time.

(A) and she was 89 years old at the time
(B) at the time when she was 89
(C) upon becoming an 89 year old
(D) when she was 89
(E) at the age of 89 years old

Ⓐ Ⓑ Ⓒ ● Ⓔ

1. Complaining that he couldn't hear hardly anything, he asked Dr. Brown, the otologist, whether he should get a hearing aid.

(A) Complaining that he couldn't hear hardly anything,
(B) Complaining that he couldn't hardly hear anything,
(C) He complained that he couldn't hear hardly anything,
(D) Complaining that he could hear hardly anything,
(E) Because he couldn't hear hardly anything,

2. Shakespeare wrote many plays, they are now being presented on public television.

(A) Shakespeare wrote many plays, they are now being presented on public television.
(B) Shakespeare wrote many plays, and they are now being presented on public television.
(C) Shakespeare wrote many plays, public television is now presenting them.
(D) The many plays Shakespeare wrote that are now being presented on public television.
(E) Shakespeare wrote many plays that are now being presented on public television.

3. Many alcoholics attempt to conceal their problem from their fellow workers, but invariably failing to keep their secret.

(A) but invariably failing to keep their secret
(B) but they invariably fail to keep their secret
(C) but fail, invariably, to keep their secret
(D) who invariably fail to keep their secret
(E) who they invariably fail to keep their secret from

4. Upon considering the facts of the case, the solution was obvious; consequently, Holmes sent for the police.

(A) Upon considering
(B) When considering
(C) Considering
(D) In consideration of
(E) When he considered

5. Familiar with the terrain from previous visits, the explorer's search for the abandoned mine site was a success.

(A) the explorer's search for the abandoned mine site was a success
(B) the success of the explorer's search for the abandoned mine site was assured
(C) the explorer succeeded in finding the abandoned mine site
(D) the search by the explorer for the abandoned mine site was successful
(E) the explorer in his search for the abandoned mine site was a success

GO ON TO THE NEXT PAGE

6. Economic conditions demand <u>not only cutting wages and prices but also to reduce</u> inflation-raised tax rates.

   (A) not only cutting wages and prices but also to reduce
   (B) we not only cut wages and prices but also reduce
   (C) to not only cut wages and prices but also to reduce
   (D) not only to cut wages and prices but also to reduce
   (E) not only a cut in wages and prices but also to reduce

7. He interviewed several candidates <u>who he thought</u> had the experience and qualifications he required.

   (A) who he thought
   (B) whom he thought
   (C) of whom he thought
   (D) he thought who
   (E) which he thought

8. It is typical of military service for a skilled technician to be inducted and <u>then you spend your whole tour of duty</u> peeling potatoes and cleaning latrines.

   (A) then you spend your whole tour of duty
   (B) to spend your whole tour of duty
   (C) then they spend their whole tour of duty
   (D) to spend their whole tour of duty
   (E) then spend her whole tour of duty

9. In years past, teenagers typically passed notes to their friends in <u>class rather than electronic instant messages today</u>.

   (A) class rather than electronic instant messages today
   (B) class, but today it is electronic instant messages
   (C) class; today they send electronic instant messages
   (D) class instead of electronic instant messages today
   (E) class; instead, teenagers today sending instant messages electronically

10. <u>George Balanchine's inspiration has had a great effect on many later choreographers who came after him</u>, including Danish-born Peter Martins.

    (A) George Balanchine's inspiration has had a great effect on many later choreographers who came after him
    (B) George Balanchine's inspiration has greatly effected many later choreographers who came after him
    (C) The inspiration of George Balanchine was great for many later choreographers who came after him
    (D) Many choreographers who came after him have been affected greatly by the inspiration of George Balanchine
    (E) George Balanchine has inspired many later choreographers

11. According to Freud, the aim of psychotherapy is to trace neurotic symptoms back to their unconscious roots and expose these roots to mature, rational <u>judgment, thereby depriving them of their compulsive power</u>.

    (A) judgment, thereby depriving them of their compulsive power
    (B) judgment; and thereby it deprives them of their compulsive power
    (C) judgment; thereby depriving them of their compulsive power
    (D) judgment, thereby it deprives them of their compulsive power
    (E) judgment, thereby it deprives them of its compulsive power

GO ON TO THE NEXT PAGE

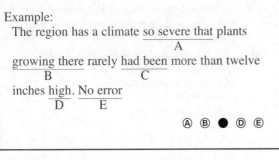

The sentences in this section may contain errors in grammar, usage, choice of words, or idioms. Either there is just one error in a sentence or the sentence is correct. Some words or phrases are underlined and lettered; everything else in the sentence is correct.

If an underlined word or phrase is incorrect, choose that letter; if the sentence is correct, select <u>No error</u>. Then blacken the appropriate space on your answer sheet.

Example:

The region has a climate <u>so severe that</u> plants
                                            A

<u>growing there</u> rarely <u>had been</u> more than twelve
       B   C

inches <u>high</u>. <u>No error</u>
        D   E

Ⓐ Ⓑ ● Ⓓ Ⓔ

12. I <u>can hardly believe</u> your tale of military intrigue;
              A

   the sophisticated secret weapons and the

   <u>increasing violent</u> actions <u>that</u> were exhibited by
            B   C

   just one man <u>seem</u> incredible. <u>No error</u>
                     D   E

13. The animals <u>who</u> were chosen <u>to represent</u> the
                    A   B

   Democratic and Republican parties, the donkey

   and the elephant, <u>were created</u> by the
                           C

   <u>renowned cartoonist</u> Thomas Nast. <u>No error</u>
            D   E

14. I <u>should like</u> you and <u>he</u> to supply the
          A   B

   <u>necessary data</u> for the annual statement that must
          C

   be prepared <u>in advance of</u> the spring meeting.
                     D

   <u>No error</u>
       E

15. <u>In the aftermath</u> of the space shuttle *Challenger*
           A

   explosion, <u>where</u> seven crew members
                  B

   were killed, the NASA program underwent a
                  C

   <u>massive examination</u> of priorities. <u>No error</u>
              D   E

16. Twenty-five <u>restless five-year-olds</u>
                        A

   were <u>throwing</u> paper clips, were drawing on
             B

   the blackboard, and <u>called to</u> one another
                            C

   <u>while their</u> teacher went searching for milk and
        D

   cookies. <u>No error</u>
               E

17. Recent medical breakthroughs, including the

   <u>discovery of</u> a vaccine to slow the AIDS virus,
        A

   <u>have encouraged</u> researchers; <u>and</u> a cure is still
          B   C

   <u>eluding</u> them. <u>No error</u>
       D   E

18. <u>Before</u> the producer took the musical to Broadway,
        A

   he <u>tried to get</u> the show with all <u>their</u> actors and
          B   C

   actresses booked in summer stock theaters for last-

   <u>minute revisions</u>. <u>No error</u>
            D   E

19. Neither the midlife career change applicant <u>nor</u>
                                                     A

   the young, inexperienced applicant <u>are finding</u> it
                                            B

   easy <u>to begin</u> a career in data processing
            C

   <u>because of</u> a shortage of job openings. <u>No error</u>
        D   E

GO ON TO THE NEXT PAGE ⟹

20. Even <u>after</u> you have endured a cold winter in
         A

    subzero weather, <u>one finds</u> <u>it</u> possible
                           B   C

    <u>to become acclimated</u> to tropical temperatures in
              D

    the summer. <u>No error</u>
                     E

21. <u>When</u> you buy a condominium, you will have
       A

    <u>less work than</u> owning a house entails, but you
           B

    <u>have not had</u> the <u>intrinsic</u> rewards. <u>No error</u>
           C   D   E

22. We have <u>come to the conclusion</u> that we can
                      A

    end hostilities in <u>that area</u> of the world by
                          B

    providing food to both sides, bringing the

    opposing forces to the <u>negotiation table</u>, and
                                  C

    <u>to guarantee</u> financial aid to both sides once peace
        D

    is established. <u>No error</u>
                         E

23. Numerous <u>collections of</u> short stories include
                    A

    works by Isaac Bashevis Singer who,

    <u>despite living</u> in the United States for more than
          B

    fifty years, <u>continued to write</u> primarily in Yiddish.
                      C   D

    <u>No error</u>
        E

24. Public television <u>has succeeded</u> <u>admirably</u> in
                            A   B

    raising money for <u>its</u> future programs through
                        C

    marathon <u>fund-raising projects</u> . <u>No error</u>
                    D   E

25. <u>By the time</u> the bank guard closed the doors,
         A

    a riot <u>had erupted</u> <u>due to</u> the long lines and
              B   C

    <u>shortage of tellers</u>. <u>No error</u>
          D   E

26. The <u>ancient concept</u> that <u>states that</u> the sun
              A   B

    <u>revolves around</u> Earth <u>is questioned by</u>
          C   D

    Copernicus in the sixteenth century. <u>No error</u>
                                              E

27. The opera company members, <u>which</u>
                                    A

    <u>ranged from</u> manager Joseph Volpe to conductor
        B

    James Levine, joined forces <u>to pay tribute</u> to
                                      C

    <u>retiring</u> tenor Luciano Pavarotti. <u>No error</u>
        D   E

28. Both major high school debate teams — <u>each</u> eager
                                              A

    <u>to dominate</u> this year's National Forensics League
        B

    competition — <u>intends</u> to review <u>thoroughly</u> the
                      C   D

    videos of last year's tournament. <u>No error</u>
                                          E

29. Improvements in the global positioning system

    (GPS) <u>will allow</u> pilots using the system to
              A

    guide aircraft <u>right down</u> to the runway
                        B

    <u>even when</u> severe weather creates <u>conditions of</u>
        C   D

    zero visibility. <u>No error</u>
                         E

GO ON TO THE NEXT PAGE

The passage below is the unedited draft of a student's essay. Parts of the essay need to be rewritten to make the meaning clearer and more precise. Read the essay carefully.

The essay is followed by six questions about changes that might improve all or part of the organization, development, sentence structure, use of language, appropriateness to the audience, or use of standard written English. In each case, choose the answer that most clearly and effectively expresses the student's intended meaning. Indicate your choice by blackening the corresponding space on the answer sheet.

[1] It is difficult to deny that the world of music has changed greatly in the past thirty years. [2] The style, sound, technology, and lyrics of music have been altered greatly. [3] In the last three decades, several new categories of music have come into being.

[4] One reason why music has changed so greatly is that artists use music as a tool to publicize certain social messages. [5] Although many artists of the 1970s used this method as well, their issues were not as severe that banning their album was possible. [6] For example, one rap-singer, Ice-T, used his album to promote "cop-killing." [7] The idea was so offensive that many believed the album should be banned. [8] The controversy caused by Ice-T made the Arista record company refuse to continue production of the album.

[9] Another way in which music has changed is lyrics. [10] When you listen to certain heavy metal or rap groups, one may notice foul and obscene language used. [11] Some of the references to sex are shocking. [12] In past eras, such language in recorded music was unheard of.

[13] Technological changes in music have occurred. [14] With the advent of highly advanced musical devices and many digital effects, the sounds of music have been completely altered. [15] Rock and roll was invented in early 1950s. [16] When you listen to heavy metal, you hear more distorted guitar sounds than in music of the 60s and 70s. [17] In the era of electronic instruments, the variety of possible sounds is incredible. [18] Present day sounds could never have been achieved in previous years because the technology was not at hand. [19] New music utilizes electronically produced sounds never heard before. [20] Computers generate everything from the human voice under water to the sound of whales. [21] There are no limits to what the music of the future will sound like.

30. Which of the following is the best revision of the underlined segment of sentence 5 below?

    Although many artists of the 1970s used this method as well, their issues were not as severe that banning their album was possible.

    (A) the issues were less severe than those which caused banning their album to be possible.
    (B) their issues were not as severe that their albums were in danger of being banned.
    (C) they never raised issues that could have caused their albums to be banned.
    (D) the issues they raised were not serious enough that banning their album was a possibility.
    (E) they raised less serious issues and banning their albums was not likely.

31. In view of the sentences that precede and follow sentence 10, which is the most effective revision of sentence 10?

    (A) Listening to certain heavy metal or rap groups, lyrics containing obscenities are often heard.
    (B) Obscene language is common in the songs of heavy metal and rap groups.
    (C) Certain heavy metal and rap groups use foul and obscene language.
    (D) Obscenities are often heard when one listens to the lyrics of certain heavy metal or rap groups.
    (E) Listening to obscene language and listening to the lyrics of certain heavy metal and rap groups.

32. In the context of the entire essay, which revision of sentence 13 provides the most effective transition between paragraphs 3 and 4?

    (A) Technological changes in music also have occurred.
    (B) Also, technology has changed musical sounds.
    (C) Noticeable changes in music's sounds have come about through technological changes.
    (D) Changes in musical technology has changed musical sound, too.
    (E) But the most noticeable change in music has been its sound.

GO ON TO THE NEXT PAGE

33. In a revision of the entire essay, which of the following sentences most needs further development?

    (A) Sentence 3
    (B) Sentence 7
    (C) Sentence 8
    (D) Sentence 19
    (E) Sentence 20

34. Which of the following sentences should be deleted to improve the unit and coherence of paragraph 4?

    (A) Sentence 14
    (B) Sentence 15
    (C) Sentence 16
    (D) Sentence 17
    (E) Sentence 18

35. With regard to the organization of the entire essay, which is the best revision of sentence 2 in the introductory paragraph?

    (A) In the past thirty years, not only the style, sound, and technology has changed, but the lyrics have, too.
    (B) Having undergone a change in the style, sound, and technology, musical lyrics have altered also.
    (C) Changes in musical sound have occurred, while the technology and lyrics have tremendously altered the style of music.
    (D) Musicians have transformed today's music in style and sound, creating new lyrics and using new technology.
    (E) Along with changes in sound and technology, the lyrics of music have changed, too.

YOU MAY GO BACK AND REVIEW THIS SECTION IN THE REMAINING TIME, BUT DO NOT WORK IN ANY OTHER SECTION UNTIL TOLD TO DO SO.   **STOP**

Test 1

SECTION 6   Time—25 Minutes   Select the best answer to each of the following questions; then
24 Questions   blacken the appropriate space on your answer sheet.

Each of the following sentences contains one or two blanks; each blank indicates that a word or set of words has been left out. Below the sentence are five words or phrases, lettered A through E. Select the word or set of words that best completes the sentence.

Example:

Fame is ----; today's rising star is all too soon tomorrow's washed-up has-been.

(A) rewarding   (B) gradual
(C) essential   (D) spontaneous
(E) transitory

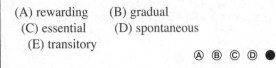

1. Because our supply of fossil fuel has been sadly ---- , we must find ---- sources of energy.

(A) stored..hoarded
(B) compensated..significant
(C) exhausted..inefficient
(D) increased..available
(E) depleted..alternative

2. He is much too ---- in his writings: he writes a page when a sentence should suffice.

(A) devious   (B) lucid   (C) verbose
(D) efficient   (E) pleasant

3. The abundance and diversity of insects is the cumulative effect of an extraordinarily low ---- rate: bugs endure.

(A) metabolic
(B) density
(C) extinction
(D) percentage
(E) standard

4. Pre-Spanish art in Mexico is not a ---- art; they are mistaken who see in its bold simplifications or wayward conceptions an inability to ---- technical difficulties.

(A) formal..ignore
(B) graphic..understand
(C) primitive..nurture
(D) crude..overcome
(E) revolutionary..instigate

5. Are we to turn into spineless ---- , afraid to take a ---- stand, unable to answer a question without pussyfooting?

(A) disciples..positive
(B) hedonists..compromising
(C) criminals..defiant
(D) critics..constructive
(E) equivocators..forthright

GO ON TO THE NEXT PAGE

6 6 6 6 6 6 6 6 6 6 6 6 6 **6**

Read the passages below, and then answer the questions that follow them. The correct response may be stated outright or merely suggested in the passages.

Questions 6–9 are based on the following passages.

Both passages relate to the career of the abolitionist Frederick Douglass. Passage 1 comes from the introduction to a collection of his short prose. Passage 2 is excerpted from Douglass's letter to his former master, written while Douglass was in England.

Passage 1

To elude slave catchers, the fugitive slave
Frederick Baily changed his name, becoming
Frederick Douglass, abolitionist spokesman and
Line author. When he published his autobiography,
(5) however, Douglass exposed himself to recapture:
federal laws gave Douglass's ex-master the right
to seize his property. Douglass traveled to Britain,
where slavery was illegal; there he worked to gain
support for America's anti-slavery movement.
(10) After two years, British friends unexpectedly
bought his freedom, allowing him to return home
to continue the fight. Some abolitionists criticized
Douglass, however, saying that by letting his freedom be bought he acknowledged his master's
(15) right to own him.

Passage 2

I have often thought I should like to explain to
you the grounds upon which I have justified
myself in running away from you…. We are distinct persons, and are each equally provided with
(20) faculties necessary to our individual existence. In
leaving you, I took nothing but what belonged to
me, and in no way lessened your means for
obtaining an *honest* living…. I therefore see no
wrong in any part of the transaction. It is true, I
(25) went off secretly; but that was more your fault
than mine. Had I let you into the secret, you
would have defeated the enterprise entirely; but
for this, I should have been really glad to have
made you acquainted with my intentions to leave.

6. In Passage 1, the word "property" (line 7) most nearly means

(A) parcel of land
(B) right of ownership
(C) characteristic trait
(D) personal possession
(E) particular virtue

7. As described in the final sentence of Passage 1, the attitude of some abolitionists to the purchase of Douglass's freedom can best be characterized as

(A) enthusiastic
(B) indifferent
(C) negative
(D) envious
(E) sympathetic

8. Compared to Passage 2, Passage 1 can be described as

(A) figurative rather than literal
(B) expository rather than argumentative
(C) rhetorical rather than unembellished
(D) descriptive rather than factual
(E) subjective rather than objective

9. The "enterprise" to which Douglass refers in the final sentence of Passage 2 is

(A) a financial transaction
(B) the letter to his former master
(C) his escape from slavery
(D) his return from England
(E) the means of earning an honest living

GO ON TO THE NEXT PAGE

Questions 10–15 are based on the following passage.

The following passage is taken from a major historical text on life in the Middle Ages.

To the world when it was half a thousand
years younger, the outlines of all things seemed
more clearly marked than to us. The contrast
Line between suffering and joy, between adversity and
(5) happiness, appeared more striking. All experience
had yet to the minds of men the directness and
absoluteness of the pleasure and pain of child-life.
Every event, every action, was still embodied in
expressive and solemn forms, which raised them
(10) to the dignity of a ritual. For it was not merely the
great facts of birth, marriage, and death which, by
their sacredness, were raised to the rank of mysteries; incidents of less importance, like a journey,
a task, a visit, were equally attended by a thou-
(15) sand formalities: benedictions, ceremonies,
formulae.

Calamities and indigence were more afflicting
than at present; it was more difficult to guard
against them, and to find solace. Illness and
(20) health presented a more striking contrast; the cold
and darkness of winter were more real evils.
Honors and riches were relished with greater
avidity and contrasted more vividly with surrounding misery. We, at the present day, can
(25) hardly understand the keenness with which a fur
coat, a good fire on the hearth, a soft bed, a glass
of wine, were formerly enjoyed.

Then, again, all things in life were of a proud
or cruel publicity. Lepers sounded their rattles
(30) and went about in processions, beggars exhibited
their deformity and their misery in churches.
Every order and estate, every rank and profession,
was distinguished by its costume. The great lords
never moved about without a glorious display of
(35) arms and liveries, exciting fear and envy. Execu-
tions and other public acts of justice, hawking,
marriages and funerals, were all announced by
cries and processions, songs and music. The lover
wore the colors of his lady; companions the
(40) emblem of their confraternity; parties and servants
the badges or blazon of their lords. Between town
and country, too, the contrast was very marked. A
medieval town did not lose itself in extensive suburbs of factories and villas; girded by its walls, it
(45) stood forth as a compact whole, bristling with
innumerable turrets. However tall and threatening
the houses of noblemen or merchants might be, in
the aspect of the town the lofty mass of the
churches always remained dominant.

(50) The contrast between silence and sound, darkness and light, like that between summer and winter, was more strongly marked than it is in our
lives. The modern town hardly knows silence or
darkness in their purity, nor the effect of a soli-
(55) tary light or a single distant cry.

All things presenting themselves to the mind in
violent contrasts and impressive forms, lent a tone
of excitement and of passion to everyday life and
tended to produce the perpetual oscillation
(60) between despair and distracted joy, between cruelty and pious tenderness which characterizes life
in the Middle Ages.

10. The author's main purpose in this passage is best
defined as an attempt to show how
(A) extremes of feeling and experience marked the
Middle Ages
(B) the styles of the very poor and the very rich
complemented each other
(C) twentieth century standards of behavior cannot
be applied to the Middle Ages
(D) the Middle Ages developed out of the Dark
Ages
(E) the medieval spirit languished five hundred
years ago

11. According to lines 10–16, surrounding an activity
with formalities makes it
(A) less important
(B) more stately
(C) less expensive
(D) more indirect
(E) less solemn

12. The author's use of the term "formulae" (line 16)
could best be interpreted to mean which of the fol-
lowing?
(A) set forms of words for rituals
(B) mathematical rules or principles
(C) chemical symbols
(D) nourishment for infants
(E) prescriptions for drugs

GO ON TO THE NEXT PAGE

6 6 6 6 6 6 6 6 6 6 6 **6**

13. The word "order" in line 32 means

   (A) command
   (B) harmony
   (C) sequence
   (D) physical condition
   (E) social class

14. According to the passage, well above the typical medieval town there towered

   (A) houses of worship
   (B) manufacturing establishments
   (C) the mansions of the aristocracy
   (D) great mercantile houses
   (E) walled suburbs

15. To the author, the Middle Ages seem to be all the following EXCEPT

   (A) routine and boring
   (B) festive and joyful
   (C) dignified and ceremonious
   (D) passionate and turbulent
   (E) harsh and bleak

Questions 16–24 are based on the following passage.

The following passage is excerpted from Hunger of Memory, *the autobiography of Mexican-American writer Richard Rodriguez, who speaks of lessons he learned as the child of working-class immigrant parents.*

I remember to start with that day in Sacramento—a California now nearly thirty years past—when I first entered a classroom, able to
Line understand some fifty stray English words.
(5)   The third of four children, I had been preceded to a neighborhood Roman Catholic school by an older brother and sister. Each afternoon they returned, as they left in the morning, always together, speaking in Spanish as they climbed the
(10) five steps of the porch. And their mysterious books, wrapped in shopping-bag paper, remained on the table next to the door, closed firmly behind them.
   An accident of geography sent me to a school
(15) where all my classmates were white, many the children of doctors and lawyers and business executives. All my classmates certainly must have been uneasy on that first day of school—as most children are uneasy—to find themselves apart
(20) from their families in the first institution of their lives. But I was astonished.

The nun said, in a friendly but oddly impersonal voice, "Boys and girls, this is Richard Rodriguez." (I heard her sound out: *Rich-heard*
(25) *Road-ree-guess*.) It was the first time I had heard anyone name me in English. "Richard," the nun repeated more slowly, writing my name down in her black leather book. Quickly I turned to see my mother's face dissolve in a watery blur behind
(30) the pebbled glass door.
   Many years later there is something called bilingual education—a scheme proposed in the late 1960s by Hispanic-American social activists, later endorsed by a congressional vote. It is a pro-
(35) gram that seeks to permit non-English-speaking children, many from lower class homes, to use their family language as the language of school. (Such is the goal its supporters announce.) I hear them and am forced to say no: It is not possible
(40) for a child—any child—ever to use his family's language in school. Not to understand this is to misunderstand the public uses of schooling and to trivialize the nature of intimate life—a family's "language."
(45)   Memory teaches me what I know of these matters; the boy reminds the adult. I was a bilingual child, a certain kind—socially disadvantaged— the son of working-class parents, both Mexican immigrants.
(50)   In the early years of my boyhood, my parents coped very well in America. My father had steady work. My mother managed at home. They were nobody's victims. Optimism and ambition led them to a house (our home) many blocks from the
(55) Mexican south side of town. We lived among *gringos* and only a block from the biggest, whitest houses. It never occurred to my parents that they couldn't live wherever they chose. Nor was the Sacramento of the fifties bent on teaching
(60) them a contrary lesson. My mother and father were more annoyed than intimidated by those two or three neighbors who tried initially to make us unwelcome. ("Keep your brats away from my sidewalk!") But despite all they achieved, perhaps
(65) because they had so much to achieve, any deep feeling of ease, the confidence of "belonging" in public was withheld from them both. They regarded the people at work, the faces in crowds, as very distant from us. They were the others,
(70) *los gringos*. That term was interchangeable in their speech with another, even more telling, *los americanos*.

GO ON TO THE NEXT PAGE

16. The family members in the passage are discussed primarily in terms of

    (A) the different personalities of each
    (B) the common heritage they shared
    (C) the ambitions they possessed
    (D) their interaction with the English-speaking world
    (E) their struggle against racial discrimination

17. The author's description of his older brother and sister's return from school (lines 7–10) suggests that they

    (A) enjoyed exploring the mysteries of American culture
    (B) were afraid to speak English at home
    (C) wished to imitate their English-speaking classmates
    (D) readily ignored the need to practice using English
    (E) regretted their inability to make friends

18. What initially confused the author on his first day of school?

    (A) His mother's departure took him by surprise.
    (B) Hearing his name in English disoriented him.
    (C) His older brother and sister had told him lies about the school.
    (D) He had never before seen a nun.
    (E) He had never previously encountered white children.

19. The word "scheme" in line 32 means

    (A) conspiracy
    (B) diagram
    (C) plan
    (D) outline
    (E) goal

20. The author rejects bilingual education on the grounds that

    (A) allowing students to use their family's language in school presents only trivial difficulties to teachers
    (B) its champions fail to see that public education must meet public needs, not necessarily personal ones
    (C) most students prefer using standard English both at home and in the classroom
    (D) the proposal was made only by social activists and does not reflect the wishes of the Hispanic-American community
    (E) it is an unnecessary program that puts a heavy financial burden upon the taxpayer

21. In lines 45–49, the author most likely outlines his specific background in order to

    (A) emphasize how far he has come in achieving his current academic success
    (B) explain the sort of obstacles faced by the children of immigrants
    (C) indicate what qualifies him to speak authoritatively on the issue
    (D) dispel any misunderstandings about how much he remembers of his childhood
    (E) evoke the reader's sympathy for socially disadvantaged children

22. The author's attitude toward his parents (lines 50–72) can best be described as

    (A) admiring   (B) contemptuous   (C) indifferent
    (D) envious   (E) diffident

23. Which of the following statements regarding Mexican-Americans in Sacramento would be most true of the author's experiences?

    (A) They were unable to find employment.
    (B) They felt estranged from the community as a whole.
    (C) They found a ready welcome in white neighborhoods.
    (D) They took an active part in public affairs.
    (E) They were unaware of academic institutions.

24. The word "telling" as used in line 71 means

    (A) outspoken
    (B) interchangeable
    (C) unutterable
    (D) embarrassing
    (E) revealing

YOU MAY GO BACK AND REVIEW THIS SECTION IN THE REMAINING TIME, BUT DO NOT WORK IN ANY OTHER SECTION UNTIL TOLD TO DO SO.

STOP

7

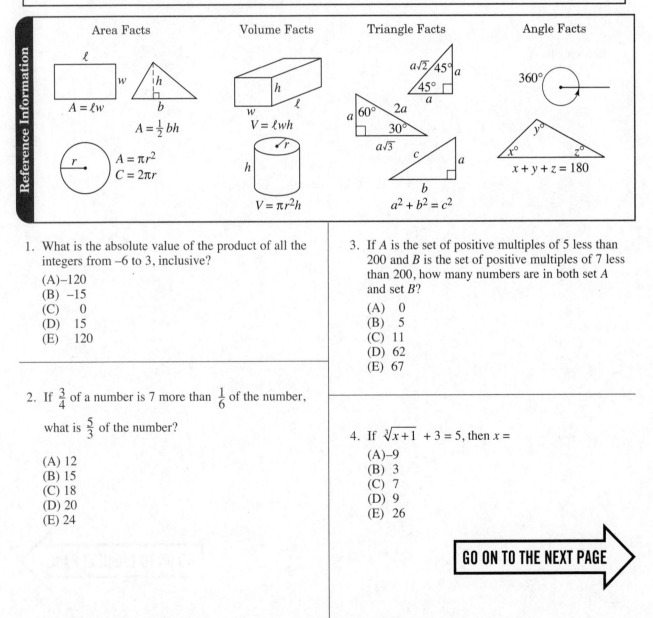

SECTION 7
Time—25 Minutes
18 Questions

You have 25 minutes to answer the 8 multiple-choice questions and 10 student-produced response questions in this section. For each multiple-choice question, determine which of the five choices is correct and blacken the corresponding choice on your answer sheet. You may use any blank space on the page for your work.

Notes:
- You may use a calculator whenever you think it will be helpful.
- Only real numbers are used. No question or answer on this test involves a complex or imaginary number.
- Use the diagrams provided to help you solve the problems. Unless you see the words "Note: Figure not drawn to scale" under a diagram, it has been drawn as accurately as possible. Unless it is stated that a figure is three-dimensional, you may assume it lies in a plane.
- For any function f, the domain, unless specifically restricted, is the set of all real numbers for which $f(x)$ is also a real number.

Reference Information

Area Facts

$A = \ell w$

$A = \frac{1}{2} bh$

$A = \pi r^2$
$C = 2\pi r$

Volume Facts

$V = \ell w h$

$V = \pi r^2 h$

Triangle Facts

$a^2 + b^2 = c^2$

Angle Facts

$360°$

$x + y + z = 180$

1. What is the absolute value of the product of all the integers from –6 to 3, inclusive?

   (A) –120
   (B) –15
   (C)   0
   (D)   15
   (E)   120

2. If $\frac{3}{4}$ of a number is 7 more than $\frac{1}{6}$ of the number, what is $\frac{5}{3}$ of the number?

   (A) 12
   (B) 15
   (C) 18
   (D) 20
   (E) 24

3. If A is the set of positive multiples of 5 less than 200 and B is the set of positive multiples of 7 less than 200, how many numbers are in both set A and set B?

   (A)   0
   (B)   5
   (C) 11
   (D) 62
   (E) 67

4. If $\sqrt[3]{x+1} + 3 = 5$, then $x =$

   (A) –9
   (B)   3
   (C)   7
   (D)   9
   (E) 26

GO ON TO THE NEXT PAGE

7

5. Let the lengths of the sides of a triangle be represented by $x + 3$, $2x - 3$, and $3x - 5$. If the perimeter of the triangle is 25, what is the length of the shortest side?

(A) 5
(B) 7
(C) 8
(D) 10
(E) It cannot be determined from the information given.

6. What is the maximum number of points of intersection between a square and a circle?

(A) less than 4
(B) 4
(C) 6
(D) 8
(E) more than 8

7. In square $ABCD$, vertex A is at $(-1, -1)$ and vertex C is at $(4, 2)$. What is the area of square $ABCD$?

(A) 9
(B) 15
(C) 17
(D) 25
(E) 34

8. If $f(x) = x + 5$, which of the following is a solution of $f(3a) + 2 = f(2a) + 3$?

(A) 1
(B) 2
(C) 5
(D) 6
(E) There are no solutions.

7

Directions for Student-Produced Response Questions (Grid-ins)

In questions 9–18, first solve the problem, and then enter your answer on the grid provided on the answer sheet. The instructions for entering your answers are as follows:

- First, write your answer in the boxes at the top of the grid.
- Second, grid your answer in the columns below the boxes.
- Use the fraction bar in the first row or the decimal point in the second row to enter fractions and decimal answers.

- Grid only one space in each column.
- Entering the answer in the boxes is recommended as an aid in gridding, but is not required.
- The machine scoring your exam can read only what you grid, so you **must grid in your answers correctly to get credit.**
- If a question has more than one correct answer, grid in only one of these answers.
- The grid does not have a minus sign, so no answer can be negative.
- A mixed number *must* be converted to an improper fraction or a decimal before it is gridded. Enter $1\frac{1}{4}$ as 5/4 or 1.25; the machine will interpret 1 1/4 as $\frac{11}{4}$ and mark it wrong.
- **All decimals must be entered as accurately as possible.** Here are the three acceptable ways of gridding

$$\frac{3}{11} = 0.272727\ldots$$

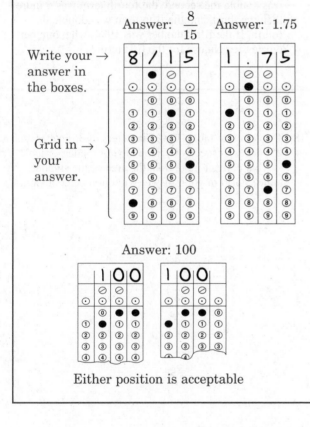

Answer: $\frac{8}{15}$ Answer: 1.75

Write your → answer in the boxes.

Grid in → your answer.

Answer: 100

Either position is acceptable

- Note that rounding to .273 is acceptable, because you are using the full grid, but you would receive **no credit** for .3 or .27, because these answers are less accurate.

---

9. If $7a = (91)(13)$, what is the value of $\sqrt{a}$?

10. If a, b, and c are positive numbers with $a = \dfrac{b}{c^2}$, what is the value of c when $a = 44$ and $b = 275$?

11. What is the area of a right triangle whose hypotenuse is 25 and one of whose legs is 15?

GO ON TO THE NEXT PAGE

7

12. If the average (arithmetic mean) of a, b, c, d, and e is 95, and the average of a, b, and e is 100, what is the average of c and d?

13. If $x + y = 10$ and $x - y = 11$, what is the value of $x^2 - y^2$?

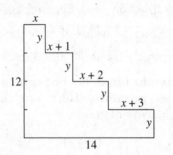

14. In the figure above, all of the line segments meet to form right angles. What is the perimeter of the figure?

15. If $a = 2b$, $3b = 4c$, and $5c = 6d$, what is the ratio of a to d?

16. In 1980, Elaine was 8 times as old as Adam, and Judy was 3 times as old as Adam. Elaine is 20 years older than Judy. How old was Adam in 1988?

17. Jessica created a sequence of five numbers. She chose a number for the first term and got each successive term by using the following rule: alternately add 6 to the preceding term and double the preceding term. The second term of Jessica's sequence was 6 more than the first, the third term was double the second, the fourth term was 6 more than the third, and the fifth term was double the fourth. If the fifth number was 1996, what number did Jessica choose for the first term?

18. Two circular tables have diameters of 35 inches and 25 inches, respectively. The area of the larger table is what percent <u>more</u> than the area of the smaller table? (Grid in your answer without a percent sign.)

YOU MAY GO BACK AND REVIEW THIS SECTION IN THE REMAINING TIME, BUT DO NOT WORK IN ANY OTHER SECTION UNTIL TOLD TO DO SO.

STOP

8 8 8 8 8 8 8 8 8 8 8

SECTION 8 | Time—20 Minutes 19 Questions | Select the best answer to each of the following questions; then blacken the appropriate space on your answer sheet.

Each of the following sentences contains one or two blanks; each blank indicates that a word or set of words has been left out. Below the sentence are five words or phrases, lettered A through E. Select the word or set of words that best completes the sentence.

Example:

Fame is ----; today's rising star is all too soon tomorrow's washed-up has-been.

(A) rewarding (B) gradual
(C) essential (D) spontaneous
(E) transitory

Ⓐ Ⓑ Ⓒ Ⓓ ●

1. In apologizing to the uncredited photographer, the editor said that he ---- that this ---- use of copyrighted photographs had taken place.

(A) deplored..legitimate
(B) conceded..inevitable
(C) regretted..unauthorized
(D) admitted..warranted
(E) acknowledged..appropriate

2. The herb Chinese parsley is an example of what we mean by an acquired taste: Westerners who originally ---- it eventually come to ---- its flavor in Oriental foods.

(A) relish..enjoy
(B) dislike..welcome
(C) savor..abhor
(D) ignore..detest
(E) discern..recognize

3. Because he was ---- in the performance of his duties, his employers could not ---- his work.

(A) derelict..quarrel over
(B) dilatory..grumble at
(C) undisciplined..object to
(D) assiduous..complain about
(E) mandatory..count on

4. British ---- contemporary art has been an obstacle even for modern artists now revered as great, such as Francis Bacon and Lucian Freud, who were ---- for years before winning acceptance.

(A) veneration of..eulogized
(B) indifference to..dismissed
(C) disdain for..lauded
(D) ignorance of..studied
(E) intolerance of..vindicated

5. The biochemistry instructor urged that we take particular care of the ---- chemicals to prevent their evaporation.

(A) insoluble (B) superficial (C) extraneous
(D) volatile (E) insipid

6. It is said that the custom of shaking hands originated when primitive men held out empty hands to indicate that they had no ---- weapons and were thus ---- disposed.

(A) lethal..clearly
(B) concealed..amicably
(C) hidden..harmfully
(D) murderous..ill
(E) secret..finally

GO ON TO THE NEXT PAGE

The questions that follow the next two passages relate to the content of both, and to their relationship. The correct response may be stated outright in the passage or merely suggested.

Questions 7–19 are based on the following passages.

The following passages are adapted from essays on detective fiction, often known as mysteries. In the first, the poet W. H. Auden discusses the detective story's magic formula. In the second, historian Robin Winks assesses what we do when we read mysteries.

Passage 1

The most curious fact about the detective story is that it makes its greatest appeal precisely to those classes of people who are most immune to
Line other forms of daydream literature. The typical
(5) detective story addict is a doctor or clergyman or scientist or artist, i.e., a fairly successful professional man with intellectual interests and well-read in his own field, who could never stomach the *Saturday Evening Post* or *True Confessions* or
(10) movie magazines or comics.

It is sometimes said that detective stories are read by respectable law-abiding citizens in order to gratify in fantasy the violent or murderous wishes they dare not, or are ashamed to, translate
(15) into action. This may be true for readers of thrillers (which I rarely enjoy), but it is quite false for the reader of detective stories. On the contrary, the magical satisfaction the latter provide (which makes them escape literature, not works
(20) of art) is the illusion of being dissociated from the murderer.

The magic formula is an innocence which is discovered to contain guilt; then a suspicion of being the guilty one; and finally a real innocence
(25) from which the guilty other has been expelled, a cure effected, not by me or my neighbors, but by the miraculous intervention of a genius from outside who removes guilt by giving knowledge of guilt. (The detective story subscribes, in fact, to
(30) the Socratic daydream: "Sin is ignorance.")

If one thinks of a work of art which deals with murder, *Crime and Punishment* for example, its effect on the reader is to compel an identification with the murderer which he would prefer not to
(35) recognize. The identification of fantasy is always an attempt to avoid one's own suffering: the identification of art is a compelled sharing in the suffering of another. Kafka's *The Trial* is another instructive example of the difference between a
(40) work of art and the detective story. In the latter it is certain that a crime has been committed and, temporarily, uncertain to whom guilt should be attached; as soon as this is known, the innocence of everyone else is certain. (Should it turn out that

(45) after all no crime has been committed, then all would be innocent.) In *The Trial*, on the other hand, it is the guilt that is certain and the crime that is uncertain; the aim of the hero's investigation is not to prove his innocence (which would
(50) be impossible for he knows he is guilty), but to discover what, if anything, he has done to make himself guilty. K, the hero, is, in fact, a portrait of the kind of person who reads detective stories for escape.

(55) The fantasy, then, which the detective story addict indulges is the fantasy of being restored to the Garden of Eden, to a state of innocence, where he may know love as love and not as the law. The driving force behind this daydream is
(60) the feeling of guilt, the cause of which is unknown to the dreamer. The fantasy of escape is the same, whether one explains the guilt in Christian, Freudian, or any other terms. One's way of trying to face the reality, on the other
(65) hand, will, of course, depend very much on one's creed.

Passage 2

Detective fiction creates for us an anonymity; within it, we may constitute the last law on earth, making decisions (to be "proved" right or wrong)
(70) as we go, responsible for them, tricked, disappointed, triumphant, joyful, honest as to our mistakes, setting the record straight. As we make leaps of faith between evidence and decision in our daily lives—to board this bus, to choose that
(75) doctor, to add these pounds—so we make leaps of faith between evidence and conclusion, through the public historiography and the private autobiography that we read. We learn how to define evidence, to use up our intellectual shoe leather in
(80) pursuit of an operable truth, to take joy from the receding horizon and pleasure in the discovery that the answer has not yet been found, that there is more work to be done. We learn that what people believe to be true is as important as the objec-
(85) tive truth defined by the researcher/detective. In Marlowe and Archer we meet people who have no *use* for their conclusions, no desire for vengeance, who know that society will supply the uses while they may engage in the happy ambigu-
(90) ity of simply finding the facts, which, inert, take on life when embedded in a context of cause and effect.

8   8 8 8 8 8 8 8 8 8   8

Ultimately one reads detective fiction because
it involves judgments—judgments made, passed
(95) upon, tested. In raising questions about purpose, it
raises questions about cause and effect. In the
end, like history, such fiction appears to, and
occasionally does, decode the environment;
appears to and occasionally does tell one what to
(100) do; appears to and occasionally does set the
record straight. Setting the record straight ought
to matter. Detective fiction, in its high seriousness, is a bit like a religion, in pursuit of truths
best left examined at a distance. As with all fine
(105) literature, history, philosophy, as with the written
word wherever employed creatively, it can lead
us to laughter in our frustration, to joy in our
experience, and to tolerance for our complexities.
It begins as Hawthorne so often does, and as the
(110) best of historians do, with a personal word, diffident, apparently modest, in search of the subject
by asking, What is the question? It ends, as historians who have completed their journey often do,
with an authoritative tone, the complex explained,
(115) the mystery revealed.

7. The word "curious" in line 1 means

   (A) inquisitive
   (B) unusual
   (C) sensitive
   (D) prying
   (E) salutary

8. The opening paragraph of Passage 1 suggests that
   the author would consider *True Confessions* and
   movie magazines to be

   (A) sources of factual data about society
   (B) worthwhile contemporary periodicals
   (C) standard forms of escapist literature
   (D) the typical literary fare of professionals
   (E) less addictive than detective fiction

9. The author of Passage 1 asserts that readers of detective fiction can most accurately be described as

   (A) believers in the creed of art for art's sake
   (B) people bent on satisfying an unconscious thirst
       for blood
   (C) dreamers unable to face the monotony of
       everyday reality
   (D) persons seeking momentary release from a
       vague sense of guilt
   (E) idealists drawn to the comforts of organized
       religion

10. The word "translate" in line 14 means

    (A) decipher
    (B) move
    (C) explain
    (D) convey
    (E) convert

11. Which best describes what the author is doing in
    citing the example of Kafka's *The Trial* (lines
    46–54)?

    (A) Dramatizing the plot of a typical detective
        story
    (B) Analyzing its distinctive qualities as a work of
        art
    (C) Refuting a common opinion about readers of
        detective fiction
    (D) Demonstrating the genius of the outside inves-
        tigator
    (E) Discrediting a theory about Kafka's narrative

12. In Passage 1, the author's attitude toward detective
    fiction can best be described as one of

    (A) fastidious distaste
    (B) open skepticism
    (C) profound veneration
    (D) aloof indifference
    (E) genuine appreciation

13. In context, "use up our intellectual shoe leather"
    (line 79) suggests that readers of mysteries

    (A) suffer in the course of arriving at the truth
    (B) are attempting to escape from overly strenuous
        intellectual pursuits
    (C) work hard mentally, much as detectives do
        physically
    (D) have only a limited supply of time to devote to
        detective fiction
    (E) grow hardened to crime in the course of their
        reading

14. In lines 78–83, the author of Passage 2 finds the
    prospect of additional work

    (A) burdensome   (B) unexpected   (C) unfounded
     (D) delightful   (E) deceptive

GO ON TO THE NEXT PAGE

8   8 8 8 8 8 8 8 8 8   8

15. Passage 2 suggests that Marlowe and Archer are most likely

   (A) murder victims
   (B) fictional detectives
   (C) prominent novelists
   (D) literary scholars
   (E) rival theorists

16. As used in line 106, the word "employed" most nearly means

   (A) hired   (B) used   (C) commissioned
    (D) remunerated   (E) labored

17. According to lines 109–112, the detective story starts by

   (A) setting the record straight
   (B) simplifying the difficulties of the case
   (C) humanizing the investigating detective
   (D) introducing the characters under suspicion
   (E) defining the problem to be solved

18. Both passages are primarily concerned with the question of

   (A) whether detective stories gratify a taste for violence
   (B) why people enjoy reading detective fiction
   (C) how detectives arrive at their conclusions
   (D) why some people resist the appeal of escapist literature
   (E) whether detective stories can be considered works of art

19. The author of Passage 1 would most likely react to the characterization of detective fiction presented in lines 93–115 by pointing out that

   (A) reading detective fiction is an escape, not a highly serious pursuit
   (B) other analyses have shown the deficiencies of this characterization
   (C) this characterization reflects the author's lack of taste
   (D) this characterization is neither original nor objective
   (E) the realities of the publishing trade justify this characterization

YOU MAY GO BACK AND REVIEW THIS SECTION IN THE REMAINING TIME, BUT DO NOT WORK IN ANY OTHER SECTION UNTIL TOLD TO DO SO.

STOP

9 9 9 9 9 9 9

9

SECTION 9

Time—20 Minutes
16 Questions

For each problem in this section determine which of the five choices is correct and blacken the corresponding choice on your answer sheet. You may use any blank space on the page for your work.

Notes:

- You may use a calculator whenever you think it will be helpful.
- Only real numbers are used. No question or answer on this test involves a complex or imaginary number.
- Use the diagrams provided to help you solve the problems. Unless you see the words "Note: Figure not drawn to scale" under a diagram, it has been drawn as accurately as possible. Unless it is stated that a figure is three-dimensional, you may assume it lies in a plane.
- For any function f, the domain, unless specifically restricted, is the set of all real numbers for which $f(x)$ is also a real number.

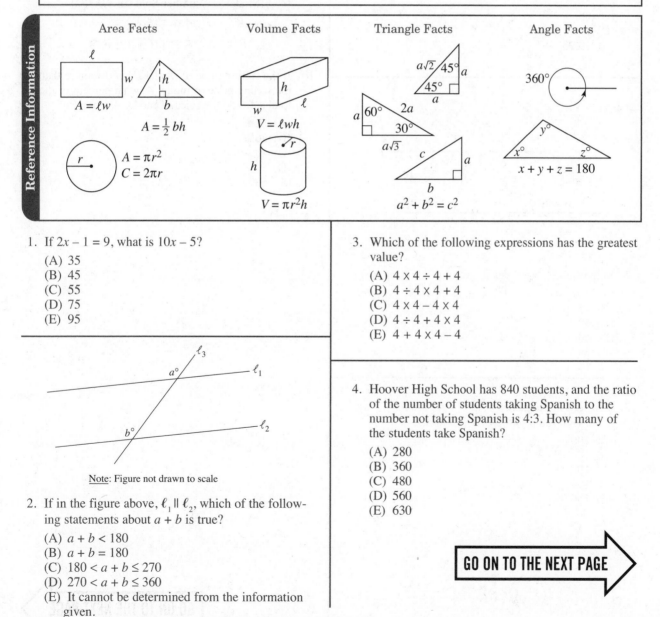

Reference Information

Area Facts — $A = \ell w$, $A = \frac{1}{2} bh$, $A = \pi r^2$, $C = 2\pi r$

Volume Facts — $V = \ell w h$, $V = \pi r^2 h$

Triangle Facts

Angle Facts — $x + y + z = 180$, $a^2 + b^2 = c^2$

1. If $2x - 1 = 9$, what is $10x - 5$?

   (A) 35
   (B) 45
   (C) 55
   (D) 75
   (E) 95

Note: Figure not drawn to scale

2. If in the figure above, $\ell_1 \parallel \ell_2$, which of the following statements about $a + b$ is true?

   (A) $a + b < 180$
   (B) $a + b = 180$
   (C) $180 < a + b \le 270$
   (D) $270 < a + b \le 360$
   (E) It cannot be determined from the information given.

3. Which of the following expressions has the greatest value?

   (A) $4 \times 4 \div 4 + 4$
   (B) $4 \div 4 \times 4 + 4$
   (C) $4 \times 4 - 4 \times 4$
   (D) $4 \div 4 + 4 \times 4$
   (E) $4 + 4 \times 4 - 4$

4. Hoover High School has 840 students, and the ratio of the number of students taking Spanish to the number not taking Spanish is 4:3. How many of the students take Spanish?

   (A) 280
   (B) 360
   (C) 480
   (D) 560
   (E) 630

GO ON TO THE NEXT PAGE

9 9 9 9 9 9 9

5. Which of the following CANNOT be expressed as the sum of three consecutive integers?

 (A) 18
 (B) 24
 (C) 28
 (D) 33
 (E) 36

6. If $\left(a^{\frac{1}{2}}\right)^3 \left(a^5\right)^{\frac{1}{2}} = a^n$, then $n =$

 (A) 2
 (B) 4
 (C) 8
 (D) 9
 (E) 19.25

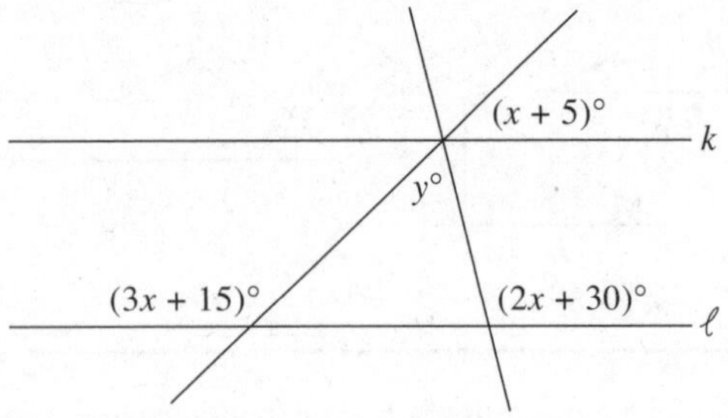

7. In the figure above, if $k \parallel \ell$, what is the value of y?

 (A) 40
 (B) 45
 (C) 50
 (D) 60
 (E) 65

8. Consider the sequence 1, 2, 3, 1, 2, 3, 1, 2, 3, ... What is the sum of the first 100 terms?

 (A) 100
 (B) 180
 (C) 198
 (D) 199
 (E) 200

9. If, for any numbers a and b, $a \circledcirc b$ represents the average (arithmetic mean) of a and b, which of the following MUST be true?

 I. $a \circledcirc (a \circledcirc a) = a$

 II. $a \circledcirc b = b \circledcirc a$

 III. $a \circledcirc (b \circledcirc c) = (a \circledcirc b) \circledcirc c$

 (A) I only
 (B) II only
 (C) I and II only
 (D) II and III only
 (E) I, II, and III

Model	Number Sold (in 1,000's)
A	⊕⊕⊕⊕⊕⊕⊕⊕⊕
B	⊕⊕⊕⊕⊕⊕⊕⊕⊕⊕

10. If the selling price of model B is 60% more than the selling price of model A, what percent of the total sales do the sales of model A represent?

 (A) 25%
 (B) 36%
 (C) 40%
 (D) 50%
 (E) 60%

GO ON TO THE NEXT PAGE ⟶

9   9   9   9   9   9   9

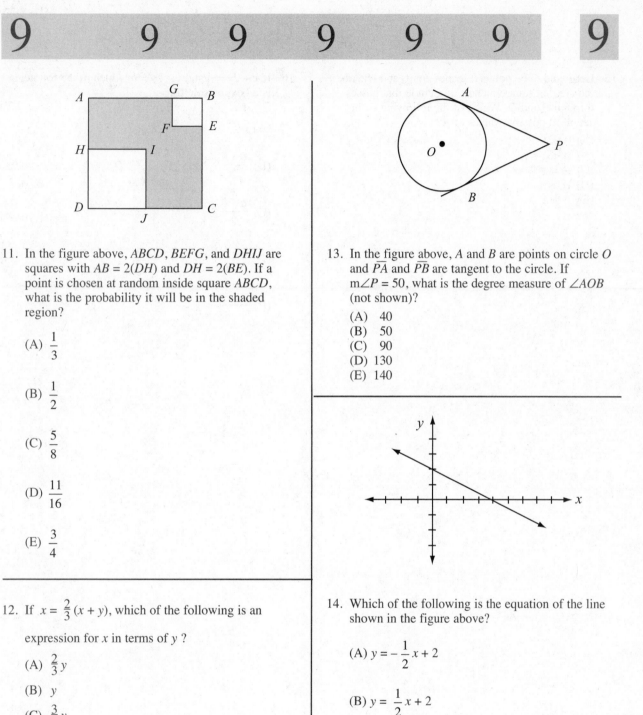

11. In the figure above, *ABCD*, *BEFG*, and *DHIJ* are squares with $AB = 2(DH)$ and $DH = 2(BE)$. If a point is chosen at random inside square *ABCD*, what is the probability it will be in the shaded region?

(A) $\dfrac{1}{3}$

(B) $\dfrac{1}{2}$

(C) $\dfrac{5}{8}$

(D) $\dfrac{11}{16}$

(E) $\dfrac{3}{4}$

12. If $x = \dfrac{2}{3}(x + y)$, which of the following is an expression for *x* in terms of *y* ?

(A) $\dfrac{2}{3}y$

(B) y

(C) $\dfrac{3}{2}y$

(D) $2y$

(E) $3y$

13. In the figure above, *A* and *B* are points on circle *O* and $\overline{PA}$ and $\overline{PB}$ are tangent to the circle. If $m\angle P = 50$, what is the degree measure of $\angle AOB$ (not shown)?

(A) 40
(B) 50
(C) 90
(D) 130
(E) 140

14. Which of the following is the equation of the line shown in the figure above?

(A) $y = -\dfrac{1}{2}x + 2$

(B) $y = \dfrac{1}{2}x + 2$

(C) $y = -\dfrac{1}{2}x + 4$

(D) $y = 2x + 4$

(E) $y = -2x + 4$

GO ON TO THE NEXT PAGE

9   9   9   9   9   9   9

15. Let P and Q be points 2 inches apart, and let A be the area, in square inches, of a circle that passes through P and Q. Which of the following is the set of all possible values of A?

    (A) $0 < A$
    (B) $0 < A \leq \pi$
    (C) $A = \pi$
    (D) $A > \pi$
    (E) $A \geq \pi$

16. If $x + 2y = a$ and $x - 2y = b$, which of the following is an expression for xy?

    (A) ab

    (B) $\dfrac{a+b}{2}$

    (C) $\dfrac{a-b}{2}$

    (D) $\dfrac{a^2 - b^2}{4}$

    (E) $\dfrac{a^2 - b^2}{8}$

YOU MAY GO BACK AND REVIEW THIS SECTION IN THE REMAINING TIME, BUT DO NOT WORK IN ANY OTHER SECTION UNTIL TOLD TO DO SO.

S T O P

10   10   10   10   10   10   10

SECTION 10   **Time—10 Minutes**
14 Questions   For each of the following questions, select the best answer from the choices provided and fill in the appropriate circle on the answer sheet.

Some or all parts of the following sentences are underlined. The first answer choice, (A), simply repeats the underlined part of the sentence. The other four choices present four alternative ways to phrase the underlined part. Select the answer that produces the most effective sentence, one that is clear and exact, and blacken the appropriate space on your answer sheet. In selecting your choice, be sure that it is standard written English, and that it expresses the meaning of the original sentence.

Example:
The first biography of author Eudora Welty came out in 1998 and she was 89 years old at the time.

(A) and she was 89 years old at the time
(B) at the time when she was 89
(C) upon becoming an 89 year old
(D) when she was 89
(E) at the age of 89 years old

Ⓐ Ⓑ Ⓒ ● Ⓔ

1. In the four chapels of Santa Croce, Giotto painted frescoes and they portrayed the lives of the saints.

   (A) frescoes and they portrayed
   (B) frescoes, being portrayals of
   (C) frescoes, they portrayed
   (D) frescoes that portrayed
   (E) frescoes because they portrayed

2. The debate coach, together with the members of the winning team, is traveling to Washington for the awards ceremony.

   (A) together with the members of the winning team, is traveling
   (B) along with the members of the winning team, they are traveling
   (C) along with the members of the winning team, are traveling
   (D) together with the members of the winning team, are traveling
   (E) together with the members of the winning team, are to travel

3. By establishing strict rules of hygiene in maternity wards, Ignaz Semmelweis saved many women from dying of childbed fever, this was a fate that many expectant mothers feared.

   (A) fever, this was a fate that many expectant mothers feared
   (B) fever, since many expectant mothers feared this was their fate
   (C) fever, it was a fate of which many expectant mothers were afraid
   (D) fever, because many expectant mothers feared this fate
   (E) fever, a fate that many expectant mothers feared

4. Veterans of World War II received greater support from the public than the Korean and Vietnam Wars.

   (A) than
   (B) than did
   (C) than did veterans of
   (D) than from the support of
   (E) than from the

5. Nowadays airport security guards have the right to search people's bags who act in a suspicious manner.

   (A) people's bags who act
   (B) persons' bags who act
   (C) the bags of people who act
   (D) the bags of persons that act
   (E) personal bags which act

6. The clipper ship was the fastest ocean-going vessel of its time; it ruled the waves only briefly, however, before the faster and more reliable steamship took its place.

   (A) time; it ruled the waves only briefly, however,
   (B) time, for it ruled the waves only briefly
   (C) time; however, ruling the waves only briefly
   (D) time, having ruled the waves only briefly, however,
   (E) time, but was ruling the waves only briefly, however,

GO ON TO THE NEXT PAGE

10   10   10   10   10   10   10

7. The real estate reporter maintained that housing prices in San Francisco were <u>higher than any other city</u> in the country.

   (A) higher than any other city
   (B) higher than every other city
   (C) the highest of those of any other city
   (D) higher than those in any other city
   (E) higher than any city

8. During the eighteenth century, inoculations against smallpox became increasingly popular among the English upper classes <u>although to the lower classes it</u> remained mysterious and therefore threatening.

   (A) although to the lower classes it
   (B) because to the lower classes it
   (C) although to the lower classes such inoculations
   (D) however, to the lower classes the inoculations
   (E) although among the lower classes it

9. With the rift between the two sides apparently widening, analysts said that they <u>considered the likelihood of a merger between the two corpora-tions to be negligible</u>.

   (A) considered the likelihood of a merger between the two corporations to be negligible
   (B) considered it was likely a merger between the two corporations being negligible
   (C) considered the two corporations' merger likely to be negligible
   (D) considered the likelihood of the two corporations merging between them to have been negligible
   (E) considered between the two corporations such a merger to be negligible

10. <u>Gold was discovered at Sutter's Mill in 1848, and</u> the prospectors who flocked to the gold fields are known not as the forty-eighters but as the forty-niners.

    (A) Gold was discovered at Sutter's Mill in 1848, and
    (B) They discovered gold at Sutter's Mill in 1848, and
    (C) Although gold was discovered at Sutter's Mill in 1848,
    (D) Upon the discovery of gold at Sutter's Mill in 1848,
    (E) Because gold was discovered at Sutter's Mill in 1848,

11. Once a leading light of the Harlem Renaissance, <u>the revived interest in African-American literary pioneers rescued Zora Neale Hurston from decades of obscurity</u>.

    (A) the revived interest in African-American liter-ary pioneers rescued Zora Neale Hurston from decades of obscurity
    (B) through the revived interest in African-American literary pioneers, Zora Neale Hurston was rescued from decades of obscurity
    (C) Zora Neale Hurston's rescue from decades of literary obscurity was due to the revived interest in African-American literary pioneers
    (D) Zora Neale Hurston was rescued from decades of literary obscurity by the revived interest in African-American literary pioneers
    (E) Zora Neale Hurston was rescued from decades of literary obscurity by reviving the interest in African-American literary pioneers

12. The historians of geography and cartography seem more interested in their maps than in the <u>explorers who went into the field, often at great risk, to get the information that these maps contain</u>.

    (A) explorers who went into the field, often at great risk, to get the information that these maps contain
    (B) explorers that went into the field, often at great risk, to get the information these maps containing
    (C) explorers going into the field, often greatly risking, and they got the information that these maps contain
    (D) explorers who went into the field to get the information that these maps often contain at great risk
    (E) explorers often at great risk that were the ones who went into the field to get the information contained in these maps

10   10   10   10   10   10   10

13. Employment statistics indicate that the percentage of <u>workers who found jobs in the fall quarter is lower than the spring</u>.

   (A) workers who found jobs in the fall quarter is lower than the spring
   (B) workers that found jobs in the fall quarter is lower than the percentage in the spring
   (C) workers who found jobs in the fall quarter is lower than the equivalent percentage in the spring
   (D) workers who had found jobs in the fall quarter is lower than the spring
   (E) workers finding jobs in the fall quarter is lower than the spring quarter

14. <u>Most of the free libraries founded by Andrew Carnegie were located in communities where there were hardly no other cultural institutions</u> available to members of the working classes.

   (A) Most of the free libraries founded by Andrew Carnegie were located in communities where there were hardly no other cultural institutions
   (B) Of the free libraries founded by Andrew Carnegie, most were located in communities in which there were hardly no other cultural institutions
   (C) Most free libraries that were founded by Andrew Carnegie he located in communities where hardly any other cultural institutions were
   (D) Andrew Carnegie founded mostly free libraries located in communities where there were hardly any other cultural institutions
   (E) Most of the free libraries founded by Andrew Carnegie were located in communities where there were hardly any other cultural institutions

YOU MAY GO BACK AND REVIEW THIS SECTION IN THE REMAINING TIME, BUT DO NOT WORK IN ANY OTHER SECTION UNTIL TOLD TO DO SO.

STOP

Answer Key

Note: The letters in brackets following the Mathematical Reasoning answers refer to the sections of Chapter 9 in which you can find the information you need to answer the questions. For example, **1. C [E]** means that the answer to question 1 is C, and that the solution requires information found in Section 9-E: Averages.

Section 2   Critical Reading

1. D	6. E	11. C	16. D	21. E
2. E	7. B	12. E	17. E	22. A
3. C	8. D	13. C	18. B	23. C
4. D	9. C	14. A	19. B	24. D
5. D	10. E	15. C	20. A	

Section 3   Mathematical Reasoning

1. C [G]	5. B [I]	9. C [C]	13. E [D, P]	17. B [M]
2. D [I]	6. B [I]	10. D [A]	14. A [K]	18. D [P]
3. E [C]	7. C [O]	11. C [K]	15. B [J, K]	19. A [H]
4. E [A]	8. B [A]	12. E [A]	16. A [D]	20. C [E]

Section 4   Writing Skills

1. D	8. E	15. B	22. D	29. E
2. E	9. C	16. C	23. E	30. C
3. B	10. E	17. C	24. E	31. B
4. E	11. A	18. C	25. C	32. E
5. C	12. B	19. B	26. D	33. A
6. B	13. A	20. B	27. A	34. B
7. A	14. B	21. C	28. C	35. D

Section 5

On this test, Section 5 was the experimental section. It could have been an extra critical reading, mathematics, or writing skills section. Remember: on the SAT you take, the experimental section may be any section from 2 to 7.

Section 6   Critical Reading

1. E	6. D	11. B	16. D	21. C
2. C	7. C	12. A	17. D	22. A
3. C	8. B	13. E	18. B	23. B
4. D	9. C	14. A	19. C	24. E
5. E	10. A	15. A	20. B	

Section 7 Mathematical Reasoning

Multiple-Choice Questions

1. **C [A]**
2. **D [G]**
3. **B [A]**
4. **C [G]**
5. **B [K, G]**
6. **D [L]**
7. **C [K, N]**
8. **A [R]**

Grid-in Questions

9. **[A]** `13`

10. **[A]** `2.5`   *or 5/2*

11. **[J]** `150`

12. **[E]** `87.5`

13. **[F, G]** `110`

14. **[K]** `52`

15. **[D]** `16/5`   *or 3.2*

16. **[H]** `12`

17. **[F, P]** `490`

18. **[C, L]** `96`

Section 8   Critical Reading

1. **C**	5. **D**	9. **D**	13. **C**	17. **E**
2. **B**	6. **B**	10. **E**	14. **D**	18. **B**
3. **D**	7. **B**	11. **B**	15. **B**	19. **A**
4. **B**	8. **C**	12. **E**	16. **B**	

Section 9   Mathematical Reasoning

1. **B [G]**	5. **C [A]**	9. **C [E]**	13. **D [L]**
2. **E [I]**	6. **B [A]**	10. **B [Q, C]**	14. **A [N]**
3. **D [A]**	7. **E [I, G]**	11. **D [K, O]**	15. **E [L]**
4. **C [D]**	8. **D [P]**	12. **D [G]**	16. **E [G]**

Section 10   Writing Skills

1. **D**	4. **C**	7. **D**	10. **C**	13. **C**
2. **A**	5. **C**	8. **C**	11. **D**	14. **E**
3. **E**	6. **A**	9. **A**	12. **A**	

Score Your Own SAT Essay

Use this table as you rate your performance on the essay-writing section of this Model Test. Circle the phrase that most accurately describes your work. Enter the numbers in the scoring chart below. Add the numbers together and divide by 6 to determine your total score. The higher your total score, the better you are likely to do on the essay section of the SAT.

Note that on the actual SAT two readers will rate your essay; your essay score will be the sum of their two ratings and could range from 12 (highest) to 2 (lowest). Also, they will grade your essay holistically, rating it on the basis of their overall impression of its effectiveness. They will *not* analyze it piece by piece, giving separate grades for grammar, vocabulary level, and so on. Therefore, you cannot expect the score you give yourself on this Model Test to predict your eventual score on the SAT with any great degree of accuracy. Use this scoring guide instead to help you assess your writing strengths and weaknesses, so that you can decide which areas to focus on as you prepare for the SAT.

Like most people, you may find it difficult to rate your own writing objectively. Ask a teacher or fellow student to score your essay as well. With his or her help you should gain added insights into writing your 25-minute essay.

	6	5	4	3	2	1
POSITION ON THE TOPIC	Clear, convincing, & insightful	Fundamentally clear & coherent	Fairly clear & coherent	Insufficiently clear	Largely unclear	Extremely unclear
ORGANIZATION OF EVIDENCE	Well organized, with strong, relevant examples	Generally well organized, with apt examples	Adequately organized, with some examples	Sketchily developed, with weak examples	Lacking focus and evidence	Unfocused and disorganized
SENTENCE STRUCTURE	Varied, appealing sentences	Reasonably varied sentences	Some variety in sentences	Little variety in sentences	Errors in sentence structure	Severe errors in sentence structure
LEVEL OF VOCABULARY	Mature & apt word choice	Competent word choice	Adequate word choice	Inappropriate or weak vocabulary	Highly limited vocabulary	Rudimentary
GRAMMAR AND USAGE	Almost entirely free of errors	Relatively free of errors	Some technical errors	Minor errors, and some major ones	Numerous major errors	Extensive severe errors
OVERALL EFFECT	Outstanding	Effective	Adequately competent	Inadequate, but shows some potential	Seriously flawed	Fundamentally deficient

Self-Scoring Chart

For each of the following categories, rate the essay from 1 (lowest) to 6 (highest)

Position on the Topic _____

Organization of Evidence _____

Sentence Structure _____

Level of Vocabulary _____

Grammar and Usage _____

Overall Effect _____

TOTAL _____

(To get a score, divide the total by 6) _____

Scoring Chart (Second Reader)

For each of the following categories, rate the essay from 1 (lowest) to 6 (highest)

Position on the Topic _____

Organization of Evidence _____

Sentence Structure _____

Level of Vocabulary _____

Grammar and Usage _____

Overall Effect _____

TOTAL _____

(To get a score, divide the total by 6) _____

Calculate Your Raw Score
Critical Reading

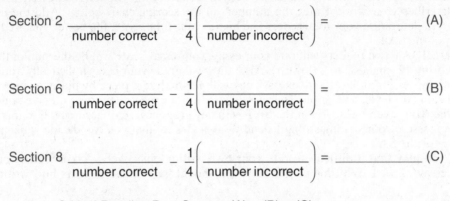

Section 2 $\underset{\text{number correct}}{\underline{\hspace{3cm}}} - \frac{1}{4}\left(\underset{\text{number incorrect}}{\underline{\hspace{3cm}}}\right) = \underline{\hspace{2cm}}$ (A)

Section 6 $\underset{\text{number correct}}{\underline{\hspace{3cm}}} - \frac{1}{4}\left(\underset{\text{number incorrect}}{\underline{\hspace{3cm}}}\right) = \underline{\hspace{2cm}}$ (B)

Section 8 $\underset{\text{number correct}}{\underline{\hspace{3cm}}} - \frac{1}{4}\left(\underset{\text{number incorrect}}{\underline{\hspace{3cm}}}\right) = \underline{\hspace{2cm}}$ (C)

Critical Reading Raw Score = (A) + (B) + (C) = $\underline{\hspace{3cm}}$

Mathematical Reasoning

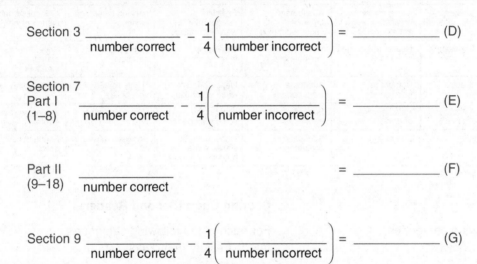

Section 3 $\underset{\text{number correct}}{\underline{\hspace{3cm}}} - \frac{1}{4}\left(\underset{\text{number incorrect}}{\underline{\hspace{3cm}}}\right) = \underline{\hspace{2cm}}$ (D)

Section 7
Part I
(1–8) $\underset{\text{number correct}}{\underline{\hspace{3cm}}} - \frac{1}{4}\left(\underset{\text{number incorrect}}{\underline{\hspace{3cm}}}\right) = \underline{\hspace{2cm}}$ (E)

Part II
(9–18) $\underset{\text{number correct}}{\underline{\hspace{3cm}}} = \underline{\hspace{2cm}}$ (F)

Section 9 $\underset{\text{number correct}}{\underline{\hspace{3cm}}} - \frac{1}{4}\left(\underset{\text{number incorrect}}{\underline{\hspace{3cm}}}\right) = \underline{\hspace{2cm}}$ (G)

Mathematical Reasoning Raw Score = (D) + (E) + (F) + (G) = $\underline{\hspace{3cm}}$

Writing Skills

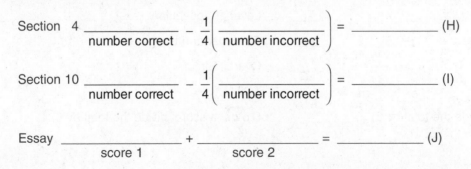

Section 4 $\underset{\text{number correct}}{\underline{\hspace{3cm}}} - \frac{1}{4}\left(\underset{\text{number incorrect}}{\underline{\hspace{3cm}}}\right) = \underline{\hspace{2cm}}$ (H)

Section 10 $\underset{\text{number correct}}{\underline{\hspace{3cm}}} - \frac{1}{4}\left(\underset{\text{number incorrect}}{\underline{\hspace{3cm}}}\right) = \underline{\hspace{2cm}}$ (I)

Essay $\underset{\text{score 1}}{\underline{\hspace{3cm}}} + \underset{\text{score 2}}{\underline{\hspace{3cm}}} = \underline{\hspace{2cm}}$ (J)

Writing Skills Raw Score = H + I (J is a separate subscore)

Evaluate Your Performance

Scaled Score	Critical Reading Raw Score	Mathematical Reasoning Raw Score	Writing Skills Raw Score
700–800	58–67	48–54	43–49
650–690	52–57	43–47	39–42
600–640	45–51	36–42	35–38
550–590	38–44	30–35	30–34
500–540	30–37	24–29	25–29
450–490	22–29	18–23	19–24
400–440	14–21	12–17	14–18
300–390	3–13	5–11	5–13
200–290	less than 3	less than 5	less than 5

Identify Your Weaknesses

Critical Reading

Question Type	Question Numbers			Chapter to Study
	Section 2	Section 6	Section 8	
Sentence Completion	1, 2, 3, 4, 5, 6, 7, 8	1, 2, 3, 4, 5	1, 2, 3, 4, 5, 6	Chapter 1
Critical Reading	9, 10, 11, 12, 13, 14, 15, 16, 17, 18, 19, 20, 21, 22, 23, 24	6, 7, 8, 9, 10, 11, 12, 13, 14, 15, 16, 17, 18, 19, 20, 21, 22, 23, 24	7, 8, 9, 10, 11, 12, 13, 14, 15, 16, 17, 18, 19	Chapter 2

Test 1

Identify Your Weaknesses

Mathematical Reasoning

Section in Chapter 9		Question Numbers			Pages to Study
		Section 3	Section 7	Section 9	
A	Basic Arithmetic Concepts	4, 8, 10, 12	1, 3, 9, 10	3, 5, 6	410–431
B	Fractions and Decimals	12, 15			432–449
C	Percents	3, 9	18	10	450–460
D	Ratios and Proportions	13, 16	15	4	461–472
E	Averages	20	12	9	473–479
F	Polynomials	10	13, 17		480–488
G	Equations and Inequalities	1	2, 4, 5, 13	1, 7, 12	489–502
H	Word Problems	19	16		503–513
I	Lines and Angles	2, 5, 6		2, 7	514–524
J	Triangles	15	11		525–542
K	Quadrilaterals	11, 14, 15	5, 14	11	543–553
L	Circles		6, 18	13, 15	554–564
M	Solid Geometry	17			565–573
N	Coordinate Geometry		7	14	574–588
O	Counting and Probability	7		11	589–600
P	Logical Reasoning	13, 18	17	8	601–608
Q	Data Interpretation			10	609–618
R	Functions and Their Graphs		8		619–628

Identify Your Weaknesses

Writing Skills

Question Type	Question Numbers		Chapter to Study
	Section 4	Section 10	
Improving Sentences	1, 2, 3, 4, 5, 6, 7, 8, 9, 10, 11	1, 2, 3, 4, 5, 6, 7, 8, 9, 10, 11, 12, 13, 14	Chapter 6
Identifying Sentence Errors	12, 13, 14, 15, 16, 17, 18, 19, 20, 21, 22, 23, 24, 25, 26, 27, 28, 29		Chapter 6
Improving Paragraphs	30, 31, 32, 33, 34, 35		Chapter 6
Essay			Chapter 7

ANSWERS EXPLAINED

Section 2 Critical Reading

1. **D.** Mitchell is optimistic about the future of African-Americans in ballet. However, he is not blindly optimistic. Instead, he is *realistic* about the problems blacks face.
Remember to watch for signal words that link one part of the sentence with another. The use of "Although" in the opening clause sets up a contrast. The missing word must be an antonym for "optimistic."   (Contrast Signal)

2. **E.** *Frustrations* or limitations are by definition not satisfying.
Again, remember to watch for signal words that link one part of the sentence with another. The use of "Despite" in the opening clause sets up a contrast. The missing word must be an antonym for "stirring and satisfying." Note, too, that you are looking for a word with negative associations.   (Contrast Signal)

3. **C.** *Derivative* means unoriginal. Unoriginal work derives from or comes from the work of others. The moviemaker is unoriginal despite his reputation for skill or *expertise*.
The word "sadly" is your clue to look for a negative word to fill in the second blank. Therefore, you can eliminate any word with positive associations.   (Definition)

4. **D.** One crowns a career with a triumph, in this case an *unsurpassable* performance. Remember, before you look at the choices, to read the sentence and think of a word that makes sense; *magnificent, superlative,* and *matchless* come to mind. Note that you are looking for a word with positive associations. Therefore, you can eliminate any word with negative ones. Choices A, B, C, and E all have negative associations. Only Choice D can be correct.   (Examples)

5. **D.** Students of genetics will have to turn or *resort to* respected journals where relevant information is *found*.
Choice A is incorrect. Excellent journals would be unlikely to ignore relevant materials.
Choice B is incorrect. An interested student of genetics would enjoy reading an excellent journal in the field. Such a student would not be likely to suffer through it.
Choice C is incorrect. Pertinent material logically would be represented in an excellent technical journal.
Choice E is incorrect. We would be unlikely to complain about excellent technical journals.   (Argument Pattern)

6. **E.** Rather than alleviating or easing problems, rent control may worsen or *exacerbate* them. The signal words "rather than" indicate that the missing word must be an antonym or near-antonym for "alleviate."

You can immediately eliminate *resolve, diminish* and *minimize,* which make no sense in the context.   (Contrast Signal)

7. **B.** This sentence sets up a contrast between Dickens's image of country dancing and Sharp's. Dickens views country dances as "lively, even *(something)*." In this context, *even* acts as an intensifier: it points up just how *very* lively these country dances could get. The first missing word must be a synonym for *very lively*.
Look at the first word of each answer choice. *Sophisticated, prudish,* and *lewd* are highly unlikely choices as synonyms for *very lively.* You can immediately eliminate Choices A, C, and D. *Enjoyable* also seems an unlikely choice: liveliness, carried to an extreme, does not by definition become more enjoyable. You probably can eliminate Choice E. Only Choice B is left. Could lively dances grow so lively that they might become disorderly, *rowdy* affairs? They could.
Consider the second word in Choice B. Sharp's image of dancing is excessively formal. It is not rowdy. It suggests more *decorum* and propriety than the behavior Dickens described. The correct answer is Choice B.   (Contrast Pattern)

8. **D.** Given treachery on the part of their allies, it is likely that the natives would seek vengeance or *retribution*. It is also likely that they would feel *justified* in doing so.
Test the first word in each answer choice. Betrayed natives who have become bitter would be unlikely to seek *acquiescence* (agreement), *magnanimity* (generosity of spirit; nobility of mind), or *exoneration* (vindication). You can immediately rule out Choices A, B, and E.   (Cause and Effect Pattern)

9. **C.** The outdoor playgrounds where the young athletes work on their game are not sheltered (they play in the heat of the afternoon sun and in the bitter cold of winter). You can eliminate Choice B. With their netless rims and lack of illumination (not to mention proper flooring), these playgrounds clearly are neither professional nor well designed. You can eliminate Choices A and D. Rather than being seldom accessible, the playgrounds are all too accessible: the young players haunt them by day and night. You can eliminate Choice E. Only Choice C is left. It is the correct answer. As basketball facilities go, these playgrounds are clearly *rudimentary* (crude; undeveloped).

10. **E.** The salvation the young players hope for would come "in the form of a contract with the NBA," that is, the National Basketball Association. Young people often look to professional sports as a way out of poverty. The salvation these basketball players dream of is their financial *deliverance*.

11. C. With comic lines such as "even the fleas would desert him for a velocipede," this portrait of the not-so-wily coyote clearly illustrates *humorous exaggeration*.

12. E. In typically exaggerated fashion, Twain claims that the meanest, *most contemptible* creature would look down on the lowly coyote.

13. C. Consider the activities Dillard describes Darwin participating in. He threw marine iguanas into the ocean, just for the sport of it; he went for rides on the backs of giant tortoises, as children today do on visits to the zoo. Thus, Dillard's initial picture of Darwin gives us a sense of his *youthful playfulness*.

14. A. In 1844, Darwin has come to the conclusion that species are *not* immutable (unable to change). He now believes that species do change. This conclusion is the *opposite* of what he originally thought. In other words, he originally viewed species as *unchanging*.
In answering questions about passages containing parenthetical comments, you may find it useful to read the passage *without* the remarks in parentheses. ("I am almost convinced . . . that species are not . . . immutable.") Once you have the basic idea, go back to the parenthetical comments to see how they modify what is being stated.
Note, by the way, the importance of negative words and prefixes here. Darwin says he almost believes that species are *not* immutable. In other words, he almost believes that species *are* mutable, able to evolve or change.

15. C. The observations that led Darwin to formulate the theory of evolution—the records Darwin made of the minute differences among the different types of finch—took place in the Galapagos. Thus, Dillard asserts that *Darwin's theory of evolution* and all it has meant to modern society began right there.

16. D. A single species of finch had been taken and modified to meet different *purposes*, to serve different ends. Again, treat this vocabulary-in-context question as if it were a sentence completion exercise. Go back to the original sentence and substitute each of the different answer choices for the word in quotes.

17. E. To say pssssssh pssssssh pssssssh pssssssh until you run out of breath is an everyday sort of thing: if you kept on breathing out that way, you'd naturally exhaust your supply of oxygen. However, to say it until an island runs out of birds—that's something else again. The idea that an island could run out of birds, that bird after bird after bird could come swooping down from the sky until there were no more birds left anywhere around—this image emphasizes the *overwhelming response of the birds*.

18. B. "Lighting" here means *landing* or coming to rest on a branch.

19. B. As each bird lands or touches down on a branch, the impact rocks the slender tree. It is the *rhythm* made by these repeated impacts that Dillard feels as "a rough pulse from the tree's thin trunk" against her hand.

20. A. Dillard spends one paragraph describing the finches as *drab*, dull creatures. In the next paragraph she shows how they can be differentiated by their distinctive beaks. Thus, her description of the finches chiefly serves to *contrast their overall drabness with their variety in one specific aspect*.

21. E. Short beaks are described as good for nabbing or catching insects. Long beaks are described as good for probing or poking deep into plants. Chisel beaks are described as good for digging grubs out of trees. What do these beaks have in common? They all *enable the birds to reach nourishment*; they have evolved to meet a particular need.

22. A. Since the Galapagos are relatively close to the mainland, some mainland birds might have *ventured* or taken the risk of flying there.

23. C. Strip down the sentence, rephrasing it in its shortest form: "You see . . . on the finches . . . a fluorescent spray of horn." *Horn* here means a hard projection, in this case a bright, shiny one. It is the author's poetic way of referring to *the birds' shiny beaks*.

24. D. Use the process of elimination to find the correct answer to this question.
In the parenthetical comment beginning "In other words" (lines 88–90), the author restates an assertion. Therefore, you can eliminate Choice A.
The author compares an archipelago to an arpeggio. Therefore, you can eliminate Choice B.
The author defines an arpeggio as "a rapid series of distinct but related notes." Therefore, you can eliminate Choice C.
In the parenthetical comment beginning "In other words" (lines 88–90), the author describes a sequence of events. Therefore, you can eliminate Choice E.
Only Choice D is left. It is the correct answer. The author never *refutes or disproves an argument*.

Section 3 Mathematical Reasoning

In each mathematics section, for many problems, an alternative solution, indicated by two asterisks (**), follows the first solution. When this occurs, one of the solutions is the direct mathematical one and the other is based on one of the tactics discussed in Chapter 8 or 9.

1. C. Use the six-step method of TACTIC G1 on the given equation, $5c + 3 = 3c + 5$:
$$5c + 3 = 3c + 5 \Rightarrow 2c + 3 = 5.$$
So, $2c = 2$ and $c = \mathbf{1}$.

**Use TACTIC 5. Backsolve, starting with C.

2. **D.** Since $\triangle ABC$ is an isosceles right triangle, $x = 45$; also, $y = 90$, since it is a corner of square $CDEF$. Therefore, $a + b = 360 - (45 + 90) = 360 - 135 = \mathbf{225}$.

   **Use TACTIC 2: trust the diagram. Clearly, 135 and 180 are too small, and 270 is too large. Guess between 210 and 225.

3. **E.** Since $74\% + 18\% = 92\%$, the \$216 spent on the party represents the other 8% of the money raised. Then
   $$0.08m = 216 \Rightarrow m = 216 \div 0.08 = \mathbf{2700}.$$

4. **E.** Here, $n\,\square\,\dfrac{1}{n} = \sqrt{n\left(\dfrac{1}{n}\right)} = \sqrt{1} = \mathbf{1}$.

   **Use TACTIC 7. Pick an easy-to-use number, say 2. (Note that 1 would *not* be a good choice because then each of the five choices would be 1.)

   Then, $2\,\square\,\dfrac{1}{2} = \sqrt{2\left(\dfrac{1}{2}\right)} = \sqrt{1} = \mathbf{1}$. Only Choice E equals 1 when $n = 2$.

5. **B.** Since vertical angles have the same measure (KEY FACT I4), $c = d$, $d = a$, and $b = a - b \Rightarrow a = 2b$. Therefore, $c = d = a = 2b$. Also, the sum of the measures of all six angles is 360° (KEY FACT I3), so $a + b + c + d + a - b + d = 2a + c + 2d = 360$. Replacing c, d, and a by $2b$ yields $10b = 360 \Rightarrow b = \mathbf{36}$.

6. **B.** Since the two angles, x and y, form a straight angle, $x + y = 180$ (KEY FACT I2). Also, it is given that $x = y + 150$. Therefore, $(y + 150) + y = 180 \Rightarrow 2y + 150 = 180$, and so $2y = 30 \Rightarrow y = \mathbf{15}$.

   **Use TACTIC 5: backsolve. Start with 20, Choice C. If $y = 20$, then $x = 170$, but $20 + 170 = 190$, which is too large. Eliminate C, D, and E, and try A and B. B works.

7. **C.** There is a total of $1 + 2 + 3 + 4 + 5 + 6 = 21$ slips of paper. Since odd numbers are written on $1 + 3 + 5 = 9$ of them, the probability of drawing an odd number is $\dfrac{9}{21} = \dfrac{\mathbf{3}}{\mathbf{7}}$.

8. **B.** The given equation can be written as $a^3 = 3a$. Since a is positive, we can divide each side by a: $a^2 = 3$. There is only **1** positive number that satisfies this equation: $\sqrt{3}$. (Note that 0

and $-\sqrt{3}$ also satisfy the original equation, but neither of these is positive.)

9. **C.** Jose made a 25% profit, so if he bought the painting for x, he sold it for
   $$x + 0.25x = 1.25x = 2000.$$
   So, $x = 2000 \div 1.25 = \mathbf{1600}$.

   **If you get stuck or don't know how to solve this problem, eliminate the absurd answer choices and guess. Selling the painting for \$2000, Jose made a profit, so he bought it for less. Eliminate choices D and E and guess.

10. **D.** Since $\dfrac{10!}{8!} = \dfrac{10 \times 9 \times (8!)}{8!}$, the fraction reduces to $10 \times 9 = 90$.
    Now, evaluate the three choices.
    I: $5! - 4! - 3! = 120 - 24 - 6 = 90$ (true).
    II: $\dfrac{5!}{4!} = 5$ (false).
    III: $15(3!) = 15(6) = 90$ (true).

    I and III only are true.

11. **C.** Use TACTIC 1: draw a diagram and label it. Use the Pythagorean theorem to find d, the length of the diagonal:
    $a^2 + (2a)^2 = d^2 \Rightarrow$
    $a^2 + 4a^2 = d^2 \Rightarrow$
    $5a^2 = d^2 \Rightarrow d = \mathbf{a\sqrt{5}}$.

    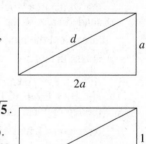

    **Use TACTIC 6. Let $a = 1$. Then use TACTIC 1, and draw the rectangle to scale; that is, let the width be 1 and the length be 2. Now use TACTIC 2: trust your eyes. Clearly, the diagonal is longer than 2 and shorter than 3 (the width plus the length is 3). The answer *must* be $\mathbf{a\sqrt{5}}$, the *only* choice between 2 and 3, when $a = 1$.

    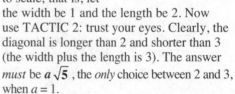

12. **E.** • Could exactly one of a, b, and c be an integer?

    Yes; $(4)\left(\dfrac{1}{2}\right)\left(\dfrac{1}{2}\right) = 1$.

    • Could exactly two of a, b, and c be integers?

    Yes; $(1)(2)\left(\dfrac{1}{2}\right) = 1$.

    • Could all three be integers? Yes again: $(1)(1)(1) = 1$. *Be careful:* the question does *not* require a, b, and c to be different numbers.

    Statements **I**, **II**, **and III** are all true.

13. E. Draw a Venn diagram. Of the 100 students taking chemistry, 20 take biology, and 80 don't; they take *only* chemistry. Similarly, of the 80 students taking biology, 20 also take chemistry, and 60 take *only* biology. The desired ratio is 80:60 = 4:3 = $\frac{4}{3}$.

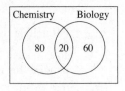

14. A. Let S be a side of the large square, and s a side of the small square. The area of the white region is just s^2, whereas the area of the shaded region is $S^2 - s^2$. Therefore,

$$S^2 - s^2 = s^2 \Rightarrow S^2 = 2s^2 \Rightarrow \frac{S^2}{s^2} = 2 \Rightarrow \frac{S}{s} = \sqrt{2}.$$

The ratio of the side of the large square to the side of the small square is $\frac{\sqrt{2}}{1}$.

**Redraw the diagram with the small square in the corner of the large one. If the ratio were 2:1, the white area would be much smaller than the shaded area, so the small square must be larger and the ratio is less than 2:1. Only $\frac{\sqrt{2}}{1}$ is less than 2:1.

15. B. $\overline{AC}$ is the hypotenuse of a 30-60-90 right triangle. By KEY FACT J11, the length of $\overline{CD}$, the leg opposite the 30° angle, is 5 (half the hypotenuse), and $AD = 5\sqrt{3}$. Then the area of the rectangle is $5 \times 5\sqrt{3} = \mathbf{25\sqrt{3}}$.

**Use TACTIC 2: trust the diagram. Side $\overline{AD}$ is surely shorter than the hypotenuse, say 8. Side $\overline{CD}$ is about half the hypotenuse, say 5. Then the area is *about* 40. Eliminate C, D, and E. Use your calculator to evaluate A (≈ 35.4) and B (≈ 43.3) and then guess.

16. A. Set up a proportion: $\frac{\text{dollars}}{\text{pounds}}$.

$$\frac{d\ \text{dollars}}{10\ \text{pounds of gold}} = \frac{d\ \text{dollars}}{10p\ \text{pounds of silver}} = \frac{x\ \text{dollars}}{1\ \text{pound of silver}}$$

Then, $\frac{d}{10p} = \frac{x}{1} \Rightarrow x = \frac{d}{\mathbf{10p}}$.

17. B. The formulas for the volumes of a rectangular solid and a cylinder are $V = \ell wh$ and $V = \pi r^2 h$, respectively. (Remember that these formulas are given to you on the first page of every SAT math section.) The volume of container I is $(4)(4)(5) = 80$ cubic inches. Since the diameter of container II is 4, its radius is 2, and so its volume is $\pi(2^2)(5) = 20\pi$. The difference in volumes is $80 - 20\pi = \mathbf{20(4 - \pi)}$.

**If you don't know, or can't use, the formulas, you must guess. If you knew the formulas, you *could* answer the question, so eliminate E. Also, D is out since $1 - \pi$ is negative. If that's all you know, guess among A, B, and C. If you know that the volume of the rectangular solid is 80, but you don't know the volume of the cylinder, eliminate C, which is over 160, and guess between A and B. *Don't leave this question out.*

18. D. Since the number of cells doubles every 30 minutes, it quadruples every hour. Since 4 hours elapsed from 8:00 A.M. to noon, the number of cells quadrupled 4 times. Therefore, at noon, the number of cells was $\mathbf{60 \times 4^4}$.

19. A. To find the average speed, in miles per hour, divide the distance, in miles, by the time, in hours. Ali drove 90 miles $\left(\frac{2}{3} \text{ of } 135\right)$ in 2.25 hours (135 minutes = 2 hours and 15 minutes = $2\frac{1}{4}$ hours). Then $90 \div 2.25 = \mathbf{40}$.

**It should be clear that there is enough information to find Ali's average speed, so eliminate E. Remember that 60 miles per hour is 1 mile per minute. Since Ali drove for 135 minutes and covered less than 135 miles, she was going slower than 60 mph. Eliminate C and D and guess.

20. C. Since the average of the five students' weights is 150.4 pounds, their total weight is $5 \times 150.4 = 752$ pounds (TACTIC E1). No student weighs less than 130 and none is within 5 pounds of another, so the least that the four lightest students can weigh is 130, 135, 140, and 145 pounds, for a total of 550 pounds. The heaviest student, therefore, cannot exceed $752 - 550 = \mathbf{202}$ pounds.

Section 4 Writing Skills

1. D. Choice D corrects the double negative found in the other four choices. Note that, grammatically, *hardly* is considered a negative word. Choice C, in addition, creates a run-on sentence.

2. E. Comma splice. Choice B is a loose, ineffective compound sentence. Choice C is a comma splice, Choice D is a sentence fragment. Choice E is the most effective sentence; it corrects the comma splice without introducing any fresh errors.

3. B. Error in parallelism. In Choice A, the conjunction *but* should be followed by a clause to parallel the clause in the first half of the sentence. Choice B provides such a clause. The awkward placement of the word *invariably* in Choice C makes the sentence very unclear. The use of *who* in Choices D and E leads to ambiguity because it may be taken to refer to *workers*.

4. E. Error in modification and word order. Choices A, B, and C are incorrect because of the dangling participle *considering*. Choice D is unidiomatic.

5. C. Error in modification and word order. In Choices A, B, and D, the modifier *familiar* is dangling. The wording in Choice E suggests that the explorer was a success, whereas the original sentence states that the search was a success—a somewhat different meaning. Choice C corrects the error and retains the original meaning of the sentence.

6. B. Error in parallelism. Choices A, C, and E do not maintain parallel structure. Choice B corrects this weakness. The infinitive *to cut* cannot be an object of *demand*, as in Choice D; a noun clause like the one in Choice B corrects this error.

7. A. Choice A is correct because the subject of the verb *had* must be *who,* not *whom. Which* in Choice E should not be used to refer to a person.

8. E. Error in pronoun-number agreement. The pronouns *you* and *your* in the second clause of the sentence refer to *technician,* which is a third person singular noun. The pronoun, therefore, should be the third person singular *her.*

9. C. Choice C corrects the ungrammatical construction by linking two independent clauses with a semicolon.

10. E. Choice E eliminates the wordiness of the original sentence. It is both clear and effective.

11. A. Sentence is correct.

12. B. Adjective and adverb confusion. Change *increasing* to *increasingly.*

13. A. Misuse of relative pronoun. Change *who* (refers to people) to *that* (refers to things).

14. B. Error in pronoun case. Change *he* to *him.*

15. B. Error in diction. Incorrect introduction to noun clause. Change *where* to *in which* to modify *explosion.*

16. C. Error in parallelism. Change *called* to *were calling.*

17. C. Error in coordination and subordination. Incorrect coordinating conjunction. Change *and* to *but.*

18. C. Error in pronoun number agreement. Change *their* to *its.*

19. B. Error in subject-verb agreement. Change *are finding* to *is finding.*

20. B. Error in tense and shift in pronoun person. Change *one finds* to *you will find.*

21. C. Error in tense. Change *have not had* to *will not have.*

22. D. Error in parallelism. Change *to guarantee* to *guaranteeing.*

23. E. Sentence is correct.

24. E. Sentence is correct.

25. C. Error in diction. Change *due to* to *as a result of.*

26. D. Error in tense. Change *is questioned by* to *was questioned by.*

27. A. Pronoun error. Change *which* (refers to things) to *who* (refers to people).

28. C. Error in subject-verb agreement. Both teams *intend* to review the videos.

29. E. Sentence is correct.

30. C. Choice A contains an awkwardly expressed clause that begins *which caused.* Choice B contains a faulty comparison: *not as severe that.* Choice C accurately revises the sentence. It is the best answer. Choice D contains an awkwardly expressed clause that begins *that banning.* Choice E contains faulty diction. The conjunction *and* is not an effective connecting word in the context.

31. B. Choice A contains a dangling participle and a weak passive construction. Choice B accurately continues the thought begun in sentence 9. It is the best answer. Choice C contains redundant language: *foul* and *obscene.* Choice D contains a weak passive construction (*Obscenities are often heard*) and is wordy. Choice E lacks a main verb; therefore, it is a sentence fragment.

32. E. Choices A and B are adequate, but dull, transitional statements. Choice C is a wordier version of A and B. Choice D contains an error in subject-verb agreement; the subject *changes* is plural, but the verb *has* is singular. Choice E serves as a good transitional statement that highlights the most important change in music discussed in the essay. It is the best answer.

33. A. Only Choice A requires development, since no mention is made in the essay of "new categories" of music. All the other choices are factual statements that require no further elaboration.

34. B. All choices except B contribute to the discussion of changes in musical sounds brought about by technology. Choice B, however, wanders from the topic.

35. D. Choice A unnecessarily repeats the phrase *in the past thirty years* and contains an error in subject-verb agreement. Choice B is awkwardly expressed and confusing. Choice C fails to list the changes in music in the proper order. Also, *technology and lyrics* appear to be a single item. Choice D succinctly and accurately states the main idea of the essay. It is the best answer. Choice E, by subordinating the initial clause, gives lyrics in music undeserved importance.

Section 6 Critical Reading

1. E. The *depletion* or exhaustion of our energy sources would lead us to seek *alternative* sources.

Remember: in double-blank sentences, go through the answer choices, testing the *first* words in each choice and eliminating those that don't fit.

Note that you are looking for a word with negative associations. Therefore, you can eliminate any word with positive ones. Choices A, B, and D all have positive associations. Only Choice C or E can be correct. Turning to the second words of these two choices, you can eliminate Choice C: it would make no sense to seek *inefficient* energy sources.

(Cause and Effect Signal)

2. C. *Verbose* means excessively wordy. The second clause of the sentence provides an example that brings the abstract term *verbose* to life.

(Examples)

3. C. Bugs are abundant or plentiful because they endure. They endure because they have an extremely low *extinction* or death rate.

(Cause and Effect Pattern)

4. D. To the author of this sentence, pre-Spanish art in Mexico is praiseworthy. It is not *crude* art but strong art. He likes its bold simplifications and asserts they are not the result of the artists' inability to *overcome* or conquer the technical difficulties involved.

Note how the second clause of the sentence serves to clarify what the author means by his assertion that pre-Spanish art is not crude.

Be careful with sentences containing negative words and prefixes. The words "not," "mistaken," and "inability" all affect the sentence's meaning.

5. E. To pussyfoot is to refrain from committing oneself, to be wary of stating one's views candidly. People unable or afraid to take *forthright* stands are, by definition, *equivocators*.

(Definition Pattern)

6. D. The "property" that Douglass's ex-master sought to reclaim was a *personal possession* that had been lost to him, namely, his former slave Frederick Douglass.

7. C. The abolitionists criticized Douglass for letting his British friends purchase his freedom. They were clearly *negative* about the action, considering it politically incorrect.

8. B. Passage 1 is clearly *expository*: it presents information about a historical figure. Passage 2, in contrast, is argumentative: in it, Douglass justifies his actions, giving his grounds for running away.

9. C. The enterprise that Douglass kept secret from his former master was his plan to *escape from slavery*.

10. A. The opening paragraph, with its talk of clearly marked outlines and contrasts "between suffering and joy," and the concluding sentence, with its mentions of "violent contrasts" and "the perpetual oscillation between despair and distracted joy," emphasize the author's main idea: the Middle Ages were marked by extremes.

Choice B is incorrect. Though the author depicts aspects of the lives of the very rich and the very poor, he does not stress the notion that their styles complemented one another.

Choice C is incorrect. The author's concern is for the Middle Ages, not for the twentieth century.

Choices D and E are incorrect. They are unsupported by the text.

Remember, when asked to find the main idea, to check the opening and the summary sentences of each paragraph.

11. B. The cloaking of minor activities (journeys, visits, etc.) with forms (line 9) "raised them to the dignity of a ritual"; in other words, the forms (fixed or formal ways of doing things) made the acts *more dignified*.

Choices A, C, D, and E are incorrect. They are not supported by the passage.

Remember: when asked about specific details in the passage, spot key words in the question and then scan the passage to find them (or their synonyms).

Key Word: formalities.

12. A. The linking of "formulae" with "ceremonies" (formal series of acts) and "benedictions" (words of blessing) suggests that these formulae are most likely *set forms of words for rituals*. Note how the use of the colon suggests that all three words that follow are examples of "formalities."

13. E. Treat this vocabulary-in-context question as if it were a sentence completion exercise. "Every ____ and estate, every rank and profession, was distinguished by its costume." Which of the answer choices best fills in the blank? *Estate* (major political or social class), *rank* (separate class in a social system), and *profession* (body of people engaged in an occupation) are all examples of groups or classes of people. Thus, in this context, an order is a *social class*. Note how the use of "and" and of the commas to group together these terms suggests that all four are similar in meaning.

14. A. The last sentence of the third paragraph states that the lofty churches, the houses of worship, towered above the town. The churches always "remained dominant."

When asked about specific details, spot the key words in the question and scan the passage to find them (or their variants).

Key Words: above, towered.

15. A. In cataloging the extremes of medieval life, the author in no way suggests that the Middle Ages were *boring*.

Choice B is incorrect. The author portrays the Middle Ages as festive and joyful; he says they were filled with vivid pleasures and proud celebrations.

Choice C is incorrect. The author portrays the Middle Ages as filled with ceremony and ritual.

Choice D is incorrect. The author portrays the Middle Ages as passionate and turbulent; he mentions the "tone of excitement and of passion" in everyday life.

Choice E is incorrect. The author suggests the Middle Ages were harsh and bleak; he portrays them as cold and miserable.

16. D.   Richard's introduction to school, his parents' reaction to their unfriendly neighbors, his brother and sister's silence about their classroom experiences—all these instances illustrate the family members' interaction with the *English-speaking world*.

17. D.   The older children return home speaking Spanish, abandoning the English taught in the classroom. What is more, "their mysterious books . . . remained on the table next to the door, closed firmly behind them." Clearly, they *readily ignored the need to practice using English* at home.

18. B.   The author's statement that it "was the first time I had heard anyone name me in English" supports Choice B. In addition to finding himself apart from his family, the usual experience of new pupils, he finds himself stripped of his name, his identity. Being addressed in such a strange and impersonal manner rattles him.
Choice A is incorrect. All the students were uneasy to find themselves separated from their families.
Choices C and D are incorrect. Nothing in the passage supports them.
Choice E is incorrect. The narrator lived in a *gringo* neighborhood; he must have seen white children.

19. C.   Bilingual education is a scheme or *plan* that seeks to permit non-English-speaking children to use their native languages in school.
Choice E is incorrect. As used in the sentence, bilingual education is a plan or program. Establishing such a plan is the goal of bilingual education's supporters.

20. B.   Bilingual education's supporters wish to have non-English-speaking children taught in the language they customarily use at home. Rodriguez feels they have missed an important point. To him, the job of public education is to teach children to function effectively in the society in which they live. To do so, they must learn to use public language, the language used *outside* the home. He believes that the champions of bilingual education *fail to see that public education must meet public needs, not necessarily personal ones*.

21. C.   Rodriguez has just given his opinion on a controversial topic. He now must convince his readers that he knows what he is talking about. To do so, he cites specific aspects of his background that prove he knows something about bilingual education. In other words, he *indicates what qualifies him to speak authoritatively on the issue*.

22. A.   The author's assertions in the last paragraph that his parents coped very well and that they were nobody's victims, indicate that his basic attitude toward them is *admiring*.

23. B.   Statement B is true to the author's experience: they *felt estranged* from the *gringos'* world.

Choice A is incorrect. Richard's father found steady work.
Choice C is incorrect. Although Sacramento as a whole was not determined to keep Mexicans out of white neighborhoods, some neighbors tried to frighten away Richard's family.
Choice D is incorrect. Lacking confidence in public, Richard's parents remained detached from community affairs.
Choice E is incorrect. Richard's parents sent their children to Roman Catholic schools; they were involved with academic institutions.

24. E.   For Richard's parents to call white people *los americanos*, "the Americans," implies that on some level they did not consider themselves Americans. This is a *telling* or *revealing* comment that points up the degree of alienation Richard's parents felt.

Section 7 Mathematical Reasoning

MULTIPLE-CHOICE QUESTIONS

1. C.   The product of any set of numbers that includes 0 is 0, and the absolute value of 0 is **0**.

2. D.   Let the number be x, and write the equation: $\frac{3}{4}x = 7 + \frac{1}{6}x$.

   Multiply both sides by 12: $9x = 84 + 2x$

   Subtract $2x$ from each side and divide by 7: $7x = 84$
   $x = 12$

   Be careful: 12 is *not* the answer. You were asked for $\frac{5}{3}$ of the number: $\frac{5}{3}(12) = \mathbf{20}$.

3. B.   A number that is a member of both A and B must be an integer that is a multiple of both 5 and 7, and so must be a multiple of 35. There are **5** multiples of 35 less than 200: 35, 70, 105, 140, 175.

4. C. $\sqrt[3]{x+1} + 3 = 5 \Rightarrow \sqrt[3]{x+1} = 2$. Cube both sides: $x + 1 = 2^3 = 8 \Rightarrow x = \mathbf{7}$.

5. B.   Write the equation and use the six-step method (TACTIC G1) to solve it:

   Set up the equation:
   $(x + 3) + (2x - 3) + (3x - 5) = 25$
   Collect like terms: $6x - 5 = 25$
   Add 5 to each side: $6x = 30$
   Divide each side by 6: $x = 5$

   Plugging in 5 for x, we get the lengths of the sides: 8, **7**, and 10.

6. D.   A circle can cross each side of a square at most twice.

   The answer is $2 \times 4 = \mathbf{8}$.

7. C. $\overline{AC}$ is a diagonal of square *ABCD*. By the distance formula

$$AC = (\sqrt{(-1-4)^2 + (-1-2)^2} =$$

$$\sqrt{(-5)^2 + (-3)^2} = \sqrt{25+9} = \sqrt{34}.$$

By KEY FACT K8, one formula for the area of a square is $\dfrac{d^2}{2}$, where *d* is the length of the diagonal. Then the area of *ABCD* is $\dfrac{(\sqrt{34})^2}{2} = \dfrac{34}{2} = \mathbf{17}$.

**Once you know that the length of diagonal $\overline{AC}$ is $\sqrt{34}$, you can find *s*, the length of a side, by dividing by $\sqrt{2}$: $\dfrac{\sqrt{34}}{\sqrt{2}} = \sqrt{17}$, and then $s^2 = \mathbf{17}$.

8. A. If $f(x) = x + 5$, then $f(3a) = 3a + 5$ and $f(2a) = 2a + 5$. Therefore,
$f(3a) + 2 = f(2a) + 3 \Rightarrow$
$3a + 5 + 2 = 2a + 5 + 3 \Rightarrow$
$3a + 7 = 2a + 8 \Rightarrow a = \mathbf{1}$.

**Use TACTIC 5: test the answer choices. When $a = 1$,
$f(3a) + 2 = f(3) + 2 = (3 + 5) + 2 = 10$
and
$f(2a) + 3 = f(2) + 3 = (2 + 5) + 3 = 10$.

GRID-IN QUESTIONS

9. (13) Use your calculator:
$$a = \frac{(19)(13)}{7} = 169 \Rightarrow \sqrt{a} = \sqrt{169} = \mathbf{13}.$$

10. $\left(2.5 \text{ or } \dfrac{5}{2}\right)$ Replace *a* by 44 and *b* by 275:
$$44 = \frac{275}{c^2} \Rightarrow 44c^2 = 275.$$
So, $c^2 = \dfrac{275}{44} = 6.25$.

Then, $c = \sqrt{6.25} = \mathbf{2.5}$.

11. (150) Draw and label the right triangle. By the Pythagorean theorem:
$15^2 + b^2 = 25^2 \Rightarrow$
$225 + b^2 = 625 \Rightarrow$
$b^2 = 400 \Rightarrow b = 20$.
The area of the triangle is $\dfrac{1}{2}(15)(20) = \mathbf{150}$.

[You can save some work if you recognize this as a 3-4-5 triangle in which each side has been multiplied by 5 (15-20-25).]

12. (87.5) If the average of 5 numbers (*a*, *b*, *c*, *d*, *e*) is 95, the sum of these numbers is 5 × 95 = 475 (TACTIC E1). Similarly, the sum of the 3 numbers *a*, *b*, and *e* whose average is 100 is 300, leaving 175 (475 – 300) as the sum of the 2 remaining numbers, *c* and *d*. The average of *c* and *d* is their sum divided by 2: 175 ÷ 2 = **87.5**.

13. (110) Here, $x^2 - y^2 = (x + y)(x - y) = 10 \times 11 = \mathbf{110}$.

**Adding the two given equations, you get $2x = 21$, so $x = 10.5$. Since $10.5 + y = 10$, then $y = -0.5$.
Evaluate using your calculator:
$x^2 - y^2 = (10.5)^2 - (0.5)^2 = 110.25 - 0.25 = \mathbf{110}$.

14. (52) Ignore the *x*'s and the *y*'s. In any "staircase" the perimeter is just twice the sum of the height and the length, so the perimeter is
$$2(12 + 14) = 2(26) = \mathbf{52}.$$

15. $\left(\dfrac{16}{5} \text{ or } 3.2\right)$ Since $a = 2b$, $b = \dfrac{4}{3}c$, and $c = \dfrac{6}{5}d$:

$$a = 2\left(\frac{4}{3}c\right) = \frac{8}{3}\left(\frac{6}{5}d\right) = \frac{16}{5}d \Rightarrow$$

$$\frac{a}{d} = \frac{16}{5} \text{ or } \mathbf{3.2}.$$

**Use TACTIC 6. If we let $d = 1$, $c = \dfrac{6}{5}$.
That's OK, but it's easier if we avoid fractions. We'll let $d = 5$. Then, $c = 6$, $b = \dfrac{4}{3}(6) = 8$, and $a = 2(8) = 16$, so $\dfrac{a}{d} = \dfrac{16}{5}$.

16. (12) Let *x* = Adam's age in 1980. Then, in 1980, Judy's age was $3x$ and Elaine's age was $8x$. Since Elaine is 20 years older than Judy, $8x = 3x + 20 \Rightarrow 5x = 20 \Rightarrow x = 4$. Therefore, in 1988, Adam was $4 + 8 = \mathbf{12}$.

**Test numbers for Adam's age in 1980 and zoom in.

Ages in 1980			Difference between Elaine and Judy
Adam	Judy	Elaine	
10	30	80	50, much too big
5	15	40	25, slightly too big
4	12	32	20, that's it

17. (490) Let *x* be the number Jessica chose. Then the other terms are as follows:

Term	2	3	4	5
Expression	$x + 6$	$2(x + 6) = 2x + 12$	$2x + 12 + 6 = 2x + 18$	$2(2x + 18) = 4x + 36$

Finally, $4x + 36 = 1996 \Rightarrow 4x = 1960 \Rightarrow x = \mathbf{490}$.
**Work backwards. Treat 1996 as the first term and alternately take half of the previous term and subtract 6 from the previous term:

$$1996 \rightarrow 998 \rightarrow 992 \rightarrow 496 \rightarrow \mathbf{490}$$

18. (96) Since the diameters of the tables are in the ratio of 35:25, or 7:5, the ratio of their areas is $7^2:5^2 = 49:25$. Convert the ratio to a percent: $49:25 = \dfrac{49}{25} = 1.96 = 196\%$. The area of the larger table is 196% of the area of the small one, or is **96%** *more* than the area of the small one.

With your calculator, actually calculate the areas. The radius of the larger table is 17.5, so its area is $\pi(17.5)^2 = 306.25\pi$. Similarly, the radius of the smaller table is 12.5, and its area is $\pi(12.5)^2 = 156.25\pi$. The difference in the areas is $306.25\pi - 156.25\pi = 150\pi$, and 150π is **96% of 156.25π:

$$\left(\frac{150\pi}{156.25\pi} = \frac{150}{156.25} = 0.96\right).$$

Section 8 Critical Reading

1. C. The publisher is apologizing for having used the photographs without the photographer's permission. He *regrets* printing them without *authorization*.
   To answer this question correctly, you *must* check the second word of each answer choice. (Definition Pattern)

2. B. To acquire a taste for something, you must originally not have that taste or even *dislike* the item; you acquire the taste by growing to like or *welcome* it.
   Note how the second clause of the sentence serves to clarify what is meant by the term "acquired taste." (Example)

3. D. *Assiduous* work, work performed industriously or diligently, should not lead employers to *complain*.
   Note that the use of *because* in the opening clause signals that a cause and effect relationship is at work here.
   (Cause and Effect Signal)

4. B. The key word here is *obstacle*. What sort of attitude toward modern art would present an *obstacle* or hindrance to artists? Clearly, a negative one. You therefore can eliminate any answer choice that is positive. *Veneration* (awed respect) is highly positive. Eliminate Choice A. *Indifference* (lack of caring), *disdain* (scorn), *ignorance*, and *intolerance* are all negative terms. You must check the second word of Choices B, C, D, and E. Bacon and Freud are now accepted, respected artists. In years past, they were viewed differently. They were *dismissed* or rejected as insignificant. The correct answer is Choice B.
   Note that a secondary meaning of *dismissed* is involved here.   (Contrast Pattern)

5. D. By definition, *volatile* substances tend to evaporate (convert from a liquid state into a vapor). Beware of Eye-Catchers. Choice A is incorrect. *Insoluble* substances cannot be dissolved in liquid. Such substances are unlikely to evaporate.   (Definition)

6. B. By showing that they had no hidden or *concealed* weapons, they were showing themselves to be friendly or *amicably* disposed.
   Because the first word of any one of these answer choices could work, you have to try out each entire pair before eliminating any of the choices.   (Cause and Effect Signal)

7. B. Auden finds it curious or *unusual* that detective fiction *most* appeals to people who are *least* likely to find other forms of escapist literature appealing.

8. C. In lines 1–4, Auden states that typical readers of detective fiction do not find other forms of daydream or escapist literature appealing. In that context he then states that the typical mystery fan could not stomach or tolerate *True Confessions* and movie magazines. This suggests that Auden considers these magazines *standard forms of escapist literature*.

9. D. In the closing paragraph of Passage 1, Auden states that readers of detective fiction indulge in a fantasy of escape or release that is prompted by a "feeling of guilt, the cause of which is unknown to the dreamer." Thus, they are *seeking momentary release from a vague sense of guilt*.
   Choice A is incorrect. Nothing in the passage supports it.
   Choice B is incorrect. Auden denies that readers of detective fiction are bent on satisfying "violent or murderous wishes."
   Choice C is incorrect. Although Auden depicts readers of detective fiction as dreamers, he depicts them as dreamers impelled by a sense of guilt, not by a sense of boredom.
   Choice E is incorrect. Nothing in the passage supports it.

10. E. To translate murderous wishes into action is to *convert* or switch from dreaming about murder to committing the actual crime.

11. B. Kafka's *The Trial* is cited as an "instructive example of the difference between a work of art and the detective story." Auden then goes on to analyze *The Trial* to point out its qualities as a work of art that distinguish it from mere detective fiction.
    Choice A is incorrect. *The Trial* is a work of art, not a detective story.
    Choice C is incorrect. Auden is not discussing readers of detective fiction in lines 46–54.
    Choice D is incorrect. The outside investigator, the genius who removes guilt by giving knowledge of guilt, is a figure out of the detective story; he has no place in the work of art. Although K investigates his situation, he is trapped inside it; he is no genius from outside.

Choice E is incorrect. There is nothing in the passage to support it.

12. E. Auden explicitly disassociates himself from the readers of thrillers (which he rarely enjoys). However, he associates himself with the readers of detective fiction ("me and my neighbors"), those who are caught up in the mystery, but, unlike the outside investigator, unable to solve it. This suggests he is a fan of detective fiction, one who views it with *genuine appreciation*.
Choices A, B, C, and D are incorrect. Nothing in the passage suggests them.

13. C. In the phrase "use up our intellectual shoe leather," the author of Passage 2 evokes a familiar image of the detective wearing out his or her shoe leather while pounding the pavements in search of clues. Readers of mysteries do not physically pound the pavements searching for clues. However, they do *work hard mentally, much as detectives do physically*.

14. D. The author writes of taking "pleasure in the discovery . . . that there is more work to be done." This suggests that he finds the prospect of additional work pleasing or *delightful*.

15. B. Throughout Passage 2 the author is discussing detective fiction. Immediately before mentioning Marlowe and Archer and their search for the facts, the author refers to the objective truth defined or discovered by the researcher/detective. This juxtaposition suggests that Marlowe and Archer are *fictional detectives*.

16. B. To employ a word is to *use* it.

17. E. The statement that the detective story begins "in search of the subject . . .(and) asking, What is the question?" suggests that the story must start by *defining the problem that is to be solved* in the course of the investigation.

18. B. In Passage 1, Auden goes on at some length about the psychological satisfaction readers of detective fiction derive from their literary "escape" from their sense of guilt. In Passage 2, Winks describes (also at some length) the pleasure readers of detective fiction get from raising questions, pursuing truths, making judgments. In both passages, the authors are primarily concerned with the question of *why people enjoy reading detective fiction*.

19. A. In characterizing detective fiction as "a bit like a religion" and linking it "with all fine literature, history, philosophy," Winks clearly goes further than Auden would. Auden stresses that detective stories are "escape literature, not works of art" (lines 19 and 20). Thus, Auden would most likely react to Winks's somewhat exalted view of detective fiction by reiterating that *reading detective fiction is an escape, not a highly serious pursuit*.

Section 9 Mathematical Reasoning

1. B. Multiplying both sides of $2x - 1 = 9$ by 5 yields $10x - 5 = \mathbf{45}$.

    **Just solve:
    $2x - 1 = 9 \Rightarrow 2x = 10 \Rightarrow x = 5 \Rightarrow$
    $10x = 50 \Rightarrow 10x - 5 = \mathbf{45}$.

2. E. Since the measures of corresponding angles are equal, $a = b$ (KEY FACT I6). Since the figure is not drawn to scale, the angles could just as well be acute as obtuse, as shown in the figure at the right. The sum $a + b$ **cannot be determined from the information given**.

3. D. Since there are no parentheses, you must be careful to follow the proper order of operations (PEMDAS). Do multiplications and divisions left to right *before* any additions and subtractions.

    A: $4 \times 4 \div 4 + 4 = 16 \div 4 + 4 = 4 + 4 = 8$
    B: $4 \div 4 \times 4 + 4 = 1 \times 4 + 4 = 4 + 4 = 8$
    C: $4 \times 4 - 4 \times 4 = 16 - 16 = 0$
    D: $\mathbf{4 \div 4 + 4 \times 4} = 1 + 16 = 17$, the greatest value
    E: $4 + 4 \times 4 - 4 = 4 + 16 - 4 = 20 - 4 = 16$

4. C. Let $4x$ and $3x$ be the numbers of students taking and not taking Spanish, respectively. Then $4x + 3x = 840 \Rightarrow 7x = 840 \Rightarrow x = 120$. The number taking Spanish is $4(120) = \mathbf{480}$.

    **Use TACTIC 5. Try choice C. If 480 students take Spanish, $840 - 480 = 360$ do not. Is $\frac{480}{360} = \frac{4}{3}$ a true proportion?

    Yes. Cross-multiply: $480 \times 3 = 360 \times 4$.

5. C. The sum of three consecutive integers can be expressed as
    $n + (n + 1) + (n + 2) = 3n + 3 = 3(n + 1)$,
    and so must be a multiple of 3. Only **28** is *not* a multiple of 3.
    **Quickly add up sets of three consecutive integers: $4 + 5 + 6 = 15$, $5 + 6 + 7 = 18$, $6 + 7 + 8 = 21$, and so on, and see the pattern (they're all multiples of 3); or cross off the choices as you come to them.

6. **B.** By KEY FACT A21, $\left(a^{\frac{1}{2}}\right)^3 = a^{\frac{3}{2}}$ and

$\left(a^5\right)^{\frac{1}{2}} = a^{\frac{5}{2}}$. Then $a^n = \left(a^{\frac{1}{2}}\right)^3 \left(a^5\right)^{\frac{1}{2}} =$

$\left(a^{\frac{3}{2}}\right)\left(a^{\frac{5}{2}}\right) = a^{\frac{3}{2}+\frac{5}{2}} = a^{\frac{8}{2}} = a^4$.

So, $n = \mathbf{4}$.

7. **E.** Since $k \parallel \ell$, in the figure below, by KEY
FACT I6, $z + (3x + 15) = 180$. But $z = x + 5$
(KEY FACT I4: vertical angles are congruent).

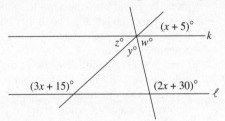

Then, $(3x + 15) + (x + 5) = 180 \Rightarrow$
$4x + 20 = 180 \Rightarrow 4x = 160 \Rightarrow x = 40$.
So $z = x + 5 = 45$. Also, $w + (2x + 30) = 180$.
But $2x + 30 = 80 + 30 = 110$, so $w = 70$.
Finally, $w + y + z = 180 \Rightarrow 70 + y + 45 = 180$.
So, $115 + y = 180$ and $y = \mathbf{65}$.

8. **D.** This is a repeating sequence with 3 terms
(1, 2, 3) in the set that repeats. Since the sum
of the 3 numbers in each set is 6, the sum of
the first 33 sets or 99 terms is $6 \times 33 = 198$.
Since the next term is 1, the sum of the first
100 terms is **199**.

9. **C.** Check each of the three statements. Since the
average of a and a is a, I is true. Clearly, the
average of a and b is the same as the average
of b and a, so II is also true. Note that
$a \odot (b \odot c)$ is *not* the average of the three
numbers a, b, and c. To calculate this average, you first take the average of b and c and
then take the average of that result and a.

Then,

$a \odot (b \odot c) = \dfrac{a + \left(\dfrac{b + c}{2}\right)}{2} = \dfrac{2a + b + c}{4}$,

whereas

$(a \odot b) \odot c = \dfrac{\left(\dfrac{a + b}{2}\right) + c}{2} = \dfrac{a + b + 2c}{4}$,

and these are equal only if $a = c$. Therefore,
III is false and **I and II only** are true.

**Use TACTIC 6: plug in some easy num-
bers. You probably don't need to do this for I
and II, but for III it may be a lot easier than
the analysis above:
$2 \odot (4 \odot 6) = 2 \odot 5 = 3.5$,
whereas
$(2 \odot 4) \odot 6 = 3 \odot 6 = 4.5$. III is false.

10. **B.** As always, with a percent problem use a
simple number such as 10 or 100. Assume that
model A sells for \$10; then, since 60% of 10
is 6, model B sells for \$16. The chart tells you
that 9000 model A's and 10,000 model B's
were sold, for a total of
$\$10(9000) + \$16(10,000) =$
$\$90,000 + \$160,000 = \$250,000$.
The sales of model A (\$90,000) represent
36% of the total sales (\$250,000).

11. **D.** Use TACTIC 7: choose a number. Let BE, the
length of a side of the smallest square, be 1.
Then $DH = 2$ and $AB = 4$; the areas of the three
squares are 1, 4, and 16, respectively. Therefore,
the shaded area is $16 - 4 - 1 = 11$, and the
probability that a point chosen at random

inside $ABCD$ is in that shaded region is $\dfrac{\mathbf{11}}{\mathbf{16}}$.

12. **D.** The best approach is to use the six-step
method from Section 12-G.
To get rid of the fractions, multiply
both sides of the equation by 3: $3x = 2(x + y)$
Use the distributive law to
get rid of the parentheses: $3x = 2x + 2y$
Subtract $2x$ from each side: $x = \mathbf{2y}$

13. **D.** Draw in radii $\overline{OA}$ and $\overline{OB}$. Then, by KEY
FACT L10, $\overline{OA} \perp \overline{PA}$ and $\overline{OB} \perp \overline{PB}$, so
quadrilateral $OAPB$ has two right angles and a
$50°$ angle. Since the sum of all four angles is
$360°$, you have
$90 + 90 + 50 + m\angle AOB = 360 \Rightarrow$
$230 + m\angle AOB = 360$, and so $m\angle AOB = \mathbf{130}$.

14. **A.** The equation of the line can be written in the
form $y = mx + b$, where b is the y-intercept
and m is the slope. Since the line crosses the
y-axis at 2, $b = 2$ and the answer must be A or
B. Since the line has a negative slope, the

answer must be A, $y = -\dfrac{1}{2}x + 2$.

**Since the line passes through (0, 2) and

$(4, 0)$, its slope $= \dfrac{0 - 2}{4 - 0} = \dfrac{-2}{4} = -\dfrac{1}{2}$.

15. **E.** If $\overline{PQ}$ is a diameter of the circle, then the radius
is 1 and A, the area, is π. This is the smallest
possible value of A, but A can actually be any
number larger than π if the radius is made arbi-
trarily large, as shown by the figures below.

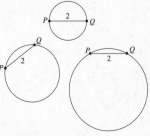

The answer is $A \geq \pi$.

16. E. The easiest way to solve this is to use TACTIC 6. Let $x = 2$ and $y = 1$. Then $xy = 2$, $a = 4$, and $b = 0$. Now, plug in 4 for a and 0 for b, and see which of the five choices is equal to 2. Only E works:

$$\frac{a^2 - b^2}{8} = \frac{4^2 - 0^2}{8} = \frac{16}{8} = 2.$$

**Here is the correct algebraic solution.

Add the two equations: $\quad\quad x + 2y = a$
$$\underline{+\ \ x - 2y = b}$$
$$2x = a + b$$

Divide by 2: $\quad\quad\quad\quad\quad x = \dfrac{a + b}{2}$

Multiply the second equation by -1, and add it to the first:
$$x + 2y = a$$
$$\underline{+\ -x + 2y = -b}$$
$$4y = a - b$$

Divide by 4: $\quad\quad\quad\quad\quad y = \dfrac{a - b}{4}$

Then $xy = \dfrac{a + b}{2} \cdot \dfrac{a - b}{4} = \dfrac{a^2 - b^2}{8}$.

This is the type of algebra you want to avoid.

Section 10 Writing Skills

1. D. Wordiness. Choice D makes the writer's point simply and concisely.

2. A. Sentence is correct. Remember: the subject's grammatical number is not changed by the addition of a phrase that begins with *along with, together with,* or a similar expression. The subject, *coach,* is singular. The verb should be singular as well.

3. E. Run-on sentence. Choice E eliminates the original comma splice to produce a balanced sentence.

4. C. Error in logical comparison. Compare veterans with veterans, not veterans with wars.

5. C. Misplaced modifier. Who are acting suspiciously? Not the bags, but the people who packed them!

6. A. Sentence is correct.

7. D. Error in logical comparison. Compare prices with prices, not prices with cities.

8. C. Error in pronoun-antecedent agreement. The subject of the sentence is *inoculations* (plural). The pronoun should be plural as well. In this particular instance, the plural pronoun *they* has been replaced by the noun phrase *such inoculations.*

9. A. Sentence is correct.

10. C. Error in subordination. The use of the conjunction *Although* in Choice C signals the contrast between what one might have expected (i.e., that the prospectors, who arrived in 1848, would become known as the forty-eighters) and what actually took place (they became known as the forty-niners).

11. D. Misplaced appositional phrase. Who was once a leading light of the Harlem Renaissance? Clearly, Hurston was. Choice D correctly positions the word being described (Hurston) closer to the descriptive phrase.

12. A. Sentence is correct.

13. C. Error in logical comparison. Compare a percentage with another percentage, not a percentage with a period of time.

14. E. Double negative. The simple change from *hardly no* to *hardly any* corrects the error without introducing new ones.

Answer Sheet–Test 2

Section 1   **ESSAY**

Essay (continued)

If a section has fewer questions than answer spaces, leave the extra spaces blank.

Section 2

1 Ⓐ Ⓑ Ⓒ Ⓓ Ⓔ	8 Ⓐ Ⓑ Ⓒ Ⓓ Ⓔ	15 Ⓐ Ⓑ Ⓒ Ⓓ Ⓔ	22 Ⓐ Ⓑ Ⓒ Ⓓ Ⓔ	29 Ⓐ Ⓑ Ⓒ Ⓓ Ⓔ
2 Ⓐ Ⓑ Ⓒ Ⓓ Ⓔ	9 Ⓐ Ⓑ Ⓒ Ⓓ Ⓔ	16 Ⓐ Ⓑ Ⓒ Ⓓ Ⓔ	23 Ⓐ Ⓑ Ⓒ Ⓓ Ⓔ	30 Ⓐ Ⓑ Ⓒ Ⓓ Ⓔ
3 Ⓐ Ⓑ Ⓒ Ⓓ Ⓔ	10 Ⓐ Ⓑ Ⓒ Ⓓ Ⓔ	17 Ⓐ Ⓑ Ⓒ Ⓓ Ⓔ	24 Ⓐ Ⓑ Ⓒ Ⓓ Ⓔ	31 Ⓐ Ⓑ Ⓒ Ⓓ Ⓔ
4 Ⓐ Ⓑ Ⓒ Ⓓ Ⓔ	11 Ⓐ Ⓑ Ⓒ Ⓓ Ⓔ	18 Ⓐ Ⓑ Ⓒ Ⓓ Ⓔ	25 Ⓐ Ⓑ Ⓒ Ⓓ Ⓔ	32 Ⓐ Ⓑ Ⓒ Ⓓ Ⓔ
5 Ⓐ Ⓑ Ⓒ Ⓓ Ⓔ	12 Ⓐ Ⓑ Ⓒ Ⓓ Ⓔ	19 Ⓐ Ⓑ Ⓒ Ⓓ Ⓔ	26 Ⓐ Ⓑ Ⓒ Ⓓ Ⓔ	33 Ⓐ Ⓑ Ⓒ Ⓓ Ⓔ
6 Ⓐ Ⓑ Ⓒ Ⓓ Ⓔ	13 Ⓐ Ⓑ Ⓒ Ⓓ Ⓔ	20 Ⓐ Ⓑ Ⓒ Ⓓ Ⓔ	27 Ⓐ Ⓑ Ⓒ Ⓓ Ⓔ	34 Ⓐ Ⓑ Ⓒ Ⓓ Ⓔ
7 Ⓐ Ⓑ Ⓒ Ⓓ Ⓔ	14 Ⓐ Ⓑ Ⓒ Ⓓ Ⓔ	21 Ⓐ Ⓑ Ⓒ Ⓓ Ⓔ	28 Ⓐ Ⓑ Ⓒ Ⓓ Ⓔ	35 Ⓐ Ⓑ Ⓒ Ⓓ Ⓔ

Section 3

1 Ⓐ Ⓑ Ⓒ Ⓓ Ⓔ	8 Ⓐ Ⓑ Ⓒ Ⓓ Ⓔ	15 Ⓐ Ⓑ Ⓒ Ⓓ Ⓔ	22 Ⓐ Ⓑ Ⓒ Ⓓ Ⓔ	29 Ⓐ Ⓑ Ⓒ Ⓓ Ⓔ
2 Ⓐ Ⓑ Ⓒ Ⓓ Ⓔ	9 Ⓐ Ⓑ Ⓒ Ⓓ Ⓔ	16 Ⓐ Ⓑ Ⓒ Ⓓ Ⓔ	23 Ⓐ Ⓑ Ⓒ Ⓓ Ⓔ	30 Ⓐ Ⓑ Ⓒ Ⓓ Ⓔ
3 Ⓐ Ⓑ Ⓒ Ⓓ Ⓔ	10 Ⓐ Ⓑ Ⓒ Ⓓ Ⓔ	17 Ⓐ Ⓑ Ⓒ Ⓓ Ⓔ	24 Ⓐ Ⓑ Ⓒ Ⓓ Ⓔ	31 Ⓐ Ⓑ Ⓒ Ⓓ Ⓔ
4 Ⓐ Ⓑ Ⓒ Ⓓ Ⓔ	11 Ⓐ Ⓑ Ⓒ Ⓓ Ⓔ	18 Ⓐ Ⓑ Ⓒ Ⓓ Ⓔ	25 Ⓐ Ⓑ Ⓒ Ⓓ Ⓔ	32 Ⓐ Ⓑ Ⓒ Ⓓ Ⓔ
5 Ⓐ Ⓑ Ⓒ Ⓓ Ⓔ	12 Ⓐ Ⓑ Ⓒ Ⓓ Ⓔ	19 Ⓐ Ⓑ Ⓒ Ⓓ Ⓔ	26 Ⓐ Ⓑ Ⓒ Ⓓ Ⓔ	33 Ⓐ Ⓑ Ⓒ Ⓓ Ⓔ
6 Ⓐ Ⓑ Ⓒ Ⓓ Ⓔ	13 Ⓐ Ⓑ Ⓒ Ⓓ Ⓔ	20 Ⓐ Ⓑ Ⓒ Ⓓ Ⓔ	27 Ⓐ Ⓑ Ⓒ Ⓓ Ⓔ	34 Ⓐ Ⓑ Ⓒ Ⓓ Ⓔ
7 Ⓐ Ⓑ Ⓒ Ⓓ Ⓔ	14 Ⓐ Ⓑ Ⓒ Ⓓ Ⓔ	21 Ⓐ Ⓑ Ⓒ Ⓓ Ⓔ	28 Ⓐ Ⓑ Ⓒ Ⓓ Ⓔ	35 Ⓐ Ⓑ Ⓒ Ⓓ Ⓔ

Section 4

1 Ⓐ Ⓑ Ⓒ Ⓓ Ⓔ	8 Ⓐ Ⓑ Ⓒ Ⓓ Ⓔ	15 Ⓐ Ⓑ Ⓒ Ⓓ Ⓔ	22 Ⓐ Ⓑ Ⓒ Ⓓ Ⓔ	29 Ⓐ Ⓑ Ⓒ Ⓓ Ⓔ
2 Ⓐ Ⓑ Ⓒ Ⓓ Ⓔ	9 Ⓐ Ⓑ Ⓒ Ⓓ Ⓔ	16 Ⓐ Ⓑ Ⓒ Ⓓ Ⓔ	23 Ⓐ Ⓑ Ⓒ Ⓓ Ⓔ	30 Ⓐ Ⓑ Ⓒ Ⓓ Ⓔ
3 Ⓐ Ⓑ Ⓒ Ⓓ Ⓔ	10 Ⓐ Ⓑ Ⓒ Ⓓ Ⓔ	17 Ⓐ Ⓑ Ⓒ Ⓓ Ⓔ	24 Ⓐ Ⓑ Ⓒ Ⓓ Ⓔ	31 Ⓐ Ⓑ Ⓒ Ⓓ Ⓔ
4 Ⓐ Ⓑ Ⓒ Ⓓ Ⓔ	11 Ⓐ Ⓑ Ⓒ Ⓓ Ⓔ	18 Ⓐ Ⓑ Ⓒ Ⓓ Ⓔ	25 Ⓐ Ⓑ Ⓒ Ⓓ Ⓔ	32 Ⓐ Ⓑ Ⓒ Ⓓ Ⓔ
5 Ⓐ Ⓑ Ⓒ Ⓓ Ⓔ	12 Ⓐ Ⓑ Ⓒ Ⓓ Ⓔ	19 Ⓐ Ⓑ Ⓒ Ⓓ Ⓔ	26 Ⓐ Ⓑ Ⓒ Ⓓ Ⓔ	33 Ⓐ Ⓑ Ⓒ Ⓓ Ⓔ
6 Ⓐ Ⓑ Ⓒ Ⓓ Ⓔ	13 Ⓐ Ⓑ Ⓒ Ⓓ Ⓔ	20 Ⓐ Ⓑ Ⓒ Ⓓ Ⓔ	27 Ⓐ Ⓑ Ⓒ Ⓓ Ⓔ	34 Ⓐ Ⓑ Ⓒ Ⓓ Ⓔ
7 Ⓐ Ⓑ Ⓒ Ⓓ Ⓔ	14 Ⓐ Ⓑ Ⓒ Ⓓ Ⓔ	21 Ⓐ Ⓑ Ⓒ Ⓓ Ⓔ	28 Ⓐ Ⓑ Ⓒ Ⓓ Ⓔ	35 Ⓐ Ⓑ Ⓒ Ⓓ Ⓔ

Section 6

1 Ⓐ Ⓑ Ⓒ Ⓓ Ⓔ	8 Ⓐ Ⓑ Ⓒ Ⓓ Ⓔ	15 Ⓐ Ⓑ Ⓒ Ⓓ Ⓔ	22 Ⓐ Ⓑ Ⓒ Ⓓ Ⓔ	29 Ⓐ Ⓑ Ⓒ Ⓓ Ⓔ
2 Ⓐ Ⓑ Ⓒ Ⓓ Ⓔ	9 Ⓐ Ⓑ Ⓒ Ⓓ Ⓔ	16 Ⓐ Ⓑ Ⓒ Ⓓ Ⓔ	23 Ⓐ Ⓑ Ⓒ Ⓓ Ⓔ	30 Ⓐ Ⓑ Ⓒ Ⓓ Ⓔ
3 Ⓐ Ⓑ Ⓒ Ⓓ Ⓔ	10 Ⓐ Ⓑ Ⓒ Ⓓ Ⓔ	17 Ⓐ Ⓑ Ⓒ Ⓓ Ⓔ	24 Ⓐ Ⓑ Ⓒ Ⓓ Ⓔ	31 Ⓐ Ⓑ Ⓒ Ⓓ Ⓔ
4 Ⓐ Ⓑ Ⓒ Ⓓ Ⓔ	11 Ⓐ Ⓑ Ⓒ Ⓓ Ⓔ	18 Ⓐ Ⓑ Ⓒ Ⓓ Ⓔ	25 Ⓐ Ⓑ Ⓒ Ⓓ Ⓔ	32 Ⓐ Ⓑ Ⓒ Ⓓ Ⓔ
5 Ⓐ Ⓑ Ⓒ Ⓓ Ⓔ	12 Ⓐ Ⓑ Ⓒ Ⓓ Ⓔ	19 Ⓐ Ⓑ Ⓒ Ⓓ Ⓔ	26 Ⓐ Ⓑ Ⓒ Ⓓ Ⓔ	33 Ⓐ Ⓑ Ⓒ Ⓓ Ⓔ
6 Ⓐ Ⓑ Ⓒ Ⓓ Ⓔ	13 Ⓐ Ⓑ Ⓒ Ⓓ Ⓔ	20 Ⓐ Ⓑ Ⓒ Ⓓ Ⓔ	27 Ⓐ Ⓑ Ⓒ Ⓓ Ⓔ	34 Ⓐ Ⓑ Ⓒ Ⓓ Ⓔ
7 Ⓐ Ⓑ Ⓒ Ⓓ Ⓔ	14 Ⓐ Ⓑ Ⓒ Ⓓ Ⓔ	21 Ⓐ Ⓑ Ⓒ Ⓓ Ⓔ	28 Ⓐ Ⓑ Ⓒ Ⓓ Ⓔ	35 Ⓐ Ⓑ Ⓒ Ⓓ Ⓔ

Remove answer sheet by cutting on dotted line

Test 2

Section 7

1 Ⓐ Ⓑ Ⓒ Ⓓ Ⓔ   3 Ⓐ Ⓑ Ⓒ Ⓓ Ⓔ   5 Ⓐ Ⓑ Ⓒ Ⓓ Ⓔ   7 Ⓐ Ⓑ Ⓒ Ⓓ Ⓔ
2 Ⓐ Ⓑ Ⓒ Ⓓ Ⓔ   4 Ⓐ Ⓑ Ⓒ Ⓓ Ⓔ   6 Ⓐ Ⓑ Ⓒ Ⓓ Ⓔ   8 Ⓐ Ⓑ Ⓒ Ⓓ Ⓔ

Section 8

1 Ⓐ Ⓑ Ⓒ Ⓓ Ⓔ   5 Ⓐ Ⓑ Ⓒ Ⓓ Ⓔ   9 Ⓐ Ⓑ Ⓒ Ⓓ Ⓔ   13 Ⓐ Ⓑ Ⓒ Ⓓ Ⓔ   17 Ⓐ Ⓑ Ⓒ Ⓓ Ⓔ
2 Ⓐ Ⓑ Ⓒ Ⓓ Ⓔ   6 Ⓐ Ⓑ Ⓒ Ⓓ Ⓔ   10 Ⓐ Ⓑ Ⓒ Ⓓ Ⓔ   14 Ⓐ Ⓑ Ⓒ Ⓓ Ⓔ   18 Ⓐ Ⓑ Ⓒ Ⓓ Ⓔ
3 Ⓐ Ⓑ Ⓒ Ⓓ Ⓔ   7 Ⓐ Ⓑ Ⓒ Ⓓ Ⓔ   11 Ⓐ Ⓑ Ⓒ Ⓓ Ⓔ   15 Ⓐ Ⓑ Ⓒ Ⓓ Ⓔ   19 Ⓐ Ⓑ Ⓒ Ⓓ Ⓔ
4 Ⓐ Ⓑ Ⓒ Ⓓ Ⓔ   8 Ⓐ Ⓑ Ⓒ Ⓓ Ⓔ   12 Ⓐ Ⓑ Ⓒ Ⓓ Ⓔ   16 Ⓐ Ⓑ Ⓒ Ⓓ Ⓔ   20 Ⓐ Ⓑ Ⓒ Ⓓ Ⓔ

Section 9

1 Ⓐ Ⓑ Ⓒ Ⓓ Ⓔ   5 Ⓐ Ⓑ Ⓒ Ⓓ Ⓔ   9 Ⓐ Ⓑ Ⓒ Ⓓ Ⓔ   13 Ⓐ Ⓑ Ⓒ Ⓓ Ⓔ   17 Ⓐ Ⓑ Ⓒ Ⓓ Ⓔ
2 Ⓐ Ⓑ Ⓒ Ⓓ Ⓔ   6 Ⓐ Ⓑ Ⓒ Ⓓ Ⓔ   10 Ⓐ Ⓑ Ⓒ Ⓓ Ⓔ   14 Ⓐ Ⓑ Ⓒ Ⓓ Ⓔ   18 Ⓐ Ⓑ Ⓒ Ⓓ Ⓔ
3 Ⓐ Ⓑ Ⓒ Ⓓ Ⓔ   7 Ⓐ Ⓑ Ⓒ Ⓓ Ⓔ   11 Ⓐ Ⓑ Ⓒ Ⓓ Ⓔ   15 Ⓐ Ⓑ Ⓒ Ⓓ Ⓔ   19 Ⓐ Ⓑ Ⓒ Ⓓ Ⓔ
4 Ⓐ Ⓑ Ⓒ Ⓓ Ⓔ   8 Ⓐ Ⓑ Ⓒ Ⓓ Ⓔ   12 Ⓐ Ⓑ Ⓒ Ⓓ Ⓔ   16 Ⓐ Ⓑ Ⓒ Ⓓ Ⓔ   20 Ⓐ Ⓑ Ⓒ Ⓓ Ⓔ

Section 10

1 Ⓐ Ⓑ Ⓒ Ⓓ Ⓔ   5 Ⓐ Ⓑ Ⓒ Ⓓ Ⓔ   9 Ⓐ Ⓑ Ⓒ Ⓓ Ⓔ   13 Ⓐ Ⓑ Ⓒ Ⓓ Ⓔ   17 Ⓐ Ⓑ Ⓒ Ⓓ Ⓔ
2 Ⓐ Ⓑ Ⓒ Ⓓ Ⓔ   6 Ⓐ Ⓑ Ⓒ Ⓓ Ⓔ   10 Ⓐ Ⓑ Ⓒ Ⓓ Ⓔ   14 Ⓐ Ⓑ Ⓒ Ⓓ Ⓔ   18 Ⓐ Ⓑ Ⓒ Ⓓ Ⓔ
3 Ⓐ Ⓑ Ⓒ Ⓓ Ⓔ   7 Ⓐ Ⓑ Ⓒ Ⓓ Ⓔ   11 Ⓐ Ⓑ Ⓒ Ⓓ Ⓔ   15 Ⓐ Ⓑ Ⓒ Ⓓ Ⓔ   19 Ⓐ Ⓑ Ⓒ Ⓓ Ⓔ
4 Ⓐ Ⓑ Ⓒ Ⓓ Ⓔ   8 Ⓐ Ⓑ Ⓒ Ⓓ Ⓔ   12 Ⓐ Ⓑ Ⓒ Ⓓ Ⓔ   16 Ⓐ Ⓑ Ⓒ Ⓓ Ⓔ   20 Ⓐ Ⓑ Ⓒ Ⓓ Ⓔ

Test 2

1 1 1 1 1 1 1 1

SECTION **1**   **Time—25 Minutes**   **ESSAY**

> The excerpt appearing below makes a point about a particular topic. Read the passage carefully, and think about the assignment that follows.

Each fresh crisis we encounter is an opportunity in disguise.

ASSIGNMENT: What are your thoughts on the statement above? Compose an essay in which you express your views on this topic. Your essay may support, refute, or qualify the view expressed in the statement. What you write, however, must be relevant to the topic under discussion. Additionally, you must support your viewpoint, indicating your reasoning and providing examples based on your studies and/or experience.

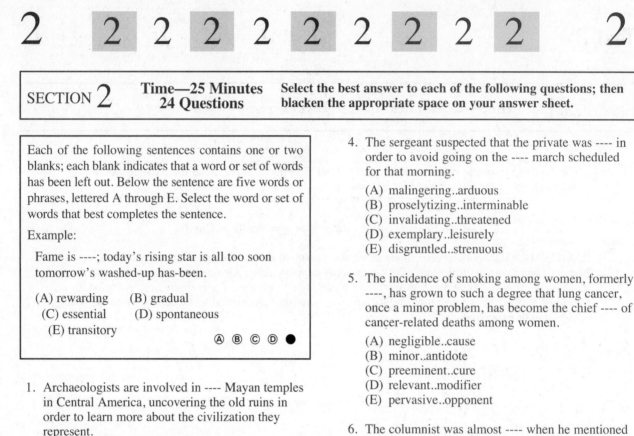

SECTION 2   **Time—25 Minutes**
24 Questions   **Select the best answer to each of the following questions; then blacken the appropriate space on your answer sheet.**

Each of the following sentences contains one or two blanks; each blank indicates that a word or set of words has been left out. Below the sentence are five words or phrases, lettered A through E. Select the word or set of words that best completes the sentence.

Example:

Fame is ----; today's rising star is all too soon tomorrow's washed-up has-been.

(A) rewarding   (B) gradual
(C) essential   (D) spontaneous
(E) transitory

Ⓐ Ⓑ Ⓒ Ⓓ ●

1. Archaeologists are involved in ---- Mayan temples in Central America, uncovering the old ruins in order to learn more about the civilization they represent.

(A) demolishing   (B) incapacitating
(C) excavating   (D) worshiping
(E) adapting

2. Afraid that the ---- nature of the plays being presented would corrupt the morals of their audiences, the Puritans closed the theaters in 1642.

(A) mediocre
(B) fantastic
(C) profound
(D) lewd
(E) witty

3. The governor's imposition of martial law on the once-peaceful community was the last straw, so far as the lawmakers were concerned: the legislature refused to function until martial law was ----.

(A) reaffirmed   (B) reiterated   (C) inaugurated
(D) rescinded   (E) prolonged

4. The sergeant suspected that the private was ---- in order to avoid going on the ---- march scheduled for that morning.

(A) malingering..arduous
(B) proselytizing..interminable
(C) invalidating..threatened
(D) exemplary..leisurely
(E) disgruntled..strenuous

5. The incidence of smoking among women, formerly ----, has grown to such a degree that lung cancer, once a minor problem, has become the chief ---- of cancer-related deaths among women.

(A) negligible..cause
(B) minor..antidote
(C) preeminent..cure
(D) relevant..modifier
(E) pervasive..opponent

6. The columnist was almost ---- when he mentioned his friends, but he was unpleasant and even ---- when he discussed people who irritated him.

(A) recalcitrant..laconic
(B) reverential..acrimonious
(C) sensitive..remorseful
(D) insipid..militant
(E) benevolent..stoical

7. An experienced politician who knew better than to launch a campaign in troubled political waters, she intended to wait for a more ---- occasion before she announced her plans.

(A) propitious
(B) provocative
(C) unseemly
(D) questionable
(E) theoretical

8. In one instance illustrating Metternich's consuming ----, he employed several naval captains to purchase books abroad for him, eventually adding an entire Oriental library to his ---- collection.

(A) foresight..indifferent
(B) altruism..eclectic
(C) bibliomania..burgeoning
(D) avarice..inadvertent
(E) egocentricity..magnanimous

GO ON TO THE NEXT PAGE

Test 2

2 2 2 2 2 2 2 2 2 2 2

Read each of the passages below, and then answer the questions that follow the passage. The correct response may be stated outright or merely suggested in the passage.

Questions 9 and 10 are based on the following passage.

After the mine owner had stripped the vegetation from twelve acres of extremely steep land at a creek head, a flash flood tumbled masses of
Line mining debris into the swollen stream. Though no
(5) lives were lost, the flood destroyed all the homes in the valley. When damage suits brought substantial verdicts favoring the victims, the company took its case to the more sympathetic tribunal at Frankfort. The state judges proclaimed
(10) that the masses of soil, uprooted trees, and slabs of rock had been harmless until set in motion by the force of water; thus they solemnly declared the damage an act of God—for which no coal operator, God-fearing or otherwise, could be held responsible.

9. As used in line 8, the word "sympathetic" most nearly means

(A) sensitive
(B) favorably inclined
(C) showing empathy
(D) humanitarian
(E) dispassionate

10. In describing the coal operator as "God-fearing or otherwise" (line 14), the author is most likely being

(A) reverent
(B) pragmatic
(C) fearful
(D) ironic
(E) naive

Questions 11 and 12 are based on the following passage.

In this excerpt from Jane Austen's The Watsons, *the elderly Mr. Watson discusses a visit to church.*

"I do not know when I have heard a discourse more to my mind," continued Mr. Watson, "or one better delivered. He reads extremely well,
Line with great propriety and in a very impressive
(5) manner; and at the same time without any theatrical grimace or violence. I own, I do not like much action in the pulpit. I do not like the studied air and artificial inflections of voice, which your very popular preachers have. A simple delivery is
(10) much better calculated to inspire devotion, and shows a much better taste. Mr. Howard read like a scholar and a gentleman."

11. The passage suggests that Mr. Watson would most likely agree with which statement?

(A) A dramatic style of preaching appeals most to discerning listeners.
(B) Mr. Howard is too much the gentleman-scholar to be a good preacher.
(C) A proper preacher avoids extremes in delivering his sermons.
(D) There is no use preaching to anyone unless you happen to catch him when he is ill.
(E) A man often preaches his beliefs precisely when he has lost them.

12. The word "studied" (line 7) most nearly means

(A) affected
(B) academic
(C) amateurish
(D) learned
(E) diligent

Test 2

GO ON TO THE NEXT PAGE

2   2 2 2 2 2 2 2 2 2   2

Questions 13–24 are based on the following passage.

Rock musicians often affect the role of social revolu-
tionaries. The following passage is taken from an
unpublished thesis on the potential of rock and roll
music to contribute to political and social change.

It should be clear from the previous arguments
that rock and roll cannot escape its role as a part
of popular culture. One important part of that role
Line is its commercial nature. Rock and roll is "big
(5) corporation business in America and around the
globe. As David De Voss has noted: 'Over fifty
U.S. rock artists annually earn from $2 million to
$6 million. At last count, thirty-five artists and
fifteen additional groups make from three to
(10) seven times more than America's highest paid
business executive.'"
Perhaps the most damning argument against
rock and roll as a political catalyst is suggested by
John Berger in an essay on advertising. Berger
(15) argues that "publicity turns consumption into a
substitute for democracy. The choice of what one
eats (or wears or drives) takes the place of significant political choice." To the extent that rock and
roll is big business, and that it is marketed like
(20) other consumer goods, rock and roll also serves
this role. Our freedom to choose the music we are
sold may be distracting us from more important
concerns. It is this tendency of rock and roll,
fought against but also fulfilled by punk, that Julie
(25) Burchill and Tony Parsons describe in *The Boy*
Looked at Johnny: The Obituary of Rock and Roll.

Never mind, kid, there'll soon be another
washing-machine/spot-cream/rock-band on
the market to solve all your problems and
(30)   keep you quiet/off the street/distracted from
the real enemy/content till the next pay-day.
Anyhow, God Save Rock and Roll. . . it
made you a consumer, a potential Moron. . .
IT'S ONLY ROCK AND ROLL AND IT'S
(35)   PLASTIC, PLASTIC, YES IT IS!!!!!!

This is a frustrating conclusion to reach, and it
is especially frustrating for rock and roll artists
who are dissatisfied with the political systems in
which they live. If rock and roll's ability to pro-
(40) mote political change is hampered by its popularity, the factor that gives it the potential to reach
significant numbers of people, to what extent can
rock and roll artists act politically? Apart from
charitable endeavors, with which rock and roll
(45) artists have been quite successful at raising
money for various causes, the potential for significant political activity promoting change appears
quite limited.

The history of rock and roll is filled with rock
(50) artists who abandoned, at least on vinyl, their
political commitment. Bob Dylan, who, by introducing the explicit politics of folk music to rock
and roll, can be credited with introducing the
political rock and roll of the sixties, quickly aban-
(55) doned politics for more personal issues. John
Lennon, who was perhaps more successful than
any other rock and roll artist at getting political
material to the popular audience, still had a hard
time walking the line between being overtly polit-
(60) ical but unpopular and being apolitical and
extremely popular. In 1969 "Give Peace a
Chance" reached number fourteen on the
Billboard singles charts. 1971 saw "Power to the
People" at number eleven. But the apolitical
(65) "Instant Karma" reached number three on the
charts one year earlier. "Imagine," which mixed
personal and political concerns, also reached
number three one year later. Lennon's most political album, *Some Time in New York City*, pro-
(70) duced no hits. His biggest hits, "Whatever Gets
You Through the Night" and "Starting Over,"
which both reached number one on the charts, are
apolitical. Jon Wiener, in his biography of
Lennon, argues that on "Whatever Gets You
(75) Through the Night," "it seemed like John was
turning himself into Paul, the person without
political values, who put out Number One songs
and who managed to sleep soundly. Maybe that's
why John (Lennon) told Elton John that 'What-
(80) ever Gets You Through the Night' was 'one of
my least favorites.'" When, after leaving music
for five years, Lennon returned in 1980 with the
best-selling *Double Fantasy* album, the subject of
his writing was "caring, sharing, and being a
(85) whole person."
The politically motivated rock and roll artist's
other option is to maintain his political commitment without fooling himself as to the ultimate
impact his work will have. If his music is not
(90) doomed to obscurity by the challenge it presents
to its listeners the artist is lucky. But even such
luck can do nothing to protect his work from the
misinterpretation it will be subjected to once it is
popular. Tom Greene of the Mekons expresses
(95) the frustration such artists feel when he says,
"You just throw your hands up in horror and try
and . . . I don't know. I mean, what can you do?

GO ON TO THE NEXT PAGE

How can you possibly avoid being a part of the power relations that exist?" The artist's challenge
(100) is to *try* to communicate with his audience. But he can only take responsibility for his own intentions. Ultimately, it is the popular audience that must take responsibility for what it does with the artist's work. The rock and roll artist cannot cause
(105) political change. But, if he is very lucky, the popular audience might let him contribute to the change it makes.

13. De Voss's comparison of the salaries of rock stars and corporate executives (lines 8–11) is cited primarily in order to

(A) express the author's familiarity with current pay scales
(B) argue in favor of higher pay for musical artists
(C) refute the assertion that rock and roll stars are underpaid
(D) support the view that rock and roll is a major industry
(E) indicate the lack of limits on the wages of popular stars

14. The word "consumption" in line 15 means

(A) supposition
(B) beginning a task
(C) using up goods
(D) advertising a product
(E) culmination

15. In the quotation cited in lines 27–35, Burchill and Parsons most likely run the words "washing-machine/spot-cream/rock-band" together to indicate that

(A) to the consumer they are all commodities
(B) they are products with universal appeal
(C) advertisers need to market them differently
(D) rock music eliminates conventional distinctions
(E) they are equally necessary parts of modern society

16. The word "plastic" in the Burchill and Parsons quotation (line 35) is being used

(A) lyrically
(B) spontaneously
(C) metaphorically
(D) affirmatively
(E) skeptically

17. Their comments in lines 32 and 33 suggest that Burchill and Parsons primarily regard consumers as

(A) invariably dimwitted
(B) markedly ambivalent
(C) compulsively spendthrift
(D) unfamiliar with commerce
(E) vulnerable to manipulation

18. The author's comments about Bob Dylan (lines 51–55) chiefly suggest that

(A) Dylan readily abandoned political rock and roll for folk music
(B) folk music gave voice to political concerns long before rock and roll music did
(C) rock and roll swiftly replaced folk music in the public's affections
(D) Dylan lacked the necessary skills to convey his political message musically
(E) Dylan betrayed his fans' faith in him by turning away from political commentary

19. Wiener's statement quoted in lines 75–81 suggests that

(A) John had no desire to imitate more successful performers
(B) John was unable to write Number One songs without help from Paul
(C) because Paul lacked political values, he wrote fewer Number One songs than John did
(D) as an apolitical performer, Paul suffered less strain than John did
(E) John disliked "Whatever Gets You Through the Night" because it had been composed by Paul

20. In lines 70–85, "Starting Over" and the *Double Fantasy* album are presented as examples of

(A) bold applications of John's radical philosophy
(B) overtly political recordings without general appeal
(C) profitable successes lacking political content
(D) uninspired and unpopular rock and roll records
(E) unusual recordings that effected widespread change

GO ON TO THE NEXT PAGE

21. The word "maintain" in line 87 means
    (A) repair   (B) contend   (C) subsidize
    (D) brace   (E) keep

22. As quoted in lines 96–99, Tom Greene of the Mekons feels particularly frustrated because
    (A) his work has lost its initial popularity
    (B) he cannot escape involvement in the power structure
    (C) his original commitment to political change has diminished
    (D) he lacks the vocabulary to make coherent political statements
    (E) he is horrified by the price he must pay for political success

23. The author attributes the success of the politically motivated rock and roll artist to
    (A) political influence
    (B) challenging material
    (C) good fortune
    (D) personal contacts
    (E) textual misinterpretation

24. In the last paragraph, the author concludes that the rock and roll artist's contribution to political change is
    (A) immediate
    (B) decisive
    (C) indirect
    (D) irresponsible
    (E) blatant

YOU MAY GO BACK AND REVIEW THIS SECTION IN THE REMAINING TIME, BUT DO NOT WORK IN ANY OTHER SECTION UNTIL TOLD TO DO SO.

STOP

3   **3** **3** **3** **3** **3** **3** **3** **3** **3** **3**   **3**

SECTION **3**

Time—25 Minutes
20 Questions

For each problem in this section determine which of the five choices
is correct and blacken the corresponding choice on your answer
sheet. You may use any blank space on the page for your work.

Notes:

- You may use a calculator whenever you think it will be helpful.
- Only real numbers are used. No question or answer on this test involves a complex or imaginary number.
- Use the diagrams provided to help you solve the problems. Unless you see the words "Note: Figure not drawn to scale" under a diagram, it has been drawn as accurately as possible. Unless it is stated that a figure is three-dimensional, you may assume it lies in a plane.
- For any function f, the domain, unless specifically restricted, is the set of all real numbers for which $f(x)$ is also a real number.

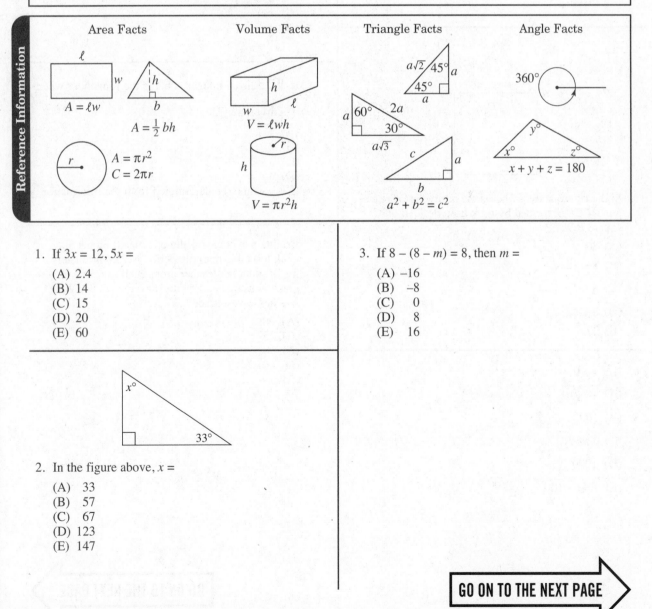

1. If $3x = 12$, $5x =$

   (A) 2.4
   (B) 14
   (C) 15
   (D) 20
   (E) 60

3. If $8 - (8 - m) = 8$, then $m =$

   (A) −16
   (B) −8
   (C)   0
   (D)   8
   (E) 16

2. In the figure above, $x =$

   (A)   33
   (B)   57
   (C)   67
   (D) 123
   (E) 147

GO ON TO THE NEXT PAGE

3   3 3 3 3 3 3 3 3 3 3   3

4. If $\frac{5}{9}$ of the members of the school chorus are boys, what is the ratio of girls to boys in the chorus?

(A) $\frac{4}{9}$

(B) $\frac{4}{5}$

(C) $\frac{5}{4}$

(D) $\frac{9}{4}$

(E) It cannot be determined from the information given.

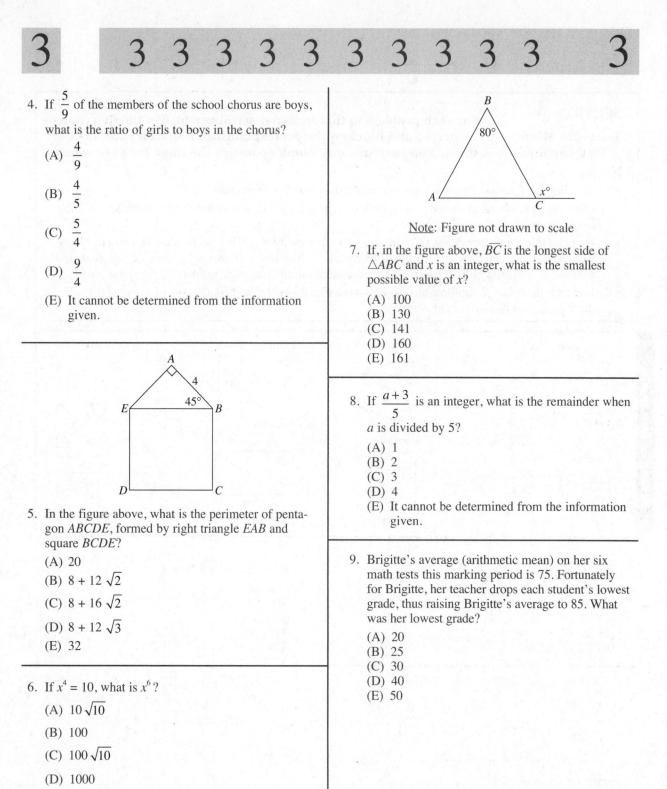

5. In the figure above, what is the perimeter of pentagon *ABCDE*, formed by right triangle *EAB* and square *BCDE*?

(A) 20

(B) $8 + 12\sqrt{2}$

(C) $8 + 16\sqrt{2}$

(D) $8 + 12\sqrt{3}$

(E) 32

6. If $x^4 = 10$, what is x^6?

(A) $10\sqrt{10}$

(B) 100

(C) $100\sqrt{10}$

(D) 1000

(E) $1000\sqrt{10}$

Note: Figure not drawn to scale

7. If, in the figure above, $\overline{BC}$ is the longest side of $\triangle ABC$ and *x* is an integer, what is the smallest possible value of *x*?

(A) 100

(B) 130

(C) 141

(D) 160

(E) 161

8. If $\frac{a+3}{5}$ is an integer, what is the remainder when *a* is divided by 5?

(A) 1

(B) 2

(C) 3

(D) 4

(E) It cannot be determined from the information given.

9. Brigitte's average (arithmetic mean) on her six math tests this marking period is 75. Fortunately for Brigitte, her teacher drops each student's lowest grade, thus raising Brigitte's average to 85. What was her lowest grade?

(A) 20

(B) 25

(C) 30

(D) 40

(E) 50

GO ON TO THE NEXT PAGE

Test 2

3   3 3 3 3 3 3 3 3 3 3   3

10. If m is an integer, which of the following could be true?

   I. $\dfrac{17}{m}$ is an even integer.

   II. $\dfrac{m}{17}$ is an even integer.

   III. $17m$ is a prime.

   (A) I only
   (B) II only
   (C) III only
   (D) I and II only
   (E) II and III only

11. Max purchased some shares of stock at $10 per share. Six months later the stock was worth $20 per share. What was the percent increase in the value of Max's investment?

   (A) 20%
   (B) 50%
   (C) 100%
   (D) 200%
   (E) The answer depends on the number of shares purchased.

12. Benjamin can type a full report in h hours. At this rate, how many reports can he type in m minutes?

   (A) $\dfrac{mh}{60}$

   (B) $\dfrac{60m}{h}$

   (C) $\dfrac{m}{60h}$

   (D) $\dfrac{60h}{m}$

   (E) $\dfrac{h}{60m}$

13. The estate of a wealthy man was distributed as follows: 10% to his wife, 5% divided equally among his three children, 5% divided equally among his five grandchildren, and the balance to a charitable trust. If the trust received $1,000,000, how much did each grandchild inherit?

   (A) $10,000
   (B) $12,500
   (C) $20,000
   (D) $62,500
   (E) $100,000

14. If A, B, C, and D lie on the same straight line, and if $AC = 2CD = 3BD$, what is the value of the ratio $\dfrac{BC}{CD}$?

   (A) $\dfrac{1}{6}$

   (B) $\dfrac{1}{3}$

   (C) $\dfrac{1}{2}$

   (D) $\dfrac{5}{3}$

   (E) It cannot be determined from the information given.

15. A car going 40 miles per hour set out on an 80-mile trip at 9:00 A.M. Exactly 10 minutes later, a second car left from the same place and followed the same route. How fast, in miles per hour, was the second car going if it caught up with the first car at 10:30 A.M.?

   (A) 45
   (B) 50
   (C) 53
   (D) 55
   (E) 60

3   3 3 3 3 3 3 3 3 3 3   3

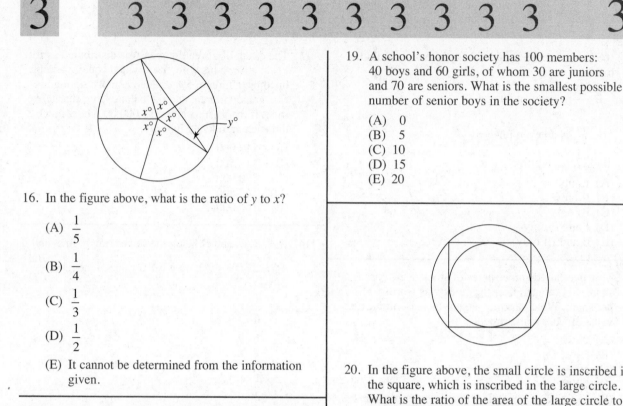

16. In the figure above, what is the ratio of *y* to *x*?

   (A) $\dfrac{1}{5}$

   (B) $\dfrac{1}{4}$

   (C) $\dfrac{1}{3}$

   (D) $\dfrac{1}{2}$

   (E) It cannot be determined from the information given.

Questions 17 and 18 refer to the following definition.

For any positive integer *n*, ⬛*n* represents the sum of the integers from 1 to *n*. For example,
⬛5 = 1 + 2 + 3 + 4 + 5 = 15.

17. Which of the following is equal to ⬛10 − ⬛9 ?
   (A) ⬛1
   (B) ⬛2
   (C) ⬛3
   (D) ⬛4
   (E) ⬛5

18. If ⬛1000 = *a* and ⬛10 = *b*, what is the value of ⬛1010 ?
   (A) *a + b*
   (B) *a + 10b*
   (C) *a + b + 1000*
   (D) *a + b + 10,000*
   (E) *a + 1000b*

19. A school's honor society has 100 members: 40 boys and 60 girls, of whom 30 are juniors and 70 are seniors. What is the smallest possible number of senior boys in the society?

   (A) 0
   (B) 5
   (C) 10
   (D) 15
   (E) 20

20. In the figure above, the small circle is inscribed in the square, which is inscribed in the large circle. What is the ratio of the area of the large circle to the area of the small circle?

   (A) $\sqrt{2}$:1

   (B) $\sqrt{3}$:1

   (C) 2:1

   (D) 2 $\sqrt{2}$:1

   (E) It cannot be determined from the information given.

YOU MAY GO BACK AND REVIEW THIS SECTION IN THE REMAINING TIME, BUT DO NOT WORK IN ANY OTHER SECTION UNTIL TOLD TO DO SO.

S T O P

4 4 4 4 4 4 4 4 4 4 4   4

SECTION **4**   Time—25 Minutes   Select the best answer to each of the following questions; then
                 35 Questions   blacken the appropriate space on your answer sheet.

Some or all parts of the following sentences are under-lined. The first answer choice, (A), simply repeats the underlined part of the sentence. The other four choices present four alternative ways to phrase the underlined part. Select the answer that produces the most effective sentence, one that is clear and exact, and blacken the appropriate space on your answer sheet. In selecting your choice, be sure that it is standard written English, and that it expresses the meaning of the original sentence.

Example:
The first biography of author Eudora Welty came out in 1998 <u>and she was 89 years old at the time</u>.

(A) and she was 89 years old at the time
(B) at the time when she was 89
(C) upon becoming an 89 year old
(D) when she was 89
(E) at the age of 89 years old

Ⓐ Ⓑ Ⓒ ● Ⓔ

---

1. By the time we arrive in Italy, <u>we have traveled through four countries</u>.

   (A) we have traveled through four countries
   (B) we had traveled through four countries
   (C) we will have traveled through four countries
   (D) four countries will have been traveled through
   (E) we through four countries shall have traveled

2. To say "My lunch was satisfactory" is <u>complimentary, to say</u> "My lunch was adequate" is not.

   (A) complimentary, to say
   (B) complementary, to say
   (C) complementary, however, to say
   (D) complimentary, but to say
   (E) complementary to saying

3. When one debates the merits of the proposed reduction in our tax base, <u>you should take into consideration the effect</u> it will have on the schools and the other public services.

   (A) you should take into consideration the effect
   (B) you should consider the effect
   (C) one should take the affect
   (D) one takes into consideration the affect
   (E) one should take into consideration the effect

4. We were afraid of the teacher's <u>wrath, due to his statement that</u> he would penalize anyone who failed to hand in his term paper on time.

   (A) wrath, due to his statement that
   (B) wrath due to his statement that,
   (C) wrath, inasmuch as his statement that,
   (D) wrath because of his statement that
   (E) wrath and his statement that,

5. Because the sports industry has become so <u>popular is the reason that some universities have created new courses in sports marketing and event planning</u>.

   (A) popular is the reason that some universities have created new courses in sports marketing and event planning
   (B) popular, some universities have created new courses in sports marketing and event planning
   (C) popular, there have been new courses in sports marketing and event planning created by some universities
   (D) popular is the reason that new courses in sports marketing and event planning have been created by some universities
   (E) popular, they have created new courses in sports marketing and event planning at some universities

6. I have discovered that the subways in New York are <u>as clean as any other city I have visited</u>.

   (A) as clean as any other city I have visited
   (B) as clean as those in any other city I have visited
   (C) as clean as those in any city I visited
   (D) cleaner than any city I visited
   (E) cleaner than any other city I have visited

GO ON TO THE NEXT PAGE

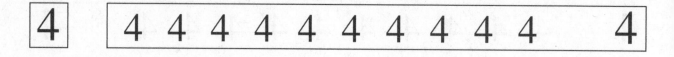

7. Inflation in the United States <u>has not and, we hope, never will reach</u> a rate of 20 percent a year.

(A) has not and, we hope, never will reach
(B) has not reached and, we hope, never will
(C) has not and hopefully never will reach
(D) has not reached and, we hope, never will reach
(E) has not reached and hopefully never will

8. *Godard* is part biography, part cultural <u>analysis, and it partly pays tribute to an artist</u> who, the author believes, is one of the most influential of his time.

(A) analysis, and it partly pays tribute to an artist
(B) analysis, and part tribute to an artist
(C) analysis, and partly a payment of tribute to an artist
(D) analysis, also it partly pays tribute to an artist
(E) analysis, but there is a part that is a tribute to an artist

9. Embarrassment over the discovery of <u>element 118, announced with great fanfare and then retracted amid accusations of scientific fraud, has left</u> the nuclear physics community feeling bruised.

(A) element 118, announced with great fanfare and then retracted amid accusations of scientific fraud, has left
(B) element 118, which was announced with great fanfare and afterwards which was retracted amid accusations of scientific fraud, has left
(C) element 118, announced with great fanfare and then retracted amid accusations of scientific fraud, have left
(D) element 118 was announced with great fanfare and then was retracted amid accusations of scientific fraud, it has left
(E) element 118, it having been announced with great fanfare and then it was retracted amidst accusations of scientific fraud, has left

10. Life on Earth has taken a tremendous range of forms, but all species arise from the same molecular <u>ingredients, these ingredients limit the chemical reactions that can occur within cells</u> and so constrain what life can do.

(A) ingredients, these ingredients limit the chemical reactions that can occur within cells
(B) ingredients, these are ingredients that limit the chemical reactions that can occur within cells
(C) ingredients, these ingredients limit the chemical reactions that could occur within cells
(D) ingredients, which limit the chemical reactions that can occur within cells
(E) ingredients; but these ingredients limit the chemical reactions that can occur within cells

11. Thompson's fictional retelling of Ignaz Semmelweis's battle to eradicate childbed fever proved to at least one adolescent reader that <u>taking a stand against the establishment, no matter the consequences, is worth the struggle.</u>

(A) taking a stand against the establishment, no matter the consequences, is worth the struggle
(B) to take a stand against the establishment, it does not matter what the consequences are, is worth the struggle
(C) taking a stand against the establishment, despite the consequences, are worth the struggle
(D) if one takes a stand against the establishment, no matter the consequences, you will find it worth the trouble
(E) taking a stand against the establishment, irregardless of the consequences, is worth the trouble

Test 2

GO ON TO THE NEXT PAGE

The sentences in this section may contain errors in grammar, usage, choice of words, or idioms. Either there is just one error in a sentence or the sentence is correct. Some words or phrases are underlined and lettered; everything else in the sentence is correct.

If an underlined word or phrase is incorrect, choose that letter; if the sentence is correct, select <u>No error</u>. Then blacken the appropriate space on your answer sheet.

Example:

The region has a climate <u>so severe that</u> plants
                     A

<u>growing</u> there rarely <u>had been</u> more than twelve
  B   C

inches <u>high</u>. <u>No error</u>
     D   E

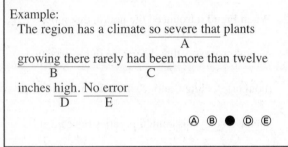

---

12. The lieutenant <u>reminded</u> his men that the only
            A

    information <u>to be given</u> to the captors was
              B

    <u>each</u> individual's name, rank, and
     C

    <u>what his serial number was</u> . <u>No error</u>
             D   E

13. <u>When</u> the teacher ordered the student <u>to go</u> to the
    A   B

    dean's office <u>as a result of</u> the class disruption, she
               C

    surprised us because she usually <u>will handle</u> her
                          D

    own discipline problems. <u>No error</u>
                 E

14. He was the author <u>whom</u> I <u>believed</u> was
              A   B

    <u>most likely</u> to receive the <u>coveted</u> award.
     C   D

    <u>No error</u>
     E

15. Please give this scholarship <u>to whoever</u> in the
                    A

    graduating class <u>has done</u> the most <u>to promote</u>
             B   C

    goodwill in the community. <u>No error</u>
     D   E

16. The two lawyers <u>interpreted</u> the statute <u>differently</u>,
               A   B

    <u>and</u> they needed a judge to settle <u>its</u> dispute.
     C   D

    <u>No error</u>
     E

17. All of the team members, except <u>him</u>, <u>has</u>
                     A   B

    anticipated <u>interest from</u> the national leagues, and
             C

    now practice twice <u>as long</u>. <u>No error</u>
                D   E

18. Everybody <u>but him</u> has paid <u>their</u> dues; we
             A   B

    <u>must seek</u> ways to make him understand the
     C

    <u>need for</u> prompt payment. <u>No error</u>
     D   E

19. In order to be sure <u>that</u> the mattress was firm
    A   B

    before placing an order, the man gingerly

    <u>sat down</u> and <u>laid back</u>. <u>No error</u>
     C   D   E

GO ON TO THE NEXT PAGE

Test 2

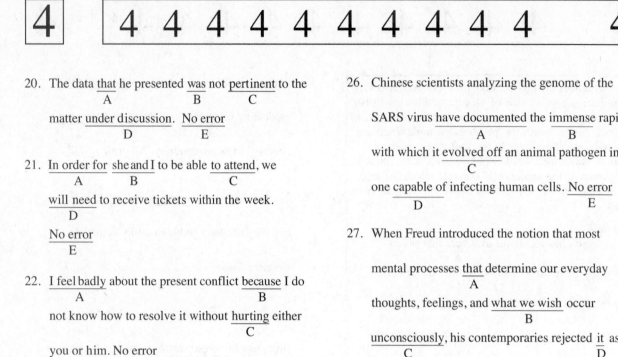

20. The data <u>that</u> he presented <u>was</u> not <u>pertinent</u> to the
    　　　　　A　　　　　　B　　　　　C
    matter <u>under discussion.</u> <u>No error</u>
    　　　　　　D　　　　　　　　　E

21. <u>In order for</u> <u>she and I</u> to be able <u>to attend,</u> we
    　　　A　　　　　　B　　　　　　　　C
    <u>will need</u> to receive tickets within the week.
    　　D
    <u>No error</u>
    　　E

22. I feel <u>badly</u> about the present conflict <u>because</u> I do
    　　　　A　　　　　　　　　　　　　　　B
    not know how to resolve it without <u>hurting</u> either
    　　　　　　　　　　　　　　　　C
    you or <u>him.</u> <u>No error</u>
    　　　　D　　　E

23. A new production of the opera *Aida* has <u>just</u> been
    　　　　　　　　　　　　　　　　　　A
    announced; <u>it</u> <u>will be sang</u> on an outdoor stage
    　　　　　　B　　C
    <u>with</u> live animals. <u>No error</u>
    　　D　　　　　　　E

24. <u>Unless</u> two or more members object to
    　　A
    <u>him</u> joining the club, we shall have <u>to accept</u> his
    　　B　　　　　　　　　　　　　C
    application <u>for</u> membership. <u>No error</u>
    　　　　　D　　　　　　　　E

25. Thurgood Marshall <u>made history</u> by <u>becoming</u> the
    　　　　　　　　　　A　　　　B
    first black Supreme Court Justice <u>when</u> he was
    　　　　　　　　　　　　　　C
    <u>appointed of</u> this position by President Lyndon
    　　D
    Johnson. <u>No error</u>
    　　　　　E

26. Chinese scientists analyzing the genome of the

    SARS virus <u>have documented</u> the <u>immense</u> rapidity
    　　　　　　A　　　　　　　　B
    with which it evolved <u>off</u> an animal pathogen into
    　　　　　　　　　　C
    one capable <u>of infecting</u> human cells. <u>No error</u>
    　　　　　　D　　　　　　　　　E

27. When Freud introduced the notion that most

    mental processes <u>that</u> determine our everyday
    　　　　　　　　A
    thoughts, feelings, and <u>what we wish</u> occur
    　　　　　　　　　　　B
    unconsciously, his contemporaries rejected <u>it</u> as
    　　　　C　　　　　　　　　　　　　D
    impossible. <u>No error</u>
    　　　　　　E

28. Artesian water <u>comes from</u> an artesian well, a well
    　　　　　　　　A
    <u>that</u> taps a water-bearing layer of rock or sand,
    　　B
    <u>in which</u> the water level <u>stands above</u> the top of the
    　　C　　　　　　　　　D
    aquifer. <u>No error</u>
    　　　　　E

29. <u>During</u> the Cultural Revolution in China,
    　　A
    Li Huayi <u>has labored</u> as a "worker-artist," painting
    　　　　　　B
    government propaganda posters, <u>while</u> in private
    　　　　　　　　　　　　　　C
    he developed <u>his own</u> artistic style. <u>No error</u>
    　　　　　　D　　　　　　　　E

4   4 4 4 4 4 4 4 4 4 4   4

The passage below is the unedited draft of a student's essay. Parts of the essay need to be rewritten to make the meaning clearer and more precise. Read the essay carefully.

The essay is followed by six questions about changes that might improve all or part of the organization, development, sentence structure, use of language, appropriateness to the audience, or use of standard written English. In each case, choose the answer that most clearly and effectively expresses the student's intended meaning. Indicate your choice by blackening the corresponding space on the answer sheet.

[1] *From the colonial times until today, the appeal of the underdog has retained a hold on Americans. [2] It is a familiar sight today to see someone rooting for the underdog while watching a sports event on television. [3] Though that only happens if they don't already have a favorite team. [4] Variations of the David and Goliath story are popular in both fact and fiction. [5] Horatio Alger stories, wondrous tales of conquering the West, and the way that people have turned rags-to-riches stories such as Vanderbilt into national myths are three examples of America's fascination with the underdog.*

[6] *This appeal has been spurred by American tradition as well as an understandably selfish desire to feel good about oneself and life. [7] Part of the aura America has held since its creation is that the humblest and poorest person can make it here in America. [8] That dream is ingrained in the history of America. [9] America is made up of immigrants. [10] Most were poor when they came here. [11] They thought of America as the land of opportunity, where any little guy could succeed. [12] All it took was the desire to lift oneself up and some good honest work. [13] Millions succeeded on account of the American belief to honor and support the underdog in all its efforts.*

[14] *The underdog goes against all odds and defeats the stronger opponent with hope. [15] It makes people feel that maybe one day they too will triumph against the odds. [16] It changes their view of life's struggles because they trust that in the end all their hardships will amount to something. [17] Despair has no place in a society where everyone knows that they can succeed. [18] It's no wonder that the underdog has always had a tight hold upon American hopes and minds.*

30. Which of the following is the best revision of the underlined sections of sentences 1 and 2 (below), so that the two sentences are combined into one?

    From the colonial times until today, <u>the appeal of the underdog has retained a hold on Americans. It is a familiar sight today to see someone rooting for the underdog</u> while watching a sports event on television.

    (A) the appeal of the underdog has retained a hold on Americans, and it is a familiar sight today to see underdogs being the one rooted for
    (B) the appeal of the underdog has retained a hold on Americans, but it is a familiar sight today to see someone rooting for the underdog
    (C) the underdog has retained a hold on Americans, who commonly root for the underdog, for example,
    (D) the underdog has retained a hold on Americans, commonly rooting for the underdog
    (E) the underdog's appeal has retained a hold on Americans, for example, they commonly root for the underdog

31. To improve the coherence of paragraph 1, which of the following sentences should be deleted?

    (A) Sentence 1
    (B) Sentence 2
    (C) Sentence 3
    (D) Sentence 4
    (E) Sentence 5

Test 2

GO ON TO THE NEXT PAGE

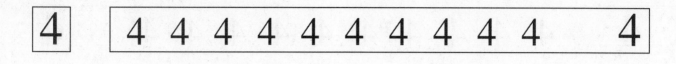

32. Considering the content of paragraph 2, which of the following is the best revision of the paragraph's topic sentence, sentence 6?

(A) This appeal got spurred by American tradition as well as by an understandably selfish desire to feel good about oneself and one's life.

(B) The appeal of the underdog has been spurred by American tradition.

(C) The appeal has been spurred by Americans' traditional and selfish desire to feel good about themselves and life.

(D) American tradition as well as Americans' desire to feel good about oneself and their life has spurred the appeal of underdogs.

(E) American traditions include an understandably selfish desire to feel good about themselves and the appeal of the underdog.

33. In the context of paragraph 2, which of the following is the best way to combine sentences 8, 9, 10, and 11?

(A) That dream is ingrained in the experience of America, a country made up of poor immigrants who believed that in this land of opportunity any little guy had a chance to succeed.

(B) That dream was ingrained in our history, a country made up of immigrants, poor and hopeful that any little guy is able to succeed in America, the land of opportunity.

(C) That dream has been ingrained America's history that poor immigrants look on America as a land of opportunity, which any little guy had been able to succeed in.

(D) The American experience has ingrained in it the dream that by immigrants coming to this country poorly could succeed because America is the land of opportunity.

(E) Ingrained in the American experience is the dream of poor immigrants that they could succeed here, after all, this is the land of opportunity.

34. In view of the sentences that precede and follow sentence 13, which of the following is the most effective revision of sentence 13?

(A) Americans believe that the underdog should be honored and supported, which led to their success.

(B) Because America believed in honoring and supporting the underdog, they succeed.

(C) And succeed they did because of America's commitment to honor and support the underdog.

(D) Honoring and supporting underdogs is a firmly held value in America, and it led to the success of underdogs.

(E) They succeeded with their efforts to be supported and honored by America.

35. Which of the following revisions of sentence 14 is the best transition between paragraphs 3 and 4?

(A) Underdogs, in addition, went against all odds and with hope defeat stronger opponents.

(B) The underdog, feeling hopeful, going against all odds, and defeating stronger opponents.

(C) It is the hope of the underdog who goes against the odds and defeats the stronger opponent.

(D) The triumph of the underdog over a strong opponent inspires hope.

(E) The underdog triumphs against all odds and defeats the stronger opponents.

YOU MAY GO BACK AND REVIEW THIS SECTION IN THE REMAINING TIME, BUT DO NOT WORK IN ANY OTHER SECTION UNTIL TOLD TO DO SO.   **S T O P**

6 6 6 6 6 6 6 6 6 6 6 6 6

SECTION 6 **Time—25 Minutes** **Select the best answer to each of the following questions; then**
24 Questions **blacken the appropriate space on your answer sheet.**

Each of the following sentences contains one or two blanks; each blank indicates that a word or set of words has been left out. Below the sentence are five words or phrases, lettered A through E. Select the word or set of words that best completes the sentence.

Example:

Fame is ----; today's rising star is all too soon tomorrow's washed-up has-been.

(A) rewarding   (B) gradual
(C) essential   (D) spontaneous
(E) transitory

Ⓐ Ⓑ Ⓒ Ⓓ ●

1. The civil rights movement did not emerge from obscurity into national prominence overnight; on the contrary, it captured the public's imagination only ----.

    (A) fruitlessly
    (B) unimpeachably
    (C) momentarily
    (D) expeditiously
    (E) gradually

2. The seventeenth-century writer Mary Astell was a rare phenomenon, a single woman who maintained and even ---- a respectable reputation while earning a living by her pen.

    (A) eclipsed   (B) impaired   (C) decimated
    (D) avoided   (E) enhanced

3. An optimistic supporter of the women's movement, Kubota contends that recent ---- by Japanese women in the business world are meaningful and indicative of ---- opportunity to come.

    (A) advances..diminished
    (B) strides..greater
    (C) innovations..marginal
    (D) retreats..theoretical
    (E) failures..hidden

4. The ---- ambassador was but ---- linguist; yet he insisted on speaking to foreign dignitaries in their own tongues without resorting to a translator's aid.

    (A) eminent..an indifferent
    (B) visiting..a notable
    (C) revered..a talented
    (D) distinguished..a celebrated
    (E) ranking..a sensitive

5. Nowadays life models—men and women who pose in the nude for artists—seem curiously ----, relics of a bygone age when art students labored amid skeletons and anatomical charts, learning to draw the human body as painstakingly as medical students learn to ---- it.

    (A) anachronistic..sketch
    (B) archaic..dissect
    (C) contemporary..diagnose
    (D) stereotyped..examine
    (E) daring..cure

GO ON TO THE NEXT PAGE

Test 2

6   6 6 6 6 6 6 6 6 6 6 6   6

Read the passages below, and then answer the questions that follow them. The correct response may be stated outright or merely suggested in the passages.

Questions 6–9 are based on the following passages.

Passage 1

It was the voyageur who struck my imagination—the canoe man who carried loads of hundreds of pounds and paddled 18 hours a day fighting
Line waves and storms. His muscle and brawn sup-
(5) plied the motive power for French-Canadian exploration and trade, but despite the harshness of his life—the privation, suffering, and constant threat of death by exposure, drowning, and Indian attack—he developed an unsurpassed noncha-
(10) lance and joy in the wilderness. These exuberant men, wearing red sashes and caps and singing in the face of disaster, were the ones who stood out.

Passage 2

The French *voyageurs* ("travelers") in essence were fur traders, commercial agents hired by a
(15) merchant company to conduct trade on its behalf. In Canada, the French fur trade in Montreal was taken over by British fur traders, who provided the capital for the enterprise. The voyageurs, for their part, supplied their knowledge of Indian
(20) tribal customs and wilderness trails, as well as their expertise in traveling by canoe. They estab-lished a system of canoe convoys between fur-trading posts that ran from Montreal to the western plains, well into the region now known as
(25) Canada's North West Territories.

6. As used in Passage 1, the word "struck" (line 1) most nearly means

 (A) picketed
 (B) inflicted
 (C) impressed
 (D) dismantled
 (E) overthrew

7. The author of Passage 1 is most affected by the voyageur's

 (A) inventiveness
 (B) hardships
 (C) strength
 (D) zest
 (E) diligence

8. Compared to the author of Passage 2, the author of Passage 1 regards the voyageurs with more

 (A) overt cynicism
 (B) objective detachment
 (C) open admiration
 (D) misguided affection
 (E) marked ambivalence

9. Unlike the author of Passage 2, the author of Passage 1 makes use of

 (A) direct quotation
 (B) historical research
 (C) literary references
 (D) statistical data
 (E) personal voice

Questions 10–15 are based on the following passage.

The following passage on the formation of oil is excerpted from a novel about oil exploration written by Alistair MacLean.

Five main weather elements act upon rock. Frost and ice fracture rock. It can be gradually eroded by airborne dust. The action of the seas,
Line whether through the constant movement of tides
(5) or the pounding of heavy storm waves, remorse-lessly wears away the coastlines. Rivers are immensely powerful destructive agencies—one has but to look at the Grand Canyon to appreciate their enormous power. And such rocks as escape
(10) all these influences are worn away over the eons by the effect of rain.

Whatever the cause of erosion, the net result is the same. The rock is reduced to its tiniest possi-ble constituents—rock particles or, simply, dust.
(15) Rain and melting snow carry this dust down to the tiniest rivulets and the mightiest rivers, which, in turn, transport it to lakes, inland seas and the coastal regions of the oceans. Dust, however fine and powdery, is still heavier than water, and
(20) whenever the water becomes sufficiently still, it will gradually sink to the bottom, not only in lakes and seas but also in the sluggish lower reaches of rivers and where flood conditions exist, in the form of silt.

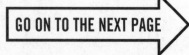
GO ON TO THE NEXT PAGE

(25) And so, over unimaginably long reaches of time, whole mountain ranges are carried down to the seas, and in the process, through the effects of gravity, new rock is born as layer after layer of dust accumulates on the bottom, building up to a *(30)* depth of ten, a hundred, perhaps even a thousand feet, the lowermost layers being gradually compacted by the immense and steadily increasing pressures from above, until the particles fuse together and reform as a new rock.

(35) It is in the intermediate and final processes of the new rock formation that oil comes into being. Those lakes and seas of hundreds of millions of years ago were almost choked by water plants and the most primitive forms of aquatic life. On *(40)* dying, they sank to the bottom of the lakes and seas along with the settling dust particles and were gradually buried deep under the endless layers of more dust and more aquatic and plant life that slowly accumulated above them. The pass- *(45)* ing of millions of years and the steadily increasing pressures from above gradually changed the decayed vegetation and dead aquatic life into oil.

Described this simply and quickly, the process sounds reasonable enough. But this is where the *(50)* gray and disputatious area arises. The conditions necessary for the formation of oil are known; the cause of the metamorphosis is not. It seems probable that some form of chemical catalyst is involved, but this catalyst has not been isolated. *(55)* The first purely synthetic oil, as distinct from secondary synthetic oils such as those derived from coal, has yet to be produced. We just have to accept that oil is oil, that it is there, bound up in rock strata in fairly well-defined areas throughout *(60)* the world but always on the sites of ancient seas and lakes, some of which are now continental land, some buried deep under the encroachment of new oceans.

10. According to the author, which of the following statements is (are) true?

I. The action of the seas is the most important factor in erosion of Earth's surface.
II. Scientists have not been able to produce a purely synthetic oil in the laboratory.
III. Gravity plays an important role in the formation of new rock.

(A) I only
(B) II only
(C) III only
(D) I and III only
(E) II and III only

11. The Grand Canyon is mentioned in the first paragraph to illustrate

(A) the urgent need for dams
(B) the devastating impact of rivers
(C) the effect of rain
(D) a site where oil may be found
(E) the magnificence of nature

12. According to the author, our understanding of the process by which oil is created is

(A) biased   (B) systematic   (C) erroneous
(D) deficient   (E) adequate

13. We can infer that prospectors should search for oil deposits

(A) wherever former seas existed
(B) in mountain streambeds
(C) where coal deposits are found
(D) in the Grand Canyon
(E) in new rock formations

14. The author does all of the following EXCEPT

(A) describe a process
(B) state a possibility
(C) cite an example
(D) propose a solution
(E) mention a limitation

15. The word "reaches" in line 23 means

(A) grasps
(B) unbroken stretches
(C) range of knowledge
(D) promontories
(E) juxtapositions

Test 2

GO ON TO THE NEXT PAGE

Questions 16–24 are based on the following passage.

The following passage is excerpted from a book on the meaning and importance of fairy tales by noted child psychologist Bruno Bettelheim.

Plato—who may have understood better what forms the mind of man than do some of our contemporaries who want their children exposed only to "real" people and everyday events—knew what
(5) intellectual experiences make for true humanity. He suggested that the future citizens of his ideal republic begin their literary education with the telling of myths, rather than with mere facts or so-called rational teachings. Even Aristotle, mas-
(10) ter of pure reason, said: "The friend of wisdom is also a friend of myth."

Modern thinkers who have studied myths and fairy tales from a philosophical or psychological viewpoint arrive at the same conclusion, regard-
(15) less of their original persuasion. Mircea Eliade, for one, describes these stories as "models for human behavior [that,] by that very fact, give meaning and value to life." Drawing on anthropological parallels, he and others suggest that myths
(20) and fairy tales were derived from, or give symbolic expression to, initiation rites or other *rites of passage*—such as metaphoric death of an old, inadequate self in order to be reborn on a higher plane of existence. He feels that this is why these
(25) tales meet a strongly felt need and are carriers of such deep meaning.

Other investigators with a depth-psychological orientation emphasize the similarities between the fantastic events in myths and fairy tales and those
(30) in adult dreams and daydreams—the fulfillment of wishes, the winning out over all competitors, the destruction of enemies—and conclude that one attraction of this literature is its expression of that which is normally prevented from coming to
(35) awareness.

There are, of course, very significant differences between fairy tales and dreams. For example, in dreams more often than not the wish fulfillment is disguised, while in fairy tales much
(40) of it is openly expressed. To a considerable degree, dreams are the result of inner pressures that have found no relief, of problems that beset a person to which he knows no solution and to which the dream finds none. The fairy tale does
(45) the opposite: it projects the relief of all pressures and not only offers ways to solve problems but promises that a "happy" solution will be found.

We cannot control what goes on in our dreams. Although our inner censorship influences what we
(50) may dream, such control occurs on an unconscious level. The fairy tale, on the other hand, is very much the result of common conscious and unconscious content having been shaped by the conscious mind, not of one particular person, but
(55) the consensus of many in regard to what they view as universal human problems, and what they accept as desirable solutions. If all these elements were not present in a fairy tale, it would not be retold by generation after generation. Only if a
(60) fairy tale met the conscious and unconscious requirements of many people was it repeatedly retold, and listened to with great interest. No dream of a person could arouse such persistent interest unless it was worked into a myth, as was
(65) the story of the pharaoh's dream as interpreted by Joseph in the Bible.

There is general agreement that myths and fairy tales speak to us in the language of symbols representing unconscious content. Their appeal is simul-
(70) taneously to our conscious mind, and to our need for ego-ideals as well. This makes it very effective; and in the tales' content, inner psychological phenomena are given body in symbolic form.

16. In the opening paragraph, the author quotes Plato and Aristotle primarily in order to

   (A) define the nature of myth
   (B) contrast their opposing points of view
   (C) support the point that myths are valuable
   (D) prove that myths originated in ancient times
   (E) give an example of depth psychology

17. The author's comment about people who wish their children exposed only to actual historic persons and commonplace events (lines 3 and 4) suggests he primarily views such people as

   (A) considerate of their children's welfare
   (B) misguided in their beliefs
   (C) determined to achieve their ends
   (D) more rational than the ancients
   (E) optimistic about human nature

GO ON TO THE NEXT PAGE

6   6 6 6 6 6 6 6 6 6 6   6

18. By "Plato . . . knew what intellectual experiences make for true humanity" (lines 1–5), the author means that

    (A) Plato comprehended the effects of the intellectual life on real human beings
    (B) Plato realized how little a purely intellectual education could do for people's actual well-being
    (C) Plato grasped which sorts of experiences helped promote the development of truly humane individuals
    (D) actual human beings are transformed by reading the scholarly works of Plato
    (E) human nature is a product of mental training according to the best philosophical principles

19. The word "persuasion" in line 15 means

    (A) enticement
    (B) convincing force
    (C) political party
    (D) opinion
    (E) gullibility

20. Lines 12–18 suggest that Mircea Eliade is most likely

    (A) a writer of children's literature
    (B) a student of physical anthropology
    (C) a twentieth century philosopher
    (D) an advocate of practical education
    (E) a contemporary of Plato

21. In line 69, the word "appeal" most nearly means

    (A) plea
    (B) wistfulness
    (C) prayer
    (D) request
    (E) attraction

22. It can be inferred from the passage that the author's interest in fairy tales centers chiefly on their

    (A) literary qualities
    (B) historical background
    (C) factual accuracy
    (D) psychological relevance
    (E) ethical weakness

23. Which of the following best describes the author's attitude toward fairy tales?

    (A) Reluctant fascination
    (B) Wary skepticism
    (C) Scornful disapprobation
    (D) Indulgent tolerance
    (E) Open approval

24. According to the passage, fairy tales differ from dreams in which of the following characteristics?

      I. The shared nature of their creation
     II. The convention of a happy ending
    III. Enduring general appeal

    (A) I only
    (B) II only
    (C) I and II only
    (D) II and III only
    (E) I, II, and III

Test 2

YOU MAY GO BACK AND REVIEW THIS SECTION IN THE REMAINING TIME, BUT DO NOT WORK IN ANY OTHER SECTION UNTIL TOLD TO DO SO.

STOP

7

SECTION 7

Time—25 Minutes
18 Questions

You have 25 minutes to answer the 8 multiple-choice questions
and 10 student-produced response questions in this section.
For each multiple-choice question, determine which of the five choices
is correct and blacken the corresponding choice on your answer
sheet. You may use any blank space on the page for your work.

Notes:

- You may use a calculator whenever you think it will be helpful.
- Only real numbers are used. No question or answer on this test involves a complex or imaginary number.
- Use the diagrams provided to help you solve the problems. Unless you see the words "Note: Figure not drawn to scale" under a diagram, it has been drawn as accurately as possible. Unless it is stated that a figure is three-dimensional, you may assume it lies in a plane.
- For any function f, the domain, unless specifically restricted, is the set of all real numbers for which $f(x)$ is also a real number.

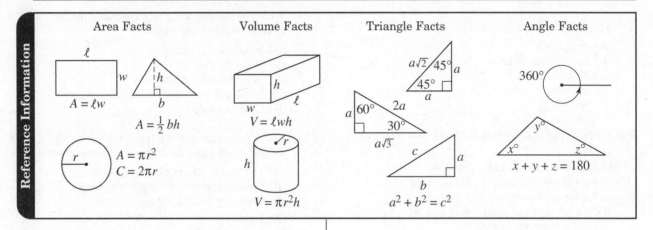

Reference Information

1. If Wally's Widget Works is open exactly 20 days each month and produces 80 widgets each day it is open, how many years will it take to produce 96,000 widgets?

   (A) less than 5
   (B) 5
   (C) more than 5 but less than 10
   (D) 10
   (E) more than 10

2. The equation $\left|10 - \sqrt{x}\right| = 7$ has two solutions. What is the sum of these solutions?

   (A)   0
   (B)   9
   (C)   18
   (D)   20
   (E)   298

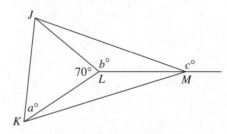

3. In the figure above, $JL = KL = LM$ and m$\angle JLK =$ 70. This information is sufficient to determine the value of which of the following?
   (A) a only
   (B) b only
   (C) a and b only
   (D) b and c only
   (E) a, b, and c

GO ON TO THE NEXT PAGE

4. *A* (5, 1) lies on a circle whose center is *O* (1, 5). If $\overline{AB}$ is a diameter, what are the coordinates of *B*?

(A) (3, 3)
(B) (6, 6)
(C) (–1, 5)
(D) (–1, 10)
(E) (–3, 9)

5. What is the volume, in cubic inches, of a cube whose total surface area is 216 square inches?

(A)   6
(B)   18
(C)   36
(D)   216
(E) 1296

6. In a class, 20 children were sharing equally the cost of a present for their teacher. When 4 of the children decided not to contribute, each of the other children had to pay $1.50 more. How much, in dollars, did the present cost?

(A)   50
(B)   80
(C) 100
(D) 120
(E) 150

7. For how many integers, *x*, is the function

$f(x) = \sqrt{x^2 - 9}$ undefined?

(A) None
(B) 4
(C) 5
(D) 7
(E) Infinitely many

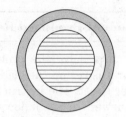

The three circles have the same center.
The radii of the circles are 3, 4, and 5.

8. If a point in the figure above is chosen at random, what is the probability that the point lies in the shaded outer ring?

(A) $\frac{1}{5}$

(B) $\frac{7}{25}$

(C) $\frac{1}{3}$

(D) $\frac{8}{25}$

(E) $\frac{9}{25}$

Test 2

GO ON TO THE NEXT PAGE

7

Directions for Student-Produced Response Questions (Grid-ins)

In questions 9–18, first solve the problem, and then enter your answer on the grid provided on the answer sheet. The instructions for entering your answers are as follows:

- First, write your answer in the boxes at the top of the grid.
- Second, grid your answer in the columns below the boxes.
- Use the fraction bar in the first row or the decimal point in the second row to enter fractions and decimal answers.

- Grid only one space in each column.
- Entering the answer in the boxes is recommended as an aid in gridding, but is not required.
- The machine scoring your exam can read only what you grid, so you **must grid in your answers correctly to get credit.**
- If a question has more than one correct answer, grid in only one of these answers.
- The grid does not have a minus sign, so no answer can be negative.
- A mixed number *must* be converted to an improper fraction or a decimal before it is gridded. Enter $1\frac{1}{4}$ as 5/4 or 1.25; the machine will interpret 1 1/4 as $\frac{11}{4}$ and mark it wrong.
- **All decimals must be entered as accurately as possible.** Here are the three acceptable ways of gridding

$$\frac{3}{11} = 0.272727...$$

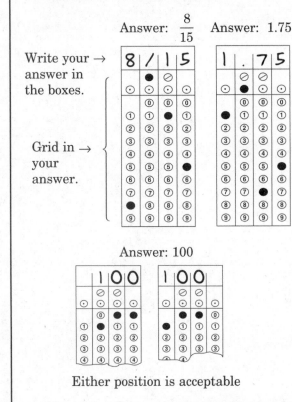

Answer: $\frac{8}{15}$ Answer: 1.75

Write your → answer in the boxes.

Grid in → your answer.

Answer: 100

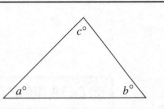

Either position is acceptable

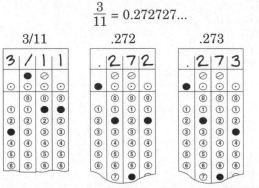

3/11   .272   .273

- Note that rounding to .273 is acceptable, because you are using the full grid, but you would receive **no credit** for .3 or .27, because these answers are less accurate.

---

9. If $a = 3$ and $b = -3$, what is the value of $3a - 2b$?

10. If $a:b:c = 6:7:11$, what is the value of $c - a$?

11. What is the perimeter of a right triangle if the lengths of its two smallest sides are 15 and 36?

GO ON TO THE NEXT PAGE

7

12. There are 250 people on a line outside a theater. If Jack is the 25th person from the front, and Jill is the 125th person from the front, how many people are between Jack and Jill?

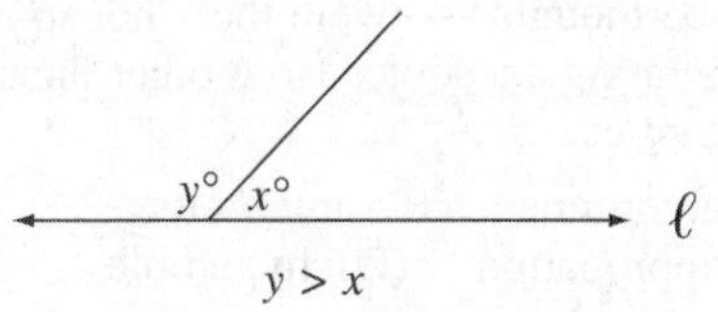

y > x

<u>Note</u>: Figure not drawn to scale

13. In the figure above, *x* and *y* are integers. What is the largest possible value of *x*?

14. Five people shared a prize of $100. Each one received a whole number of dollars, and no two people received the same amount. If the largest share was $30 and the smallest share was $15, what is the most money that the person with the third largest share could have received? (Grid in your answer without a dollar sign.)

15. The average (arithmetic mean) of a set of 9 numbers is 99. After one of the numbers is deleted from the set, the average of the remaining numbers is 89. What number was deleted?

16. The sum of three different positive integers is 12. Let *g* be the greatest possible product of the three integers, and let ℓ be the least possible product of the integers. What is the value of $g - \ell$?

17. In a right triangle, $\dfrac{1}{4}$ of the length of the longer leg is equal to $\dfrac{3}{5}$ of the length of the shorter leg. What is the ratio of the length of the hypotenuse to the length of the shorter leg?

18. If *x* varies inversely with *y* and varies directly with *z*, and if *y* and *z* are both 12 when *x* = 3, what is the value of *y* + *z* when *x* = 4?

YOU MAY GO BACK AND REVIEW THIS SECTION IN THE REMAINING TIME, BUT DO NOT WORK IN ANY OTHER SECTION UNTIL TOLD TO DO SO.

S T O P

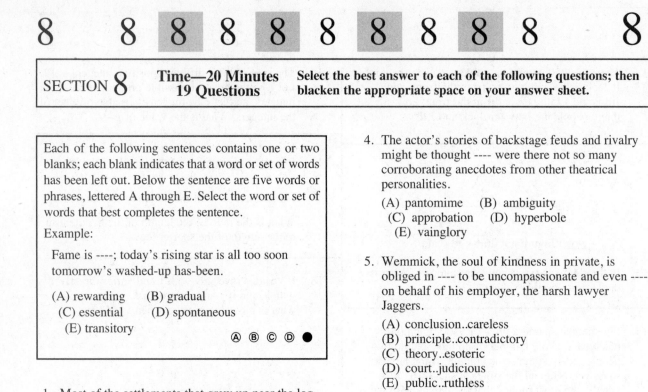

Test 2

SECTION 8   **Time—20 Minutes**   **19 Questions**   Select the best answer to each of the following questions; then blacken the appropriate space on your answer sheet.

Each of the following sentences contains one or two blanks; each blank indicates that a word or set of words has been left out. Below the sentence are five words or phrases, lettered A through E. Select the word or set of words that best completes the sentence.

Example:

Fame is ----; today's rising star is all too soon tomorrow's washed-up has-been.

(A) rewarding   (B) gradual
(C) essential   (D) spontaneous
  (E) transitory

Ⓐ Ⓑ Ⓒ Ⓓ ●

1. Most of the settlements that grew up near the logging camps were ---- affairs, thrown together in a hurry because people needed to live on the job.
   (A) protracted   (B) unobtrusive   (C) nomadic
   (D) ramshackle   (E) banal

2. Quick-breeding and immune to most pesticides, cockroaches are so ---- that even a professional exterminator may fail to ---- them.
   (A) vulnerable..eradicate
   (B) widespread..discern
   (C) fragile..destroy
   (D) hardy..eliminate
   (E) numerous..detect

3. The patient bore the pain ----, neither wincing nor whimpering when the incision was made.
   (A) histrionically   (B) stoically
   (C) sardonically   (D) poorly
     (E) marginally

4. The actor's stories of backstage feuds and rivalry might be thought ---- were there not so many corroborating anecdotes from other theatrical personalities.
   (A) pantomime   (B) ambiguity
   (C) approbation   (D) hyperbole
     (E) vainglory

5. Wemmick, the soul of kindness in private, is obliged in ---- to be uncompassionate and even ---- on behalf of his employer, the harsh lawyer Jaggers.
   (A) conclusion..careless
   (B) principle..contradictory
   (C) theory..esoteric
   (D) court..judicious
   (E) public..ruthless

6. Although Roman original contributions to government, jurisprudence, and engineering are commonly acknowledged, the artistic legacy of the Roman world continues to be judged widely as ---- the magnificent Greek traditions that preceded it.
   (A) an improvement on
   (B) an echo of
   (C) a resolution of
   (D) a precursor of
   (E) a consummation of

8   8 8 8 8 8 8 8 8 8   8

> The questions that follow the next two passages relate to the content of both, and to their relationship. The correct response may be stated outright in the passage or merely suggested.

Questions 7–19 are based on the following passages.

The following passages are taken from memoirs by two young American writers, each of whom records his reaction to the prospect of visiting his ancestral homeland.

Passage 1

Thomas Wolfe said that going home again is like stepping into a river. You cannot step into the same river twice; you cannot go home again.
Line After a very long time away, you will not find the
(5) same home you left behind. It will be different, and so will you. It is quite possible that home will not be home at all, meaningless except for its sentimental place in your heart. At best it will point the long way back to where you started, its value
(10) lying in how it helped to shape you and in the part of home you have carried away.

Alex Haley went to Africa in the mid-sixties. Somehow he had managed to trace his roots back to a little village called Juffure, upriver from
(15) Banjul in the forests of The Gambia. It was the same village from which his ancestors had been stolen and forced into slavery. In some way Haley must have felt he was returning home: a flood of emotions, an awakening of the memories hidden
(20) in his genes.

Those were the two extremes between which I was trapped. I could not go home again, yet here I was. Africa was so long ago the land of my ancestors that it held for me only a symbolic sig-
(25) nificance. Yet there was enough to remind me that what I carry as a human being has come in part from Africa. I did not feel African, but was beginning to feel not wholly American anymore either. I felt like an orphan, a waif without a
(30) home.

I was not trying to find the village that had once been home to my people, nor would I stand and talk to people who could claim to be my relatives, as Haley had done. The thought of running
(35) into someone who looked like a relative terrified me, for that would have been too concrete, too much proof. My Africanism was abstract and I wanted it to remain so. I did not need to hear the names of my ancient ancestors or know what they
(40) looked like. I had seen the ways they loved their children in the love of my father. I would see their faces and their smiles one day in the eyes of my children.

Haley found what he was seeking. I hardly
(45) knew what I was looking for, except perhaps to know where home once was, to know how much of me is really me, how much of being black has been carried out of Africa.

Passage 2

I am a *Sansei*, a third-generation Japanese-
(50) American. In 1984, through luck and through some skills as a poet, I traveled to Japan. My reasons for going were not very clear.

At the time, I'd been working as an arts administrator in the Writers-in-the-Schools pro-
(55) gram, sending other writers to grade schools and high schools throughout Minnesota. It wasn't taxing, but it didn't provide the long stretches needed to plunge into my own work. I had applied for a U.S./Japan Creative Artist Exchange
(60) Fellowship mainly because I wanted time to write.

Japan? That was where my grandparents came from; it didn't have much to do with my present life.

(65) For me Japan was cheap baseballs, Godzilla, weird sci-fi movies like *Star Man,* where you could see the strings that pulled him above his enemies, flying in front of a backdrop so poorly made even I, at eight, was conscious of the fakery. Then
(70) there were the endless hordes storming GI's in war movies. Before the television set, wearing my ever-present Cubs cap, I crouched near the sofa, saw the enemy surrounding me. I shouted to my men, hurled a grenade. I fired my gun. And the
(75) Japanese soldiers fell before me, one by one.

So, when I did win the fellowship, I felt I was going not as an ardent pilgrim, longing to return to the land of his grandparents, but more like a contestant on a quiz show who finds himself win-
(80) ning a trip to Bali or the Bahamas. Of course, I was pleased about the stipend, the plane fare for me and my wife, and the payments for Japanese lessons, both before the trip and during my stay. I was also excited that I had beat out several
(85) hundred candidates in literature and other fields for one of the six spots. But part of me wished the prize was Paris, not Tokyo. I would have preferred French bread and Brie over *sashimi* and rice, Baudelaire and Proust over Basho and
(90) Kawabata, structuralism and Barthes over Zen and D. T. Suzuki.

GO ON TO THE NEXT PAGE ⟶

8   8   8   8   8   8   8   8   8   8   8

This contradiction remained. Much of my life I
had insisted on my Americanness, had shunned
most connections with Japan and felt proud I
knew no Japanese; yet I *was* going to Japan as a
(95)   poet, and my Japanese ancestry was there in my
poems—my grandfather, the relocation camps,
the *hibakusha* (victims of the atomic bomb), a
picnic of *Nisei* (second-generation Japanese-
Americans), my uncle who fought in the 442nd.
(100)   True, the poems were written in blank verse,
rather than *haiku*, *tanka*, or *haibun*. But perhaps
it's a bit disingenuous to say that I had no longing
to go to Japan; it was obvious my imagination
had been traveling there for years, unconsciously
(105)   swimming the Pacific, against the tide of my family's emigration, my parents' desire, after the
internment camps, to forget the past.

7. Wolfe's comment referred to in lines 1–6 represents

(A) a digression from the author's thesis
(B) an understatement of the situation
(C) a refutation of the author's central argument
(D) a figurative expression of the author's point
(E) an example of the scientific method

8. According to lines 8–11, the most positive outcome
of attempting to go home again would be for you to

(A) find the one place you genuinely belong
(B) recognize the impossibility of the task
(C) grasp how your origins have formed you
(D) reenter the world of your ancestors
(E) decide to stay away for shorter periods of time

9. Throughout Passage 1, the author seeks primarily
to convey

(A) his resemblance to his ancestors
(B) his ambivalence about his journey
(C) the difficulties of traveling in a foreign country
(D) his need to deny his American origins
(E) the depth of his desire to track down his roots

10. The statement "I could not go home again, yet here
I was" (lines 22 and 23) represents

(A) a paradox
(B) a prevarication
(C) an interruption
(D) an analogy
(E) a fallacy

11. The word "held" in line 24 means

(A) grasped
(B) believed
(C) absorbed
(D) accommodated
(E) possessed

12. By "my own work" (line 58), the author of Passage
2 refers to

(A) seeking his ancestral roots
(B) teaching in high school
(C) writing a travel narrative
(D) creating poetry
(E) directing art programs

13. The word "taxing" in lines 56 and 57 means

(A) imposing
(B) obliging
(C) demanding
(D) accusatory
(E) costly

14. The author's purpose in describing the war movie
incident (lines 70–74) most likely is to

(A) indicate the depth of his hatred for the
Japanese
(B) show the extent of his self-identification as an
American
(C) demonstrate the superiority of American films
to their Japanese counterparts
(D) explore the range of his interest in contempo-
rary art forms
(E) explain why he had a particular urge to travel
to Japan

15. By "a trip to Bali or the Bahamas" (line 79) the
author wishes to convey

(A) his love for these particular vacation sites
(B) the impression that he has traveled to these
places before
(C) his preference for any destination other than
Japan
(D) his sense of Japan as just another exotic desti-
nation
(E) the unlikelihood of his ever winning a second
trip

GO ON TO THE NEXT PAGE

Test 2

8   8   8   8   8   8   8   8   8   8   8

16. The author's attitude toward winning the fellow-
    ship can best be described as one of

    (A) graceful acquiescence
    (B) wholehearted enthusiasm
    (C) unfeigned gratitude
    (D) frank dismay
    (E) marked ambivalence

17. The author concludes Passage 2 with

    (A) a rhetorical question
    (B) a eulogy
    (C) an epitaph
    (D) an extended metaphor
    (E) a literary allusion

18. Both passages are concerned primarily with the
    subject of

    (A) ethnic identity
    (B) individual autonomy
    (C) ancestor worship
    (D) racial purity
    (E) genealogical research

19. For which of the following statements or phrases
    from Passage 1 is a parallel idea not conveyed in
    Passage 2?

    (A) Africa "held for me only a symbolic signifi-
        cance" (lines 24 and 25)
    (B) "I did not feel African" (line 27)
    (C) "I felt like an orphan, a waif without a home"
        (lines 29 and 30)
    (D) "I hardly knew what I was looking for" (lines
        44 and 45)
    (E) "An awakening of the memories hidden in his
        genes" (lines 19 and 20)

Test 2

YOU MAY GO BACK AND REVIEW THIS SECTION IN THE REMAINING TIME,
BUT DO NOT WORK IN ANY OTHER SECTION UNTIL TOLD TO DO SO.

STOP

9   **9**   **9**   **9**   **9**   **9**   **9**

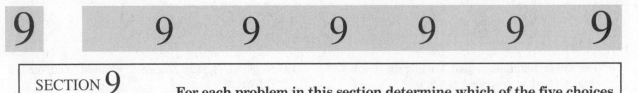

SECTION 9

Time—20 Minutes
16 Questions

For each problem in this section determine which of the five choices is correct and blacken the corresponding choice on your answer sheet. You may use any blank space on the page for your work.

Notes:

- You may use a calculator whenever you think it will be helpful.
- Only real numbers are used. No question or answer on this test involves a complex or imaginary number.
- Use the diagrams provided to help you solve the problems. Unless you see the words "Note: Figure not drawn to scale" under a diagram, it has been drawn as accurately as possible. Unless it is stated that a figure is three-dimensional, you may assume it lies in a plane.
- For any function f, the domain, unless specifically restricted, is the set of all real numbers for which $f(x)$ is also a real number.

Test 2

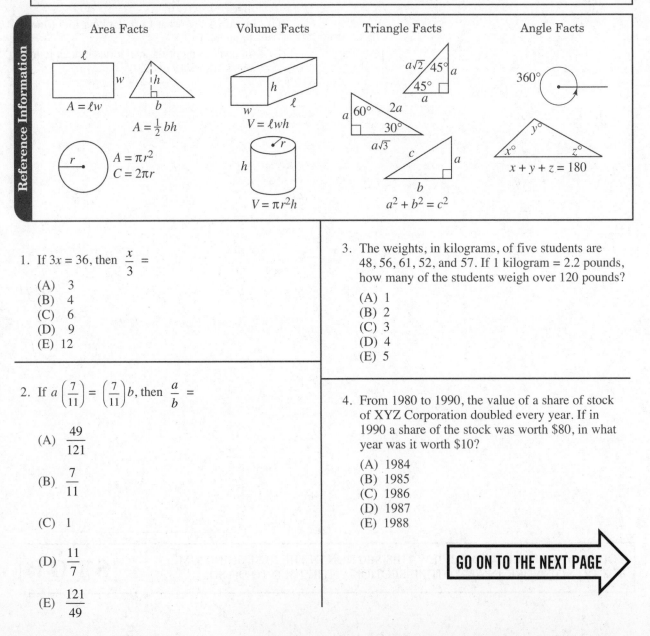

Reference Information

1. If $3x = 36$, then $\dfrac{x}{3} =$

(A) 3
(B) 4
(C) 6
(D) 9
(E) 12

2. If $a\left(\dfrac{7}{11}\right) = \left(\dfrac{7}{11}\right)b$, then $\dfrac{a}{b} =$

(A) $\dfrac{49}{121}$

(B) $\dfrac{7}{11}$

(C) 1

(D) $\dfrac{11}{7}$

(E) $\dfrac{121}{49}$

3. The weights, in kilograms, of five students are 48, 56, 61, 52, and 57. If 1 kilogram = 2.2 pounds, how many of the students weigh over 120 pounds?

(A) 1
(B) 2
(C) 3
(D) 4
(E) 5

4. From 1980 to 1990, the value of a share of stock of XYZ Corporation doubled every year. If in 1990 a share of the stock was worth $80, in what year was it worth $10?

(A) 1984
(B) 1985
(C) 1986
(D) 1987
(E) 1988

GO ON TO THE NEXT PAGE

9   9   9   9   9   9   9

5. The average (arithmetic mean) of two numbers is
    a. If one of the numbers is 10, what is the other?

    (A) $2a + 10$
    (B) $2a - 10$
    (C) $2(a - 10)$
    (D) $\dfrac{10 + a}{2}$
    (E) $\dfrac{10 - a}{2}$

6. The chart below shows the value of an investment
    on January 1 of each year from 1990 to 1995.
    During which year was the percent increase in the
    value of the investment the greatest?

Year	Value
1990	$150
1991	$250
1992	$450
1993	$750
1994	$1200
1995	$1800

    (A) 1990
    (B) 1991
    (C) 1992
    (D) 1993
    (E) 1994

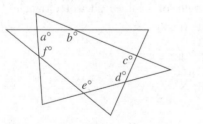

7. In the figure above, what is the value of
    $a + b + c + d + e + f$?

    (A) 360
    (B) 540
    (C) 720
    (D) 900
    (E) It cannot be determined from the information
        given.

8. If the circumference of a circle is equal to the
    perimeter of a square whose sides are π, what is
    the radius of the circle?

    (A) 1
    (B) 2
    (C) 4
    (D) π
    (E) 2π

9. The first term of a sequence is 1 and every term
    after the first one is 1 more than the square of the
    preceding term. What is the fifth term?

    (A) 25
    (B) 26
    (C) 256
    (D) 676
    (E) 677

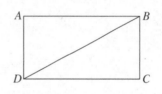

Note: Figure not drawn to scale

10. If the perimeter of rectangle $ABCD$ above is 14,
    what is the perimeter of $\triangle BCD$?

    (A) 7
    (B) 12
    (C) $7 + \sqrt{29}$
    (D) $7 + \sqrt{37}$
    (E) It cannot be determined from the information
        given.

11. Jordan has taken five math tests so far this
    semester. If he gets a 70 on his next test, that
    grade will lower his test average (arithmetic
    mean) by 4 points. What is his average now?

    (A) 74
    (B) 85
    (C) 90
    (D) 94
    (E) 95

GO ON TO THE NEXT PAGE

Test 2

Test 2

12. If $f(x) = x^2 - 3x$ and $g(x) = f(3x)$, what is $g(-10)$?

(A) 210
(B) 390
(C) 490
(D) 810
(E) 990

13. The expression $\dfrac{12a^2 b^{-\frac{1}{2}} c^6}{4a^{-2} b^{\frac{1}{2}} c^2}$ is equivalent to which of the following?

(A) $\dfrac{3a^4 c^4}{b}$

(B) $\dfrac{3c^3}{ab}$

(C) $\dfrac{3bc^4}{a^4}$

(D) $\dfrac{a^4 c^3}{3b}$

(E) $3c^4$

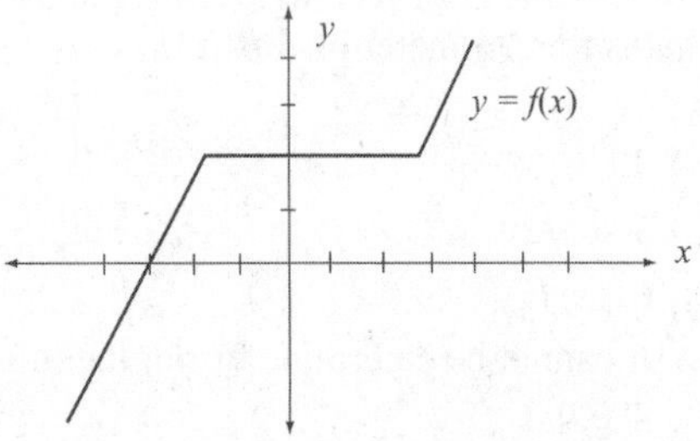

$y = f(x)$

14. The figure above is the graph of the function $y = f(x)$. What are the x-coordinates of the points where the graph of $y = f(x - 2)$ intersects the x-axis?

(A) Only -5
(B) Only -1
(C) -5 and -1
(D) All numbers between -2 and 3
(E) The graph of $y = f(x - 2)$ does not intersect the x-axis.

15. Store 1 is a full-service retail store that charges regular prices. Store 2 is a self-service factory-outlet store that sells all items at a reduced price. In January 2004, each store sold three brands of DVD players. The numbers of DVD players sold and their prices are shown in the following tables.

Number of DVD Players Sold

	Store 1	Store 2
Brand A	10	30
Brand B	20	40
Brand C	20	20

Prices of DVD Players

	Brand A	Brand B	Brand C
Store 1	$80	$100	$150
Store 2	$50	$80	$120

What was the difference between Store 1 and Store 2 in the dollar values of the total sales of the three brands of DVD players?

(A) 40
(B) 80
(C) 140
(D) 330
(E) 1300

16. $A = \{2, 3\}$ $B = \{4, 5\}$ $C = \{6, 7\}$

In how many ways is it possible to pick 1 number from each set, so that the 3 numbers could be the lengths of the three sides of a triangle?

(A) 0
(B) 2
(C) 4
(D) 6
(E) 8

YOU MAY GO BACK AND REVIEW THIS SECTION IN THE REMAINING TIME, BUT DO NOT WORK IN ANY OTHER SECTION UNTIL TOLD TO DO SO.

STOP

10   10   10   10   10   10   10

SECTION **10**   Time—10 Minutes
14 Questions

For each of the following questions, select the best answer from the choices provided and fill in the appropriate circle on the answer sheet.

Some or all parts of the following sentences are underlined. The first answer choice, (A), simply repeats the underlined part of the sentence. The other four choices present four alternative ways to phrase the underlined part. Select the answer that produces the most effective sentence, one that is clear and exact, and blacken the appropriate space on your answer sheet. In selecting your choice, be sure that it is standard written English, and that it expresses the meaning of the original sentence.

Example:

The first biography of author Eudora Welty came out in 1998 <u>and she was 89 years old at the time.</u>

(A) and she was 89 years old at the time
(B) at the time when she was 89
(C) upon becoming an 89 year old
(D) when she was 89
(E) at the age of 89 years old

Ⓐ Ⓑ Ⓒ ● Ⓔ

1. Jane Austen wrote <u>novels and they depicted</u> the courtships and eventual marriages of members of the middle classes.

    (A) novels and they depicted
    (B) novels, being depictions of
    (C) novels, they depicted
    (D) novels that depict
    (E) novels, and depictions in them

2. The princess, <u>together with the members of her retinue, are scheduled</u> to attend the opening ceremonies.

    (A) together with the members of her retinue, are scheduled
    (B) together with the members of her retinue, were scheduled
    (C) along with the members of the retinue, are scheduled
    (D) together with the members of her retinue, is scheduled
    (E) being together with the members of her retinue, is scheduled

3. Dog experts describe the chihuahua as <u>the smallest dog, and also the most truculent of them</u>.

    (A) the smallest dog, and also the most truculent of them
    (B) the smallest and yet the most truculent of dogs
    (C) the smallest dog at the same time it is the most truculent dog
    (D) not only the smallest dog, but also more truculent than any
    (E) the smallest of dogs in spite of being the most truculent of them

4. Painters of the Art Deco period took motifs from the art of Africa, South America, and the Far East <u>as well as incorporating</u> them with the sleek lines of modern industry.

    (A) as well as incorporating
    (B) they also incorporated
    (C) and incorporated
    (D) likewise they incorporated
    (E) furthermore incorporating

5. The university reserves the right to sublet <u>students' rooms who are</u> away on leave.

    (A) students' rooms who are
    (B) students whose rooms are
    (C) the rooms of students who are
    (D) the rooms of students which are
    (E) students' rooms which are

6. High school students at the beginning of the twenty-first century ate more fast food <u>than</u> the middle of the twentieth century.

    (A) than
    (B) than the high schools during
    (C) than occurred in
    (D) than did students in
    (E) than did

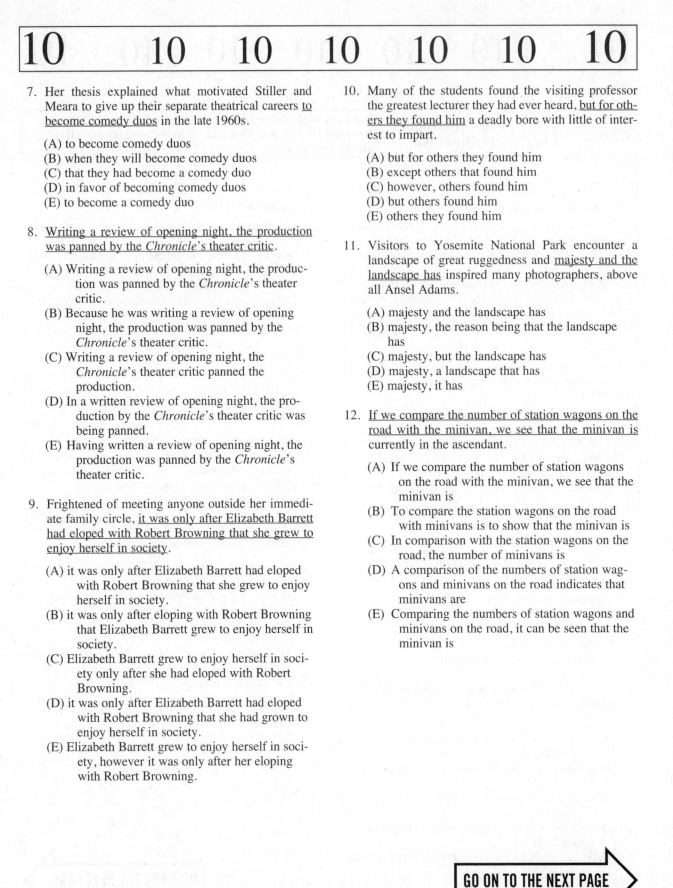

7. Her thesis explained what motivated Stiller and Meara to give up their separate theatrical careers <u>to become comedy duos</u> in the late 1960s.

(A) to become comedy duos
(B) when they will become comedy duos
(C) that they had become a comedy duo
(D) in favor of becoming comedy duos
(E) to become a comedy duo

8. <u>Writing a review of opening night, the production was panned by the *Chronicle*'s theater critic.</u>

(A) Writing a review of opening night, the production was panned by the *Chronicle*'s theater critic.
(B) Because he was writing a review of opening night, the production was panned by the *Chronicle*'s theater critic.
(C) Writing a review of opening night, the *Chronicle*'s theater critic panned the production.
(D) In a written review of opening night, the production by the *Chronicle*'s theater critic was being panned.
(E) Having written a review of opening night, the production was panned by the *Chronicle*'s theater critic.

9. Frightened of meeting anyone outside her immediate family circle, <u>it was only after Elizabeth Barrett had eloped with Robert Browning that she grew to enjoy herself in society.</u>

(A) it was only after Elizabeth Barrett had eloped with Robert Browning that she grew to enjoy herself in society.
(B) it was only after eloping with Robert Browning that Elizabeth Barrett grew to enjoy herself in society.
(C) Elizabeth Barrett grew to enjoy herself in society only after she had eloped with Robert Browning.
(D) it was only after Elizabeth Barrett had eloped with Robert Browning that she had grown to enjoy herself in society.
(E) Elizabeth Barrett grew to enjoy herself in society, however it was only after her eloping with Robert Browning.

10. Many of the students found the visiting professor the greatest lecturer they had ever heard, <u>but for others they found him</u> a deadly bore with little of interest to impart.

(A) but for others they found him
(B) except others that found him
(C) however, others found him
(D) but others found him
(E) others they found him

11. Visitors to Yosemite National Park encounter a landscape of great ruggedness and <u>majesty and the landscape has</u> inspired many photographers, above all Ansel Adams.

(A) majesty and the landscape has
(B) majesty, the reason being that the landscape has
(C) majesty, but the landscape has
(D) majesty, a landscape that has
(E) majesty, it has

12. <u>If we compare the number of station wagons on the road with the minivan, we see that the minivan is</u> currently in the ascendant.

(A) If we compare the number of station wagons on the road with the minivan, we see that the minivan is
(B) To compare the station wagons on the road with minivans is to show that the minivan is
(C) In comparison with the station wagons on the road, the number of minivans is
(D) A comparison of the numbers of station wagons and minivans on the road indicates that minivans are
(E) Comparing the numbers of station wagons and minivans on the road, it can be seen that the minivan is

GO ON TO THE NEXT PAGE ➡

Test 2

10   10   10   10   10   10   10

13. Despite all his attempts <u>to ingratiate himself with his prospective father-in-law, the young man found he could hardly do nothing to please him</u>.

(A) to ingratiate himself with his prospective father-in-law, the young man found he could hardly do nothing to please him
(B) to ingratiate himself to his prospective father-in-law, the young man found he could hardly do nothing to please him
(C) to ingratiate himself with his prospective father-in-law, the young man found he could hardly do anything to please him
(D) to be ingratiating toward his prospective father-in-law, the young man found he could hardly do nothing to please him
(E) to ingratiate himself with his prospective father-in-law, the young man had found he could hardly do nothing to please him

14. Of all the cities competing to host the 2012 Olympic Games, <u>the mayor of New York was the only one to lack the funds</u> to build a new stadium.

(A) the mayor of New York was the only one to lack the funds
(B) New York's mayor only lacked the funds
(C) New York was the only one whose mayor lacked the funds
(D) the mayor of New York lacked only the funds
(E) New York had a mayor who was the only one who was lacking the funds

YOU MAY GO BACK AND REVIEW THIS SECTION IN THE REMAINING TIME, BUT DO NOT WORK IN ANY OTHER SECTION UNTIL TOLD TO DO SO.   **S T O P**

Test 2

Answer Key

<u>Note:</u> The letters in brackets following the Mathematical Reasoning answers refer to the sections of Chapter 9 in which you can find the information you need to answer the questions. For example, **1. C [E]** means that the answer to question 1 is C, and that the solution requires information found in Section 9-E: Averages.

Section 2   Critical Reading

1. C	6. B	11. C	16. C	21. E
2. D	7. A	12. A	17. E	22. B
3. D	8. C	13. D	18. B	23. C
4. A	9. B	14. C	19. D	24. C
5. A	10. D	15. A	20. C	

Section 3   Mathematical Reasoning

1. D [G]	5. B [J, K]	9. B [E]	13. B [C]	17. D [A, P]
2. B [J]	6. A [A]	10. E [A]	14. E [D, I]	18. D [A, P]
3. D [G]	7. E [J]	11. C [C]	15. A [D, H]	19. C [O]
4. B [D]	8. B [A, G]	12. C [D]	16. B [I, J]	20. C [J, L]

Section 4   Writing Skills

1. C	8. B	15. E	22. A	29. B
2. D	9. A	16. D	23. C	30. C
3. E	10. D	17. B	24. B	31. C
4. D	11. A	18. B	25. D	32. B
5. B	12. D	19. D	26. C	33. A
6. B	13. D	20. B	27. B	34. C
7. D	14. A	21. B	28. E	35. D

Section 5

On this test, Section 5 was the experimental section. It could have been an extra critical reading, mathematics, or writing skills section. Remember: on the SAT you take, the experimental section may be any section from 2 to 7.

Section 6   Critical Reading

1. E	6. C	11. B	16. C	21. E
2. E	7. D	12. D	17. B	22. D
3. B	8. C	13. A	18. C	23. E
4. A	9. E	14. D	19. D	24. E
5. B	10. E	15. B	20. C	

Section 7   Mathematical Reasoning

Multiple-Choice Questions

1. **B [A]**
2. **E [A, G]**
3. **A [J]**
4. **E [N]**
5. **D [M]**
6. **D [G]**
7. **C [R]**
8. **E [L]**

Grid-in Questions

9. [A] **1 5**

10. [D, J] **3 7 . 5**

11. [J] **9 0**

12. [O] **9 9**

13. [I] **8 9**

14. [A, P] **1 9**

15. [E] **1 7 9**

16. [A] **4 2**

17. [D, J] **1 3 / 5**

or 2.6

18. [D] **2 5**

Section 8   Critical Reading

1.	**D**	5.	**E**	9.	**B**	13.	**C**	17.	**D**
2.	**D**	6.	**B**	10.	**A**	14.	**B**	18.	**A**
3.	**B**	7.	**D**	11.	**E**	15.	**D**	19.	**C**
4.	**D**	8.	**C**	12.	**D**	16.	**E**		

Section 9   Mathematical Reasoning

1.	**B [G]**	5.	**B [E, G]**	9.	**E [P]**	13.	**A [A]**
2.	**C [G]**	6.	**B [C, Q]**	10.	**E [J, K]**	14.	**B [R]**
3.	**C [D]**	7.	**C [K]**	11.	**D [E, G]**	15.	**E [Q]**
4.	**D [B]**	8.	**B [K, L]**	12.	**E [R]**	16.	**C [J]**

Section 10   Writing Skills

1.	**D**	4.	**C**	7.	**E**	10.	**D**	13.	**C**
2.	**D**	5.	**C**	8.	**C**	11.	**D**	14.	**C**
3.	**B**	6.	**D**	9.	**C**	12.	**D**		

Test 2

Score Your Own SAT Essay

Use this table as you rate your performance on the essay-writing section of this Model Test. Circle the phrase that most accurately describes your work. Enter the numbers in the scoring chart below. Add the numbers together and divide by 6 to determine your total score. The higher your total score, the better you are likely to do on the essay section of the SAT.

Note that on the actual SAT two readers will rate your essay; your essay score will be the sum of their two ratings and could range from 12 (highest) to 2 (lowest). Also, they will grade your essay holistically, rating it on the basis of their overall impression of its effectiveness. They will *not* analyze it piece by piece, giving separate grades for grammar, vocabulary level, and so on. Therefore, you cannot expect the score you give yourself on this Model Test to predict your eventual score on the SAT with any great degree of accuracy. Use this scoring guide instead to help you assess your writing strengths and weaknesses, so that you can decide which areas to focus on as you prepare for the SAT.

Like most people, you may find it difficult to rate your own writing objectively. Ask a teacher or fellow student to score your essay as well. With his or her help you should gain added insights into writing your 25-minute essay.

	6	**5**	**4**	**3**	**2**	**1**
POSITION ON THE TOPIC	Clear, convincing, & insightful	Fundamentally clear & coherent	Fairly clear & coherent	Insufficiently clear	Largely unclear	Extremely unclear
ORGANIZATION OF EVIDENCE	Well organized, with strong, relevant examples	Generally well organized, with apt examples	Adequately organized, with some examples	Sketchily developed, with weak examples	Lacking focus and evidence	Unfocused and disorganized
SENTENCE STRUCTURE	Varied, appealing sentences	Reasonably varied sentences	Some variety in sentences	Little variety in sentences	Errors in sentence structure	Severe errors in sentence structure
LEVEL OF VOCABULARY	Mature & apt word choice	Competent word choice	Adequate word choice	Inappropriate or weak vocabulary	Highly limited vocabulary	Rudimentary
GRAMMAR AND USAGE	Almost entirely free of errors	Relatively free of errors	Some technical errors	Minor errors, and some major ones	Numerous major errors	Extensive severe errors
OVERALL EFFECT	Outstanding	Effective	Adequately competent	Inadequate, but shows some potential	Seriously flawed	Fundamentally deficient

Self-Scoring Chart

For each of the following categories, rate the essay from 1 (lowest) to 6 (highest)

Position on the Topic _____

Organization of Evidence _____

Sentence Structure _____

Level of Vocabulary _____

Grammar and Usage _____

Overall Effect _____

TOTAL _____

(To get a score, divide the total by 6) _____

Scoring Chart (Second Reader)

For each of the following categories, rate the essay from 1 (lowest) to 6 (highest)

Position on the Topic _____

Organization of Evidence _____

Sentence Structure _____

Level of Vocabulary _____

Grammar and Usage _____

Overall Effect _____

TOTAL _____

(To get a score, divide the total by 6) _____

Calculate Your Raw Score

Critical Reading

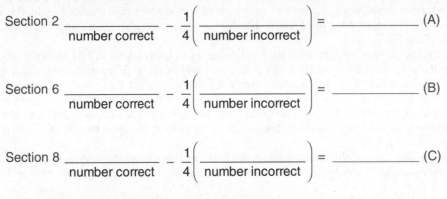

Section 2 $\rule{2cm}{0.4pt}$ $-$ $\frac{1}{4}$ $\left(\rule{2cm}{0.4pt} \right)$ = $\rule{2cm}{0.4pt}$ (A)
number correct   number incorrect

Section 6 $\rule{2cm}{0.4pt}$ $-$ $\frac{1}{4}$ $\left(\rule{2cm}{0.4pt} \right)$ = $\rule{2cm}{0.4pt}$ (B)
number correct   number incorrect

Section 8 $\rule{2cm}{0.4pt}$ $-$ $\frac{1}{4}$ $\left(\rule{2cm}{0.4pt} \right)$ = $\rule{2cm}{0.4pt}$ (C)
number correct   number incorrect

Critical Reading Raw Score = (A) + (B) + (C) = $\rule{2cm}{0.4pt}$

Mathematical Reasoning

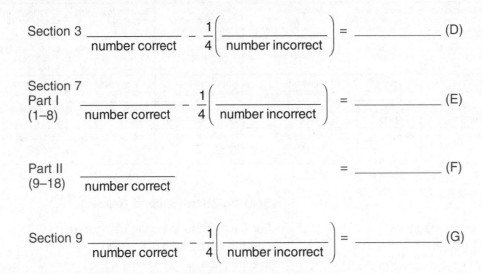

Section 3 $\rule{2cm}{0.4pt}$ $-$ $\frac{1}{4}$ $\left(\rule{2cm}{0.4pt} \right)$ = $\rule{2cm}{0.4pt}$ (D)
number correct   number incorrect

Section 7
Part I $\rule{2cm}{0.4pt}$ $-$ $\frac{1}{4}$ $\left(\rule{2cm}{0.4pt} \right)$ = $\rule{2cm}{0.4pt}$ (E)
(1–8)   number correct   number incorrect

Part II $\rule{2cm}{0.4pt}$ = $\rule{2cm}{0.4pt}$ (F)
(9–18)   number correct

Section 9 $\rule{2cm}{0.4pt}$ $-$ $\frac{1}{4}$ $\left(\rule{2cm}{0.4pt} \right)$ = $\rule{2cm}{0.4pt}$ (G)
number correct   number incorrect

Mathematical Reasoning Raw Score = (D) + (E) + (F) + (G) = $\rule{2cm}{0.4pt}$

Writing Skills

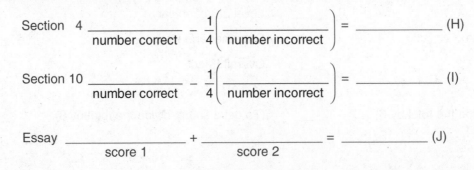

Section 4 $\rule{2cm}{0.4pt}$ $-$ $\frac{1}{4}$ $\left(\rule{2cm}{0.4pt} \right)$ = $\rule{2cm}{0.4pt}$ (H)
number correct   number incorrect

Section 10 $\rule{2cm}{0.4pt}$ $-$ $\frac{1}{4}$ $\left(\rule{2cm}{0.4pt} \right)$ = $\rule{2cm}{0.4pt}$ (I)
number correct   number incorrect

Essay $\rule{2cm}{0.4pt}$ $+$ $\rule{2cm}{0.4pt}$ = $\rule{2cm}{0.4pt}$ (J)
score 1   score 2

Writing Skills Raw Score = H + I (J is a separate subscore)

Test 2

Evaluate Your Performance

Scaled Score	Critical Reading Raw Score	Mathematical Reasoning Raw Score	Writing Skills Raw Score
700–800	58–67	48–54	43–49
650–690	52–57	43–47	39–42
600–640	45–51	36–42	35–38
550–590	38–44	30–35	30–34
500–540	30–37	24–29	25–29
450–490	22–29	18–23	19–24
400–440	14–21	12–17	14–18
300–390	3–13	5–11	5–13
200–290	less than 3	less than 5	less than 5

Identify Your Weaknesses

Critical Reading

Question Type	Question Numbers			Chapter to Study
	Section 2	Section 6	Section 8	
Sentence Completion	1, 2, 3, 4, 5, 6, 7, 8	1, 2, 3, 4, 5	1, 2, 3, 4, 5, 6	Chapter 1
Critical Reading	9, 10, 11, 12, 13, 14, 15, 16, 17, 18, 19, 20, 21, 22, 23, 24	6, 7, 8, 9, 10, 11, 12, 13, 14, 15, 16, 17, 18, 19, 20, 21, 22, 23, 24	7, 8, 9, 10, 11, 12, 13, 14, 15, 16, 17, 18, 19	Chapter 2

Test 2

Identify Your Weaknesses

Mathematical Reasoning

Section in Chapter 9	Question Numbers			Pages to Study
	Section 3	Section 7	Section 9	
A Basic Arithmetic Concepts	6, 8, 10, 17, 18	1, 2, 9, 14, 16	13	410–431
B Fractions and Decimals			4	432–449
C Percents	11, 13		6	450–460
D Ratios and Proportions	4, 12, 14, 15	10, 17, 18	3	461–472
E Averages	9	15	5, 11	473–479
F Polynomials				480–488
G Equations and Inequalities	1, 3, 8	6, 2	1, 2, 5, 11	489–502
H Word Problems	15			503–513
I Lines and Angles	14, 16	13		514–524
J Triangles	2, 5, 7, 16	3, 10, 11, 17	10, 15, 16	525–542
K Quadrilaterals	5, 20		7, 8, 10	543–553
L Circles	20	8	8, 15	554–564
M Solid Geometry		5		565–573
N Coordinate Geometry		4		574–588
O Counting and Probability	19	12		589–600
P Logical Reasoning	18	14	9	601–608
Q Data Interpretation		7	15	609–618
R Functions and Their Graphs			12, 14	619–628

Identify Your Weaknesses

Writing Skills

Question Type	Question Numbers		Chapter to Study
	Section 4	Section 10	
Improving Sentences	1, 2, 3, 4, 5, 6, 7, 8, 9, 10, 11	1, 2, 3, 4, 5, 6, 7, 8, 9, 10, 11, 12, 13, 14	Chapter 6
Identifying Sentence Errors	12, 13, 14, 15, 16, 17, 18, 19, 20, 21, 22, 23, 24, 25, 26, 27, 28, 29		Chapter 6
Improving Paragraphs	30, 31, 32, 33, 34, 35		Chapter 6
Essay			Chapter 7

ANSWERS EXPLAINED

Section 2 Critical Reading

1. **C.** To uncover buried ruins is to *excavate* them. Notice the use of the comma to set off the phrase that defines the missing word.
(Definition)

2. **D.** Puritans (members of a religious group following a pure standard of morality) would be offended by *lewd* (lecherous, obscene) material and would fear it might corrupt theatergoers.   (Argument Pattern)

3. **D.** *Rescind* means to cancel or withdraw. The lawmakers were so angered by the governor's enactment of martial law that they refused to work until it was canceled.
The phrase "the last straw" refers to the straw that broke the camel's back. *Because* the governor had exceeded his bounds, the lawmakers essentially went on strike.
(Cause and Effect Pattern)

4. **A.** *Malingering* means pretending illness to avoid duty. Faced with an *arduous* (hard) march, a private might well try to get out of it.
(Argument Pattern)

5. **A.** What was once a minor problem is now a major cause of death; what was formerly *negligible* (insignificant; minor and thus of no consequence) has become the chief *cause* of cancer-related deaths. Note how the two phrases set off by commas ("formerly..."; "once...") balance one another and are similar in meaning.
Remember: in double-blank sentences, go through the answer choices, testing the *first* word in each choice and eliminating the ones that don't fit.   (Argument Pattern)

6. **B.** The columnist was almost *reverential* (worshipful) in what he wrote about those he liked, but he savagely attacked those he disliked. "Even" here serves as an intensifier.
Acrimonious (stinging or bitter in nature) is a stronger word than *unpleasant*. It emphasizes how *very* unpleasant the columnist could become.   (Contrast Signal)

7. **A.** *Propitious* means favorable. It would be sensible to wait for a favorable moment to reveal plans. Remember: before you look at the choices, read the sentence and think of a word that makes sense.
Likely Words: appropriate, fitting, favorable.
(Examples)

8. **C.** Metternich hires ships' captains to buy books to add to his growing (*burgeoning*) collection. This is an example of his great passion for books (*bibliomania*).
Word Parts Clue: *Biblio-* means book; *mania* means passion or excessive enthusiasm.
(Example)

9. **B.** The coal-mining company naturally sought a court that it expected to be *favorably inclined* toward its case.

10. **D.** The author, alluding to the judges' ruling that the damage had been an act of God, is being *ironic* in describing the coal operator as God-fearing or perhaps not so God-fearing after all. Certainly the coal operator does not fear God enough to recompense the people who suffered because of his actions.

11. **C.** Mr. Watson dislikes theatricality and violence in sermons. His notion of a proper preacher is one who *avoids extremes in delivering his sermons.*

12. **A.** Mr. Watson likes simplicity in preaching. Thus, he condemns artificiality and a studied or *affected* (phony, pretentious) attitude.

13. **D.** The sentence immediately preceding the De Voss quotation asserts that rock and roll is "big corporation business." The De Voss quote is used to support this view that *rock and roll is a major industry*, for, by showing that many rock stars earn far more than major corporate executives do, it indicates the impact that the music business has on America's economy.

14. **C.** *Consumption* here refers to *using up* [*consumer*] *goods*, such as foodstuffs, clothes, and cars.

15. **A.** The washing machine, spot cream, and rock band are all "on the market" (lines 28 and 29): they are all being marketed as *commodities*, and they all serve equally well to distract the consumer from more essential concerns.

16. **C.** "Plastic" here is being used *metaphorically* or figuratively. It creates an image of rock and roll as somehow synthetic, dehumanized, even mercenary, as in *plastic smiles* or *plastic motel rooms* or *plastic money*.

17. **E.** To Burchill and Parsons, the consumer is "a potential Moron" who can be kept quiet and content by being handed consumer goods as a distraction. Thus, the consumer is someone who is *vulnerable to manipulation* by the enemy.

18. **B.** Dylan is given credit for "introducing the explicit politics of folk music to rock and roll." Clearly, this implies that, at the time Dylan introduced politics to rock, folk music was already an openly political medium through which artists expressed their convictions. It was only after Dylan's introduction of political ideas into his lyrics that other rock and roll artists began to deal with political materials. In other words, *folk music gave voice to political concerns long before rock and roll music did.*

19. **D.** Wiener makes three points about Paul: he lacked political values (was *apolitical*), wrote highly successful nonpolitical songs ("Number One hits"), and managed to sleep

soundly. Clearly, this suggests that John, who attempted to express his political values through his songs and as a result had difficulty putting out Number One hits, didn't always sleep soundly. This in turn implies that, as *an apolitical performer* who had a relatively easy time turning out hits, *Paul suffered less strain than John did.*

20. C.   The author describes Lennon's apolitical "Starting Over" as one of his "biggest hits" (line 70). Similarly, she describes the highly personal *Double Fantasy* album as "best-selling" (line 83). Thus, she clearly offers them as examples of *profitable successes lacking political content.*

21. E.   The artist's task is to *keep* or preserve his political commitment without deluding himself about how much influence his songs will have.
         Treat vocabulary-in-context questions as if they are sentence completion exercises. Always substitute each of the answer choices in place of the quoted word in the original sentence.

22. B.   Greene asks how one can "possibly avoid being a part of the power relations that exist." He feels trapped. The more popular his music is, the more his work is subject to misinterpretation, and the more he is involved in the power relations of the music industry. As a politically committed artist, he is frustrated because *he cannot escape involvement* in the very power relations he condemns.

23. C.   Throughout the last paragraph, the author reiterates that the politically motivated artist, given the difficulty of his material, is lucky to gain any degree of popular success. She clearly attributes any such success to pure luck or *good fortune*.

24. C.   The author states that the "rock and roll artist cannot cause political change" (lines 104 and 105). In other words, he has no direct, immediate effect on the political situation. However, he may be able to make an *indirect* contribution to political change by influencing his audience and thus contributing to any change it makes.

Section 3 Mathematical Reasoning

In each mathematics section, for many problems, an alternative solution, indicated by two asterisks (**), follows the first solution. When this occurs, one of the solutions is the direct mathematical one and the other is based on one of the tactics discussed in Chapter 8 or 9.

1. D. $3x = 12 \Rightarrow x = 4 \Rightarrow 5x = \mathbf{20}$.

2. B.   The sum of the measures of the three angles in any triangle is 180° (KEY FACT J1), so
        $90 + 33 + x = 180 \Rightarrow 123 + x = 180 \Rightarrow x = \mathbf{57}$.

3. D.   Clearing the parentheses in the original equation gives $8 - 8 + m = 8$, so $m = \mathbf{8}$.
        **Use TACTIC 5: backsolve. Replace m by 0, choice C: $8 - (8 - 0) = 8 - 8 = 0$. This is too small; eliminate A, B, C. Let $m = \mathbf{8}$, choice D. It works!

4. B.   Use TACTIC 7: pick an easy-to-use number. Since $\frac{5}{9}$ of the members are boys, assume there are 9 members, 5 of whom are boys. Then the other 4 are girls, and the ratio of girls to boys is 4 to 5, or $\frac{\mathbf{4}}{\mathbf{5}}$.

5. B.   Triangle EAB is a 45-45-90 triangle; so, by KEY FACT J8, $AE = 4$ and $BE = 4\sqrt{2}$. Since $BCDE$ is a square, each of its other sides is also equal to $4\sqrt{2}$, so the perimeter is
        $4 + 4 + 4\sqrt{2} + 4\sqrt{2} + 4\sqrt{2} = \mathbf{8 + 12\sqrt{2}}$
        Use TACTIC 2: trust the diagram. $\overline{BC}$ is clearly longer than $\overline{AB}$, which is 4, but not nearly twice as long. A good guess would be between 5 and 6. Then the perimeter is between 23 and 26. Now, use your calculator; to the nearest whole number, the five choices are: 20, 25, 31, 29, 32. Obviously, the right one is **B.

6. A.   If $x^4 = 10$, then (taking the square root of each side) $x^2 = \sqrt{10}$, and $x^6 = x^4 \cdot x^2 = \mathbf{10\sqrt{10}}$.
        **If $x^4 = 10$, then $x^8 = x^4 \cdot x^4 = 10 \times 10 = 100$, so x^6 is surely less. Of the five choices, only A, $10\sqrt{10}$, is less than 100.
        **Use your calculator. The fourth root of 10, $(10^{.25})$, is approximately 1.78, which, when raised to the sixth power (1.78^6), is approximately 32. Only $\mathbf{10\sqrt{10}}$ is anywhere near 32.

7. E.   Since by KEY FACT J2 the measure of an exterior angle of a triangle is equal to the sum of the measures of the two opposite interior angles, $x = 80 + y$. But, since $BC > AC$, by KEY FACT J3 $y > 80$. So, x must be greater than 160. Since x is an integer, it must be at least **161**.
        **Use TACTIC 5: backsolve. Start with 100, the smallest choice. If $x = 100$, then $z = 80$, which would leave only 20° for y. This is *way too small*, since y is supposed to be the largest angle. Try something much bigger for x.

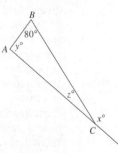

8. **B.** Pick an integer, 2 say. Then

$$\frac{a+3}{5} = 2 \Rightarrow a + 3 = 10 \Rightarrow a = 7,$$

and 5 goes into 7 once with a remainder of **2**.

9. **B.** On six tests combined, Brigitte earned a total of $6 \times 75 = 450$ points (TACTIC E1). The total of her five best grades is $5 \times 85 = 425$ points, so her lowest grade was $450 - 425 = \mathbf{25}$.

10. **E.** Check each statement independently.
   - The only factors of 17 are ± 1 and ± 17. If m is any of these, $\frac{17}{m}$ is an odd integer. (I is false.)
   - Could $\frac{m}{17}$ be an even integer? Sure, it could be *any* even integer; for example, if $m = 34$, $\frac{m}{17} = 2$, and if $m = 170$, $\frac{m}{17} = 10$. (II is true.)
   - Could $17m$ be a prime? Yes, if $m = 1$. (III is true.)

   The true statements are **II and III only**.

11. **C.** The percent increase in Max's investment is $\frac{\text{actual increase}}{\text{original value}} \times 100\%$. Each share was originally worth $10, and the actual increase in value of each share was $10. Max's percent increase in value $= \frac{10}{10} \times 100\% = \mathbf{100\%}$.

12. **C.** The number, n, of reports Benjamin can type is equal to the rate, in reports *per minute*, at which he types times the number of minutes he types. Then

$$n = \frac{1 \text{ report}}{h \text{ hours}} \times m \text{ minutes}$$
$$= \frac{1 \text{ report}}{60h \text{ minutes}} \times m \text{ minutes} = \frac{m}{60h} \text{ reports.}$$

   **Use TACTIC 7: pick some easy-to-use numbers. Suppose Benjamin can type 1 report every 2 hours, and he types for 60 minutes; he will complete half of a report. Which of the five choices equals $\frac{1}{2}$ when $h = 2$ and $m = 60$? Only $\frac{m}{60h}$.

13. **B.** The trust received 80% of the estate (10% went to the man's wife, 5% to his children, and 5% to his grandchildren). If E represents the value of the estate, then

$$0.80E = 1{,}000{,}000$$
$$E = 1{,}000{,}000 \div 0.80 = 1{,}250{,}000.$$

   Each grandchild received 1% (one-fifth of 5%) of the estate, or **$12,500**.

14. **E.** Use TACTIC 1: draw a diagram. Since this is a ratio problem, immediately plug in a number (TACTIC 6). To avoid fractions, use 6, the LCM of the numbers in the question. Let $AC = 6$; then $CD = 3$, with D on either side of C. $BD = 2$, but B could be on either side of D, and so we have no way of knowing length BC. The value of the ratio $\frac{BC}{CD}$ **cannot be determined from the information given.**

15. **A.** At 10:30 A.M. the first car had been going 40 miles per hour for 1.5 hours, and so had gone $40 \times 1.5 = 60$ miles. The second car covered the same 60 miles in 1 hour and 20 minutes, or $1\frac{1}{3} = \frac{4}{3}$ hours. Therefore, its rate was

$$60 \div \frac{4}{3} = 60 \times \frac{3}{4} = \mathbf{45} \text{ miles per hour.}$$

16. **B.** Since $5x = 360$ (KEY FACT I3), $x = 72$ and $m\angle AOB = 2x = 144$. Since $OA = OB$ (they are both radii), $\triangle AOB$ is isosceles:

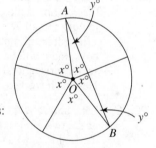

$$2y + 144 = 180 \Rightarrow 2y = 36 \Rightarrow y = 18.$$

   Then $\frac{y}{x} = \frac{18}{72} = \mathbf{\frac{1}{4}}$.

   **It should be clear that the values of x and y can be determined, so eliminate E, and use TACTIC 2: trust the diagram; x appears to be about 70 and y about 20. Then,

$$\frac{y}{x} \approx \frac{20}{70} = \frac{1}{3.5}, \text{ and you should } \textit{guess}$$

   between $\frac{1}{3}$ and $\frac{1}{4}$.

17. **D.** It's not hard to calculate $\boxed{10}$ and $\boxed{9}$, but you don't have to. Here, $\boxed{10} - \boxed{9} = (1 + 2 + \cdots + 9 + 10) - (1 + 2 + \cdots + 9) = 10$. Now, calculate the choices: Only $\boxed{4} = 1 + 2 + 3 + 4 = 10$.

18. D. $\boxed{1010} = (1 + 2 + \cdots + 1000) + (1001 + 1002 + \cdots + 1010)$. The sum in the first parentheses is just $\boxed{1000} = a$. The sum in the second parentheses is $(1000 + 1) + (1000 + 2) + \cdots + (1000 + 10)$, which can be written as $(1000 + 1000 + \cdots + 1000) + (1 + 2 + \cdots + 10) = 10{,}000 + b$. The total is
$$a + 10{,}000 + b = \boldsymbol{a + b + 10{,}000}.$$

19. C. Draw a Venn diagram and label each region.

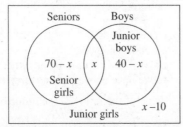

Let x be the number of senior boys. Then $40 - x$ is the number of boys who are not seniors (i.e., are juniors), and $70 - x$ is the number of seniors who are not boys (i.e., are girls). Then number of junior girls =
$$100 - [(40 - x) + x + (70 - x)] =$$
$$100 - [110 - x] = x - 10.$$
Since the number of junior girls must be at least 0, $x - 10 \ge 0$ and so $x \ge \boldsymbol{10}$.
Use TACTIC 5: backsolve; but since you want the smallest number, start with A. If there are no senior boys, then all 40 boys are juniors and all 70 seniors are girls; but that's 110 people. Eliminate A. If there are 5 senior boys, there will be 35 junior boys and 65 senior girls, a total of 105. Finally, check **10, which works.

20. C. Let r and R be the radii of the two circles. From the figure, you can see that $\triangle OAB$ is a 45-45-90 right triangle, and so $R = r\sqrt{2}$ (KEY FACT J8). Therefore,

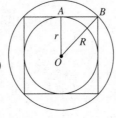

$$\frac{\text{area of large circle}}{\text{area of small circle}} = \frac{\pi R^2}{\pi r^2} = \frac{\pi (r\sqrt{2})^2}{\pi r^2} = \frac{2\pi r^2}{\pi r^2} = 2.$$
The ratio is **2:1**.
**Do exactly the same thing except use TACTIC 6. Let $r = 1$; then $R = \sqrt{2}$, and the ratio is $\dfrac{\pi(\sqrt{2})^2}{\pi(1)^2} = \dfrac{2\pi}{\pi} = \boldsymbol{2:1}.$

Section 4 Writing Skills

1. C. Error in sequence of tenses. This sentence illustrates the use of the future perfect tense. The present perfect tense, as used in Choice A, and the past perfect tense, as used in Choice B, are incorrect. Choice C correctly indicates that an anticipated event will be completed before a definite time in the future. Choice D is weak because of the use of the passive voice and the consequent vagueness as to who is performing the action. Choice E is awkward because of the needless separation of subject (*we*) from verb (*shall have traveled*).

2. D. Choices A, B, and C are examples of comma splice sentences. Choices B, C, and E also confuse the meanings of *complementary* and *complimentary*. Choice E leaves the verb *is not* without a subject. Choice D corrects the comma splice and adds no other errors.

3. E. Shift of personal pronoun. In Choices A and B there is an unwarranted shift from the third person pronoun *one* to the second person pronoun *you*. Choices C and D improperly use *affect* instead of *effect*.

4. D. Error in diction. Choices A and B illustrate the incorrect use of *due to*. The change to *inasmuch* in Choice C creates a sentence fragment. Choice E is poor because it omits the causal relationship implied by the original sentence.

5. B. Wordiness. Choice B cuts out the unnecessary words and creates a clear, effective sentence.

6. B. Error in logical comparison. Choices A, D, and E compare two things that cannot be directly compared—subways and cities. In Choice D, the omission of *other* changes the meaning of the sentence.

7. D. Choices A, B, and E omit important parts of the verb. *Hopefully* in Choices C and E is wrong; although many people use it this way, most grammarians do not accept it as a substitute for *we hope*. (Strictly speaking, *hopefully* should only be used to mean *in a hopeful way*, as in *The farmer searched the skies hopefully looking for signs of rain.*)

8. B. Lack of parallelism. Change *it partly pays tribute* to *part tribute*.

9. A. Sentence is correct.

10. D. Run-on sentence. Choice D provides a replacement that is both grammatical and concise.

11. A. Sentence is correct.

12. D. Error in parallelism. Change the clause *what his serial number was* to a noun (*serial number*) to match the other items in the list.

13. D. Error in tense. Change *will handle* to *handled*.

14. A. Error in pronoun case. Change *whom* to *who*.

15. E. Sentence is correct.

16. D. Error in pronoun number agreement. Since the antecedent of the pronoun is *lawyers,* change *its* to *their*.

17. B. Error in tense. Delete the word *has* to make the verb *anticipated*.

18. B. Error in pronoun number agreement. *Everybody* is a singular pronoun. Change *their* to *his* or *her*.

19. D. Error in diction. The verb *to lay* (past tense is *laid*) means to put or to place; the verb *to lie* (past tense is *lay*) means to recline. Therefore, change *laid back* to *lay back*.

20. B. Error in subject-verb agreement. *Data* is a plural noun. Change *was* to *were*.

21. B. Error in pronoun case. Change *she and I* to *us*.

22. A. Adjective and adverb confusion. The verb *feels* should be followed by an adjective (*bad*).

23. C. Error in verb form. Change *will be sang* to *will be sung*.

24. B. Error in pronoun case. Gerunds (verb forms ending in *-ing* that function as nouns) take the possessive pronoun. Change *him joining* to *his joining*.

25. D. Error in idiom. Change *appointed of* to *appointed to*.

26. C. Unidiomatic preposition choice. The verb *evolve* customarily is paired with the preposition *from*. Change *evolved off* to *evolved from*.

27. B. Lack of parallelism. Change *what we wish* to the plural noun *wishes*.

28. E. Sentence is correct.

29. B. Error in sequence of tenses. Change *has labored* to *labored*.

30. C. Choice A contains the extremely awkward phrase *to see underdogs being the one rooted for*. Choice B uses the coordinating conjunction *but*, which makes no sense in the context. It also contains the redundant phrase "sight . . . to see." Choice C clearly and concisely combines the thoughts contained in the two sentences. It is the best answer. Choice D contains a clause and a phrase that have no grammatical relationship. Choice E contains a comma splice between *Americans* and *for example*.

31. C. All sentences except 3 contribute to the discussion of the underdog. Sentence 3 is an unnecessary digression. Therefore, Choice C is the best answer.

32. B. Choice A is grammatically correct, but it refers to Americans' desire to feel good, a topic not discussed in paragraph 2. Choice B accurately introduces the topic of the paragraph. It is the best answer. Choices C and D are similar to A. Choice E is awkwardly expressed and contains the pronoun *themselves*, which refers grammatically to *traditions* instead of to *Americans*.

33. A. Choice A clearly and accurately combines the sentences. It is the best answer. Choice B is awkward and cumbersome. Choice C contains an awkward shift in verb tense from present (*look*) to past perfect (*had been*). Choice D contains the adverb *poorly*, which should be an adjective and should modify *immigrants* instead of *coming*.

34. C. Choice A is not an effective revision. It changes the focus of the discussion and contains the pronoun *their*, which refers grammatically to *Americans* instead of to *underdog*. Choice B contains an awkward shift in verb tense from past (*believed*) to present (*succeed*). Choice C follows naturally from the preceding sentence and is accurately expressed. It is the best answer. Choice D is grammatical, but it shifts the focus of the discussion. Choice E is confusing and contains the pronouns *they* and *their*, which lack a specific referent.

35. D. Choice A contains some transitional material but shifts verb tenses from past (*went*) to present (*defeat*). Choice B, which lacks a main verb, is a sentence fragment. Choice C, although grammatically correct, seems incomplete because the pronoun *it* lacks a specific referent. Choice D provides a smooth transition between paragraphs and introduces the topic of paragraph 3. It is the best answer. Choice E lacks any meaningful transitional material.

Section 6 Critical Reading

1. E. The first clause states that the movement did not become famous instantly or "overnight." Instead, it gained fame step by step, or *gradually*.
Remember to watch for signal words that link one part of the sentence to another. The use of "on the contrary" here sets up a contrast. The missing word must be an antonym for *overnight*.   (Contrast Signal)

2. E. The intensifier "even" indicates that Astell did more than merely maintain a good reputation; she improved or *enhanced* it.
(Intensifier Signal)

3. B. Kubota is hopeful about the success of the women's movement. Thus, she maintains that the recent forward steps or *strides* made by Japanese women in business mean even *greater* chances for women in future days.
(Support Signal)

4. A. This is a case in which you can't eliminate any of the answer choices by checking the first word of each answer pair: all are terms that could describe an ambassador. In this case, the *eminent* ambassador was only an *indifferent* (mediocre) linguist; nevertheless, he insisted on trying to speak foreign languages without help. Remember to watch for signal words that link one part of the sentence to another. The use of "yet" in the second clause sets up a contrast. Note that "but" here means "only." That's your clue to be on the lookout for a belittling or negative word.   (Contrast Signal)

5. B. To the author, nude models seem *archaic*, suited to an earlier day when art students spent as much time learning to draw the human body as medical students today spend learning to *dissect* or cut it up.

Remember: in double-blank sentences, go through the answer choices, testing the *first* word in each choice and eliminating the ones that don't fit. By definition, a relic or remnant of a bygone age is outdated or old-fashioned. You can immediately eliminate Choices C and E.   (Definition)

6. **C.** In stating that the voyageur struck his imagination, the narrator indicates that the voyageur *impressed* him.

7. **D.** Although the narrator comments on the voyageur's strength and on the hardships and dangers he faces on the trail, the narrator is most impressed by the voyageur's "unsurpassed nonchalance and joy in the wilderness." To the narrator, this exuberance or *zest* is the voyageur's outstanding quality.

8. **C.** Although both authors clearly appreciate the contribution of the voyageur to Canadian exploration and trade, the author of Passage 1 shows a greater degree of *open admiration* of the voyageur than does the author of Passage 2. Beware of eye-catchers. While the author of Passage 1 may feel some degree of affection for the colorful voyageur, nothing in Passage 1 suggests that such affection may be *misguided*.

9. **E.** The author of Passage 1 describe the personal impression made upon him by the voyageur: "It was the voyageur who struck my imagination." Compared to the author of Passage 2, he writes personally rather than impersonally, making use of his *personal voice.*

10. **E.** You can arrive at the correct answer by the process of elimination.
Statement I is false. While sea action plays a part in erosion, the author does not say it is the most important factor in erosion. Therefore, you can eliminate Choices A and D.
Statement II is true. "The first purely synthetic oil . . . has yet to be produced." Therefore, you can eliminate Choice C.
Statement III is true. New rock is born or created "through the effects of gravity." Therefore, you can eliminate Choice B.
Only Choice E is left. It is the correct answer.

11. **B.** The author mentions the Grand Canyon while speaking of rivers as "immensely powerful destructive agencies." The dramatic canyon illustrates the *devastating impact* a river can have.

12. **D.** In the last paragraph the author states that "the cause of the metamorphosis" of decayed vegetation and dead aquatic life into oil is not known. We lack full understanding of the process by which oil is created; therefore, our understanding is *deficient.*
Choice C is incorrect. Our knowledge is not *erroneous* or false; it is simply incomplete.

13. **A.** The last sentence states that oil is always found "on the sites of ancient seas and lakes."

14. **D.** The author describes several processes (erosion, rock formation, oil formation). He states the

possibility that a chemical catalyst is involved in oil formation. He cites the Grand Canyon as an example of what a river can do to the land. He mentions the limitation of our ability to produce oil synthetically. However, he never proposes a solution to any problem.

15. **B.** The term "reaches" here refers to the vast, *unbroken stretches* of time required for the mountains to erode and, out of their dust, for new rock to be formed at the bottom of the sea.

16. **C.** The author presents these favorable comments about myths in order to support his general thesis that myths and fairy tales perform valuable psychological and educational functions, that is, *are valuable.*

17. **B.** The author looks on contemporary parents who want their children exposed only to "real" people and everyday events as mistaken. Stating that Plato may have known more about what shapes people's minds than these modern parents do, he suggests that his contemporaries may be *misguided in their beliefs.*

18. **C.** As used in this sentence, "make for" means help to promote or maintain. The author is asserting that Plato understood which sorts of experiences worked to *promote the development of* true humanity.

19. **D.** No matter what they originally believe—regardless of their original persuasion or *opinion*—contemporary theorists who study myths and fairy tales come to the same conclusion. Remember: when answering a vocabulary-in-context question, test each answer choice by substituting it in the sentence for the word in quotes.

20. **C.** The opening sentences of the second paragraph suggest that Eliade is a modern thinker who has studied myths from a philosophical or psychological view.
Note the use of the phrase "for one" in the sentence describing Eliade. "For one" indicates that Eliade is one of a group. In this case he is one example of the group of *twentieth century philosophers* who have explored the nature of myths.

21. **E.** The author has been discussing what there is about fairy tales that attracts and holds an audience's interest. He concludes that their *attraction* or appeal is at one and the same time to our conscious mind and to our unconscious mind as well.
Again, when answering a vocabulary-in-context question, test each answer choice by substituting it in the sentence for the word in quotes.

22. **D.** Like Eliade and other modern thinkers, the author is concerned with the tales' meeting strongly felt needs and providing desirable solutions to human problems—in other words, their *psychological relevance.*

23. **E.** The author's citation of the favorable comments of Plato, Aristotle, and Eliade (and his lack of

citation of any unfavorable comments) indicates his attitude is one of *approval*.

24. E. Use the process of elimination to answer this question.
Characteristic I illustrates a way in which fairy tales differ from dreams. Fairy tales are shaped by the conscious minds of many people (*shared creation*). Dreams, however, are created by an individual's unconscious mind. Therefore, you can eliminate Choices B and D.
Characteristic II illustrates a second way in which fairy tales differ from dreams. Fairy tales promise a happy solution to problems (*happy ending*). Dreams, on the other hand, do not necessarily offer any solutions to problems. Therefore, you can eliminate Choice A.
Characteristic III illustrates a third way in which fairy tales differ from dreams. Unlike dreams, which usually interest only the dreamer, fairy tales arouse persistent interest in many people (*general appeal*). Therefore, you can eliminate Choice C.
Only Choice E is left. It is the correct answer.

Section 7 Mathematical Reasoning

MULTIPLE-CHOICE QUESTIONS

1. B. Wally produces 80 widgets per day × 20 days per month × 12 months per year = 19,200 widgets per year; 96,000 ÷ 19,200 = **5.**

2. E. If $|10 - \sqrt{x}| = 7$, then either

$$10 - \sqrt{x} = 7 \quad \text{or} \quad 10 - \sqrt{x} = -7$$
$$-\sqrt{x} = -3 \quad \text{or} \quad -\sqrt{x} = -17$$
$$\sqrt{x} = 3 \quad \text{or} \quad \sqrt{x} = 17$$
$$x = 9 \quad \text{or} \quad x = 289$$

The sum of the two solutions is 9 + 289 = **298.**

3. A. Since $JL = KL$, the angles opposite them have the same measure (KEY FACT J3). Then, $d = a$, and we *can* find the value of a ($a + a + 70 = 180$), but that's it. Since b and e are not necessarily equal (see the diagram), we *cannot* determine b or c. The answer is a **only.**

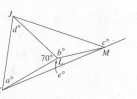

4. E. O is the midpoint of $\overline{AB}$. Let B have coordinates (x, y). Then by KEY FACT N3,

$$(1, 5) = \left(\frac{x+5}{2}, \frac{y+1}{2} \right). \text{ Therefore,}$$

$$1 = \frac{x+5}{2} \Rightarrow 2 = x + 5 \Rightarrow x = -3, \text{ and}$$

$$5 = \frac{y+1}{2} \Rightarrow 10 = y + 1 \Rightarrow y = 9.$$

Therefore, B has coordinates **(–3, 9).**

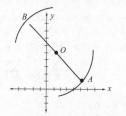

Even a rough sketch will indicate that B is in Quadrant II, and y is surely greater than 5. Only choices D and E are even plausible. A *good* sketch will lead to choice **E.

5. D. If the total surface area of the cube is 216, then the area of each of the 6 faces is 216 ÷ 6 = 36. Since each face is a square of area 36, each edge is 6. Finally, the volume of the cube is $6^3 = $ **216.**

6. D. Let x be the amount, in dollars, that each of the 20 children was going to contribute; then $20x$ represents the cost of the present. When 4 children dropped out, the remaining 16 each had to pay $(x + 1.50)$ dollars, so
$$16(x + 1.5) = 20x \Rightarrow 16x + 24 = 20x \Rightarrow$$
$$24 = 4x \Rightarrow x = 6,$$
and so the cost of the present was 20 × 6 = **120** dollars.
Use TACTIC 5: backsolve. Try choice C, 100. If the present cost $100, then each of the 20 children would have had to pay $5. When 4 dropped out, the remaining 16 would have had to pay $100 ÷ 16 = $6.25 apiece, an increase of $1.25. Since the actual increase was $1.50, the gift was more expensive. Eliminate A, B, and C. Try D, **120; it works.

7. C. The function $f(x) = \sqrt{x^2 - 9}$ is defined for all real numbers except those that cause $x^2 - 9$ to be negative.
$$x^2 < 9 \Rightarrow -3 < x < 3.$$
Five integers satisfy this inequality: $-2, -1, 0, 1, 2$.

8. E The area of the shaded ring is the area of the large circle, 25π, minus the area of the middle circle, 16π:
Area of shaded ring = $25\pi - 16\pi = 9\pi$.
The probability that the point is in that ring is $\dfrac{9\pi}{25\pi} = \dfrac{\mathbf{9}}{\mathbf{25}}$.

GRID-IN QUESTIONS

9. (15) Evaluate $3a - 2b$:
$3(3) - 2(-3) = 3(3) + 2(3) = 9 + 6 = \mathbf{15}$.

10. (37.5) Use TACTIC D1. In a ratio problem write the letter x after each number. Then, $a = 6x$, $b = 7x$, and $c = 11x$; and since the sum of the measures of the angles of a triangle is 180°:
$6x + 7x + 11x = 180 \Rightarrow 24x = 180 \Rightarrow x = 7.5$.
Then $c - a = 11x - 6x = 5x = 5(7.5) = \mathbf{37.5}$.
[Note that we did *not* have to find the value of any of the angles (TACTIC 10).]

11. (90) Draw a right triangle and label the two legs 15 and 36. To calculate the perimeter, you need only find the length of the hypotenuse and then add the lengths of the three sides. Before using the Pythagorean theorem, ask yourself whether this is a multiple of one of the basic right triangles you know: 3-4-5 or 5-12-13. It is: $15 = 3 \times 5$ and $36 = 3 \times 12$, so the hypotenuse is $3 \times 13 = 39$. The perimeter is $3(5 + 12 + 13) = 3 \times 30 = \mathbf{90}$.
**If you don't recognize the triangle, use the Pythagorean theorem and your calculator:
$15^2 + 36^2 = c^2 \Rightarrow c^2 = 225 + 1296 = 1521$.
So $c = \sqrt{1521} = 39$.
The perimeter is $15 + 36 + 39 = \mathbf{90}$.

12. (99) From the 124 people in front of Jill, remove Jack plus the 24 people in front of Jack:
$124 - 25 = \mathbf{99}$.
**It may be easier for you to see this if you draw a diagram (TACTIC 1):

13. (89) Since $y > x$, then y must be greater than 90 and x less than 90. The largest integer less than 90 is **89**.

14. (19) Draw a diagram. For the third-place share to be as large as possible, the fourth-place share must be as small as possible. However, it must be more than \$15, so let it be \$16. Then the amount, in dollars, left for second and third places is $100 - (30 + 16 + 15) = 100 - 61 = 39$. The second-place share could be \$20, and the third-place share **\$19**.

Use TACTIC 7. Try a number. Third place must be less than 30 and more than 15; try 20. Then second place must be at least 21 and fourth place at least 16. But $30 + 21 + 20 + 16 + 15 = 102$, which is a *little* too big. Try a little smaller number, such as **19, which works.

15. (179) If the average of a set of 9 numbers is 99, their sum is $9 \times 99 = 891$. If deleting 1 number reduces the average of the remaining 8 numbers to 89, the sum of those 8 numbers must be $8 \times 89 = 712$. The deleted number was $891 - 712 = \mathbf{179}$.

16. (42) Use TACTIC 14. Systematically list all the ways of expressing 12 as the sum of three different positive integers, and calculate each product.

Integers	Product	Integers	Product
9, 2, 1	18	6, 5, 1	30
8, 3, 1	24	6, 4, 2	48
7, 4, 1	28	5, 4, 3	60
7, 3, 2	42		

Then $g = 60$, $\ell = 18$, and $g - \ell = \mathbf{42}$.

17. $\left(\dfrac{13}{5} \text{ or } 2.6\right)$ Use TACTIC 1.
Draw a right triangle, and label the shorter leg a, the longer leg b, and the hypotenuse c.
Then $\dfrac{1}{4}b = \dfrac{3}{5}a \Rightarrow b = \dfrac{12}{5}a$. *Stop*.
This is a question about right triangles, so if the 12 and the 5 in that fraction make you think of a 5-12-13 triangle, check it out: $\dfrac{1}{4}(12) = 3$ and $\dfrac{3}{5}(5) = 3$. It works. The ratio is $\dfrac{\mathbf{13}}{\mathbf{5}}$.

**If you didn't see that, use the Pythagorean theorem:

$$c^2 = a^2 + \left(\frac{12}{5}a\right)^2 =$$

$$a^2 + \frac{144}{25}a^2 = \frac{25}{25}a^2 + \frac{144}{25}a^2 = \frac{169}{25}a^2 \Rightarrow$$

$$c = \sqrt{\frac{169}{25}a^2} = \frac{13}{5}a \Rightarrow \frac{c}{a} = \frac{\mathbf{13}}{\mathbf{5}}.$$

18. (25) Since x varies inversely with y, there is a constant k such that $xy = k$. Then $k = (3)(12) = 36$, and, when $x = 4$, $4y = 36 \Rightarrow y = 9$. Also, since x varies directly with z, there is a constant m

such that $\dfrac{x}{z} = m$. Then $m = \dfrac{3}{12} = \dfrac{1}{4}$, and when

$x = 4$, $\dfrac{4}{z} = \dfrac{1}{4} \Rightarrow z = 16$. Finally, $9 + 16 = \mathbf{25}$.

Section 8 Critical Reading

1. D. Buildings constructed in such a hurry would tend to be *ramshackle* (loosely held together) affairs. (Definition)

2. D. Immune to most pesticides, cockroaches are thus tough or *hardy* and hard to *eliminate*. Remember: in double-blank sentences, go through the answer choices, testing the *first* word in each choice and eliminating those that don't fit. You can immediately eliminate Choices A and C. (Cause and Effect Pattern)

3. B. *Stoically* means that a person bears pain with great courage.
Note how the part of the sentence after the comma describes the patient, and thus provides enough context to clarify how the patient bore or endured pain. (Context Clue)

4. D. Note the use of "might." Without the support of other stories, the actor's stories might not be believed. If people need such supporting testimony, their first response to the stories must be disbelief. They must think them exaggerations or *hyperbole*. "Were there not" is a short way of saying "If there were not."
(Argument)

5. E. Wemmick's private kindness is contrasted with his *public* harshness. Note here the use of "even" as an intensifier: to be *ruthless* or relentless is more blameworthy than merely to be *uncompassionate* or hard-hearted. (Contrast Pattern)

6. B The view of Rome's contributions to government, law, and engineering is wholly positive: these additions to human knowledge are generally acknowledged. *In contrast,* Rome's original contributions to art are *not* recognized: they are seen as just *an echo* or imitation *of* the art of ancient Greece.
Note that "although" sets up a contrast.
(Contrast Signal)

7. D. Wolfe is making a point through a simile, a type of *figurative expression*. Going home again, he says, is *like* stepping into a river, through which new water constantly flows. Each time you step into the river, it will be different; each time you try to return home, it too will be different.

8. C. The author of Passage 1 states that *at best* the journey home will point you to your origins, "to where you started," and will let you know how your origins have "helped to shape you." In other words, the most positive outcome of

your attempting to go home would be for you to *grasp how your origins have formed you.*

9. B. The author feels trapped between Wolfe's certainty that one cannot go home again and Haley's certainty that one *can* do so, that one can find the way back to one's ancestral homeland and return to one's roots. He is torn between extremes, uncertain about just what he is looking for—his conflicting desires clearly show his *ambivalence about his journey.*
Choice A is incorrect. The author has no desire to know what his ancestors looked like. He is not seeking to convey his resemblance to them.
Choices C and D are incorrect. Nothing in the passage supports them.
Choice E is incorrect. Though on one level the author deeply desires to trace his roots (as Haley did), on another he feels attempting to do so is a meaningless exercise. Thus, he chiefly conveys his ambivalence about his journey.

10. A. A *paradox* is a seemingly contradictory statement that may perhaps be true in fact. Here the author was, in Africa, his ancestral homeland, but it did not feel like home to him. He clearly found his situation paradoxical.

11. E. Africa held or *possessed* symbolic significance for the author of this passage.
Remember: when answering a vocabulary-in-context question, try substituting each answer choice in the original sentence for the word in quotes.

12. D. Though the author earns his living as an arts administrator, he thinks of himself as a poet, a creative artist. When he says he needed time for his own work, he is referring to his *creating poetry.*

13. C. The author essentially looks down on his administrative work. Though it is time-consuming, leaving him with little time to compose poetry, it is not a taxing or *demanding* job.

14. B. The author describes a scene in which he, a Japanese-American child watching old World War II movies, playacted being an American G.I. shooting down Japanese soldiers. Rather than siding with the Japanese soldiers whom he physically resembled, he took the part of their opponents. This episode serves to show how much he *identified himself as an American.*
Choice A is incorrect. The author had no particular hatred for Japan or the Japanese. He merely felt they did not have much to do with his life.
Choice C is incorrect. Though he has mentioned the fakery of Japanese films, he does not describe the American-made war movies in order to show that they are better than Japanese films.

Choice D is incorrect. Nothing in the passage supports it.

Choice E is incorrect. Childhood experiences playing soldiers would be unlikely to motivate anyone to travel to Japan.

15. D. Bali is in the South Pacific. The Bahamas are in the Caribbean. The primary thing these islands have in common is that they are classic *exotic destinations* for vacationers.

16. E. Like the author of Passage 1, the author of Passage 2 feels *marked ambivalence* about his prospective journey. He is happy to have won the fellowship, but unhappy at the prospect of having to spend a year in a country he finds relatively unappealing.

17. D. In the final lines of Passage 2, the author creates a picture of his imagination as a swimmer, "unconsciously swimming the Pacific" toward Japan, going against the tide of his family's earlier movement from Japan to America. This picture is *an extended metaphor* or image.

18. A. In both passages, the authors are concerned about their racial or *ethnic identity*. The author of Passage 1 is seeking to discover "how much of being black" comes from his African origins. The author of Passage 2 has to a degree denied his ethnic identity ("Much of my life I had insisted on my Americanness, had shunned most connections with Japan and felt proud I knew no Japanese") and yet has celebrated his Japanese heritage in his verse.

Choice B is incorrect. The authors are not seeking to establish their independence as individuals. They are seeking to discover the nature of their ties to their ancestral homelands.

Choice C is incorrect. While the authors may wish to learn more about their ancestors, they do not worship them.

Choice D is incorrect. There is nothing in either passage to support it.

Choice E is incorrect. While Passage 1 mentions Haley's attempts to trace his roots, its author has no such attempts in mind. Passage 2's author never mentions genealogical research.

19. C. Use the process of elimination to arrive at the correct answer to this question.

The author of Passage 2 insists that Japan "didn't have much to do with" his present life. This parallels the statement in Passage 1 that Africa held "only a symbolic significance" to the author. Therefore, Choice A is incorrect. The author of Passage 2 asserts that he "had insisted on" his Americanness and "felt proud" of knowing no Japanese. Like the author of Passage 1, who "did not feel African," the Japanese-American author of Passage 2 did not feel Japanese. Therefore, Choice B is incorrect. The author of Passage 2 states that his "reasons for going [to Japan] were not very clear." He hardly knew why he was going there. This parallels the comment in Passage 1 that its

author "hardly knew what" he was looking for in Africa. Therefore, Choice D is incorrect. The image of "memories hidden in [one's] genes" awakening in Passage 1 has its counterpart in Mura's image of how his poetic imagination had been returning to his ancestral past, "unconsciously swimming the Pacific." Therefore, Choice E is incorrect.

Only Choice C is left. It is the correct answer. Passage 1's author is so torn between Africa and America that he comes to feel like a "waif without a home." There is nothing corresponding to this idea in Passage 2. Throughout Passage 2, its author insists on his Americanness, identifies with the GI's in World War II movies. He clearly feels America is his home.

Section 9 Mathematical Reasoning

1. B. $3x = 36 \Rightarrow x = 12 \Rightarrow \dfrac{x}{3} = \mathbf{4}$.

2. C. If $\dfrac{7}{11} a = \dfrac{7}{11} b$, then $a = b$, and $\dfrac{a}{b} = \mathbf{1}$.

3. C. Set up a proportion:

$$\frac{2.2 \text{ pounds}}{1 \text{ kilogram}} = \frac{120 \text{ pounds}}{x \text{ kilograms}}. \text{ Then}$$

$$2.2x = 120 \Rightarrow x = \frac{120}{2.2} = 54.54....$$

Therefore, the **3** students weighing more than 120 pounds are the 3 who weigh more than 54.54 kilograms.

**Quickly multiply by 2.2: $56 \times 2.2 = 123.2$, so 56, 57, and 61 kilograms are all more than 120 pounds. The other two weights are less.

4. D. Since the value of a share doubled every year, each year it was worth *half* as much as the following year. In 1990 a share was worth $80, so in 1989 it was worth half as much, or $40; in 1988 it was worth $20; and in **1987** it was worth $10.

Use TACTIC 5: backsolve, starting with C, 1986. If a share was worth $10 in 1986, then it was worth $20 in 1987, $40 in 1988, $80 in 1989. That's a year too soon. Start a year later—1987**.

5. B. If a is the average of 10 and some other number, x, then

$$a = \frac{10 + x}{2} \Rightarrow 2a = 10 + x \Rightarrow x = \mathbf{2a - 10}.$$

**Use TACTIC 6. Pick a number for a, say 5. Since 5 is the average of 10 and 0, check the five choices to see which one equals 0 when $a = 5$. Only B: $2(5) - 10 = 0$.

6. **B.** The percent increase in a quantity is

$$\frac{\text{actual increase}}{\text{original}} \times 100\% \text{ (KEY FACT C5).}$$

For *each* year calculate the actual increase and divide. For example, in 1990 the increase was \$100 (from \$150 to \$250), so the percent increase was $\frac{100}{150} \times 100\% = 66.66\%$. In **1991** the increase was \$200 and the percent increase was $\frac{200}{250} \times 100\% = 80\%$. Check the other choices; this is the greatest.

7. **C.** The interior of the star is a hexagon, a six-sided polygon. By KEY FACT K2, the sum of the six angles in a hexagon is $(6 - 2)180 = 4(180) = $ **720**.
   Use TACTIC 2: trust the diagram. Since each of the six angles clearly measures more than 100° but less than 150°, the total is more than 600 but less than 900. Only **720 is in that range.

8. **B.** If each side of the square is π, then its perimeter is 4π. Since the circumference of the circle is equal to the perimeter of the square, $C = 4\pi$. But $C = 2\pi r$, and so $2\pi r = 4\pi \Rightarrow r = $ **2**.

9. **E.** Just calculate the first 5 terms: $a_1 = 1$; $a_2 = 1^2 + 1 = 2$; $a_3 = 2^2 + 1 = 5$; $a_4 = 5^2 + 1 = 26$; $a_5 = 26^2 + 1 = $ **677**.

10. **E.** The perimeter, P, of $\triangle BCD = $ $BC + CD + BD$. Since $BC + CD = 7$ (it is one-half the perimeter of rectangle $ABCD$), $P = 7 + BD$. But BD cannot be determined, since it depends on the length of sides $\overline{BC}$ and $\overline{CD}$. Both rectangles in the figure have perimeters that are 14, but the values of BD are different. The perimeter of $\triangle BCD$ **cannot be determined from the information given.**

11. **D.** If a represents Jordan's average after five tests, then he has earned a total of $5a$ points (TACTIC E1). A grade of 70 on the sixth test will lower his average 4 points to $a - 4$. Therefore

$$a - 4 = \frac{5a + 70}{6} \Rightarrow 6(a - 4) = 5a + 70. \text{ So,}$$
$$6a - 24 = 5a + 70 \Rightarrow 6a = 5a + 94 \Rightarrow a = \mathbf{94}.$$

**Use TACTIC 5: backsolve, starting with choice C, 90. If Jordan's five-test average is 90, he has 450 points and a 70 on the sixth test will give him a total of 520 points, and an average of $520 \div 6 = 86.666$. The 70 lowered his average 3.3333 points, which is not enough. Eliminate A, B, and C. Try D, 94. It works.

12. **E.** $g(-10) = f(3(-10)) = f(-30) = (-30)^2 - 3(-30) = 900 - (-90) = 900 + 90 = 990$
   $g(x) = f(3x) = (3x)^2 - 3(3x) = 9x^2 - 9x$. Then $g(-10) = 9(-10)^2 - 9(-10) = 900 + 90 = $ **990.

13. **A.** $\dfrac{12a^2 b^{-\frac{1}{2}} c^6}{4a^{-2} b^{\frac{1}{2}} c^2} = 3a^{2-(-2)} b^{-\frac{1}{2}-\frac{1}{2}} c^{6-2} = 3a^4 b^{-1} c^4 = $

$$\frac{3a^4 c^4}{b}.$$

14. **B.** The graph of $y = f(x - 2)$ is obtained by shifting the graph of $y = f(x)$ 2 units to the right. Therefore the x-intercept $(-3, 0)$ shifts 2 units to $(-1, 0)$; the **only** x-coordinate is **–1**.

15. **E.** Store 2 sold 30 DVDs at \$50, 40 DVDs at \$80, and 20 DVDs at \$120. Store 2: $(30 \times \$50) + (40 \times \$80) + (20 \times \$120) = \$7100$. Store 1 sold 10 DVDs at \$80, 20 DVDs at \$100, and 20 DVDs at \$150. Store 1: $(10 \times \$80) + (20 \times \$100) + (20 \times \$150) = \$5800$. Finally, $\$7100 - \$5800 = $ **\$1300**.

16. **C.** According to the triangle inequality (KEY FACT J10), the sum of the lengths of two sides of a triangle must be greater than the length of the third side. There is only one way to pick a number, a, from A and a number, b, from B so that their sum is greater than 7: $a = 3$ and $b = 5$. There are three ways to choose a and b so that their sum is greater than 6: $a = 2$ and $b = 5$; $a = 3$ and $b = 4$; and $a = 3$ and $b = 5$. Therefore, in all there are **4** ways to pick the lengths of the three sides.

Section 10 Writing Skills

1. **D.** Wordiness. Choice D makes the writer's point simply and concisely.
2. **D.** Error in subject-verb agreement. Remember: the subject's grammatical number is not changed by the addition of a phrase that begins with *along with, together with,* or a similar expression. The subject, *princess,* is singular. The verb should

be singular as well. Only Choice D corrects the error without introducing fresh errors.

3. B. Lack of parallelism. Choice B tightens the original loose sentence, neatly linking its similar elements (*the smallest* and *the most truculent*) with the connective *yet* to produce a balanced sentence.

4. C. Lack of parallelism. Choice C balances the past tense verb *took* with a similar verb in the past tense (*incorporated*), linking them with the connective *and*.

5. C. Misplaced modifier. Who are away on leave? Not the rooms, but the students!

6. D. Error in logical comparison. Compare students with students, not students with a time period ("the middle of the twentieth century").

7. E. Error in usage. A comedy duo by definition consists of two comedians.

8. C. Error in modification. Ask yourself who was writing the review. Was it the production? No, the production was *being* reviewed: the reviewer was the paper's theater critic. Only Choice C

rewrites the sentence so that the phrase *Writing a review of opening night* correctly modifies *critic*.

9. C. Dangling modifier. Who was afraid of meeting strangers? Obviously, Elizabeth Barrett. Choice C rearranges the sentence to eliminate the dangling modifier. (While choice E also rearranges the sentence so that the opening phrase modifies Barrett, it introduces a comma splice.)

10. D. Wordiness. Choice D eliminates the unnecessary words *for* and *they*.

11. D. The suggested revision tightens this ineffective compound sentence in two ways: first, it eliminates the connective *and;* second, it repeats *a landscape* to emphasize its importance.

12. D. Error in logical comparison. Compare numbers with numbers, not numbers with minivans.

13. C. Double negative. Change *could hardly do nothing* to *could hardly do anything*.

14. C. Error in logical comparison. Compare cities with cities, not cities with mayors.

Answer Sheet—Test 3

Section 1   ESSAY

Essay (continued)

If a section has fewer questions than answer spaces, leave the extra spaces blank.

Section 2

1 Ⓐ Ⓑ Ⓒ Ⓓ Ⓔ	8 Ⓐ Ⓑ Ⓒ Ⓓ Ⓔ	15 Ⓐ Ⓑ Ⓒ Ⓓ Ⓔ	22 Ⓐ Ⓑ Ⓒ Ⓓ Ⓔ	29 Ⓐ Ⓑ Ⓒ Ⓓ Ⓔ
2 Ⓐ Ⓑ Ⓒ Ⓓ Ⓔ	9 Ⓐ Ⓑ Ⓒ Ⓓ Ⓔ	16 Ⓐ Ⓑ Ⓒ Ⓓ Ⓔ	23 Ⓐ Ⓑ Ⓒ Ⓓ Ⓔ	30 Ⓐ Ⓑ Ⓒ Ⓓ Ⓔ
3 Ⓐ Ⓑ Ⓒ Ⓓ Ⓔ	10 Ⓐ Ⓑ Ⓒ Ⓓ Ⓔ	17 Ⓐ Ⓑ Ⓒ Ⓓ Ⓔ	24 Ⓐ Ⓑ Ⓒ Ⓓ Ⓔ	31 Ⓐ Ⓑ Ⓒ Ⓓ Ⓔ
4 Ⓐ Ⓑ Ⓒ Ⓓ Ⓔ	11 Ⓐ Ⓑ Ⓒ Ⓓ Ⓔ	18 Ⓐ Ⓑ Ⓒ Ⓓ Ⓔ	25 Ⓐ Ⓑ Ⓒ Ⓓ Ⓔ	32 Ⓐ Ⓑ Ⓒ Ⓓ Ⓔ
5 Ⓐ Ⓑ Ⓒ Ⓓ Ⓔ	12 Ⓐ Ⓑ Ⓒ Ⓓ Ⓔ	19 Ⓐ Ⓑ Ⓒ Ⓓ Ⓔ	26 Ⓐ Ⓑ Ⓒ Ⓓ Ⓔ	33 Ⓐ Ⓑ Ⓒ Ⓓ Ⓔ
6 Ⓐ Ⓑ Ⓒ Ⓓ Ⓔ	13 Ⓐ Ⓑ Ⓒ Ⓓ Ⓔ	20 Ⓐ Ⓑ Ⓒ Ⓓ Ⓔ	27 Ⓐ Ⓑ Ⓒ Ⓓ Ⓔ	34 Ⓐ Ⓑ Ⓒ Ⓓ Ⓔ
7 Ⓐ Ⓑ Ⓒ Ⓓ Ⓔ	14 Ⓐ Ⓑ Ⓒ Ⓓ Ⓔ	21 Ⓐ Ⓑ Ⓒ Ⓓ Ⓔ	28 Ⓐ Ⓑ Ⓒ Ⓓ Ⓔ	35 Ⓐ Ⓑ Ⓒ Ⓓ Ⓔ

Section 3

1 Ⓐ Ⓑ Ⓒ Ⓓ Ⓔ	8 Ⓐ Ⓑ Ⓒ Ⓓ Ⓔ	15 Ⓐ Ⓑ Ⓒ Ⓓ Ⓔ	22 Ⓐ Ⓑ Ⓒ Ⓓ Ⓔ	29 Ⓐ Ⓑ Ⓒ Ⓓ Ⓔ
2 Ⓐ Ⓑ Ⓒ Ⓓ Ⓔ	9 Ⓐ Ⓑ Ⓒ Ⓓ Ⓔ	16 Ⓐ Ⓑ Ⓒ Ⓓ Ⓔ	23 Ⓐ Ⓑ Ⓒ Ⓓ Ⓔ	30 Ⓐ Ⓑ Ⓒ Ⓓ Ⓔ
3 Ⓐ Ⓑ Ⓒ Ⓓ Ⓔ	10 Ⓐ Ⓑ Ⓒ Ⓓ Ⓔ	17 Ⓐ Ⓑ Ⓒ Ⓓ Ⓔ	24 Ⓐ Ⓑ Ⓒ Ⓓ Ⓔ	31 Ⓐ Ⓑ Ⓒ Ⓓ Ⓔ
4 Ⓐ Ⓑ Ⓒ Ⓓ Ⓔ	11 Ⓐ Ⓑ Ⓒ Ⓓ Ⓔ	18 Ⓐ Ⓑ Ⓒ Ⓓ Ⓔ	25 Ⓐ Ⓑ Ⓒ Ⓓ Ⓔ	32 Ⓐ Ⓑ Ⓒ Ⓓ Ⓔ
5 Ⓐ Ⓑ Ⓒ Ⓓ Ⓔ	12 Ⓐ Ⓑ Ⓒ Ⓓ Ⓔ	19 Ⓐ Ⓑ Ⓒ Ⓓ Ⓔ	26 Ⓐ Ⓑ Ⓒ Ⓓ Ⓔ	33 Ⓐ Ⓑ Ⓒ Ⓓ Ⓔ
6 Ⓐ Ⓑ Ⓒ Ⓓ Ⓔ	13 Ⓐ Ⓑ Ⓒ Ⓓ Ⓔ	20 Ⓐ Ⓑ Ⓒ Ⓓ Ⓔ	27 Ⓐ Ⓑ Ⓒ Ⓓ Ⓔ	34 Ⓐ Ⓑ Ⓒ Ⓓ Ⓔ
7 Ⓐ Ⓑ Ⓒ Ⓓ Ⓔ	14 Ⓐ Ⓑ Ⓒ Ⓓ Ⓔ	21 Ⓐ Ⓑ Ⓒ Ⓓ Ⓔ	28 Ⓐ Ⓑ Ⓒ Ⓓ Ⓔ	35 Ⓐ Ⓑ Ⓒ Ⓓ Ⓔ

Section 4

1 Ⓐ Ⓑ Ⓒ Ⓓ Ⓔ	8 Ⓐ Ⓑ Ⓒ Ⓓ Ⓔ	15 Ⓐ Ⓑ Ⓒ Ⓓ Ⓔ	22 Ⓐ Ⓑ Ⓒ Ⓓ Ⓔ	29 Ⓐ Ⓑ Ⓒ Ⓓ Ⓔ
2 Ⓐ Ⓑ Ⓒ Ⓓ Ⓔ	9 Ⓐ Ⓑ Ⓒ Ⓓ Ⓔ	16 Ⓐ Ⓑ Ⓒ Ⓓ Ⓔ	23 Ⓐ Ⓑ Ⓒ Ⓓ Ⓔ	30 Ⓐ Ⓑ Ⓒ Ⓓ Ⓔ
3 Ⓐ Ⓑ Ⓒ Ⓓ Ⓔ	10 Ⓐ Ⓑ Ⓒ Ⓓ Ⓔ	17 Ⓐ Ⓑ Ⓒ Ⓓ Ⓔ	24 Ⓐ Ⓑ Ⓒ Ⓓ Ⓔ	31 Ⓐ Ⓑ Ⓒ Ⓓ Ⓔ
4 Ⓐ Ⓑ Ⓒ Ⓓ Ⓔ	11 Ⓐ Ⓑ Ⓒ Ⓓ Ⓔ	18 Ⓐ Ⓑ Ⓒ Ⓓ Ⓔ	25 Ⓐ Ⓑ Ⓒ Ⓓ Ⓔ	32 Ⓐ Ⓑ Ⓒ Ⓓ Ⓔ
5 Ⓐ Ⓑ Ⓒ Ⓓ Ⓔ	12 Ⓐ Ⓑ Ⓒ Ⓓ Ⓔ	19 Ⓐ Ⓑ Ⓒ Ⓓ Ⓔ	26 Ⓐ Ⓑ Ⓒ Ⓓ Ⓔ	33 Ⓐ Ⓑ Ⓒ Ⓓ Ⓔ
6 Ⓐ Ⓑ Ⓒ Ⓓ Ⓔ	13 Ⓐ Ⓑ Ⓒ Ⓓ Ⓔ	20 Ⓐ Ⓑ Ⓒ Ⓓ Ⓔ	27 Ⓐ Ⓑ Ⓒ Ⓓ Ⓔ	34 Ⓐ Ⓑ Ⓒ Ⓓ Ⓔ
7 Ⓐ Ⓑ Ⓒ Ⓓ Ⓔ	14 Ⓐ Ⓑ Ⓒ Ⓓ Ⓔ	21 Ⓐ Ⓑ Ⓒ Ⓓ Ⓔ	28 Ⓐ Ⓑ Ⓒ Ⓓ Ⓔ	35 Ⓐ Ⓑ Ⓒ Ⓓ Ⓔ

Section 6

1 Ⓐ Ⓑ Ⓒ Ⓓ Ⓔ	8 Ⓐ Ⓑ Ⓒ Ⓓ Ⓔ	15 Ⓐ Ⓑ Ⓒ Ⓓ Ⓔ	22 Ⓐ Ⓑ Ⓒ Ⓓ Ⓔ	29 Ⓐ Ⓑ Ⓒ Ⓓ Ⓔ
2 Ⓐ Ⓑ Ⓒ Ⓓ Ⓔ	9 Ⓐ Ⓑ Ⓒ Ⓓ Ⓔ	16 Ⓐ Ⓑ Ⓒ Ⓓ Ⓔ	23 Ⓐ Ⓑ Ⓒ Ⓓ Ⓔ	30 Ⓐ Ⓑ Ⓒ Ⓓ Ⓔ
3 Ⓐ Ⓑ Ⓒ Ⓓ Ⓔ	10 Ⓐ Ⓑ Ⓒ Ⓓ Ⓔ	17 Ⓐ Ⓑ Ⓒ Ⓓ Ⓔ	24 Ⓐ Ⓑ Ⓒ Ⓓ Ⓔ	31 Ⓐ Ⓑ Ⓒ Ⓓ Ⓔ
4 Ⓐ Ⓑ Ⓒ Ⓓ Ⓔ	11 Ⓐ Ⓑ Ⓒ Ⓓ Ⓔ	18 Ⓐ Ⓑ Ⓒ Ⓓ Ⓔ	25 Ⓐ Ⓑ Ⓒ Ⓓ Ⓔ	32 Ⓐ Ⓑ Ⓒ Ⓓ Ⓔ
5 Ⓐ Ⓑ Ⓒ Ⓓ Ⓔ	12 Ⓐ Ⓑ Ⓒ Ⓓ Ⓔ	19 Ⓐ Ⓑ Ⓒ Ⓓ Ⓔ	26 Ⓐ Ⓑ Ⓒ Ⓓ Ⓔ	33 Ⓐ Ⓑ Ⓒ Ⓓ Ⓔ
6 Ⓐ Ⓑ Ⓒ Ⓓ Ⓔ	13 Ⓐ Ⓑ Ⓒ Ⓓ Ⓔ	20 Ⓐ Ⓑ Ⓒ Ⓓ Ⓔ	27 Ⓐ Ⓑ Ⓒ Ⓓ Ⓔ	34 Ⓐ Ⓑ Ⓒ Ⓓ Ⓔ
7 Ⓐ Ⓑ Ⓒ Ⓓ Ⓔ	14 Ⓐ Ⓑ Ⓒ Ⓓ Ⓔ	21 Ⓐ Ⓑ Ⓒ Ⓓ Ⓔ	28 Ⓐ Ⓑ Ⓒ Ⓓ Ⓔ	35 Ⓐ Ⓑ Ⓒ Ⓓ Ⓔ

Section 7

1 Ⓐ Ⓑ Ⓒ Ⓓ Ⓔ   3 Ⓐ Ⓑ Ⓒ Ⓓ Ⓔ   5 Ⓐ Ⓑ Ⓒ Ⓓ Ⓔ   7 Ⓐ Ⓑ Ⓒ Ⓓ Ⓔ
2 Ⓐ Ⓑ Ⓒ Ⓓ Ⓔ   4 Ⓐ Ⓑ Ⓒ Ⓓ Ⓔ   6 Ⓐ Ⓑ Ⓒ Ⓓ Ⓔ   8 Ⓐ Ⓑ Ⓒ Ⓓ Ⓔ

Grid-in answer boxes numbered 9, 10, 11, 12, 13, 14, 15, 16, 17, 18.

Section 8

1 Ⓐ Ⓑ Ⓒ Ⓓ Ⓔ   5 Ⓐ Ⓑ Ⓒ Ⓓ Ⓔ   9 Ⓐ Ⓑ Ⓒ Ⓓ Ⓔ   13 Ⓐ Ⓑ Ⓒ Ⓓ Ⓔ   17 Ⓐ Ⓑ Ⓒ Ⓓ Ⓔ
2 Ⓐ Ⓑ Ⓒ Ⓓ Ⓔ   6 Ⓐ Ⓑ Ⓒ Ⓓ Ⓔ   10 Ⓐ Ⓑ Ⓒ Ⓓ Ⓔ   14 Ⓐ Ⓑ Ⓒ Ⓓ Ⓔ   18 Ⓐ Ⓑ Ⓒ Ⓓ Ⓔ
3 Ⓐ Ⓑ Ⓒ Ⓓ Ⓔ   7 Ⓐ Ⓑ Ⓒ Ⓓ Ⓔ   11 Ⓐ Ⓑ Ⓒ Ⓓ Ⓔ   15 Ⓐ Ⓑ Ⓒ Ⓓ Ⓔ   19 Ⓐ Ⓑ Ⓒ Ⓓ Ⓔ
4 Ⓐ Ⓑ Ⓒ Ⓓ Ⓔ   8 Ⓐ Ⓑ Ⓒ Ⓓ Ⓔ   12 Ⓐ Ⓑ Ⓒ Ⓓ Ⓔ   16 Ⓐ Ⓑ Ⓒ Ⓓ Ⓔ   20 Ⓐ Ⓑ Ⓒ Ⓓ Ⓔ

Section 9

1 Ⓐ Ⓑ Ⓒ Ⓓ Ⓔ   5 Ⓐ Ⓑ Ⓒ Ⓓ Ⓔ   9 Ⓐ Ⓑ Ⓒ Ⓓ Ⓔ   13 Ⓐ Ⓑ Ⓒ Ⓓ Ⓔ   17 Ⓐ Ⓑ Ⓒ Ⓓ Ⓔ
2 Ⓐ Ⓑ Ⓒ Ⓓ Ⓔ   6 Ⓐ Ⓑ Ⓒ Ⓓ Ⓔ   10 Ⓐ Ⓑ Ⓒ Ⓓ Ⓔ   14 Ⓐ Ⓑ Ⓒ Ⓓ Ⓔ   18 Ⓐ Ⓑ Ⓒ Ⓓ Ⓔ
3 Ⓐ Ⓑ Ⓒ Ⓓ Ⓔ   7 Ⓐ Ⓑ Ⓒ Ⓓ Ⓔ   11 Ⓐ Ⓑ Ⓒ Ⓓ Ⓔ   15 Ⓐ Ⓑ Ⓒ Ⓓ Ⓔ   19 Ⓐ Ⓑ Ⓒ Ⓓ Ⓔ
4 Ⓐ Ⓑ Ⓒ Ⓓ Ⓔ   8 Ⓐ Ⓑ Ⓒ Ⓓ Ⓔ   12 Ⓐ Ⓑ Ⓒ Ⓓ Ⓔ   16 Ⓐ Ⓑ Ⓒ Ⓓ Ⓔ   20 Ⓐ Ⓑ Ⓒ Ⓓ Ⓔ

Section 10

1 Ⓐ Ⓑ Ⓒ Ⓓ Ⓔ   5 Ⓐ Ⓑ Ⓒ Ⓓ Ⓔ   9 Ⓐ Ⓑ Ⓒ Ⓓ Ⓔ   13 Ⓐ Ⓑ Ⓒ Ⓓ Ⓔ   17 Ⓐ Ⓑ Ⓒ Ⓓ Ⓔ
2 Ⓐ Ⓑ Ⓒ Ⓓ Ⓔ   6 Ⓐ Ⓑ Ⓒ Ⓓ Ⓔ   10 Ⓐ Ⓑ Ⓒ Ⓓ Ⓔ   14 Ⓐ Ⓑ Ⓒ Ⓓ Ⓔ   18 Ⓐ Ⓑ Ⓒ Ⓓ Ⓔ
3 Ⓐ Ⓑ Ⓒ Ⓓ Ⓔ   7 Ⓐ Ⓑ Ⓒ Ⓓ Ⓔ   11 Ⓐ Ⓑ Ⓒ Ⓓ Ⓔ   15 Ⓐ Ⓑ Ⓒ Ⓓ Ⓔ   19 Ⓐ Ⓑ Ⓒ Ⓓ Ⓔ
4 Ⓐ Ⓑ Ⓒ Ⓓ Ⓔ   8 Ⓐ Ⓑ Ⓒ Ⓓ Ⓔ   12 Ⓐ Ⓑ Ⓒ Ⓓ Ⓔ   16 Ⓐ Ⓑ Ⓒ Ⓓ Ⓔ   20 Ⓐ Ⓑ Ⓒ Ⓓ Ⓔ

Test 3

SECTION **1**   **Time—25 Minutes**   **ESSAY**

> The excerpt appearing below makes a point about a particular topic. Read the passage carefully, and think about the assignment that follows.

Nature (one's genetic inheritance) affects one's character and behavior more than nurture (one's life experiences).

ASSIGNMENT: What are your thoughts on the statement above? Do you agree or disagree with the writer's assertion that nature or biological inheritance has a greater effect on one's character and behavior than nurture or life experience does? Compose an essay in which you express your views on this topic. Your essay may support, refute, or qualify the views expressed in the statement. What you write, however, must be relevant to the topic under discussion. Additionally, you must support your viewpoint, indicating your reasoning and providing examples based on your studies and/or experience.

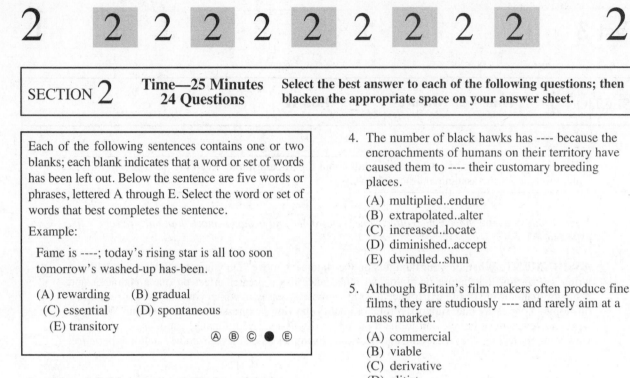

2 2 2 2 2 2 2 2 2 2 2

Each of the following sentences contains one or two blanks; each blank indicates that a word or set of words has been left out. Below the sentence are five words or phrases, lettered A through E. Select the word or set of words that best completes the sentence.

Example:

Fame is ----; today's rising star is all too soon tomorrow's washed-up has-been.

(A) rewarding   (B) gradual
(C) essential   (D) spontaneous
   (E) transitory

     Ⓐ Ⓑ Ⓒ ● Ⓔ

1. Although in his seventies at the time of the interview, Picasso proved alert and insightful, his faculties ---- despite the inevitable toll of the years.

   (A) atrophied   (B) diminished   (C) intact
   (D) useless   (E) impaired

2. While the 1940s are most noted for the development of black modern dance, they are also ---- because they were the last gasp for tap dancing.

   (A) irrelevant
   (B) unfounded
   (C) significant
   (D) speculative
   (E) contemporary

3. People who take megadoses of vitamins and minerals should take care: though beneficial in small quantities, in large amounts these substances may have ---- effects.

   (A) admirable
   (B) redundant
   (C) intangible
   (D) toxic
   (E) minor

4. The number of black hawks has ---- because the encroachments of humans on their territory have caused them to ---- their customary breeding places.

   (A) multiplied..endure
   (B) extrapolated..alter
   (C) increased..locate
   (D) diminished..accept
   (E) dwindled..shun

5. Although Britain's film makers often produce fine films, they are studiously ---- and rarely aim at a mass market.

   (A) commercial
   (B) viable
   (C) derivative
   (D) elitist
   (E) collaborative

6. MacDougall's former editors remember him as a ---- man whose ---- and exhaustive reporting was worth the trouble.

   (A) domineering..wearisome
   (B) congenial..pretentious
   (C) popular..supercilious
   (D) fastidious..garbled
   (E) cantankerous..meticulous

7. The opossum is ---- the venom of snakes in the rattlesnake subfamily and thus views the reptiles not as ---- enemies but as a food source.

   (A) vulnerable to..natural
   (B) conscious of..mortal
   (C) impervious to..lethal
   (D) sensitive to..deadly
   (E) defenseless against..potential

8. Breaking with established musical conventions, Stravinsky was ---- composer whose heterodox works infuriated the traditionalists of his day.

   (A) a derivative
   (B) an iconoclastic
   (C) an uncontroversial
   (D) a venerated
   (E) a trite

GO ON TO THE NEXT PAGE

Test 3

Read each of the passages below, and then answer the questions that follow the passage. The correct response may be stated outright or merely suggested in the passage.

Questions 9 and 10 are based on the following passage.

Today, more than ever, Hollywood depends on adaptations rather than original screenplays for its story material. This is a far cry from years ago
Line when studio writers created most of a producer's
(5) scripts. To filmmakers, a best-selling novel has a peculiar advantage over an original script: already popular with the public, the story *must* be a potential box-office success. Furthermore, it is usually easier and less time-consuming for a
(10) script writer to adapt a major work than to write one. The rub for producers is that they pay such extravagant prices for these properties that the excess load on the budget often puts the movie into the red.

9. The word "peculiar" (line 6) most nearly means

(A) quaint
(B) bizarre
(C) unfortunate
(D) particular
(E) artistic

10. The primary drawback to basing a screenplay on a best-selling novel is

(A) the amount of time required to create a script based on a novel
(B) the public's resentment of changes the script writer makes to the novel's story
(C) the degree of difficulty involved in faithfully adapting a novel for the screen
(D) the desire of studio writers to create their own original scripts
(E) the financial impact of purchasing rights to adapt the novel

Questions 11 and 12 are based on the following passage.

This excerpt from Jack London's Call of the Wild *describes the sled dog Buck's attempt to rescue his master from the rapids.*

When Buck felt Thornton grasp his tail, he headed for the bank, swimming with all his splendid strength. From below came the fatal roaring
Line where the wild current went wilder and was rent
(5) in shreds and spray by the rocks that thrust through like the teeth of an enormous comb. The suck of the water as it took the beginning of the last steep pitch was frightful, and Thornton knew that the shore was impossible. He scraped furi-
(10) ously over a rock, bruised across a second, and struck a third with crushing force. He clutched its slippery top with both hands, releasing Buck, and above the roar of the churning water shouted: "Go, Buck! Go!"

11. In line 8, the word "pitch" most nearly means

(A) high tone
(B) viscous substance
(C) recommendation
(D) intensity
(E) slope

12. The tone of the passage is best described as

(A) lyrical
(B) informative
(C) urgent
(D) ironic
(E) resigned

GO ON TO THE NEXT PAGE

Test 3

Questions 13–24 are based on the following passage.

In this adaptation of an excerpt from a short story set in Civil War times, a man is about to be hanged. The first two paragraphs set the scene; the remainder of the passage presents a flashback to an earlier, critical encounter.

Line

(5)

(10)

(15)

(20)

A man stood upon a railroad bridge in Northern Alabama, looking down into the swift waters twenty feet below. The man's hands were behind his back, the wrists bound with a cord. A rope loosely encircled his neck. It was attached to a stout cross-timber above his head, and the slack fell to the level of his knees. Some loose boards laid upon the sleepers supporting the metals of the railway supplied a footing for him and his executioners—two private soldiers of the Federal army, directed by a sergeant, who in civil life may have been a deputy sheriff. At a short remove upon the same temporary platform was an officer in the uniform of his rank, armed. He was a captain. A sentinel at each end of the bridge stood with his rifle in the position known as 'support'—a formal and unnatural position, enforcing an erect carriage of the body. It did not appear to be the duty of these two men to know what was occurring at the center of the bridge; they merely blockaded the two ends of the foot plank which traversed it.

(25)

(30)

(35)

The man who was engaged in being hanged was apparently about thirty-five years of age. He was a civilian, if one might judge from his dress, which was that of a planter. His features were good—a straight nose, firm mouth, broad forehead, from which his long, dark hair was combed straight back, falling behind his ears to the collar of his well-fitting frock coat. He wore a moustache and pointed beard, but no whiskers; his eyes were large and dark grey and had a kindly expression that one would hardly have expected in one whose neck was in the hemp. Evidently this was no vulgar assassin. The liberal military code makes provision for hanging many kinds of people, and gentlemen are not excluded.

(40)

(45)

Peyton Farquhar was a well-to-do planter, of an old and highly respected Alabama family. Being a slave-owner, and, like other slave-owners, a politician, he was naturally an original secessionist and ardently devoted to the Southern cause. Circumstances had prevented him from taking service with the gallant army that had fought the disastrous campaigns ending with the fall of Corinth, and he chafed under the inglorious restraint, longing for the release of his energies, the larger life of the soldier, the opportunity for distinction. That opportunity, he felt, would come,

(50)

(55)

as it comes to all in war time. Meanwhile, he did what he could. No service was too humble for him to perform in aid of the South, no adventure too perilous for him to undertake if consistent with the character of a civilian who was at heart a soldier, and who in good faith and without too much qualification assented to at least a part of the frankly villainous dictum that all is fair in love and war.

(60)

(65)

One evening while Farquhar and his wife were sitting near the entrance to his grounds, a grey-clad soldier rode up to the gate and asked for a drink of water. Mrs. Farquhar was only too happy to serve him with her own white hands. While she was gone to fetch the water, her husband approached the dusty horseman and inquired eagerly for news from the front.

(70)

"The Yanks are repairing the railroads," said the man, "and are getting ready for another advance. They have reached the Owl Creek bridge, put it in order, and built a stockade on the other bank. The commandant has issued an order, which is posted everywhere, declaring that any civilian caught interfering with the railroad, its bridges, tunnels, or trains, will be summarily hanged. I saw the order."

(75)

"How far is it to the Owl Creek bridge?" Farquhar asked.

"About thirty miles."

"Is there no force on this side of the creek?"

(80)

"Only a picket post half a mile out, on the railroad, and a single sentinel at this end of the bridge."

(85)

"Suppose a man—a civilian and a student of hanging—should elude the picket post and perhaps get the better of the sentinel," said Farquhar, smiling, "what could he accomplish?"

(90)

The soldier reflected. "I was there a month ago," he replied. "I observed that the flood of last winter had lodged a great quantity of driftwood against the wooden pier at the end of the bridge. It is now dry and would burn like tow."

(95)

The lady had now brought the water, which the soldier drank. He thanked her ceremoniously, bowed to her husband, and rode away. An hour later, after nightfall, he repassed the plantation, going northward in the direction from which he had come. He was a Yankee scout.

GO ON TO THE NEXT PAGE

Test 3

2   2   2   2   2   2   2   2   2   2   **2**

13. The word "civil" in line 11 means

   (A) polite
   (B) individual
   (C) legal
   (D) collective
   (E) nonmilitary

14. In cinematic terms, the first two paragraphs most nearly resemble

   (A) a wide-angle shot followed by a close-up
   (B) a sequence of cameo appearances
   (C) a trailer advertising a feature film
   (D) two episodes of an ongoing serial
   (E) an animated cartoon

15. In lines 30–33, by commenting on the planter's amiable physical appearance, the author suggests that

   (A) he was innocent of any criminal intent
   (B) he seemed an unlikely candidate for execution
   (C) the sentinels had no need to fear an attempted escape
   (D) the planter tried to assume a harmless demeanor
   (E) the eyes are the windows of the soul

16. The author's tone in discussing "the liberal military code" (line 34) can best be described as

   (A) approving
   (B) ironic
   (C) irked
   (D) regretful
   (E) reverent

17. Peyton Farquhar would most likely consider which of the following a good example of how a citizen should behave in wartime?

   (A) He should use even underhanded methods to support his cause.
   (B) He should enlist in the army without delay.
   (C) He should turn to politics as a means of enforcing his will.
   (D) He should avoid involving himself in disastrous campaigns.
   (E) He should concentrate on his duties as a planter.

18. The word "consistent" in line 52 means

   (A) unfailing
   (B) agreeable
   (C) dependable
   (D) constant
   (E) compatible

19. In line 55, the word "qualification" most nearly means

   (A) competence
   (B) eligibility
   (C) restriction
   (D) reason
   (E) liability

20. It can be inferred from lines 61 and 62 that Mrs. Farquhar is

   (A) sympathetic to the Confederate cause
   (B) uninterested in news of the war
   (C) too proud to perform menial tasks
   (D) reluctant to ask her slaves to fetch water
   (E) inhospitable by nature

21. Farquhar's inquiry about what a man could accomplish (lines 82–85) illustrates which aspect of his character?

   (A) Morbid longing for death
   (B) Weighty sense of personal responsibility
   (C) Apprehension about his family's future
   (D) Keenly inquisitive intellect
   (E) Romantic vision of himself as a hero

22. From Farquhar's exchange with the soldier (lines 75–90), we can infer that Farquhar most likely is going to

   (A) sneak across the bridge to join the Confederate forces
   (B) attempt to burn down the bridge to halt the Yankee advance
   (C) remove the driftwood blocking the Confederates' access to the bridge
   (D) attack the stockade that overlooks the Owl Creek bridge
   (E) undermine the pillars that support the railroad bridge

23. As used in the next-to-last paragraph, "tow" is

   (A) an act of hauling something
   (B) a tugboat
   (C) a railroad bridge
   (D) a highly combustible substance
   (E) a picket post

24. We may infer from lines 93–96 that

   (A) the soldier has deserted from the Southern army
   (B) the soldier has lost his sense of direction
   (C) the scout has been tempting Farquhar into an unwise action
   (D) Farquhar knew the soldier was a Yankee scout
   (E) the soldier returned to the plantation unwillingly

YOU MAY GO BACK AND REVIEW THIS SECTION IN THE REMAINING TIME, BUT DO NOT WORK IN ANY OTHER SECTION UNTIL TOLD TO DO SO.   **STOP**

3 3 3 3 3 3 3 3 3 3 3 **3**

SECTION **3**

Time—25 Minutes
20 Questions

For each problem in this section determine which of the five choices is correct and blacken the corresponding choice on your answer sheet. You may use any blank space on the page for your work.

<u>Notes:</u>

- You may use a calculator whenever you think it will be helpful.
- Only real numbers are used. No question or answer on this test involves a complex or imaginary number.
- Use the diagrams provided to help you solve the problems. Unless you see the words "<u>Note</u>: Figure not drawn to scale" under a diagram, it has been drawn as accurately as possible. Unless it is stated that a figure is three-dimensional, you may assume it lies in a plane.
- For any function f, the domain, unless specifically restricted, is the set of all real numbers for which $f(x)$ is also a real number.

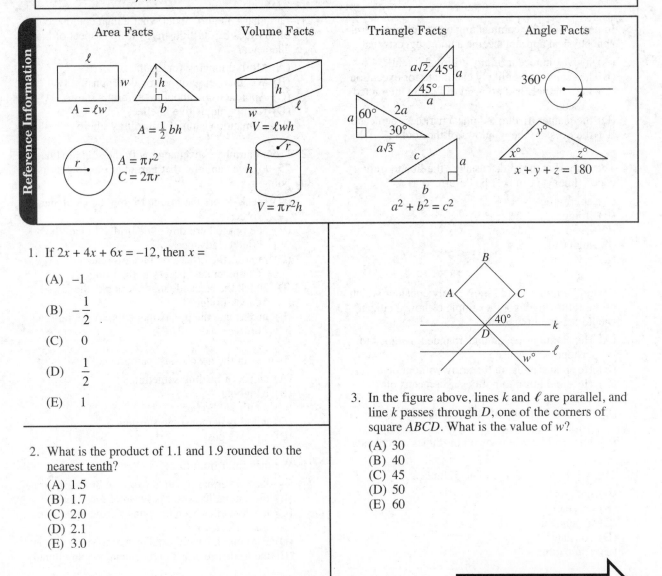

Reference Information

Area Facts

$A = \ell w$

$A = \frac{1}{2}bh$

$A = \pi r^2$
$C = 2\pi r$

Volume Facts

$V = \ell wh$

$V = \pi r^2 h$

Triangle Facts

$a^2 + b^2 = c^2$

Angle Facts

$360°$

$x + y + z = 180$

1. If $2x + 4x + 6x = -12$, then $x =$

 (A) -1

 (B) $-\dfrac{1}{2}$

 (C) 0

 (D) $\dfrac{1}{2}$

 (E) 1

2. What is the product of 1.1 and 1.9 rounded to the <u>nearest tenth</u>?

 (A) 1.5
 (B) 1.7
 (C) 2.0
 (D) 2.1
 (E) 3.0

3. In the figure above, lines k and ℓ are parallel, and line k passes through D, one of the corners of square $ABCD$. What is the value of w?

 (A) 30
 (B) 40
 (C) 45
 (D) 50
 (E) 60

GO ON TO THE NEXT PAGE

Test 3

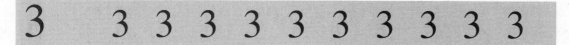

Questions 4 and 5 refer to the following table.

The data show the number of students in each of the five fifth-grade classes at Taft Elementary School and, for each class, the number of students in the school band.

Class	Number of Students	Number in Band
A	20	5
B	30	7
C	23	5
D	27	6
E	25	6

4. What is the average (arithmetic mean) number of students per class?

    (A) 23
    (B) 24
    (C) 24.5
    (D) 25
    (E) 26

5. Which class has the highest percent of students in the band?

    (A) A
    (B) B
    (C) C
    (D) D
    (E) E

6. Steve took a bike trip in which he covered half the total distance on Monday. After going 100 kilometers on Tuesday, he determined that he still had 10% of the trip to complete. What was the total length, in kilometers, of the trip?

    (A) 200
    (B) 250
    (C) 400
    (D) 500
    (E) 600

7. A number, x, is chosen at random from the set of positive integers less than 10. What is the probability that $\dfrac{9}{x} > x$?

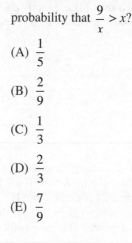

    (A) $\dfrac{1}{5}$

    (B) $\dfrac{2}{9}$

    (C) $\dfrac{1}{3}$

    (D) $\dfrac{2}{3}$

    (E) $\dfrac{7}{9}$

8. The members of the French Club conducted a fund-raising drive. The average (arithmetic mean) amount of money raised per member was $85. Then Jean joined the club and raised $50. This lowered the average to $80. How many members were there before Jean joined?

    (A) 4
    (B) 5
    (C) 6
    (D) 7
    (E) 8

9. R, S, and T are points with $RT = 2RS$. Which of the following could be true?

    I. R, S, and T are the vertices of a right triangle.
    II. R, S, and T are three of the vertices of a square.
    III. R, S, and T all lie on the circumference of a circle.

    (A) I only
    (B) III only
    (C) I and II only
    (D) I and III only
    (E) I, II, and III

 **GO ON TO THE NEXT PAGE**

Test 3

3   3   3   3   3   3   3   3   3   3   3   3

10. There are 12 men on a basketball team, and in a game 5 of them play at any one time. If the game is 1 hour long, and if each man plays exactly the same amount of time, how many minutes does each man play?

   (A) 10
   (B) 12
   (C) 24
   (D) 25
   (E) 30

11. The volume of pitcher I is A ounces, and the volume of pitcher II is B ounces, with $B > A$. If pitcher II is full of water and pitcher I is empty, and if just enough water is poured from pitcher II to fill pitcher I, what fraction of pitcher II is now full?

   (A) $\dfrac{1}{2}$

   (B) $\dfrac{1}{B}$

   (C) $\dfrac{A}{B}$

   (D) $\dfrac{A - B}{B}$

   (E) $\dfrac{B - A}{B}$

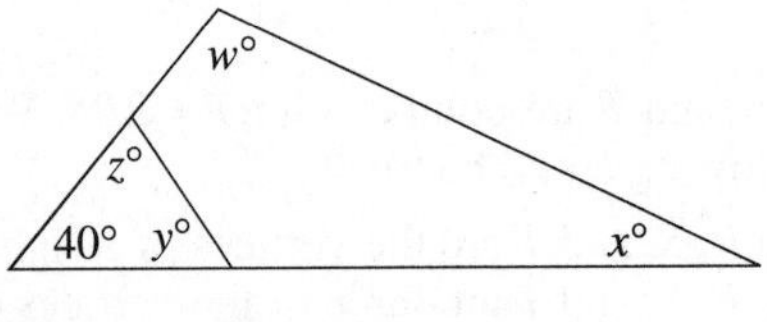

12. In the figure above, $w + x + y + z =$

   (A) 140
   (B) 280
   (C) 300
   (D) 320
   (E) 360

13. What is the greatest value of x that is a solution of the following equation?

$$|x - 5| + 10 = 15$$

   (A) 0
   (B) 5
   (C) 10
   (D) 20
   (E) 30

$$x + y = 10 \qquad y + z = 15 \qquad x + z = 17$$

14. What is the average (arithmetic mean) of $x, y,$ and z?

   (A) 7
   (B) 14
   (C) 15
   (D) 21
   (E) It cannot be determined from the information given.

15. A number of people boarded a bus at the terminal. At the first stop, half of the passengers got off and 1 got on. At the second stop, $\dfrac{1}{3}$ of the passengers on the bus got off and 1 got on. If the bus then had 15 passengers, how many were there when the bus left the terminal?

   (A) 40
   (B) 48
   (C) 58
   (D) 60
   (E) 62

16. Thirty years ago, Mr. and Mrs. Lopez purchased a house. On average, the value of the house has doubled every 6 years. If the house is worth $320,000 today, what did they pay for it 30 years ago?

   (A) $ 5,000
   (B) $ 10,000
   (C) $ 64,000
   (D) $160,000
   (E) $320,000 \times 2^5$

GO ON TO THE NEXT PAGE

3   3 3 3 3 3 3 3 3 3 3   3

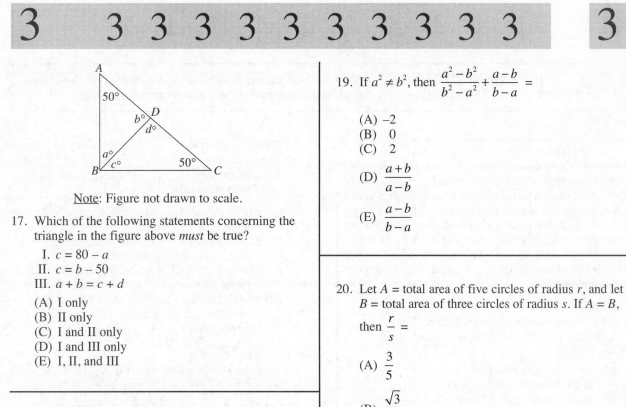

Note: Figure not drawn to scale.

17. Which of the following statements concerning the triangle in the figure above *must* be true?

I. $c = 80 - a$
II. $c = b - 50$
III. $a + b = c + d$

(A) I only
(B) II only
(C) I and II only
(D) I and III only
(E) I, II, and III

18. If c carpenters can build a garage in d days, how many days will it take e carpenters, working at the same rate, to build 2 garages?

(A) $\dfrac{2cd}{e}$

(B) $\dfrac{2d}{ce}$

(C) $\dfrac{2e}{cd}$

(D) $\dfrac{cd}{2e}$

(E) $\dfrac{ce}{2d}$

19. If $a^2 \neq b^2$, then $\dfrac{a^2 - b^2}{b^2 - a^2} + \dfrac{a - b}{b - a} =$

(A) -2
(B) 0
(C) 2

(D) $\dfrac{a + b}{a - b}$

(E) $\dfrac{a - b}{b - a}$

20. Let A = total area of five circles of radius r, and let B = total area of three circles of radius s. If $A = B$,

then $\dfrac{r}{s} =$

(A) $\dfrac{3}{5}$

(B) $\dfrac{\sqrt{3}}{\sqrt{5}}$

(C) $\dfrac{3\pi}{5}$

(D) $\dfrac{\sqrt{3\pi}}{\sqrt{5}}$

(E) $\dfrac{\sqrt{3}}{\sqrt{5}}\pi$

YOU MAY GO BACK AND REVIEW THIS SECTION IN THE REMAINING TIME, BUT DO NOT WORK IN ANY OTHER SECTION UNTIL TOLD TO DO SO.

S T O P

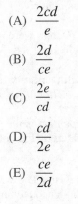

Test 3

4   4 4 4 4 4 4 4 4 4 4   4

Some or all parts of the following sentences are under-lined. The first answer choice, (A), simply repeats the underlined part of the sentence. The other four choices present four alternative ways to phrase the underlined part. Select the answer that produces the most effec-tive sentence, one that is clear and exact, and blacken the appropriate space on your answer sheet. In select-ing your choice, be sure that it is standard written English, and that it expresses the meaning of the orig-inal sentence.

Example:

The first biography of author Eudora Welty came out in 1998 and she was 89 years old at the time.

(A) and she was 89 years old at the time
(B) at the time when she was 89
(C) upon becoming an 89 year old
(D) when she was 89
(E) at the age of 89 years old

Ⓐ Ⓑ Ⓒ ● Ⓔ

1. Unable to see more than three inches in front of her nose without corrective lenses, Mary's search for her missing glasses was frantic.

   (A) Mary's search for her missing glasses was frantic
   (B) Mary's frantic search was for her missing glasses
   (C) Mary frantically searched for her missing glasses
   (D) her missing glasses were what Mary frantically searched for
   (E) her missing glasses was that for which Mary frantically searched

2. Ron liked to play word games, of which he found crossword puzzles particularly satisfying.

   (A) games, of which he found crossword puzzles particularly satisfying
   (B) games, and it was crossword puzzles that par-ticularly found satisfaction
   (C) games, particularly satisfying to him were crossword puzzles
   (D) games; he found crossword puzzles particularly satisfying
   (E) games; the satisfaction of crossword puzzles particularly

3. Martin Luther King Jr.'s influence had a strong impact on the members of the Southern Christian Leadership Conference, especially Jesse Jackson and Ralph Abernathy.

   (A) Martin Luther King Jr.'s influence had a strong impact on the members
   (B) Martin Luther King Jr.'s influence had a strong impact regarding the members
   (C) Martin Luther King Jr. strongly influenced members
   (D) The influence of Martin Luther King Jr. was strong on the members
   (E) Martin Luther King Jr.'s influence strongly impacted members

4. *Raise High the Roofbeam, Carpenters* is a novel written by the notoriously reclusive J. D. Salinger.

   (A) *Raise High the Roofbeam, Carpenters* is a novel written by the notoriously reclusive J. D. Salinger.
   (B) *Raise High the Roofbeam, Carpenters* were a novel written by the notorious reclusive J. D. Salinger.
   (C) *Raise High the Roofbeam, Carpenters* were a novel that the notoriously reclusive J. D. Salinger wrote.
   (D) As a notorious recluse, J. D. Salinger has writ-ten a novel that is called *Raise High the Roofbeam, Carpenters*.
   (E) *Raise High the Roofbeam, Carpenters* is the name of a novel that was written by the noto-rious reclusive J. D. Salinger.

5. Fans of Donald Trump's reality television show *The Apprentice* have described it as simultaneously infu-riating because of Trump's arrogance but Trump's shrewdness still has a fascination.

   (A) but Trump's shrewdness still has a fascination
   (B) and Trump's shrewdness still is fascinating
   (C) and Trump is fascinatingly shrewd
   (D) and fascinating because of Trump's shrewdness
   (E) while Trump is so shrewd that he fascinates them

GO ON TO THE NEXT PAGE

6. That it is deemed necessary to shield television view-ers from ads concerning pressing public issues while they are being bombarded with commercial pitches for beer and sports utility vehicles is a sad commen-tary on the state of our culture and of our democracy.

(A) they are being bombarded with commercial pitches for beer and sports utility vehicles is a sad commentary on the state of our culture and of our democracy
(B) they had been bombarded with commercial pitches for beer and sports utility vehicles sadly is a commentary on the state of our culture and of our democracy
(C) it is bombarded with commercial pitches for beer and sports utility vehicles is a sad com-mentary on the state of our culture and of our democracy
(D) they are being bombarded with commercial pitches for beer and sports utility vehicles are sad commentaries on the state of our culture and of our democracy
(E) they are bombarding with commercial pitches for beer and sports utility vehicles is a sad commentary on the state of our culture and of our democracy

7. There is simply no way one can avoid conflict; hence, if you must fight, fight to win.

(A) There is simply no way one can avoid conflict; hence,
(B) In no way can one simply avoid conflict; hence,
(C) You cannot avoid conflict; hence,
(D) There is simply no way one can avoid conflict; however,
(E) There is simply no way in which you may avoid conflict; consequently,

8. The federal Fish and Wildlife Service is expected to rule this week on whether to protect beluga sturgeon under the Endangered Species Act.

(A) is expected to rule this week on whether to pro-tect beluga sturgeon under the Endangered Species Act
(B) are expected to rule this week on whether to protect beluga sturgeon under the Endangered Species Act
(C) have been expected to rule this week on whether to protect beluga sturgeon under the Endangered Species Act
(D) is expected to rule this week about the protect-ing of beluga sturgeon by means of the Endangered Species Act
(E) is being expected to rule this week on whether or not they should protect beluga sturgeon under the Endangered Species Act

9. In most states where local property taxes fund the public schools, communities with strong tax bases from commercial property can support its schools while maintaining low property tax rates.

(A) with strong tax bases from commercial prop-erty can support its schools while maintain-ing low property tax rates
(B) that have strong tax bases from commercial property can support their schools and main-taining low property tax rates
(C) with strong tax bases from commercial prop-erty could have supported its schools while maintaining low property tax rates
(D) with strong tax bases from commercial prop-erty can support their schools while maintain-ing low property tax rates
(E) with strong tax bases from commercial property could of supported its schools and the main-tenance of low property tax rates

10. The drop in interest rates, especially for home mort-gages, have encouraged prospective buyers and applied for loans.

(A) have encouraged prospective buyers and applied for loans
(B) have encouraged prospective buyers and loans have been applied for
(C) have encouraged prospective buyers; therefore, they applied for loans
(D) has encouraged prospective buyers, that they applied for loans
(E) has encouraged prospective buyers to apply for loans

11. The bridge between San Francisco and Marin County, California, is actually painted a reddish orange, while being called the Golden Gate.

(A) is actually painted a reddish orange, while being
(B) although actually painted a reddish orange, is
(C) whose paint is actually a reddish orange, while it is
(D) being actually painted a reddish orange caused it to be
(E) which is actually painted a reddish orange, while being

The sentences in this section may contain errors in grammar, usage, choice of words, or idioms. Either there is just one error in a sentence or the sentence is correct. Some words or phrases are underlined and lettered; everything else in the sentence is correct.

If an underlined word or phrase is incorrect, choose that letter; if the sentence is correct, select <u>No error</u>. Then blacken the appropriate space on your answer sheet.

Example:
The region has a climate <u>so severe that</u> plants
A
<u>growing there rarely</u> <u>had been</u> more than twelve
B C
inches <u>high</u>. <u>No error</u>
D E

Ⓐ Ⓑ ● Ⓓ Ⓔ

12. <u>Although</u> many people are <u>unfamiliar with</u> the Web
A B
site, <u>it is</u> well known to shoppers <u>desirous for</u>
C D
comparing prices before they make purchases
online. <u>No error</u>
E

13. A hard-hitting and highly <u>focused</u> competitor, John
A
is <u>known as</u> one of those players <u>which</u> always give
B C
total commitment <u>to</u> a team. <u>No error</u>
D E

14. What <u>may</u> be the world's largest rodent is the
A B
capybara, a <u>water-loving</u> mammal found
C
throughout <u>much of</u> South America. <u>No error</u>
D E

15. <u>While</u> rain has long been used as a water source in
A
areas <u>where</u> well water is unavailable <u>or</u> tainted, the
B C
amounts collected are usually small and rarely
<u>suitable to</u> consumption without treatment.
D
<u>No error</u>
E

16. Though <u>barely</u> <u>mentioned</u> in popular histories
A B
of World War II, black soldiers fought <u>beside</u>
C
whites in the war's final year <u>for the first time since</u>
D
the American Revolution. <u>No error</u>
E

17. Joan of Arc had a <u>hunger to save</u> France, a
A
<u>knack for performing miracles</u>, and <u>was willing to</u>
B C
endure great suffering <u>rather than to deny</u> her faith.
D
<u>No error</u>
E

18. Despite the <u>thorough</u> investigation after the
A
assassination, <u>surprising</u> little is <u>known of</u> the
B C
motivations of the killer who <u>struck</u> down the prime
D
minister. <u>No error</u>
E

19. Cream, like other dairy products that <u>spoil</u> <u>easily</u>,
A B
<u>need</u> to be kept <u>under</u> refrigeration. <u>No error</u>
C D E

GO ON TO THE NEXT PAGE

4   4 4 4 4 4 4 4 4 4 4   4

20. In many respects, California's Tevis Cup race and
    _____
         A
    Australia's Quilty Cup are very similar equestrian

    events, but the Tevis Cup poses the greatest
    ____   _____
     B   C   D
    challenge to both horses and riders. No error
                                         _____
                                            E

21. During the 1920s, members of the white literary

    establishment began to show much interest in the
                       _____   ____
                         A   B
    movement of black writers who came to be
                              _____
                                C
    known as the Harlem Renaissance. No error
    _____   _____
      D   E

22. Clearly, Whitman's verses, unlike Kipling, are
    _____   _____
       A   B
    wholly unconventional in their absence of rhyme.
    _____   _____
             C   D
    No error
    _____
       E

23. Her interest in fine food led her to visit ethnic
                            ___ ___
                             A   B
    foodmarkets throughout the region as well as
                                      _____
                                          C
    an apprenticeship at the nearby Culinary Institute.
    _____
          D
    No error
    _____
       E

24. The perspective advantages this proposed merger
        _____
             A
    can bring to our firm greatly outweigh any of the
    _____   _____
        B   C
    potential disadvantages predicted by opponents of
                            _____
                                D
    the consolidation. No error
                       _____
                          E

25. Initially, the candidate made heavy use of the
    _____   _____
        A   B
    Internet to raise funds for his campaign; latter he
                                              _____
                                                 C
    went on to more conventional fund-raising
                ____
                 D
    methods. No error
             _____
                E

26. A sudden downpour that drenched the poolside area
      _____   _____
        A   B
    where the sunbathers had been laying caused
                         _____
                               C
    everyone to scatter. No error
    _____   _____
       D   E

27. It is likely that the Coen brothers' latest movie,

    originally scheduled to be released in time for
    _____   _____
        A   B
    Thanksgiving, would be postponed until summer
                 _____
                       C
    because of unforeseen postproduction difficulties.
               _____
                           D
    No error
    _____
       E

28. During his lifetime, Degas exhibited only one piece
                               _____ ____
                                  A   B
    of sculpture, *Little Dancer, Aged Fourteen*, which
                                                 _____
                                                   C
    was shown in 1881 in the sixth exhibition of
    _____
        D
    Impressionist art in Paris. No error
                                _____
                                   E

29. The differences between Locke's world view and

    that of Hobbes arise less from a dispute about the
    _____ _____
          A   B
    function of government but from a dispute about
                           _____
                                C
    the nature of mankind. No error
    _____   _____
        D   E

GO ON TO THE NEXT PAGE

Test 3

4   4 4 4 4 4 4 4 4 4 4 4   4

The passage below is the unedited draft of a student's essay. Parts of the essay need to be rewritten to make the meaning clearer and more precise. Read the essay carefully.

The essay is followed by six questions about changes that might improve all or part of the organization, development, sentence structure, use of language, appropriateness to the audience, or use of standard written English. In each case, choose the answer that most clearly and effectively expresses the student's intended meaning. Indicate your choice by blackening the corresponding space on the answer sheet.

[1] Although some people believe that certain celebrations have no point, celebrations are one of the few things that all people have in common. [2] They take place everywhere. [3] Listing all of them would be an impossible task. [4] People of all kinds look forward to celebrations for keeping traditions alive for generation after generation. [5] Those who criticize celebrations do not understand the human need to preserve tradition and culture.

[6] In the Muslim religion, the Ead is a celebration. [7] It begins as soon as Ramadan (the fasting month) is over. [8] During the Ead, families gather together. [9] New clothes are bought for children, and they receive money from both family and friends. [10] Also, each family, if they can afford it, slaughters a sheep or a cow. [11] They keep a small fraction of the meat, and the rest must give to the poor. [12] They also donate money to a mosque.

[14] Many celebrations involve eating meals. [15] In the United States, people gather together on Thanksgiving to say thank you for their blessings by having a huge feast with turkey, sweet potatoes, and cranberry sauce. [16] Christmas and Easter holiday dinners are a custom in the Christian religion. [17] They have a roast at Christmas. [18] At Easter they serve ham. [19] The Jewish people celebrate Passover with a big meal called a seder. [20] They say prayers, drink wine, and sing songs to remember how Jews suffered centuries ago when they escaped from slavery in Egypt.

[21] A celebration is held each year to honor great people like Dr. Martin Luther King. [22] His birthday is celebrated because of this man's noble belief in equality of all races. [23] People wish to remember not only his famous speeches, including "I Have A Dream," but also

about him being assassinated in Memphis in 1968. [24] He died while fighting for the equality of minorities. [25] Unlike religious celebrations, celebrations for great heroes like Martin Luther King are for all people everywhere in the world. [26] He is a world-class hero and he deserved the Nobel Prize for Peace that he won.

30. To improve the unity of the first paragraph, which of the following is the best sentence to delete?

(A) Sentence 1
(B) Sentence 2
(C) Sentence 3
(D) Sentence 4
(E) Sentence 5

31. Which is the best revision of sentence 9 below?

New clothes are bought for children, and they receive money from both family and friends.

(A) New clothes are bought for children, and they receive money from both family and friends.
(B) The children receive new clothes and gifts of money from family and friends.
(C) Receiving new clothes, money is also given by family and friends.
(D) Gifts are given to the children of new clothes and money by family and friends.
(E) Parents buy new clothes for their children, and family and friends also give money to them.

32. In the context of the third paragraph, which is the best way to combine sentences 16, 17, and 18?

(A) A roast at Christmas, ham at Easter—that's what Christians eat.
(B) Christians customarily serve a roast for Christmas dinner, at Easter ham is eaten.
(C) At customary holiday dinners, Christians eat a roast at Christmas and ham is for Easter dinner.
(D) Christians often celebrate the Christmas holiday with a roast for dinner and Easter with a traditional ham.
(E) Christmas and Easter dinners are the custom in the Christian religion, where they have a roast at Christmas and ham at Easter.

GO ON TO THE NEXT PAGE

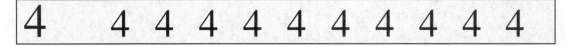

33. In an effort to provide a more effective transition between paragraphs 3 and 4, which of the following would be the best revision of sentence 21 below?

A celebration is held each year to honor great people like Dr. Martin Luther King.

(A) There are also some celebrations to honor great people like Dr. Martin Luther King.

(B) Martin Luther King is also celebrated in the United States.

(C) In the United States, celebrating to honor great people like Dr. Martin Luther King has become a tradition.

(D) In addition to observing religious holidays, people hold celebrations to honor great leaders like Dr. Martin Luther King.

(E) Besides holding religion-type celebrations, celebrations to honor great people like Dr. Martin Luther King are also held.

34. Which is the best revision of the underlined segment of sentence 23 below?

People wish to remember not only his famous speeches, including "I Have A Dream," but also about him being assassinated in Memphis in 1968.

(A) that his assassination occurred

(B) about his being assassinated

(C) the fact that he was assassinated

(D) about the assassination, too,

(E) his assassination

35. In the context of the essay as a whole, which one of the following best explains the main function of the last paragraph?

(A) To summarize the main idea of the essay

(B) To refute a previous argument stated in the essay

(C) To give an example

(D) To provide a solution to a problem

(E) To evaluate the validity of the essay's main idea

YOU MAY GO BACK AND REVIEW THIS SECTION IN THE REMAINING TIME, BUT DO NOT WORK IN ANY OTHER SECTION UNTIL TOLD TO DO SO.   **S T O P**

Test 3

| SECTION 6 | Time—25 Minutes 24 Questions | Select the best answer to each of the following questions; then blacken the appropriate space on your answer sheet. |

Each of the following sentences contains one or two blanks; each blank indicates that a word or set of words has been left out. Below the sentence are five words or phrases, lettered A through E. Select the word or set of words that best completes the sentence.

Example:

Fame is ----; today's rising star is all too soon tomorrow's washed-up has-been.

(A) rewarding   (B) gradual
(C) essential   (D) spontaneous
  (E) transitory

Ⓐ Ⓑ Ⓒ Ⓓ ●

1. The critics were distressed that an essayist of such glowing ---- could descend to writing such dull, uninteresting prose.

   (A) obscurity   (B) ill-repute   (C) shallowness
   (D) promise   (E) amiability

2. Although Henry was not in general a sentimental man, occasionally he would feel a touch of ---- for the old days and would contemplate making a brief excursion to Boston to revisit his childhood friends.

   (A) exasperation   (B) chagrin   (C) nostalgia
   (D) lethargy   (E) anxiety

3. We had not realized how much people ---- the library's old borrowing policy until we received complaints once it had been ----.

   (A) enjoyed..continued
   (B) disliked..administered
   (C) respected..imitated
   (D) ignored..lauded
   (E) appreciated..superseded

4. Even though the basic organization of the brain does not change after birth, details of its structure and function remain ---- for some time, particularly in the cerebral cortex.

   (A) plastic   (B) immutable   (C) essential
   (D) unavoidable   (E) static

5. Lavish in visual beauty, the film *Lawrence of Arabia* also boasts ---- of style: it knows how much can be shown in a shot, how much can be said in a few words.

   (A) extravagance   (B) economy   (C) autonomy
   (D) frivolity   (E) arrogance

Test 3

GO ON TO THE NEXT PAGE

Read the passages below, and then answer the questions that follow them. The correct response may be stated outright or merely suggested in the passages.

Questions 6–9 are based on the following passages.

Passage 1

In 1979, when the World Health Organization declared that smallpox had finally been eradicated, few, if any, people recollected the efforts
Line of an eighteenth-century English aristocrat to
(5) combat the then-fatal disease. As a young woman, Lady Mary Wortley Montagu had suffered severely from smallpox. In Turkey, she observed the Eastern custom of inoculating people with a mild form of the pox, thereby immunizing them, a
(10) practice she later championed in England. The Turks, she wrote home, even held house parties during which inoculated youngsters played together happily until they came down with the pox, after which they convalesced together.

Passage 2

(15) Who was Onesimus? New Testament students say that Onesimus was a slave converted to Christianity by the apostle Paul. In doing so, they ignore the claims of another slave named Onesimus, an African, who in 1721 helped stem a
(20) smallpox epidemic threatening the city of Boston. Asked by his owner, Cotton Mather, whether he had ever had smallpox, Onesimus responded, "Yes, and no," for as a child he had been intentionally infected with smallpox in a process called
(25) inoculation and had become immune to the disease. Emboldened by Onesimus's account, Mather led a successful campaign to inoculate Bostonians against the dread disease.

6. The primary purpose of both passages is to

(A) celebrate the total eradication of smallpox
(B) challenge the achievements of Lady Mary Wortley Montagu
(C) remind us that we can learn from foreign cultures
(D) show that smallpox was a serious problem in the eighteenth century
(E) call attention to neglected historical figures

7. According to Passage 1, Lady Mary's efforts to combat smallpox in England came about

(A) as a direct result of her childhood exposure to the disease
(B) as part of a World Health Organization campaign against the epidemic
(C) in response to the migration of Turks to England
(D) as a consequence of her travels in the East
(E) in the face of opposition from the medical profession

8. In Passage 1, the author uses the word "even" (line 11) primarily to

(A) exaggerate the duration of the house parties
(B) emphasize the widespread acceptance of the inoculation procedure
(C) indicate the most appropriate setting for treatment
(D) encourage her readers to travel to Turkey
(E) underscore the dangers of English methods for treating the disease

9. Lady Mary Wortley Montagu (lines 7–14, Passage 1) and Cotton Mather (lines 21–28, Passage 2) serve as examples of

(A) scientists who were authorities on epidemiology
(B) individuals who advocated a foreign medical practice
(C) travelers who brought back word of new therapeutic techniques
(D) slave owners who had the wisdom to learn from their slaves
(E) writers whose works reveal an ignorance of current medical traditions

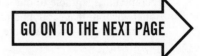

Test 3

Questions 10–15 are based on the following passage.

Are Americans today overworked? The following passage is excerpted from a book published in 1991 on the unexpected decline of leisure in American life.

Faith in progress is deep within our culture. We have been taught to believe that our lives are better than the lives of those who came before us.
Line The ideology of modern economics suggests that
(5) material progress has yielded enhanced satisfaction and well-being. But much of our confidence about our own well being comes from the assumption that our lives are easier than those of earlier generations. I have already disputed the
(10) notion that we work less than medieval European peasants, however poor they may have been. The field research of anthropologists gives another view of the conventional wisdom.

The lives of so-called primitive peoples are
(15) commonly thought to be harsh—their existence dominated by the "incessant quest for food." In fact, primitives do little work. By contemporary standards, we'd have to judge them very lazy. If the Kapauku of Papua work one day, they do no
(20) labor on the next. !Kung Bushmen put in only two and a half days per week and six hours per day. In the Sandwich Islands of Hawaii, men work only four hours per day. And Australian aborigines have similar schedules. The key to
(25) understanding why these "stone age peoples" fail to act like us—increasing their work effort to get more things—is that they have limited desires. In the race between wanting and having, they have kept their wanting low—and, in this way, ensure
(30) their own kind of satisfaction. They are materially poor by contemporary standards, but in at least one dimension—time—we have to count them richer.

I do not raise these issues to imply that we
(35) would be better off as Polynesian natives or medieval peasants. Nor am I arguing that "progress" has made us worse off. I am, instead, making a much simpler point. We have paid a price for prosperity. Capitalism has brought a dra-
(40) matically increased standard of living, but at the cost of a much more demanding worklife. We are eating more, but we are burning up those calories at work. We have color televisions and compact disc players, but we need them to unwind after a
(45) stressful day at the office. We take vacations, but we work so hard throughout the year that they become indispensable to our sanity. The conventional wisdom that economic progress has given us more things *as well as* more leisure is difficult
(50) to sustain.

10. According to the author, we base our belief that American people today are well off on the assumption that

(A) America has always been the land of opportunity
(B) Americans particularly deserve to be prosperous
(C) people elsewhere have an inferior standard of living
(D) people elsewhere envy the American way of life
(E) our faith in progress will protect us as a nation

11. The author regards "the conventional wisdom" (line 13) with

(A) resentment
(B) skepticism
(C) complacency
(D) apprehension
(E) bewilderment

12. In lines 18–22, the Kapauku tribesmen and the !Kung Bushmen are presented as examples of

(A) malingerers who turn down opportunities to work
(B) noble savages with little sense of time
(C) people who implicitly believe in progress
(D) people unmotivated by a desire for consumer goods
(E) people obsessed by their constant search for food

13. The word "raise" in line 34 means

(A) elevate
(B) increase
(C) nurture
(D) bring up
(E) set upright

14. The primary purpose of the passage is to

(A) dispute an assumption
(B) highlight a problem
(C) ridicule a theory
(D) answer a criticism
(E) counter propaganda

GO ON TO THE NEXT PAGE

6 6 6 6 6 6 6 6 6 6 6 6   **6**

15. The last four sentences of the passage (lines 41–50) provide

(A) a recapitulation of a previously made argument
(B) an example of the argument that has been proposed earlier
(C) a series of assertions and qualifications with a conclusion
(D) a reconciliation of two opposing viewpoints
(E) a reversal of the author's original position

Questions 16–24 are based on the following passage.

The following passage, written in the twentieth century, is taken from a discussion of John Webster's seventeenth-century drama "The Duchess of Malfi."

The curtain rises; the Cardinal and Daniel de
Bosola enter from the right. In appearance, the
Cardinal is something between an El Greco cardi-
Line nal and a Van Dyke noble lord. He has the tall,
(5) spare form—the elongated hands and features—of
the former; the trim pointed beard, the imperial
repose, the commanding authority of the latter.
But the El Greco features are not really those of
asceticism or inner mystic spirituality. They are
(10) the index to a cold, refined but ruthless cruelty in
a highly civilized controlled form. Neither is the
imperial repose an aloof mood of proud detachment. It is a refined expression of satanic pride of
place and talent.
(15)   To a degree, the Cardinal's coldness is artificially cultivated. He has defined himself against
his younger brother Duke Ferdinand and is the
opposite to the overwrought emotionality of the
latter. But the Cardinal's aloof mood is not one of
(20) bland detachment. It is the deliberate detachment
of a methodical man who collects his thoughts
and emotions into the most compact and formidable shape—that when he strikes, he may strike
with the more efficient and devastating force. His
(25) easy movements are those of the slowly circling
eagle just before the swift descent with the
exposed talons. Above all else, he is a man who
never for a moment doubts his destined authority
as a governor. He derisively and sharply rebukes
(30) his brother the Duke as easily and readily as he
mocks his mistress Julia. If he has betrayed his
hireling Bosola, he uses his brother as the tool to
win back his "familiar." His court dress is a long
brilliant scarlet cardinal's gown with white cuffs
(35) and a white collar turned back over the red, both
collar and cuffs being elaborately scalloped and
embroidered. He wears a small cape, reaching
only to the elbows. His cassock is buttoned to the
ground, giving a heightened effect to his already

(40) tall presence. Richelieu would have adored his
neatly trimmed beard. A richly jeweled and orna-
mented cross lies on his breast, suspended from
his neck by a gold chain.
     Bosola, for his part, is the Renaissance "famil-
(45) iar" dressed conventionally in somber black with
a white collar. He wears a chain about his neck, a
suspended ornament, and a sword. Although a
"bravo," he must not be thought of as a leather-
jacketed, heavy-booted tough, squat and swarthy.
(50) Still less is he a sneering, leering, melodramatic
villain of the Victorian gaslight tradition. Like his
black-and-white clothes, he is a colorful contradiction, a scholar-assassin, a humanist-hangman;
introverted and introspective, yet ruthless in
(55) action; moody and reluctant, yet violent. He is a
man of scholarly taste and subtle intellectual discrimination doing the work of a hired ruffian. In
general effect, his impersonator must achieve sup-
pleness and subtlety of nature, a highly complex,
(60) compressed, yet well restrained intensity of temperament. Like Duke Ferdinand, he is inwardly
tormented, but not by undiluted passion. His dominant emotion is an intellectualized one: that of
disgust at a world filled with knavery and folly,
(65) but in which he must play a part and that a lowly,
despicable one. He is the kind of rarity that
Browning loved to depict in his Renaissance
monologues.

16. The primary purpose of the passage appears to be to

(A) provide historical background on the Renaissance church
(B) describe ecclesiastical costuming and pageantry
(C) analyze the appearances and moral natures of two dramatic figures
(D) explain why modern audiences enjoy *The Duchess of Malfi*
(E) compare two interpretations of a challenging role

17. The word "spare" in line 5 means

(A) excessive
(B) superfluous
(C) pardonable
(D) lean
(E) inadequate

GO ON TO THE NEXT PAGE

18. In lines 24–27, the author most likely compares the movements of the Cardinal to those of a circling eagle in order to emphasize his

(A) flightiness
(B) love of freedom
(C) eminence
(D) spirituality
(E) mercilessness

19. The Cardinal's "satanic pride of place" (lines 13 and 14) refers to his glorying in his

(A) faith
(B) rank
(C) residence
(D) immobility
(E) wickedness

20. As used in the third paragraph, the word "bravo" most nearly means

(A) a courageous man
(B) a national hero
(C) a clergyman
(D) a humanist
(E) a mercenary killer

21. In describing Bosola (lines 44–68), the author chiefly uses which of the following literary techniques?

(A) Rhetorical questions
(B) Unqualified assertions
(C) Comparison and contrast
(D) Dramatic irony
(E) Literary allusion

22. The word "discrimination" in lines 56 and 57 means

(A) prejudice
(B) villainy
(C) discretion
(D) favoritism
(E) discernment

23. According to lines 61–66, why does Bosola suffer torments?

(A) His master, the Cardinal, berates him for performing his duties inadequately.
(B) He feels intense compassion for the pains endured by the Cardinal's victims.
(C) He is frustrated by his inability to attain a higher rank in the church.
(D) He feels superior to the villainy around him, yet must act the villain himself.
(E) He lacks the intellectual powers for scholarly success, but cannot endure common fools.

24. The author of the passage assumes that the reader is

(A) familiar with the paintings of El Greco and Van Dyke
(B) disgusted with a world filled with cruelty and folly
(C) ignorant of the history of the Roman Catholic Church
(D) uninterested in psychological distinctions
(E) unacquainted with the writing of Browning

YOU MAY GO BACK AND REVIEW THIS SECTION IN THE REMAINING TIME, BUT DO NOT WORK IN ANY OTHER SECTION UNTIL TOLD TO DO SO.

STOP

7

SECTION 7
Time—25 Minutes
18 Questions

You have 25 minutes to answer the 8 multiple-choice questions and 10 student-produced response questions in this section.
For each multiple-choice question, determine which of the five choices is correct and blacken the corresponding choice on your answer sheet. You may use any blank space on the page for your work.

Notes:
- You may use a calculator whenever you think it will be helpful.
- Only real numbers are used. No question or answer on this test involves a complex or imaginary number.
- Use the diagrams provided to help you solve the problems. Unless you see the words "Note: Figure not drawn to scale" under a diagram, it has been drawn as accurately as possible. Unless it is stated that a figure is three-dimensional, you may assume it lies in a plane.
- For any function f, the domain, unless specifically restricted, is the set of all real numbers for which $f(x)$ is also a real number.

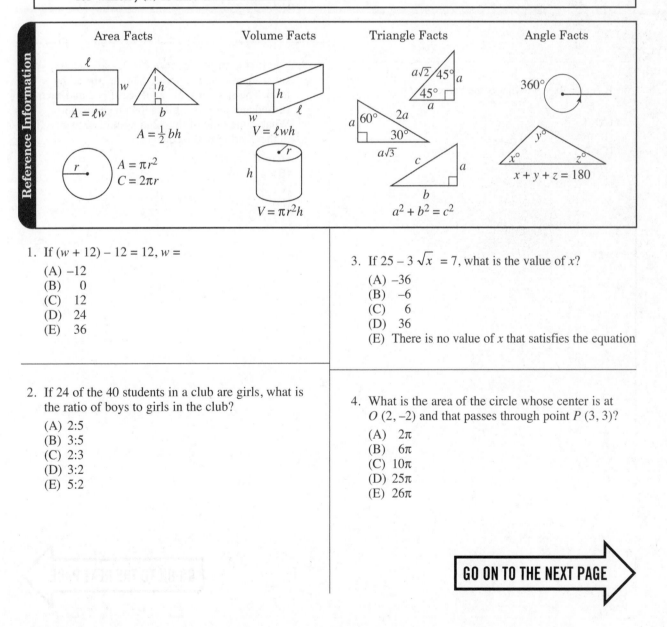

Reference Information

1. If $(w + 12) - 12 = 12$, $w =$

   (A) −12
   (B)   0
   (C)   12
   (D)   24
   (E)   36

2. If 24 of the 40 students in a club are girls, what is the ratio of boys to girls in the club?

   (A) 2:5
   (B) 3:5
   (C) 2:3
   (D) 3:2
   (E) 5:2

3. If $25 - 3\sqrt{x} = 7$, what is the value of x?

   (A) −36
   (B)   −6
   (C)   6
   (D)   36
   (E) There is no value of x that satisfies the equation

4. What is the area of the circle whose center is at O (2, −2) and that passes through point P (3, 3)?

   (A) 2π
   (B) 6π
   (C) 10π
   (D) 25π
   (E) 26π

GO ON TO THE NEXT PAGE

7

5. At Music Outlet the regular price for a CD is *d* dollars. How many CDs can be purchased for *m* dollars when the CDs are on sale at 50% off the regular price?

(A) $\dfrac{m}{50d}$

(B) $\dfrac{md}{50}$

(C) $\dfrac{md}{2}$

(D) $\dfrac{m}{2d}$

(E) $\dfrac{2m}{d}$

6. If $f(x) = 9x + 9^x$, what is the value of $f\left(\dfrac{1}{2}\right)$?

(A) 3
(B) 6
(C) 7.5
(D) 9
(E) 9.9

7. Which of the following is equivalent to $\dfrac{2x^2 - 8}{x^2 - 4x + 4}$?

(A) 2

(B) $\dfrac{2(x+2)}{x-2}$

(C) $\dfrac{2(x+4)}{x-4}$

(D) $\dfrac{2x+2}{x-2}$

(E) $\dfrac{6}{4x-4}$

8. The first term of sequence I is 2, and each subsequent term is 2 more than the preceding term. The first term of sequence II is 2 and each subsequent term is 2 times the preceding term. What is the ratio of the 32nd term of sequence II to the 32nd term of sequence I?

(A) 1
(B) 2
(C) 2^{26}
(D) 2^{27}
(E) 2^{32}

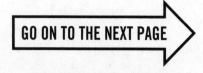

7

Directions for Student-Produced Response Questions (Grid-ins)

In questions 9–18, first solve the problem, and then enter your answer on the grid provided on the answer sheet. The instructions for entering your answers are as follows:

- First, write your answer in the boxes at the top of the grid.
- Second, grid your answer in the columns below the boxes.
- Use the fraction bar in the first row or the decimal point in the second row to enter fractions and decimal answers.

Answer: $\frac{8}{15}$ Answer: 1.75

Write your → answer in the boxes.

Grid in → your answer.

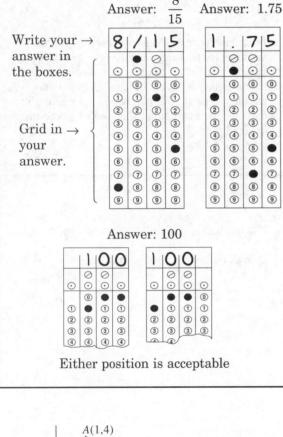

Answer: 100

Either position is acceptable

- Grid only one space in each column.
- Entering the answer in the boxes is recommended as an aid in gridding, but is not required.
- The machine scoring your exam can read only what you grid, so you **must grid in your answers correctly to get credit.**
- If a question has more than one correct answer, grid in only one of these answers.
- The grid does not have a minus sign, so no answer can be negative.
- A mixed number *must* be converted to an improper fraction or a decimal before it is gridded. Enter $1\frac{1}{4}$ as 5/4 or 1.25; the machine will interpret 1 1/4 as $\frac{11}{4}$ and mark it wrong.
- **All decimals must be entered as accurately as possible.** Here are the three acceptable ways of gridding

$$\frac{3}{11} = 0.272727...$$

3/11   .272   .273

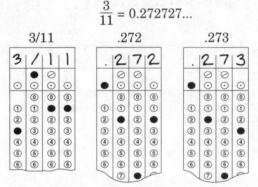

- Note that rounding to .273 is acceptable, because you are using the full grid, but you would receive **no credit** for .3 or .27, because these answers are less accurate.

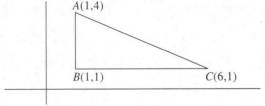

9. In the figure above, what is the area of $\triangle ABC$?

10. If $a \otimes b = (a^2 + b^2) - (a^2 - b^2)$, what is the value of $6 \otimes 7$?

GO ON TO THE NEXT PAGE

Test 3

7

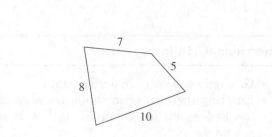

11. A square, not shown, has the same perimeter as the quadrilateral above. What is the length of a side of the square?

12. A factory can produce 1 gizmo every 333 seconds. How many <u>hours</u> will it take to produce 40 gizmos?

13. If the average (arithmetic mean) of a, b, and 10 is 100, what is the average of a and b?

14. If the rent on an apartment goes up 10% every year, next year's rent will be how many times last year's rent?

15. Boris was 26 years old in 1970, when his daughter, Olga, was born. In what year was Boris exactly 3 times as old as Olga?

16. When 25 students took a quiz, the grades they earned ranged from 2 to 10. If exactly 22 of them passed, by earning a grade of 7 or higher, what is the highest possible average (arithmetic mean) the class could have earned on the quiz?

17. Jason has twice as many red marbles as blue marbles. He puts them in two jars in such a way that the ratio of the number of red marbles to blue marbles in jar I is 2:7 and there are only red marbles in jar II. The number of red marbles in jar II is how many times the number of red marbles in jar I?

18. If a and b are positive integers and their product is 3 times their sum, what is the value of $\dfrac{1}{a}+\dfrac{1}{b}$?

YOU MAY GO BACK AND REVIEW THIS SECTION IN THE REMAINING TIME, BUT DO NOT WORK IN ANY OTHER SECTION UNTIL TOLD TO DO SO.

S T O P

8 8 8 8 8 8 8 8 8 8 8

SECTION 8 | Time—20 Minutes 19 Questions | Select the best answer to each of the following questions; then blacken the appropriate space on your answer sheet.

Each of the following sentences contains one or two blanks; each blank indicates that a word or set of words has been left out. Below the sentence are five words or phrases, lettered A through E. Select the word or set of words that best completes the sentence.

Example:

Fame is ----; today's rising star is all too soon tomorrow's washed-up has-been.

(A) rewarding   (B) gradual
 (C) essential   (D) spontaneous
  (E) transitory

Ⓐ Ⓑ Ⓒ Ⓓ ●

1. Famous in her time and then forgotten, the seventeenth-century Dutch painter Judith Leyster was ---- obscurity when, in 1993, the Worcester Art Museum organized the first retrospective exhibition of her work.

   (A) resigned to
   (B) rewarded with
   (C) rescued from
   (D) indifferent to
   (E) worthy of

2. The testimony of eyewitnesses is notoriously ----; emotion and excitement all too often cause our minds to distort what we see.

   (A) judicious
   (B) interdependent
   (C) credible
   (D) unreliable
   (E) gratifying

3. During the Dark Ages, hermits and other religious ---- fled the world to devote themselves to silent contemplation.

   (A) renegades   (B) skeptics   (C) altruists
    (D) recluses   (E) convictions

4. No real-life hero of ancient or modern days can surpass James Bond with his nonchalant ---- of death and the ---- with which he bears torture.

   (A) contempt..distress
   (B) disregard..fortitude
   (C) veneration..guile
   (D) concept..terror
   (E) ignorance..fickleness

5. A code of ethics governing the behavior of physicians during epidemics did not exist until 1846 when it was ---- by the American Medical Association.

   (A) rescinded
   (B) promulgated
   (C) presupposed
   (D) depreciated
   (E) implied

6. Unlike the highly ---- Romantic poets of the previous century, Arnold and his fellow Victorian poets were ---- and interested in moralizing.

   (A) rhapsodic..lyrical
   (B) frenetic..distraught
   (C) emotional..didactic
   (D) sensitive..strange
   (E) dramatic..warped

GO ON TO THE NEXT PAGE

Test 3

8   8   8   8   8   8   8   8   8   8   8   8

The questions that follow the next two passages relate to the content of both, and to their relationship. The correct response may be stated outright in the passage or merely suggested.

Questions 7–19 are based on the following passages.

The following passages deal with the exotic world of subatomic physics. Passage 1, written by a popularizer of contemporary physics, was published in 1985. Passage 2 was written nearly 15 years later.

Passage 1

    The classical idea of matter was something with solidity and mass, like wet stone dust pressed in a fist. If matter was composed of
Line atoms, then the atoms too must have solidity and
(5) mass. At the beginning of the twentieth century the atom was imagined as a tiny billiard ball or a granite pebble writ small. Then, in the physics of Niels Bohr, the miniature billiard ball became something akin to a musical instrument, a finely
(10) tuned Stradivarius 10 billion times smaller than the real thing. With the advent of quantum mechanics, the musical instrument gave way to pure music. On the atomic scale, the solidity and mass of matter dissolved into something light and
(15) airy. Suddenly physicists were describing atoms in the vocabulary of the composer—"resonance," "frequency," "harmony," "scale." Atomic electrons sang in choirs like seraphim, cherubim, thrones, and dominions. Classical distinctions
(20) between matter and light became muddled. In the new physics, light bounced about like particles, and matter undulated in waves like light.
    In recent decades, physicists have uncovered elegant subatomic structures in the music of mat-
(25) ter. They use a strange new language to describe the subatomic world: *quark, squark, gluon, gauge, technicolor, flavor, strangeness, charm.* There are *up* quarks and *down* quarks, *top* quarks and *bottom* quarks. There are particles with *truth*
(30) and *antitruth*, and there are particles with *naked beauty.* The simplest of the constituents of ordinary matter—the proton, for instance—has taken on the character of a Bach fugue, a four-part counterpoint of matter, energy, space, and time.
(35) At matter's heart there are arpeggios, chromatics, syncopation. On the lowest rung of the chain of being, Creation dances.
    Already, the astronomers and the particle physicists are engaged in a vigorous dialogue.
(40) The astronomers are prepared to recognize that the large-scale structure of the universe may have

been determined by subtle interactions of particles in the first moments of the Big Bang. And the particle physicists are hoping to find confirmation
(45) of their theories of subatomic structure in the astronomers' observations of deep space and time. The snake has bitten its tail and won't let go.

Passage 2

    Consider a dew drop, poised at the tip of a grass blade. Only one millimeter in diameter, this
(50) tiny dew drop is composed of a billion trillion molecules of water, each consisting of two hydrogen atoms and one oxygen atom (H_2O). At the onset of the twentieth century, this was the accepted view of the nature of matter. Atoms
(55) were seen as matter's basic building blocks, elementary or fundamental particles that could not be divided into anything smaller.
    This relatively simple picture, however, changed drastically as physicists came to explore
(60) the secrets of the subatomic world. The once-indivisible atom, split, was revealed to consist of a nucleus made up of protons and neutrons around which electrons orbited. Protons and neutrons, in turn, were composed of even smaller subatomic
(65) particles whimsically dubbed quarks. At first, theorists claimed that all matter was made of three fundamental particles: electrons and paired up and down quarks. Later, however, experiments with powerful accelerators and colliding particle beams
(70) suggested the existence of other pairs of quarks, three generations in all, whose mass increased with each generation. Lightest of all were the first generation quarks, up and down, which combined to create the basic protons and neutrons; some-
(75) what heavier were the second generation quarks, strange and charm, the building blocks of the more esoteric particles produced in the physicists' labs. Then in 1977 a team headed by Fermilab physicist Leon Lederman uncovered the possibil-
(80) ity of a third generation of quarks. Using new accelerators with higher energies, they produced a short-lived heavy particle, the upsilon, whose properties suggested it could not be made of the four quarks then known. They concluded it must
(85) be made of a fifth quark, which they named bottom, whereupon scientists throughout the world set off in hot pursuit of bottom's hypothetical partner, top.

GO ON TO THE NEXT PAGE

8   8   8   8   8   8   8   8   8   8   8

The hunt for the top quark consumed the
(90) world's particle physicists for nearly twenty
years. It was their Grail, and they were as determined as any knight of King Arthur's court to
succeed in their holy quest. To Harvard theorist
Sheldon Glashow in 1994, it was "not just
(95) another quark. It's the last blessed one, and the
sooner we find it, the better everyone will feel."
Indeed, they had to find it, for the Standard
Model of particle physics, the theoretical synthesis that reduced the once-maddening hordes of
(100) particles (the so-called "particle zoo") to just a
few primary components, hinged upon its existence. Physicists likened the missing quark to the
keystone of an arch: the Standard Model, like an
arch, was supported by all its constituents, but it
(105) was the keystone, the last piece to go in, that
ensured the structure's stability.

In 1995 the physicists found the keystone to
their arch, and with it, new questions to answer.
Surprisingly the top quark was far heavier than
(110) theorists had predicted, nearly twice as heavy in
fact. Fermilab physicist Alvin Tollestrup originally had estimated top to weight at least as much
as a silver atom. At the hunt's end, top was determined to have a mass similar to that of an atom of
(115) gold. (With an atomic weight of 197, a gold atom
is made up of hundreds of up and down quarks.)
The question thus remains, why is top so massive? Why does any fundamental particle have
mass? With its astonishing heft, the top quark
(120) should help clarify the hidden mechanisms that
make some particles massive while others have
no mass at all.

7. Which of the following would be the most appropriate title for Passage 1?

(A) Linguistic Implications of Particle Physics
(B) The Influence of Music on Particle Interactions
(C) Matter's Transformation: The Music of
     Subatomic Physics
(D) Trends in Physics Research: Eliminating the
     Quark
(E) The Impossible Dream: Obstacles to Proving
     the Existence of Matter

8. The author of Passage 1 refers to quarks, squarks,
and charms (paragraph 2) primarily in order to

(A) demonstrate the similarity between these parti-
     cles and earlier images of the atom
(B) make a distinction between appropriate and
     inappropriate terms
(C) object to suggestions of similar frivolous names
(D) provide examples of idiosyncratic nomencla-
     ture in contemporary physics
(E) cite preliminary experimental evidence sup-
     porting the existence of subatomic matter

9. The author's tone in the second paragraph of
Passage 1 can best be described as one of

(A) scientific detachment
(B) moderate indignation
(C) marked derision
(D) admiring wonder
(E) qualified skepticism

10. "Matter's heart" mentioned in line 35 is

(A) outer space
(B) the subatomic world
(C) the language of particle physics
(D) harmonic theory
(E) flesh and blood

11. In line 47, the image of the snake biting its tail is
used to emphasize

(A) the dangers of circular reasoning
(B) the vigor inherent in modern scientific
     dialogue
(C) the eventual triumph of the classical idea of
     matter
(D) the unity underlying the astronomers' and
     particle physicists' theories
(E) the ability of contemporary scientific doctrine
     to swallow earlier theories

12. The word "properties" in line 83 of Passage 2 most
nearly means

(A) lands
(B) titles
(C) investments
(D) civilities
(E) characteristics

GO ON TO THE NEXT PAGE

Test 3

8   8 8 8 8 8 8 8 8 8   8

13. Glashow's comment in lines 94–96 reflects his

    (A) apprehension
    (B) impatience
    (C) imagination
    (D) jubilation
    (E) spirituality

14. The references to the "keystone" of an arch (lines 103 and 105) serve to

    (A) diminish the top quark's status to that of a commodity
    (B) provide an accurate physical description of the elusive particle
    (C) highlight the contrast between appearance and reality
    (D) give an approximation of the top quark's actual mass
    (E) illustrate the importance of the top quark to subatomic theory

15. The word "hinged" (line 101) most nearly means

    (A) folded
    (B) vanished
    (C) remarked
    (D) depended
    (E) weighed

16. The author of Passage 2 does all of the following EXCEPT

    (A) cite an authority
    (B) use a simile
    (C) define a term
    (D) pose a question
    (E) deny a possibility

17. The author of Passage 2 mentions the gold atom (lines 114 and 115) primarily to

    (A) clarify the monetary value of the top quark
    (B) explain what is meant by atomic weight
    (C) illustrate how hefty a top quark is compared to other particles
    (D) suggest the sorts of elements studied in high-energy accelerators
    (E) demonstrate the malleability of gold as an element

18. As Passage 2 suggests, since the time Passage 1 was written, the Standard Model has

    (A) determined even more whimsical names for the subatomic particles under discussion
    (B) taken into account the confusion of the particle physicists
    (C) found theoretical validation through recent experiments
    (D) refuted significant aspects of the Big Bang theory of the formation of the universe
    (E) collapsed for lack of proof of the existence of top quarks

19. The author of Passage 2 would most likely react to the characterization of the constituents of matter in lines 31–37 by pointing out that

    (A) this characterization has been refuted by prominent physicists
    (B) the characterization is too fanciful to be worthwhile
    (C) the most recent data on subatomic particles support this characterization
    (D) this characterization supersedes the so-called Standard Model
    (E) the current theoretical synthesis is founded on this characterization

YOU MAY GO BACK AND REVIEW THIS SECTION IN THE REMAINING TIME, BUT DO NOT WORK IN ANY OTHER SECTION UNTIL TOLD TO DO SO.

S T O P

9 9 9 9 9 9 9

SECTION 9

Time—20 Minutes
16 Questions

For each problem in this section determine which of the five choices is correct and blacken the corresponding choice on your answer sheet. You may use any blank space on the page for your work.

Notes:

- You may use a calculator whenever you think it will be helpful.
- Only real numbers are used. No question or answer on this test involves a complex or imaginary number.
- Use the diagrams provided to help you solve the problems. Unless you see the words "<u>Note</u>: Figure not drawn to scale" under a diagram, it has been drawn as accurately as possible. Unless it is stated that a figure is three-dimensional, you may assume it lies in a plane.
- For any function f, the domain, unless specifically restricted, is the set of all real numbers for which $f(x)$ is also a real number.

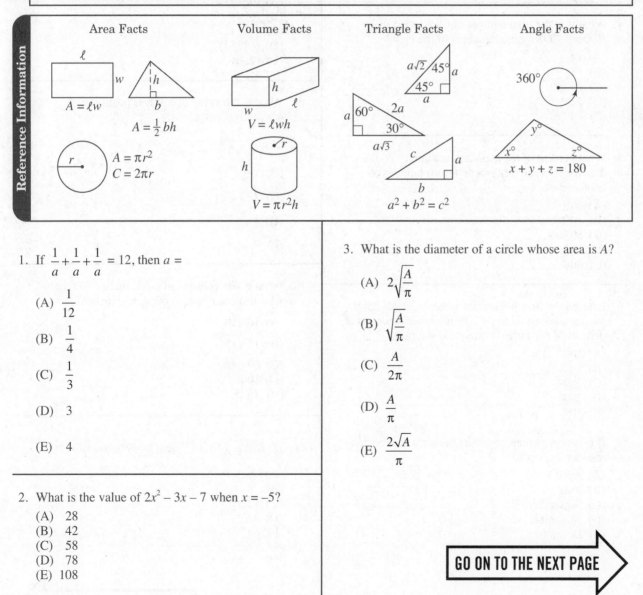

1. If $\dfrac{1}{a} + \dfrac{1}{a} + \dfrac{1}{a} = 12$, then $a =$

   (A) $\dfrac{1}{12}$

   (B) $\dfrac{1}{4}$

   (C) $\dfrac{1}{3}$

   (D) 3

   (E) 4

2. What is the value of $2x^2 - 3x - 7$ when $x = -5$?

   (A) 28
   (B) 42
   (C) 58
   (D) 78
   (E) 108

3. What is the diameter of a circle whose area is A?

   (A) $2\sqrt{\dfrac{A}{\pi}}$

   (B) $\sqrt{\dfrac{A}{\pi}}$

   (C) $\dfrac{A}{2\pi}$

   (D) $\dfrac{A}{\pi}$

   (E) $\dfrac{2\sqrt{A}}{\pi}$

GO ON TO THE NEXT PAGE

9   9   9   9   9   9   9

Questions 4 and 5 refer to the following bar graph.

The graph shows the number of books read in January 1995 by the five members of a book club.

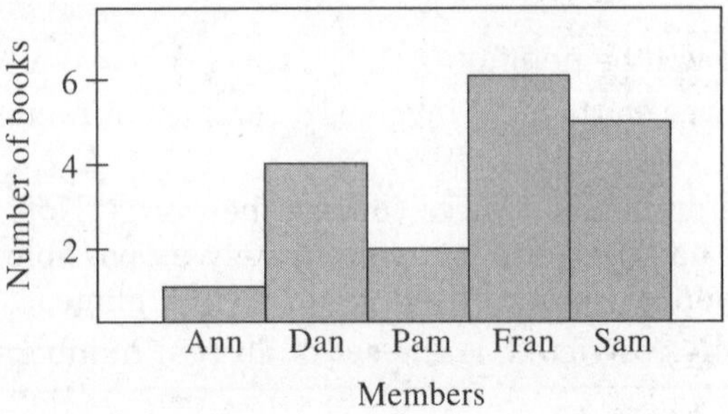

4. What was the total number of books read in January 1995 by the members of the club?

    (A) 14
    (B) 15
    (C) 16
    (D) 17
    (E) 18

5. What percent of the members read more books than the average (arithmetic mean) number of books read?

    (A) 20%
    (B) 40%
    (C) 50%
    (D) 60%
    (E) 80%

6. Laurie inherited 40% of her father's estate. After paying a tax equal to 30% of her inheritance, what percent of her father's estate did she own?

    (A) 10%
    (B) 12%
    (C) 25%
    (D) 28%
    (E) 30%

7. If it is now September, what month will it be 555 months from now?

    (A) April
    (B) June
    (C) September
    (D) November
    (E) December

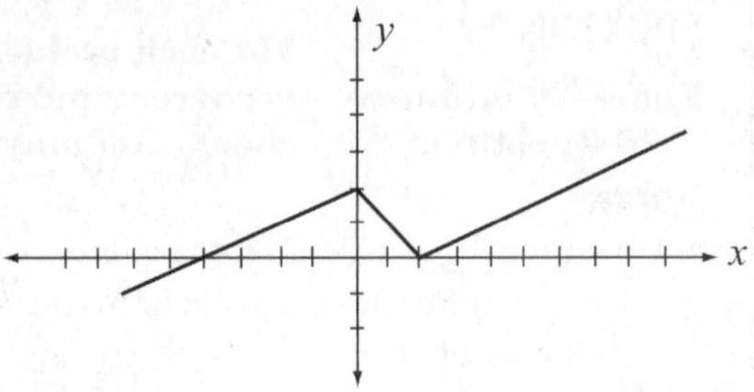

8. The graph of $y = f(x)$ is shown in the figure above. Which of the following is a point on the graph of $y = -f(x)$?

    (A) $(0, -4)$
    (B) $(0, 2)$
    (C) $(-1, 1)$
    (D) $(-1, -1)$
    (E) $(2, 0)$

9. What is the value of a if a is positive and $a \times a \times a = a + a + a$?

    (A) $\dfrac{1}{3}$

    (B) $\sqrt{3}$

    (C) 3

    (D) $3\sqrt{3}$

    (E) 9

10. What is the volume, in cubic inches, of a cube whose surface area is 60 square inches?

    (A) $10\sqrt{10}$
    (B) $15\sqrt{15}$
    (C) $60\sqrt{60}$
    (D) 1000
    (E) 3375

11. If $f(x) = x^{\frac{1}{2}} + x^{\frac{1}{4}}$, what is the value of $f(16)$?

    (A) 6
    (B) 8
    (C) 12
    (D) 32
    (E) 64

GO ON TO THE NEXT PAGE

9 9 9 9 9 9 9

12. If the circumference of circle I is equal to the diameter of circle II, what is the ratio of the area of circle II to the area of circle I?

(A) $\dfrac{1}{\pi^2}$

(B) $\sqrt{\pi}$

(C) π

(D) π^2

(E) $4\pi^2$

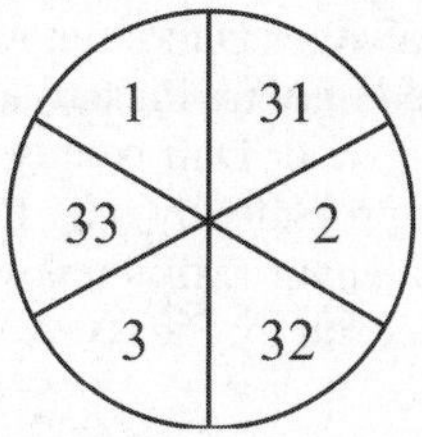

13. The dartboard shown above is divided into 6 regions, all the same size. If a dart lands randomly on the board, what is the probability that it lands on a prime number?

(A) $\dfrac{1}{6}$

(B) $\dfrac{1}{3}$

(C) $\dfrac{1}{2}$

(D) $\dfrac{2}{3}$

(E) $\dfrac{5}{6}$

14. If A is the set of integers between −50 and 50, and a number is in set B if it is the cube of a number in set A, how many elements of set B are in set A?

(A) 2
(B) 6
(C) 7
(D) 11
(E) 101

15. If A is 25 kilometers east of B, which is 12 kilometers south of C, which is 9 kilometers west of D, how far, in kilometers, is A from D?

(A) 20

(B) $5\sqrt{34}$

(C) $5\sqrt{41}$

(D) $10\sqrt{13}$

(E) 71

16. If a, b, and c are positive numbers such that $3a = 4b = 5c$, and if $a + b = kc$, what is the value of k?

(A) $\dfrac{12}{35}$

(B) $\dfrac{5}{7}$

(C) $\dfrac{10}{7}$

(D) $\dfrac{7}{5}$

(E) $\dfrac{35}{12}$

YOU MAY GO BACK AND REVIEW THIS SECTION IN THE REMAINING TIME, BUT DO NOT WORK IN ANY OTHER SECTION UNTIL TOLD TO DO SO.

S T O P

10   10   10   10   10   10   10

SECTION 10   Time—10 Minutes
14 Questions

For each of the following questions, select the best answer from the choices provided and fill in the appropriate circle on the answer sheet.

Some or all parts of the following sentences are underlined. The first answer choice, (A), simply repeats the underlined part of the sentence. The other four choices present four alternative ways to phrase the underlined part. Select the answer that produces the most effective sentence, one that is clear and exact, and blacken the appropriate space on your answer sheet. In selecting your choice, be sure that it is standard written English, and that it expresses the meaning of the original sentence.

Example:
The first biography of author Eudora Welty came out in 1998 and she was 89 years old at the time.

(A) and she was 89 years old at the time
(B) at the time when she was 89
(C) upon becoming an 89 year old
(D) when she was 89
(E) at the age of 89 years old

Ⓐ Ⓑ Ⓒ ● Ⓔ

1. Into her shopping basket she placed her favorite vegetables, an assortment of fresh fruit, and she included a loaf of French bread.

(A) and she included a loaf of French bread
(B) and a loaf of French bread
(C) and she also included a loaf of French bread
(D) a loaf of French bread as well
(E) and she includes a loaf of French bread

2. Heather Hurst's paintings and architectural renderings of the pre-Columbian Americas not only recover records that were previously lost, but these are works of art in their own right.

(A) not only recover records that were previously lost, but these are works of art
(B) not only recover records that had been previously lost, but these are works of art
(C) not only recover previously lost records but also are works of art
(D) do not recover only records that were previously lost, but these are works of art
(E) not only recovers records that were previously lost, but they are works of art

3. Today, among twentieth-century artists, Salvador Dali's renown is probably exceeded only by Picasso.

(A) artists, Salvador Dali's renown is probably exceeded only by Picasso
(B) artists, Salvador Dali is probably exceeded in renown only by Picasso's
(C) artists, Salvador Dali's renown is probably exceeded only by Picasso's
(D) artists, Salvador Dali is only exceeded in renown probably by only Picasso
(E) artists, Salvador Dali's renown is only probably exceeded by Picasso's

4. So many of the internal workings of the lungs change at night that lung diseases, particularly asthma, has become the best studied of the nighttime illnesses.

(A) asthma, has become the best studied of the nighttime illnesses
(B) asthma, has become the best studied nighttime illnesses
(C) asthma, has become the better studied of the nighttime illnesses
(D) asthma, have become the best studied of the nighttime illnesses
(E) asthma, have been becoming the better studied out of all the nighttime illness

5. There are a long list of causes of air pollution, ranging from automobile exhaust to methane emissions from livestock.

(A) There are a long list of causes of air pollution,
(B) There were a long list of things causing air pollution,
(C) There are a lengthy list of causes of air pollution,
(D) There have been a long list of causes of air pollution,
(E) There is a long list of causes of air pollution,

GO ON TO THE NEXT PAGE

Test 3

6. <u>Acupuncture has been widely used for years to ease chronic pain conditions, studies</u> have repeatedly endorsed its usefulness.

   (A) Acupuncture has been widely used for years to ease chronic pain conditions, studies

   (B) Although acupuncture having been been widely used for years to ease chronic pain conditions, studies

   (C) Acupuncture has been widely used for years to ease chronic pain conditions, and studies

   (D) Due to the fact that acupuncture has been widely used for years to ease chronic pain conditions, studies

   (E) Because acupuncture has been widely used for years to ease chronic pain conditions is the reason why studies

7. Lower Manhattan was a seasonal home for the Lenni Lenape <u>Indians, who granted the Dutch settlers land-use rights to Manhattan, but</u> did not actually sell it for $24 in trinkets.

   (A) Indians, who granted the Dutch settlers land-use rights to Manhattan, but

   (B) Indians, which granted the Dutch settlers land-use rights to Manhattan, but

   (C) Indians, who granted the Dutch settlers land-use rights to Manhattan, however they

   (D) Indians, and they granted the Dutch settlers land-use rights to Manhattan, but

   (E) Indians, where they granted the Dutch settlers land-use rights to Manhattan; but they

8. From papayas in Hawaii to canola in Canada, the spread of pollen or seeds from genetically engineered <u>plants are evolving from an abstract scientific worry into</u> a significant practical problem.

   (A) plants are evolving from an abstract scientific worry into

   (B) plants are evolving from an abstractly scientific worry into

   (C) plants are in process of evolving from an abstract scientific worry into

   (D) plants is evolving from an abstract scientific worry into

   (E) plants having evolved from an abstract scientific worry into

9. <u>After removing their skins,</u> the children sliced the carrots into sticks for dipping.

   (A) After removing their skins,

   (B) After they removed their skins,

   (C) After they had removed their skins,

   (D) After removing the carrots' skins,

   (E) After they had removed the skins from the carrots,

10. Opinion polls show the public <u>has about as dim a view of pharmaceutical companies as tobacco companies</u>.

    (A) has about as dim a view of pharmaceutical companies as tobacco companies

    (B) have about as dim a view of pharmaceutical companies as tobacco companies

    (C) has about as dim a view of pharmaceutical companies as it does of tobacco companies

    (D) has almost so dim a view of pharmaceutical companies as of tobacco companies

    (E) has approximately as dim a view of pharmaceutical companies as tobacco companies

11. The adjacent homes were dissimilar enough <u>to justify their radically different prices</u>.

    (A) to justify their radically different prices

    (B) to justify its radically different prices

    (C) to be justified by their radically different prices

    (D) to justify there radically different prices

    (E) to be a justification for their radically different prices

12. The pale white petals of the gardenia possess a scent of great sweetness and <u>subtlety and the scent has</u> intrigued many perfume-makers.

    (A) subtlety and the scent has

    (B) subtlety, that being the reason why the scent has

    (C) subtlety, but the scent has

    (D) subtlety, a scent that has

    (E) subtlety, it has

GO ON TO THE NEXT PAGE

13. <u>Attempting to maximize the income-producing potential of her pension plan by investing a substantial amount</u> in so-called junk bonds.

(A) Attempting to maximize the income-producing potential of her pension plan by investing a substantial amount

(B) Attempting to maximize the income-producing potential of her pension plan by substantially investing an amount

(C) She made an attempt to produce the maximum potentiality in income out of her pension plan and she invested a substantial amount

(D) In an attempt to produce the maximum income-producing potential from her pension plan by investing a substantial amount

(E) She attempted to maximize the income-producing potential of her pension plan by investing a substantial amount

14. <u>Seldom do the barriers between the races seem less in evidence than on this league-leading high school football team</u>.

(A) Seldom do the barriers between the races seem less in evidence than on this league-leading high school football team

(B) More so than on other teams, they seem to be less evident barriers between the races on this league-leading high school football team

(C) On this league-leading high school football team, more so than on other teams, the barriers between the races are less in evidence, it seems

(D) The barriers between the races do seem fewer in evidence seldom on this league-leading high school football team

(E) Seldom less than on this league-leading high school football team does the barriers between the races seem less in evidence

YOU MAY GO BACK AND REVIEW THIS SECTION IN THE REMAINING TIME, BUT DO NOT WORK IN ANY OTHER SECTION UNTIL TOLD TO DO SO.

S T O P

Answer Key

<u>Note:</u> The letters in brackets following the Mathematical Reasoning answers refer to the sections of Chapter 9 in which you can find the information you need to answer the questions. For example, **1. C [E]** means that the answer to question 1 is C, and that the solution requires information found in Section 9-E: Averages.

Section 2   Critical Reading

1. C	6. E	11. E	16. B	21. E
2. C	7. C	12. C	17. A	22. B
3. D	8. B	13. E	18. E	23. D
4. E	9. D	14. A	19. C	24. C
5. D	10. E	15. B	20. A	

Section 3   Mathematical Reasoning

1. A [G]	5. A [Q, C]	9. D [J, K, L]	13. C [A, G]	17. E [J]
2. D [B]	6. B [C]	10. D [A]	14. A [E]	18. A [D]
3. D [I]	7. B [A, O]	11. E [B, M]	15. A [G]	19. A [F]
4. D [Q, E]	8. C [E, G]	12. B [J]	16. B [H]	20. B [L]

Section 4   Writing Skills

1. C	8. A	15. D	22. B	29. C
2. D	9. D	16. E	23. D	30. C
3. C	10. E	17. C	24. A	31. B
4. A	11. B	18. B	25. C	32. D
5. D	12. D	19. C	26. C	33. D
6. A	13. C	20. D	27. C	34. E
7. C	14. E	21. C	28. E	35. C

Section 5

On this test, Section 5 was the experimental section. It could have been an extra critical reading, mathematics, or writing skills section. Remember: on the SAT you take, the experimental section may be any section from 2 to 7.

Section 6   Critical Reading

1. D	6. E	11. B	16. C	21. C
2. C	7. D	12. D	17. D	22. E
3. E	8. B	13. D	18. E	23. D
4. A	9. B	14. A	19. B	24. A
5. B	10. C	15. C	20. E	

Section 7 Mathematical Reasoning

Multiple-Choice Questions

1. **C [G]**
2. **C [D]**
3. **D [G]**
4. **E [L, N]**
5. **E [C, D]**
6. **C [R]**
7. **B [F]**
8. **C [P]**

Grid-in Questions

9. [J,N] 7 . 5

10. [F] 9 8

11. [K] 7 . 5

12. [K,D] 3 . 7

13. [E] 1 4 5

14. [C] 1 . 2 1

15. [H] 1 9 8 3

16. [E] 9 . 3 6

17. [D, H] 6

18. [B] 1 / 3

Section 8   Critical Reading

1. C	5. B	9. D	13. B	17. C
2. D	6. C	10. B	14. E	18. C
3. D	7. C	11. D	15. D	19. B
4. B	8. D	12. E	16. E	

Section 9   Mathematical Reasoning

1. B [B, G]	5. D [C, E, Q]	9. B [A]	13. C [A, O]
2. C [A, F]	6. D [C]	10. A [M]	14. C [A]
3. A [L]	7. E [R]	11. A [A, R]	15. A [J, K]
4. E [Q]	8. E [R]	12. D [D, L]	16. E [G]

Section 10   Writing Skills

1. B	4. D	7. A	10. C	13. E
2. C	5. E	8. D	11. A	14. A
3. C	6. C	9. D	12. D	

Score Your Own SAT Essay

Use this table as you rate your performance on the essay-writing section of this Model Test. Circle the phrase that most accurately describes your work. Enter the numbers in the scoring chart below. Add the numbers together and divide by 6 to determine your total score. The higher your total score, the better you are likely to do on the essay section of the SAT.

Note that on the actual SAT two readers will rate your essay; your essay score will be the sum of their two ratings and could range from 12 (highest) to 2 (lowest). Also, they will grade your essay holistically, rating it on the basis of their overall impression of its effectiveness. They will *not* analyze it piece by piece, giving separate grades for grammar, vocabulary level, and so on. Therefore, you cannot expect the score you give yourself on this Model Test to predict your eventual score on the SAT with any great degree of accuracy. Use this scoring guide instead to help you assess your writing strengths and weaknesses, so that you can decide which areas to focus on as you prepare for the SAT.

Like most people, you may find it difficult to rate your own writing objectively. Ask a teacher or fellow student to score your essay as well. With his or her help you should gain added insights into writing your 25-minute essay.

	6	**5**	**4**	**3**	**2**	**1**
POSITION ON THE TOPIC	Clear, convincing, & insightful	Fundamentally clear & coherent	Fairly clear & coherent	Insufficiently clear	Largely unclear	Extremely unclear
ORGANIZATION OF EVIDENCE	Well organized, with strong, relevant examples	Generally well organized, with apt examples	Adequately organized, with some examples	Sketchily developed, with weak examples	Lacking focus and evidence	Unfocused and disorganized
SENTENCE STRUCTURE	Varied, appealing sentences	Reasonably varied sentences	Some variety in sentences	Little variety in sentences	Errors in sentence structure	Severe errors in sentence structure
LEVEL OF VOCABULARY	Mature & apt word choice	Competent word choice	Adequate word choice	Inappropriate or weak vocabulary	Highly limited vocabulary	Rudimentary
GRAMMAR AND USAGE	Almost entirely free of errors	Relatively free of errors	Some technical errors	Minor errors, and some major ones	Numerous major errors	Extensive severe errors
OVERALL EFFECT	Outstanding	Effective	Adequately competent	Inadequate, but shows some potential	Seriously flawed	Fundamentally deficient

Self-Scoring Chart

For each of the following categories, rate the essay from 1 (lowest) to 6 (highest)

Position on the Topic   _____

Organization of Evidence   _____

Sentence Structure   _____

Level of Vocabulary   _____

Grammar and Usage   _____

Overall Effect   _____

TOTAL   _____

(To get a score, divide the total by 6)   _____

Scoring Chart (Second Reader)

For each of the following categories, rate the essay from 1 (lowest) to 6 (highest)

Position on the Topic   _____

Organization of Evidence   _____

Sentence Structure   _____

Level of Vocabulary   _____

Grammar and Usage   _____

Overall Effect   _____

TOTAL   _____

(To get a score, divide the total by 6)   _____

Calculate Your Raw Score

Critical Reading

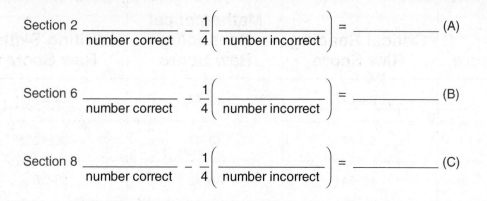

Section 2 $\frac{}{\text{number correct}} - \frac{1}{4}\left(\frac{}{\text{number incorrect}}\right) = \underline{}$ (A)

Section 6 $\frac{}{\text{number correct}} - \frac{1}{4}\left(\frac{}{\text{number incorrect}}\right) = \underline{}$ (B)

Section 8 $\frac{}{\text{number correct}} - \frac{1}{4}\left(\frac{}{\text{number incorrect}}\right) = \underline{}$ (C)

Critical Reading Raw Score = (A) + (B) + (C) = $\underline{}$

Mathematical Reasoning

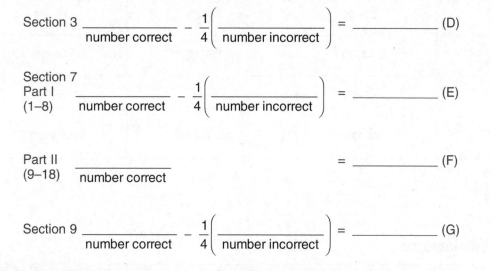

Section 3 $\frac{}{\text{number correct}} - \frac{1}{4}\left(\frac{}{\text{number incorrect}}\right) = \underline{}$ (D)

Section 7
Part I
(1–8) $\frac{}{\text{number correct}} - \frac{1}{4}\left(\frac{}{\text{number incorrect}}\right) = \underline{}$ (E)

Part II
(9–18) $\frac{}{\text{number correct}}$ $= \underline{}$ (F)

Section 9 $\frac{}{\text{number correct}} - \frac{1}{4}\left(\frac{}{\text{number incorrect}}\right) = \underline{}$ (G)

Mathematical Reasoning Raw Score = (D) + (E) + (F) + (G) = $\underline{}$

Writing Skills

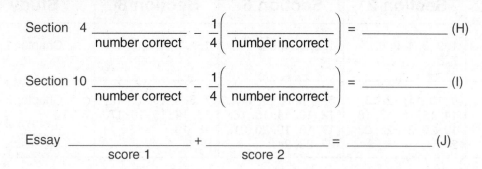

Section 4 $\frac{}{\text{number correct}} - \frac{1}{4}\left(\frac{}{\text{number incorrect}}\right) = \underline{}$ (H)

Section 10 $\frac{}{\text{number correct}} - \frac{1}{4}\left(\frac{}{\text{number incorrect}}\right) = \underline{}$ (I)

Essay $\frac{}{\text{score 1}} + \frac{}{\text{score 2}} = \underline{}$ (J)

Writing Skills Raw Score = H + I (J is a separate subscore)

Test 3

Evaluate Your Performance

Scaled Score	Critical Reading Raw Score	Mathematical Reasoning Raw Score	Writing Skills Raw Score
700–800	58–67	48–54	43–49
650–690	52–57	43–47	39–42
600–640	45–51	36–42	35–38
550–590	38–44	30–35	30–34
500–540	30–37	24–29	25–29
450–490	22–29	18–23	19–24
400–440	14–21	12–17	14–18
300–390	3–13	5–11	5–13
200–290	less than 3	less than 5	less than 5

Identify Your Weaknesses

Critical Reading

Question Type	Question Numbers			Chapter to Study
	Section 2	Section 6	Section 8	
Sentence Completion	1, 2, 3, 4, 5, 6, 7, 8	1, 2, 3, 4, 5	1, 2, 3, 4, 5, 6	Chapter 1
Critical Reading	9, 10, 11, 12, 13, 14, 15, 16, 17, 18, 19, 20, 21, 22, 23, 24	6, 7, 8, 9, 10, 11, 12, 13, 14, 15, 16, 17, 18, 19, 20, 21, 22, 23, 24	7, 8, 9, 10, 11, 12, 13, 14, 15, 16, 17, 18, 19	Chapter 2

Identify Your Weaknesses

Mathematical Reasoning

Section in Chapter 9	Question Numbers			Pages to Study
	Section 3	**Section 7**	**Section 9**	
A Basic Arithmetic Concepts	1, 7, 10		2, 9, 11, 13, 14	410–431
B Fractions and Decimals	4, 11	18	1	432–449
C Percents	3, 6	5, 14	4, 6	450–460
D Ratios and Proportions	18	2, 5, 12, 17	12	461–472
E Averages	2, 8, 14	13, 16	4	473–479
F Polynomials	19	7, 9	2	480–488
G Equations and Inequalities	8, 15	1, 3	1, 13, 16	489–502
H Word Problems	16	15, 17		503–513
I Lines and Angles	5			514–524
J Triangles	9, 12, 17	10	15	525–542
K Quadrilaterals	9	11, 12	15	543–553
L Circles	9, 20	4, 13	5, 12	554–564
M Solid Geometry	11		10	565–573
N Coordinate Geometry		4	8	574–588
O Counting and Probability	7			589–600
P Logical Reasoning	13	8	7	601–608
Q Data Interpretation	2, 3		3, 4	609–618
R Functions and Their Graphs		6	8, 11	619–628

Identify Your Weaknesses

Writing Skills

Question Type	Question Numbers		Chapter to Study
	Section 4	**Section 10**	
Improving Sentences	1, 2, 3, 4, 5, 6, 7, 8, 9, 10, 11	1, 2, 3, 4, 5, 6, 7, 8, 9, 10, 11, 12, 13, 14	Chapter 6
Identifying Sentence Errors	12, 13, 14, 15, 16, 17, 18, 19, 20, 21, 22, 23, 24, 25, 26, 27, 28, 29		Chapter 6
Improving Paragraphs	30, 31, 32, 33, 34, 35		Chapter 6
Essay			Chapter 7

ANSWERS EXPLAINED

Section 2 Critical Reading

1. **C.** If one is alert and insightful, one's faculties (mental powers) are *intact* (sound or whole). Note how the phrase set off by the comma restates and clarifies the idea that Picasso has continued to be perceptive and alert.
(Contrast Signal)

2. **C.** *While* suggests a contrast between the fates of the two dance forms during the 1940s. The decade was *most* noted for the growth of Black modern dance. However, it was also noteworthy or *significant* for the decline of tap dancing. (Contrast Signal)

3. **D.** Something beneficial or helpful in small amounts may be *toxic* (poisonous) in large amounts.
Remember to watch for signal words that link one part of the sentence to another. The use of "though" in the second clause sets up a contrast. The missing word must be an antonym or near-antonym for *beneficial*.
(Argument Pattern)

4. **E.** The encroachments or trespassing of human beings on the hawk's territory would frighten the birds, leading them to *shun* or avoid their usual locations for breeding. Frightened away from their nests, disturbed in their breeding routines, the hawks would have fewer offspring. Thus, their numbers would diminish or *dwindle*. You can immediately eliminate Choices A, B, and C. Choices A and C you can rule out on the basis of general knowledge: when humans come close, wild birds abandon their nests (and their eggs): they have fewer offspring. Choice B you can rule out on the basis of usage. People may *extrapolate* or make projections on the basis of known data about the number of hawks. The "number of black hawks," however, doesn't extrapolate anything. (Argument Pattern)

5. **D.** To aim at a mass market is to try to appeal to the lowest common denominator. British films, which rarely aim at the masses, instead try to appeal to the elite. They are thus *elitist*. (Contrast Signal)

6. **E.** The key phrase here is "worth the trouble." What sort of person creates trouble for his employers? Not a *congenial* (agreeable) or *popular* one. You can immediately eliminate Choices B and C. A *cantankerous* (bad-tempered) employee creates problems. However, if he turns in *meticulous* (very careful and exact) work, his employers may think he's worth the trouble he makes.
Note that, after eliminating the answer choices whose first word does not work in the sentence, you must check the second words of the remaining answer choices. A *domineering* (bossy) or *fastidious* (fussy) employee might create problems around the newspaper office. However, he would not get on his employers' good side by turning in *wearisome* (boring) or *garbled* (confused) stories. (Argument)

7. **C.** Because the opossum is *impervious* to (unharmed by) the poison, it can treat the rattlesnake as a potential source of food and not as a *lethal* or deadly enemy.
Note the cause and effect signal *thus*. The nature of the opossum's response to the venom explains *why* it can look on a dangerous snake as an easy prey.
(Cause and Effect Signal)

8. **B.** By definition, someone who breaks with established convention is *iconoclastic* or nonconformist. Go through the answer choices, eliminating those you can.
Choices A and E are incorrect. Someone who departs from tradition is unlikely to be *derivative* (lacking originality) or *trite* (commonplace; timeworn).
Choices C and D are incorrect. Someone who infuriates (enrages) the traditionalists is controversial, not *uncontroversial*, and is unlikely to be *venerated* (deeply respected) by them. This is one of the last sentence completion questions, so its answer is an extremely difficult word. (Definition Pattern)

9. **D.** The "peculiar" advantage that a best-selling novel has over an original script is its *particular*, special advantage: the story's popularity with a substantial segment of the population is guaranteed.

10. **E.** The final sentence of the passage explains the difficulty involved in working with best-selling novels: filmmakers have to pay so much money to get the screen rights that the producers often wind up losing money on the movie. In other words, the problem is *the financial impact of purchasing rights to adapt the novel*.

11. **E.** The pitch is the steep *slope* of the rapids into which Thornton has fallen.

12. **C.** With its forceful descriptive phrases ("suck of the water," "last steep pitch, "scraped... bruised... struck") and its sharp exclamations, the passage has a strongly *urgent* tone.

13. **E.** Substitute the answer choices in the original sentence. The sergeant is a person who might have been a deputy sheriff before he joined the army—that is, in his civil or *nonmilitary* life.

14. **A.** Paragraph 1 presents a general picture of the man on the bridge, the executioners and the officer standing nearby, the sentinels at the far ends of the bridge. Cinematically, it is like *a wide-angle shot* of the whole panorama. Paragraph 2 takes a closer look at the man, examining his clothes, his face, his expression. It is as if the camera has moved in for *a close-up* shot.

15. B.   The author's comment that the man "had a kindly expression that one would hardly have expected in one whose neck was in the hemp" suggests that he is *an unlikely candidate for execution* and that some unusual circumstances must have brought him to this fate.

16. B.   In calling the military code "liberal" because it doesn't exclude members of the upper classes from being executed, the author is being highly *ironic*. Generally, people would like regulations to be interpreted liberally to permit them to do the things they want. Here, the liberal military code is permitting the man to be hanged. Clearly, the gentleman facing execution would have preferred the code to be less liberal in this case.

17. A.   Farquhar agrees readily with the saying that all is fair in love and war. This implies he is willing to use *underhanded* or unfair *methods to support his* [the Southern] *cause*.

18. E.   Farquhar has no objection to performing humble errands or undertaking dangerous tasks as long as these tasks are appropriate to someone who sees himself as a sort of "undercover soldier," a secret agent of the Confederacy. Anything he does must be consistent or *compatible* with his image of himself in this role.

19. C.   At heart a soldier, Farquhar fundamentally agrees that all's fair in war. He doesn't particularly qualify or restrict his commitment to this viewpoint: he's ready to go out and do something underhanded for his cause without much *restriction* as to what he's willing to do.

20. A.   Mrs. Farquhar's readiness to fetch water for the gray-clad Confederate soldier suggests some degree of sympathy on her part for the Confederate cause.
Choices B and D are incorrect. There is nothing in the passage to suggest either of them. Choices C and E are incorrect. Mrs. Farquhar's action, in hospitably fetching water "with her own white hands," contradicts them.

21. E.   Earlier in the passage, Farquhar is described as frustrated by "the inglorious restraint" preventing his serving the Southern cause. He sees the life of the soldier as larger than that of the civilian, a life filled with opportunities for distinction, for renown. Thus, when he speaks about someone managing to sneak past the guards and accomplishing something for the cause, he is *envisioning himself as a hero*.

22. B.   Farquhar wishes to prevent the Yankee advance. To do so, he must somehow damage the railroad, its bridges, its tunnels, or its trains. The soldier tells him that some highly flammable driftwood is piled up at the base of the wooden railroad bridge. Clearly, it would make sense for Farquhar to try to set fire to the driftwood in *an attempt to burn down* the bridge.

23. D.   The phrase "burn like tow" and the reference to dry driftwood suggest that tow *is highly combustible*. Remember: when asked to give the meaning of an unfamiliar word, to look for nearby context clues.

24. C.   The scout is a Yankee soldier disguised as a member of the enemy. By coming to the Farquhars' plantation in Confederate disguise, he is able to learn they are sympathetic to the enemy. By telling Farquhar of the work on the bridge, stressing both the lack of guards and the abundance of fuel, he is *tempting Farquhar* into an attack on the bridge (and into an ambush). The scout's job is to locate potential enemies and draw them out from cover.

Section 3 Mathematical Reasoning

In each mathematics section, for many problems, an alternative solution, indicated by two asterisks(**), follows the first solution. When this occurs, one of the solutions is the direct mathematical one and the other is based on one of the tactics discussed in Chapter 8 or 9.

1. A.   If $2x + 4x + 6x = -12$, then $12x = -12$ and $x = -1$.
**Note that x *must* be negative, so only A and B are possible. Test these choices.

2. D.   Use your calculator: $1.1 \times 1.9 = 2.09$, which, to the nearest tenth, is **2.1**.

3. D.   Since *ABCD* is a square, $y = 90$. Then $x + 90 + 40 = 180$ and so $x = 50$.

Then $x = z = u = w = $ **50** [When parallel lines are cut by a transversal, the four acute angles have the same measure (KEY FACT I6)].
**Use TACTIC 2: trust the diagram; w appears to be slightly more than a 45° angle.

4. D.   The average is just the sum of the number of students in the five classes (125) divided by 5: $125 \div 5 = $ **25**.

5. A.   In class **A**, one-fourth, or 25% (5 of 20), of the students are in the band. In each of the other classes, the number in the band is *less than* one-fourth of the class.

6. B.   Since 50% of the trip was completed on Monday and 10% of the trip is left, the 100 kilometers traveled on Tuesday represents the other 40% of the total distance, *d*, so

$$0.40d = 100 \Rightarrow d = 100 \div 0.40 = \textbf{250}.$$

Estimate. Since half of the trip was completed Monday, the 100 kilometers traveled on Tuesday plus the 10% still to go constitutes the other half. The 100 kilometers by itself is slightly less than half, and 200 kilometers would be slightly less than the whole distance. Of the choices, only **250 is possible.

7. B. There are nine positive integers less than 10: 1, 2, ... , 9. For which of them is $\dfrac{9}{x} > x$? Only 1 and 2: $\dfrac{9}{1} > 1$ and $\dfrac{9}{2} > 2$. When $x = 3$, $\dfrac{9}{x} = x$, and for all the others $\dfrac{9}{x} < x$. The probability is $\dfrac{2}{9}$.

8. C. Let n represent the number of members of the club before Jean joined. These members raised a total of $85n$ dollars (KEY FACT E1). After Jean was in the club, the total raised was $85n + 50$, the average was 80, and the number of members was $n + 1$:

$$\dfrac{85n + 50}{n + 1} = 80$$

Cross-multiply: $85n + 50 = 80(n + 1)$
Distribute: $85n + 50 = 80n + 80$
Subtract $80n$ and 50
from each side $5n = 30$
Divide by 5: $n = 6$

**Backsolve, starting with 6, Choice C. If there were 6 members, they would have raised $6 \times \$85 = \$510$. After Jean joined and raised $50, there would have been 7 members who raised a total of $510 + \$50 = \$560$. And $560 \div 7 = \$80$. Choice C works.

9. D. Draw pictures.
 • R, S, T *could be* the vertices of a right triangle. (I is true.)
 • R, S, T *could not be* the vertices of a square: if $\overline{RS}$ is a side of the square, then $RT = \sqrt{2}\,RS$, so $RT \neq 2RS$. (II is false.)

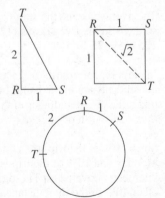

 • R, S, T *could* all lie on a circle. (III is true.)
Statements **I and III only** are true.

10. D. Since the game takes 1 hour, or 60 minutes, and there are always 5 men playing, there is a total of $5 \times 60 = 300$ man-minutes of playing time. If that amount of time is evenly divided among the 12 players, each one plays $300 \div 12 = \mathbf{25}$ minutes.
**Estimate. If 5 men played the first 10 or 12 minutes, and 5 other men played the next 10 or 12 minutes, who would be left to play the rest of the game? Since 10 and 12 are much too small, eliminate A and B. If 5 men played for 30 minutes, and 5 other men played the next 30 minutes, the game would be over and 2 men wouldn't have played at all. Since 30 is too large, eliminate E. The answer must be 24 or 25. Guess.

11. E. When A ounces of water are removed from pitcher II, that pitcher will contain $B - A$ ounces. Since its capacity is B, pitcher II will be $\dfrac{B - A}{B}$ full.
**Use TACTIC 7: plug in easy-to-use numbers. Suppose pitcher II holds 10 ounces and pitcher I holds 3. Then, if 3 ounces are poured from pitcher II into pitcher I, pitcher II will have 7 ounces and be $\dfrac{7}{10}$ full. Which of the choices equals $\dfrac{7}{10}$ when $B = 10$ and $A = 3$?
Only $\dfrac{B - A}{B}$.

12. B. In $\triangle ABC$, $w + x + 40 = 180 \Rightarrow w + x = 140$. Similarly, in $\triangle ADE$, $y + z + 40 = 180 \Rightarrow y + z = 140$. Then $w + x + y + z = 140 + 140 = \mathbf{280}$.

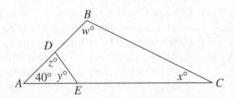

Use TACTIC 2: trust the diagram; $w, x, y,$ and z appear to be *about* 100, 45, 60, and 80, respectively, for a total of 285. Your estimate may well be slightly more or less, but should surely be between 240 and 310. With anything less than 300, guess **280; if your estimate is over 300, you might pick 320.

13. C. $|x - 5| + 10 = 15 \Rightarrow |x - 5| = 5 \Rightarrow$
  $x - 5 = 5$ or $x - 5 = -5 \Rightarrow$
  $x = 10$ or $x = 0$
The greatest value is **10**.

14. A. Use TACTIC 17:
when you have more
than two equations,
add them.

$$x + y = 10$$
$$y + z = 15$$
$$\underline{+\ x + z = 17}$$
$$2x + 2y + 2z = 42$$

Divide by 2: $x + y + z = 21$

To get the average,
divide the sum by 3: $\dfrac{x+y+z}{3} = \dfrac{21}{3} = \mathbf{7}$

(Note: You *could* solve for x, y, z, but you
shouldn't.)

15. A. Let x = the number of passengers originally on
the bus, and keep track of the comings and
goings. At the first stop half the people got

off, leaving $\dfrac{1}{2}x$ on the bus, and 1 more got

on: $\dfrac{1}{2}x + 1$. At the second stop $\dfrac{1}{3}$ of the

passengers got off, leaving two-thirds on the

bus, and 1 person got on: $\dfrac{2}{3}\left(\dfrac{1}{2}x + 1\right) + 1$.

This simplifies to $\dfrac{1}{3}x + \dfrac{2}{3} + 1$, which

equals 15, so

$$\dfrac{1}{3}x + \dfrac{2}{3} = 14 \Rightarrow x + 2 = 42 \Rightarrow x = \mathbf{40}.$$

**Work backwards. At the end there were 15
passengers, so before the last one got on, there

were 14, which was $\dfrac{2}{3}$ of the number before

any got off at the second stop. At that point
there were 21 passengers, meaning that, before
1 person got on at the first stop, there were 20,
which is half of **40**, the original number.
**Use TACTIC 5: backsolve. Start with C, 58:
29 got off and 1 got on; then there were 30; 10
got off and 1 got on; then there were 21, but we
should have only 15. Since 58 is too big, eliminate C, D, and E. Try A or B; A works.

16. B. Since the value of the house doubled every
6 years, in the past 30 years it has doubled
5 times. If the original price of the house
was d dollars, the value today would be $d(2^5)$
dollars.
$2^5 d = \$320,000 \Rightarrow 32d = \$320,000$, and so
$d = \mathbf{\$10,000}$.
**You can just work backwards. Six years
ago, the house was worth one half of
$320,000, or $160,000. Six years earlier, it
was worth $80,000. Continue dividing by 2:
$320,000 → $160,000 → $80,000 →
$40,000 → $20,000 → **$10,000**.

17. E.

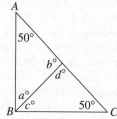

Check each statement to see if it *must* be true.
• In $\triangle ABC$, $\angle B$ measures 80°, so $a + c = 80$
and $c = 80 - a$. (I is true.)
• Since the measure of an exterior angle of a
triangle equals the sum of the measures of
the two opposite interior angles (KEY
FACT J2), $b = c + 50 \Rightarrow c = b - 50$.
(II is true.)
• Since $a + b = 130$ and $c + d = 130$, then
$a + b = c + d$. (III is true.)
Statements **I**, **II**, and **III** are true.

18. A. If c carpenters can build a garage in d days,
then 1 carpenter will take c times as long,
or cd days, and $2\ cd$ days to build 2 garages.
Finally, if the work is divided up among e

carpenters, they will take $\dfrac{2cd}{e}$ days.

**Use TACTIC 6: plug in easy-to-use
numbers. If 2 carpenters can build a garage
in 10 days, they will take 20 days to build
2 garages. It will take 4 carpenters half as
long: 10 days. Which choice is equal to 10
when $c = 2$, $d = 10$, and $e = 4$? Only

$\dfrac{2cd}{e}$. Remember: test each choice with your

calculator, and eliminate a choice as soon as
you can see that it is not equal to 10.

19. A. This question is easier than it seems at first.
In each fraction, the numerator is the negative
of the denominator, so each fraction equals -1
and the sum of the fractions is **–2**.
**Of course, you can use TACTIC 6: plug in
numbers. If $a = 1$ and $b = 2$, then each fraction
is equal to -1.

20. B. Here $A = 5\pi r^2$ and $B = 3\pi s^2$, so $5\pi r^2 = 3\pi s^2$
Divide both sides by π: $5r^2 = 3s^2$

Divide both sides by $5s^2$: $\dfrac{r^2}{s^2} = \dfrac{3}{5}$

Take the square root of each side: $\dfrac{r}{s} = \dfrac{\sqrt{3}}{\sqrt{5}}$.

Section 4 Writing Skills

1. C. Error in modification. The opening phrase
("Unable to see more than three inches in front
of her nose without corrective lenses")
describes *Mary*, not Mary's search or Mary's
glasses.

2. D. The original sentence is both wordy and unidiomatic. Choice B is also wordy and changes the meaning of the original. Choice C introduces a comma splice error. Choice E introduces a sentence fragment after the semicolon. Only Choice D is an effective, idiomatic sentence.

3. C. The original sentence, while grammatically correct, is wordy. Choice C eliminates the wordiness without introducing new errors.

4. A. Sentence is correct. Choices B and C introduce errors in subject-verb agreement. Choices D and E are wordy and awkward.

5. D. Lack of parallelism. In Choice D, the phrase *fascinating because of Trump's shrewdness* exactly parallels the earlier phrase *infuriating because of Trump's arrogance.*

6. A. Sentence is correct. Choice B introduces an error in tense. Choice D introduces an error in subject-verb agreement (the verb should not be plural). Choices C and E are wholly confusing.

7. C. Shift of personal pronoun. Remember: everything in the sentence that has *not* been underlined is correct. Therefore, the pronoun *you* is correct; the pronoun *one* is incorrect. Choice C corrects the error in person economically.

8. A. Sentence is correct. Choices B and C introduce errors in subject-verb agreement and tense. Choices D and E are wordy and awkward.

9. D. Error in pronoun-antecedent agreement. The antecedent is the plural noun *communities*; the appropriate pronoun, therefore, is *their*, not *its*.

10. E. Errors in subject-verb agreement and in idiom. The subject is *drop* (singular); the verb should be singular as well. Replace *have encouraged* with *has encouraged*. Additionally, note that the buyers are encouraged to do something, namely, *to apply* for loans.

11. B. The change in subordination emphasizes the built-in contrast between the bridge's actual color and its name.

12. D. Error in idiom. Use the preposition *of* with the adjective *desirous*: the shoppers are *desirous of* comparing prices.

13. C. Incorrect pronoun. Players are people. John is one of those players *who* always give total commitment to the team.

14. E. Sentence is correct.

15. D. Error in idiom. Use the preposition *for* with the adjective *suitable*: the amounts of water collected are rarely *suitable for* consumption without treatment.

16. E. Sentence is correct.

17. C. Lack of parallelism. *Hunger* and *knack* are both nouns. The third item in this series should also be a noun. Substitute *a willingness* for *was willing*.

18. B. Adjective and adverb confusion. Change the adjective *surprising* to the adverb *surprisingly,* which then correctly modifies the adjective *little.*

19. C. Error in subject-verb agreement. The verb should be *needs* to agree with the singular subject *cream*.

20. D. Error in comparison. Only two events are being compared. Of the two, the Tevis Cup presents the *greater* challenge.

21. C. Incorrect pronoun. The clause modifies *movement*, not *writers*. It was the movement *that* came to be known as the Harlem Renaissance.

22. B. Error in logical comparison. The sentence is comparing Whitman's poetry with Kipling's poetry, not with Kipling the poet. The sentence should begin "Clearly, Whitman's verses, *unlike Kipling's*, are wholly unconventional."

23. D. Error in parallelism. Change *an apprenticeship* to *to apprentice*, paralleling *to visit*.

24. A. Error in word usage. *Perspective* is a noun meaning viewpoint or vista; *prospective* is an adjective meaning expected or future. The sentence is discussing the proposed merger's future or *prospective* advantages.

25. C. Error in word usage. *Latter*, an adjective or noun, refers to the second of two persons or things; *later*, an adverb, refers to time. Initially (at first) the candidate raised funds via the Internet; *later* he tried other methods.

26. C. Error in word usage. *Laying* is nonstandard English for *lying*, meaning reclining or resting. The sunbathers had been *lying* near the pool.

27. C. Error in tense. Replace *would be* with *will be*.

28. E. Sentence is correct.

29. C. The problem here involves a fusion of idioms. It is correct to say that the differences arise *less from* a dispute about the function of government *than from* a dispute about the nature of mankind. It would also be correct to say that the differences arise *not from* a dispute about the function of government *but from* a dispute about the nature of mankind. Do not mix the two constructions.

30. C. All sentences except sentence 3 contribute to the paragraph's main point, that celebrations help to unite people and keep traditions alive. Therefore, Choice C is the best answer.

31. B. Choice A is grammatically correct, but the first clause is awkwardly expressed in the passive voice. Choice B is clearly written and to the point. It is the best answer.
    Choice C contains a dangling participle. The phrase *Receiving new clothes* should modify *children*, not *money*.
    Choice D is awkwardly expressed.
    Choice E is wordy and awkward.

32. D. Choice A is fresh, but its tone is not consistent with the rest of the essay.
    Choice B contains a comma splice between *dinner* and *at*.
    Choice C emphasizes the idea properly, but lacks parallel construction.

Choice D places the emphasis where it belongs and expresses the idea effectively. It is the best answer.

Choice E is repetitious, and it contains an error in pronoun reference. The pronoun *they* has no specific antecedent.

33. D. Choice A does not provide a significantly better transition.

Choice B does nothing to improve the relationship between paragraphs 3 and 4.

Choice C is awkwardly worded and does not include transitional material.

Choice D provides an effective transition between paragraphs. It is the best answer.

Choice E tries to provide a transition, but it is wordy and it contains a dangling participle.

34. E. Choice A places emphasis on the location of the assassination instead of on the event itself, an emphasis that the writer did not intend.

Choice B contains a nonstandard usage: the phrase *to remember about*.

Choice C is grammatically correct but wordy.

Choice D is the same as B.

Choice E is a succinct and proper revision. It is the best answer.

35. C. The main purpose of the last paragraph is to provide an example of a celebration that unites people and preserves tradition. Therefore, Choice C is the best answer.

Section 6 Critical Reading

1. D. The critics would regret any lapse on the part of a *promising* writer.

The adjective *glowing* is your clue that you are looking for a word with positive associations. Therefore, you can eliminate any word with negative ones. Choices A, B, and C have negative associations. Only Choice D or E can be correct.   (Cause and Effect Pattern)

2. C. A longing for old friends and familiar scenes is *nostalgia* or homesickness.

Remember: before you look at the choices, read the sentence and think of a word that makes sense.

Likely Words: homesickness, nostalgia, yearning.   (Definition)

3. E. Borrowers would complain that an old, *appreciated* borrowing policy had been set aside or *superseded*.

Remember: in double-blank sentences, go through the answer choices, testing the *first* words in each choice and eliminating those that don't fit. The fact that the new policy has received complaints indicates that the old policy was viewed positively. You can immediately eliminate Choice B, *disliked*, and Choice D, *ignored*. Both are negative terms.   (Contrast Pattern)

4. A. *Even though* signals a contrast. The brain's fundamental organization does not change. However, the details of the brain's organization do change: they remain *plastic*, pliable, capable of being molded or shaped.   (Contrast Signal)

5. B. The key phrase here is "in a few words." Although the movie is lavish in its beauty, it is not lavish in its use of words or film. Instead, it demonstrates *economy* of style. (Definition)

6. E. The opening sentence of Passage 1 states that few, if any, people recalled Lady Mary's efforts to fight smallpox. Her efforts have largely been forgotten. Likewise, the opening sentences of Passage 2 assert that some people "ignore the claims" of the African slave Onesimus, who played a small but important part in the battle against the deadly disease. Thus, both passages attempt to *call attention to neglected historical figures*.

7. D. Without her travels in the East, where she encountered the Eastern custom of inoculation, Lady Mary would not have been inspired to bring back this procedure to England. Thus, her smallpox-fighting efforts in England came about *as a consequence of her travels in the East*.

8. B. Not only did the Turks practice the custom of inoculation, they "even" held house parties so that inoculated youngsters could convalesce in company and in comfort. Clearly the procedure enjoyed *widespread acceptance*.

9. B. Both Montagu and Mather *advocated* inoculation, a *foreign medical practice* well known in Turkey and in parts of Africa.

10. C. According to the author, "We have been taught to believe that our lives are better than the lives of those who came before us" and the lives of those today who live in similarly "primitive" circumstances. We base our belief that we Americans are well off today on the assumption that people in earlier generations and people now living in "primitive" circumstances have an *inferior standard of living*.

11. B. The conventional wisdom is that the lives of primitive peoples are filled with toil. The author, however, states that primitives do little work. Thus, she regards the conventional wisdom with *skepticism* or doubt.

12. D. According to the author, these "stone age peoples" have limited desires. They are not motivated by any particular *desire for consumer goods* or other material comforts.

13. D. To raise an issue is to *bring it up* for discussion.

14. A. Throughout the passage the author *disputes the assumption* made by the conventional wisdom that our economic progress has been an unmitigated blessing. She argues instead that we "have paid a price for prosperity."

15. C. The author makes an assertion: "We are eating more." She then qualifies or limits her asser-

tion: "but we are burning up those calories at work." She repeats this pattern of assertion followed by qualification. She then draws her conclusion: it is hard to support the conventional wisdom that economic progress has been an unmixed blessing for us.

16. C. The author provides the reader both with physical details of dress and bearing (*appearances*) and with comments about the motives and emotions (*moral natures*) of the Cardinal and Bosola.

    Choice A is incorrect. The passage scarcely mentions the church. Choice B is incorrect. The description of ecclesiastical costumes is only one item in the description of the Cardinal. Choice D is incorrect. While audiences today might well enjoy seeing the characters acted as described here, the author does not cite specific reasons why the play might appeal to modern audiences. Choice E is incorrect. The author's purpose is to describe two separate roles, not to compare two interpretations of a single role.

17. D. "Spare" is being used to describe the Cardinal's physical appearance. He is tall and *lean*.

18. E. The eagle is poised to strike "with exposed talons." It, like the Cardinal, poises itself to strike with greater force. The imagery suggests the Cardinal's *mercilessness*.

    Choice A is incorrect. The Cardinal is not *flighty* (light-headed and irresponsible); he is cold and calculating. Choice B is incorrect. He loves power, not *freedom*. Choice C is incorrect. An eagle poised to strike with bare claws suggests violence, not *eminence* (fame and high position). Choice D is incorrect. Nothing in the passage suggests he is *spiritual*.

    Beware of Eye-Catchers. "Eminence" is a title of honor applied to cardinals in the Roman Catholic church. Choice C may attract you for this reason.

19. B. The Cardinal glories in his place in the hierarchy of the Church: his *rank* or status as an ecclesiastical lord.

20. E. Although Bosola is not a "leather-jacketed" hoodlum, he is a hired "assassin," a "hangman," a mercenary killer (despite his scholarly taste and humanist disposition).

21. C. Answer this question by the process of elimination.

    Choice A is incorrect. In describing Bosola the author makes no use of *rhetorical questions* (questions asked solely to produce an effect). Choice B is incorrect. Though the author makes many assertions about Bosola, he limits or *qualifies* many of them. For example, the author asserts that Bosola "is inwardly tormented." He then immediately qualifies his assertion, adding "but not by undiluted passion." Thus, the author does not chiefly use *unqualified assertions* in describing Bosola.

Choice D is incorrect. *Dramatic irony* is irony built in to a speech or a situation, which the audience understands, but which the characters onstage have yet to grasp. The author does not use this literary technique in describing Bosola. Choice E is incorrect. The author makes one brief literary allusion (to Browning's verse monologues). He does not chiefly use *literary allusions* in describing Bosola.

Only Choice C is left. It is the correct answer. Throughout the passage's final paragraph, the author describes Bosola through *comparisons* ("Like his black-and-white clothes," "Like Duke Ferdinand") and *contrasts* ("not . . . a leather-jacketed, heavy-booted tough," "Still less . . . a sneering, leering, melodramatic villain").

22. E. The author is contrasting the two sides of Bosola, the scholar and the assassin. As a scholar, he is a man of perceptive intellect, noted for discrimination or *discernment*.

23. D. Lines 61–66 state that Bosola "is inwardly tormented . . . (by) disgust at a world filled with knavery and folly, . . . in which he must play a part and that a lowly, despicable one." The villainy and foolishness around him disgust him. He feels intellectually superior to the evil around him, *yet must act the villain himself*.

24. A. The casual references to the elongated hands and features of El Greco's work and to the trim beards and commanding stances in the work of Van Dyke imply that the author assumes the reader is familiar with both painters' art.

Section 7 Mathematical Reasoning

MULTIPLE-CHOICE QUESTIONS

1. C. The left-hand side of $(w + 12) - 12 = 12$ is just w, so $w = \mathbf{12}$.
   **Of course, you can use TACTIC 5: backsolve, starting (and ending) with C.

2. C. If 24 of the students are girls, then $40 - 24 = 16$ are boys. The ratio of boys to girls is 16:24 which reduces to **2:3**.
   **Even if you can't do the above, there are clearly fewer boys than girls, and so the ratio must be less than 1:1. Eliminate D and E and guess.

3. D. $25 - 3\sqrt{x} = 7 \Rightarrow -3\sqrt{x} = -18 \Rightarrow$
   $\sqrt{x} = 6 \Rightarrow x = \mathbf{36}$.
   If you want to avoid the algebra, use TACTIC 5: backsolve. First eliminate choices A and B, since you can't take the square root of a negative number. Then use your calculator to test the other choices. Only **36, choice D, works:
   $25 - 3\sqrt{36} = 25 - 3(6) = 25 - 18 = 7$.

4. E. Since the formula for the area of a circle is $A = \pi r^2$, to calculate the area you need to know the radius, which is just the distance from the center, O, to the point, P. Use the distance formula:

$$r = \sqrt{(3-2)^2 + (3-(-2))^2} = \sqrt{1^2 + 5^2} =$$

$$\sqrt{1 + 25} = \sqrt{26}.$$

The area is $\pi\left(\sqrt{26}\right)^2 = \mathbf{26\pi}$.

5. E. At the regular price, a CD costs d dollars, so at 50% off it costs $\dfrac{d}{2}$ dollars. To find out how many you can buy, divide the amount of money, m, by the price per CD, $\dfrac{d}{2}$:

$$m \div \frac{d}{2} = m \times \frac{2}{d} = \boldsymbol{\frac{2m}{d}}.$$

**Use TACTIC 6: plug in easy-to-use numbers. If a CD regularly costs \$10, then on sale at 50% off, they cost \$5 each. How many can be purchased on sale for \$20? The answer is 4. Which of the choices equals 4 when $d = 10$ and $m = 20$?

Only $\boldsymbol{\dfrac{2m}{d}}$.

6. C. $f\left(\dfrac{1}{2}\right) = 9\left(\dfrac{1}{2}\right) + 9^{\frac{1}{2}} = 4.5 + \sqrt{9} = 4.5 + 3 = \mathbf{7.5}.$

7. B. $\dfrac{2x^2 - 8}{x^2 - 4x + 4} = \dfrac{2(x^2 - 4)}{(x-2)(x-2)} =$

$$\frac{2\cancel{(x-2)}(x+2)}{\cancel{(x-2)}(x-2)} = \boldsymbol{\frac{2(x+2)}{x-2}}$$

**Use TACTIC 6: plug in a number for x. For example, if $x = 3$:

$\dfrac{2x^2 - 8}{x^2 - 4x + 4}$ is $\dfrac{2(3)^2 - 8}{3^2 - 4(3) + 4} = \dfrac{18 - 8}{9 - 12 + 4} =$

$$\frac{10}{1} = 10.$$

Only choice B is 10 when $x = 3$:

$$\frac{2(3+2)}{3-2} = \frac{2(5)}{1} = 10.$$

8. C. Sequence I: 2, 4, 6, 8, 10, ...
The nth term is $2n$, so the 32nd term is 64.
Sequence II: 2, 4, 8, 16, 32, ...
The nth term is 2^n, so the 32nd term is 2^{32}.

Finally, $\dfrac{2^{32}}{64} = \dfrac{2^{32}}{2^6} = \mathbf{2^{26}}.$

GRID-IN QUESTIONS

9. (7.5) Here, $\triangle ABC$ is a right triangle and its area is given by $\dfrac{1}{2}(AB)(BC)$. Since $\overline{AB}$ is vertical, find its length by subtracting the y-coordinates: $AB = 4 - 1 = 3$. Similarly, since $\overline{BC}$ is horizontal, find its length by subtracting the x-coordinates: $BC = 6 - 1 = 5$. Then

$$\text{area of } \triangle ABC = \frac{1}{2}(3)(5) = \frac{15}{2} = \mathbf{7.5}.$$

10. (98) The easiest way is to simplify first: $(a^2 + b^2) - (a^2 - b^2) = 2b^2$. Then $6 \otimes 7 = 2(7^2) = 2(49) = \mathbf{98}$.
**If you don't think to simplify (or you can't), just do the arithmetic:

$$(6^2 + 7^2) - (6^2 - 7^2) = (36 + 49) - (36 - 49) =$$
$$85 - (-13) = 85 + 13 = \mathbf{98}.$$

11. (7.5) The perimeter of the quadrilateral in the figure is 30 $(5 + 7 + 8 + 10)$. Then $4s = 30$, where s is a side of the square, and $s = \mathbf{7.5}$.

12. (3.7) To produce 40 gizmos takes $40 \times 333 = 13{,}320$ seconds. Since there are 60 seconds in a minute and 60 minutes in an hour, there are $60 \times 60 = 3600$ seconds in an hour; $13{,}320 \div 3600 = \mathbf{3.7}$ hours.
**13,320 seconds $\div$ 60 = 222 minutes, and 222 minutes $\div$ 60 = $\mathbf{3.7}$ hours.

13. (145) Since the average of a, b, and 10 is 100, their sum is 300 (TACTIC E1). Then

$$a + b + 10 = 300 \Rightarrow a + b = 290.$$

So, $\dfrac{a+b}{2} = \dfrac{290}{2} = \mathbf{145}.$

14. (1.21) Use TACTIC 7. Since this is a percent problem, assume the rent *last year* was \$100. Since 10% of 100 is 10, this year the rent went up \$10 to \$110. Now, 10% of 110 is 11, so next year the rent will go up \$11 to \$121. Finally, 121 is $\mathbf{1.21} \times 100$.

15. (1983) Let x be the number of years after 1970 when Boris is 3 times as old as Olga.

Year	Boris's Age	Olga's Age
1970	26	0
1970 + x	26 + x	x

The equation is $26 + x = 3x \Rightarrow 26 = 2x \Rightarrow x = 13$. Boris was 3 times as old as Olga 13 years after 1970, in **1983** (when they were 39 and 13, respectively).

16. (9.36)   The class average will be highest when all the grades are as high as possible. Assume that all 22 students who passed earned 10's. Of the 3 who failed, 1 received a grade of 2; but assume that the other 2 students had 6's, the highest failing grade. Then the total is $22 \times 10 + 2 + 2 \times 6 = 220 + 2 + 12 = 234$, so the highest possible class average is $234 \div 25 = \mathbf{9.36}$.

17. (6)   Let $2x$ and $7x$ represent the number of red and blue marbles, respectively, in jar I. Then in total there are $7x$ blue marbles and $14x$ red ones. Since there are $2x$ red marbles in jar I, there are $12x$ red marbles in jar II. Then there are **6** times as many red marbles in jar II as there are in jar I.
   **Do the same analysis, except let $x = 1$. Then jar I contains 2 red and 7 blue marbles, whereas jar II contains 12 red ones.

18. ($\frac{1}{3}$)   Adding the fractions, we get $\dfrac{1}{a} + \dfrac{1}{b} = \dfrac{a+b}{ab}$.

   But it is given that ab is 3 times $(a + b)$.

   Therefore, $\dfrac{a+b}{ab} = \dfrac{1}{3}$.

Section 8 Critical Reading

1. C.   To be the subject of a major exhibition would surely *rescue* a forgotten artist from obscurity (the state of being unknown).
   (Cause and Effect Pattern)

2. D.   If we see things in a distorted or altered fashion, our testimony is *unreliable*.
   Note how the second clause serves to clarify or define the meaning of the missing word. Remember: before you look at the choices, read the sentence and think of a word that makes sense.
   Likely Words: undependable, misleading.
   (Definition)

3. D.   People who shut themselves away from society are, by definition, hermits or *recluses*.
   (Definition)

4. B.   Heroic virtues include *disregard* or ignoring of death and *fortitude* or courage in the face of torture. Through it all, Bond remains nonchalant or cool.   (Examples)

5. B.   If the code did not exist until 1846, it could not have been *rescinded* (canceled), *presupposed* (required as an already existing condition), or *depreciated* (disparaged) at that time. It makes most sense that the code was *promulgated* or made known to the public by the AMA at that time.   (Definition)

6. C.   The Romantic poets can be described as *emotional*; Arnold and the later "moralizing" Victorian era poets can be described as *didactic* (interested in teaching). Remember to watch for signal words that link one part of the sentence to another. The use of *unlike* in the opening clause sets up a contrast. The missing words must be antonyms or near-antonyms. You can immediately eliminate Choices A and B as synonyms or near-synonym pairs.   (Contrast Signal)

7. C.   The opening paragraph discusses changes in the idea of matter, emphasizing the use of musical terminology to describe the concepts of physics. The second paragraph then goes on to develop the theme of the *music of subatomic particles.*
   Choice B is incorrect. Music does not directly influence the interactions of particles; physicists merely use musical terms to describe these interactions.

8. D.   The author mentions these terms as examples of what he means by the strange new language or *idiosyncratic nomenclature* of modern particle physics.

9. D.   In his references to the elegance of the newly discovered subatomic structures and to the dance of Creation, the author conveys his *admiration* and *wonder*.

10. B.   "Matter's heart," where the physicist can observe the dance of Creation, is *the subatomic world*, the world of quarks and charms.

11. D.   The image of the snake swallowing its tail suggests that the astronomers' and physicists' theories are, at bottom, one and the same. In other words, there is an *underlying unity* connecting them.

12. E.   The properties of the upsilon particle that implied it could not be made of up, down, strange, or charm quarks were its *characteristics* or attributes.

13. B.   Glashow is eager for the end of the hunt. His words ("last blessed one," "the sooner...the better") reflect his *impatience*.

14. E.   The keystone of the arch (the wedge-shaped block that is inserted last into the arch and locks the other pieces in place) completes the arch. By comparing the top quark to the keystone, the author of Passage 2 *illustrates the importance of the top quark to subatomic theory.*

15. D.   The physicists had to find the top quark because their theory *depended* on the top's existence.

16. E.   The author of Passage 2 cites authorities (Glashow, Tollestrup) and uses similes ("like an arch"). She defines the Standard Model as the theoretical synthesis that reduced the zoo of subatomic particles to a manageable number. She poses a question about what makes certain particles more massive than others. However, she *never denies a possibility*.

17. C.   Physicists are familiar with the weight of a gold atom. In stating that the top was determined to weigh about as much as a gold atom,

the author is illustrating just *how hefty* or massive a top quark is.

18. **C.** The 1995 experiments succeeded: The physicists found the keystone to their arch. From this we can infer that the Standard Model was not disproved but instead received its *validation*.

19. **B.** In lines 31–37, the author of Passage 1 develops a fanciful metaphor for the nature of matter. To him, subatomic matter is like a Bach fugue, filled with arpeggios. While the author of Passage 2 resorts to some figurative language ("Grail," "keystone") in attempting to describe the top quark, she is more factual than figurative: she never uses any metaphor as extended as the metaphor "the music of matter." Thus, her most likely reaction to lines 31–37 would be to point out that this metaphor *is too fanciful to be worthwhile*.

Section 9 Mathematical Reasoning

1. **B.** Solve the given equation: $\dfrac{1}{a} + \dfrac{1}{a} + \dfrac{1}{a} = 12$

   Add the fractions: $\dfrac{3}{a} = 12$

   Multiply both sides by a: $3 = 12a$

   Divide both sides by 12: $a = \dfrac{3}{12} = \dfrac{1}{4}$.

   **You can use TACTIC 5: backsolve; try choice C. If $a = \dfrac{1}{3}$, then $\dfrac{1}{a} = 3$, so the left-hand side equals 9. That's too small. Now, *be careful*: a fraction gets bigger when its denominator gets *smaller* (KEY FACT B4). Eliminate C, D, and E, and try a smaller value for a: $\dfrac{1}{4}$ works.

2. **C.** If $x = -5$, then

   $2x^2 - 3x - 7 = 2(-5)^2 - 3(-5) - 7$
   $= 2(25) + 15 - 7 = \mathbf{58}$.

3. **A.** The formula for the area of a circle is: $A = \pi r^2$

   Divide both sides by π: $r^2 = \dfrac{A}{\pi}$

   Take the square root of each side: $r = \sqrt{\dfrac{A}{\pi}}$

   The diameter is twice the radius: $d = 2r = \mathbf{2\sqrt{\dfrac{A}{\pi}}}$

   **Let the radius of the circle be 1. Then the area is π, and the diameter is 2. Which of the five choices is equal to 2 when $A = \pi$? Only $2\sqrt{\dfrac{A}{\pi}}$.

4. **E.** Carefully read the values from the chart. Ann, Dan, Pam, Fran, and Sam read 1, 4, 2, 6, and 5 books, respectively. The sum is **18**.

5. **D.** The average number of books read by the five members is the sum, 18 (calculated in the solution to question 3), divided by 5: 3.6. Three of the five members, or **60%**, read more than 3.6 books.

6. **D.** If Laurie had to pay 30% of the value of her inheritance in taxes, she still owned 70% of her inheritance: 70% of 40% is **28%** ($0.70 \times 0.40 = 0.28$).
   Assume the estate was worth \$100. Laurie received 40%, or \$40. Her tax was 30% of \$40, or \$12. She still had \$28, or **28%, of the \$100 estate.

7. **E.** The months of the year form a repeating sequence with 12 terms in the set that repeats. By KEY FACT P2, the nth term is the same as the rth term, where r is the remainder when n is divided by 12.
   $555 \div 12 = 46.25 \Rightarrow$ the quotient is 46.
   $46 \times 12 = 552$ and $555 - 552 = 3 \Rightarrow$ the remainder is 3.
   Therefore, 555 months from September will be the same month as 3 months from September, namely **December**.

8. **E.** The graph of $y = -f(x)$ is the reflection in the x-axis of the graph of $y = f(x)$.

   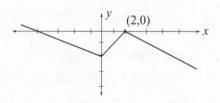

   Of the five choices, only **(2, 0)** is on this graph.

9. **B.** Write the given equation as: $a^3 = 3a$
   Since a is positive, divide both sides by a: $a^2 = 3$
   Take the square root of each side: $a = \mathbf{\sqrt{3}}$

   **Use TACTIC 5: test the choices, starting with C.

10. **A.** If e is the edge of the cube, the surface area, A, is $6e^2$ and the volume, V, is e^3 (KEY FACTS M1 and M2). Then

   $$A = 6e^2 = 60 \Rightarrow e^2 = 10 \Rightarrow e = \sqrt{10}$$

   $$V = \left(\sqrt{10}\right)^3 = \left(\sqrt{10}\right)\left(\sqrt{10}\right)\left(\sqrt{10}\right) = \mathbf{10\sqrt{10}}.$$

11. A. $f(16) = (16)^{\frac{1}{2}} + (16)^{\frac{1}{4}} = \sqrt{16} + \sqrt[4]{16} = 4 + 2 = \mathbf{6}$.

**If you use your calculator, you don't need to change $16^{\frac{1}{2}}$ to $\sqrt{16}$. Just enter $(16)^{\left(\frac{1}{2}\right)} + (16)^{\left(\frac{1}{4}\right)}$. If you prefer, you can enter the exponents as .5 and .25.

12. D. Let r = radius of circle I, and let R = radius of circle II. Then $2R$ is the diameter of circle II, and $2\pi r$ is the circumference of circle I.

It is given that: $2\pi r = 2R$
Divide both sides by 2: $R = \pi r$

Then $\dfrac{\text{area of circle II}}{\text{area of circle I}} = \dfrac{\pi R^2}{\pi r^2} = \dfrac{\pi (\pi r)^2}{\pi r^2}$

$= \dfrac{\pi^3 r^2}{\pi r^2} = \pi^2$

**Use TACTIC 6. Pick some easy-to-use number, such as 1, for the radius of circle I. Then the circumference of circle I is 2π, which is the diameter of circle II, and the radius of circle II is π (one-half its diameter). The area of a circle is given by $A = \pi r^2$, so the area of circle I is $\pi(1) = \pi$, and the area of circle II is $\pi(\pi^2) = \pi^3$. Finally, the ratio of their areas is $\dfrac{\pi^3}{\pi} = \pi^2$.

13. C. Exactly 3 of the numbers on the dart board are prime: 2, 3, and 31. Therefore, the probability that a dart lands on a prime is $\dfrac{3}{6} = \dfrac{1}{2}$. (Remember: 1 is *not* a prime.)

14. C. The elements of B that are in A are the perfect cubes between –50 and 50. There are **7** of them: –27, –8, –1, 0, 1, 8, 27.

15. A. Use TACTIC 1: draw a diagram.

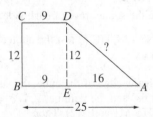

Form rectangle $BCDE$ by drawing $\overline{DE} \perp \overline{AB}$. Then, $BE = 9$, $AE = 16$, and $DE = 12$. Finally, $DA = \mathbf{20}$, because right triangle AED is a 3-4-5 triangle in which the length of each side is multiplied by 4. If you don't realize that, use the Pythagorean theorem to get DA:

$(DA)^2 = (AE)^2 + (DE)^2 = 16^2 + 12^2 = 256 + 144 = 400$
so, $DA = \mathbf{20}$.

16. E. If $3a = 4b = 5c$, then $a = \dfrac{5}{3}c$ and $b = \dfrac{5}{4}c$, so

$a + b = \dfrac{5}{3}c + \dfrac{5}{4}c = \left(\dfrac{5}{3} + \dfrac{5}{4}\right)c = \dfrac{35}{12}c$.

Then $k = \dfrac{\mathbf{35}}{\mathbf{12}}$.

**Use TACTIC 6: plug in easy-to-use numbers. The factors 3, 4, 5 suggest the number 60. Let $a = 20$, $b = 15$, $c = 12$. Then $a + b = 35$, so $35 = 12k$ and $k = \dfrac{\mathbf{35}}{\mathbf{12}}$.

Section 10 Writing Skills

1. B. Lack of parallelism. Choice B demonstrates proper parallel structure: *vegetables*, *assortment*, and *loaf*.

2. C. Lack of parallelism. The correlatives, *not only ... but also* typically connect parallel structures. Choice C reflects the appropriate parallel construction.

3. C. Error in logical comparison. Compare renown with renown, not with a renowned painter.

4. D. Error in subject-verb agreement. The subject, *diseases*, is plural. The verb should be plural as well. Change *has become* to *have become*.

5. E. Error in subject-verb agreement. Do not be misled because the subject follows the verb. Here, the subject, *list*, is singular; the verb should be singular as well. Change *There are* to *There is*.

6. C. Run-on sentence. Do not link two independent clauses with a comma. The addition of the connective *and* in Choice C corrects the error.

7. A. Sentence is correct.

8. D. Error in subject-verb agreement. The subject, *spread*, is singular; the verb should be singular as well. Change *are evolving* to *is evolving*.

9. D. Ambiguous reference. The children were removing the carrots' skins, not their own skins.

10. C. Lack of parallelism. Choice C supplies the appropriate parallel structure.

11. A. Sentence is correct.

12. D. Wordiness. The suggested revision tightens this ineffective compound sentence in two ways: first, it eliminates the connective *and*; second, it repeats the phrase *a scent* to emphasize its importance.

13. E. Sentence fragment. The introduction of a subject (*She*) and the substitution of a main verb (*attempted*) for the participle *Attempting* result in a complete sentence.

14. A. Sentence is correct.

Answer Sheet—Test 4

Section 1   **ESSAY**

Essay (continued)

If a section has fewer questions than answer spaces, leave the extra spaces blank.

Section 2

1 Ⓐ Ⓑ Ⓒ Ⓓ Ⓔ	8 Ⓐ Ⓑ Ⓒ Ⓓ Ⓔ	15 Ⓐ Ⓑ Ⓒ Ⓓ Ⓔ	22 Ⓐ Ⓑ Ⓒ Ⓓ Ⓔ	29 Ⓐ Ⓑ Ⓒ Ⓓ Ⓔ
2 Ⓐ Ⓑ Ⓒ Ⓓ Ⓔ	9 Ⓐ Ⓑ Ⓒ Ⓓ Ⓔ	16 Ⓐ Ⓑ Ⓒ Ⓓ Ⓔ	23 Ⓐ Ⓑ Ⓒ Ⓓ Ⓔ	30 Ⓐ Ⓑ Ⓒ Ⓓ Ⓔ
3 Ⓐ Ⓑ Ⓒ Ⓓ Ⓔ	10 Ⓐ Ⓑ Ⓒ Ⓓ Ⓔ	17 Ⓐ Ⓑ Ⓒ Ⓓ Ⓔ	24 Ⓐ Ⓑ Ⓒ Ⓓ Ⓔ	31 Ⓐ Ⓑ Ⓒ Ⓓ Ⓔ
4 Ⓐ Ⓑ Ⓒ Ⓓ Ⓔ	11 Ⓐ Ⓑ Ⓒ Ⓓ Ⓔ	18 Ⓐ Ⓑ Ⓒ Ⓓ Ⓔ	25 Ⓐ Ⓑ Ⓒ Ⓓ Ⓔ	32 Ⓐ Ⓑ Ⓒ Ⓓ Ⓔ
5 Ⓐ Ⓑ Ⓒ Ⓓ Ⓔ	12 Ⓐ Ⓑ Ⓒ Ⓓ Ⓔ	19 Ⓐ Ⓑ Ⓒ Ⓓ Ⓔ	26 Ⓐ Ⓑ Ⓒ Ⓓ Ⓔ	33 Ⓐ Ⓑ Ⓒ Ⓓ Ⓔ
6 Ⓐ Ⓑ Ⓒ Ⓓ Ⓔ	13 Ⓐ Ⓑ Ⓒ Ⓓ Ⓔ	20 Ⓐ Ⓑ Ⓒ Ⓓ Ⓔ	27 Ⓐ Ⓑ Ⓒ Ⓓ Ⓔ	34 Ⓐ Ⓑ Ⓒ Ⓓ Ⓔ
7 Ⓐ Ⓑ Ⓒ Ⓓ Ⓔ	14 Ⓐ Ⓑ Ⓒ Ⓓ Ⓔ	21 Ⓐ Ⓑ Ⓒ Ⓓ Ⓔ	28 Ⓐ Ⓑ Ⓒ Ⓓ Ⓔ	35 Ⓐ Ⓑ Ⓒ Ⓓ Ⓔ

Section 3

1 Ⓐ Ⓑ Ⓒ Ⓓ Ⓔ	8 Ⓐ Ⓑ Ⓒ Ⓓ Ⓔ	15 Ⓐ Ⓑ Ⓒ Ⓓ Ⓔ	22 Ⓐ Ⓑ Ⓒ Ⓓ Ⓔ	29 Ⓐ Ⓑ Ⓒ Ⓓ Ⓔ
2 Ⓐ Ⓑ Ⓒ Ⓓ Ⓔ	9 Ⓐ Ⓑ Ⓒ Ⓓ Ⓔ	16 Ⓐ Ⓑ Ⓒ Ⓓ Ⓔ	23 Ⓐ Ⓑ Ⓒ Ⓓ Ⓔ	30 Ⓐ Ⓑ Ⓒ Ⓓ Ⓔ
3 Ⓐ Ⓑ Ⓒ Ⓓ Ⓔ	10 Ⓐ Ⓑ Ⓒ Ⓓ Ⓔ	17 Ⓐ Ⓑ Ⓒ Ⓓ Ⓔ	24 Ⓐ Ⓑ Ⓒ Ⓓ Ⓔ	31 Ⓐ Ⓑ Ⓒ Ⓓ Ⓔ
4 Ⓐ Ⓑ Ⓒ Ⓓ Ⓔ	11 Ⓐ Ⓑ Ⓒ Ⓓ Ⓔ	18 Ⓐ Ⓑ Ⓒ Ⓓ Ⓔ	25 Ⓐ Ⓑ Ⓒ Ⓓ Ⓔ	32 Ⓐ Ⓑ Ⓒ Ⓓ Ⓔ
5 Ⓐ Ⓑ Ⓒ Ⓓ Ⓔ	12 Ⓐ Ⓑ Ⓒ Ⓓ Ⓔ	19 Ⓐ Ⓑ Ⓒ Ⓓ Ⓔ	26 Ⓐ Ⓑ Ⓒ Ⓓ Ⓔ	33 Ⓐ Ⓑ Ⓒ Ⓓ Ⓔ
6 Ⓐ Ⓑ Ⓒ Ⓓ Ⓔ	13 Ⓐ Ⓑ Ⓒ Ⓓ Ⓔ	20 Ⓐ Ⓑ Ⓒ Ⓓ Ⓔ	27 Ⓐ Ⓑ Ⓒ Ⓓ Ⓔ	34 Ⓐ Ⓑ Ⓒ Ⓓ Ⓔ
7 Ⓐ Ⓑ Ⓒ Ⓓ Ⓔ	14 Ⓐ Ⓑ Ⓒ Ⓓ Ⓔ	21 Ⓐ Ⓑ Ⓒ Ⓓ Ⓔ	28 Ⓐ Ⓑ Ⓒ Ⓓ Ⓔ	35 Ⓐ Ⓑ Ⓒ Ⓓ Ⓔ

Section 4

1 Ⓐ Ⓑ Ⓒ Ⓓ Ⓔ	8 Ⓐ Ⓑ Ⓒ Ⓓ Ⓔ	15 Ⓐ Ⓑ Ⓒ Ⓓ Ⓔ	22 Ⓐ Ⓑ Ⓒ Ⓓ Ⓔ	29 Ⓐ Ⓑ Ⓒ Ⓓ Ⓔ
2 Ⓐ Ⓑ Ⓒ Ⓓ Ⓔ	9 Ⓐ Ⓑ Ⓒ Ⓓ Ⓔ	16 Ⓐ Ⓑ Ⓒ Ⓓ Ⓔ	23 Ⓐ Ⓑ Ⓒ Ⓓ Ⓔ	30 Ⓐ Ⓑ Ⓒ Ⓓ Ⓔ
3 Ⓐ Ⓑ Ⓒ Ⓓ Ⓔ	10 Ⓐ Ⓑ Ⓒ Ⓓ Ⓔ	17 Ⓐ Ⓑ Ⓒ Ⓓ Ⓔ	24 Ⓐ Ⓑ Ⓒ Ⓓ Ⓔ	31 Ⓐ Ⓑ Ⓒ Ⓓ Ⓔ
4 Ⓐ Ⓑ Ⓒ Ⓓ Ⓔ	11 Ⓐ Ⓑ Ⓒ Ⓓ Ⓔ	18 Ⓐ Ⓑ Ⓒ Ⓓ Ⓔ	25 Ⓐ Ⓑ Ⓒ Ⓓ Ⓔ	32 Ⓐ Ⓑ Ⓒ Ⓓ Ⓔ
5 Ⓐ Ⓑ Ⓒ Ⓓ Ⓔ	12 Ⓐ Ⓑ Ⓒ Ⓓ Ⓔ	19 Ⓐ Ⓑ Ⓒ Ⓓ Ⓔ	26 Ⓐ Ⓑ Ⓒ Ⓓ Ⓔ	33 Ⓐ Ⓑ Ⓒ Ⓓ Ⓔ
6 Ⓐ Ⓑ Ⓒ Ⓓ Ⓔ	13 Ⓐ Ⓑ Ⓒ Ⓓ Ⓔ	20 Ⓐ Ⓑ Ⓒ Ⓓ Ⓔ	27 Ⓐ Ⓑ Ⓒ Ⓓ Ⓔ	34 Ⓐ Ⓑ Ⓒ Ⓓ Ⓔ
7 Ⓐ Ⓑ Ⓒ Ⓓ Ⓔ	14 Ⓐ Ⓑ Ⓒ Ⓓ Ⓔ	21 Ⓐ Ⓑ Ⓒ Ⓓ Ⓔ	28 Ⓐ Ⓑ Ⓒ Ⓓ Ⓔ	35 Ⓐ Ⓑ Ⓒ Ⓓ Ⓔ

Section 6

1 Ⓐ Ⓑ Ⓒ Ⓓ Ⓔ	8 Ⓐ Ⓑ Ⓒ Ⓓ Ⓔ	15 Ⓐ Ⓑ Ⓒ Ⓓ Ⓔ	22 Ⓐ Ⓑ Ⓒ Ⓓ Ⓔ	29 Ⓐ Ⓑ Ⓒ Ⓓ Ⓔ
2 Ⓐ Ⓑ Ⓒ Ⓓ Ⓔ	9 Ⓐ Ⓑ Ⓒ Ⓓ Ⓔ	16 Ⓐ Ⓑ Ⓒ Ⓓ Ⓔ	23 Ⓐ Ⓑ Ⓒ Ⓓ Ⓔ	30 Ⓐ Ⓑ Ⓒ Ⓓ Ⓔ
3 Ⓐ Ⓑ Ⓒ Ⓓ Ⓔ	10 Ⓐ Ⓑ Ⓒ Ⓓ Ⓔ	17 Ⓐ Ⓑ Ⓒ Ⓓ Ⓔ	24 Ⓐ Ⓑ Ⓒ Ⓓ Ⓔ	31 Ⓐ Ⓑ Ⓒ Ⓓ Ⓔ
4 Ⓐ Ⓑ Ⓒ Ⓓ Ⓔ	11 Ⓐ Ⓑ Ⓒ Ⓓ Ⓔ	18 Ⓐ Ⓑ Ⓒ Ⓓ Ⓔ	25 Ⓐ Ⓑ Ⓒ Ⓓ Ⓔ	32 Ⓐ Ⓑ Ⓒ Ⓓ Ⓔ
5 Ⓐ Ⓑ Ⓒ Ⓓ Ⓔ	12 Ⓐ Ⓑ Ⓒ Ⓓ Ⓔ	19 Ⓐ Ⓑ Ⓒ Ⓓ Ⓔ	26 Ⓐ Ⓑ Ⓒ Ⓓ Ⓔ	33 Ⓐ Ⓑ Ⓒ Ⓓ Ⓔ
6 Ⓐ Ⓑ Ⓒ Ⓓ Ⓔ	13 Ⓐ Ⓑ Ⓒ Ⓓ Ⓔ	20 Ⓐ Ⓑ Ⓒ Ⓓ Ⓔ	27 Ⓐ Ⓑ Ⓒ Ⓓ Ⓔ	34 Ⓐ Ⓑ Ⓒ Ⓓ Ⓔ
7 Ⓐ Ⓑ Ⓒ Ⓓ Ⓔ	14 Ⓐ Ⓑ Ⓒ Ⓓ Ⓔ	21 Ⓐ Ⓑ Ⓒ Ⓓ Ⓔ	28 Ⓐ Ⓑ Ⓒ Ⓓ Ⓔ	35 Ⓐ Ⓑ Ⓒ Ⓓ Ⓔ

Test 4

SECTION **1**   **Time—25 Minutes**   **ESSAY**

> The excerpt appearing below makes a point about a particular topic. Read the passage carefully, and think about the assignment that follows.

We most resent in others the very flaws that we ourselves possess.

ASSIGNMENT: What are your thoughts on the statement above? Do you agree or disagree with the writer's assertion? Compose an essay in which you express your views on this topic. Your essay may support, refute, or qualify the view expressed in the statement. What you write, however, must be relevant to the topic under discussion. Additionally, you must support your viewpoint, indicating your reasoning and providing examples based on your studies and/or experience.

2   2 2 2 2 2 2 2 2 2   2

SECTION 2   Time—25 Minutes   Select the best answer to each of the following questions; then
24 Questions   blacken the appropriate space on your answer sheet.

Each of the following sentences contains one or two blanks; each blank indicates that a word or set of words has been left out. Below the sentence are five words or phrases, lettered A through E. Select the word or set of words that best completes the sentence.

Example:

Fame is ----; today's rising star is all too soon tomorrow's washed-up has-been.

(A) rewarding   (B) gradual
(C) essential   (D) spontaneous
  (E) transitory

Ⓐ Ⓑ Ⓒ Ⓓ ●

1. He felt that the uninspiring routine of office work was too ---- for someone of his talent and creativity.

(A) diverse   (B) insatiable   (C) exacting
  (D) enthralling   (E) prosaic

2. The museum arranged the fossils in ---- order, placing the older fossils dating from the Late Ice Age on the first floor and the more recent fossils on the second floor.

(A) alphabetical
(B) chronological
(C) random
(D) arbitrary
(E) retrospective

3. With the evolution of wings, insects were able to ---- to the far ecological corners, across deserts and bodies of water, to reach new food sources and inhabit a wider variety of promising environmental niches.

(A) relate   (B) disperse   (C) transgress
  (D) revert   (E) ascend

4. Having recently missed out on the Matisse retrospective, which has taken Paris and New York by storm, and on the tour of great paintings from Philadelphia's Barnes collection, London is becoming ---- in the competition to show ---- international art exhibitions.

(A) a trend-setter..major
(B) an also-ran..blockbuster
(C) a world-beater..itinerant
(D) a mecca..distinguished
(E) a connoisseur..esoteric

5. What most ---- the magazine's critics is the manner in which its editorial opinions are expressed—too often as if only an idiot could see things any other way.

(A) belies
(B) impedes
(C) riles
(D) placates
(E) identifies

6. Despite her compassionate nature, the new nominee to the Supreme Court was single-minded and ---- in her strict ---- the letter of the law.

(A) merciful..interpretation of
(B) uncompromising..adherence to
(C) dilatory..affirmation of
(D) vindictive..deviation from
(E) lenient..dismissal of

7. Although he generally observed the adage "Look before you leap," in this instance he was ---- acting in an unconsidered fashion.

(A) chary of
(B) impervious to
(C) precipitate in
(D) hesitant about
(E) conventional in

8. Crabeater seal, the common name of *Lobodon carcinophagus*, is a ----, since the animal's staple diet is not crabs, but krill.

(A) pseudonym
(B) misnomer
(C) delusion
(D) digression
(E) compromise

GO ON TO THE NEXT PAGE

Read each of the passages below, and then answer the questions that follow the passage. The correct response may be stated outright or merely suggested in the passage.

Questions 9 and 10 are based on the following passage.

In the 1880's, when the commercial theater had ceased to be regarded as a fit medium for serious writers, British intellectuals came to
Line champion the plays of an obscure Norwegian
(5) dramatist. Hungry for a theater that spoke to their intellects, they wholeheartedly embraced the social realist dramas of Henrik Ibsen. Eleanor Marx, daughter of Karl Marx, went so far as to teach herself Norwegian in order to translate
(10) Ibsen's *A Doll's House*, which she presented in an amateur performance in a Bloomsbury drawing room.

9. The word "embraced" (line 6) most nearly means

(A) clasped
(B) adopted
(C) comprised
(D) incorporated
(E) hugged

10. The discussion of Eleanor Marx in lines 7–12 ("Eleanor . . . room") serves primarily to

(A) propose a counterexample
(B) correct an inaccurate statement
(C) introduce a questionable hypothesis
(D) support an earlier assertion
(E) acknowledge a factual discrepancy

Questions 11 and 12 are based on the following passage.

According to reports from psychologists world-wide, measures of personal happiness hardly change as the national income rises. This finding
Line has led many social critics to maintain that income
(5) growth has ceased to foster well-being. A moment's recollection suggests otherwise. I remember years ago when our car clanked and juddered and limped into a garage, warning lights ablaze. "Threw a rod," said the mechanic. "Junk her." I remember
(10) interminable trips to used-car lots, sleepless nights worrying about debt, calls to friends about possible leads. Recently, my wife suggested we get a new car. "Great!" I said. "What about a hybrid?"
Money can't buy happiness, but having money
(15) sure takes the pressure off.

11. In lines 6–13, the author uses a personal anecdote to

(A) warn about the dangers of consumer debt
(B) explain what caused the author's engine trouble
(C) suggest the range of the author's tastes in automobiles
(D) express an unorthodox view about psychology
(E) contradict the social critics' conclusion

12. The author's tone in the closing lines of the passage (lines 14 and 15) can best be characterized as

(A) breezy
(B) objective
(C) cautionary
(D) ambivalent
(E) nostalgic

Questions 13–24 are based on the following passage.

The writer John Updike muses on the significance of Mickey Mouse.

Cartoon characters have soul as Carl Jung defined it in his *Archetypes and the Collective Unconscious*: "soul is a life-giving demon who
Line plays his elfin game above and below human
(5) existence." Without the "leaping and twinkling of the soul," Jung says, "man would rot away in his greatest passion, idleness." The Mickey Mouse of the thirties shorts was a whirlwind of activity, with a host of unsuspected skills and a reluctant
(10) heroism that rose to every occasion. Like Chaplin and Douglas Fairbanks and Fred Astaire, he acted out our fantasies of endless nimbleness, of perfect weightlessness. Yet withal, there was nothing aggressive or self-promoting about him, as there
(15) was about Popeye. Disney, interviewed in the thirties, said, "Sometimes I've tried to figure out why Mickey appealed to the whole world. Everybody's tried to figure it out. So far as I know, nobody has. He's a pretty nice fellow who
(20) never does anybody any harm, who gets into scrapes through no fault of his own, but always manages to come up grinning." This was perhaps Disney's image of himself: for twenty years he

GO ON TO THE NEXT PAGE

did Mickey's voice in the films, and would often
(25) say, "There's a lot of the Mouse in me." Mickey
was a character created with his own pen, and
nurtured on Disney's memories of his mouse-rid-
den Kansas City studio and of the Missouri farm
where his struggling father tried for a time to
(30) make a living. Walt's humble, scrambling begin-
nings remained embodied in the mouse, whom
the Nazis, in a fury against the Mickey-inspired
Allied legions (the Allied code word on D-Day
was "Mickey Mouse"), called "the most miser-
(35) able ideal ever revealed...mice are dirty."
But was Disney, like Mickey, just "a pretty
nice fellow"? He was until crossed in his driving
perfectionism, his Napoleonic capacity to marshal
men and take risks in the service of an artistic and
(40) entrepreneurial vision. He was one of those great
Americans, like Edison and Henry Ford, who
invented themselves in terms of a new technology. The technology—in Disney's case, film
animation—would have been there anyway, but
(45) only a few driven men seized the full possibilities
and made empires. In the dozen years between
Steamboat Willie and *Fantasia*, the Disney stu-
dios took the art of animation to heights of ambition and accomplishment it would never have
(50) reached otherwise, and Disney's personal zeal
was the animating force. He created an empire of
the mind, and its emperor was Mickey Mouse.
The thirties were Mickey's conquering decade.
His image circled the globe. In Africa, tribesmen
(55) painfully had tiny mosaic Mickey Mouses inset
into their front teeth, and a South African tribe
refused to buy soap unless the cakes were
embossed with Mickey's image. Nor were the
high and mighty immune to Mickey's elemental
(60) appeal—King George V and Franklin Roosevelt
insisted that all film showings they attended
include a dose of Mickey Mouse. But other popular phantoms, like Felix the Cat, have faded,
where Mickey has settled into the national collec-
(65) tive consciousness. The television program
revived him for my children's generation, and the
theme parks make him live for my grandchildren's. Yet survival cannot be imposed through
weight of publicity. Mickey's persistence springs
(70) from something unhyped, something timeless in
the image that has allowed it to pass in status
from a fad to an icon.
To take a bite out of our imaginations, an icon
must be simple. The ears, the wiggly tail, the red
(75) shorts, give us a Mickey. Donald Duck and
Goofy, Bugs Bunny and Woody Woodpecker are
inextricably bound up with the draftsmanship of
the artists who make them move and squawk, but
Mickey floats free. It was Claes Oldenburg's pop

(80) art that first alerted me to the fact that Mickey
Mouse had passed out of the realm of commercially generated image into that of artifact. A new
Disney gadget, advertised on television, is a cam-
era-like box that spouts bubbles when a key is
(85) turned; the key consists of three circles, two
mounted on a larger one, and the image is unmistakably Mickey. Like yin and yang, like the
Christian cross and the star of Israel, Mickey can
be seen everywhere—a sign, a rune, a hiero-
(90) glyphic trace of a secret power, an electricity we
want to plug into. Like totem poles, like African
masks, Mickey stands at that intersection of
abstraction and representation where magic
connects.

13. The author's attitude toward Popeye in lines 13–15
is primarily
(A) nostalgic
(B) deprecatory
(C) apathetic
(D) vindictive
(E) reverent

14. By describing Mickey's skills as "unsuspected" and
his heroism as "reluctant" (line 9), the author pri-
marily conveys Mickey's
(A) unassuming nature
(B) unrealistic success
(C) contradictory image
(D) ignominious failings
(E) idealistic character

15. The word "scrapes" in line 21 means
(A) abrasions
(B) harsh sounds
(C) small economies
(D) discarded fragments
(E) predicaments

16. By saying "There's a lot of the Mouse in me" (line
25), Disney revealed
(A) his inability to distinguish himself as an
individual
(B) the extent of his identification with his creation
(C) the desire to capitalize on his character's
popularity
(D) his fear of being surpassed by a creature he
produced
(E) his somewhat negative image of himself

GO ON TO THE NEXT PAGE

17. The reference to the Nazis' comments on Mickey (lines 32–35) can best be described as

    (A) a digression
    (B) a metaphor
    (C) an analysis
    (D) an equivocation
    (E) a refutation

18. The word "crossed" in line 37 means

    (A) traversed
    (B) confused
    (C) intersected
    (D) encountered
    (E) opposed

19. The author views Disney as all of the following EXCEPT

    (A) a self-made man
    (B) a demanding artist
    (C) an enterprising businessman
    (D) the inventor of film animation
    (E) an empire-builder

20. The references to the African tribesmen (lines 54–58) and to Franklin Roosevelt (line 60) serve primarily to

    (A) demonstrate the improbability of Mickey's reaching such disparate audiences
    (B) dispel a misconception about the nature of Mickey's popularity
    (C) support the assertion that people of all backgrounds were drawn to Mickey Mouse
    (D) show how much research the author has done into the early history of Disney cartoons
    (E) answer the charges made by critics of Disney's appeal

21. The distinction made between a "fad" and an "icon" (lines 68–72) can best be summarized as which of the following?

    (A) The first is a popular fashion, the second attracts only a small group.
    (B) The first involves a greater degree of audience involvement than the second.
    (C) The first is less likely to need publicity than the second.
    (D) The first is less enduring in appeal than is the second.
    (E) The first conveys greater prestige than the second.

22. The phrase "take a bite out of our imaginations" (line 73) most nearly means

    (A) injure our creativity
    (B) reduce our innovative capacity
    (C) cut into our inspiration
    (D) capture our fancies
    (E) limit our visions

23. The author's description of the new Disney gadget (lines 82–87) does which of the following?

    (A) It suggests that popular new product lines are still being manufactured by Disney.
    (B) It demonstrates that even a rudimentary outline can convey the image of Mickey.
    (C) It illustrates the importance of television advertising in marketing new products.
    (D) It disproves the notion that Disney's death has undermined his mercantile empire.
    (E) It refutes the author's assertion that Mickey's survival springs from something unhyped.

24. Which of the following most resembles the new Disney gadget (lines 82–87) in presenting Mickey as an artifact?

    (A) A comic book presenting the adventures of Mickey Mouse
    (B) A rubber mask realistically portraying Mickey's features
    (C) A Mickey Mouse watch on which Mickey's hands point at the time
    (D) A Mickey Mouse waffle iron that makes waffles in the shape of three linked circles
    (E) A framed cell or single strip from an original Mickey Mouse animated film

YOU MAY GO BACK AND REVIEW THIS SECTION IN THE REMAINING TIME, BUT DO NOT WORK IN ANY OTHER SECTION UNTIL TOLD TO DO SO.   **S T O P**

SECTION 3

Time—25 Minutes
20 Questions

For each problem in this section determine which of the five choices is correct and blacken the corresponding choice on your answer sheet. You may use any blank space on the page for your work.

Notes:

- You may use a calculator whenever you think it will be helpful.
- Only real numbers are used. No question or answer on this test involves a complex or imaginary number.
- Use the diagrams provided to help you solve the problems. Unless you see the words "Note: Figure not drawn to scale" under a diagram, it has been drawn as accurately as possible. Unless it is stated that a figure is three-dimensional, you may assume it lies in a plane.
- For any function f, the domain, unless specifically restricted, is the set of all real numbers for which $f(x)$ is also a real number.

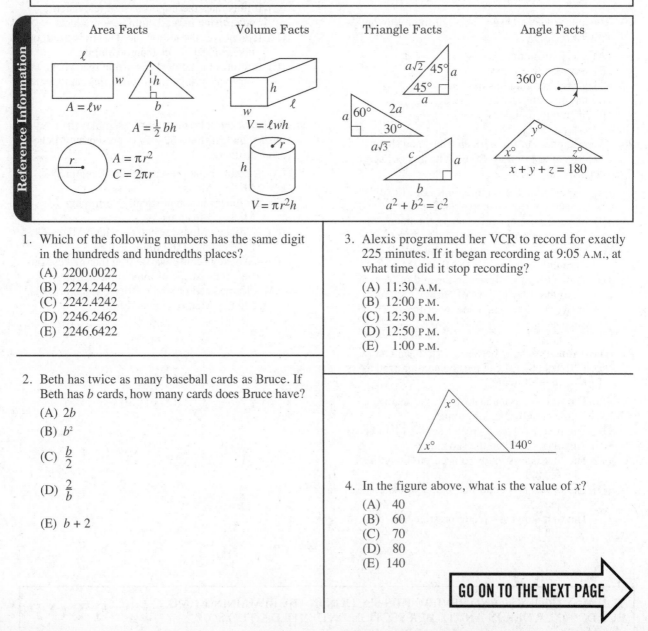

Reference Information

Area Facts

$A = \ell w$

$A = \frac{1}{2} bh$

$A = \pi r^2$
$C = 2\pi r$

Volume Facts

$V = \ell w h$

$V = \pi r^2 h$

Triangle Facts

$a^2 + b^2 = c^2$

Angle Facts

$360°$

$x + y + z = 180$

1. Which of the following numbers has the same digit in the hundreds and hundredths places?

(A) 2200.0022
(B) 2224.2442
(C) 2242.4242
(D) 2246.2462
(E) 2246.6422

2. Beth has twice as many baseball cards as Bruce. If Beth has b cards, how many cards does Bruce have?

(A) $2b$

(B) b^2

(C) $\frac{b}{2}$

(D) $\frac{2}{b}$

(E) $b + 2$

3. Alexis programmed her VCR to record for exactly 225 minutes. If it began recording at 9:05 A.M., at what time did it stop recording?

(A) 11:30 A.M.
(B) 12:00 P.M.
(C) 12:30 P.M.
(D) 12:50 P.M.
(E) 1:00 P.M.

4. In the figure above, what is the value of x?

(A) 40
(B) 60
(C) 70
(D) 80
(E) 140

GO ON TO THE NEXT PAGE

3   3   3   3   3   3   3   3   3   3   3   3

5. If the difference of two numbers is greater than the sum of the numbers, which of the following *must* be true?

(A) Neither number is negative.
(B) At least one of the numbers is negative.
(C) Exactly one of the numbers is negative.
(D) Both numbers are negative.
(E) None of these statements *must* be true.

6. $(3a^2b^3)^3 =$

(A) $9a^5b^6$
(B) $9a^6b^9$
(C) $27a^5b^6$
(D) $27a^6b^9$
(E) $27a^8b^{27}$

7. Anne-Marie was x years old y years ago. How old will she be in z years?

(A) $x + y + z$
(B) $x - y + z$
(C) $z - x - y$
(D) $y - x + z$
(E) $x - y - z$

8. 10 is what percent of A?

(A) $10A\%$

(B) $\dfrac{1}{10A}\%$

(C) $\dfrac{10}{A}\%$

(D) $\dfrac{100}{A}\%$

(E) $\dfrac{1000}{A}\%$

9. A rectangle has a perimeter equal to the circumference of a circle of radius 3. If the width of the rectangle is 3, what is its length?

(A) $3\pi - 3$
(B) $4.5\pi - 3$
(C) $6\pi - 6$
(D) $9\pi - 3$
(E) $9\pi - 6$

10. If Anthony had 3 times as many marbles as he actually has, he would have $\frac{1}{3}$ as many marbles as Billy has. What is the ratio of the number of marbles Anthony has to the number of marbles Billy has?

(A) 1:9
(B) 1:3
(C) 1:1
(D) 3:1
(E) 9:1

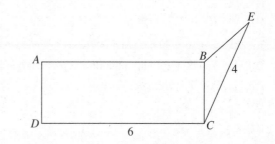

11. In the figure above, $\overline{BC} \cong \overline{BE}$. If R represents the perimeter of rectangle $ABCD$, and T represents the perimeter of $\triangle CBE$, what is the value of $R - T$?

(A) 2
(B) 8
(C) 20
(D) $12 - 4\sqrt{2}$
(E) It cannot be determined from the information given.

12. Two cylindrical tanks have the same height, but the radius of one tank equals the diameter of the other. If the volume of the larger is $k\%$ more than the volume of the smaller, $k =$

(A) 50
(B) 100
(C) 200
(D) 300
(E) 400

GO ON TO THE NEXT PAGE

Test 4

13. For any positive numbers a, b, c, d, is defined to be a number box if $ac = bd$ and $a = b + c + d$.

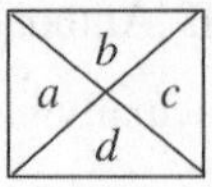

If 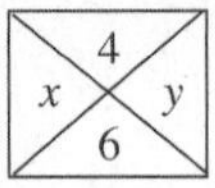 is a number box, then $x + y =$

(A) 8
(B) 10
(C) 12
(D) 14
(E) 24

14. If $f(x) = 3x + 8$, for what value of a is $f(a) = a$?

(A) −4
(B) −2
(C) $-\frac{3}{8}$
(D) 0
(E) $\frac{3}{8}$

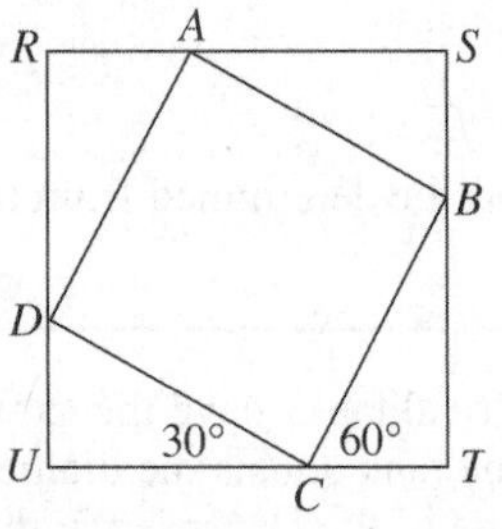

15. In the figure above, if the perimeter of square $ABCD$ is 8, what is the perimeter of square $RSTU$?

(A) $4 + 4\sqrt{3}$
(B) $8\sqrt{3}$
(C) 12
(D) 16
(E) It cannot be determined from the information given.

16. If $x + y = a$, $y + z = b$, and $x + z = c$, what is the average (arithmetic mean) of x, y, and z?

(A) $\dfrac{a + b + c}{2}$
(B) $\dfrac{a + b + c}{3}$
(C) $\dfrac{a + b + c}{4}$
(D) $\dfrac{a + b + c}{6}$
(E) $\dfrac{a + b + c}{12}$

17. A circular grass field has a circumference of $120\sqrt{\pi}$ meters. If Eric can mow 400 square meters of grass per hour, how many hours will he take to mow the entire field?

(A) 4
(B) 5
(C) 6
(D) 8
(E) 9

18. If $X = \dfrac{ab^2}{c}$, what is the result on X of doubling a, tripling b, and quadrupling c?

(A) X is multiplied by 1.5.
(B) X is multiplied by 3.
(C) X is multiplied by 4.5.
(D) X is multiplied by 6.
(E) X is multiplied by 9.

GO ON TO THE NEXT PAGE

19. A sequence of numbers begins 1, 1, 1, 2, 2, 3 and then repeats this pattern of six numbers forever. What is the sum of the 135th, 136th, and 137th numbers in the sequence?

(A) 3
(B) 4
(C) 5
(D) 6
(E) 7

20. The measures of the three angles of a triangle are in the ratio of 5:5:10, and the length of the longest side is 10. From this information, which of the following can be determined?

   I. The area of the triangle

   II. The perimeter of the triangle

   III. The length of each of the three altitudes

(A) I only
(B) II only
(C) III only
(D) I and II only
(E) I, II, and III

SECTION 4 **Time—25 Minutes** Select the best answer to each of the following questions; then
35 Questions blacken the appropriate space on your answer sheet.

Some or all parts of the following sentences are underlined. The first answer choice, (A), simply repeats the
underlined part of the sentence. The other four choices
present four alternative ways to phrase the underlined
part. Select the answer that produces the most effective sentence, one that is clear and exact, and blacken
the appropriate space on your answer sheet. In selecting your choice, be sure that it is standard written
English, and that it expresses the meaning of the original sentence.

Example:

The first biography of author Eudora Welty
came out in 1998 and she was 89 years old at
the time.

(A) and she was 89 years old at the time
(B) at the time when she was 89
(C) upon becoming an 89 year old
(D) when she was 89
(E) at the age of 89 years old

Ⓐ Ⓑ Ⓒ ● Ⓔ

1. Are psychiatrists unusually vulnerable to mental
   illness, or are they merely more aware of their problems than the rest of us?

   (A) problems than the rest of us
   (B) problems as us
   (C) problems than they are aware of us
   (D) problems like we are
   (E) problems like ours are

2. When used undiluted, you can irritate your skin with
   liquid bleach.

   (A) you can irritate your skin with liquid bleach
   (B) liquid bleach can irritate your skin
   (C) bleach, it being liquid, could irritate your skin
   (D) you could be irritating your skin with liquid
       bleach
   (E) then liquid bleach could be irritating to your
       skin

3. The authors, taking on a formidable and sensitive
   subject, has largely conquered it, thanks to indefatigable research and a rigorous analysis of the data.

   (A) taking on a formidable and sensitive subject,
       has largely conquered it, thanks to indefatiga-
       ble research
   (B) took on a formidable and sensitive subject; but
       has largely conquered it, thanks to indefatiga-
       ble research
   (C) taking on a formidable and sensitive subject,
       have largely conquered it, thanks to indefati-
       gable research
   (D) taking on a formidable and sensitive subject,
       have largely conquered them, thanks to
       indefatigable research
   (E) taking on a formidably sensitive subject, has
       largely conquered it, due to indefatigable
       research

4. Paul Bertolli followed a typically meandering route
   for a contemporary American chef, earning a degree
   in music at Berkeley, working in restaurants in
   California and Italy, and took time off to study history in Canada before becoming the chef at Oliveto.

   (A) working in restaurants in California and Italy,
       and took time off to study history in Canada
       before becoming
   (B) working in restaurants in California and Italy,
       and taking time off to study history in
       Canada before becoming
   (C) and he worked in restaurants in California and
       Italy, and took time off to study history in
       Canada before becoming
   (D) working in restaurants in California and Italy,
       and took time off to study history in Canada
       before he had become
   (E) he worked in restaurants in California and Italy,
       and he took time off to study history in
       Canada before becoming

GO ON TO THE NEXT PAGE

5. Many of the innovations in the early compositions of Charles Ives were adaptations of musical experiments performed by his father, particularly that of polytonality.

   (A) Ives were adaptations of musical experiments performed by his father, particularly that of polytonality
   (B) Ives, and in particular polytonality, was an adaptation of musical experiments performed by his father
   (C) Ives being adapted, and polytonality in particular, from musical experiments performed by his father
   (D) Ives, these were adaptations of musical experiments performed by his father, particularly that of polytonality
   (E) Ives, particularly polytonality, were adaptations of musical experiments performed by his father

6. There is a great deal of practical advice on antiques that readers may find useful in the mystery novels of Jonathan Gash.

   (A) There is a great deal of practical advice on antiques that readers may find useful in the mystery novels of Jonathan Gash.
   (B) There are great deals of practical advice regarding antiques that readers may find useful in Jonathan Gash's mystery novels.
   (C) Readers may find useful the great deal of practical advice on antiques in Jonathan Gash's mystery novels.
   (D) A great deal of practical and useful advice on antiques are offered to readers by Jonathan Gash in his mystery novels.
   (E) In his mystery novels, Jonathan Gash offers readers a great deal of practical advice on antiques.

7. Of the three Fates, the weavers Clotho, Lachesis, and Atropos, the latter was most frightening, for she cut the "thread" of life, thus determining the individual's moment of death.

   (A) the latter was most frightening
   (B) the latter was more frightening
   (C) the latter is most frightening
   (D) the last was most frightening
   (E) the last are more frightening

8. A popular lecturer who spoke as eloquently on Christianity as literature, Lewis combined faith and fiction in his allegorical tales of Narnia.

   (A) as eloquently on Christianity as literature
   (B) with eloquence on Christianity and literature also
   (C) eloquently on Christianity so much as on literature
   (D) so eloquently on Christianity plus literature
   (E) as eloquently on Christianity as on literature

9. Administration officials have consistently sought to stonewall, undermine, or intimidating anyone who might try to check up on their performance.

   (A) undermine, or intimidating anyone who might try to check up on their performance
   (B) undermine, or intimidating those who might try to check up on their performance
   (C) undermine, or intimidating anyone who might try to check up about their performance
   (D) undermine, or intimidate anyone who might try to check up on their performance
   (E) undermine, or to be intimidating anyone who might be trying to check up on their performance

10. Although I understand why airlines have to serve frozen foods to their passengers, I do not understand why I was served a meal by a flight attendant that had been only partially defrosted.

    (A) a meal by a flight attendant that had been only partially defrosted
    (B) an only partially defrosted meal by a flight attendant
    (C) a meal that had been only partially defrosted by a flight attendant
    (D) by a flight attendant a meal that had been only partially defrosted
    (E) by a flight attendant of a partially defrosted meal

11. An important factor in the spread of disease is when people fail to practice proper hygiene.

    (A) An important factor in the spread of disease is when
    (B) An important factor in spreading disease is when
    (C) An important factor in the spread of disease is that
    (D) Much of the spread of disease results from when
    (E) Much of the spread of disease is due to the fact that when

GO ON TO THE NEXT PAGE ▷

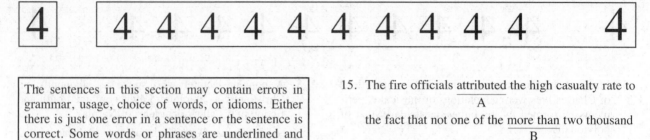

The sentences in this section may contain errors in grammar, usage, choice of words, or idioms. Either there is just one error in a sentence or the sentence is correct. Some words or phrases are underlined and lettered; everything else in the sentence is correct.

If an underlined word or phrase is incorrect, choose that letter; if the sentence is correct, select <u>No error</u>. Then blacken the appropriate space on your answer sheet.

Example:

The region has a climate <u>so severe that</u> plants
                      A

<u>growing</u> there <u>rarely had been</u> more than twelve
  B   C

inches <u>high</u>. <u>No error</u>
     D   E

Ⓐ Ⓑ ● Ⓓ Ⓔ

12. Irregardless of the danger, the outnumbered
      A   B
soldiers of the Light Brigade obeyed the orders of

their commander and <u>charged</u> the enemy forces.
  C   D
<u>No error</u>
   E

13. The President has <u>designated</u> Senator Frank <u>as one</u>
              A   B
of the Congressmen who are <u>going</u> to attend the
                      C
conference <u>on</u> nuclear waste disposal. <u>No error</u>
         D   E

14. In American history, we studied <u>the reasons that</u>
                                A
the American colonists <u>came</u> to oppose the British,
                  B
the formation of the Continental Congress,
              C
and how <u>they organized the militia</u>. <u>No error</u>
              D   E

15. The fire officials <u>attributed</u> the high casualty rate to
             A
the fact that not one of the <u>more than</u> two thousand
                  B
rooms in the hotel <u>were equipped</u> with sprinklers
                 C
<u>or</u> smoke detectors. <u>No error</u>
 D   E

16. The students in the audience <u>became</u> restive and
                     A
noisy <u>when</u> the curtain failed to <u>raise</u> at the
     B   C
<u>scheduled time</u>. <u>No error</u>
    D   E

17. There <u>have been</u> <u>remarkable</u> progress in the
     A   B
biological sciences since Crick and Watson <u>jointly</u>
                              C
discovered the <u>structure of DNA</u>. <u>No error</u>
            D   E

18. If one follows the discipline of Hatha Yoga,

<u>you know</u> the <u>critical</u> importance of purificatory
  A   B
processes, the regulation of breathing, and the

adoption of certain <u>bodily</u> postures, such as
      C   D
the lotus position. <u>No error</u>
            E

19. Oprah Winfrey <u>has</u> the <u>distinction of</u> having
          A   B
promoted the sales <u>of more</u> serious contemporary
            C
novels than <u>any</u> talk show host. <u>No error</u>
     D   E

GO ON TO THE NEXT PAGE

4　　4　4　4　4　4　4　4　4　4　4　| 4

20. The new inspector general's office in Iraq

    $\underset{A}{\underline{\text{operates under}}}$ $\underset{B}{\underline{\text{most unique}}}$ rules that $\underset{C}{\underline{\text{greatly limit}}}$

    both its powers and $\underset{D}{\underline{\text{its}}}$ independence. $\underset{E}{\underline{\text{No error}}}$

21. Chinese scientists analyzing the genome of the

    SARS virus $\underset{A}{\underline{\text{have documented}}}$ the immense rapidity

    $\underset{B}{\underline{\text{with which}}}$ it $\underset{C}{\underline{\text{evolved from}}}$ an animal pathogen into

    one $\underset{D}{\underline{\text{capable to}}}$ infecting human cells. $\underset{E}{\underline{\text{No error}}}$

22. Also in the program $\underset{A}{\underline{\text{is}}}$ a taped $\underset{B}{\underline{\text{discussion with}}}$ the

    $\underset{C}{\underline{\text{late}}}$ choreographer George Balanchine and a

    $\underset{D}{\underline{\text{performance by}}}$ Patricia McBride and Edward

    Villella of the pas de deux from "Diana and

    Acteon." $\underset{E}{\underline{\text{No error}}}$

23. Fifty years ago, movies $\underset{A}{\underline{\text{on}}}$ biblical themes,

    $\underset{B}{\underline{\text{far from being}}}$ the $\underset{C}{\underline{\text{more}}}$ controversial Hollywood

    offerings, $\underset{D}{\underline{\text{were among}}}$ the least. $\underset{E}{\underline{\text{No error}}}$

24. *The Bronte Myth,* Lucasta Miller's study of the

    three British novelists, $\underset{A}{\underline{\text{attempts}}}$ to trace the

    historical route $\underset{B}{\underline{\text{by which}}}$ Charlotte and Emily

    Bronte (and, $\underset{C}{\underline{\text{to a less degree,}}}$ Anne) became

    $\underset{D}{\underline{\text{popular}}}$ cultural icons. $\underset{E}{\underline{\text{No error}}}$

25. Religion $\underset{A}{\underline{\text{is}}}$, $\underset{B}{\underline{\text{like}}}$ sex and politics, one of those

    subjects traditionally $\underset{C}{\underline{\text{to be avoided}}}$ at dinner

    parties or family reunions, $\underset{D}{\underline{\text{lest inflamed}}}$ passions

    disrupt civility. $\underset{E}{\underline{\text{No error}}}$

26. Opinions on Charles Ives as a composer

    have always been split, $\underset{A}{\underline{\text{with some}}}$ listeners

    regarding him as, at best, an entertaining eccentric,
    $\underset{B}{\underline{}}$

    $\underset{C}{\underline{\text{while others lauding}}}$ him as the $\underset{D}{\underline{\text{most influential}}}$

    composer of his age. $\underset{E}{\underline{\text{No error}}}$

27. Reviewing the ballet, the *Times* dance critic

    expressed her $\underset{A}{\underline{\text{liking for}}}$ Damian Woetzel's

    affecting performance, $\underset{B}{\underline{\text{which}}}$, she wrote, was

    $\underset{C}{\underline{\text{more compelling}}}$ $\underset{D}{\underline{\text{than}}}$ the other dancers. $\underset{E}{\underline{\text{No error}}}$

28. The annual guest lecture, originally $\underset{A}{\underline{\text{scheduled for}}}$

    fall semester, is $\underset{B}{\underline{\text{liable}}}$ to be $\underset{C}{\underline{\text{postponed}}}$ until spring

    because of the visiting lecturer's $\underset{D}{\underline{\text{extended}}}$ illness.

    $\underset{E}{\underline{\text{No error}}}$

29. In the nineteenth century, photography was a

    $\underset{A}{\underline{\text{window on}}}$ the world for curious members of

    the public, $\underset{B}{\underline{\text{few of which}}}$ $\underset{C}{\underline{\text{could ever hope}}}$ to visit

    exotic lands $\underset{D}{\underline{\text{in person}}}$. $\underset{E}{\underline{\text{No error}}}$

GO ON TO THE NEXT PAGE ⟶

The passage below is the unedited draft of a student's essay. Parts of the essay need to be rewritten to make the meaning clearer and more precise. Read the essay carefully.

The essay is followed by six questions about changes that might improve all or part of the organization, development, sentence structure, use of language, appropriateness to the audience, or use of standard written English. In each case, choose the answer that most clearly and effectively expresses the student's intended meaning. Indicate your choice by blackening the corresponding space on the answer sheet.

[1] At the beginning of the twentieth century, no one knew the technological developments that would be made by the 1990s. [2] The area of communication media is one of the significant developments in the twentieth century. [3] Also nuclear energy and great advancements in medicine and the treatment of disease.

[4] One important development was the invention of communication satellites which allow images and messages to be sent wirelessly around the world. [5] One advantage is that current events can be sent worldwide in seconds. [6] News used to travel by boat and take weeks or months to get overseas. [7] When a disaster struck the World Trade Center, the world saw it immediately and condemned the terrorists' actions. [8] One weak aspect of communication satellites is that they are launched from a space shuttle, and that is an extremely costly operation. [9] They also cost millions of dollars to build and operate. [10] Therefore, many poor countries are left out of the so-called "Global Village."

[11] The invention and use of nuclear energy is another important technological development. [12] One positive feature of nuclear energy is that energy is cheaper, and can be made easy. [13] This is important in countries like France where almost all of the electricity is nuclear. [14] A negative consequence of nuclear energy is the probability of major nuclear accidents. [15] Watch out for human error and careless workmanship. [16] They were the cause of the meltdown in Chernobyl, which killed hundreds or maybe even thousands, and radiated half the Earth.

[17] There have been many significant technological advances in medicine in the twentieth century. [18] One development was the invention of the CAT scan. [19] The CAT scan allows doctors to make a picture of your brain to see if there is a growth on it. [20] One positive effect of the CAT scan is that doctors can diagnose brain tumors and brain cancer at an early stage. [21] One negative effect is that CAT scans are costly, so they are not used in third world countries.

30. In view of the main idea of the whole essay, which of the following is the best revision of sentence 1?

   (A) In 1900 no one could anticipate the technological developments in the 1990s.
   (B) Recent technological achievements would blow the minds of people at the beginning of the twentieth century.
   (C) The twentieth century has seen remarkable technological achievements, but there has also been a price to pay for progress.
   (D) No one knows if the twenty-first century will produce as much technological progress as the twentieth century did.
   (E) Technological progress in communications, nuclear energy, and medicine is wonderful, but in the process we are destroying ourselves and our environment.

31. Which is the best revision of the underlined segment of sentence 12 below?

   One positive feature of nuclear energy is that <u>*energy is cheaper, and can be made easy.*</u>

   (A) energy is cheaper and can be made easily
   (B) energy is made cheaper and more easily made
   (C) it is cheap and easy to make
   (D) it is both cheap as well as made easily
   (E) it's more cheaper and easier to make

32. To improve the coherence of paragraph 2, which of the following is the best sentence to delete from the essay?

   (A) Sentence 5
   (B) Sentence 6
   (C) Sentence 7
   (D) Sentence 8
   (E) Sentence 9

33. In the context of the sentences that precede and follow sentence 15, which is the best revision of sentence 15?

   (A) Human error and careless workmanship are almost unavoidable.
   (B) Especially human error and careless workmanship.
   (C) There's hardly no foolproof way to prevent human error and careless workmanship.
   (D) You must never put down your guard against human error and careless workmanship.
   (E) Accidents can happen accidentally by human error and careless workmanship.

GO ON TO THE NEXT PAGE

34. With regard to the entire essay, which of the following best explains the writer's intention in paragraphs 2, 3, and 4?

    (A) To compare and contrast three technological achievements
    (B) To provide examples of the pros and cons of technological progress
    (C) To analyze the steps needed for achievement in three areas
    (D) To convince the reader to be open to technological change
    (E) To advocate more funds for technological research and development

35. Assume that sentences 17 and 18 were combined as follows: *A significant advance in medicine has been the invention of the CAT scan.* Which of the following is the best way to continue the paragraph?

    (A) The CAT scan allows your doctors to make pictures of a brain to see if it has a growth on it, a cancer is growing, or tumors at an early stage.
    (B) The CAT scan permits your doctors to make a picture and see if your brain has a growth on it, or whether or not you have brain tumors or brain cancer at an early stage.
    (C) Taking pictures with a CAT scan, your brain is studied by doctors for growths, brain tumors, and cancer at an early stage.
    (D) Doctors may make pictures of your brain to see if there is a growth, a tumor, or cancer at an early stage on it.
    (E) With this device a doctor may look into a patient's brain to check for growths and to detect cancerous tumors at an early stage.

SECTION 6   **Time—25 Minutes**
24 Questions

Select the best answer to each of the following questions; then blacken the appropriate space on your answer sheet.

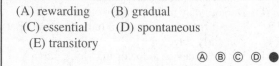

Each of the following sentences contains one or two blanks; each blank indicates that a word or set of words has been left out. Below the sentence are five words or phrases, lettered A through E. Select the word or set of words that best completes the sentence.

Example:

Fame is ----; today's rising star is all too soon tomorrow's washed-up has-been.

(A) rewarding   (B) gradual
(C) essential   (D) spontaneous
(E) transitory

Ⓐ Ⓑ Ⓒ Ⓓ ●

1. She pointed out that his resume was ---- because it merely recorded his previous positions and failed to highlight the specific skills he had mastered in each job.

(A) disinterested
(B) inadequate
(C) conclusive
(D) obligatory
(E) detailed

2. Because it was already known that retroviruses could cause cancer in animals, it seemed only ---- to search for similar cancer-causing viruses in human beings.

(A) culpable   (B) charitable   (C) hypothetical
(D) logical   (E) negligent

3. Ms. Ono ---- gives interviews because she believes the news media have ---- her and treated her badly.

(A) frequently..publicized
(B) rarely..misrepresented
(C) seldom..eulogized
(D) reluctantly..acclaimed
(E) gradually..evaded

4. Totem craftsmanship reached its ---- in the nineteenth century, when the introduction of metal tools enabled carvers to execute more sophisticated designs.

(A) roots
(B) conclusion
(C) antithesis
(D) reward
(E) apex

5. For those who admire realism, Louis Malle's recent film succeeds because it consciously ---- the stuff of legend and tells ---- story as it might actually unfold with fallible people in earthly time.

(A) rejects..a derivative
(B) anticipates..an antiquated
(C) shuns..an unembellished
(D) emulates..an ethereal
(E) exaggerates..a mythic

Read the passages below, and then answer the questions that follow them. The correct response may be stated outright or merely suggested in the passages.

Questions 6–9 are based on the following passages.

Passage 1

Exquisitely adapted for life in one of Earth's harshest environments, polar bears can survive for 20 years or more on the Arctic Circle's glacial
Line ice. At home in a waste where temperatures reach
(5) minus 50 degrees Fahrenheit, these largest members of the bear family are a striking example of natural selection at work. With two layers of fur over a subcutaneous layer of blubber, polar bears are well adapted to resist heat loss. Their broad,
(10) snowshoe-like paws and sharp, curved claws enable them to traverse the ice with ease. Formidable hunters, these monarchs of the icy waste even possess the capacity to scent prey from a distance of 20 miles.

Passage 2

(15) Top predator of the arctic ecosystem, the polar bear preys on beluga whales, narwhals, musk oxen, walruses, hares, geese, and seals. In the mid-twentieth century this fearsome killer became the prey of even more deadly killers, trophy
(20) hunters and commercial hide hunters who came close to decimating the polar bear population. For a time, the 1973 signing of the international Polar Bear Agreement, which prohibited the capture and killing of polar bears and protected their habi-
(25) tats, reduced the danger of polar bear extinction. Today, however, polar bears face a new threat, as increasing arctic pollution fouls their environment with chemical toxins.

6. In the final sentence of Passage 1, "capacity" most nearly means

(A) ability
(B) stature
(C) quantity
(D) spaciousness
(E) intelligence

7. Unlike Passage 2, Passage 1 is concerned primarily with the

(A) harsh living conditions in the Arctic Circle
(B) polar bear's effect on its environment
(C) increasing decline of the polar bear population
(D) physical characteristics of polar bears
(E) mechanics of natural selection

8. Unlike the author of Passage 1, the author of Passage 2 does which of the following?

(A) proposes a solution
(B) explains a study
(C) quotes an authority
(D) poses a question
(E) establishes a time frame

9. Which generalization about polar bears is supported by both passages?

(A) They are vulnerable to chemical toxins.
(B) They are well adapted to a changing environment.
(C) They are notable predators.
(D) They move at a rapid rate.
(E) They are threatened by other predators.

GO ON TO THE NEXT PAGE

6 6 6 6 6 6 6 6 6 6 6 6 6 **6**

Questions 10–15 are based on the following passage.

The following passage is taken from Jane Austen's novel Persuasion. *In this excerpt we meet Sir Walter Elliot, father of the heroine.*

Vanity was the beginning and end of Sir Walter Elliot's character: vanity of person and of situation. He had been remarkably handsome in
Line his youth, and at fifty-four was still a very fine
(5) man. Few women could think more of their personal appearance than he did, nor could the valet of any new-made lord be more delighted with the place he held in society. He considered the blessing of beauty as inferior only to the blessing of a
(10) baronetcy; and the Sir Walter Elliot, who united these gifts, was the constant object of his warmest respect and devotion.

His good looks and his rank had one fair claim on his attachment, since to them he must have
(15) owed a wife of very superior character to anything deserved by his own. Lady Elliot had been an excellent woman, sensible and amiable, whose judgment and conduct, if they might be pardoned the youthful infatuation which made her Lady
(20) Elliot, had never required indulgence afterwards. She had humored, or softened, or concealed his failings, and promoted his real respectability for seventeen years; and though not the very happiest being in the world herself, had found enough in
(25) her duties, her friends, and her children, to attach her to life, and make it no matter of indifference to her when she was called on to quit them. Three girls, the two eldest sixteen and fourteen, was an awful legacy for a mother to bequeath, an awful
(30) charge rather, to confide to the authority and guidance of a conceited, silly father. She had, however, one very intimate friend, a sensible, deserving woman, who had been brought, by strong attachment to herself, to settle close by her,
(35) in the village of Kellynch; and on her kindness and advice Lady Elliot mainly relied for the best help and maintenance of the good principles and instruction which she had been anxiously giving her daughters.
(40) This friend and Sir Walter did not marry, whatever might have been anticipated on that head by their acquaintance. Thirteen years had passed away since Lady Elliot's death, and they were still near neighbors and intimate friends, and
(45) one remained a widower, the other a widow.

That Lady Russell, of steady age and character, and extremely well provided for, should have no thought of a second marriage, needs no apology to the public, which is rather apt to be unrea-
(50) sonably discontented when a woman *does* marry

again, than when she does *not;* but Sir Walter's continuing in singleness requires explanation. Be it known, then, that Sir Walter, like a good father (having met with one or two disappointments in
(55) very unreasonable applications), prided himself on remaining single for his dear daughters' sake.

10. According to the passage, Sir Walter Elliot's vanity centered on his

 I. physical attractiveness
 II. possession of a title
 III. superiority of character

 (A) I only
 (B) II only
 (C) I and II
 (D) I and III
 (E) I, II, and III

11. The narrator speaks well of Lady Elliot for all of the following EXCEPT

 (A) her concealment of Sir Walter's shortcomings
 (B) her choice of an intimate friend
 (C) her guidance of her three daughters
 (D) her judgment in falling in love with Sir Walter
 (E) her performance of her wifely duties

12. It can be inferred that over the years Lady Elliot was less than happy because of

 (A) her lack of personal beauty
 (B) her separation from her most intimate friend
 (C) the disparity between her character and that of her husband
 (D) the inferiority of her place in society
 (E) her inability to teach good principles to her wayward daughters

13. Lady Elliot's emotions regarding her approaching death were complicated by her

 (A) pious submissiveness to her fate
 (B) anxieties over her daughters' prospects
 (C) resentment of her husband's potential remarriage
 (D) lack of feeling for her conceited husband
 (E) reluctance to face the realities of her situation

14. The phrase "make it no matter of indifference to her when she was called on to quit them" (lines 26 and 27) is an example of

 (A) ironic understatement
 (B) effusive sentiment
 (C) metaphorical expression
 (D) personification
 (E) parable

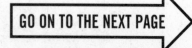

GO ON TO THE NEXT PAGE

15. The "applications" made by Sir Walter (line 55) were most likely

(A) professional
(B) insincere
(C) marital
(D) mournful
(E) fatherly

Questions 16–24 are based on the following passage.

The following passage is excerpted from a text on Native American history. Here, the author describes how certain major Indian nations related to the European powers during the 1700s.

By the end of the seventeenth century the coastal tribes along most of the Atlantic seaboard had been destroyed, dispersed, or subjected
Line directly to European control. Yet the interior
(5) tribes—particularly those who had grouped themselves into confederations—remained powers (and were usually styled nations) who dealt with Europeans on a rough plane of equality. Throughout the eighteenth century, the Creeks,
(10) Choctaws, Chickasaws, Cherokees, and Iroquois, as well as the tribes of the Old Northwest, alternately made war and peace with the various European powers, entered into treaties of alliance and friendship, and sometimes made cessions of
(15) territory as a result of defeat in war. As the imperial power of France and Great Britain expanded into the interior, those powerful Indian nations were forced to seek new orientations in their policy. For each Indian nation the reorientation was
(20) different, yet each was powerfully affected by the growth of European settlements, population, and military power. The history of the reorientation of Iroquois policy toward the Europeans may serve as an example of the process that all the interior
(25) nations experienced in the eighteenth century.

The stability that had marked the Iroquois Confederacy's generally pro-British position was shattered with the overthrow of James II in 1688, the colonial uprisings that followed in Massachu-
(30) setts, New York, and Maryland, and the commencement of King William's War against Louis XIV of France. The increasing French threat to English hegemony in the interior of North America was signalized by French-led or French-
(35) inspired attacks on the Iroquois and on outlying colonial settlements in New York and New England. The high point of the Iroquois response was the spectacular raid of August 5, 1689, in which the Iroquois virtually wiped out the French
(40) village of Lachine, just outside Montreal. A coun-

terraid by the French on the English village of Schenectady in March, 1690, instilled an appropriate measure of fear among the English and their Iroquois allies.
(45) The Iroquois position at the end of the war, which was formalized by treaties made during the summer of 1701 with the British and the French, and which was maintained throughout most of the eighteenth century, was one of "aggressive neu-
(50) trality" between the two competing European powers. Under the new system the Iroquois initiated a peace policy toward the "far Indians," tightened their control over the nearby tribes, and induced both English and French to support their
(55) neutrality toward the European powers by appropriate gifts and concessions.

By holding the balance of power in the sparsely settled borderlands between English and French settlements, and by their willingness to
(60) use their power against one or the other nation if not appropriately treated, the Iroquois played the game of European power politics with effectiveness. The system broke down, however, after the French became convinced that the Iroquois were
(65) compromising the system in favor of the English and launched a full-scale attempt to establish French physical and juridical presence in the Ohio Valley, the heart of the borderlands long claimed by the Iroquois. As a consequence of the ensuing
(70) Great War for Empire, in which Iroquois neutrality was dissolved and European influence moved closer, the play-off system lost its efficacy and a system of direct bargaining supplanted it.

16. The author's primary purpose in this passage is to

(A) denounce the imperialistic policies of the French
(B) disprove the charges of barbarism made against the Indian nations
(C) expose the French government's exploitation of the Iroquois balance of power
(D) describe and assess the effect of European military power on the policy of an Indian nation
(E) show the inability of the Iroquois to engage in European-style diplomacy

GO ON TO THE NEXT PAGE

17. Which of the following best captures the meaning of the word "styled" in line 7?

    (A) Arranged
    (B) Designated
    (C) Brought into conformity with
    (D) Dismissed as
    (E) Made fashionable

18. In writing that certain of the interior tribes "dealt with Europeans on a rough plane of equality" (lines 7 and 8), the author

    (A) agrees that the Europeans treated the Indians with unnecessary roughness
    (B) concedes that the Indians were demonstrably superior to the Europeans
    (C) acknowledges that European-Indian relations were not those of absolute equals
    (D) emphasizes that the Europeans wished to treat the Indians equitably
    (E) suggests that the coastal tribes lacked essential diplomatic skills

19. The author most likely has chosen to discuss the experience of the Iroquois because he regards it as

    (A) singular
    (B) colorful
    (C) representative
    (D) ephemeral
    (E) obscure

20. It can be inferred from the passage that the author's attitude toward the Iroquois leadership can best be described as one of

    (A) suspicion of their motives
    (B) respect for their competence
    (C) indifference to their fate
    (D) dislike of their savagery
    (E) pride in their heritage

21. With which of the following statements would the author be LEAST likely to agree?

    (A) The Iroquois were able to respond effectively to French acts of aggression.
    (B) James II's removal from the throne caused dissension to break out among the colonies.
    (C) The French begrudged the British their alleged high standing among the Iroquois.
    (D) Iroquois negotiations involved playing one side against the other.
    (E) The Iroquois ceased to hold the balance of power early in the eighteenth century.

22. The author attributes such success as the Iroquois policy of aggressive neutrality had to

    (A) the readiness of the Iroquois to fight either side
    (B) the Iroquois' ties of loyalty to the British
    (C) French physical presence in the borderlands
    (D) the confusion of the European forces
    (E) European reliance on formal treaties

23. The word "compromising" in line 65 means

    (A) humiliating   (B) jeopardizing   (C) revealing
    (D) yielding   (E) conceding

24. The final three paragraphs of the passage provide

    (A) an instance of a state of relationships described earlier
    (B) a modification of a thesis presented earlier
    (C) a refutation of an argument made earlier
    (D) a summary of the situation referred to earlier
    (E) an allusion to the state of events depicted earlier

YOU MAY GO BACK AND REVIEW THIS SECTION IN THE REMAINING TIME, BUT DO NOT WORK IN ANY OTHER SECTION UNTIL TOLD TO DO SO.

STOP

7

SECTION 7
Time—25 Minutes
18 Questions

You have 25 minutes to answer the 8 multiple-choice questions and 10 student-produced response questions in this section.

For each multiple-choice question, determine which of the five choices is correct and blacken the corresponding choice on your answer sheet. You may use any blank space on the page for your work.

Notes:

- You may use a calculator whenever you think it will be helpful.
- Only real numbers are used. No question or answer on this test involves a complex or imaginary number.
- Use the diagrams provided to help you solve the problems. Unless you see the words "Note: Figure not drawn to scale" under a diagram, it has been drawn as accurately as possible. Unless it is stated that a figure is three-dimensional, you may assume it lies in a plane.
- For any function f, the domain, unless specifically restricted, is the set of all real numbers for which $f(x)$ is also a real number.

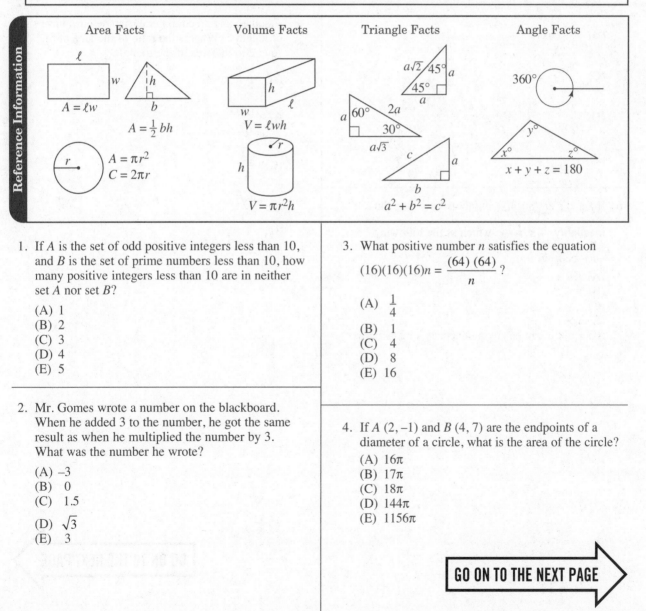

Reference Information

Area Facts — $A = \ell w$, $A = \frac{1}{2}bh$, $A = \pi r^2$, $C = 2\pi r$

Volume Facts — $V = \ell w h$, $V = \pi r^2 h$

Triangle Facts — $a^2 + b^2 = c^2$

Angle Facts — $x + y + z = 180$

1. If A is the set of odd positive integers less than 10, and B is the set of prime numbers less than 10, how many positive integers less than 10 are in neither set A nor set B?

   (A) 1
   (B) 2
   (C) 3
   (D) 4
   (E) 5

2. Mr. Gomes wrote a number on the blackboard. When he added 3 to the number, he got the same result as when he multiplied the number by 3. What was the number he wrote?

   (A) −3
   (B) 0
   (C) 1.5
   (D) $\sqrt{3}$
   (E) 3

3. What positive number n satisfies the equation
   $$(16)(16)(16)n = \frac{(64)(64)}{n}\,?$$

   (A) $\frac{1}{4}$
   (B) 1
   (C) 4
   (D) 8
   (E) 16

4. If $A\,(2, -1)$ and $B\,(4, 7)$ are the endpoints of a diameter of a circle, what is the area of the circle?

   (A) 16π
   (B) 17π
   (C) 18π
   (D) 144π
   (E) 1156π

GO ON TO THE NEXT PAGE

7

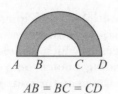

$A \quad B \qquad C \quad D$

$AB = BC = CD$

<u>Note:</u> Figure not drawn to scale.

5. In the figure above, arcs $\overset{\frown}{AD}$ and $\overset{\frown}{BC}$ are semicircles. If a point is chosen at random inside the figure, what is the probability that the point lies in the shaded region?

(A) $\dfrac{4}{9}$

(B) $\dfrac{5}{9}$

(C) $\dfrac{2}{3}$

(D) $\dfrac{7}{9}$

(E) $\dfrac{8}{9}$

6. If r and s are positive numbers satisfying the inequality $\dfrac{r}{s} < \dfrac{r+1}{s+1}$, which of the following *must* be true?

(A) $r < s$
(B) $s < r$
(C) $r > 1$
(D) $s > 1$
(E) r and s can be any numbers as long as $r \neq s$.

7. If $f(x) = 3 + \dfrac{5}{x}$, which of the following CANNOT be a value of $f(x)$?

(A) $-\dfrac{5}{3}$

(B) $-\dfrac{3}{5}$

(C) 0

(D) $\dfrac{5}{3}$

(E) 3

8. A square and an equilateral triangle each have sides of length 5. What is the ratio of the area of the square to the area of the triangle?

(A) $\dfrac{4}{3}$

(B) $\dfrac{16}{9}$

(C) $\dfrac{\sqrt{3}}{4}$

(D) $\dfrac{4\sqrt{3}}{3}$

(E) $\dfrac{16\sqrt{3}}{9}$

7

Directions for Student-Produced Response Questions (Grid-ins)

In questions 9–18, first solve the problem, and then enter your answer on the grid provided on the answer sheet. The instructions for entering your answers are as follows:

• First, write your answer in the boxes at the top of the grid.
• Second, grid your answer in the columns below the boxes.
• Use the fraction bar in the first row or the decimal point in the second row to enter fractions and decimal answers.

Answer: $\frac{8}{15}$ Answer: 1.75

Write your → answer in the boxes.

Grid in → your answer.

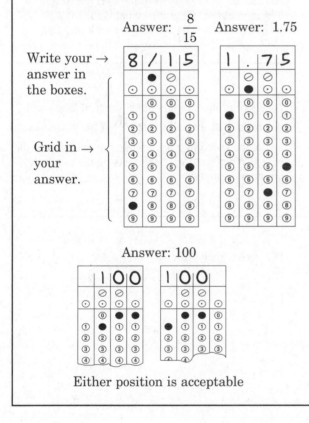

Answer: 100

Either position is acceptable

• Grid only one space in each column.
• Entering the answer in the boxes is recommended as an aid in gridding, but is not required.
• The machine scoring your exam can read only what you grid, so you **must grid in your answers correctly to get credit.**
• If a question has more than one correct answer, grid in only one of these answers.
• The grid does not have a minus sign, so no answer can be negative.
• A mixed number *must* be converted to an improper fraction or a decimal before it is gridded. Enter $1\frac{1}{4}$ as 5/4 or 1.25; the machine will interpret 1 1/4 as $\frac{11}{4}$ and mark it wrong.
• **All decimals must be entered as accurately as possible.** Here are the three acceptable ways of gridding

$$\frac{3}{11} = 0.272727...$$

3/11   .272   .273

• Note that rounding to .273 is acceptable, because you are using the full grid, but you would receive **no credit** for .3 or .27, because these answers are less accurate.

9. Two white cards each measuring 3" × 5" are placed on a 9" × 12" piece of red construction paper so that they do not overlap. What is the area, in square inches, of the uncovered part of the red paper?

10. If 80% of the adult population of a village are registered to vote, and 60% of those registered actually voted in a particular election, what percent of the adults in the village did NOT vote in that election?

GO ON TO THE NEXT PAGE

7

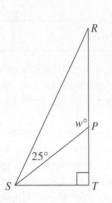

11. In the figure above, if $\overline{PS}$ bisects $\angle RST$, what is the value of w?

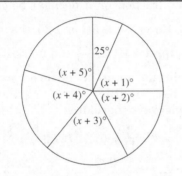

12. What is the value of x in the figure above?

13. If Henry drove 198 kilometers between 10:00 A.M. and 1:40 P.M., what was his average speed, in kilometers per hour?

14. The first term of a sequence is 1. Starting with the second term, each term is 1 less than 3 times the preceding term. What is the smallest number greater than 100 in the sequence?

15. Each stockholder of XYZ Corporation belongs to either Group A or Group B. Exactly 10% of the stockholders are in Group A, and collectively they own 80% of the stock. Let a represent the average number of shares of stock owned by the members of Group A, and b represent the average number of shares of stock owned by the members of Group B. If $a = kb$, what is the value of k?

16. In a jar containing only red and blue marbles, 40% of the marbles are red. If the average weight of a red marble is 40 grams and the average weight of a blue marble is 60 grams, what is the average weight, in grams, of all the marbles in the jar?

17. A school group charters three identical buses and occupies $\frac{4}{5}$ of the seats. After $\frac{1}{4}$ of the passengers leave, the remaining passengers use only two of the buses. What fraction of the seats on the two buses are now occupied?

18. If $a^{-4} = 16$, then $(2a)^{\frac{1}{2}} =$

YOU MAY GO BACK AND REVIEW THIS SECTION IN THE REMAINING TIME, BUT DO NOT WORK IN ANY OTHER SECTION UNTIL TOLD TO DO SO.

STOP

8 8 8 8 8 8 8 8 8 8 8

SECTION 8 | Time—20 Minutes 19 Questions | Select the best answer to each of the following questions; then blacken the appropriate space on your answer sheet.

Each of the following sentences contains one or two blanks; each blank indicates that a word or set of words has been left out. Below the sentence are five words or phrases, lettered A through E. Select the word or set of words that best completes the sentence.

Example:

Fame is ----; today's rising star is all too soon tomorrow's washed-up has-been.

(A) rewarding   (B) gradual
(C) essential   (D) spontaneous
(E) transitory

Ⓐ Ⓑ Ⓒ Ⓓ ●

---

1. Her ---- is always a source of irritation: she never uses a single word when she can substitute a long clause or phrase in its place.

   (A) frivolity   (B) verbosity   (C) ambivalence
   (D) cogency   (E) rhetoric

2. It is ---- to try to destroy pests completely with chemical poisons, for as each new chemical pesticide is introduced, the insects gradually become ---- to it.

   (A) useless..drawn
   (B) pointless..vulnerable
   (C) futile..resistant
   (D) wicked..indifferent
   (E) worthwhile..immune

3. As delicate and ---- as insect bodies are, it is remarkable that over the ages enough of them have ----, preserved in amber, for scientists to trace insect evolution.

   (A) beautiful..disappeared
   (B) fragile..survived
   (C) impervious..multiplied
   (D) refined..awakened
   (E) indestructible..evolved

4. Unfortunately, the current Broadway season offers some ---- fare that sounds markedly like imitations of previous hits.

   (A) epic
   (B) radical
   (C) formulaic
   (D) incongruous
   (E) challenging

5. Surrounded by a retinue of sycophants who invariably ---- her singing, Callas wearied of the constant adulation and longed for honest criticism.

   (A) orchestrated
   (B) thwarted
   (C) assailed
   (D) extolled
   (E) reciprocated

6. There is nothing ---- or provisional about Moore's early critical pronouncements; she deals ---- with what were then radical new developments in poetry.

   (A) tentative..confidently
   (B) positive..expertly
   (C) dogmatic..arbitrarily
   (D) shallow..superficially
   (E) imprecise..inconclusively

GO ON TO THE NEXT PAGE

8   8   8   8   8   8   8   8   8   8   8

Test 4

The questions that follow the next two passages relate to the content of both, and to their relationship. The correct response may be stated outright in the passage or merely suggested.

Questions 7–19 are based on the following passages.

The following passages are excerpted from popular articles on dolphins, the first dating from the 1960s, the second written in 1990.

Passage 1

Most of the intelligent land animals have prehensile, grasping organs for exploring their environment—hands in human beings and their
Line anthropoid relatives, the sensitive inquiring trunk
(5) in the elephant. One of the surprising things about the dolphin is that his superior brain is unaccompanied by any type of manipulative organ. He has, however, a remarkable range-finding ability involving some sort of echo-sounding. Perhaps
(10) this acute sense—far more accurate than any that human ingenuity has been able to devise artificially—brings him greater knowledge of his watery surroundings than might at first seem possible. Human beings think of intelligence as
(15) geared to things. The hand and the tool are to us the unconscious symbols of our intellectual attainment. It is difficult for us to visualize another kind of lonely, almost disembodied intelligence floating in the wavering green fairyland of the
(20) sea—an intelligence possibly near or comparable to our own but without hands to build, to transmit knowledge by writing, or to alter by one hairsbreadth the planet's surface. Yet at the same time there are indications that this is a warm, friendly,
(25) and eager intelligence quite capable of coming to the assistance of injured companions and striving to rescue them from drowning. Dolphins left the land when mammalian brains were still small and primitive. Without the stimulus provided by agile
(30) exploring fingers, these great sea mammals have yet taken a divergent road toward intelligence of a high order. Hidden in their sleek bodies is an impressively elaborated instrument, the reason for whose appearance is a complete enigma. It is as
(35) though both the human being and the dolphin were each part of some great eye which yearned to look both outward on eternity and inward to the sea's heart—that fertile entity like the mind in its swarming and grotesque life.

Passage 2

(40)   Nothing about dolphins has been more widely or passionately discussed over the centuries than their supposed intelligence and communicative abilities. In fact, a persistent dogma holds that dolphins are among the most intelligent of ani-
(45) mals and that they communicate with one another in complex ways. Implicit in this argument is the belief that dolphin cultures are at least as ancient and rich as our own. To support the claim of high intelligence amongst dolphins, proponents note
(50) that they have large brains, live in societies marked as much by co-operative as by competitive interactions and rapidly learn the artificial tasks given to them in captivity. Indeed, dolphins are clearly capable of learning through observa-
(55) tion and have good memories. People who spend time with captive dolphins are invariably impressed by their sense of humor, playfulness, quick comprehension of body language, command of situations, mental agility, and emotional
(60) resilience. Individual dolphins have distinctive personalities and trainers often speak of being trained by their subjects, rather than the other way round.

The extremely varied repertoires of sounds
(65) made by dolphins are often invoked as *prima facie* evidence of advanced communication abilities. In addition, some "scientific" experiments done by John Lilly and his associates during the 1950s and 1960s were claimed to show that dol-
(70) phins communicate not only with one another but also with humans, mimicking human speech and reaching out across the boundaries that divide us.

These conclusions about dolphin intelligence and communication have not withstood critical
(75) scrutiny. While they have fueled romantic speculation, their net impact has been to mislead. Rather than allowing dolphins to be discovered and appreciated for what they are, Lilly's vision has forced us to measure these animals' value
(80) according to how close they come to equalling or exceeding our own intelligence, virtue, and spiritual development.

The issues of dolphin intelligence and communication have been inseparable in most people's
(85) minds, and the presumed existence of one has

GO ON TO THE NEXT PAGE

8   8 8 8 8 8 8 8 8 8   8

been taken as proof of the other, a classic case of
begging the question. Not surprisingly then, most
experiments to evaluate dolphin intelligence have
measured the animals' capacity for cognitive pro-
(90) cessing as exhibited in their understanding of the
rudiments of language.

From the early work of researchers like
Dwight Batteau and Jarvis Bastian through the
more recent work of Louis Herman and associ-
(95) ates, dolphins have been asked to accept simple
information, in the form of acoustic or visual
symbols representing verbs and nouns, and then
to act on the information following a set of commands from the experimenter.
(100) The widely publicized results have been somewhat disappointing. Although they have demonstrated that dolphins do have the primary skills
necessary to support understanding and use of a
language, they have not distinguished the dol-
(105) phins from other animals in this respect. For
example, some seals, animals we do not normally
cite as members of the intellectual or communicative elite, have been found to have the same basic
capabilities.
(110) What, then, do the results of experiments to
date mean? Either we have not devised adequate
tests to permit us to detect, measure, and rank
intelligence as a measure of a given species' ability to communicate, or we must acknowledge that
(115) the characteristics that we regard as rudimentary
evidence of intelligence are held more commonly
by many "lower" animals than we previously
thought.

7. According to Passage 1, which of the following
statements about dolphins is true?

   (A) They have always been water-dwelling
       creatures.
   (B) They at one time possessed prehensile organs.
   (C) They lived on land in prehistoric times.
   (D) Their brains are no longer mammalian in nature.
   (E) They developed brains to compensate for the
       lack of a prehensile organ.

8. The author of Passage 1 suggests that human
failure to understand the intelligence of the dolphin
is due to

   (A) the inadequacy of human range-finding
       equipment
   (B) a lack of knowledge about the sea
   (C) the want of a common language
   (D) the primitive origins of the human brain
   (E) the human inclination to judge other life by
       our own

9. In Passage 1, the author's primary purpose is
apparently to

   (A) examine the dolphin's potential for surpassing
       humankind
   (B) question the need for prehensile organs in
       human development
   (C) refute the theory that dolphins are unable to
       alter their physical environment
   (D) reassess the nature and extent of dolphin
       intelligence
   (E) indicate the superiority of human intelligence
       over that of the dolphin

10. The word "acute" in line 10 means

   (A) excruciating
   (B) severe
   (C) keen
   (D) sudden and intense
   (E) brief in duration

11. The "impressively elaborated instrument" referred
to in line 33 is best interpreted to mean which of
the following?

   (A) A concealed manipulative organ
   (B) An artificial range-finding device
   (C) A complex, intelligent brain
   (D) The dolphin's hidden eye
   (E) An apparatus for producing musical sounds

12. According to the author's simile in lines 38 and 39,
the human mind and the heart of the sea are alike
in that both

   (A) teem with exotic forms of life
   (B) argue in support of intelligence
   (C) are necessary to the evolution of dolphins
   (D) are directed outward
   (E) share a penchant for the grotesque

13. Which of the following best characterizes the tone
of Passage 1?

   (A) Restrained skepticism
   (B) Pedantic assertion
   (C) Wondering admiration
   (D) Amused condescension
   (E) Ironic speculation

GO ON TO THE NEXT PAGE

14. The author of Passage 2 puts quotation marks around the word "scientific" in line 67 to indicate he

    (A) is faithfully reproducing Lilly's own words
    (B) intends to define the word later in the passage
    (C) believes the reader is unfamiliar with the word as used by Lilly
    (D) advocates adhering to the scientific method in all experiments
    (E) has some doubts as to how scientific those experiments were

15. The author of Passage 2 maintains that the writings of Lilly and his associates have

    (A) overstated the extent of dolphin intelligence
    (B) been inadequately scrutinized by critics
    (C) measured the worth of the dolphin family
    (D) underrated dolphins as intelligent beings
    (E) established criteria for evaluating dolphin intelligence

16. By calling the argument summarized in lines 83–86 a classic case of begging the question, the author of Passage 2 indicates he views the argument with

    (A) trepidation
    (B) optimism
    (C) detachment
    (D) skepticism
    (E) credulity

17. Which of the following would most undercut the studies on which the author bases his conclusion in lines 110–118?

    (A) Evidence proving dolphin linguistic abilities to be far superior to those of other mammals
    (B) An article recording attempts by seals and walruses to communicate with human beings
    (C) The reorganization of current intelligence tests by species and level of difficulty
    (D) A reassessment of the definition of the term "lower animals"
    (E) The establishment of a project to develop new tests to detect intelligence in animals

18. The author of Passage 2 would find Passage 1

    (A) typical of the attitudes of Lilly and his associates
    (B) remarkable for the perspective it offers
    (C) indicative of the richness of dolphin culture
    (D) supportive of his fundamental point of view
    (E) intriguing for its far-reaching conclusions

19. Compared to Passage 2, Passage 1 is

    (A) more figurative
    (B) less obscure
    (C) more objective
    (D) more current
    (E) less speculative

YOU MAY GO BACK AND REVIEW THIS SECTION IN THE REMAINING TIME, BUT DO NOT WORK IN ANY OTHER SECTION UNTIL TOLD TO DO SO.

STOP

9   9   9   9   9   9   9

SECTION 9

Time—20 Minutes
16 Questions

For each problem in this section determine which of the five choices is correct and blacken the corresponding choice on your answer sheet. You may use any blank space on the page for your work.

Notes:

- You may use a calculator whenever you think it will be helpful.
- Only real numbers are used. No question or answer on this test involves a complex or imaginary number.
- Use the diagrams provided to help you solve the problems. Unless you see the words "Note: Figure not drawn to scale" under a diagram, it has been drawn as accurately as possible. Unless it is stated that a figure is three-dimensional, you may assume it lies in a plane.
- For any function f, the domain, unless specifically restricted, is the set of all real numbers for which $f(x)$ is also a real number.

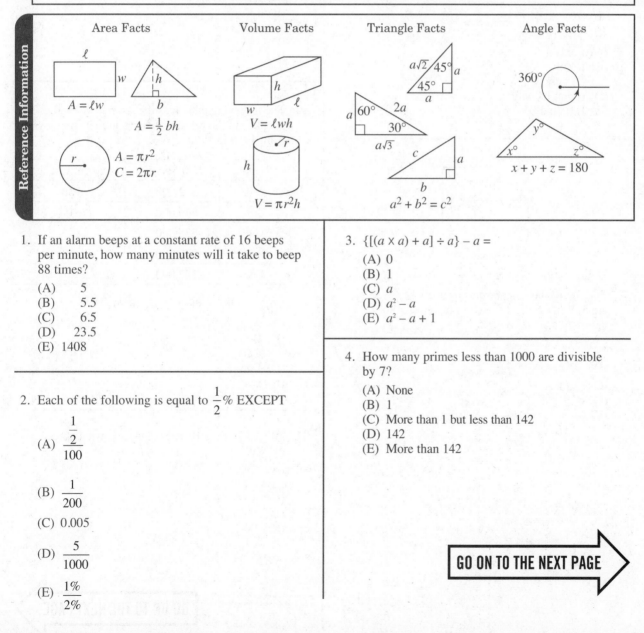

Reference Information

Area Facts — $A = \ell w$; $A = \frac{1}{2}bh$; $A = \pi r^2$, $C = 2\pi r$

Volume Facts — $V = \ell w h$; $V = \pi r^2 h$

Triangle Facts — $a^2 + b^2 = c^2$

Angle Facts — $x + y + z = 180$

1. If an alarm beeps at a constant rate of 16 beeps per minute, how many minutes will it take to beep 88 times?

    (A)   5
    (B)   5.5
    (C)   6.5
    (D)   23.5
    (E)   1408

2. Each of the following is equal to $\frac{1}{2}$% EXCEPT

    (A) $\dfrac{\frac{1}{2}}{100}$

    (B) $\dfrac{1}{200}$

    (C) 0.005

    (D) $\dfrac{5}{1000}$

    (E) $\dfrac{1\%}{2\%}$

3. $\{[(a \times a) + a] \div a\} - a =$

    (A) 0
    (B) 1
    (C) a
    (D) $a^2 - a$
    (E) $a^2 - a + 1$

4. How many primes less than 1000 are divisible by 7?

    (A) None
    (B) 1
    (C) More than 1 but less than 142
    (D) 142
    (E) More than 142

GO ON TO THE NEXT PAGE

Test 4

5. If the average (arithmetic mean) of the measures of two angles of a quadrilateral is 60°, what is the average of the measures of the other two angles?

(A) 60°
(B) 90°
(C) 120°
(D) 180°
(E) 240°

6. If m is an integer and m, $m + 1$, and $m + 2$ are the lengths of the sides of a triangle, which of the following could be the value of m?

   I. 1
   II. 10
   III. 100

(A) I only
(B) II only
(C) III only
(D) II and III only
(E) I, II, and III

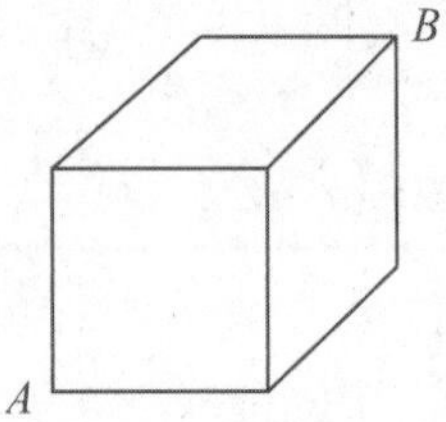

7. The figure above represents a cube whose edges are 3. What is the distance from vertex A to vertex B?

(A) 3
(B) $3\sqrt{2}$
(C) $3\sqrt{3}$
(D) 6
(E) 9

8. In a certain sequence the difference between any two consecutive terms is 5. If the 20th term is 63, what is the 2nd term?

(A) −32
(B) −27
(C) −22
(D) 32
(E) 37

9. What is the measure, in degrees, of the smaller angle formed by the hour hand and the minute hand of a clock at 11:20?

(A) 120
(B) 130
(C) 135
(D) 140
(E) 150

10. The following table lists the salaries in 1980 of five people and the percent changes in their salaries from 1980 to 1990.

Name	1980 Salary	Percent Change
Ada	$32,000	+35
Bob	$40,000	+11
Cal	$35,000	+25
Dan	$50,000	−12
Eve	$42,000	+6

Who had the highest salary in 1990?

(A) Ada
(B) Bob
(C) Cal
(D) Dan
(E) Eve

11. 10% more than 10% less than x is what percent of $10x$?

(A) 9%
(B) 9.9%
(C) 10%
(D) 99%
(E) 100%

GO ON TO THE NEXT PAGE

9   9   9   9   9   9   9

12. If $2 - 3\sqrt{x} = 8$, what is the value of x?

(A) 0
(B) 2
(C) 4
(D) 9
(E) There is no value of x that satisfies the equation

13. If $x \neq -1$, 1, or 3, which of the following is

equivalent to $\dfrac{x^2 - x}{2x - 6} \cdot \dfrac{x^2 - 2x - 3}{x^2 - 1}$?

(A) $\dfrac{x}{2}$

(B) $\dfrac{x + 3}{2(x - 3)}$

(C) $\dfrac{x - 1}{2x - 6}$

(D) $\dfrac{x^2 - 3x - 3}{2x - 7}$

(E) $\dfrac{x^2 - x - 3}{-7}$

14. If $f(x) = x^2 + \sqrt{x}$ and $g(x) = f(4x)$, what is the value of $g(4)$?

(A) 18
(B) 36
(C) 72
(D) 144
(E) 260

15. So far this year, Adam has played 30 games of chess and has won only 6 of them. What is the minimum number of additional games he must play, given that he is sure to lose at least one-third of them, so that for the year he will have won more games than he lost?

(A) 25
(B) 34
(C) 57
(D) 87
(E) It is not possible for Adam to do this.

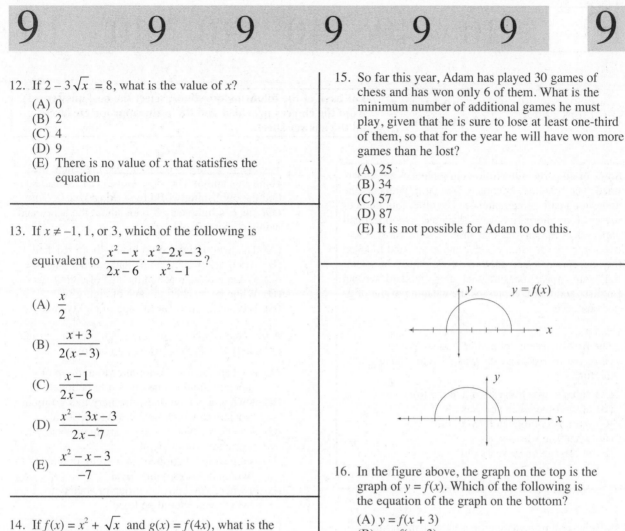

16. In the figure above, the graph on the top is the graph of $y = f(x)$. Which of the following is the equation of the graph on the bottom?

(A) $y = f(x + 3)$
(B) $y = f(x - 3)$
(C) $y = f(x) + 3$
(D) $y = f(x) - 3$
(E) $y = f(3x)$

YOU MAY GO BACK AND REVIEW THIS SECTION IN THE REMAINING TIME, BUT DO NOT WORK IN ANY OTHER SECTION UNTIL TOLD TO DO SO.   **S T O P**

Test 4

SECTION **10** Time—10 Minutes
14 Questions

For each of the following questions, select the best answer from the choices provided and fill in the appropriate circle on the answer sheet.

Some or all parts of the following sentences are underlined. The first answer choice, (A), simply repeats the underlined part of the sentence. The other four choices present four alternative ways to phrase the underlined part. Select the answer that produces the most effective sentence, one that is clear and exact, and blacken the appropriate space on your answer sheet. In selecting your choice, be sure that it is standard written English, and that it expresses the meaning of the original sentence.

Example:
The first biography of author Eudora Welty came out in 1998 <u>and she was 89 years old at the time</u>.

(A) and she was 89 years old at the time
(B) at the time when she was 89
(C) upon becoming an 89 year old
(D) when she was 89
(E) at the age of 89 years old

Ⓐ Ⓑ Ⓒ ● Ⓔ

1. <u>Helen is a trained veterinarian, and she has a specialization in the treatment of feline diseases</u>.

   (A) Helen is a trained veterinarian, and she has a specialization in the treatment of feline diseases.
   (B) Helen is a trained veterinarian, moreover, she has a specialization in the treatment of feline diseases.
   (C) Helen, a trained veterinarian, she has a specialization in treating feline diseases.
   (D) As a trained veterinarian, Helen has got a specialization in how she should treat feline diseases.
   (E) A trained veterinarian, Helen specializes in treating feline diseases.

2. <u>The age of eighty-two having been reached</u>, the children's author Theodore Geisel (Dr. Seuss) startled the publishing world by writing *You're Only Old Once*, a lighthearted book about the aches and pains of growing old.

   (A) The age of eighty-two having been reached
   (B) At eighty-two, when he had reached that age
   (C) When having reached the age of eighty-two
   (D) When he reached the age of eighty-two
   (E) Having reached for the age of eighty-two

3. A turncoat <u>is when someone is a traitor to a group or society to which he owes it to be loyal</u>.

   (A) is when someone is a traitor to a group or society to which he owes it to be loyal
   (B) is when a person does treachery to a group or society to which he owes it to be loyal
   (C) is someone who betrays a group or society to which he owes loyalty
   (D) is a person which betrays a group or society to which he owes being loyal
   (E) is where you betray a group or society to which you should be loyal

4. Like general contractors, writers <u>are notorious optimistic when it comes to estimating how long a project will take</u>.

   (A) are notorious optimistic when it comes to estimating how long a project will take
   (B) are notorious optimistic at estimating how long a project will take
   (C) are notoriously optimistic when it comes to estimating how long a project will take
   (D) are notoriously optimistic when they come to make an estimate of how long a project will take
   (E) are notorious optimistic when it comes to estimating how long a project is liable to take

GO ON TO THE NEXT PAGE

10   10   10   10   10   10   10

5. Bioengineered crops seem to have a way of turning up where they are not wanted, <u>through cross-pollination, intermingling of seed, or other routes</u>.

(A) through cross-pollination, intermingling of seed, or other routes
(B) through cross-pollination, intermingling of seed, and there are other routes
(C) by means of cross-pollination, and perhaps intermingling of seed, other routes
(D) through cross-pollination, they intermingle their seed, or taking other routes
(E) through cross-pollination, intermingling of seed, or there are other routes

6. <u>Having exceptional talent in fencing, ballet, as well as debate</u>, Benjamin was considered to be a likely candidate for admission to Harvard.

(A) Having exceptional talent in fencing, ballet, as well as debate
(B) Because of his exceptional talent in fencing, ballet, and debate
(C) Having exceptional talent in fencing, ballet, and in debate as well
(D) By being an exceptional talent in both fencing and ballet, and also debate
(E) With his exceptional talent in fencing and ballet and being good in debating

7. The movie's unlikely happy ending <u>came to pass as the result of an incredulous series</u> of lucky accidents.

(A) came to pass as the result of an incredulous series
(B) came past as the result of an incredulous series
(C) came about through an incredulous series
(D) resulted from an incredulous series
(E) resulted from an incredible series

8. Although the folk singer specializes in singing British sea chanteys, <u>he has never visited England and has no experience at sea</u>.

(A) he has never visited England and has no experience at sea
(B) he has never visited England and also has never experienced being at sea
(C) it is without ever having visited England or ever having experienced being at sea
(D) he has never visited England nor has he had no experience at sea
(E) it is without ever visiting England and having experience at sea

9. The recent increase in the number of applicants to medical schools <u>have encouraged hospital administrators, many of whom had bemoaned</u> the lack of potential interns and physicians.

(A) have encouraged hospital administrators, many of whom had bemoaned
(B) have encouraged hospital administrators, whom many had bemoaned of
(C) has encouraged hospital administrators, many of them had bemoaned
(D) have encouraged hospital administrators, many of whom bemoaning
(E) has encouraged hospital administrators, many of whom had bemoaned

10. <u>Having command of ballet, modern dance, as well as jazz</u>, Jerome Robbins is regarded as an outstanding American choreographer.

(A) Having command of ballet, modern dance, as well as jazz
(B) Because of his command of ballet, modern dance, and jazz
(C) Because of him having a command of ballet, modern dance, and jazz
(D) With his command of ballet and modern dance and knowing jazz
(E) Being in command of ballet and modern dance and also his jazz side

11. Some people believe that one day <u>we will create not only a universal health care system, but also the revitalized social security system will exist</u>.

(A) we will create not only a universal health care system, but also the revitalized social security system will exist
(B) not only a universal health care system will be established but also the revitalized social security system will be in existence
(C) we will not only create a universal health care system, but we will revitalize the social security system in addition
(D) we will not only create a universal health care system, but also revitalize the social security system
(E) we will create not only a universal health care system, but a revitalized social security system also

10   10   10   10   10   10   10

12. Jane Smiley makes a convincing case that horses, like people, have their own natures, and that one can learn about them <u>the same way you can learn about human beings</u>: through observation, reading, and empathy.

(A) the same way you can learn about human beings

(B) in the same way you can learn about human beings

(C) the same way you could learn about human beings

(D) the same way one can learn about human beings

(E) only the same way one learns about human beings

13. Brought up in a homogeneous, all-white suburb, <u>it was only when I moved to San Francisco that I realized how exciting life in an ethnically diverse community can be</u>.

(A) it was only when I moved to San Francisco that I realized how exciting life in an ethnically diverse community can be

(B) I did not realize how exciting life in an ethnically diverse community can be until I moved to San Francisco

(C) when I moved to San Francisco I realized how exciting life in an ethnically diverse community can be

(D) an exciting life in an ethnically diverse community was unrealized by me until I moved to San Francisco

(E) moving to San Francisco made me realize how exciting life in an ethnically diverse community can be

14. For an overtly political cartoonist like Aaron McGruder, <u>being free to criticize contemporary American society is more important than</u> winning a large and admiring audience.

(A) being free to criticize contemporary American society is more important than

(B) there is greater importance in the freedom to criticize contemporary American society than in

(C) having freedom for criticism of contemporary American society is more important than

(D) to have the freedom to criticize contemporary American society is more important than

(E) freedom to criticize contemporary American society has more importance than does

YOU MAY GO BACK AND REVIEW THIS SECTION IN THE REMAINING TIME, BUT DO NOT WORK IN ANY OTHER SECTION UNTIL TOLD TO DO SO.

S T O P

Answer Key

Note: The letters in brackets following the Mathematical Reasoning answers refer to the sections of Chapter 9 in which you can find the information you need to answer the questions. For example, **1. C [E]** means that the answer to question 1 is C, and that the solution requires information found in Section 9-E: Averages.

Section 2   Critical Reading

1.	E	6.	B	11.	E	16.	B	21.	D
2.	B	7.	C	12.	A	17.	A	22.	D
3.	B	8.	B	13.	B	18.	E	23.	B
4.	B	9.	B	14.	A	19.	D	24.	D
5.	C	10.	D	15.	E	20.	C		

Section 3   Mathematical Reasoning

1.	C [A]	5.	B [A]	9.	A [K, L]	13.	D [G]	17.	E [H, L]
2.	C [G]	6.	D [A]	10.	A [D, H]	14.	A [R]	18.	C [A]
3.	D [A]	7.	A [H]	11.	B [K, G]	15.	A [J, K]	19.	C [P]
4.	C [J]	8.	E [C]	12.	D [M, C]	16.	D [E, G]	20.	E [J]

Section 4   Writing Skills

1.	A	8.	E	15.	C	22.	A	29.	B
2.	B	9.	D	16.	C	23.	C	30.	C
3.	C	10.	B	17.	A	24.	C	31.	C
4.	B	11.	C	18.	A	25.	E	32.	B
5.	E	12.	A	19.	D	26.	C	33.	A
6.	E	13.	E	20.	B	27.	D	34.	B
7.	D	14.	D	21.	D	28.	B	35.	E

Section 5

On this test, Section 5 was the experimental section. It could have been an extra critical reading, mathematics, or writing skills section. Remember: on the SAT you take, the experimental section may be any section from 2 to 7.

Section 6   Critical Reading

1.	B	6.	A	11.	D	16.	D	21.	E
2.	D	7.	D	12.	C	17.	B	22.	A
3.	B	8.	E	13.	B	18.	C	23.	B
4.	E	9.	C	14.	A	19.	C	24.	A
5.	C	10.	C	15.	C	20.	B		

Section 7   Mathematical Reasoning

Multiple-Choice Questions

1.	C [A]	3.	B [G]	5.	E [L, O]	7.	E [R]
2.	C [G]	4.	B [L, N]	6.	A [A, D]	8.	D [J, K]

Grid-in Questions

9. [K] 78

10. [C] 52

11. [J] 115

12. [I,G] 64

13. [D, H] 54

14. [P] 122

15. [C, E] 36

16. [E] 52

17. [B] 9/10   or .9

18. [A] 1

Section 8   Critical Reading

1. **B**	5. **D**	9. **D**	13. **C**	17. **A**
2. **C**	6. **A**	10. **C**	14. **E**	18. **A**
3. **B**	7. **C**	11. **C**	15. **A**	19. **A**
4. **C**	8. **E**	12. **A**	16. **D**	

Section 9   Mathematical Reasoning

1. **B [D]**	5. **C [K]**	9. **D [I, P]**	13. **A [F]**
2. **E [B, C]**	6. **D [J]**	10. **E [C, Q]**	14. **E [R]**
3. **B [A]**	7. **C [M]**	11. **B [C]**	15. **C [G, H]**
4. **B [A]**	8. **B [P]**	12. **E [G]**	16. **A [R]**

Section 10   Writing Skills

1. **E**	4. **C**	7. **E**	10. **B**	13. **B**
2. **D**	5. **A**	8. **A**	11. **D**	14. **A**
3. **C**	6. **B**	9. **E**	12. **D**	

Score Your Own SAT Essay

Use this table as you rate your performance on the essay-writing section of this Model Test. Circle the phrase that most accurately describes your work. Enter the numbers in the scoring chart below. Add the numbers together and divide by 6 to determine your total score. The higher your total score, the better you are likely to do on the essay section of the SAT.

Note that on the actual SAT two readers will rate your essay; your essay score will be the sum of their two ratings and could range from 12 (highest) to 2 (lowest). Also, they will grade your essay holistically, rating it on the basis of their overall impression of its effectiveness. They will *not* analyze it piece by piece, giving separate grades for grammar, vocabulary level, and so on. Therefore, you cannot expect the score you give yourself on this Model Test to predict your eventual score on the SAT with any great degree of accuracy. Use this scoring guide instead to help you assess your writing strengths and weaknesses, so that you can decide which areas to focus on as you prepare for the SAT.

Like most people, you may find it difficult to rate your own writing objectively. Ask a teacher or fellow student to score your essay as well. With his or her help you should gain added insights into writing your 25-minute essay.

	6	5	4	3	2	1
POSITION ON THE TOPIC	Clear, convincing, & insightful	Fundamentally clear & coherent	Fairly clear & coherent	Insufficiently clear	Largely unclear	Extremely unclear
ORGANIZATION OF EVIDENCE	Well organized, with strong, relevant examples	Generally well organized, with apt examples	Adequately organized, with some examples	Sketchily developed, with weak examples	Lacking focus and evidence	Unfocused and disorganized
SENTENCE STRUCTURE	Varied, appealing sentences	Reasonably varied sentences	Some variety in sentences	Little variety in sentences	Errors in sentence structure	Severe errors in sentence structure
LEVEL OF VOCABULARY	Mature & apt word choice	Competent word choice	Adequate word choice	Inappropriate or weak vocabulary	Highly limited vocabulary	Rudimentary
GRAMMAR AND USAGE	Almost entirely free of errors	Relatively free of errors	Some technical errors	Minor errors, and some major ones	Numerous major errors	Extensive severe errors
OVERALL EFFECT	Outstanding	Effective	Adequately competent	Inadequate, but shows some potential	Seriously flawed	Fundamentally deficient

Self-Scoring Chart

For each of the following categories,
rate the essay from 1 (lowest)
to 6 (highest)

Position on the Topic _____

Organization of Evidence _____

Sentence Structure _____

Level of Vocabulary _____

Grammar and Usage _____

Overall Effect _____

TOTAL _____

(To get a score, divide the total by 6) _____

Scoring Chart (Second Reader)

For each of the following categories,
rate the essay from 1 (lowest)
to 6 (highest)

Position on the Topic _____

Organization of Evidence _____

Sentence Structure _____

Level of Vocabulary _____

Grammar and Usage _____

Overall Effect _____

TOTAL _____

(To get a score, divide the total by 6) _____

Test 4

Calculate Your Raw Score

Critical Reading

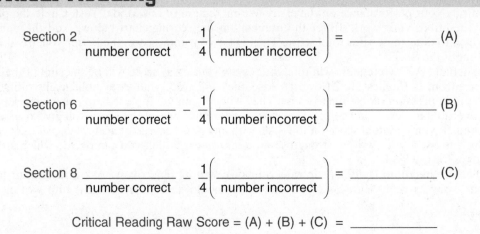

Section 2 _____ – $\frac{1}{4}$ (_____) = _____ (A)
number correct   number incorrect

Section 6 _____ – $\frac{1}{4}$ (_____) = _____ (B)
number correct   number incorrect

Section 8 _____ – $\frac{1}{4}$ (_____) = _____ (C)
number correct   number incorrect

Critical Reading Raw Score = (A) + (B) + (C) = _____

Mathematical Reasoning

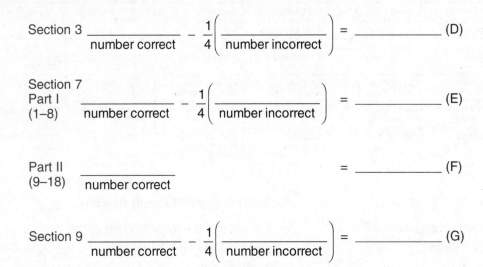

Section 3 _____ – $\frac{1}{4}$ (_____) = _____ (D)
number correct   number incorrect

Section 7
Part I   _____ – $\frac{1}{4}$ (_____) = _____ (E)
(1–8)   number correct   number incorrect

Part II   _____   = _____ (F)
(9–18)   number correct

Section 9 _____ – $\frac{1}{4}$ (_____) = _____ (G)
number correct   number incorrect

Mathematical Reasoning Raw Score = (D) + (E) + (F) + (G) = _____

Writing Skills

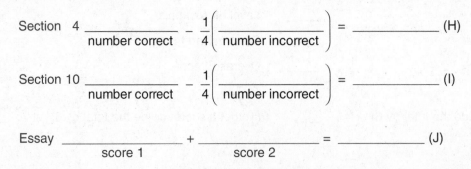

Section 4 _____ – $\frac{1}{4}$ (_____) = _____ (H)
number correct   number incorrect

Section 10 _____ – $\frac{1}{4}$ (_____) = _____ (I)
number correct   number incorrect

Essay _____ + _____ = _____ (J)
score 1   score 2

Writing Skills Raw Score = H + I (J is a separate subscore)

Evaluate Your Performance

Scaled Score	Critical Reading Raw Score	Mathematical Reasoning Raw Score	Writing Skills Raw Score
700–800	58–67	48–54	43–49
650–690	52–57	43–47	39–42
600–640	45–51	36–42	35–38
550–590	38–44	30–35	30–34
500–540	30–37	24–29	25–29
450–490	22–29	18–23	19–24
400–440	14–21	12–17	14–18
300–390	3–13	5–11	5–13
200–290	less than 3	less than 5	less than 5

Identify Your Weaknesses

Critical Reading

Question Type	Question Numbers			Chapter to Study
	Section 2	Section 6	Section 8	
Sentence Completion	1, 2, 3, 4, 5, 6, 7, 8	1, 2, 3, 4, 5	1, 2, 3, 4, 5, 6	Chapter 1
Critical Reading	9, 10, 11, 12, 13, 14, 15, 16, 17, 18, 19, 20, 21, 22, 23, 24	6, 7, 8, 9, 10, 11, 12, 13, 14, 15, 16, 17, 18, 19, 20, 21, 22, 23, 24	7, 8, 9, 10, 11, 12, 13, 14, 15, 16, 17, 18, 19	Chapter 2

Identify Your Weaknesses

Mathematical Reasoning

Section in Chapter 9	Question Numbers			Pages to Study
	Section 3	Section 7	Section 9	
A Basic Arithmetic Concepts	1, 3, 5, 6, 18	1, 6, 18	3, 4	410–431
B Fractions and Decimals		17	2	432–449
C Percents	8, 12	12, 15	2, 10, 11	450–460
D Ratios and Proportions	10	6, 13	1	461–472
E Averages	16	15, 16		473–479
F Polynomials			13	480–488
G Equations and Inequalities	2, 11, 13, 16	2, 3, 10	12, 15	489–502
H Word Problems	7, 10, 17	13	15	503–513
I Lines and Angles		10	7, 9	514–524
J Triangles	4, 15, 20	8, 9	6	525–542
K Quadrilaterals	9, 11, 15	8, 11	5	543–553
L Circles	9, 17	4, 5		554–564
M Solid Geometry	12		7	565–573
N Coordinate Geometry		4		574–588
O Counting and Probability		5		589–600
P Logical Reasoning	19	14	8, 9	601–608
Q Data Interpretation			10	609–618
R Functions and Their Graphs	14	7	14, 16	619–628

Identify Your Weaknesses

Writing Skills

Question Type	Question Numbers		Chapter to Study
	Section 4	Section 10	
Improving Sentences	1, 2, 3, 4, 5, 6, 7, 8, 9, 10, 11	1, 2, 3, 4, 5, 6, 7, 8, 9, 10, 11, 12, 13, 14	Chapter 6
Identifying Sentence Errors	12, 13, 14, 15, 16, 17, 18, 19, 20, 21, 22, 23, 24, 25, 26, 27, 28, 29		Chapter 6
Improving Paragraphs	30, 31, 32, 33, 34, 35		Chapter 6
Essay			Chapter 7

ANSWERS EXPLAINED

Section 2 Critical Reading

1. E. The subject considers himself talented and creative and thinks office work is uninspiring, dull—in a word, *prosaic*.
   Note that the missing word must be a synonym or near-synonym for "uninspiring." Connected by the linking verb *was*, both words describe or define the office routine.
   (Definition)

2. B. A *chronological* order is one arranged in order of time. The missing word is an adjective describing the order in which the museum arranged the fossils. The second part of the sentence defines that order: from older to more recent in time.
   Word Parts Clue: *Chron-* means time.
   (Definition)

3. B. Thanks to the development of wings, insects were able to *disperse* or scatter over Earth's surface. Thus, they were able to reach new habitats and untapped sources of nourishment.
   (Cause and Effect Pattern)

4. B. For London to miss out on (fail to attract) two major international art exhibitions marks it as a failure or *also-ran* in the blockbuster-hungry world of international art museums.
   (Cause and Effect Pattern)

5. C. The critics are *riled* or irritated by the condescending, superior tone of the magazine's editorials.
   Note how the section of the sentence following the blank illustrates what aspect of the magazine annoys its critics. (Example)

6. B. *Although* the Supreme Court nominee had a compassionate nature, nevertheless she was strict and unbending (*uncompromising*) in sticking or *adhering* to the law.
   Note that "although" signals a contrast. Look at the first word of each answer choice to see if it is an antonym for "compassionate by nature." You can immediately eliminate Choices A, C, and E.
   Choice D is incorrect. Someone *truly* compassionate by nature would not be *vindictive* or vengeful. (Contrast Signal)

7. C. To observe the adage "Look before you leap" is to be cautious. In this instance, however, the subject did *not* look before he leaped. Instead, he was *precipitate* (hasty, rash) in acting in a thoughtless, unconsidered manner.
   Again, "although" signals a contrast. Look at each answer choice to see if it is an antonym for being cautious. (Contrast Signal)

8. B. Because these seals eat far more krill than crabs, to call them crabeater seals is to *misname* them. The term is thus a *misnomer*, a name that's wrongly applied to someone or something.

Beware of Eye-Catchers. Choice A is incorrect. A *pseudonym* isn't a mistaken name; it's a false name that someone, especially an author, adopts.
   Remember: this is the last sentence completion question of a set of eight. If you have to guess, try the *least* familiar word among the answers. (Cause and Effect Signal)

9. B. By embracing Ibsen's controversial dramas, the British intellectuals *adopted* them, making them their own.

10. D. The author states that Marx "went so far as" to teach herself Norwegian in order to translate Ibsen. This action on Marx's part demonstrates her ardent championing of the Norwegian dramatist. It *supports the earlier assertion* that British intellectuals "wholeheartedly embraced" Ibsen's works.

11. E. The author is *contradicting the social critics' conclusion* that income growth no longer promotes well-being. He points to his personal experience to show that his increased income has led to a greater sense of well-being on his part.

12. A. The author's use of the colloquial exclamation "Great!," his casual suggestion of purchasing a hybrid vehicle, and his slangy, informal wording ("having money sure takes the pressure off") all contribute to the *breezy*, carefree tone.

13. B. The author contrasts Popeye with Mickey, referring to Popeye as "aggressive" and "self-promoting." These relatively negative terms indicate that the author's attitude toward Popeye is *deprecatory* or disparaging.

14. A. Unlike Popeye, Mickey does not promote or boast about himself: he lets his skills remain unsuspected. Similarly, when danger strikes, Mickey does not push himself forward: he is a reluctant hero. These traits reveal Mickey's modest, *unassuming nature*.

15. E. The scrapes Mickey gets into are *predicaments* (difficult situations).

16. B. Immediately before quoting Disney's assertion that there was a lot of the Mouse in him, the author states that the image of Mickey as a pretty nice, harmless, good-natured sort of guy "was perhaps Disney's image of himself." Disney pictured himself as Mickey, scrambling and struggling and yet always managing to come up grinning. Thus, by saying "There's a lot of the Mouse in me," Disney revealed *the extent of his identification with his creation*.

17. A. The author has been developing Disney's positive image of Mickey as a pretty nice fellow, showing how Disney's background led to his identifying himself with the humble, scrambling mouse. He then suddenly goes off on a side topic, explaining why the Nazis during World War II had a negative image of Mickey. Clearly, he is *digressing*, straying from the subject at hand.

18. E. Disney is described as being nice "until crossed." If someone *opposed* him and stood in the way of his reaching his artistic and business goals, he quit being nice.

19. D. Disney was *not* the inventor of film animation. As the passage indicates, the technology "would have been there anyway."

20. C. Both President Roosevelt, who insisted on being shown Mickey Mouse cartoons, and the African tribesmen, who had Mickey's image set into their teeth, are examples of people around the globe who enjoyed Mickey Mouse. The author uses these examples to *support the assertion* that Mickey's image was known around the world—it was popular all over Africa as well as in the United States—and that powerful people as well as primitive tribesmen, *people of all backgrounds, were drawn to Mickey Mouse*.

21. D. According to the passage, "something timeless in the image" transforms the status of a fad or passing fancy to that of an icon (a sign that stands for the object it represents because of some resemblance between the two; often a sacred image venerated by people). *The fad is clearly less enduring in appeal than is the icon*.

22. D. The author wishes to show how strong a hold Mickey has on America's collective awareness. To do so, he revitalizes a familiar cliché. Mickey does not simply grab our imaginations; he takes a bite out of them. In other words, he forcefully *captures our fancies*.

23. B. The key shaped out of three connected circles does not present a realistic, detailed likeness of Mickey Mouse. It fails to show his nose, his eyes, his mouth—the usual identifying features. Nevertheless, this simple, bare outline is *unmistakably* Mickey: anyone who looks at it knows it is an image of Mickey Mouse. This clearly shows that *even a rudimentary outline can convey the image of Mickey*.

24. D. The new Disney gadget is described as representing Mickey's image in the simplest, most rudimentary fashion: "three circles, two mounted on a larger one, [whose] image is unmistakably Mickey." Only the *waffle iron*, turning out its three-ringed, featureless (but unmistakable) Mickey Mouse waffles, presents Mickey as an artifact, a manufactured object, rather than as the commercially generated, representational image of the familiar cartoon figure in red shorts.

Section 3 Mathematical Reasoning

In each mathematics section, for many problems, an alternative solution, indicated by two asterisks (**), follows the first solution. When this occurs, one of the solutions is the direct mathematical one and the other is based on one of the tactics discussed in Chapter 8 or 9.

1. C. Just look at each number carefully. The hundreds place is the third from the left of the decimal point, and the hundredths place is the second to the right of the decimal point: 2**2**42.4**2**42.

2. C. If Beth has twice as many cards as Bruce, Bruce has half as many as Beth: $\frac{b}{2}$.

   **This is so easy that you shouldn't have to plug in a number, but you could: If Beth has 10 cards, Bruce has 5, and only $\frac{b}{2}$ equals 5 when b is 10.

3. D. To convert 225 minutes to hours, divide by 60: the quotient is 3 and the remainder is 45. Therefore, 225 minutes from 9:05 is 3 hours and 45 minutes from 9:05 A.M., that is, **12:50 P.M.**

   **If you divide 225 by 60 on your calculator, you get 3.75; then you have to convert 0.75, or $\frac{3}{4}$, of an hour to 45 minutes.

4. C. By KEY FACT J2, the measure of an exterior angle of a triangle is equal to the sum of the measures of the two opposite interior angles, so $140 = x + x = 2x \Rightarrow x = $ **70**.
   **If you don't remember this fact, label the third angle in the triangle y. Then $140 + y = 180$, and so $y = 40$. Now solve the equation $40 + x + x = 180$:
   $$40 + 2x = 180 \Rightarrow 2x = 140 \Rightarrow x = 70.$$

5. B. Let x and y be the two numbers: $x - y > x + y \Rightarrow -y > y \Rightarrow 0 > 2y \Rightarrow y$ is negative. Therefore, **at least one of the numbers is negative**. [Note that there are no restrictions on x: $x - (-1) = x + 1$, which is greater than $x + (-1) = x - 1$, no matter what x is.]

6. D. By the laws of exponents (KEY FACT A16), $(3a^2b^3)^3 = 3^3(a^2)^3(b^3)^3 = $ **$27a^6b^9$**.

   Use TACTIC 6: substitute numbers. If a and b are 1, $(3a^2b^3)^3 = 3^3 = 27$. Eliminate A and B. If $a = 1$ and $b = 2$, $(3a^2b^3)^3 = (3 \cdot 1 \cdot 8)^3 = 24^3$. Use your calculator to evaluate $24^3 = 13,824$; then test choices C (which doesn't work) and D: **$27a^6b^9$.

7. A. If y years ago Anne-Marie was x years old, she is now $x + y$, and in z years she will be **$x + y + z$**.

   **Use TACTIC 6: substitute numbers. If 2 years ago Anne-Marie was 10, how old will she be in 3 years? She is now 12 and in 3 years will be 15. Only $x + y + z$ (A) equals 15 when $x = 10$, $y = 2$, and $z = 3$.

8. E. Solve the equation, $10 = \frac{x}{100}A$:

$$1000 = xA \Rightarrow x = \frac{1000}{A}\%.$$

**Use TACTIC 6: substitute an easy-to-use number. 10 is 100% of 10. Which choices are equal to 100% when $A = 10$? Both A and E. Eliminate B, C, and D, and try another number: 10 is 50% of 20. Of A and E, only $\frac{1000}{A}$ equals 50 when $A = 20$.

9. A. Refer to the figures below.

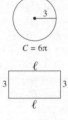

Since the formula for the circumference of a circle is $2\pi r$, the circumference of this circle is 6π (KEY FACT L4). By KEY FACT K7, the perimeter of a rectangle is $2(\ell + w)$, so here $P = 2(\ell + 3)$.

$$6\pi = 2(\ell + 3) \Rightarrow$$
$$\ell + 3 = 3\pi \Rightarrow \ell = \mathbf{3\pi - 3}.$$

10. A. Let x be the number of marbles that Anthony has. Then $3x$ is $\frac{1}{3}$ the number of marbles Billy has, so Billy has $9x$ marbles. The ratio is $x:9x$ or **1:9**.

Use TACTIC 7: pick an easy-to-use number. Assume that Anthony has 1 marble. If he had 3 times as many, he would have 3; and if 3 is $\frac{1}{3}$ the number that Billy has, Billy has 9. The ratio is **1:9.

11. B. It is given that $\overline{BE} \cong \overline{BC}$; also $\overline{BC} \cong \overline{AD}$, since they are opposite sides of a rectangle. Label each of them w, as shown in the figure.

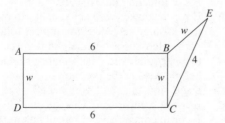

Then $R = 12 + 2w$ and $T = 4 + 2w$, so $R - T = \mathbf{8}$.

12. D. The volume of the small tank is $\pi r^2 h$, and the volume of the large tank is $\pi (2r)^2 h$, which equals $4\pi r^2 h$, so the large tank is 4 times the size of the small one. *Be careful!* This is an *increase* of 300%, not 400%. (4 is 3 more than 1, so is 300% more than 1.) Therefore, $k = \mathbf{300}$.

13. D. Since 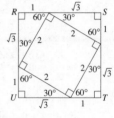 is a number box,

$xy = 4 \times 6 = 24$ and $x = 4 + y + 6$, so
$$x = 10 + y \Rightarrow y = 2 \text{ and } x = 12.$$
Therefore, $x + y = 12 + 2 = \mathbf{14}$.

14. A. $f(a) = a \Rightarrow 3a + 8 = a \Rightarrow 8 = -2a \Rightarrow a = \mathbf{-4}$.

15. A. If the hypotenuse of a 30-60-90 right triangle is 2, the legs are 1 and $\sqrt{3}$. Therefore, each side of square *RSTU* is $1 + \sqrt{3}$, and the perimeter is 4 times that value:

$$\mathbf{4 + 4\sqrt{3}}.$$

16. D. Use TACTIC 17. When you have three equations, add them:

$$
\begin{array}{r}
x + y = a \\
y + z = b \\
+\quad x + z = c \\
\hline
2x + 2y + 2z = a + b + c
\end{array}
$$

Divide by 2: $x + y + z = \dfrac{a + b + c}{2}$

Divide by 3: $\dfrac{x + y + z}{3} = \dfrac{a + b + c}{6}$

**Use TACTIC 6: substitute for the variables. Let $x = 1$, $y = 2$, and $z = 3$. Then the average of x, y, and z is 2. When $a = 1 + 2 = 3$, $b = 2 + 3 = 5$, and $c = 1 + 3 = 4$, which of the choices equals 2? Only $\dfrac{a + b + c}{6}$.

17. E. Since $C = 2\pi r$ (KEY FACT L4),

$$2\pi r = 120\sqrt{\pi} \Rightarrow r = \frac{120\sqrt{\pi}}{2\pi} = \frac{60\sqrt{\pi}}{\pi}.$$

Then, by KEY FACT L8, the area of the field is $\pi\left(\dfrac{60\sqrt{\pi}}{\pi}\right)^2 = \pi\,\dfrac{3600\pi}{\pi^2} = \dfrac{3600\pi^2}{\pi^2} =$

3600 square meters.

Finally, since Eric can mow 400 square meters of grass per hour, he will take $3600 \div 400 = \mathbf{9}$ hours to mow the entire field.

18. C. Replacing *a* by 2*a*, *b* by 3*b*, and *c* by 4*c* gives
$$\frac{(2a)(3b)^2}{4c} = \frac{2a(9b^2)}{4c} = \frac{9}{2}\left(\frac{ab^2}{c}\right) = \frac{9}{2}X = 4.5X.$$
In words, **X is multiplied by 4.5**.

**Use TACTIC 6. Let *a* = 1, *b* = 2,
and *c* = 3. Then $X = \frac{1(2)^2}{3} = \frac{4}{3}$. Now let
a = 2, *b* = 6, and *c* = 12; what will *X* be?
$\frac{2(6)^2}{12} = \frac{72}{12} = 6$. By what must $\frac{4}{3}$ be multiplied
to get 6? The calculation is as follows:
$$6 \div \frac{4}{3} = 6 \times \frac{3}{4} = \frac{18}{4} = \mathbf{4.5}.$$

19. C. Since the pattern has six digits, divide 135 by 6. The quotient is 22, and the remainder is 3. Since 22 × 6 = 132, the 132nd number completes the pattern for the 22nd time. Then the 133rd, 134th, and <u>135</u>th numbers are 1's, and the <u>136</u>th and <u>137</u>th are 2's; and their sum is <u>1</u> + <u>2</u> + <u>2</u> = **5**.

20. E. If you think to reduce the ratio 5:5:10 to 1:1:2, fine; if not, just write
$$180 = 5x + 5x + 10x = 20x \Rightarrow x = 9,$$
and so the angles measure 45°, 45°, and 90°. By KEY FACT J8, if you know the length of any side of a 45-45-90 right triangle, you can find the other sides and hence the area (I), the perimeter (II), and the lengths of the altitudes (III), two of which are the legs. Statements **I**, **II, and III** are true. (*Note*: You should not waste any time actually finding the area, the perimeter, or the altitudes.)

Section 4 Writing Skills

1. A. Sentence is correct.
2. B. The original sentence contains a dangling modifier, as does Choice D. Choices C and E are wordy and awkward. Only Choice B corrects the error and is an effective, concise sentence.
3. C. Error in subject-verb agreement. The authors (plural) *have* largely conquered their subject (singular). Only Choice C corrects the error in subject-verb agreement without introducing a fresh error.
4. B. Error in parallelism. Choice B repairs the lack of parallel structure without introducing fresh errors.
5. E. Error in placement. The concluding phrase in the original is both misplaced and awkwardly worded.
6. E. Lack of conciseness. The original sentence is unnecessarily wordy. Choice E cuts out the needless words and substitutes an active verb for the linking verb *is*.
7. D. Error in usage. When three or more persons are named, use *last* instead of *latter*. (Although Choice E does substitute *last* for *latter*, it introduces an error in subject-verb agreement.)
8. E. Error in parallelism. To make the parallel clear, repeat the preposition. Lewis spoke as eloquently *on* Christianity as *on* literature.
9. D. Error in parallelism. To correct the error, change *intimidating* to *intimidate*. Remember: all items in a series should have the same form.
10. B. Dangling modifier. What was only partially defrosted, the meal or the attendant? Clearly, it was the meal. Choice B clears up the confusion economically.
11. C. Do not use *when* after *is* unless you are making a statement about time ("3:00 P.M. is when I take my next pill"). Replace "A factor...is when" with "A factor...is that."
12. A. Error in word usage. *Irregardless* is nonstandard. Substitute *Regardless*.
13. E. Sentence is correct.
14. D. Error in parallelism. Change *and how they organized the militia* to *and the organization of the militia*.
15. C. Error in subject-verb agreement. Not one of the more than two thousand rooms *was equipped* with sprinklers.
16. C. Error in word usage. *Raise,* a transitive verb, means to lift something upward; *rise,* an intransitive verb, means simply to move upward. Backstage, stagehands pull on ropes to *raise* the curtain. From the viewpoint of the audience out front, the curtain simply *rises*.
17. A. Error in subject-verb agreement. The subject, *progress*, is singular; the verb should be singular as well. Change *have been* to *has been*.
18. A. Shift of personal pronoun. Do not switch person from *one* to *you*.
19. D. Error in logical comparison. Change *any* to *any other*.
20. B. Error in comparison. *Unique* is an absolute adjective, one without degrees of comparison. Do not describe something as *most unique*; either it is unique (one of a kind) or it is not unique.
21. D. Error in idiom. The animal pathogen is *capable of* infecting human cells.
22. A. Error in subject-verb agreement. Remember that in some sentences the subject follows the verb. Here the subject is plural: *discussion* and *performance*. The sentence should begin "Also in the program *are* a taped discussion...and a performance."
23. C. Error in comparison. Change *more* to *most*.
24. C. Error in comparison. Change *less* to *lesser* (the comparative form of the adjective).
25. E. Sentence is correct.
26. C. Incorrect conjunction. Change *while* to *and*.

27. D.   Incomplete comparison. Compare perfor-
         mances with performances, not performances
         with dancers. Change "than the other dancers"
         to "than those of the other dancers."
28. B.   Error in diction. Substitute *likely* for *liable*.
29. B.   Incorrect pronoun. Replace *few of which* with
         few of whom.
30. C.   Choice A implies that the essay's purpose is to
         admire the technological achievements of the
         twentieth century. The essay, however, has
         another purpose. Choice B is similar to A and
         also contains an inappropriate colloquialism.
         Choice C accurately captures the essay's
         theme—that technological progress is neither
         all good nor all bad. It is the best answer.
         Choice D suggests that the essay will discuss
         the prospects for continued technological
         progress, but the essay has a different purpose.
         Choice E names the three areas discussed in
         the essay but, contrary to the point of the
         essay, suggests that we would be better off
         without technological progress.
31. C.   Choice A unnecessarily repeats *energy* and
         contains an incomplete comparison. Energy
         is cheaper than what? Choice B contains an
         incomplete comparison. Energy is cheaper than
         what? It also contains an error in parallel con-
         struction. Choice C is succinct and accurately
         expressed. It is the best answer. Choice D con-
         tains an error in parallel construction. Choice E
         also contains a faulty comparison. Cheaper and
         easier than what?
32. B.   Although related to communications, the
         information contained in sentence 6 is not
         germane to the discussion of communication
         satellites. Therefore, B is the best answer.
33. A.   Choice A is consistent in style and tone to the
         sentences preceding and following sentence
         15. It is the best answer. Choice B is a sen-
         tence fragment. Choice C contains the non-
         standard usage, *hardly no*, which is a double
         negative. Choice D contains a sudden shift to
         second person, which does not fit the tone and
         style of the preceding and following sen-
         tences. Choice E is needlessly repetitious.
34. B.   Choice A does not accurately describe either
         the paragraph structure or the point of the
         essay. Choice B precisely describes the struc-
         ture of each paragraph. It is the best answer.
         Choices C and D describe neither the para-
         graph structure nor the point of the essay.
         Choice E is an inference that might be drawn
         from the essay, but the writer never directly
         advocates greater funding.
35. E.   Choice A unnecessarily repeats *CAT scan* and
         contains faulty parallelism. Choice B unneces-
         sarily repeats *CAT scan* and is needlessly
         wordy. Choice C contains a dangling partici-
         ple. The phrase that begins *Taking pictures*
         should modify *doctors,* not *brain*. Choice D
         does not make a clear, explicit connection

with the preceding sentence. Choice E is a
succinct and error-free follow-up to the preceding sentence. It is the best answer.

Section 6 Critical Reading

1. B.   The words "merely" and "failed to highlight"
        indicate that the woman is dissatisfied with the
        job-seeker's resume. It lacks some qualities
        she thinks it needs. It is *inadequate*, not up to
        standards, deficient.
        Note that you are looking for a word with neg-
        ative associations. Therefore, you can elimi-
        nate any word with positive ones. Choices C
        and E both have positive associations. Only
        Choice A, B, or D can be correct.
                                              (Examples)
2. D.   Most medical research is aimed at helping
        human beings. Therefore, having discovered
        something about the cause of a disease
        affecting animals, it would be perfectly rea-
        sonable or *logical* for researchers to wish to
        apply their findings to the treatment of
        humans.
        Remember: before you look at the choices,
        read the sentence and think of a word that
        makes sense.
        Watch for signal words that link one part of
        the sentence to another. The use of "Because"
        in the opening clause is a cause signal. Ask
        yourself what would be a logical next step
        after finding out that a kind of virus caused
        cancer in animals.   (Cause and Effect Signal)
3. B.   The key phrase here is "treated her badly."
        Because the news media have *misrepresented*
        her, distorting or misstating her comments,
        Ms. Ono does not like to give interviews.
        Therefore, she gives them *rarely*.
        Remember to watch for signal words that link
        one part of the sentence to another. The use of
        "because" introducing the second clause sets up
        a pattern of cause and effect. Note also the use
        of the support signal *and*, here letting you know
        that the second missing word must be a syn-
        onym or near-synonym for "treated her badly."
              (Cause and Effect Signal/Support Signal)
4. E.   The introduction of metal tools significantly
        improved totem craftsmanship: *because* the
        carvers had better tools, they could do better,
        "more sophisticated" or advanced work. Thus,
        thanks to the introduction of metal tools,
        totem craftsmanship reached its high point or
        apex.   (Cause and Effect Pattern)
5. C.   Admirers of realism would not esteem "the
        stuff of legend"; they prefer fallible, ordinary
        people to mythic figures who seem larger-
        than-life. They thus prefer a film that *shuns* or
        rejects make-believe in order to tell a plain,
        unembellished tale.
        Note the cause-and-effect signal *because*. The
        sentence explains why Malle's realistic film
        succeeds.   (Cause and Effect Signal)

6. A. The capacity in question is the bear's remarkable *ability* to smell its prey from a phenomenal distance away.

7. D. Passage 1 describes the polar bear's layers of blubber and fur, its broad paws, its sharp claws—in other words, its *physical characteristics*.

8. E. The author of Passage 2 *establishes a time frame*. First, she cites a threat to polar bear survival that occurred "In the mid-twentieth century." Then, she refers to a 1973 agreement that diminished that threat. Finally, she mentions a new threat that exists "Today."

9. C. Passage 1 describes polar bears as formidable hunters; Passage 2 terms them top predators and fearsome killers. Both passages support the generalization that polar bears *are notable predators*.

10. C. Choice C is correct. You can arrive at it by the process of elimination.
Statement I is true. Sir Walter's vanity was "vanity of person." He was vain about his personal appearance, his *physical attractiveness*. Therefore, you can eliminate Choice B.
Statement II is true. Sir Walter's vanity was also vanity "of situation." He was vain about his position in society, his titled rank. Therefore, you can eliminate Choices A and D.
Statement III is untrue. Sir Walter's wife, not Sir Walter, was superior in character. Therefore, you can eliminate Choice E.
Only Choice C is left. It is the correct answer.

11. D. The narrator does *not* commend Lady Elliot for falling in love with Sir Walter, calling it a "youthful infatuation," the only misjudgment in an otherwise blameless life. Therefore, Choice D is correct.
The narrator speaks well of Lady Elliot for concealing Sir Walter's shortcomings: she has "promoted his real respectability." Choice A is supported by the passage. Therefore, it is incorrect.
The narrator commends Lady Elliot for her choice of a friend: she has chosen "a sensible, deserving woman," one who even moves into the neighborhood to be near her. Choice B is supported by the passage. Therefore, it is incorrect.
The narrator speaks well of the way Lady Elliot guides her daughters: she has given them "good principles and instruction." Choice C is supported by the passage. Therefore, it is incorrect.
Choice E is incorrect. The narrator clearly commends Lady Elliot in her performance of her duties as a wife.

12. C. The narrator's statement that Lady Elliot was "not the very happiest being in the world herself" is preceded by a list of all Lady Elliot had to do to cover up for her "conceited, silly" husband. Thus we can infer that the cause of her unhappiness was the difference or *disparity* between her character and that of her husband.
Choice A is incorrect. Nothing in the passage suggests Lady Elliot lacks beauty. Indeed, we suspect that Sir Walter, so conscious of his own beauty, would not have chosen an unattractive wife.
Choice B is incorrect. Lady Elliot's best friend had moved to be near her; they were not separated.
Choice D is incorrect. Lady Elliot's social position was, at least in Sir Walter's eyes, superior, not inferior.
Choice E is incorrect. Nothing in the passage suggests that Lady Elliot's daughters were wayward.

13. B. Choice B is correct. The narrator tells little directly of Lady Elliot's feelings about dying. However, such phrases as "Three girls...was an awful legacy to bequeath" and "anxiously giving her daughters [instruction]" show us something of her mind. Her concern centers not on herself but on those she must leave behind: her daughters. Her emotions as she faces death are complicated by *anxieties over her daughters' prospects*.
Choice A is incorrect. Nothing in the passage suggests resignation or pious submissiveness on her part.
Choices C and D are incorrect. Both are unsupported by the passage.
Choice E is also incorrect. Lady Elliot clearly has faced the reality of her approaching death: she realizes that she is leaving her daughters to the care of her conceited, silly husband.

14. A. Lady Elliot in "quitting" her family is not simply taking a trip: she is dying. We expect a person facing death to react strongly, emotionally. Instead, the narrator states that Lady Elliot was merely attached enough to life to make dying "no matter of indifference to her." That is clearly an *understatement*. It is an example of *irony*, the literary technique that points up the contradictions in life, in this case the contradiction between the understated expression and the deeply felt reality.

15. C. Sir Walter's applications have been *marital* ones. In his conceit, he has applied for the hand in marriage of some women who were far too good for him (his applications were *unreasonable*). Sensibly enough, these women have turned him down (he has been *disappointed* in his proposals of matrimony). However, his conceit is undiminished: he prides himself on remaining single for his dear daughters' sake.

16. D. The opening sentence describes the shattering of the Iroquois leadership's pro-British policy. The remainder of the passage describes how Iroquois policy changed to reflect changes in European military goals.

Choice A is incorrect. The passage is expository, not accusatory.

Choice B is incorrect. Nothing in the passage suggests that such charges were made against the Iroquois.

Choice C is incorrect. It is unsupported by the passage.

Choice E is incorrect. The passage demonstrates the Iroquois were able to play European power politics.

Remember: when asked to find the main idea, be sure to check the opening and summary sentences of each paragraph.

17. **B.** The Europeans *designated* or called these confederations of Indian tribes nations, giving them the same title they used for European states.

18. **C.** In this sentence, "rough" means approximate, as in "a rough guess." The tribes dealt with Europeans as approximate equals, not as *exact* or *absolute equals*.

19. **C.** The author presents the Iroquois Confederacy's experience "as an example of the process that *all* the interior nations experienced." Thus, he regards what happened to the Iroquois as *representative* or typical of the experiences of the other interior tribes.

20. **B.** In lines 61–63, the author states that the Iroquois "played the game of European power politics with effectiveness." Thus, he shows *respect for their competence*.

None of the other choices is supported by the passage.

Remember: when asked to determine the author's attitude or tone, look for words that convey value judgments.

21. **E.** Lines 45–63 indicate that in the early 1700s and through most of the eighteenth century the Iroquois *did* hold the balance of power. Therefore, Choice E is the correct answer.

Choice A is incorrect. The raid on Lachine was an effective response to French aggression, as was the Iroquois-enforced policy of aggressive neutrality.

Choice B is incorrect. James II's overthrow was followed by colonial uprisings.

Choice C is incorrect. In response to the Iroquois leaders' supposed favoring of the British (lines 63–69), the French went to war.

Choice D is incorrect. This sums up the policy of aggressive neutrality.

22. **A.** Lines 57–60 indicate that the Iroquois played the game of power politics with effectiveness "by their willingness to use their power against one or the other nation." In other words, they were *ready to fight either side*.

Choice B is incorrect. Ties of loyalty may actually have hampered the Iroquois; the French fear that the Iroquois were compromising the system in favor of the British led to the eventual breakdown of the policy of neutrality.

Choice C is incorrect. French presence in the borderlands would have been a challenge to Iroquois power.

Choices D and E are incorrect. They are unsupported by the passage.

23. **B.** The French believed that the Iroquois were *jeopardizing* or undermining the system of Iroquois neutrality by making decisions that favored the English.

24. **A.** The opening paragraph describes the changing state of relationships between the European powers and the tribes of the interior during the eighteenth century. As more and more French and English settlers moved into the interior, the Indian nations had to find new ways of dealing with the encroaching French and English populations. The paragraph concludes by stating: "The history of the reorientation of Iroquois policy toward the Europeans may serve as an example of the process that all the interior nations experienced in the eighteenth century." Thus, the next three paragraphs, which sum up the Iroquois' experience, provide *an instance of a state of relationships described earlier*.

Section 7 Mathematical Reasoning

MULTIPLE-CHOICE QUESTIONS

1. **C.** $A = \{1, 3, 5, 7, 9\}$ and $B = \{2, 3, 5, 7\}$. The positive integers less than 10 that are in neither A nor B are 4, 6, and 8. There are **3** of them.

2. **C.** Let x be Mr. Gomes's number.
   Then $x + 3 = 3x \Rightarrow 3 = 2x \Rightarrow x = \mathbf{1.5}$.

   **Use TACTIC 5: backsolve. Start with C:
   $1.5 + 3 = 4.5$ and $1.5 \times 3 = 4.5$. It works.

3. **B.** The easiest solution is to quickly reduce, either by dividing by 16 (if you recognize that $64 = 4 \times 16$) or by repeatedly dividing each

   side by 8: $\dfrac{\cancel{(16)}\cancel{(16)}\cancel{(16)} n}{} = \dfrac{\cancel{(64)}\overset{1}{\cancel{(64)}}\overset{4}{\cancel{(64)}}}{n}$.

   Then $n = \dfrac{1}{n} \Rightarrow n = \mathbf{1}$.

   **Of course, you can rewrite the equation as
   $$n^2 = \frac{(64)(64)}{(16)(16)(16)}$$
   and use your calculator: $n^2 = \mathbf{1}$.

4. **B.** By the distance formula (KEY FACT N2),

   the length of diameter $\overline{AB}$ is

   $$\sqrt{(2-4)^2 + (-1-7)^2} = \sqrt{(-2)^2 + (-8)^2} =$$
   $$\sqrt{4 + 64} = \sqrt{68}.$$

Then the radius of the circle is $\dfrac{\sqrt{68}}{2}$, and the

area of the circle is $\pi\left(\dfrac{\sqrt{68}}{2}\right)^2 = \pi\left(\dfrac{68}{4}\right) = \mathbf{17\pi}$.

5. **E.** Since no numbers were given, choose a simple value for the length of diameter $\overline{BC}$ of the small semicircle, say 2. Then the small semicircle has a radius of 1, and its area is

$\dfrac{1}{2}\pi(1)^2 = \dfrac{\pi}{2}$. Since $AB = BC = CD = 2$,

then $\overline{AD}$, the diameter of the large semicircle, has length 6, and so the radius is 3. Then the

area of the large semicircle is $\dfrac{1}{2}\pi(3)^2 = \dfrac{9\pi}{2}$.

Finally, the area of the shaded region is

$\dfrac{9\pi}{2} - \dfrac{\pi}{2} = \dfrac{8\pi}{2} = 4\pi$, and the probability

that the point lies in the shaded region is

$\dfrac{4\pi}{\frac{9\pi}{2}} = 4\pi \times \dfrac{2}{9\pi} = 4 \times \dfrac{2}{9} = \dfrac{\mathbf{8}}{\mathbf{9}}$.

**Since the ratio of the radii is $\dfrac{1}{3}$, the ratio of

the areas is $\dfrac{1}{9}$. Then the white semicircle is $\dfrac{1}{9}$

and the shaded region is $\dfrac{\mathbf{8}}{\mathbf{9}}$ of the entire figure.

6. **A.** Cross-multiply: $r(s + 1) < s(r + 1) \Rightarrow$
$rs + r < rs + s \Rightarrow \mathbf{r < s}$.
(Note that, since s is positive, the order of the inequality is preserved. Also, if r and s are integers, then $s > 1$, but they need not be integers.)
**Use Tactic 6: Try some numbers.
If $r = 1$ and $s = 1$, the inequality is false.
If $r = 1$ and $s = 2$, only A, D, and E are satisfied, so eliminate B and C. If trying one or two more numbers doesn't eliminate any other choices, guess.

7. **E.** $f(x) = 3 \Rightarrow 3 + \dfrac{5}{x} = 3 \Rightarrow \dfrac{5}{x} = 0$, which is

impossible, so **3** cannot be a value of $f(x)$.
(A fraction can equal 0 only if its numerator is 0.) Note that x cannot be 0, but

$f(x)$ can be: $f(x)$ is 0 if $x = -\dfrac{5}{3}$.

8. **D.** Since you need a ratio, the length of the side is irrelevant. The area of a square is s^2, and the

area of an equilateral triangle is $\dfrac{s^2\sqrt{3}}{4}$

(KEY FACT J15). Then the ratio is

$s^2 \div \dfrac{s^2\sqrt{3}}{4} = s^2 \times \dfrac{4}{s^2\sqrt{3}} = \dfrac{4}{\sqrt{3}} = \dfrac{\mathbf{4\sqrt{3}}}{\mathbf{3}}$.

Of course, you could have used 5 instead of s; and if you forgot the formula for the area of an equilateral triangle, you could have used

$A = \dfrac{1}{2}bh$.

GRID-IN QUESTIONS

9. (78) The area of the red paper is $9 \times 12 = 108$ square inches. The area of each 3×5 card is 15 square inches, so the area of the uncovered part of the red paper is $108 - 15 - 15 = \mathbf{78}$ square inches.

10. (52) If there are x adults in the village, then $.8x$ of them are registered and $.6(.8x) = .48x$ voted. Therefore, $x - .48x = .52x$, or **52%**, of the adults did not vote.

    **The above solution is straightforward, but there is no reason to use x. Use TACTIC 6, and assume there are 100 adults. Then 80 of them are registered and 60% of 80 = 48 of them voted; 52 did not vote, which is

    $\dfrac{52}{100}$ or **52%**.

11. (115) We can find any or all of the angles in the figure. First, note that the measure of $\angle PST = 25°$. Then, since the measure of an exterior angle of a triangle is equal to the sum of the measures of the two opposite interior angles (KEY FACT J2), $w = 25 + 90 = \mathbf{115}$.
    **Alternatively, $25 + 90 + x = 180 \Rightarrow$ $115 + x = 180 \Rightarrow x = 65$.
    Then $x + w = 180 \Rightarrow 65 + w = 180 \Rightarrow$ $w = \mathbf{115}$.

12. (64) Since the sum of the six angles is 360° (KEY FACT I3), combining like terms, we get $5x + 40 = 360 \Rightarrow 5x = 320 \Rightarrow x = \mathbf{64}$.

13. (54) To find Henry's average speed, in kilometers per hour, divide the distance he went, in kilometers (198), by the time it took, in hours. Henry drove for 3 hours and 40

minutes, which is $3\frac{2}{3}$ hours

(40 minutes = $\frac{40}{60}$ hour = $\frac{2}{3}$ hour). Henry's

average speed, in kilometers per hour, was

$198 \div 3\frac{2}{3} = 198 \div \frac{11}{3} = 198 \times \frac{3}{11} = \mathbf{54}$.

14. (122)   Write out the first few terms, being careful
to follow the directions. The first term is 1.
The second term is 1 less than 3 times the
first term: $3(1) - 1 = 2$. The third term is 1
less than 3 times the second term:
$3(2) - 1 = 5$. Continue: $3(5) - 1 = 14$;
$3(14) - 1 = 41$; $3(41) - 1 = \mathbf{122}$.

15. (36)   Use TACTIC 6. Assume there are 100
stockholders and a total of 100 shares of
stock. Then Group A has 10 members and
Group B has 90. The 10 members of Group
A own 80 shares, an average of 8 shares per
member. The 90 members of Group B own
the other 20 shares, an average of $\frac{20}{90} = \frac{2}{9}$
shares per member.
Then, $8 = \frac{2}{9}k \Rightarrow k = 8 \times \frac{9}{2} = \mathbf{36}$.

16. (52)   This is a weighted average (KEY FACT E6):
$$\frac{40\%(40) + 60\%(60)}{100\%} = \frac{16 + 36}{1} = \mathbf{52}.$$

**If you prefer, assume there are 100
marbles, 40 of which are red and 60 of
which are blue:

$$\frac{40(40) + 60(60)}{100} = \frac{1600 + 3600}{100} = \mathbf{52}.$$

17. ($\frac{9}{10}$ or .9)   If there are x seats on each bus, then the
group is using $\frac{4}{5}(3x) = \frac{12}{5}x$ seats. After

$\frac{1}{4}$ of passengers get off, $\frac{3}{4}$ of them, or

$\frac{3}{4}(\frac{12}{5}x) = \frac{9}{5}x$, remain. The fraction of

the $2x$ seats now being used on the two

buses is $\dfrac{\frac{9}{5}x}{2x} = \dfrac{\frac{9}{5}}{2} = \dfrac{\mathbf{9}}{\mathbf{10}}$.

**Again, you can use TACTIC 6 to
avoid working with x. Assume there are
20 seats on each bus. At the beginning,
the group is using 48 of the 60 seats on

the three buses [$\frac{4}{5}(60) = 48$]. When 12

people left [$\frac{1}{4}(48) = 12$], the 36 remaining

people used $\frac{36}{40} = \frac{\mathbf{9}}{\mathbf{10}}$ of the 40 seats on two
buses.

18. (1) $a^{-4} = 16 \Rightarrow \dfrac{1}{a^4} = \dfrac{16}{1} \Rightarrow 16a^4 = 1.$

So, $a^4 = \dfrac{1}{16} \Rightarrow a = \dfrac{1}{2}.$

$(2a)^{\frac{1}{2}} = \left(2\left(\frac{1}{2}\right)\right)^{\frac{1}{2}} = (1)^{\frac{1}{2}} = \sqrt{1} = \mathbf{1}.$

Section 8 Critical Reading

1. B.   The subject's *verbosity*, her tendency to use
too many words, is what's irritating. The second clause defines the first.   (Definition)

2. C.   It would be useless or *futile* to try to poison
pests chemically if the creatures eventually
became *resistant* to or able to withstand the
effect of each new poison you introduced.
Choice C is correct.
Remember: watch for signal words that link
one part of the sentence to another. The conjunction *for* connecting the two halves of the
sentence signals you to expect a *cause and
effect* relationship between them.
                    (Cause and Effect Signal)

3. B.   *Because* insect bodies are *fragile* or breakable,
it is surprising that enough of them have *survived* (lasted in an unbroken condition) for scientists to draw conclusions about the way
insect species changed over time.
The key word here is "remarkable." It signals
a built-in contrast between what one might
expect to have happened and what actually did
happen.   (Implicit Contrast Signal)

4. C.   There are two key words here, "unfortunately"
and "imitations." "Unfortunately" indicates
that the missing word has negative connotations: the plays currently showing on
Broadway are pretty poor. "Imitations"
defines in just what way these plays are poor.
They are copies of hit plays, imitations trying
to follow a once-sucessful *formula* or pattern
that no longer works. In other words, they are
formulaic fare.   (Definition)

5. D.   Callas longed for honest criticism. She had
grown tired of *adulation* (praise) because she
had been surrounded by a group of people
who constantly *extolled* (praised) her singing.
(A retinue of sycophants is a group of flatter-
ers in attendance on an important personage.)
Remember, before you look at the choices, to
read the sentence and think of a word that
makes sense.
Likely Words: praised, admired.   (Examples)

6. A. Moore's criticism was *not* unsure (*tentative*) or provisional. It was sure or confident: she wrote *confidently*.

Remember to watch for signal words that link one part of the sentence to another. The presence of *or* linking a pair or a series of items indicates that the missing word may be a synonym or near-synonym for "provisional," the other linked word.

This sentence contrasts two ideas *without* using a signal word. The contrast is implicit in the juxtaposition of the two clauses.

(Contrast Pattern)

7. C. Passage 1 states: "Dolphins left the land when mammalian brains were still small and primitive" (lines 27–29). This indicates that dolphins were once *land* animals, mammals like ourselves, whose evolutionary development took them back into the sea.

8. E. The passage indicates that human beings think of intelligence in terms of our own ability to manipulate our environment—our ability to build and do all sorts of things with our hands. Since dolphins have no hands, we have trouble appreciating their high level of intelligence because of our *inclination to judge other life by our own*.

9. D. Passage 1 attempts to *reassess the nature and extent of dolphin intelligence*, first giving reasons why human beings may have trouble appreciating how intelligent dolphins really are and then, in the concluding sentence, reflecting how dolphin intelligence (that looks "inward to the sea's heart") may complement human intelligence (that looks "outward on eternity").

10. C. The dolphin's acute echo-sounding sense is a sharp, *keen* sense that enables the dolphin to sound or measure the ocean depths by using echoes.

11. C. The entire passage has concentrated on the dolphin's brain, so it is safe to assume that this is what is meant by "impressively elaborated instrument." The items listed in the other answer choices have not been mentioned. Note that Choice B, an artificial range-finding device, is incorrect because the dolphin's range-finding ability is entirely natural, not artificial.

12. A. The sea's heart is like the human mind in that it swarms or *teems* (abounds) with grotesque or *exotic forms of life*.

13. C. The author's tone is distinctly *admiring*. The passage speaks of the dolphins' "remarkable range-finding ability," mentions their care for each other, and repeatedly praises dolphin intelligence.

14. E. The quotation marks here indicate that the word in quotes is being used in a special sense (often an ironic one). In this case, as the next paragraph makes abundantly clear, the author

is critical of both the results and the influence of Lilly's experiments. He *has some doubts as to how scientific those experiments were*.

15. A. According to the author of Passage 2, by claiming that "dolphins communicate not only with one another but also with humans, mimicking human speech and reaching out across the boundaries that divide us" (lines 69–72), Lilly and his associates have *overstated* their case, misrepresenting *the extent of dolphin intelligence*. Choice B is incorrect. In stating that Lilly's conclusions have not withstood (stood up against) critical scrutiny, the author indicates that they *have* been critically scrutinized to an appropriate degree.

16. D. "Begging the question" refers to assuming the truth of the very point whose truth or falsehood you're trying to establish. The author of Passage 2 considers the reasoning in this argument flawed; he views it with doubt or *skepticism*.

17. A. Proof that dolphins are *far superior in linguistic capability* to seals and other mammals clearly would contradict the results of the studies the author cites and would thus *undercut* or weaken their impact.

18. A. In its glorification of dolphin intelligence as something that equals or possibly exceeds human intelligence, the author of Passage 2 would find Passage 1 *typical of the attitudes of Lilly and his associates*.

19. A. Passage 1 is filled with images. The sea is a "wavering green fairyland." The dolphin's brain is an "impressively elaborated instrument." Mammals take "a divergent road." The passage concludes with an elaborate simile. It is clearly *more figurative* than Passage 2.

Choice B is incorrect. With its enigmatic references to some "impressively elaborated instrument" and to a "great eye" staring at eternity, Passage 1 is far more *obscure* than Passage 2.

Choice C is incorrect. Passage 1 is heavily slanted in favor of the superiority of dolphin intelligence. It is not *more objective* or impartial than Passage 2, which attempts to give a short survey of research on dolphin intelligence, summing up current experiments and providing historical background.

Choice D is incorrect. The italicized introduction indicates that Passage 2 was written almost thirty years after Passage 1. By definition, it presents a more *current*, up-to-date view of the topic. *Always pay attention to information contained in the introductions to the reading passages.*

Choice E is incorrect. Passage 1's conclusion is sheer conjecture or *speculation*.

Section 9 Mathematical Reasoning

1. **B.** 88 beeps ÷ 16 beeps per minute = **5.5** minutes. If you prefer, set up a ratio and cross-multiply:

$$\frac{16 \text{ beeps}}{1 \text{ minute}} = \frac{88 \text{ beeps}}{x \text{ minutes}}.$$

2. **E.** $\frac{1}{2}\%$ means $\frac{1}{2}$ (or 0.5) divided by 100, which equals 0.005. With your calculator verify that choices A through D all equal 0.005, or $\frac{1}{2}\%$, whereas choice E, $\frac{1\%}{2\%} = \frac{1}{2}$.

3. **B.** $\{[(a \times a) + a] \div a\} - a =$
$\{[a^2 + a] \div a\} - a =$
$\dfrac{a^2 + a}{a} - a = a + 1 - a = \mathbf{1}.$

   **Use TACTIC 6. Let $a = 2$; then
$\{[(2 \times 2) + 2] \div 2\} - 2 =$
$\{[4 + 2] \div 2\} - 2 = \{6 \div 2\} - 2 = 3 - 2 = \mathbf{1}.$

4. **B.** There is *only* **1** prime divisible by 7, namely, 7.

5. **C.** The sum of the measures of the four angles of any quadrilateral is 360° (KEY FACT K1). If the average of the measures of two of them is 60°, then they total 120° (TACTIC E1), leaving 240° for the other two angles, so their average is **120°**.

   **Draw a quadrilateral, two of whose angles measure 60°, and estimate the measures of the other angles. None of the wrong choices is even close.

6. **D.** Just check each choice. Is there a triangle whose sides are 1, 2, 3? No, the sum of any two sides of a triangle must be *greater* than the third side (KEY FACT J12). (I is false.) Are there triangles whose sides are 10, 11, 12 and 100, 101, 102? Yes. (II and III are true.) Statements **II and III only** are true.

7. **C.** By KEY FACT M4, the diagonal of a box whose dimensions are ℓ, w, h is

$$\sqrt{\ell^2 + w^2 + h^2}. \text{ Here, } \ell = w = h = 3,$$

   so $AB = \sqrt{3^2 + 3^2 + 3^2} = \sqrt{27} = \mathbf{3\sqrt{3}}.$

   **If you get stuck on a question like this, use TACTIC 8: eliminate absurd choices and guess. Since each edge is 3, clearly $AB > 3$, and going around the edges from A to B would give you 9, which is clearly too big. Then, at the very least, eliminate choices A and E.

8. **B.** If you know the formula for an arithmetic sequence (KEY FACT P2), you can use it with $a_{20} = 63$ and $d = 5$.
$63 = a_{20} = a_1 + 19(5) \Rightarrow 63 = a_1 + 95$, and so $a_1 = -32$. Since the first term is -32, the 2nd term is $-32 + 5 = \mathbf{-27}$.

   **To get from the 2nd term to the 20th term, you need to add the common difference (5) 18 times.
$a_2 + 18(5) = 63 \Rightarrow a_2 + 90 = 63 \Rightarrow a_2 = \mathbf{-27}.$

9. **D.** Draw a diagram. The minute hand, of course, is pointing right at 4. The hour hand, however, is *not* pointing at 11. It was pointing at 11 at 11:00, 20 minutes, or $\frac{1}{3}$ hour, ago. The hour

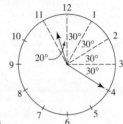

   hand is now one-third of the way between 11 and 12, so there are 20 degrees between the hour hand and 12 and another 120 degrees to 4, a total of **140** degrees.

   **If you can't figure the answer out exactly, guess. From the diagram, you should see that the angle is considerably more than 120. Eliminate at least A and B, and probably see that E is too big.

10. **E.** Calculate each 1990 salary by multiplying each 1980 salary by (1 + the percent change). **Eve** had the highest 1990 salary, $42,000(1.06) = \$44,520$.

11. **B.** Use TACTIC 6: substitute a simple number for x. Since this is a percent problem, choose 10 or 100. Let $x = 10$: 10% less than 10 is 9, and 10% more than 9 is 9.9. Now, what percent of 100 ($10x$) is 9.9? The answer is **9.9%**.

12. **E.** $2 - 3\sqrt{x} = 8 \Rightarrow -3\sqrt{x} = 6 \Rightarrow \sqrt{x} = -2.$ Since the square root of a number can never be negative, **there is no value of x that satisfies the equation.**

   **$\sqrt{x}$, and hence $3\sqrt{x}$, must be positive, and subtracting a positive number from 2 cannot yield 8.

   **Use TACTIC 5: backsolve. Test choices A through D. None of them works.

13. **A.** Factor each numerator and denominator and simplify.

$$\frac{x^2 - x}{2x - 6} \cdot \frac{x^2 - 2x - 3}{x^2 - 1} =$$

$$\frac{x\cancel{(x-1)}}{2\cancel{(x-3)}} \cdot \frac{\cancel{(x-3)}\cancel{(x+1)}}{\cancel{(x-1)}\cancel{(x+1)}} = \frac{x}{2}.$$

**Use TACTIC 6: plug in a simple number for x, say 2. Then

$$\frac{2^2 - 2}{2(2) - 6} \cdot \frac{2^2 - 2(2) - 3}{2^2 - 1} = \frac{2}{-2} \cdot \frac{-3}{3} = 1.$$

Only choice A equals 1 when $x = 2$.

14. E. $g(4) = f(4 \cdot 4) = f(16) = 16^2 + \sqrt{16} = 256 + 4 = \mathbf{260}$.

15. C. Assume Adam loses the minimum number, one-third, of the remaining games. Say he loses x games and wins $2x$ games. Then, in total, he will have $6 + 2x$ wins and $24 + x$ losses. Finally,

$$6 + 2x > 24 + x \Rightarrow 2x > 18 + x \Rightarrow x > 18$$

and so x is at least 19. He has at least 19 additional losses and 38 additional wins, for a total of **57** more games.

Avoid the algebra and zoom in by trial and error. If Adam plays 30 more games, losing 10 and winning 20, he'll have 34 losses and 26 wins—not enough. If he plays 60 more games, losing 20 and winning 40, he'll have 46 wins and 44 losses. Close enough, pick **57.

16. A. The graph on the bottom is the result of shifting the graph on the top 3 units to the left. Therefore, by KEY FACT R2, its equation is $f(x + 3)$.

Section 10 Writing Skills

1. E. Wordiness. Choice E omits the unnecessary words without committing fresh errors.

2. D. Unnatural construction. The subject of the sentence is Dr. Seuss; the underlined portion should be modified to refer directly to Seuss. Choice D does so, replacing the original construction with a subordinate clause.

3. C. Error in usage. Do not use *when* after *is* in making a definition.

4. C. Adjective-adverb confusion. Change *notorious optimistic* to *notoriously optimistic*.

5. A. Sentence is correct.

6. B. Lack of parallelism. Choice B supplies the desired parallel structure.

7. E. Wordiness and error in usage. *Incredulous* means disbelieving; only people can be incredulous ("When Shelby heard that she had scored a perfect 2400 on the SAT, she was momentarily incredulous; then she was ecstatic.") The series of accidents was *incredible* (unbelievable), not incredulous. Choice E avoids this usage error and eliminates unnecessary words.

8. A. Sentence is correct.

9. E. Errors in subject-verb agreement. The suject is *increase* (singular); the verb should be singular as well. Replace *have encouraged* with *has encouraged*.

10. B. Lack of parallelism. Replace *as well as* with *and*.

11. D. Lack of parallelism. The use of "not only ... but also" indicates a need for parallel structure. In Choice D, *revitalize the social security system* exactly parallels *create a universal health care system*.

12. D. Error in pronoun choice. Avoid shifting from one pronoun to another within a single sentence. Change *you can learn* to *one can learn*.

13. B. Dangling participial phrase. Who was brought up in an all-white suburb? *I* was. Choice B corrects the dangling participial phrase by rearranging the sentence so that "Brought ... suburb" clearly refers to the pronoun "I."

14. A. Sentence is correct.

Answer Sheet—Test 5

Section 1   ESSAY

Remove answer sheet by cutting on dotted line

Test 5

Essay (continued)

If a section has fewer questions than answer spaces, leave the extra spaces blank.

Section 2

1 Ⓐ Ⓑ Ⓒ Ⓓ Ⓔ	8 Ⓐ Ⓑ Ⓒ Ⓓ Ⓔ	15 Ⓐ Ⓑ Ⓒ Ⓓ Ⓔ	22 Ⓐ Ⓑ Ⓒ Ⓓ Ⓔ	29 Ⓐ Ⓑ Ⓒ Ⓓ Ⓔ
2 Ⓐ Ⓑ Ⓒ Ⓓ Ⓔ	9 Ⓐ Ⓑ Ⓒ Ⓓ Ⓔ	16 Ⓐ Ⓑ Ⓒ Ⓓ Ⓔ	23 Ⓐ Ⓑ Ⓒ Ⓓ Ⓔ	30 Ⓐ Ⓑ Ⓒ Ⓓ Ⓔ
3 Ⓐ Ⓑ Ⓒ Ⓓ Ⓔ	10 Ⓐ Ⓑ Ⓒ Ⓓ Ⓔ	17 Ⓐ Ⓑ Ⓒ Ⓓ Ⓔ	24 Ⓐ Ⓑ Ⓒ Ⓓ Ⓔ	31 Ⓐ Ⓑ Ⓒ Ⓓ Ⓔ
4 Ⓐ Ⓑ Ⓒ Ⓓ Ⓔ	11 Ⓐ Ⓑ Ⓒ Ⓓ Ⓔ	18 Ⓐ Ⓑ Ⓒ Ⓓ Ⓔ	25 Ⓐ Ⓑ Ⓒ Ⓓ Ⓔ	32 Ⓐ Ⓑ Ⓒ Ⓓ Ⓔ
5 Ⓐ Ⓑ Ⓒ Ⓓ Ⓔ	12 Ⓐ Ⓑ Ⓒ Ⓓ Ⓔ	19 Ⓐ Ⓑ Ⓒ Ⓓ Ⓔ	26 Ⓐ Ⓑ Ⓒ Ⓓ Ⓔ	33 Ⓐ Ⓑ Ⓒ Ⓓ Ⓔ
6 Ⓐ Ⓑ Ⓒ Ⓓ Ⓔ	13 Ⓐ Ⓑ Ⓒ Ⓓ Ⓔ	20 Ⓐ Ⓑ Ⓒ Ⓓ Ⓔ	27 Ⓐ Ⓑ Ⓒ Ⓓ Ⓔ	34 Ⓐ Ⓑ Ⓒ Ⓓ Ⓔ
7 Ⓐ Ⓑ Ⓒ Ⓓ Ⓔ	14 Ⓐ Ⓑ Ⓒ Ⓓ Ⓔ	21 Ⓐ Ⓑ Ⓒ Ⓓ Ⓔ	28 Ⓐ Ⓑ Ⓒ Ⓓ Ⓔ	35 Ⓐ Ⓑ Ⓒ Ⓓ Ⓔ

Section 3

1 Ⓐ Ⓑ Ⓒ Ⓓ Ⓔ	8 Ⓐ Ⓑ Ⓒ Ⓓ Ⓔ	15 Ⓐ Ⓑ Ⓒ Ⓓ Ⓔ	22 Ⓐ Ⓑ Ⓒ Ⓓ Ⓔ	29 Ⓐ Ⓑ Ⓒ Ⓓ Ⓔ
2 Ⓐ Ⓑ Ⓒ Ⓓ Ⓔ	9 Ⓐ Ⓑ Ⓒ Ⓓ Ⓔ	16 Ⓐ Ⓑ Ⓒ Ⓓ Ⓔ	23 Ⓐ Ⓑ Ⓒ Ⓓ Ⓔ	30 Ⓐ Ⓑ Ⓒ Ⓓ Ⓔ
3 Ⓐ Ⓑ Ⓒ Ⓓ Ⓔ	10 Ⓐ Ⓑ Ⓒ Ⓓ Ⓔ	17 Ⓐ Ⓑ Ⓒ Ⓓ Ⓔ	24 Ⓐ Ⓑ Ⓒ Ⓓ Ⓔ	31 Ⓐ Ⓑ Ⓒ Ⓓ Ⓔ
4 Ⓐ Ⓑ Ⓒ Ⓓ Ⓔ	11 Ⓐ Ⓑ Ⓒ Ⓓ Ⓔ	18 Ⓐ Ⓑ Ⓒ Ⓓ Ⓔ	25 Ⓐ Ⓑ Ⓒ Ⓓ Ⓔ	32 Ⓐ Ⓑ Ⓒ Ⓓ Ⓔ
5 Ⓐ Ⓑ Ⓒ Ⓓ Ⓔ	12 Ⓐ Ⓑ Ⓒ Ⓓ Ⓔ	19 Ⓐ Ⓑ Ⓒ Ⓓ Ⓔ	26 Ⓐ Ⓑ Ⓒ Ⓓ Ⓔ	33 Ⓐ Ⓑ Ⓒ Ⓓ Ⓔ
6 Ⓐ Ⓑ Ⓒ Ⓓ Ⓔ	13 Ⓐ Ⓑ Ⓒ Ⓓ Ⓔ	20 Ⓐ Ⓑ Ⓒ Ⓓ Ⓔ	27 Ⓐ Ⓑ Ⓒ Ⓓ Ⓔ	34 Ⓐ Ⓑ Ⓒ Ⓓ Ⓔ
7 Ⓐ Ⓑ Ⓒ Ⓓ Ⓔ	14 Ⓐ Ⓑ Ⓒ Ⓓ Ⓔ	21 Ⓐ Ⓑ Ⓒ Ⓓ Ⓔ	28 Ⓐ Ⓑ Ⓒ Ⓓ Ⓔ	35 Ⓐ Ⓑ Ⓒ Ⓓ Ⓔ

Section 4

1 Ⓐ Ⓑ Ⓒ Ⓓ Ⓔ	8 Ⓐ Ⓑ Ⓒ Ⓓ Ⓔ	15 Ⓐ Ⓑ Ⓒ Ⓓ Ⓔ	22 Ⓐ Ⓑ Ⓒ Ⓓ Ⓔ	29 Ⓐ Ⓑ Ⓒ Ⓓ Ⓔ
2 Ⓐ Ⓑ Ⓒ Ⓓ Ⓔ	9 Ⓐ Ⓑ Ⓒ Ⓓ Ⓔ	16 Ⓐ Ⓑ Ⓒ Ⓓ Ⓔ	23 Ⓐ Ⓑ Ⓒ Ⓓ Ⓔ	30 Ⓐ Ⓑ Ⓒ Ⓓ Ⓔ
3 Ⓐ Ⓑ Ⓒ Ⓓ Ⓔ	10 Ⓐ Ⓑ Ⓒ Ⓓ Ⓔ	17 Ⓐ Ⓑ Ⓒ Ⓓ Ⓔ	24 Ⓐ Ⓑ Ⓒ Ⓓ Ⓔ	31 Ⓐ Ⓑ Ⓒ Ⓓ Ⓔ
4 Ⓐ Ⓑ Ⓒ Ⓓ Ⓔ	11 Ⓐ Ⓑ Ⓒ Ⓓ Ⓔ	18 Ⓐ Ⓑ Ⓒ Ⓓ Ⓔ	25 Ⓐ Ⓑ Ⓒ Ⓓ Ⓔ	32 Ⓐ Ⓑ Ⓒ Ⓓ Ⓔ
5 Ⓐ Ⓑ Ⓒ Ⓓ Ⓔ	12 Ⓐ Ⓑ Ⓒ Ⓓ Ⓔ	19 Ⓐ Ⓑ Ⓒ Ⓓ Ⓔ	26 Ⓐ Ⓑ Ⓒ Ⓓ Ⓔ	33 Ⓐ Ⓑ Ⓒ Ⓓ Ⓔ
6 Ⓐ Ⓑ Ⓒ Ⓓ Ⓔ	13 Ⓐ Ⓑ Ⓒ Ⓓ Ⓔ	20 Ⓐ Ⓑ Ⓒ Ⓓ Ⓔ	27 Ⓐ Ⓑ Ⓒ Ⓓ Ⓔ	34 Ⓐ Ⓑ Ⓒ Ⓓ Ⓔ
7 Ⓐ Ⓑ Ⓒ Ⓓ Ⓔ	14 Ⓐ Ⓑ Ⓒ Ⓓ Ⓔ	21 Ⓐ Ⓑ Ⓒ Ⓓ Ⓔ	28 Ⓐ Ⓑ Ⓒ Ⓓ Ⓔ	35 Ⓐ Ⓑ Ⓒ Ⓓ Ⓔ

Section 6

1 Ⓐ Ⓑ Ⓒ Ⓓ Ⓔ	8 Ⓐ Ⓑ Ⓒ Ⓓ Ⓔ	15 Ⓐ Ⓑ Ⓒ Ⓓ Ⓔ	22 Ⓐ Ⓑ Ⓒ Ⓓ Ⓔ	29 Ⓐ Ⓑ Ⓒ Ⓓ Ⓔ
2 Ⓐ Ⓑ Ⓒ Ⓓ Ⓔ	9 Ⓐ Ⓑ Ⓒ Ⓓ Ⓔ	16 Ⓐ Ⓑ Ⓒ Ⓓ Ⓔ	23 Ⓐ Ⓑ Ⓒ Ⓓ Ⓔ	30 Ⓐ Ⓑ Ⓒ Ⓓ Ⓔ
3 Ⓐ Ⓑ Ⓒ Ⓓ Ⓔ	10 Ⓐ Ⓑ Ⓒ Ⓓ Ⓔ	17 Ⓐ Ⓑ Ⓒ Ⓓ Ⓔ	24 Ⓐ Ⓑ Ⓒ Ⓓ Ⓔ	31 Ⓐ Ⓑ Ⓒ Ⓓ Ⓔ
4 Ⓐ Ⓑ Ⓒ Ⓓ Ⓔ	11 Ⓐ Ⓑ Ⓒ Ⓓ Ⓔ	18 Ⓐ Ⓑ Ⓒ Ⓓ Ⓔ	25 Ⓐ Ⓑ Ⓒ Ⓓ Ⓔ	32 Ⓐ Ⓑ Ⓒ Ⓓ Ⓔ
5 Ⓐ Ⓑ Ⓒ Ⓓ Ⓔ	12 Ⓐ Ⓑ Ⓒ Ⓓ Ⓔ	19 Ⓐ Ⓑ Ⓒ Ⓓ Ⓔ	26 Ⓐ Ⓑ Ⓒ Ⓓ Ⓔ	33 Ⓐ Ⓑ Ⓒ Ⓓ Ⓔ
6 Ⓐ Ⓑ Ⓒ Ⓓ Ⓔ	13 Ⓐ Ⓑ Ⓒ Ⓓ Ⓔ	20 Ⓐ Ⓑ Ⓒ Ⓓ Ⓔ	27 Ⓐ Ⓑ Ⓒ Ⓓ Ⓔ	34 Ⓐ Ⓑ Ⓒ Ⓓ Ⓔ
7 Ⓐ Ⓑ Ⓒ Ⓓ Ⓔ	14 Ⓐ Ⓑ Ⓒ Ⓓ Ⓔ	21 Ⓐ Ⓑ Ⓒ Ⓓ Ⓔ	28 Ⓐ Ⓑ Ⓒ Ⓓ Ⓔ	35 Ⓐ Ⓑ Ⓒ Ⓓ Ⓔ

Section 7

1 Ⓐ Ⓑ Ⓒ Ⓓ Ⓔ   3 Ⓐ Ⓑ Ⓒ Ⓓ Ⓔ   5 Ⓐ Ⓑ Ⓒ Ⓓ Ⓔ   7 Ⓐ Ⓑ Ⓒ Ⓓ Ⓔ
2 Ⓐ Ⓑ Ⓒ Ⓓ Ⓔ   4 Ⓐ Ⓑ Ⓒ Ⓓ Ⓔ   6 Ⓐ Ⓑ Ⓒ Ⓓ Ⓔ   8 Ⓐ Ⓑ Ⓒ Ⓓ Ⓔ

Test 5

Section 8

1 Ⓐ Ⓑ Ⓒ Ⓓ Ⓔ	5 Ⓐ Ⓑ Ⓒ Ⓓ Ⓔ	9 Ⓐ Ⓑ Ⓒ Ⓓ Ⓔ	13 Ⓐ Ⓑ Ⓒ Ⓓ Ⓔ	17 Ⓐ Ⓑ Ⓒ Ⓓ Ⓔ
2 Ⓐ Ⓑ Ⓒ Ⓓ Ⓔ	6 Ⓐ Ⓑ Ⓒ Ⓓ Ⓔ	10 Ⓐ Ⓑ Ⓒ Ⓓ Ⓔ	14 Ⓐ Ⓑ Ⓒ Ⓓ Ⓔ	18 Ⓐ Ⓑ Ⓒ Ⓓ Ⓔ
3 Ⓐ Ⓑ Ⓒ Ⓓ Ⓔ	7 Ⓐ Ⓑ Ⓒ Ⓓ Ⓔ	11 Ⓐ Ⓑ Ⓒ Ⓓ Ⓔ	15 Ⓐ Ⓑ Ⓒ Ⓓ Ⓔ	19 Ⓐ Ⓑ Ⓒ Ⓓ Ⓔ
4 Ⓐ Ⓑ Ⓒ Ⓓ Ⓔ	8 Ⓐ Ⓑ Ⓒ Ⓓ Ⓔ	12 Ⓐ Ⓑ Ⓒ Ⓓ Ⓔ	16 Ⓐ Ⓑ Ⓒ Ⓓ Ⓔ	20 Ⓐ Ⓑ Ⓒ Ⓓ Ⓔ

Section 9

1 Ⓐ Ⓑ Ⓒ Ⓓ Ⓔ	5 Ⓐ Ⓑ Ⓒ Ⓓ Ⓔ	9 Ⓐ Ⓑ Ⓒ Ⓓ Ⓔ	13 Ⓐ Ⓑ Ⓒ Ⓓ Ⓔ	17 Ⓐ Ⓑ Ⓒ Ⓓ Ⓔ
2 Ⓐ Ⓑ Ⓒ Ⓓ Ⓔ	6 Ⓐ Ⓑ Ⓒ Ⓓ Ⓔ	10 Ⓐ Ⓑ Ⓒ Ⓓ Ⓔ	14 Ⓐ Ⓑ Ⓒ Ⓓ Ⓔ	18 Ⓐ Ⓑ Ⓒ Ⓓ Ⓔ
3 Ⓐ Ⓑ Ⓒ Ⓓ Ⓔ	7 Ⓐ Ⓑ Ⓒ Ⓓ Ⓔ	11 Ⓐ Ⓑ Ⓒ Ⓓ Ⓔ	15 Ⓐ Ⓑ Ⓒ Ⓓ Ⓔ	19 Ⓐ Ⓑ Ⓒ Ⓓ Ⓔ
4 Ⓐ Ⓑ Ⓒ Ⓓ Ⓔ	8 Ⓐ Ⓑ Ⓒ Ⓓ Ⓔ	12 Ⓐ Ⓑ Ⓒ Ⓓ Ⓔ	16 Ⓐ Ⓑ Ⓒ Ⓓ Ⓔ	20 Ⓐ Ⓑ Ⓒ Ⓓ Ⓔ

Section 10

1 Ⓐ Ⓑ Ⓒ Ⓓ Ⓔ	5 Ⓐ Ⓑ Ⓒ Ⓓ Ⓔ	9 Ⓐ Ⓑ Ⓒ Ⓓ Ⓔ	13 Ⓐ Ⓑ Ⓒ Ⓓ Ⓔ	17 Ⓐ Ⓑ Ⓒ Ⓓ Ⓔ
2 Ⓐ Ⓑ Ⓒ Ⓓ Ⓔ	6 Ⓐ Ⓑ Ⓒ Ⓓ Ⓔ	10 Ⓐ Ⓑ Ⓒ Ⓓ Ⓔ	14 Ⓐ Ⓑ Ⓒ Ⓓ Ⓔ	18 Ⓐ Ⓑ Ⓒ Ⓓ Ⓔ
3 Ⓐ Ⓑ Ⓒ Ⓓ Ⓔ	7 Ⓐ Ⓑ Ⓒ Ⓓ Ⓔ	11 Ⓐ Ⓑ Ⓒ Ⓓ Ⓔ	15 Ⓐ Ⓑ Ⓒ Ⓓ Ⓔ	19 Ⓐ Ⓑ Ⓒ Ⓓ Ⓔ
4 Ⓐ Ⓑ Ⓒ Ⓓ Ⓔ	8 Ⓐ Ⓑ Ⓒ Ⓓ Ⓔ	12 Ⓐ Ⓑ Ⓒ Ⓓ Ⓔ	16 Ⓐ Ⓑ Ⓒ Ⓓ Ⓔ	20 Ⓐ Ⓑ Ⓒ Ⓓ Ⓔ

Test 5

SECTION 1   Time—25 Minutes   ESSAY

> The excerpt appearing below makes a point about a particular topic. Read the passage carefully, and think about the assignment that follows.

In her novel Sense and Sensibility, *Jane Austen wrote, "It is not time or opportunity that is to determine intimacy. Seven years would be insufficient to make some people acquainted with each other, and seven days are more than enough for others." Now Austen may have been writing somewhat tongue in cheek, for she attributes these sentiments to the excessively romantic Marianne Dashwood, whose extreme sensibility or emotional susceptibility gets its comeuppance by the novel's end. Nonetheless, the point that young Miss Dashwood makes is valid. No amount of time spent in another person's company can guarantee that the two of you will become friends.*

ASSIGNMENT: What are your thoughts on the idea that neither time nor opportunity can determine intimacy? What causes two people to become friends? Compose an essay in which you express your views on this topic. Your essay may support, refute, or qualify the views expressed in the excerpt. What you write, however, must be relevant to the topic under discussion. Additionally, you must support your viewpoint, indicating your reasoning and providing examples based on your studies and/or experience.

Test 5

Each of the following sentences contains one or two blanks; each blank indicates that a word or set of words has been left out. Below the sentence are five words or phrases, lettered A through E. Select the word or set of words that best completes the sentence.

Example:

Fame is ----; today's rising star is all too soon tomorrow's washed-up has-been.

(A) rewarding   (B) gradual
(C) essential   (D) spontaneous
 (E) transitory

Ⓐ Ⓑ Ⓒ Ⓓ ●

1. His critical reviews were enjoyed by many of his audience, but the subjects of his analysis dreaded his comments; he was vitriolic, devastating, irritating and never ----.

(A) analytic   (B) personal   (C) constructive
 (D) uncharitable   (E) controversial

2. Despite the team members' resentment of the new coach's training rules, they ---- them as long as he did not ---- them too strictly.

(A) embraced..follow
(B) condemned..formulate
(C) questioned..interpret
(D) challenged..implement
(E) tolerated..apply

3. Given the ---- state of the published evidence, we do not argue here that exposure to low-level microwave energy is either hazardous or safe.

(A) inconclusive
(B) satisfactory
(C) definitive
(D) immaculate
(E) exemplary

4. Tacitus' descriptions of Germanic tribal customs were ---- by the ---- state of communications in his day, but they match the accounts of other contemporary writers.

(A) defined..inconsequential
(B) limited..primitive
(C) enriched..antiquated
(D) contradicted..thriving
(E) muddled..suspended

5. No matter how ---- the revelations of the coming years may be, they will be hard put to match those of the past decade, which have ---- transformed our view of the emergence of Mayan civilization.

(A) minor..dramatically
(B) profound..negligibly
(C) striking..radically
(D) bizarre..nominally
(E) questionable..possibly

6. Because of its inclination to ----, most Indian art is ---- Japanese art, where symbols have been minimized and meaning has been conveyed by the merest suggestion.

(A) exaggerate..related to
(B) imitate..superior to
(C) understate..reminiscent of
(D) overdraw..similar to
(E) sentimentalize..supportive of

7. Irony can, after a fashion, become a mode of escape: to laugh at the terrors of life is in some sense to ---- them.

(A) overstate   (B) revitalize   (C) corroborate
 (D) evade   (E) license

8. The campus police who monitored the demonstrations had little respect for the student protesters, generally speaking of them in ---- terms.

(A) hyperbolic
(B) euphemistic
(C) pejorative
(D) derivative
(E) uncertain

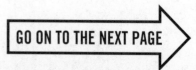
GO ON TO THE NEXT PAGE

Read each of the passages below, and then answer the questions that follow the passage. The correct response may be stated outright or merely suggested in the passage.

Questions 9 and 10 are based on the following passage.

> Did she or didn't she? From the 1950s popu-
> lar song lyrics proclaiming that
> *Captain Smith and Pocahontas*
Line   *Had a very mad affair*
 (5) to the 1995 Walt Disney animated film, the legend of Pocahontas has been widely popular in
 American culture. But the romance between John
 Smith and the Indian chieftain's daughter appears
 to have been a total fabrication. True, young
(10) Matoaka, whose pet name was Pocahontas
 ("favorite daughter"), interceded to save Smith's
 life, but she was only 11 at the time; and though
 she eventually married an Englishman named
 John, his surname was Rolfe, not Smith.

9. The author's primary purpose in this paragraph is to

(A) debunk a common myth
(B) refute a challenge to an argument
(C) encourage us to identify with historical figures
(D) celebrate a legendary romance
(E) distinguish between history and drama

10. The word "True" in line 9 primarily serves to acknowledge the

(A) existence of a relationship between Pocahontas and Smith
(B) high esteem in which Pocahontas was held by her father
(C) lack of information about Matoaka's actual emotions
(D) authoritative nature of the Disney animated version
(E) enduring popularity of legendary heroic figures

Questions 11 and 12 are based on the following passage.

> The Mayans and Aztecs considered chocolate
> the food of the gods, but today's lovers of sweets
> would not find the earliest chocolate heavenly.
Line Chocolate is made from the roasted and ground
 (5) seeds of the cacao tree. Until the sixteenth century, ground chocolate was mixed with water and
 spices, including chili peppers, to make a bitter,
 frothy beverage that Spanish explorers termed fitter for hogs than men. Not until Cortez brought
(10) chocolate back to Spain in 1526 was sugar added
 to the mix, but once it was, European royalty
 prized hot chocolate drinks. Over the next two
 centuries, hot chocolate became fashionable;
 chocolate houses (like coffeehouses) sprang up
(15) throughout Europe.

11. The opening sentence of the passage makes use primarily of which of the following?

(A) Humorous understatement
(B) Classical allusion
(C) Personification
(D) Allegory
(E) Simile

12. The initial attitude of the Spaniards toward the Aztec chocolate beverage can best be characterized as

(A) appreciative
(B) indifferent
(C) objective
(D) derisive
(E) nostalgic

GO ON TO THE NEXT PAGE

Test 5

Questions 13–24 are based on the following passage.

In this excerpt from his autobiographical Narrative of the Life of an American Slave, *the abolitionist Frederick Douglass tells how he, as a young child, learned the value of learning to read and write.*

Mr. and Mrs. Auld were both at home, and met me at the door with their little son Thomas, to take care of whom I had been given. And here I
Line saw what I had never seen before; it was a white
(5) face beaming with the most kindly emotions; it was the face of my new mistress, Sophia Auld. I wish I could describe the rapture that flashed through my soul as I beheld it. It was a new and strange sight to me, brightening up my pathway
(10) with happiness. Little Thomas was told, there was his Freddy, and I was told to take care of little Thomas; and thus I entered upon the duties of my new home with the most cheering prospect ahead.
(15) My new mistress proved to be all she appeared when I first met her at the door—a woman of the kindest heart and feelings. She had never had a slave under her control previously to myself, and prior to her marriage she had been dependent
(20) upon her own industry for a living. She was by trade a weaver; and by constant application to her business, she had been in a good degree preserved from the blighting and dehumanizing effects of slavery. I was utterly astonished at her goodness.
(25) I scarcely knew how to behave towards her. My early instruction was all out of place. The crouching servility, usually so acceptable a quality in a slave, did not answer when manifested toward her. Her favor was not gained by it; she seemed to
(30) be disturbed by it. She did not deem it impudent or unmannerly for a slave to look her in the face. The meanest slave was put fully at ease in her presence, and none left without feeling better for having seen her. But alas! this kind heart had but
(35) a short time to remain such. The fatal poison of irresponsible power was already in her hands, and soon commenced its infernal work.
Very soon after I went to live with Mr. and Mrs. Auld, she very kindly commenced to teach
(40) me the A, B, C. After I had learned this, she assisted me in learning to spell words of three or four letters. Just at this point of my progress, Mr. Auld found out what was going on, and at once forbade Mrs. Auld to instruct me further, telling
(45) her that it was unlawful, as well as unsafe, to teach a slave to read. Further, he said, "If you give a slave an inch, he will take an ell. A slave should know nothing but to obey his master—to do as he is told to do. Learning would *spoil* the
(50) best slave in the world. Now," said he, "if you teach that boy (speaking of myself) how to read, there would be no keeping him. It would forever unfit him to be a slave. He would at once become unmanageable, and of no value to his master. As
(55) to him, it could do him no good, but a great deal of harm. It would make him discontented and unhappy." These words sank deep into my heart, stirred up sentiments within that lay slumbering, and called into existence an entirely new train of
(60) thought. I now understood what had been to me a most perplexing difficulty—to wit, the white man's power to enslave the black man. From that moment I understood the pathway from slavery to freedom. Though conscious of the difficulty of
(65) learning without a teacher, I set out with high hope, and a fixed purpose, at whatever cost of trouble, to learn how to read. The very decided manner with which my master spoke, and strove to impress his wife with the evil consequences of
(70) giving me instruction, served to convince me that he was deeply sensible of the truths he was uttering. It gave me the best assurance that I might rely with the utmost confidence on the results which, he said, would flow from teaching me to
(75) read. What he most dreaded, that I most desired. What he most loved, that I most hated. That which to him was a great evil, to be carefully shunned, was to me a great good, to be diligently sought; and the argument which he so warmly
(80) urged, against my learning to read, only served to inspire me with a desire and determination to learn. In learning to read, I owe almost as much to the bitter opposition of my master, as to the kindly aid of my mistress. I acknowledge the
(85) benefit of both.

13. According to the opening paragraph, the author's initial reaction toward joining the Aulds' household was primarily one of

(A) absolute astonishment
(B) marked pleasure
(C) carefree nonchalance
(D) quiet resignation
(E) subdued nostalgia

GO ON TO THE NEXT PAGE

14. To some degree, the author attributes Mrs. Auld's freedom from the common attitudes of slave owners to her

    (A) abolitionist upbringing
    (B) personal wealth
    (C) indifference to her husband
    (D) experiences as a mother
    (E) concentration on her trade

15. Which of the following best explains why the author felt his "early instruction was all out of place" (line 26)?

    (A) It failed to include instruction in reading and writing.
    (B) It did not prepare him to take adequate care of the Aulds' son Thomas.
    (C) It did not train him to assist Mrs. Auld with her weaving.
    (D) It had been displaced by the new instructions he received from the Aulds.
    (E) It insisted on an obsequiousness that distressed his new mistress.

16. The word "answer" in line 28 most nearly means

    (A) acknowledge
    (B) retort
    (C) reply
    (D) serve
    (E) atone

17. By "this kind heart had but a short time to remain such" (lines 34 and 35) the author primarily intends to convey that Mrs. Auld

    (A) had only a brief time in which to do her work
    (B) was fated to die in the near future
    (C) was unable to keep her temper for extended periods of time
    (D) had too much strength of will to give in to the softer emotions
    (E) was destined to undergo a change of character shortly

18. It can be inferred from the passage that all of the following were characteristic of Mrs. Auld at the time the author first met her EXCEPT

    (A) diligence in labor
    (B) dislike of fawning
    (C) gentleness of spirit
    (D) disdain for convention
    (E) benevolent nature

19. For which of the following reasons does Mr. Auld forbid his wife to educate her slave?

    I. Providing slaves with an education violates the law.
    II. He believes slaves lack the capacity for education.
    III. He fears education would leave the slave less submissive.

    (A) I only
    (B) III only
    (C) I and II only
    (D) I and III only
    (E) I, II, and III

20. We can assume on the basis of Mr. Auld's comment in lines 46 and 47 that

    (A) he is willing to give his slaves the inch they request
    (B) he uses the term *ell* to signify a letter of the alphabet
    (C) Mrs. Auld is unfamiliar with standard forms of measurement
    (D) an ell is a much larger unit of length than an inch
    (E) slaves are far less demanding than he realizes

21. The author's main purpose in this passage is to

    (A) describe a disagreement between a woman and her husband
    (B) analyze the reasons for prohibiting the education of slaves
    (C) describe a slave's discovery of literacy as a means to freedom
    (D) dramatize a slave's change in attitude toward his mistress
    (E) portray the moral downfall of a kindhearted woman

22. The word "sensible" in line 71 means

    (A) logical
    (B) prudent
    (C) intelligent
    (D) conscious
    (E) sensory

GO ON TO THE NEXT PAGE

Test 5

23. The tone of the author in acknowledging his debt to his master (lines 82–85) can best be described as

    (A) sentimental and nostalgic
    (B) cutting and ironic
    (C) petulant and self-righteous
    (D) resigned but wistful
    (E) angry and impatient

24. Which of the following definitions of "education" is closest to the author's view of education as presented in the passage?

    (A) Education makes people easy to govern, but impossible to enslave.
    (B) Education is the best provision for old age.
    (C) Education has for its object the formation of character.
    (D) Education has produced a vast population able to read but unable to distinguish what is worth reading.
    (E) Education begins and ends with the knowledge of human nature.

YOU MAY GO BACK AND REVIEW THIS SECTION IN THE REMAINING TIME, BUT DO NOT WORK IN ANY OTHER SECTION UNTIL TOLD TO DO SO.   **STOP**

Test 5

3   3 3 3 3 3 3 3 3 3 3   3

SECTION 3

Time—25 Minutes
20 Questions

For each problem in this section determine which of the five choices is correct and blacken the corresponding choice on your answer sheet. You may use any blank space on the page for your work.

Notes:

- You may use a calculator whenever you think it will be helpful.
- Only real numbers are used. No question or answer on this test involves a complex or imaginary number.
- Use the diagrams provided to help you solve the problems. Unless you see the words "Note: Figure not drawn to scale" under a diagram, it has been drawn as accurately as possible. Unless it is stated that a figure is three-dimensional, you may assume it lies in a plane.
- For any function f, the domain, unless specifically restricted, is the set of all real numbers for which $f(x)$ is also a real number.

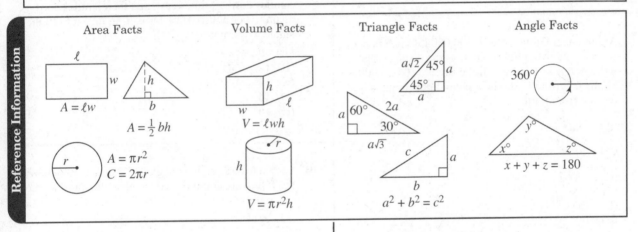

Reference Information

1. If $a - 5 = 0$, what is the value of $a + 5$?

(A) −10
(B) −5
(C) 0
(D) 5
(E) 10

2. What is 50% of 50% of 50?

(A) 0.125
(B) 0.5
(C) 1.25
(D) 5.0
(E) 12.5

3. Which of the following is an expression for "the product of 5 and the average (arithmetic mean) of x and y"?

(A) $\dfrac{5x + y}{2}$

(B) $\dfrac{5x + 5y}{2}$

(C) $\dfrac{5 + x + y}{3}$

(D) $5 + \dfrac{x + y}{2}$

(E) $\dfrac{5 + 5x + 5y}{3}$

GO ON TO THE NEXT PAGE

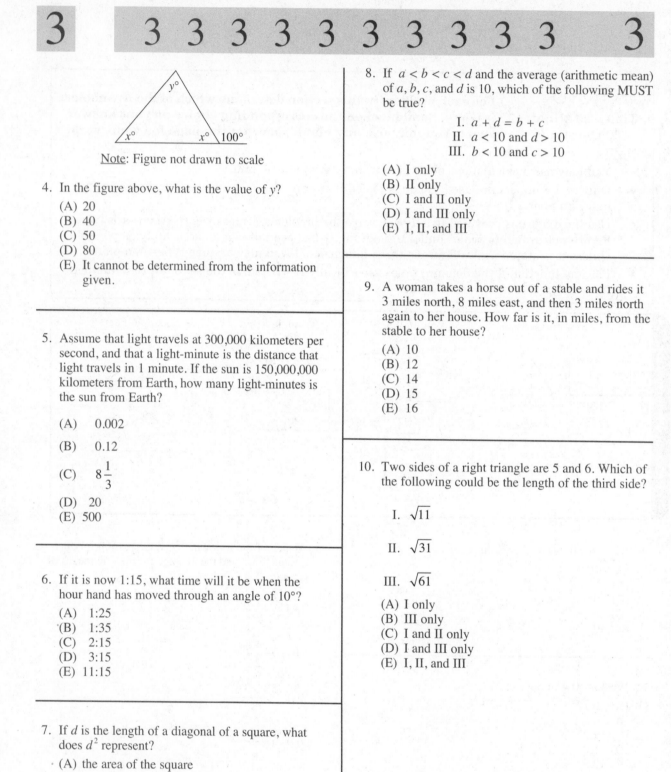

Note: Figure not drawn to scale

4. In the figure above, what is the value of *y*?

   (A) 20
   (B) 40
   (C) 50
   (D) 80
   (E) It cannot be determined from the information given.

5. Assume that light travels at 300,000 kilometers per second, and that a light-minute is the distance that light travels in 1 minute. If the sun is 150,000,000 kilometers from Earth, how many light-minutes is the sun from Earth?

   (A)   0.002

   (B)   0.12

   (C) $8\frac{1}{3}$

   (D)   20
   (E)   500

6. If it is now 1:15, what time will it be when the hour hand has moved through an angle of 10°?

   (A)   1:25
   (B)   1:35
   (C)   2:15
   (D)   3:15
   (E)   11:15

7. If *d* is the length of a diagonal of a square, what does d^2 represent?

   (A) the area of the square
   (B) twice the area of the square

   (C) $\frac{1}{2}$ the area of the square

   (D) 4 times the area of the square

   (E) $\frac{1}{4}$ the area of the square

8. If $a < b < c < d$ and the average (arithmetic mean) of $a, b, c,$ and d is 10, which of the following MUST be true?

       I. $a + d = b + c$
      II. $a < 10$ and $d > 10$
     III. $b < 10$ and $c > 10$

   (A) I only
   (B) II only
   (C) I and II only
   (D) I and III only
   (E) I, II, and III

9. A woman takes a horse out of a stable and rides it 3 miles north, 8 miles east, and then 3 miles north again to her house. How far is it, in miles, from the stable to her house?

   (A) 10
   (B) 12
   (C) 14
   (D) 15
   (E) 16

10. Two sides of a right triangle are 5 and 6. Which of the following could be the length of the third side?

        I. $\sqrt{11}$

       II. $\sqrt{31}$

      III. $\sqrt{61}$

    (A) I only
    (B) III only
    (C) I and II only
    (D) I and III only
    (E) I, II, and III

GO ON TO THE NEXT PAGE

Questions 11 and 12 refer to the following definition.

For any numbers a, b, and c,

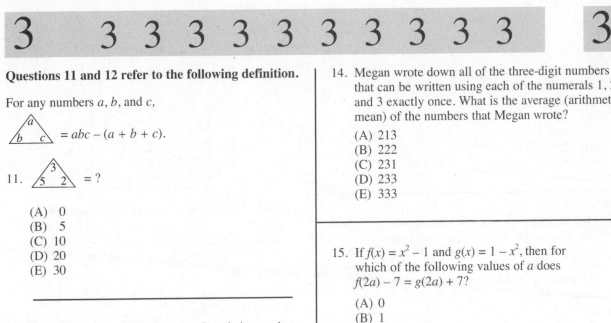

$= abc - (a + b + c)$.

11. $= ?$

(A) 0
(B) 5
(C) 10
(D) 20
(E) 30

12. For which of the following equations is it true that there is exactly one positive integer that satisfies it?

I. △(a / 0 −a) $= 0$

II. △(a / a a) $= 0$

III. △(a / 2a 3a) $= 0$

(A) None
(B) I only
(C) III only
(D) I and III only
(E) I, II, and III

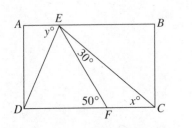

Note: Figure not drawn to scale

13. In the figure above, rectangle $ABCD$ has been partitioned into four triangles. If $DF = EF$, what is the value of $x + y$?

(A) 60
(B) 75
(C) 85
(D) 90
(E) 105

14. Megan wrote down all of the three-digit numbers that can be written using each of the numerals 1, 2, and 3 exactly once. What is the average (arithmetic mean) of the numbers that Megan wrote?

(A) 213
(B) 222
(C) 231
(D) 233
(E) 333

15. If $f(x) = x^2 - 1$ and $g(x) = 1 - x^2$, then for which of the following values of a does $f(2a) - 7 = g(2a) + 7$?

(A) 0
(B) 1
(C) $\sqrt{2}$
(D) $\sqrt{7}$
(E) 7

16. The population density of a region is the number of people living in the region per square mile. Jackson County is a rectangle whose length is ℓ miles and whose width is w miles. How many people live in Jackson County if its population density is d?

(A) $d\ell w$

(B) $\dfrac{\ell w}{d}$

(C) $\dfrac{d}{\ell w}$

(D) $\dfrac{2(\ell + w)}{d}$

(E) $\dfrac{\ell + w}{2d}$

GO ON TO THE NEXT PAGE

Test 5

3 3 3 3 3 3 3 3 3 3 3 3

17. If A is point $(-4,1)$ and B is point $(2,1)$, what is the area of the circle that has $\overline{AB}$ as a diameter?

(A) 3π
(B) 6π
(C) 9π
(D) 12π
(E) 36π

18. Mrs. James gave a test to her two geometry classes. The 24 students in her first-period class had a class average (arithmetic mean) of 78. The average of the 26 students in her second-period class was 83. What was the average for all students taking the exam?

(A) 79.4
(B) 80.5
(C) 80.6
(D) 81.2
(E) 81.4

19. If $x = 2y - 5$ and $z = 16y^3$, what is z in terms of x?

(A) $\left(\dfrac{x+5}{2}\right)^3$

(B) $\dfrac{(x+5)^3}{2}$

(C) $2(x+5)^3$
(D) $4(x+5)^3$
(E) $8(x+5)^3$

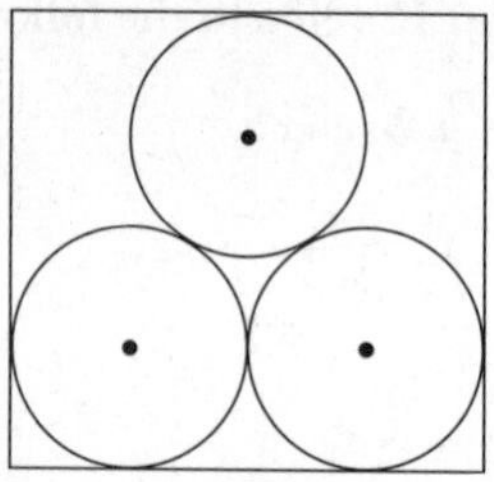

20. In the figure above, each circle is tangent to the other two circles and to the sides of the rectangle. If the diameter of each circle is 10, what is the area of the rectangle?

(A) 300
(B) 400
(C) $100 + 200\sqrt{3}$
(D) $200 + 100\sqrt{3}$
(E) It cannot be determined from the information given.

Test 5

YOU MAY GO BACK AND REVIEW THIS SECTION IN THE REMAINING TIME, BUT DO NOT WORK IN ANY OTHER SECTION UNTIL TOLD TO DO SO.

S T O P

4   4   4   4   4   4   4   4   4   4   4   4

SECTION 4   Time—25 Minutes   Select the best answer to each of the following questions; then
             35 Questions   blacken the appropriate space on your answer sheet.

Some or all parts of the following sentences are underlined. The first answer choice, (A), simply repeats the
underlined part of the sentence. The other four choices
present four alternative ways to phrase the underlined
part. Select the answer that produces the most effective sentence, one that is clear and exact, and blacken
the appropriate space on your answer sheet. In selecting your choice, be sure that it is standard written
English, and that it expresses the meaning of the original sentence.

Example:
The first biography of author Eudora Welty
came out in 1998 <u>and she was 89 years old at
the time.</u>

(A) and she was 89 years old at the time
(B) at the time when she was 89
(C) upon becoming an 89 year old
(D) when she was 89
(E) at the age of 89 years old

                 Ⓐ Ⓑ Ⓒ ● Ⓔ

1. Nowhere do <u>the problems of urban decay seem
more evident than in this dying city.</u>

   (A) Nowhere do the problems of urban decay seem
       more evident than in this dying city.
   (B) Nowhere more than in this dying city is there
       evidence of the problems of urban decay.
   (C) In this dying city, more so than in other places,
       they evidently seem to have problems of
       urban decay.
   (D) The problems of urban decay do seem more
       evident in this dying city than other places.
   (E) In this dying city, more so than elsewhere, the
       problems of urban decay are evident, it
       seems.

2. The average citizen today is surprisingly knowledgeable about landmark court decisions concerning such questions as affirmative action,
reproductive <u>rights, and whether students can pray
in school.</u>

   (A) rights, and whether students can pray in school
   (B) rights, and whether students could pray in
       school
   (C) rights, or whether students can pray in school
   (D) rights, and the issue of praying in school
   (E) rights, and school prayer

3. <u>Georgette Heyer is best known for her two dozen
romances set in the Regency era, and</u> her novel *The
Conqueror* takes place over seven hundred years
earlier at the time of the Battle of Hastings.

   (A) Georgette Heyer is best known for her two
       dozen romances set in the Regency era, and
   (B) Georgette Heyer is best known for her two
       dozen romances set in the Regency era,
       nevertheless
   (C) Although Georgette Heyer is best known for
       her two dozen romances set in the Regency
       era,
   (D) Georgette Heyer is best known for her two
       dozen romances set in the Regency era,
   (E) Insofar as Georgette Heyer is best known for
       her two dozen romances set in the Regency
       era,

4. <u>At an early stage in his travels, Henry James, writ-
ing</u> from abroad, described the subtle differences
distinguishing Americans from Europeans.

   (A) At an early stage in his travels, Henry James
       writing
   (B) At an early stage in his travels, Henry James
       wrote
   (C) At an early stage in his travels, Henry James
       was written
   (D) At an early stage in his travels, Henry James
       was writing
   (E) Henry James, whose writing at an early stage in
       his travels

5. Fame as well as <u>fortune were his goals in life.</u>

   (A) Fame as well as fortune were his goals in life.
   (B) Fame as well as fortune was his goals in life.
   (C) Fame as well as fortune were his goal in life.
   (D) Fame and fortune were his goals in life.
   (E) Fame also fortune were his goals in life.

6. For recreation I like to watch <u>these kind of</u> programs
in the evening.

   (A) these kind of
   (B) these sort of
   (C) these kinds of
   (D) them kinds of
   (E) this kind of a

GO ON TO THE NEXT PAGE ⟶

7. Whatever the surface appearances at the moment may be, modern men are fundamentally <u>less tolerant of despots then men of old</u>.

(A) less tolerant of despots then men of old
(B) less tolerant of despots than of older men
(C) more intolerant of despots than of men of old
(D) more intolerant of despots then men in former years
(E) less tolerant of despots than were men of old

8. The method <u>of how different viruses being transmitted</u> from one patient to another depends on the particular viruses involved.

(A) of how different viruses being transmitted
(B) whereby the transmission of different viruses is
(C) by which different viruses are transmitted
(D) for different viruses that are being transmitted
(E) when different viruses being transmitted

9. The fierce competition for grades among premed students <u>is because of wanting to be accepted by a top medical school</u>.

(A) is because of wanting to be accepted by a top medical school
(B) is because of a desire to be accepted by a top medical school
(C) stems out of wanting to be accepted by a top medical school
(D) stems from the desire to be accepted by a top medical school
(E) is because of the desire for acceptance at a top medical school

10. <u>Born in the days when no modest woman would admit to writing novels, Jane Austen's name</u> was allowed to appear on her books only after her death.

(A) Born in the days when no modest woman would admit to writing novels, Jane Austen's name
(B) Because Jane Austen was born in the days when no modest woman would admit to writing novels, her name
(C) Although born in the days when no modest woman would admit to writing novels, Jane Austen's name
(D) Having been born in the days when no modest woman would have admitted to writing novels, Jane Austen
(E) Born in the days when a modest woman would not have admitted to writing novels, Jane Austen's name

11. For a politically committed filmmaker like Michael Moore, <u>being free to denounce society's ills is more important than</u> gaining commercial success.

(A) being free to denounce society's ills is more important than
(B) there is greater importance in the freedom to denounce the ills of society than there is in
(C) being free to denounce society's illnesses is more important, and then
(D) freedom to denounce society's ills has more importance than does
(E) the free denunciation of society's ills importantly is more than

GO ON TO THE NEXT PAGE

12. This multimedia exhibition, <u>part of a</u> worldwide
                                   A

 <u>celebration of</u> the centenary of Balanchine's birth,
     B

 <u>includes</u> photographs, designs, costumes, and set
   C

 models, <u>complimented by</u> videotapes and excerpts
          D

 from oral histories in the Library of Performing

 Arts. <u>No error</u>
        E

13. *The Mozart Myths* <u>looks at</u> <u>how</u> scholars have
                        A   B

 revised their predecessors' findings, selecting

 material that might support their own pet theories,

 and depicting Mozart, <u>variously</u>, <u>as</u> a childish
                        C   D

 victim, a Romantic genius, and an Enlightenment

 rebel. <u>No error</u>
         E

14. <u>Following</u> the example of the Orpheus chamber
     A

 orchestra, this <u>recently</u> formed <u>ensemble of</u> young
                  B   C

 conservatory graduates <u>performing</u> without a
                          D

 conductor. <u>No error</u>
             E

15. To <u>most</u> Americans, the notion that free markets
        A

 and democracy are <u>essential to</u> curing the world's
                     B

 ills <u>is</u> an <u>article of</u> faith. <u>No error</u>
       C   D   E

16. What better word <u>than</u> *serendipity* <u>could define</u> the
                      A   B

 collectors' triumphs, in which accidentally <u>found</u>
                                              C

 objects <u>discovered</u> to have extraordinary value?
          D

 <u>No error</u>
  E

17. <u>Contrary to what</u> moviegoers have <u>for so long</u>
     A   B

 regarded as absolute truth, the mutiny of the

 Bounty's seamen <u>was</u> not <u>provoked from</u> any
                    C   D

 unreasonable harshness on the part of Captain

 Bligh. <u>No error</u>
         E

GO ON TO THE NEXT PAGE

4 4 4 4 4 4 4 4 4 4 4 4

18. Since the sociologist Max Weber wrote about the
    <u>A</u>

    Protestant work ethic and the <u>spirit of</u> capitalism,
    <u>B</u>

    social scientists have argued that culture, including

    religious habits, <u>are</u> part of the complex mix that
    <u>C</u>

    determines a country's economic health. <u>No error</u>
    <u>D</u>   <u>E</u>

19. J. D. Salinger <u>had had</u> many offers
    <u>A</u>

    <u>to be interviewed</u> by <u>reporters, but</u> the
    <u>B</u>   <u>C</u>

    reclusive author <u>invariably</u> refuses to meet
    <u>D</u>

    the press. <u>No error</u>
    <u>E</u>

20. <u>To find</u> employment at a time when companies
    <u>A</u>

    are <u>laying</u> off employees, one must be <u>diligent in</u>
    <u>B</u>   <u>C</u>

    following up leads and ingenious in

    <u>your</u> pursuit of fresh contacts. <u>No error</u>
    <u>D</u>   <u>E</u>

21. The black bear presents <u>such</u> a danger to
    <u>A</u>

    homeowners in some New Jersey areas that it

    <u>has become</u> imperative <u>to discover</u> methods to
    <u>B</u>   <u>C</u>

    prevent <u>their</u> encroaching on human territory.
    <u>D</u>

    <u>No error</u>
    <u>E</u>

22. Although many literary critics <u>have written</u> about
    <u>A</u>

    the Bronte family, <u>never before</u> <u>has</u> the differences
    <u>B</u>   <u>C</u>

    in style of the three novelist sisters been

    <u>so clearly</u> delineated. <u>No error</u>
    <u>D</u>   <u>E</u>

23. Our parents did <u>their</u> best to ignore the <u>ongoing</u>
    <u>A</u>   <u>B</u>

    rivalry between my <u>brother and I</u> because they
    <u>C</u>

    believed we would <u>only</u> be encouraged if they
    <u>D</u>

    attempted to intervene. <u>No error</u>
    <u>E</u>

24. Because James had <u>disobeyed</u> computer lab
    <u>A</u>

    regulations <u>by</u> downloading games, the computer
    <u>B</u>

    science teacher penalized him <u>by taking away</u>
    <u>C</u>

    his computer privileges for an <u>indecisive</u> period.
    <u>D</u>

    <u>No error</u>
    <u>E</u>

25. If one is <u>concerned</u> <u>with improving</u> conditions in
    <u>A</u>   <u>B</u>

    the Third World, <u>you should</u> consider volunteering
    <u>C</u>

    for the Peace Corps. <u>No error</u>
    <u>D</u>   <u>E</u>

GO ON TO THE NEXT PAGE

4 4 4 4 4 4 4 4 4 4 4

26. The steaks that Karl and Kathy ordered online

    to be delivered to their brother were less tender and
           A   B

    far more costly than the Chelsea Meat Market.
       C   D

    No error
      E

27. Perspective visitors to tropical countries should
         A   B

    plan to start taking antimalaria pills one to two

    weeks prior to their setting out on their trips.
       C   D

    No error
      E

28. Gold, like other soft metals that bend easily,
          A   B

    are widely used in jewelry-making. No error
     C   D   E

29. Given the long-standing bias against Victorian art,
                      A

    it is unsurprising that British artists of the later
                         B

    nineteenth century are poorly represented in the
             C   D

    museum's collections. No error
           E

Test 5

GO ON TO THE NEXT PAGE

Test 5

The passage below is the unedited draft of a student's essay. Parts of the essay need to be rewritten to make the meaning clearer and more precise. Read the essay carefully.

The essay is followed by six questions about changes that might improve all or part of the organization, development, sentence structure, use of language, appropriateness to the audience, or use of standard written English. In each case, choose the answer that most clearly and effectively expresses the student's intended meaning. Indicate your choice by blackening the corresponding space on the answer sheet.

[1] Members of our community have objected to the inclusion of various pieces of art in the local art exhibit. [2] They say that these pieces offend community values. [3] The exhibit in its entirety should be presented.

[4] The reason for this is that people have varied tastes, and those who like this form of art have a right to see the complete exhibit. [5] An exhibit like this one gives the community a rare chance to see the latest modern art nearby, and many people have looked forward to it with great anticipation. [6] It would be an unfortunate blow to those people for it not to be shown.

[7] The exhibit may contain pieces of art that tend to be slightly erotic, but what is being shown that most people haven't already seen? [8] So, give it an R or an X rating and don't let small children in. [9] But how many small children voluntarily go to see an art exhibit? [10] The exhibit includes examples of a new style of modern art. [11] The paintings show crowds of nude people. [12] The exhibit is at the library's new art gallery. [13] For centuries artists have been painting and sculpting people in the nude. [14] Why are these works of art different? [15] Perhaps they are more graphic in some respects, but we live in a entirely different society than from the past. [16] It is strange indeed for people in this day and age to be offended by the sight of the human anatomy.

[17] If people don't agree with these pieces, they simply should just not go. [18] But they should not be allowed to prevent others from seeing it.

30. With regard to the sentences that precede and follow sentence 3, which of the following is the best revision of sentence 3?

(A) On the other hand, the whole exhibit should be presented.

(B) The exhibit, however, should be presented in its entirety.

(C) The exhibit should be entirely presented regardless of what the critics say.

(D) But another point of view is that the exhibit should be presented in its entirety.

(E) Still other members also say the whole exhibit should be presented in its entirety.

31. In the context of paragraph 3, which of the following is the best revision of sentence 8?

(A) So, an R or X rating will warn people with small children to keep them out.

(B) Therefore, giving it an R or an X rating and not letting small children in.

(C) To satisfy everyone objecting to the exhibit, perhaps the exhibit could be given an R or an X rating to advise parents that some of the art on exhibit may not be suitable for young children.

(D) Let an R or an X rating caution the public that some of the art may be offensive and be unsuitable for young children.

(E) In conclusion, small children will be kept out by giving it an R or an X rating.

32. In the context of paragraph 3, which of the following is the best revision of sentences 10, 11, and 12?

(A) Paintings on exhibit at the library showing crowds of nude people and done in a new style of modern art.

(B) The exhibit, on display at the library, includes paintings of crowds of nude people done in a new style of modern art.

(C) The exhibit includes paintings in a new style of modern art, which shows crowds of nude people at the library.

(D) The library is the site of the exhibit which shows a new style of modern art, with paintings showing crowds of nude people.

(E) The new style of modern art includes examples of paintings showing crowds of nude people on exhibit in the library.

GO ON TO THE NEXT PAGE

33. To improve the clarity and coherence of the whole essay, where is the best place to relocate the ideas contained in sentences 10, 11, and 12?

    (A) Before sentence 1
    (B) Between sentences 1 and 2
    (C) Between sentences 8 and 9
    (D) Between sentences 15 and 16
    (E) After sentence 18

34. Which of the following is the best revision of the underlined segment of sentence 15 below?

    Perhaps they are more graphic in some respects, but we live in an entirely different society than from the past.

    (A) an entirely different society than of the past
    (B) a completely different society than the past
    (C) a society completely different than from past societies
    (D) a society that is entirely different from the way societies have been in the past
    (E) an entirely different society from that of the past

35. Which of the following revisions of sentence 17 provides the best transition between paragraphs 3 and 4?

    (A) If anyone doesn't approve of these pieces, they simply should not go to the exhibit.
    (B) Anyone disagreeing with the pieces in the exhibit shouldn't go to it.
    (C) Anyone who disapproves of nudity in art simply shouldn't go to the exhibit.
    (D) If anyone dislikes the sight of nudes in art, this show isn't for them.
    (E) Don't go if you disapprove of nudity in art.

Test 5

YOU MAY GO BACK AND REVIEW THIS SECTION IN THE REMAINING TIME, BUT DO NOT WORK IN ANY OTHER SECTION UNTIL TOLD TO DO SO.

STOP

6   6 6 6 6 6 6 6 6 6 6 6   6

SECTION 6   **Time—25 Minutes**
24 Questions   **Select the best answer to each of the following questions; then blacken the appropriate space on your answer sheet.**

Each of the following sentences contains one or two blanks; each blank indicates that a word or set of words has been left out. Below the sentence are five words or phrases, lettered A through E. Select the word or set of words that best completes the sentence.

Example:

Fame is ----; today's rising star is all too soon tomorrow's washed-up has-been.

(A) rewarding   (B) gradual
(C) essential   (D) spontaneous
(E) transitory

Ⓐ Ⓑ Ⓒ Ⓓ ●

1. Either the Polynesian banquets at Waikiki are ----, or the one I visited was a poor example.

(A) delicious   (B) impeccable   (C) overrated
(D) untasted   (E) unpopular

2. The college librarian initiated a new schedule of fines for overdue books with the ----, if not the outright encouragement, of the faculty library committee.

(A) skepticism   (B) acquiescence   (C) scorn
(D) applause   (E) disapprobation

3. At first ---- were simply that: straightforward first-hand testimonials about the ---- of a product.

(A) trademarks..contents
(B) creeds..excellence
(C) prejudices..flaws
(D) reprimands..benefits
(E) endorsements..virtues

4. He was habitually so docile and ---- that his friends could not understand his sudden ---- his employers.

(A) accommodating..outburst against
(B) incorrigible..suspicion of
(C) truculent..virulence toward
(D) erratic..envy of
(E) hasty..cordiality toward

5. That Mr. Willis's newest film is No. 1 at the box office this week is a testament to the star's ---- power and not to the reviews, which were ---- at best.

(A) waning..indifferent
(B) ongoing..glowing
(C) drawing..modest
(D) increasing..matchless
(E) unique..superb

GO ON TO THE NEXT PAGE ⟶

Test 5

Read the passages below, and then answer the questions that follow them. The correct response may be stated outright or merely suggested in the passages.

Questions 6–9 are based on the following passages.

Passage 1

Thomas Hobbes, who lived during the English Civil War (1642–1646), believed that a world without government would inevitably be a war of
Line every man against every man. His view of human
(5) nature was so bleak that he could not imagine people living in peace without an all-powerful government to constrain their actions. John Locke, writing nearly forty years later, had a more optimistic impression of human nature. While he, like
(10) Hobbes, envisioned that a world without government would suffer disorder, he described this disorder as merely an "inconvenience."

Passage 2

What motivates a political philosopher? In the case of Thomas Hobbes, the driving force was
(15) fear. In his autobiography, Hobbes says as much, for it was fear that accompanied him into the world. On Good Friday of 1588, Hobbes's mother heard that the Spanish Armada had set sail for England. Hobbes relates what ensued: "The
(20) rumour went everywhere through our towns that the last day for our nation was coming by fleet. At that point my mother was filled with such fear that she bore twins, me together with fear." In Hobbes's philosophy, fear, especially fear of war,
(25) plays a central role.

6. The first two sentences of Passage 1 (lines 1–7) serve primarily to

(A) illustrate the physical damage done by the Civil War to Thomas Hobbes
(B) demonstrate the need for government to function as a restraining influence
(C) present the thinking of a political theorist
(D) argue in favor of the world view held by John Locke
(E) emphasize the author's pacifist beliefs

7. The author of Passage 1 does all of the following EXCEPT

(A) establish a time frame
(B) contrast two differing viewpoints
(C) make an assertion
(D) refute an argument
(E) quote a source

8. Both passages support which of the following conclusions about Hobbes's world view?

(A) It is more pragmatic than the world view expressed by John Locke.
(B) It provides an insightful perspective despite its evident inconsistencies.
(C) It met with little opposition in his lifetime.
(D) It cannot be easily ascertained, given its lack of documentation.
(E) It is inherently pessimistic in its outlook.

9. Which of the following best describes the relationship between the two passages?

(A) Passage 1 draws a contrast that is weakened by examples in Passage 2.
(B) Passage 2 presents a hypothesis that is disproved by Passage 1.
(C) Passage 2 gives an anecdote that confirms a statement made in Passage 1.
(D) Passage 1 poses a question that is explicitly answered in Passage 2.
(E) Passage 2 attacks an opinion that is supported by Passage 1.

Test 5

Questions 10–15 are based on the following passage.

The following passage is taken from Civilisation, *a book based on the scripts for the television series of the same name. In this excerpt, author Kenneth Clark introduces the audience to the Europe of the thirteenth to fifteenth centuries: the Gothic world.*

    I am in the Gothic world, the world of chivalry, courtesy, and romance; a world in which serious things were done with a sense of play—
Line where even war and theology could become a sort
(5) of game; and when architecture reached a point of extravagance unequalled in history. After all the great unifying convictions that inspired the medieval world, High Gothic art can look fantastic and luxurious—what Marxists call conspicu-
(10) ous waste. And yet these centuries produced some of the greatest spirits in the history of man, amongst them St. Francis of Assisi and Dante. Behind all the fantasy of the Gothic imagination there remained, on two different planes, a sharp
(15) sense of reality. Medieval man could see things very clearly, but he believed that these appearances should be considered as nothing more than symbols or tokens of an ideal order, which was the only true reality.
(20)   The fantasy strikes us first, and last; and one can see it in the room in the Cluny Museum in Paris hung with a series of tapestries known as *The Lady with the Unicorn*, one of the most seductive examples of the Gothic spirit. It is poet-
(25) ical, fanciful and profane. Its ostensible subject is the four senses. But its real subject is the power of love, which can enlist and subdue all the forces of nature, including those two emblems of lust and ferocity, the unicorn and the lion. They kneel
(30) before this embodiment of chastity, and hold up the corners of her cloak. These wild animals have become, in the heraldic sense, her supporters. And all round this allegorical scene is what the medieval philosophers used to call *natura natu-*
(35) *rans*—nature naturing—trees, flowers, leaves galore, birds, monkeys, and those rather obvious symbols of nature naturing, rabbits. There is even nature domesticated, a little dog, sitting on a cushion. It is an image of worldly happiness at its
(40) most refined, what the French call the *douceur de vivre*, which is often confused with civilization.
    We have come a long way from the powerful conviction that induced medieval knights and ladies to draw carts of stone up the hill for the
(45) building of Chartres Cathedral. And yet the notion of ideal love, and the irresistible power of gentleness and beauty, which is emblematically

conveyed by the homage of these two fierce beasts, can be traced back for three centuries, to
(50) days long before these tapestries were conceived.

10. The author distinguishes the medieval imagination from the Gothic on the basis of the latter's
    (A) heraldic sense
    (B) respect for tradition
    (C) elaborateness of fancy
    (D) philosophical unity
    (E) firm belief

11. The word "point" in line 5 means
    (A) tip   (B) component   (C) message
    (D) motive   (E) degree

12. The author cites St. Francis and Dante (line 12) primarily in order to
    (A) identify the inspiration for the design of the Unicorn tapestries
    (B) illustrate the source of the great convictions that animated the Medieval world
    (C) demonstrate his acquaintance with the writings of great thinkers of the period
    (D) refute the notion that the Gothic period produced nothing but extravagance
    (E) support his contention that theology could become a sort of game

13. The author thinks of the Unicorn tapestries as exemplifying the essence of the Gothic imagination because
    (A) their allegorical nature derives from medieval sources
    (B) their use as wall hangings expresses the realistic practicality of the Gothic mind
    (C) they demonstrate the wastefulness and extravagance of the period
    (D) they combine worldly and spiritual elements in a celebration of love
    (E) they confuse the notion of civilization with worldly happiness

14. By "this embodiment of chastity" (line 30) the author is referring to
    (A) the unicorn
    (B) the Gothic spirit
    (C) St. Francis
    (D) the lady
    (E) the Cluny Museum

GO ON TO THE NEXT PAGE

15. According to the final paragraph, in the Middle Ages some members of the nobility demonstrated the depth of their faith by

(A) designing tapestries symbolic of courtly love
(B) paying homage to aristocratic ladies
(C) choosing to refine their notions of worldly happiness
(D) hauling stones used to construct Chartres Cathedral
(E) following the Franciscan ideal of living in harmony with nature

Questions 16–24 are based on the following passage.

This passage is from a book written by a contemporary American surgeon about the art of surgery.

One holds the knife as one holds the bow of a cello or a tulip—by the stem. Not palmed nor gripped nor grasped, but lightly, with the tips of
Line the fingers. The knife is not for pressing. It is for
(5) drawing across the field of skin. Like a slender fish, it waits, at the ready, then, go! It darts, followed by a fine wake of red. The flesh parts, falling away to yellow globules of fat. Even now, after so many times, I still marvel at its power—
(10) cold, gleaming, silent. More, I am still struck with dread that it is I in whose hand the blade travels, that my hand is its vehicle, that yet again this terrible steel-bellied thing and I have conspired for a most unnatural purpose, the laying open of the
(15) body of a human being.
  A stillness settles in my heart and is carried to my hand. It is the quietude of resolve layered over fear. And it is this resolve that lowers us, my knife and me, deeper and deeper into the person
(20) beneath. It is an entry into the body that is nothing like a caress; still, it is among the gentlest of acts. Then stroke and stroke again, and we are joined by other instruments, hemostats and forceps, until the wound blooms with strange flowers whose looped
(25) handles fall to the sides in steely array.
  There is a sound, the tight click of clamps fixing teeth into severed blood vessels, the snuffle and gargle of the suction machine clearing the field of blood for the next stroke, the litany of monosylla-
(30) bles with which one prays his way down and in: *clamp, sponge, suture, tie, cut.* And there is color. The green of the cloth, the white of the sponges, the red and yellow of the body. Beneath the fat lies the fascia, the tough fibrous sheet encasing the
(35) muscles. It must be sliced and the red beef of the muscles separated. Now there are retractors to

hold apart the wound. Hands move together, part, weave. We are fully engaged, like children absorbed in a game or the craftsmen of some place
(40) like Damascus.
  Deeper still. The peritoneum, pink and gleaming and membranous, bulges into the wound. It is grasped with forceps, and opened. For the first time we can see into the cavity of the abdomen.
(45) Such a primitive place. One expects to find drawings of buffalo on the walls. The sense of trespassing is keener now, heightened by the world's light illuminating the organs, their secret colors revealed—maroon and salmon and yellow. The
(50) vista is sweetly vulnerable at this moment, a kind of welcoming. An arc of the liver shines high and on the right, like a dark sun. It laps over the pink sweep of the stomach, from whose lower border the gauzy omentum is draped, and through which
(55) veil one sees, sinuous, slow as just-fed snakes, the indolent coils of the intestine.
  You turn aside to wash your gloves. It is a ritual cleansing. One enters this temple doubly washed. Here is man as microcosm, representing
(60) in all his parts the Earth, perhaps the universe.
  I must confess that the priestliness of my profession has ever been impressed on me. In the beginning there are vows, taken with all solemnity. Then there is the endless harsh novitiate of
(65) training, much fatigue, much sacrifice. At last one emerges as a celebrant, standing close to the truth lying curtained in the ark of the body. Not surplice and cassock but mask and gown are your regalia. You hold no chalice, but a knife. There is no wine,
(70) no wafer. There are only the facts of blood and flesh.

16. The passage is best described as

(A) a definition of a concept
(B) an example of a particular method
(C) a discussion of an agenda
(D) a description of a process
(E) a lesson on a technique

17. The "wake of red" to which the author refers (line 7) is

(A) a sign of embarrassment
(B) an infectious rash
(C) a line of blood
(D) the blade of the knife
(E) a trail of antiseptic

GO ON TO THE NEXT PAGE →

18. In line 7, "parts" most nearly means

    (A) leaves
    (B) splits
    (C) rushes
    (D) shares
    (E) quivers

19. The "strange flowers" with which the wound blooms (line 24) are

    (A) clots of blood
    (B) severed blood vessels
    (C) scattered sponges
    (D) gifts of love
    (E) surgical tools

20. In writing of the "strange flowers" with which the wound blooms (lines 22–25), the author is being

    (A) technical
    (B) derogatory
    (C) ambivalent
    (D) metaphorical
    (E) didactic

21. The word "engaged" in line 38 most nearly means

    (A) compromised
    (B) engrossed
    (C) delighted
    (D) determined
    (E) betrothed

22. In lines 45–46, the comment "One expects to find drawings of buffalo on the walls" metaphorically compares the abdominal cavity to

    (A) an art gallery
    (B) a zoological display
    (C) a natural history museum
    (D) a prehistoric cave
    (E) a Western film

23. In creating an impression of abdominal surgery for the reader, the author makes use of

    (A) comparison with imaginary landscapes
    (B) contrast to other types of surgery
    (C) description of meteorological processes
    (D) evocation of the patient's emotions
    (E) reference to religious observances

24. One aspect of the passage that may make it difficult to appreciate is the author's apparent assumption throughout that readers will

    (A) have qualms about reading descriptions of major surgery
    (B) be already familiar with handling surgical tools
    (C) be able to visualize the body organs that are named
    (D) relate accounts of specific surgical acts to their own experience of undergoing surgery
    (E) remember their own years of medical training

YOU MAY GO BACK AND REVIEW THIS SECTION IN THE REMAINING TIME, BUT DO NOT WORK IN ANY OTHER SECTION UNTIL TOLD TO DO SO.

STOP

7

SECTION 7

Time—25 Minutes
18 Questions

You have 25 minutes to answer the 8 multiple-choice questions and 10 student-produced response questions in this section.
For each multiple-choice question, determine which of the five choices is correct and blacken the corresponding choice on your answer sheet. You may use any blank space on the page for your work.

Notes:

- You may use a calculator whenever you think it will be helpful.
- Only real numbers are used. No question or answer on this test involves a complex or imaginary number.
- Use the diagrams provided to help you solve the problems. Unless you see the words "Note: Figure not drawn to scale" under a diagram, it has been drawn as accurately as possible. Unless it is stated that a figure is three-dimensional, you may assume it lies in a plane.
- For any function f, the domain, unless specifically restricted, is the set of all real numbers for which $f(x)$ is also a real number.

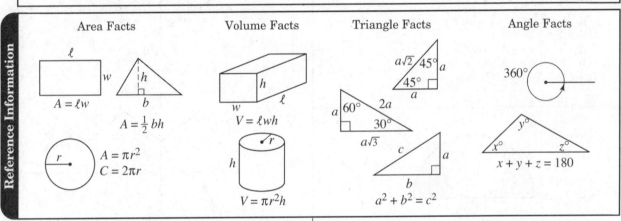

Reference Information

Area Facts   Volume Facts   Triangle Facts   Angle Facts

$A = \ell w$

$A = \frac{1}{2}bh$

$A = \pi r^2$
$C = 2\pi r$

$V = \ell wh$

$V = \pi r^2 h$

$a^2 + b^2 = c^2$

$x + y + z = 180$

1. What is the length of each of the five equal sides of a regular pentagon if the perimeter of the pentagon is equal to the perimeter of a square whose area is 25?

(A) 4
(B) 5
(C) 10
(D) 20
(E) 25

2. How many minutes did John take, driving at 20 miles per hour, to go the same distance that Mary took 30 minutes to drive at 60 miles per hour?

(A) 10
(B) 30
(C) 60
(D) 90
(E) 180

3. If $x \neq 0, 1$, which of the following is equivalent to $\dfrac{x^2 - 1}{x^2 - x}$?

(A) $\dfrac{1}{x}$

(B) $\dfrac{x+1}{x-1}$

(C) $\dfrac{x+1}{x}$

(D) $\dfrac{x-1}{x+1}$

(E) $\dfrac{x-1}{x}$

GO ON TO THE NEXT PAGE

7

4. The volume of a cylinder whose height is 4 and whose radius is 2 is how many times the volume of a cylinder whose height is 2 and whose radius is 4?

   (A) $\dfrac{1}{4}$

   (B) $\dfrac{1}{2}$

   (C) 1
   (D) 2
   (E) 4

5. If x is an even number, then each of the following must be true EXCEPT

   (A) $2x + 7$ is odd
   (B) $3x^2 + 5$ is odd
   (C) $x^3 - x^2 + x - 1$ is odd
   (D) $3x + 4$ is even
   (E) $(3x - 5)(5x - 3)$ is even

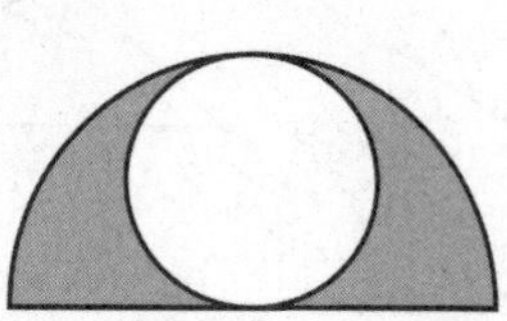

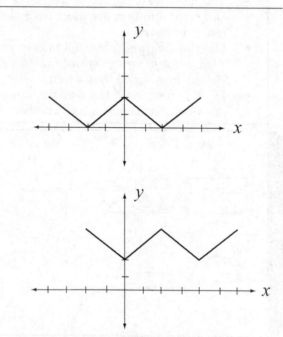

6. The figure above shows a circle inscribed in a semicircle. If a point is chosen at random inside the semicircle, what is the probability that the point is in the shaded region?

   (A) $\dfrac{1}{\pi}$

   (B) $\dfrac{1}{3}$

   (C) $\dfrac{1}{2}$

   (D) $\dfrac{2}{3}$

   (E) $\dfrac{2}{\pi}$

7. What is the area of the quadrilateral whose vertices are at $(1, 1)$, $(5, 1)$, $(5, 5)$ and $(3, 5)$?

   (A) 8
   (B) 12
   (C) 16
   (D) 24
   (E) $10 + 2\sqrt{2}$

8. In the figure above, the graph on the top is the graph of $y = f(x)$. Which of the following is the equation of the graph on the bottom?

   (A) $y = f(x + 2)$
   (B) $y = f(x - 2)$
   (C) $y = f(x + 2) + 2$
   (D) $y = f(x - 2) + 2$
   (E) $y = f(x + 2) - 2$

Test 5

GO ON TO THE NEXT PAGE

7

Directions for Student-Produced Response Questions (Grid-ins)

In questions 9–18, first solve the problem, and then enter your answer on the grid provided on the answer sheet. The instructions for entering your answers are as follows:

- First, write your answer in the boxes at the top of the grid.
- Second, grid your answer in the columns below the boxes.
- Use the fraction bar in the first row or the decimal point in the second row to enter fractions and decimal answers.

- Grid only one space in each column.
- Entering the answer in the boxes is recommended as an aid in gridding, but is not required.
- The machine scoring your exam can read only what you grid, so you **must grid in your answers correctly to get credit.**
- If a question has more than one correct answer, grid in only one of these answers.
- The grid does not have a minus sign, so no answer can be negative.
- A mixed number *must* be converted to an improper fraction or a decimal before it is gridded. Enter $1\frac{1}{4}$ as 5/4 or 1.25; the machine will interpret 1 1/4 as $\frac{11}{4}$ and mark it wrong.
- **All decimals must be entered as accurately as possible.** Here are the three acceptable ways of gridding

$$\frac{3}{11} = 0.272727...$$

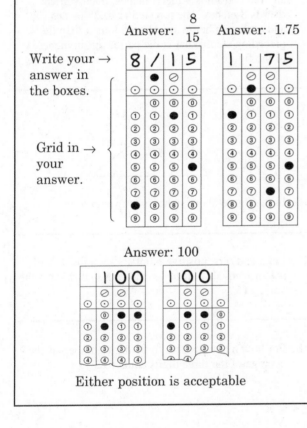

Answer: $\frac{8}{15}$ Answer: 1.75

Write your → answer in the boxes.

Grid in → your answer.

Answer: 100

Either position is acceptable

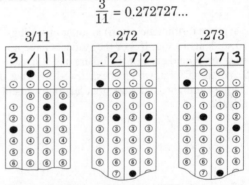

3/11   .272   .273

- Note that rounding to .273 is acceptable, because you are using the full grid, but you would receive **no credit** for .3 or .27, because these answers are less accurate.

9. What is the value of $\dfrac{1}{5} + \dfrac{2}{10} + \dfrac{3}{15} + \dfrac{4}{20} + \dfrac{5}{25}$?

10. If $ab = 20$ and $a = -5$, what is the value of $a^2 - b^2$?

GO ON TO THE NEXT PAGE

7

11. If $\frac{2}{3}$ of x equals $\frac{3}{4}$ of x, what is $\frac{4}{5}$ of x?

12. A clock chimes every hour to indicate the time, and also chimes once every 15 minutes on the quarter-hour and half-hour. For example, it chimes 3 times at 3:00, once at 3:15, once at 3:30, once at 3:45, and 4 times at 4:00. What is the smallest number of times the clock can chime in an interval of $2\frac{1}{2}$ hours?

13. Each integer from 1 to 50 whose units digit is 7 is written on a separate slip of paper. If the slips are placed in a box and one is picked at random, what is the probability that the number picked is prime?

14. The average (arithmetic mean) amount of savings of 10 students is $60. If 3 of the students have no savings at all, and each of the others has at least $25, including John, who has exactly $130, what is the largest amount, in dollars, that any one student can have?

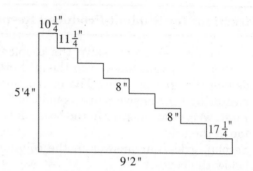

15. In the stair unit in the figure above, all the angles are right angles. The left side is 5 feet 4 inches, and the bottom is 9 feet 2 inches. Each vertical riser is 8 inches. The top step is 10.25 inches, and each step below it is 1 inch longer than the preceding step. What is the perimeter, in inches, of the figure?

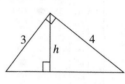

16. In the figure above, what is the value of h?

17. Let a and b be positive numbers such that $a\%$ of $a\%$ of b equals c. If $a^2\%$ of b equals kc, what is the value of k?

18. For how many positive three-digit numbers is the average of the three digits equal to 2?

Test 5

8   8   8   8   8   8   8   8   8   8   8

Each of the following sentences contains one or two blanks; each blank indicates that a word or set of words has been left out. Below the sentence are five words or phrases, lettered A through E. Select the word or set of words that best completes the sentence.

Example:

Fame is ----; today's rising star is all too soon tomorrow's washed-up has-been.

(A) rewarding   (B) gradual
(C) essential   (D) spontaneous
(E) transitory

Ⓐ Ⓑ Ⓒ Ⓓ ●

1. Given the ---- nature of wood, the oldest totem poles of the Northwest Coast Indians eventually fell to decay; only a few still stand today.

   (A) resilient   (B) combustible   (C) malleable
   (D) perishable   (E) solid

2. Lee, who refrained from excesses in his personal life, differed markedly from Grant, who ---- notorious drinking bouts with his cronies.

   (A) deprecated
   (B) minimized
   (C) indulged in
   (D) shunned
   (E) compensated for

3. By nature Toshiro was ----, given to striking up casual conversations with strangers he encountered at bus stops or check-out stands.

   (A) diffident
   (B) observant
   (C) reticent
   (D) gregarious
   (E) laconic

4. In the absence of native predators to stop their spread, imported deer ---- to such an inordinate degree that they overgrazed the countryside and ---- the native vegetation.

   (A) thrived..threatened
   (B) propagated..cultivated
   (C) suffered..abandoned
   (D) flourished..scrutinized
   (E) dwindled..eliminated

5. The contract negotiations were often surprisingly ----, deteriorating at times into a welter of accusations and counteraccusations.

   (A) perspicacious
   (B) phlegmatic
   (C) sedate
   (D) acrimonious
   (E) propitious

6. Black religion was in part a protest movement—a protest against a system and a society that was ---- designed to ---- the dignity of a segment of God's creation.

   (A) unintentionally..reflect
   (B) explicitly..foster
   (C) inevitably..assess
   (D) deliberately..demean
   (E) provocatively..enhance

8 8 8 8 8 8 8 8 8 8 8

The questions that follow the next two passages relate to the content of both, and to their relationship. The correct response may be stated outright in the passage or merely suggested.

Questions 7–19 are based on the following passages.

The following passages deal with the importance of money to Americans. The first is taken from a commencement address made by American philosopher George Santayana in 1904. The second is taken from an essay written by British poet W. H. Auden in 1963.

Passage 1

American life, everyone has heard, has extraordinary intensity; it goes at a great rate. This is not due, I should say, to any particular urgency in
Line the object pursued. Other nations have more
(5) pressing motives to bestir themselves than America has: and it is observable that not all the new nations, in either hemisphere, are energetic. This energy can hardly spring either from unusually intolerable conditions which people wish to
(10) overcome, nor from unusually important objects which they wish to attain. It springs, I should venture to say, from the harmony which subsists between the task and the spirit, between the mind's vitality and the forms which, in America,
(15) political and industrial tradition has taken on. It is sometimes said that the ruling passion in America is the love of money. This seems to me a complete mistake. The ruling passion is the love of *business*, which is something quite different. The
(20) lover of money would be jealous of it; he would spend it carefully; he would study to get out of it the most he could. But the lover of business, when he is successful, does not much change his way of living; he does not think out what further
(25) advantages he can get out of his success. His joy is in that business itself and in its further operation, in making it greater and better organized and a mightier engine in the general life. The adventitious personal profit in it is the last thing he
(30) thinks of, the last thing he is skillful in bringing about; and the same zeal and intensity is applied in managing a college, or a public office, or a naval establishment, as is lavished on private business, for it is not a motive of personal gain
(35) that stimulates to such exertions. It is the absorbing, satisfying character of the activities themselves; it is the art, the happiness, the greatness of them. So that in beginning life in such a society, which has developed a native and vital tradition
(40) out of its practice, you have good reason to feel that your spirit will be freed, that you will begin to realize a part of what you are living for.

Passage 2

Political and technological developments are rapidly obliterating all cultural differences and it
(45) is possible that, in a not remote future, it will be impossible to distinguish human beings living on one area of the earth's surface from those living on any other, but our different pasts have not yet been completely erased and cultural differences
(50) are still perceptible. The most striking difference between an American and a European is the difference in their attitudes towards money. Every European knows, as a matter of historical fact, that, in Europe, wealth could only be acquired at
(55) the expense of other human beings, either by conquering them or by exploiting their labor in factories. Further, even after the Industrial Revolution began, the number of persons who could rise from poverty to wealth was small; the vast majority
(60) took it for granted that they would not be much richer nor poorer than their fathers. In consequence, no European associates wealth with personal merit or poverty with personal failure.
To a European, money means power, the free-
(65) dom to do as he likes, which also means that, consciously or unconsciously, he says: "I want to have as much money as possible myself and others to have as little money as possible."
In the United States, wealth was also acquired
(70) by stealing, but the real exploited victim was not a human being but poor Mother Earth and her creatures who were ruthlessly plundered. It is true that the Indians were expropriated or exterminated, but this was not, as it had always been in
(75) Europe, a matter of the conqueror seizing the wealth of the conquered, for the Indian had never realized the potential riches of his country. It is also true that, in the Southern states, men lived on the labor of slaves, but slave labor did not make
(80) them fortunes; what made slavery in the South all the more inexcusable was that, in addition to being morally wicked, it didn't even pay off handsomely.
Thanks to the natural resources of the country,
(85) every American, until quite recently, could reasonably look forward to making more money than his father, so that, if he made less, the fault must

GO ON TO THE NEXT PAGE

8 8 8 8 8 8 8 8 8 8 8

be his; he was either lazy or inefficient. What an
American values, therefore, is not the possession
(90) of money as such, but his power to make it as a
proof of his manhood; once he has proved himself
by making it, it has served its function and can be
lost or given away. In no society in history have
rich men given away so large a part of their for-
(95) tunes. A poor American feels guilty at being poor,
but less guilt than an American *rentier** who has
inherited wealth but is doing nothing to increase
it; what can the latter do but take to drink and
psychoanalysis?

*A *rentier* lives on a fixed income from rents and
investments.

7. In Passage 1, the word "spring" in line 8 means

   (A) leap
   (B) arise
   (C) extend
   (D) break
   (E) blossom

8. The lover of business (lines 22–38) can be
described as all of the following EXCEPT

   (A) enthusiastic
   (B) engrossed
   (C) enterprising
   (D) industrious
   (E) mercenary

9. The author of Passage 1 maintains that Americans
find the prospect of improving business organizations

   (A) pleasurable
   (B) problematic
   (C) implausible
   (D) wearing
   (E) unanticipated

10. In line 28, "engine" most nearly means

   (A) artifice
   (B) locomotive
   (C) mechanical contrivance
   (D) financial windfall
   (E) driving force

11. The author of Passage 1 contends that those who
grow up in American society will be influenced by
its native traditions to

   (A) fight the intolerable conditions afflicting their
country
   (B) achieve spiritual harmony through meditation
   (C) find self-fulfillment through their business
activities
   (D) acknowledge the importance of financial
accountability
   (E) conserve the country's natural resources

12. In lines 43–48 the author of Passage 2 asserts that
technological advances

   (A) are likely to promote greater divisions between
the rich and the poor
   (B) may eventually lead to worldwide cultural
uniformity
   (C) can enable us to tolerate any cultural differences between us
   (D) may make the distinctions between people
increasingly easy to discern
   (E) destroy the cultural differences they are
intended to foster

13. The word "striking" in line 50 means

   (A) attractive
   (B) marked
   (C) shocking
   (D) protesting
   (E) commanding

14. In taking it for granted that they will not be much
richer or poorer than their fathers (lines 59–61),
Europeans do which of the following?

   (A) They express a preference.
   (B) They refute an argument.
   (C) They qualify an assertion.
   (D) They correct a misapprehension.
   (E) They make an assumption.

Test 5

GO ON TO THE NEXT PAGE

8   8   8   8   8   8   8   8   8   8   8

15. Until quite recently, according to lines 84–88, to Americans the failure to surpass one's father in income indicated

(A) a dislike of inherited wealth
(B) a lack of proper application on one's part
(C) a fear of the burdens inherent in success
(D) the height of fiscal irresponsibility
(E) the effects of a guilty conscience

16. The author's description of the likely fate of the American *rentier* living on inherited wealth is

(A) astonished
(B) indulgent
(C) sorrowful
(D) sympathetic
(E) ironic

17. In Passage 2 the author does all of the following EXCEPT

(A) make a categorical statement
(B) correct a misapprehension
(C) draw a contrast
(D) pose a question
(E) cite an authority

18. The authors of both passages most likely would agree that Americans engage in business

(A) on wholly altruistic grounds
(B) as a test of their earning capacity
(C) only out of economic necessity
(D) regardless of the example set by their parents
(E) for psychological rather than financial reasons

19. Compared to the attitude toward Americans expressed in Passage 1, the attitude toward them expressed in Passage 2 is

(A) more admiring
(B) less disapproving
(C) more cynical
(D) less patronizing
(E) more chauvinistic

YOU MAY GO BACK AND REVIEW THIS SECTION IN THE REMAINING TIME, BUT DO NOT WORK IN ANY OTHER SECTION UNTIL TOLD TO DO SO.

STOP

9   9   9   9   9   9   9

SECTION 9

**Time—20 Minutes
16 Questions**

For each problem in this section determine which of the five choices is correct and blacken the corresponding choice on your answer sheet. You may use any blank space on the page for your work.

Notes:

- You may use a calculator whenever you think it will be helpful.
- Only real numbers are used. No question or answer on this test involves a complex or imaginary number.
- Use the diagrams provided to help you solve the problems. Unless you see the words "Note: Figure not drawn to scale" under a diagram, it has been drawn as accurately as possible. Unless it is stated that a figure is three-dimensional, you may assume it lies in a plane.
- For any function f, the domain, unless specifically restricted, is the set of all real numbers for which $f(x)$ is also a real number.

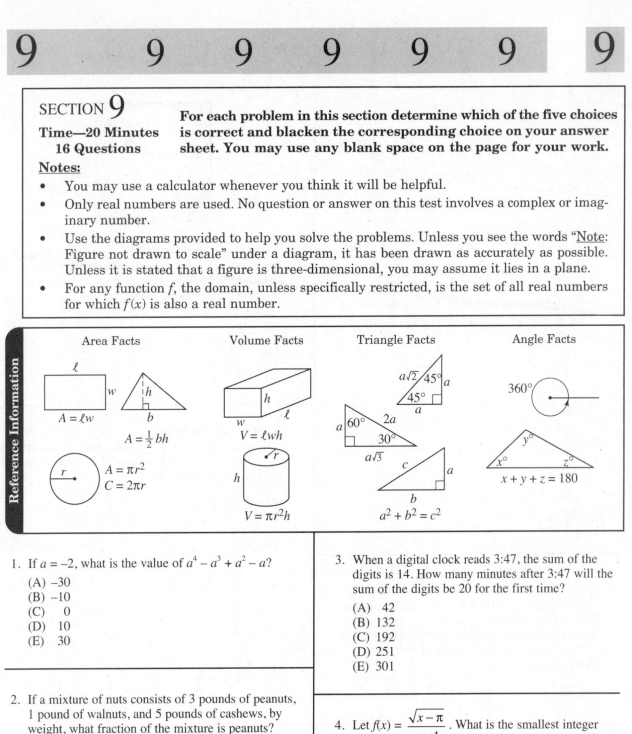

Reference Information

Area Facts

$A = \ell w$

$A = \frac{1}{2} bh$

$A = \pi r^2$
$C = 2\pi r$

Volume Facts

$V = \ell wh$

$V = \pi r^2 h$

Triangle Facts

$a^2 + b^2 = c^2$

Angle Facts

$360°$

$x + y + z = 180$

1. If $a = -2$, what is the value of $a^4 - a^3 + a^2 - a$?

   (A) -30
   (B) -10
   (C) 0
   (D) 10
   (E) 30

2. If a mixture of nuts consists of 3 pounds of peanuts, 1 pound of walnuts, and 5 pounds of cashews, by weight, what fraction of the mixture is peanuts?

   (A) $\dfrac{1}{9}$

   (B) $\dfrac{1}{5}$

   (C) $\dfrac{1}{3}$

   (D) $\dfrac{3}{8}$

   (E) $\dfrac{1}{2}$

3. When a digital clock reads 3:47, the sum of the digits is 14. How many minutes after 3:47 will the sum of the digits be 20 for the first time?

   (A) 42
   (B) 132
   (C) 192
   (D) 251
   (E) 301

4. Let $f(x) = \dfrac{\sqrt{x - \pi}}{x - 4}$. What is the smallest integer for which $f(x)$ is defined?

   (A) 0
   (B) 1
   (C) 3
   (D) 4
   (E) 5

GO ON TO THE NEXT PAGE

9   9   9   9   9   9   9

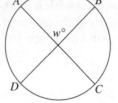

$\overline{AC}$ and $\overline{BD}$ are diameters.

Note: Figure not drawn to scale

5. In the figure above, if $w = 40$, what is the ratio of the total length of arcs $\overset{\frown}{AB}$ and $\overset{\frown}{CD}$ to the circumference?

(A) $\dfrac{1}{9}$

(B) $\dfrac{2}{9}$

(C) $\dfrac{1}{4}$

(D) $\dfrac{2}{5}$

(E) $\dfrac{1}{2}$

6. Phil's Phone Shop sells three models of cellular phones, priced at \$100, \$125, and \$225. In January, Phil sold exactly the same number of each model. What percent of the total income from the sales of cellular phones was attributable to sales of the cheapest model?

(A) $22\dfrac{2}{9}\%$

(B) $28\dfrac{4}{7}\%$

(C) $33\dfrac{1}{3}\%$

(D) $44\dfrac{4}{9}\%$

(E) It cannot be determined from the information given.

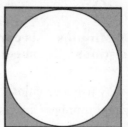

7. In the figure above, a circle is inscribed in a square. If a point is chosen at random inside the square, which of the following is closest to the probability that the point is in the shaded region?

(A) 0.1
(B) 0.15
(C) 0.2
(D) 0.25
(E) 0.3

8. Gilda drove 650 miles at an average speed of 50 miles per hour. How many miles per hour faster would she have had to drive in order for the trip to have taken 1 hour less?

(A) $6\dfrac{2}{3}$

(B) $4\dfrac{2}{3}$

(C) $4\dfrac{1}{3}$

(D) $4\dfrac{1}{6}$

(E) $3\dfrac{1}{3}$

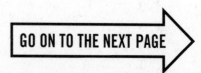

GO ON TO THE NEXT PAGE

9   **9**   **9**   **9**   **9**   **9**   **9**

9. If a team played g games and won w of them, what fraction of the games played did the team lose?

(A) $\dfrac{w-g}{w}$

(B) $\dfrac{w-g}{g}$

(C) $\dfrac{g-w}{g}$

(D) $\dfrac{g}{g-w}$

(E) $\dfrac{g-w}{w}$

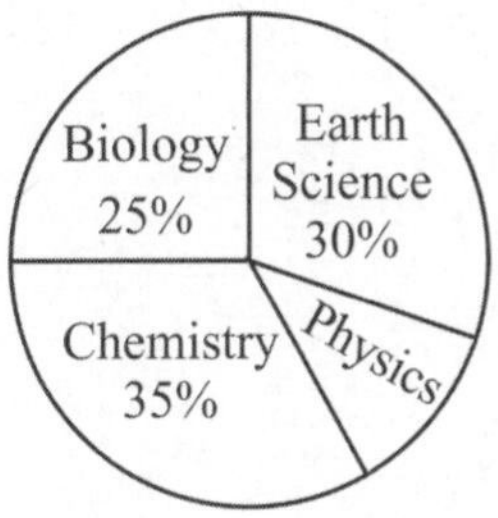

10. The chart above shows the percent of students at Central High School taking each of the four science courses offered. If every student takes exactly one science course, and if 20% of the students taking chemistry switch to physics, what percent of the students will be taking physics?

(A) 7%
(B) 17%
(C) 20%
(D) 25%
(E) 30%

11. In 1980, the cost of p pounds of potatoes was d dollars. In 1990, the cost of $2p$ pounds of potatoes was $\dfrac{1}{2} d$ dollars. By what percent did the price of potatoes decrease from 1980 to 1990?

(A) 25%
(B) 50%
(C) 75%
(D) 100%
(E) 400%

12. If a square and an equilateral triangle have equal perimeters, what is the ratio of the area of the triangle to the area of the square?

(A) $\dfrac{4\sqrt{3}}{9}$

(B) $\dfrac{3}{4}$

(C) $\dfrac{1}{1}$

(D) $\dfrac{4}{3}$

(E) It cannot be determined from the information given.

13. If A is at $(3, -1)$ and B is at $(5, 6)$, what is the slope of the perpendicular bisector of segment $\overline{AB}$?

(A) $-\dfrac{7}{2}$

(B) $-\dfrac{2}{5}$

(C) $-\dfrac{2}{7}$

(D) $\dfrac{2}{7}$

(E) $\dfrac{2}{5}$

GO ON TO THE NEXT PAGE

9 9 9 9 9 9 9

14. In the sequence 1, 2, 3, –4, 1, 2, 3, –4, …, the numbers 1, 2, 3, –4 repeat indefinitely. What is the sum of the first 150 terms?

(A) 0
(B) 3
(C) 37
(D) 77
(E) 300

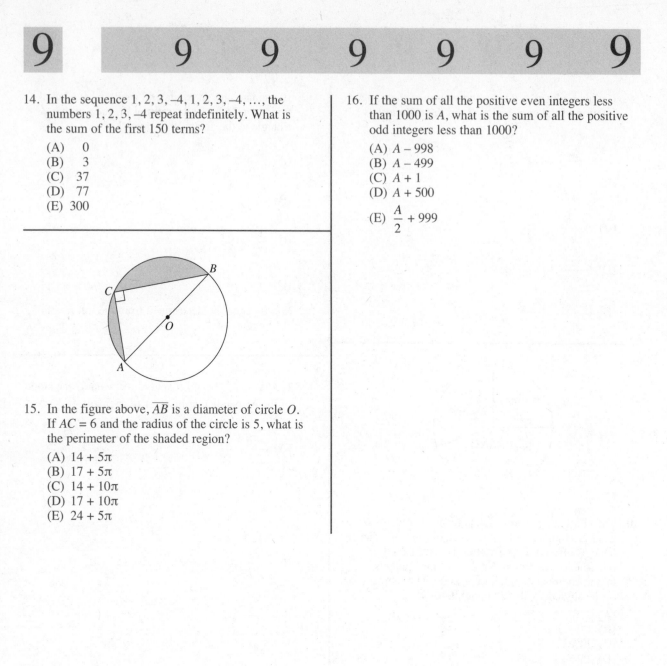

15. In the figure above, $\overline{AB}$ is a diameter of circle O. If $AC = 6$ and the radius of the circle is 5, what is the perimeter of the shaded region?

(A) $14 + 5\pi$
(B) $17 + 5\pi$
(C) $14 + 10\pi$
(D) $17 + 10\pi$
(E) $24 + 5\pi$

16. If the sum of all the positive even integers less than 1000 is A, what is the sum of all the positive odd integers less than 1000?

(A) $A - 998$
(B) $A - 499$
(C) $A + 1$
(D) $A + 500$
(E) $\dfrac{A}{2} + 999$

YOU MAY GO BACK AND REVIEW THIS SECTION IN THE REMAINING TIME, BUT DO NOT WORK IN ANY OTHER SECTION UNTIL TOLD TO DO SO.

S T O P

10   10   10   10   10   10   10

SECTION **10** **Time—10 Minutes**
14 Questions

For each of the following questions, select the best answer
from the choices provided and fill in the appropriate circle
on the answer sheet.

Some or all parts of the following sentences are underlined. The first answer choice, (A), simply repeats the
underlined part of the sentence. The other four choices
present four alternative ways to phrase the underlined
part. Select the answer that produces the most effective sentence, one that is clear and exact, and blacken
the appropriate space on your answer sheet. In selecting your choice, be sure that it is standard written
English, and that it expresses the meaning of the original sentence.

Example:
The first biography of author Eudora Welty
came out in 1998 <u>and she was 89 years old at
the time</u>.

(A) and she was 89 years old at the time
(B) at the time when she was 89
(C) upon becoming an 89 year old
(D) when she was 89
(E) at the age of 89 years old

Ⓐ Ⓑ Ⓒ ● Ⓔ

---

1. Experts predict that global warming <u>will cause sea
   levels to raise and lead to flooding</u> from tidal surges.

   (A) will cause sea levels to raise and lead to
       flooding
   (B) would cause sea levels to raise and lead to
       flooding
   (C) will result in raising sea levels and leading to
       floods
   (D) will be the cause of sea levels' rising and
       flooding
   (E) will raise sea levels and lead to flooding

2. <u>When one realizes how very different caterpillars
   and spiders are</u>, you too will find it remarkable that
   they produce silks that are similar.

   (A) When one realizes how very different caterpil-
       lars and spiders are
   (B) If one should realize the great differences
       between caterpillars and spiders
   (C) If one realizes how greatly caterpillars and
       spiders differ
   (D) When you realize how very different caterpil-
       lars and spiders are
   (E) Upon the realization of how very different
       caterpillars and spiders are

3. <u>The della Robbias created many sculptural reliefs of
   the Virgin and Child surrounded by garlands, and
   they</u> traditionally worked in terra-cotta.

   (A) The della Robbias created many sculptural
       reliefs of the Virgin and Child surrounded by
       garlands, and they
   (B) The della Robbias, who created many sculp-
       tural reliefs of the Virgin and Child sur-
       rounded by garlands,
   (C) Creating many sculptural reliefs of the Virgin
       and Child surrounded by garlands were the
       della Robbias, and they
   (D) The della Robbias created many sculptural
       reliefs of the Virgin and Child surrounded by
       garlands, and doing this they
   (E) In the creation of many sculptural reliefs of the
       Virgin and Child surrounded by garlands, the
       della Robbias they

4. <u>An egotist is when a person thinks the entire universe revolves around him or her.</u>

   (A) An egotist is when a person thinks the entire
       universe revolves around him or her.
   (B) Egotists think the entire universe revolves
       around them.
   (C) An egotist is when a person thinks the entire
       universe is revolving around them.
   (D) An egotist is a person which thinks the entire
       universe revolves around him or her.
   (E) An egotistical person thinks the entire universe
       revolves around himself or herself.

5. Harold <u>Brodkey's eager anticipated first novel was so long in coming</u>—more than three decades, as it turned out—that he actually became famous for not writing a book.

   (A) Brodkey's eager anticipated first novel was so long in coming
   (B) Brodkey's eager anticipated first novel took so long to come
   (C) Brodkey eagerly anticipated his first novel, it was so long in coming
   (D) Brodkey eagerly anticipated his first novel, and it took so long to come
   (E) Brodkey's eagerly anticipated first novel was so long in coming

6. <u>Studies demonstrate the beneficial effects of keeping pets, many</u> senior housing centers are adopting strays from local humane societies.

   (A) Studies demonstrate the beneficial effects of keeping pets, many
   (B) Though studies demonstrate the beneficial effects from keeping pets, many
   (C) Because studies demonstrate the beneficial effects of keeping pets, many
   (D) Studies demonstrate the beneficial effects of keeping pets, and many
   (E) Studies demonstrate that there are beneficial effects from keeping pets, therefore many

7. <u>Having excelled in football, baseball, as well as track</u>, Jim Thorpe is hailed by many as the greatest athlete of the twentieth century.

   (A) Having excelled in football, baseball, as well as track
   (B) With his excellence in football and baseball and being a track star
   (C) Because he excelled in football, baseball, and track
   (D) Having excelled in football and baseball, what is more, track
   (E) By being excellent in football and baseball and also track

8. Running an insurance agency left Charles Ives little time for composition, yet he <u>nevertheless developed a unique musical idiom</u>.

   (A) nevertheless developed a unique musical idiom
   (B) nevertheless developed a very unique musical idiom
   (C) therefore developed a uniquely musical idiom
   (D) nevertheless developed his musical idiom uniquely
   (E) however developed a very unique and idiomatic music

9. <u>While some scientists are absorbed by the philosophical question of what consciousness is,</u> but others restrict themselves to trying to understand what is going on at the neurological level when consciousness is present.

   (A) While some scientists are absorbed by the philosophical question of what consciousness is,
   (B) Although some scientists are absorbed by the philosophical question of what consciousness is,
   (C) Some scientists are absorbed by the philosophical question of what consciousness is,
   (D) Some scientists being absorbed by the philosophical question of what consciousness is,
   (E) While some scientists absorbed the philosophical question of what consciousness is,

10. <u>Given the difficulties inherent in bringing up children, it is remarkable that</u> so many single parents succeed in raising happy, healthy youngsters

    (A) Given the difficulties inherent in bringing up children, it is remarkable that
    (B) Given the difficulties inherent in bringing up children, it seems remarkably that
    (C) If you give the difficulties inherent and bring up children, it is remarkable that
    (D) Giving the difficulties inherent in the upbringing of children, they are remarkable in that
    (E) Having been given the difficulties inherent in bringing up children, one is able to remark that

11. Music journalism at its highest level is a valid literary <u>genre, not a</u> vicarious alternative to mastering an instrument.

    (A) genre, not a
    (B) genre, it is not a
    (C) genre; not a
    (D) genre, but is not a
    (E) genre; and it is not a

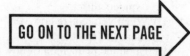
GO ON TO THE NEXT PAGE

10   10   10   10   10   10   10

12. Although his fantasy trilogy, *The Lord of the Rings*, was far better known than his linguistic research on Anglo-Saxon verse, Professor Tolkien refused to grant interviews about the novels he <u>had written or otherwise to promote</u> his nonacademic work.

    (A) had written or otherwise to promote
    (B) had written or otherwise promoting
    (C) wrote nor otherwise promoting
    (D) has written nor otherwise to have promoted
    (E) wrote or otherwise promoting

13. Many of us attempt to rewrite our personal stories to present ourselves in the best light; indeed, <u>there is an almost universal inclination to this</u>.

    (A) there is an almost universal inclination to this
    (B) our inclination for it is almost universal
    (C) our having this inclination is an almost universal condition
    (D) we are almost universally inclined to do so
    (E) doing so is almost universal as an inclination within us

14. The best known Iban <u>textiles, large ceremonial cloths called *pua kumbu*, whose designs depict</u> the flora and fauna of Borneo as well as figures from the spirit realm.

    (A) textiles, large ceremonial cloths called *pua kumbu*, whose designs depict
    (B) textiles, large ceremonial cloths called *pua kumbu*, in whose designs are depicted
    (C) textiles are large ceremonial cloths called *pua kumbu*, whose designs depict
    (D) textiles are large ceremonial cloths called *pua kumbu*, their designs depict
    (E) textiles, large ceremonial cloths, are called *pua kumbu*, in their designs are depicted

Test 5

YOU MAY GO BACK AND REVIEW THIS SECTION IN THE REMAINING TIME, BUT DO NOT WORK IN ANY OTHER SECTION UNTIL TOLD TO DO SO.

STOP

Answer Key

<u>Note:</u> The letters in brackets following the Mathematical Reasoning answers refer to the sections of Chapter 9 in which you can find the information you need to answer the questions. For example, **1. C [E]** means that the answer to question 1 is C, and that the solution requires information found in Section 9-E: Averages.

Section 2   Critical Reading

1. C	6. C	11. A	16. D	21. C
2. E	7. D	12. D	17. E	22. D
3. A	8. C	13. B	18. D	23. B
4. B	9. A	14. E	19. D	24. A
5. C	10. A	15. E	20. D	

Section 3   Mathematical Reasoning

1. E [G]	5. C [D, H]	9. A [J]	13. C [I, J]	17. C [L, N]
2. E [C]	6. B [I, D]	10. D [J]	14. B [E]	18. C [E]
3. B [A, E]	7. B [J, K]	11. D [A]	15. C [R]	19. C [G]
4. A [J]	8. B [E]	12. C [G]	16. A [D]	20. D [K, L]

Section 4   Writing Skills

1. A	8. C	15. E	22. C	29. E
2. E	9. D	16. D	23. C	30. D
3. C	10. B	17. D	24. D	31. D
4. A	11. A	18. C	25. C	32. B
5. D	12. D	19. A	26. D	33. A
6. C	13. E	20. D	27. A	34. E
7. E	14. D	21. D	28. C	35. C

Section 5

On this test, Section 5 was the experimental section. It could have been an extra critical reading, mathematics, or writing skills section. Remember: on the SAT you take, the experimental section may be any section from 2 to 7.

Section 6   Critical Reading

1. C	6. C	11. E	16. D	21. B
2. B	7. D	12. D	17. C	22. D
3. E	8. E	13. D	18. B	23. E
4. A	9. C	14. D	19. E	24. C
5. C	10. C	15. D	20. D	

Section 7   Mathematical Reasoning

Multiple-Choice Questions

1. **A [K]**
2. **D [D]**
3. **C [F]**
4. **B [M]**
5. **E [A, G]**
6. **C [L, O]**
7. **B [K, N]**
8. **D [R]**

Grid-in Questions

9. [B] — **1**

10. [A] — **9**

11. [A, B] — **0**

12. [P] — **11**

13. [A, O] — **4/5** *or* **.8**

14. [E] — **345**

15. [K] — **348**

16. [J] — **12/5** *or 2.4*

17. [C] — **100**

18. [E, P] — **21**

Section 8   Critical Reading

1. **D**	5. **D**	9. **A**	13. **B**	17. **E**
2. **C**	6. **D**	10. **E**	14. **E**	18. **E**
3. **D**	7. **B**	11. **C**	15. **B**	19. **C**
4. **A**	8. **E**	12. **B**	16. **E**	

Section 9   Mathematical Reasoning

1. **E [A]**	5. **B [L]**	9. **C [B]**	13. **C [N]**
2. **C [B]**	6. **A [C]**	10. **B [C, Q]**	14. **D [P]**
3. **C [P]**	7. **C [K, L, O]**	11. **C [C, D]**	15. **A [J, L]**
4. **E [R]**	8. **D [M]**	12. **A [J, K]**	16. **D [A, P]**

Section 10   Writing Skills

1. **E**	4. **B**	7. **C**	10. **A**	13. **D**
2. **D**	5. **E**	8. **A**	11. **A**	14. **C**
3. **B**	6. **C**	9. **C**	12. **A**	

Test 5

Score Your Own SAT Essay

Use this table as you rate your performance on the essay-writing section of this Model Test. Circle the phrase that most accurately describes your work. Enter the numbers in the scoring chart below. Add the numbers together and divide by 6 to determine your total score. The higher your total score, the better you are likely to do on the essay section of the SAT.

Note that on the actual SAT two readers will rate your essay; your essay score will be the sum of their two ratings and could range from 12 (highest) to 2 (lowest). Also, they will grade your essay holistically, rating it on the basis of their overall impression of its effectiveness. They will *not* analyze it piece by piece, giving separate grades for grammar, vocabulary level, and so on. Therefore, you cannot expect the score you give yourself on this Model Test to predict your eventual score on the SAT with any great degree of accuracy. Use this scoring guide instead to help you assess your writing strengths and weaknesses, so that you can decide which areas to focus on as you prepare for the SAT.

Like most people, you may find it difficult to rate your own writing objectively. Ask a teacher or fellow student to score your essay as well. With his or her help you should gain added insights into writing your 25-minute essay.

	6	5	4	3	2	1
POSITION ON THE TOPIC	Clear, convincing, & insightful	Fundamentally clear & coherent	Fairly clear & coherent	Insufficiently clear	Largely unclear	Extremely unclear
ORGANIZATION OF EVIDENCE	Well organized, with strong, relevant examples	Generally well organized, with apt examples	Adequately organized, with some examples	Sketchily developed, with weak examples	Lacking focus and evidence	Unfocused and disorganized
SENTENCE STRUCTURE	Varied, appealing sentences	Reasonably varied sentences	Some variety in sentences	Little variety in sentences	Errors in sentence structure	Severe errors in sentence structure
LEVEL OF VOCABULARY	Mature & apt word choice	Competent word choice	Adequate word choice	Inappropriate or weak vocabulary	Highly limited vocabulary	Rudimentary
GRAMMAR AND USAGE	Almost entirely free of errors	Relatively free of errors	Some technical errors	Minor errors, and some major ones	Numerous major errors	Extensive severe errors
OVERALL EFFECT	Outstanding	Effective	Adequately competent	Inadequate, but shows some potential	Seriously flawed	Fundamentally deficient

Self-Scoring Chart

For each of the following categories, rate the essay from 1 (lowest) to 6 (highest)

Position on the Topic _____

Organization of Evidence _____

Sentence Structure _____

Level of Vocabulary _____

Grammar and Usage _____

Overall Effect _____

TOTAL _____

(To get a score, divide the total by 6) _____

Scoring Chart (Second Reader)

For each of the following categories, rate the essay from 1 (lowest) to 6 (highest)

Position on the Topic _____

Organization of Evidence _____

Sentence Structure _____

Level of Vocabulary _____

Grammar and Usage _____

Overall Effect _____

TOTAL _____

(To get a score, divide the total by 6) _____

Calculate Your Raw Score

Critical Reading

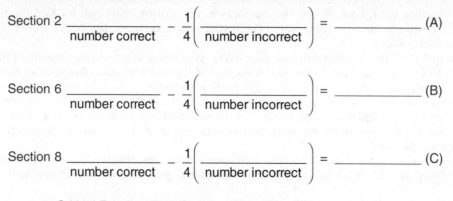

Section 2 $\underline{}$ $-$ $\dfrac{1}{4}$ $\left(\underline{} \right)$ $=$ $\underline{}$ (A)
 number correct number incorrect

Section 6 $\underline{}$ $-$ $\dfrac{1}{4}$ $\left(\underline{} \right)$ $=$ $\underline{}$ (B)
 number correct number incorrect

Section 8 $\underline{}$ $-$ $\dfrac{1}{4}$ $\left(\underline{} \right)$ $=$ $\underline{}$ (C)
 number correct number incorrect

Critical Reading Raw Score = (A) + (B) + (C) = $\underline{}$

Mathematical Reasoning

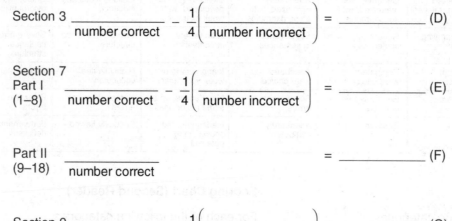

Section 3 $\underline{}$ $-$ $\dfrac{1}{4}$ $\left(\underline{} \right)$ $=$ $\underline{}$ (D)
 number correct number incorrect

Section 7
Part I $\underline{}$ $-$ $\dfrac{1}{4}$ $\left(\underline{} \right)$ $=$ $\underline{}$ (E)
(1–8) number correct number incorrect

Part II $\underline{}$ $=$ $\underline{}$ (F)
(9–18) number correct

Section 9 $\underline{}$ $-$ $\dfrac{1}{4}$ $\left(\underline{} \right)$ $=$ $\underline{}$ (G)
 number correct number incorrect

Mathematical Reasoning Raw Score = (D) + (E) + (F) + (G) = $\underline{}$

Writing Skills

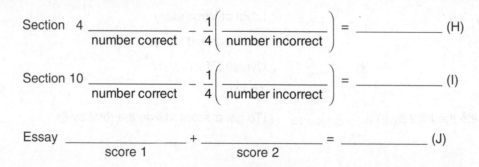

Section 4 $\underline{}$ $-$ $\dfrac{1}{4}$ $\left(\underline{} \right)$ $=$ $\underline{}$ (H)
 number correct number incorrect

Section 10 $\underline{}$ $-$ $\dfrac{1}{4}$ $\left(\underline{} \right)$ $=$ $\underline{}$ (I)
 number correct number incorrect

Essay $\underline{}$ $+$ $\underline{}$ $=$ $\underline{}$ (J)
 score 1 score 2

Writing Skills Raw Score = H + I (J is a separate subscore)

Test 5

Evaluate Your Performance

Scaled Score	Critical Reading Raw Score	Mathematical Reasoning Raw Score	Writing Skills Raw Score
700–800	58–67	48–54	43–49
650–690	52–57	43–47	39–42
600–640	45–51	36–42	35–38
550–590	38–44	30–35	30–34
500–540	30–37	24–29	25–29
450–490	22–29	18–23	19–24
400–440	14–21	12–17	14–18
300–390	3–13	5–11	5–13
200–290	less than 3	less than 5	less than 5

Identify Your Weaknesses

Critical Reading

Question Type	Question Numbers			Chapter to Study
	Section 2	Section 6	Section 8	
Sentence Completion	1, 2, 3, 4, 5, 6, 7, 8	1, 2, 3, 4, 5	1, 2, 3, 4, 5, 6	Chapter 1
Critical Reading	9, 10, 11, 12, 13, 14, 15, 16, 17, 18, 19, 20, 21, 22, 23, 24	6, 7, 8, 9, 10, 11, 12, 13, 14, 15, 16, 17, 18, 19, 20, 21, 22, 23, 24	7, 8, 9, 10, 11, 12, 13, 14, 15, 16, 17, 18, 19	Chapter 2

Identify Your Weaknesses

Mathematical Reasoning

Section in Chapter 9		Question Numbers			Pages to Study
		Section 3	**Section 7**	**Section 9**	
A	Basic Arithmetic Concepts	3, 11	5, 10, 11, 13	1, 16	410–431
B	Fractions and Decimals		9, 11	2, 9	432–449
C	Percents	2	17	6, 10, 11	450–460
D	Ratios and Proportions	5, 7, 16	2	11	461–472
E	Averages	3, 8, 14, 18	14, 18		473–479
F	Polynomials		3		480–488
G	Equations and Inequalities	1, 12, 19	5, 9		489–502
H	Word Problems	5		4	503–513
I	Lines and Angles	6, 13			514–524
J	Triangles	4, 7, 9, 10, 13	16	12, 15	525–542
K	Quadrilaterals	7, 20	1, 7, 15	7, 12	543–553
L	Circles	17, 20	6	5, 7, 15	554–564
M	Solid Geometry		4		565–573
N	Coordinate Geometry	17	7	13	574–588
O	Counting and Probability		6, 13	7	589–600
P	Logical Reasoning		12, 18	3, 14, 16	601–608
Q	Data Interpretation			10	609–618
R	Functions and Their Graphs	15	8	8	619–628

Identify Your Weaknesses

Writing Skills

Question Type	Question Numbers		Chapter to Study
	Section 4	**Section 10**	
Improving Sentences	1, 2, 3, 4, 5, 6, 7, 8, 9, 10, 11	1, 2, 3, 4, 5, 6, 7, 8, 9, 10, 11, 12, 13, 14	Chapter 6
Identifying Sentence Errors	12, 13, 14, 15, 16, 17, 18, 19, 20, 21, 22, 23, 24, 25, 26, 27, 28, 29		Chapter 6
Improving Paragraphs	30, 31, 32, 33, 34, 35		Chapter 6
Essay			Chapter 7

ANSWERS EXPLAINED

Section 2 Critical Reading

1. **C.** The reviewer was vitriolic (as biting as acid), devastating (destructive), and irritating (annoying). He was not *constructive* or helpful. *Never* signals a contrast. The missing word must be an antonym or near-antonym for the three adjectives in the series.
Note that you are looking for a word with positive associations. Therefore, you can eliminate any word with negative ones. Choices D and E have negative associations. Only Choice A, B, or C can be correct. Choice C is preferable.   (Contrast Signal)

2. **E.** The team members *tolerated* or put up with the coach's rules as long as the coach was not too strict in *applying* them.
Despite signals a contrast. You expect people who resent rules to fight them or disobey them. Instead, the team members put up with them. Remember: in double-blank sentences, go through the answer choices, testing the *first* word in each choice and eliminating the ones that don't fit. You can immediately eliminate Choices B, C, and D.   (Contrast Signal)

3. **A.** If we still cannot make up our minds whether low-level microwave radiation is dangerous or safe, our evidence must be too weak for us to be able to decide; it must be *inconclusive*. Remember: before you look at the choices, read the sentence and think of a word that makes sense.
Likely Words: incomplete, uncorroborated, unverified.   (Argument Pattern)

4. **B.** Tacitus' descriptions were *limited* or hindered by the crude (*primitive*) state of communications.
But signals a contrast. The fact that Tacitus' descriptions match those of other writers of his time implies that they are reasonable descriptions for that period. They are adequate *in spite of* the limitations they suffered from.
(Contrast Signal)

5. **C.** If future archaeological discoveries will be "hard put to match" the revelations of the past ten years, the past decade's discoveries must have been truly remarkable ones, ones that *radically* or fundamentally changed the field. Even *striking* or dramatic discoveries could not compare with such revelations.
(Argument Pattern)

6. **C.** Indian art recalls (is *reminiscent of*) Japanese art because, like Japanese art, it minimizes; it *understates*.
The clause following "Japanese art" gives *examples* of what Japanese art is like: it suggests; it does not state directly or overstate.

Look at the first word of each answer pair. If the first word means states directly or overstates, then the second word must mean "is unlike," because it is unlike Japanese art to overstate. If the first word means suggests or understates, then the second word must mean "is like," because it is like Japanese art to understate.   (Examples)

7. **D.** If irony has become a way of escape, then its job is to help people escape or *evade* life's terrors.
Note that the second clause defines what is meant by irony as a *mode of escape*. It clarifies the phrase's meaning.   (Definition)

8. **C.** Looking down on the demonstrators (viewing them with "little respect"), the police would most likely talk about them in *pejorative* (negative) terms.   (Definition)

9. **A.** By denying the existence of a love affair between Pocahontas and John Smith, the author is *debunking* (exposing the falseness of) *a common myth*.

10. **A.** By saying "True," the author admits that there was some sort of relationship between Pocahontas and John Smith, even if it was not the passionate relationship that lovers of romantic tales would prefer.

11. **A.** To say that today's chocolate lovers would not find the Aztec's "food of the gods" heavenly is a *humorous understatement*. More likely, their reaction would be like that of the Spanish explorers who described the unsweetened chocolate beverage as food for pigs!

12. **D.** In describing the Aztec beverage as "fitter for hogs than men," the explorers were being scornful or *derisive*.

13. **B.** The author describes his rapture or great joy when he first saw his new owner's smiling face. Clearly, his immediate response to the prospect of living with the Aulds was chiefly one of *marked* (distinct) *pleasure*.

14. **E.** Lines 21–24 state that "by constant application to her business, she [Mrs. Auld] had been in a good degree preserved from the blighting and dehumanizing effects of slavery." Mrs. Auld has applied herself to her business or trade of weaving. She has *concentrated on this trade*. Because she has not owned slaves but has kept herself busy with her own work, she has been relatively unaffected by slavery and has not adopted the inhumane attitudes typical of slave owners.

15. **E.** The sentences immediately following Douglass's comment about his early instruction clarify what he had been taught. He had been taught to behave in a slavish, *obsequious* fashion. However, "her favor was not gained by it [crouching servility]; she seemed to be disturbed by it" (lines 29 and 30). In other words, the *obsequiousness in which Douglass had been drilled distressed his new mistress.*

16. D. Fawning and cringing did not *serve* the purpose of pleasing Mrs. Auld; such slavish behavior did not do at all in this particular situation.

17. E. According to Douglass, at the time he met her Mrs. Auld was a kind, loving woman who had not yet had the experience of owning slaves. Thus, she had been kept free of "the blighting and dehumanizing effects of slavery" (lines 23 and 24). However, she now owned a slave—Douglass himself—and would inevitably be affected by her power over him. Her kind heart would cease to be kind: she *was destined to undergo a change of character* as she became corrupted by her participation in the institution of slavery.

18. D. The passage does not suggest that a *disdain* (scorn) *for convention* is typical of Mrs. Auld. Therefore, Choice D is correct.
Mrs. Auld was noted for "constant application to her business" (lines 21 and 22). This implies that *diligence in labor* was one of her characteristics. Therefore, Choice A is incorrect.
Mrs. Auld seemed "disturbed" by "crouching servility" (lines 26 and 27). This implies that a *dislike of fawning* was one of her characteristics. Therefore, Choice B is incorrect.
Mrs. Auld was kindhearted (lines 16 and 17) and able to put people at ease (lines 32 and 33). This implies that *gentleness of spirit* was one of her characteristics. Therefore, Choice C is incorrect.
Mrs. Auld voluntarily began to teach the narrator. She wished him well. This implies that a *benevolent nature* was one of her characteristics. Therefore, Choice E is incorrect.

19. D. Choice D is correct. You can arrive at it by the process of elimination.
Statement I is true. In line 45 Mr. Auld tells his wife that instructing slaves is unlawful: it *violates the law*. Therefore, you can eliminate Choice B.
Statement II is untrue. Since Mr. Auld is so concerned that education would spoil his slaves, he must believe that slaves *can* be taught. Therefore, you can eliminate Choices C and E.
Statement III is true. Mr. Auld states that a slave who was able to read would become "unmanageable" (line 54). Therefore, you can eliminate Choice A.
Only Choice D is left. It is the correct answer.

20. D. Mr. Auld is arguing that Mrs. Auld should not give Douglass reading lessons. To convince her, he cites a variant of the proverb "If you give him an inch, he'll take a mile." (In other words, he'll take a lot *more* than you originally planned to give him.) A mile

is a much larger unit of length than an inch. We can assume that *an ell is a much larger unit of length than an inch*, also.

21. C. The author's purpose in this passage is to show how he discovered that learning to read was vital for him if he wanted to be free. The bulk of the passage deals with learning to read—the author's introduction to it, his master's arguments against it, his own increased determination to succeed in it.
Choice A is incorrect. It is the cause of the disagreement that is central, not the existence of the disagreement.
Choice B is incorrect. The author lists, but does not analyze, the master's reasons for forbidding his wife to teach her slave.
Choice D is incorrect. It is unsupported by the passage.
Choice E may seem a possible answer, but it is too narrow in scope. Only the last two sentences of the first paragraph stress Mrs. Auld's moral downfall.

22. D. Douglass states that his master "was deeply sensible of the truths he was uttering." In other words, his master was highly *conscious* that he was saying the truth; he felt sure that only evil consequences would come from teaching a slave to read.

23. B. The author's tone is strongly ironic. He knows full well that, in opposing his education, his master did not intend to benefit him. Thus, by acknowledging his "debt" to his master, the author is underlining his master's defeat. His tone is *cutting and ironic*.
Choice A is incorrect. The author is not filled with loving sentiment and warmth when he thinks of his harsh master.
Choice C is incorrect. The author neither whines nor congratulates himself on his own moral superiority.
Choice D is incorrect. The author is not resigned or submissive; he certainly is not wistful or longing for the days gone by.
Choice E is incorrect. Although the author still feels anger at the institution of slavery, when he thinks of his master's defeat he feels triumphant as well.

24. A. The author wholly believes his master's statement that learning would make him unmanageable. In other words, education would make him *impossible to enslave*.
Choice B is incorrect. The author is concerned with education for freedom, not for old age.
Choices C, D, and E are incorrect. They are unsupported by the passage.

Section 3 Mathematical Reasoning

In each mathematics section, for many problems, an alternative solution, indicated by two asterisks (**), follows the first solution. When this occurs, one of the solutions is the direct mathematical one and the other is based on one of the tactics discussed in Chapter 8 and 9.

1. **E.** $a - 5 = 0 \Rightarrow a = 5 \Rightarrow a + 5 = \mathbf{10}$.

2. **E.**   Use your calculator *only* if you don't realize that $50\% = \dfrac{1}{2}$. Otherwise, just say $\dfrac{1}{2}$ of 50 is 25, and $\dfrac{1}{2}$ of 25 is **12.5**.

3. **B.**   The average of x and y is $\dfrac{x+y}{2}$, and the product of that fraction and 5 is

   $$5\left(\frac{x+y}{2}\right) = \frac{5x+5y}{2}.$$

   **It's easier and quicker to do this directly, so substitute for x and y only if you get stuck or confused. If $x = 2$ and $y = 4$, their average is 3; and the product of 5 and 3 is 15. Only $\dfrac{5x+5y}{2}$ is equal to 15 when $x = 2$ and $y = 4$.

4. **A.**   Since $x + 100 = 180$, $x = 80$; also,
   $$180 = y + x + x = y + 80 + 80 = y + 160$$
   $$\Rightarrow y = \mathbf{20}.$$

5. **C.**   In 1 minute light will travel
   $(300{,}000 \text{ km/s})(60 \text{ s}) = 18{,}000{,}000$ km. Therefore, light will travel 150,000,000 kilometers in $\dfrac{150{,}000{,}000}{18{,}000{,}000} = \mathbf{8\dfrac{1}{3}}$ light minutes.

6. **B.**   Every hour the hour hand moves through 30° $\left(\dfrac{1}{12} \text{ of } 360°\right)$ It will move through 10° in $\dfrac{1}{3}$ hour, or 20 minutes; and 20 minutes after 1:15 the time is **1:35**.

7. **B.**   Draw a square, and let the sides be 1. Then, by KEY FACTS J8 and J10, the diagonal, d, is $\sqrt{2}$, and $d^2 = 2$. Since the area of the square is 1, d^2 is **twice the area of the square**.
   **By KEY FACT K8, one formula for the area of a square is $A = \dfrac{d^2}{2}$.

8. **B.**   Since the average of a, b, c, and d is 10, their sum is 40. The only other condition is that they be in increasing order. The numbers could be 1, 2, 3, and 34, in which case both I and III are false. This guarantees that the answer is **II only**, but let's just verify that II is true: in any set of numbers that are not all equal, the smallest number in the set is less than the average of the numbers, and the greatest number is more than their average.

9. **A.**   Use TACTIC 1: draw a diagram, and label all the line segments. Now add two segments to create a right triangle. Since the legs are 6 and 8, the hypotenuse is **10**.

   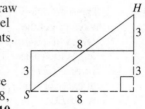

   **Use TACTIC 8: eliminate the absurd choices and guess. The woman rode 14 miles. Clearly, the direct path is shorter; eliminate C, D, and E. Since it's probably *much* shorter, eliminate B, as well.

10. **D.**   There are only two possibilities. Either (i) 5 and 6 are the lengths of the two legs, or (ii) 5 is the length of a leg, and 6 is the hypotenuse. In either case use the Pythagorean theorem:

    (i) $5^2 + 6^2 = c^2 \Rightarrow$
    $\quad c^2 = 61 \Rightarrow c = \sqrt{61}$;
    or
    (ii) $a^2 + 5^2 = 6^2 \Rightarrow$
    $\quad a^2 = 36 - 25 = 11 \Rightarrow$
    $\quad a = \sqrt{11}$.

    Statements **I and II only** are true.

11. **D.**   By definition, $\overset{5}{\underset{3 \quad 2}{\triangle}} = $
    $(5)(3)(2) - (5 + 3 + 2) = 30 - 10 = \mathbf{20}$.

12. **C.**   Check each choice to see which of the equations has (have) *exactly one positive integer solution*.

    I. For *every* number a: $(0)(a)(-a) = 0$ and $0 + a + (-a) = 0$, so for *every* positive integer a, $\overset{a}{\underset{0 \quad -a}{\triangle}} = 0 - 0 = 0$. (I is false.)

    II. 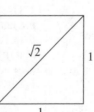 $= a \cdot a \cdot a - (a + a + a) = a^3 - 3a = a(a^2 - 3)$.

    So, if $\overset{a}{\underset{a \quad a}{\triangle}} = 0$, then $a = 0$ or $a^2 - 3 = 0$, in which case $a = \pm\sqrt{3}$, none of which is a positive integer.

III. 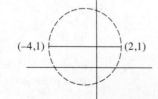 $= a \cdot 2a \cdot 3a - (a + 2a + 3a) =$

$6a^3 - 6a = 6a(a^2 - 1)$

So, if ⟨triangle⟩ $= 0$, then $a = 0$ or $a^2 = 1 = 0$, in which case $a = 1$ or $a = -1$. So, this equation has *one* positive integer solution, $a = 1$. (III is true.)

Statement **III only** is true.

13. **C.** There are many ways to get the values of x and y; here's the easiest. Since $\angle EFD$ is an exterior angle of $\triangle FEC$,

$50 = 30 + x \Rightarrow x = 20$ (KEY FACT J2). Since in $\triangle DEF$, $DF = EF$, then $a = b$ and

$$a + b + 50 = 180 \Rightarrow a + b = 130,$$

so a and b are 65 each. But since the opposite sides of a rectangle are parallel, $b = y$, so $y = 65$ and $x + y = 20 + 65 = \mathbf{85}$.

14. **B.** It's possible to reason the answer out without writing down and adding up all the numbers, but it won't save any time. Systematically list them: 123, 132, 213, 231, 312, 321. Use your calculator: the sum is 1332, and the average is $1332 \div 6 = \mathbf{222}$.

15. **C.** $f(2a) = (2a)^2 - 1 = 4a^2 - 2$ and $g(2a) = 1 - (2a)^2 = 1 - 4a^2$. Then $f(2a) - 7 = 4a^2 - 1 - 7 = 4a^2 - 8$ and $g(2a) + 7 = 1 - 4a^2 + 7 = 8 - 4a^2$. So $4a^2 - 8 = 8 - 4a^2 \Rightarrow 8a^2 = 16$. So, $a^2 = 2 \Rightarrow a = \sqrt{2}$ (or $-\sqrt{2}$, which isn't an answer choice).

16. **A.** Write the equation from the definition given:

$$\text{density} = \frac{\text{population}}{\text{area}}.$$ The area of Jackson County is ℓw, so if the population is p, then

$$d = \frac{p}{\ell w} \Rightarrow p = d\ell w.$$

**Use TACTIC 6: replace the letters with easy-to-use numbers. Let $\ell = 2$ and $w = 3$. Then the area is 6; and if the population is 60, the density is 10 people per square mile. Only $d\ell w$ equals 60 when $\ell = 2$, $w = 3$, and $d = 10$.

17. **C.** Use TACTIC 1: draw a diagram. Since the distance between $(-4,1)$ and $(2,1)$ is 6, the

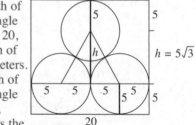

diameter of the circle is 6 and the radius is 3. Then the area is $\pi(3)^2 = \mathbf{9\pi}$.

18. **C.** This question calls for a weighted average. The students in the first-period class earned a total of $24 \times 78 = 1872$ points, and the students in the second-period class earned $26 \times 83 = 2158$ points. In total, the 50 students earned $1872 + 2158 = 4030$ points, so their average was

$$\frac{4030}{50} = \mathbf{80.6}.$$

The average of 78 and 83 is 80.5. However, since the group of students averaging 83 is *slightly* larger than the group with the 78 average, the average must be *slightly* greater than 80.5. Eliminate A and B and guess. There's no guarantee, but certainly, **80.6 is *slightly* greater than 80.5.

19. **C.** $x = 2y - 5 \Rightarrow 2y = x + 5 \Rightarrow y = \dfrac{x+5}{2}$, so

$$z = 16y^3 = 16\left(\frac{x+5}{2}\right)^3$$

$$= \overset{2}{\cancel{16}}\,\frac{(x+5)^3}{\underset{1}{\cancel{8}}} = 2(x+5)^3.$$

**Use TACTIC 6: replace the letters with numbers. Let $y = 2$; then $x = -1$ and $z = 16(2)^3 = 16(8) = 128$. Which of the five choices equals 128 when $x = -1$? Only $\mathbf{2(x+5)^3}$.

20. **D.** The length of the rectangle is clearly 20, the length of two diameters. The width of the rectangle is $10 + h$, where h is the height of the equilateral triangle formed by joining the centers of the three circles. Since the sides of that triangle are 10, the height is $5\sqrt{3}$ (KEY FACT J11). Then the width of the rectangle is $10 + 5\sqrt{3}$ and its area is

$20(10 + 5\sqrt{3}) = \mathbf{200 + 100\sqrt{3}}$.
**Use TACTIC 2: trust the diagram. Clearly, the length is 20, and the width is much more than 10, but less than 20. You should even see that the width must be more than 15, so the area is between 300 and 400. Only Choice D is between 300 and 400.

Section 4 Writing Skills

1. **A.** Sentence is correct.
2. **E.** The original sentence lacks parallel structure. Choices B and C are wordy and awkward. Choice D is wordy. Only Choice E both

corrects the error and produces an effective, concise sentence.

3. C. Lack of needed subordination. The sentence establishes a contrast. Most of Heyer's books are set in the eighteenth century; one, however, is set in the eleventh century. Only Choice C establishes this contrast without introducing any fresh errors.

4. A. Sentence is correct.

5. D. Error in subject-verb agreement. Do not use *as well as* as a synonym for *and*. Only Choice D corrects the error.

6. C. Error in number. Because *programs* is plural, *kind* should be plural as well. The preferred form is *these kinds of programs*.

7. E. Errors in word usage and in parallelism. Do not use *then*, referring to time, in place of the function word *than*. The basic sentence states that modern men *are* less tolerant than men of old *were*. The revision in Choice E clarifies the meaning of the sentence.

8. C. Errors in verb form and idiom. Choice C both provides the noun clause with a verb (*are transmitted*) and introduces the noun clause properly with the preposition *by*.

9. D. The original sentence is both informal and redundant. By substituting *stems from the desire* for *is because of wanting*, you create a stronger, more effective sentence.

10. B. Dangling modifier. Ask yourself *who* was born in the days when no modest woman would admit to writing novels. The answer is *Jane Austen*. Choice B corrects the error by making *Jane Austen* the subject of a dependent clause.

11. A. Sentence is correct.

12. D. Error in word usage. *Complimented* means praised. The videotapes did not praise the exhibition; they made it complete. In other words, they *complemented* it.

13. E. Sentence is correct.

14. D. Sentence fragment. Change *performing* to *performs*. The ensemble *performs* without a conductor.

15. E. Sentence is correct.

16. D. Error in verb form. The passive voice is necessary here. The accidentally found objects do not discover anything. Instead they *are discovered* to be amazingly valuable.

17. D. Error in word usage. Change *provoked from* to *provoked by*.

18. C. Error in subject-verb agreement. A singular subject requires a singular verb. Culture *is* part of the complex mix.

19. A. Error in sequence of tenses. Since *refuses* is present tense, change *had had* to *has had*.

20. D. Errors in parallelism and in shift of pronoun. Change *your pursuit of* to *pursuing*.

21. D. Error in pronoun-antecedent agreement. Who is encroaching on human territory? The black bear is. The antecedent is singular; the pronoun should be singular as well. Change *their* to *its*.

22. C. Error in subject-verb agreement. Do not let the unusual word order confuse you. The subject of the main clause is *differences*, plural. Replace *has* with *have*.

23. C. Error in pronoun case. Here, the pronoun is the object of the preposition *between*. The sentence should read "between my brother and *me*," not "between my brother and I."

24. D. Error in word usage. People are *indecisive* (unable to make a decision); periods of time are *indefinite* (without a fixed or defined end). Replace *indecisive* with *indefinite*.

25. C. Shift in personal pronoun. Replace *you should* either with *one should* or with *he or she should*.

26. D. Error in logical comparison. Compare steaks with steaks, not steaks with meat markets. Change *Chelsea Meat Market* to *those at Chelsea Meat Market*.

27. A. Error in word usage. *Perspective* is a noun meaning viewpoint or vista; *prospective* is an adjective meaning expected or future. The visitors are *prospective* or future tourists.

28. C. Error in subject-verb agreement. The subject *Gold* is singular; the verb should be singular as well. Replace *are* with *is*.

29. E. Sentence is correct.

30. D. Choices A, B, and C abruptly state the contrasting point of view without regard to the context.
Choice D takes the context into account and provides for a smooth progression of thought. It is the best answer.
Choice E is confusing. It is unclear until the end of the sentence whether the *other members* support or oppose the exhibit.

31. D. Choice A is not consistent in style and mood with the rest of the paragraph.
Choice B is a sentence fragment.
Choice C is excessively wordy.
Choice D fits the context of the paragraph and expresses the idea correctly. It is the best answer.
Choice E inappropriately uses *in conclusion* and contains the pronoun *it*, which lacks a specific antecedent.

32. B. Choice A lacks a main verb; therefore, it is a sentence fragment.
Choice B accurately combines the sentences. It is the best answer.
Choice C expresses the idea in a way that the writer could not have intended.
Choice D subordinates important ideas and emphasizes a lesser one.
Choice E restates the idea in a manner that changes the writer's intended meaning.

33. A. Choice A is the best answer because sentences 10–12 contain basic information about the topic. Readers are left in the dark unless the information appears as early as possible in the essay.

34. E. Choice A contains faulty idiom; the phrase *than of the past* is nonstandard usage.
Choice B contains a faulty comparison; *society* and *the past* cannot be logically compared.
Choice C contains an error in idiom; *than from* is redundant.
Choice D is correct but excessively wordy.
Choice E is the best answer.

35. C. Choice A provides a reasonable transition, but it contains an error in pronoun-antecedent agreement. The pronoun *they* is plural; its antecedent *anyone* is singular.
Choice B contains an error in diction. One can *disapprove of* but not *disagree with* a piece of art.
Choice C alludes to the content of the preceding paragraph and is clearly and succinctly expressed. It is the best answer.
Choice D contains an error in pronoun-antecedent agreement. The pronoun *them* is plural; the antecedent *anyone* is singular.
Choice E is inconsistent in tone and mood with the rest of the essay.

Section 6 Critical Reading

1. C. The sentence implies that Polynesian banquets are usually reputed to be good. The speaker was disappointed by the banquet. Two possibilities exist: either this banquet was a poor one, or the banquets in general are *overrated* (too highly valued).
Note how the "either...or" structure sets up a contrast between the two clauses.
                                    (Contrast Signal)

2. B. The librarian has the committee's *acquiescence* or agreement; they assent but do not go so far as to encourage or spur on the librarian. Their support is of a lesser degree.
Note how the "with the...if not the" structure signals that the missing word and the noun *encouragement* must differ in meaning to some degree.
Remember: before you look at the choices, read the sentence and think of a word that makes sense.
Likely Words: agreement, permission, consent, approval

3. E. An *endorsement* is a testimonial or statement recommending a product for its *virtues* or good qualities.
Beware of Eye-Catchers. Choice A is incorrect. Though products have trademarks, trademarks are not statements of a product's contents; they are names or logos manufacturers use to identify their products. (Definition)

4. A. His friends could not understand his *outburst against* his employers because he was usually dutiful (*docile*) and helpful (*accommodating*).

Remember: watch for signal words that link one part of the sentence to another. The presence of *and* linking a pair of items indicates that the missing word may be a synonym or near-synonym for the other linked word. In this case, *docile* and *accommodating* are near-synonyms.   (Support Signal)

5. C. To be No. 1 at the box office, a film must attract or draw a large audience. Such popularity attests to its star's *drawing* power, particularly if the film didn't receive especially good reviews.
To say that the film's reviews were *modest* at best is *not* high praise. It indicates that even the best of the reviews were lukewarm or middling.   (Contrast Pattern)

6. C. The opening sentences simply present Hobbes's thoughts on the nature of government.

7. D. You can answer this question by using the process of elimination.
Does the author of Passage 1 establish a time frame? Yes. She states that the English Civil War took place between 1642 and 1646; she also states that Locke wrote forty years after Hobbes did. You can eliminate (A).
Does the author contrast two differing viewpoints? Definitely. You can eliminate (B).
Does the author make an assertion? Yes. She asserts that Hobbes had a bleak view of human nature, that Locke had a more optimistic view, and so on. You can eliminate (C).
Does the author refute an argument? No. She merely states the arguments or beliefs of others. This is probably the correct answer. Just to be sure, check (E).
Does the author quote a source? Yes. She quotes Locke, citing his description of the disorder created by the absence of government. You can eliminate (E).
Only (D) is left. It is the correct answer.

8. E. Passage 1 describes Hobbes's view of human nature as "fearful and bleak." Passage 2 states that fear of war plays a central role in his philosophy. Both passages indicate that his world view *is inherently pessimistic*.

9. C. The anecdote in Passage 1 about Hobbes's premature birth (which was brought on by his mother's fear of an attack by the Spanish fleet) *confirms the statement* in Passage 1 that his view of human nature was "fearful and bleak."

10. C. In the opening paragraph the writer speaks of the Gothic world in terms of play and extravagance, of the fantastic and the luxurious. In other words, he speaks of it in terms of its *elaborateness of fancy* or fantasy.
Choices A and B are incorrect. They are unsupported by the passage.

Choices D and E are incorrect. They are attributes of the medieval imagination, not of the Gothic.

11. E. For architecture to reach "a point of extravagance unequalled in history" is for it to achieve an unparalleled *degree* of lavishness and excess.

12. D. The author has just described the extraordinary degree of wastefulness and excess in the Gothic period. He then notes something somewhat paradoxical. Despite the worldly extravagance of the period, it produced the saintly Francis of Assisi and the religious poet Dante. By citing these two great spirits, the author corrects a potential misapprehension. He thus *refutes the notion that the Gothic period produced nothing but extravagance.*

13. D. The tapestries combine worldly elements (mythological beasts that symbolize lust and ferocity, wild creatures that symbolize fertility) with spiritual ones (the lady who embodies chastity) to express "the power of love." Choice A is incorrect. It is unsupported by the passage.
Choice B is incorrect. Though the Gothic imagination has a "sharp sense of reality" (lines 14 and 15), it is more inclined to be playful than to be practical.
Choice C is incorrect. Nothing in the passage suggests that wall hangings are wasteful.
Choice E is incorrect. It is unsupported by the passage.

14. D. The tapestries are known as *The Lady with the Unicorn*. In the central tapestry, the lion and the unicorn kneel before *the lady*, who gently, irresistibly, subdues the forces of nature.

15. D. "To draw carts of stones up the hill for the building of Chartres Cathedral" is to *haul the stones used to construct the cathedral*. In doing such hard manual labor, the noble knights and ladies showed the depth of their conviction or belief.

16. D. Step by step, the author traces the course of a surgical procedure, from the initial grasping of the scalpel through the opening incision to the eventual sensory exploration of the internal organs. In doing so, he is *describing a process*.

17. C. As the surgeon draws the knife across the skin, it leaves a thin *line of blood* in its wake (path or track passed over by a moving object).

18. B. To part the flesh is to *split* or separate the skin.

19. E. The "strange flowers" with their looped handles are the hemostats, forceps, and other *surgical tools* attached to the opening.

20. D. To write of one object by using a term that normally indicates a different object, suggesting a likeness between them, is to make an implicit comparison, that is, to be *metaphorical*.

21. B. The simile "like children absorbed in a game" indicates that in this context "engaged" means *engrossed* or deeply involved.

22. D. Primitive drawings of buffalo and other wild beasts still exist in *caves* in which *prehistoric* humans dwelled.

23. E. Writing of "ritual cleansing," entering the "temple" of the human body, the truth hidden in the "ark" or holy place, the author is referring to priestly or *religious observances* (rites).

24. C. The author freely uses technical names for various *body organs* — "fascia," "peritoneum," "omentum" — tossing in occasional descriptive adjectives or phrases as if he assumes the reader is already *able to visualize* these organs in some detail. Readers without much background in anatomy might well feel the need for additional information about these organs (size, function, specific location) in order to appreciate the passage fully.

Section 7 Mathematical Reasoning

MULTIPLE-CHOICE QUESTIONS

1. A. Since the area of the square is 25, its sides are 5, and its perimeter is 20. Since the perimeter of the pentagon is also 20, each of its sides is **4**.

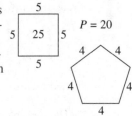

2. D. Going at $\frac{1}{3}$ of Mary's speed, John took 3 times as long: $3 \times 30 = \mathbf{90}$ minutes.

3. C. $\dfrac{x^2 - 1}{x^2 - x} = \dfrac{(x+1)(x-1)}{x(x-1)} = \dfrac{x+1}{x}$.

   **Use TACTIC 6: plug in a number for x. If $x = 2$, then $\dfrac{x^2 - 1}{x^2 - x} = \dfrac{2^2 - 1}{2^2 - 2} = \dfrac{3}{2}$. Only choice C is equal to $\dfrac{3}{2}$, where $x = 2$: $\dfrac{2+1}{2} = \dfrac{3}{2}$.

4. B. The formula for the volume of a cylinder, which is given to you in the reference box, is $V = \pi r^2 h$. The first cylinder has a height of 4 and a radius of 2. Its volume is $\pi(2^2)4 = 16\pi$. The second cylinder has a height of 2 and a radius of 4. Its volume is $\pi(4^2)2 = 32\pi$. The volume of the first cylinder is $\dfrac{16\pi}{32\pi} = \dfrac{1}{2}$ the volume of the second cylinder.

5. **E.** If x is even, then every multiple of x is even and x^n is even for any positive integer n. So, x, $2x$, $3x$, $5x$, x^2, $3x^2$, and x^3 are all even. Finally, the sum of any two even numbers is even, and the sum of an even number and an odd number is odd. Therefore, choices A–D are all true. **Choice E** is the product of two odd numbers and so is odd.

**Use TACTIC 6 and replace x with a simple even number, such as 2. Then evaluate each of the choices to see which one is not true. When $x = 2$, $(3x - 5)(5x - 3) = (1)(7) = 7$, which is odd. Choice E is not true.

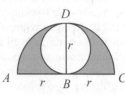

6. **C.** $\overline{AB}$, $\overline{BC}$, and $\overline{BD}$ are all radii of the semicircle. If r is the radius, then the area of the semicircle is $\frac{1}{2}\pi r^2$. Since r is the diameter of the circle, the circle's radius is $\frac{1}{2}r$ and its area is $\pi\left(\frac{1}{2}r\right)^2 = \frac{1}{4}\pi r^2$. Then the area of the shaded region is $\frac{1}{2}\pi r^2 - \frac{1}{4}\pi r^2 = \frac{1}{4}\pi r^2$.

The area of the shaded region and the area of the unshaded region are equal. Therefore, the probability that the point is in the shaded region is $\frac{1}{2}$.

**Do exactly the same thing but let $r = 2$. Then the total area is 2π and the shaded area is π.

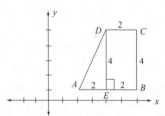

7. **B.** Sketch quadrilateral $ABCD$, and draw $\overline{DE}$ perpendicular to $\overline{AB}$. Then the area of rectangle $BCDE$ is $2 \times 4 = 8$, and the area of right $\triangle AED$ is $\frac{1}{2}(2)(4) = 4$. The total area is **12**.

8. **D.** To get the graph on the bottom, the graph on the top was shifted 2 units to the right and 2 units up. By KEY FACT R2 its equation is $y = f(x - 2) + 2$.

GRID-IN QUESTIONS

9. (1) $\dfrac{1}{5} + \dfrac{2}{10} + \dfrac{3}{15} + \dfrac{4}{20} + \dfrac{5}{25} =$

   $\dfrac{1}{5} + \dfrac{1}{5} + \dfrac{1}{5} + \dfrac{1}{5} + \dfrac{1}{5} = \dfrac{5}{5} = \mathbf{1}$.

10. (9) $ab = 20$ and $a = -5 \Rightarrow -5b = 20 \Rightarrow b = -4$, so $a^2 - b^2 = (-5)^2 + (-4)^2 = 25 - 16 = \mathbf{9}$.

11. (0) If $a \ne b$ and $ax = bx$, then x must be 0. Therefore

   $$\frac{2}{3}x = \frac{3}{4}x \Rightarrow x = 0 \Rightarrow \frac{4}{5}x = \mathbf{0}.$$

12. (11) Between 12:10 A.M. and 2:40 P.M., for example, the clock chimes once every 15 minutes, beginning at 12:15 and continuing to 2:30, except twice at 2:00: a total of **11** times.

13. $\left(\dfrac{4}{5} \text{ or } 0.8\right)$ There are five integers less than 50 whose units digit is 7: 7, 17, 27, 37, and 47. Of these, four (all but 27) are prime. Then, the probability of drawing a prime is $\dfrac{4}{5}$.

14. (345) Since the average amount of savings for the 10 students is $60, the total amount they have all saved is $600 (TACTIC E1). John has $130, and 3 students have no savings at all. If 5 other students have $125 total ($25 each, the least possible), then the tenth student will have $600 – $130 – $125 = **$345**.

15. (348) You don't need to add up the lengths of the steps. Together, all the horizontal steps are equal to the bottom, and all the vertical risers are equal to the left side. The sum of the left side, 5 feet 4 inches, or 64 inches, and the bottom, 9 feet 2 inches, or 110 inches, is half the perimeter. The perimeter is $2(64 + 110) = 2(174) = \mathbf{348}$.
   **Of course, if you don't see this, you can just use your calculator to add everything.

16. $\left(\dfrac{12}{5} \text{ or } 2.4\right)$ Since the area of a right triangle is $\dfrac{1}{2}$ the product of its legs, the area is $\dfrac{1}{2}(3)(4) = 6$.

   But the area can also be calculated as $\dfrac{1}{2}bh$.

Test 5

Since this is a 3-4-5 triangle, the base is 5, so

$$6 = \frac{1}{2}(5)h \Rightarrow 5h = 12 \Rightarrow h = \frac{12}{5} \text{ or } \mathbf{2.4}.$$

**There are *several* other ways to get this answer if you know more than the basic geometry required for the SAT. For example, the little triangle on the left in the figure is similar to the large one, and the ratio of the hypotenuse of the small triangle to the hypotenuse of the large triangle is 3:5. Then, $3:5 = h: 4 \Rightarrow h = \mathbf{2.4}$.

17. (100) $c = a\%$ of $a\%$ of $b = \dfrac{a}{100} \times \dfrac{a}{100} \times b =$

$\dfrac{a^2 b}{10{,}000}$, and $kc = a^2\%$ of $b = \dfrac{a^2}{100}b$. Then

$$\frac{a^2 b}{100} = kc = k\frac{a^2 b}{10{,}000} \Rightarrow \frac{1}{100} = \frac{k}{10{,}000} \Rightarrow$$
$$100k = 10{,}000 \Rightarrow k = \mathbf{100}.$$

**Use TACTIC 6: replace the variables with numbers. If $a = 10$ and $b = 100$, 10% of (10% of 100) = 10% of 10 = 1, so $c = 1$; but $(10)^2\%$ of 100 = 100% of 100 = 100. Then $kc = 100 \Rightarrow k = \mathbf{100}$.

18. (21) Since the average of the three digits is 2, the sum of the digits is 6. The simplest thing is to list them. If there are only a few, list them all; if it seems that there will be too many to list, look for a pattern. The list starts this way: 105, 114, 123, 132, 141, 150, so there are 6 positive three-digit numbers in the 100's. Continue: 204, 213, 222, 231, 240; there are 5 in the 200's. You can conclude, correctly, that there are 4 in the 300's, 3 in the 400's, 2 in the 500's, and 1 in the 600's. The total is $6 + 5 + 4 + 3 + 2 + 1 = \mathbf{21}$. If you don't spot the pattern, just continue the list: 303, 312, ... , 501, 510, 600.

Section 8 Critical Reading

1. D. If something falls into decay or disintegrates, by definition it must be *perishable* or subject to decay.   (Cause and Effect)

2. C. Since Lee avoided or refrained from excesses, Grant, his opposite, must have *indulged in* or satisfied his taste for excesses.
   The key words in this sentence are "differed markedly." They set up the contrast between the two men.
   Note that you are looking for a word that suggests Grant enjoyed drinking. Therefore, you can eliminate any word that suggests he disliked or disapproved of it. Choices A, B, and D all suggest dislike or disapproval. They are clearly incorrect. Choice E, *compensated for*, suggests neither disapproval nor dislike.

However, it makes no sense in the context. Choice C is the correct answer.
                              (Contrast Pattern)

3. D. Someone given to starting casual conversations with total strangers is by definition *gregarious* or sociable.   (Definition)

4. A. With no enemies to stop their spread, the deer *thrived*. In fact, they did so well that they "overgrazed" or ate too much grass. This *threatened* (was bad for) the vegetation. Note how the "to such an inordinate degree...that" structure signals cause and effect.
   Remember: in double-blank sentences, go through the answer choices, testing the *first* word in each choice and eliminating the ones that don't fit. You can immediately eliminate Choices C and E.   (Cause & Effect Signal)

5. D. The negotiations have degenerated or deteriorated; they have become *acrimonious* (bitter). The phrase following the blank gives an example of what the sessions are like. They are degenerating into a welter or turmoil of accusations and countercharges.
   Note that you are looking for a word with negative associations. Therefore, you can eliminate any word with positive ones. Choices A, C, and E all have positive associations. Only Choice B or Choice D can be correct. Choice C, *phlegmatic* (slow and stolid; undemonstrative), is an inappropriate word to describe a wild turmoil of accusations. By process of elimination, the correct answer must be *acrimonious*, Choice D.   (Examples)

6. D. One would protest a system *deliberately* or intentionally designed to *demean* (degrade or debase) human dignity.
   Choices A, B, and E are incorrect. One would be unlikely to protest a system that reflected, fostered (nourished), or enhanced (improved) human dignity.
   Choice C is also incorrect. *Assess* (evaluate) is inappropriate in the context.   (Definition)

7. B. The energy of American life springs or *arises* from various factors enumerated by the author.
   Remember: when answering a vocabulary-in-context question, test each answer choice, substituting it in the sentence for the word in quotes.

8. E. Use the process of elimination to answer this question.
   Choice A is incorrect. The lover of business is *enthusiastic*; he applies zeal or enthusiasm to the task at hand.
   Choice B is incorrect. The lover of business is *engrossed* in his work because of its "absorbing, satisfying character" (lines 35 and 36).
   Choice C is incorrect. The lover of business is *enterprising*, industriously devoting himself to

making the business "greater and better organized" (line 27).

Choice D is incorrect. The lover of business is *industrious*; he applies himself to the task at hand with "zeal and intensity" (line 31).

Only Choice E is left. It is the correct answer. The lover of business is *not* ruled by the love of money or material advantages. He is clearly not *mercenary*.

9. A. Lines 25–28 plainly state that American lovers of business find joy or pleasure in making businesses greater and better organized. Thus, Americans clearly must find the prospect of improving business organizations *pleasurable*.

10. E. The word "engine" here is used metaphorically to indicate a *driving force* in society. The lover of business wants his organization to be a powerful force in the world.

11. C. The concluding sentence of Passage 1 states that "in beginning life in such a society, which has developed a native and vital tradition" of business, young people will come to "realize a part of what [they] are living for." In other words, they will be influenced to *find self-fulfillment* or self-realization *through their business activities*.

12. B. The author states that technological advances have wiped out cultural differences so thoroughly that the time may come when "it will be impossible to distinguish human beings living on one area of the earth's surface from those living on any other." In other words, he asserts that these advances *may eventually lead to worldwide cultural* sameness or *uniformity*.

13. B. A striking difference is *marked* or noticeable; it immediately strikes the eye.

14. E. To take something for granted is to accept it without question or objection, in other words, to *assume* it.

15. B. If a man made less money than his father did, Americans assumed the fault was his. A son's failure to surpass his father in income was proof that the son had not worked hard enough ("was lazy") or had not worked effectively ("was...inefficient"). In other words, he had not *applied himself properly* to the task.

16. E. If the *rentier* is doing nothing to increase his inherited wealth, he is "doomed" to a life of drunkenness or psychoanalysis. Clearly, the author feels no sympathy for the sufferings of this poor little rich man. Instead, he views the *rentier* with sardonic *irony*.

17. E. Use the process of elimination to answer this question.

Choice A is incorrect. The assertion "In no society in history have rich men given away so large a part of their fortunes" is a *categorical statement*.

Choice B is incorrect. The author *corrects a misapprehension* about how profitable slave labor was to Southern slave owners.

Choice C is incorrect. Throughout the passage the author *contrasts* the European and American attitudes toward money.

Choice D is incorrect. In the passage's final sentence, the author *poses a question*.

Only Choice E is left. It is the correct answer. Throughout the passage, the author never refers to or *cites an authority*.

18. E. The author of Passage 1 asserts that American men engage in business for the sheer love of business activities. The author of Passage 2 asserts they do so out of a sense of Oedipal rivalry with their fathers. However, both authors would agree that Americans engage in business *for psychological rather than financial reasons*.

19. C. The author of Passage 1 is making a commencement address to students about to graduate from an American college. Appropriately enough, he addresses them positively, expressing an optimistic view of American traditions and society. The British author of Passage 2, however, has a far *more cynical* view of Americans, who are (in his opinion) far less rational than their European counterparts.

Section 9 Mathematical Reasoning

1. E. *Be careful* with the minus signs and the negatives:
$$(-2)^4 - (-2)^3 + (-2)^2 - (-2) =$$
$$16 - (-8) + 4 - (-2) = 16 + 8 + 4 + 2 = \mathbf{30}.$$

2. C. The weight of the mixture is 9 (3 + 1 + 5) pounds, of which 3 pounds are peanuts.

Hence, the desired fraction is $\dfrac{3}{9} = \dfrac{1}{3}$.

3. C. The largest possible sum of the digits *for the minutes* is 14, when the time is 59 minutes after the hour. Therefore, the first time that the sum of *all* the digits can be 20 occurs when the hour is 6: at 6:59 we have 6 + 5 + 9 = 20. Since 6:59 is 3 hours and 12 minutes after 3:47, and since 3 hours is 180 minutes, this sum of 20 will occur after 180 + 12 = **192** minutes.

4. E. The expression $\sqrt{x-\pi}$ is defined only if $x - \pi \geq 0$, so $x \geq \pi$. The smallest integer greater than π is 4. But if x were 4, the denominator

of $\dfrac{\sqrt{x-\pi}}{x-4}$ would be 0, and $f(4)$ is not defined. The smallest integer for which $f(x)$ is defined is **5**.

5. B. Since $w = 40$, arc $\overarc{AB}$ is $\dfrac{40}{360} = \dfrac{1}{9}$ of the circumference. Arc $\overarc{CD}$ is the same length, so the total length of the two arcs is $\dfrac{2}{9}$ of the circumference.

**The two arcs add up to 80°, which is less than 90°, a quarter of the circle. Therefore, the answer is less than $\dfrac{1}{4}$: eliminate C, D, and E.

Also, since $\dfrac{1}{9} = 0.111...$, which is much too small, eliminate A.

**Use TACTIC 3: redraw the diagram.

Clearly, the two arcs take up more than $\dfrac{1}{9}$, but much less than $\dfrac{1}{2}$, of the circumference; even $\dfrac{2}{5}$ is way too big.

Eliminate A, D, and E,

and guess between $\dfrac{2}{9} = 0.222$ and $\dfrac{1}{4} = 0.25$, which are too close to distinguish just by looking.

6. A. Assume Phil sold only one phone of each model. Then his total sales were $450 ($100 + $125 + $225), so $\dfrac{100}{450} = \dfrac{2}{9}$ of the total sales were attributable to the cheapest phone.

Changing to percents gives:

$\dfrac{2}{9} = \dfrac{2}{9}(100)\% = \mathbf{22\dfrac{2}{9}}\%$.

7. C. Pick a value for a side of the square, say 2. Then the area of the square is 4. Since the diameter of the circle is also 2, the radius is 1, and the area of the circle is π. Then the area of the unshaded region is $4 - \pi$, and the probability that the chosen part is in the shaded region is $\dfrac{4 - \pi}{4} \approx 0.214$. Of the choices, **0.2** is the closest.

8. D. Driving at 50 miles per hour, Gilda took $650 \div 50 = 13$ hours for the trip. In order for the trip to have taken only 12 hours, she would have had to drive at a rate of

$650 \div 12 = 54\dfrac{1}{6}$ miles per hour, or

$4\dfrac{1}{6}$ miles per hour faster.

9. C. If a team won w of the g games it played, it lost the rest: $g - w$. The fraction is $\dfrac{g - w}{g}$.

**Use TACTIC 6: plug in easy-to-use numbers. If the team won 2 of its 3 games, it lost $\dfrac{1}{3}$ of them. Only $\dfrac{g - w}{g}$ equals $\dfrac{1}{3}$ when $g = 3$ and $w = 2$.

10. B. Currently, $25\% + 30\% + 35\% = 90\%$ of the students are taking a course other than physics, so 10% are taking physics. Since 20% of 35% is 7%, if 20% of the chemistry students transfer to physics, the percent of students taking physics will be $10\% + 7\% = \mathbf{17\%}$.

**Assume there are 100 students at Central High School. Then 35 of them are taking chemistry, and 10 are taking physics. Since 20% of 35 = 7, there will be 17 students taking physics.

11. C. Since, in 1990, $2p$ pounds of potatoes cost $\dfrac{1}{2}d$ dollars, p pounds cost half as much: $\dfrac{1}{2}\left(\dfrac{1}{2}d\right)$ or $\dfrac{1}{4}d$. This is $\dfrac{1}{4}$, or 25%, as much as the cost in 1980, which represents a decrease of **75%**.

**In this type of problem it is often easier to use TACTIC 6. Assume that 1 pound of potatoes cost $100 in 1980. Then in 1990, 2 pounds cost $50, so 1 pound cost $25. This is a decrease of $75 in the cost of 1 pound of potatoes, and

$$\text{percent decrease} = \dfrac{\text{decrease}}{\text{original cost}}(100\%)$$

$$= \dfrac{75}{100}(100\%) = \mathbf{75\%}.$$

12. A. Use TACTIC 7. Choose an appropriate number for the common perimeter. Any number will work; but since a triangle has 3 sides and a square has 4 sides, 12 is a good choice. Then, each side of the square is 3, and its area is $3^2 = 9$. Each side of the equilateral triangle is 4, and its area is $\dfrac{4^2\sqrt{3}}{4} = 4\sqrt{3}$ (KEY FACT J15). The ratio is $\dfrac{4\sqrt{3}}{9}$.

13. **C.** The slope of $\overline{AB}$ is $\dfrac{6-(-1)}{5-3} = \dfrac{7}{2}$. Then the slope of *any* line perpendicular to $\overline{AB}$ is the negative reciprocal of $\dfrac{7}{2}$, namely, $-\dfrac{2}{7}$.

14. **D.** Since there are 4 numbers (1, 2, 3, –4) in the repeating set, divide 150 by 4: $150 \div 4 = 37.5$. This means that in the first 150 terms there are 37 complete groups of the 4 numbers. The sum of the numbers in each group is $1 + 2 + 3 - 4 = 2$, so the sum of the numbers in the 37 groups is $37 \times 2 = 74$. Finally, note that $37 \times 4 = 148$. Then the sum of the first 148 terms is 74. The next 2 terms are 1 and 2, so the sum of the first 150 terms is $74 + 1 + 2 = \mathbf{77}$.

15. **A.** Since the radius of circle O is 5, $AB = 10$. Also, since $\triangle ACB$ is a right triangle whose hypotenuse, $\overline{AB}$, is 10 and one of whose legs is 6, the other leg, $\overline{BC}$, is 8. (If you don't recognize this as a 6-8-10 triangle, use the Pythagorean theorem.) The circumference of a circle whose diameter is 10 is 10π, so the length of the semicircle is 5π. The perimeter is the sum of the lengths of the semicircle and the two legs of the triangle: $6 + 8 + 5\pi = \mathbf{14 + 5\pi}$.

16. **D.** Let B be the sum of all the positive odd integers less than 1000.

$$A = 2 + 4 + 6 + 8 + \cdots + 996 + 998$$
$$\downarrow \quad \downarrow \quad \downarrow \quad \downarrow \qquad\quad \downarrow \qquad \downarrow$$
$$B = (1 + 3 + 5 + 7 + \cdots + 995 + 997) + 999$$

A is the sum of 499 even integers, each of which is 1 more than the corresponding odd integer in B. Then $(1 + 3 + 5 + \cdots + 997) = A - 499$, and $B = (A - 499) + 999 = \mathbf{A + 500}$.

Section 10 Writing Skills

1. **E.** Error in usage. The verb *raise* means *cause to move upward, lift, increase*. It is transitive, as in "Raise your hand!" The verb *rise* means *get up, move up, ascend*. It is intransitive, as in "Rise up and sing!" When manufacturers *raise* prices, our expenses *rise*. Choice E uses *raise* correctly.

2. **D.** Error in pronoun choice. Avoid shifting from one pronoun to another within a single sentence. Change *When one realizes* to *When you realize*.

3. **B.** Ineffective sentence. Do not string two main clauses together with *and* unless both clauses deserve equal emphasis. Choice B, through its use of subordination, effectively emphasizes the idea that the della Robbias worked in terra-cotta.

4. **B.** Wordiness. Do not use *when* after *is* when you are defining a term. Choice B eliminates unnecessary words to create a strong, effective sentence.

5. **E.** Adjective-adverb confusion. Change *eager anticipated* to *eagerly anticipated*.

6. **C.** Run-on sentence. Use a comma between main clauses *only* when they are linked by a coordinating conjunction (*and, but,* etc.). Choice C corrects the error by replacing the original construction with a subordinate clause.

7. **C.** Choice C strengthens the sentence by correcting the error in parallelism and clarifying the cause-and-effect relationship: *because* Thorpe excelled in sports, *therefore* people acclaim him.

8. **A.** Sentence is correct. *Unique* means being without a like or equal. Avoid phrases like *very unique* and *more unique* that imply there can be degrees of uniqueness.

9. **C.** Remember: any sentence elements that are *not* underlined are by definition correct. Here, the coordination conjunction *but* is not underlined. Coordinating conjunctions connect sentence elements that are grammatically equal. In this case, *but* should connect the main clause beginning "others restrict themselves" with another main clause. However, *while*, a subordinating conjunction, introduces a subordinate, not a main, clause. To correct the error, delete *While* and begin the sentence with *Some scientists are absorbed*.

10. **A.** Sentence is correct.

11. **A.** Sentence is correct.

12. **A.** Sentence is correct.

13. **D.** The revised sentence is stronger and less vague than the original both because it eliminates the weak *there is* construction and introduces the pronoun *we*.

14. **C.** Sentence fragment. Choice C corrects the fragment by providing a verb, *are*, without introducing any new errors.

Pronunciation Key*

ă	as in pat	ĕ	as in pet and cherry	ə	as in above and cactus
ā	as in play and maid	ē	as in see	û(r)	as in purr and pert
ah	as in bother and hot	ēr	as in ear and peer	o͞o	as in school and mule
ahr	as in car	ĭ	as in pit	o͝o	as in full and good
â(r)	as in Mary and fair	ī	as in pie and my	ng	as in Ping-Pong
aw	as in paw	ō	as in toe and grow		
ow	as in how and cloud	oi	as in point and toy		

*Note: Pronunciation often tends to be regional and you may find that you pronounce a word differently than what is shown. These guidelines are meant to give you a general idea of the pronunciation (to distinguish between the adjective, verb, or noun forms of the word, for example), and are based primarily on the first-listed pronunciation in *Merriam Webster's Collegiate Dictionary*, Eleventh Edition.

v. waver; fluctuate.

Uncertain which suitor she ought to marry, the princess *vacillated*, saying now one, now the other.

---

v. slander.

Waging a highly negative campaign, the candidate attempted to *vilify* his opponent's reputation.

---

n. fanatic; person who shows excessive zeal.

Though Glenn was devout, he was no *zealot* who tried to force his beliefs on friends.

---

v. seize another's power or rank.

The revolution ended when the victorious rebel general succeeded in his attempt to *usurp* the throne.

---

adj. wordy.

Someone mute can't talk; someone *verbose* can hardly stop talking.

---

adj. changeable; explosive; evaporating rapidly.

The political climate today is extremely *volatile*: no one can predict what the electorate will do next.

---

v. weaken; sap.

The recent scandals have *undermined* many people's faith in the government. The heavy rains have washed away much of the cliffside, threatening to *undermine* the pillars supporting several houses at its edge.

---

v. revere.

In Tibet today, the common people still *venerate* their traditional spiritual leader, the Dalai Lama.

---

n. highly skilled artist.

The child prodigy Yehudi Menuhin grew into a *virtuoso* whose violin performances thrilled millions.

Fold along perforation before detatching cards

undermine **(əN dû(r) mīn)**	**usurp** **(yo͞o SəRP)**	**vacillate** **(VĂ sə lāt)**
venerate **(VĚ nə rāt)**	**verbose** **(vû(r) BŌS)**	**vilify** **(vĭ lə fī)**
virtuoso **(vû(r) cho͞o Ō sō)**	**volatile** **(VAH lə t(ə)l)**	**zealot** **(ZĚ lət)**

v. exceed.

Her SAT scores *surpassed* our expectations.

---

adj. habitually silent; talking little.

The stereotypical cowboy is a *taciturn* soul, answering lengthy questions with a "Yep" or "Nope."

---

n. state of violent agitation.

Warned of approaching *turbulence* in the atmosphere, the pilot told the passengers to fasten their seat belts.

---

adj. unnecessary; excessive; overabundant.

Betsy lacked the heart to tell June that the wedding present was *superfluous*; they had already received five toasters.

---

n. servile flatterer; bootlicker; yes-man.

The King believed the flattery of his *sycophants* and refused to listen to warnings.

---

adv. momentary; temporary; staying for a short time.

Lexy's joy at finding the perfect gift for Phil was *transient*; she still had to find presents for all the cousins.

Located near the airport, this hotel caters to a largely *transient* trade.

---

adj. trivial; shallow.

Since your report gave only a *superficial* analysis of the problem, I cannot give you more than a passing grade.

---

adj. secret; furtive; sneaky; hidden.

Hoping to discover where his mom had hidden the Christmas presents, Timmy took a *surreptitious* peek into the closet.

---

adj. concise; abrupt; pithy.

There is a fine line between speech that is *terse* and to the point and speech that is too abrupt.

Fold along perforation before detatching cards

superficial
(sŏŏ pər FĬ shəl)

superfluous
(sŏŏ PŪ(R) flŏŏ əs)

surpass
(sər PĂS)

surreptitious
(sû(r) əp TĬ shəs)

sycophant
(SĬ kə fənt)

taciturn
(TĂ sə tû(r)n)

terse
(TÛ(R)S)

transient
(TRĂN(T) sh(ē) ənt)

turbulence
(TÛ(R) byə lən(t)s)

v. examine closely and critically.

Searching for flaws, the sergeant *scrutinized* every detail of the private's uniform.

---

adj. gloomy; depressing; dark; drab.

From the doctor's grim expression, I could tell he had *somber* news.

---

adj. brief; terse; compact.

Don't bore your audience with excess verbiage: be *succinct*.

---

adj. conscientious; extremely thorough.

Though Alfred is *scrupulous* in fulfilling his duties at work, he is less conscientious about his obligations at home.

---

n. doubter; person who suspends judgment until the evidence supporting a point of view has been examined. skepticism, *n.*

I am a *skeptic* about the new health plan; I want some proof that it can work.

---

v. establish by evidence; verify; support.

These endorsements from satisfied customers *substantiate* our claim that Barron's *How to Prepare for the SAT* is the best SAT-prep book on the market.

---

adj. mocking.

The humor of cartoonist Gary Trudeau is often *satirical.*

---

adj. slavish; cringing.

Constantly fawning on his employer, humble Uriah Heep was a *servile* individual.

---

adj. motionless; stale; dull.

Mosquitoes commonly breed in ponds of *stagnant* water.

Fold along perforation before detatching cards

scrutinize
(SKRŌŌ t(ə)n īz)

somber
(SAHM bər)

succinct
(sək SĬNG(K)T)

scrupulous
(SKRŌŌ pyə ləs)

skeptic
(SKĔP tĭk)

substantiate
(səb STĔN(T) shē āt)

satirical
(sə TĬR ĭ kəl)

servile
(SÛ(R) vəl)

stagnant
(STĂG nənt)

v. reprove severely; rebuke. also n.

Every time Ermengarde made a mistake in class, she was afraid that Miss Minchin would *reprimand* her and tell her father how badly she was doing in school.

---

n. reserve; uncommunicativeness; inclination to silence.

Fearing his competitors might get advance word about his plans from talkative staff members, Hughes preferred *reticence* from his employees to loquacity.

---

v. approve; ratify.

Nothing will convince me to *sanction* the engagement of my daughter to such a worthless young man.

---

adj. deserving blame.

Shocked by the viciousness of the bombing, politicians of every party uniformly condemned the terrorists' *reprehensible* deed.

---

v. disown; disavow.

On separating from Tony, Tina announced that she would *repudiate* all debts incurred by her soon-to-be-ex-husband.

---

adj. pertaining to effective communication; insincere in language.

To win his audience, the speaker used every *rhetorical* trick in the book.

---

v. abandon; disown; repudiate.

Joan of Arc refused to *renounce* her belief that her voices came from God.

---

v. censure; rebuke.

The principal severely *reproved* the students whenever they talked in the halls.

---

v. withdraw; take back.

When I saw how Fred and his fraternity brothers had trashed the frat house, I decided to *retract* my offer to let them use our summer cottage.

Fold along perforation before detaching cards

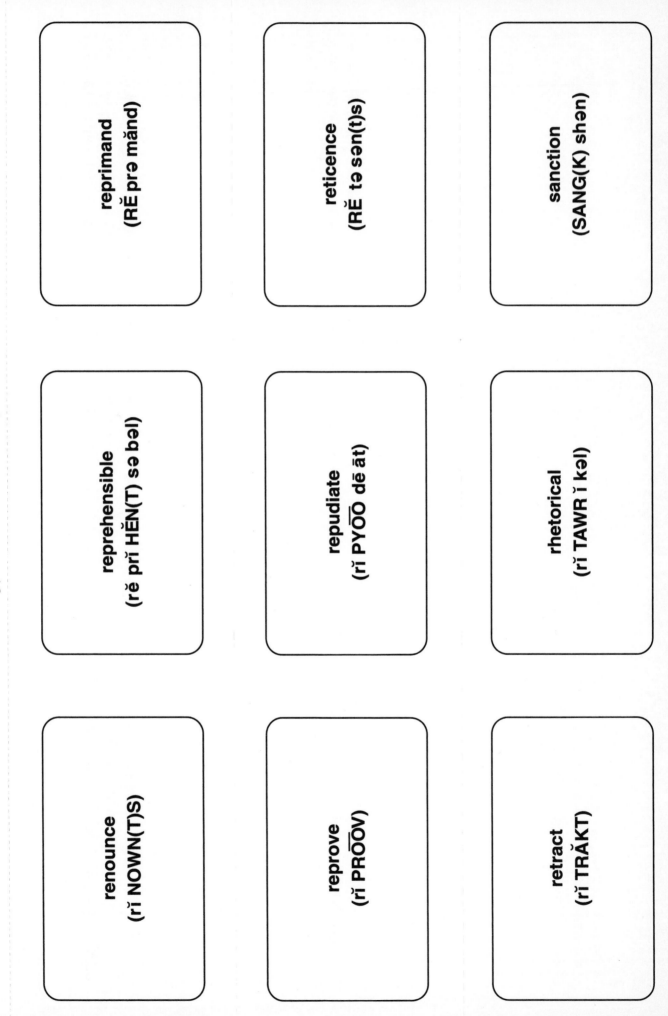

reprimand
(RĔ prə mănd)

reticence
(RĔ tə sən(t)s)

sanction
(SANG(K) shən)

reprehensible
(rĕ prĭ HĔN(T) sə bəl)

repudiate
(rĭ PYOO dē āt)

rhetorical
(rĭ TAWR ĭ kəl)

renounce
(rĭ NOWN(T)S)

reprove
(rĭ PROOV)

retract
(rĭ TRĂKT)

n. bitterness; hatred.

Thirty years after the war, she could not let go of the past but was still consumed with *rancor* against the foe.

---

v. set right; correct.

You had better send a check to *rectify* your account before American Express cancels your credit card.

---

v. banish to an inferior position; delegate; assign.

After Ralph dropped his second tray of drinks that week, the manager *relegated* him to a minor post, cleaning behind the bar.

---

n. dilemma.

When both Harvard and Stanford accepted Laura, she was in a *quandary* as to which school she should attend.

---

n. hermit; loner.

Disappointed in love, Miss Emily became a *recluse*; she shut herself away in her empty mansion.

---

v. disprove.

The defense called several respectable witnesses who were able to *refute* the false testimony of the prosecution's sole witness.

---

adj. cautious; careful. prudence, *n.*

A miser hoards money not because he is *prudent* but because he is greedy.

---

n. refutation; response with contrary evidence.

The defense lawyer confidently listened to the prosecutor sum up his case, sure that she could answer his arguments in her *rebuttal*.

---

adj. superfluous; repetitious; excessively wordy.

The bottle of wine I brought to Bob's was certainly *redundant*; how was I to know he owned a winery?

Fold along perforation before detatching cards

prudent (PRŌŌ dənt)	**quandary** (KWAHN d(ə) rē)	**rancor** (RĂNG kər)
rebuttal (rĭ Bə t(ə)l)	**recluse** (RĔ klōōs)	**rectify** (RĔK tə fī)
redundant (rĭ DəN dənt)	**refute** (rĭ FYŌŌT)	**relegate** (RĔ lə gāt)

adj. wasteful; reckless with money. also *n.*

Don't be so *prodigal* spending my money; when you've earned some money yourself, you can waste it as much as you want!

---

n. overabundance; lavish expenditure.

Seldom have I seen food and drink served in such *profusion* as at the wedding feast.

---

n. nearness.

Blind people sometimes develop a compensatory ability to sense the *proximity* of objects around them.

---

adj. widespread; generally accepted.

Reed had no patience with the conservative views *prevalent* in the America of his day.

---

adj. deep; not superficial; complete.

Freud's remarkable insights into human behavior caused his fellow scientists to honor him as a *profound* thinker.

---

adj. abundantly fruitful.

My editors must assume I'm a *prolific* writer; they expect me to revise six books this year.

---

adj. ostentatious; pompous; making unjustified claims; overly ambitious.

None of the other prize winners are wearing their medals; isn't it a bit *pretentious* of you to wear yours?

---

v. violate; desecrate; treat unworthily.

Tourists are urged not to *profane* the sanctity of holy places by wearing improper garb.

---

n. rapid growth; spread; multiplication. proliferate, *v.*

Times of economic hardship inevitably encourage the *proliferation* of countless get-rich-quick schemes.

Fold along perforation before detatching cards

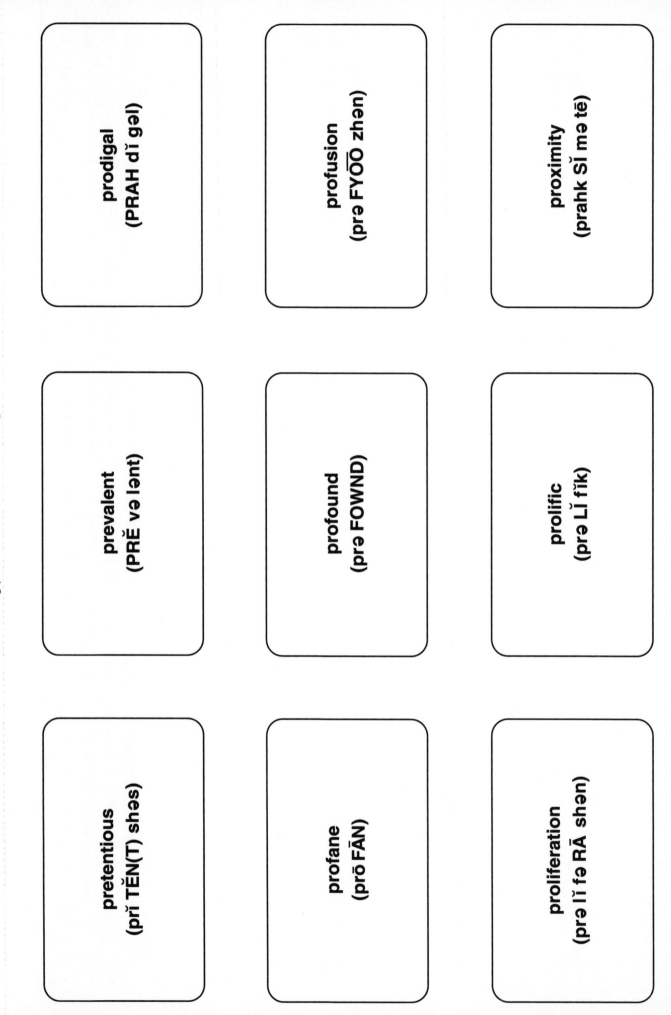

prodigal
(PRAH dǐ gəl)

profusion
(prə FYOO zhən)

proximity
(prahk SǏ mə tē)

prevalent
(PRĚ və lənt)

profound
(prə FOWND)

prolific
(prə LǏ fǐk)

pretentious
(prǐ TĚN(T) shəs)

profane
(prō FĀN)

proliferation
(prə lǐ fə RĀ shən)

v. pacify; conciliate.

The store manager tried to *placate* the angry customer, offering to replace the damaged merchandise.

---

v. make impossible; eliminate.

The fact that the band was already booked to play in Hollywood on New Year's Eve *precluded* their accepting the New Year's Eve gig in London.

---

adj. overconfident; impertinently bold; taking liberties.

Matilda thought it was *presumptuous* of the young man to have addressed her without first having been introduced. Perhaps manners were freer here in the New World.

---

n. religious devotion; godliness.

The nuns in the convent were noted for their *piety*, spending their days in worship and prayer.

---

adj. practical; concerned with the practical worth or impact of something.

The coming trip to France should provide me with a *pragmatic* test of the value of my conversational French class.

---

n. former occupant of a post.

I hope I can live up to the fine example set by my late *predecessor* in this office.

---

n. lover of mankind; doer of good.

In his role as a *philanthropist* and public benefactor, John D. Rockefeller, Sr. donated millions to charity.

---

adj. weighty; unwieldy.

His humor lacked the light touch; his jokes were always *ponderous*.

---

adj. advanced in development.

Listening to the grown-up way the child discussed serious topics, he couldn't help remarking how *precocious* she was.

Fold along perforation before detatching cards

philanthropist
(fĭ LĂN(T) thrə pĭst)

piety
(PĪ ə tē)

placate
(PLĀ kāt)

ponderous
(PAHN d(ə) rəs)

pragmatic
(prăg MĂ tĭk)

preclude
(prĭ KLŌŌD)

precocious
(prĭ KŌshəs)

predecessor
(PRĔ də sĕ sər)

presumptuous
(prĭ ZəM(P) chə wəs)

n. extreme wealth; luxuriousness; abundance. *opulent, adj.*

The glitter and *opulence* of the ballroom took Cinderella's breath away.

---

adj. one-sided; prejudiced; committed to a party.

On certain issues of principle, she refused to take a *partisan* stand, but let her conscience be her guide.

---

n. belief that life is basically bad or evil; gloominess.

Considering how well you have done in the course so far, you have no real reason for such *pessimism* about your final grade.

---

n. individual who sacrifices principles for expediency by taking advantage of circumstances.

Joe is such an *opportunist* that he tripled the price of bottled water at his store as soon as the earthquake struck.

---

n. one opposed to force; antimilitarist.

Shooting his way through the jungle, Rambo was clearly not a *pacifist*.

---

adj. pervading; spread throughout every part.

Despite airing them for several hours, Martha could not rid her clothes of the *pervasive* odor of mothballs that clung to them.

---

adj. dark; not transparent.

The *opaque* window shade kept the sunlight out of the room.

---

adj. showy; pretentious; trying to attract attention.

Trump's latest casino in Atlantic City is the most *ostentatious* gambling palace in the East.

---

adj. marginal; outer.

We lived, not in central London, but in one of those *peripheral* suburbs that spring up on the outskirts of a great city.

Fold along perforation before detatching cards

opaque
(ō PĀK)

ostentatious
(ahs tən TĀ shis)

peripheral
(pə RĬ f(ə) rəl)

opportunist
(ah pū̆(r) TOŌ nĭst)

pacifist
(PĂ sə fĭst)

pervasive
(pər VĂ sĭv)

opulence
(AH pyə lən(t)s)

partisan
(PAHR tə zən)

pessimism
(PĔ sə mĭ ĕz)

adj. stingy; mean.

Transformed by his vision on Christmas Eve, mean old Scrooge ceased being *miserly* and became a generous, kind old man.

---

adj. worldly as opposed to spiritual; everyday.

Uninterested in philosophical or spiritual discussion, Tom talked only of *mundane* matters such as the daily weather forecast.

---

n. obscurity; forgetfulness.

After a decade of popularity, his works had fallen into *oblivion*; no one bothered to read them anymore.

---

adj. excessively careful; painstaking.

Martha Stewart was a *meticulous* housekeeper, fussing about each and every detail that went into making up her perfect home.

---

adj. ill-humored; sullen; melancholy.

Forced to take early retirement, Bill acted *morose* for months.

---

v. nourish; educate; foster.

The Head Start program attempts to *nurture* prekindergarten children so they will do well when they enter public school.

---

n. preoccupation with physical comforts and things.

By its nature, *materialism* is opposed to idealism, for where the materialist emphasizes the needs of the body, the idealist emphasizes the needs of the soul.

---

v. appease; moderate.

Nothing Jason did could *mitigate* Medea's anger; she refused to forgive him for betraying her.

---

n. disrepute; ill fame.

If the starlet couldn't have a good reputation, she'd settle for *notoriety*.

Fold along perforation before detatching cards

miserly
(mī zŭ(r) lē)

mundane
(mən DĀN)

oblivion
(ə BLĬ vē ən)

meticulous
(mə TĬ kyə ləs)

morose
(mə RŌS)

nurture
(NÛ(R) chŭ(r))

materialism
(mə TĬR ē ə lĭ zəm)

mitigate
(MĬ tə gāt)

notoriety
(nō tə RĪ ə tē)

v. overwhelm; flood; submerge.

This semester I am *inundated* with work: you should see the piles of paperwork flooding my desk. Until the great dam was built, the waters of the Nile used to *inundate* the river valley like clockwork every year.

---

adj. drowsy; dull.

The stuffy room made her *lethargic*; she felt as if she was about to nod off.

---

adj. hateful; spiteful. malice, *n.*

Jealous of Cinderella's beauty, her *malicious* stepsisters expressed their spite by forcing her to do menial tasks.

---

adj. fearless.

For her *intrepid* conduct nursing the wounded during the war, Florence Nightingale was honored by Queen Victoria.

---

v. praise.

The NFL *lauded* Boomer Esiason's efforts to raise money to combat cystic fibrosis.

---

adj. lacking in spirit or energy.

We had expected him to be full of enthusiasm and were surprised by his *listless* attitude.

---

v. urge; start; provoke.

Rumors of police corruption led the mayor to *instigate* an investigation into the department's activities.

---

adj. resulting in an unexpected and contrary outcome.

It is *ironic* that his success came when he least wanted it.

---

n. lack of seriousness; lightness.

Stop giggling and wriggling around in the pew; such *levity* is improper in church.

Fold along perforation before detatching cards

inundate
(Ĭ nən dāt)

lethargic
(lə THAHR jĭk)

malicious
(mə LĬ shəs)

intrepid
(ĭn TRĔ pəd)

laud
(LAWD)

listless
(LĬST ləs)

instigate
(ĬN(T) stə gāt)

ironic
(ī RAH nĭk)

levity
(LĔ və tē)

v. persuade; bring about. inducement, *n.*

After the quarrel, Tina said nothing could *induce* her to talk to Tony again.

---

adj. inborn.

Mozart's parents soon recognized young Wolfgang's *innate* talent for music.

---

adj. lacking in flavor; dull.

Flat prose and flat ginger ale are equally *insipid*; both lack sparkle.

---

v. charge.

If the grand jury *indicts* the suspect, he will go to trial.

---

adj. firmly established by nature or habit.

Katya's *inherent* love of justice caused her to champion anyone she considered treated unfairly by society.

---

n. change; introduction of something new. innovate, *v.*

Although Richard liked to keep up with all the latest technological *innovations*, he didn't always abandon tried and true techniques in favor of something new.

---

adj. not correctable.

Miss Watson called Huck *incorrigible* and said he would come to no good end.

---

adj. clever; resourceful.

She admired the *ingenious* way that her computer keyboard opened up to reveal the built-in CD-ROM below.

---

adj. harmless.

An occasional glass of wine with dinner is relatively *innocuous* and should have no ill effect on you.

Fold along perforation before detatching cards

induce
(ĭn DŌOS)

innate
(ĭ NĀT)

insipid
(ĭn SĬ ped)

indict
(ĭn DĪT)

inherent
(ĭn HĔR ent)

innovation
(ĭ ne VĀ shen)

incorrigible
(ĭn KAWR e je bel)

ingenious
(ĭn JĒN yes)

innocuous
(ĭ NAH kye wes)

adj. based on assumptions or hypotheses; supposed.

Why do we have to consider *hypothetical* cases when we have actual case histories that we may examine?

---

v. hinder; block; delay.

A series of accidents *impeded* the launching of the space shuttle.

---

adj. not fitting; absurd.

Dave saw nothing *incongruous* about wearing sneakers with his tuxedo.

---

v. arouse to action.

He *incited* his fellow students to go on strike to protest the university's anti-affirmative action stand.

---

v. injure; hurt.

Drinking alcohol can *impair* your ability to drive safely; if you're going to drink, don't drive.

---

adj. pretending to be virtuous; deceiving.

Believing Eddie to be interested only in his own advancement, Greg resented his *hypocritical* posing as a friend.

---

adj. silly; senseless.

There's no point to what you're saying. Why are you bothering to make such *inane* remarks?

---

adj. unchangeable.

All things change over time; nothing is *immutable*.

---

adj. of the same kind.

Because the student body at the prep school was so *homogeneous*, they decided to send their daughter to a school that offered greater cultural diversity.

Fold along perforation before detatching cards

hypothetical
(hī pə THĚ tĭ kəl)

impede
(ĭm PĒD)

incongruous
(ĭn KAHNG grə wəs)

hypocritical
(hĭ pə KRĬ tĭ kəl)

impair
(ĭm PÂ(R))

incite
(ĭn SĪT)

homogeneous
(hō mə JĒ nē us)

immutable
(ĭ(m) MYO̅O̅ tə bəl)

inane
(ĭ NĀN)

adj. sociable.

Typically, partygoers are *gregarious*; hermits are not.

---

n. pride; arrogance.

I resent his *haughtiness* because he is no better than we are.

---

n. seriousness.

We could tell we were in serious trouble from the *gravity* of the principal's expression.

---

n. arrangement by rank or standing; authoritarian body divided into ranks.

To be low man on the totem pole is to have an inferior place in the *hierarchy*.

---

v. obstruct.

The new mother didn't realize how much the effort of caring for an infant would *hamper* her ability to keep an immaculate house.

---

adj. loquacious; wordy; talkative. garrulity, n.

My uncle Henry can out-talk any three people I know. He is the most *garrulous* person in Cayuga County.

---

n. opinion contrary to popular belief; opinion contrary to accepted religion.

He was threatened with excommunication because his remarks were considered to be pure *heresy*.

---

n. deceit; duplicity; wiliness; cunning.

Iago uses considerable *guile* to trick Othello into believing that Desdemona has been unfaithful.

---

n. one who believes that pleasure is the sole aim in life.

A thoroughgoing *hedonist*, he considered only his own pleasure.

Fold along perforation before detatching cards

garrulous
(GĂR ə ləs)

gravity
(GRĂ və tē)

gregarious
(grĭ GÂ(R) ē əs)

guile
(Gī(ə)L)

hamper
(HĂM pər)

haughtiness
(HAW tē nəs)

hedonist
(HĔ d(ə)n ĭst)

heresy
(HĔR ə sē)

hierarchy
(Hī (ə) rahr kē)

n. excessive zeal; extreme devotion to a belief or cause.

The leader of the group was held responsible even though he could not control the *fanaticism* of his followers.

---

adj. false; misleading.

Your reasoning must be *fallacious* because it leads to a ridiculous answer.

---

n. overflowing abundance; joyful enthusiasm; lavishness; flamboyance.

I was bowled over by the *exuberance* of Amy's welcome. What an enthusiastic greeting!

---

adj. conspicuously wicked; blatant; outrageous.

The governor's appointment of his brother-in-law to the State Supreme Court was a *flagrant* violation of the state laws against nepotism.

---

n. glowing ardor; intensity of feeling.

At the protest rally, the students cheered the strikers and booed the dean with equal *fervor*.

---

adj. difficult to please; squeamish.

Bobby was such a *fastidious* eater that he would eat a sandwich only if his mother first cut off every scrap of crust.

---

adj. stealthy; sneaky.

Noticing the *furtive* glance the customer gave the diamond bracelet on the counter, the jeweler wondered whether he had a potential shoplifter on his hands.

---

n. thrift; economy. frugal, *adj.*

In economically hard times, anyone who doesn't learn to practice *frugality* risks bankruptcy.

---

adj. lacking in seriousness; self-indulgently carefree; relatively unimportant.

Though Nancy enjoyed Bill's *frivolous*, lighthearted companionship, she sometimes wondered whether he could ever be serious.

Fold along perforation before detatching cards

fanaticism
(fə NǍ tə sĭ zəm)

flagrant
(FLĀ grənt)

furtive
(FŪ(R) tĭv)

fallacious
(fə LĀ shəs)

fervor
(FŪ(R) vū(r))

frugality
(fro͞o GĂ lə tē)

exuberance
(ĭg ZO͞O b(ə) rən(t)s)

fastidious
(fă stĭ dē əs)

frivolous
(FRǏ vəl əs)

adj. thorough; comprehensive.

We have made an *exhaustive* study of all published SAT tests and are happy to share our research with you.

---

adj. totally clear; definite; outspoken.

Don't just hint around that you're dissatisfied; be *explicit* about what's bugging you.

---

v. free; disentangle.

Icebreakers were needed to *extricate* the trapped whales from the icy floes that closed them in.

---

adj. serving as a model; outstanding.

At commencement, the dean praised Ellen for her *exemplary* behavior as class president.

---

adj. suitable; practical; politic.

A pragmatic politician, he was guided by what was *expedient* rather than by what was ethical.

---

adj. not essential; superfluous.

No wonder Ted can't think straight! His mind is so cluttered up with *extraneous* trivia, he can't concentrate on the essentials.

---

v. worsen; embitter.

The latest bombing *exacerbated* England's already existing bitterness against the IRA, causing the prime minister to break off the peace talks abruptly.

---

v. acquit; exculpate.

The defense team feverishly sought evidence that might *exonerate* their client.

---

v. praise; glorify.

The president *extolled* the astronauts, calling them the pioneers of the Space Age.

Fold along perforation before detatching cards

exhaustive
(ĭg ZAW stiv)

explicit
(ĭk SPLĬ sət)

extricate
(EK strə kāt)

exemplary
(ĭg ZĔM plə rē)

expedient
(ĭk SPĒ dē ənt)

extraneous
(ĕk STRĀ nē əs)

exacerbate
(ĭg ZĂ sər bāt)

exonerate
(ĭg ZAH nə rāt)

extol
(ĭk STŌL)

n. puzzle; mystery.

"What do women want?" asked Dr. Sigmund Freud. Their behavior was an *enigma* to him.

---

adj. learned; scholarly.

Though his fellow students thought him *erudite*, Paul knew he would have to spend many years in serious study before he could consider himself a scholar.

---

n. mild expression in place of an unpleasant one.

The expression "he passed away" is a *euphemism* for "he died."

---

v. increase; improve.

You can *enhance* your chances of being admitted to the college of your choice by learning to write well; an excellent essay can *enhance* any application.

---

adj. ambiguous; intentionally misleading.

Rejecting the candidate's *equivocal* comments on tax reform, the reporters pressed him to state clearly where he stood on the issue.

---

n. expression of praise, often on the occasion of someone's death.

Instead of delivering a spoken *eulogy* at Genny's memorial service, Jeff sang a song he had written in her honor.

---

v. imitate; rival.

In a brief essay, describe a person you admire, someone whose virtues you would like to *emulate*.

---

adj. short-lived; fleeting.

The mayfly is an *ephemeral* creature; its adult life lasts little more than a day.

---

adj. hard to understand; known only to the chosen few.

The New Yorker short stories often include *esoteric* allusions to obscure people and events.

Fold along perforation before detatching cards

enigma
(ĭ NĬG mə)

erudite
(ĔR yə dīt)

euphemism
(YŌŌ fə mĭ zəm)

enhance
(ĭn HĂN(T)S)

equivocal
(ĭ KWĬ və kəl)

eulogy
(YŌŌ lə jē)

emulate
(ĔM yə lāt)

ephemeral
(ĭ FĔM rəl)

esoteric
(ĕ sə TĔR ĭk)

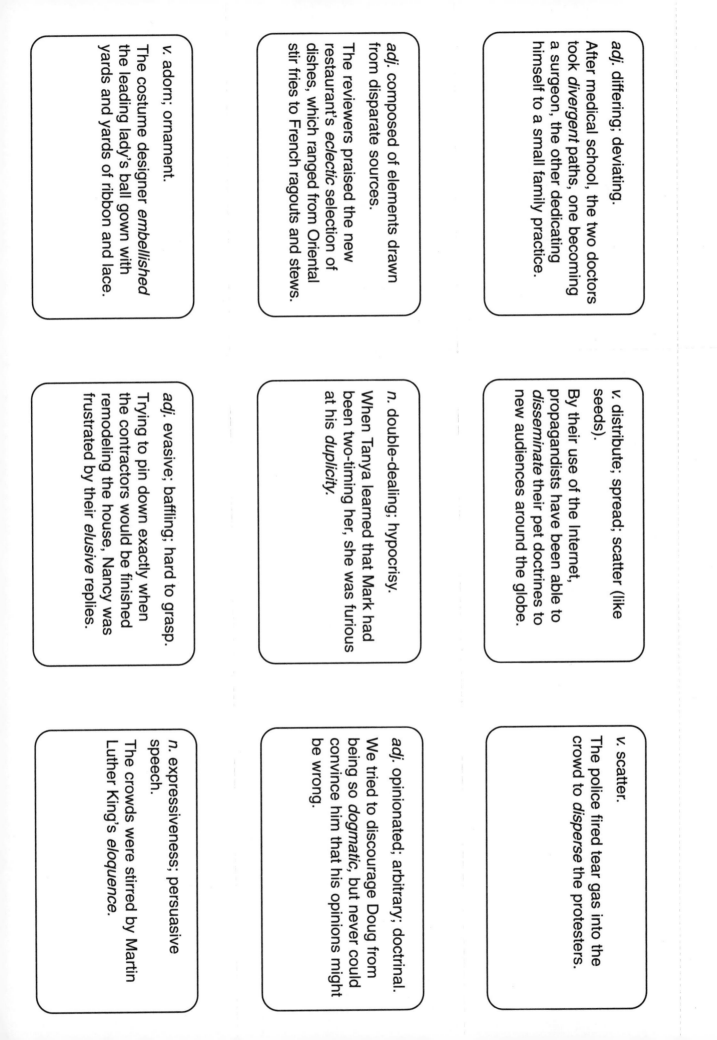

adj. differing; deviating.
After medical school, the two doctors took *divergent* paths, one becoming a surgeon, the other dedicating himself to a small family practice.

adj. composed of elements drawn from disparate sources.
The reviewers praised the new restaurant's *eclectic* selection of dishes, which ranged from Oriental stir fries to French ragouts and stews.

v. adorn; ornament.
The costume designer *embellished* the leading lady's ball gown with yards and yards of ribbon and lace.

v. distribute; spread; scatter (like seeds).
By their use of the Internet, propagandists have been able to *disseminate* their pet doctrines to new audiences around the globe.

n. double-dealing; hypocrisy.
When Tanya learned that Mark had been two-timing her, she was furious at his *duplicity*.

adj. evasive; baffling; hard to grasp.
Trying to pin down exactly when the contractors would be finished remodeling the house, Nancy was frustrated by their *elusive* replies.

v. scatter.
The police fired tear gas into the crowd to *disperse* the protesters.

adj. opinionated; arbitrary; doctrinal.
We tried to discourage Doug from being so *dogmatic*, but never could convince him that his opinions might be wrong.

n. expressiveness; persuasive speech.
The crowds were stirred by Martin Luther King's *eloquence*.

Fold along perforation before detatching cards

disperse
(dĭ SPÛ(R)S)

dogmatic
(dawg MĂ tĭk)

eloquence
(Ĕ lə kwən(t)s)

disseminate
(dĭ SĔ mə nāt)

duplicity
(do͞o PLĬ sə tē)

elusive
(ē Lo͞osĭv)

divergent
(də VÛ(R) jənt)

eclectic
(ĕ KLĔK tĭk)

embellish
(ĭm BĔ lĭsh)

adj. not harmonious; conflicting.

Nothing is quite so *discordant* as the sound of a junior high school orchestra tuning up.

---

n. unwillingness.

Some mornings I feel a great *disinclination* to get out of bed.

---

n. difference; condition of inequality.

Their *disparity* in rank made no difference at all to the prince and Cinderella.

---

adj. mentally quick and observant; having insight.

Though no genius, the star was sufficiently *discerning* to tell her true friends from the countless phonies who flattered her.

---

v. view with scorn or contempt.

In the film *Funny Face*, the bookish heroine *disdained* fashion models for their lack of intellectual interests.

---

v. belittle.

A doting mother, Emma was more likely to praise her son's crude attempts at art than to *disparage* them.

---

n. lessening; reduction in size.

Old Jack was as sharp at eighty as he had been at fifty; increasing age led to no *diminution* of his mental acuity.

---

n. lack of consistency; difference.

The police noticed some *discrepancies* in his description of the crime and did not believe him.

---

v. put away from consideration; reject.

Believing in John's love for her, she *dismissed* the notion that he might be unfaithful. (secondary meaning)

Fold along perforation before detatching cards

diminution
(dĭ mə NŌŌ shən)

discerning
(dĭ SÛ(R) nĭng)

discordant
(dĭs KAWR d(ə)nt)

discrepancy
(dĭs KRĔ pən sē)

disdain
(dĭs DĀN)

disinclination
(dĭ sin klə NĀ shən)

dismiss
(dĭs MĬS)

disparage
(dĭ SPĂR ĭj)

disparity
(dĭ SPĂR ə tē)

v. condemn; criticize. denunciation, *n.*

The reform candidate *denounced* the corrupt city officers for having betrayed the public's trust.

---

v. ridicule; make fun of. derision, *n.*

The critics *derided* his pretentious dialogue and refused to consider his play seriously.

---

n. wandering away from the subject. digress, *v.*

Nobody minded when Professor Renoir's lectures wandered away from their official theme; his *digressions* were always more fascinating than the topic of the day.

---

n. portray.

He is a powerful storyteller, but he is weakest when he attempts to *delineate* character.

---

v. express disapproval of; protest against; belittle.

A firm believer in old-fashioned courtesy, Miss Post *deprecated* the modern tendency to address new acquaintances by their first names.

---

n. something that discourages; hindrance.

Does the threat of capital punishment serve as a *deterrent* to potential killers?

---

n. propriety; orderliness and good taste in manners. decorous, *adj.*

Even the best-mannered students have trouble behaving with *decorum* on the last day of school.

---

n. extreme corruption; wickedness.

The *depravity* of Caligula's behavior came to sicken even those who had willingly participated in his earlier, comparatively innocent orgies.

---

adj. depressed; gloomy. despondency, *n.*

To the dismay of his parents, William became seriously *despondent* after he broke up with Jan; they despaired of finding a cure for his gloom.

Fold along perforation before detatching cards

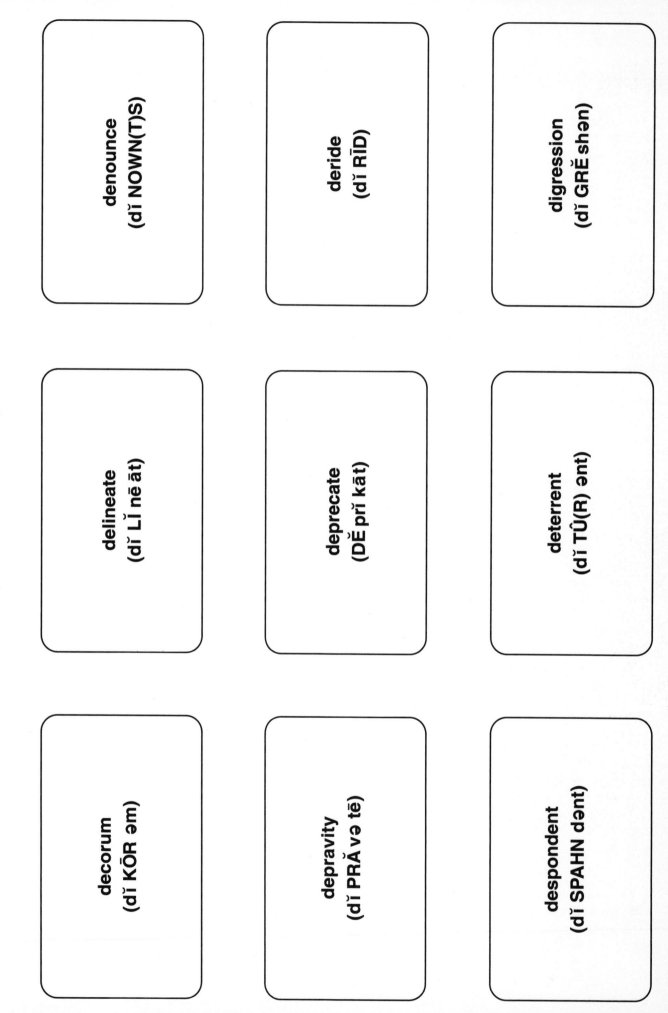

denounce
(dĭ NOWN(T)S)

deride
(dĭ RĪD)

digression
(dĭ GRĔ shən)

delineate
(dĭ LĬ nē āt)

deprecate
(DĔ prĭ kāt)

deterrent
(dĭ TÛ(R) ənt)

decorum
(dĭ KŌR əm)

depravity
(dĭ PRĂ və tē)

despondent
(dĭ SPAHN dənt)

adj. quarrelsome.

Disagreeing violently with the referees' ruling, the coach became so *contentious* that they threw him out of the game.

---

n. belief on slight evidence; gullibility; naiveté.

Con artists take advantage of the *credulity* of inexperienced investors to swindle them out of their savings.

---

adj. casual; hastily done.

Because a *cursory* examination of the ruins indicates the possibility of arson, we believe the insurance agency should undertake a more extensive investigation of the fire's cause.

---

n. compulsion; repression of feelings. constrain, *v.*

There was a feeling of *constraint* in the room because no one dared to criticize the speaker.

---

v. confirm; support.

Though Huck was quite willing to *corroborate* Tom's story, Aunt Polly knew better than to believe either of them.

---

adj. mysterious; hidden; secret.

Thoroughly baffled by Holmes's *cryptic* remarks, Watson wondered whether Holmes was intentionally concealing his thoughts about the crime.

---

n. general agreement.

The *consensus* indicates that we are opposed to entering into this pact.

---

n. judgment that someone is guilty of a crime; strongly held belief.

Even her *conviction* for murder did not shake Peter's *conviction* that Harriet was innocent of the crime.

---

n. standard used in judging.

What *criterion* did you use when you elected this essay as the prizewinner?

Fold along perforation before detatching cards

consensus
(kən SĔN(T) səs)

constraint
(kən STRĀNT)

contentious
(kən TĔN(T) shəs)

conviction
(kən VĬK shən)

corroborate
(kə RAH bə rāt)

credulity
(krĭ DYŌŌ lə tē)

criterion
(krī TĬR ē ən)

cryptic
(KRĬP tĭk)

cursory
(KÛ(R) sə rē)

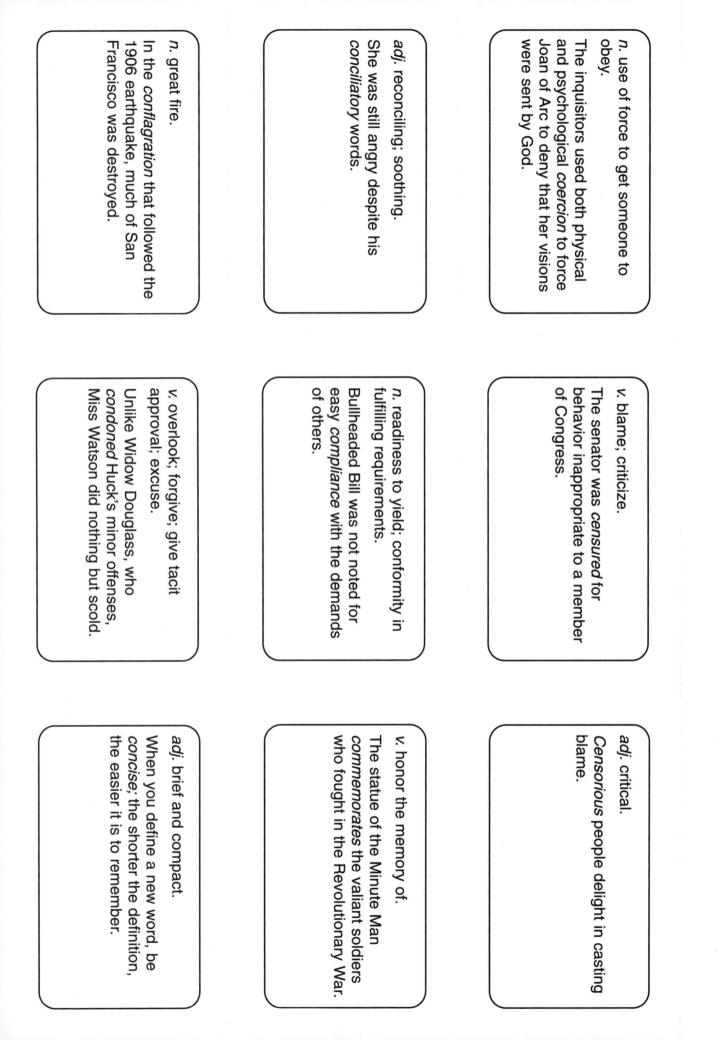

n. use of force to get someone to obey.
The inquisitors used both physical and psychological *coercion* to force Joan of Arc to deny that her visions were sent by God.

adj. reconciling; soothing.
She was still angry despite his *conciliatory* words.

n. great fire.
In the *conflagration* that followed the 1906 earthquake, much of San Francisco was destroyed.

v. blame; criticize.
The senator was *censured* for behavior inappropriate to a member of Congress.

n. readiness to yield; conformity in fulfilling requirements.
Bullheaded Bill was not noted for easy *compliance* with the demands of others.

v. overlook; forgive; give tacit approval; excuse.
Unlike Widow Douglass, who *condoned* Huck's minor offenses, Miss Watson did nothing but scold.

adj. critical.
Censorious people delight in casting blame.

v. honor the memory of.
The statue of the Minute Man *commemorates* the valiant soldiers who fought in the Revolutionary War.

adj. brief and compact.
When you define a new word, be *concise;* the shorter the definition, the easier it is to remember.

Fold along perforation before detatching cards

censorious
(sĕn SAWR ē əs)

censure
(SĔN(T) shər)

coercion
(ko Û(R) zhən)

commemorate
(kə MĔ mə rāt)

compliance
(kəm PLĪ ən(t)s)

conciliatory
(kən SĬL yə tawr ē)

concise
(kən SĪS)

condone
(kən DŌN)

conflagration
(kahn flə GRĀ shən)

adj. forbiddingly stern; severely simple.

The headmaster's *austere* demeanor tended to scare off the more timid students, who never visited his study willingly.

---

adj. wise; shrewd; keen.

The painter was an *astute* observer, noticing every tiny detail of her model's appearance.

---

adj. practicing self-denial; austere. also n.

The wealthy, self-indulgent young man felt oddly drawn to the strict, *ascetic* life led by members of some monastic orders.

---

adj. generous; charitable.

Mr. Fezziwig was a *benevolent* employer who wished to make Christmas merrier for young Scrooge and his other employees.

---

v. contradict; give a false impression.

His coarse, hard-bitten exterior *belied* his inner sensitivity.

---

adj. self-governing. autonomy, *n.*

Although the University of California at Berkeley is just one part of the state university system, in many ways Cal Berkeley is *autonomous,* for it runs several programs that are not subject to outside control.

---

adj. unpredictable; fickle.

The storm was *capricious*; it changed course constantly.

---

v. coax; wheedle.

Diane tried to *cajole* her father into letting her drive the family car.

---

n. conciseness.

Brevity is essential when you send a telegram or cablegram; you are charged for every word.

Fold along perforation before detatching cards

ascetic
(ə SĔ tĭ k)

astute
(ə STŌŌT)

austere
(aw STĒR)

autonomous
(aw TAH nə məs)

belie
(bĭ LĪ)

benevolent
(bə NĔV ə lənt)

brevity
(BRE və tē)

cajole
(kə JŌL)

capricious
(kə PRĬ shəs)

adj. unclear or doubtful in meaning.

His *ambiguous* instructions misled us; we did not know which road to take.

---

n. lack of caring; indifference.

A firm believer in democratic government, she could not understand the *apathy* of people who never bothered to vote.

---

n. controlling influence; domination.

Leaders of religious cults maintain *ascendancy* over their followers by methods that can verge on brainwashing.

---

adj. unselfishly generous; concerned for others.

In providing college scholarships for economically disadvantaged youths, Eugene Lang performed a truly *altruistic* deed.

---

n. person who seeks to overturn the established government; advocate of abolishing authority.

Denying she was an *anarchist*, Katya maintained she wished only to make changes in our government, not to destroy it entirely.

---

adj. effective; distinct.

Her *articulate* presentation of the advertising campaign impressed her employers.

---

v. relieve.

This should *alleviate* the pain; if it does not, we shall have to use stronger drugs.

---

n. the state of having contradictory or conflicting emotional attitudes.

Torn between loving her parents one minute and hating them the next, she was confused by the *ambivalence* of her feelings.

---

adj. capricious; randomly chosen; tyrannical.

Tom's *arbitrary* dismissal angered him; his boss had no reason to fire him.

Fold along perforation before detatching cards

alleviate
(ə LĒ vē āt)

altruistic
(ăl tro͞o ĬS tĭk)

ambiguous
(ăm BĬ gyə wəs)

ambivalence
(ăm BĬ və lən(t)s)

anarchist
(Ă nər kĭst)

apathy
(Ă pə thē)

arbitrary
(ĂHR bə trĕr ē)

articulate
(ahr TĬ kyə lət)

ascendancy
(ə SĔN dən(t) sē)

v. applaud; announce with great approval. also *n.*

The NBC sportscasters *acclaimed* every American victory in the Olympics and decried every American defeat.

---

n. poverty; misfortune.

We must learn to meet *adversity* gracefully.

---

n. positive assertion; confirmation; solemn pledge by one who refuses to take an oath.

Despite Tom's *affirmations* of innocence, Aunt Polly still suspected he had eaten the pie.

---

adj. theoretical; not concrete; nonrepresentational.

To him, hunger was an *abstract* concept; he had never missed a meal.

---

n. opponent.

The young wrestler struggled to defeat his *adversary*.

---

adj. artistic; dealing with or capable of appreciation of the beautiful. aesthete, *n.*

The beauty of Tiffany's stained glass appealed to Esther's *aesthetic* sense.

---

v. condense or shorten.

Because the publishers felt the public wanted a shorter version of *War and Peace*, they proceeded to *abridge* the novel.

---

n. flattery; admiration.

The rock star thrived on the *adulation* of his groupies and yes-men.

---

v. urge; plead for.

The abolitionists *advocated* freedom for the slaves.

Fold along perforation before detatching cards

abridge
(ə BRĬJ)

abstract
(ăb STRĂKT)

acclaim
(ə KLĀM)

adulation
(ă jə LĀ shən)

adversary
(ĂD vû(r) sĕr ē)

adversity
(ăd VÛ(R) sə tē)

advocate
(ĂD və kāt)

aesthetic
(ĕs THĔ tĭk)

affirmation
(ă fər MĀ shun)